MW00806253

The Interpreted New Testament

An Expanded Paraphrase with In-line Commentary

The Interpreted New Testament

An Expanded Paraphrase with In-line Commentary

DANIEL M. BOERGER

שמע ישראל יהוה אלהינו יהוה אחד

Hear and respond, people of Israel!
Yahweh is our God who created us!
Yahweh is the only God that exists, and is one divine collective unity
He is calling us to love him with all our
heart, thoughts, personality, and determination!
❖ *For our intended destiny is nothing less than to be his eternal lover and companion.*
[Deuteronomy 6:4-5]

FONTES PRESS

The Interpreted New Testament:
An Expanded Paraphrase with In-line Commentary

Copyright © 2020 by Daniel M. Boerger

ISBN: 978-1-948048-24-8 (hardback)

ISBN: 978-1-948048-25-5 (paperback)

All rights reserved. No part of this publication may be reproduced, stored in a retrieval system, or transmitted in any form or by any means—electronic, mechanical, photocopy, recording, or any other—except for brief quotations in printed reviews, without the prior permission of the publisher.

FONTES PRESS

DALLAS, TX

www.fontespress.com

To my wife and other Bible Translation colleagues
who have dedicated their lives to making the Scriptures
easily accessible and understandable to all speakers of the
7350+ languages and 400+ sign languages in this world.

The task is far from complete.

See **www.ethnologue.com** and
www.wycliffe.net/resources/scripture-access-statistics
and **www.deafbiblesociety.com**
for more information.
*(The above URLs do not imply any endorsement of this book by these organizations,
but do express my endorsement of their work.)*

This book is also available in its entirety as a free Android phone app.
Go to **https://play.google.com/store/apps**
Search for "The Interpreted New Testament" within quote marks.

Contents

Preface

About the Author

For 20 years, my wife and I were full-time Scripture translation advisors with an international mission agency that specializes in translating the Bible into minority languages. We worked among a language group of about 5000 speakers on the island of Santa Cruz in the Solomon Islands in the Southwestern Pacific. Directing a New Testament translation and vernacular literacy project team, we provided expertise and guidance in biblical exegesis, Bible translation principles, and literacy material production.

The language group we worked with were largely unfamiliar with the Scriptures except for the gospel stories. In the process of discovering local misconceptions and barriers to accurately understanding the New Testament text, I realized that many Americans today are also unfamiliar with Bible history, first-century Jewish culture and religious beliefs, ancient Roman culture and other knowledge necessary to properly understand much of New Testament.

The vernacular translation we helped produce was limited in what extra information could be included in picture captions, section headings, footnotes and glossary articles. So I decided to write, in my spare time, an expanded paraphrase with commentary that incorporated all the kinds of information I was learning in the process of exegeting the New Testament—for my own benefit, and also for the benefit of others who find the New Testament difficult in places because they also lack some of this information. The result is this book.

Concerning Exegetical Source Citations

The Interpreted New Testament (INT) is aimed at a popular audience, and citing sources for every comment and footnote would have made it less readable for my intended readers. But to acknowledge that 99 + % of the content of the commentary and footnotes are not my own creation, I include a bibliography of the exegetical resources I used, divided by New Testament book. Most of the notes in this book are found in many commentaries and study Bibles. Pastors typically know most of this material so I didn't feel it necessary to provide citations for interpretations and insights that are more or less "common knowledge" among those with theological training. But where I included an interpretation or insight that I believed was not as universally known, or depended heavily on one particular exegetical source, I give credit to a specific author so others can find it.

What this Book Is

The INT is an easy-to-understand interpreted paraphrase of the New Testament text—with additional explanatory notes and commentary. Its main goal is to enable almost any American adult reader who knows nothing at all about the Bible to be able to quickly and easily gain an in-depth understanding of the entire New Testament—without encountering obscure references, words, customs, and intents of a speaker in the text, or of the original writer, that are not clearly explained. I don't want any reader to give up reading in frustration because the text is too hard to understand. Nor do I want readers to misinterpret the meaning of a passage because they are unaware of cultural and historical information that clarifies the meaning communicated to the original readers nearly 2000 years ago.

My hope is that after reading this book, the reader will be able to pick up and read any literal translation of the Bible with nearly as much understanding as someone who has been familiar with the New Testament for years. *The INT* is sufficiently in-depth that mature believers and even some clergy will find it helpful, but it is also sufficiently self-explanatory that any adult should be able to understand it.

What this Book Is Not

While *The INT* is written in such a way that it appears to be a "paraphrase"—like *The Living Bible*—it is neither a translation nor an ordinary paraphrase because various kinds of information have been added to the text itself—such as background, implied and explanatory information—which is not in the original Greek text. In expressing the meaning of the text, no effort has been taken to reflect the form (i.e. words, word order, or grammar) of the original Greek text. This means you cannot use it to know what the Bible "literally says." For that, you need to have a literal translation on hand. I *strongly* recommend that you do have such a literal translation open alongside this book if you are doing any serious Bible study. For *The INT* is an accessory, like a commentary or other Bible reference book. It presents one or more understandings of the way theologically conservative scholars interpret the originally intended meaning of every verse—and focuses on making that meaning easily accessible rather than presenting what the original text actually says. This has advantages and disadvantages when compared with translations.

The INT is NOT intended to be used as a stand-alone Bible, or to substitute for real translations, nor is it meant to be used alone for Bible study purposes. I strongly recommend that you DO NOT use it for memorizing Scripture. It is not intended for public reading of Scripture lessons. It is not to be regarded as the "authoritative Word of God." It is one fallible person's interpretation—based on interpretations put forth by theologically conservative scholars who are also fallible. Consider it to be on par with a theologically conservative expository sermon—on every verse in the New Testament.

The INT's Advantages

1) Background information that the Biblical writers assumed their readers knew—but is not known by many people today—is included in the interpreted text as if the original author had penned it for a 21st-century American audience.

2) ❖ *The relatively brief background information included in the interpreted text is often not sufficient to explain everything the reader should know. So, commentary is included in this typeface. Note that sometimes the commentary refers to words and phrases found in literal translations that are not found in the interpreted text. This book is meant to be used alongside a literal translation for serious Bible-study purposes.* ➤ All of this kind of information can be found in commentaries and study Bibles, but in this "interpretation," it's mostly included in the body of the text and in commentary notes—rather than in footnotes—to make it more accessible.

3) Scriptural references *[e.g. John 1:1]* are put immediately after the text that they would clarify or amplify for a more-in-depth study, and also following Old Testament quotes.

4) Footnotes include interpretational reasoning, textual variants, and other notes less necessary for the understanding of the passage, but containing information some readers will be interested in.

The INT's Disadvantages

The INT will not tell you what the Bible actually says, only what many theologically conservative scholars think it means. For serious Bible study, it should always be used with a literal translation. The Greek text, or a literal translation of the Greek, is the basis for discovering the meaning. In the original text, the actual words that the author used often tie together concepts and passages—and these ties can only be seen in a very literal translation. Deviating from the literal words or phrasing obscures these ties. The literal text often has secondary meanings that are lost when the interpretation rewords the text to clearly express the primary meaning.

Bible scholars have differing opinions on the interpretation of some passages. True translations try as much as possible to not interpret the text—leaving that to the reader with the help of the Holy Spirit. But in order to make a passage clear and meaningful, *The INT* provides an explicit interpretation of the original writer's intended meaning. ❖ *Alternate interpretations are often mentioned in* commentary notes. ➤ That has the disadvantage of inherently obscuring other possible interpretations. Only by studying a literal translation will you know what the text actually says, and only by reading commentaries can you find out the range of interpretations held by scholars—though this book is a good start.

Another disadvantage to *The INT* is that there are a few places where the original text is ambiguous. In some of these places, some Bible scholars believe the author was purposefully ambiguous—intending more than one possible meaning to be true at the same time. But in presenting one meaning clearly, other possibilities can be obscured. Often, more than one of the commonly held interpretations are mentioned, but in many places it wasn't practical to include every possibility. So to explore these areas more adequately, you will have to consult scholarly commentaries.

Then there are a very few passages where Bible scholars admit that no one really knows with any high degree of confidence what the author originally meant to say. For these passages, *The INT* presents one of the more reasonable interpretations so there are no places where the text seems obscure and difficult. There is usually a commentary note to indicate that the rendered interpretation is just one among many offered by scholars.

In places where the original text uses figurative language that may not be clear to the modern reader, different words or even a different illustration is substituted to make the same point. In a couple of places an illustration is dropped completely, and *The INT* just tells the reader what the speaker or author meant by what he said. There is always an accompanying note to indicate when this is done.

For example, in Luke 14:26 (NIV) Jesus said, "If anyone comes to me and does not hate his father and mother, his wife and children, his brothers and sisters—yes, even his own life—he cannot be my disciple." Jesus was using a common Semitic idiom of comparison. Literal hatred was never intended. (Scholars agree about this.)

The INT renders his statement like this: Jesus said, "If you want to be one of my followers but cannot place your loyalty and obedience to me above your loyalty to your parents, spouse, siblings, children, and even your own desires for your life, then I will not accept you." Then there is a note which informs the reader: ❖ *Jesus actually said, "If anyone wants to follow me, and does not hate his own father and mother and wife and children and brothers and sisters and even his own life, he cannot be my follower." The people listening to him were Jews, and Jewish teachers (rabbis) often used a figure of speech called "hyperbole," (exaggeration to make a strong point). Jesus' listeners knew that the Torah commands us to respect and love all these people, and that Jesus was not advocating going against God's commands. They would have easily understood this Semitic idiom and the point he was making about the relative degree of loyalty he was requiring, as expressed in the interpreted translation above.* ➤

Please understand that when such an interpretation appears in quotes, it does not mean that Jesus said these exact words. All it means is that he said something that meant approximately what appears in the quotes. You should be aware that the original manuscripts of the New Testament in the Greek language don't have quotation marks, punctuation, or even spaces between words—and sometimes scholars disagree where quotes end and what punctuation should be used. There's some scholarly "guess work" in any translation. It's good to realize that even the "exact words" in the original Greek text of the Gospels are a translation—and not the exact words Jesus used himself—because he almost certainly spoke in Aramaic when he taught his fellow Jews. (Aramaic is a Semitic language closely related to Hebrew, and was the everyday language of Jews in Israel during the first century AD.)

So *The INT* is an "easy-to-understand interpretation." ❖ *with added commentary for clarification* ➤ That limits its usefulness for some purposes, but I hope that its value and strength will be to introduce the New Testament to many readers who lack the background knowledge to easily understand many sections of most English translations. The interpretations presented in this book were chosen from among those found in commentaries written by theologically conservative scholars. So even though *The INT* is worded very freely and deliberately interprets the text, it should convey the "essence" of the New Testament message as much as any conservative pastor's preaching on a passage does. And that is all I claim it does.

Differences from Most English Translations

"Messiah" is used instead of "Christ" because for most people, "Christ" sounds like a name rather than the title it actually is—and it thereby loses some of the intended meaning and force in certain contexts.

When quoting some Old Testament Scripture passages, I used "Yahweh" instead of "the Lord" where the Tetragrammaton—the four Hebrew consonants representing God's name—is in the original passage in Hebrew. Contrary to popular belief, neither "God" nor "Lord" are names. ("God" is a classifier, and "Lord" is a title.) "Yahweh" is God's name (or at least his most commonly-used name—used over 6000 times in the Hebrew Scriptures). Also contrary to tradition, the name "Jehovah" is a mistake and a distortion of "Yahweh." For Jewish readers who—out of respect and in order to follow their tradition—wish to refrain from saying God's name and choose to substitute "the Lord" or "Adonai," this is easily done when reading aloud. But just as "the Name" is found in the Hebrew text and is visible to the reader's eyes, it is kept in writing in this book—since removing "the Name" would be a significant violation and misrepresentation of the original text. Because it has been removed from most English translations, many Christians are unaware that God's name is "Yahweh"—and that his name actually appears in the original Scripture manuscripts where God caused it to be written and where he intended his people to see it.

"Assembly" is used instead of "church" —which many people mistake to refer to a building. There are also several other changes I've made in terminology to avoid words and expressions that would have negative connotations for some Jewish readers.

These changes were made in *The INT* because one fact has been lost on many people today: Jesus is a Jew. He lived as a Jew, taught as a Jewish rabbi, had to a large extent a Jewish worldview (although his was not limited to that of the common Jew of his day), and almost exclusively spoke to other Jews in a Jewish context. If these things are not kept in mind when reading the New Testament, some things can easily be misinterpreted. Using "Messiah," and "Yahweh" may help to keep that Jewish background in mind. If these conventions make you overly uncomfortable, I'm sorry, but you are not part of the intended audience for this book.

There are undoubtedly places where knowledgeable readers will disagree with some of the interpretations expressed in this book. That is to be expected. Where scholars disagree or are not sure themselves, by choosing to express one interpretation from among more than one possibility, it will often be judged "wrong" by those who interpret the meaning differently. Yet the message conveyed is well within the range of teachings of conservative Christian "orthodoxy"—and should not lead anyone away from Jesus himself. It is my hope and prayer that because *The INT* is easy to understand, it will bring many closer to an understanding of the Truth than they have ever been before.

One final note: Even though I've said that some passages have more than one interpretation, you should know that these variations of interpretation are mostly minor nuances. It's not as if there are many significantly different understandings of the main points of the text. Most of the uncertainties are on minor points that have little or no effect on the teachings held in common by all theologically conservative believers. In fact, the differences in interpretation that are mentioned in the notes of this book are very representative of the minor differences of interpretation that exist. I use the phrase "theologically conservative" to indicate those who take the

Biblical text at face value, and who assume it is a reliable account without significant distortions from what was originally written, and who accept it as the authoritative message (or "Word") from God to humanity. Many people who call themselves believers deny that the Bible has been reliably transmitted through the centuries—claiming that God has allowed it to become full of significant contradictions, errors, and additions—and they deny that it conveys his authoritative message to humanity. Such "theologically liberal" believers—having different working assumptions—of course often have very different interpretations of the Bible from what is presented in this book.

A Way to Use this Book for Bible Study

Since it would be overly repetitive to provide complete background information every place it might be needed, the first-time New Testament reader will gain the most benefit from this book by initially reading it through—cover to cover—twice. The first time will hopefully be clear and informative, but there may be places where adequate background information was not included in a particular place, and so leave some gaps in the reader's understanding. However, during the second read-through, the reader will have already been exposed to every bit of background information provided in the book, and this should help to make every passage more fully understandable the second time through.

For the first-time New Testament reader, I recommend that you read this book through twice before doing the following steps in comparing it to a real translation. The reader who is already familiar with the New Testament would, of course, not need the double read-through. For serious study, this book is meant to be used along with a literal translation. Commentary notes often mention words and phrases that can be found in a literal translation that are not in the interpreted text. The reader might become confused about such comments unless he or she also has a literal translation open.

I suggest that you use this book prayerfully—asking for the Holy Spirit's help in understanding—in the following manner:

1) Read a passage in a literal translation to find out what the text actually says. Some commonly available translations that are literal to various degrees are (in alphabetical order, no ranking intended):

CJB (Complete Jewish Bible)
ESV (English Standard Version)
GW (God's Word)
HCSB (Holman Christian Standard Bible)
NASB (New American Standard Bible)
NET (New English Translation)
NIV (New International Version)
NJB (New Jerusalem Bible)
NKJV (New King James Version)
NRSV (New Revised Standard Version).

There are also many other good translations available. I don't recommend the KJV—King James Version—for new Bible readers, only because of the archaic language which is difficult for modern speakers of English to accurately understand without considerable instruction. Once a reader has a proper background understanding of the biblical cultures, and has learned enough about the meanings of many archaic words in the KJV, the KJV is a perfectly good literal translation to use for serious study.

2) Read the same passage in *The INT* to fill in any gaps in your knowledge of background information, and to gain an understanding of ONE common conservative interpretation of the passage. Also read through notes from any study Bibles you have on hand.

3) Read the same passage again in a literal translation, and understand it in the light of the added information you now have, and the interpretation you just read.

4) Read the same passage again in the literal translation and notice places where the literal text might suggest other meanings and interpretations in addition to, or different from, the one you read in this book. Note any ambiguities in the literal translation. Ask the Holy Spirit to show you things he wants you to notice. Ask him to show you how the passage applies to your life. Make notes about questions you have, and other

possible meanings and interpretations that come to mind that you would like to investigate.

5) Consult as many commentaries and other exegetical resources as you have access to—including mature believers you respect, and books and sermons on a passage or topic—in order to explore other possible meanings and interpretations, and the arguments for and against them.

6) Make summary notes on the interpretation(s) you have noted or chosen for this passage. Record what commentary, book, or person shares your interpretation, and what some of the main arguments are for or against it. You may later want to know where you got that interpretation from and not remember unless you record the source—especially if someone asks you in a Bible study, "Where did you get that idea?"

7) Make your own "freely-worded easy-to-understand interpretation" of the passage—or perhaps only those parts of a passage which don't seem transparent to you in a literal translation to reflect your understanding of it. Put it in a computer file to use as a personal Bible-study resource. Include notes about where you got your interpretation, and about arguments for and against it. Share your interpretation during Bible studies to help others benefit from your study of the meaning of the passage.

8) DO NOT depend on *The INT* as your main Bible! Use it only as a resource to help fill in your knowledge and understanding. If you rely on this book exclusively, you will be too dependent on reading one view that excludes other possibilities! You will also deny yourself access to the authoritative Word of God—which this book is not! While the beginner might initially think this book is more informative, the reality is that mature believers—who have internalized the kind of background information available here—will eventually get more out of serious study and contemplation of a real translation. This interpretation just brings out the most-basic meaning of teachings in the New Testament—and not many of the deeper meanings or applications. [Hebrews 5:12-14] So please, don't use this interpretation for memorizing Scripture. Don't publicly read it as "the authoritative Word of God" in your assembly meetings. If you do quote it to others, please do so only after quoting the same passage from a real translation first, and better yet—also afterward.

A Brief Introduction
to the Hebrew Scriptures

History and Facts You Should Know
Before Reading the New Testament

Before you start reading the New Testament for the first time, you should know some background from the Jewish Bible (the Hebrew Scriptures **A**) if you really want to understand many of the things talked about in the New Testament. Considering the material to be covered, the overview provided in this introduction is extremely brief. Please consider it the barest outline, and realize that for a more in-depth understanding of the New Testament, reading and understanding much of the Hebrew Scriptures is essential. Together, the Hebrew Scriptures and the New Testament tell us the story of God's plan for humanity. Don't complain that it's too complicated. Life is complicated, and if you want to understand life well enough to get ahead, you need to be willing to spend some time learning the "ins and outs" of things. God's plan isn't overly complicated, but it is true that it can't all be absorbed in a day. In fact, there's enough truth and depth in what the Scriptures have to teach us about God and his ways that a lifetime isn't enough. Since the known universe is as "infinite" in size and complexity as modern science has revealed, it shouldn't be a surprise that its creator is even more complex and infinite. Once you fall in love with him, you will never need fear boredom in exploring the depths of the revelation he has given us about himself in the Bible.

What does the word "Testament" mean? Before that can be answered, we need to talk about another important Bible word— i.e., "covenant." A covenant is an ancient kind of formal agreement between two parties that was binding for life, and usually pledged that the two parties involved made all of their resources available to each other. There were promises to each other—often for mutual protection—and usually penalties threatened if the covenant was broken. The Bible talks about several covenants, but two major covenants, called the "Mosaic Covenant" (called the "Old Covenant" by Gentiles) and the "New Covenant" (or "Renewed Covenant") are about the terms of God's relationship with his chosen people. The Mosaic Covenant is covered in detail in the Hebrew Scriptures—as well as some tantalizing prophecies giving details about the New Covenant. The main details of the Mosaic Covenant are found in the Torah— which is a name for the first five books of the Bible (Genesis, Exodus, Leviticus, Numbers, and Deuteronomy). "Torah" means "Teaching." **B** This Mosaic Covenant—as detailed in the Torah—is often referred to in

---

A The Hebrew Scriptures are those Scriptures which were originally written in Hebrew—though some small portions were written in Aramaic—called the "Tanakh" by Jews, and called the "Old Testament" by Christians. The main difference between the Jewish Tanakh and the Christian Old Testament is the ordering of the books and some minor differences in verse numbering. Otherwise they are identical in content.

B Gentile believers refer to the first five books of the Bible—the Torah—as "the Pentateuch." The Greek translation of "Torah" in the New Testament is νόμος

(nomos) which means "law." But a better general translation of "Torah" by a single word into English is "Teaching." Since most Gentiles are not comfortable with the word "Torah" and are not familiar with its meaning, it is often rendered by the redundant phrase "Torah teachings" in this book, or some variation with "Torah" or "Teaching(s)" in it. For those not familiar with the Bible, the word "Law" by itself may be misunderstood, and even "God's Law" or the "Law of Moses" can be misleading—because the Torah is much more than just a collection of Laws.

English translations of the New Testament as "the Law" or "the Law of Moses" or "the Law given to Moses" or "God's Law."

The word "testament" is very similar in meaning to "covenant," but is more one sided. Since the covenants between God and humanity were initiated and maintained mostly or entirely by God, some Gentiles think "testament" is a better term than "covenant." "Testament" can also mean "testimony"—and the Old and New Testaments are God's testimony concerning his Old (Mosaic) and New Covenants. As you read on in this introduction, some details of the Mosaic Covenant will be made clear. Details of the New Covenant are what the New Testament is all about.

Genesis

Genesis—the first book of the Bible—means "beginnings," and it tells the story of creation, the fall of humanity into a state of sin and rebellion against God, and a very brief and selective history of the world for the first 2,000 years after creation—focusing mainly on the lives of five men: Noah, Abraham, Isaac, Jacob, and Joseph. Genesis is, in general, a fairly-easy book to understand in any translation. I highly recommend that you read it even before you continue reading this book. But knowing that many readers won't do that, here are a few essential details taught in Genesis that you need to know to understand the New Testament.

The Bible teaches that God first existed by himself and that everything else that exists he created. That includes all galaxies, stars, planets, all animal and plant life, people, and angels. When he created everything, it was all "good"—reflecting his own nature and perfection. But he created angels and humans with the ability to choose for themselves. This capability is usually called "free will." If God had created humanity in such a way that they didn't have the ability or freedom to choose against him, then their love and friendship would not be freely given or real. (If your spouse or friends were forced to like or love you, their friendship and love wouldn't be "real" and would have

much less value to you.) God created humans differently than all other forms of life. Everything he created he "spoke" into being. But he formed man from the dust of the ground and made him "in his own image." Then he breathed his own "breath of life" into him. What all is included in being made "in God's image" we don't entirely know. But it includes the ability to reason, to love, to make decisions, and to create. God created humanity for the purpose of having a close relationship with us. He also put humanity in charge of this planet and everything on it. Humanity was God's representative in this world. We don't know a lot about the angels, but they were created as God's servants. The highest, most powerful, and most beautiful of those angels—Lucifer—became proud and rebelled against God's authority. Hints in the Bible lead many to believe that he convinced about a third of the angels to rebel with him. For this they were cast out of Heaven, and some were imprisoned in a place of punishment created specifically for them—which we now call "Hell." Lucifer—more commonly known as "Satan" or "the Devil"—enticed Eve (the first woman) to rebel against God, and she in turn enticed Adam (the first man). Some theologians believe that the reason God did not immediately imprison Satan and all the other rebellious angels—commonly referred to as "demons" or "evil spirits" or "unclean spirits"—was that he wants to prove a point about his nature to them. Satan tried to ruin God's plan by enticing humans to also rebel, but God was not taken by surprise. He had planned what he was going to do even before he created the world—because he knew all that would happen.

When Adam and Eve rebelled, they died "spiritually." Just as physical death makes a body consciously unresponsive to the physical world, "spiritual death" means that a person is consciously unresponsive (in general) to the spirit world, and specifically unresponsive to God. Their close relationship with God was severed because God is spirit, and humans relate to him through their human spirit—which is now "dead" and self-oriented, rather than God-oriented. God is holy and will not tolerate sin in his presence for long. God had warned Adam and Eve that they would die if they disobeyed his command. But spiritual death and physical death are only part of the story. The just penalty for sin is eternal death—which is eternal separation from God, the source of all life. Man's soul—i.e., mind, emotions, memory, personality, and will—is eternal and does not cease to exist after the body dies. Since all that exists that is good is from God, to be totally separated from God for all eternity means to be totally separated from all that is good—and also separated from his presence—and yet still existing. Realize that having friends is "good." So logically, where there is no "good" there will be no friends. Many people think they will join their friends in Hell and have a "good" time. But they fail to realize that all "good" comes from God, and to live completely without God means there will be no "good" and no "pleasure" in Hell. This is the nature of Hell. This was not God's plan or desire for humanity, yet he had a purpose that could not be accomplished without allowing humankind the freedom to rebel. And God will accomplish his purpose in creating a new redeemed humanity that is perfect, holy, and that freely chooses to have a close relationship with him. The price of accomplishing this is, apparently, the suffering of all those who freely choose to reject him. Since God has given humanity free will, he respects our decisions and does not force people to decide to love and obey him. To do so would mean that their relationship with him was forced—and therefore of no real value to him.

Physical and spiritual death entered the world when Adam and Eve sinned. This event is commonly called the "Fall" of humanity. God placed all of the physical creation under a curse of decay so that people would learn to recognize the consequences of rebellion against God—and not be blithely content in a temporary paradise on earth while unaware of the fate of Hell awaiting them after death, and unaware of their need for God to save them.

Suffering entered this world because humanity chose to rebel, but in one sense, part of that suffering is a blessing in disguise. For those who will realize it, suffering teaches us that all is not right in the universe and that every person has a need for God. Suffering is intended to drive us to God so he can save us from the fate of eternal suffering and death in Hell. Almost nobody realizes their need for God and turns to him when everything is going well. Many people reject a God who would permit suffering and evil, and who would send anyone to Hell. They don't understand that 1) God did not himself desire or create evil and suffering, 2) they are rejecting a very real God who must permit suffering and evil if humans are to have free will (and he actually does limit suffering and evil in some ways—especially for those who have a relationship with him), and who allows them the dignity of freely rejecting him, and 3) God by his very nature cannot ultimately allow sinful and rebellious people to ruin his plan for a perfect universe where there will be no evil. That universe did exist for a short time when he first created it—until Satan and his angels and humanity rebelled. But at a definite point in time—which many believers think is not very far away—God will in effect say, "You have had enough time to choose, and I have redeemed enough people who have chosen to follow me to fulfill my plan, so the rest of you will have to leave." After all, it's his universe. If you choose to ignore the God of this universe, you will suffer the consequences. It's entirely your choice—and God will not listen to excuses on Judgment Day. He has clearly said in the Bible that everyone deep down knows enough of the truth to choose to turn to him—if they want to. He doesn't want to spend eternity with people who don't want him.

Immediately after the Fall, God promised Adam and Eve that he would send a savior to save humankind from the fate of eternal death in Hell. Although the Bible doesn't say this explicitly in Genesis, it is apparent that God also explained to Adam and Eve a way to approach him and to be saved. He taught them that the penalty for sin is death, and that God's nature allowed a substitute death to pay the death penalty. Animal sacrifices were instituted to remind humanity that the penalty for sin is death, and that only after sin is punished in death can sin be forgiven and humankind allowed to approach God. The animal sacrifices themselves did not actually pay for sin, because human sin requires a human death in payment. But they were a teaching tool and a pattern that would allow people to eventually recognize the one death that *would* pay for humanity's sins. That being the death of his son who became the man Jesus.

Because Adam and Eve had rebelled against God, something in their nature changed. They were no longer able to choose to obey God because their very nature became self-oriented. The Bible calls this our "sinful nature" or our "fallen nature." This fallen condition is passed on from parent to child. Even before a child is consciously able to rebel against God and his will, the child's very nature is focused on itself. All people are born with a "bent" nature that is totally inclined to selfishness and rebellion against God. That is not to say that people are totally evil—at least by human standards. We were created in God's image and part of that image remains in our nature—even though it is "tarnished." Thus properly raised and taught, people are capable of great selflessness and love and much beauty. At the same time, all people are capable of much evil. There is a lot of good and a lot of bad in most people. Yet from God's perspective, even the "good" in humanity is tainted because nothing we do is from 100% pure motives in relation to loving and serving him. So even our "good" deeds and love can't really earn us any merit in God's eyes. Everything we do is tarnished—even our very best. Of course to us things appear very different since we have never experienced sinless perfection—and we are incapable of understanding things from his perspective unless he teaches us about it.

This may seem extremely unfair to some people. After all, we didn't choose to be born. We didn't have the freedom of choice to become sinners or not like Adam and Eve did. But God does offer us an out. He offers us a way to be free from sin and to regain our lost position and to enjoy all the benefits of a close relationship with him that he intended for humanity all along. If we choose to reject his offer, that's our choice. Even though we didn't choose to be this way, we came into existence spoiled. The creator looks at us and says we are unacceptable. He will not tolerate having an eternal relationship with such flawed selfish creatures. He created humanity for his own purposes, and if it doesn't suit him, he has every right to destroy or uncreate them and start over. For reasons that we can only guess at, he has chosen a different response. He instead offers us a chance to be changed into what we were meant to be in the first place. But we have to choose this and meet his conditions. Those who reject his conditions will experience an eternal existence of ruin in Hell. But God will have accomplished his purpose with those who do respond.

I said earlier that we are incapable of choosing to obey him, yet we have the freedom to choose. This may sound like a contradiction, and is one area where there is some disagreement among believers. Because our self-orientation prevents us from being able to choose to obey God, he has to help us. He sends his Holy Spirit to work in the hearts and minds of every person—or some believe only in selected individuals—to give them the ability to choose to obey him that our self-oriented sinful nature inherently lacks. Those who do so choose, come to realize it was only because God enabled them to do so—and not anything that they can claim credit for.

Returning to Genesis: Initially after the Fall of humanity into sin, people lived incredibly-long lifetimes. The genetic perfection of humankind in its youth enabled people to live, on average, 10 times as long as they do now. But life is like a path that you follow. People either choose to follow a path leading toward God or one leading away from him. Knowing the evil that people are capable of when they live only 60-90 years on this planet—as we have seen in the past century and can see all around us—imagine how good and how evil people could become if they were able to live and follow their path for 10 times as long. There would be great saints and utterly evil monsters. Unfortunately, history has shown that statistically a majority of people choose paths away from God. In the ten generations after the Fall, humanity became mostly very evil. Their evil was so great that God almost regretted creating humankind. He decided he would destroy the world with a flood and start all over again. But at that time, he found one man who had chosen the path of having a relationship with God. That man was Noah, and he and his immediate family were saved from the flood—and they became the originators of all of subsequent humanity.

Noah and his sons continued to live extremely long lives after the flood, but in the course of several generations the lifespan of people was reduced to something on the order it is today. This may have been due to God's direct intervention, or due to increased radiation after the world's climate changed in the worldwide flood, or it may have come from genetic degradation starting from a small imperfect gene pool.

At any rate, after several generations when the world's population had again increased to relatively-large numbers, God chose a man named Abram—whose name he changed to Abraham. Abraham lived about 2000 BC. God decided that he would raise up a special group of people—descended from Abraham—who would learn about him and his ways and requirements, and represent him to the world. Because of Abraham's incredible trust in God's promises in the face of their seeming impossibility, God declared that Abraham was acceptable to him—and forgave his sin. Abraham's trust in God's promises became a pattern for humanity to follow if they want to be restored to a close relationship with God. This restoration is based on trust or "faith"—in what God has said and promised. Abraham's son was Isaac, and Isaac's son was Jacob. Jacob also came to know God

personally, and God changed his name to Israel. The families of Jacob's twelve sons developed into the twelve tribes of Israel.

When God chose Abraham, he promised him that through his descendants—and through one of them in particular—that all the people of the world would be blessed. It was always God's intention to offer his way of salvation to all of humanity. Unfortunately, Abraham's descendants usually neglected their God-intended mission to represent him to the rest of humanity, and focused selfishly on themselves—as is typical of all fallen humanity.

A Digression About Creation And Evolution

Many people today have been taught and are convinced that the theory of evolution is a fact, and if they also happen to believe in God, they believe that he created the world by means of evolution. Therefore, they believe the creation story in Genesis is a "myth." If you are one of those people, there is nothing I can say at this point to convince you otherwise, so I won't try. I merely ask you to put that issue aside for the time being. Get to know who Jesus is through reading this book. That's the first important step. Then, if you become convinced he is who the Bible says he is, and choose to enter into an experiential faith relationship with him as your Master and Savior, he will lead you to the understanding he wants you to have about creation and evolution. Try not to worry about it now. But having an understanding about the fall of mankind into sin as taught in Genesis is essential to understanding the message of the New Testament.

Exodus

The Israelites found themselves eventually enslaved in Egypt. God used a man named Moses to free his people from slavery. The experiences that the Israelites went through with Moses in becoming free, and their journey to the promised land of Canaan (modern-day Israel) is not only history, but a picture with remarkable parallels to God's freeing people from their slavery to sin. That subject itself would take a book to explore in depth. Suffice it to say that the experiences of God's people recorded in the Hebrew Scriptures very often have spiritual parallels for us to learn from in our getting close to God.

Leviticus, Numbers, Deuteronomy

During their time of wandering in the Sinai wilderness after being freed from slavery in Egypt—and before they entered the land of Canaan that God had promised to give them—God made a covenant agreement with the people of Israel known as the "Mosaic Covenant"—which is now known by Gentile believers as the "Old Covenant." He gave the details of this covenant to them through Moses. He promised to be their God and to protect them and make them prosper if they would obey him and follow his requirements as specified in the system of Teachings that he dictated to Moses. God instructed them to construct a holy tent—which was their primary place of worship and sacrifice. This tent was called the "Tabernacle." He promised to live among them in the Tabernacle. In his covenant, he also promised dire consequences if his people disobeyed the terms of the covenant.

Judges, 1 & 2 Samuel, 1 & 2 Kings, 1 & 2 Chronicles

God led his chosen people—the Israelites—to conquer the land of Canaan because the peoples living there were particularly corrupt by his standards. They "worshipped" their idols with sexual acts forbidden by God—and even offered their children as sacrifices to them. People today like to stress that part of God's nature which is "love." But the God who created this world is also a God of justice. He hates what is evil and will punish those who refuse to turn away from evil to follow his ways. Many of us might like to "create" in our minds our own version of a God who is "pure love"—who has no anger and who wouldn't create a Hell. But our desires can't change the reality of who God is. Either we reject him completely—and suffer any consequences of that decision if he really exists—or we turn toward him and learn what he is really like from what he has told us about himself in the Bible.

After the Israelites conquered Canaan, they lived there for several hundred years without a hereditary leader. God appointed individuals called "judges" to help lead the Israelites in times of crisis—which happened mainly when they strayed from following the terms of their covenant agreement with God, and thus came under his discipline. His discipline took the form of allowing hostile neighboring peoples to attack, conquer, and oppress them. After some generations of living this way, the Israelites protested this kind of leadership. They wanted a king like the other countries around them. God granted them their request and chose a young man named "Saul" as King. Saul didn't follow God's commands very long and lost favor with him. God then appointed another young man to be king whose name was "David." David lived about 1000 BC and was a man who loved God with all his heart. For all but one brief episode in his life where he stumbled in serious sin, he was always obedient and close to God his entire life. Because of David's faithfulness, God caused David's kingdom to prosper and promised him that one of his descendants would always be a king over his chosen people, the Israelites, forever.

David's son, Solomon, became the next king, and the nation of Israel entered its golden age. Solomon built a grand Temple in Jerusalem to replace the Tabernacle as the place where God would live among his people, and where they would offer sacrifices as required in God's Torah teachings. But in his later years, Solomon started worshipping false gods, so God told him he would split the kingdom in two and that the larger part would be taken away from his descendants' rule. But because David had been so faithful, he would not do this until after Solomon died. After Solomon died, his son took power. But because of his greed and poor leadership, the kingdom was split in two (about 920 BC) with 10 tribes (really eight tribes and the two half-tribes descended from Joseph) following another king and forming the northern kingdom of

Israel. Solomon's son was king over two tribes (Judah and Benjamin) in the kingdom called Judah. (The tribe of Levi was not counted because they didn't own land, and some Levites lived in Judah and others in Israel.)

Most of the next several hundred years found most of the kings of Israel and of Judah and their citizens to be unfaithful to following the requirements of their covenant with God. Injustice and immorality were common—and worst of all was their worship of false gods. God sent prophets to warn the kings and the people that if they didn't repent and return to following his Torah teachings, that he would punish them by having another country destroy them. Finally, God caused the Assyrian Empire to conquer the northern kingdom of Israel in about 723 BC. The 10 tribes of Israel were led off into exile where they eventually intermarried with their conquerors and lost their identity as God's chosen people (though some returned and became part of the kingdom of Judah, so there were people from all 12 tribes represented in Judah). Judah as a kingdom lasted somewhat longer because there were a few godly kings who instituted reforms for short periods, so God mercifully withheld his punishment for a time.

Isaiah, Jeremiah, and the Other Prophets

During the centuries when God sent his prophets to warn his people about his coming punishment if they would not repent, he also had his prophets give more details about the promised savior that he intended to send them. This same savior was promised to Adam and Eve, and to Abraham, and also to David. This promised savior went by the title "Messiah"—which means "Anointed One." Anointing was the ritual of pouring sacred oil over a person—the oil being symbolic of the Spirit of God and a sign of God's choosing and empowering that person for leadership, either as king or as a spiritual leader. The prophets also talked about a New Covenant that God would someday make with his people that would be different from the current one they were under.

Daniel, Ezra, Nehemiah, Esther

But despite the warnings of all the prophets, finally the kingdom of Judah too was so consistently wicked that God cause the Babylonian Empire to conquer them about 586 BC. Much of the population of Judah was taken into exile in Babylon—and Jerusalem and the Temple were destroyed. But God had predicted through his prophets that this exile would only last 70 years, and that he would then bring a remnant of his people who had remained faithful to him back to Jerusalem, and that he would again bless his people. After 70 years, a remnant did return—and they rebuilt the Temple and the city walls of Jerusalem.

Inter-Testamental Period

After the experience of their exile in Babylon, the returning remnant of God's people, now called "Jews"—derived from the name of the kingdom and tribe of Judah—finally learned to shun false gods and remain at least outwardly faithful to their covenant relationship with God. After this, there was a 400-year period when they were conquered by the Greeks (about 333 BC), then had a short time of independence, and then were conquered by the Romans in 63 BC. This 400-year period is called the "inter-testamental period" because the events of that time are not recorded in either the Old or New Testaments—though there are non-biblical books that record some of the events of that period.

Important Revelations About God Revealed in the Hebrew Scriptures

Over the centuries, through his interactions with people and through the prophets, God revealed much about himself that he wants people to know.

Of first importance is that Yahweh is the one and only God and the creator and sustainer of all that is. There are no other gods and never have been. There is no other being remotely like him. The many deities worshipped by people are either powerless man-made idols, or sometimes demons (angels that followed Satan in rebelling against God).

Secondly, Yahweh is a holy God—perfect and just. He cannot ignore sin. He does—in his mercy—often delay punishment, but ultimately sin has to be punished. He hates sin but he loves people.

Yahweh desires a relationship with people and has provided a way to overcome the problem of humankind's sinful rebellion. In the Hebrew Scriptures, all the details of his plan to save people were not given, but as long as people obeyed his covenant requirements and trusted in his promises, he accepted them as his people and forgave their sins.

Yahweh is a patient, loving, and merciful God—who is very slow to get angry. To humans, he often just seems slow, period, in doing what he says he will do, but his apparent slowness is due to his patience and his perfect timing.

Yahweh desires to forgive people, yet he requires repentance. The Biblical concept of repentance is more than just being sorry for having done wrong. It is also a decision to change—a determination to cease doing wrong and to try to do what is right in God's sight. He knows we are weak and imperfect and that we will stumble in sin, but he has made provision for that. As long as we are willing to continue to genuinely repent, he will forgive us—even for the same sin over and over and over.

Yahweh has told us about himself in the Scriptures. He inspired the men who wrote them and he guarantees that they are basically accurate and reliable despite millennia of copying and transmission. (Modern archaeological discoveries in the 20th century confirmed the accuracy and preservation of the Scriptures without significant change—i.e., without change that changes the message.) He always keeps his promises—even though some have been waiting thousands of years to be fulfilled. His main criterion for people to be acceptable to him and have a relationship with him—aside from repentance—is that they believe that everything he has said in his Word, i.e., everything that is in the Scriptures, is true—and

that he will keep all his promises and prophecies. We must realize that he doesn't intend to keep all his promises as we interpret them—insofar as our interpretation is different from what he intended. Thus sometimes our imperfect understanding may make it seem that God is not faithful to his Word. But he is faithful, and he doesn't intend to be difficult, tricky, or obscure. Our understanding is often imperfect because of our own stubbornness and willful rebellion.

Yahweh is in total control of history on the large scale, and also of all events on the smallest scale. Yet he allows for individual free will—even when people choose to sin—but he never tempts or causes anyone to sin. He allows people to suffer the results of their own sin and also the consequences of the sins of others. Yet he is in total control and sets limits. Even Satan and his demons have boundaries and rules set by him beyond which they cannot go in their trying to deceive and harm us. Suffering is meant to drive us to God. He has made no blanket promises about freedom from suffering in this life, but he does promise that there will be no suffering in Heaven—and that all injustices will be set right through punishments, rewards, and compensations in the life to come after Judgment Day.

All that is good in this world and this life ultimately comes from him. God has never originated evil, and according to his standards he does no evil. Since he is the all-powerful creator, only his standards really matter in the long run.

God answers prayers offered by his people that are in accordance with his will. But he does so in his own way and in his own time. We do not control God. However, God has given management of this world to humanity, and he often waits for his people to ask him to do something he would like done before he will do it. This is because he wants to work in partnership with us.

One major purpose of the Scriptures is to record how God has interacted with his people in the past so we can learn from these examples. God does not change. His nature and character are constant. In addition to the revelations about himself, his promises, his prophecies, and his laws—we are to learn how to relate to God by studying the examples of how people related to him in the past and how he responded.

People who physically die are still alive and aware but without mortal physical bodies of the type we now have. Those who respond properly to God in this life go to live with him in Heaven. Those who reject his overtures in this life go to Hell. There will be a Last Day when Jesus will return to Earth in power—and the current stage of human history where evil exists in this world will end. All who have died will be resurrected with new immortal physical bodies—and everyone will be judged according to how they lived their lives. Those who have rejected God's offer of salvation in this life will be judged by their deeds to determine the severity of their punishment in Hell. Those who have received God's salvation— and thus have been forgiven—will not be punished for any of the sins they have done in this life, since the punishment for their sins was paid for by God's Son. But their deeds will be judged to determine their rewards and status in Heaven. All inequalities and injustices will be righted. While the poor usually have no opportunity for riches and power in this world, their responses to God in this life give them equal opportunities—or perhaps even more than the rich and powerful have—to gain eternal riches and status in Heaven.

A common misconception among people is that God is a killjoy. They think he creates a lot of rules that serve no other purpose than to spoil our pleasure in this life. But there is another way of looking at these things. God knows that certain desires and behaviors are inherently destructive because they lead us away from him. He designed human beings, so he knows what will ultimately satisfy us and what will not. He designed us to delight in knowing him above all else. All the wonderful pleasures of this life are but pale shadows of the joys to be found in knowing him—who created all those pleasures. He knows that some very pleasurable things—like some drugs or improper sexual behavior—will in the long

run trap us and destroy us. They either destroy our bodies, or our minds, or our relationships with others, or our relationship with him. So when God prohibits something, he is not wanting to ruin your fun. He is trying to guide you to ultimate permanent pleasure and to preserve your life. When a sign says "stay on this side of the fence" and on the other side of the fence is a treacherous cliff, the writer of that sign isn't trying to restrict you or destroy your fun. He's trying to tell you that on this side of the fence is life—on the other side is death. All of God's rules have this purpose. Since the only things we can know about God and spiritual reality are what he tells us, we have to trust that he knows best about what leads to true joy and eternal life—and what leads to eternal death. There is plenty of evidence in enough areas that he does indeed love us and wants the very best for us. So in the areas where we don't understand his reasons for his rules and prohibitions, we need to learn to trust him that they are for our ultimate good and pleasure.

This is some of the general background knowledge you should be acquainted with in order to more fully understand the contents of the New Testament.

The New Testament

By the time of Jesus (2000 years ago), the Jews were desperately wanting the promised Messiah to come because they were living under the oppression of their Roman conquerors. But their idea of the Messiah's role had transformed into that of a political savior who would free them from Roman rule. They believed he would become a king and make the kingdom of Israel as great again as it had been during the golden age of King Solomon—nearly a thousand years earlier. Their expectations of the Messiah were different from what God really intended and had promised.

Also at that time were two main groups of people who were leaders among the Jews. The Sadducees were members of the priesthood—who were wealthy and collaborators with the Romans. The Sadducees did not accept many of the writings of the prophets as God's word—only the Torah (Pentateuch). They didn't believe in a life after death or in angels. In this they were similar to many people today. The other group of leaders were the Pharisees. Pharisees were mostly laymen (non-priests) who lived very religious lives and made it a point to follow God's Torah teachings to the letter. In fact, they were so zealous to not disobey God's Torah teachings that they added hundreds of additional rules—which they insisted Jews follow who wanted to be godly. They reasoned that if people followed all of these additional rules, they were certain not to break any of God's laws, and so would be accepted as righteous in God's sight. Unfortunately, they became so focused on the outward detail of keeping their rules that they totally neglected their inner attitudes—which in God's mind are of equal or greater importance. They were highly regarded by the common people as holy and good men, but many of their hearts were actually far from God. Jesus publicly called some of them "hypocrites." They elevated their set of man-made rules to be on equal authority with the Torah teachings given by God. This is one area where Jesus often clashed with them because Jesus had no regard for man-made rules that were stricter than God's commands—and thus made life even harder for people. Because Jesus refused to follow their rules, many Pharisees considered him to be an evil person. And because of his popularity, he was a threat to their authority and way of life. Since the common people were so anxious for a Messiah to free them from Roman rule, over the years they followed several self-proclaimed Messiahs in revolt against Roman rule. The result of these revolts was always violent suppression by the Roman legions. Because the Sadducees were Roman collaborators and part of the status quo, any potential Messiah figure who might lead the people into revolt was considered a threat to their position. So when Jesus became popular among the people and had a big following—and people started speculating that he might be the Messiah—both the Sadducees and the Pharisees had strong reasons to get rid of him.

The Four Gospels

The word "gospel" means "good news." The four gospels were written by four different men—each to different audiences with different emphases—although the first three (written by Matthew, Mark, and Luke) have a lot of overlap in content. Some of them were compiled from oral stories handed down over the years, and they probably were not written until several decades after the events happened. (That does not mean, however, that the stories were not accurately preserved. When they were written down, many people were still alive who experienced those events.) The "Good News" that they tell about presupposes you first know the "bad news" revealed in the Hebrew Scriptures—namely that people are sinners and under threat of eternal punishment for their sins of rebellion against a holy God who created them. The Good News is that God has provided a way for people to be forgiven and made holy themselves and to have an intimate relationship with him—which is what he intended when he created humanity. The four gospels tell the story of Jesus—who is the Messiah that God promised to send to save humanity from the fate of damnation.

The four gospels are included individually in this book, but for the first-time reader they have also been put together in what is called a "harmony" of the gospels. The four accounts are combined into one story that includes almost all of the details recorded in the four gospels, but without the duplication.

The attempt is to provide a "chronological type" account—although this is not entirely possible because the exact order of events in the four gospels is not always clear. The writers of the gospels had a different purpose in mind than to provide us with a modern-style chronological history. You may be frustrated by what they left out. But their main purpose was to introduce the man named "Jesus" to you, to tell you what he taught and what he did, so that you can become convinced that he is who he said he is—God's Son and the Messiah. The "harmony" of the four gospels is at the beginning of "*The Interpreted NT*" and is an excellent way to introduce you to Jesus. Later, you can read the four gospels individually and learn how four different men portrayed Jesus. But after you read the "harmony," you might find it more interesting to skip on to the book of Acts—which continues the story where the gospels leave off.

Introduction to the Gospel Harmony

Before introducing this harmony—which is intended to be an introduction to the life and teachings of Jesus the Messiah—I would like to apologize to any reader who has ever been offended by people who claim to be Christians. I hope you can distance yourself emotionally from such negative experiences and determine to evaluate the person of Jesus for who he claims to be—and not get side-tracked by the words and actions of people who claim to be his followers. You will see that Jesus exhorted his followers to obey his teachings. You will come to the understanding that if his followers were really faithful to his teachings, they would never deliberately do or say something that would be intended to hurt or offend you or anyone else. Those who do so are disobeying him. However, if you read through this entire book, you will see that Jesus does not promise to perfect his followers in this life. That perfection is promised, but not until we die. Yes, it is easy to criticize many who claim to be his followers, for some of them are not really trying to follow his teachings at all, and so are not really his followers. And others who are trying, often don't succeed. That does not excuse their bad behavior. But you will find that Jesus promises to eventually right all wrongs—including those done against you. We are all citizens of a country, and it is easy to find fellow citizens who you wish you could say were not true citizens. The problem is that citizenship does not automatically convey good character. That doesn't mean your country or its ideals are bad—only that some of the citizens don't live up to them. So as a follower of Jesus, I want to apologize for the bad behavior and hurt caused to you and others by people who claim to be followers of Jesus. All I can say is, Jesus' concern is with you and your response to his claims. He will deal with those who claim to be his followers but do not obey his commands or reflect his character. And he will deal with you too—based on your response to him. So

I ask you to separate the issue of his followers who have done wrong, from the claims and character of Jesus himself—and his demands on your life. Yes, that sounds rather strong, but he does make demands. The other side of the coin is that you will never find anyone in this universe more loving, gentle, kind, considerate, and fair than he is—so his commands are actually a delight to obey, and he promises to help you obey. His exercise of his authority over his followers is easy and light. If after getting to know about him you submit to him as the Lord and Master of your life, he will change you and make you *want* to obey and please him. You will not need to 'work up the desire to obey' in yourself. So please focus on Jesus and his character and claims—and for the moment try to forget the gross imperfections of too many who claim to follow him.

This harmony is an attempt at weaving the four gospels into a single narrative in chronological order—as much as that is possible. Unfortunately, the exact chronology of all the parts is not known for certain. The gospels were not written as a modern historian would write—with the view of chronological accuracy. The gospel writers had other purposes—mainly to tell people about this unique individual named Jesus who claimed to be the eternally-existing Son of God who became a human being. So each gospel writer chose from his memories or the stories he heard from others and wove a narrative fitting his particular audience. Obviously some of the writers, or even all four of them, didn't stick to strict chronological sequence. However in comparing them, if one assumes that Mark's gospel is entirely in chronological sequence, there is the least amount of reordering needed among the other gospels to mesh with it. If you assume any other gospel as being entirely chronological, there is always significantly more reordering needed overall among the other three. Of course it may be that none of the gospels are completely chronological. But for most of the stories about Jesus and his teachings, the exact order is not critical.

The sections are numbered for easy reference. The Harmony Chart shows which verses from the different gospels were combined in each section. But there are no chapter or verse numbers in the Harmony text since that would appear disjointed and distracting.

The original Greek manuscripts didn't have chapter or verse divisions, or paragraph breaks, or unequivocal sentence breaks, or markings for where direct quotes began or ended. There weren't even word breaks (no spaces between words) or a difference between capital and lower-case letters. So how to mark all these wonderful tools of modern writing is somewhat debatable and not terribly important. None of these things are part of the inspired Word of God—and they vary considerably at times among translations.

In making this Harmony I have operated under several principles and assumptions:

1. I'm assuming for the most part that Mark's account is entirely in chronological order and the other gospel accounts need to bend to fit it.

2. I assume that when two gospels indicate that two subsequent events are in the same order, that they were in that order. An exception is with the material from Luke 9:51—19:48—which Luke arranged in a chiastic structure, moving some stories out of chronological sequence for the purpose of symmetry. (See the Introduction to Luke to see this chiastic structure outlined.) So when the narrative in this section of Luke didn't seem to fit the location or sequence, it was moved elsewhere.

3. I assume the that same story in different accounts sometimes have different details stated in each account, yet are the same story. I allow for the discrepancies in details by the fact that different eye-witness accounts almost never match exactly. So when one writer says there were two angels at Jesus' tomb on Easter Sunday morning, and another writer mentions only one, I don't assume they were separate incidents

or that one is wrong. I assume that the fuller account is accurate, and that the writer who mentioned only one angel didn't consider the other one important to mention for his purposes when he wrote the story. For example, if only one of the angels spoke, the writer may have considered it immaterial to mention the other one. Minor differences of details like these would not have bothered people 2000 years ago—as they seem to bother some people today. Such details missing from one account and present in another are not errors. Nobody will report all the details of an event. Everyone chooses details they think are important and leave out some they think are not worth mentioning. That does not mean that the accounts with missing details are wrong. They are just less complete.

4. Based on the last assumption, when I assume that two accounts are really talking about the same event, I try to include all the details from each account and weave them all together into one narrative.

5. There are several stories in different gospels that may or may not be the same event. Similar incidents could have happened at separate times. Sometimes I will assume they are the same event and combine them and the details in the various accounts, and other times I assume they are different and tell them at different times. Timing and ordering as they appear in the individual Gospel accounts may help in making the decision—but sometimes it's just guesswork.

6. Where short phrases or certain sentences from one gospel don't fit well into a combined account, I haven't felt compelled to include them for completeness. They can be found in the individual gospel accounts. Their omission in the Harmony does not diminish the overall story. For example, to include Luke's introduction to his gospel in the Harmony—which is addressed to Theophilus—would make it sound like he wrote the entire Harmony for Theophilus. Since that would be misleading, I left it out of the Harmony.

7. There are a few discrepancies of detail between different accounts that are difficult

to reconcile. I don't worry about them too much—and some have been omitted or glossed over in the Harmony to avoid making the story too confusing. Such issues are more appropriately treated elsewhere. I believe there are reasonable explanations for all of the discrepancies without resorting to the assumption that there was an "error" in the recording of the account. The goal of this Harmony is to provide a relatively complete combined narrative without the repetition and incompleteness of detail found when reading the four gospels sequentially. It is meant to be a single overall story of the life of Jesus—to introduce him to people who don't know him. Yet keep in mind that some of the stories could have been organized and combined differently. Stick to the individual gospels for serious study.

The individual gospel accounts have numerous cross references and footnotes for study purposes. To make it read more smoothly, almost none of these are included in the Harmony. The individual gospels also have numerous commentary notes. These have been mostly eliminated in the Harmony, but a few basic ones are included to increase the comprehension of the first-time reader. Those familiar with the Bible can skip them entirely when reading the Harmony and miss nothing.

The gospel accounts are quite sketchy except for the accounts of Jesus' last week on Earth before his death—and they are not intended to be a biography or an exhaustive record of what he said and did during his ministry. These stories are recorded so you can get to know him and be convinced that he is real—not a legend—and more than human. He is God—who became a human being so we could comprehend what God is like.

Also note that the way Jews and other ancient peoples taught moral lessons and truth was by telling stories. These accounts were not meant to be just entertaining stories. They were meant to teach lessons about Jesus and God. They are examples of truths that go far beyond the stories themselves. Ask the Holy Spirit to help you to understand what the truths are that can be learned from them. There are so many truths and they are so deep that you can mine through these stories your entire life and not get everything out of them. So read deeply and ponder—asking God to teach you through them.

Harmony Chart

#	Event	Probable Location	MT	MK	LK	JN
1	Jesus Is the Creator					1:1-5
2	Genealogy of the Messiah		1:1-17		3:23-38	
3	An Angel Foretells the Birth and Significance of John the Baptizer	Jerusalem			1:5-25	
4	The Angel Gabriel Appears to Miriam	Nazareth			1:26-38	
5	Miriam Visits Elizabeth	Hill country of Judea			1:39-45	
6	Miriam's Song of Praise	Hill country of Judea			1:46-56	
7	The Birth of John the Baptizer	Hill country of Judea			1:57-66	
8	Zechariah's Prophecy	Hill country of Judea			1:67-80	
9	An Angel Appears to Yosef	Nazareth	1:18-25			
10	The Birth of Jesus	Bethlehem			2:1-7	
11	Angels Announce the Messiah's Birth	Bethlehem			2:8-20	
12	The Baby Messiah Is Named	Bethlehem			2:21	
13	Baby Jesus Is Dedicated in the Temple	Jerusalem			2:22-38	
14	God Reveals the Messiah to Gentiles	Jerusalem & Bethlehem	2:1-12			
15	Yosef and His Family Flee to Egypt	Bethlehem & Egypt	2:13-15			
16	The Slaughter in Bethlehem	Bethlehem	2:16-18			
17	Yosef and His Family Return from Egypt to Israel	Egypt & Nazareth	2:19-23		2:39-40	
18	The Boy Jesus in the Temple	Jerusalem			2:41-52	
19	John the Baptizer Prepares God's People to Receive the Messiah	Judean wilderness	3:1-12	1:1-8	3:1-18	1:6-28
20	Jesus Is Baptized and Empowered by the Holy Spirit	Jordan River near Lake Galilee	3:13-17	1:9-11	3:21-23	
21	Satan Tempts Jesus	Judean wilderness	4:1-11	1:12-13	4:1-13	
22	John Proclaims Jesus as God's Sacrificial Lamb	Jordan River near Lake Galilee				1:29-34
23	Jesus' First Followers	Galilee				1:35-42
24	Jesus Calls Philip to Follow Him	Galilee				1:43-51
25	Jesus' First Miraculous Sign	Cana in Galilee				2:1-11
26	Passover at the Start of Jesus' Ministry, the First Temple Cleansing	Jerusalem				2:13-25
27	Nicodemus and the New Birth	Jerusalem				3:1-21
28	John's Testimony About Jesus	Judea				3:22-36
29	Crossing Cultural & Social Barriers to Evangelize (The Woman at the Well)	Samaria				4:1-42
30	Herod Imprisons John, and Jesus Starts His Public Ministry in Galilee	Galilee	4:12-17	1:14-15	3:19-20 4:14-15	4:43-45
31	Jesus Heals an Official's Son at a Distance	Cana				4:46-54
32	Jesus Is Rejected in Nazareth	Nazareth			4:16-30	
33	Jesus Calls Four Fishermen to Be His Followers	Capernaum	4:18-22	1:16-20	5:1-11	
34	Jesus Expels Demons from a Man in the Capernaum Synagogue	Capernaum		1:21-28	4:31-37	
35	Jesus Heals Simon's Mother-in-law and All Who Are Brought to Him	Capernaum	8:14-17	1:29-34	4:38-41	
36	Jesus Preaches and Heals in Galilee	Galilee	4:23-25	1:35-39	4:42-44	
37	Jesus Wants to Heal	Galilee	8:1-4	1:40-45	5:12-16	
38	Jesus Heals a Paralyzed Man to Prove He Has Authority to Forgive Sin	Capernaum	9:1-8	2:1-12	5:17-26	

#	Event	Probable Location	MT	MK	LK	JN
39	Jesus Associates with Disreputable People	Capernaum	9:9-13	2:13-17	5:27-32	
40	Jesus Answers a Question About Fasting	Capernaum	9:14-17	2:18-22	5:33-39	
41	The Healing at Bethesda	Jerusalem				5:1-16
42	Jesus Claims to Be Equal with God	Jerusalem				5:17-47
43	Jesus Is Master over Sabbath Regulations	to Galilee	12:1-8	2:23-28	6:1-5	
44	Jesus Heals a Man with a Crippled Hand on a Sabbath	Galilee	12:9-14	3:1-6	6:6-11	
45	Jesus' Ministry Fulfilled Prophecy About the Messiah	Lake Galilee	12:15-21	3:7-12	6:17-19	
46	Jesus Appoints Twelve Apostles	near Capernaum		3:13-19	6:12-16	
	SERMON ON THE MOUNT (Sections 47-63)	near Capernaum	5:1–7:29		6:20-49	
47	The Attitudes We Should Have	near Capernaum	5:1-12		6:20-26	
48	We Are Meant to Attract Others to Him	near Capernaum	5:13-16			
49	Jesus' View of Moses' teachings	near Capernaum	5:17-20			
50	The Importance of Good Relationships	near Capernaum	5:21-26			
51	Thoughts Are as Important as Actions	near Capernaum	5:27-30			
52	God's View of Divorce	near Capernaum	5:31-32		16:18	
53	Always Speak Truthfully Without Invoking Oaths	near Capernaum	5:33-37			
54	Showing Self-Sacrificial Love	near Capernaum	5:38-48		6:27-36	
55	How to Gain Heavenly Rewards	near Capernaum	6:1-8			
56	On prayer	near Capernaum	6:9-18			
57	A Proper Attitude About Riches and Possessions	near Capernaum	6:19-34		12:22-34	
58	Jesus Forbids Us to Criticize or Condemn Others	near Capernaum	7:1-6		6:37-42	
59	We Often Don't Have Because We Haven't Bothered to Ask	near Capernaum	7:7-12			
60	Only a Relative Few Find the Way to Heaven	near Capernaum	7:13-14			
61	Beware of False Religious Teachers and Prophets	near Capernaum	7:15-20		6:43-45	
62	Many Who Consider Themselves Believers Will Not Enter Heaven	near Capernaum	7:21-23			
63	Two Ways to Respond to Jesus' Teaching	near Capernaum	7:24-29		6:46-49	
64	The Power of Faith in Jesus	Capernaum	8:5-13		7:1-10	
65	Jesus Resurrects a Widow's Son	Nain			7:11-17	
66	John the Baptizer Sends Messengers to Jesus	Galilee	11:2-19		7:18-35	
67	Jesus at the House of Simon the Pharisee	Capernaum			7:36-50	
68	Women Who Helped Jesus	Galilee			8:1-3	
69	Beware of Saying the Spirit's Work Is of Satan	Capernaum	12:22-37	3:20-30	11:14-23	
70	Those Who Reject Jesus Will Have No Excuse	Capernaum	12:38-45		11:24-36	
71	Jesus' True Relatives	Capernaum	12:46-50	3:31-35	8:19-21	
72	Parable of the Four Soils	by Lake Galilee	13:1-9	4:1-9	8:4-8	
73	Why Jesus Teaches in Parables	by Lake Galilee	13:10-17	4:10-12	8:9-10	
74	Jesus Explains the Parable of the Four Soils	by Lake Galilee	13:18-23	4:13-20	8:11-15	
75	Parable About the Weeds	by Lake Galilee	13:24-30			
76	God Intends to Reveal His Truth to Everyone	by Lake Galilee		4:21-25	8:16-18	
77	The Parable About How God Causes His Kingdom to Grow	by Lake Galilee		4:26-29		
78	Parable of the Mustard Seed	by Lake Galilee	13:31-32	4:30-34	13:18-19	
79	Parable of the Yeast	by Lake Galilee	13:33		13:20-21	
80	Jesus' Teaching in Parables Fulfilled Prophecy	by Lake Galilee	13:34-35			
81	Jesus Explains the Parable About the Weeds	by Lake Galilee	13:36-43			
82	Two Parables About How to Regard Citizenship in God's Kingdom	by Lake Galilee	13:44-46			

#	Event	Probable Location	MT	MK	LK	JN
83	Parable of the Fish Net	by Lake Galilee	13:47-52			
84	Jesus Demonstrates Authority Over Weather	Lake Galilee	8:23-27	4:35-41	8:22-25	
85	Jesus Demonstrates Authority Over Demons	Lake Galilee Eastern shore	8:28-34	5:1-20	8:26-39	
86	A Woman's Faith Heals Her; and Jesus Demonstrates Power over Death	Capernaum	9:18-26	5:21-43	8:40-56	
87	Two Blind Men and a Man Made Mute by a Demon	Galilee	9:27-34			
88	Jesus is Rejected in Nazareth a Second Time	Nazareth	13:53-58	6:1-6		
89	Pray for More Kingdom Workers	Galilee	9:35-38			
90	Jesus Sends Out the Twelve to Minister	Galilee	10:1-15	6:6-13	9:1-6	
91	Those Who Do God's Work Will Be Persecuted	Galilee	10:16-33		12:4-12	
92	The Price of Being Jesus' True Follower	Galilee	10:34-39			
93	God Rewards Those Who Help His Workers	Galilee	10:40-11:1			
94	John the Baptizer's Death	Galilee	14:1-12	6:14-29	9:7-9	
95	Jesus Demonstrates Power to Multiply Resources	near Bethsaida	14:13-21	6:30-44	9:10-17	6:1-14
96	Jesus and Peter Walk on Water	Lake Galilee	14:22-33	6:45-52		6:15-21
97	Jesus Heals in Gennesaret	Gennesaret	14:34-36	6:53-56		
98	Jesus' Discourse on 'The Bread of Life'	Capernaum				6:22-71
99	Defiles Us in God's Sight and What Does Not	Galilee	15:1-20	7:1-23		
100	The Persistent Faith of a Gentile Woman	Phoenicia	15:21-28	7:24-30		
101	Jesus Heals a Deaf-Mute	Decapolis		7:31-37		
102	Jesus Multiplies Resources to Feed 4000 Men	Decapolis	15:29-39	8:1-10		
103	Interpreting the Signs of the Times	Magdala	16:1-4	8:11-13	12:54-56	
104	Jesus Warns About the Influence of the Pharisees and Sadducees		16:5-12	8:14-21		
105	Jesus Heals a Blind Man	Bethsaida		8:22-26		
106	Peter Recognizes That Jesus Is the Messiah	near Caesarea Philippi	16:13-20	8:27-30	9:18-21	
107	Jesus Predicts His Suffering and Death	near Caesarea Philippi	16:21-23	8:31-33	9:22	
108	The High Cost of Following Jesus		16:24-28	8:34-9:1	9:23-27	
109	God Reveals Jesus' True Glory (the Transfiguration)	unnamed mountain	17:1-13	9:2-13	9:28-36	
110	Jesus' Followers Fail to Expel a Demon	near unnamed mountain	17:14-21	9:14-29	9:37-42	
111	Jesus Talks About His Death a Second Time	Galilee	17:22-23	9:30-32	9:43-45	
112	Jesus Miraculously Pays the Temple Tax	Capernaum	17:24-27			
113	How to Be Important in God's Sight	Capernaum	18:1-5	9:33-37	9:46-48	
114	Jesus' Followers Try to Exclude Others	Capernaum		9:38-41	9:49-50	
115	Jesus Teaches About Temptation and Sin	Capernaum	18:6-11	9:42-50	17:1-4	
116	All People Are Important to God	Capernaum	18:12-14			
117	How to Handle Unrepented Sin Among Believers	Capernaum	18:15-20			
118	The Consequences of Unforgiveness	Capernaum	18:21-35			
119	The Relationship Between Faith and the Release of God's Power	Capernaum			17:5-6	
120	The Cost of Following Jesus	Capernaum	8:18-22		9:57-62	
121	Jesus Rejects His Brother's Advice	Galilee	19:1			7:2-10
122	Jesus Answers a Question About Divorce	trip to Jerusalem	19:1-12	10:1-12		
123	Jesus Blesses children	Perea	19:13-15	10:13-16	18:15-17	
124	The Stumbling Stone of Being Rich	Perea	19:16-30	10:17-31	18:18-30	
125	A Parable About God's Generosity	Perea	20:1-16			
126	The Festival of Shelters (Sukkot)	Jerusalem				7:11-52
127	The Woman Caught in Adultery	Jerusalem				7:53–8:11

#	Event	Probable Location	MT	MK	LK	JN
128	Jesus Claims to Be God's Light Sent to the Sinners of This World	Jerusalem				8:12-59
129	Jesus Gives Sight to a Man Born Blind	Jerusalem				9:1-41
130	The Good Shepherd	Jerusalem				10:1-21
131	Parable of the Good Samaritan	Jerusalem			10:25-37	
132	Jesus Visits Martha and Mary	Bethany			10:38-42	
133	How to Pray	Jerusalem area			11:1-13	
134	Parable of the Widow and the Corrupt Judge	Jerusalem area			18:1-8	
135	Parable of the Pharisee and the Tax Collector	Jerusalem area			18:9-14	
136	Jesus Warns the Pharisees and Scripture Teachers	Jerusalem area	23:29-36		11:37-54	
137	Jesus Warns About Hypocrisy	Jerusalem area			12:1-3	
138	Parable About the Rich Fool	Jerusalem area			12:13-21	
139	Being Shrewd in Getting Ahead	Jerusalem area			16:1-17	
140	The Rich Man and Lazarus	Jerusalem area			16:19-31	
141	Always Be Ready for Jesus' Return	Jerusalem area			12:35-48	
142	Loyalty to Jesus Will Cause People to Reject You	Jerusalem area			12:49-53	
143	A Call to Repentance and a Warning	Jerusalem area			13:1-5	
144	Parable of the Barren Fig Tree	Jerusalem area			13:6-9	
145	Jesus Heals a Crippled Woman on the Sabbath	Jerusalem area			13:10-17	
146	Jesus Claims to Be God, and Jewish Leaders Attempt to Stone Him	Jerusalem				10:22-42
147	The Story of Lazarus	Perea to Bethany				11:1-45
148	Jewish Leaders Plot to Kill Jesus	Jerusalem				11:45-54
	JESUS RETURNS TO GALILEE					
149	A Samaritan Village Refuses Jesus Hospitality	Start of final trip to Jerusalem			9:51-56	
150	Jesus Heals Ten Men with Leprosy	Galilee, Samaria			17:11-19	
151	Jesus Sends Out 72 as Evangelists	going to Jerusalem			10:1-12	
152	Jesus Laments for Towns That Rejected Him	going to Jerusalem	11:20-24		10:13-16	
153	The Return of the 72	going to Jerusalem			10:17-20	
154	Jesus Rejoices	going to Jerusalem	11:25-30		10:21-24	
155	The Narrow Door to Heaven	going to Jerusalem			13:22-30	
156	Jesus' Love for the People of Jerusalem	going to Jerusalem			13:31-35	
157	Jesus Heals on a Sabbath	going to Jerusalem			14:1-6	
158	Humility	going to Jerusalem			14:7-14	
159	Parable of the Great Banquet in Heaven	going to Jerusalem			14:15-24	
160	The Price of Being Jesus' True Follower	going to Jerusalem			14:25-35	
161	The Good Shepherd and the Lost Sheep	going to Jerusalem			15:1-7	
162	The Good Woman and the Lost Coin	going to Jerusalem			15:8-10	
163	The Good Father and His Two Lost Sons	going to Jerusalem			15:11-32	
164	The Proper Attitude to Have in Serving Jesus	going to Jerusalem			17:7-10	
165	The Coming of God's Kingdom	going to Jerusalem			17:20-21	
166	Jesus Speaks About His Death a Third Time	going to Jerusalem	20:17-19	10:32-34	18:31-34	
167	Kingdom Authority	going to Jerusalem	20:20-28	10:35-45		
168	Jesus Heals Bar Timaeus & Another Blind Man	Jericho	20:29-34	10:46-52	18:35-43	
169	Zaccheus	Jericho			19:1-10	
170	Parable of the Minas	Jericho			19:11-27	
171	People Wonder if Jesus Will Dare to Appear in Jerusalem During Passover	Jerusalem				11:55-57

#	Event	Probable Location	MT	MK	LK	JN
	JESUS' FINAL WEEK BEFORE HIS DEATH	Jerusalem area				
172	Jesus' Triumphal Entry into Jerusalem on "Palm Sunday"	Bethany, Jerusalem, Bethany	21:1-11	11:1-11	19:28-44	12:12-19
173	A Hypocritical Fig Tree	Bethany to Jerusalem	21:18-19	11:12-14		
174	Jesus Cleanses the Temple a Second Time	Jerusalem	21:12-17	11:15-19	19:45-48	
175	Jesus Again Talks About His Death	Jerusalem				12:20-36
176	Most Jews Refused to Accept Jesus as the Messiah	Jerusalem				12:37-43
177	People Will Be Condemned by Their Rejecting Jesus' Teaching	Jerusalem				12:44-50
178	The Relationship Between Faith and the Release of God's Power	Bethany to Jerusalem	21:20-22	11:20-26		
179	Jesus' Authority Is Questioned	Jerusalem	21:23-27	11:27-33	20:1-8	
180	A Parable About the Response of Two Sons to Their Father	Jerusalem	21:28-32			
181	Parable About the Evil Tenants	Jerusalem	21:33-46	12:1-12	20:9-19	
182	Parable of the Great Banquet in Heaven	Jerusalem	22:1-14			
183	The Question About Paying Taxes to Rome	Jerusalem	22:15-22	12:13-17	20:20-26	
184	The Question About Life After Death	Jerusalem	22:23-33	12:18-27	20:27-40	
185	God's Most Important Command	Jerusalem	22:34-40	12:28-34		
186	A Question About the Messiah	Jerusalem	22:41-46	12:35-37	20:41-44	
187	The Hypocrisy of the Religious Leaders	Jerusalem	23:1-28, 37-39	12:38-40	20:45-47	
188	Sacrificial Giving	Jerusalem		12:41-44	21:1-4	
189	Jesus Predicts the Destruction of the Temple	Mount Olivet	24:1-2	13:1-2	21:5-6	
190	Signs of Jesus' Returning	Mount Olivet	24:3-14	13:3-13	21:7-19	
191	Jesus Predicts the Destruction of Jerusalem	Mount Olivet			21:20-24	
192	Jesus Predicts the Great Tribulation	Mount Olivet	24:15-28	13:14-23	17:23-24	
193	The Coming of the Son of Man	Mount Olivet	24:29-31	13:24-26	21:25-28	
194	Learn to Observe the Signs	Mount Olivet	24:32-35	13:27-31	21:29-33	
195	Always Be Ready for Jesus' Return	Mount Olivet	24:36-51	13:32-37	17:22, 25-37, 21:34-38	
196	Parable of the Ten Young Bridesmaids	Mount Olivet	25:1-13			
197	Parable of the Talents	Mount Olivet	25:14-30			
198	Jesus Judges the Righteous and the Cursed	Mount Olivet	25:31-46			
199	Make Peace with God Before It's Too Late	Mount Olivet			12:57-59	
200	The Plot to Arrest Jesus	Jerusalem	26:1-5	14:1-2	22:1-2	
201	Mary Anoints Jesus	Bethany	26:6-13	14:3-9		12:2-8
202	Judas Agrees to Betray Jesus	Jerusalem	26:14-16	14:10-11	22:3-6	
203	Jesus Prepares to Eat the Passover	Jerusalem	26:17-19	14:12-16	22:7-13	
204	Jesus Models the Role of a Servant Leader, the Start of Passover	Upper room	26:20	14:17	22:14-16	13:1-17
205	How to Be Among the Greatest in God's Kingdom	Upper room			22:24-30	
206	Jesus Predicts His Betrayal	Upper room	26:21-25	14:18-21	22:21-23	13:18-30
207	Jesus Establishes the Lord's Supper	Upper room	26:26-29	14:22-25	22:17-20	
208	Jesus Predicts Peter's Denial	Upper room	26:31-35	14:27-31	22:31-34	13:31-38
209	Jesus Warns That Difficult Times Are Coming	Upper room			22:35-38	
210	Jesus Is the Only Way to the Father	Upper room				14:1-14
211	Jesus Promises the Holy Spirit	Upper room				14:15-31
212	We Relate to Jesus like Branches to a Vine	Upper room				15:1-17

g#	Event	Probable Location	MT	MK	LK	JN
213	Those Who Reject Jesus Will Also Hate His Followers	Upper room				15:18–16:4
214	Jesus Talks About Leaving them	Upper room				16:5-33
215	Jesus Prays for His Followers	Upper room				17:1-26
216	In Gethsemane	Mount Olivet	26:30, 36-46	14:26, 32-42	22:39-46	18:1
217	Jesus Is Arrested	Gethsemane	26:47-56	14:43-52	22:47-53	18:2-12
218	Jesus Is Questioned by Annas	Jerusalem				18:12-14, 19-24
219	Jesus Before the Sanhedrin	Jerusalem	26:57, 59-68	14:53, 55-65	22:54, 63-65	
220	Peter Denies Knowing Jesus	Jerusalem	26:58, 69-75	14:54, 66-72	22:54-62	18:15-18, 25-27
221	Jesus Is Condemned by the Sanhedrin & Handed Over to Roman Authority for Execution	Jerusalem	27:1-2	15:1	22:66-71	
222	Judas Commits Suicide	Jerusalem	27:3-10			
223	First Appearance Before Pilate	Jerusalem	27:11-14	15:1-5	23:1-7	18:28-38
224	Jesus Before Herod	Jerusalem			23:6-12	
225	Jesus Is Sentenced to Die	Jerusalem	27:15-31	15:6-19	23:13-25	18:39–19:16
226	The Crucifixion	Jerusalem to Golgotha	27:32-44	15:20-32	23:26-43	19:17-27
227	Jesus' Death	Golgotha	27:45-50	15:33-37	23:44-46	19:28-30
228	Events at Jesus' Death	Jerusalem	27:51-56	15:38-41	23:47-49	
229	Jesus' Burial	outside Jerusalem	27:57-60	15:42-46	23:50-54	19:31-42
230	Jesus' Tomb Is Sealed	outside Jerusalem	27:61-66	15:47	23:55-56	
231	God Makes Jesus Alive Again	outside Jerusalem	28:1-10	16:1-8	24:1-12	20:1-10
232	Jesus Appears to Mary from Magdala	outside Jerusalem		16:9-11		20:11-18
233	The Guards Report to the Chief Priests	Jerusalem	28:11-15			
234	Jesus Appears on the Road to Emmaus	road to Emmaus		16:12-13	24:13-35	
235	Jesus Appears to Ten Apostles Without Thomas	Jerusalem		16:14	24:36-43	20:19-23
236	Thomas' Response to the Resurrection	Jerusalem				20:24-29
237	Jesus Appears to His Followers at Lake Galilee	Galilee				21:1-23
238	Jesus Appears to Others [1 Corinthians 15:6]					
239	Jesus' Last Instructions to His Followers	Mount Olivet	28:16-20	16:15-18	24:44-49	
240	Jesus Ascends to Heaven [Acts 1:4-11]	Mount Olivet		16:19 20	24:50-53	
241	The Record of Jesus' Ministry Is Far from Complete					20:30-31, 21:25

Gospel Harmony

The Life and Teachings of Jesus the Messiah

1. Jesus is the Creator

Before God created anything, the "Word of God" existed as a person. This person—the Word or Expression of God—has always existed in unity of essence with God the Father, and so is himself also God. Since he was already with God when time was created, he is not a created being. In fact, it was the Word of God who created all that was created—including everything that lives. Eternal self-existing life is part of his essence and he is the source of all life for every living thing. He is also the person who reveals eternal truths about God and the way to obtain eternal life. So he is a spiritual "Light" to those who live in the darkness of sin—under the threat of eternal death—and the demonic powers of darkness have never overcome this Light.

2. Genealogy of the Messiah

Adam

Cain Abel **Seth**

Enosh

Kenan *(Cainen)*

Mahalalel *(or Mahalaleel)*

Jared

Enoch

Methuselah

Lamech

Noah *- Flood*

Shem *Ham Japheth*

Arphaxad

Cainan

Shelah

Eber

Peleg

Reu

Serug

Nahor

Terah

Abram *(God changed his name to Abraham) approx. 2000 BC*

Ishmael **Isaac**

Esau Jacob *(God changed his name to Israel)*

Reuben Simeon Levi **Judah** *Dan Naphtali Gad Asher Issachar Zebulun Joseph Benjamin*

Perez

Hezron

Ram *(or Aram)*

(Admin)

Amminadab

Nahshon

Salmon *(or Sala)*

Boaz

Obed
Jesse
King David *(7th son of Jesse) - approx. 1000 BC*

Matthew's Account:	**Luke's Account:**
(Royal line of Yosef)	*(Miriam's line)*
King Solomon *(son of King David)*	Nathan *(son of King David)*
King Rehoboam	Mattatha
King Abijah	Menna
King Asa	Melea
King Jehoshaphat	Eliakim
King Jehoram (or Joram)	Jonam
*	Joseph
*	Judah
*	Simeon
King Uzziah (or Azariah)	Levi
King Jotham	Matthat
King Ahaz	Jorim
King Hezekiah	Eliezer
King Manasseh	Joshua
King Amon	Er
King Josiah	Elmadam
*	Cosam
King Jeconiah *(or Jehoiachin or Coniah)*	Addi
Shealtiel	Melki
	Neri
Zerubbabel	Shealtiel
	Zerubbabel
Abiud	Rhesa
	Joanan
Eliakim	Joda
	Josech
Azor	Semein
	Mattathias
Zadok	Maath
	Naggai
Akim	Esli
	Nahum
Eliud	Amos
	Mattathias
Eleazar	Joseph
	Jannai
Matthan	Melki
	Levi
Jacob	Matthat
	Heli
Yosef - *(married Miriam)*	(Yosef) - Miriam

Jesus the Messiah

❖ *Luke's genealogy has 42 generations after David—spanning 1,000 years—which is an average of 23.8 years per generation. This is likely a complete genealogy from Nathan— a son of David—to Miriam. Miriam would not be mentioned since women were not generally included in genealogies in Jewish culture. ¶ Matthew's genealogy is clearly shortened.*

There are 4 Kings listed in the Hebrew Scriptures that are left out by Matthew (their places indicated by * in the list). Matthew's genealogy shows the royal line of descent from Solomon—the son of David who inherited the crown—to Yosef. Even though Yosef was not Jesus' biological father, he was his legal father. So this shows Jesus' legal right to reign as king over Israel as a legal descendant of King David within the royal line. ➤

3. An Angel Foretells the Birth and Significance of John the Baptizer
(~7 BC)

When Herod the Great was king over the Roman province of Judea (in Israel), there lived a Jewish priest named Zechariah who was a member of Abijah's division of priests. His wife Elizabeth—being the daughter of a priest—was also a descendant of Aaron. God considered them to be righteous because they conscientiously followed all the requirements of Yahweh's Torah teachings. But Elizabeth was barren so they were childless, and they were also both quite elderly by the time of this story.

During one of the weeks that Zechariah was on duty in the Temple, he was chosen by lot for the honor of burning incense on the altar in the Temple's "Holy Place." While he was doing this, people were gathered outside in the Temple courtyard praying.

Suddenly, an angel appeared to Zechariah, standing to the right of the incense altar. When Zechariah saw him, he was startled and frightened. But the angel said, "Don't be afraid, Zechariah! God has heard your prayer that he send the Messiah soon—and he is answering it. As part of his plan, your wife will have a son whom you must name John. Many will rejoice with you because of his birth, for this child is important in Yahweh's plan. You must instruct him to never drink wine or other alcoholic beverages, and he will be filled with the Holy Spirit even before he is born. When he is grown, his preaching will convince many Israelites to turn away from their sins and be reconciled to Yahweh—their God. John will preach with the power of the Holy Spirit as the prophet Elijah did long ago. Then, people will see Yahweh himself. ❖ *This refers to Jesus.* ➤ John will

reconcile children with their fathers and lead those who have been rebelling against God to repent and live righteously. He will prepare the Jewish people—who are chosen by God—to recognize and receive the Messiah when he comes."

Zechariah skeptically replied, "I don't see how that's possible since I'm old and my wife is well past her childbearing years."

The angel replied, "My name is Gabriel, and I've come from the very presence of God who sent me to bring you this good news. But since you don't believe it, as a sign that what I've said is true, you will be deaf and unable to speak from now until it happens. For God will bring it about in his perfect timing."

Meanwhile, the people were waiting for Zechariah in the Temple courtyard, wondering why he was taking so long in the sanctuary. When he finally came out, he was unable to speak. But they understood that he had seen a vision while burning the incense because he communicated this with gestures. His inability to speak continued, and when his week of service at the Temple was finished, he returned to his hometown in the hill country of Judea.

Sometime after this, his wife Elizabeth became pregnant. But for five months, she stayed secluded so people wouldn't laugh at her if she said she was pregnant. When she finally did go out, she said, "Look what the Lord has done! He has enabled me to become pregnant! He has blessed me and removed the shame people assigned to me because I've been childless!" ❖ *The Jews of that time commonly—and inaccurately—believed the inability to have children was punishment from God for some secret sin.* ➤

4. The Angel Gabriel Appears to Miriam
(~7–6 BC)

During the sixth month of Elizabeth's pregnancy, God sent an angel named Gabriel to the village of Nazareth in Galilee Province. He took a message to a virgin named Miriam who was engaged to a man named Yosef—a descendant of King David. The angel appeared to her and said, "Greetings, Miriam! Yahweh is with you and has chosen you to receive a special honor."

Miriam was flustered by the angel's words and wondered what this appearance might mean. So the angel reassured her, "Don't be frightened, because God has chosen to greatly favor you. Listen carefully! You will become pregnant and have a son. When he is born, you must name him "Jesus." He will be a great man and will also be God's Son. Yahweh will establish him as the rightful king and heir of his ancestor David. He will reign over all of Israel forever, and his Kingdom will never come to an end."

Miriam replied, "I'm not married and I'm still a virgin. So how will this happen?"

The angel answered, "The Holy Spirit will come on you and God's power will cover you to make you pregnant. Therefore, the baby will be holy and God's Son. As a sign that what I say is true, your relative Elizabeth is now six months pregnant—even though she is elderly and has been barren all her life. For nothing is impossible for God and everything I've told you will happen."

Miriam replied, "I am the Lord's willing servant and I submit to his will as you've revealed it." Then the angel left.

5. Miriam Visits Elizabeth
(~ 6 BC)

Soon afterward, Miriam got ready and hurried to the village in the hill country of Judea where Elizabeth lived. When she arrived, she entered Zechariah's house and greeted Elizabeth. When Elizabeth heard Miriam's greeting, the baby in her womb kicked hard because the Holy Spirit within the baby recognized the presence of the Messiah in Miriam. Then, Elizabeth too was filled with the Holy Spirit who moved her to prophetically exclaim, "God has blessed you more than any other woman in the world! His blessing will also be upon your son! I'm amazed that the mother of my Lord should come to visit someone as unimportant as me! The moment I heard you speak, the baby in my womb jumped for joy. The Lord has greatly blessed you because you believed what his angel told you."

6. Miriam's Song of Praise

Then Miriam said, "I praise the Lord for his greatness, and in my spirit, I rejoice that he is my Savior. For he has shown me great kindness—I who am no more than a servant. From now till the end of time, people will know that I've been blessed because Almighty God has done this wonderful thing for me. He is holy! He has compassion on those in every generation who fear and worship him! He has demonstrated his power, scattering the proud and haughty. He overthrows evil rulers and exalts those who humble themselves before him. He satisfies the hungry and needy with all that they need, but strips the wicked of their wealth. He has come to help his chosen people—the Israelites—fulfilling his promise to our ancestors that he would demonstrate his mercy to Abraham and all his descendants forever."

Miriam stayed with Elizabeth about three months until John was born, and then returned to Nazareth.

7. The Birth of John the Baptizer

Now Elizabeth's due date arrived and her son was born. Her neighbors and relatives heard how Yahweh had finally blessed her with a child and they all celebrated with her.

When the baby was a week old, their relatives and friends came for the circumcision ceremony required by the Teachings of Moses to mark him as belonging to God. They intended to name him "Zechariah" after his father, but his mother said, "No. His name will be John."

They protested, "But you don't have any relatives named John!" So they made gestures asking Zechariah what he wanted the boy's name to be.

Zechariah motioned for something to write with and wrote, "His name is John"—surprising everyone. As soon as he wrote this, he was able to speak and hear again and began to praise and thank God. A sense of awe and fear came upon all the neighbors, and news of these events spread throughout the hill country of Judea. Everyone who heard about it wondered, "What will this child become?" For it was evident that Yahweh's favor, direction, and power was with him.

8. Zechariah's Prophecy

Then, Zechariah was filled with the Holy Spirit and began to prophesy about the Messiah and his son John. He said, "We must praise the Lord God of Israel! For he is coming to set his people free from the power of their enemies. He is raising up a mighty Savior among the descendants of his exalted servant King David. God promised long ago through his holy prophets that he would save us from the power of our enemies who hate us. He did this to demonstrate his compassion to our ancestors—just as he promised in his Holy Covenant. He made an oath to our ancestor Abraham that we—his descendants—would be rescued from the power of our enemies so that we would be able to worship and serve him without fear of persecution, and so we might live right-eous and holy lives in God's presence all the days of our lives."

Then Zechariah prophesied about the in-fant John, "My son, you will be God's prophet and will go ahead of the Lord God, telling people that they must prepare them-selves for his coming. You will tell his people that they can be saved from his judgment through their sins being forgiven—because our God is tender and compassionate. He is sending the Messiah to us who will be like a sunrise from Heaven dispelling the spiritual darkness. The Messiah comes to shine on those who are living in the darkness of their sin—under the threat of eternal death. He will reveal the way to be saved and how to live in peace with God."

So the child, John, grew spiritually strong; and when he became a man, he went to live in the wilderness areas of Judea until the day he appeared in public as a prophet— about 30 years after his birth.

9. An Angel Appears to Yosef

These are the circumstances surrounding the birth of Jesus the Messiah: Miriam—who later bore him—was betrothed to Yosef. But before they were married, and when they had not yet had sexual relations, Miriam became pregnant by the power of the Holy Spirit. Yosef always tried to do what was right, so he mercifully decided to divorce her quietly—rather than shame her with a public accusation of immorality. But after he had decided to do this, he had a dream in which an angel appeared and told him, "Yosef, descendant of King David, don't hesitate to take Miriam into your home as your wife. She has done nothing wrong. The child she carries was miraculously conceived by the Holy Spirit—not by any man. She will have a son and you are to name him "Jesus" ❖ *His name in Aramaic is "Yeshua"—which means "Yahweh saves"* ➤ because he will save his people from the penalty of their sins."

It happened this way so the Lord's prophecy would be fulfilled: "A virgin will become pregnant and have a son who will be 'Immanuel' "—which means "God with us." When Yosef woke up, he realized this was not a mere dream, but a command from God. So when the period of their betrothal was finished, they had the wedding party and he took Miriam to his home as his wife, obeying the angel's directions. But he had no sexual relations with her until after her first child—a son—was born.

10. The Birth of Jesus
(~ 6–5 BC)

Around the time that John was born, the Roman Emperor—Caesar Augustus— decreed that everyone in the empire was to be registered in a census for tax purposes. This was the first such census ordered by Rome and it happened while Quirinius was governor of the Roman province of Syria. Every man had to go to his ancestral hometown in order register.

So Yosef set out from his home in Nazareth in Galilee and traveled south to Bethlehem in Judea—which was known as "David's town" because it had been King David's home. Yosef was a direct descendant of David, and he took Miriam with him to be registered because she was his legal wife and was pregnant. While they were in Bethlehem, her due date arrived and her first child—a son—was born. They wrapped him in strips of cloth, but his cradle was only a feeding trough for animals in a stable behind a relative's house. They stayed there since there was no space in the guest room.

11. Angels Announce the Messiah's Birth

That same night, there were shepherds looking after their sheep in the fields outside Bethlehem. Suddenly, they were terrified by the appearance of an angel and the brilliant light of Yahweh's glory shining all around him. But the angel said, "Don't be afraid! I've come to bring you wonderful news that will cause all Israelites to rejoice. Today, a Savior was born in David's town. This baby is the long-promised Messiah who is also Yahweh himself. This is how you can recognize him and be sure that I'm telling the truth. You will find the baby wrapped in strips of cloth, lying in an animals' feeding trough."

Then suddenly, a huge number of angels appeared with the first one and they all praised God, saying, "All honor and glory belong to God who lives in the highest Heaven! Let there be shalom here on earth among all those whom God chooses to favor!" ❖ *Shalom means: peace, calmness, success, comfort, contentment, safety, health, wholeness, prosperity, integrity, well-being, and good relationships with God and people.* ➤

Then the angels left, returning to Heaven. The shepherds said to each other, "Let's go to Bethlehem right away to find this newborn Messiah that the Lord has told us about through his angel."

So they went as quickly as they could and found Miriam and Yosef with the baby—which was lying in a feeding trough just as the angel had described it. When the shepherds saw the baby, they told Yosef and Miriam and others in Bethlehem what the angel had said about him. Everyone who heard their story was amazed by it. Later, Miriam often recalled their story and her own angelic encounter and thought about them. The shepherds returned to their sheep, praising God because of all the things they had heard from the angel and had confirmed with their own eyes.

12. The Baby Messiah Is Named

When the baby was a week old, it was time for him to be circumcised according to the Torah's requirement, thus marking him as an heir of God's promise to Abraham. At that time, they named him "Jesus"—which means "Yahweh saves"—following the instructions the angel gave Miriam before he was conceived.

13. Baby Jesus Is Dedicated in the Temple

Forty days after Jesus' birth, it was time for Miriam to undergo the ceremony for "ritual purification after childbirth" following the requirements in the Teachings of Moses. So they took the infant to the Temple in Jerusalem to dedicate him to Yahweh's service at the same time. In doing this, they were obeying the Torah command that says, "Every family's first child—if it is a male—must be dedicated to Yahweh's service." They also offered the sacrifice for ritual purification after childbirth required by the command that says, "If a woman can't afford a lamb, she may bring two doves or two pigeons—one for a burnt offering and one for a sin offering."

At that time, an old man named Simeon lived in Jerusalem. He was righteous in God's sight and very devout. He was waiting expectantly for the coming of the Messiah to save the Israelites, because the Holy Spirit was on him and had told him that he would live to see Yahweh's Messiah with his own eyes. Now, the same day that Miriam and Yosef brought Jesus to the Temple to pay for his redemption, the Holy Spirit prompted Simeon to go there too. When Simeon saw the baby, he took him in his arms and praised God, saying, "Lord, you may now allow your humble servant to die. I'm content because you've fulfilled your promise to me. I've finally seen with my own eyes the promised Savior you've sent, whom you will reveal to all the people groups in this world. He's a light that will show your way of salvation to the Gentiles. ❖ *A Gentile is a non-Jew.* ➤ He will also bring honor to your chosen people—the descendants of Israel."

Jesus' parents were astonished at Simeon's prayer. Then, he prayed that God would bless them, and prophesied to Miriam, "This child has been chosen by God. Because of his life, many Israelites will come under God's judgment and many others will be saved. He will be a sign from God that many will oppose and reject. What people really believe about him will be seen in their actions. And what some will do to him will bring you grief as painful as a sword piercing your heart."

There was also an old woman there—a prophetess named Anna. Her father was Phanuel of the Israelite tribe of Asher. She had been married for seven years when she was young, but had now been a widow for 84 years. She was almost always in the Temple worshipping with fasting and prayer, both night and day. While Simeon was there with Yosef and Miriam, Anna came up to them and thanked God for sending his Messiah. Later, she continued to speak about the infant Jesus to anyone who was still waiting for God's Messiah to come to save the people of Jerusalem and all of Israel.

14. God Reveals the Messiah to Gentiles

Some months after Jesus was born in Bethlehem in Judea Province—where King Herod the Great reigned—astrological scholars from the east arrived in Jerusalem and asked the local authorities, "Where is the child who has recently been born to be King of the Jews? We saw the new star that proclaims his birth rise in the east—and so have come to worship him."

When Herod heard about this, he was upset; and everyone in Jerusalem feared he might go on a killing rampage. Herod summoned all the chief priests and Scripture teachers and asked them where—according to prophecy—the Messiah was to be born.

They told him, "In Bethlehem of Judea Province. For the prophet Micah wrote this: 'You, Bethlehem of Judah, even though you are a small village, the leaders of Judah consider you important because it is from you that a ruler will come who will be the spiritual shepherd for my people Israel.'"

So Herod summoned the astrologers to a secret audience and found out from them when the star had first appeared. Then he sent them to Bethlehem and said, "Go find the young child and come back to tell me where he is so I too can go and worship him."

After their audience with the king, they started on their way to Bethlehem. Then the star—which they had first seen in the east—appeared again moving before them. When they saw it, they joyfully exulted and followed it until it stopped over the house where the child was living. When they entered the house, they saw the child with his mother Miriam and bowed down to worship him. Then, they brought out the treasures they had brought with them and gave the child kingly gifts of gold, frankincense, and myrrh.

Afterward, the astrologers started on the trip back to their own country, but they didn't go through Jerusalem for God warned them in a dream that they shouldn't return to Herod.

15. Yosef and His Family Flee to Egypt

After these men had left, an angel appeared to Yosef in a dream. He told him, "Get up immediately! Take the child and his mother and flee to Egypt. Stay there until I tell you to return. For Herod wants to find the child to kill him."

So Yosef immediately got up and, while it was still night, left for Egypt with Miriam and the child. They stayed in Egypt until Herod died. This fulfilled the prophecy that Yahweh gave through the prophet Hosea, "I called my Son to come out of Egypt."

16. The Slaughter in Bethlehem

When Herod realized that the astrologers had tricked him and were not returning, he was furious. Remembering the time they had said the star had first appeared, he ordered his soldiers to kill all the baby boys that were two years of age and younger in Bethlehem and the surrounding area.

This fulfilled Jeremiah's prophecy that says, "The sound of funeral songs and wailing and mourning is heard in the village of Ramah. It's Rachel crying for her children.

She refuses to be comforted because they are no longer there."

17. Yosef and His Family Return from Egypt
(4 BC)

❖ *We know from historical sources that Herod the Great died in the Spring of 4 BC. So we also know that a mistake was made in calculating the year of Jesus' birth. We don't know exactly when he was born, but it was probably about 6-5 BC.* ➤

A short time later, Herod died, and an angel appeared to Yosef in a dream telling him, "Get up and take the child and his mother back to Israel because the people who wanted to kill him are dead." So Yosef did as the angel said and returned to Israel with his family.

But when he heard that Herod's son, Archelaus, had become king over Judea after his father, he was afraid to settle there. After being warned with further instructions in another dream, he took them to Galilee Province. There, they settled in the village of Nazareth. This happened so what the prophets said about the Messiah would be fulfilled, "He will be called a Nazarene." There, the boy grew up and became strong. He became very wise and was greatly blessed by God.

18. The Boy Jesus in the Temple
(AD 7)

It was the custom of Jesus' parents to travel together to Jerusalem every year to observe the Passover Festival. When Jesus was twelve years old, he was old enough to go with them so the three of them made the pilgrimage to Jerusalem to observe it. Now, when the eight days of the back-to-back festivals of Passover and Unleavened Bread were over, his parents set out on the journey back to their home in Nazareth. But young Jesus stayed behind in Jerusalem without telling his parents. They were traveling with others from their area and assumed that he was somewhere among the group of travelers. So they walked an entire day before starting to search for him among their relatives and acquaintances in the group. When they didn't find him, they returned to Jerusalem spending the entire next day searching for him on the way. On the following day, they found him in the Temple sitting with Scripture teachers. He was listening to their teaching and asking and answering questions. All who heard the answers he gave to the teachers' questions were amazed at his understanding. When his parents saw him there, they were astonished. His mother said, "My son, why did you do this to us? Your father and I have been searching and worrying about you!"

Jesus answered, "Why didn't you know where I'd be? Didn't you know that I had to be involved in my Father's affairs?" But they didn't understand what he was talking about.

Then, he went back with them to their home in Nazareth and was always obedient. But his mother remembered all the unusual things connected with his birth and childhood and often thought about them. As the years passed, Jesus grew, continued to increase in wisdom, and gained favor with God and the people who knew him.

19. John the Baptizer Prepares God's People to Receive the Messiah
(AD 26–28)

After Jesus was an adult, in the 15th year of the reign of the Roman Emperor Tiberius Caesar, Pontius Pilate was the Roman governor over Judea, Herod Antipas—son of Herod the Great—ruled the Roman province of Galilee, Antipas' brother—Herod Philip—ruled the Roman provinces of Iturea and Trachonitis northeast of Galilee, and Lysanias ruled the province of Abilene northwest of Damascus. Caiaphas was High Priest, although he effectively shared his authority with his father-in-law Annas. ❖ *Annas had been High Priest but was forced out of office by Roman authority. According to the Teachings of Moses, a High Priest held his position for life; so in the eyes of the Jews, Annas was still the legitimate High Priest.* ➤

It was at this time that God's word of commission came to Zechariah's son John—while he was living in the wilderness just north of the Dead Sea—to become a prophet to the Jews—who were chosen by God as his own special people. In obedience to God's command, John preached all around the wilderness area near the Jordan river.

His mission was to tell what God had shown him about the divine Light whom God was sending into this world in the person of the Messiah. So as a result of his testimony, many would be open to listening to and trusting the Light when he was introduced to them. John wasn't the Light—as some thought. But he did come to tell people what God wanted them to know about the Light—who was yet to be introduced.

Now, the genuine Light of God came into this world where all humanity was in rebellion against their creator. He came to reveal the truth about spiritual realities to all who were willing to listen. He came and lived in this sinful world as a man, but those in rebellion against God didn't recognize him as their creator. He was born among God's chosen people—the Jews—but most of them rejected him and his message. Yet to those who believed his claims and put their confidence in him, he gave the right and ability to enter into a new relationship with God as his children. They were spiritually born into this new relationship by God's power—not because they had a particular human ancestry and not as a result of human-initiated decision or desire.

That person—who is the Word (or Expression) of God and an eternal spirit—became flesh and blood by being born as a human being, and lived among us for a time. We—his apostles—have seen his divine glory which is uniquely his as the one and only eternally existing Son of God. He came to us from God the Father and his glory—reflected in his character—is full of truth and willingness to freely offer undeserved divine favor and power. All of us who believe in him have received a never-ending flow of undeserved blessings from the fullness of the divine favor, power, and truth that he freely offers. Through Moses, God offered undeserved favor and truth to the nation of Israel in his holy Torah teachings—which enabled them to have a relationship with him. But a superior expression of God's undeserved favor and truth is offered to all humanity through Jesus the

Messiah. No human living in this world has ever seen God as is really is. But the only Son of God—whose eternal divine nature comes from his eternal divine Father, and who has the most intimate possible relationship with God the Father—is the one who has revealed to us what the Father is like.

John's main message was, "Turn away from sinning and start obeying God if you want to be part of his Kingdom. For he is starting to establish his rule in a new way among his people in this world." John exhorted people to publicly confess their sins and then be immersed in water (baptized) as a sign of their decision to turn away from their sinful way of life—and God would forgive them.

Like the prophet Elijah hundreds of years earlier had done, John wore a leather belt and coarse clothing made from woven camel hair. He lived in the wilderness as a poor ascetic, eating mainly locusts and wild honey. Many people came out to the wilderness to hear him preach and to be baptized. They came from Jerusalem and everywhere else in Judea Province, and also from the areas on both sides of the Jordan River. In response to his message, many publicly confessed their sins, and then John baptized them in the Jordan River.

The crowds asked him, "What should we do to show that we've repented?"

He answered, "Live unselfishly like this—whoever has two coats must share with someone who has none. And whoever has food must share it too."

Some tax collectors ❖ *the very dregs of Jewish society* ➤ also came to be baptized. They asked, "Rabbi, what should we do to show our repentance?"

John answered, "Don't steal by collecting more than your Roman masters require."

Some Jewish soldiers also asked, "And what about us? What should we do?"

John answered, "Don't use your authority to threaten people with violence or false accusations in order to extort money. Just be content with your legitimate pay."

But when John noticed many Pharisees and Sadducees coming to be baptized, he lashed out at them, "You hypocritical sons of vipers! ❖ *He was saying that they pretended to be good, but were, in fact, evil.* ➤ I find it hard to believe you are finally admitting that *you*—like everyone else—need to repent and turn from your sins in order to escape God's righteous wrath and judgment! Well, don't think that getting baptized without genuinely repenting will do you any good at all! True repentance must be clearly demonstrated in the way you live. Don't deceive yourselves by thinking, 'We are saved because Abraham is our ancestor, so we are automatically God's favored people.' I assure you, God could make righteous descendants for Abraham from these stones. He doesn't need you to fulfill his plans and promises! God's judgment ax is poised at the roots of his trees ❖ *i.e., his people, the Jews* ➤ and every tree that doesn't bear good fruit as a result of true repentance will be cut down and thrown in Hell's fire!" ❖ *Trees are frequently used in the Scriptures as figures to show how God will punish evil people.* ➤

Now, the Jews had been waiting for the Messiah to come and John's preaching raised their expectations. Many wondered if he was the Messiah himself. John realized what people were saying and addressed the issue by declaring, "I only baptize you with water. But the Messiah—whose authority and power far exceed mine—is coming soon. He is so much greater than me that I'm not worthy to be his servant and untie his sandals. He will immerse you in the Holy Spirit who will purify you like fire purifies silver. The Messiah will come with his winnowing pitchfork of judgment, separating the righteous from the wicked—just like people separate wheat from worthless chaff—and he will then clear the threshing floor of this world of all worthless chaff. He will gather the righteous 'wheat' in his barn in Heaven, but the wicked 'chaff' he will burn in Hell's eternal fire."

In many other ways, he warned and exhorted the people as he preached the Good News about God's way of salvation and the coming Messiah.

When John had gained some public notoriety, the Jewish leaders in Jerusalem sent priests and Levites to ask him, "What claims do you make about yourself?" This is what he said about himself. He didn't refuse to answer but openly declared, "I'm not claiming to be the Messiah, if that's what you're thinking." So they asked, "Then, are you the prophet Elijah whom God promised to send back from Heaven before the Messiah comes?" He said, "No, I'm not." They asked again, "Are you the prophet whom Moses said God would send—who would be like Moses?" He answered, "No." Then they said, "We have to take some answer back to our superiors. So what claims do you make about yourself and your ministry?" John replied by quoting the prophet Isaiah, "I am the person in the wilderness who can be heard calling out to God's people, 'Prepare the way for the coming of Yahweh! Every sinful valley in your heart must be filled in and every mountain and hill of pride must be leveled. The crooked ways in your life must be made straight and the rough areas made smooth to receive him with proper humility and submission. Then, all humanity will see the Messiah who is God's way of salvation.' "

Now, some of those in this group who had been sent to John were Pharisees. They asked him, "If you aren't the Messiah or Elijah or the prophet that Moses spoke about, then where do you get your authority to baptize people?" John's reply was, "I only baptize people in water to prepare them to welcome the Messiah. He is living among you right now but you don't know who he is yet. He is the one you should be asking about. He's the one who comes after me, but is my superior. Compared to him, I'm not even worthy to be his slave and untie his sandals." These events happened near a town named Bethany on the eastern bank of the Jordan River where John was baptizing people.

20. Jesus Is Baptized and Empowered by the Holy Spirit
(early AD 27 or 28)

When John was still ministering in this way, Jesus came from the village of Nazareth in Galilee to where John was baptizing in the Jordan River and asked to be baptized. But John objected, "Why are you coming to be baptized as a sign of repentance when you don't need it? I should be asking you to baptize me instead!" Jesus replied, "For the present, I want you to minister to me, for this is what God wants." Then, John agreed to do it.

As soon as he was baptized, Jesus came out of the water. While he was praying, he saw the sky appear to open. He saw God's Holy Spirit fly down in the visible bodily form of a dove and alight on him. Then, God's voice thundered out of Heaven, "You are my only Son and I'm very pleased with you."

21. Satan Tempts Jesus

Now from his baptism onward, Jesus was filled with the Holy Spirit. And the Spirit immediately led him up into the dangerous unpopulated highlands of the Judean wilderness so he would be tempted by Satan. He stayed there 40 days without eating anything, and at the end of that period he was very hungry.

Satan came to tempt him through his hunger, "Since you are God's Son, why not just command these stones to become bread for you?" Jesus replied, "No, I won't. God's Torah says, 'The way for a person to have true life is not by eating ordinary food, but by obeying Yahweh in everything he commands.' "

Then Satan instantly transported him to Jerusalem—the holy city—onto the highest point of the Temple. ❖ *It was about 450 feet to the bottom of the Kidron Valley below.* ➤ He said, "Since you are God's Son, prove it to the people by jumping down from here. The Scriptures say that you won't be harmed because, 'God will command his angels to take care of you and guard you from harm. They will carry you in their arms to prevent even your foot from scraping against a stone.' " Jesus countered, "No, I won't. God's Torah also says, 'Do not deliberately test the patience and promises of Yahweh, your God.' "

Then Satan transported him to the top of a very high mountain and in an instant of time, showed him all the kingdoms of the world in all their beauty and splendor. He said, "I can give you complete authority over all these kingdoms and their glory. For they were all handed over to me by Adam through

his disobedience, and I can give them to whomever I wish. If you will only bow down and submit to me in worship, they will be yours to rule." But Jesus replied, "Get out of here, Satan! God's Teaching says, 'Only worship and serve Yahweh, your God.' "

So after trying every kind of temptation on Jesus without success, Satan left him, waiting for an opportune time to try again.

There were also wild animals there in the wilderness, but angels came to take care of him and provide for his needs.

22. John Proclaims That Jesus Is God's Sacrificial Lamb

The next day, John saw Jesus coming and said to those present, "That man is the one God has chosen to be his sacrificial Lamb. He will die as a substitute for all of humanity to take away our sin and it's penalty. This is the person I was speaking about when I said, 'Someone is coming after me who is greater than I am because he existed long before I did.' At first, I didn't realize he was the Messiah. But God sent me to baptize people in water so they would be prepared for his coming and so I could point him out to the people of Israel. God told me, 'You will see the Holy Spirit come down from Heaven and remain on a man. That man is the one who will baptize people in the Holy Spirit.' I've seen the Spirit come down from Heaven in the form of a dove and remain on this man. Otherwise, I wouldn't have recognized him as the Messiah. So I'm declaring to you that I've seen this happen, and this man is God's Son."

23. Jesus' First Followers

The next day, John was in the same place with two of his followers. When Jesus walked by, John said to them, "Look, that man is the one God has chosen to be his sacrificial Lamb!" When they heard this, they went after Jesus. He turned around and saw them coming so he asked, "What do you want?" They said, "Rabbi (a respectful title given Jewish religious teachers), where are you staying?" He answered, "Come and see for yourselves." So they went with him, saw where he was staying, and spent the rest of the day with him since it was already about four in the afternoon.

One of these men was Andrew—the brother of Simon Peter. The first thing he did after leaving Jesus was to find his brother Simon and tell him, "We've found the Messiah!" (Messiah means "Anointed One.") Then, he took him to meet Jesus. Jesus looked at him and said, "You are Simon, son of John. But I will call you 'Rock.'"

❖ *"Peter"—i.e., "Petros" in Greek—means "rock."* ➤

24. Jesus Calls Philip to Follow Him

The next day, Jesus decided to go into Galilee Province. There, he found Philip and said, "Come be one of my followers!" So he did. Philip was from Bethsaida, the same village as Andrew and Peter (Rock). Then, Philip went and found Nathanael and told him, "We have found the Messiah who Moses wrote about in the Torah, and who is written about in the books of the Prophets. He is Jesus from Nazareth—the son of Yosef." Nathanael replied, "How can anyone of significance come from Nazareth?" Philip said, "Come and find out." When Jesus saw Nathanael approaching, he said, "Now here comes an Israelite who is honest and has pure motives!" Nathanael asked, "How do you know about me?" Jesus replied, "Even before Philip called you to come, I saw you under the fig tree." Nathanael said, "Rabbi, you are God's Son! You are the King of Israel!" Jesus said, "You believe that just because I said that I saw you under the fig tree? You will see greater evidence than this. I solemnly assure all of you that you will have clear revelation from God that he has appointed me to be the Son of Man." ❖ *"Son of Man" was an obscure Messianic title that avoided the political overtones of other Messianic titles used by Jesus' contemporaries. He didn't want to encourage false expectations. It was an allusion to Daniel 7:13-14 and was not understood by the Jews of that time to be a Messianic title at all. But if someone were to recognize the allusion to the description of the "son of man" in Daniel 7:13-14, they would realize that he was claiming these things about himself—he came from Heaven, he was worthy to enter into the very presence of God, God gave him authority, glory, and power over all people and nations, he is worshipped, and his Kingdom will never end.* ➤

25. Jesus' First Miraculous Sign

Two days later, there was a wedding in the village of Cana in Galilee. Jesus' mother was there, and he and his followers were also invited. When the wine ran out—sometime during the seven-day celebration following the wedding—Jesus' mother told him, "They're out of wine." Jesus replied, "What business is that of ours? It isn't my time yet." But his mother told the servants, "Do whatever he tells you to do." There were six stone containers there, used to hold water for Jewish ritual washing. Each one could hold about 20-30 gallons. Jesus told the servants, "Fill the containers with clean water." So they filled them all to the brim. Then he told them, "Now draw some out and take it to the man in charge." When the man in charge tasted it, it had become wine. He didn't know where it came from, but the servants knew. He called the groom and said, "Everyone else serves his best wine first, and when people have been drinking quite awhile, then they bring out the cheap stuff. But you've kept the best wine until now!"

So Jesus' first miraculous sign was performed in the village of Cana in Galilee. This sign revealed his glory to those who had faith to perceive it, and his followers believed that he was the Messiah.

After this, Jesus, his mother, brothers, and his followers made the one-day journey down from the hill country of Cana to Capernaum and stayed there a few days.

26. The Passover at the Start of Jesus' Ministry When He First Cleansed the Temple
(First Passover – Spring AD 27 or 28)

When the time for the Passover Festival approached, Jesus went up to Jerusalem. When he arrived in the outer courtyard of the Temple—which is the court of the Gentiles—he saw people selling cattle, sheep, and doves for sacrifice, and money changers doing business at tables. ❖ *The money changers exchanged foreign coins into those acceptable to be used to pay the Temple tax. These people were all providing needed services, but it was where they were doing it that was inappropriate. One main reason Jesus was upset was that by making the court of the Gentiles a marketplace, they were robbing the Gentiles of a place to worship the one true God—and God had specifically intended the Temple to be a place of prayer for people from every people group.* ➤

So he made a multi-stranded whip of cords and drove them all out of the Temple court with their sheep and cattle. He overturned the money changers' tables, scattering their coins. To those who were selling doves, he said, "Take these birds out of here! Stop making my Father's house into a place of business!" And his followers remembered the Scripture that says, "Zeal for the purity of your house will consume me." Then, the Jewish leaders demanded, "Can you show us a sign from God to prove that you have his authority to do these things in his Temple?" Jesus replied, "Destroy this Temple, and I will raise it up again in three days." They exclaimed incredulously, "It took forty-six years to build this Temple! You're going to rebuild it in three days?" But he was speaking cryptically about the Temple of his body. ❖ *Jesus' and all believers' bodies are temples—i.e., dwelling places of God— through the indwelling Holy Spirit.* ➤ Some three years later—when he was alive again after having died—his followers remembered that he had said this. Then, they believed the things the Scriptures said about the Messiah, and also this statement that he would "raise it up again in three days."

During that Passover Festival in Jerusalem, Jesus performed some miraculous signs—and many who saw them believed that he was the Messiah. But Jesus understood what people are like, so he didn't trust them to continue to believe in him. No one had to tell him about human motivations and ways since he knew what went on inside them.

27. Nicodemus and the New Birth

Now, there was a Pharisee named Nicodemus who was a member of the Sanhedrin. ❖ *The Sanhedrin was the council—headed by the High Priest—which ruled the religious lives of the Jews. Pharisees were a sect of laymen devoted to the strict keeping of the Scriptures and Jewish traditions.* ➤ Coming to see Jesus secretly one night, he said, "Rabbi, we know that God has sent you to teach us since no one can do miraculous signs like you do unless God enables him." Going straight to Nicodemus' unrecognized need, Jesus said, "I'm going to tell you a very important fact. No one can be part of God's Kingdom without being born again." Nicodemus said, "How can an old man be born again? He can't enter his mother's womb a second time to be born, can he?" ❖ *Since he was a Jewish elder, used to speaking, teaching, and debating in figures, and he focuses on an "old" man being reborn (whereas it's equally impossible for anyone to be physically reborn, regardless of age), it seems likely that he understood Jesus and was saying that it would be very difficult for an old person, set in his ways, to start all over again on a new spiritual journey.* ➤ Jesus replied, "I'm telling you the way it is. Unless you are born of water and Spirit you can't enter God's Kingdom. The physical gives birth to a physical body, but the Holy Spirit gives birth to a new spirit in a person. You shouldn't be surprised at my saying, 'People must be born again.' You can hear the wind blowing and observe its effects, but where it blows is unpredictable and you can't control it. It's the same with the Holy Spirit. You can observe his effect on those in whom he births new spirits, but you can neither control him nor predict his ways." Nicodemus asked, "How can people be born of the Spirit?" Jesus exclaimed, "You are one of the most respected rabbis in Israel, yet you don't understand these things? I'm telling you the truth. We are only able to talk about and confirm what we've seen and known, and that is what I'm doing. Yet you, and many like you, refuse to accept what John the Baptizer and I say. If you don't believe me about basic truths that happen here on earth—like the new birth—how can you believe me if I tell you about Heaven? No one has ascended into Heaven and returned to tell about it. Only I, the Son of Man, have come from Heaven and can do so. Just as Moses lifted up the bronze snake in the wilderness to save people's lives, in a similar way, I, the Son of Man, must be lifted up on a cross to die so anyone who believes in me can have eternal life.

"Since God loves people despite their sin and rebellion, he sent me—his only Son— into this world to die in their place. So everyone who really believes in me will not perish in Hell, but instead will have eternal life. God didn't send me into this world to condemn people, but to save them through me. God will not condemn those who believe in me. But all who refuse to believe in me remain condemned because they have rejected God's only Son. People are condemned on this basis: I came into this world as God's spiritual Light to enable people to know him. But many people love the darkness of spiritual ignorance because their ways are evil and they don't want to change. Everyone whose way is evil hates me because I am the spiritual Light that reveals God's truth. They avoid his Light because they are afraid that their evil ways will be exposed. But those whose ways are good are attracted to the Light so everyone can see that their good ways have come about by God's power."

28. John's Testimony About Jesus

After this, Jesus and his followers left Jerusalem and went out into the rural areas of Judea where he spent some time with them and had them baptize people. At the same time, John was also baptizing at Aenon near Salim because of the many springs there, and people were constantly coming to him to be baptized. One day, John's followers had an argument with a certain Jew about ritual washing for purification. Afterward, they went to John and said, "Rabbi, you know the man you testified about who was with you when you were baptizing on the other side of the Jordan river? Well, now he's baptizing people too, and it seems like everyone is going to him instead!" John replied, "Everything good that a man has, even success, comes from God. You heard me declare that I'm not the Messiah and have only been sent ahead of him to prepare his way.

"I'm like the groom's best man. I rejoice to hear the groom's voice and when I see the bride go to him, my joy is complete. ❖ *In the Hebrew Scriptures, God refers to his people as his "bride." In the New Testament, those who are saved are the Messiah's bride.* ➤ His prominence must increase and mine must decrease.

"People of this world can only speak authoritatively about the things of this world. But Jesus came from Heaven and is greater than any other human being. He authoritatively tells us about what he has seen and heard in Heaven, yet almost no one believes what he says. But those who do believe him are only acknowledging that God's words are always true, because it was God who sent him, and his message came from God. We can be sure of this because God gave him his Holy Spirit without limit, as can be seen by the healings and miracles he does. God the Father loves his Son, Jesus, and has given him power and authority over everything that exists. Those who really believe in the Son have eternal life. But those who don't obey the Son will not experience eternal life, and they remain under God's sentence of punishment for sin in Hell." ❖ *Note that the opposite of "believing in Jesus" is "not obeying him."* ➤

29. Crossing Cultural & Social Barriers to Evangelize
(The Woman at the Well)

The news went around that Jesus was baptizing more people and had more followers than John the Baptizer, though in fact, it was Jesus' followers who did the actual baptizing. When Jesus learned that the Pharisees had heard this, he and some of his followers left Judea and made the three-day journey to Galilee, passing through Samaria. On the way, they came to the Samaritan town of Sychar around noon. Jesus was tired from the journey and sat down by the famous well that Jacob had dug. This was near the plot of land Jacob had given to his son Joseph more than 1500 years earlier.

His followers went into the village to buy food, so he was alone when a Samaritan woman came to draw water from the well. Jesus asked her, "Would you give me a drink?" ❖ *The well was deep and he had no way of getting water from it for himself.* ➤ Now, Jews normally wouldn't even use the same cup as a Samaritan. ❖ *And a Jewish man normally wouldn't speak to a female stranger.* ➤ So the woman incredulously asked, "Now why does a Jew ask me, a woman and a Samaritan, for water?" Jesus said, "If you knew who I was and what gift God is offering you, you would be asking me for life-giving water and I would give it to you." She replied, "Sir, the well is more than 100 feet deep and you've nothing to draw with. So just where would you get this life-giving water? Do you think you're greater than our ancestor Jacob who dug this well? Do you offer better water than this, which he and his sons and cattle drank?" Jesus answered, "Everyone who drinks water from this well gets thirsty again. But once people drink the water I give, they never thirst again. For the water I give becomes a spring within them, out of which flows life-giving water, giving them eternal life." ❖ *He was speaking of the Holy Spirit who is often referred to in the Scriptures using figurative language about water. But she takes him literally.* ➤ The woman replied, "Sir, then give me this kind of water so I will never be thirsty or need to come all the way here from town to the well."

Jesus told her, "Go get your husband and bring him here." She replied, "I don't have a husband." Jesus said, "You answered truthfully when you said you don't have a husband. You have had five husbands and you aren't married to the man you are now living with. So you've at least told the truth." The woman said, "Sir, it's apparent that you're a prophet. My Samaritan ancestors worshipped here on Mount Gerizim, but you Jews claim Jerusalem is the proper place to worship." Jesus answered her, "You Samaritans don't really know the God you worship. ❖ *The Samaritans only accepted the five books of Moses as Scripture—known as the "Torah" or "Pentateuch." So they lacked the further revelation about God and his will given in the rest of the Hebrew Scriptures.* ➤ We Jews have a much better understanding of the God we submit to in worship because he decided to use the Jews to bring salvation to this world. But the truth is, that in just a short time you Samaritans will no longer worship the Father on this mountain nor even in Jerusalem. The time is coming—and for some it has already started—when true worshipers will submissively worship the Father in spirit and truth. The Father is seeking people who will truly worship him in this way. God is an infinite spiritual being, not confined to one place. So those who would really submit to him in worship him

must worship him by means of the Holy Spirit, and worship him as he really is." The woman said, "I know that God's Anointed One—the Messiah—is coming. When he comes, he will make all these things clear to us." Jesus replied, "I am the Messiah and I'm telling you these things right now."

Right then, his followers returned from town and they were shocked to find him speaking with a woman. But none of them dared ask him what he wanted from her or why he was speaking with her. Then, the woman left her water jar and hurried back to town. She told people there, "Come and see a man who told me everything I've ever done! He might even be the Messiah!" So many of them headed out to the well to see him.

Meanwhile, after the woman left, Jesus' followers were urging him to eat. But he told them, "I have food that you don't know about." ❖ *Physical food is sometimes used as a metaphor for spiritual food.* ➤ So they started asking each other, "Did someone else bring him something to eat?" Jesus explained, "My sustenance comes from doing my Father's will and finishing the work that he has given me. Don't you commonly say just after planting, 'There are four more months until harvest, so there's no urgency to do anything?' But take a good look at the people over there coming this way. I've just today planted, and already they're like a field that's ready for harvesting. Those who are doing God's work of gathering a harvest of souls into eternal life are already earning eternal rewards. So now, those who plant God's word as seed and those who harvest souls can work and rejoice together. The saying, 'One person plants and another harvests,' is true. I've commissioned you to harvest souls where you didn't plant. Others have planted and labored before you, and now you join in their work to finish it and benefit from it."

Merely on the basis of the woman's testimony that, "He told me everything I've ever done," many of the Samaritans in that town believed in Jesus as the Messiah. So when they came to him at the well, they begged him to stay with them, and he ended up staying there two days. During that time, many more of them believed in him because of the things he said. Then, they told the woman, "Now it's no longer only on the basis of your testimony that we believe in him. For we've heard him ourselves and know for sure that he is the Savior of the world."

30. Herod Imprisons John, and Jesus Starts His Public Ministry in Galilee

After those two days in the town of Sychar, Jesus and his followers continued on into Galilee. Unlike the Samaritans—who believed in him without seeing miracles—Jesus knew it was difficult for his fellow Jews to believe that he was the Messiah. He, himself, said that a prophet is generally not honored in his own country. Therefore, when he arrived in Galilee, the people welcomed him mainly because they had been at the Passover Festival in Jerusalem and had seen all the miraculous signs he had done there.

Meanwhile, in addition to exhorting the crowds, John also rebuked the tetrarch Herod Antipas, exhorting him to repent of his adulterous marriage to his brother's wife, Herodias, while his brother still lived, and to repent of other evils that he had done. But Herod refused and compounded his sins by having John arrested.

After Jesus heard that Herod had arrested John, he decided to start his ministry in Galilee. But instead of basing in the small village of Nazareth where he had grown up, he moved 20 miles northeast to the much larger town of Capernaum on the north shore of Lake Galilee, in the area of the lands originally allotted to the Israelite tribes of Zebulun and Naphtali. His moving there fulfilled Isaiah's prophecy about the Messiah that says, "The people living in the lands of Zebulun and Naphtali—that are on the way to the sea, to the west of the Jordan River, which is the region called Galilee where many Gentiles live—are people who live in spiritual darkness. But they will see the Messiah who—like a bright light—will reveal to them the way of salvation. He will shine the light of God's truth on those who live in a land of spiritual shadow and who walk on the road toward eternal death."

From that time on, Jesus was empowered for ministry by the Holy Spirit and began doing miracles. News about him spread throughout the surrounding region. He also began to publicly preach and teach God's message in the synagogues about how to be saved, and was praised by all who heard him. The core of his message was, "Today is your appointed opportunity to turn away from sinful ways, start obeying God, and believe that he will freely accept you into his Kingdom!"

31. Jesus Heals an Official's Son at a Distance

During his time in Galilee, Jesus returned to the village of Cana where he had turned water into wine. While he was there, the son of a royal official in Capernaum was sick. When he heard that Jesus had returned to Galilee Province from Judea Province, he went to him in Cana and begged him to come down to Capernaum to heal his son who was near death. Jesus said, "Unless you people see miraculous signs and wonders you refuse to believe in me." The man pleaded, "Sir, please come quickly before my child dies." Jesus replied, "You can go home. Your son will live." The man believed what Jesus told him and left. On his way home the next day, his servants met him on the road and told him that his son was alive and well. So he asked them when he had begun to get better, and they said, "The fever broke about one o'clock yesterday afternoon." The father knew it was about one o'clock that Jesus had said to him, "Your son will live." As a result of this, he and his whole household came to believe that Jesus was the Messiah.

This was the second miraculous sign that Jesus performed in Galilee after returning from Judea.

32. Jesus is Rejected in Nazareth

Now in the course of his ministry, Jesus came to the village of Nazareth where he had been raised as a child. As was his practice on the Sabbath, ❖ *i.e., Saturday* ➤ he went to the local synagogue. He stood in front to read from the Scriptures and was handed the scroll of the prophet Isaiah which he had requested. He opened it and read from the place where it says, "The Spirit of Yahweh is upon me, for he has anointed me to preach to the poor about the Good News of God's way of salvation. He has sent me to proclaim the way of freedom for all who are bound as slaves to sin, to enable those who are spiritually blind to see God's truth, to free those who are oppressed by the physical and emotional consequences of sin, and to announce that the time has arrived when Yahweh will show undeserved favor to his people and save them from the fate of eternal death."

After reading that, Jesus rolled up the scroll, handed it back to the keeper of the scrolls, and sat down to teach. Everyone had their eyes fixed on him to listen to his commentary. He began by saying, "The prophecy in the Scripture you just heard me read was fulfilled in me today while I was reading it." The people were amazed at his elegant manner of speaking, yet were indignant at what they perceived as his presumption. They said to each other, "Who does he think he is? He's only Yosef's boy! We've known him all his life!"

So Jesus said to them, "I expect you would like to quote me the proverb, 'Doctor, prove your ability by healing yourself!' and also say, 'Demonstrate the kinds of things we've heard you did in Capernaum. If you want us to believe you, do the same kinds of things here where you belong.'

"But instead, I will quote you the saying, 'No prophet is accepted as such in his hometown.'

"So I tell you, in the prophet Elijah's time, there was no rain for three and a half years, resulting in severe famine everywhere in Israel. But even though there were many needy widows in Israel, God didn't send him to any of them. Rather, he was sent to a pagan widow in the Phoenician town of Zarephath—on the Mediterranean coast near the city of Sidon. And again, in the prophet Elisha's time, there were many lepers in Israel but he didn't heal any of them. He only healed Naaman—a pagan from Syria." ❖ *By these examples, Jesus was saying that their unbelief and rejection of him made them unworthy so* *they would be passed over from receiving miraculous help in favor of pagan Gentiles—just as their ancestors had been passed over in the times of Elijah and Elisha because of their unbelief and unfaithfulness.* ➤

When the people heard this, they were furious. They became a mob and drove him outside of town to the edge of a cliff on the hill where the town was built, intending to push him over the edge. But because it wasn't yet his appointed time to die, Jesus calmly turned and walked through the middle of the crowd and went on his way.

33. Jesus Calls Four Fishermen to Follow Him

One day, when Jesus stood on the shore of Lake Galilee, throngs of people were crowding in close to hear him teach God's message. He noticed two empty fishing boats pulled up on the shore and the fishermen who owned them nearby, washing their nets. So Jesus got into the boat belonging to Simon and asked him to put the boat out a little from shore so people could see and hear him more easily. He did so, and Jesus sat down and taught the crowd from the boat.

When he finished teaching, he told Simon, "Move the boat out into deep water and let down your nets to catch some fish."

Simon replied, "Master, we worked hard all night and caught nothing. But since you command it, we will let the nets down." When they did, they caught a huge number of fish. They were so heavy that the nets started to break, so they signaled to their partners in the other boat for help. They came out and together filled the boats with so many fish that both started to sink. When Simon saw this, he recognized that Jesus was a prophet. Prostrating himself before him, he exclaimed, "You should leave me, sir! For I am a sinful man and not worthy to be in your presence!" For he, along with his fishing partners James and John—the sons of Zebedee—and all their other companions were astounded at the huge number of fish they had caught. Then Jesus said to him, "Don't be afraid! From now on, you will be 'catching' people and bringing them to me, instead of catching fish."

And when they had pulled their boats up on shore, Simon, James, and John left their profession behind and became followers of Jesus. ❖ *"Followers" is usually translated "disciples." It means they were followers, students, and apprentices. Jesus had many disciples, not just twelve. Anyone today who believes that Jesus is the Messiah and follows his teachings is his follower and disciple.* ➤

34. Jesus Expels Demons from a Man in the Capernaum Synagogue

They went to the town of Capernaum on the north shore of Lake Galilee, and as soon as the Sabbath arrived, Jesus began to teach in the synagogue there. The people marveled at his teaching because unlike the Scripture teachers—who always quoted other authorities—he spoke from personal authority.

Then, a man came into the synagogue who was defiled with demons. He yelled at Jesus, "Arrrgh! Get out of here Jesus of Nazareth! Just leave us alone! You've come to destroy us! I know who you are! You are God's special Holy One!"

But Jesus commanded, "Be silent and come out of him!" The demons made the man convulse and shout on the floor in front of everyone, and then came out without injuring him. The people were awed and exclaimed, "This is certainly a new kind of authoritative teaching! He simply commands demons, and they obey!" Thus reports about him spread like wildfire throughout the surrounding area of Galilee.

35. Jesus Heals Simon's Mother-In-Law and All Who Are Brought to Him

Afterward, Jesus, James, and John left the synagogue and went with Simon and Andrew to their house for the Sabbath meal. When they arrived, he learned that Simon's mother-in-law had a high fever, and her family asked him to heal her. So he went to where she was lying, stood over her, touched her hand, and rebuked the fever. It left her, and she got right up and began to serve them the meal.

When the Sabbath was over at sunset, everyone in town who was sick with any kind of ailment was brought to him. It seemed like the entire town was gathered outside the doorway to that house. He laid his hands on them and healed every one of them. He also expelled demons from many. They would start to yell, "You are God's Son!" But he rebuked them and didn't allow them to speak—because they knew he was the Messiah, and he didn't want it proclaimed openly. In doing these things, Jesus was fulfilling the prophecy about him written by the prophet Isaiah that says, "He lifted the burden of our sicknesses and carried away our diseases."

36. Jesus Preaches and Heals in Galilee

Long before daylight the next morning, Jesus got up and left the house to find a place outside of Capernaum where he could be alone to pray. Later, when they discovered he was gone, Simon and Jesus' other followers went out searching for him. When they found him, they said, "Everyone is searching for you!" And the people of Capernaum tried to keep him from leaving their village. But he told them, "I have to proclaim the Good News about God's Kingdom in other towns too, since that's what he sent me to do."

So Jesus traveled through every part of Galilee Province, teaching in the synagogues and proclaiming the Good News that God was inviting people who would submit to him into his wonderful Kingdom. Wherever he went, he also healed people from every kind of sickness and disorder. News about his ability to heal spread among the Jewish communities in Syria Province—north of Galilee. Many people were brought to him who were sick with all kinds of diseases, pain, and other disorders, including those who were demonized, epileptics, and those with paralysis. He healed all who were brought to him. Because of this, a large crowd started following him wherever he went. They came from Galilee, from the Gentile Decapolis area southeast of Lake Galilee, from Jerusalem and the rest of Judea Province, and from other areas on the eastern side of the Jordan River.

37. Jesus Wants to Heal

One day, a man with a contagious skin disease came and knelt in front of Jesus and said, "Sir, I know you can heal me if you want to." Jesus felt deep compassion for the man, and despite the prohibition against touching such a person—and the fact that he would become ritually unclean by doing so—Jesus reached out and touched him. He said, "Of course I want to. I command you to be healed!" Instantly, he was visibly cured.

Then Jesus sent him on his way with these instructions, "Don't tell anyone about my healing you. But go immediately to a priest so he can examine you as the Teachings of Moses require. Then make all the required sacrificial offerings so the priest will be able to publicly announce that you have been healed and are ritually clean."

Despite the admonition not to talk about it, he spread the story everywhere. Jesus attracted so many people who wanted to be healed that he couldn't enter a village openly without being mobbed. So he tended to stay out in the unpopulated areas, but people still found out where he was and came to him from everywhere. But even though he had these constant demands placed on him, Jesus frequently made it a priority to slip away by himself into the wilderness to pray.

38. Jesus Heals a Paralyzed Man to Prove He Has Authority to Forgive Sin

Sometime later, Jesus returned to Capernaum, and the news that he was home again spread quickly throughout the area. One day, there were so many people packed into the house where he was teaching that there was no room for more, and there was even a crowd outside gathered around the door to hear him. Then, four men arrived carrying a man who was paralyzed. They were intending to bring him to Jesus for healing. But since the crowd made it impossible to get inside, they went around to the outside steps and carried him up onto the house's flat roof. There, they made an opening in the tiles of the roof and lowered the man on his stretcher right into the center of the house in front of Jesus. At that time, Yahweh's power was with Jesus, enabling him to heal. So when he saw their faith in him, he said to the man, "My son, I declare that your sins are forgiven."

But some Pharisees and Scripture teachers who had come from Jerusalem were there observing Jesus, and thought to themselves, "How dare this man blaspheme God by claiming he forgives sins made against God himself? Only God can forgive sins!"

❖ *To blaspheme means to talk impiously, irreverently, or disrespectfully about God. Blasphemy was considered a serious sin, punishable by death. In this instance, they thought Jesus was presumptuously taking upon himself the authority to speak for God. To do such a thing was disrespectful of God's authority, and hence blasphemous.* ➤

Right away, Jesus was aware in his spirit what they were thinking and asked, "Why are you thinking such evil things about me? Which do you think is less likely that I'm able to do—forgive this man's sins or enable him to stand up and walk? You correctly believe that only God has the power to do either of these things. So I will demonstrate I have power and approval from God to heal, in order that you may know for sure that I, the Son of Man, also have his authority to forgive people's sins." Jesus said to the paralyzed man, "I command you to get up, pick up your stretcher, and go home."

Immediately, the man got up, picked up his stretcher, carried it out in full view of everyone there, and went home praising God. All the people who witnessed this were astonished and also began to praise God for giving such authority to people. They were filled with awe and said, "We've seen an incredible thing today!"

39. Jesus Associates with Disreputable People

After this, Jesus went down to walk along the shore of Lake Galilee. A large crowd followed so he began to teach them. As he was going along, he saw Matthew Levi—the son of Alphaeus—sitting in his tax collector's booth. Jesus went up to him and said, "Come be one of my followers." Matthew—having heard a lot about Jesus—immediately left behind his lucrative job and everything he owned and began to follow him.

Later, Jesus and his close followers dined at Matthew's house with many of his tax collector friends and other disreputable people—for many of them were Jesus' avid followers. When some Scripture teachers—who were also Pharisees—saw the company Jesus kept, they complained indignantly to his close followers, "Why do you and your Rabbi pollute yourselves by eating and drinking with tax collectors and other such sinners!"

But when Jesus heard this, he said, "A doctor doesn't tend to people who are well. It's sick people who need his attention. Go study the Scriptures and try to understand what God meant when he said, 'It's more important to me that you show mercy to others than to offer me sacrifices.' I didn't come to call righteous people to follow me, but to invite those who know they are sinners to repent and change their way of life."

40. Jesus Answers a Question about Fasting

Now it was the practice of John the Baptizer's followers and the Pharisees to fast twice a week. One day, some of them came to Jesus and asked, "Why is it that we and the Pharisees fast, but you don't have your followers do the same?"

To explain that it wasn't appropriate for his followers to fast while he was with them, Jesus replied, "Nobody would think of suggesting that a grooms' close friends fast and mourn while he's with them at his wedding banquet. But the time will come when I'm taken away from them, and then they will fast."

And to explain that the Pharisees' teachings and legalistic fasting couldn't be mixed with his new teachings without ruining both, Jesus gave these illustrations, "No one rips a piece of cloth out of a new garment and uses it as a patch on an old one, since he would needlessly ruin the new one, and the patch wouldn't match the old garment's pattern. And after washing, the new patch would shrink and rip the old garment even more. Also, no one puts new wine into rigid old wineskins since the pressure from the fermenting wine would burst the already-stretched skins. It would ruin them and spill the wine on the ground. New wine must be put into new wineskins, then both the new wine and wineskins are preserved.

"And it's hard for someone who has tasted aged wine to desire un-aged new wine since he will think, 'The old wine is better.' "

❖ *The following events occurred at either the Feast of Shelters in the Fall of AD 27, or at the Second Passover recorded in the Gospels in the Spring of AD 28. We don't know which of these festivals it was.* ➤

41. The Healing at Bethesda

Sometime after these events, Jesus and his followers went up to Jerusalem for one of the Jewish festivals. Now there's a pool in Jerusalem, near the Sheep Gate, which in Aramaic is called "Bethesda." It has five pillared pavilions. In these pavilions, large crowds of sick people used to lie. They included people who were blind, lame, and paralyzed who were waiting for an angel that occasionally came to stir up the water. After that happened, the first person to step into the water was healed. At that time, there was a man there who had been an invalid for years. When Jesus saw him lying there and knew he had been this way for a long time, he asked him, "Do you want to be well?" The man said, "Sir, I don't have anyone here to help me get me into the pool first when the water is stirred. While I'm trying to get in, someone else always gets in ahead of me." Jesus told him, "Stand up! Pick up your sleeping mat and walk!" Immediately, the man was completely healed. He picked up his mat and began to walk normally.

Now, this incident took place on a Sabbath. So when some Jewish leaders saw the man, they said, "Today is the Sabbath and you're not allowed to carry your mat!" He replied, "The man who healed me told me to pick up my mat and walk." So they asked, "Who is this man who told you to carry it?" But he didn't know who Jesus was, and he was unable to point him out because Jesus had slipped away into the crowd.

Later, Jesus saw him in the Temple and said, "You are healthy now, so stop sinning lest something worse happens to you." Then, the man went and told the Jewish leaders that it was Jesus who had healed him. So because Jesus was healing on the Sabbath, the Jewish leaders started persecuting him.

42. Jesus Claims to be Equal with God

But Jesus' reply to their accusation of working on the Sabbath was, "My Father is always working and so must I." The Jewish leaders recognized that Jesus was calling God his Father—thus clearly implying that he was deity and equal with God. So they became even more intent on killing him, since this crime of blasphemy was more serious than breaking the Sabbath rules.

Jesus said, "I will tell you this important truth. As God's Son, I can do nothing on my own initiative. I can only do what I see my Father doing. Whatever the Father does, I must also do. I can do these things because my Father loves me and shows me everything he is doing. And he will show me even greater miraculous works for me to do than those you've seen, such that you will be astonished. For I can give life to anyone I wish—just like my Father brings dead people back to life. And contrary to what you believe, my Father doesn't judge anyone in this world, but has delegated all authority to judge people to me—his Son—so that all will honor me equally with my Father. Those who refuse to honor me are, in fact, refusing to honor my Father who sent me.

"I will tell you an important truth. Those who hear and obey my words which I get from my Father, and believe in my Father who sent me—and therefore believe in me—have eternal life right now and will not be condemned on Judgment Day. ❖ *Judgment Day is when Jesus will judge everyone who has ever lived and assign them their eternal fate.* ➤ They have already crossed over from being spiritually dead and under the sentence of eternal death, into being spiritually alive and possessing eternal life. I want to emphasize this truth. The time has been long in coming and has finally arrived, when many who are spiritually dead will hear and respond to the voice of God's Son and thereby become spiritually alive. For just as my Father is the self-existing source of all life, in my unity with him as his Son, I too am this self-existing source of all life and can give life to others. And since I'm also the Son of Man—having become human—he has given me all authority to pass judgment on humanity. Don't be surprised at these things. The time is coming when all who have died will hear my voice and they will become alive again with new physical bodies. Those who have done what is good will be made alive to live forever. Those who have done evil will be made alive to be condemned.

"I can do nothing on my own authority. I only judge according to what I hear from my Father. So my judgment is fair and just because I'm not following my own will, but my Father's will—just as he sent me to do.

"If my testimony about myself is the only thing backing up my claims, then it's not true. But someone else does testify about me, and I know that his testimony is true. You sent many people to John the Baptizer and he told the truth about me. Now, the testimony that I accept is directly from God—and not from a man. But I remind you of John's testimony so you might believe what he said about me and be saved. John was like a lamp that gave out the prophetic light of God's message—and for a while you all enjoyed his message.

"But I have much more authoritative testimony than John's—which are the words, deeds, and miraculous signs my Father has given me to do. These all demonstrate that God the Father sent me and approves of me and is working through me.

"He has testified to you, revealing the truth about who I am, and he is still testifying about me. But you've never heard him or seen him, and in your hearts you reject his words and message because you refuse to believe me—whom he sent to you.

"You diligently study the Scriptures because you think that by knowing them and legalistically following their commands you will gain eternal life. But these very Scriptures point to me as the source of the life you seek. Yet you refuse to come and learn from me so I can give you eternal life.

"I'm not seeking approval or honor from people, for I only care about what my Father thinks of me. But I know that you really have no love for God at all in your hearts. I've come representing my Father with his authority—as he attests by the miracles he does through me—and you refuse to accept me. Yet if someone else comes having no authority backing him at all, you will accept him as the Messiah. It's no wonder you reject me and will accept those who aren't from God. Because you are clearly more concerned with flattery and praise from people than approval from the only one who counts—God himself.

"On Judgment Day, I won't be the one standing before the Father accusing you of rejecting his Messiah. You've set your hopes on obeying the Teachings of Moses to gain favor with God, rather than by believing in the one he wrote about. But you will be surprised to hear Moses using his Torah teachings to accuse you of rejecting me. For if you really believed what Moses wrote in the Torah, you would believe me—because he wrote about me. But since you don't correctly understand and believe what he wrote about, of course you won't believe me either."

43. Jesus is Master over Sabbath Regulations

One Sabbath, while Jesus and his followers were walking along a path that went through some grain fields, his followers were picking some of the grain, rubbing it in their hands to remove the chaff, and eating it. Some Pharisees who saw them do this accused them, "Your followers are breaking the Teachings of the Torah by working on the Sabbath!"

Jesus counter argued, "Don't tell me you aren't familiar with the example David set in the Scriptures when he and his men were hungry! He entered God's house ❖ *i.e., the Tabernacle* ➤ when Abiathar was high priest, and he and his men ate consecrated bread which only priests are allowed to eat—and God didn't condemn them. Haven't you ever realized that the Torah commands priests who are on duty in the Temple to, in effect, break the Sabbath rules by working on the Sabbath? Yet God considers them innocent of disobeying any command because the Temple regulations supersede the Sabbath command. And there is someone ranking even higher than the Temple here. If you really understood what God meant when he said, 'It's more important to me that you

show mercy to others than to offer me sacrifices,' then you wouldn't condemn my followers for what they've done. They are, in fact, innocent of doing wrong. God made the Sabbath to benefit people. It's not more important than they are, and he certainly didn't intend it to make life more difficult for them. So I, the Son of Man, am Master of the Sabbath and its regulations."

44. Jesus Heals a Man with a Crippled Hand on a Sabbath

Moving on from that place, Jesus went into their synagogue where a man with a crippled hand was present. The Pharisees watched him carefully to see if he might heal him, since they considered this to be work that was forbidden on the Sabbath and they were looking for grounds to accuse him of disobeying the Torah. But Jesus knew what they were thinking and told the man with the crippled hand, "Come and stand here." The man got up and stood with Jesus.

Jesus then said to those present, "I ask you, what do the Teachings in our Torah allow us to do on the Sabbath? Are we allowed to do good works, or should do we allow harm to come through our inaction? Does it allow us to save life, or does it command us to allow life to be destroyed through inaction?" But they remained sullenly silent. Jesus looked around at them and was righteously angry and deeply upset at their self-righteous, uncaring, and even murderous attitudes.

Then Jesus said, "If any of you had a sheep that fell into a deep hole on the Sabbath, no one among you would refuse to help it just because it was the Sabbath! And a human being is much more valuable than a sheep! So yes, God does allow us to do good on the Sabbath."

He told the man, "Straighten out your hand." As he did so, his hand became completely normal, just like the other. The Pharisees were furious because he had publicly discredited their Sabbath rules, and they began plotting with some of King Herod's men how they could kill him.

45. Jesus' Ministry
Fulfilled Prophecy About the Messiah

Jesus was aware of this, so he and his close followers left there and went to the shore of Lake Galilee. But many followed after him, and he healed all who were sick—though he ordered them not to tell others he had done so.

They had come from Galilee and Judea Provinces, Jerusalem, Idumea Province—south of Judea—and also from the Gentile areas east of the Jordan River, and around the Gentile cities of Tyre and Sidon on the Mediterranean coast—northeast of Galilee. They came to hear Jesus teach and to be healed, for they had all heard about the miracles and healings he was doing and came to see for themselves.

He told his close followers to get a boat ready for him so he could sit in it a little offshore and not be crushed by the crowd while he taught them. For they had seen him heal so many people that those who were sick kept pushing their way through the crowd just to touch him. They did this because power was going out from him and healing all who did so. Whenever demonized people came close, the demons would make them prostrate themselves in front of him and shout, "You are God's Son!" But Jesus would always sternly command the demons not to say that about him, and then freed the people from their demonic affliction.

The nature of his ministry fulfilled the prophecy made by the prophet Isaiah about the Messiah which says: "Here is my chosen servant, the one I specially love who delights me. I will empower him with my Spirit, and he will proclaim to every people group the truth about the way to be righteous in my sight. He will not be one to shout or argue with others, or try to publicly rally people to himself. He will be gentle and kind to those who are spiritually weak, battered, fragile, and about ready to give up believing. He will carefully work to heal and restore them to strong faith and vitality until his goodness overcomes evil and its consequences. In the end, people from every people group will put their trust in him to save them."

46. Jesus Appoints Twelve Apostles

It was about that time—early in his ministry—that Jesus went up a mountain by himself to pray. He spent the entire night praying to God the Father for guidance. In the morning, he called all of his followers to him and selected twelve of them to be appointed apostles. ❖ *"Apostle" means "someone who is sent as a messenger."* ➤ They were to always be with him, as he intended to train them to go out on their own to preach the Good News and to have authority to expel demons. These are the names of the twelve he chose:

Simon, to whom he also gave the name Peter (sometimes called Cephas),
Andrew (Simon's brother),
James (son of Zebedee),
John (James' younger brother), (Jesus called James and John, "Boanerges," which means "sons of thunder.")
Philip ,
Bartholomew (who might also have been called Nathanael),
Matthew Levi ,
Thomas ,
James (son of Alpheus),
Judas Thaddeus (son of James),
Simon (who was called the Zealot), and
Judas Iscariot who would later betray Jesus to his enemies.

JESUS TEACHES ON A HILLSIDE

(The Sermon on the Mount)
(Sections 47-63)

47. Attitudes We Should Have

One day, Jesus saw the crowd following him and headed up a hill. He sat down, ready to teach, and his regular followers came to sit near him. He began to teach them these things:

"Those who humbly recognize their own spiritual poverty and have renounced all desire for riches in this world in order to seek God and his help are indeed in his good favor. They are already citizens of his Kingdom.

"Those who turn to God when they are sad or grieving are in his good favor because he has promised to comfort them.

"Those who weep in repentance over their sin in this life are in God's good favor because in the life to come, he will certainly make them laugh with joy.

"Those who humbly depend on God to take care of their rights as he sees fit—instead of asserting themselves—are in his good favor. For they will certainly receive all that he has promised, which includes a position of authority in his Kingdom.

"Those who continually yearn to please God by living the way he wants them to live are in his good favor. For he will help them do it, and their desires will certainly be satisfied.

"Those who routinely demonstrate compassion, mercy, leniency, and kindness to others are in God's good favor. For he will certainly treat them the same way, both in this life and on Judgment Day.

"Those who are completely dedicated to God and keep even their innermost thoughts undividedly devoted to him are indeed in his good favor.

"Those who strive to promote peace and harmony are in God's good favor, for he will call them his children.

"Those who are unjustly persecuted because they strive to please God are indeed in his good favor, for they are already citizens of his Kingdom.

"Those of you who are hated, excluded, verbally abused, insulted, treated badly, slandered, and falsely accused of doing all kinds of evil because you are trying to be faithful to me, the Son of Man, are very much in God's good favor. You should be thrilled and joyfully exult because you can rest assured that God has a great reward waiting for you in Heaven. Their persecution proves that you are his faithful servants. You're in good company. Consider that he allowed people to persecute his favored prophets in the same way, long ago.

"But how terrible it will be for those who are rich or want to be rich, believing that possessions are able to make them happy and give them satisfaction and meaning in life. In this life, they are enjoying all the comfort they will ever have, for there will be no comfort for them in Hell!

"How terrible it will be for those who are well fed and content with their sinful lives, having no desire to change or submit to God's will. For when they are in Hell, they will hunger for contentment they can't have!

"How terrible it will be for those who laugh and only think about enjoying life in the present, having no concern about their sins. For when they are in Hell, they will mourn and weep forever!

"How terrible it will be for those who seek fame and praise in this life. Praise from people is not to be equated with God's approval. On the contrary, it was the false prophets who were always praised by your rebellious ancestors!"

48. We are Meant to Attract Others to Him

Speaking to his followers, Jesus continued, "You are God's expression of his wisdom in this world for the benefit of others. But if you were to become morally foolish, you would be worthless for his purposes and be thrown out of the Kingdom where everyone would also consider you worthless. You are God's revelatory light to the people of this world, showing them his truth and way of salvation. You know it is ridiculous to try to hide a city that is built on a hill. Neither can you hide the fact that you are different from unbelievers—because God's light of truth is in you. No one lights a lamp and then tries to hide its light under a basket. Instead, they elevate the lamp so it can illuminate the entire room. God intends for everyone to see your light, so don't try to hide it. Let people see that you are different and help them to understand the truth that you know. Then, they will understand the good things you do and praise your Heavenly Father for putting his light in you."

49. Jesus' View of Moses' Teachings

Jesus said, "Never think that my purpose is to disobey, reject, weaken, or abolish the Teachings of Moses or any of the rest of the Scriptures. My purpose is to keep them, fulfill them, explain them, and make them more completely and correctly established among God's people. Yes, may it be so! I'm telling you an important truth when I say that until all of God's purposes are accomplished—and the currently existing Heaven and Earth disappear—not even a single letter in the Torah will be invalidated or abolished. Therefore, those who disregard even the least important of God's commands in the Scriptures and also teach others to do so will be among those of lowest status in God's Kingdom. But those who keep all of God's commands and teach others to obey them will be among those of highest status in Heaven. I'm warning you that your righteousness needs to far exceed that of the Pharisees and Scripture teachers—or you will never enter God's Kingdom.

50. The Importance of Good Relationships

"For example, you know that long ago, Moses told our ancestors that God's Torah says, 'Never commit murder. Those who do so will be sentenced to death by the court.' But I'm telling you that the true meaning of this command is much broader. Even being angry with someone without a truly righteous cause is sufficient for you to be found guilty of sin. And if your anger causes you to insult someone, you will be found guilty before the Heavenly court on Judgment Day. If you are so angry that you pronounce someone cursed and worthy of Hell, then you yourself are in danger of being sent there. With this in mind, if you find yourself about to present a sacrifice to God to be reconciled with him or as a fellowship offering, and it comes to mind that someone is angry with you for something you've done, you need to be reconciled with that person first before God will accept your offering. So put your sacrifice aside and go be reconciled with that person. *Then* return and offer your sacrifice to God.

"You should be reconciled with someone you've wronged as soon as possible or you may find yourself being sued. If you don't make amends before he hauls you into court, it will be too late. The court may have you thrown into prison until you've paid the court's judgment against you in full. Being reconciled with people is extremely important in terms of the consequences, both with God and with people."

51. Thoughts Are as Important as Actions

"You know that the Torah says, 'Never commit adultery.' But I'm telling you that the true meaning of this command is much broader. For a man to even look at a woman married to someone else and desire to have sex with her violates this command. In God's view, he is already guilty of adultery with her in his mind and heart.

"You need to understand just how serious sin is. If your best eye entices you to sin, you would actually be better off getting rid of it than to keep it and end up in Hell. Even if your right hand were to entice you to sin, you would still be better off getting rid of it than to end up in Hell."

52. God's View of Divorce

"Interpreters of the Torah have said that a man who divorces his wife must give her documentary proof that he has released her from her marriage vows. But I'm telling you that a man who divorces his wife and marries a different woman is guilty of adultery—violating his marriage vows. He also causes his ex-wife to become guilty of adultery when she remarries, unless he divorced her because she was already guilty of adultery. And a man that marries such a divorced woman will also be guilty of violating her marriage vows."

53. Always Speak Truthfully Without Invoking Oaths

"You know that God's Torah says, 'Do not break your oaths. Any oath that you've made invoking God as a witness he expects you to keep by telling the truth.' But I'm telling you that you shouldn't make any kind of oath at all to convince others that you're telling the truth. Even swearing 'by Heaven' invokes God since Heaven is where he rules as King. So don't do it. And don't swear by the Earth for it's his footstool, or by Jerusalem for it's his capital city. Don't even swear by your own head for you lack the power to make even one gray hair turn black again. Just always speak truthfully and mean what you say. Any additional oath you invoke to prop up an appearance of truthfulness is inspired by evil."

54. Show Self-Sacrificial Love

"You know that the Torah says, 'Don't sentence people to punishments that are excessive or unjust. The severity of their punishment should match their crime. If they caused a person to lose an eye, put out one of theirs. If they knocked out a tooth, knock out one of theirs.' But I say that God has shown you extreme favor and mercy that you don't deserve by forgiving your sins and saving you; so he wants you to go beyond the idea of merely seeking justice with appropriate legal punishment for those who wrong you. He wants you to also be merciful and not seek legal action against those who do evil to you. If someone publicly insults and humiliates you by slapping your right cheek, don't retaliate, but offer the other one to him to show your love and forbearance. If someone steals your only coat, offer him your shirt too in order to win him for the Kingdom by showing him love. If someone sues you for the clothes off your back, voluntarily give him everything you have. If someone steals from you, don't necessarily seek to get it back. If someone makes a demand of you—even one he can legally enforce—don't resist or do it grudgingly, but willingly do more than he demands—even twice as much—in order to demonstrate God's love.

"Give to those in need who ask you for help; and don't be reluctant to lend to those who—from genuine need—ask to borrow from you just because you're afraid they won't be able to return what they borrow.

"You know that the Torah says, 'Love your neighbor,' and that others teach it is acceptable to love your enemies less. But I'm saying that you should treat everyone as if they were your neighbor. Therefore, you should show love to everyone—including your enemies and those who hate you. Ask God to bless those who curse you; do good to those who hate you and pray for those who deliberately mistreat you and persecute you. This is the way God the Father expects his true sons and daughters to live for it reflects his character. This is seen in the way he generously provides sunshine and rain not only for his own people, but also for those who reject him.

"Do you think God will reward you for only showing love to those who are likely to love you back? Certainly not! Even unbelievers and those tax collectors you despise do that much. Do you think God will count it in your favor if you only have friendly greetings for your own people? Everyone does that much, even unbelieving pagans. Do you think God counts it in your favor if you only do good for those who will likely respond in kind? Certainly not! Even selfish sinners do that! Do you really think God approves if you are only willing to lend to people that you are sure will return what they borrow? Most certainly not! Even the worst kind of sinners are willing to lend with the expectation that they will get back what they lend. You are to live differently! You must demonstrate love to your enemies and do good to them. Lend and give generously to all in need while expecting to get nothing back. If you live like this, your reward in Heaven will be great, and you will be known as God's true sons and daughters who reflect his character. For he is always kind—even to ungrateful and evil people—and he expects his children to do the same. You are to show mercy to the undeserving in the same way that your Heavenly Father does to you. Your Father expects your love to be perfectly mature by loving everyone without discrimination, just as his love is perfect.

"So the kind and loving things you would like people to do for you, you should always do for others first—even for those who aren't nice to you or are hostile. For this is the essence of the teachings in the Torah and in the rest of the Scriptures."

55. How to Gain Heavenly Rewards

"When you pray, fast, give to the poor, or serve in other ways make sure your motive is not to have others notice how 'spiritual' you are. For if your goal is a good reputation among people, then you will receive no reward for such deeds from your

Heavenly Father. So for example, whenever you help the poor, don't do anything to draw attention to what you are doing. Those who make displays of their 'generosity' in the synagogue and other public places so others will notice them are hypocrites. Any human approval they obtain for their public piety is all the reward they will get. When you help those in need, don't tell anyone what you're doing—not even your close friends. You should try to keep others from knowing about your generosity, for then God the Father who sees everything will openly reward you in Heaven.

"Or when you pray, don't make a display of it like those hypocrites who stand in the synagogue or other public places. The only reward they will get is the public attention they crave. But you should go where you can be alone when you pray to your invisible Heavenly Father. Then, he who sees everything will reward you for your prayers.

"And don't pray like pagans do—who think that long repetitive prayers of empty flowery phrases will get their deity's attention. Your Father knows what you need and wants to help you even before you ask him—so don't be like them.

56. The Way to Pray

"When you pray, make it simple like this and for these kinds of things: Our Heavenly Father, cause more and more people to honor your name and submit to your Kingship. Cause your will to be accomplished as perfectly in this world as it is in Heaven. Provide us with the food and other things we need for today. Forgive our sins in the same way that we've forgiven those who have wronged us. Help us so we won't yield to temptation—rescuing us from the power and influence of evil. For you are the great eternal and glorious King who has power over everything. Yes, may it be so!"

Jesus continued, "Be aware that if you forgive others who wrong you, then your Heavenly Father will also forgive you. But if you refuse to forgive someone, then your Father will also refuse to forgive you.

"When you fast in order to help your prayers, don't draw attention to what you're doing. Those who make it obvious that they are fasting are hypocrites. I guarantee you the only reward they will get for their fasting is the notice of those they are trying to impress. When you fast, groom yourself to appear as you normally do so others won't notice anything unusual. But your invisible Heavenly Father who sees everything will note what you're secretly doing and will reward you for it.

57. A Proper Attitude About Riches and Possessions

"This is how to store up treasure in Heaven that you will have forever: Sell what you own and give the money to those in need. Don't waste your time amassing riches in this world where they can be stolen or destroyed in various ways. Instead, you should invest your time and effort to accumulate wealth in Heaven that you can enjoy for all eternity. Such wealth can't be stolen or destroyed. And unlike accumulating earthly wealth, it's good for you to acquire the eternal kind because if this is your focus, your attention and commitment will be in the right place.

"Your desires reveal your true self. If your only desire is to please God through demonstrating love and generosity to others, then you will truly understand and serve him. But if you are distracted by desires for personal earthly wealth, you cannot understand God or serve him.

"No one can serve two masters at the same time. You will either have lesser loyalty to the first and be completely devoted to the second, or the other way around. In the same way, you have to choose in this life between being devoted to God and serving him with your money, or being devoted to acquiring money for your own purposes. You can't do both.

"So what I'm telling you is this: Don't worry about having enough to eat or drink or having decent clothes to wear, because there are much more important things than food and clothing in this life. Consider birds. They don't plant crops or harvest them or even store food. Yet, God sees to it that they eat what they need. And you are much more valuable to God than birds, so he will certainly meet your needs. All the worrying in the world can't add a single moment to your life or improve it in any way, so why bother?

"Why worry about what you will wear? Consider how wildflowers grow. They don't have to work or make their beautiful petals. But not even King Solomon in all his splendor looked as good as they do. Think about it. If God so beautifully clothes field grass with wildflowers—grass that grows for only a short time before it is cut and burned—he will be even more concerned to provide you with clothing! Your faith in his provision is too small!

"Don't worry about what you will eat and drink or what you will wear today or tomorrow. Those who don't know God worry about such things. But you have a Heavenly Father who knows your needs. So submit to him and concentrate on the affairs of his Kingdom in your life and on what he wants you to do for him. Do that, and he will provide you with the necessities. Don't worry about what might happen tomorrow or whether your needs will be met. Tomorrow is in God's hands. There are enough problems for you to deal with today without anticipating tomorrow's too, for every day has its own set. Don't be afraid, my children. Your Father delights to give you all that is in his Kingdom."

58. Jesus Forbids Us to Criticize or Condemn Others

Jesus continued, "If you condemn others, God will condemn you. If you criticize others, God will hold you accountable for all your faults. If you want God to forgive you, you must forgive everyone who wrongs you. The same manner and attitude you have toward others is the one that God will have toward you. He will judge you by your own standards and return your harshness or mercy toward others back to you.

"Help people who are in need, and in return you will receive your reward from God in Heaven. The generous way that he will pay you back is like a basket of grain that's filled with a full measure, then tightly packed, pressed down, and shaken to settle the contents and even more heaped on top to overflowing. The same standard of generosity—or lack of it—that you follow in giving to people in need is the standard that God will follow in rewarding you."

Then Jesus told a parable to say that we shouldn't criticize others because there are many times we don't recognize our own faults. He said, "A person who is blind to his own sin can't successfully lead others away from theirs. If he tries, they will all fall into a sinful trap. It should be obvious that a student can't become better than his rabbi. But a student who is fully trained can hope to be just like his rabbi. ❖ *Jesus was saying that if we aspire to be like him, we must not criticize others.* ➤

"Why do you get fixated on the tiny speck of sin in another's life, but don't notice the major sin in your own? How can you dare to tell someone, 'Allow me to point out the small sin I see in your life and help you get rid of it,' when you refuse to recognize your own major sins! If you do this, you're a self-righteous hypocrite! First, remove the major sins and pride from your own life, then you will have the humility and sensitivity to help others with the small sins in their lives.

"But on the other hand, be wise in how you approach people who are vicious or clearly content in their evil lifestyles. Don't attempt to share holy and valuable truths with those who will obviously despise them or turn on you."

59. We Often Don't Have Because We Haven't Bothered to Ask

Jesus said, "When you ask God for something you need, keep on asking, and at the proper time he will give it. Keep on seeking him and you will find him. Keep on knocking on his door in prayer, and he will open it to you. Everyone who asks will receive. No exceptions. Everyone who seeks will find what he's seeking. Also, the door will open to everyone who knocks. You fathers, if your little boy asks you for bread, would you give him a stone? Or if he asks you for a fish, would you give him a poisonous snake? If you are willing to give good things to your children—even though you are sinners—it should be clear that your Heavenly Father is even more willing to give good things to those who ask for them.

60. Only a Few Find the Way to Heaven

"In order to reach Heaven you must go the way that is narrow and more difficult—which most people ignore or reject. ❖ *This narrow way (narrow gate, in the literal text) is true faith in Jesus the Messiah—which results in repentance and obedience.* ➤ The obvious easy-to-find gate is broad and attractive, but leads to destruction in Hell. Many chose that way. Relatively few make the effort to find the narrow way that leads to eternal life.

61. Beware of
False Religious Teachers and False Prophets

"Watch out for false religious teachers who say they come from God. They will say things to make you think they are fellow believers, but their intention is to greedily satisfy their own desires and to establish their own agenda at the expense of God's people. You can recognize them by the results of their teaching and ministry in their own lives and lifestyles, and also in the lives of those who follow them. Anyone can identify a tree by the fruit it bears—and you obviously don't get grapes or figs from thorn bushes. So you can identify good trees by the good fruit they bear, and good teachers by the good influences they have on those who follow them. But just as a bad tree bears bad fruit, bad teachers will not produce spiritually mature believers who faithfully follow the Lord's commands. A good tree cannot fail to produce good fruit, and a bad tree is incapable of bearing good fruit. In the same way, from the abundance of goodness that fills the heart of a righteous person proceeds the fruit of good words and actions. And from the evil that fills the heart of an evil person proceeds the fruit of evil words and deeds. What a person speaks and does reflects his innermost character. That's how righteous and evil people can be identified. The same is true of religious teachers and their followers. God examines the fruit that every person produces, and those who do not bear good fruit will be cut down and burned in Hell. Therefore, you can recognize if they are true teachers or false by looking at the results of their ministry.

62. Many Who Consider Themselves Believers Will Not Enter Heaven

"Don't be deceived! Not everyone who calls me 'Lord' will enter God's Kingdom in Heaven. Only those who live in obedience to the will of my Father will enter. On Judgment day, many will appeal to me, 'Lord, we prophesied in your name and expelled demons from people in your name and even did miracles in your name!' But my answer will be, 'We've never had a real relationship where you were submitted to me. Go away and don't come back! You are not welcome because you are evil!' "

63. Two Ways to Respond to Jesus' Teaching

Jesus said, "Why do some of you call me 'Lord and Master,' but ignore my commands concerning the way you are to live? I will tell you what someone is like who comes to me, hears my teaching, and lives by it. That person is like a man who digs down to bedrock for a firm foundation on which to build his house. ❖ *In this illustration, a person's house represents his life. All a person does in this life contributes to building his "house."* ➤ Later, when it rains and the flood of death comes and smashes against that house, it isn't even shaken because it was firmly built on a proper foundation. ❖ *If our lives are built on submissive obedience to Jesus' teaching, then all the good things we do will have lasting value beyond our deaths, and we will be rewarded for them in Heaven.* ➤ But those who hear my teaching and refuse to live by it are like a foolish man who built his house on top of sand with no foundation at all. Then the rain came, the river flooded, and the winds blew and smashed against that house, causing it to collapse and destroying it completely."
❖ *Even though people do good works in this life, if their lives aren't based on the foundation of submissive obedience to Jesus, ultimately, all those good works will count for nothing after their deaths—and they themselves will experience an eternal existence of ruin in Hell.* ➤

When Jesus finished speaking, the people were in awe of his teaching because unlike the Scripture teachers, he spoke from personal authority rather than quoting others.

64. The Power of Faith

When Jesus finished preaching these things, he went to Capernaum. Stationed there was a Roman centurion who had a slave he thought highly of that was near death from sickness. The centurion had heard about Jesus. So when he learned that Jesus was in Capernaum, he sent some friends who were Jewish elders to him with a message asking him to come and heal his slave. When these elders came to Jesus, they urged him to grant the centurion's request, saying, "Even though he's a Gentile, he's a good and worthy person, and you should consider granting his request. For he loves our people and he practically built our synagogue by himself with his contributions."

So Jesus went with them. As he was nearing the house, the centurion saw him and sent some friends out to meet him with a message. They said on his behalf, "Sir, don't trouble yourself to come any further. For I am not a Jew, and therefore I'm not worthy to have you enter my house. I don't want you to ritually defile yourself by doing so. That's why I didn't presume to come to you in person. But I ask you to command that my slave be healed, and I know it will happen. For I'm a man under authority and I understand how authority works. I have soldiers under my command, and when I tell one, 'Go!' he goes, and to another, 'Come!' and he comes, and to my slave, 'Do this!' and he does it."

When Jesus heard this, he was amazed at his faith and understanding. He turned and said to those following him, "I tell you, I haven't encountered such great faith even among God's chosen people! It's a fact that many Gentiles from everywhere in the world will come and be welcomed to eat with Abraham, Isaac, and Jacob in God's Kingdom in Heaven. But many Jews who should be in the Kingdom will be banished outside of it in the darkness of Hell where people will cry in great agony and defiant rage." So Jesus commanded that the slave be healed, and when the messengers returned to the centurion's house, they found the slave completely well.

65. Jesus Resurrects a Widow's Son

Soon after this, Jesus made the nine-hour walk to the town of Nain, southwest of Capernaum. His followers and a large crowd went with him. As he approached the town entrance, a large funeral procession was coming out the gate. They were carrying the body of a man who had been the only son of a widow—who would now have no male relative to take care of her. When the Lord saw the woman, he felt compassion for her. Approaching her, he said, "You don't need to cry anymore." Then ignoring the fact that it would make him ritually unclean, he touched the bier, and the bearers came to a halt. He said, "Young man, I command you to get up!" The man who had been dead sat up and started talking. Jesus then presented him to his mother.

Those who witnessed this were filled with fear and awe, and they began to praise God and exclaim, "After so long a time, a great prophet has been sent to us!" and "God has come to help his people through this prophet!"

The news about this incident spread throughout the provinces of Galilee and Judea and the surrounding areas.

66. John the Baptizer
Sends Messengers to Jesus

Now by this time, John the Baptizer was in prison, so his followers were reporting all these things about Jesus to him. But since Jesus was not initiating the end-time judgment which John had prophesied, he summoned two of his followers and sent them to Jesus. When they arrived, they asked him, "Are you really the long-awaited Messiah or should we be looking for someone else?"

Jesus replied, "Go and tell John what you've seen and heard me do. Those who were blind can see, those who were crippled can walk, those with contagious skin diseases are cured, those who were deaf can hear, some who have died live again, and the poor are hearing the Good News about God inviting them into his Kingdom. May God bless anyone who doesn't reject me for not fulfilling their preconceived ideas of what the Messiah will do."

As John's messengers were leaving, Jesus spoke to the crowds about the Baptizer. "When you went out to John in the wilderness, what did you expect to see? A man who goes with the flow of popular opinion—like a reed that bends in any direction the wind blows? Hardly. Who would listen to such a man? Then why did you go out to see him? To see a man who knows how to ingratiate himself with the king so as to be rewarded with royal favors, and who wears soft clothing? Those who wear rich apparel and live in luxury are found in palaces, not in the wilderness. So tell me, what did you hope to find? A prophet sent from God? Yes, you went to hear God's prophet! But I tell you that he is more than just a prophet, for his work surpasses that of all previous prophets. John is the messenger who announced the arrival of the Messiah. This Scripture was written about him, 'I will send my messenger in advance to prepare the way for you to be accepted by my people.' I tell you, from the beginning of creation until now, there has been no one who has had a more important role than John. And yet even the lowest-ranking person in God's Kingdom is greater than he is.

"From the time that John started preaching his message of repentance until now, God has been drawing people to himself with great power—and many people are exerting their utmost to enter his Kingdom. God's word and will was proclaimed in the Torah and the writings of the prophets until John came. When all the people heard him preach, many believed God's message that they were sinners and needed to repent—and they demonstrated this by having John baptize them. Even tax collectors responded. But the Pharisees and Scripture teachers refused to acknowledge their need for repentance or their need for John to baptize them—and in doing this, they rejected God's will for them. If you are willing to accept what I say, John is the 'prophet like Elijah' who the Scriptures said would come first—before the Messiah. If your hearts are attuned to God, try to understand what this means!

"How can I characterize the leaders and many of the people living today? Do you know what they're like? They are never satisfied with God's messengers. They're like children sitting in the market who complain to one another, 'We played a happy tune, but you wouldn't dance. Then we sang a song of mourning, but you wouldn't cry.' For John the Baptizer came as an ascetic and didn't eat bread or drink wine like most people, so they rejected him, claiming he was demonized. Then I, the Son of Man, came and was willing to dine and drink as a guest in people's homes, and they say, 'Look at that glutton and drunkard, hanging around with tax collectors and other sinful outcasts!' But a proverb says, 'Wisdom is vindicated by all her children.' So those who accept that God sent us will have their faith vindicated by the good fruit produced in their lives."

67. Jesus at the House of Simon the Pharisee

One day, a Pharisee named Simon invited Jesus to dine with him. So he went into the Pharisee's house and, as was the custom, reclined on his side on a dining couch at the table. Now, a woman who lived in the city and was known to have lived an immoral life heard that he was a guest there. Much to the indignation of the Pharisees present, she barged in with an alabaster flask of expensive perfume. She stood behind him at the end of the couch near his feet, crying out of gratitude for his message of God's love and forgiveness. Her tears fell and wet his feet, and in her anxious state, she forgot propriety—further shocking the guests—and immodestly let down her hair and dried his feet with it. She also kissed his feet in reverence and gratitude and then broke the flask and poured the perfume on them. When Simon saw this, he despised her as a worthless sinner, refusing to believe that she had repented, and thought to himself, "If this man were really a prophet, he would know what kind of person is touching and defiling him and wouldn't allow it."

Answering his thoughts, Jesus bluntly said, "Simon, I would say something to you." With insincere politeness and apparent reluctance he replied, "Go ahead, Rabbi."

Jesus said, "A certain money lender was owed money by two men, one who owed five hundred days wages, and the other who owed fifty. When he learned that they were unable to repay their debts, he graciously canceled both of them. Now tell me, which of the two would be more grateful?" Simon answered, "I suppose the one who had the larger debt."

Jesus said, "You've come to the correct conclusion." Turning to face the woman—dignifying her presence—he said to Simon, "Do you see this woman? I entered your house as a guest, and you failed to offer me the common courtesy of water—normally offered to all guests—so I could wash my feet. But she wet my feet with her tears and dried them with her hair. As a direct insult seen by everyone here, you didn't welcome me with a customary kiss of greeting, but ever since I came in, she hasn't stopped kissing my feet. You didn't even offer the customary hospitality of anointing my head with inexpensive olive oil, but she has anointed my feet with costly perfume.

"Therefore I must tell you, her great love clearly reveals that she has repented, and her many sins have already been forgiven. But he who has been forgiven little—because he hasn't recognized his own sinfulness—shows little love."

Then Jesus said to the woman, "Your sins really have been forgiven."

The people at the table with him were indignant and said to each other, "Who does he think he is to claim that he forgives sin?"

But ignoring them, Jesus said to the woman, "Your faith has saved you. Go in peace."

68. Women Who Helped Jesus

Not long after this, Jesus went around to many towns and villages preaching the Good News that God was wanting a new relationship with those who would submit to him as King. His twelve apostles went with him, and also some women he had healed or from whom he had expelled demons. Among them were Mary of Magdala village (from whom he had expelled seven demons), Joanna (whose husband, Chuza, was an administrator for the tetrarch Herod Antipas), Susanna, and many other women who supported Jesus and his followers financially from their own resources.

69. Beware of Saying that the Spirit's Work Is of Satan

Then, Jesus returned home to Capernaum, but such a large crowd gathered there to be healed and to hear his teaching that neither he nor his close followers had time to even eat. When Jesus' family in Nazareth heard about this, they set out to rescue him and bring him home because—from the things they heard people say about him—they thought he wasn't behaving rationally.

Someone brought him a demonized man who was blind and mute. When Jesus expelled the demon, the man could both speak and see. The people were amazed and asked, "Could he possibly be the Son of David?"

❖ *"Son of David" was a common title for the Messiah.* ➤

But when some Pharisees heard this, they tried to discourage this kind of thinking by saying, "He can only expel demons because he has Satan—the prince of demons—helping him!" Others wanted to test Jesus to make him prove that his power came from God and not from Satan. So they demanded he perform some miraculous sign that was clearly from God.

Jesus called the people together and began to counter this accusation, using these illustrations, "How could it profit Satan to expel his own demons from people? Any kingdom divided by civil war won't last long, and a divided household fighting against each other will fall apart. If Satan is fighting against his own demons, how can his kingdom continue? And if I'm expelling them with Satan's power, then what about your own followers? They expel demons too. Whose power do they use? They will judge the reasonableness of your accusation! But if I'm expelling demons by God's power, then this proves that God's Kingdom is being established among you."

Comparing Satan to a strongman, Jesus continued, "No one can rob a strongman of his possessions unless he is first overpowered. If someone stronger does this and ties him up, then he can rob the strongman's house. ❖ *Jesus' point was that he was able to expel demons because he is mightier than Satan. The strongman's "possessions" are the people he had under the control or influence of his demons.* ➤

"You have to choose sides. Those who aren't helping me are against me. And those who don't help me lead people to God are helping to drive them away. So I'm warning you to be careful about the accusations you make. God will forgive every sin and blasphemy—except blasphemy against the Holy Spirit. Anyone who speaks against me—the Son of Man—in any way, can be forgiven if he or she repents. But anyone who blasphemes against the Holy Spirit will not be forgiven." He was warning them because people were saying that the Spirit within him was demonic.

"If the fruit of a tree is good, you have to conclude that the tree itself is good. If the fruit of a tree is bad, then you must conclude the tree itself is bad, for the kind of tree and it's health is recognized by its fruit. ❖ *Therefore, if the deeds I do are good, you should recognize that the source of those deeds is also good.* ➤ But you Pharisees are a bunch of evil deceivers! So how can anything you say be good? What a person speaks and does reflects his innermost character. From the goodness that fills the heart of a righteous person proceeds the fruit of good words and actions. And from the evil that fills the heart of an evil person proceeds the fruit of evil words and deeds. That's how righteous and evil people can be identified.

"It's a fact that on Judgment Day, God will hold you responsible for everything you have said—even words you've said without thinking first. You will be judged innocent or guilty based on what you've said in this life."

70. Those Who Reject Jesus Will Have No Excuse

Then, some Pharisees and Scripture teachers said, "Rabbi, we want to see you perform a miraculous sign—that only God could do—to prove that he sent you." He replied, "Many people living today are evil.

They want me to perform spectacular miraculous signs to prove that my power comes from God, but I won't do it. The only sign I will give is similar to the sign that happened to the prophet Jonah. Jonah's reprieve from death after three days in the stomach of a large fish was a sign to the people of Nineveh long ago. And what will happen to me, the Son of Man, will be the same kind of sign to people living today. ❖ *Jesus was speaking cryptically about his future resurrection—after being in the grave for parts of three days.* ➤ On Judgment Day, the people of Nineveh will stand up and condemn you because they listened to Jonah's message and repented. And now someone greater than Jonah is here, yet you refuse to repent. ❖ *Jesus was speaking of himself as greater than Jonah.* ➤ On Judgment Day, the Queen of the South will stand and condemn those living today because she traveled from a distant land to listen to Solomon's wisdom. But you are unable to recognize that someone greater than Solomon is here that you refuse to listen to.

"When a demon is expelled from a man, it travels through arid places looking for a new resting place in someone's body. If it doesn't find such a place, it says to itself, 'I will return to my former house.' When it returns, it finds the house unoccupied, clean, and in order. ❖ *i.e., The man's body is vacant of any demons.* ➤ Then, it goes and brings seven worse demons and they all enter the man to live there—so he is worse off than before. The same kind of thing will happen to you evil people living today. You are worse off now than you were before I came. Since you've rejected me, you have left a vacancy in your lives that Satan will fill."

When Jesus had said this, a woman in the crowd called out, "God blessed your mother who birthed and nursed you!" But Jesus replied, "Those really blessed by God are people who hear his word and obey it."

He continued, "No one lights a lamp and then hides it or covers it up. Instead, he puts it on a stand so all who enter the room can see by the light. ❖ *His point is that he hasn't at all hidden the truth about where his power comes from. Rather, his teaching and miracles have all been out in the open so everyone could see them and recognize the obvious fact that God sent him and gave him his power as a clear sign of his approval.* ➤ The eye of spiritual discernment is the window to your mind. If your eye is clear, your mind will be filled with the light of truth. If your discerning eye is bad, your mind will be filled with the darkness of error. Be sure that what you think is light in you isn't actually darkness! If your mind is filled with truth, then you won't be deceived by error and will have proper understanding." ❖ *Jesus was implying: If you've come to proper conclusions from what you've seen, then it's obvious that God has sent me and no further miracles as proof are necessary. Anyone really wanting to know the truth of the matter can do so.* ➤

71. Jesus' True Relatives

While Jesus was still speaking to the crowd, his mother and brothers arrived from Nazareth to see him. But they but they couldn't get in the house where he was teaching because it was crammed with people. So they passed a message inside asking him to come out. Someone told him, "Your mother and brothers are outside, wanting to see you."

But using this as a teaching opportunity, Jesus asked, "Who is my mother and who are my brothers?" Looking around at all those sitting there who were wanting to learn from him, he said, "These people are as mothers and brothers to me! Those who accept God's word and obey it are as close to me as my brother and sister and mother."

72. Parable of the Four Soils

Later, Jesus again went down to the shore of Lake Galilee to teach. Such a large crowd gathered that he got into a boat and sat in it just offshore so the entire crowd on land could see and hear him. Then, he taught them many spiritual truths in parables. One went like this: "Pay attention to this! A farmer went out to sow seed in his field. As he scattered the seed, some fell on a hard-packed path where people walked on it, and it was eaten by birds. Some of it fell where the soil was merely a thin layer over rock. These seeds sprouted quickly because the soil was shallow. ❖ *The shallow soil was easily warmed by the sun, so the seeds would grow more quickly than in deeper cooler soil.* ➤ But the sun quickly scorched the

young plants, and they withered because the rock beneath the shallow soil did not allow them to develop a deep root system to collect water. Some seed fell on ground where thorn bushes had grown and their roots still remained. Those also sprouted and were able to grow for a while. But the young plants weren't able to compete for light and water with the thorn bushes that also grew. So they were choked, produced no grain, and died. And some seed fell on good soil. These sprouted, grew strong, and bore more seed in varying amounts—some 30, some 60, and others 100."

Then, Jesus said with emphasis, "If your hearts are attuned to God, try to understand what this parable means!"

73. Why Jesus Taught in Parables

Later, when only Jesus' usual followers were with him, they asked, "Why do you only speak to the people in parables?"

He answered, "You have the privilege of being the first to learn about Kingdom truths that haven't been revealed before. But for the present, they do not have this privilege. People like you, who have some understanding of God and his Kingdom—because you are submitted to him and have a sincere desire to learn more—will be given more understanding by God. But those who have little understanding of spiritual truth—because they aren't really interested in it and are unwilling to submit to God—will have even what little understanding they possess taken away from them. That is why I only teach others about spiritual truths in parables. Those who aren't interested in learning more about them will hear the parables but not understand the spiritual truth being taught. Just as they see the miraculous signs but don't see the spiritual reality and implications behind them—because they refuse to believe in me. ❖ *Implied: But those who do seek to understand will be able to do so.* ➤ This is to fulfill Isaiah's prophecy that records God saying, 'Even though they hear, they don't understand. Even though they look, they don't perceive. For they've become close minded and uninterested in hearing from me. They ignore the things I do to get their attention that are plainly evident to their eyes. If this wasn't true about them, they would perceive what I'm showing them and hear what I'm saying and understand what I'm trying to teach them—and turn away from their sinful ways. If they did that, I would spiritually heal them.'

"But God is specially blessing you that your eyes get to see the signs I do—and you perceive spiritual truth behind them—and you get to listen to my teachings and learn. For it's a fact that many of God's prophets and others in the past who were fully submitted to him yearned to see the things you are seeing me do and to hear the truths I'm teaching you, but they didn't have the opportunity in their lifetimes."

74. Jesus Explains the Parable of the Four Soils

His followers asked him the meaning of the parable of the four soils. Jesus said, "Don't you understand even this simple parable? If you don't understand it, how will you possibly understand any of my other parables? The seed represents God's message about the way of salvation being preached to people, and the farmer is anyone who proclaims that message. The path illustrates people whose hearts are hard and whose minds are closed toward God's message. They may hear his truth, but it can't enter their hardened hearts. And just like the birds ate the seed, Satan snatches the memory of it away from them. The layer of shallow soil over rock illustrates people who hear God's message and happily receive it at first. But just like a plant in shallow soil can't develop the roots it needs to survive, God's message doesn't go deep in their hearts because they aren't willing to fully surrender themselves to him. Their shallow faith lasts for only a short time until the first real testing of their faith or persecution occurs. Then it quickly dies. The ground with thorn bushes illustrates people who initially accept God's message into their lives, but they never give it first priority. So other concerns and higher priorities—such as worries, materialism, and pleasure—don't allow his word to produce good fruit in them. Eventually, their faith is smothered

and dies. But the good soil illustrates people who hear God's message, grab onto it, recognize its worth, and allow it to take deep root in their hearts and minds. They surrender themselves to God and make him first priority in their lives. So their faith matures and their lives cause God's Kingdom to increase and prosper to varying degrees." ❖ *The implication is that individuals can determine what kind of "soil" their hearts are by how they respond to God's message.* ➤

75. Parable About the Weeds

Jesus also told this parable, "God's Kingdom in this world can be illustrated by the story of a farmer who planted good wheat seed in his field. But while everyone was sleeping, his enemy came and planted poisonous darnel weeds in the same field ❖ *which closely resembles wheat until the heads of wheat appear* ➤ and then went away. When the wheat grew to the point that it was bearing grain, then the presence of the darnel weeds became apparent. The farmer's workers went to him and asked, 'Sir, how did these weeds get there? Wasn't the seed you planted good?' He told them, 'It was an enemy that did this!' His workers asked, 'Do you want us to go weed them out?' He replied, 'No. If you uproot the weeds, you may also uproot some of the wheat with them. Allow them both to grow unhindered until harvest time, when I will tell the harvesters, "First collect all the weeds together and tie them in bundles to be burned. Then, gather all the wheat and put it in my barn." ' "

76. God Intends to Reveal His Truth to Everyone

Jesus continued, "No one lights a lamp and then hides it under a bed or covers it so its light can't be seen. Instead, they put it where the light can illuminate as much of the room as possible. Then, everything that was hidden in darkness will be clearly seen in its light. ❖ *He meant that God fully intends for the light of his truth to be seen and understood by people. He would never want it hidden, as that would defeat its purpose.* ➤ If your hearts are attuned to God, try to understand what this means!

"That is why you should pay close attention to the spiritual light of God's teaching that I'm giving you. For God will increase the understanding of those who receive it with proper regard in order to understand and obey it. But those who don't receive it properly with such a desire, even the understanding they think they have will be taken away from them."

77. Parable About the Growth of God's Kingdom

Jesus continued his teaching, "The way God causes his Kingdom to grow can be illustrated by a farmer who scatters wheat seed on the ground. He does nothing further that aids the growth of the seed. Day and night he goes about his daily work and sleeps, but the seeds grow of their own accord without his understanding how. The soil causes the plants to grow all by itself. First the stalk appears, then the head, then the mature grain on the head. And when the grain is ripe, it's time for it to be harvested."
❖ *In this parable, the farmer is anyone who proclaims God's Word, and the seed is that Word or message. The growth of the plants and production of grain represents new believers and their spiritual growth and maturity, and the harvest time represents Judgment Day.* ➤

78. Parable of the Mustard Seed

Jesus said, "How can I teach you what God's Kingdom is like in this world? What can I compare it to? It is like a mustard seed. Even though it's one of the smallest seeds, once it is planted, it grows into one of the largest garden plants and becomes a tree large enough for birds to come and nest in its branches." ❖ *God's Kingdom starts in a small way in people's hearts. But it grows in influence, eventually becoming quite large and a blessing to those around it.* ➤

Jesus told many of these kinds of parables to teach truths about God's Kingdom. But since he only taught in parables, the people understood only as much truth as they were ready to believe and understand. But afterward, when he was alone with his close followers, he explained the parables to them.

79. Parable of the Yeast

Again Jesus said, "How can I teach you what God's Kingdom is like? What can I compare it to? It's like a little yeast that a woman mixes with a large amount of flour until it's worked through the whole lump of dough." ❖ *That little bit of yeast affects all of the dough. In the same way, God's people may be few, but their quiet slow influence in the world can be far reaching and have large effects.* ➤

80. Jesus' Teaching in Parables Fulfilled Prophecy

Jesus taught all these things to the crowds only in parables. He never taught them anything plainly. He did this to fulfill the prophecy that says, "I will speak in parables to explain things unknown to people since God first created the world."

81. Jesus Explains the Parable About the Weeds

After teaching the crowd, Jesus went into a house. His followers came to him and asked, "Would you please explain the parable of the weeds to us?" Jesus answered, "The farmer who plants the good seed is me, the Son of Man. The field is this world, and the good seeds are my people who belong to God's Kingdom. The weeds are those who belong to Satan. Satan is the enemy who planted his people among mine. The harvest is Judgment Day, and the harvesters are my angels. Just as the weeds were gathered and burned in the parable, on Judgment day I, the Son of Man, will send my angels to gather together all those who do evil and cause others to sin. They will be removed from my Kingdom and thrown into the fire of Hell where people will cry in great agony and defiant rage. Then, my people will live in their Heavenly Father's Kingdom, shining with joy and glory. If your hearts are attuned to God, try to understand what this means!"

82. Two Parables About How to Regard Citizenship in God's Kingdom

Jesus said, "Citizenship in God's Kingdom is to be desired as a supremely valuable treasure. If a man were to accidentally find such a treasure in a field that he didn't own, he would hide it and joyfully sell all he had to be able to buy the field and legally possess the treasure.

"Again, you should seek citizenship in God's Kingdom like a merchant seeks fine pearls. If he were to find one of surpassing value, he would sell all he had so he could acquire it."

83. Parable of the Fish Net

Jesus then told this parable, "God's Kingdom in this world attracts all kinds of people. It is like a net that is thrown into a lake by some fishermen, which then catches all kinds of sea creatures. When it's full, they pull it up on shore and sit down to separate their catch. They gather the good fish and put them in their baskets, but the worthless ones are thrown away. That's the way it will be on Judgment Day. The angels will separate those whom God approves of from those that reject him. The latter will be thrown into the fire of Hell where people will cry in great agony and defiant rage."

Jesus asked his followers, "Have you understood these parables?" They answered, "Yes." Then Jesus said, "Each of you now is like the owner of a house who is able to bring out both old and new treasures from his storeroom to show to others. Knowing the teachings in God's Torah, and being my followers who understand about God's Kingdom, you are now able to teach others about spiritual truths in the Scriptures and about the new things that I've taught you."

84. Jesus Demonstrates Authority over Weather

Late afternoon on that same day, Jesus said to the twelve, "Let's sail to the other side of the lake." So right away, they got into the boat with Jesus and set out, leaving the crowd behind—although there were some that followed in other boats that were there. As they were crossing, a sudden storm came up which was so severe that waves were breaking over the boat and quickly filling it. But Jesus was asleep with his head on a cushion in the elevated back of the boat. His men were afraid, so they woke him and said, "Rabbi, don't you care that we're about to drown?" Jesus got up and commanded the wind and waves to calm down. The storm quickly dissipated and the water became flat. Then he said, "Why were you so frightened? Why didn't you trust God to protect you? Your trust in him is too small!" They were utterly amazed and awed, and asked each other, "Who is he? He even has authority over the wind and waves!"

85. Jesus Demonstrates Authority over Demons

They arrived on the eastern shore of the lake in the region of Gergesa. When Jesus went ashore, right away, he was met by two severely demonized men from the city who came out of the tombs where they had been living naked for a long time. The demons had taken control of them many times and made them supernaturally strong so that no one could keep them bound, not even with chains. The authorities had repeatedly tried keeping them chained under guard. But they were able to break the chains, and no one was strong enough to control them. So they always got away, and the demons drove them into the wilderness. They could be heard among the tombs in the hills yelling day and night because the demons made them cut themselves with sharp stones. They were known to be so violent that no one dared pass near that place.

They had first seen Jesus from a distance, then ran up and bowed down in front of him. As Jesus was commanding the demons to come out of them, the men shouted, "Arrrgh! Get out of here, Jesus, Son of God Most High! Just leave us alone! We adjure you by God, do not torment us!" ❖ *It's not entirely clear what the word rendered as "adjure" means in this context. Some commentators think they are putting Jesus under oath before God as a witness that he would not harm them.* ➤ Then Jesus asked, "What's your name?" They replied, "Our name is Legion because we are many." And the demons in the men kept on begging Jesus not to force them away from that region to the abyss in Hell.

Since there was a large herd of pigs feeding on a nearby hillside, they begged him, "If you expel us, send us to that herd of pigs." Jesus gave them permission, so they left the men and entered the pigs. Then, the herd of about 2000 ran down the steep hillside into the lake and drowned.

The pig herders ran off into town and reported what they had seen, and many came out to see for themselves what had happened. When they arrived, they found Jesus with the previously demonized men sitting near him, clothed and sane. When they realized what had happened, they became afraid of Jesus—for he obviously had great power. The eyewitnesses kept telling the newcomers exactly how the demonized men had been delivered and what had happened to the pigs. Then motivated by fear, the people respectfully asked Jesus to leave their district.

So Jesus got in the boat to return to the other side of the lake. But the men he had delivered begged to go with him.

Jesus told them, "No. I want you to go home and tell your people how God showed you great mercy and what he did for you." So the men went throughout the entire Decapolis District telling everyone they met what Jesus had done for them. All who heard it were amazed and awed.

86. A Woman's Faith Heals Her, and Jesus Demonstrates Power over Death

When Jesus arrived on the Capernaum side of the lake, a large crowd gathered around him on the shore because they had all been waiting for him to return. Then, a leader of the local synagogue named Jairus came, and when he saw Jesus, he prostrated himself in front of him and pleaded, "My 12-year-old daughter is dying. Please come and lay your hands on her so she will live." Jesus agreed to come, and as they walked through the narrow streets, the crowd following them pressed in on every side.

In the crowd was a woman who suffered from chronic uterine bleeding. She had had this problem for twelve years and had spent all she owned on doctors whose treatments caused additional suffering with no positive results. Her condition had only gotten worse. Since she had heard about the things Jesus could do, she came up behind him in the crowd and unobtrusively touched a symbolic tassel hanging from his robe. She was thinking, "If I can just touch a tassel on his robe, I will be healed." Immediately, the bleeding stopped, and she knew from the way her body felt that she was completely healed. At the same instant, Jesus sensed that healing power had flowed out from him, so he abruptly stopped, turned around, and asked, "Who touched my robe?" His close followers said, "Master, everyone's crowding around you. Anyone could've accidentally touched you." But Jesus said, "I know that someone deliberately touched me because I felt power go out from me." So he kept looking around to find out who had done it. When the woman realized that she hadn't gotten away unnoticed, she came forward—trembling with fear—and prostrated herself before him. Then in front of everyone, she confessed what she had done, and why, and how she had immediately been healed. Jesus said to her gently, "My daughter, your faith in me has healed you. Go home in wholeness and peace—and don't be afraid."

While Jesus was still speaking to her, someone arrived from Jairus' house and reported, "Jairus, your daughter has died. There's no reason the Rabbi should bother to come." But Jesus overheard and told him, "Don't be afraid. Continue to trust in me and she will be OK." Then, Jesus didn't allow anyone from the crowd to follow him any farther toward the house except Peter, John, and James. When they arrived, Jesus saw a crowd of people surrounding the house, mourning and wailing. Since Jesus knew that he was going to wake her back to life, he told the mourners, "You shouldn't be making all this commotion and wailing. The girl isn't dead, she is only sleeping." They ridiculed him because they knew she was dead. But he made all the mourners leave. Then with the girl's parents and his three companions, he entered the room where the girl was. Holding her hand, he said in ordinary Aramaic, "*Talitha koum!*" which means, "Little girl, stand up!"

Her life returned and she immediately sat up. Then Jesus told her parents to give her something to eat. Everyone there was astounded. Jesus sternly commanded them not to tell anyone what had happened. But the news about this was rapidly spread throughout the region anyway.

87. Two Blind Men and a Man Made Mute by a Demon

As Jesus went on from there, two blind men followed some way behind him, shouting, "Son of David, have mercy and help us!" Jesus reached the house where he was staying and went inside, and the blind men caught up and entered too. He asked them, "Do you believe I can make you see?" They answered, "Yes, Lord!" He touched their eyelids and said, "Since you believe, you will be able to see!" And immediately, they could see. Jesus gave them firm instructions, "I don't want you telling anyone about this!" But they were so excited that they went out and told everyone anyway, so the story spread throughout the region.

As they were on their way out, a demonized man who couldn't speak was brought in to him. But as soon as Jesus commanded the demon to leave, the man was able to speak. The crowd was amazed and said, "There has never been anything like this in Israel before!"

But the Pharisees were saying, "He is only able to expel demons because he has the help of Satan who rules them!"

88. Jesus Is Rejected in Nazareth a Second Time

When Jesus finished telling all these parables, he left Capernaum and came to his hometown of Nazareth where he had been raised as a child. As was his practice on the Sabbath, he went to the local synagogue and taught. All who heard him were shocked. They indignantly asked each other, "Where did he get this wisdom and the power to do miracles? He's just the carpenter's son, isn't he? Isn't Miriam his mother, and his brothers are James, Joseph, Simon, and Judas? Aren't his sisters living here too? What makes him think he can be a prophet?" So they were offended and rejected him. Then Jesus said, "No prophet is accepted as such in his hometown, or among his own family." And because of their active disbelief in him, he was unable to do any miracles there

except heal a few people through laying his hands on them. He was astonished at their lack of faith.

89. Pray for More Kingdom Workers

Jesus went to every town and village in the region, teaching in the synagogues and proclaiming the Good News about how people could enter into a new relationship with God as their King. Everywhere he went, he healed every kind of disease and illness. He felt compassion for the people because they had troubles and felt helpless. They were like sheep without a shepherd to care for them. He told his close followers, "The potential harvest of people ready to enter God's Kingdom is great, but the number of people ready to help bring them in are few. So pray to the owner of the harvest who has been preparing these people to believe, and ask him to send out more workers to proclaim the Good News to help bring them in."

90. Jesus Sends Out the Twelve to Minister

Jesus continued his ministry to visit and teach from village to village. Then, he summoned his twelve apostles together and gave them power and authority to expel any demon and to heal every kind of disease and illness.

❖ *The names of the twelve are given in section 46.* ➤

He organized them in pairs and sent them out to various places to minister after giving them the following instructions: "Don't go to any Gentile areas or to any Samaritans. Your mission is to go to Israelites who are not following God's ways. Wherever you go, preach this message: 'God is inviting people to submit to him as their King. Now is when you have the opportunity to do so.' Also heal those who are sick, raise dead people back to life, heal those with contagious skin diseases, and expel demons from people. Minister in these ways without accepting pay beyond room, board, and basic necessities since you've received the power and authority to do these things without charge.

"Don't take money of any amount with you. Don't take a beggars bag or extra clothing or even a walking stick, but you may wear sandals. Basically, you are to trust that

God will provide what you need through the people you minister to. For a worker deserves to be supported by those who benefit from his labor.

"When you enter a town or village, find someone there who is willing to accept you and your message and to be your host. Then stay with that person until you move on to the next town. Whenever you enter a house, greet them with 'shalom.' If the people in that house welcome you, allow your blessing of shalom to remain. Don't seek better accommodations or move from house to house. But if they do not welcome you or your message, tell them that God withdraws his blessing of shalom from them. In that case, pointedly shake off the dust from your feet as you leave. ❖ *This was a non-verbal rebuke in that culture, implying that even the dust of their house (or town) was defiling and offensive because they were no better than pagans. It was also a warning that they had better repent or they would face God's judgment.* ➤ It's a fact that on Judgment Day, the sinners of Sodom and Gomorrah will be punished less than those people.

91. Those Who Do God's Work Will Be Persecuted

"Be aware that though I'm sending you out to minister, you're as defenseless as lambs among wolves. So you need to be wise, sensible, shrewd, and cautious, yet at the same time be totally pure and innocent of doing any wrong. Be on guard against men who will try to arrest you because you are my followers. They will hand you over to local authorities and have you beaten in their synagogues. You will be put on trial before rulers and kings, but God will allow this so you can have the opportunity to tell about the things you've see me do and heard me teach. You will even have opportunity to tell these things to Gentiles. But when they arrest you and bring you to trial, don't worry about what you should say to defend yourself, and don't think about how to say it ahead of time. For at the time you need to speak, God will give you the words he wants you to say. It won't be you who is actually speaking, but the Spirit of your Heavenly Father who will be speaking through you.

"Be aware that some of you will even be betrayed to the authorities to be executed by your siblings, your parents, or your children. Many will hate you because you are my followers. But those of you who patiently endure all these things to the end of their lives—while remaining faithful to me—will be saved. When they persecute you in one town, do your best to escape to another. Be sure to know this: You won't finish going through all the towns of Israel preaching the message of the Good News before I, the Son of Man, return.

"A follower isn't any more important than his master, just as a slave isn't more important than his owner. So a follower should be content to be treated like his master, and the slave should be content to be treated like his owner. Since people have said that I'm in league with Satan and treat me accordingly, you would be wise to expect the same—and even worse.

"But don't be afraid of them. Reveal to them all the things that I've told you but so far have not taught the public. What I tell you in private, you must proclaim for all to hear. Don't be afraid of those who might kill you. They can kill your body, but they can't touch your soul. But I will tell you who you should have a healthy fear of—and that's God. He not only has power over your life in this world, but after you die, he decides if you will be sent to Hell or not. If you have any sense at all, you should realize he is the one to be afraid of—not people.

"You know that sparrows are so common they are nearly worthless. Two of them can be bought for next to nothing. But even creatures as unimportant as sparrows are noticed by God. He is aware of each and every one of them and what happens to them. I assure you, you are far more important to him than mere sparrows! God's awareness and care for you is so great that he even knows how many hairs are on your head every moment. Nothing takes him by surprise and nothing can defeat his power, so there is no reason for any of his children to ever be afraid of what people can do to them.

"So don't be afraid to publicly proclaim your allegiance to me from fear of persecution or even death. I want you to know that all who are willing to publicly declare they are my followers—regardless of the consequences—will find on Judgment Day that I will publicly declare before my Heavenly Father and his angels that they belong to me. But those who publicly deny they belong to me—even if it's only because they're afraid of persecution or death—will find that I too will publicly deny before my Heavenly Father and his angels that they belong to me.

92. The Price of Being Jesus' True Follower

"Did you think that I came to bring peace to this world? Not at all! I came to bring division between those who follow me and those who continue to reject me. Your enemies might even be the members of your own family. Families will divide, father against son, mother against daughter, mother-in-law against daughter-in-law, and every other possible relationship.

"If you want to be one of my followers but can't place your loyalty and obedience to me above your loyalty to your parents or children—then I won't accept you. If you aren't willing to give up your own plans and desires in order to obey my will for you—even if it means you must suffer or die for me—then you can't be one of my true followers. Those who try to save their lives by denying that they belong to me will not have eternal life in Heaven. But those who are willing to die in order to faithfully follow me will find that they have eternal life.

93. God Rewards Those Who Help His Workers

"Those who welcome you because they recognize that you are my followers, my Father and I consider as also welcoming us. Those who welcome God's prophets because they recognize they are such, God will reward. And those who welcome godly people because they recognize their relationship to me will receive the same reward that God gives godly people. Those who give one of my humble followers as little as a cup of cold water to drink because they recognize that they belong to me, God will certainly reward."

When Jesus finished giving all these instructions to his twelve apostles, he sent them off to minister while he continued on alone to teach and preach in their towns. So the apostles set out and went through many towns and villages, preaching that people should turn away from their sins and submit to God's rule over their lives. They also expelled many demons and anointed the sick with oil for healing—and many were healed.

94. John the Baptizer's Death

This is how John died. Herod had married Herodias—who was still legally the wife of his younger brother Philip. John the Baptizer kept telling Herod that God's Torah forbade such a relationship, and this made Herodias want him dead. So Herod had John put in prison to silence his public criticism. But he respected John—knowing that he was a good and holy man—and protected him so Herodias couldn't have her way. Herod liked to have John brought in so he could listen to him preach, even though he became very upset every time he did so. But one day, an opportunity presented itself for Herodias to have John killed.

On Herod's birthday, he gave a banquet for all his high-ranking military and administrative officers and some of the important leaders in Galilee. Herodia's daughter came in and danced erotically for Herod and his guests. She pleased them all so much that Herod imprudently told the girl in front of everyone, "As a reward, ask me for anything and I will give it to you. I make a solemn oath before everyone here that I will give you anything at all—up to half of my kingdom." So she went to ask advice from her mother, "What should I ask for?" Her mother said, "John the Baptizer's head." The girl immediately returned to the king and said, "I want John the Baptizer's head on a platter, right now." Herod then regretted his oath, but would lose face in front of his guests if he refused to keep it. So he immediately ordered an executioner to bring him John's head. The man did as he was told and soon brought the head on a platter. It was given to the girl, who took it to her mother.

When John's followers heard about it, they retrieved his body and placed it in a tomb. Then they went to tell Jesus what had happened.

The news about Jesus and the things he was doing spread everywhere. People were saying that Jesus was John the Baptizer come back from the dead, and that was why he had the power to do these miracles. Others said that he was the prophet Elijah. Still others thought he was a prophet of the same caliber as the great prophets from long ago.

About the same time that Jesus was sending out his twelve apostles to minister, all this came to the notice of Herod Antipas, tetrarch over Galilee Province. When he heard about it, he started saying, "This is John—the man I had beheaded—come back to life! That's why there's power in him to do miracles." And he made unsuccessful efforts to see Jesus.

95. Jesus Demonstrates Power to Multiply Resources
(Just Before Passover in the Spring of AD 29)

It was nearly time for the Passover Festival when the apostles returned from their tour of ministry and reported to Jesus all that they had done. But there were so many people coming for healing that they hardly had a chance to eat. Also about this same time, Jesus learned what had happened to John (who was a relative). So he got into a boat with his close followers and tried to withdraw to the eastern shore of Lake Galilee (also known as Lake Tiberius) where he could have some privacy from the public. But people from many villages heard where he was headed and hiked there along the shore of the lake. When Jesus arrived, he saw a large crowd waiting for him and felt compassion for them. They were like helpless sheep with no one to care for them. So he started to teach them many spiritual truths that they needed to know and went about healing all among them who were sick.

As it was getting on toward evening, his close followers came to him and said, "This place is pretty remote, and it's already getting late. You should send the people away so they have time to reach some village or farm to find lodging and something to eat

before night falls." But Jesus replied, "They don't need to leave. I want you to feed them." Then Jesus asked Philip, "Where can we buy enough bread to feed all these people?" But he knew what he was going to do and was simply testing Philip's faith. Philip replied, "Even eight months' wages wouldn't be enough to feed everyone just a little!" Then another of his followers—Simon Peter's brother Andrew—said, "There's a boy here with five small loaves of barley bread and two small fish—but they are nothing for so many." Jesus replied, "Well, bring them to me."

He directed all the people to recline on the green spring grass in groups, and they did so in groups of fifty or a hundred. He then took the five rolls and the two fish, looked up toward Heaven in an attitude of prayer, and thanked God for the food. Then he broke them into small pieces and kept giving them to his followers. And they distributed the pieces—which were miraculously multiplied and never ran out—to all the people. Everyone in the crowd ate as much as they wanted and were fully satisfied.

When everyone was full, he told his followers, "Gather up the leftovers so nothing will be wasted." So they gathered all the leftovers and filled twelve baskets with bread. When the people saw the miraculous sign that Jesus had done, they said to each other, "He must be the Prophet that Moses promised would come!" But Jesus perceived that they intended to come and force him to be a king behind whom they would rally and overcome the Romans. So he decided to withdraw by himself higher up into the hills.

96. Jesus and Peter Walk on Water

Jesus told his close followers to get back in the boat and proceed to the other side of the lake ahead of him while he convinced the people to go home. After dismissing the people, Jesus went up the mountain by himself to pray. He stayed there all alone until well after sunset. By that time, the boat with his followers was quite a ways out on the lake, but they were hindered by a strong wind blowing against them which was also causing large waves. They fought to make headway against the wind for hours; and during the fourth watch of the night,

❖ *i.e., sometime between 3 and 6 a.m.—but before dawn* ➤ Jesus came walking across the lake toward them on the water, intending to pass by them. But when his followers saw him, they were terrified. They cried out, "It's a ghost!"

But Jesus immediately reassured them, "Don't worry! It's me! There's nothing to be afraid of!"

Peter called out to him, "Lord, if it's really you, command me to come out to you on the water."

Jesus said, "Come!" So Peter got out of the boat and started walking on the water toward Jesus. But then he was distracted by the wind and the waves and became frightened. Focusing on the impossibilities—instead of remembering to trust Jesus—he began doubt and to sink. But immediately he cried out, "Lord, save me!"

Jesus quickly reached out and grabbed him. He said to Peter, "Your faith is so small! Why did you start to doubt me?"

Then, they both climbed into the boat, and the wind suddenly died down. His followers recognized the significance of all this and bowed down to worship him. They exclaimed, "You really are God's Son!"

97. Jesus Heals in Gennesaret

When they finished their crossing, they landed in Gennesaret and tied the boat up there. As soon as they got out of the boat, people recognized Jesus and ran to spread the news to everyone in the area that he was there. As a result, many sick people were carried to him on their sleeping mats. Wherever he went in towns, villages, or fields people brought the sick and laid them on the ground for him to heal. The sick begged him for permission to just touch one of the symbolic tassels of his robe as he passed by, and all who did so were healed.

98. Jesus' Teaching on 'The Bread of Life'

The next day, the crowd that had stayed on the other side of the lake were waiting to see Jesus because they knew there had only been one boat and that his followers had left in it without him. Then, some boats from Tiberius came to shore, near the place where the crowd had eaten the miraculously multiplied bread. So when the crowd realized that neither Jesus nor his followers were there, they got into the boats and went looking for him in Capernaum. When they found him there, they asked him, "Rabbi, when and how did you get here?"

Jesus replied, "The truth is, you are only following me because you know that I have the power to feed you, not because you understand the significance of this miraculous sign. You shouldn't be nearly as concerned about obtaining food to sustain this temporary life as you should be about obtaining spiritual food that gives eternal life. I, the Son of Man, am the one who gives this spiritual food and eternal life. This should be clear because God the Father has put his sign of approval on me." So they asked him, "What work does God want us to do to obtain eternal life?" Jesus replied, "The only work that God requires of you to gain eternal life is to believe in me, whom he sent to you." They demanded, "What miraculous sign will you do to convince us that he sent you so we can believe in you? Moses gave our ancestors manna in the wilderness, just as it's written, 'He gave them bread from Heaven to eat.' " Jesus replied, "The truth is, it was my Father—not Moses—who gave them the bread from Heaven called 'manna.' It's also my Father who offers you the 'True Bread from Heaven' that gives eternal life. For God's 'Bread' comes down from Heaven and gives eternal life to the people of this world." They said, "Sir, give us that bread every day!"

Jesus told them, "I am the 'Bread from Heaven' that gives eternal life. Those who believe in me and follow me will never again have spiritual hunger or thirst, for they will be satisfied with eternal life. But as I've said before, you've seen me and the signs I've done, yet you still refuse to believe that God sent me. However, the people that my Father gives me will believe in me, and I will always keep them close to me. For I came from Heaven to do his will, not my own, and his will is that of all the people he gives me to be my true followers, none will be lost.

They will all persevere in faith, and I will give them eternal life on the Last Day. For my Father's will is that all who look to me—his Son—for eternal life and believe in me will gain eternal life. And on the Last Day, I, myself, will raise them up and usher them into that new life."

Then, the people started to grumble and complain against Jesus because he said, "I am the Bread from Heaven that gives eternal life." They were saying, "How can he claim to have come down from Heaven? We know who his parents are. He's just the son of Yosef!" Jesus told them, "Stop grumbling about what I said. No one can believe in me unless my Father who sent me first draws them and enables them to believe. And those I will indeed raise up on the Last Day. As it's written in the prophets about those who come to God, 'They will all be taught by Yahweh.' So everyone who listens to the Father and learns from him will come to believe in me. Not that anyone has ever seen the Father except me—whom he sent into this world. I've seen him, and you can only get to know him through me. I'm telling you an important truth. Those who believe in me have eternal life. I am the Bread that gives eternal life. Your ancestors ate manna in the wilderness—a miraculous bread from Heaven—and they still died. But those who eat the 'Bread that comes down from Heaven' that I'm talking about, won't die. And I am that eternal-life-giving Bread that came down from Heaven. Those who eat this Bread will live forever. And the Bread that I offer up in sacrifice for the lives of everyone in this world is my flesh."

These words offended the people and made them angry. They began to argue about what he meant. They asked, "How can he give us his flesh to eat?" So Jesus said, "This is an important truth. I am the Son of Man, and you can't have eternal life unless you eat my flesh and drink my blood. But those who eat my flesh and drink my blood have eternal life. And on the Last Day, I, my-self, will raise them up and usher them into that new life. Food and drink are necessary for life, but my flesh and blood are the true food and drink that are necessary for eternal life. Those who eat my flesh and drink my blood are spiritually united with me. I live in them, and they live in me. Just as the Father who sent me is the source of all life, I too am the source of life because of my relationship with him. So those who feed on me will live forever because I am the source of eternal life.

"So I am the 'Bread that came down from Heaven.' Your ancestors ate manna from Heaven and later died. But those who feed on me will live forever." Jesus said these things while teaching at the synagogue in Capernaum.

When many who had been following him heard this, they said, "This teaching is offensive! Who can accept it?" But Jesus was aware that his followers were grumbling about this, so he said, "Do my words offend you and cause you to reject me? Then what would your reaction be if you were to see me, the Son of Man, ascend back up into Heaven? It is God's Holy Spirit who gives eternal life. Physical efforts cannot produce it. The things I've been saying to you have been about spiritual truths, and come from him. They will impart eternal life to those who receive them. But some of you don't believe me." Jesus knew right from the beginning when they started following him, which of them didn't believe in him and who would betray him. Then he added, "That's why I told you nobody can believe in me unless my Father who sent me first draws them and enables them to believe." As a result of this teaching, many of his followers left him and no longer desired to associate themselves with him.

So Jesus challenged his twelve closest followers, "You're not going to leave me too, are you?" Simon Peter answered, "Lord, who else could we go to? You are the one with God's message about eternal life. We believe in you and are convinced that you are the Holy One sent by God." Jesus replied, "Each of you twelve were hand-picked by me, yet one of you is Satan's henchman!" He was referring to Judas—son of Simon Iscariot—because even though he was one of Jesus' twelve closest followers, he would later betray him.

99. What Defiles Us in God's Sight and What Does Not

One day, some Pharisees and Scripture teachers from Jerusalem approached Jesus. They had noticed that Jesus' close followers didn't ritually wash their hands before eating to "purify" themselves, as the traditions of the Jewish elders required. They taught that when people came home from the marketplace, they must ritually wash before eating. There were also many other traditions that they religiously observed, such as the proper ritual washing of cups, pitchers, copper pots, and dining couches (upon which they reclined when they ate). So these Pharisees and Scripture teachers indignantly said, "You are responsible for the behavior of your followers. Why do you allow them to break the traditions established by the elders? They don't ritually wash their hands before eating!"

Jesus retorted, "You are a bunch of hypocrites! God was speaking about people just like you when he had Isaiah write, 'These people say they honor me and they make a show of it, but in their hearts they don't really love me at all. I consider their worship to be worthless since they teach their followers to keep their man-made rules as if they were my commands!' You even consider your own man-made traditions more important than the teachings in the Torah given by God, and are perfectly willing to break his commands in order to follow your petty rules! As an example, God says, 'Honor your parents,' and also, 'Someone who curses his parents is to be executed.' But you say a person can inform his parents that he has dedicated his resources to God, and then he doesn't have to use those resources to support them in their old age. Your tradition thus circumvents God's command and it's intent that a man should honor and help his parents. And that's only one example among many such ways you have to avoid doing what God requires."

Then, Jesus called everyone's attention to what he was about to say. He said, "Listen carefully and try to understand this! It is what comes out of a person's mouth that defiles him—not what goes in as the Pharisees teach! If your minds are attuned to God, try to understand what this means!"

Afterward, his followers came and said, "You realize that the Pharisees were highly offended by what you just said, don't you?"

Jesus contemptuously replied, "My Heavenly Father will completely destroy any teaching that doesn't come from him. I want you to ignore them and their teachings. They claim to be spiritual guides to those who are ignorant of God's truth. But in reality, they are themselves blind to it. They lead those who follow them to destruction."

Peter asked him, "Would you please explain what you said about being defiled?"

Jesus was exasperated. He replied, "Don't you understand either? What goes in your mouth goes down to your stomach, then through your bowels, and is eventually eliminated from your body, cleansing all food. **A** Don't you see that eating something with unwashed hands doesn't affect how God views you? 'What comes out of your mouth,' is what you say. Your words come from your mind, and if they are sinful, then they defile you in God's sight. An evil heart produces evil thoughts and desires: to murder, to commit adultery or sexual immorality, to steal, to do evil deeds, to covet, to envy, to be stingy, to deceive, to lust, to be indecent, to falsely testify or slander, to blaspheme, to be proud, to be arrogant, to be morally foolish, and other such sins. These are the kinds of things that defile a person in God's sight. Eating without ritually washing your hands doesn't affect your heart or mind at all and can't make your heart evil. And ritually washing your hands can't make or keep your mind pure. It's the things of your mind and thoughts that God cares about, not meaningless outward ceremonies."

A 99 See the note at Mark 7:19 about what the phrase "cleansing all food" means and does not mean.

100. The Persistent Faith of a Gentile Woman

After that, Jesus left Galilee and traveled north to the region around the Gentile port cities of Tyre and Sidon. He stayed in a particular house and didn't want people to know where he was. But as usual, he was recognized and news of his location spread quickly.

A Gentile woman from that area heard about him and immediately went to find him. Then, she prostrated herself in front of him and loudly pleaded, "Lord, Son of David, have mercy and help me for my daughter is severely demonized." Surprisingly, Jesus ignored her. So his followers said to him, "She is just going to continue to follow us and shout. Please send her away." But instead, he said to the woman, "God only sent me to minister to Israelites who are lost in their sin." Instead of being put off, the woman pleaded, "Lord, please help me!" He replied, "It wouldn't be right to take food that's meant for God's children and give it to the pet dogs." She replied, "Yes, Lord. But even dogs are allowed to eat bits from the children's food that fall under the master's table." Then Jesus exclaimed, "My dear woman, you have strong faith indeed! I will grant your request. You may go home for the demon has left your girl." And her daughter was healed right then. When she arrived at her house, she found her little girl lying peacefully in bed because the demon was gone.

101. Jesus Heals a Deaf mute

Then Jesus left the area near Tyre and passed through Sidon and down to Lake Galilee and then on to the Gentile Decapolis district. Some people there brought him a man who was deaf and mute and begged him to lay his hands on him for healing. Jesus led the man off away from the crowd, put his fingers in the man's ears, then spit on his own fingers and touched the man's tongue with the saliva. He looked up toward Heaven in prayer and sighed deeply. Then he said in ordinary Aramaic, "Effatha!" which means, 'Open!' Immediately, the man could hear and speak clearly. Jesus told the people who had brought him not to tell anyone what he had done. But it seemed that the more strictly he forbade this, the more people proclaimed what they knew. They were completely astonished at this healing and said, "Everything he does turns out good. He even enables the deaf and mute to hear and speak."

102. Jesus Multiplies Resources to Feed 4000 Men

Returning to Lake Galilee, Jesus went up a hill and sat down, ready to teach. A large crowd followed him and brought people to be healed from being lame, crippled, blind, mute, and many other disorders. They would lay them at Jesus' feet, and he healed each one of them. The people were constantly amazed as they saw the formerly mute speak, those who had been crippled made normal, those who had been lame walking, and they praised the God of Israel for doing it through Jesus.

After spending some days there, any food that they had brought with them was finished. Jesus summoned his close followers and told them, "I feel sorry for these people. They've been with me for three days and their food is gone. I don't want to send them away without something to eat for some of them might faint from hunger on their way home."

His followers said, "But this crowd is so huge! Where could we find enough bread in this remote place to feed them, even if we could afford it?"

Jesus asked them, "How many loaves of bread do you have?" They answered, "Only seven, plus a few small fish."

Then, Jesus told the people to recline on the ground and he took the seven loaves and the fish. He thanked God for them, broke them, and gave them to his followers to distribute. Everyone ate all they that could desire and were full. When the leftovers were gathered, they filled seven large baskets. That crowd included about 4000 men—not counting the women and children.

After Jesus sent the people home, he and his close followers got into the boat and went to the region of Magadan and Dalmanutha.

103. Interpreting the Signs of the Times

Some Pharisees and Sadducees came to test Jesus. They asked him for an unmistakable miraculous sign that God had sent him. Jesus sighed deeply in his spirit and said, "Some evenings you predict, 'Tomorrow's weather will be fair since the sky is red.' And some mornings you predict, 'Today, there will be a rainstorm since the sky is overcast and red.' Or when you see a rain cloud coming out of the west from the Mediterranean Sea, you say, 'It's going to rain,' and you're right. And when you notice a wind out of the south from the desert, you say, 'It's going to be hot,' and that's exactly how it turns out. You hypocrites! You're observant enough to interpret the weather signs, but you seem incapable of interpreting the equally obvious signs that are happening in these times. ❖ *They were hypocrites because they claimed to know God and understand his ways, yet they refused to understand that Jesus was the Messiah sent by God. And they refused to accept his teaching despite the miraculous signs he did. They chose to ignore these signs because they didn't want to conclude that Jesus was the Messiah. If they did so, they would have to give up their own cherished beliefs and status as interpreters of God's Torah and will. The meaning of the signs and the message he preached were as obvious as the weather signs.* ➤ This generation is evil and unfaithful to God. You want a miraculous sign before you will believe, but none will be granted you except the sign of Jonah!" Then he left them, got back into the boat with his followers, and crossed the lake.

104. Jesus Warns About the Evil Influence of the Pharisees and Sadducees

As they were crossing, his men realized that they had forgotten to bring bread along. All they had was one small loaf with them. Jesus, still thinking about his confrontation with the Pharisees and Sadducees, said, "Guard yourselves against the leaven of the Pharisees and Sadducees." ❖ *"Leaven" was a piece of unused dough that had been set aside to use to raise another batch of bread. The natural yeast in that piece multiplied as the dough sat for a few days. Leaven was a metaphor meaning influence, sometimes positive, but usually negative. It represented* *impure influence when they rid their houses of it during the preparation for Passover and the Feast of Unleavened Bread. They should have understood his meaning, yet they were focused on their own concerns.* ➤ His followers started discussing the meaning of his statement among themselves and concluded, "He said it because we forgot to bring bread along."

But Jesus was aware of their discussion and said, "Why are you talking about not having any bread? Are you so resistant to truth that you still don't understand the things you've seen and heard? Or are your memories faulty? When I fed the crowd of 5000 men with five loaves of bread, how many baskets of leftovers did you gather?" They answered, "Twelve." Jesus continued, "And when I fed the crowd of 4000 men with seven loaves of bread, how many large baskets of leftovers did you gather?" They answered, "Seven." He asked them, "Don't you understand the significance of those miracles is that I can provide you with any food you need, so I wasn't concerned about your not bringing bread along? What I said was, guard yourselves against the leaven of the Pharisees and the Sadducees!" Then, they finally understood that he wasn't talking about the leaven in bread, but about the teachings of the Pharisees and Sadducees.

105. Jesus Heals a Blind Man

They arrived at the town of Bethsaida where some people brought a blind man to Jesus and begged him to touch him for healing. Jesus took him by the hand and led him outside of town away from the people. He spit in the man's eyes and lay his hands on him, then asked, "Are you able to see anything now?" The man looked around and said, "Yes, I can see people, but not clearly. They look like trees walking around." So Jesus put his hands over the man's eyes again. Afterward, the man stared intently and his sight was fully restored. He saw everything clearly. Then Jesus sent him on his way home but told him, "Don't go into the town to tell others about this on your way home."

106. Peter Recognizes That Jesus Is the Messiah

Afterwards, Jesus and his close followers walked north about 25 miles to the villages near Caesarea Philippi. On the way, he asked them, "Who do people think I am?" They answered, "Some say that you're John the Baptizer come back to life. Some say you're the prophet Elijah. And some say that you're some other prophet from long ago who has returned."

Then he asked, "What about you? Who do you think I am?" Simon Peter immediately answered, "You are God's Anointed One—the Messiah—the Son of the only living God!"

Jesus said to him, "I bless you, Simon son of John, because no human being could tell you this. It was my Heavenly Father who revealed it to you. I will also say that you are like a rock. And upon this rock foundation— the confession of faith in me that you've just made—I will build my Assembly of Believers which the power of death will never overcome nor silence. I will give you, Peter, the keys to God's Kingdom. Whatever you prohibit or allow here on earth will correspondingly be prohibited or allowed in Heaven." Then Jesus sternly ordered his followers not to tell anyone yet that he was the Messiah because he didn't want to force people to make a decision at this time about who they believed he was.

107. Jesus Predicts His Suffering and Death

Starting at that time, Jesus began to explain to his close followers that he had to go to Jerusalem where he would be arrested and suffer under the power of the Jewish religious leaders, be killed, and then come back to life on the second day after his death. **A** He explained it all very plainly. But Peter spoke to Jesus privately and rebuked him for saying that these things would happen. He said, "Lord! May God forbid that anything like that should happen to you! It must not happen!" Jesus turned away from Peter and said, "Get out of my way, Adversary! You are tempting me to stumble in sin. Avoiding what must happen is your human response, but it's not what God wants me to do."

108. The High Cost of Following Jesus

Then Jesus told his followers, "If you want to be one of my true followers, you must put aside your own desires and be willing to suffer and even die in order to follow and obey me. Those who want to retain control of their own lives and protect them ❖ *as opposed to submitting to God's authority and risk suffering for him* ➤ will ultimately lose them. But those who are willing to give up all that they are and have in order to follow me—even their own lives— will ultimately gain their true lives in Heaven. What benefit have you gained if you acquire everything you desire in this temporary world but in the process lose your chance at eternal life in Heaven? What is the opportunity to live forever in Heaven and avoid eternity in Hell worth to you? Isn't it worth more than anything else, even over saving your temporary life in this world?

"For I, the Son of Man, will return to this world with the glorious power and majesty I have in union with my Father. I will come with his angels and will reward each person based on what they've done in their earthly lives. Those who are ashamed to be associated with me and my message because they fear persecution, I, the Son of Man, will reject when I return. I assure you that some of you standing here right now will see, before they die, the glory of God's Kingdom manifest in power, and me, the Son of Man, coming as King."

109. God Reveals Jesus' True Glory

About six days later, Jesus took just Peter, James, and James' younger brother John up a high mountain so they could pray by themselves. While they were there, his appearance changed before their very eyes. His face started to shine like the sun and his clothing became whiter than anything man can make, shining with a brilliant light.

A 107 See the note at Matthew 16:21 for the reasoning behind not using the traditional phrase, "the third day."

Then, Moses and the prophet Elijah suddenly appeared from Heaven. They too shone with the light of God's glory. They spoke with Jesus about his upcoming departure from this world and what would soon happen to him in Jerusalem. As Moses and Elijah were about to leave, Peter blurted out, "Rabbi, it's good that we're here. If you want, I will make three shelters here, one for you, one for Moses, and one for Elijah." (He didn't really know what to say, as he and his companions were so frightened.)

While he was saying this, a cloud appeared around them like a thick fog—making everything look shadowy—and frightening them. Then they heard God's voice saying, "This is my Son, my Chosen One who pleases me greatly in all that he says and does. *He* is the one you should listen to and obey!" ❖ *i.e., The authority of God's Son exceeds that of Moses and his Teachings and the prophets and their writings.* ➤ When the three followers heard this, they were terrified and prostrated themselves on the ground in worship. Jesus came over, touched them, and said, "There's nothing to be afraid of. Get up." When they raised their heads to look around, they only saw Jesus as he normally was.

While they were going down the mountain together, Jesus commanded them, "Don't tell anyone about the vision you saw until after I, the Son of Man, have died and come back from death." So they kept this as a secret among themselves, but discussed what Jesus might have meant about "coming back from death."

Since they had just seen Elijah, they asked him, "Why do the Scripture teachers say that Elijah must come before the Messiah comes?" Jesus replied, "That prophecy is certainly true. Elijah did come, and he inaugurated events that will restore everything to be as it should be. Elijah came, but no one recognized him. Instead, they mistreated a prophet from God any way they liked, just as the Scriptures say about him." Then they understood that he was saying John the Baptizer was the one who fulfilled that prophecy. Jesus added, "In a similar way, the Scriptures say that I, the Son of Man, must suffer many things and be despised and rejected."

110. Jesus' Followers Fail to Expel a Demon

When they reached the bottom of the mountain where they had left the rest of Jesus' close followers, they saw them surrounded by a large crowd, and they were arguing with some Scripture teachers. The people were surprised when they saw Jesus coming and they all ran to greet him. Jesus asked his followers, "What are you arguing with them about?"

Then a man came and prostrated himself in front of Jesus and said, "Rabbi! I beg you to look at my only son. A demon keeps seizing control of him, making him unable to speak. It makes him scream and convulse. It often makes him fall on the ground, foam at the mouth, grind his teeth, and become entirely rigid. It hardly ever leaves him alone and it's continually injuring him. I begged your followers to expel it, but they couldn't."

Jesus said to his apostles, "You are stubborn and have no faith! How long will I have to be with you and put up with you before you learn how to use my power?" Then he said to the man, "Bring your son here." ❖ *Jesus had already trained his apostles and had given them power and authority over every demon. Since the man came to them for help, it is clear that they had a reputation for expelling demons. But they had failed to learn the lesson well enough.* ➤

They brought the boy, but when the demon saw Jesus, it immediately caused the boy to have a violent seizure. He collapsed on the ground, writhing and foaming at the mouth. Jesus asked the father, "How long has he been having these seizures?" He answered, "Ever since he was a child. The demon makes him fall into fires and water, trying to kill him. If you can do anything at all, please have pity and help us!" Jesus replied, "Why do you express doubt by saying, 'If I can?' God can do anything for the person who believes in his power and love." The man immediately replied, "I do believe, but help me overcome my doubts!" When Jesus noticed that the crowd was quickly getting larger, he said to the demon, "You demon that's causing this boy to be deaf and mute, I command you to leave him and never enter him again!" In fury, the demon made the boy scream and have one last violent seizure, then it left him. The boy lay unmoving on the ground as if he were dead, and many in the crowd thought he was. But Jesus took his hand and helped him stand up. He healed the boy and presented him back to his father. All who saw it were awed by this display of God's power.

Later, Jesus' followers came to him in private and asked, "Why couldn't we expel that demon?" He answered, "Because of your unbelief. You must understand this. If you have even a small amount of genuine faith, you can overcome even seemingly impossible obstacles. Nothing that God wants you to do will be impossible for you. But this kind of demon does not leave easily with just a command. You also need to fast and pray."

111. Jesus Talks a Second Time About His Death

Jesus and his close followers left that place, and though they were traveling through Galilee, he didn't want people to know where he was. He wanted to be alone with his close followers so he could teach them, and he was trying to tell them, "Listen carefully to what I tell you and remember it. I, the Son of Man, will be handed over to the authorities by men who hate me. They will kill me, and on the second [A] day after my death, God will make me alive again." When they heard this, they were greatly distressed. But they were blinded by their cultural expectations about the Messiah and they didn't understand what he was talking about, for God prevented them. And they were too timid to ask him what he meant.

112. Jesus Miraculously Pays the Temple Tax

When Jesus and his close followers arrived in Capernaum, those who were collecting the annual two-drachma Temple tax came to Peter and asked, "Your Rabbi pays the Temple tax, doesn't he?" He answered, "Yes." Later, he entered the house where Jesus was, but Jesus spoke first, "Simon, I'd like to hear your opinion on a matter. Do the kings of this world collect taxes from their own sons or from others?" Peter answered, "From others." Jesus replied, "Then you agree that the king's sons are exempt. But we don't want to offend the tax collectors who wouldn't understand that we are exempt. So go down to the lake and throw in a fishing line. Inside the mouth of the first fish you catch, you will find a shekel. ❖ worth four drachmas ➤ Take it, and give it to the tax collector for your tax and mine."

113. How to Be Important in God's Sight

One day, Jesus' followers were arguing about which of them was most important in God's Kingdom. Later when they were with Jesus indoors, he asked them, "What were you discussing before we arrived here?" They were too embarrassed to answer him, but Jesus already knew what they had been talking about. So he called them all to gather round. He brought a child and had him stand in front of the men. Jesus took the child in his arms and told the adults, "It's important you understand this. Unless you change your attitudes and become humble and forget about status, you will never enter God's Kingdom. So those who humble themselves like this child will be among the greatest in God's Kingdom. Those who humbly welcome and serve others out of loving obedience to me—even someone as low in status as this child—I will consider them as having done it to me. And my Father who sent me will also consider them as having done it to him. For whoever is the most humble in serving all others as if he were the least important among them—has the highest status in God's sight."

114. Jesus' Followers Try to Exclude Others

John told Jesus, "Rabbi, we saw someone expelling demons using your name as if you had given him your authority, and we tried to stop him since he isn't associated with us." But Jesus responded, "You shouldn't stop such people! Those who do miracles using my name won't be among those who slander me. Anyone who isn't against us is on our side. Anyone who helps

---

A 111 See the note at Matthew 16:21 for the reasoning behind not using the traditional phrase, "the third day."

one of you because you're my follower—even if it's as small a thing as giving a cup of water to drink—will most certainly be rewarded for it.

115. Jesus Teaches About Temptation and Sin

"And on the other hand, anyone who tempts someone who believes in me to sin or to reject me will be severely punished—even if the person he so leads is as low in status as this child. It's inevitable that people will be tempted to sin. But the one who deliberately tempts others to sin would be better off by far if his only punishment were to have a huge stone tied around his neck and he were thrown into the sea to drown. The punishment in Hell for those who tempt or cause my people to sin will indeed be terrible!

"Take care not to consider any of my humble people—such as these small children—as insignificant. Their guardian angels are always in my Heavenly Father's presence and will report any way that you mistreat them. For I, the Son of Man, have come to save people who are spiritually lost. None of them are insignificant to me.

"The consequences of sin are serious! If your hand or foot or eye entices you to sin, you would be better off getting rid of it and enter eternal life maimed or crippled than to be whole and end up in the eternal fire of Hell—where there's no relief from the torment of fire that burns but does not consume, or from the maggots that eat your decaying flesh.

"Do your utmost to resist temptation, for everyone will have to endure the fires of testing that result in purification and stronger faith. Salt is good, but if it loses its flavor, it can't be made salty again. So don't foolishly give in to temptation and lose your ability to positively influence those around you. And strive to live in harmony with each other.

116. All People Are Important to God

"Think about this. If a man has 100 sheep and one of them gets lost, don't you think he would leave the other 99 grazing and go look for the one that was lost? And if he then finds it, he would certainly be far happier about that one sheep he found than over the 99 that didn't get lost. So in a similar way, your Heavenly Father doesn't want anyone—not even a supposedly insignificant child—to be lost. Everyone is important to him."

117. How to Handle Unrepented Sin Among Believers

Jesus told his followers, "If your fellow believer sins against you, lovingly confront him in private about it. If he listens to you and repents, then you've restored your relationship. But if he refuses to listen to you, take one or two other believers along with you as witnesses to confront him again. This way, any accusation you need to make against him later will have two or three witnesses to confirm your story. But if he refuses to listen to them too, then bring the matter before the local assembly of believers. And if he refuses to listen even to the assembly, then treat him as a nonbeliever who is not part of the assembly.

"It's important for you to understand this. Whatever you prohibit or allow here on earth with regard to order, practice, and discipline in the Assembly of Believers will correspondingly be prohibited or allowed in Heaven. And furthermore, if two of you agree about anything you ask for in prayer, my Heavenly Father will do it for you. For even if as few as two or three believers have come together to submit to me in worship or pray, I will be there to give them my attention.

"So if fellow believers sin, lovingly rebuke them. And if they repent, forgive them. Even if someone sins against you the same way seven times in a day and every time comes to you saying he is sorry and will try to change, then you must forgive him."

118. The Consequences of Unforgiveness

Then Peter came and asked Jesus, "Lord, how many times should I forgive a fellow believer who sins against me? As many as seven times?" Jesus answered, "Not just seven times! Don't place a limit—not even seventy times seven times! Always be willing to forgive. Here's a parable that teaches how God views someone who is unwilling to forgive.

"There was a king who decided to see how his servants were handling his finances. He had just started the process when one servant who owed him 10,000 talents was brought before him. ❖ *A talent was a heavy weight of gold or silver. We don't know exactly what a talent was worth, but 10,000 talents was a staggering amount that no individual could ever hope to pay.* ➤ Since the servant could not possibly pay his debt, the king ordered him and his wife and children to be sold as slaves, and all he had to be sold to help repay part of the debt. But the servant prostrated himself before the king and begged, 'Please have patience with me and I will find a way to repay you everything.' The king felt compassion for the man and decided to cancel his debt and allow him to go free.

"But that same servant then went and found one of his fellow servants who owed him only a hundred days wages. He grabbed him around the neck and started choking him and demanded, 'Pay what you owe me immediately!' Then that fellow servant prostrated himself and begged, 'Please have patience with me and I will find a way to repay you everything.' But he refused to wait. Instead, he had the man arrested and put in debtor's prison until the debt was paid in full. ❖ *Someone in debtor's prison would have no means of acquiring money to pay his debt. He would be at the mercy of friends and relatives who would want to pay his debt for him.* ➤ When some of the other servants saw what had happened, the injustice distressed them. So they went to the king and told him everything. Then, the king summoned the servant and said, 'You are evil! I had pity on you and forgave you your entire debt just because you pleaded with me for mercy. Since I granted you great mercy, you should have also been willing to grant your fellow servant mercy for a much smaller debt!' The king was so angry that he had the man tortured until his debt was paid in full.

"That's exactly the attitude my Heavenly Father will have toward you if you refuse to sincerely and completely forgive someone who sins against you, especially a fellow believer."

119. The Relationship Between Faith and the Release of God's Power

The apostles recognized that they would find it difficult to forgive in this way, so they said, "Lord, help us to increase our faith."

The Lord answered, "If you have faith that's only as large as a mustard seed, it's enough that you could say to this mulberry tree, 'Be uprooted and planted in the sea,' and God would make it obey you." ❖ *Jesus isn't saying that God will be our magic genie doing anything we wish, if we have faith. He was using hyperbole to make a point. The point he made here is that it's God's power that works mighty miracles, not our great faith. In fact, only a little faith on our part is needed before God will release his power to do great things. What needs to be understood is this only happens when what we request or command is in alignment with God's will. In this context, Jesus said it is God's will for us to forgive, no matter how hard it may seem to do so. All we need is a little faith, and he will give us all the power we need to forgive. See Section 3. F. Forgiving Other People, in the Appendix to this book.* ➤

120. The Cost of Following Jesus [A]

One time, a man came to Jesus and said, "I will follow you wherever you go." But Jesus replied, "Do you realize what's involved in following me? Foxes have their dens, and birds have their nests. But I, the Son of Man, am rejected by the leaders of this nation. If you follow me, they will also reject you. Are sure you want to follow me?"

Jesus said to a different man, "Come and be my follower." But he replied, "Sir, I must first fulfill my duty to serve my father as long as he lives—as tradition demands and society expects. After my father dies, I will be free to follow you." Jesus replied, "Let those who are spiritually dead take care of themselves. I'm calling you to go and proclaim the Good News about God's Kingdom." ❖ *Jesus demands loyalty from his followers that is above loyalty to tradition, cultural norms, or the expectations of others.* ➤

[A] **120** Commentary for section 120 comes from Kenneth E. Bailey's book "Through Peasant Eyes," pp. 22-32.

Another man said, "I'd like to follow you, sir. But first I must ask permission from my family." Jesus replied, "A man who starts plowing a field and keeps looking back isn't fit for God's Kingdom." ❖ *The task of plowing required complete concentration ahead to do it properly, lest adjacent furrows were damaged by a crooked course, making the job harder. Jesus demands absolute loyalty from his followers, even over that of their own family. This illustration means that anyone who sets his mind to follow Jesus and then has second thoughts and keeps looking back to his former life or can't resolve the tension of conflicting loyalties isn't fully committed. He will be judged as useless for the purposes of God's Kingdom.* ➤

121. Jesus Rejects His Brother's Advice
(September, AD 29)

Now, the time for the Jewish Festival of Shelters approached. So Jesus' brothers—who didn't believe in him—sarcastically told him, "If you want to be known, you can't remain here working in obscurity. Leave Galilee and go to Judea so people can see you do your miracles publicly and become your followers. Since you're doing these things, why not let everyone see them?" Jesus replied, "The time that God has appointed for me to go there hasn't come yet. But you can go any time you want because the sinful people of this world don't hate you. They hate me because I tell them what they do is evil. So go up to the festival without me, for it's not the right time for me to go yet." So he remained in Galilee awhile longer.

But after his brothers had left for the festival, he and his close followers also went without letting others know about it.

122. Jesus Answers a Question About Divorce

Jesus and his close followers left Galilee and traveled to Judea along the eastern side of the Jordan River. As usual, a large crowd gathered around him so he taught them spiritual truths—as he did at every opportunity—and he healed all who were sick among them. Some Pharisees came to try to trap Jesus with a question that they thought he couldn't possibly answer to anyone's satisfaction. They asked, "Does the Torah allow a man to divorce his wife for any reason

he wishes?" Jesus responded, "What do you understand Moses as having commanded concerning divorce in the Torah?" They said, "Moses allowed a man to give his wife a written document indicating that he had divorced her, and then he could send her away." Jesus said, "Moses allowed that only because men are so stubborn and unteachable. But I tell you that if someone divorces his wife for anything less than the fact that she was unfaithful to him, then he commits adultery if he marries another woman. God's original plan for marriage is clear. When he first made people, he never intended divorce to happen. For the Scriptures say that he 'created them as one male and one female,' and 'that is why a man will leave his parents and be united to his wife, and the two will become one.' So God has joined them and in his sight they are no longer two, but a permanent unity. That is why man should not separate what God has joined."

Later, when only his close followers were indoors with him, they asked him about this topic again. Jesus told them, "Any man that divorces his wife and marries a different woman is guilty of committing adultery against her. And if a woman divorces her husband and remarries, she is guilty of committing adultery against him."

Then Jesus' close followers said, "If the marriage relationship is this binding in God's sight, perhaps it's better to remain single." Jesus replied, "Not everyone can be content to remain unmarried, only those whom God has called to be that way. Some men are born deformed and are physically incapable of having relations with a woman. Others are celibate because they are castrated. And some decide to be celibate so they can devote all their time and energy to serving God's Kingdom. Those who are able to do this should do so."

123. Jesus' Attitude Toward Little Children

One day, some people were bringing their small children and infants to Jesus so he would lay his hands on them and pray a blessing on them. When his followers saw this, they rebuked the people, telling them not to bother the Rabbi. But Jesus was displeased when he noticed them doing this and called the children to come to him. He told his followers, "Don't stop children from coming to me! These are the kind of people that God loves to have in his Kingdom—those who are humble and trusting. And remember this! Anyone who isn't humble and trusting like a child will never enter God's Kingdom at all." Then, he held the children in his arms, placed his hands on them, and blessed them.

124. The Stumbling Stone of Being Rich

As Jesus and his followers were starting out on a journey to another village, a rich young Jewish religious leader came running up, knelt down in front of him, and asked, "Good Rabbi, what good thing do I need to do in order to live forever?" Jesus replied, "Why do you call me 'good?' No one is good except God himself. So do you realize what you're saying about me when you call me good? If you want to live forever, obey all the commandments perfectly." The man asked, "But which ones?" Jesus replied, "You know the ones: Don't murder, don't commit adultery, don't steal, don't lie about others, don't cheat others, honor your parents, and love your neighbor in the same way you love yourself." The young man replied, "But Rabbi, I've kept all of those commandments ever since I was young, but I feel that's not enough. What else do I need to do?"

Jesus looked at him and felt God's pure love for him, wanting to bring him into a proper relationship with himself. But he knew that the man didn't recognize his sin and the biggest thing hindering him from wholeheartedly following God was his idolatrous love for his riches. So he told him, "If you want to be completely dedicated to God, sell everything you have and give the money to the poor so you will have riches in Heaven. Then come and be one of my followers." But when the man heard this, he was dejected and went away sad because he was very rich and unwilling to surrender his wealth and put his life in Jesus' hands.

Jesus saw him go and said to all his followers there, "It's very difficult for the rich to enter God's Kingdom!" When his followers heard this, they were astonished. But Jesus continued to emphasize his statement. "My children, it is extremely difficult for anyone to enter God's Kingdom! I will reiterate the difficulty. It would be easier for a camel to go through the eye of a sewing needle than for a rich man to enter God's Kingdom." His followers were even more astonished at this and asked him, "If it's so hard for even people whom God has clearly blessed with riches to be saved, then who can hope to be saved?" Jesus looked at them and said, "It may be impossible for people to enter on their own, but with God's help, anything is possible."

Then Peter said, "We've left our homes and everything we have to follow you, just like you told that man. So what can we expect from God?" Jesus answered, "You can be sure of this: When I, the Son of Man, sit on my throne in all my glory, then you who have followed me will also sit on twelve thrones and rule the twelve tribes of Israel. And all who leave home or brothers or sisters or parents or children or livelihood to obey me and to proclaim the Good News about how people can be saved, will receive from God in this life a hundred times as much as he has given up—including homes and brothers and sisters and mothers and children and means of living—but in addition should expect to be persecuted. And in the next age after I return, they will receive eternal life in Heaven. But many who are important in this life will be among the least important in Heaven, and many who are least important in this life will be among the most important in Heaven."

125. A Parable About God's Generosity

Jesus continued, "The reward of receiving eternal life in God's Kingdom is illustrated by a landowner who went at dawn one morning to hire laborers to work in his vineyard. After he agreed with the men he found to pay them each a denarius for working all day, he sent them to work. ❖ *A denarius was the common wage for a full day's work at that time.* ➤ About midmorning, he noticed some more men standing in the market waiting for someone to hire them. He told them, 'Go work in my vineyard for the rest of the day, and I will pay you an appropriate wage for your time.' They agreed and went to work. He went to the market again at noon and also about midafternoon and did the same thing with more men. About an hour before the end of the work day, he again went and found still more men standing around. He asked them, 'Why have you been standing here all day with nothing to do?' They replied, 'Only because no one has hired us.' He told them, 'You go work in my vineyard for the rest of the day.' When evening came, the landowner told his foreman, 'Call all the workers in from the vineyard and pay them their wages. Start with the last group I hired and end with the first group.' Those who started working only one hour before the end of the day were each paid a denarius. When those who had been hired first came to be paid, they expected to receive more since they had worked much longer. But they also were each paid a single denarius, as had been agreed. When they received their money, they complained to the landowner, 'Those men worked only one hour, and you gave them the same wage you gave us. We worked under the hot sun all day. It's not fair!' But the landowner answered one of them. 'My friend, you agreed to work for me all day for a denarius, didn't you? I've paid you that and have done you no wrong. So take it and go home. It was my desire to pay those last workers the same as you. It's not against the teachings in the Torah for me to do what I want with my own money. Are you ungrateful and envious just because I'm generous to others?' " Jesus concluded, "In the same way that you find this equal treatment unexpected, you will also be surprised that many who are important in this life will be among the least important in Heaven, and many who are least important in this life will be among the most important in Heaven. Just as it's also true that God calls everyone to turn to him and be saved, but only a few are chosen."

126. The Festival of Shelters
(October, AD 29)

Now, the time for the Festival of Shelters arrived, and the Jewish leaders were watching for Jesus at the festival. They kept asking around if anyone had seen him. There was a lot of whispering about him among the crowds. Some said he was a good man; others said he led people astray from following the Torah's teachings and their traditions. But no one would openly support him because they were afraid of persecution from the Jewish leaders.

In the middle of the week-long festival, Jesus went up to the Temple and openly taught in the courtyard there. The leaders were astonished by the quality of his teaching and asked, "How did this man become so knowledgeable, since he has no formal rabbinical education?" Jesus told them, "The things I teach aren't based on my own knowledge. They come straight from God who sent me. Those who are committed to following the will of God will know whether what I say comes from God or if I'm speaking from my own authority. Someone who speaks from his own authority will say things to gain the praise of others. But someone who only seeks honor for the one who sent him has pure motives and speaks the truth. You would agree with me that Moses gave you God's Teachings. Yet none of you obeys all that the Torah commands. If you did, you wouldn't want to kill me." The crowd replied, "You must have a demon deluding you! Who do you think wants to kill you?" Jesus said, "I did one particular miracle on the Sabbath and you were all shocked that I disobeyed your Sabbath traditions. But you break the Sabbath command too. Moses commanded you to circumcise your sons a week after their birth—though the command really started with Abraham, not Moses. So you routinely circumcise boys on the Sabbath. But if you can circumcise on the Sabbath in order to obey the Teachings of Moses, and it takes precedence over your own Sabbath traditions, why are you angry with me for healing a man on the Sabbath? Stop judging by superficial legalistic criteria and judge correctly."

Some of the people who lived in Jerusalem were saying, "This is the man our leaders wanted to kill, isn't he? Here he is teaching in public, and they are not opposing him! Could they have decided he really is the Messiah? But we know where he comes from—and when the Messiah comes, nobody will know where he came from." Then, while Jesus was still teaching in the Temple, he called out, "You think that you know me and where I'm from? I'm not here on my own authority. I was really sent by God, but you don't know him. I know him because I came from him, and he sent me to you."

Then some of the people tried to seize him for saying that he came from God, but no one was able to lay a hand on him because it was not yet God's time for him to be arrested. But many in the crowd believed in him and said, "He must be the Messiah! Surely no one could perform more miraculous signs than he has!" When some Pharisees heard these whisperings in the crowd, they went to the chief priests and had them send some Temple guards to arrest him. Jesus said, "I will only be with you for a little while longer and then I will return to my Father who sent me. At that time, you will search for me, but you won't find me because I'm going where you can't go." The Jewish leaders were puzzled and asked each other, "Where does he plan to go that we won't be able to find him? Certainly he isn't intending to go live among our people in Gentile countries and teach Gentiles! What does he mean by, 'we will search for him and not find him because he's going where we can't go?' "

Now this was the climactic last day of the festival, and Jesus stood up and shouted to the crowds, "All who are spiritually thirsty should come to me and drink. Those who believe in me will discover that, 'From out of his innermost being will flow rivers of living water,' just as the Scriptures say." Jesus meant that those who believed in him would later receive the Holy Spirit to live in them. But at that time, the Spirit had not yet been given because Jesus was not yet glorified.

When the people heard this, some of them said, "Surely he is the 'Prophet like Moses.' " Others said, "He's the Messiah." But others responded to this, "But the Messiah isn't going to be from Galilee! The Scriptures say that the Messiah will be a descendant of King David and be born in Bethlehem where David lived!" So public opinion was quite divided on who he really was. There were also some who wanted to arrest him, but no one laid a hand on him.

Later, the Temple guards returned to the chief priests and Pharisees who had sent them to arrest Jesus. Their superiors demanded, "Why haven't you arrested him?" The guards replied, "No one has ever spoken the way he speaks." The Pharisees sneered, "Are you so credulous that you're deceived too? Have you heard of even one of the ruling council or the Pharisees who has believed in him? Of course not! But those uneducated rabble know nothing of the Torah's teachings! They are under God's curse for listening to him!" Then Nicodemus—who had met with Jesus before—spoke up. He said, "You know that our Torah doesn't allow us to condemn a man without first listening to him and investigating what he's done." They retorted contemptuously, "Are you a Galilean sympathizer now too? Go back and search the Scriptures, and you will see that no prophet ever comes from Galilee!" After that, they all went home.

127. The Woman Caught in Adultery

Jesus spent the night on Mount Olivet which overlooks the city. Early in the morning, he again returned to the Temple courtyard. Many people came to listen to him, and he sat down to teach.

While he was teaching, some Scripture teachers and Pharisees brought in a woman who had been caught committing adultery. They made her stand in the middle of the crowd and said to Jesus, "Rabbi, this woman was caught in the act of adultery. The Teachings of Moses say an adulteress must be stoned to death. What do you think we should do?" The question was intended to trap him into saying something they could use against him. ❖ *If he advocated stoning her, they could report him to the Roman authorities who didn't allow the Jewish leaders to execute anyone except for Temple violations. If he said to let her go, he would be breaking God's command in the Torah, which would prove that he had no regard for God or his commands, and thus make him unpopular with the people.* ➤ Jesus stooped down and wrote in the dust on the ground with his finger. But they kept on questioning him about this, so he stood up and said, "The one to throw the first stone must be someone who is not guilty of the same sin." Then he stooped down and wrote on the ground again.

When her accusers heard this, they began to leave one by one, the older ones first, until only Jesus and the woman were left in the middle of the crowd. Jesus stood up and spoke gently to her, "Miss, where are those who accused you? Didn't anyone remain to condemn you?" She answered, "No, sir." Then Jesus said, "And I don't condemn you either. So you may go, but keep yourself from sinning."

128. Jesus Claims to Be God's Light Sent to the Sinners of This World

Later, Jesus taught the people again. He said, "I am God's Light sent into this sinful world to illuminate his path to salvation. Those who follow me will never walk in the spiritual darkness of sin and death, but will possess the Light that gives true life."

The Pharisees objected, "You're simply making claims about yourself. Without someone to back you up, your claims are insufficient grounds for us to accept them." Jesus replied, "You are wrong that my claims are unsupported. And even though I'm making claims about myself, they are still true because I know where I came from and where I'm going. But you don't know these things about me. You are judging based on limited human understanding without insight from God. But I don't judge anyone that way. If I do judge people, my judgment is true because I don't make judgments on my own, but with the help of my Father who sent me. In your Torah it states that the testimony of two men is to be accepted as fact if their testimonies agree. I am one witness who tells you about myself, and

my Father who sent me is the other who testifies about me."

They responded, "Where is your father?" Jesus replied, "It's clear that you don't know me or my Father, since if you really knew me, you would also know him." This interaction took place in the Temple near the treasury where he had been teaching. But he wasn't arrested because the time God had set for it to happen hadn't yet arrived.

Once more Jesus told them, "I'm going away, and you will look for me, and you will die without your sins being forgiven. You won't be able to come where I'm going." So they were asking each other, "What does he mean that we can't go where he's going? He can't be thinking of killing himself, can he?" Jesus said, "You're from this world which is below. I am not from this world, but from above. If you don't believe that I am He, ❖ *i.e., the Messiah,* ➤ you will die with your sins unforgiven."

They asked him, "Who do you say you are?" Jesus replied, "Just who I've been claiming to be all along. I have much I could say to you and there's much for which I could condemn you, but I don't. I only represent the one who sent me. His words are entirely trustworthy and true so I only tell people what I hear from him." They still didn't catch on that he was speaking about God the Father as the one who sent him. So Jesus said, "After you have lifted up the Son of Man, then you will know that I am He. I do nothing from my own initiative. I only say what my Father instructs me to say. And he who sent me hasn't left me on my own. He is always with me because I only do what pleases him." While Jesus was saying these things, many of those listening started to believe in him.

Jesus said to those who believed, "If you continue to faithfully follow my teachings, then you are my true followers. In doing this, you will know what God says about absolute truth, and that truth will set you free." They replied, "We are descendants of Abraham and have never been in spiritual slavery. What do you mean we will be 'set free'?"

Jesus said, "I'm telling you an important truth. Everyone who sins is enslaved by sin. A slave has no permanent place in a family, but a son or daughter is part of the family forever. So if God's Son sets you free, you will really be free. I know that you are Abraham's physical descendants, but you want to kill me because you can't accept my teaching. The things I'm telling you are what my Father has revealed to me. In the same way, you are also doing the things that you learned from your father."

They retorted, "Abraham is our forefather!" Jesus said, "If you were true spiritual descendants of Abraham, then you would do the righteous things he did. But instead, you want to kill me, when all I've done is tell you truths I've heard from God. Abraham's way was to listen to God—so you aren't imitating him. You are following the example of your true father." They replied, "We're not illegitimate! The only father we have is God!"

Jesus said, "If God were your true father, then you would love me for I came from him into this world. I didn't come on my own authority. He is the one who sent me. Why aren't you getting what I'm saying? It's simply because you are not willing to accept my message. It's clear that you belong to Satan. He is your true father because you have the same desires he does. He was a murderer from the beginning of this world and he completely rejects God's truth so there is no truth in him. Thus lying is his native language and reflects his true nature. He is both a liar and the originator of all lies. So you don't believe me because what I tell you is true and comes from God. Can anyone prove that I have in any way sinned? If not, then what I say must be true. So why don't you believe me? Those who really belong to God listen to what he says. The reason you don't accept his message through me is because you are not really his children."

Those Jews insultingly replied, "We were right all along to say that you're a demonized Samaritan!" Jesus replied, "I don't have a demon. I'm simply honoring my Father in what I say, and you are dishonoring me. I'm not seeking honor for myself. But there is one who honors me and he is the one who judges between us.

"This is most certainly true: Those who obey my teaching will never die." They exclaimed, "Now we know that you're demonized! Abraham died and so did the prophets. It's clear that no one is exempt from dying. Yet you say that if people obey your teaching they won't die! Who do you think you are? Do you think you're greater than our patriarch Abraham or God's prophets?"

Jesus replied, "If I honored myself, it would be meaningless. But it's my Father who honors me. He is the one who you call your God, even though you don't really know him. But I do know him. If I said I didn't, I would be a liar like you are. But I do know him and I obey his instructions.

"Even your ancestor Abraham rejoiced when he foresaw the day that I would come to this world." They scornfully retorted, "You aren't even fifty years old, and you claim to have seen Abraham!" Jesus replied, "The truth is, I existed before Abraham was even born because I AM." They assumed that he was blaspheming so they picked up some stones to stone him, but Jesus hid and slipped out of the Temple.

129. Jesus Gives Sight to a Man Born Blind

As Jesus and his followers were walking along, they saw a man who had been born blind. His followers asked him, "Rabbi, what caused this man to be born blind? Was it due to his sin or his parents' sin?" Jesus answered, "His blindness is not due to any sin—neither his nor his parents'. He was born this way so that God's power could be clearly demonstrated in his life. As long as it's still daytime, we must do the work of my Father who sent me. Night is coming when no one can work. While I'm on earth, I am the Light that enables sinners to see the truth about God."

Having made this point, Jesus spat on the ground, making some mud which he smeared on the man's eyelids. Then he told the man, "Go to the Pool of Siloam and wash off your eyes." (In Hebrew, "Siloam" means "sent.") So he went there, washed, and went home able to see. His neighbors and others who had always seen him when he was begging asked, "Isn't this the man who used to sit on the side of the street and beg?" Some said that he was, but others claimed he only looked like the beggar. But he kept telling them, "Yes, I am that beggar!" So they asked him, "What happened that enabled you to see?" He replied, "The man people call 'Jesus' made some mud and put it on my eyelids. He told me to go wash it off in Siloam. So I went there and washed and then I was able to see." They asked, "Where is he now?" He said, "I don't know."

Then some of them took him to the Pharisees. Now, the day Jesus made the mud and enabled the man to see was a Sabbath. So the Pharisees questioned the man about how he received the ability to see. He told them, "He put mud on my eyelids, I washed it off, and I was able to see." Then some of the Pharisees said, "The man who did this is not God's messenger because he breaks the rule about working on the Sabbath." But other Pharisees said, "It wouldn't be possible for a sinner do such miraculous signs as these." So they were divided in their opinion of Jesus. Then they asked the man again, "Since he enabled you to see, what do you think about him?" He said, "I believe he is a genuine prophet from God."

The Jewish leaders were unwilling to believe that he had been born blind and was now able to see for the first time. So they summoned his parents and asked them, "Is this your son? Is it true that he was born blind? If so, then how did it come about that he can now see?" His parents answered, "We know that he's our son and that he was born blind. But we don't have any idea who enabled him to see or how it was done. He's of legal age to testify, so ask him." Now, the Jewish leaders had already threatened to expel anyone from the synagogue who said that Jesus was the Messiah. So they were afraid to say anything that would make the leaders expel them. That's why they said, "He's of legal age to testify, so ask him."

So the man who had been blind was summoned again and they told him, "Glorify God by telling us the truth about what happened. For we know that this man Jesus—who you claimed healed you—is a sinner." He replied, "As to whether or not he's a sinner as you claim, I don't know. But one thing I do know: I was blind, but now I can see because of him!" So they asked him again, "What did he do to you? How did he make you able to see?" He sarcastically retorted, "I've already told you, but you apparently didn't listen! Why do you want to hear it again? Do you want to become his followers too?" They responded to this with anger and insults, "You are clearly one of his followers! But we follow the teachings of Moses! We know that God spoke to Moses, but as for that Jesus, we don't even know where he comes from, let alone whether he has authority from God." The man exclaimed, "That's incredible! He enabled me to see, yet you're unsure of his credentials! We all know that God doesn't listen to unrepentant sinners. He only answers the prayers of those who are properly in awe of him and who do his will. Since the beginning of time, no one has ever heard of anyone that could enable a person to see who was born blind. He wouldn't be able to do miracles like this if he didn't have God's authority!" The leaders blasted him, "Who do you think you are, trying to lecture us! You were born in such sin that God caused you to be born blind!" Then they expelled him from the synagogue—and thus from fellowship with the Jewish community.

When Jesus heard that the man had been expelled in this way, he went to find him and asked, "Do you put your trust in the Son of Man?" He replied, "Sir, tell me who he is so I can." Jesus answered, "You have already seen him and have been talking with him. I am he." The man declared, "Lord, I believe you are the Messiah!" Then he bowed down and worshipped Jesus.

Jesus said, "I came into this sinful world to expose sin and precipitate decisions that will determine the way people will be judged. I came to enable the spiritually blind to see God's truth and way of salvation, and to show those who think they have spiritual sight that they are blind to the truth." Some Pharisees overheard him and said, "Are you saying that we are spiritually blind?" Jesus replied, "If you were blind in the sense of being genuinely ignorant of God's truth but were humbly seeking it, then he wouldn't hold you accountable. But since you proudly claim to have spiritual insight and knowledge of the truth, you will be judged guilty for rejecting the real thing."

130. The Good Shepherd

Jesus continued, "Let me talk about a self-evident truth to make a point. Someone who enters a sheep pen by climbing over the wall instead of going through the gate is clearly a thief and a vandal. But the shepherd enters through the gate, and the watchman recognizes him and lets him in. The sheep respond to his voice when he calls them by name and leads them out to pasture. When he has called out all of his own sheep, he walks ahead of them and they follow him because they recognize his voice. But they would never follow a stranger. Instead, they would run away from him because they didn't recognize his voice."

Jesus used this image to make his point, but they didn't understand what he was getting at. So he spoke again to clarify, "This is an important truth for you to understand. I am the gate for the sheep. All false teachers and messianic pretenders who came before me were thieves and vandals. But my sheep didn't respond to them. I am the gate. Those who come in through me will be saved. They will come in and go out and find good pasture. Thieves come to steal and destroy the sheep. But I come so they may obtain eternal life and enjoy all it has to offer.

"I am also the Good Shepherd who is so dedicated to taking care of the sheep that he willingly sacrifices his life to save them. A hired hand who doesn't own the sheep will abandon them and run away when he sees a wolf coming. He will run away, allowing the wolf to attack and scatter them because he isn't concerned about the sheep, since they don't belong to him. But I'm the Good Shepherd and owner of the sheep. In the same way that my Father knows me and I know my Father, I know which sheep belong to me and they know me. So I am willing to sacrifice my own life for the sake of my sheep. I also have other sheep that aren't part of this fold. I must bring them in too. They will respond to my voice, and then there will be only one flock under one shepherd.

"My Father loves me because I always obey him, even to the point of sacrificing my life—which I will do so I can afterward take it back again. Following my Father's plan and command, I will lay down my life of my own free will. No one can take it from me without my consent. I have the authority to lay it down in sacrifice and I have the authority to take it up again."

The Jews were again divided in their opinions about Jesus as a result of what he said. Many of them exclaimed, "He has a demon which has made him insane. Why bother listening to him?" But some countered, "Demonized people don't talk like this! And you certainly don't believe that a demon has the power to give sight to a man born blind, do you?"

131. Parable of the Good Samaritan

One day, a Scripture teacher stood up and asked a question to see what kind of answer Jesus would give. He said, "Rabbi, what must I do to gain eternal life?"

Jesus answered, "What do the Teachings of Moses say? What's your understanding of their requirements?"

He answered, "You must love Yahweh, your God, with your entire being—all your heart, thoughts, personality, and determination. You must also love your neighbor in the same tolerant accepting way that you love yourself."

Jesus said, "You have answered correctly. If you really love God and your neighbor in this way, you will gain eternal life."

But the teacher wanted to justify himself, so he asked, "Who exactly is my neighbor?"

Jesus replied by telling this story, "A man was walking down the road from Jerusalem to Jericho when he was attacked by robbers. They beat him up, stripped him of his clothes and possessions, and left him half dead. It happened that a priest came down that same road. When he saw the man, he passed by on the other side. In the same way, a Levite also came by, saw the man, and passed by on the other side. But then a Samaritan came along on his journey; and when he saw the man, he felt compassion for him. He went to him and poured wine and oil on his wounds and then bandaged him. Then he put the man on his donkey, took him to an inn, and cared for him there. In the morning, he gave the innkeeper money equivalent to two-days' wages and said, 'Continue to look after him, and when I return, I will reimburse you for any additional cost.' "

Addressing the teacher, Jesus asked, "Which of these three men acted as a neighbor to the man who was attacked by robbers?"

Unwilling to utter the word "Samaritan," he answered, "The one who showed him mercy."

Then Jesus told him, "Go and love others in the same way."

132. Jesus Visits Martha and Mary

As Jesus and his followers traveled along, they entered Bethany village—just outside of Jerusalem—where a woman named Martha offered them hospitality in her home. While she was working, her sister Mary sat on the floor near Jesus, listening to him teach—hanging on his every word. But Martha was mainly concerned with all the preparations needed to feed her guests. She came to Jesus and said, "Lord, don't you care that my sister has left me to do all the work myself? Please tell her to come and help me!"

But he told her, "My dear Martha, you worry too much about too many things. There's only one thing you should really be concerned about—and Mary has chosen it by sitting here listening to me. I will not make her give it up."

133. How to Pray

One day, Jesus had been praying in a certain place. When he finished, one of his followers came to him and said, "Lord, teach us how to pray, just like John the Baptizer taught his followers."

Jesus said, "When you pray, do it simply like this and for these kinds of things: 'Father, cause people to honor your name and submit to your kingship. Provide us with the food and other things we need today. Forgive our sins in the same way that we forgive those who wrong us. And help us so we won't yield to temptation.' "

Then he said, "Imagine this situation: A friend of yours has been traveling and just arrived at your home at midnight for a visit, but you have no food in the house to offer him. So you go to the house of a neighbor who is a friend and wake him. You say, 'A friend has just arrived for a visit, and I've nothing to feed him. Would you please loan me three loaves of bread?' Can you imagine him answering like this? 'Don't bother me! I've already locked the door, and my children are in bed with me. I can't get up to give you anything!' Of course he would never refuse! ❖ *Middle-Eastern culture considered hospitality to be one of the highest obligations—with the entire village's honor at stake. A neighbor would never refuse such a request.* ➤ I tell you, the man might not want to get up and give you something for the sake of friendship, but to avoid spoiling his good reputation in the village he will get up and give you everything you want—not just the bread you asked for." ❖ *Jesus' point was: If a mere man will do this for the sake of his integrity and reputation, you can be certain that your Heavenly Father who loves you is even more willing to give you what you ask for in prayer.* ➤ **A**

Jesus continued, "When you ask God for something that you need, keep on asking, and at the proper time you will receive it. Keep on seeking him and you will find him. Keep on knocking on his door in prayer, and he will open it to you. Everyone who asks will receive. Everyone who seeks will find what he's seeking. And the door will open to everyone who knocks. You fathers, if your son asks you for a fish, would you give him a snake? Or if he asks for an egg, would you give him a scorpion? Since you know how to give good things to your children—even though you're sinners—you can be sure that your Heavenly Father is even more willing to give the Holy Spirit to those who ask him!"

A 133 Insight for interpreting this parable comes from Kenneth E. Bailey's book "Poet & Peasant," pp. 119-141.

134. Parable of
the Widow and the Corrupt Judge

Then Jesus told them a parable to teach that we need to persist in prayer until God answers. He said, "There was a judge in a certain town who didn't believe in God and he didn't care what people thought about him. But a widow living in that town was constantly begging him to help her. She would say, 'Please grant me justice against my adversary!' For a long time he refused, but eventually said to himself, 'Even though I don't believe in God and I don't care what people think about me, I will do what she asks because her constant begging is getting on my nerves. I will do it just to have some peace and quiet!' "

Jesus said, "Note what the corrupt judge said. If even a corrupt judge like that will grant justice just to stop a woman from bothering him, you can be sure that God—who loves his people—is even more willing to help them when they cry out to him in prayer, day and night! He will not delay long in helping them. I assure you, he will bring about justice for them quickly. But when I—the Son of Man—return, will I find people who still believe in me?"

135. Parable of
the Pharisee and the Tax Collector

Jesus also told this parable to those who think they are better than others, or believe that God thinks more highly of them than others, "Two men went up to the Temple to pray. One was a Pharisee and the other a tax collector.

"The Pharisee stood and prayed to himself. He said, 'Thank you, God, that I'm not evil like other people who are greedy and rob others, or who are unjust, or adulterers, or like that tax collector over there. I fast twice a week and I give you a tenth of everything I get.'

"But the tax collector stood some distance away and didn't even look up toward Heaven because he was ashamed. Instead, he beat his chest and said, 'God, have mercy on me, for I am a sinner!' " Jesus said, "I tell you, this man went back to his home accepted by God—and not the Pharisee. For God will humble anyone who exalts himself, and he exalts those who humble themselves before him."

136. Jesus Warns
the Pharisees and Scripture Teachers

When Jesus finished speaking, a Pharisee invited him to have lunch. So Jesus went with him, entered his house, and reclined at the table. His host was surprised that Jesus didn't ritually wash his hands first before reclining for the meal—according to Jewish custom. Since Jesus knew what the Pharisee was thinking, he said, "You Pharisees are so concerned about externals—such as carefully washing the outside of cups and dishes. But you totally neglect internal motives and attitudes which are more important. Outwardly, you are ritually clean and meticulous about keeping rules. But your hearts are full of greed and evil. You are morally depraved! Didn't God make the inside as well as the outside? If you really want to be 'clean' in God's sight, then motivated by love for him, give what you have to the poor. If you do this, he will count everything about you as 'clean.'

"You Pharisees are in real trouble with God! You meticulously give one tenth of all your income, crops, animals, and material increase to God—even down to a tenth of the herbs from your garden—but you totally ignore the major issues of justice and loving God. It's these more important laws that you should be most anxious to keep—without neglecting the minor ones. It's going to be bad for you Pharisees on the Last Day! Your main desires are to sit in the seats of honor in the synagogue and for people to kowtow to you in public. You are going to be judged harshly! You are like unmarked defiling graves in a field that people walk over without being aware of it."

A Scripture teacher said, "Rabbi, what you're saying insults us too!"

Jesus replied, "Yes, God's judgment of you Scripture teachers is going to be terrible as well! Your man-made rules and regulations crush people under a burden they can't and shouldn't have to carry—and you don't even lift a finger to help them. You yourselves don't even follow all those rules! Your punishment will be severe! You build monuments on the tombs of the prophets murdered by your ancestors and decorate the graves of godly people that they also killed. But you are no different than your ancestors were. You sanctimoniously claim, 'If we had lived in those times, we certainly would not have helped them kill God's prophets!' Your words and deeds testify against you. You admit that you are 'sons of' those who murdered God's prophets—and you are just like them. You reject God's prophets just like they did. This shows that you approve of what they did and are as guilty as they are. ❖ *Two prophets that they rejected were John the Baptizer and Jesus the Messiah.* ➤ So go ahead and do what you intend. Finish what your ancestors started—if you have no fear of God! Don't think that you will escape condemnation in Hell if your ancestors didn't—you hypocritical sons of vipers!

"This is what God in his wisdom said, 'I will send prophets and apostles to them. They will kill some of them and persecute others.' Since this is the way that it's happened over and over, I will continue to send you prophets and men of wisdom and those who teach God's ways, and you will continue to kill and crucify some of them, and to flog others in your synagogues, hounding them from town to town. That is why God will hold you responsible for the murders of all his prophets from the beginning of creation until now, starting with Cain's killing of Abel ❖ *the first murder* ➤ and ending with the murder of Zechariah who was killed between the altar and the Holy Place. ❖ *This was the last murder mentioned in the Tanakh (i.e., the Jewish Scriptures, whose books are ordered differently than in the Old Testament of the Christian Bible).* ➤ I guarantee that you will be held accountable for all of their deaths!

"I pity you Scripture teachers because of the punishment waiting for you! People look up to you as teachers, yet you hide from them the key which opens the way to knowing God's truth. You yourselves refuse to submit to God so you could enter his Kingdom—and you do your best to prevent others from entering too!"

When Jesus left there, the Pharisees and Scripture teachers hated him. After this, they often interrogated him in public on many subjects and plotted to trap him into saying something they could use against him in court.

137. Jesus Warns About Hypocrisy

In the meantime, thousands of people had gathered around Jesus to hear him—to the point that they were stepping on each other's feet. Jesus first addressed his followers, "Beware of the infectious influence of the Pharisees—particularly their hypocritical pretense of holiness. Don't think that any pretense will ultimately succeed. Remember that Judgment Day will come when all hidden thoughts, attitudes, motives, and deeds will be publicly revealed. Whatever you've said in darkness will be heard in broad daylight. Whatever you've whispered in secret will be shouted from the housetops for all to hear. All your secret sins will be exposed."

138. Parable About the Rich Fool

A man in the crowd said to him, "Rabbi, please tell my older brother to fairly divide the inheritance he got from our father with me."

Jesus replied, "I wasn't sent to be an arbiter or judge between you."

Then using this request as a topic to teach on, he said to the crowd, "Be careful to guard against every kind of greed in your life. Quality of life is not determined by what you have—not even when a person is wealthy." Then he told them this parable, "There was a rich farmer whose land was very productive. He began to reason with himself like this, 'I don't have enough storage capacity for all my crops. What should I do?' Then he said to himself, 'This is what I will do. I will tear down my old barns and build new ones big enough to store everything I have. Then I will say to myself, "Take it easy and enjoy life! Eat, drink, and be merry! You've got enough stored up to last for years!" ' But God said to him, 'You are a fool because tonight you will die and you've made no preparations at all for that event. So what good will all this wealth you've accumulated do you?'

"That is the fate of those who are mainly interested in acquiring wealth for themselves in this life, but haven't used it to serve God."

139. Being Shrewd in Getting Ahead A

Jesus said to his followers, "A rich man had a general manager that looked after his estate and all his business. It was reported to him that his manager was wasting his resources. So he summoned him and said, 'What's the truth about what I've been hearing? Have you been mismanaging my estate? Prepare me a report accounting for all your transactions and business on my behalf. If what I've heard is true, you will no longer be working for me!' The manager said to himself, 'My employer is going to fire me! What will I do for a living? No one will hire me for such a job again. I'm not strong enough to do manual labor, and would be too ashamed to become a beggar... I know what I will do! By the time I'm fired, I will have plenty of friends indebted to me who will help me out.'

"So before the rumor got out that he was about to lose his job, he summoned all the people who owed his employer. He asked the first one, 'How much do you owe my master?' He said, '800 gallons of olive oil.' The manager said, 'Here's the original bill. Let's write out a new one for only 400.' ❖ *Since he was still the rich man's general manager, those who owed him would assume that he was doing this with his master's knowledge and blessing. He may also have insinuated that he had convinced his master to display such generosity, which would only make both the rich man and the manager very popular among those who were indebted to him.* ➤ He said to another, 'And how much do you owe?' He said, 'A thousand bags of wheat.' The manager said, 'Here's the original bill. Let's write out a new one for only 800.'

"When the rich man found out about this, he praised the dishonest manager for his shrewdness." ❖ *The rich man was unlikely to want undo what his manager had done and so destroy the good reputation of generosity that these actions had given him in the community. He admired the shrewdness of the manager's*

actions in knowing how to get ahead, even though he had been dishonest. Jesus doesn't say if he ended up firing him or not. He wasn't saying that the manager's actions were right or good, but that he was shrewd—and his point was: It is good to be shrewd.* ➤

Jesus continued to say, "I tell this story because unbelievers often surpass believers in their shrewdness in getting ahead, each toward their respective goals. ❖ *Unbelievers know how to use money to get ahead and make themselves rich and powerful in this world—which is their goal. But most believers are not nearly as shrewd in getting ahead in God's Kingdom—which should be their goal.* ➤

"I'm saying that you should be using your resources to help people in this life. That way, you earn their friendship and also have God's favor. So when you are broke, they will help you; and when your life in this world is ended, they will welcome you into their homes in Heaven. God knows that a person who is faithful in minor responsibilities will also be faithful in larger ones. And the person who is dishonest in minor matters will also be dishonest in major things. So if he doesn't find you being faithful in your use of such minor things as money in this world, he certainly isn't going to trust you to administer more important things in Heaven. And if you haven't been responsible to use the resources he has put into your hands in this life for his purposes and to advance his Kingdom, then don't expect to be given much in the way of your own resources in Heaven.

"No one can serve two masters at the same time. For you will either be less loyal to the first and completely devoted to the second, or the other way around. In the same way, you have to choose in this life between loving God and serving him with your money, or loving money and trying to acquire it for your own purposes. You can't do both."

Some Pharisees heard all this and made fun of Jesus because they loved money. They believed that riches were a sign of God's blessing for their being righteous and were theirs to do with as they pleased. Jesus said to them, "You want to look good in the

---

A **139** The interpretation of the parable in section 139 follows the analysis of Kenneth E. Bailey in "Poet & Peasant," pp. 86-118.

eyes of others, but God knows what's in your minds. Many of the things in this life that are highly esteemed and admired by people are despised by God.

"God's word and will was proclaimed in the Torah and the writings of the prophets until John the Baptizer came. Since then, the Good News about how to enter God's Kingdom has been openly preached, and many are exerting their utmost to enter it. But the Teachings of Moses in the Torah and the writings of the prophets are still God's holy word and remain in force. It would be easier to destroy Heaven and Earth than for a single letter in the Torah or other Scriptures to be made invalid."

140. The Rich Man and Lazarus

To conclude his teaching on the proper use of money, Jesus told the following story which also teaches that one purpose of the Scriptures is to warn people that they need to repent and change their way of living. He said, "There was a certain rich man who wore only the best clothing and daily indulged himself in every luxury. There was also a poor man named Lazarus whose body was covered with sores from lack of proper nutrition and treatment. Every day, those who cared about him carried him to the rich man's gate, for he was hoping to be fed scraps that the rich man's servants would throw away. But he was consistently ignored by the rich man, and was a pathetic sight, with dogs licking his sores as the only relief he received in his suffering.

"So it came about that the poor man died, and angels carried his spirit to Paradise to be with Abraham and others rewarded by God. The rich man too eventually died and was buried, but he ended up in Hell—the place of eternal torment for all who have rejected God. There, he was able to look up and see Abraham far away and Lazarus with him. So he called out, 'Father Abraham! Grant me a small mercy. Send Lazarus to dip his finger in some water to cool my tongue because I'm in agony in this fire!'

"But Abraham said, 'Remember, my son, that during your life on earth, God gave you plenty of good things, but Lazarus only experienced hunger and suffering. Now he is being comforted here and you are suffering in agony as you deserve. Anyway, it's impossible for us to help you because there's a great chasm between us that no one can cross.' The rich man said, 'Then I beg of you, Father Abraham, that you send Lazarus to my father's household. For I have five brothers, and I want him to warn them to repent and change their ways so they don't end up in this place of torment too.'

"But Abraham said, 'Your brothers have the writings of Moses and the other prophets in the Scriptures to warn them. They must listen to them and heed their warnings.' The rich man answered, 'That's not enough, Father Abraham! They have heard the Scriptures, but haven't believed them. But if someone from the dead were to go to them, then they would believe and repent!' Abraham replied, 'If they won't heed the warnings of Moses and the prophets in the Scriptures, then they also won't believe even if someone were to rise from the dead.' "

141. Always Be Ready for Jesus' Return

Jesus said, "Always be ready for my return on the Last Day, like servants who are dressed, alert, and keeping their oil lamps lit while they wait for their master to return from a wedding feast. They will want to be ready to open the door for him the moment he returns. He will give special rewards to those he finds alert when he arrives. I assure you, he will prepare himself to serve, have them sit down to dine, and then wait on them. They will, indeed, be in his good favor if he finds them ready—even if he returns late at night or in the wee hours of the morning.

"To use another illustration, if a homeowner knew when a burglar planned to break in, he would be awake and ready at the time he expected him. But of course, nobody can anticipate such things. I, the Son of Man, will also return at a time you can't anticipate. So you always need to be ready." Peter asked, "Lord, does this illustration only apply to us, or is it for everyone?"

The Lord answered, "I'm talking to anyone who wants to be a faithful and wise manager that has been given the responsibilities of supervising the master's household and feeding his other servants. Such a manager will, indeed, be in a good position with his master if he finds him faithfully doing his duties when he returns. As a reward, the master will put him in charge of everything he owns.

"But what if such a manager thinks to himself, 'My master won't be returning for quite a while,' and then starts to beat the other servants, and party and get drunk? He will find the time of His master's return totally unexpected. The master will severely punish him and throw him outside the Kingdom with others who aren't faithful and the disobedient.

"The servant who knows what his master wants him to do but doesn't do it will be severely punished. But the servant who doesn't know what his master expects will be punished lightly for doing wrong. God requires a lot from those he has blessed with much in this life. And if he has entrusted someone with many resources, he expects proportionally more from them."

142. Loyalty to Jesus Will Cause People to Reject You

Jesus continued, "I've come to ignite a fire in this world, and I wish it were already burning. ❖ *Jesus meant the heat of division between those who choose to follow him and those who reject him. Fire also often represents purification—and he may also have been thinking about the purification of those who choose to follow him. His purpose in coming into this world was to call out those who are willing to be purified and are wanting to enter into a close relationship with him so they can be saved. He yearns for this to be accomplished.* ➤ But first, I have to undergo a baptism of suffering—and it's a difficult thing for me to contemplate until it's finally over. ❖ *Baptism, in this sense, means "complete immersion." Jesus knew all about the suffering that awaited him in Jerusalem and was not looking forward to it. Yet he was determined to go through with it.* ➤ Did you think that I came to bring peace to this world? Not at all! I came to bring division between those who follow me and those who continue to reject me. Families will divide, three who reject me against two who follow me, and all other possible combinations. They will divide father

against son, mother against daughter, mother-in-law against daughter-in-law, and between every other possible relationship."

143. A Call to Repentance and a Warning

At that time, some people told Jesus about Pilate ordering some Galileans to be killed while they were offering sacrifices. Jesus said to them, "Do you think these Galileans were worse sinners than others because this happened to them? Not at all! But I warn you, unless you repent of your sin and turn to God, you too will suffer violent destruction. And what about those eighteen men who died when the tower of Siloam fell on them? Do you think that they were the worst sinners living in Jerusalem? I say they were not! But if you don't repent, you too will suffer violent destruction."

144. Parable of the Barren Fig Tree

Then Jesus told this parable, "A man had a fig tree in his vineyard and he kept coming round to look for fruit on it—but never found any. So he told his gardener, 'For three years I've waited for this tree to bear fruit and I haven't seen any yet. Chop it down; it's wasting good space.' But the gardener said, 'Sir, let it stay for one more year. I will loosen the soil and fertilize it. If it bears fruit next year, you can keep it. If not, then you can have it chopped down.' "
❖ *The fig tree in the Scriptures sometimes symbolizes the people of Israel. Jesus' parable was a warning. God found no fruit in their lives. i.e., They weren't living the way he meant for them to live. They are under threat of destruction if they don't repent and start producing the fruit of obedience. They have been given a short reprieve to see if they will respond to special attention and feeding. Jesus' ministry would be that season of special attention. Unfortunately, most of the nation of Israel did not repent and accept Jesus as God's Messiah— and in AD 70, they were destroyed as a nation as a result of their rebelling against Rome, and against God.* ➤

145. Jesus Heals a Crippled Woman on a Sabbath

One Sabbath, Jesus was teaching in a synagogue. A woman was there who had been sick for eighteen years because of an afflicting demon. She was bent over and unable to stand up straight. When Jesus saw her, he called her forward and said, "You are free from your sickness!" Then he placed his hands on her, and she immediately straighten up normally and started praising God.

But the leader of the synagogue was angry that Jesus had healed her on the Sabbath. So he took it out on the people, saying, "There are six work days in a week! Come on one of those days to be healed—but not on the Sabbath!"

The Lord replied to him and others who agreed with him, "You self-righteous hypocrites! Every one of you work on the Sabbath when you untie your ox or donkey and lead them out to drink. You know it's necessary to take care of them this way and that the teachings in the Torah allow it. Isn't a human being much more important than a dumb animal? And she's a descendant of Abraham, thus a rightful heir to the blessings God promised him! Satan has held her in bondage for eighteen years, and you are saying it isn't right that she be set free from this bondage today, even if it is the Sabbath?" When he said this, those who had opposed him were humiliated because it was clear that he was right. And the people were thrilled at all the wonderful things he did.

146. Jesus Again Claims to Be God, so the Jewish Leaders Attempt to Stone Him
(December, AD 29)

A couple of months later, it was winter and time for the eight-day Festival of Dedication in Jerusalem. This festival is also called Hanukkah or the Festival of Lights. Jesus was walking in the Temple courtyard in the roofed area called "Solomon's Portico." Many Jewish leaders gathered around him and said, "How long are you going to keep us in suspense? If you are the Messiah, then tell us clearly." Jesus answered, "I have already, in effect, told you, but you refuse to believe me. The miracles I've done using my Father's authority and power are sufficiently clear testimony about who I am. But you don't believe me because you're not my sheep. I know my own sheep. They respond to my voice and follow me. I give them eternal life, and they will never die because no one has the power to snatch them away from me. My Father is the one who gave them to me, and his power is greater than everything. No one can snatch them away from him. My Father and I are a unity."

They immediately picked up stones to execute him. But Jesus said to them, "You've seen me do many good works that my Father told me to do. For which of these are you intending to kill me?" They replied, "We don't execute you for doing good works, but for blaspheming by claiming you, a mere man, are God." Jesus retorted, "Isn't it written in your own Teachings that God said to the people of Israel, 'You are gods'? ❖ *The word for "god" that Jesus would have quoted from the Hebrew Scriptures is "el," and "gods" is "elohim." The range of meaning of this word is broad. It usually refers to God himself but is also used in the Hebrew Scriptures to refer to false gods, and angels, and even men who are in authority. So the meaning of the word is determined by context. Jesus uses this ambiguity to his advantage.* ➤ Since he called the people who received his Teachings 'gods'—and Scripture is always true—it must be even more true of me, whom the Father set apart and sent into this world for his purposes. So how can you accuse me of blaspheming him because I said I'm God's Son? If the works I do are not clearly from my Father, then don't believe me. But if I'm doing works that clearly originate with my Father, even though you don't accept my witness that I am God's Son, at least accept the witness of my Father through these works. Then you will recognize that the Father is in me, and I am in the Father." But they weren't convinced, so once again they tried to seize him. But he miraculously eluded them.

He and his close followers went and stayed on the east side of the Jordan River where John had first baptized people—outside of the jurisdiction of the Jerusalem leaders. Many came to hear him teach. They were saying to each other, "Even though John the Baptizer never did any miraculous signs, everything he said about Jesus is true." So many there believed that Jesus was the Messiah.

147. The Story of Lazarus

Jesus had friends who lived in Bethany—less than two miles from

Jerusalem on the east side of Mount Olivet—named Lazarus and his sisters Mary and Martha. Mary was the one who later anointed the Lord with expensive perfume and wiped his feet with her hair. Now, Lazarus became very sick so the sisters sent a messenger to Jesus with this message, "Lord, your close friend is very sick."

But when Jesus heard this, he said, "This sickness will not result in his death. God has allowed it in order to reveal his glory and so I, his Son, may receive glory through the situation." Now, Jesus loved Martha and her sister and Lazarus. Yet, when he heard Lazarus was sick, he stayed where he was for two more days.

Then after the two days, he said to his followers, "Let's return to Judea." They replied, "Rabbi, our leaders tried to kill you, and you want to risk going back there?" Jesus answered, "Every day has twelve hours of light. Those who walk during the day won't stumble because they can see by the light. But those who walk at night stumble because they don't have light."

Then he went on to say, "Our friend Lazarus has fallen asleep. I'm going there to wake him." His followers said, "Lord, if he's sleeping, it's a good sign that he will recover." Jesus had been speaking euphemistically and meant that Lazarus was dead, but his followers had taken his words literally. So he told them plainly, "What I meant was, Lazarus is dead. But I'm glad for your sakes that I wasn't there to heal him, so your faith in me may increase. Let's go to him now." Then Thomas, whose nickname was "Twin," said to the others, "Let's go too so we can die with him."

When they approached Bethany, they heard news that Lazarus had already been entombed for four days. Since Bethany was less than two miles from Jerusalem, many of the Jewish leaders had come to Martha and Mary's house to console them over their brother's death. When Martha heard that Jesus was approaching, she went out to meet him, but Mary stayed home. Martha said to Jesus, "Lord, if only you had been here, my brother wouldn't have died! But even now I know that God will grant you whatever you ask of him." Jesus replied, "Your brother will come back to life again." Martha said, "Yes, I know that will happen on the Last Day when everyone is resurrected from death." Jesus said, "I am the source of resurrection power and eternal life. Those who believe in me will live forever—even if their bodies die. And those who believe in me—and thus have eternal life—will never experience death. Do you believe me?" Martha answered, "Yes Lord. I believe you are the Messiah who was prophesied would come, and are also God's Son." After she said this, she went back to the house and called her sister Mary aside. She told her secretly, "The Rabbi is nearby and he wants you to go to him." When Mary heard it, she quickly got up and went out to meet him. Now, Jesus hadn't yet entered the village but was still where Martha had met him. When the Jewish leaders—who had been trying to console Mary—saw her leave so quickly, they followed her, thinking she was going to cry at the tomb. When Mary reached Jesus, she fell at his feet and cried, "Lord, if only you had been here, I know my brother wouldn't have died!" When Jesus saw her grief and also the grief of those who followed her, he was deeply moved and angered. Then he asked, "Where have you put him?" They answered, "Lord, come and we will show you." Then Jesus also expressed his grief by crying. People noticed this and said to each other, "See how much he loved him!" But some of them said, "He had the power to give sight to a blind man. Why couldn't he have kept this man from dying?"

Jesus arrived at the tomb and was deeply moved again. The tomb was a cave with a stone covering the entrance. Jesus said, "Remove the stone!" Martha replied, "Lord, he's been in there for four days. There will be a terrible stench." Jesus responded, "Didn't I tell you that you would see God's glory if you believed?" So they removed the stone from the entrance. Then Jesus looked up to Heaven in an attitude of prayer and said, "Father, I thank you that you listen to my prayers and answer them. I know you always do this, but I'm saying this for the benefit of those listening so they will be able to believe that you really sent me with your authority." Then he shouted into the tomb, "Lazarus! Come out!" The dead man came out of the tomb, his hands and feet still bound with strips of linen and his face still wrapped with a cloth. Jesus said, "Unbind him and let him go."

Many of the people who had come to comfort Mary saw what Jesus did and believed in him. But some of them returned to Jerusalem to tell the Pharisees the latest thing that Jesus had done.

148. Jewish Leaders Plot to Kill Jesus

In response to this latest report about Jesus, the Pharisees and the chief priests convened a session of the Sanhedrin. The question was brought up, "What are we accomplishing in our efforts to squash the popularity of Jesus? He keeps performing all these miraculous signs! If we allow him to go on like this, everyone will believe that he's the Messiah, there will be a revolt, the Romans will destroy our Temple, and we will lose our positions as rulers over the nation!" Then Caiaphas—who was High Priest at that time—spoke up, "You don't know what you're talking about! You should realize it is expedient for us that this one man die for the people so the whole nation won't be destroyed."

He didn't realize it, but these words weren't his own. As High Priest, God caused him to prophesy that Jesus was going to die for the nation. And not only for that nation, but for all of God's people all over the world to make them one in spiritual union with him. So from that day on, they were resolved to kill Jesus. Therefore, he no longer traveled publicly, but he and his close followers left the vicinity of Jerusalem to stay in the village of Ephraim near the wilderness.

❖ *There's a gap of a couple of months in the gospel accounts here at the beginning of AD 30 when Jesus apparently returned to Galilee.* ➤

149. A Samaritan Village
Refuses Jesus Hospitality
(Before Passover – Spring, AD 30)

Jesus knew the time was approaching when he would have to die and then be taken up to Heaven. So he resolutely started out toward Jerusalem to face his time of trial. He sent messengers ahead to make arrangements for him and his traveling companions to spend the night in a village in Samaria. But the Samaritans there refused to take him in because it was clear that they were Jews who were going to Jerusalem for the Passover Festival. When James and John heard this, they were furious and said, "Master, do you want us to command fire to come down from Heaven to destroy them?" But Jesus turned and rebuked them, "You don't realize that a demon is influencing you to say this! I didn't come to destroy people; I came to save them!" Then they went on to a different village.

150. Jesus Heals Ten Men with Leprosy

On his way to Jerusalem, Jesus traveled for a ways along the border between Galilee and Samaria. As he was entering a certain village, ten men with leprosy came to meet him but kept their distance. They shouted, "Jesus! Master, have mercy on us and heal us!"

When Jesus saw them, he commanded, "Go and show yourselves to the priests." Then as they were on their way to find a priest, they were completely healed. One of them, when he saw that he was healed, returned to Jesus and loudly praised God on the way. When he found him, he prostrated himself at Jesus' feet and thanked him profusely. Now, the man who did this was a Samaritan. Jesus said to those around him, "Weren't there ten who were healed? Where are the other nine? Was the only one who was thankful and thought to turn back and give praise to God this foreigner?" Then Jesus said to the man, "Stand up and go where I told you to go. Your faith has healed you."

151. Jesus Sends Out 72 Followers
as Evangelists

Later, as he had sent out the twelve apostles to preach before, Jesus now chose 72 more men from among his followers and sent them out in pairs. He sent them ahead of himself to minister in all the towns and villages he was planning to pass through on his way to Jerusalem. He told them, "Many are ready to enter God's Kingdom. They are like a field that promises a plentiful harvest. But the number of harvest workers are few, so ask God to send out more workers. Get ready to go, but be aware that there are people who will attack you. You are as helpless as lambs among wolves, but trust God to take care of you. Don't take any money with you or a bag or extra footwear. God will provide what you need. Go quickly and don't allow people you meet on the way to delay you. Whatever house you enter, greet them with a blessing, saying, 'May God bless you with peace, health, and wholeness.' If they are worthy and accept your blessing, it will remain on them. Otherwise, your blessing will not be effective. If they accept you, stay in their house as long as you are in that town instead of moving from house to house. Don't hesitate to accept whatever they offer you to eat and drink because you are working for God and a worker should be compensated. Whenever you enter a town and they welcome you, be content to eat whatever they set before you. Heal those who are sick in that town and tell them, 'God's Kingdom has touched you, and you may join it if you are willing to submit to him as your King.' But if you go to a town and they refuse to welcome you, go out in the streets and warn them that God is displeased with them and they are the same as pagans in his sight. Say, 'We are wiping off even the dust of your town from our feet as a sign that God rejects you because you have rejected us, his messengers! God's Kingdom was offered to you today, but you rejected it!' " Jesus said to his followers, "I assure you that on Judgment Day, God will show more mercy to the citizens of Sodom than to the citizens of that town."

152. Jesus Laments for Towns That Rejected Him

Then Jesus began to lament for the people of the towns who had seen him do most of his miracles because they had not responded with repentance. "O how terrible it will be for you citizens of Chorazin and Bethsaida! ❖ *These are Jewish towns just north of Lake Galilee, near Capernaum.* ➤ God will punish you because you refused to repent in spite of the miracles you've seen. If the miracles which were done for you had been done for the pagans in the cities of Tyre and Sidon, they would have repented long ago and would have demonstrated their sorrow by wearing sackcloth and ashes. On Judgment Day, the wicked pagans of Tyre and Sidon will be better off than you because you saw God's miracles and you heard the Good News, but you rejected it. And you people of Capernaum! Do you think you will be honored in Heaven? No, you will be cast down to the world of the dead! If the people of Sodom had seen the miracles you've seen, they would have repented and that city would still exist. So on Judgment Day, God will assign you a punishment even greater than theirs!"

Then Jesus said to the 72, "Anyone who accepts your message is accepting me. And anyone who rejects you is also rejecting me. And anyone who rejects me is also rejecting God who sent me." Then they went on their way.

153. The Return of the 72

Days later, the 72 returned from their mission and joyfully reported to Jesus, "Lord, even the demons obeyed us when we commanded them in your name!"

Jesus said, "Yes, while you were ministering, I saw Satan fall from the heights of power like a flash of lightning. Your work was defeating him. I gave you authority so you can trample on demonic serpents and scorpions with impunity and can overcome all the power of Satan. There is nothing they can do to harm you if you use my authority over them. But don't center your joy on the fact that demons obey you. Rather, focus your joy on the fact that your names are written in the 'Book of Life' in Heaven."

154. Jesus Rejoices

Then Jesus was filled with the Holy Spirit and exulted, "Yes! O Father! Lord of Heaven and earth! I praise and thank you for hiding your truths from those who think much of themselves, and for revealing them to the humble! Yes, Father, I know this is what pleases you!"

To his followers, he said, "My Father has given me power and authority over everything. No one really knows me, God's Son, except my Father in Heaven. And no one knows the Father except me, his Son, and those to whom I choose to reveal him.

"All of you who are burdened with emotional and spiritual cares and worries and are weary of bearing them, come to me! I will give you relief and rest. Submit yourselves to obey me and allow me to teach you. You will find me a humble and gentle master, and you will find the emotional and spiritual rest you desire. You will learn that it isn't hard at all to be under my lordship. The things that I require of you will not be difficult."

When they were in private, Jesus turned to his followers and said, "You really are fortunate to be seeing the things you see! For many prophets and kings longed to see the things you see and to hear what you hear, but they didn't happen in their lifetimes."

155. The Narrow Door to Heaven

Afterward, Jesus traveled through villages and towns on his way to Jerusalem and taught as he went. Someone asked, "Lord, is it true that only a few people will be saved and go to Heaven?"

Jesus replied, "Try hard to enter Heaven through the narrow door now because many will try to enter when it's too late ❖ *i.e., after death, or after he returns* ➤ and not succeed because the door will be shut. The time will come when I—the master of the house—will shut the door to Heaven. Then you will stand outside knocking and pleading, 'Lord, open the door for us!' But I will answer, 'I don't have a relationship with you, so I won't.' Then you will say, 'But we ate and drank with you, and you taught in our village!' But I will reply, 'I don't have any relationship with you. Go away and don't come back! You are not welcome because you are evil!' Then you will wail with grief and defiant rage when you see Abraham and Isaac and Jacob and all the prophets present in God's Kingdom—with yourselves banished! But Gentiles will have come from every nation in the world to take their places at the feast in God's Kingdom. And note this, some who are the lowliest in this world will be the most important in the Kingdom. Also, some who are the most important in this world will be the lowliest in Heaven."

156. Jesus' Love for the People of Jerusalem

At that time, some Pharisees came to Jesus and told him, "You should leave here and go somewhere else because Herod Antipas says he is going to kill you!"

Jesus replied, "You go and tell that vicious and destructive fox that I will continue to expel demons and heal people today and tomorrow ❖ *meaning for the near future,* ➤ and on the third day ❖ *some special day not too far off, or perhaps the day of his resurrection* ➤ I will finish my work. Regardless of what Herod intends, for now, I must continue on to Jerusalem. It just wouldn't do for a prophet to be killed anywhere but in Jerusalem!

"O my people in Jerusalem! You kill the prophets and stone God's messengers! Many times I wanted to shield you from God's coming punishment. I wanted to gather you in together to protect you like a hen gathers her chicks under her wings. But you didn't want me. Take notice! God will leave you and turn his back on you. He will no longer protect you from your enemies. And you won't see me again until you say, 'Blessed is the he who comes in the name of the Lord.' "

157. Jesus Heals on a Sabbath

One Sabbath, Jesus accepted an invitation eat with a prominent Pharisee, but they were actually watching him closely to see if they could catch him in some violation of a Torah command that they could use against him. A man with a serious illness that caused swelling in his arms and legs came to Jesus. So Jesus said to the Pharisees and Scripture teachers present, "Do the Teachings of Moses allow healing on the Sabbath, or not?"

But they sat in stony silence. So Jesus touched the man, healed him, and sent him away. Then he said, "Is there anyone here who would even hesitate to help his son or ox if one fell into a well on the Sabbath?"

There was nothing they could say to refute this, nevertheless they hated him for justifying this public violation of their Sabbath rule.

158. Humility

Jesus noticed that many of the guests had maneuvered to sit in seats of honor, so he began to teach them, "When you're invited to a wedding reception, don't presume to sit in the seat of honor. It might be reserved for someone else and your host would be forced to embarrass you by asking you to move. You could end up in whatever seat is still available—possibly the worst one in the house. So when you're invited, take the worst seat in the house, and your host is likely to honor you by asking you to move to a more prominent position. This is the way God rules in his Kingdom. Those who try to exalt themselves will be humbled, and those who humble themselves will be honored."

Then Jesus said to his host, "If you invite people to a meal and want God's approval, don't invite only—or mainly—your friends, brothers, relatives, or rich neighbors. Because they will just invite you back and their return invitation will be your only reward. Instead, invite those who are poor, crippled, and blind. Then God will bless you in this life and also reward you when he raises his people from death on the Last Day because you've unselfishly blessed those he loves who are unable to pay you back."

159. Parable of the Great Banquet in Heaven

When one of the men sitting at the table heard this, he said to Jesus, "Those who will feast in God's Kingdom are indeed in a good position!"

So Jesus told this parable, "A man planned a big banquet and sent out many invitations. When the banquet was ready, he sent out his servant to tell all the invited guests, 'Everything is ready, so come right now!' But one after another—in grave insult and offense to their host—they all made extremely lame excuses why they couldn't come. The first guest said, 'I just bought some land I haven't seen yet seen so I have to go inspect it. Please excuse me.' Another one said, 'I just bought five pair of oxen and I need to try them out to see how well they plow. Please excuse me.' Another said, 'I just got married last week so I can't come.'

"The servant returned and reported this to his master who became very angry. So he told his servant, 'Hurry and go down all the streets and alleys in town and bring back those who are poor, crippled, and blind to attend my banquet.' After doing as he was told, he reported, 'Master, I've done as you ordered, but there is still room for more people.' The master said, 'Go and search the country roads and paths for more people and urge them all to come. I want my house to be filled. But I can guarantee you that none of the invited guests will get even a taste of my banquet!' "

160. The Cost of Being Jesus' True Follower

Now, large crowds were traveling with Jesus on the way to Jerusalem for the upcoming Passover Festival. He turned to them and said, "If you want to be one of my followers, but can't place your loyalty and obedience to me above your loyalty to your parents, spouse, siblings, children, and even your own desires for your life—then I won't accept you. If you aren't willing to give up your own plans and desires in order to obey my will for you—even if it means you must suffer or die for me—then you can't be one of my true followers.

"If you wanted to build a tower, you would of course carefully plan it out first, determine how much it would cost, and make sure that you had enough resources to finish the project. If you didn't, you might only get the foundation laid, run out of funds, and become the laughing stock of everyone who found out. You would become known as someone who doesn't finish what he starts.

"Or, suppose a king decides to wage war against another king. If he's smart, he will carefully evaluate whether his 10,000 men are really able to defeat his enemy's 20,000 men. And if he decides that he can't, he had better send ambassadors to negotiate a peace treaty before it's too late.

"The point of all this is—if you want to be one of my true followers, you need to consider what it will cost you and if you can go through with it to the very end of your life. Because you have to be willing to give up everything in your life that will hinder you from following and obeying me."

Jesus continued, "Salt is good, but if it loses its flavor, it can't be made salty again. It's not fit for anything—not even for the ground or a pile of manure. It will be thrown away. If you have your ears attuned to God, try to understand what I'm saying!" ❖ *Salt was a valuable commodity in Jesus' time. But even something good and valuable can become worthless. His point is that people who start out following him are valuable to him. But if they lose their commitment, they become worthless to his Kingdom. They will be rejected and cast out and nothing will be able to restore them.* ➤

161. The Good Shepherd and the Lost Sheep

Many tax collectors and other notorious sinners were always coming to listen to Jesus. But the Pharisees and Scripture teachers complained, "This man welcomes habitual sinners and even eats with them!" So Jesus told this parable to show that God is concerned about people who are "lost" and can't find the way to have a proper relationship with him.

Jesus began, "Which of you, if you had a hundred sheep and had lost one of them, wouldn't leave the other 99 grazing in the pasture and search for the lost one until you found it? When you found it, you would put it on your shoulders and carry it back again, rejoicing. When you got home, you would call your friends and neighbors together and say, 'Celebrate with me because I've found my lost sheep!' I'm telling you, it is just like that in Heaven. God rejoices more over one sinner who repents and turns back to him than over 99 godly people who have no need to repent." ❖ *Jesus is equating "accepting being found" with "repentance" in this illustration. The sheep cannot save itself, but the shepherd (God) must come and find it. There can be no repentance without God reaching out to find. This is his offering of undeserved favor (also known as "grace").* ➤

162. The Good Woman and the Lost Coin

Then Jesus told a second story with the same point. He said, "Or what woman who has ten silver coins—each worth a day's wage—and loses one wouldn't light a lamp and thoroughly sweep the dirt floor of her house, searching until she finds it? When she does find it, she would call her friends and neighbors and say, 'Celebrate with me for I've found the coin that I lost!' I'm telling you, it is just like that in Heaven. God rejoices in front of his angels over even one sinner who repents."

163. The Good Father and His Two Lost Sons A

Then Jesus told a third story in which he contrasted God's welcoming attitude toward repentant sinners versus the unforgiving attitude of those who are self-righteous. He said, "There was a man who had two sons. The younger one grievously insulted his father by saying, 'Father, right now I want the share of your estate that I will get when you die.' So the man divided his land between his two sons. Within a few days, the younger son sold his share of the estate and left home with the money. He went to a distant country where he squandered it all in wasteful living. When all his money was gone, a severe famine spread throughout the region and he had nothing to live on. So in desperation, he got a job from one of the citizens of that country, feeding pigs in the fields. Because of the famine, food was scarce and no one would feed him. He was so hungry that he would have gladly eaten the carob pods that he fed to the pigs, but these are not digestible by people. Finally, he came to his senses and said to himself, 'My father's hired workers have more than enough to eat, and here I am starving to death! I will go back to my father and— playing on his soft heart—say, "Father, I've sinned against both God and you. I'm not worthy to be treated as a son, but please make me one of your hired workers." ' ❖ *He was not repentant since he did not intend to ask for forgiveness. He was only doing this because he was starving and saw no alternative. If this was repentance, Jesus would be saying that the lost son could take the initiative and repent*

A **163** The insight for interpreting the three parables in sections 161-163 comes from Kenneth E. Bailey's books: "Finding The Lost – Cultural Keys to Luke 15" and "Jacob & the Prodigal – How Jesus retold Israel's story." More of Bailey's insights are presented in the account in Luke chapter 15.

on his own. But in fact, it is the father who takes the initiative to restore the relationship. ➤ So he went to his father. But while he was still a long way off, his father—who had already planned what he would do if his son returned and had been looking for him every day—saw him and was filled with compassion. He ran to his son, embraced him, and repeatedly kissed him. ❖ *A middle-eastern father would never run, nor would he go out to meet a son who had humiliated him. He was publicly sacrificing his dignity because of his great love for his son. He had to reach him and publicly welcome him back before others officially banned him from the community for his disgraceful behavior. The father was freely offering undeserved forgiveness.* ➤ The son contritely said, 'Father, I've sinned against both God and you. I'm not worthy to be treated as a son.' ❖ *It was his father's public self-humiliation in order to help him and restore the relationship that shocked him and touched his heart. He became ashamed of what he had put his father through, so he didn't finish his speech but genuinely confessed his sin. To go through with his plan would imply that he didn't believe in or accept his father's forgiveness.* ➤ But the father said to his slaves, 'Hurry! Bring out my best robe and put it on him. And put my signet ring on his finger as a sign of his authority to transact business in my name. And put sandals on his feet to show that he is neither a slave nor a servant, but my son. And slaughter a calf that's been fattened especially for feasting. Then let's have a party to celebrate because it was like my son was dead to me, but now he's alive again; he was lost to me, but now I've found him!' ❖ *The father "found" him in restoring him to his position as a son. The son was restored by "accepting being found," i.e., accepting his father's undeserved favor and forgiveness.* ➤ Then they began to celebrate.

"Now, the older son had been working in the fields and when he approached the house, he heard music and dancing. So he summoned one of the young boys and asked him what was happening. He answered, 'Your brother has returned, and your father had a fat calf slaughtered for a feast to celebrate because he has welcomed him in shalom and restored their relationship.' The older son became angry; and in a display of rebellion and deliberate public insult to his father, he refused to enter the house. His father—publicly sacrificing his own dignity because of his love for his son—came out and pleaded with him to come in and join the celebration. But further humiliating his father in front of everyone, the son loudly protested, 'Look! All these years I served you like a slave and never disobeyed a single one of your commands. You've never given me even so much as a young goat so I could have a party and celebrate with my friends—let alone a calf! But this son of yours comes home after wasting your money on prostitutes, and you honor him by killing a calf and having a party for him!'

"His father—again motivated by his love for his son and ignoring the display of rebellion and the resulting public shame to himself—appealed to him, 'My son, you have always been with me, and everything I now own is your inheritance. But we had to celebrate and rejoice because your brother was dead to me and now he's alive; he was lost to me, but now I've found him again!' " ❖ *Jesus doesn't tell the final response of the older brother—who represents the self-righteous religious leaders—in hope of urging a response from them. By telling this parable, Jesus was pleading with them to forgive sinners and join him in celebrating the restoration of their brothers.* ➤

164. The Proper Attitude to Have in Serving Jesus

On another occasion, Jesus said, "Suppose one of you has a slave that's hoeing a garden, or perhaps looking after sheep. When he comes in from his work, would you say, 'Sit down and eat, you deserve a break'? You would not because it's his job to serve you your meal before his work for the day is finished. You would tell him, 'Prepare my evening meal then get out of your outdoor work clothes and dress for serving. Wait on me until I've finished eating and then you may be dismissed to eat your own meal.' You also don't go out of your way to praise a slave just for adequately doing his normal duties, do you? Of course not. So you ought to have a similar attitude in serving God. When you have done everything that you are commanded to do, don't think that you've earned some big reward for just doing your duty. Instead, have the attitude, 'We are unworthy slaves. We have only done our duty.' "

165. The Coming of God's Kingdom

Some Pharisees asked Jesus just when the Kingdom of God was coming. He answered, "You can't observe it by looking for outward signs. And you can't rely on people that say, 'Look, here it is!' or, 'There it is!' For the Kingdom of God—where he rules—is inside the hearts and minds of those who are submitted to him."

166. Jesus Speaks a Third Time About His Death

Now, Jesus and his followers were heading toward Jerusalem with Jesus walking quickly and determined in the lead. They were amazed that he was so eager to go there since they knew that the Jewish leaders were plotting against him, and they feared what might happen. On the way, Jesus took the twelve apostles aside and once again told them what was going to happen to him. He said, "We are going up to Jerusalem and when we get there, all the things the prophets wrote about the Son of Man in the Scriptures will happen to me. I, the Son of Man, will be betrayed and handed over to the custody of the chief priests and Scripture teachers. They will sentence me to death and hand me over to the Roman authorities for execution. The Romans will mock me and spit on me, then whip and execute me. But on the second **A** day after my death, God will bring me back to life again."

But his followers didn't understand any of what he was trying to tell them because their expectations for the Messiah were entirely different—and they couldn't see beyond them. So they completely failed to understand what he was saying.

167. Kingdom Authority

Then Zebedee's wife came to Jesus in private with her sons, James and John. She bowed down and said, "Rabbi, we want you to grant us a favor." He asked her, "What do you want me to do for you?" She said, "Grant that my two sons will sit on either side of you when you become King—the two highest positions under you." Jesus replied, "You have no idea what the implications are of what you're asking. Are the two of you willing to endure the suffering that I'm about to go through?" They answered, "Yes, we are." Jesus said, "Then you will indeed share in my suffering. But I don't have the authority to decide who will have the top two positions under me. My Father has decided who will have them."

When the other ten apostles heard about this request, they were indignant with James' and John's presumption that they were above the rest of them. Jesus called them all together and said, "You know the way of earthly rulers and men of authority. They use their positions to order others around or even tyrannize them, and they make sure that their status and privileges remain clearly above those under them. But that's not the way it's going to be among my people. Whoever wants God to consider them as being important or wants to become a leader over my people must become everyone else's servant. If you want to attain the highest rank, then you must be a slave to everyone else. I, the Son of Man, am your example. For I came into this world to serve people and to give my life to redeem them— not to be served by them."

168. Jesus Heals Bar-Timaeus and Another Blind Man

As Jesus and his followers were just outside of Jericho on their way to Jerusalem (15 miles away), a large crowd was following him. There were two blind men sitting by the road, one whose name was Bar-Timaeus (which means son of Timaeus). When they heard the crowd walking past, they asked what was happening. People in the crowd told them that Jesus of Nazareth was passing by. When they heard this, they started shouting, "Jesus, Son of David! Have mercy on us!" Some in the crowd told them to be quiet and know their place, but they just shouted even louder, "Son of David!

A 166 See note at Matthew 16:21 for the reasoning behind not using the traditional phrase, "the third day."

Have mercy and help us!" When Jesus heard them, he stopped and commanded that they be brought to him. So those nearby said, "Stand up and get yourselves together. He's calling for you to come to him!" Immediately, they threw aside the robes in their laps, got quickly to their feet, and went in the direction of Jesus' voice. When they arrived, Jesus asked them, "What do you want me to do for you?" Bar-Timaeus and the other man said, "Rabbi, we want to see again." Jesus felt compassion for them and touched their eyes. He said, "Receive your sight. You may go on your way because your faith in me has saved you." Immediately, they could see again and began following Jesus as he continued on the road—all the while praising God. When the people in the crowd saw what had happened, they too praised God.

169. Zaccheus

Jesus entered Jericho with the crowd following behind him and was passing through the town. A man named Zaccheus lived there who was the chief tax collector and hence quite rich. He had heard about Jesus and desperately wanted to see him, but he was short and unable to see above the heads of the crowd. So he ran ahead of the crowd and climbed a Sycamore tree to see Jesus as he passed by on the road. But when Jesus reached that spot, he stopped, looked up, and said, "Zaccheus, hurry down because I must stay at your house today."

Zaccheus came down quickly and was thrilled to host him at his house. The people in the crowd who saw this grumbled because Jesus was honoring a collaborator with their Roman conquerors who had become rich by abusing his office. They said, "He has gone to be the guest of a sinner!"

While Jesus stayed with him, Zaccheus' heart attitude changed and he repented. He stood up and publicly announced, "Lord, I'm going to give half of all my possessions to the poor. And those whom I've defrauded, I will pay back four times as much."

Jesus said to those listening, "It's clear that God has saved this man because in faith, he has given his life to God, just like his ancestor Abraham did. It was for this very reason that I, the Son of Man, came to this world—to look for and save people like him who are lost in sin and have turned their backs on God."

170. Parable of the Minas

❖ *A mina was a gold coin worth about 100 days' wages.* ➤

While the people were listening to this, Jesus went on and told a parable. He was nearing Jerusalem in his journey and he knew they were expecting him to visibly establish God's Kingdom there very shortly. He said, "A certain nobleman went to a distant country, intending to receive authority to become a king, and planning to return to his home to rule. But before he left, he summoned ten of his slaves and gave each of them a mina. He instructed them, 'Invest this and see what profit you can make for me while I'm gone.' Then he left on his journey. But some of the citizens in that country hated him and sent a delegation to the high king—where the nobleman was headed—to tell him, 'We don't want this man to become our king.'

"But eventually, the nobleman did return as their rightful king, and he sent for his slaves to whom he had entrusted his money. He summoned them in one at a time to find out what they had accomplished with it. The first one entered and reported, 'Master, I've earned ten additional minas from the one you left in my charge.' The king said, 'Well done! You are a good slave! Because you were faithful in this small matter, I'm placing you in authority over ten of my cities.' The second slave entered and reported, 'Master, I've earned five additional minas from the one you left in my charge.' The king told him, 'And I'm placing you in authority over five of my cities.'

"A third slave entered and reported, 'Master, here is your mina which I kept hidden safely in a cloth. I was afraid of failing to earn anything with it and of losing it all because I know that you're a strict businessman. You easily make a profit from the work of others and reap where others have sown.' His master replied, 'You are a worthless slave! By your own words, you are condemned because you didn't obey my command to invest it. You didn't even try. You know that I'm a strict businessman and that I make a profit from the work of others and reap where others have sown. So why didn't you at least put my money in a bank so I could have collected interest on it?'

"So then he told the people gathered there, 'Take the mina away from him and give it to the slave who earned ten minas.' They said, 'But Master, he already has ten minas!' He replied, 'I assure you, everyone who has demonstrated that he is responsible with what I've given him will be given even more responsibility. But someone who has shown no responsibility, even what little he has will be taken away from him. And now, as for my enemies who didn't want me to be their king, bring them here and kill them in my presence!' "

171. People Wonder if Jesus Will Dare to Appear in Jerusalem During Passover

When it was nearly time for the Passover Festival, many people came to Jerusalem from the hill country to go through the week-long purification rites before the festival began, using the purification pools in the Temple courts. They kept looking for Jesus while they were in the Temple courtyard, asking each other, "Do you think he will show up for the festival, or not?" Because they wanted to arrest him, the chief priests and Pharisees had announced that anyone who knew where Jesus was had to report it to them.

172. Jesus' Triumphal Entry into Jerusalem on 'Palm Sunday'
(The week before Passover, Spring, AD 30)

As Jesus and his followers approached Mount Olivet near the villages of Bethany and Bethphage—only a mile or two from Jerusalem—he sent two of his close followers ahead and told them, "Go to that village. When you enter, you will see a donkey tethered with her colt next to her which has never been ridden. Untie them and bring them here. If anyone asks what you're doing, just tell them that the Lord needs them, and they will allow you to take them."

So they went and found them in the street, tied to a door. They started to untie them, and some people standing nearby said, "What do you think you're doing untying those donkeys? They don't belong to you!" They gave the answer that Jesus had told them to say, and they allowed the men to take them.

They brought the donkey and the colt to him, put their outer robes on the colt, and then and helped Jesus onto it. This was a fulfillment of the Scripture that says, "Have no fear, people of Jerusalem, for your King is coming riding on a young donkey." At that time, his followers didn't realize that this event was a fulfillment of prophecy. But after Jesus' resurrection, they remembered the prophecies written about the Messiah and realized that they had been a part of their fulfillment.

As he rode toward Jerusalem, Jesus cried because he loved God's people who lived there, but he knew that most of them and the city would be destroyed because of their rejecting him. ❖ *This happened about 40 years later in AD 70 when the Roman army destroyed the Temple and the city and killed most of the people.* ➤ He said, "If even today you would realize how you could repent and be at peace with God, it wouldn't be too late to escape his judgment. But because of your stubborn hearts, it's hidden from you. The day will come when your enemies will surround you and build an embankment to breech your walls. You will be hemmed in on every side with no chance of escape. The city will be leveled. Not a single stone will remain on top of another. Everyone inside will be destroyed. All this will happen because you've rejected your Messiah. You didn't recognize your own God when he visited you."

As he approached Jerusalem, many in the crowd spread their outer robes on the road and others cut tree branches and spread them on the road. As he approached the place where the road descends Mount Olivet toward Jerusalem, the entire crowd started rejoicing and loudly praising God for all the miracles they had seen Jesus do. They shouted, "Hosanna to the Son of David! May God bless the one he sent with his authority!

All glory and praise be to God in the highest Heaven! May there be peace between God and his people! May God bless the Messiah—King David's descendant—as he re-establishes the reign of his Kingdom! May God bless the King of Israel!"

Some Pharisees in the crowd were angry because the people were proclaiming him to be the Messiah and they didn't believe it. So they told Jesus, "Rabbi, rebuke your followers!"

But Jesus replied, "I assure you, if they were quiet, then the stones themselves would cry out!"

The people that had come with him from Bethany—who had also been with him when he called Lazarus out of the tomb and raised him back to life—started telling this story to everyone they met. As a result of hearing about this miraculous sign, many others flocked to Jesus. So the Pharisees exclaimed in frustration to each other, "Our efforts have been useless! The whole world is following him now!"

By the time Jesus entered Jerusalem, everyone in the city knew something was happening. When they saw Jesus on the donkey, many asked, "Who is he?" And the crowd that was accompanying him answered, "This is the prophet Jesus, from Nazareth in Galilee." So it was in this way that Jesus arrived in Jerusalem. Then he went into the Temple courtyard and observed everything that was there, but soon left again with his close followers to spend the night in Bethany—since it was already late in the day.

173. A Hypocritical Fig Tree
(Monday)

The next morning as he left Bethany on his way back to Jerusalem, Jesus was hungry. Noticing a fig tree with leaves by the road some distance away, he went to it to find some fruit. Even though it wasn't yet the season for ripe figs, he expected to find some immature fruit. But when he reached it, he found nothing but leaves. Then his followers heard him say to the tree, "No one will ever eat fruit from you again!" ❖ *When the leaves are fully grown, there should be young figs on the tree. This tree with its leaves promised fruit from afar, but didn't*

have any. Such trees were called "hypocrites." In the Scriptures, the fig tree is sometimes a figure for Israel itself. [Hosea 9:10; Joel 1:7] Commentators believe Jesus cursed the fig tree as a prophetic sign that the nation of Israel could expect the same judgment if they didn't start bearing the fruit of repentance and obedience. ➤

174. Jesus Cleanses the Temple a Second Time
(Monday)

When Jesus and his followers arrived back in Jerusalem, he entered the court of the Gentiles at the Temple and drove out everyone who was doing business there. He overturned tables used by the money changers and the seats of those who sold doves for sacrifices. He also stopped people who were disregarding the sanctity of the Temple by carrying merchandise through the courtyard as if it were an ordinary thoroughfare. Later, Jesus entered the Temple and drove out those who were selling animals for sacrifices within the area set aside for worship. He said to them, "It's written in the Scriptures that God said, 'My house will be a house of prayer for people of all nations.' But you have turned it into a den of thieves!" ❖ *The merchants were providing needed services for pilgrims coming to Jerusalem for the Passover festival who couldn't bring sacrificial animals with them from far away. They also operated currency exchanges. One problem was that they were turning the Temple into a marketplace. But even more significant is the fact that they were doing this in the outer Court of the Gentiles, thus robbing the Gentiles of a place to worship the one true God.* ➤

After that, people who were blind and lame came to him there in the Temple courtyard, and he healed them. The chief priests and Scripture teachers observed Jesus heal people, and the children shouting, "Hosanna to the Son of David," and they were indignant. They approached Jesus and demanded, "Do you hear what these children are saying!" Jesus replied, "Yes, I do. Haven't you ever read the Scripture that says, 'You, Lord, have caused infants and children to speak words of perfect praise'?"

When it was near the end of the day, Jesus and his close followers left the city and returned to spend the night in Bethany.

Then for the next several days, Jesus taught in the Temple while the chief priests and Scripture teachers and other leaders of the people became desperate for a plan to get rid of him. They were afraid of his influence with the crowds who were mesmerized by his teaching and miracles and believed that he was the Messiah. But they could never find an opportunity to arrest him because there were always crowds around him, hanging on his every word. Any attempt to arrest him in public would have caused a riot.

175. Jesus Again Talks About His Death
(Sometime between Monday and Thursday)

Now, there were some God-fearing Gentiles among those who came to Jerusalem to worship during the festival. They came to Philip who was from Bethsaida in Galilee and said, "Sir, we would like to meet Jesus." Philip went and told Andrew, and together they went and told Jesus. Jesus replied, "The time has come for me, the Son of Man, to be glorified. This is an important truth for you to understand: Unless a grain of wheat is put in the ground and dies, it remains just a single grain. But if it dies, it will produce many grains. Those who love their lives in this world more than they love me will end up losing them. But those who consider their lives in this world less important than living in obedience to God will end up exchanging them for eternal life. Those who want to serve me must obey me and follow my leading. If they do this, then they will remain with me wherever I am. And my Father will honor all those who serve me.

"But now my emotions are rebelling loudly within me. Yet is it right for me to ask my Father to let me escape the suffering that's almost upon me? Not at all, since the very reason I came into this world was to suffer and die! Father, I ask that you enable me to go through with what you sent me to endure—and so bring you great glory!" Then God spoke audibly from Heaven, "I've already revealed my glorious character through your work—and I will do so again." The crowd standing nearby heard the voice. Some, not discerning the words, said it was thunder. But others said, "It was an angel speaking to him!" Jesus told them, "The voice wasn't so much for my benefit as for yours—to let you know that God sent me. The time for God's judgment has come, and Satan—the prince of this world—will be overthrown. When I am lifted up from the earth, I will draw all people to myself." He talked about being "lifted up" to indicate that the way he would die was on a cross. The crowd asked him, "We've heard that the Torah teaches the Messiah will stay here forever. So how can you say that the Son of Man must be 'lifted up'? What kind of Son of Man are you talking about?" Jesus responded, "My light will be with you for just a short time. Walk in the spiritual light that I give while it's here to guide you so that spiritual darkness won't conquer you. Those who walk in spiritual darkness have no idea where they're going. While I'm still with you, put your trust in me so you can become heirs who follow the Light." After saying this, Jesus left them and secluded himself from the public.

176. Most Jews Refused to Accept Jesus as the Messiah

Despite the many miraculous signs he had done by the Father's power, most of the Jews didn't believe that he was the Messiah. This fulfilled the prophecy of Isaiah which says, "Yahweh, who among those who have seen your mighty power have believed our message?" But the people couldn't believe in him because Isaiah also said, "God has blinded them to truth and closed their minds so they have no spiritual insight and no under-standing. Hence they don't turn to me for spiritual healing." Isaiah wrote this because of the vision he had of Jesus' glory. Even though most of the people rejected him, there were quite a few who did believe he was the Messiah, even many who were leaders. But they were unwilling to profess their belief publicly because they were afraid the Pharisees would expel them from the synagogue and community. For even though they believed that Jesus was the Messiah, they still valued public acceptance more than God's.

177. People Will Be Condemned Because They Rejected Jesus' Teaching
(Sometime between Monday and Thursday)

One other time in public before the Passover, Jesus shouted out to the crowd, "Those who believe in me aren't only believing in me, but also in God who sent me. When you look at me, you are also looking at the One who sent me. I've come as a spiritual Light shining in this sinful world, revealing the way of salvation so that all who believe in me will not remain in the spiritual darkness of sin and death. I don't condemn those who hear my teaching but choose not to follow it because I didn't come to judge people—I came to save them. But there is a judge who will—on the Last Day—condemn those who reject me and my teaching. Their rejection of the words I've said will condemn them because the words I've spoken aren't my own, but come from my Father who always tells me exactly what to say. I know that his words and commands lead those who receive them to eternal life—so I always say exactly what my Father tells me to say."

178. The Relationship Between Faith and the Release of God's Power
(Tuesday)

The next morning, as they were returning to the city, Jesus' followers noticed that the fig tree he had spoken to the morning before was withered all the way down to its roots. Peter remembered what Jesus had said to the tree and spoke up, "Rabbi, look! The fig tree you cursed yesterday is completely withered!" His followers were amazed to see this and asked him, "How could it wither so quickly?" Jesus replied, "It's important that you understand this. You need to have faith in God's will and power. If you have faith and don't doubt, you can do even more than this. You can overcome great obstacles and accomplish the seemingly impossible—if it's within God's will. So when you ask for something in prayer and you know that it is within God's will, firmly believe that he has already said yes to your request, and you will receive it if you have faith. ❖ *Note there is no promise about how quickly you will receive your answer. Most people give up far too quickly. You need to persist in faith.* ➤ But a condition is that when you are praying, first forgive anyone you haven't yet forgiven so your Father in Heaven will forgive you too. But if you refuse to forgive others, then your Heavenly Father will not forgive your sins either."

179. Jesus' Authority Is Questioned
(Tuesday)

Jesus and his followers once again arrived in Jerusalem and went to the Temple. As he was walking in the Temple courtyard, the chief priests, Scripture teachers, and Jewish elders boldly approached him and demanded, "What right do you have to do things like you did here in the Temple yesterday? Who gave you this authority?" Jesus replied, "I will answer that if you first answer this question. When John was baptizing and preaching, was his authority from God or did he do it on his own authority?" They debated among themselves what to answer. "If we acknowledge that his authority was from God, then he will ask why we didn't believe his message and his witness that Jesus is the Messiah. But if we say that his authority wasn't from God, this crowd will reject us and stone us since they are convinced that John was a prophet." So they finally answered, "We don't know where John's authority came from." Jesus replied, "If you are unwilling to answer that question, then I'm not going to tell you where my authority comes from either."

180. Parable About the Response of Two Sons to Their Father
(Tuesday)

Still talking to the religious leaders, Jesus said, "But what is your opinion about this? There was a man who had two sons. He went to his firstborn and said, 'Son, I want you to go work in the vineyard today.' His son replied, 'No, I don't want to!' But later, he changed his mind and went to work there. Then the father went to his second son and said the same thing. This son respectfully replied, 'I will, sir,' but he didn't. Which of the two sons obeyed his father?" They answered, "The first one."

Jesus then said, "This is something you need to understand. Tax collectors and prostitutes are entering God's Kingdom, and you are not. For John the Baptizer came to you and taught you the way that God wants you to live, but you rejected him. Many tax collectors and prostitutes did believe and repented and changed their ways, but even after seeing this good fruit from his ministry, you refused to repent and believe him."

181. Parable About the Evil Tenants
(Tuesday)

Still speaking to the religious leaders, Jesus said, "Listen to another parable. There was a landowner who planted a vineyard, built a wall around it, dug a winepress, and built a watchtower. Then he rented it out to some tenant farmers and went on a journey for a long time. ❖ *The vineyard represents Israel, the owner represents God, and the farmers represent the leaders of Israel.* ➤ When it came time for the grapes to be harvested, the owner sent a servant to collect a portion of the crop—which was the agreed upon payment for their rent. But the farmers beat him and sent him away empty handed. ❖ *The servants represent the prophets that God sent to his people over the years.* ➤ The owner sent another servant, and they beat him too, treated him shamefully, and sent him away with nothing. So he sent a third servant, and this one they murdered. So it went with many other servants that the owner sent. Some they killed and others they beat severely. Now, the owner said to himself, 'What should I do? I will send my son whom I love. Perhaps they will respect him and pay what they owe me.' But when the farmers saw the son, they reasoned, 'This is the owner's heir. If we kill him, we can keep the vineyard for ourselves!' So they captured him, killed him, and threw his body outside the vineyard.

"So when the owner of the vineyard comes, what do you think he will do to those tenant farmers? He will come and kill those evil men and will rent the vineyard to other tenants who will give him his share of the crop at harvest time."

The people fully recognized what Jesus' parable meant, that their leaders would kill God's Messiah, and that God would take the Kingdom away from the Jews and give it to Gentiles. Both ideas were abhorrent to them and they exclaimed, "May it never be!"

Jesus looked at them and asked, "Then what do you think this Scripture means, 'The stone that the builders rejected became the cornerstone. This is Yahweh's doing, and it's a marvel to see.'? ❖ *Jesus is speaking of himself as that stone.* ➤ All who stumble over that stone will be broken into pieces, and it will crush to dust those it falls on. So I'm telling you that God will take his Kingdom away from you and give it to people who will produce the fruit that he wants."

The chief priests and Pharisees there realized that Jesus was speaking about them as the evil tenant farmers in his parable. They wanted to arrest him immediately, but they were afraid the crowd would riot in protest so they did nothing for the time being.

182. Parable of the Great Banquet in Heaven
(Tuesday)

Then Jesus told the leaders another parable, "God's inviting people to submit to him as their King can be illustrated by a king who prepared a wedding banquet for his son. When the banquet was ready, he sent his servants to the invited guests to tell them it was time to come. But they didn't want to come! So he tried again, sending out different servants to the invited guests with the message, 'The banquet is ready. I've butchered bulls and fattened cattle, and everything is ready for you. Come quickly to the wedding banquet.' But the invited guests ignored the summons and went to work, some to their farms, others to their businesses, while others physically attacked the servants and killed them. The king was outraged and sent his army to kill those murderers and burn their city. Then he told his servants, 'The wedding banquet is ready but the invited guests were not worthy. So go to the crossroads and invite as many people as you can to my banquet.' His servants went out in the streets and gathered everyone they could find, both good and bad, and finally the banquet hall was filled with guests.

"But when the king entered to view his guests, he saw a man who wasn't wearing the special wedding garment that he provided for all of them. The king said to him, 'Sir, you are not wearing a wedding garment. Why did you refuse one?' But the man couldn't think of anything to say. Then the king said to his servants, 'Tie him up and throw him outside where it's dark and others like him are crying in great agony and defiant rage.' " Jesus concluded, "For God calls everyone into his Kingdom, but only a few are chosen."

183. The Question About Paying Taxes to Rome
(Tuesday)

Then the Pharisees went off and plotted a way to trick Jesus into saying something they could use against him. They sent some of their followers to him, accompanied by some men loyal to King Herod. They tried to put him off his guard by flattering him, "Rabbi, we know you speak with integrity and teach God's way based on the truth of his word—not on what you think people want to hear. You don't try to hedge your teaching so that it won't offend certain people because you aren't trying to please any particular group. You just teach the plain truth. We are looking for a clear definitive answer to this question. Is it right for Jews to pay taxes to Caesar, or not?" But Jesus knew their evil intent and said, "You're a bunch of lying hypocrites! Do you really think you can trap me? ❖ *He knew that if he answered "Yes," then the Jewish leaders could accuse him of being a Roman collaborator—which would destroy his popularity with the people. If he answered "No," then they could accuse him of sedition to the Roman authorities.* ➤ Show me one of the coins that's used to pay the tax you're talking about." They produced a denarius. Then he asked them, "Whose face and name are on it?" They answered, "Caesar's." Then Jesus said, "So give to Caesar what he rightfully demands, and give to God what rightfully belongs to him."

They were dumbfounded at his answer. They weren't able to catch him saying anything in public that they could use against him—so they just went away.

184. The Question About Life after Death
(Tuesday)

That same day, some Sadducees—who deny there will be a resurrection—came to Jesus with a question. They said, "Rabbi, Moses wrote in the Torah that if a man's brother dies and leaves a widow with no children, he must take her to be his wife—and the first son they have will be considered the son of the dead brother. Now, there were seven brothers among us. The oldest married and died with no child. Then the second brother married her and also died childless, and then a third did the same. In the same way, all seven men married her and died leaving no children. Last of all, the wife died too. So on the day when God raises the dead back to life—if there is such a day—whose wife will she be since she was married to all seven brothers?" ❖ *They reasoned that God would never command people to do anything that violated one of his other commands. But a woman being married to more than one man violated the teachings in God's Torah. Therefore, there couldn't be any resurrection because the command requiring a brother to marry his dead brother's childless widow would force some women to be illegally married to more than one husband after the resurrection.* ➤

Jesus replied, "Your understanding is faulty because you are ignorant of both the Scriptures and God's power. People living in this age—before the day of resurrection—marry. But it won't be like that in the age to come. Those who God judges worthy to participate in the resurrection and live with him in Heaven will neither marry nor be married. And they will never die again. They will be like the angels who never marry nor procreate, and they will be God's children because they will have risen from death to live forever. As for the resurrection, even Moses gave you evidence for it in his account of the burning bush where he recorded that Yahweh said, 'I am the God of Abraham, the God of Isaac, and the God of Jacob.' It should be obvious that Yahweh is not the God of people who no longer exist. He is God of those having a living existence. Your belief about there being no resurrection is entirely wrong and is a serious doctrinal error." When the crowd heard this, they were amazed at his teaching.

Some Scripture teachers spoke up and said, "Rabbi, that was well argued!" Then the Sadducees were all afraid to ask him any more questions to try to trap him—lest he publicly shame them again.

185. God's Most Important Command
(Tuesday)

One of the Scripture teachers who had heard this discussion recognized that Jesus had answered the Sadducees question well, from a proper knowledge of the Scriptures. So he asked Jesus, "Rabbi, which command in the Teachings of Moses is the most important?" Jesus answered, "The most important command God has given is this: 'Hear and respond, people of Israel! Yahweh is your God who created you! He is the only one that really exists and he is calling you to love him with all your heart, thoughts, personality, and determination!' The next most important one is this: 'You must love all other people that you come in contact with in the same tolerant accepting way that you love yourself.' There is no other command more important than these two. All the teachings in the Torah written by Moses and in the writings of the Prophets are based on these two commands."

The Scripture teacher said, "You are correct, Rabbi. You have correctly declared that there is only one God—and none other like him—and that to love him with all your heart, thoughts, personality, and determination, and to love others in the same way you love yourself is more important than all the commands about offerings and sacrifices."

When Jesus heard that man's understanding, he told him, "If you really believe that, then you are very close to having a proper relationship with God as your King." After that, the Jewish leaders realized it was futile to try to trap Jesus into saying something in public that they could use against him, so they gave up asking him questions.

186. A Question About the Messiah
(Tuesday)

While the Pharisees were still gathered there, Jesus asked them a question, "Who do you think the Messiah is descended from?" They answered, "He will be a descendant of King David." Jesus said, "If that's the case, then why did the Spirit inspire David to call him his Lord? For David himself—under the inspiration of the Holy Spirit—prophetically wrote about the Messiah in a Psalm, 'Yahweh said to my Lord, the Messiah, "Sit here in the place of highest honor at my right side until I've humiliated all your enemies and put them under your power." ' David calls the Messiah, 'Lord,' so how can also be his descendant?" No one was able to give him an answer. After that, none of them dared ask him any more questions because they were afraid of further public humiliation. But the crowd loved to listen to him.

187. The Hypocrisy of the Religious Leaders
(Tuesday)

Then Jesus said to the crowd and his followers there, "The Scripture teachers and the Pharisees have taken it upon themselves to be the official interpreters of the teachings in the Torah. So you should carefully obey what they tell you to do. But don't allow yourselves to have attitudes like the Scripture teachers; and don't follow the example of their own behavior because they don't follow their own teachings. They require you to obey an unending list of burdensome rules but they make no effort to help people successfully follow them. Everything they do is for the purpose of making sure people notice how 'holy' they supposedly are. That's why they make their phylacteries and symbolic tassels more prominent. They like to dress in expensive long fancy robes to impress people. They love to sit in the seats of honor at banquets and in the most important seats in synagogues. They are also greedy and take advantage of helpless widows, taking their homes and lands from them—leaving them destitute. And purely for show, they recite long prayers, trying to impress others with their spirituality. God isn't taken in by them, and on Judgment Day, their punishment will be all the greater because of their hypocrisy.

"They love to hear people greet them respectfully in public and call them 'Rabbi.' But I don't want you to allow others to call you 'Rabbi' because I am your only master, and you are all to be on the same level as brothers and sisters to one another. And don't call anyone in this world 'Father'—as someone who is your spiritual superior—for your only spiritual Father is your Heavenly Father. And don't allow others to call you 'Teacher' because the Messiah is your only teacher. Those who want to be important leaders among you must become everyone else's servant.

"You hypocritical Scripture teachers and Pharisees are in real trouble with God! People look up to you as teachers, yet you hide from them the key which opens the way to knowing God's truth. You yourselves refuse to submit to God so you could enter his Kingdom, and you do your best to prevent others from entering too!

"God is going to punish you hypocritical Scripture teachers and Pharisees! You go to great efforts to convert a person and then make him twice as deserving of punishment in Hell as yourselves!

"You blind guides are going to be punished harshly! You teach people that swearing by the Temple means nothing, but that swearing by the gold of the Temple makes them bound by their oath. You spiritually blind fools always have wrong values and priorities! You should know that the Temple is more important than the gold— for it is what makes the gold sacred. You also teach that swearing by the altar means nothing, but swearing by the offering on the altar makes them bound by their oath. You are blind to what's important. It's the altar that makes the offering sacred! So in God's sight, those who swear by the altar also swear by everything on it. And those who swear by the Temple also swear by God who lives in it. Swearing by Heaven is to swear by God's throne and the one who sits on it.

"It's going to be bad for you hypocritical Scripture teachers and Pharisees on the Last

Day! You are like immaculately clean tombs that look nice on the outside but are full of decay, corruption, and foul stench on the inside. So outwardly you appear to others as good and holy, but inwardly, God sees that you are full of hypocrisy and evil rebellion."

188. Sacrificial Giving
(Tuesday)

Jesus sat facing the treasury box in the Temple and observed wealthy people putting their gifts into it. Many of them clearly put in large amounts, as everyone could hear the clinking of the many coins they dropped in. Then he saw an obviously poor widow put in two small copper coins.

Getting his followers attention, he told them, "I assure you that by God's standard, that poor widow contributed far more than anyone else. For everyone else put in offerings out of what they could easily spare, but she put in everything she had and has nothing left to even live on."

189. Jesus Predicts the Temple's Destruction
(Tuesday)

Jesus left the courtyard and was walking away from the Temple when his followers came to him and pointed out the beauty and greatness of the Temple buildings and the adornments of intricate gold work that had been given as special offerings. Jesus unexpectedly replied, "The day will come when all the things you see here are destroyed. The destruction will be so complete than not even one stone will be left standing on top of another."

190. Signs of Jesus' Returning
(Tuesday)

Later, as Jesus was sitting on Mount Olivet, his followers approached him privately and said, "Tell us when this destruction will happen, and what sign we should look for in connection with your coming again and the end of the age." Jesus answered, "Be careful that you are not deceived, for many men will come to prominence saying they are the Messiah and that the time of judgment is almost here. Many false prophets will claim their messages are from God and they will deceive many people into following them. You will hear about wars happening nearby, and reports of wars far away, but don't be afraid. These things need to happen first, but the end of all things doesn't follow immediately after them. Ethnic groups will fight against each other, and entire countries will war against each other. There will be major earthquakes and famines in various places. All this is just like the beginning of birth pains. They will last for a while before I return. There will be terrifying things happening and great signs in the sky.

"But before all these things happen, you need to watch out for your own safety because people will hate you, arrest you, persecute you, and kill you just because you are my followers. They will deliver you before courts in synagogues and before kings and other legal authorities, and imprison you. This will be an opportunity for you to testify about the things that you've heard and seen me do. When you are arrested, don't be concerned ahead of time about what you will say in your defense. But when the time comes, just say whatever comes to your mind, for it will be the Holy Spirit speaking through you. The words will not be your own. I will put words of wisdom in your mouth that none of your opponents will be able to contradict or refute.

"At that time, many professing believers will deny their faith because of their fear of persecution. They will hate true believers and betray them to the authorities. You will be betrayed by parents, siblings, relatives, friends, and even your own children—and some of you will be executed. But they can't really harm you as far as eternity is concerned—not even slightly. Their power is only over your physical bodies—and even that is in God's hands.

"Most people will find it difficult to love God or anyone else because they will increasingly reject all rules and authority, allowing every sinful impulse to run wild. But those who stand firm in their faith and obedience to the end of their lives—or until I return—will be saved.

"The Good News message about how to be saved and become a part of God's Kingdom will be preached to every people group in the world to let them know what God has done for them—and then the end of the age will come."

191. Jesus Predicts Jerusalem's Destruction
(Tuesday)

Jesus continued, "When you see Jerusalem surrounded by armies, then you can be sure that her destruction is imminent. When you see that army coming, those who are in Judea should flee to hide in the mountains. Those in the city should escape. And those in the county shouldn't try to enter the city for any reason because that will be the time of God's vengeance against the people of Jerusalem for their rejection of his Messiah. That time fulfills all the prophecies in the Scriptures about God's vengeance on those who rebel against him. The people will experience disaster, panic, grief, and horror because of God's judgment. Many will be killed and others will be captured and taken into exile as slaves, scattered all over the Gentile world. Jerusalem will be oppressed under the power of Gentiles until the time God has set for their control over it to end."

192. Jesus Predicts the Great Tribulation
(Tuesday)

Jesus continued, "The prophet Daniel prophesied about an 'abomination that causes destruction.' (The reader of this book should look carefully into the matter as prophesied by Daniel and try to understand what this means.) When you see it in the holy place of the Temple, then terrible things will soon happen. ❖ *Such a thing happened in the Temple before Jesus was born—in the second century BC. It might have happened again in AD 66 when zealots killed priests in the Temple. It might have happened again with Roman standards—which bore the insignia of Caesar who was submitted to in worship as a god—when Jerusalem and the Temple were destroyed by the Romans in the year AD 70. And it may happen again when the Jews in Israel rebuild the Temple in the last days.* ➤ So those who are in Judea should flee to hide in the mountains. If you are on the roof of your house, don't take the time to get your things from inside. Flee from the city. And those working in their fields shouldn't try to go back to their house for any reason. They should flee to the mountains. It will be terrible for pregnant women and for those still nursing babies because it will be hard for them to run and escape to the mountains. Pray that this will not occur on a Sabbath or in the winter for that would add to your difficulties. For there will be a great tribulation—a time of calamities with great distress—far worse than anything that has ever happened anywhere in the world before that time. And there will never be anything like it again. God has limited the number of days that this will last. If he didn't, nobody in the world would survive. But for the sake of his elect people, he has limited the number of days.

"And during those difficult times, if anyone says, 'I know where the Messiah is,' or 'The Messiah is in such a place,' don't believe it. For false messiahs and false prophets will become prominent, and they will perform such great miraculous signs to deceive people that even God's elect might be tempted to believe in them. Now you have advance warning—so be on your guard. So if anyone says, 'The Messiah is in the wilderness,' don't go out looking for me. Or if they say, 'The Messiah is in a particular house,' don't believe them. For when I, the Son of Man, return, it will be as obvious as lightning flashing across the entire sky. Nobody will miss it."

193. The Coming of the Son of Man
(Tuesday)

Jesus continued, "Immediately after those days of tribulation, the sun will be darkened and the moon will not shine. There will be great dread among the countries of the world at the roaring and tossing of the sea. People will lose heart, faint, and even die from terror when they think about the things happening in the world because the stars will fall from the sky and the spiritual principalities and powers of the heavens will be shaken. Then the sign of the Son of Man will appear in the sky, and all the

unbelievers in all the people groups of the world will mourn the fate they know is coming to them for having rejected me. They will see me, the Son of Man, in the sky coming on clouds with great glory and power. Signaling with a loud trumpet call, I will send my angels to gather my elect people from everywhere on earth.

"When these last things start to happen, rejoice and look up expectantly because the time of your complete redemption and transformation is extremely near.

194. Learn to Observe the Signs
(Tuesday)

"Learn the lesson that you should watch for these signs from what you know about the fig tree. You already know that when young green shoots start growing on its branches and it starts to grow leaves, summer is near. In the same way, when you see the signs I just told you about, you can know that my return and the manifestation of God's Kingdom in all its glory is very near. I assure you that all these things will happen before all the people of the generation that sees these signs die. Heaven and earth will end, but my words are always true and all will happen as I've said."

195. Always Be Ready for Jesus' Return
(Tuesday)

Then he said to his followers, "The time will come when you will long to see me, the Son of Man, return in power as King, but you will not see it because it isn't yet time. First, I must suffer many things and be rejected by most of those living today.

"But no one knows the exact day or hour that I will return. Even I do not yet know. Only the Father knows. When I, the Son of Man, do return, it will be just as it was in Noah's time when most people didn't pay any attention to God's word. In the days just before the flood, life went on as usual. Every day, people ate, drank, and were married right up to the time that Noah entered the Ark, and they didn't understand what was happening until the flood came and destroyed them all. The same thing happened in Lot's time. Life went on as usual with nobody listening to God's warnings to repent. They ate and drank, and bought and sold, planted and built. On the day that God's angels led Lot out of Sodom, fire and burning sulfur rained down on them from the sky and destroyed them all. It will be just like that on the day that I, the Son of Man, return in glory. Unbelievers will not understand what is happening and will be completely taken by surprise.

"On that day, if a man is outside his house, he must not take the time to go inside to get anything to take with him. And someone working in the field must not take time to go to his house. They must go immediately. Remember Lot's wife who failed to listen to the instructions given to her by the angels who were trying to help her. She looked back and died. Whoever tries to keep control over his own life will ultimately lose it forever. But whoever is willing to lose his life for my sake will in the end preserve it forever.

"On the night I return it will be like this: Two people will be sleeping in the same bed; one will be taken to be with me and the other will be left behind. Two men will be working in a field; one will be taken and the other left behind. Two women will be working together grinding flour; one will be taken and the other left behind. So watch for the signs and always be prepared because you don't know when your Lord will be returning.

"As an illustration, if a homeowner knew when a burglar planned to break in, he would be awake and ready at the time he expected him. But of course nobody can anticipate such things. I, the Son of Man, will also return at a time you can't anticipate. So you always have to be ready. Watch for the signs and always be prepared.

"As another illustration, my going and returning again is like a man who went on a trip. He left his servants to be in charge of his household while he was away and assigned each one specific duties. He instructed the guard at the gate to be continually on watch for his return. You always have to be ready because you don't know when your master is returning. It could be in the evening, or at midnight, in the wee hours of the morning when roosters crow, or after dawn. If I were to return suddenly and unexpectedly, it would not be good for you to be caught asleep, neglecting your duties. Take care not to allow yourselves to be distracted from prayer and preparation for my return, or allow your emotions to be weighed with worry, which could lead to your seeking escape in drunkenness and various kinds of intoxication that cloud your thinking. If you do, you will not be ready for my return. It will spring on you as suddenly as a trap, and you will be caught in your folly. It will happen at the same time to everyone living in the world, without warning. So keep spiritually alert and pray that your faith will endure all the things that are about to happen so that you can escape condemnation at the judgment and stand before me, the Son of Man, as one whom I approve.

"I am exhorting you all ahead of time to always be alert to signs and be completely ready for my return." His followers asked, "Where will you be, Lord?" Jesus answered, "Wherever there's a dead body, that's where the vultures gather." ❖ *This probably means that just like the circling of vultures makes it obvious where something has died, it will be equally obvious at the time where he can be found.* ➤

Now, for those last few days before his arrest, Jesus was teaching in the Temple during the day. But in the evening, he went out of the city and spent the night on Mount Olivet. Early each morning all the people would get up and go to the Temple to listen to his teaching.

196. Parable of the Ten Young Bridesmaids
(Tuesday)

Jesus also told this parable, "When I return as King, some who are waiting for me will be ready and others will not. It will be like ten young bridesmaids who went to the bride's house to wait for the groom to arrive and lead them to his house for the wedding ceremony and celebration. They had their torches with them, ready to light the way for the procession to the groom's house when he arrived. ❖ *The torches were sticks with rags tied to one end. They poured olive oil on the rags and lit them. Their weddings were at night. While they waited, the groom was haggling over the bride price which was paid in gifts, not money. This often went on a long time.* ➤ Five of these young women were foolish and the other five were wise. For the foolish ones took their torches but took no extra oil with them. ❖ *They would light their torches when the groom arrived, but they would burn out after about 15 minutes and then they would have to pour on more oil to keep them burning.* ➤ But the wise ones took jars of oil along with their torches. Now the groom was delayed so they all became drowsy and fell asleep.

"At midnight, someone shouted, 'Here comes the groom! Come out to meet him!' Then the bridesmaids woke up and lit their torches. The foolish ones said to the others, 'Give us some of your oil, or our torches will go out before we get to the groom's house.' ❖ *It was their responsibility to have enough oil for their torches to burn during the procession to the groom's house and during the ceremony and celebration.* ➤ But the wise bridesmaids replied, 'If we do that, there won't be enough for all of us. Go and buy some somewhere.' ❖ *If all the torches ran out before the end of the festivities, it would ruin the celebration. Despite the announcement that the groom was coming, there was still a little time before he arrived and the entire village would be awake for the wedding, so it might be possible to find someone to sell them oil.* ➤ But while they were away, the groom arrived, and those who were ready processed through the streets with him to the wedding banquet. All the guests went in and the door was shut. Later, the other bridesmaids came to the house and called out, 'Sir! Please let us in!' But he answered them from the other side of the door, 'I don't know you. My friends are already here. Go away!' " ❖ *They had missed the most important part of the wedding, which was an insult to the groom.* ➤

Jesus concluded, "So always be ready for my return because you have no way of knowing when I will come."

197. Parable of the Talents
(Tuesday)

Jesus told this parable, "My leaving you and going to Heaven—later to return as King on the Last Day—can be illustrated by a man who planned to go on a journey. Before he left, he called his servants together and told them to take care of his possessions while he was gone. To one of them he gave five talents, two talents to another, and one talent to a third servant—according to his estimate of their abilities. ❖ *A talent was a heavy unit of weight of gold or silver.* ➤ Then he left on his journey. The man with the five talents used them for trading and eventually doubled his capital. The man with the two talents did the same and doubled his capital. But the man with only one talent buried it in the ground to keep it safe from theft.

"After a considerable length of time, the master of those men returned and called them together to find out what they had been doing on his behalf while he was away. The first servant brought in his ten talents and reported, 'Master, you entrusted five talents to me, and I've doubled it for you.' His master said, 'Well done. You are a good steward! And because you were faithful in managing this small amount, I'm going to put you in charge of much greater things. Come into my banquet and celebrate with me!' Then the second servant brought in his four talents and reported, 'Master, you entrusted two talents to me, and I've doubled it for you.' His master said, 'Well done. You are a good steward! And because you were faithful in managing this small amount, I'm going to put you in charge of much greater things. Come into my banquet and celebrate with me!' Then the third servant brought in his one talent and reported, 'Master, I knew you are a shrewd businessman and that you easily make a profit from the work of others and reap where others have sown. I was afraid of failing to earn anything with it and losing it all, so I buried it in the ground to keep it hidden and safe. Here is what belongs to you.' His master said, 'You shiftless lazy good-for-nothing servant! You knew that I'm a shrewd businessman and easily make a profit from the work of others. So you should have known that I expected you to earn a profit for me. You should have at least put my money in the bank so I would get it back with interest!' Speaking to other servants present, he said, 'Take the talent away from him and give it to the man who has ten. He has had his chance to make use of it. For everyone who has demonstrated that he is responsible with what I've given him, will be given even more responsibility. But someone who has demonstrated no responsibility, even what little he has will be taken away from him. Throw this worthless servant outside in the dark where he will cry in agony and defiant rage.' "

198. Jesus Judges the Righteous and the Cursed
(Tuesday)

Jesus continued, "When I, the Son of Man, return to this world with my angels in all my glory and majesty, I will sit on my glorious throne to judge all humanity. All humanity from every people group of the world will be gathered in front of me, and I will separate them into two groups like a shepherd separates sheep from goats. I will put people who are my righteous sheep in a group on my right side, and people who are the cursed goats in a group on my left side. Then as Sovereign King of the universe I will say to those on my right, 'All you who are blessed by my Father, come and receive your inheritance in my Kingdom which has been prepared for you since I created this world. For you fed me when I was hungry, you gave me something to drink when I was thirsty, and you offered the hospitality of your home to me even though I was a stranger to you. You gave me clothing when I needed it, you took care of me when I was sick, and visited me in prison.' Then God's people will ask, 'Lord, when did we see you hungry and feed you, or see you thirsty and give you something to drink? When did we see you as a stranger and offer you hospitality in our home, or see you had need of clothes and provide them? When did we see you sick or in prison and visit you?' Then I will tell them, 'The truth is, whatever kindness you showed to one of those who believe in me—even those who seemed to have no status or worth—you did it to me.'

"Then I will say to those on my left, 'All you who are cursed by God, leave my presence and enter the eternal fire of Hell that was originally prepared for Satan and his demons! For you gave me nothing to eat or drink when I was hungry or thirsty. When I was a stranger, you never offered me hospitality, you never gave me clothing I needed, and you never visited me when I was sick or in prison.' Then they will ask, 'Lord, when did we ever see you hungry or thirsty or a stranger or needing clothing or sick or in prison and did not help you?' Then I will tell them, 'The truth is, whatever kindness you failed to give to one of those who believe in me—even those who seemed to have no status or worth—you failed to give to me.' And those cursed people will be sent to eternal punishment in Hell, but my righteous ones will enter into eternal life."

199. Make Peace with God Before It's Too Late
(Tuesday)

"Why don't you judge for yourselves what is right? ❖ *i.e., Why don't you recognize your need to repent and get right with God, instead of ignoring what he is saying to you?* ➤ If someone brings a legitimate lawsuit against you, it's in your own best interest to make peace with him before it gets to court. If you are convicted, the judge will hand you over to an officer, and you will be thrown in debtor's prison. And if that happens, I guarantee that you won't get out until you've paid the last penny you owe." ❖ *Jesus' picture and point may seem obscure since we no longer have debtor prisons. The judge represents God. The one who brings the lawsuit against you is also God. He will play two roles in our lives, accuser and judge. The point is, we need to make peace with God before we die or before the final judgment—whichever comes first. If we don't, then when we stand before him as judge it will be too late to do anything about our fate. The picture of paying the last penny of your debt has no parallel with our lives since it is impossible for us to pay off our debt of sin to God. The point of that part of the story is that you will never get out—your punishment will be forever. Jesus offers us the way to be at peace with God before it's too late.* ➤

200. The Plot to Arrest Jesus
(Tuesday)

When Jesus finished talking about all these things, he told his close followers, "You are all aware that Passover begins in two days, and that I, the Son of Man, will be handed over to the power of my enemies who will have me crucified."

About that time, the chief priests and Jewish elders were meeting in the palace of Caiaphas, the High Priest. They were plotting how to arrest Jesus without the general public knowing about it, and then quickly execute him before the common people could protest. They said, "It can't happen during the Passover Festival or the people might riot."

201. Mary Anoints Jesus
(Wednesday)

On a Saturday, six days before the Passover, Jesus and his close followers had arrived in Bethany, the village where Lazarus lived—whom he had raised back to life. When people heard that Jesus was in Bethany, a large crowd came to see him and Lazarus. But the chief priests decided to kill Lazarus as well as Jesus because many had started to believe that Jesus was the Messiah as a result of Lazarus' resurrection.

Four days later on Wednesday, a dinner was prepared in Jesus' honor, and Martha helped serve while Lazarus reclined at the table with Jesus and the other guests. This was at the house of a man named Simon— who had been cured of a contagious skin disease. While Jesus was reclining at the meal, Mary came in with an alabaster jar of very expensive perfume made of pure nard. She broke the neck of the flask open and poured the perfume over his head. She also anointed his feet with it and then wiped his feet with her hair. The entire house was filled with the fragrance.

But Judas Iscariot—one of Jesus' close followers who later betrayed him—protested, "Why didn't she sell this perfume and give the money to the poor? It's worth nearly a year's wages!" Now, he didn't say this because he was overly concerned about helping the poor. In reality, he was a thief and as their treasurer, he often helped himself from the funds they held in common. Jesus' other close followers who observed what Mary did also thought it was totally inappropriate and were indignant. They muttered among themselves, "That was a thoughtless waste!"

But Jesus heard them and said, "Leave her alone! Why are you criticizing her for doing such a beautiful thing to me? She did the only thing she was able to do for me. Allow her to remember what she has done without regret, for it was done in preparation for my burial. There will always be poor people around that you can minister to, but I won't always be here with you. The truth of the matter is, her act of extreme devotion is such a good example that it will be recounted everywhere the message of salvation is preached throughout the world."

202. Judas Agrees to Betray Jesus
(Wednesday)

Judas—also called Iscariot—was one of Jesus' twelve apostles. Satan entered his heart to influence him, so he went to the chief priests and Temple guards and discussed how he might hand Jesus over to them. They were glad for the opportunity and agreed to pay him if he did this. He asked them, "How much will you pay me if I help you find a time and a place where you can arrest him away from public notice?" They showed him thirty silver coins. Judas consented to the arrangement and began seeking an opportunity to betray Jesus to them when no crowd was around.

203. Jesus Prepares to Eat the Passover
(Thursday)

The first day of the festival arrived— the preparation day when the Passover lambs were sacrificed. Jesus told Peter and John, "Go prepare the Passover meal for us." They asked, "Where do you want us to prepare it?" He said, "When you enter Jerusalem, you will meet a man carrying a pitcher of water. Follow him until he enters a house. Then say to the owner of that house, 'The Rabbi says his appointed time is near and he wants to celebrate the Passover with his close followers at your house.'"

So they went and found everything just as Jesus had described it—and they prepared the Passover meal.

204. Jesus Models the Role of a Servant Leader, and Passover Begins
(Thursday Evening – Friday Night)

❖ *Note that the way Jews divide the day, a day starts at sunset—so the night portion of a day precedes the day-light portion of a day. Thursday "evening" was the hour or so before sunset, and Friday night began immediately after sunset Thursday.* ➤

When sunset was approaching—at which time the actual day of Passover would begin—Jesus arrived at that room with his twelve apostles. He knew the time had come when he would be leaving this sinful world and return to his Father in Heaven. His followers had always been very dear to him, and now he demonstrated the full extent of his love for them. The Passover meal was being set out before them, and Satan had already tempted Judas Iscariot to betray Jesus. Jesus was fully aware that his Father had given him complete authority and power over everything—and that he had originally come from God and would soon return to him. So he got up from the table, took off his outer garment, and wrapped a towel around himself—now dressed as a low-level slave. Then he poured some water in a basin and began to wash his followers' feet and drying them with the towel. When he came to Simon Peter, Peter asked, "Lord, do you intend to wash my feet?" Jesus responded, "You don't have to understand right now what I'm doing. Just submit—and later you will understand." Peter objected, "No, it's not right! I will never have my master wash my feet!" Jesus replied, "If you don't allow me to wash you, then you can't have anything to do with me." With that at stake, Peter capitulated and said, "Lord, if washing me enables me to remain with you, don't just wash my feet, but my hands and head too!" Jesus replied, "A person who has bathed is completely clean. And all but one of you are clean." He said one of them wasn't clean because he knew that Judas was going to betray him.

When he finished washing their feet, he put on his outer garment again and resumed his place at the table. Then he asked them, "Do you understand what I was doing for you? You appropriately call me your Rabbi and Lord, for that is what I am to you. So since your Lord and Rabbi has washed your feet, you should follow my example and be humble enough to wash each other's feet. I've given you an example of a leader humbly serving those who follow him, so you must be willing to be as humble with those who will follow you. This is an important truth: A slave can't be greater than his master, nor is a messenger greater than the one who sent him. Now that you know this, God will bless you if you put it into practice!"

When the sun had set, Jesus reclined at the table to eat the Passover meal with them. He said, "I've been looking forward to eating this Passover with you before I suffer and die. I will not eat it again until what it represents has been completely fulfilled in God's Kingdom."

205. How to Be Among the Greatest in God's Kingdom
(Friday Night)

While they were dining, the apostles began to dispute among themselves who of them would be the greatest in God's Kingdom. Then Jesus admonished them, "The kings in this world exercise power over their people. And those in authority often force those under them to call them 'Benefactors of the people'—when they're really oppressors. But this isn't how I intend it to be among you! You who consider yourselves among the most important should act as if you are the least important—being willing to do the lowliest things. And if you want to lead, you should do so by serving others.

"Who is greater, the one who dines or the waiter? In human society, it's the one who dines. But I've set an example for you as a leader who serves, rather than one who makes demands.

"You are the ones who have stood by me through thick and thin; so just as my father has given me authority to rule, I too will give you the privilege of dining at my table in the Kingdom and will make you rulers over the twelve tribes of Israel.

206. Jesus Predicts His Betrayal
(Friday Night)

"But I'm not including all of you in the things I've been saying. I knew the hearts and minds of each of you when I chose you to be my close followers. But I made my choice to fulfill the prophecy in Scripture that says, 'My close friend whom I trusted and who ate with me has turned against me.' I'm telling you about this beforehand so when it does happen, you may believe even more that I am the Messiah. And it's important to understand this: Those who welcome you—whom I send to represent me—in effect also welcome me. Consequently, they also welcome God who sent me."

After this, Jesus felt anguish over what he knew was about to happen and exclaimed, "This is something you should know. One of you who is eating with me tonight as a sign of his loyalty and friendship to me is going to betray me." This upset them, and they started to discuss among themselves which of them it might be. Thinking that one of them might do something without intending to, they each asked him, "Lord, it won't be me, will it?" Jesus replied, "It will be one of you twelve who are eating with me now. I, the Son of Man, will die just as the Scriptures predict, but it will be terrible for the one who deliberately betrays me! He would have been much better off having never been born." Then Judas—who had already agreed to betray him—said, "Rabbi, it won't be me, will it?" Jesus answered him, "I haven't accused you in particular. You are the one asking the question."

Reclining just in front of Jesus was John, his closest friend. Simon Peter caught John's eye, nodded toward Jesus, and mouthed the message, "Ask him who it is." So John leaned back until his head was touching Jesus' chest and he could see him eye to eye and quietly asked, "Lord, who is it?" Jesus quietly answered, "After I dip this piece of bread in the sauce, I will give it to him." Then he dipped the bread and—as an indication of his love—gave it to Judas, son of Simon Iscariot. As soon as Judas ate the bread, Satan entered him. Aware of this, Jesus told him, "Be quick about what you are going to do." But no one else at the table knew why he said this to him. Since Judas was their treasurer, some of them thought Jesus was telling him to buy what they needed for the Feast of Unleavened Bread—which began the next day—or to go out and give money to the poor. Then Judas left immediately, heading out into spiritual darkness.

207. Jesus Establishes the Lord's Supper
(Friday Night)

During the course of the meal, Jesus took some bread, thanked God for it, broke it, and handed it around to his followers. He told them, "I want you all to eat from this bread. It is my body that I'm offering up as a sacrifice for you. From now on, this is the way that I want you to remember my death." After they had eaten, he took a cup of wine, thanked God for it, and passed it around to his followers. He told them, "I want each of you to drink from this cup. For the wine in it is my blood that I will shed in my dying—which will establish the New Covenant so God can forgive the sins of many people. But I will not drink wine again until the Kingdom of God comes in its fullness—when I will drink it with you with a new meaning at the great banquet in my Father's Heavenly Kingdom."

208. Jesus Predicts Peter's Denial
(Friday Night)

When Judas was gone, Jesus said, "The time has come for my glory as the Son of Man to be revealed, and through me, God's glory too. And since God's glory will be revealed through me, God will also very soon reveal the glory that belongs to me as the Son of Man because I am one with God. My sons, I will only be with you for a little while longer. You will still seek me out, but as I told the leaders, you won't be able to go where I'm going—at least not right away. And now I'm giving you a new command: Love each other to the same extent and in the same manner that I have loved you. This is what will prove to outsiders that you are my true followers—when they see your great love for each other."

Simon Peter asked, "Lord, where are you going?" Jesus replied, "You won't be able to follow me where I'm going right away, but only later." Peter asked, "Lord, why can't I follow you right away? I'm willing to go anywhere with you, even if it costs me my life!" Then Jesus told them, "Tonight you will all have a temporary lapse of faith and run away because of what will happen to me. The Scriptures prophesy, 'I will strike down the shepherd, and his flock will be scattered.' But after my Father has made me alive again, I will go to Galilee where you will see me.

"Simon, my friend! You must know this: Satan has demanded permission from God to severely test all of you. He will try to destroy your faith. And God has granted him permission to try. But I have prayed especially for you, Simon, that your faith won't be destroyed. When you have composed yourself, help to comfort and strengthen the faith of your brothers here." Peter protested, "But Lord, I'm prepared to be imprisoned with you and to even die with you! I will never run away—even if everyone else does." Jesus replied, "The truth is that before you hear a rooster crow two separate times tonight, you will three times publicly deny having any association with me in order to save your own life." But Peter asserted, "I will never deny that I'm your follower, even if it means I have to die with you!" And all the others said the same thing.

209. Jesus Warns That Difficult Times Are Coming
(Friday Night)

Jesus asked them, "When I first sent you out to minister without money or spare clothes, did you ever lack for anything you needed?" They replied, "No." He said, "But from now on, things will be different. If you have money or extra clothing and a bag, take them along when you travel to minister. And if you don't own a sword, you should sell your cloak and buy one because the Scripture about me must be fulfilled that says, 'He was considered a criminal.' "

They said, "Look, Lord, here are two swords." He replied, "That's enough."

210. Jesus Is the Only Way to the Father
(Friday Night)

Jesus said to all of them, "Don't worry. Trust God to take care of you and trust me too. There are many dwelling places in Heaven where my Father lives, and I am going there to prepare a permanent place for each of you. If it were otherwise, I would tell you. Since I'm going away to prepare your places, I will return to receive you into spiritual union with myself so you can always be with me. And you know the way to where I'm going." Thomas spoke up, "Lord, since we don't know where you're going, how can we know the way?" Jesus answered, "I'm going to my Father in Heaven, and I am the only way for anyone to get there. I am the only Way to get there because I am God's ultimate revelation of Truth, and I am the only source of eternal Life.

"Since you have known me, you now know my Father too. Starting now, you can realize that you both know him and have seen him." Philip said, "Lord, show us God the Father, and we will be content." Jesus replied, "Philip! Don't you know who I am by now? How can you ask me to show you God the Father? I've been with you all for so long, and you still don't understand! Anyone who sees me sees the Father too! Don't you believe that I only exist in unity with the Father and that he reveals himself through me? None of the words I've said to all of you were my own, but they came from the Father who lives in me and does his work through me. Please believe me when I say that I only exist in unity with the Father and that he reveals himself through me. Or at least believe it's true because of the miraculous works you've seen—which only the Father could do. I will tell you an important truth. Those who believe in me will do the same kinds of miraculous works I've been doing. Through me, they will do even greater ones than these because I am going to my Father to be glorified. Anything you ask me to do that's in line with my will, I will do so I can reveal the greatness of my Father's character and bring him praise. Ask me to do anything at all that's in line with my will, and I will do it for you!"

211. Jesus Promises the Holy Spirit
(Friday Night)

Jesus continued to say, "If you first love me, then out of that love will naturally flow your desire and ability obey my commands. I'm going to ask my Father to send you another person who will be to you what I have been to you—who will always be in and with you. He is the Holy Spirit who will lead you to understand all the spiritual truth that my Father wants you to know. Those who follow the sinful ways of this world can't submit to him because they are unable to spiritually perceive him or understand him. But you know him because he lives *with* you now, and later he will be *in* you. I will not abandon you and leave you as helpless as orphans. Through the Spirit, I will come back to be with you. In a short time, those who follow the ways of this sinful world will no longer see me. But through the spiritual insight that the Spirit will give you, you will see me. And because I live eternally, you too will live eternally with me. When the Spirit lives in you, then you will know without a doubt that I exist in unity with the Father, and that you exist in spiritual unity with me, and that I am living in you and revealing myself to others through you. Those who understand my commands and obey them are the ones who really love me. My Father and I will love them, and I will reveal myself to each of them." Then Judas Thaddeus (not Iscariot, who had already left) said, "But Lord, what has happened to change what the Scriptures say about the Messiah, such that now you are only going to reveal yourself to your followers and not to the rest of the world?" Jesus answered, "I'm speaking of a special revelation that is only for those who love me and live in obedience to my teachings. Those are the ones my Father will love, and we will both come to them and live with them. But those who don't love me won't live in obedience to my teachings. My

teachings didn't originate with me, but are my Father's—and he sent me to give them to you.

"I'm telling you all this while I'm still physically with you. But my Father will send the Holy Spirit to you as my emissary to help you. The Spirit will teach you everything you need to know and will also remind you of all the things I've taught you.

"I'm leaving you with shalom **A**—real shalom that comes from me—not the superficial peace that this world offers. So don't be afraid or worried about what will happen. You heard me say that I'm leaving and will later return to you spiritually, through the Holy Spirit. If your love for me was less selfish, you would rejoice that I'm returning to my Father to again share in his glory—for his glory is greater than mine while I'm here. I'm telling you these things before they happen so that when they do happen, you will continue to believe in me. I won't be able to speak with you much longer, for Satan—the prince of this sinful world—is coming to kill me. He has no legal hold or power over me. But I will do exactly what my Father has told me to do so the world can know that I love my Father."

212. We Relate to Jesus like Branches to a Vine
(Friday Night)

Jesus continued, "*I am* the true vine, and my Father is the gardener. He cuts off any of my branches that don't bear fruit. And he prunes every branch that does bear fruit so it will be even more fruitful. You are like already-pruned branches who will produce much fruit because you have believed my message and responded with obedience. Stay spiritually joined to me and I will continue to live in and through you as your source of life. Just as a branch can't produce fruit unless it's attached to the vine, you can't bear the spiritual fruit that comes from obedience unless you stay joined to me in a vital living relationship and allow me to live through you.

A 211 Shalom means peace, calmness, success, comfort, contentment, safety, health, wholeness, prosperity, integrity, well-being and good relationships with God and people.

"I am the source of spiritual life, and you relate to me as branches do to a vine. Only those who stay in vital relationship with me will produce abundant spiritual fruit because separated from me, you can accomplish nothing of eternal value. Those who don't continue in a vital relationship with me are rejected and cut off as useless unproductive branches. They dry up and die and are only fit to be burned. But those who continue in a vital relationship with me and live according to the truths I've taught may ask God for anything they wish—and he will grant it. When you bear abundant fruit in this way, my Father's glorious character and power is revealed and praised—and this proves that you belong to me.

"I love you in the same way that my Father loves me. So continue to live in relationship with me and receive my love. You do this by living in obedience to the things I've told you to do. This is the same way that I continue in relationship with my Father and receive his love, by doing what he wants me to do. I've told you this so you will experience the same joy I have and that you may be entirely filled with this perfect joy.

"The most important command I give you is to demonstrate love to each other in the same selfless self-sacrificial way that I have loved you. This is the standard of my love for you—and there is no greater love than this—that a person is willing to sacrifice his life for his friends. And the main characteristic of my friends is that they obey me. I will no longer call you servants because a servant isn't taken into his master's confidence. You are my friends so I've told you everything that I've heard from my Father. I was the one who took the initiative in choosing you. Your choice was only a response. And I have chosen you for the task of producing results that will last eternally. To enable you to accomplish this, my Father will grant you anything that you ask of him with my authorization. So remember to obey my command to demonstrate your love for each other."

213. Those Who Reject Jesus Will Also Hate His Followers
(Friday Night)

Jesus continued, "Don't be shocked when people of this sinful world hate and reject you. Remember that they hated and rejected me first. The people of this world live in rebellion against God. If you were still like them, they would accept you as their own. But you are no longer like them because I chose you to be mine—and that's why they will hate you. Remember I told you, 'A slave can't be greater than his master.' So don't expect them to treat you any better than they do me. If they persecute me, they will persecute you too. But those who follow my teaching will also follow you. The people of this world don't know God who sent me. So they reject me and they will persecute you because you follow me. If I hadn't come and revealed God's truth to them, then they wouldn't be held accountable for not following it because of their ignorance. But now they have no excuse for not living the way he wants them to. Since my words and deeds come from my Father, he considers their hating and rejecting me the same as hating and rejecting him. If I hadn't performed miraculous signs among them unlike any ever done before, they wouldn't be held accountable for not recognizing that the Father sent me. But they have seen these things and still reject me and my Father. So they will be held accountable. Their doing this fulfills the prophecies written in the Torah that say, 'They hated me without valid cause.'

"But I will send the Spirit of Truth to help you. He will come from my Father and will tell you things from me. Then you will tell others about me, and also tell them the things I've said—because you've been with me from the beginning of my ministry.

"I'm giving you advance warning about the persecution you will face so when it happens, you won't lose faith from surprise and discouragement. They will expel you from synagogues, making you outcasts from Jewish society. It will come to the point where some Jews will think that they are serving God by killing you. But they will do these things because they have never really known my Father or me—despite their show of religious fervor. I'm warning you now in advance so when that time comes, you will remember that I told you it would happen and you can take comfort knowing that all these things are still in God's hand. I didn't tell you about these things earlier because they mainly attacked me while I've been with you. But now they will attack you.

214. Jesus Talks About Leaving Them
(Friday Night)

"Soon, I'm going back to God who sent me, yet none of you are asking me where I'm going or how it will affect our relationship. Instead, you are full of self-pity from the things I've been saying. But the truth is, it will be better for you when I leave because I will send the Holy Spirit to help you. But if I stayed, you wouldn't have the benefit of his help. When he comes, he will continue my work of convicting people of their sin, and of the imperfection and inadequacy of their self-righteousness, and of their false standards of judgment—in order to bring them to repentance. He will also convict them of their main sin—which is not believing in me. Since I'm returning to my Father and I will no longer be seen, he will be the one who will continue my work of convicting people of their inadequate righteousness through the witness of your righteous lives. And because Satan— the prince of this sinful world—will have been defeated, the Spirit will convict people of their wrong judgment concerning me. There are many more things that I have to tell you that you aren't yet able to bear hearing. But when the Spirit of Truth comes, he will help you to understand all of God's truth that he desires you to know. He won't tell you things on his own authority, but will tell you what he hears from the Father—just as I have. He will also tell you about some events before they happen. He will bring me praise and honor by revealing to you knowledge that I have. Everything that my Father has also belongs to me. That's why I said the Spirit will reveal

knowledge to you that I have—because it all comes from my Father.

"In just a very short time, you won't see me. Then a short time after that, you will see me again." Some of his followers asked each other, "What does he mean by, 'In just a very short time, you won't see me. Then a short time after that, you will see me again,' and that he won't be seen 'because I'm returning to my Father'? What does 'a short time' mean? What's he talking about?" Jesus knew they wanted to ask him some questions, so he said, "Are you trying to figure out the meaning of what I've just said? This is very important. You will grieve and cry over what's about to happen, but others will rejoice. You will grieve for a time, but then your grief will be transformed into great joy.

"It will be for you like a woman going through childbirth. During her labor she suffers great pain. But immediately after giving birth, the pain is forgotten because of her joy in seeing her new child. In a similar way, you are experiencing emotional pain right now. But later when you see me again, you will rejoice—and no one will be able to steal your joy from you. When that time comes, you won't need to ask me about—or for—anything. It's important for you to understand that if you ask my Father for anything with my authorization, he will give it to you. Until now, you haven't asked my Father for anything with my authorization. Go ahead and start asking for things in this way. Then you will receive and be filled with joy.

"I've been speaking to you in cryptic terms, but the time is coming when I will be able to explain things about my Father clearly. Then I won't need to ask my Father to help you. He wants you to ask him directly with my authorization because he loves you. He loves you because you love me and believe that he sent me. It's true that I came from my Father into this sinful world, but now I'm going to leave it and return to him."

Then his followers overconfidently said, "Finally, you're speaking clearly without obscure figures! Now we realize that you know everything, even what we are about to ask. This helps us believe that you came from God." Jesus replied, "You think you believe this? You say it, but your belief is weak. This very night, you will all be frightened for your lives and scatter, leaving me alone. But I won't really be alone since my Father is always with me. I've been telling you all these things that will happen so that later you can have peace, knowing you are one with me. While you live in this sinful world, you will have trials and persecution. But take courage because I have defeated every evil power, and you will experience that victory through your relationship with me."

215. Jesus Prays for his Followers
(Friday Night)

After he was done saying these things, Jesus looked up toward Heaven in an attitude of prayer and said, "Father, the time has finally come for me to suffer and die. I ask you to reveal your glorious character of self-sacrificial love, holiness, and righteousness in me, your Son, as I carry out your will—so I will bring you great praise and honor. I ask you to do this since according to your plan in eternity past, you gave me authority over all humanity so I could give eternal life to those you enable to be my people. For eternal life comes from entering into a vital and intimate relationship with you and with me—the Messiah you sent to them. This relationship happens through their belief in the revelatory knowledge we have given them, and through their response of loving obedience. I have revealed the glory of your character here on earth by doing everything that you've given me to do—and so have brought you great praise. And now, Father, I ask you to accomplish your plan and then bring me into your presence, restoring to me the fullness of the glory I had with you from eternity past— which I temporarily laid aside in coming to this world.

"I've revealed your true character to those that you separated from the unbelievers in this sinful world and gave to me. They were your people and you have given them to me. They have responded to your message with obedience. Now they've come to realize that everything I've said, done, and

have really comes directly from you. I passed on your teachings to them, and they have welcomed them. They really believe that I came from you and that it was you who sent me to earth.

"It's for them that I'm making my requests. I'm not asking on behalf of the unbelievers in this world, but on behalf of those you have given to me because they are your own people. For everything I have belongs to you, and everything that is yours belongs to me. And the glory of my character has been revealed through them to others too. I'm going to be returning to you and will no longer be in this world, but they will remain here for a while. So, Holy Father, I'm asking you to keep them united with your holy and loving character—the same character that you've given me—so they may be spiritually united as one just as we are one. While I've been with them, I have kept them united with your character which you've given me, and I've guarded their faith. None of them have fallen into unbelief except Judas—the one destined to an eternal existence of ruin in Hell so the prophecy in Scripture about him would be fulfilled.

"But now I'm returning to you and I've said these things to my followers this evening so they may be filled with the same joy that I have in serving you. I've passed on your message to them, and they have believed it. So now the unbelievers of this world hate them, for my followers are no longer anymore a part of this sinful world than I am. I'm not asking you to take them out of this world yet, but that you will keep their faith safe from the Evil One. For like me, they don't belong to this world or to the one who rules it. Set them apart and consecrate them to exclusively serve you. Purify them and equip them for this service by transforming them to think and live in conformity to your truth and revelation— which is the truth of your word. Just as you sent me into this sinful world to reveal your truth about sin, death, and the only way to be saved—and to bring people into your Kingdom—in the same way I am sending them out with the same message and mission. I'm consecrating myself to do your will to redeem them so that they will be able to consecrate themselves to do your will through the transforming power of your truth.

"I'm not asking these things only for these men with me right now, but also for all those who will later come to believe in me through the message that they will preach. Father, I ask that you would make them all one in faith, purpose, love, and action—just like you and I are united. I ask that they may be joined spiritually as one in union with us, so that we may be seen in their lives and the people of this world will be convinced that you really sent me and that we live in them. Your glorious, loving, and righteous character that you've given me, I have also given to them so they can be one just like we are. I live in them, and you live in me so they can be brought into perfect unity with us. Then the people of this world will have to realize that you sent me and that you love my followers just like you love me. Father, it's my desire that the people you have given me will eventually be with me in Heaven so they can see the glorious splendor you've given me because you loved me even before anything was created.

"Righteous Father, even though the unbelievers in this world don't know you, I know you, and my people know that you sent me. So I've enabled them to know you—and your loving character too—and will continue to enable others to know you who will believe in me later. For I want them all to experience the great love you have for me living in them too. And I also want to live in them."

After this prayer, he said to his followers, "Come, let's be on our way." Then they sang a hymn and went out of the city making the 15-minute walk to Mount Olivet.

216. In Gethsemane
(Friday Night)

Jesus and his followers arrived at an olive grove on Mount Olivet called Gethsemane. (Now, Judas—who had left to betray Jesus—was familiar with that grove because Jesus often met there with his followers.)

Jesus told most of those with him, "You all sit here for a while. I'm going over there a little farther to pray." But he took Peter and Zebedee's two sons—James and John—with him. As he contemplated the sufferings that awaited him later that day, he was overcome with grief and distress. He told his three companions, "I feel so oppressed that I could want to die to escape it. Stay here and keep me company while I pray. And pray for yourselves so you will be able to resist the temptation that you will soon face."

Then he went about a stone's throw away from them and prostrated himself on the ground. He asked his Father if it was possible for him to avoid the suffering and tortuous death that was ahead of him. He said, "Daddy! My Father! You can do anything! Please don't tell me to go through with this painful plan! But more than anything, I want to follow your will and not my own desires."

While he was praying, God sent an angel to minister to him and strengthen him. He was in great emotional distress over the suffering and torture that he faced, and he struggled to remain submitted to his Father's will that he go through it. He was praying so intensely and was in such distress that he sweated profusely and the sweat fell from him like drops of blood on the ground.

When he finally got up from praying, he went over to his followers and found them sleeping. Their own sadness had drained them and made them tired. He woke Peter and said, "Simon, don't you three have the strength to stay awake with me for even an hour? You should be praying for God's help to resist the temptation you will soon face! Your spirits are willing enough to do what's right, but your own ability to resist temptation is weak."

Then he went and prayed a second time in the same way, saying basically the same words, "Father, if I cannot avoid this suffering and it's your will that I go through it, then I want to follow your will." Again, when he returned to his three companions, he found them asleep. They were just unable to keep their eyes open. When he woke them again, they were so embarrassed that they didn't know what to say to him.

So he left them to sleep and went to pray a third time, saying essentially the same things he had prayed before. Then he returned to them and said, "Now is not the time to be sleeping! Get up and come with me! The time has finally come for me, the Son of Man, to be betrayed and handed over to the power of evil men. See, here comes the traitor!"

217. Jesus Is Arrested
(Friday Night)

While he was still speaking, Judas arrived at the grove leading part of a cohort of soldiers and officials. They came with lanterns, torches, swords, and clubs and were sent with the authority of the chief priests and Jewish elders to arrest Jesus. The traitor had told them, "Arrest the man that I greet with a kiss. He is the one you want. Seize him and take him away." Going straight to Jesus, Judas said, "Greetings, Rabbi!" and kissed him. Jesus replied, "My friend, what have you come for? Are you betraying me with a kiss?"

Jesus already knew everything that was going to happen to him. So he went up to them and asked, "Who are you looking for?" They replied, "Jesus of Nazareth." He said, "I am he." When he said this, they all stepped back and fell to the ground. Jesus asked them again, "Who are you looking for?" Again they replied, "Jesus of Nazareth." Jesus said, "I've told you that I am he. So if it's me you want, let these others go free." He said this to fulfill the prophecy he had made in his prayer that none of his people would be lost.

Then the men with Judas arrested and held Jesus. When his followers saw this, they asked, "Lord, should we fight with our swords?" Simon Peter had a sword, so he drew it and struck at Malchus—the High Priest's servant—cutting off his right ear.

But Jesus commanded, "Stop! No more of this! Put away your sword! All who fight with swords will just end up getting killed. You should realize that if I wanted, I could ask my Father for help, and he would

instantly send more than twelve legions of angels to rescue me. But if I resisted, then how could the Scriptures be fulfilled that say this must happen? I must go through with this because it is my Father's will for me." Then he touched the man's ear and healed it.

Jesus confronted the chief priests and Temple officers and elders who had come to arrest him, "Why have you come armed with swords and clubs to arrest me as if I were a violent criminal? I've been with you every day in the Temple, and you could have easily arrested me there. But now is the time that God has appointed for this to happen and for the forces of spiritual darkness to have a free hand. Things have happened this way to fulfill the prophecies in the Scriptures."

When his close followers realized that he didn't intend to resist, they became afraid for their own lives and ran away. A certain young man had been following Jesus and his close followers that night. The crowd that arrested Jesus tried to seize him too, but he was only wearing a linen tunic and wriggled out of it—leaving his captors holding it while he ran away naked into the darkness.

218. Jesus Is Questioned by Annas
(Friday Night)

Then the soldiers and the commander and Jewish officers who had arrested Jesus tied him so he couldn't escape. They took him to Annas—the father-in-law of Caiaphas who was High Priest that year. It was Caiaphas who had advised the Jewish leaders that it would be expedient for one man to die for the people so that the whole nation wouldn't be destroyed.

Inside the house, Annas—the former High Priest—questioned Jesus about his followers and what he had taught them. Jesus answered, "I have always spoken publicly for all to hear and I've said nothing in private that is different from what I've taught openly. All my teachings have been presented in synagogues and in the Temple court. Why are you questioning me? Ask those who have listened to me. They know what I've said." When he said this, one of the guards standing there backhanded him across his face, saying, "Is that the proper way to answer the High Priest?" Jesus responded, "If I have said anything wrong, tell us what it was. But if I've spoken the truth, why do you strike me?" Then Annas sent him to Caiaphas, still bound.

219. Jesus Before the Sanhedrin
(Friday Night)

Jesus was taken to the house of Caiaphas, where he and the Scripture teachers and elders were assembled waiting for him.

Inside the house, the chief priests and the entire Sanhedrin were questioning witnesses—many who gave false testimony—to try to find sufficient evidence against him that they could have him executed. But they couldn't find any—even though many witnesses came forward and told lies about him—for their testimony did not agree. ❖ *The court required two witnesses to agree without contradiction in order for their testimony to be accepted as fact. When two witnesses contradicted each other under questioning, their testimony was invalidated and technically someone should have been severely punished for giving false testimony. Evidently, procedure required these witnesses to testify separately so they couldn't hear each other.* ➤ Finally, some men testified, "We heard this man say, 'I will destroy God's Temple—which was built by men—and miraculously build another.'" But even in this matter their testimonies did not agree in every detail. Then the High Priest stood and asked Jesus, "Aren't you going to say something? Don't you want to rely to this accusation?" But Jesus remained silent.

The High Priest demanded, "If you are the Messiah, tell us plainly!" He responded, "If I do tell you, you won't believe me. And if I ask you questions, you will refuse to answer me. We've been over this before."

Then the High Priest said, "I'm putting you under oath before the Living God. Tell us whether or not you are the Messiah—God's Son." Jesus answered, "Yes—though not exactly as you interpret that. But it is true that you will see me, the Son of Man, sitting in the place of highest honor at the right hand of God Almighty and coming with the clouds of Heaven." Then the High Priest tore his robes and said, "He has blasphemed God! We don't need any more

witnesses! You are all witnesses to his blasphemy! What is your verdict?" And they unanimously condemned him to death. They then proceeded to spit in his face, slap him, and beat him with fists. They blindfolded him and then took turns hitting him and taunting, "Prophesy for us, Messiah! Tell us who hit you!" They also ridiculed and insulted him in many other ways.

220. Peter Denies Knowing Jesus
(Friday Night)

After they had run off, Peter and John had followed at a distance behind those who arrested Jesus, hidden in the darkness. John knew the High Priest, so he was allowed to enter the courtyard of his house along with those who had arrested Jesus, but Peter waited outside the gate. So John, who was known in the household, a little later came back and spoke to the woman in charge of the gate, and she allowed Peter in too. The woman who was the gatekeeper said to Peter, "Aren't you one of Jesus' followers too?" Peter replied, "I don't know such a person and have no idea what you're talking about." While Jesus' interrogation was going on inside, Peter was sitting outside in the courtyard. Now, it was cold so the servants and guards lit a charcoal fire in the middle of the house's courtyard to keep warm, and Peter joined those sitting around it.

A serving girl came by and noticed him warming himself by the fire. She looked at him closely and said, "You are one of those who were with Jesus of Nazareth!" But Peter denied it vehemently. He said, "I swear before God, I don't even know the man!" Then he got up and went to the area near the entrance of the courtyard. He heard a rooster crow, but was barely aware of it.

After about an hour passed, one of the High Priest's servants—a relative of Malchus whose ear Peter had cut off—said, "Didn't I see you in the olive grove with Jesus? It's clear that you are one of those who follow him. Your Galilean accent gives you away." Fearing for his life, Peter declared, "May the Lord curse me if I'm telling a lie! I swear before the Lord of Heaven that I do not know that man!"

Immediately after he said it, for the second time that night he heard a rooster crow. The Lord Jesus—who was visible inside the house from the courtyard—turned and looked straight at Peter. Then Peter remembered what Jesus had told him earlier, "Before you hear a rooster crow two separate times tonight, you will three times publicly deny having any association with me." He was overcome with remorse and went outside the courtyard into the darkness, weeping bitterly because of what he had done.

221. Jesus Is Condemned by the Sanhedrin and Handed Over to Roman Authority for Execution
(Friday Morning)

When it became light, all the chief priests and Jewish elders conferred together in an official session of the Sanhedrin and planned how they would have Jesus executed. ❖ *They didn't have the authority to execute him because the Roman government reserved that power for themselves. So they had to plan how to present the case to the Roman governor.* ➤

Then they bound him, took him to the Roman authorities, and handed him over to be dealt with by Pilate, the governor.

222. Judas Commits Suicide
(Friday Morning)

When the traitor, Judas, saw that Jesus was sentenced to death, he felt remorse over what he had done and took the money he had received for the betrayal back to the chief priests and elders who had paid him. He told them, "I have sinned by betraying an innocent man to his death." They replied, "That's no concern of ours; you are responsible for your own actions." Judas threw the money on the Temple floor and went outside the city and hung himself. The chief priests picked up the coins and said, "It's against the Teachings of the Torah to put money used for evil purposes in the Temple treasury." So they discussed what to do with it and decided to purchase a potter's field to be used as a cemetery for strangers who died while visiting Jerusalem. This is why that field has been called the "Field of Blood" even to this day. These events fulfilled the prophecy made by Jeremiah which says, "They took the 30 silver coins—the price some of the men of Israel had placed on him—and they used them to purchase a potter's field, as Yahweh commanded me."

223. Jesus Is Questioned by Pilate
(Friday Morning)

Very early in the morning after the Sanhedrin had met, they all took Jesus from Caiaphas to the palace being used by the Roman governor in Jerusalem. They didn't enter the palace proper so that they wouldn't be ritually defiled and could continue to participate in all the Passover feasts. So Pilate—the Roman governor—went outside to meet them and asked, "What are the charges you're bringing against this man?" The Jewish leaders replied, "If he weren't a criminal, we wouldn't have brought him to you." Pilate replied, "Then take him and try him according to your own laws." The Jewish leaders answered, "But we're not allowed to put him to death." This happened in fulfillment of Jesus' prophecy about how he would die.

They started accusing him, "We have found this man guilty of stirring up trouble and encouraging people not to pay their taxes. He also calls himself 'the Messiah'—which means he intends to set himself up as a king."

Pilate went back inside the palace and summoned Jesus for questioning. He asked, "Are you king of the Jews?" Jesus replied, "Did others accuse me of this, or are you asking for reasons of your own?" Pilate retorted, "Do you think I'm a Jew and know or care about these things? It's your own people who have handed you over to me and brought this charge! What have you done that they want to kill you?" Jesus answered, "My Kingdom is not someplace in this world—in rival to the emperor. If I were such a king, then my followers would have fought to prevent my arrest. But my authority doesn't originate in this world." Pilate said, "So you are a king, then." Jesus replied, "You're the one calling me a king. Yes, I'm a king, but not in the way you think. I came into this world for one purpose—which is to reveal what is absolutely true. Those who really want to know about absolute truth are the ones who listen to me and follow me." Pilate cynically retorted, "What is truth?" Then he went outside again and told the Jewish leaders, "I don't find this man guilty of breaking any Roman law."

Then the chief priests started shouting all sorts of accusations against Jesus. Pilate demanded, "Aren't you going to respond to all these charges they are bringing against you?" Jesus amazed the governor by remaining totally silent. But the Jewish leaders kept insisting, "He is always stirring up the people—all the way from Galilee down through Judea." When Pilate heard this, he asked, "Is this man from Galilee?" And when he found out that Jesus came from Herod's jurisdiction, he sent him off to Herod—who happened to be in Jerusalem for the festival.

224. Jesus Before Herod
(Friday Morning)

Now, Herod was thrilled to see Jesus because he had been hearing about his miracles and popularity for a long time and wanted to see him perform a miracle. Herod questioned him at length, but Jesus just stood there silently. When given the opportunity, the chief priests and Scripture teachers angrily accused him of many crimes. Since he got neither miracles nor answers from him, Herod and his soldiers got their entertainment by mocking and humiliating Jesus. Then they put a fancy robe on him and sent him back to Pilate. It was because of that occasion—when Pilate and Herod deferred to each other with regard to judging Jesus—that they became friends, even though prior to this they had been unfriendly rivals.

225. Jesus Is Sentenced to Die
(Friday Morning)

After receiving Jesus into his custody again, Pilate summoned together the chief priests and Jewish leaders and said, "You have accused this man of inciting the people to rebel against Rome. But I've interrogated him in your presence and find no basis for the charges you've brought against him. And

neither did Herod since he sent him back to me. He has certainly broken no Roman law deserving the death penalty. But he has obviously caused trouble for you; so I will have him whipped as a warning against making any further trouble and let him go." Then Pilate ordered that Jesus be whipped.

❖ *Romans had three levels of flogging: 1) the fustigatio, the least severe of the three, given for small offenses, 2) the flagellatio, a severe flogging given to criminals for serious offenses, 3) the verberatio, the most severe scourging, often given before crucifixion. This whipping was one of the first two, designed to make the crowd feel pity for him.* ➤

Then the soldiers took Jesus into the governor's palace—called the "Praetorium"—and gathered the entire Roman cohort around him. They stripped him and whipped him. Then in order to mock the claim that he was a king, they dressed him in a purple robe and made him a crown by twisting some thorn branches together—making a mock wreath crown as vassal kings wore—and put it on his head. Then they put a stick in his right hand as a mockery of a scepter and made fun of him. They began to bow and kneel before him in mock homage and saluted him, saying, "Hail, King of the Jews!" They also beat the thorns into his head with a stick and spit on him.

Pilate went outside to the crowd again and said, "Look, I'm bringing him out to you, but I haven't found him guilty of any capital crime!" When Jesus was brought out wearing the crown of thorns and the purple robe, Pilate announced, "Here is the man!" But when the chief priests and Jewish officials saw him, they yelled, "Crucify him! Crucify him!" Pilate taunted them, "You take him and crucify him yourselves! You brought him to me, and I find him innocent!" Expressing their frustration, the Jewish leaders replied, "According to our laws he must die because he claims to be God's Son!" When Pilate heard this, he became afraid. He went back inside the palace and asked Jesus, "Where do you really come from?" But Jesus didn't answer. In irritation, Pilate exclaimed, "Why won't you answer me? Don't you see I have the power to release you or crucify you?" Jesus replied, "This situation—where you have the power to make that decision about me—wouldn't have arisen if God hadn't allowed it to happen. That is why Caiaphas—who decided to hand me over to you for execution—is guilty of a greater sin than you are." When Pilate heard this, he tried to find a way to set him free.

He had a custom where he would set free a prisoner of the crowd's choosing during the Passover Festival. At that time, he had a well-known troublemaker in custody named Barabbas—who was awaiting execution for a murder he committed during a revolt. The Jewish crowd gathered outside of Pilate's palace started demanding that he release a prisoner for them as he always did at Passover. So Pilate asked them, "Do you want me to release Barabbas to you this Passover, or Jesus who is called 'Messiah?'" He was aware that the chief priests had handed Jesus over to him out of envy of his popularity and was expecting the crowd to ask for Jesus' release—thereby relieving him of this matter. But the chief priests persuaded the crowd—which consisted mostly of their followers—to instead ask for Barabbas' release.

While Pilate was sitting there presiding over Jesus' fate, his wife sent him a note that said, "Don't have anything to do with condemning that innocent man to death. For I just had a dream about him that has upset me a lot." ❖ *Romans thought that such dreams were warnings from their gods and took them seriously.* ➤

The governor asked the crowd again, "Which of the two do you want released?" They shouted, "Barabbas!" Then Pilate asked, "And what should I do with Jesus who is called 'Messiah?'" They all shouted, "Crucify him!"

Pilate taunted the Jewish leaders by proclaiming, "Here is your king!" But they shouted, "Away with him! Crucify him!" Pilate responded, "You want me to crucify your king?" The chief priests replied, "The only king we have is Caesar!"

For the third time, Pilate said, "But why crucify him? What evil has he done? I haven't been able to find any reason according to Roman law that says he should be executed. So I will only punish him and then release him." But the Jewish leaders shouted, "If you release this man, you are no friend of Caesar! Anyone who claims to be a king is Caesar's enemy!"

When Pilate heard their implied threat, he had Jesus brought outside and then sat on the judgment seat to pass sentence. This was in a place called the "Stone Pavement." (Or *"Gabbatha"* in Aramaic.) It was nearing midday on Friday—the day of preparation for the Sabbath. Pilate realized that he wouldn't get the crowd to listen to him and they were on the verge of rioting, so he ritually washed his hands in front of them and declared, "I refuse to take responsibility for killing this innocent man. The guilt will be yours." They answered, "We take responsibility for his death. Let any consequences come to us and our children!" So Pilate reluctantly released Barabbas to them and ordered that Jesus be whipped again in preparation for his crucifixion. ❖ *This whipping was the verberatio.* ➤

226. The Crucifixion
(Friday Morning)

Some soldiers took charge of Jesus and they made him carry on his back the crossbeam of the cross on which he would be executed. As the soldiers were leading Jesus out of the city to the execution site, they forced a bystander named Simon—from the city of Cyrene in North Africa—to carry the crossbeam for Jesus since he was too weak from the whippings to continue bearing it himself.

A large crowd was following this procession through the streets of Jerusalem, and many were wailing in mourning for him—especially the women. But Jesus turned to them and said, "Women of Jerusalem, don't cry for me but cry for yourselves and your children because of God's judgment that will come upon this city. The time will come when people in Jerusalem say, 'Normally, barren women are pitied, but now they are the lucky ones because they don't have to see their children suffering.' Things will be so terrible that people will wish for an earthquake to bury them under landslides and put them out of their misery. For if men do these things to a righteous man, God will certainly punish those who are guilty!"

There were also two revolutionaries being led out to be executed with Jesus at the same time. They took them to a hill outside the city wall called the "skull"—which in Aramaic is *"Golgotha."* That's where they crucified Jesus and the two revolutionaries—one on each side of him.

They offered Jesus some wine mixed with myrrh, but after tasting it and discovering what it was, he refused to drink it.

After they had stripped him and nailed him to the cross, they cast lots to see who would get his clothing. It was shortly before noon when they crucified him. Then they sat nearby to keep guard as he hung there. The two revolutionaries were crucified at the same time—one on each side of Jesus. This fulfilled the Scripture which says, "He was considered to be just another law breaker."

Pilate had the usual sign made and hung over Jesus which publicly proclaimed his crime. Jesus' read, "Jesus of Nazareth—King of the Jews." The place of execution was near the city so many people could see and read the sign which was written in Aramaic—the common language of Judea, Latin—the language of Rome and the army, and Greek—the language of wider communication in the Roman empire. The chief priests protested to Pilate, "Don't allow it to say, 'King of the Jews,' but that he claimed to be King of the Jews!" But Pilate, enjoying their frustration, said, "What I've already written, stands!"

After the soldiers had crucified Jesus, they divided his outer clothing among the four of them. But his long tunic was woven in one piece without any seams. So they said, "Let's not tear it, but cast lots to determine who gets it." This fulfilled the prophecy in Scripture that reads, "They divided my garments among them, casting lots for my clothing."

While he was hanging on the cross, Jesus prayed, "Father, forgive them. They don't really know what they are doing."

Many who passed by blasphemed him and shook their heads in scorn. They said things like, "And you were going to destroy the Temple and rebuild it in three days! If you are God's Son, come down from the cross and save yourself!" People stood nearby, watching his suffering while the chief priests and Scripture teachers and the Jewish elders also made it a point to come and ridicule him. They said, "He had the power to save others but can't even save himself. If he really is the Messiah—the King of Israel—let's see him come down from the cross! Then we will believe in him! He said that he's God's Son and trusts in God. So let God rescue him now, if he really approves of him!"

The soldiers also made fun of him. They said, "If you are the king of the Jews, save yourself! Come on down and we will share our wine with you!"

One of the revolutionaries hanging next to him also mocked him, "Aren't you supposed to be the Messiah? Then save yourself and us too!"

But the other revolutionary rebuked the mocker. He said, "Have you no fear of God since you too are about to die and meet your maker? We deserve what we're getting, but this man has done nothing wrong. By mocking a righteous man you are only adding to your list of sins and the punishment that God will give you." Then he said, "Jesus, when you do become King, please remember me and have mercy!"

Jesus replied, "I assure you, today you will join me in Paradise!"

Standing near Jesus' cross were his mother, his mother's sister, Mary the wife of Clopas, and Mary of Magdala. When Jesus saw his mother and his close friend John standing there, he said to his mother, "Mother, he will be as a son to you." Then he said to John, "She is to be as a mother to you." So from that day on, John took her care of her in his own home.

227. Jesus' Death
(Friday Afternoon)

Then from midday until midafternoon, the entire land—as far as could be seen—was shrouded in darkness. About the middle of the afternoon, Jesus shouted in Aramaic, *"Eloi, eloi, lama sabachthani!"*

which means, "My God, my God, why have you left me!"

Some who were nearby heard him say this and thought, "He's calling for Elijah to help him." One of them ran to get a sponge. He soaked it in sour wine, put in on a stick, and raised it to Jesus' lips so he might drink it. But the others said, "Wait! Let's see if Elijah will come to save him first."

After this, when Jesus knew that he had accomplished everything his Father had sent him to do, he fulfilled one last prophecy from Scripture by saying, "I am thirsty." The soldiers had a jar of cheap wine there, so they put a sponge soaked with the cheap wine on a hyssop stalk and elevated it to Jesus' mouth. When he had sucked some of the wine, Jesus said, "It is finished!" Then he shouted "Father! I give my spirit into your hands!" He bowed his head and died.

228. Events at Jesus' Death
(Friday afternoon)

At that moment, the thick curtain in the Temple that closed off the Holy of Holies was torn in two from top to bottom. There was also an earthquake so severe that rocks were split. Tombs broke open and many of the bodies of God's holy people buried in them were raised back to life. They came out of the tombs, and after God made Jesus alive again, they went into Jerusalem and showed themselves to many who knew them.

When the centurion in charge of the execution and the other soldiers guarding Jesus saw the earthquake and all the other things that had happened while Jesus hung on the cross, they exclaimed in terror, "Truly this was the son of a god!" The centurion said, "I'm certain this man was innocent of any wrong!"

Many women—who had traveled with Jesus from Galilee to help support him and his ministry financially—observed all these things while standing some distance away. Among those watching were Mary of Magdala village, Salome, the mother of James and John (Zebedee's wife), and Miriam, who was the mother of James and Joseph. There were many other women there too who had traveled to Jerusalem with him.

Then all who had gathered to watch the spectacle began to return home, beating their chests in sorrow after having seen all that had happened, and believing an innocent man had died.

229. Jesus' Burial
(Friday Evening)

Since it was Friday, the preparation day for the Sabbath during the Passover Festival, the Jewish leaders didn't want bodies left hanging on the crosses when the Sabbath began at sunset. So they asked Pilate to have the legs of the men on the crosses broken in order to speed their deaths—so their bodies could be removed and buried before sunset. When Pilate gave the order, soldiers went and broke the legs of the two men crucified on both sides of Jesus. But when they reached Jesus, they saw that he was already dead so they didn't bother to break his legs. But to be sure he was dead, one of the soldiers stabbed a spear into Jesus' side, and immediately blood and water flowed out. It happened this way to fulfill the prophecy in Scripture that says, "None of his bones will be broken." And another prophecy says, "They will look at me—at him whom they pierced."

There was a member of the Sanhedrin named Joseph who was from the town of Arimathea. He was a good man who was eagerly looking forward to the establishment of God's Kingdom as taught by Jesus—and he had not agreed with the Council's plans or their actions. He boldly went to Pilate and asked permission to remove Jesus' dead body from the cross for burial. Pilate was surprised to hear that he was already dead, and sent a centurion to verify that it was true. When the centurion confirmed it, Pilate granted Joseph permission to take the body. Joseph bought some linen cloth for a burial shroud. Then he went and took the body, aided by Nicodemus—the same one who had visited Jesus at night. Nicodemus and his servants brought about 75 pounds of burial spices—a mixture of myrrh and aloes. They wrapped Jesus' body with the spices in strips of linen, following Jewish burial custom. Near the place of crucifixion was Joseph's own unused tomb which he had recently had cut out of rock in the side of a cliff. Since it was nearly sunset when the Sabbath would begin, they were in a hurry and they put Jesus' body in this tomb because it was so close by. Then they rolled a large disk-shaped stone to block the tomb's entrance.

230. Jesus' Tomb Is Sealed
(Friday Evening, Saturday Morning)

The women who had come with Jesus from Galilee followed after Joseph and saw the tomb and where he laid Jesus' body to rest. Mary from Magdala and Miriam—the mother of James and Joseph—were sitting nearby facing the tomb, observing where Joseph placed Jesus' body. Then they returned to where they were staying because they had to rest on the Sabbath—as the Teachings of Moses required—before they could return to finish the details of Jesus' burial.

The next day, the chief priests and Pharisees went to see Pilate. They said to him, "Sir, we recall that the charlatan Jesus claimed, 'God will make me alive again the second [A] day after my death.' So we are formally requesting that you order the grave to be guarded until the second day after his death, to prevent his followers from stealing the body during the night and claiming he has come back to life. If that happened, this last fraud would be worse than the one where he claimed to be the Messiah." Pilate replied, "You have a guard. Go make things as secure as you can." So they went and made sure the grave was securely guarded, and a seal was placed on the stone covering the entrance such that they would know if the tomb was opened.

231. God Makes Jesus Alive Again
(Sunday Morning)

When the Sabbath was over at sunset Saturday, Mary of Magdala and Salome and Miriam the mother of James went and bought burial spices so they could use them to anoint Jesus' body.

About dawn on Sunday morning—the first day of the week—these women headed toward Jesus' tomb. On their way there, they were discussing with each other how they would find someone to roll the heavy stone away from the tomb entrance.

Suddenly, an angel appeared at the tomb, and there was a violent earthquake. The angel then rolled away the stone that sealed the tomb in order to show that it was empty—and sat on it. The angel's clothes were snow white and as bright as a flash of lightning. The guards trembled and fell to the ground, paralyzed with fear as if they were dead.

When the women arrived, they saw no angel but went in the tomb and saw that Jesus' body was gone. Mary of Magdala immediately ran back to the city to Simon Peter and John and told them, "Someone has removed the Lord's body from the tomb where it was buried, and we don't know where they've taken it!" So Peter and John hurried to the tomb to see for themselves.

Meanwhile, the other women were confused as they stood in the tomb when two angels suddenly appeared near them. They looked like men, but their clothes radiated a brilliant light. Terrified, the women crouched down with their faces touching the ground, and one of the angels said, "There is no need to be afraid! I know you are looking for Jesus who was crucified. But why are you looking in a tomb for someone who is alive? He's not here! God has made him alive again! Don't you remember? He told you all this would happen when he was still teaching in Galilee. He said that the Son of Man would be handed over to sinful men, that he would be crucified, and on the second day after his death he would come back to life again. Come and look at the place where they put his body and see that it's gone. Then hurry to tell his close followers and Peter that God has made him alive again, and that Jesus is planning to meet you all in Galilee—just as he told you. This is the message I've been instructed to give you." So

---

A 230 See note at Matthew 16:21 for the reasoning behind not using the traditional phrase, "the third day."

after looking around the empty tomb, the women—shocked and trembling with fear—ran away from the tomb and were too frightened to say anything about this to anyone they met on the way. They were both afraid and joyful at the same time. They headed back into the city where the eleven apostles and others of Jesus' followers were staying to report what they had seen and heard.

While they were still on their way to the city, Jesus suddenly met them and said, "Rejoice!" The women came up to him and knelt down at his feet, grabbing hold of them—both to be sure he was real and as an act of worship. Then Jesus said, "There is no reason to be afraid! Go tell my followers to meet me in Galilee."

Meanwhile, they missed encountering Peter and John who arrived at the tomb with John getting there first. He bent over to look inside the tomb and saw the linen cloths that had been wrapped around the body lying there. But he didn't go in. Then Peter arrived and ducked inside the entrance. He also saw the linen cloths lying there and the cloth that had been around Jesus' head—which was rolled up and lying separately from the linen strips. Then John went inside too and saw these same things and believed that Jesus had risen from death. But even then they didn't understand that the Scriptures said it was necessary for the Messiah to die and rise again. Then they returned to the place where they were staying in the city.

Among the group of women that reported all these things were Mary of Magdala, Joanna, Miriam the mother of James, as well as some other women. But most of the men considered their report to be hysterical nonsense and wouldn't believe them.

232. Jesus Appears to Mary of Magdala
(Sunday Morning)

After Mary of Magdala—who had missed the angels the first time—reported to Peter and John, she headed back to the tomb too and stood outside it crying. While she was crying, she bent over to look inside and saw two angels clothed in white—one sitting at the head and one at the foot of where Jesus' body had been. They asked her, "Miss, why are you crying?" She replied, "Someone has taken my Lord's body, and I don't know what they've done with it!" Turning around, she saw a man standing there, but didn't recognize that he was Jesus. Jesus asked her, "Miss, why are you crying? Are you looking for someone?" Mary assumed that he was a gardener and said, "Sir, if you took him away, please tell me where you've put him and I will go take him to be properly buried!" Jesus said, "Mary!" She turned, and realizing it was Jesus, said in Aramaic, "Rabboni!"—which means "my teacher." Jesus told her, "You don't need to keep on clinging to me because I'm not returning to my Father yet. But go to my brothers and tell them I said, 'I am ascending to my Father and God—who is also your Father and God.'" She then went and reported this to his followers and said, "I've seen the Lord, and he is alive!" And she told them what he said to her. But most of them refused to believe her.

233. The Guards Report to the Chief Priests
(Sunday Morning)

While the women were taking the message to Jesus' followers, some of the guards who had been at the tomb went into the city and reported to the chief priests everything that had happened. After hearing this report, the chief priests met with the Jewish elders and they agreed upon a course of action. They gave a large bribe to the soldiers and told them, "You are to say that Jesus' followers came during the night and stole his body while you slept. And if this story gets to the governor's ears, we will persuade him to not give you any trouble." So the soldiers took the bribe and spread the story as they were instructed. And it's widely circulated among the Jews even to this day.

234. Jesus Appears on the Road to Emmaus
(Sunday Afternoon)

Later that same day, two of Jesus' followers were walking the seven miles from Jerusalem to the village of Emmaus. They were talking about all the things that had happened to Jesus, and now the confusion about what had happened to his body. While they were walking and discussing this, Jesus approached them from behind. And when he had caught up to them, he started walking along with them. But they were prevented from recognizing him. Jesus asked, "What have you two been talking about as you've been walking?" They stopped and stared at him with very sad expressions on their faces. The one named Cleopas exclaimed, "Are you the only person that's been in Jerusalem who doesn't know what has been happening there these past few days?" Jesus asked, "What things do you mean?"

They said, "The things that have happened to Jesus of Nazareth. He was a mighty prophet of God who performed miracles and taught God's message, and was popular with most of the people. But the chief priests and other rulers delivered him over to the Romans and got him sentenced to death—and they crucified him on Friday. We were hoping that he was the Messiah who was going to save Israel. Today is the second [A] day since he died, and we've all been depressed. And now, some of the women in our group went to his tomb early this morning and they came back with a crazy story of seeing angels and that his body was gone and that he's alive again. So some of the men went to the tomb and confirmed it was empty, but they didn't see Jesus or any angels."

Then Jesus said, "Why are you so muddle headed and slow to believe the things written by the prophets in the Scriptures? Didn't they clearly write that the Messiah had to suffer these things before entering into his glory?" Then he began to explain to them all the predictions about the Messiah in the Scriptures, starting with the writings of Moses and continuing through the writings of all the other prophets.

As they approached the village where they were going, Jesus acted like he was going to continue farther on the road. But they begged him, "Please stay with us for the night. After all, it will be dark soon." So he went with them to their lodging. And while they were reclining at the table ready to eat, Jesus took some bread, thanked God for it, and broke it. As he was passing it to them, it was like their eyes were newly opened and they recognized who he was. But then he vanished before their very eyes. They exclaimed to each other, "While he was explaining the Scriptures to us on the road, didn't your heart burn with joy? How could we not have recognized him!"

They were so excited that they left within the hour to hurry back to Jerusalem to tell the eleven apostles and the others. When they arrived, even before they could tell their story the others said, "The Lord really is alive again! He came to Simon!"

Then they started to tell their story about Jesus' walking with them on the road and how they didn't recognize him until he broke the bread.

235. Jesus Appears to Ten Apostles Without Thomas
(Sunday Late Afternoon)

Late afternoon on that same Sunday, many of Jesus' close followers were in a house behind locked doors because they were still afraid that the Jewish leaders might be searching to arrest them. While those two men were telling their story, Jesus suddenly appeared standing among them and said, "I bless you with shalom!"

But they were startled and frightened and thought they were seeing a ghost. Jesus said, "Why are you afraid? And why do you continue to doubt that I'm really alive, or who I am? Look at the nail scars in my arms and feet from my crucifixion. It's really me! Touch me and confirm for yourselves that I'm a living human being—not an insubstantial apparition."

When he had said this, he showed all of them the scars of the wounds in his arms near his wrists and his feet. They were thrilled, stunned, and so overwhelmed that it was still difficult for them to fully believe he was alive. So Jesus asked, "Do you have

---

A **234** See note at Matthew 16:21 for the reasoning behind not using the traditional phrase, "the third day."

anything here to eat?" They gave him a piece of broiled fish, and he ate it while they watched—to prove that he wasn't a ghost.

He rebuked them for their stubborn refusal to accept the witness of others concerning his being alive and for their persistent unbelief despite his having told them ahead of time that all this would happen.

Afterwards, he told them, "I'm sending you to minister to the people of this world in the same way that my Father sent me to minister to them." Then he breathed on them and said, "Receive the Holy Spirit. If you forgive someone, then God has forgiven their sins too. If you withhold forgiveness from someone, then God also withholds his forgiveness."

236. Thomas' Response to the Resurrection
(One Week After the Resurrection)

Now, Thomas—one of the original twelve apostles who was nicknamed "Twin"—was not with the other followers of Jesus when he appeared to them on that first Sunday. When the others told him, "We have seen the Lord and he's alive!" he said, "I refuse to believe it! The only thing that could convince me is to see the scars of the nail prints in his arms and actually feel them with my finger, and to put my hand into the wound in his side to feel its reality."

On the next Sunday, Jesus' followers were again together in the same house behind locked doors—as they had been when Jesus first appeared to them—and this time, Thomas was with them. Once again, Jesus suddenly appeared standing among them and said, "I bless you with shalom!" Then speaking to Thomas, he said, "See my arms. Come and touch the scars with your fingers. Come and feel the wound in my side. Then stop exercising your unbelief and believe that I really have physically come back to life!" Thomas was awe struck and exclaimed, "You are my Lord—and now I know that you are also my God!" Jesus said, "You believe I'm alive because you've seen me. But God will accept and bless all those who believe the same—even though they haven't seen me."

237. Jesus Appears to His Followers at Lake Galilee

Some days later, Jesus once again appeared to some of his followers on the shore of Lake Tiberius (a.k.a. Lake Galilee). This is the story. Simon Peter, Thomas—known as "Twin", Nathanael from Cana in Galilee, James and John—the sons of Zebedee—and two other followers were together.

Peter said to the others, "I'm going fishing." They all responded, "We'll come with you." So they went out in a boat to do some net fishing that night, but didn't catch a single fish. At daybreak, Jesus was standing on the shore, but his followers didn't recognize who he was. He called out to them, "Hey guys! Haven't you caught anything?" They called back, "Nothing!" Then he said, "Cast your net on the right side of the boat and you will get some!" So they did—and the net became so heavy with fish that they couldn't haul it into the boat.

Then John exclaimed to Peter, "It's the Lord!" When Peter heard this, he wrapped his outer garment around his waist—for he didn't wear it while he worked—dove into the water and swam to Jesus. The others followed in the boat, dragging the net full of fish. They were only about 100 yards from shore. When they came ashore, they saw a charcoal fire with some fish already cooking and some bread. Jesus told them, "Bring some of your catch." Peter went back up into the boat to help drag the net ashore. It wasn't torn, even though it contained 153 large fish. Then Jesus said, "Come and have some breakfast." None of the men dared ask him who he was because they knew he was their Lord. Then Jesus took the bread and divided it among them and did the same with the fish he had cooked. This was the third time that Jesus appeared to a group of his followers after his resurrection.

When they had finished eating, Jesus said, "Simon, son of John, do you love me more than these other followers do?" Peter replied, "Yes Lord, you know that I love you." Jesus said, "Then take care of my lambs." ❖ *Lambs and sheep are figures representing Jesus' followers.* ➤ Then Jesus asked him a second time, "Simon, son of John, do you love me?" Peter replied, "Yes Lord, you know that I love you." Jesus said, "Then watch over my sheep." A third time, Jesus asked, "Simon, son of John, do you love me?" Peter was grieved because he asked the same thing a third time. He said, "Lord, you know everything, so you must know that I love you!" Jesus told him a third time, "Then take care of my sheep.

"This truth is for you: When you were younger, you dressed yourself and went wherever you wanted. But when you are old, you will stretch out your hands. Others will dress you and take you where you don't want to go." ❖ *The phrase "stretch out your hands" was widely used to refer to crucifixion, and this is how tradition says that Peter died.* ➤ Jesus said this to indicate how Peter would die and bring glory to God. Then Jesus told him, "Follow in my footsteps."

Peter turned and saw John following them—Jesus' special friend who had leaned back against his chest at the last supper and asked who would betray him. When he saw John, he asked Jesus, "Lord, what will happen to him?" Jesus answered, "If I want him to live until I return again, that should be of no concern to you. You are only to concern yourself with following me!" So a rumor spread among the believers that John wouldn't die. But that isn't what Jesus said. He meant that whether or not John died before Jesus returned wasn't Peter's business. ❖ *According to tradition, John did live to old age, dying a natural death around the year AD 100—while all or most of the other apostles died as martyrs.* ➤

238. Jesus Appears to Others

After that, he appeared to more than five hundred believers at once—and most of those eyewitnesses are still alive at the time of my writing, ❖ *about 23-26 years after his resurrection* ➤ even though some have died. Then he appeared to his brother James, and then to all the apostles. Finally, years after his ascension, he also appeared to the Apostle Paul.

239. Jesus' Last Instructions to His Followers

Jesus' eleven close followers went to Galilee to a hill where Jesus had told them to go. When he met them there, some of them worshipped him, but some still had doubts.

Then Jesus said, "I want to go over with you again the things that I taught you while we were together before all this happened. I told you that all the things written about me in the Teachings of Moses and in the writings of the prophets and in the Psalms had to be fulfilled." Then he enabled them to clearly understand how all the different prophecies about him had come true. Afterwards, in conclusion he said, "And so it was written that the Messiah would suffer and die and rise from death on the second **A** day after his death."

Jesus came closer and told them, "God the Father has given me absolute authority over everything and everyone in Heaven and on earth. Therefore from that position of authority, I am commanding you to go to every people group in the world and preach the Good News about how to be saved. I want you to fully train people from each group to be my faithful followers because you are eyewitnesses to all these things. Baptize each of them in the name of the Father and the Son and the Holy Spirit. And I want you to teach each of them to obey all of the commands that I gave you while I was with you. Those who believe your message and are baptized will be saved. But those who reject your message will be damned in Hell. Those who believe will find that these miraculous signs will happen to verify their message: They will expel demons from people, they will speak in unknown languages, they will safely pick up poisonous snakes, if they unknowingly drink poison it won't harm them, and they will lay their hands on the sick to pray for them— and they will get well. I will soon send the Holy Spirit to come upon you—just as my Father promised. But you are to wait in Jerusalem until he comes and fills you with

---

A 239 See note at Matthew 16:21 for the reasoning behind not using the traditional phrase, "the third day."

his power. And believe that I am always spiritually with you until I return again physically at the end of the age."

240. Jesus Ascends to Heaven
(40 Days After the Resurrection)

Later, they were in Jerusalem again. One of those times while he was eating with them, he said, "Don't leave Jerusalem yet, but wait here for the gift of the Holy Spirit to come to you that my Father promised and whom I've told you about before. For John baptized people with water, but in just a few days, you will be baptized with the Holy Spirit."

When they met together with Jesus on the 40th day after his resurrection, he led them out of Jerusalem until they approached Bethany. They asked him, "Lord, are you now going to restore the glory of the Kingdom of Israel and get rid of the Romans?" He answered, "The time for such things has been set by my Father—and he doesn't want you to know when it will happen. But what you should be expecting is that the Holy Spirit will come on you and give you access to his power. Then you will tell everyone what you know about me—all that I've done and taught. You will start here in Jerusalem, move out to all of Judea and Samaria, and some of you will even go to the remotest parts of the earth."

After he told them these things, he raised his hands and blessed them. And while he was blessing them and as they watched, he rose high into the air until finally a cloud prevented them from seeing him any longer. And while they were still staring up in the sky as he was going, two angels suddenly appeared standing with them in the form of men dressed in white. They said, "Men of Galilee, why are you just standing there staring into the sky? Jesus has been taken up into Heaven, and he will someday return on a cloud in exactly the same manner that you saw him leave." So they returned to Jerusalem full of joy, and every day after that, they met together in the Temple to worship and praise God.

Jesus now sits in the position of highest authority and power at the right side of God the Father in Heaven. Later, his followers did go and preach the message of the Good News in as many places as they could—while the Lord worked in and through them and confirmed their message with the miraculous signs that he had promised they would do. Yes, that's the way it was—and may it continue to be so!

241. The Record of Jesus' Ministry is Far from Complete

Jesus' followers saw him perform many other miraculous signs that aren't recorded in this book. But these were recorded so you may come to believe that Jesus really is the Messiah—God's Son—and gain eternal life by trusting in him to save you and submitting to him as Lord over your life.

The Good News About Jesus the Messiah

as Told by

Matthew

The apostle Matthew—son of Alphaeus, [Mark 2:14] also known as Levi the tax collector—wrote this book. Most Jews considered tax collectors to be traitors for collaborating with their Roman conquerors. They extorted money from people so were viewed as corrupt, evil, and among the worst of sinners. The fact that Jesus choose Matthew to be his follower demonstrates that he considers no one to be too great a sinner to be saved. Matthew probably wrote this book sometime between AD 45–68. He wrote it to fellow Jews and his main purpose was to show that Jesus was the promised Messiah—descended from King David—who would rule over God's people forever. To do this, he frequently quoted prophecies about the Messiah that Jesus fulfilled. He also frequently quoted Jesus referring to himself as "the Son of Man," an allusion to Daniel 7:13-14. The Jews of his day did not understand this to be a Messianic title, and Jesus probably used it because: 1) it didn't have the political overtones that Jews associated with other Messianic titles, and 2) if someone recognized the allusion to Daniel 7:13-14, they would realize he was claiming these things about himself: He came from Heaven, he was worthy to enter God's presence, God gave him authority, glory, and power over all people and nations, all people serve him, and his Kingdom will never end.

Some Important Passages in This Book:

How Jesus' followers are to live. [chapters 5—7]
Parables about God's Kingdom. [chapter 13]
The last days before Jesus' return and the final judgment. [chapters 24—25]
Jesus' final instructions to his followers. [28:18-20]

1

Jesus' Royal Ancestry
Through Solomon to Yosef

¹ This book is a history of Jesus the Messiah who is descended from King David and Abraham. ❖ *In genealogies of this time, not every person in the line was necessarily mentioned. Saying a person was the "father" of someone merely meant he was an ancestor, and often only the more prominent people in the line were listed. This genealogy is abridged. Four names are listed in this genealogical line in 1 Chronicles chapter 3 that Matthew leaves out. Matthew's genealogy from David to Yosef mentions only 28 generations, averaging about 36 years per generation. Luke's genealogy mentions 42 generations after David, averaging 24 years per generation. The generations from Judah to Boaz are shortened, as there are only 13 generations mentioned from Isaac to David, spanning a period of 900 years. Jewish genealogical records were kept in the Temple in Jerusalem and could be inspected there before its*

destruction in AD 70. After that, no Jew was able to prove his ancestry. Since prophecy said the Messiah was to descend from King David, he had to make his claim before the Temple's destruction to be able to prove his ancestry. Even though Yosef was not Jesus' biological father, he was his legal father. And this genealogy shows Jesus' legal line of descent in the royal line of the kings of Judah, directly from David, thus fulfilling prophecy. King Jeconiah (a.k.a. Jehoiachin or Coniah) in Yosef's line did evil in the sight of the Lord. [2 Chronicles 36:9] God promised that none of his descendants would reign as a king descended from David. [Jeremiah 22:24-30] Thus Yosef, who was Jeconiah's descendant, could not be Jesus' biological father since Jesus does reign as a king descended from David. The genealogy in Luke shows his biological descent through his mother Miriam's line. It deviates from the one Matthew recorded in the generations after King David, showing him descended from David's son Nathan, rather than Solomon. (See the Harmony for a comparison of the two genealogies side by side.) ➤

² Abraham's descendants were: ❖ *He lived about 2000 BC.* ➤

Isaac

Jacob (whom God renamed "Israel")

❖ *Jacob was second born.* ➤

Judah and his 11 brothers whose descendants became the 12 tribes of Israel. ❖ *Judah was fourth born.* ➤

3 Perez and his twin brother Zerah (His mother was Judah's daughter-in-law, Tamar.) ❖ *[Genesis 38:1-30; 1 Chronicles 2:4] Judah had three sons by his wife who was a Gentile, but they were not part of the ancestry of the Messiah. Many commentators believe Tamar was a Gentile, and that was Matthew's reason for mentioning her.* ➤

Hezron *[Ruth 4:18; 1 Chronicles 2:5]*

Ram *[Ruth 4:19; 1 Chronicles 2:9]* ❖ *a.k.a. Aram. Ram was second born. Luke's genealogy has Hezron the ancestor of Arni, Arni the ancestor of Admin, Admin the ancestor of Ram. But there are manuscript variations in these few names between Hezron and Ram in Luke.* ➤

4 Amminadab *[Ruth 4:19; 1 Chronicles 2:10]*

Nahshon *[Numbers 1:7; Ruth 4:20; 1 Chronicles 2:10]*

Salmon (or Salma) who married Rahab ❖ *the Gentile prostitute [Joshua 2:1-21; 6:17-25; Ruth 4:20; 1 Chronicles 2:11]* ➤

5 Boaz, who married Ruth *[Ruth 4:21; 1 Chronicles 2:11]* ❖ *Ruth was a Gentile from Moab. See Deuteronomy 23:3 about Moabites becoming part of the people of Israel.* ➤

Obed *[Ruth 4:13-21; 1 Chronicles 2:12]*

Jesse *[Ruth 4:22; 1 Chronicles 2:12]*

6 David, the second king of Israel. *[Ruth 4:22; 1 Samuel 16:1-13; 2 Samuel 2:1-7; 5:1-5; 1 Chronicles 2:13-15]* ❖ *David was seventh and last born and lived around 1000 BC. All the other kings of Judah were descended from him. David's life is recorded in 1 Samuel chapters 16—31; all of 2 Samuel, and 1 Kings 1:1—2:11.* ➤

King Solomon, son of Bathsheba (Uriah's wife). *[2 Samuel chapter 11; 1 Chronicles 3:4-5]* ❖ *Many commentators think Bathsheba was a Gentile. We know Uriah was a Hittite. Solomon's life is recorded in 1 Kings chapters 1—11; 1 Chronicles chapters 28—29; and 2 Chronicles chapters 1—9.* ➤

7 King Rehoboam, who reigned when Israel split into the kingdoms of

Judah and Israel. *[1 Chronicles 3:10]*

❖ *Rehoboam's life is recorded in 1 Kings 11:43—14:31 and 2 Chronicles 9:31—12:16.* ➤

King Abijah *[1 Chronicles 3:10]* ❖ *Abijah's life is recorded in 1 Kings 14:1—15:8 and 2 Chronicles 11:20—14:1.* ➤

King Asa *[1 Chronicles 3:10]* ❖ *a.k.a. Asaph—but not the Psalmist. Asa's life is recorded in 1 Kings 15:8—15:24 and 2 Chronicles 14:1—16:14.* ➤

8 King Jehoshaphat *[1 Chronicles 3:10]* ❖ *Jehoshaphat's life is recorded in 1 Kings 22:41-50 and 2 Chronicles 17:1—21:1.* ➤

King Jehoram **A** *[1 Chronicles 3:11]* ❖ *a.k.a. Joram. Jehoram's life is recorded in 1 Kings 22:50; 2 Kings 8:16-24 and 2 Chronicles 21:1-20. 1 Chronicles 3:11-12 lists three Kings not mentioned by Matthew. Jehoram was the father of King Ahaziah.* **B** *[2 Kings 8:25—9:29; 2 Chronicles 22:1-9] Ahaziah was the father of King Joash. [2 Kings 11:1—12:21; 2 Chronicles 22:10—24:25] Joash was the father of King Amaziah. [2 Kings 12:21; 14:1-20; 2 Chronicles 24:27—25:28] Amaziah was the father of King Uzziah.* ➤

King Uzziah *[1 Chronicles 3:12]* ❖ *a.k.a. Azariah. Uzziah's life is recorded in 2 Kings 14:21-22; 15:1-7 and 2 Chronicles 26:1-23.* ➤

9 King Jotham *[1 Chronicles 3:12]* ❖ *Jotham's life is recorded in 2 Kings 15:7; 15:32-38 and 2 Chronicles 26:23—27:9.* ➤

King Ahaz *[1 Chronicles 3:13]* ❖ *Ahaz's life is recorded in 2 Kings 15:38—16:20 and 2 Chronicles 27:9—28:27.* ➤

King Hezekiah *[1 Chronicles 3:13]* ❖ *Hezekiah's life is recorded in 2 Kings 16:20; 18:1—20:21 and 2 Chronicles 28:27—2:33.* ➤

10 King Manasseh *[1 Chronicles 3:13]* ❖ *Manasseh's life is recorded in 2 Kings 20:21—21:18 and 2 Chronicles 32:33—33:20.* ➤

King Amon *[1 Chronicles 3:14]* ❖ *Amon's life is recorded in 2 Kings 21:18-26 and 2 Chronicles 33:20-24.* ➤

King Josiah *[1 Chronicles 3:14]* ❖ *1 Chronicles 3:15-16 says that Josiah was the father of King Jehoiakim (or Jehoiachim, a.k.a. Eliakim) (second born) [2 Kings 23:34—24:6; 2 Chronicles 36:4-8], Jehoiakim was the father of King Jeconiah (Jehoiakin). 2 Kings 23:30-34 and 2 Chronicles*

A **1:8** There was another King Jehoram (a.k.a. Joram) of the northern kingdom of Israel, son of Ahab. [2 Kings 1:17; 3:1—9:24]

B **1:8** There was another King Ahaziah of the northern kingdom of Israel [1 Kings 22:51-53; 2 Kings 1:2-18]

36:1-4 say Josiah's son, Jehoahaz, was king after him, and then Jehoiachim. Josiah's life is recorded in 2 Kings 21:26—23:30 and 2 Chronicles 33:25—35:27. ➤

11 King Jeconiah (a.k.a. Jehoiakin, Jehoiachin or Coniah) and his brothers. Jehoiakin was King when Nebuchadnezzar conquered Judah and took its people to Babylon. *[1 Chronicles 3:14-17; Esther 2:6; Jeremiah 24:1; 27:20; 28:4; 29:2]* ❖ *The exile lasted 70 years from 605 BC to 537 BC. Jeconiah's life is recorded in 2 Kings 24:6-15; 25:27-30 and 2 Chronicles 36:8-10.* ➤

12 After the deportation to Babylon, Jeconiah became the father of Shealtiel . *[1 Chronicles 3:17]*
Zerubbabel *[1 Chronicles 3:19; Ezra 3:2, 8; 5:2; Nehemiah 12:1; Haggai 1:1, 12-13; 2:2, 23]* ❖ *Matthew was using the Septuagint (the Greek translation of the Hebrew Scriptures) as a source. The Septuagint lists Zerubbabel as the son of Shealtiel, but the Hebrew text mentions Pedaiah as the son of Shealtiel and the father of Zerubbabel.* ➤

13 Abiud (Abihud)
Eliakim
Azor
14 Zadok
Akim (Achim)
Eliud
15 Eleazar
Matthan
Jacob
16 Yosef (Joseph), husband of Miriam (Mary) who bore
Jesus (Yeshua) the Messiah. ❖ *Note the literal text does not say Yosef fathered Jesus, in contrast to every other pair of names. The period from Zerubbabel until Jesus was about 500 years.* ➤

17 So there are 14 generations in this list from Abraham to David (inclusive), and 14 from David to the exile in Babylon (David to Josiah inclusive) and another 14 from the exile to the birth of the Messiah (Jeconiah to Jesus inclusive). ❖ *We can't be sure why Matthew tailored his list into three groups of 14 (though David has to be used twice in order to claim there are 14 in the second group).*

Commentators speculate several reasons, one being that it made the genealogy easier to memorize, another that it highlighted Abraham (Israel's most revered ancestor) and David (whose reign was the highlight of Israel's history) and the exile in Babylon (which was the lowest point in Israel's history) and the Messiah. Fourteen was the number of High Priests from Aaron to the establishment of Solomon's Temple, and also from the establishment of the Temple until the last High Priest mentioned in the Hebrew Scriptures. 14 is two times seven, and seven (in the Bible) symbolizes completeness. In Hebrew, each letter stands for a number and the numerical value for David's name in Hebrew is 14. So by emphasizing David in the list and the number 14, Matthew was in some manner emphasizing that Jesus was descended from David and thus was qualified to be the Messiah. ➤

The Messiah's Birth

18 These are the circumstances surrounding the birth of Jesus the Messiah: Miriam, who later bore him, was betrothed to Yosef. ❖ *Their betrothal was less than a marriage, yet more of a commitment than a modern-day engagement. They were called "husband and wife" even though they were not yet living together. The betrothal typically lasted for one year before the wedding.* ➤ But before they married and before they had sexual relations, Miriam became pregnant by the power of the Holy Spirit. 19 Yosef always tried to do what was right, so he mercifully decided to divorce her quietly rather than shame her with a public accusation of immorality. ❖ *Breaking the betrothal was called a "divorce," and he only had to give her a certificate of divorce before two witnesses to do this. The penalty of death by stoning [Deuteronomy 22:20-21] was rarely executed by that time. If he went through with the divorce, it is unlikely anyone else would ever marry her.* ➤ 20 But after he had decided to do this, an angel **A** appeared to him in a dream and said, "Yosef, descendant of King David, don't hesitate to take Miriam into your home as your wife. She has done nothing wrong. The child she carries was miraculously conceived by the Holy Spirit, not by any man. 21 She will have a son, and you are to name him 'Jesus' ❖ *which in Hebrew is "Yeshua" and means "Yahweh saves"* ➤ because he will save his people from the penalty of

---

A 1:20 Literally: "messenger of the Lord"

their sins." ❖ *By naming the child, Yosef legally accepted him as his own.* ➤

22 It happened this way so that God's prophecy about this miraculous sign would be fulfilled: **23** **"A virgin will become pregnant and—while still a virgin—have a son who will be** *'Immanuel,'* **"** *[Isaiah 7:14]* **which means, "God with us."** *[Isaiah 8:10]* ❖ *The fulfillment of the first part is clearly the birth of Jesus to the virgin Miriam. The fulfillment of the second part is not as obvious. It sounds like "Immanuel" should be a name, but Jesus was never called by this name. In Luke 1:32 the angel tells Miriam, "He will be called the 'Son of the Most High God.'" But the phrase "he will be called" clearly didn't refer to what people would call him during his earthly life. It meant "He will be the Son of the Most High God," just like the literal phrase "they will call him" in this verse means "he will be." In both cases the literal text became true after he ascended into Heaven.* ➤ **24** When Yosef woke up, he realized this was not an ordinary dream but a command from God. So when their betrothal period ended, they married and he took Miriam to his home as his wife, obeying the angel's directions. **25** But he had no sexual relations with her until after her first **A** child was born, who was a son. And he named the boy, "Jesus." ❖ *Roman Catholics believe that Miriam remained a virgin—never having sexual relations with Yosef—and that Jesus' brothers, mentioned elsewhere, [Matthew 12:47; 13:55-56; Mark 3:32; Luke 8:19-20; John 2:12; 7:3-10; Acts 1:14; 1 Corinthians 9:5] were Yosef's children by a previous marriage. Most Protestants and Jews think this is extremely unlikely. Jesus was born sometime around 7–5 BC. This oddity is due to a mistake made by those in the sixth century who developed the system*

of dating years "BC" and "AD." ¶ *More details about Jesus' birth are in Luke 1:5—2:38.* ➤

2

God Reveals the Messiah to Gentiles

1 Jesus was born in Bethlehem in Judea Province ❖ *Another Bethlehem was in Galilee Province near Nazareth.* ➤ where King **B** Herod the Great reigned. Sometime later, astrological scholars **C** from the east ❖ *probably Babylon or Persia* ➤ arrived in Jerusalem asking the authorities, **2** "Where is the child who has recently been born as **D** King of the Jews? Where we lived in the east, we saw a new star rise that proclaims his birth and have come to worship him."

3 When Herod heard about this he was upset, and everyone in Jerusalem feared he might go on a killing rampage. ❖ *Herod was called "the Great" because of his building achievements, but he was also a ruthless tyrant who killed anyone he thought threatened his throne, including family members. Herod clearly believed the astrologers' report that a king had been born and considered him a threat.* ➤ **4** Herod summoned all the chief priests and Scripture teachers and asked them where, according to prophecy, the Messiah would be born. ❖ *Though not mentioned previously, the astrologers and Herod considered the star a sign of no ordinary king, but of the Messiah himself.* ➤

5 They told him, "In Bethlehem of Judea. For the prophet Micah wrote: **6** 'You, village of Bethlehem in the land of Judah, **E** even though you are small, the leaders of Judah

---

A 1:25 Some manuscripts have "firstborn son," others only "son."

B 2:1 Herod the Great was under the authority of the Roman Emperor but was allowed to have the title "king." Later, Augustus Caesar would not allow Herod's sons to use that title. From historical sources, we know that Herod died in 4 BC, hence we know Jesus was born before that year. (Note: Recently, there has been some debate about the date of Herod's death. I have retained the more traditional scholarly dates concerning Jesus' date of birth, but some now think Herod might have died in 1 BC. The interested reader can research this debate online.)

C 2:1 Astrologers at that time were highly educated and not in the same class as present-day astrologists. Though modern science ridicules the idea that signs in the sky portend important events, there are places in the Scriptures

which say that God does place such signs in the sky. [Luke 21:25; Acts 2:19-20] But at the same time, God has forbidden his people from doing divination (i.e., attempting to foretell the future or gain knowledge through occult means). [Deuteronomy 18:10, 14] These scholars probably also studied the meaning of dreams. Some commentators think they may have been descended from students of Daniel. [Daniel 2:48] If so, they might even have been aware they were seeking the Messiah.

D 2:2 The Greek text does not specify whether the child was born "as" king or "to become" king. In some sense, both meanings are true.

E 2:6 "Judea" was the name of the Roman province at the time of the story. "Judah" was the name of that area when the Israelites settled it, and when the prophecy was given.

consider you important. Because it is from you that a king will come who will be the shepherd for my people Israel.' " *[Micah 5:2, 4; 2 Samuel 5:2; 1 Chronicles 11:2]* ❖ *Micah wrote this prophecy around 700 BC.* ➤ 7 So Herod summoned the astrologers to a secret audience and found out when the star had first appeared. ❖ *He assumed that the date of its first appearance indicated when the Messiah had been born, so he would know how old the child was.* ➤ 8 Then he told them, "Go to Bethlehem. Find the child and come back to tell me where he is so I too can go and worship him."

9-10 After this, they started on their way to Bethlehem which is about six miles south of Jerusalem. And the star, which they had first seen in their own country to the far east of Jerusalem, appeared again moving before them. When they saw it, they joyfully exulted and followed it until it stopped over the house where the child was staying. ❖ *This could not be a real star, planet, alignment of planets, or even a comet. Such lights could not possibly guide them to a particular house. Only something less than a mile above the ground could do so.* ➤ 11 When they entered the house, they saw the child with his mother Miriam and bowed down to worship him. Then they brought out the treasures they had brought and gave the child kingly gifts of gold, frankincense, and myrrh. ❖ *Frankincense was an expensive sweet-smelling incense from Arabia, made from the resin of frankincense trees. The Torah said to use it as part of the offerings to God. [Leviticus 2:2, 15-16; 6:15] Myrrh was also expensive and made from the sap of myrrh bushes. People used it as a perfume and also for medicinal purposes. [Mark 15:23] They also used it to prepare bodies for burial [John 19:39] and in making holy oil for anointing priests and sacred objects. [Exodus 30:23-33] Each of these gifts were fit for a king. Some people see symbolic meanings for these gifts: gold for a king, frankincense for God, and myrrh for suffering and death. Because of the three gifts, some people think there were three astrologers, and tradition calls them "kings" without basis. We know from Luke 2:22-24 that 40 days after Jesus' birth, Miriam and Yosef were still poor and had to offer two doves, rather than a lamb, as a sacrifice for purification after childbirth. So it's clear that they received these gifts after that time. The astrologers (traditionally called "wise men") did not see the infant in a stable. By this time, Miriam and Yosef were staying in a house. [verse 11] From verses 7 and 16, it's possible that the astrologers didn't arrive until nearly two years after Jesus' birth.* ➤

12 Then the astrologers started on the trip back to their own country. But they didn't go through Jerusalem, for God warned them in a dream that they shouldn't return to Herod. ❖ *They had to go far out of their way to avoid Jerusalem without being noticed.* ➤

Yosef and His Family Flee to Egypt

13 After these men had left, an angel appeared to Yosef in a dream. He told him, "Get up immediately! Take the child and his mother and flee to Egypt. Stay there until I tell you to return. For Herod wants to find the child to kill him." ❖ *The trip to Egypt would take 10-12 days. The gold from the astrologers enabled them to afford to make this journey and supported them while in Egypt.* ➤

14 So Yosef immediately got up and— while it was still night—left for Egypt with Miriam and the child. 15 They stayed in Egypt until Herod died. This fulfilled the prophecy that God said through the prophet Hosea, **"I called my Son to come out of Egypt."** *[Hosea 11:1]* ❖ *The prophecy originally referred to the people of Israel, but the Jews often interpreted the coming of the Messiah in terms of their ancestors' experience in coming out of Egypt.* ➤

The Slaughter in Bethlehem

16 When Herod realized that the astrologers had tricked him and were not returning, he was furious. Remembering the time that they said the star had first appeared, he ordered his soldiers to kill all the boys two years of age and younger in Bethlehem and the surrounding area.

17 This fulfilled Jeremiah's prophecy that says, 18 **"The sound of funeral songs A and wailing and mourning is heard in the village of Ramah. It's Rachel crying for her children. She refuses to be comforted because they are no longer alive."** *[Jeremiah 31:15]* ❖ *Ramah was a village five miles north of Jerusalem, which is in the same general area of Israel as Bethlehem (which is about six miles south of Jerusalem). David Stern says there is a place called Ramah just outside of Bethlehem where Rachel was buried. Rachel was Jacob's favorite wife*

A 2:18 Many manuscripts do not have "funeral songs and."

and symbolically is the mother of all Israelites or represented all Israelite mothers. She was buried near the village of Ephrath which was later called Bethlehem. [Genesis 35:19] The prophecy (made about 600 BC) was originally about the mourning for those whom the Babylonians took into captivity, but the Holy Spirit inspired Matthew to apply it to this situation. It's possible Jesus himself told his followers that this event was a fulfillment of this prophecy. [Luke 24:27, 44-45] ➤

Yosef and His Family Return from Egypt

19 A short time later, Herod died ❖ this happened in the Spring of 4 BC, probably within months of their fleeing to Egypt. ➤ and an angel appeared to Yosef in a dream, telling him, 20 "Get up and take the child and his mother back to Israel because the people who wanted to kill him are dead." ❖ Matthew only reports that Herod died, but the angel (or Matthew) may have used the plural to bring to mind the quote in Exodus 4:19 spoken to Moses. Matthew's Jewish readers would have noted the parallels between Jesus' and Moses' early lives. Herod's killing the children is parallel to Pharaoh's ordering the baby Israelite boys killed. Both were saved from that fate. Both fled to another country for safety. The Jews were expecting a great prophet like Moses. [Deuteronomy 18:15, 18] The parallels with Moses that Matthew points out in Jesus' life would prepare his Jewish readers to accept Jesus as that prophet. ➤ 21 So Yosef did as the angel said and returned to Israel with his family.

22 But when he heard that Herod's son, Archelaus, had become king over Judea after his father died, Yosef was afraid to settle there. After God warned him in another dream with further instructions, Yosef took them to Galilee. ❖ Archelaus ruled over the Roman provinces of Judea, Samaria, and Perea from 4 BC to AD 6. He was as cruel as his father had been, and the Romans deposed him. After Herod the Great died, his son Herod Antipas ruled Galilee province. We know from Luke 1:26 and 2:4 that Yosef and Miriam had lived in Nazareth in Galilee before Jesus was born. They probably had wanted to settle in Bethlehem since the people there would not know about Miriam's pregnancy before they were married, and living in Nazareth would be socially more difficult for that reason. ➤ 23 There they settled in the village of Nazareth. This fulfilled what the prophets said about the Messiah, "He will be called a Nazarene." ❖ (i.e., a person from Nazareth) We don't know where Matthew got this prophecy. Nazareth was an insignificant village that is never mentioned in the Hebrew Scriptures. Commentators have several suggestions to

explain Matthew's assertion. One of the better ones notes that Matthew writes that this was said about him through "the prophets," plural, and does not cite a particular prophet as he usually does. Nor does he introduce this with "saying," as he does other places when quoting the Scriptures. This suggests it is not a specific prophecy but a general teaching found in more than one place in the writings of the prophets. That teaching is that the Messiah was prophesied to be someone who was despised and rejected. [e.g., Psalm 22:6-7; Isaiah 53:3] Nazareth had a poor reputation, and Jews looked down on people who came from there. In Jesus' day, to call someone a "Nazarene" was an insult. This is hinted at in John 1:46 and Acts 24:5. Other attempts to explain this prophecy say that Matthew was pointing to the similarities of sound between "Nazareth" or "Nazarene" and some other word in Hebrew, like "netser" which means "branch" and is a title for the Messiah, [Jeremiah 23:5; 33:15; Zechariah 3:8; 6:12; Isaiah 11:1] or "nazirite" which is a class of people dedicated to God, [Numbers 6:1-21] , or "zera" which means "seed" or "descendant" and refers to the Messiah in Genesis 3:15; 21:12; and 22:18. ➤

3

John the Baptizer Prepares God's People to Receive the Messiah

1 About 30 years later—but while Jesus was still living in Nazareth—John the Baptizer started to preach in the Judean wilderness, west of the Dead Sea. His main message was, 2 "Turn away from sinning and start obeying God if you want to be part of his Kingdom. For he is establishing his rule in a new way among his people in this world." ❖ In the literal text, Matthew uses the phrase "Kingdom of Heaven" which is identical in meaning to Mark and Luke's "Kingdom of God." As a sign of respect, Jews of that time preferred to avoid saying the word "God" and often substituted "Heaven"—God's dwelling place—but meaning "God" himself. This is a figure of speech called "metonymy." ¶ John also literally said that "the Kingdom of Heaven has come near." The Kingdom of God is where God rules. Until the Messiah came, God was distant—approached only through priests and sacrifices—and ruled over his people through a covenant of laws. But the New Covenant—which God had promised to establish in Jeremiah 31:31-33—was now near in time, and God would now be near his people, ruling over them as an approachable loving Father through his indwelling Holy Spirit. ➤ 3 John was the one whom the prophet Isaiah referred to when he wrote, "A voice can be heard of someone in the

wilderness calling out to God's people, 'Prepare the way for the coming of Yahweh! Be prepared to welcome him properly.' " *[Isaiah 40:3]* ❖ *See the footnote at John 1:23. To prepare for Yahweh's coming and to welcome him properly means to repent, i.e., to turn away from sinning and to start obeying God, as in verse 2 above.* ➤ 4 Like the prophet Elijah hundreds of years earlier, John wore a leather belt and coarse clothing made from woven camel hair. *[2 Kings 1:8]* He lived in the wilderness as a poor ascetic, eating mainly locusts and wild honey. 5 Many people went out to the wilderness to hear him preach. They came from Jerusalem and everywhere else in Judea Province and also from the areas on both sides of the Jordan River. 6 Many publicly confessed their sins, and then John baptized them in the Jordan River. ❖ *Their confessions may have been a general admission that they were sinners rather than a detailed list of sins, but we don't know. Their confession of sin implies that they were seeking forgiveness from God, and in fact, John had promised that would happen. [Mark 1:4] Jews traditionally baptized Gentile converts but John was baptizing Jews who supposedly already had a relationship with the one true God. See the note at John 1:25. John's baptism for repentance was not the same as baptism in the name of Jesus that believers began to do after Jesus returned to Heaven. [Matthew 28:19; Acts 2:38; 8:16; 10:48; 18:25; Romans 6:3; Galatians 3:27; Colossians 2:11-12]* ➤

7 But when John noticed many Pharisees and Sadducees coming to be baptized, he lashed out at them, "You hypocritical sons of vipers! ❖ *The desert viper sometimes appeared harmless—looking like a stick—but was deadly. John meant that they pretended to be good but were, in fact, evil. Jews considered snakes to be cunning demonic creatures that led people astray. [Genesis 3:1-13; Job 20:16; Psalm 58:3-4; 140:1-3]* ➤ I find it hard to believe you are really admitting that *you,* like everyone else, need to repent and turn from your sins in order to escape God's righteous anger and judgment! ❖ *John knew that their coming to be baptized was not from a genuine desire to repent. Many Pharisees considered themselves entirely righteous and holy. They didn't recognize their own sins and so would not have publicly*

repented. Why were these Jewish leaders coming to be baptized when they clearly (as is seen elsewhere) didn't accept John as a genuine prophet from God? Probably because they knew the common people believed John was a prophet and they wanted to do the things people thought were proper to do to be "holy" and in a good relationship with God. It was all for appearance's sake. But after John denounced them, they more or less openly showed their contempt for him. ➤ 8 Well don't think that getting baptized without genuinely repenting will do you any good at all! True repentance must be demonstrated by the way you live. 9 Don't deceive yourselves by thinking, 'We are saved because Abraham is our ancestor and we are automatically God's favored people.' ❖ *This was the common assumption of many Jews at that time.* ➤ I assure you, God could make righteous descendants for Abraham from these stones. He doesn't need you to fulfill his plans and promises! 10 ❖ *John is now probably talking to the crowd in general, not just to the Pharisees and Sadducees.* ➤ God's judgment ax is poised at the roots of his trees, ❖ *i.e., the Jews* ➤ and every tree that doesn't bear good fruit as a result of true repentance he will cut down and throw into Hell's fire! *[Matthew 7:19; Luke 3:9]* ❖ *In the Hebrew Scriptures, trees are frequently used as a figure to show how God will punish evil people. [Isaiah 10:18-19, 33-34; Jeremiah 11:16-17; Ezekiel 31:2-18; Daniel 4:23-27]* 11 I only baptize you with water as a sign that you have turned away from your sins. But the Messiah—whose authority and power far exceed mine—is coming soon. He is so much greater than me that I'm not worthy to be his servant who unties his sandals. He will baptize you in the Holy Spirit who will purify you like fire purifies silver. ❖ *This could refer to painful trials and afflictions that God uses to purify us. [Isaiah 1:25; 4:4; Zechariah 13:9; Malachi 3:2] Alternately, many commentators believe the "and fire" in the literal text refers to a different baptism (i.e., immersion) of fire that is God's punishment for those who do not repent. [Isaiah 26:11; 66:15-16, 24]* ➤ 12 The Messiah will come with his winnowing **A** pitchfork of judgment, separating the righteous from the wicked, like people

---

A 3:12 A bundle of wheat was trampled by oxen or beaten (this is called "threshing") to loosen the inedible dry outer husk (called "chaff") from the wheat grains. Then a winnowing pitchfork was used to toss the wheat stalks into the air where the wind would blow the light-weight "chaff" away, and the wheat grains *(continued next page)* would fall to the ground. The seedless stalks would be removed, leaving only the edible wheat behind.

separate wheat from worthless chaff. Then he will clear the threshing floor of this world of all worthless chaff. He will gather the righteous 'wheat' in his barn in Heaven, but the wicked 'chaff' he will burn in Hell's eternal fire."

Jesus Comes to Be Baptized

13 About that time, Jesus came from Galilee to where John was in the Jordan River and asked to be baptized. 14 But John objected, "Why are you coming to be baptized as a sign of repentance when you don't need it? I should be asking you to baptize me instead!" 15 Jesus replied, "For the present, please do this for me as this is what God wants me to do." Then John agreed to do it. ❖ *Jesus was probably identifying with sinful humanity. [Isaiah 53:12] He may also have been repenting on behalf of the nation of Israel as a way of interces-sion as Daniel, Ezra, and Nehemiah did for sins that were not their own. [Daniel 9:4-19; Ezra 9:6-15; Nehemiah 1:5-11]* ➤

16 As soon as he was baptized, Jesus came out of the water and saw the heavens opened. *[Isaiah 64:1]* ❖ *Literally: "the heavens were opened to him." A few manuscripts lack "to him." The plural "heavens" is deliberate. See the note at 2 Corinthians 12:2.* ➤ He saw God's Spirit come down in the form of a dove and rest on him. ❖ *Luke 3:22 says the Spirit took the physical form of a dove. This event means that the Holy Spirit came upon Jesus in a way that he was not previously present. Many believe it was for the purpose of empowering his ministry and was similar to the baptism of the Holy Spirit his followers would later experience at Pentecost, after his return to Heaven. [Acts 1:1-5; 2:1-4, 38-39]* ➤ 17 Then God said, ❖ *apparently to everyone there* ➤ "This is my Son whom I love, and I'm very pleased with him." *[Isaiah 42:1]* ❖ *Matthew literally wrote "a voice out of the heavens" but Jews of that time would know he meant "God's voice." The phrase "whom I love" is literally, "the beloved" and some commentators think it's a Messianic title. In Psalm 2, which the Jews recognized as being about the Messiah, God calls his Messiah—the Anointed One— "my Son" in verse 7 and again as "the Son" in verse 12. Thus this verse is a proclamation that Jesus is the Messiah, as well as God's Son.* ➤

4

Satan Tempts Jesus

1 Immediately after coming upon Jesus, the Holy Spirit led him into the dangerous unpopulated highlands of the Judean wilderness so Satan could tempt him. 2 He stayed there 40 days without eating and at the end of that period he was hungry. ❖ *In the Scriptures, the number 40 is often figurative for a time of testing. [Deuteronomy 8:1-2; 1 Kings 19:4-8] But that doesn't mean he wasn't out there a full 40 days. The literal text says he was fasting, which implies it was a time of prayer and communion with God. Moses also fasted 40 days on the mountain. [Exodus 24:18; 34:28] Matthew often points out similarities between Jesus and Moses since Jesus is replacing the Moses as the final authority from God.* ➤ 3 Satan tempted him through his hunger, saying, "Since you are God's son, why not command these stones to become bread?" ❖ *The Greek word εἰ (ei), commonly translated here as "if" can also mean "since." Since demons elsewhere recognize who he is, Satan certainly does here. So it's unlikely he was trying to provoke Jesus to prove who he was. The temptation was to use God's power for his own needs and purposes without the direction of his Father. Jesus only did what his Father told him to do. [John 5:19]* ➤ 4 Jesus replied, "No, I won't. It is written in God's Torah that, **'People will not have true life by eating food, but by obeying everything Yahweh commands.'** " *[Deuteron-omy 8:3]* ❖ *"No, I won't" is not in the literal text but is clearly implied.* ➤ 5 Then Satan transported him to the holy city of Jerusalem onto the highest point of the Temple. ❖ *which was about 450 feet above the Kidron Valley below* ➤ 6 He said, "Since you are God's son, prove it to the people by jumping down from here. The Scriptures say you won't be harmed because, **'God will command his angels to guard you from harm. They will carry you in their arms to prevent even your foot from scraping on a stone.'** " *[Psalm 91:11-12]* ❖ *Satan easily quotes Scripture for his own purpose. The temptation may have been to make God prove his love, or to test God's word, or to prove to the people that he was more than a mere man.* ➤ 7 Jesus countered, "No, I won't. God's Torah also commands, **'Do not deliberately test the patience and promises of Yahweh, your God.'** *[Deuteronomy 6:16]* ❖ *In some way, this was a real temptation to Jesus. Note that he always countered*

Satan's temptations by quoting Scripture. See the note at Ephesians 6:17. ➤

8 Then Satan transported him to a high mountaintop and showed him all the kingdoms of the world in all their beauty and splendor. **9** He said, "I will give you all these kingdoms to rule if you will only bow down and submit to me in worship." ❖ *It was Satan's pride and desire to be like God that caused him to rebel in the first place. To have God's Son bow down to him in worship (which means in submission to him) would enable him to claim victory over God. He was offering Jesus a shortcut to becoming King over the world. He could offer it because he is the temporary "ruler of this world." [John 12:31]* ➤ **10** But Jesus replied, "Get out of here, Satan! God's Torah commands, **'Only worship and serve Yahweh, who is your God.'** " *[Deuteronomy 6:13]* ❖ *In the previous verses, the original text refers to Satan as "the devil." "Devil" comes from the Greek word* διάβολος *(diabolos) meaning "slanderer" or "false accuser." "Satan" comes from Hebrew and means "enemy" or "adversary." David Stern notes in his Jewish New Testament Commentary that Satan used the same three kinds of temptation with Eve in the Garden of Eden. 1) tempting the desires of the body (for Eve, the good fruit; for Jesus, food when he was hungry), 2) tempting the desires of the eye (for Eve, the attractiveness of the fruit; for Jesus, the splendor of the world), 3) the desire of self-aggrandizement (for Eve, the desire to be like God; for Jesus, the desire to have people recognize that he was God). Eve and Adam, the first man, did not resist these temptations, but Jesus, the "last Adam," did. [1 Corinthians 15:45-49] Also, the three texts Jesus quotes from the Torah were commands that God gave to the people of Israel when he tested them in the wilderness for 40 years. Unlike Israel at that time, Jesus— as Israel's representative, the Son of Man—kept those commands.* ➤ **11** So Satan left him, and angels came to provide for his needs.

Jesus Starts His Public Ministry in Galilee

12 After Jesus heard that Herod Antipas had arrested John the Baptizer, he returned to Galilee. ❖ *More about John's arrest can be found in Matthew 14:3-4; Mark 6:17-18; and Luke 3:19-20.* ➤ **13** But instead of basing in Nazareth where he had grown up, he moved 20 miles northeast to the much larger town of Capernaum on the north shore of Lake Galilee, in the region originally allotted to the Israelite tribes of Zebulun and Naphtali. *[Joshua 19:10-16, 32-39]* ❖ *Naphtali borders Lake Galilee, and Nazareth was in Zebulun. The tribal areas of Zebulun and Naphtali correspond*

roughly with the area known in Jesus' time as "Galilee." Lake Galilee is a freshwater lake with the Jordan River flowing into the north end and out at the south end. The lake is about seven miles wide by 13 miles long, very deep, and about 700 feet below sea level. It was traditionally called the "sea" of Galilee because the Greek word θάλασσα *(thalassa) means any large body of water, whether ocean, sea, or freshwater lake. Capernaum was on a major trade route and was a strategic center at which to base in the heavily populated Galilee Province. Capernaum means "Nahum's village."* ➤ **14** He did this to fulfill Isaiah's prophecy about the Messiah that says, **15** "**The people in Zebulun and Naphtali (on the way to the sea, west of the Jordan River, the region called "Galilee" where many Gentiles live) 16 live in spiritual darkness. But they will see the Messiah who, like a bright light, will reveal the way of salvation. He will shine the light of God's truth on those living in spiritual shadow and walking the road to eternal death.**" *[Isaiah 9:1-2]* ❖ *The original prophecy, written about 600 BC, is in the past tense. This simply indicated it was certain to happen, not that it had already happened when the prophet spoke it. The prophecy as quoted by Matthew doesn't match up with the Hebrew text as it exists today or with the Septuagint (the Greek translation of the Hebrew Scriptures). He may have used a different Hebrew manuscript or adjusted the quotation for his purpose, as Jewish teachers of his time often did. Commentators do not agree on what the phrase "on the way to the sea" means, or which sea (Galilee or the Mediterranean) that it refers to. They also do not agree what the phrase "across the Jordan" means. It depends on which side of the river the speaker is situated. In the New Testament, "across the Jordan" usually means the east side of the river, but Jesus spent relatively little time there. The interpretation above assumes the speaker is east of the Jordan, thus uniformly referring to the lands of Zebulun and Naphtali—later called Galilee—to the west of the Jordan on the way to the Mediterranean sea. Jesus did spend most of his ministry in Galilee, and in his time it contained many Gentile villages.* ➤

17 From then on, Jesus preached publicly and his core message was, "Turn away from your sinful ways and start obeying God if you want to be in his Kingdom. For he is establishing his rule among his people in a new way." ❖ *This would sound like a warning of imminent judgment to the Jews of his day.* ➤

Jesus Calls Four Fishermen to Be His Followers

18 One day while walking along the shore of Lake Galilee, Jesus saw two fishermen casting their net into the lake. One was Simon, who was later also called Peter, and the other was his younger brother Andrew. 19 Jesus called to them, "Come be my followers, and I will teach you how to catch people for God's Kingdom." 20 They immediately left behind their nets and livelihood as fishermen and became his followers. ❖ *Matthew gives no indication as to whether or not they knew Jesus before this. Such details were not important for his purpose. But it seems unlikely that they would have done what they did had he been a total stranger. "Followers" is traditionally rendered "disciples." It means that they were his students, companions, and apprentices. At that time, students usually chose their own teacher, but for his followers, Jesus did the choosing, just as God chooses who are to be his people.* ➤

21 A little further along the shore, Jesus saw two more brothers—James and John— in a boat working on their nets with their father Zebedee. He called to the two brothers. 22 Immediately, they left their father in the boat along with their livelihood and became his followers. ❖ *Luke 5:10 says that James and John were fishing partners with Simon and Andrew. Their cultural responsibility was to stay with their father, be submissive to him, and take care of him as long as he lived. Their leaving him put their status in the community at risk. But Jesus always demands loyalty to himself above that to family and cultural expectations.* ➤

Jesus Preaches and Heals in Galilee

23 Jesus traveled through every part of Galilee Province, teaching in the synagogues. He proclaimed the Good News that God was inviting people—who would submit to him—into his wonderful Kingdom. Wherever he went, he also healed people from every kind of sickness and disorder. 24 News about his ability to heal spread among the Jewish communities in Syria Province, north of Galilee. Many people were brought to him who were sick with all kinds of diseases, pain, and other disorders, including those who were demonized, epileptics, and those with paralysis. He healed all who were brought to him. 25 Because of this, a large crowd started following him wherever he went. They came from Galilee, from the Gentile Decapolis area southeast of Lake Galilee, from

Jerusalem and the rest of Judea Province, and from other areas on the eastern side of the Jordan River.

5

Jesus' Teaching on the Hillside

❖ *This is commonly referred to as the "Sermon on the Mount." Note that the Greek word ὄρος (oros) can mean either "hill" or "mountain." It doesn't distinguish between these as English does. And having been to the traditional location, it is more of a hillside than a mountain.* ➤

1 One day, Jesus saw a crowd following him so he headed up a hill. He sat down to teach, and his regular followers came to sit near him. ❖ *Jewish rabbis generally sat while they taught.* ➤ 2 He taught them these things: ❖ *In 5:3—7:27 Jesus is mainly speaking to his committed followers, describing how citizens of God's Kingdom must live. There is no message about repenting, which he included when teaching the general public. But there were many others listening in as well. We don't know if this is the complete message he gave on this occasion or if it's just a summary.* ➤

3 "Those who humbly recognize their own spiritual poverty and have renounced all desire for riches in this world in order to seek God and his help are indeed in his good favor. They are already citizens of his Kingdom. ❖ *To some, being in God's Kingdom may not sound attractive. Consider all that is good and enjoyable in this world. All of that will be even greater in his Kingdom. If you have the idea that being in his Kingdom implies restriction and no fun, you've got the wrong picture. It's pure joy.* ➤

4 "Those who turn to God when they're sad or grieving are in his good favor because he has promised to comfort them. [Isaiah 61:2] ❖ *The Greek word μακάριος (makarios) is usually translated "blessed," mainly because many translators think a single word in the Greek must be translated by a single word in English, so "blessed" is the best choice of those available. Some translators say that this word means "happy," but they ignore the fact that context determines the precise meaning a word has. Another meaning assigned to this word is "fortunate." It's not the point of this passage that God has already blessed people who have these attitudes (which is why some translators want to move away from "blessed"). And it should be obvious that people who are poor (in spirit or otherwise), or hungry (whether physically or spiritually), or mourning, or who are being persecuted are probably not "happy." "Fortunate" can be misinterpreted to mean "lucky" which implies chance and ignores the fact that God is in*

control of all circumstances. So "in God's good favor" (i.e., their attitudes or situation put them in a position where God favors them and wants to bless them) is an attempt to clarify the sense in which such people are "blessed." ➤

5 "Those who humbly depend on God to take care of their rights as he sees fit—instead of asserting themselves—are in his good favor. For they will certainly receive all he has promised, which includes a position of authority in his Kingdom on the New Earth. *[Psalm 37:11]* ❖ *The original Psalm focused on inheriting the land of Israel, but Jesus was focusing on those who will ultimately obtain a position of authority in God's Kingdom. It won't be those who are aggressive and self-assertive in this life, contrary to human expectations.* ➤

6 "Those who continually yearn to please God by living the way he wants them to live are in his good favor. For he will help them do it, and their desires will certainly be satisfied.

7 "Those who routinely demonstrate compassion, mercy, leniency, and kindness to others are in God's good favor. For he will treat them the same way, both in this life and on Judgment Day.

8 "Those who are completely dedicated to God and keep their thoughts undividedly devoted to him are indeed in his good favor. *[Psalm 24:3-5]* ❖ *It literally says "pure in heart" instead of "keep their thoughts undividedly devoted to him." But to Hebrews, the heart was the center of thinking, not emotions. Purity of heart referred to singleness of devotion, not moral purity—as our culture would interpret the expression. Also "to see God" in the literal text, or "to see his face" in the Hebrew Scriptures meant to "have his favor." When you could "see his face," he was paying attention to you because he was pleased with you.* ➤

9 "Those who strive to promote peace and harmony are in God's good favor, for he will call them his children.

10 "Those who are unjustly persecuted because they strive to please God are indeed in his good favor, for they are already citizens of his Kingdom. *[1 Peter 3:14]*

11 "Those of you who are verbally abused, badly treated, and falsely accused of doing all kinds of evil because you are trying to be faithful to me, are very much in God's good favor. *[1 Peter 4:14]* 12 You should be thrilled and joyfully exult because you can be sure that God has a great reward waiting for you in Heaven. *[James 1:2]* The actions of your persecutors prove you are his faithful servants. You are in good company. Consider that he allowed people to persecute his favored prophets in the same way, long ago." *[2 Chronicles 36:16; Acts 7:52]*

God's People
Are Meant to Attract Others to Him

13 Speaking to his followers, Jesus continued, "You are the expression of God's wisdom for others in this world to see. But if you become morally foolish, you will be worthless for his purpose. He will expel you from his Kingdom, and people will abuse you. ❖ *The meaning of the salt metaphor in the literal text is debated, with commentators offering several possible interpretations. The Greek verb often translated "lose its flavor" can also mean "were to become foolish." So salt can be a figure for "wisdom" and some Jewish writings use it that way. [See Colossians 4:6] Another possible meaning of "salt" is "a preserving and saving influence." Some believe that it's impossible for a true believer to become worthless and be expelled from God's kingdom, just like it's impossible for real salt to lose its saltiness. But Jesus is clearly giving a warning here with this figure, not reassurance.* ➤ 14 You are God's light to humanity, revealing his truth and way of salvation. *[Isaiah 42:6; 49:6; John 8:12; 9:5]* It's impossible to hide a city that was built on a hill. Nor can you hide the fact that you are different from unbelievers because your character displays the light of God's truth. 15 No one lights a lamp and then hides its light under a covering. Instead they elevate it to illuminate the entire room. ❖ *First-century Jewish houses were typically only one room.* ➤ God wants everyone to see your light, so don't try to hide it. 16 Let people see that you are different and help them to understand the truth that you know. Then they will see the good things you do and praise your Heavenly Father for them."

Jesus' View of Moses' Teachings

17 Jesus said, "Never think that God sent me to disobey, reject, weaken, or abolish the Teachings of Moses ❖ *i.e., the commands and teachings in the first five books of the Hebrew Scriptures, written by Moses* ➤ or any of the rest of the Hebrew Scriptures. ❖ *He said this because people had seen him reject some of the Pharisees' teachings that were incorrect interpretations of the Torah's intent. He healed*

on the Sabbath, which the Pharisees condemned as illegal work. He also refused to ritually wash his hands before eating, which they insisted righteous people must do. So Jesus taught the correct way to understand the Torah's teachings. He submitted to them completely in the way that God intended them to be followed. This also means that while Jesus is not recorded as having explicitly taught on some subjects, he fully agreed that everything in the Torah and Old Testament Scriptures was still God's will and he intended for his followers to follow those teachings. ➤ My purpose is to keep them, fulfill them, explain them, and make them more completely and correctly established among God's people. Yes, may it be so! ❖ *Six senses in which he "fulfilled" the Torah and the other Scriptures are: 1) He kept all God's commands perfectly, thus showing he believed that they taught God's will. 2) He fulfilled all the prophecies about his first coming and will fulfill the rest in his second coming. 3) He came to fulfill all of God's promises to his people, especially those about providing a way of salvation. The remaining promises he will fulfill at his second coming. 4) He explained the proper meaning of God's commands, especially in so far as the Jews of his time had misunderstood them. 5) He completed God's teachings in the Torah and other Scriptures by filling in any remaining details of God's will for humanity. He did this in his teaching, some of which is recorded in the Gospels, and some of which he passed on to his apostles who passed it on to us in the epistles (Paul's letters) and in the book of Revelation. 6) He fulfilled some of the Torah's requirements in such a way that some teachings were changed. For example, he fulfilled the requirement for a sacrifice to remove sin. Therefore, the regulations pertaining to animal sacrifices for sin have been fulfilled and are no longer applicable. Not because God's will changed—it didn't—but because it was forever fulfilled in Jesus' death and resurrection. Jesus' teaching now reveals the way to continue to obey God's will in obtaining forgiveness, and that is to trust that Jesus' finished sacrifice is sufficient. The next verses clarify that God's Torah—as Jesus explained, amended, and fulfilled it—is still valid. Keeping its commands is not a means of salvation, as some Jews of his time thought. It never was. But it teaches the proper response for saved people who want to please their Savior. Those who disregard the Torah and its teachings, disregard God's revealed will for his people. It's not a legalistic way to attain righteousness, but it is the way God wants his people to live. In fact, the entire New Testament and the rest of the Hebrew Scriptures are an integral part of God's amended "Torah," which means "teaching."* ➤ 18 I'm telling you an important truth when I say that until all of God's purposes are accomplished and the current Heaven and Earth disappear, not even a single letter in the ❖ *amended* ➤ Torah will be invalidated or abolished. *[Luke 16:17; 2 Peter 3:10-13; Revelation 21:1]* 19 Therefore, those who disregard even the least important of God's commands in the Scriptures and also teach others to disregard them will have the lowest status in God's Kingdom. But those who keep all of God's commands and teach others to obey them will have the highest status in Heaven. 20 And I'm warning you that your righteousness needs to far exceed that of the Pharisees and Scripture teachers or you will never even enter God's Kingdom." ❖ *This is because the righteousness of these Jewish leaders was based on a legalistic outward keeping of the Torah's commands, which Jesus elsewhere teaches is no righteousness at all. Only people having God's righteousness—which he gives to those who trust and obey Jesus—will enter Heaven. Since Jesus' listeners considered the Pharisees and Scripture teachers to be among the most holy people alive, Jesus' statement would have shocked them and caused them to inquire why.* ➤

The Importance of Good Relationships

21 "For example, you know that long ago Moses told our ancestors that God commanded, **'Never commit murder. The court will sentence murderers to death.'** *[Exodus 20:13; Deuteronomy 5:17; 17:8-13]* ❖ *He meant murder or any kind of illegal killing by individuals, not all kinds of killing. God himself commanded that people be executed for certain crimes. [Exodus 19:13; 21:12, 15-17, 29; 22:19; 31:14-15; 32:27-28; 35:2; Leviticus 19:20; 20:2, 9-16, 27; 24:16-17, 21, 23; Numbers 1:51; 3:10, 38; 15:35-36; 18:7; 35:16-21, 30-31; Deuteronomy 13:5-10; 17:6, 12; 18:20; 22:22, 25; 24:7, 16; Joshua 7:15, 25] Those legally executing the death sentence are not committing murder. God also commanded Israel's armies to kill and they were not committing murder. [e.g., Numbers 21:34-35; 31:1-17; Joshua 6:2, 21, 24; 8:1-2, 18-26; 10:8-10; 11:6-8] The Apostle Paul also taught that governments have God's authority to use deadly force to punish and defend. [Romans 13:1-5]* ➤ 22 But I'm telling you that the intent of this command is much broader. Even being angry with someone {without a righteous cause} **A** makes you guilty of this sin. And if

---

A **5:22** Many manuscripts lack these words, but most commentators think that they're implied anyway.

Jesus himself was angry with those who sold goods in the court of the Gentiles in the Temple, and with

your anger leads you to insult someone, the Heavenly court will find you guilty on Judgment Day. If you are so angry that you curse someone and say that they deserve to go to Hell, then you are in danger of God sending *you* there. 23 Therefore, if you are about to offer God a sacrifice and you remember that someone is still angry with you, 24 you must first reconcile with that person before God will accept your offering. *[Proverbs 15:8; Isaiah 1:10-15; Jeremiah 6:20; Amos 5:21-24]* So put your sacrifice aside and go get right with that person. Then God will accept your sacrifice.

25-26 "Be reconciled with those you've wronged as soon as possible, before they sue you. If they haul you into court, it will be too late. The judge may sentence you to prison until you have paid the judgment in full. Consequences for not reconciling with people can be severe, both with God and people. ❖ *Jesus used this same illustration in Luke 12:57-59 where the emphasis is on reconciling with God before Judgment Day. Here, the focus is on reconciling with those you've wronged before it's too late to avoid earthly consequences.* ➤

Thoughts Are as Important as Actions

27 "You know that the Torah commands, **'Never commit adultery.'** *[Exodus 20:14; Deuteronomy 5:18]* ❖ *Adultery involves a sexual relationship where at least one of the persons is married. It's more serious than fornication—where both persons are unmarried— because adultery breaks a vow of faithfulness to one's spouse. Marriage is meant to illustrate Jesus' spiritual relationship with his people. [Ephesians 5:25-32] So he views violations of marriage vows as corrupting something holy that he created for his own purposes.* ➤ 28 But I'm telling you that this command's true intent is much broader. If a person merely desires sex with someone else's spouse, it violates this command. In God's view, that person has already committed adultery in his or her mind. 29 You must understand the seriousness of sin. If your stronger eye entices you to sin, you would actually be better off getting rid of it than to keep it and end up in Hell. 30 Even if your dominant hand entices you to sin, you would still be better

off getting rid of it than to end up in Hell. *[Mark 9:43-47; Matthew 18:8-9]* ❖ *Jesus didn't think that eyes or hands are real sources of sinful desires. His point is that sin is serious and you should do whatever is necessary to avoid it. No option is too extreme if it enables you to avoid Hell."* ➤

God's View of Divorce

31 "Interpreters of the Torah say that a man who divorces his wife must give her documentary proof that he releases her from her marriage vows. *[Deuteronomy 24:1]* ❖ *With this, she could prove that her divorce was legal and could marry again. In that culture, an unmarried woman would find it difficult to live on her own since she could not own land. Without the ability to remarry (and no one would do so without proof she was no longer legally married) she would become destitute. A man could easily divorce his wife but a woman could not divorce her husband. Jewish teachers pointed to Deuteronomy 24:1 as saying that the Torah allowed such a divorce. But a careful look at Deuteronomy 24:1-4 shows that the Torah does not say this is what a man should do, nor does it give overt permission for him to do so. The Torah allows divorce in this manner only in the sense that it doesn't expressly prohibit this practice, which existed before God gave the Torah. The passage assumes that the man divorces his wife due to her being "indecent" which implies adultery (based on Jesus' teaching in verse 32 below). The point of legislation in Deuteronomy 24:4 prohibits the first husband from remarrying the same woman after she has been married to someone else, even if her second husband dies. This would be a perversion in God's sight because she is defiled. Yet many Jewish Rabbis pointed to this passage and allowed divorce for almost any reason, as did the Romans. In Jesus' time, there were two schools of thought on how to interpret "indecent" in Deuteronomy 24:1. One school—headed by Rabbi Shammai—thought it implied adultery, and the other school— headed by Rabbi Hillel—interpreted it to mean almost any reason the man found the wife unsatisfactory. To use this passage as divine permission for divorce (as long as a certificate is issued) was a wrong interpretation of its intent. They also had Malachi 2:16 and Deuteronomy 22:13-19 to help them interpret it.* ➤ 32 But I'm telling you that a man who divorces his wife causes her to commit adultery when she remarries, unless he divorced her because she was already guilty of adultery. And a man that marries such a divorced woman will also commit

---

the Pharisees. So it's possible to be angry and not sin. [Ephesians 4:26]

adultery." ❖ *A marriage is still binding in God's sight—even if the couple has legally divorced—unless one of the partners has broken the marriage vow of faithfulness. This means that the man also commits adultery if he remarries and his first wife is innocent of adultery. Note that this passage, which allows divorce under the circumstance of adultery, does not encourage it. In the Hebrew Scriptures, God portrayed his relationship with Israel as a marriage. He likened their worshipping other gods to adultery, yet God always pleaded with his adulterous "wife" to come back to him. This shows that God strongly prefers forgiveness and restoration of the relationship over divorce, even in the case of adultery. [e.g. Jeremiah 3:6-22; Ezekiel 16:8-63; 20:27-30; Hosea 1:2-9; 2:14-23; 4:15; 5:3; 9:1-9; 11:1-11; 14:1-7] Also see the footnote at 1 Corinthians 7:11.* ➤

Always Speak Truthfully Without Invoking Oaths

33 "You know that God's Torah commands, 'Do not break your oaths. Any oath you have made—invoking God as a witness—he expects you to tell truthfully and keep.' [Exodus 20:7; Leviticus 19:12]** ❖ *Commentators are divided on what Jesus meant. Some say it only refers to invoking God as a witness to the truthfulness of what you say (meaning he will punish you if you lie). This view goes well with verses 35-37 that follow. Most believe this does not apply to oaths in court since the High Priest put Jesus under oath, and he didn't object. [Matthew 26:63-64] Others say it can also refer to vows made to God. [Numbers 30:2; Deuteronomy 23:21, 23]* ➤ **34** But I'm saying that you shouldn't make any kind of oath at all to convince others that you are telling the truth. Even swearing 'by Heaven' does not avoid invoking God since Heaven is where he rules as King. So don't do it. [Isaiah 66:1] 35** And don't swear by the Earth for it's his footstool, or by Jerusalem for it's his capital city. **36** Don't even swear by your own head for you lack the power to turn even one gray hair black again. **37** Just speak truthfully and say what you mean. Any additional oath you invoke to appear truthful is inspired by evil." [James 5:12]** ❖ *"Evil" could refer to Satan, known as the "Evil One," or to evil intentions. The practice of using oaths was often abused, with the belief that in an improperly made oath—that the listener didn't catch was improper—it was acceptable to lie and God would not punish the person making it. Jesus' command is that everything we say should be true and binding because God holds us accountable for all that we say. [Matthew 12:36-37]* ➤

Demonstrating Self-Sacrificial Love

38 "You know that God's Torah commands, 'Don't give out punishments that are excessive or unjust. A punishment's severity should match the crime. If the offender caused the loss of an eye, put out one of his. If he knocked out a tooth, knock out one of his.' [Exodus 21:24; Leviticus 24:20; Deuteronomy 19:21]** ❖ *This referred to official court-imposed sentences and was meant to limit the harshness of punishment. In ancient times, even minor crimes were often punished by slavery or death.* ➤ **39** But I say that God has shown you extreme favor and mercy—which you didn't deserve—by forgiving your sins and saving you. So he wants you to go beyond the idea of merely seeking justice for those who wrong you. He wants you to be merciful and *not* seek legal action against them. [Romans 12:19] If someone insults you by slapping your right cheek, offer him the other cheek to slap too, showing you will not retaliate. [Luke 6:29]** ❖ *In that culture, a slap was the greatest possible insult and was prosecutable under both Roman and Jewish law. This verse refers to retaliation by legal means. Jesus' listeners already knew that the Torah prohibits all personal revenge and that all vengeance belongs to God. [Leviticus 19:18; Deuteronomy 32:35, 43] This is also made clear in Romans 12:18-20 and Hebrews 10:30.* ➤ **40** If someone sues you for the clothes off your back, voluntarily give him everything you have. ❖ *The text literally talks about a tunic and an outer robe. Someone suing you for your tunic implies you have nothing more valuable to sue for. The opponent could not legally sue for a person's outer robe. Even the poorest person had the right to keep that garment, which was more valuable than a tunic and was more important for keeping warm. If your opponent took your tunic and you gave him your robe, you would literally own nothing but the skin on your back. Jesus' illustration is hyperbole (exaggeration to make a point). Offering more than your opponent demands shows that he has no power over you because you are trusting God to take care of you. It also demonstrates how much you are willing to sacrifice in order to show him God's love. Don't gloss over this command. Are you really willing to obey it?* ➤ **41** If someone forces you to do something, don't resist or do it grudgingly. Instead, demonstrate God's love by cheerfully doing much more than required. ❖ *Roman soldiers could legally demand that a civilian carry something for a certain distance, perhaps the one Roman mile mentioned in* the literal text (which was 1,000 paces, or 4,854 feet). An example of this is when Simon of Cyrene was forced to carry the crossbeam to Jesus' cross. [Matthew 27:32; Mark 15:21; Luke 23:26] The point Jesus made goes beyond this situation. It is the principle of demonstrating self-sacrificial love by submitting and doing more than required. ➤ **42** Give to those in need who ask you for help and don't be reluctant to lend to those who—from genuine need—ask to borrow from you.

❖ i.e., Don't be reluctant to lend because you think they won't return what they borrow. Beggars and the extremely poor were common at that time. [Deuteronomy 15:9-11; Psalm 112:5, 9; Proverbs 19:17; 21:13; 22:9] These Scriptures make it clear that Jesus was referring to people in genuine need. He doesn't require that you give to everyone who asks, even if they have no need. His point is to be generous and not horde your possessions just so you can live more comfortably. He doesn't mean to give away all you have to the detriment of your dependents. Yet this implies more than giving only out of your plentiful surplus. If you have basic shelter, clothing, and food, anything beyond that is not a "need." [1 Timothy 6:8] You should be willing to give anything you have beyond those basics to help those in genuine need. So if you tie up all your excess wealth in expensive homes, cars, clothing, food, and luxuries, and therefore don't have any money available to help the needy, you are not properly using the resources God gave you. The level of generosity that you show others will be reflected in the rewards that God gives you in Heaven. [Luke 6:38] Also see the note at Luke 19:26. ➤

43 "You know that the Torah commands you to, **'Love your neighbor,'** [Leviticus 19:18] and that others teach it's OK to hate your enemies. ❖ There is no explicit command in the Scriptures to "hate your enemies." [Proverbs 25:21-22] Yet that attitude was allowed and in some sense encouraged. [e.g. Deuteronomy 30:7; Psalm 18:37-42; 55:15; 59:10-13; 69:22-25; 70:2; 71:13; 109:6-20; 137:8-9; 139:19-22; 143:12; Jeremiah 11:20; 15:17; 17:18; 18:23; 20:12] Though in all these verses the writer is asking God to take action against the enemies, rather than taking vengeance himself. These passages do not encourage individuals to take revenge but, rather, to depend on God to do so. In general, Jews would have considered other Jews as their "neighbors" and Gentiles as their "enemies." It was also a common Semitic idiom that "hate" meant "to love less" in a comparison, [e.g. Malachi 1:2-3; Luke 14:26; Romans 9:13] so it's possible Jesus was using it in that sense, i.e., that some teach it's OK to love your enemies less than your neighbors. ➤ **44** But I'm saying that you should treat everyone as if they were your neighbor. Therefore, you should demonstrate love to your enemies by {asking God to bless those who curse you, by doing good to those who hate you, [Luke 6:27-28] and by} **A** praying for those who {deliberately mistreat and} persecute you. **45** For God the Father expects his redeemed sons and daughters to live this way, reflecting his character. ❖ Jesus was not excluding females when he said "sons" in the literal text. In that culture, sons inherited wealth from their father and daughters did not. That's why in other places the Scriptures say you will be a "son"—even if you are female—for it means you will be an heir. [Galatians 3:28-29] ➤ God's way is to generously provide sunshine and rain not only for his own people but also for those who reject him. **46** Do you think God will reward you when you only show love to those likely to love you back? Certainly not! Even tax collectors—whom you despise—do that much. ❖ Tax collectors were hated as traitors because they oppressed their own people—getting rich from extorted excess taxes—and they collaborated with their Roman conquerors. ➤ **47** Do you think God will count it in your favor if you only have friendly greetings for your own people? **B** Everyone does that much, even pagans. **C** ❖ Jesus implied that God doesn't give Heavenly rewards for ordinary kindnesses that all people naturally do for their loved ones. But he does reward those who demonstrate love to the "unlovable." Note that he doesn't say that you have to "feel" love before you show it. It is not hypocritical to do loving deeds for others when you don't feel love for them, because it is God in you who is doing it and in doing so you are obeying him. ➤ **48** God the Father expects you to love everyone with undivided devotion to him, just as his love is perfect."

❖ "Perfectly," in the literal text, does not mean "sinless

A **5:44** The sections in { } are in many Greek manuscripts but not in many others. Most scholars believe they weren't were a part of the original text. But the first is in Luke and the second is contained within the meaning of "persecution" so they are validly Jesus' teaching.

B **5:47a** Most manuscripts have "brothers" (instead of "own people") which in this context meant "fellow Jews," but some manuscripts have "friends." The point is the same.

C **5:47b** Most manuscripts have "Gentiles," instead of "pagans," but some manuscripts have "tax collectors." The point is the same.

perfection." It means "with undivided devotion to God"
which results in self-sacrificial love for the undeserving,
without discrimination.

6

How to Gain Heavenly Rewards

1 "When you pray, fast, give to the poor, or serve in other ways, make sure that your motive is not to have others notice how 'spiritual' you are. For if your goal is a good reputation, then your Heavenly Father will not reward you for such deeds. ❖ *It's implied that God will reward his people for doing these things from the proper motives of loving others and wanting to please him.* ➤ 2 So when you help the poor, don't draw attention to yourself. Those who publicly display their 'generosity' in the synagogue and elsewhere are hypocrites. Any human approval they obtain for their piety is all the reward they will get. 3 When you help those in need, don't tell anyone what you are doing, not even your close friends. ❖ *Commentators agree that the expression in the literal text "don't let your left hand know what your right hand is doing" was an idiom with the meaning just given. It might, however, be necessary to be open with your spouse about such things.* ➤ 4 You should hide your generosity from others for then God the Father, who sees everything, will {openly} A reward you in Heaven. ❖ *Some commentators say we shouldn't be motivated by eternal rewards when we give. We are supposed to do it out of pure love. But Jesus here encourages us to be secretively generous in order to please God who will reward us. Wanting to please God is a pure motive.* ➤ 5 "And don't make a display of your prayers, like those hypocrites do while standing in the synagogue or other public places. The only reward they will get is the public attention they crave. 6 But you should go where you are alone when you pray to your invisible Heavenly Father. Then he, who sees everything, will reward you for your prayers.

7 "Don't pray like pagans do, who think long repetitive prayers of empty flowery phrases will get their deity's attention. 8 Your Father knows what you need and wants to help you even before you ask, so don't be like them.

9 "Pray simply, like this and for these kinds of things: Our Heavenly Father, cause more and more people to honor your name 10 and submit to your Kingship. Cause your will to be carried out in this world as perfectly as it's followed in Heaven. 11 Provide us with today's food and necessities. 12 Forgive our sins in the same way that we've forgiven those who've wronged us. 13 Help us to resist temptation, and rescue us from the power and influence of evil. B {For you are the great eternal and glorious King who has power over everything. Yes, may it be so!"} C

14 Jesus continued, "Be aware that if you forgive others who wrong you, then your Heavenly Father will also forgive you. 15 But if you refuse to forgive someone, then your Father will also refuse to forgive you. *[Mark 11:25-26]* ❖ *This is a serious warning. If God does not forgive you, you will not enter Heaven. See Luke 17:3-6 and the note at verse 6 on how to forgive others.* ➤ 16 When you fast in order to help your prayers, D don't draw attention to what you are doing. Those who make it obvious that they're

---

A **6:4** Some manuscripts have "openly," but most do not.

B **6:13a** Or: the Evil One, i.e., Satan.

C **6:13b** The section in { } is not in the older manuscripts. Scholars assume it was added for use in liturgical worship.

D **6:16** Fasting is a spiritual discipline that Jesus expects all his people to practice. [Matthew 6:16-18; 9:15; Mark 2:19-20; Luke 5:34-35] God commands us to fast. [Joel 2:12] Moses fasted, [Exodus 34:28] Daniel fasted, [Daniel 9:3] the believers in the first century fasted, and Jesus fasted. [Matthew 4:2; Luke 4:2] Fasting helps us in our prayers in various ways. It makes us more sensitive to discerning God's will and more resistant to temptation. When Jesus fasted in the wilderness after his baptism, he knew his father's will and was able to resist Satan's temptations. Fasting is a way to prepare for doing God's work [Matthew 4:1-2] or to prepare us to pray for those who do God's work. [Acts 13:3; 14:23] Prayer and fasting is a way to worship. When fasting, you demonstrate that your desire to meet with God in prayer exceeds your desire to eat, and this pleases him. [Luke 2:36-37; Acts 13:2] It's a way to humble ourselves so he will answer our prayers, [Psalm 69:10-13; 109:24-26] especially prayers for others. [Psalm 35:13; Isaiah chapter 58] When we fast and pray on behalf of others, he will also help us. [Isaiah 58:11-12] We should fast when we need guidance for ourselves, for our family,

fasting are hypocrites. I guarantee you that the only reward they will get is the notice of those they're trying to impress. 17 When you fast, groom yourself to appear as you normally do 18 so others won't notice anything unusual. But your invisible Heavenly Father who sees everything will reward you for it.

19 "Don't waste your time amassing riches in this world where they can be stolen or destroyed in various ways. *[James 5:2-3]* 20 Instead, you should invest your time and effort in accumulating wealth in Heaven that you can enjoy for eternity. Such wealth can't be stolen or destroyed. 21 And unlike accumulating earthly wealth, it's good to accumulate the eternal kind. For if this is your focus, your heart and mind will be in the right place.

22 "Your desires reveal your true self. If you desire to please God by demonstrating love and generosity to others, then you will truly understand and serve him. 23 But if you have divided loyalties and are distracted from God by desires for earthly wealth, you cannot understand or serve him. ❖ *The literal figure given in verses 22-23 rarely communicates to modern audiences. A good or sound or "single" eye (i.e., an eye focused on one thing) was a figure meaning generosity. A bad or "divided" eye (i.e., one focused on more than one thing) was a figure meaning stinginess. Light represents knowledge and understanding of truth, especially in relation to God. The body is the person. The ancients believed that an eye provided light for seeing, like a lamp, not that it took light in. An eye focused on one thing (on pleasing God) provided understanding of him, so one could serve him.* ➤ 24 No one can serve two masters at the same time. For he will either hate the first and love the second, or the other way around. So you have to choose between loving and serving God with your money, or loving money and acquiring it for your own purposes. You can't do both." *[Luke 16:13]*

The Proper Attitude Toward Possessions

25 "So what I'm telling you is this: Don't worry about having enough to eat or drink or having decent clothes to wear because there are much more important things in this life than food and clothing. 26 Consider birds. They neither plant nor harvest crops and don't store food. Yet God sees to it that they eat what they need. You are much more valuable to God than birds, so he will certainly provide for your needs. 27 All the worrying in the world can't add a single moment to your life, so why bother?

28 "Why worry about what you will wear? Consider how wildflowers grow. They don't work or make their beautiful adornment. 29 But not even King Solomon in all his splendor looked as good as they do. 30 Think about it. If God so beautifully clothes the grass in the fields with wildflowers, even though it grows for only a short time and then is cut and burned, he will certainly provide *you* with clothing! Your faith in God's provision is too small!

31 "Don't worry about what you will eat, drink, and wear today or tomorrow. 32 Those who don't know God worry about such things. But you have a Heavenly Father who knows you need them. 33 So submit to him and mainly be concerned about the affairs of his Kingdom and about what he requires you to do for him. Do that, and he will provide you with the necessities. 34 Don't worry about what might happen tomorrow or whether or not your needs will be met. Tomorrow is in God's hands. There are enough problems to be concerned about today without anticipating tomorrow's too, for every day has its own set." ❖ *Jesus didn't mean that we shouldn't make plans for the future. He was exhorting us not to worry about things beyond our control. Those things are in God's hands and he will take care of us.* ➤

---

or for what to do with our money and resources. [Judges 20:26-28; Ezra 8:21-23] We should fast when we intercede for a group of people or for a country. [2 Chronicles 20:3; Esther 4:1-3, 16; Daniel 9:3] We should fast when praying for someone who's sick. [2 Samuel 12:15-22] We must fast and pray if a demon refuses to leave a person when commanded. [Matthew 17:21; Mark 9:29] Fasting is also a way to show repentance. [1 Samuel 7:5-6; 1 Kings 21:27-29; Nehemiah 1:4-7; 9:1-2; Jonah 3:5-10] But God will not be impressed with our fasting if we are not also obeying him. [Jeremiah 14:12; Zechariah 7:1-13]

7

Jesus Forbids Us to Criticize or Condemn Others

1 Jesus continued, "Don't criticize or condemn others, or else God will do the same to you. ❖ *This doesn't mean that we don't recognize wrong actions. But we don't take it upon ourselves to criticize them in person or to other people, or punish them, except in cases when we have legitimate responsibility to do so such as with our children or employees. But in those cases, it must be done in a loving manner to help them, not to put them down. When we recognize that someone has done wrong, we should pray for them to realize it and repent. Only if you have an appropriate relationship with that person should you go to them in humility and love to talk about it. If you are unwilling to do that or don't have an appropriate relationship, you should keep your thoughts to yourself.* ➤ 2 The same manner and attitude you have toward others is how God will treat you. He will judge you by your own standards and will give back to you the harshness or mercy that you show others. *[Matthew 18:23-35]* 3 Why do you fixate on the speck of sin in another's life but ignore your own major sin of pride? 4 You should be afraid to tell someone, 'Allow me to point out the small sin I see in your life and help you get rid of it,' when you refuse to recognize your own major sins. 5 If you do this, you are a self-righteous hypocrite! First remove pride and other major sins from your own life and then you will have the necessary humility and sensitivity to help others with small sins in their lives. ❖ *Jesus' original illustration was of a speck of dirt in your brother's eye, and a log in your own. The eye is the most sensitive part of our body. When we do correct others, we must be sure that we aren't being self-righteous and failing to recognize our own faults. We must also be careful not to hurt the person we're trying to help, just as we would take great care in removing something from their eye. We must be loving and not act superior.* ➤ 6 But on the other hand, be wise in how you approach people who are vicious or content in their sinful lifestyles. Don't share holy and valuable truths with people who will despise them or turn on you.

We Often Don't Have Because We Haven't Bothered to Ask

7 "When you ask God for something you need, persist in asking and at the proper time he will give it. Never give up seeking him, and you will find him. Persist in knocking on his door in prayer, and he will open it to you. 8 He will give to everyone who asks. No exceptions. Everyone who seeks long enough will find what he is seeking. And the door will open for everyone who persists in knocking. 9 You fathers, if your little boy asks you for bread, would you give him a stone? 10 Or if he asks you for a fish, would you give him a poisonous snake? 11 If you want to give good things to your children, even though you are sinners, you can be certain that your Heavenly Father wants to give good things to his children who ask for them.

12 "So the kind and loving things you would like people to do for you, you should do for them first. For this is the essence of God's teachings in the Torah and the rest of the Hebrew Scriptures. *[Luke 6:31]*

Relatively Few Find the Way to Heaven

13 "You need to enter Heaven through the narrow and difficult way, which most people reject or choose to ignore. ❖ *This narrow "gate," in the literal text, is faith in Jesus as the Messiah which results in repentance and obeying him.* ➤ The obvious and easy-to-find way that many think leads to Heaven is broad and attractive, but it leads to destruction in Hell. ❖ *See the note at 2 Thessalonians 1:9 on "destruction in Hell."* ➤ Many chose that way. ❖ *The easy and broad way is doing your own thing, believing whatever you want to believe and not caring that it doesn't match up with God's revelation about Jesus in the Scriptures.* ➤ 14 But relatively few make the effort to find the narrow way that leads to eternal life. *[Luke 13:24]*

Beware of False Religious Teachers and Prophets

15 "Watch out for religious teachers who claim to be preaching God's message but their teaching doesn't conform to the Scriptures. *[Acts 17:11]* They may appear to be true believers

but they intend to establish their own agenda at the expense of God's people. 16 You can recognize them by their lives and lifestyles and by the results of their teachings in the lives of their followers. ❖ *i.e., Do they honor Jesus and the Scriptures? Are they bringing people to faith in Jesus? Are those people maturing and living in obedience to Scriptural teaching? Or are they self-focused and do little to increase the Kingdom? Does their lifestyle honor God or themselves?* ➤ Anyone can identify a tree by the fruit it bears, for you don't get grapes or figs from thorn bushes. *[Luke 6:43-44]* 17 So you can identify good trees by the good fruit they bear, and good teachers by the good influences they have in the lives of their followers. But just as a bad tree bears bad fruit, bad teachers will not produce spiritually mature believers who obey God. 18 A good tree cannot fail to produce good fruit, and a bad tree is incapable of bearing good fruit. The same is true of religious teachers and their followers. 19 God examines the fruit produced in everyone's life, and those who do not bear good fruit for his Kingdom will burn in Hell. *[Matthew 3:10; Luke 3:9]* 20 Therefore, you can recognize if they are true teachers or false by looking at their lives and the results of their ministry. *[Matthew 12:33]*

Many Who Think They Are Saved Will Not Enter Heaven

21 "Don't be deceived! Not everyone who calls me 'Lord' will enter God's Kingdom in Heaven. Only those who obey my Father's will as revealed in the Scriptures will enter. ❖ *Entrance is not **earned** by obedience. However, those who have genuine faith will submit to God's will by obeying him. Those who don't obey do not have a faith that saves. Their "faith" is in something that contradicts God's truth as revealed in the Scriptures.* ➤ 22 On Judgment day, many will appeal to me ❖ *Jesus will be the judge* ➤ saying, 'Lord, we prophesied in your name and expelled demons from people in your name and even did miracles in your name!' 23 But my answer will be, '**I've never known you to be submitted to me. Go away and don't come back! You are not welcome because you are evil!'** *[Psalm 6:8; Luke 13:25-27]* ❖ *Their evil was in being self-centered, following their own will and ideas.*

It's not enough to be sincere and do good deeds and call yourself a follower of Jesus. You must obey his commands as taught in the Scriptures and be in a genuine relationship with him, following his will for your life as he reveals it to you. True faith will lead you into this relationship, and he will give you the desire to please and obey him. ➤

Two Ways to Respond to Jesus' Teaching

24 "Therefore, those who hear my teaching and live by it are like a man who dug down to bedrock for a firm foundation on which to build his house. ❖ *In this illustration, a person's house represents his life. All a person does in this life contributes to building his "house."* ➤ 25 When the rain came, the river flooded, and the winds blew against that house, it didn't collapse because its foundation was on bedrock. ❖ *The rain, flood, and wind represent hard times in this life, and also death. That his house was not destroyed means that his life and work was not destroyed. If our lives are built on obedience to Jesus' teaching, then all the good things we do will have lasting value beyond our deaths, and God will reward us for them in Heaven.* ➤

26 "But those who hear my teaching and refuse to live by it are like a foolish man that built his house on top of sand with no foundation at all. 27 Then the rain came, the river flooded, and the winds blew and smashed against that house, causing it to collapse and completely destroying it." ❖ *Even though people do good works in this life, if their lives aren't based on the foundation of obedience to Jesus, ultimately all those good works will count for nothing after their deaths. And they themselves will experience an eternal existence of ruin in Hell. [2 Thessalonians 1:9]* ➤

28 When Jesus finished speaking, the people were in awe of his teaching 29 because unlike the Scripture teachers who always quoted other authorities, he spoke from personal authority. *[Mark 1:22; Luke 4:31-32]*

8

Jesus Wants to Heal

1 When Jesus had finished teaching, he went down the hillside and large crowds followed after him. 2 A man with a contagious skin disease **A** came and knelt in

---

A 8:2 "Leprosy," in the literal text, does not necessarily mean Hansen's disease which is commonly called

"leprosy" today. Many different contagious skin diseases were covered by that term in *[Continued next page]*

front of him. He said to Jesus, "Sir, I know you can heal me if you want to."

3 Despite the prohibition against touching such a person, and knowing he would become ritually unclean by doing so, Jesus reached out and touched him. ❖ *This was unnecessary, as he healed without touching at other times. But it ministered to the man's emotional need for acceptance.* ➤ Jesus said, "Of course I want to. I command you to be healed!" And instantly he was visibly cured. ❖ *See Malachi 3:6 and Hebrews 13:8—God does not change and Jesus does not change. Therefore, he still wants to heal today.* ➤ 4 Jesus ordered him not to tell anyone about the healing and then said, "Go immediately to a priest so he can examine you as the Torah requires. [Leviticus 14:1-32] Then make the required sacrifices so the priest can publicly announce you are well and ritually clean." ❖ *Jesus often commanded people to not talk about his healing them. He healed out of compassion, [Matthew 14:14; 20:34; Mark 1:41] but the fame associated with his healing miracles made it difficult to lead a normal life.* ➤

How Jesus Responds to Faith in His Power

5 When Jesus reached Capernaum, a centurion came to plead for his help, 6 "Sir, my servant boy is paralyzed in bed and in agony." ❖ *A centurion was a Roman officer who had authority over 100 soldiers. Most Jews despised their Roman conquerors.* ➤

7 Jesus responded, "I will come with you and heal him."

8 But the centurion replied, "Sir, I'm not a Jew and therefore, not worthy to have you enter my house, and I don't want you to ritually defile yourself by doing so. But I ask you to command my slave to be healed, and I know it will happen. 9 For I'm a man under authority and I understand how authority works. I have soldiers under my command and when I tell one, 'Go!' he goes, and to another, 'Come!' he comes, and to my slave, 'Do this!' he does it." ❖ *He recognized that Jesus had divine authority to make such a command work.* ➤

10 When Jesus heard this, he was amazed at his faith and understanding since he was a Gentile who hadn't grown up learning

about the one true God. Jesus said to those following him, "I tell you, I haven't encountered such great faith even among God's chosen people! 11 It's a fact that many Gentiles from everywhere in the world will come to God, and he will welcome them to dine with Abraham, Isaac, and Jacob in his Heavenly Kingdom. ❖ *Jews of that time didn't think any Gentiles would be in Heaven. Abraham, Isaac, and Jacob are the three great patriarchs of the Jews.* ➤ 12 But many Jews who should be in the Kingdom will be banished outside of it in the darkness of Hell where people will cry in great agony and defiant rage." ❖ *Commentators say "gnashing of teeth," in the literal text, means having great pain or grief or rage or perhaps all of them.* ➤

13 The Jesus told the centurion, "Go home. I will do it just as you believe I can." And his servant was instantly healed.

Jesus Heals All Who Are Brought to Him

14 When Jesus came to Peter's house in Capernaum, he saw that Peter's mother-in-law was in bed with a fever. 15 He touched her hand and the fever left her. She immediately got up and began to serve him a meal.

16 When the sun set, people in the village brought many who were demonized to Jesus, and he expelled the demons with a single word. He also healed all the sick they brought to him. ❖ *From Luke 4:38-40, we know that this sunset marked the end of the Sabbath. That's why people waited until then to bring the sick. The Torah forbids working on the Sabbath and they considered carrying the sick to be work.* ➤

17 In doing these things, Jesus was fulfilling Isaiah's prophecy about him that says, **"He lifted the burden of our sicknesses and carried away our diseases."** [Isaiah 53:4] ❖ *This is an inspired commentary on Isaiah 53:4, which many wrongly think refers to our sins. Matthew says it literally refers to our sicknesses. The passage in Isaiah clearly connects the Messiah's healing ministry with his self-sacrificial death, [James 5:16; 1 Peter 2:24] just as his death also provided for our salvation, as is taught elsewhere. [Romans 5:8-10]* ➤

The Cost of Following Jesus

18 When Jesus noticed the large crowd around him, he told his close followers

---

the Scriptures. See Leviticus chapters 13—14 for more information about this condition as defined in the Torah.

they were going to cross Lake Galilee. ¹⁹ Just then, a Scripture teacher came up to him and said, "Rabbi, I will follow you wherever you go."

²⁰ But Jesus replied, "Do you realize what that involves? Foxes have dens and birds have nests. But I, the Son of Man, am rejected by our nation's leaders. If you follow me, they will also reject you. Can you live with that?" ❖ *Jesus called Herod, who was a half-foreign ruler, a fox, [Luke 13:32] and birds sometimes were figures for Gentiles, [Ezekiel 31:5-6] which here could refer to the Romans. Both Herod and Romans were foreigners and in power, and the Sadducees collaborated with them. But the Jewish leaders rejected their own Messiah. Jesus tells potential followers to consider the consequences of following him and to expect rejection by society if they choose to do so.* ➤

²¹ Another who wanted to follow him said, "Sir, I must first fulfill my duty to serve my father as long as he lives, as tradition demands and society expects. After my father dies, I will be free to follow you."

²² Jesus replied, "I'm calling you to follow me right now, so let those who are spiritually dead take care of themselves." ❖ *Jesus requires loyalty from his followers that's above loyalty to tradition, cultural norms, or the expectations of others.* ➤

Jesus Demonstrates Authority over Weather

²³ Then Jesus and his close followers got into a boat to cross the lake. ²⁴ While they were crossing, a violent storm came up and waves were breaking over the boat. ❖ *Sudden storms are common on Lake Galilee.* ➤ But Jesus was asleep. ²⁵ So his followers woke him and said, "Lord, save us! We're going to sink!"

²⁶ He said, "Why are you so frightened? Your trust in God is too small!" Then he got up and rebuked the wind and waves. The storm quickly dissipated and the water became calm. ²⁷ They were utterly amazed and awed, and asked each other, "What kind of a man is he? He even has authority over the wind and waves!" *[Psalm 65:7; 89:8-9; 93:3-4; 107:25, 28-29; Jonah 1:15-16]* ❖ *Jews believed only God could control these things.* ➤

Jesus Demonstrates Authority over Demons

²⁸ When they arrived on the eastern shore in the region of Gergesa, **A** two demonized men came out of tombs in the cliffs, straight to Jesus. They were known to be so violent that no one dared pass near that place. ²⁹ They shouted at him, "Arrrgh! Get out of here, Son of God! Just leave us alone! **B** Have you come to torment us before Judgment Day?"

³⁰ A large herd of pigs was feeding on the hillside nearby, ³¹ and the demons begged Jesus, "If you are going to expel us, send us to that herd of pigs." ³² He replied, "Go!" So they left the men and entered the pigs. Then the herd ran down the steep hillside into the lake and drowned.

³³ The pig herders ran into the town and reported what they'd seen, including all that had happened to the demonized men. ❖ *This was clearly a Gentile area since the Torah categorized pigs as "unclean," and Jews never raised them.* ➤ ³⁴ Then most of the people in that town went out to meet Jesus. When they saw him and the situation, they were frightened by his power and begged him to leave their area.

9

Jesus Heals a Paralyzed Man
to Prove His Authority to Forgive Sin

¹ Jesus and his followers got back into the boat and crossed the lake again to Capernaum, where he lived. ² There, some men carried a paralyzed man on a stretcher to Jesus. When Jesus discerned their faith in him, he said to the paralyzed man, "Don't worry, my son. I declare that your sins are forgiven."

A 8:28 The name of this town varies among manuscripts and the Gospels. Some say it was the region of Gadara (8 miles from the lake). Others say it was the region of Gerasa (about 30 miles southeast of the lake). Both were in the same general region of the Decapolis, a predominantly Gentile area. Others say it was the region of Gergesa on the lake shore where there are cliffs in the vicinity, and this one seems to fit the story best.

B 8:29 Literally, "What to us to you," the sense of hostility carried by this idiomatic expression is rendered above, rather than the more literal, "What have you to do with us?"

3 Some Scripture teachers heard him say this and thought, "This man is blaspheming God!" ❖ *To blaspheme means to talk impiously, irreverently, or disrespectfully about God. Blasphemy was considered a serious sin, punishable by death. [Leviticus 24:16] In this instance, they thought that Jesus was presumptuously speaking for God. To do so was disrespectful of God's authority and, therefore, blasphemous.* ➤

4 Jesus knew what they were thinking ❖ *via a "word of knowledge" [1 Corinthians 12:8]* ➤ and asked them, "Why are you thinking evil about me? 5 Which do you think is less likely that I'm able to do—forgive this man's sins or enable him to stand up and walk? 6 You correctly believe that only God has the power to do either of these things. So I will demonstrate that I have power and approval from God to heal, in order that you may know for sure that I, the Son of Man, also have his authority to forgive sins." Jesus said to the paralyzed man, "I command you to get up, pick up your stretcher, and go home." ❖ *The Jews correctly believed that God would only do miracles through a person if he had a proper relationship with God. God would never give a blasphemer the power to heal. Thus the healing proved that he was not a blasphemer, and so what he said about forgiving sins was true. They believed that only God could do such a healing and never attributed healings to Satan. (Although Jesus' detractors claimed his power to expel demons came from Satan.)* ➤

7 The man immediately got up and walked home, entirely healed. 8 All the people who witnessed this were astonished and also began to praise God for giving such authority to people.

Jesus Associates with Disreputable People

9 As Jesus went on from there, he noticed a man named Matthew Levi sitting in a tax collector's booth. ❖ *Matthew later wrote this gospel. Tax collectors were social outcasts because they collaborated with their Roman conquerors and also got rich by extorting excess tax from people and pocketing the difference.* ➤ Jesus went up to him and said, "Come and be one of my followers." Matthew, having heard a lot about Jesus, immediately left behind his lucrative job and everything he owned and began to follow him.

10 Later, while Jesus and his followers were dining at Matthew's house, many of his tax collector friends and other disreputable people came and joined them. 11 When some Pharisees saw this, they indignantly asked Jesus' close followers, "Why does your rabbi pollute himself by eating and drinking with tax collectors and other such sinners?" *[Luke 15:1-2]* ❖ *They believed that Jesus' eating with sinners meant he approved of their godless way of life, and that it made him ritually unclean in God's sight.* ➤

12 But when Jesus heard this, he said, "Healthy people don't need a doctor, only the sick do. 13 Go study the Scriptures and discover what God meant when he said, 'It's **more important to me that you show mercy to others than to offer me sacrifices.'** *[Hosea 6:6]* ❖ *Telling Pharisees to go study and learn from the Scriptures was a rebuke since they considered themselves to be experts at knowing and interpreting them.* ➤ I didn't come to call righteous people to follow me but to invite those who know that they are sinners to repent and change their way of life." ❖ *The word "righteous" is used in different senses in the Bible. When referring to God, it means sinless perfection. But when used of people, it means someone God has forgiven and accepted into relationship with himself. Jesus may have meant that He didn't come to invite righteous people because no one is sinless. He could also have meant that those who God accepts as righteous don't need to be invited since they are already obediently following him. In any case, the Pharisees and Scripture teachers thought that God accepted them as righteous because they legalistically followed all of the Mosaic Laws. And they believed that God cared for no other kind of person. But their "self-righteousness" made them "unrighteous" in God's view because they refused to acknowledge their own sin and need for forgiveness. They saw no need for a Savior for themselves. So ironically, it was the social outcasts who had no pride and knew they were sinners who were most open to Jesus' invitation.* ➤

Jesus Answers a Question About Fasting

14 Then some of John the Baptizer's followers came to Jesus and asked him, "Why is it that we and the Pharisees fast but you don't tell your followers to do the same?" ❖ *Pharisees fasted as often as twice a week, even though the Torah only required fasting once a year on the Day of Atonement. See the footnote on fasting at Matthew 6:16.* ➤

15 To explain that it wasn't appropriate for his followers to fast while he was with them, Jesus replied, "Nobody would suggest that a groom's friends fast and mourn while he is with them at his wedding banquet. But

the time will come when I'm not with them, and then they will fast." ❖ *Jesus assumed his followers will fast. Do you?* ➤

16 And to explain that the Pharisees' teachings and legalistic fasting couldn't be mixed with his teachings without ruining both, Jesus gave these illustrations, "No one rips a piece of cloth out of a new garment and uses it as a patch on an old one. Doing so would needlessly ruin the new one and after washing, the new patch would shrink and rip the old garment even more. 17 Also, no one puts new wine into rigid old wineskins since the pressure from the fermenting wine would burst the already-stretched skins. It would ruin the wineskins and spill the wine. New wine must be put into new wineskins, then both the wine and wineskins are preserved."

❖ *Jesus' teaching about how to join God's Kingdom was incompatible with the Pharisees' emphasis on the legalistic observance of many man-made rules. Their focus was on outward behavior only, while Jesus stressed humility and attitudes of the mind, as well as behavior. A person could not follow Jesus and maintain all the legalistic rules the Pharisees taught because their focus would ruin what Jesus was trying to teach. His teachings were much more than a new patch on the Old Covenant's way of approaching God. It was about an entirely New Covenant.* ➤

A Woman's Faith Heals Her, and Jesus Demonstrates Power over Death

18 While he was saying this, a leader of the local synagogue came and prostrated **A** himself in front of Jesus. He said, "My daughter has just died, but if you come and touch her, she will live."

19 Jesus and his followers got up and went with the man to his home.

20 In the crowd, was a woman who had suffered from chronic bleeding for twelve years. She came up behind Jesus and touched a tassel **B** hanging from his robe. ❖ *Her condition made her ritually unclean, and anyone she* touched would become unclean until evening and have to go through ritual washing. This was a terrible burden to bear and a constant embarrassment. She hoped no one would notice her. [Leviticus 15:19-30] ➤ 21 She was thinking to herself, "If I just touch a tassel on his robe, I will be healed."

22 But Jesus turned and seeing her, said, "Don't worry, my daughter. Your faith in me has saved **C** you." And God instantly healed her.

23 When Jesus arrived at the man's house, he saw the funeral musicians playing and mourners wailing. 24 He told them, "Everyone go away! The girl isn't dead, she's only sleeping." But they ridiculed him.

❖ *Unbelief could prevent Jesus from performing a miracle. [Matthew 13:58; Mark 6:5-6] He may have wanted them away from there and said what he did to minimize the unbelief present.* ➤ 25 When the crowd finally left, he went in and held the girl's hand and raised her back to life. 26 The news about this spread rapidly throughout the region.

Two Blind Men and a Man Made Mute by a Demon

27 As Jesus went on from there, two blind men followed a ways behind him shouting, "Son of David, have mercy and help us!" ❖ *"Son of David" was a messianic title, indicating that these men believed Jesus was the Messiah.* ➤

28 Jesus reached the house where he was staying and went in, and the blind men caught up and entered too. He asked them, "Do you believe that I can make you see?" They answered, "Yes, Lord!"

29 He touched their eyelids and said, "Since you believe, you *will* be able to see!" 30 And immediately they could see. Jesus gave them firm instructions, "I don't want you telling anyone about this!" ❖ *This was probably an attempt to minimize his notoriety. He couldn't go anywhere without a large crowd following, and it was getting worse all the time.* ➤

A 9:18 The word translated as "prostrated himself" means "to bow down in worship." But it most likely was an attitude of humility and pleading, not true worship. Unless he recognized Jesus as God, a devout Jew would never worship a man.

B 9:20 The Greek word κράσπεδον (kraspedon) can also mean "fringe" or "edge," but here it probably corresponds to the Hebrew word "tzitzit," which is a special kind of tassel and the holiest part of a Jewish man's robe. The plural of "tzitzit" is "tzitziyot." The Torah commands Jewish men to wear tzitziyot (symbolic tassels) on the corners of their outer garments. [Numbers 15:38-40]

C 9:22 The word σώζω (sōzō), commonly translated "healed," can also mean "saved."

31 But they were so excited that they went out and told everyone anyway. So the story spread throughout the region.

32 As they were about to leave the house, a demonized man who couldn't speak was brought in to him. 33 But as soon as Jesus commanded the demon to leave, the man was able to speak. The crowds were amazed and said, "There's never been anything like this in Israel before!"

34 But the Pharisees were saying, "He's only able to expel demons because he has the help of Satan who rules them!"

We Must Pray for More People to Spread the Good News

35 Jesus went to every town and village in the region, teaching in the synagogues and proclaiming the Good News about how people could have a new relationship with God as their Kin. Everywhere he went, he healed every kind of disease and illness. 36 He always felt compassion for people because they had troubles and felt helpless. They were like sheep without a shepherd to care for them. 37 He told his close followers, "The potential harvest of people ready to enter God's Kingdom is great, but the number of people ready to help bring them in is few. 38 So ask God—who has been preparing these people to believe—to send out more workers to proclaim the Good News and help bring them in." ❖ *What kind of worker was Jesus thinking of for them to ask God to send out? Remember that there were no section headings or chapter breaks in the original text. He wants to send out the same kind of workers he sent out just a few verses later in chapter 10 verses 7-8 who will obey the same command, i.e., those who know they have his authority and commission to share the Good News, heal the sick, raise the dead, and expel demons. Lest you try to let yourself off the hook by saying this command was only given to the apostles, or only for his followers 2000 years ago, Jesus gave this command again in Mark 16:16-18 to those who would go everywhere in the world to every people group. The command to heal the sick, raise the dead, and expel demons is still as valid today as the part of the command to share the Good News to people from every people group everywhere in the world.* ➤

10

Jesus Sends Out the Twelve to Minister

1 Jesus summoned his twelve apostles together and gave them power and authority to expel any demon and to heal every kind of disease and illness. ❖ *"Apostle" means "someone who is sent as a messenger." He intended to train them and give them authority to be his representatives after he returned to Heaven.* ➤ 2 The names of those apostles are:

Simon, whom he also called Peter
  ❖ *or Cephas (In Hebrew: Kefa [Kay-fah]). Peter, from the Greek "Petros," and Kefa (Cephas), both mean "rock."* ➤
Andrew, Simon's brother
James, son of Zebedee
John, James' younger brother
3 Philip
Bartholomew, son of Tolmai ❖ *who might have also been called Nathanael* ➤
Thomas
Matthew the tax collector,
  also called Levi
James, son of Alpheus
Judas, son of James,
  also called Thaddeus
4 Simon (called the Zealot because of
  his former association with the left-
  wing Zealot group that wanted to
  free Israel from Roman rule by
  revolution), and
Judas Iscariot, who would later betray
  Jesus to his enemies.

❖ *Jesus' apostles included uneducated fishermen, a social outcast who collaborated with the enemy (Matthew), a violent political fanatic (Simon the Zealot), and a man who Jesus knew would betray him. Anyone can become a follower of Jesus, although it does involve leaving behind your former sinful ways.* ➤

5 Jesus sent them out to minister after giving them the following instructions: "Don't go to any Gentile areas or to any Samaritans. 6 Your mission is to go to those Israelites who are not following God's ways. 7 Wherever you go, preach this message: 'God invites you to submit to him as your King. You have the opportunity to do this right now.' 8 Also heal the sick, raise the dead, heal those with contagious skin

diseases, and expel demons. Minister in these ways without accepting pay beyond room and board since you have received the power and authority to do these things without charge. ❖ *The New Testament model of evangelism always included healing ministry. Why is this neglected today?* ➤ 9 Don't take any money with you. 10 Don't take a beggars bag, **A** or extra clothing, or even a walking stick. Go just as you are, totally dependent on God's provision. For workers deserve to be supported by those who spiritually benefit from their labor. ❖ *These instructions were for a short-term ministry tour. Jesus later gave different instructions for after he left them. [Luke 22:35-36]* ➤

11 "When you enter a town or village, find someone who accepts you and your message and wants to be your host. Then stay with that person until you move on to the next town. 12 Whenever you enter a house, greet them with 'shalom.' ❖ *"Shalom" was a greeting and a leave taking. It was a one-word prayer of blessing, that the person would have peace, calmness, comfort, contentment, safety, health, wholeness, success, prosperity, integrity, well-being, and good relationships with God and people.* ➤ 13 If that household welcomes you, allow your blessing of shalom to remain. But if they do not welcome you or your message, tell them that God withdraws his blessing of shalom from them. 14 In every household or town that doesn't welcome you or your message, shake the dust off your feet as you leave. ❖ *This was a figurative action of rebuke, meaning that even the dust of their house or town was defiling and offensive and they were no better than pagans. It was a warning that they had better repent or face God's judgment.* ➤ 15 It's a fact that on Judgment Day, God will punish the sinners of Sodom and Gomorrah less than such people. ❖ *God destroyed the cities of Sodom and Gomorrah for their evil ways and immorality, and the names of their cities came to be used to represent the epitome of evil. [Genesis 18:16—19:29] Yet in God's view, rejecting his message of salvation and his messengers is worse and will be punished more severely.* ➤

Those Who Do God's Work Will Be Persecuted

16 "Understand that even though I'm sending you out to minister, you are as defenseless as lambs among wolves. *[Luke 10:3]* So you need to be wise, sensible, shrewd, and cautious, yet at the same time, be totally pure and innocent of doing any wrong. 17 Be on guard against men who will try to arrest you because you are my followers. They will hand you over to the local authorities and have you beaten in their synagogues. *[John 16:2]* 18 You will be put on trial before rulers and kings, but God will allow this so you can have the opportunity to tell about the things you have seen me do and heard me teach. You will even have opportunity to tell these things to Gentiles. 19 But when they arrest you and bring you to trial, don't worry about what you should say to defend yourself or think about how to say it ahead of time. For at the time you need to speak, God will put in your mind the words he wants you to say. 20 It won't be you who speaks, but the Spirit of your Heavenly Father will speak through you. ❖ *i.e., the Holy Spirit* ➤

21 "Be aware that some of you will even be betrayed to the authorities for execution by your siblings, children, or parents. 22 Many will hate you because you are my followers. But God will save those who patiently endure all these things to the end of their lives—while remaining faithful to me. *[Matthew 24:13; Mark 13:13; 1 Timothy 4:16; 2 Timothy 2:10-12; Hebrews 10:36; 12:1-7; James 1:12; 5:7-11]* 23 When they persecute you in one town, do your best to escape to another. Be sure to know this: You won't finish going through all the towns of Israel preaching the message of the Good News before I, the Son of Man, return. ❖ *The interpretation of this time frame varies widely. Most recent commentators think he is talking about his second coming. But others think it refers to his resurrection, or his coming in judgment in AD 70 to destroy Jerusalem. They also posit several other ideas.* ➤

24 "A follower isn't more important than his master, just as a slave isn't more important than his owner. 25 So a follower should be content to be treated like his master, and the slave should be content to be treated like his owner. Since people say

---

A 10:10 The word πήρα (pēra) translated "beggar's bag" could also mean any kind of bag to put things in.

Scholars do not agree on its meaning in this context.

that I'm in league with 'Satan' and treat me accordingly, you would be wise to expect even worse. *[John 15:18-21]*

26 "But don't be afraid of them. Instead, tell them all the things that I've told you but have not yet taught the public. 27 What I tell you in private, you must proclaim for all to hear. 28 Don't be afraid of those who might kill you. They can't touch your soul, only your body. But you *should* have a healthy fear of God. He not only has power over your life in this world, but after you die, he decides if you will go to Hell or not. If you have any sense at all, you should realize that he is the one to be afraid of, not people. 29-31 You know that sparrows are so common they are nearly worthless. You can buy two for next to nothing. But God even pays attention to creatures as unimportant as sparrows. He's aware of each and every one of them and what happens to them. I assure you, you are far more important to him than mere sparrows! God's knows you so intimately that he even knows how many hairs are on your head every moment. Nothing takes him by surprise and nothing can defeat his power. There's no reason for you to ever fear what people can do to you. ❖ *Jesus explicitly taught that people are much more important than animals, contrary to modern American attitudes. He implies here that nothing happens to God's people except what God allows. God is in control of our lives. If bad things happen to us, he has allowed them for his reasons and purposes which are always for our ultimate good. See Romans 8:28.* ➤

32 "So don't allow persecution or a death threat to stop you from proclaiming your allegiance to me. If you publicly declare that you follow me, then on Judgment Day I will tell my Father that you belong to me. 33 But if you deny that you are my follower, even to avoid dying, then I will tell my Father that you do not belong to me.

The Price of Being a True Follower

34 "Did you think that I came to bring peace to this world? Not at all! I came to bring division between those who will follow me and those who reject me. 35-36 Your enemies might even be family members. Families will divide, father against son, mother against daughter, mother-in-law against daughter-in-law, and between every other possible relationship." *[Micah 7:6]* ❖ *Jesus doesn't desire division, but his purpose is to draw those who want to have a love relationship with him. Since he wants people to choose this of their own free will, he won't coerce anyone. Thus the inevitable conflict is, in his eyes, entirely due to those who reject him because he is their creator and rightful master.* ➤

37 "If you want to be my follower but can't place your loyalty and obedience to me above loyalty to your parents or children, then I won't accept you. A 38 If you aren't willing to give up your own plans and desires in order to obey me, even if it means you must suffer or die, then you can't be my follower. 39 Those who try to save their earthly lives by denying they belong to me will not live in Heaven. But those who are willing to die in order to faithfully follow me will have eternal life.

God Rewards Those Who Help His Workers

40 "When people welcome you because they know that you follow me, my Father and I count it as welcoming us. 41 Those who welcome God's prophets because they know what they are, God will reward the same way he rewards his prophets. And those who welcome godly people because they recognize their relationship to me will receive the same reward that God gives godly people. *[e.g., Rahab in Joshua chapter 2; 6:15-25; Matthew 10:41]* 42 Even those who give one of my humble followers a cup of cold water because they recognize that they belong to me will certainly be rewarded." ❖ *The*

A 10:37 Jesus actually said, "If anyone wants to follow me and does not hate his own father and mother and wife and children and brothers and sisters and even his own life, he cannot be my follower." The people listening to him were Jews, and Jewish rabbis often used a figure of speech called "hyperbole" which is an exaggeration to make a strong point. They knew that the Torah commands us to respect and love all these people and that Jesus was not telling them to disobey God's Torah. They would have properly

example implies that they only give a cup of cold water because they are so poor that is all they are able to give. This statement would not apply if the giver were well-off and stingily gave a cup of water when his resources and the need were greater. ➤

11

1 When Jesus finished instructing his twelve apostles, he sent them off to minister and he continued on without them to teach and preach in their towns. ❖ *Most commentators think "their towns" mean the towns of Galilee or of Israel.* ➤

John the Baptizer Sends Messengers to Jesus

2 Now by this time, John the Baptizer was in prison and was receiving reports from his followers about Jesus' activities. But since Jesus was not initiating the end-time judgment that John had prophesied the Messiah would do, *[Luke 3:17]* John summoned two of his followers and sent them to Jesus. 3 When they arrived, they asked him, "Are you really the long-awaited Messiah or should we be looking for someone else?"

4 Jesus replied, "Tell John what you have seen me do and heard me preach. 5 The blind can see, the crippled can walk, those with contagious skin diseases are cured, the deaf can hear, some who had died now live again, and the poor are hearing the Good News about God inviting them into his Kingdom. ❖ *These things fulfilled the prophecies in Isaiah 26:19; 29:18-19; 35:5-6; 61:1-2; about what the Messiah would do.* ➤ 6 And God will bless those who don't reject me for not fulfilling their preconceived ideas of what the Messiah will and should do."

Jesus Talks About John the Baptizer

7 As John's men were leaving, Jesus spoke to the crowd about the Baptizer. "When you went out to John in the wilderness, what did you expect to see? A man who goes with the flow of popular opinion, like a reed that bends in any direction the wind blows? 8 Hardly. Who would listen to such a man? Then why did you go out to see

him? To see a man who wears luxurious clothing? Those who wear rich apparel and live in luxury are found in palaces, not in the wilderness. 9 So tell me, what did you hope to find? A genuine prophet from God like the prophets of old? Yes, you went to hear God's prophet! But I tell that you he is more than just a prophet for his work surpassed that of all previous prophets. John proclaimed the coming of the Messiah. 10 This Scripture was written about John, '**I will send my messenger in advance to prepare the way for you to be accepted by my people.**' *[Malachi 3:1]* 11 I tell you, from the beginning of creation until now no one has had a more important role than John. Yet even the lowest-ranking person in God's Kingdom is greater than he is. ❖ *As great as John was, he lived in the time of promise before Jesus' resurrection and the coming of the Holy Spirit on all of God's people. Those who enter God's Kingdom are indwelt by the Holy Spirit and are adopted as God's children so they achieve a higher status than John ever did in his life on Earth. Of course, after his death, he joined God's people in Heaven and certainly has high status there.* ➤ 12 From the time John started preaching his message of repentance until now, God has been drawing people to himself with great power, and many are exerting their utmost to enter his Kingdom. *[Luke 16:16]* ❖ *Whatever Jesus is talking about in this verse pertains mainly to the period between John's first starting to preach and this point in Jesus' ministry. Noting this fact and the immediate context makes the above interpretation the most likely one to be true. Some other interpretations are: 1) God's Kingdom has suffered violent attacks and violent people are trying to destroy it. 2) God's Kingdom has been triumphantly advancing, and determined people are eagerly entering it. 3) Violent people (like the zealots) have been attempting to establish God's Kingdom by force.* ➤ 13 God's word and will was proclaimed in his Torah and in the writings of the prophets ❖ *i.e., the Hebrew Scriptures* ➤ until John came. ❖ *i.e., These were the authorities over God's people until John came, when he started proclaiming the coming of the Messiah who would be the new authority for those who would accept him. [Matthew 17:5; Mark 9:7; Luke 9:35]* ➤ 14 And if you are willing to accept what I say, ❖ *OR: what the prophecies say* ➤ John is the prophet like Elijah who

---

understood this Semitic idiom and the point he was making about the relative degree of loyalty he was

requiring, as has been expressed in the interpreted translation above.

the Scriptures said would come before the Messiah. *[Malachi 4:5; Matthew 17:10-13; Mark 9:11-13]* 15 If your minds are attuned to God, try to understand what this means!

16 "How can I characterize most of the religious leaders and people of this generation? Do you know what they're like? They're never satisfied with God's messengers. They're like children sitting in the market who complain to one another, 17 'We played a happy tune but you wouldn't dance. Then we sang a sad song but you wouldn't cry.' 18 For John came as an ascetic and didn't eat bread or drink wine like most people, so they rejected him and said he was demonized. 19 Then I, the Son of Man, came and was willing to dine and drink as a guest in people's homes, and they say, 'Look at that glutton and drunkard who hangs around with tax collectors and other sinful outcasts!' ❖ *The Jewish leaders at that time were unwilling to accept anyone who rocked the status quo. They were interested in their own power more than God's truth. It didn't matter what kind of prophet God sent. If the prophet criticized them or didn't submit to their authority, he was rejected.* ➤ But as the proverb says, 'Wisdom is vindicated by what she does.' **A** So we will be vindicated by the good fruit that God produces in the lives those of those who follow our teaching."

Jesus Talks About Those Who Reject Him

20 Then Jesus began to reprimand the people of the towns who had seen him do most of his miracles because they had not responded with repentance. 21 "How terrible it will be for you citizens of Chorazin and Bethsaida! ❖ *These Jewish towns were just north of Lake Galilee near Capernaum.* ➤ God will punish you because you refused to repent in spite of the miracles you have seen. If the wicked pagans who lived in Tyre and Sidon long ago had seen these same miracles, they would have repented and demonstrated their sorrow by wearing sackcloth and ashes. *[Isaiah 23:1-18; Ezekiel 26:1—28:26; Joel 3:4-8; Amos 1:9-10; Zechariah 9:2-4]* ❖ *Wearing sackcloth and ashes was a cultural expression of sorrow and repentance.* ➤ 22 On

Judgment Day, those citizens of Tyre and Sidon will be better off than you because you saw God's miracles and heard the Good News but rejected it. ❖ *Pagans who were ignorant of God's message will be punished less than those who hear and reject it. [John 15:22-24]* ➤ 23 And you people of Capernaum! Do you think you will be honored in Heaven? No, you will be cast down to Hell with the spiritually dead! *[Isaiah 14:13-15]* If the people of Sodom had seen the miracles you have seen, they would have repented and that city would still exist. *[Genesis 19:24-28]* 24 So on Judgment Day, God will assign you a punishment even greater than theirs!" *[Matthew 10:15; Luke 10:12]* ❖ *See the note at Matthew 10:15.* ➤

Those Who Know Jesus

25 Then Jesus exulted, "Yes, Father! Lord of Heaven and earth! I praise and thank you for hiding your truths from those who think much of themselves and for revealing them to the humble! 26 Yes, Father, I know this is what pleases you!"

27 To his followers he said, "My Father has given me power and authority over everything. No one really knows me, God's Son, except my Father in Heaven. And no one knows the Father except me, his Son, and those to whom I choose to reveal him. *[John 1:18; 10:15]* 28 All of you who are burdened with emotional and spiritual cares and worries and are weary of bearing them, come to me! I will give you relief and rest. 29 Submit to obeying me and allow me to teach you. You will find me a humble and gentle master and you will find the emotional and spiritual rest you desire. *[Jeremiah 6:16]* 30 You will discover it isn't hard to be under my lordship and care for I will not require difficult things of you." ❖ *This is true if we submit and allow him to live his life through us. If we try in our own strength to do what he requires, then his requirements are impossible.* ➤

12

Jesus Is Master over Sabbath Regulations

1 One Sabbath, while Jesus and his followers were walking on a path through

---

A 11:19 Some manuscripts say Wisdom is vindicated "by her deeds," others say "by her children." This same variation occurs in manuscripts of Luke 7:35. These phrases mean the same thing.

some grain fields, his followers were picking the grain and eating it. ❖ *The Torah allowed hand picking of grain while walking in another man's field, but forbade cutting it with a sickle. [Deuteronomy 23:25] So they were not stealing.* ➤ 2 Some Pharisees who saw this accused them, saying, "Your followers are disobeying the Torah by working on the Sabbath!" ❖ *They considered picking the grain to be the work of harvesting. See Exodus 20:8-10; 31:14-17; 35:1-3; Leviticus 23:3; Deuteronomy 5:12-14; and Jeremiah 17:21-27 about Sabbath regulations. The Pharisees were stretching the definition of work with man-made rules. No such details about what they claimed to be work were in the Torah.* ➤

3 Jesus counter argued, "Don't tell me you aren't familiar with the example David set in the Scriptures when he and his men were hungry! *[1 Samuel 21:1-6]* 4 He entered the Tabernacle and he and his men ate consecrated bread which only priests are allowed to eat. *[Leviticus 24:9]* ❖ *Jesus used David as an example because he knew the Pharisees thought highly of him. His point was: There's no mention or implication in the Scriptures of God condemning David or the priest who gave him the bread for breaking this command in order to meet the needs of David's men. So God wasn't going to condemn Jesus' followers for breaking the Pharisees' man-made Sabbath rules in order to satisfy their hunger. The Pharisees, who were proud of their detailed knowledge of the Scriptures, should have been able to see the implications of this story and not demand more from people than God does.* ➤ 5 And haven't you ever realized that the Torah commands the priests on duty in the Temple to, in effect, break the Sabbath law by working on the Sabbath? *[Numbers 28:9-10]* Yet God considers them innocent of breaking any command. 6 The Temple regulations supersede the Sabbath command. And there is someone ranking even higher than the Temple here. ❖ *Jesus was referring to himself as having more authority than the Temple, and so also having authority over the Sabbath command. He didn't overtly mention himself as having the authority since Jewish culture did not approve of someone honoring himself.* ➤ 7 If you really understood what God meant when he said, 'It's more important to me that you show mercy to others than to offer me sacrifices,' *[Hosea 6:6; also Psalm 40:6; 50:13-14; 51:16-17]* then you wouldn't condemn my

followers for what they've done. They are, in fact, innocent of doing wrong. 8 For I, the Son of Man, am Master of the Sabbath and its regulations."

Jesus Heals a Man with a Crippled Hand on a Sabbath

9 Moving on from that place, Jesus entered their synagogue. 10 A man with a crippled hand **A** was present. Looking for grounds to accuse Jesus of disobeying Torah commands, the Pharisees asked him, "Do you think the Torah allows healing on the Sabbath?" 11 He replied, "If any of you had a sheep fall into a deep hole on the Sabbath, would you refuse to help it because it was the Sabbath? ❖ *Even the most legalistic of them would disobey the Sabbath command in such a case.* ➤ 12 And a human being is certainly much more valuable than a sheep! So yes, God does allow us to do good on the Sabbath." 13 Then he told the man, "Straighten out your hand." The man did so and his hand became completely normal, just like the other. 14 But the Pharisees were furious because he had publicly discredited their interpretation of the Sabbath rules, so they began plotting how to kill him. ❖ *They ignored the fact that Jesus only said a few words, which isn't work by any definition, and that only God's power could heal so they were angry at what God had done. They were also blind to their own disobeying of the Torah's commands to not kill. [Exodus 20:13; 23:7; Deuteronomy 5:17] Their only concern was their authority as interpreters of the Scriptures.* ➤

Jesus' Ministry Fulfilled Prophecy About the Messiah

15 Jesus was aware of this so he went away from there. But many followed after him and he healed all who were sick, 16 though he ordered them not to tell others that he had healed them. 17 His ministry fulfilled Isaiah's prophecy about the Messiah that says: 18 **"Here is my chosen servant, the one I specially love who delights me. I will empower him with my Spirit and he will**

A 12:10 The Greek word χείρ (cheir), commonly translated "hand," can include the wrist and forearm. It's possible it was more than what we would call his "hand" that was crippled or "withered."

proclaim to every people group the truth about how to be righteous in my sight. 19 He will not shout or argue with others or publicly rally people to follow him. 20 He will be gentle and kind to those who are spiritually weak, battered, fragile, and about ready to give up believing. He will work to heal and restore them to strong faith and vitality until his goodness overcomes evil and its consequences. 21 In the end, people from every people group will trust him to save them." *[Isaiah 42:1-4]*
❖ *Matthew's quotation doesn't follow either the Masoretic Hebrew text or the Septuagint (the Greek translation of the Hebrew Scriptures that Jesus and his contemporaries mainly used). He may have quoted a different translation or made up his own. The IVP commentary says that "my servant," in the context of the book of Isaiah, clearly refers to Israel. It was a later Jewish tradition that applied it to the Messiah.* ➤

Beware of Saying the Spirit's Work Is of Satan

22 After that, someone brought a blind and mute demonized man to Jesus. When Jesus expelled the demon, the man could both speak and see. 23 Those who saw it were amazed and asked, "Could he possibly be the Son of David?" ❖ *"Son of David" was a common Messianic title.* ➤

24 But when some Pharisees heard this, they tried to discourage this kind of thinking by saying, "He can only expel demons because he has Beelzebul, the prince of demons, helping him." ❖ *Beelzebul was a Jewish name for Satan.* ➤

25 Knowing what they were thinking, Jesus replied to this accusation, "Any kingdom divided in civil war won't last long, and a divided household will fall apart. 26 If Satan is fighting against his own demons, how can his kingdom continue? 27 And if I'm expelling them with Beelzebul's power, then what about your own followers? They expel demons too. Whose power do they use? They will judge the reasonableness of your accusation! 28 But if I'm expelling demons by the power of God's Spirit, then that proves he is establishing his Kingdom among you."

29 Comparing Satan to a strongman, Jesus continued, "You can't rob a strongman of his possessions unless you first overpower him. If someone stronger than the strongman ties him up, then he can rob his house. ❖ *Jesus' point was that he is able to expel demons because he is mightier than Satan. The strongman's "possessions" are the people he had under the control or influence of his demons.* ➤

30 "You have to choose sides. Those who aren't helping me are against me. And those who don't help me lead people to God are helping to drive them away. 31 So I'm warning you to be careful about the accusations you make. God will forgive every sin and blasphemy except blasphemy against the Holy Spirit. 32 Anyone who in any way speaks against me, the Son of Man, can be forgiven if he or she repents. But God will not forgive anyone who blasphemes against the Holy Spirit. ❖ *It's the Holy Spirit who enables us to repent, and without repentance there is no forgiveness. If a person rejects the Holy Spirit so he leaves, that person will never again desire to repent. So anyone who is worried about having committed this sin, hasn't. The Pharisees said that the power that worked through Jesus was Satan's power. Therefore, they were in danger of committing this unforgivable sin by insulting the Holy Spirit. Some believers today are in danger of doing the same thing if they accuse believers, who are using the Holy Spirit's power to do miraculous things, of doing them by Satan's power. Genuine skepticism does not justify such a dangerous accusation.* ➤

33 "If a tree's fruit is good, you have to conclude that the tree itself is good. If a tree's fruit is bad, then you must conclude the tree itself is bad, for a tree's health can be recognized by its fruit. *[Matthew 7:20; Luke 6:43-44]* Therefore, if the deeds I do are good, you should conclude that the source of those deeds is also good. 34 But you Pharisees are a bunch of evil deceivers! So how can anything you say be good? What a person speaks and does reflect the character of his innermost heart and thoughts. *[Matthew 15:18-19; Luke 6:45]* 35 From the goodness that fills the heart and mind of a righteous person proceeds the fruit of good words and actions. And from the evil that fills the heart and mind of an evil person proceeds the fruit of evil words and deeds. That's how righteous and evil people can be identified.

36 "It's a fact that on Judgment Day, God will hold you responsible for everything you have said, even words you have said without thinking. 37 He will judge you innocent or

guilty based on what you say in this life."

❖ *He doesn't mean this will be the only basis of judgment, but that our words will certainly be judged as well as our actions.* ➤

Those Who Reject Jesus Will Have No Excuse

38 Then some Pharisees and Scripture teachers said, "Rabbi, we want to see you perform a miraculous sign that only God could do to prove that he sent you." *[Matthew 16:1; Luke 11:16]* 39 He replied, "Many people living today are evil. They want me to perform spectacular signs to prove my power comes from God, but I won't. *[Matthew 16:4; Luke 11:29-32]* The only sign I will give is like the sign that happened to the prophet Jonah. 40 Just as he spent three days in the stomach of a large fish, *[Jonah 1:17—2:10]* I, the Son of Man, will spend parts of three days in the grave. ❖ *Jesus was speaking cryptically about his future resurrection which would be all the proof they needed that God had sent him. Literally, he said "three days and three nights." Matthew also refers to his resurrection "on the third day" [16:21] and "after three days." [27:63] Leon Morris points out that these three expressions, all written by the same author, must all mean the same thing. But we shouldn't interpret them as if a modern English speaker wrote them. First-century Jews counted time differently than we do. Any part of a day was counted as a day. So a full day with part of a day on either side, as short a period as 26 hours, was counted as three days. Even the fact that three nights were mentioned doesn't mean that Matthew meant three 24-hour days. It has to be interpreted according to the standards of the culture when and where it was written.* ➤ 41 On Judgment Day, the people of Nineveh will stand and condemn you because they listened to Jonah's message and repented. *[Jonah 3:5]* And someone greater than Jonah is here, yet you refuse to repent. ❖ *Jesus was speaking of himself as greater than Jonah.* ➤ 42 On Judgment Day, the Queen of Sheba who visited Solomon *[1 Kings 10:1-10; 2 Chronicles 9:1-12]* will stand and condemn those living today because she traveled from a distant land to listen to Solomon's wisdom. But someone greater than Solomon is here whom you refuse to listen to.

43 "When a demon is expelled from a man, it travels through arid places looking for a new place to rest in someone's body. 44 If it doesn't find such a place, it says to itself, 'I will return to my former house.' When it returns, it finds the house unoccupied by any demons, clean, and in order. 45 Then it goes and brings seven worse demons and they all enter the man to live, so he is worse off than before. The same kind of thing will happen to you evil people living today. You are worse off now than you were before I came. Since you have rejected me, you've left a vacancy in your lives that Satan will fill."

Jesus' True Relatives

46 While Jesus was still speaking to the crowd, his mother and brothers *[Matthew 13:55]* arrived from Nazareth to see him. But they couldn't enter the house where he was teaching because it was crammed with people. 47 Someone told him, "Your mother and brothers are outside wanting to see you."

48 Using this as a teaching opportunity, Jesus asked the one who said this, "Who is my mother and who are my brothers?" 49 Pointing to his followers, he said, "These people are as mothers and brothers to me! 50 Those who obey my Heavenly Father are as close to me as my brother and sister and mother."

13

Parable of the Four Soils

1 Later that same day, Jesus went down to sit by the lake. 2 But such a large crowd gathered around him that he got into a boat and moved a little offshore so those on land could hear him better. 3 Then he taught them many spiritual truths in parables. One went like this: "A farmer went to sow seed in his field. ❖ *He scattered the seed on the ground and later plowed it under.* ➤ 4 As he scattered the seed, some fell on a hard-packed path and birds ate them. 5 Some fell where the soil was just a thin layer over rock. These sprouted quickly because the soil was shallow. ❖ *The sun rapidly warmed the shallow soil so the seed grew faster there than in deeper soil.* ➤ 6 But the sun scorched the young plants and they withered because the underlying rock blocked their roots from reaching water. 7 Some seed fell on ground where thorn bushes had grown and their roots still remained. These sprouted and grew for a while, but the young plants

couldn't compete for light and water with the thorn bushes that also grew and choked them. So they produced no grain and died. 8 And some seed fell on good soil. These sprouted, grew strong, and bore more seed in varying amounts, some 100, some 60, and others 30. 9 If your minds are attuned to God, try to understand this parable!"

Why Jesus Taught in Parables

10 Later when only Jesus' usual followers were with him, they asked, "Why do you only speak to the public in parables?"

11 He said, "You have the privilege of being the first to learn about Kingdom truths that God hasn't revealed before. But for the present, they do not have this privilege. 12 You have some understanding of God and his Kingdom because you are submitted to him and have a sincere desire to learn more. So God will give you more understanding. But many understand little about spiritual truth because of their disinterest and unwillingness to submit to God. So even the little understanding that they possess will be taken from them. ❖ *Probably through demonic deception. [Matthew 25:29; Mark 4:25; Luke 8:18]* ➤ 13 Therefore, I only teach others about spiritual truths in parables. Those who aren't interested in God will hear the parables but not understand the spiritual truth being taught. They also see the miraculous signs but don't see the spiritual reality and implications behind them because they refuse to believe in me. ❖ *God never forces truth on anyone in this life. His hiding truth in parables actually protected the disinterested because God holds people responsible for things they know. They will be punished for rejecting Jesus but will not receive additional punishment for rejecting truth they did not understand.* ➤ But God will reveal the meaning to those who seek to understand. 14 This fulfills Isaiah's prophecy where God said, 'Even though they hear, they don't understand. Even though they look, they don't perceive. 15 For they've become close-minded and uninterested in hearing from me. They ignore things I do to get their attention that are before their very eyes. If this wasn't true about them, they would perceive what I'm showing them and hear what I'm saying and understand what I'm trying to teach, and then turn away from their sinful ways. If they did that, I would spiritually heal them.' *[Isaiah 6:9-10]*

16 "But it is God's special blessing that you get to see the signs I do and perceive the spiritual truths behind them, and you get to listen to my teachings and learn. 17 For it's a fact that many of God's prophets and other godly people in the past yearned to see the things you are seeing me do and to hear the truths I'm teaching you, but they didn't have the opportunity."

Jesus Explains the Parable of the Four Soils

18 Jesus said, "This is what the parable means. ❖ *He called it the "Parable of the Sower."* ➤ 19 The seed represents God's message about the way of salvation. The farmer is anyone who preaches this message. The hard-packed path illustrates people whose minds are closed toward God's message. They may hear his truth but it can't enter their hardened minds. Just like the birds ate the seed, Satan snatches the memory of the message away from them. 20 The layer of shallow soil over rock illustrates people who hear God's message and happily receive it at first. 21 But just like a plant in shallow soil can't develop the roots it needs to survive, God's message doesn't go deep in their minds and hearts because they aren't willing to fully surrender themselves to him. Their shallow faith lasts for only a short time until the first real testing of their faith or persecution occurs. Then it quickly dies. 22 The ground with thorn bushes illustrates people who initially accept God's message but they never give it first priority. So other concerns and higher priorities, such as worries, materialism, and pleasure, keep his word from producing good fruit in their lives. Eventually, their faith is smothered and dies. ❖ *Some commentators believe the plants did not die but were merely unproductive. Jesus taught elsewhere that trees producing no fruit were only fit to be burned. [Matthew 3:10; 7:19; Luke 3:9; John 15:4-6] The focus in this parable is on how the seed is received and the resulting fruit. Only good soil results in fruit, and Jesus' point is that good soil is the only acceptable kind. Just as in your own garden, plants that don't produce are rejected as worthless.* ➤ 23 But the good soil illustrates those people who hear God's message,

recognize its worth, grab onto it, and allow it to take deep root in their hearts and minds. They surrender themselves to God and make him first priority in their lives. So their faith matures and their lives cause God's Kingdom to increase and prosper to varying degrees." ❖ *The implication is that individuals can determine what kind of "soil" their hearts and minds are by how they respond to God's message.* ➤

Parable of the Weeds

24 Jesus also told this parable, "God's Kingdom in this world can be illustrated by a farmer who planted good wheat seed in his field. 25 But while everyone slept, his enemy came and planted poisonous darnel weeds ❖ *which closely resemble wheat until the heads of wheat appear* ➤ in the same field and then went away. 26 When the wheat began to bear grain, the darnel weeds became apparent. 27 The farmer's workers went to him and asked, 'Sir, how did those weeds get there? Wasn't the seed you planted good?' 28 He told them, 'It was an enemy who did this!' They asked, 'Do you want us to pull them out?' 29 He replied, 'No. If you uproot the weeds you may also uproot some of the wheat with them. 30 Allow them both to grow unhindered until harvest time. Then I will tell the harvesters, "First collect all the weeds and tie them in bundles to be burned. Then gather all the wheat and put it in my barn." ' "

Parable of the Mustard Seed

31 Jesus also told this parable, "God's Kingdom in this world can be illustrated by a mustard seed that a farmer planted in his field. 32 Even though it's one of the smallest seeds, it grows into one of the largest garden plants and becomes a tree large enough for birds to nest in its branches." *[Psalm 104:12; Ezekiel 17:23; 31:6; Daniel 4:12]* ❖ *God's Kingdom starts in a small way in people's hearts. But it grows in influence, eventually becoming quite large and a blessing to those around it. Jesus may also have had in mind that birds often represented Gentiles, and the Kingdom would even take in Gentiles under its sway, which was a radical thought for the Jews of his day.* ➤ A

Parable of the Yeast

33 Jesus told them yet another parable, "God's Kingdom in this world can be illustrated by a little bit of yeast that a woman mixes in a large amount of flour until it permeates all the dough." ❖ *That little bit of yeast affects all the dough. In the same way, God's people may be few but their quiet slow influence in this world can be far reaching and have large effects.* ➤ B

Jesus' Teaching in Parables Fulfilled Prophecy

34 Jesus only taught these things to the public in parables. He never taught them anything plainly. 35 He did this to fulfill the prophecy that says, **"I will speak in parables**

A 13:32 Some interpret the birds nesting in the branches as representing false believers and corruption entering the church. It is true that in a majority of cases, Gentiles (frequently referred to in the Hebrew Scriptures as "the nations") are referred to as evil and pagan, and in many places the Scriptures talk about their evil influence on God's people. But in this parable, it seems more likely that the birds (Gentiles) which nest in the branches go along with the numerous prophecies about Gentiles (nations) being blessed by God's people and becoming a part of them, as in: Genesis 18:18; 22:18; 26:4; Deuteronomy 15:6; 32:1; 1 Chronicles 16:24, 31; Psalm 2:8; 22:27-28; 46:10; 67:2-4; 72:11, 17; 86:9; 102:15; 117:1; Isaiah 2:2; 9:1-2; 11:10; 25:3; 42:6-7; 49:6; 60:1-3; Jeremiah 3:17; 4:3; Zechariah 2:11; 8:22-23; 9:10. Jesus' focus in this parable—and in the following one about the yeast—seems to be about the positive characteristics of the kingdom and how it grows, not on how it is corrupted. The presence of false believers among God's people has already been addressed in the previous parable about the weeds, which shows how God deals with that problem.

B 13:33 Some interpret the dough as representing the church and the leaven (or yeast) as evil influence that will permeate the church. Their assumption is that leaven, when used figuratively, always depicts evil influence, as in Exodus 12:14-19; 13:7; Leviticus 2:11; 6:17; Deuteronomy 16:4; Matthew 16:5-12; Mark 8:15; Luke 12:1; 1 Corinthians 5:6-8; and Galatians 5:9. But Jesus literally says, "the kingdom of Heaven is like leaven" (not like dough—so also in Luke 13:21) so their conclusion about leaven always representing evil is incorrect. Leaven in the Scriptures when it is a figure represents influence, usually evil influence, but in a few contexts, good influence. See also Leviticus 23:17 where leaven is not seen as something impure. Figures in Scripture must be interpreted according to context. They do not necessarily always mean the same thing in every context. E.g., The Devil prowls like a roaring lion, [1 Peter 5:8] and Jesus is the lion of Judah. [Revelation 5:5]

to explain things unknown to people since God first created the world." *[Psalm 78:2]*

Jesus Explains the Parable of the Weeds

36 After teaching the crowd, Jesus went into a house. His followers came and asked, "Would you please explain the parable of the weeds to us?"

37 Jesus answered, "The farmer who plants the good seed is me, the Son of Man. 38 The field is this world and the good seeds are my people who belong to God's Kingdom. The weeds are those who belong to Satan, 39 who planted his people among mine. The harvest is Judgment Day and the harvesters are my angels. 40 Just as the weeds were gathered and burned in the parable, on Judgment day, 41 I, the Son of Man, will send my angels to gather all those who do evil and cause others to sin. They will be removed from my Kingdom 42 and thrown into Hell's fire where people will cry in great agony and defiant rage. 43 Then my people will live in their Heavenly Father's Kingdom, shining with joy and glory. If your minds are attuned to God, try to understand what this means!"

Two Parables About How to Regard Citizenship in God's Kingdom

44 Jesus said, "Citizenship in God's Kingdom is to be desired as a supremely valuable treasure. If a man were to accidentally find such a treasure in a field he didn't own, he would hide it and joyfully sell all he had to be able to buy the field and legally possess the treasure.

45 "Again, you should seek citizenship in God's Kingdom like a merchant seeks fine pearls. 46 If he were to find one of surpassing value, he would sell all he had so he could acquire it." ❖ *These parables tell us there is nothing in this world more valuable than being part of God's Kingdom. We should be willing to give up everything in order to become one of his people.* ➤

Parable of the Fish Net

47 Jesus then told this parable, "God's Kingdom in this world attracts all kinds of people. It can be illustrated by some fishermen who threw their net into the lake and caught all kinds of sea creatures. 48 When it was full, they pulled it up on shore and sat down to separate their catch. They gathered the good fish and put them in their baskets, but the worthless ones they threw away. 49 That's the way it will be on Judgment Day. The angels will separate God's people from those that reject him. 50 The latter they will throw into Hell's fire where people will cry in great agony and defiant rage."

51 Jesus asked his followers, "Have you understood these parables?" They answered, "Yes." 52 Then Jesus said, "Each of you now are like the owner of a house who can bring out both old and new treasures from his storeroom to show to others. Knowing the Torah's teachings and understanding about God's Kingdom, you are now able to teach others about spiritual truths in the Hebrew Scriptures and about the new things that I've taught you."

Jesus Is Rejected in Nazareth

53 When Jesus finished telling these parables, he left Capernaum 54 and went to his hometown of Nazareth where he had been raised. He taught in their synagogue and the people were shocked. They indignantly asked each other, "Where did *he* get this wisdom and the power to do miracles? 55 He's just the carpenter's son, isn't he? Isn't Miriam his mother, and his brothers James, Joseph, **A** Simon, and Judas? ❖ *Though none of his brothers believed in him before his resurrection, James became the leader of the assembly in Jerusalem, and Judas (a.k.a. Jude) became a missionary and wrote "Jude's Letter." We don't know anything more of Joseph and Simon or his sisters. Protestants assume these are younger brothers and sisters born to Miriam and Yosef after Jesus' birth. Catholics believe they are older brothers and sisters who his father Yosef had from a previous marriage.* ➤ 56 Aren't his sisters living here too? What makes him think he can be a prophet?" ❖ *In many cultures, people are expected to remain in the class, station, or occupation in life into which they were born. To do otherwise is considered presumptuous.* ➤ 57 So they were

---

A 13:55 Most manuscripts have "Joseph," but some have "John" and some have "Joses" which is a shortened form of "Joseph" that was used in Galilee.

offended and rejected him. Then Jesus said, "No prophet is accepted as such in his hometown or among his own family." *[John 4:44]* 58 So he was unable to do many miracles there because they refused to believe in him. *[Mark 6:4-5]* ❖ *Unbelief will hinder God's working in the miraculous. The text in Mark says he was "unable," not "unwilling." Therefore, it is not surprising that people who do not believe God works in certain ways anymore fail to see him do so, even if he wants to. This doesn't mean that God is really unable, but that he has chosen to work only in response to faith and so constrains himself. Do you have unbelief that actively inhibits God from working miracles in your life?* ➤

14

The Story of the Baptizer's Death

1 About that same time, Herod Antipas— ruler of Galilee Province—heard about the things Jesus and his followers were doing. 2 He said to his servants, "This must be John the Baptizer come back to life! That's why there's power in him to do miracles." ❖ *It's odd that Herod had not heard of Jesus' miracles while John was alive, and also odd that he would think this is John since John never did any miracles. [John 10:41] He obviously thought highly of John as a prophet from God and felt guilt over his ordering him beheaded. Such guilt can torment a person with irrational thoughts.* ➤

3 Now sometime before this, Herod had ordered John arrested at the insistence of Herodias, his brother Philip's former wife. ❖ *Herod and Herodias had an affair and then divorced their spouses to marry each other.* ➤ 4 For John had been telling Herod, "God's Torah forbids you from having her." *[Leviticus 18:15-16; 20:21]* 5 Herod wanted to execute John, but he feared the reaction of the people who believed John was a prophet.

6 But at Herod's birthday celebration, Herodias' daughter performed a seductive dance for his guests. She pleased Herod so much 7 that he imprudently vowed before his guests to give her whatever she asked. 8 Her mother urged her to say, "I want John the Baptizer's head on a platter."

9 Herod regretted his vow but granted her request to save face in front of his guests. ❖ *"Saving face" was very important in that Near Eastern culture.* ➤ 10 He had his soldiers behead John in the prison 11 and they brought his head in on a platter and gave it to the girl who took it to her mother. 12 John's followers came and took his body for burial. Then they went to tell Jesus what had happened.

Jesus Demonstrates Power to Multiply Resources

13 When Jesus heard about John's death, ❖ *Tradition says John was his cousin.* ➤ he and his close followers got in a boat and tried to withdraw from the public to have some privacy. But their plans were overheard, and people from many villages hiked along the shore of the lake to Jesus' destination. 14 When Jesus got out of the boat, he saw that a large crowd had arrived ahead of him. He felt compassion for them and went about healing all who were sick.

15 As evening approached, his close followers came to him and said, "This place is pretty remote and it's already getting late. You should send them away so they have time to walk to a village for something to eat before night falls."

16 Jesus replied, "They don't need to leave. I want you to feed them."

17 Incredulously, they said, "But we only have five bread rolls and two fish!"

18 He instructed, "Well, bring them to me." 19 Jesus had all the people recline on the grass. ❖ *Reclining while propping themselves up on one elbow was the way they normally ate, following Roman custom.* ➤ Then he took the five bread rolls and two fish, looked up toward Heaven, thanked God for the food, and broke the rolls and fish into pieces that he gave to his followers. ❖ *If Jesus followed the common form of Jewish thanksgiving, he said something like this: "You are to be blessed (i.e., praised), O Lord our God, King of the universe, who brings forth bread from the earth."* ➤ They then distributed the pieces—which were miraculously multiplied—to all the people. 20 Everyone ate as much as they wanted and were fully satisfied. Afterward, the leftovers were gathered and filled twelve baskets. ❖ *Even miraculous provision is not to be wasted. This is the only miracle recorded in all four Gospels, and all four record the twelve baskets so the number must be significant. Most take it to mean that he is able to supply all the needs of the twelve tribes of Israel, which are symbolic of all of God's people.* ➤ 21 They had fed about 5000 men,

not counting women and children. *[2 Kings 4:42-44]* ❖ *In that culture, women, and children were not commonly counted. There were easily 10,000 to 20,000 people who were fed.* ➤

Jesus and Peter Walk on Water

22 Right after that, Jesus told his close followers to get back in the boat and proceed to the other side of the lake ahead of him while he convinced the people to go home. 23 After dismissing the crowd, Jesus went up a nearby mountain alone to pray. He stayed there until well after sunset. 24 By that time, the boat with his followers was quite a ways out on the lake, but a strong wind blowing against them hindered their progress and caused large waves.

25 They fought to make headway for hours, and during the fourth watch of the night, ❖ *sometime between 3 and 6 a.m., but before dawn* ➤ Jesus came to them walking on the water. *[Job 9:8]* 26 When his followers saw him coming toward them on the water in the darkness, they were terrified. They cried out, "It's a ghost!"

27 But Jesus immediately reassured them, "Don't worry! It's me! There's nothing to be afraid of!" ❖ *The Greek text literally has him saying, "I am," which is the natural way in Greek to say "It's me." But Jesus probably didn't speak Greek to his followers (their everyday language was Aramaic) so Matthew might have been putting in a subtle clue to the observant reader that Jesus claimed to be the great "I AM," i.e., Yahweh. [Exodus 3:14]* ➤

28 Peter called to him, "Lord, if **A** it's really you, command me to come out to you on the water." ❖ *Peter had faith for the miraculous but was not presumptuous. He didn't try to walk on the water without his Lord's command. But when Jesus gave the command, Peter knew he would also give the power to obey it. If we lack the faith to ask or to follow through when he directs us, then we won't experience miracles.* ➤

29 Jesus said, "Come!" So Peter got out of the boat and started walking on the water toward Jesus. ❖ *Many don't give Peter enough credit. How many of us would be willing to first ask and then obey such a command?* ➤ 30 But then the wind and waves distracted him and he became

frightened. Focusing on the impossibilities, instead of remembering to trust Jesus, he began to doubt and to sink. But then he immediately cried out, "Lord, save me!"

31 Jesus quickly reached out, grabbed him *[Psalm 18:16; 144:7]* and said, "Your faith is so small! Why did you start to doubt me?"

32 Then they both climbed into the boat and the wind suddenly died down. 33 Those in the boat recognized the significance of all this and bowed down in submission to worship him. They exclaimed, "You really are God's Son!"

Jesus Heals in Gennesaret

34 They finished their crossing by landing in Gennesaret. ❖ *There was a village named Gennesaret, but this was likely the area of that name which was located on the northwest shore of Lake Galilee, southwest of Capernaum.* ➤ 35 When the people there recognized Jesus, they spread the news of his location to everyone in the area. As a result, they brought many sick people to him. 36 People begged for permission just to touch the tassel **B** of his robe, and God healed everyone who did so.

15

What Defiles Us in God's Sight and What Does Not

1 Then some Pharisees and Scripture teachers from Jerusalem came to Jesus and indignantly said, 2 "You are responsible for the behavior of your followers. Why do you allow them to disregard the traditions established by the elders? They don't ritually wash their hands before eating!" ❖ *They were referring to man-made rules that had become traditions and were considered by the Pharisees and Scripture teachers to be as important as God's commands in the Torah. Their traditions built a "hedge" around the Torah. They believed that a person who kept all of their traditions would never disobey God's commands, for these traditions were more rigorous in their demands on outward behavior than the Torah required. Jesus rejected these traditions and claimed they placed an unnecessary burden on people. He also rejected them because the religious leaders claimed that breaking these*

A 14:28 The word εἰ (ei) could mean "since" instead of "if," and some commentators take it that way.

B 14:36 Or fringe, or edge. See the footnote at Matthew 9:20.

man-made traditions was sin. These rules also encouraged people to think that God was mainly concerned with outward behavior more than attitudes of the heart and mind. Concerning ritual washing, they believed that many of the things they touched in everyday life ritually defiled them in God's sight. So if they touched their food with defiled hands, the food would become defiled, and eating defiled food would defile the entire person. ➤

3 Jesus retorted, "And why do you consider your own man-made traditions more important than the teachings of God's Torah, so you are willing to disobey his commands in order to follow your petty rules? 4 As an example, the Torah says, 'Honor your parents,' and also, 'Someone who curses his parents is to be executed.' [Exodus 20:12; 21:17; Leviticus 20:9; Deuteronomy 5:16] 5 But you say that a man can inform his parents he has dedicated his resources to God 6 and then he doesn't have to use those resources to support them in their old age. Your tradition circumvents God's command and its intention that a man should honor and help his parents. You pretend to honor God while you disobey his command in order to honor your own traditions! 7 The prophet Isaiah correctly prophesied about hypocrites like you when he recorded God saying, 8 'These people say they honor me and they make a show of it, but in their hearts they don't love me at all. 9 I consider their worship to be worthless since they teach people to follow their man-made rules above my commands!' " [Isaiah 29:13]

10 Then Jesus drew everyone's attention to himself and said, "Listen carefully and try to understand this! 11 It's what comes out of people's mouths that defiles them in God's sight, not what goes in as the Pharisees teach!"

12 Then his followers came and said, "You do realize that the Pharisees were highly offended by what you just said, don't you?"

13 Jesus contemptuously replied, "My Heavenly Father will destroy any teaching that doesn't come from him! 14 I want you to ignore them and their teachings. They claim to be spiritual guides to those who are ignorant of God's truth. But in reality, they themselves are blind to it. They lead those who follow them to destruction."

15 Peter asked him, "Would you please explain what you said about being defiled?"

16 Jesus was exasperated, "Don't you understand either? 17 What goes in your mouth goes down into your stomach and then is eventually eliminated from your body. Don't you see that eating something with unwashed hands doesn't affect how God views you? ❖ *The topic in this passage is "eating without ritually washing one's hands," not "eating non-kosher food," which was never mentioned and was certainly not even being considered by those involved in this conversation. All the food in question is kosher. It never would have occurred to Jews in Jesus' time to consider non-kosher food as something fit to eat. While this passage might—with other Scriptural support—be interpreted to apply to non-kosher food, that is not the point Jesus was making here.* ➤ 18 What "comes out of your mouth" is what you say. Your words express what is in your heart and mind. If they are sinful, they defile you in God's sight. 19 An evil mind produces evil thoughts and desires to murder, to commit adultery, to indulge in sexual immorality, to steal, to lie while testifying, and to slander. 20 These are the kinds of things that defile a person in God's sight. Eating without ritually washing your hands doesn't affect your heart or mind at all and can't make your mind evil. And ritually washing your hands can't make or keep your heart and mind pure. It's the things of your heart and mind that God cares about, not meaningless outward ceremonies."

The Persistent Faith of a Gentile Woman

21 After that, Jesus left Galilee and went to the region near the Gentile cities of Tyre and Sidon on the Mediterranean coast. 22 A Gentile woman from that area came to him and loudly pleaded, "Lord, Son of David, have mercy and help me, for my daughter is severely demonized." 23 Surprisingly, Jesus ignored her. So his followers said to him, "She's just going to continue following us and shouting. Please send her away." ❖ *Some commentators think his followers meant: help her and send her away.* ➤ 24 But instead, he said to the woman, ❖ *Or to his followers* ➤ "God only sent me to minister to Israelites who are lost in their sin." 25 Instead of being put off, the woman bowed down in front of him and

pleaded, "Lord, please help me!" 26 He replied, "It wouldn't be right to take food that's meant for God's children and give it to the dogs." ❖ *Jesus immediately recognized her great faith. So instead of quickly granting her request, he extended his interaction with her in order to showcase her faith to his followers. He knew that his apparent harshness would not deter her and would provide her with the opportunity to demonstrate persistence in the face of adversity. So this incident is an example for us to follow when we bring our requests to the Lord.* ➤ 27 She replied, "Yes, Lord. But even dogs are allowed to eat the bits that fall under the master's table." 28 Then Jesus exclaimed, "My dear woman, you have strong faith indeed! I will grant your request." And God immediately healed her daughter.

Jesus Heals

29 Returning to Lake Galilee, Jesus went up a hill and sat down. 30 A large crowd followed him and brought people who were lame, crippled, blind, mute, and had many other disorders. They laid them at Jesus' feet and he healed each one of them. 31 The people were constantly amazed as they saw the formerly mute able to speak, those who had been crippled made normal, those who had been lame now able to walk, and they praised the God of Israel for doing it through Jesus.

Jesus Multiplies Resources Again to Feed 4000 Men

32 Jesus summoned his close followers and told them, "I feel sorry for these people. They've been with me for three days and their food is gone. I don't want to send them away without something to eat, or some of them might faint from hunger on their way home."

33 His followers said, "But this crowd is so huge! Where could we find enough bread in this remote place to feed them, even if we could afford it?"

34 Jesus asked them, "How many bread rolls do you have?" They answered, "Only seven, plus a few small fish."

35 Then, Jesus told the people to recline on the ground 36 and took the seven rolls and the fish. He thanked God for them, broke them, and gave them to his followers to distribute to the people. 37 Everyone ate all they could desire and were full. When the leftovers were gathered, they filled seven large baskets. 38 That crowd included about 4000 men, not counting the women and children who were also there.

39 After Jesus sent the people home, he and his close followers got into the boat and went to the region of Magadan. ❖ *Mark 8:10 says they went to Dalmanutha. These may have been two villages close together or different names for the same village. But today, the location is unknown.* ➤

16

Interpreting the Signs of the Times

1 One day, some Pharisees and Sadducees came to Jesus to test him. They asked him to show them miraculous proof that God had sent him. ❖ *And they expected him to fail to produce it.* ➤ 2 But his reply was, "Some evenings you predict, 'Tomorrow's weather will be fair, since the sky is red.' 3 And some mornings you predict, 'Today there will be a rainstorm, since the sky is overcast and red.' You are observant enough to interpret the signs in the sky, but you seem incapable of interpreting the equally obvious signs that are happening in these times. ❖ *They had seen and heard about many of Jesus' miracles and healings, yet they chose to ignore these signs because they didn't want to conclude that Jesus was the Messiah. If they did so, they would have to give up their own cherished beliefs and status as interpreters of the Torah.* ➤ 4 Many in this generation are evil and unfaithful to God. You want a miraculous sign before you will believe, but none will be granted except the sign of Jonah!" Then he turned and left them. ❖ *The sign of Jonah was a cryptic reference to his resurrection. Just as the prophet Jonah spent parts of three days in the belly of a fish and then was spit out alive, [Jonah chapters 1—2] Jesus would spend parts of three days dead in the grave and then come back to life. This was the only sign they would be given and the only one they should need. Many Pharisees and priests did believe after the resurrection, but many others did not.* ➤

Jesus Warns About the Evil Influence of the Pharisees and Sadducees

5 Later, when Jesus and his followers arrived on the opposite shore, they

discovered that they had forgotten to bring any bread along. ❖ *Bread was their main staple food, eaten at every meal, so it was usually mentioned as representing food in general.* ➤ 6 Still thinking about his confrontation with the Jewish leaders, Jesus said, "Guard yourselves against the leaven of the Pharisees and the Sadducees." ❖ *"Leaven" was a piece of dough that was set aside to use to leaven another batch of bread. The natural yeast in that piece multiplied as the dough sat for a few days. Leaven is often used in the Scriptures as a symbol of influence, sometimes positive, and often negative. It represented impure influence when they rid their houses of it during the preparation for the Passover and Feast of Unleavened Bread. They should have easily understood his meaning, yet they were focused on their own concerns.* ➤ 7 His followers started discussing the meaning of his statement among themselves and concluded, "He said it because we forgot to bring bread along."

8 But Jesus was aware of their discussion and said, "Why are you talking about not having any bread? Do you have so little faith that you forget I can provide it for you? 9 Don't you understand the significance of 5000 men being fed from only five rolls of bread? Do you remember how much was left over? 10 And what about the 4000 men fed from only seven rolls? Do you remember how much was left over that time? 11 So why do you think I'd be concerned about you forgetting a little bread? What I said was, guard yourselves against the leaven of the Pharisees and the Sadducees!"

12 Then they finally understood that he wasn't talking about the leaven in bread, but about the teachings and influence of the Pharisees and Sadducees.

Peter Recognizes That Jesus Is the Messiah

13 Jesus was in the area near Caesarea Philippi ❖ *about 25 miles north of Lake Galilee at the base of Mt. Hermon* ➤ when he asked his close followers, "Who do people say that I, the Son of Man, am?" 14 They answered, "Some say you are John the Baptizer, others say you are the prophet Elijah, and others that you are

the prophet Jeremiah or one of the other prophets from long ago." *[2 King 2:1-12; Malachi 4:5; Matthew 14:1-2; Mark 6:14-15; Luke 9:7-8]* 15 Then he asked, "And what about you? Who do you think I am?" 16 Simon Peter immediately answered, "You are God's Anointed One, the Messiah, the Son of the only living God!" *[2 Samuel 7:14; Psalm 2:7; 89:27]* 17 Jesus said to him, "I bless you, Simon son of John, A because no human being could tell you this. It was my Heavenly Father who revealed it to you. 18 I will also say that you are like a rock ❖ *Or: you are Peter—"petros" in Greek—which means "rock"* ➤ And on this rock foundation, *[Isaiah 51:1-2; Ephesians 2:20]* which is the confession of faith in me you have just made, I will build my Assembly of Believers. And the defenses of Satan's kingdom will not prevail against ❖ *the onslaught of* ➤ my Assembly. ❖ *The meaning of verse 18 is highly debated in all its aspects. The "rock" upon which Jesus builds his assembly (church) is variously interpreted as 1) Peter himself (the view of the Roman Catholic church), 2) Peter's confession (the view of most Protestants), 3) all of Jesus' followers [Ephesians 2:20; Revelation 21:14], 4) Jesus himself [1 Corinthians 3:11; 10:4; 1 Peter 2:6-8], 5) Jesus' teaching [Matthew 7:24-25; Luke 6:47-49], 6) Any combination of the preceding options. ¶ The traditional interpretation of the last sentence is, "And the gates of Hades will not overcome or silence my Assembly." The "gates of Hades" in the Hebrew Scriptures are associated with the realm of the dead and the power of death. [Job 38:17; Psalm 9:13; Revelation 20:13] But despite the term "gates of Hades" meaning the realm or power of death, "gates" as a figure implies defenses, not an attacking force. Elsewhere in the Scriptures, it is clear that Jesus has defeated Satan and his demons, and the Messiah's followers—his Assembly— have authority over all the power of the enemy. [Matthew 10:1, 8; Mark 3:15; 6:7, 13; Luke 9:1; 10:17] In a struggle against Satan and his demons for the salvation of people under his influence, we will prevail. They will not prevail against our efforts to make followers of Jesus. And in any struggle against believers to discourage or destroy our faith or in other ways defeat us, we have victory because of our spiritual union with the Messiah. [1 Corinthians 15:57; 2 Corinthians 2:14; 1 John 2:13] The traditional translation and interpretation of this sentence, while it is the almost-universal interpretation given*

A **16:17** Literally he called him "Bar-Yonah," which is a transliteration into Greek from Aramaic for "son of Yonah" (Jonah). But in John 1:42 he is called "son of John," and there is no record of anyone having the name "Jonah" for

hundreds of years before or after Jesus' time. In Aramaic, John is "Yochanan" (Johanan). Yonah (Jonah) might be a short form for Yochanan (John), or one might have been his Greek name and the other his Aramaic name.

by commentators and does express truth, implies a defensive posture on the part of the assembly of believers that is at odds with Scriptural teaching on the victory of the cross and the aggressive evangelistic posture we are exhorted to boldly assume, and the spiritual warfare we are meant to wage. ➤ 19 I will give you, Peter, ❖ *Every "you" in verse 19 is singular in Greek, referring to Peter alone.* ➤ the keys to God's Kingdom. Whatever you prohibit or allow here on earth will correspondingly be prohibited or allowed in Heaven." [Isaiah 22:22] ❖ *This is also a highly controversial verse. First is the issue of who possesses the keys: 1) Peter himself, 2) all the apostles, 3) the assembly of believers corporately, 4) every individual believer [Matthew 18:18 (the you is plural in 18:18), 28:20] , 5) assembly leaders only. Most commentators conclude number 4) from Matthew 18:18 and its context. Secondly, what do the keys represent? 1) the power to decide who will be saved and not saved, 2) the power to forgive sin or not forgive it [John 20:22-23], 3) power over demons, 4) the power for the assembly leaders to decide what practices are allowed or not allowed, 5) more general power over spiritual realities. [Matthew 18:15-20], 6) all of the above. Some denominations say it is limited to 2) or 4). Many Charismatics and Pentecostals go with number 6).* ➤ 20 Then Jesus sternly ordered his followers not to tell anyone yet that he was the Messiah. ❖ *If Jesus or his followers openly pressed the point with people at that time, some would have immediately rejected him and hardened their hearts against him. But if they were not forced to make a decision at that time, they might later respond positively after the evidence of the resurrection.* ➤

Jesus Predicts His Suffering and Death

21 Starting at that time, Jesus began to explain to his close followers that he had to go to Jerusalem. There, he would be arrested and suffer under the power of the Jewish leaders, be killed, and then come back to life on the second day after his death. ❖ *The "third day" (in the literal text) is confusing for modern readers because of the inclusive way Jews of that day counted time. The day of his death they called "the first day of his death." The "third day of his death" we more naturally phrase in English as "the second day after his death." But tradition strongly preserves the phrase "the third day," usually without adequate explanation, leading to confusion or wrong conclusions by people who think the phrase means the same in modern English as it did in first-century Greek written by a*

Jewish author. It does not. Also see the note at Matthew 12:40. ➤ 22 But Peter spoke to Jesus privately and rebuked him for saying that these things would happen. He said, "Lord! May God forbid that anything like that should happen to you! It must not happen!" 23 Jesus turned away from Peter ❖ *others think he turned toward him* ➤ and said, "Get out of my way, Adversary! You are tempting me to stumble in sin. Avoiding what must happen is your human response, but it's not what God wants me to do." ❖ *It's worth noting that the same person can one minute speak revelatory truth from God, and the next minute speak lies from the enemy. We need to take care how we interpret any revelation the Lord gives us. The Father showed Peter that Jesus was the Messiah, but he interpreted what this must imply from his own cultural expectations about the Messiah, which were wrong.* ➤

The High Cost of Following Jesus

24 Then Jesus told his followers, "If you want to be one of my true followers, you must put aside your own desires and be willing to suffer and even die in order to obey me. 25 Those who want to retain control of their own lives **A** and protect them, as opposed to submitting to God's authority and risk suffering for him, will ultimately lose them. But those who are willing to give up all that they are and have—even their own lives—in order to follow me, will ultimately gain their true lives and live forever. 26 What benefit have you gained if you acquire everything you desire in this temporary world but in the process lose your chance at eternal life in Heaven? [Psalm 49:7-9] What is the opportunity to live forever in Heaven and avoid eternity in Hell worth to you? 27 For I, the Son of Man, will return to this world possessing the glorious power and majesty I have in unity with my Father. I will come with his angels and **will reward each person based on what they have done in their earthly lives.** [Psalm 62:12; Matthew 25:31-46; Romans 2:6; Ephesians 6:8; Revelation 22:12] 28 I assure you that some of you standing here right now will see me, the Son of Man, coming as King before they die." [Mark 9:1; Luke

---

A 16:25 The word ψυχή (psuchē) translated "life" in this verse and in verse 26 also means "soul."

9:27; 2 Peter 1:16-18] ❖ *Jesus may have been referring to the event that Matthew reports next. Or he may have meant those who would see him after his resurrection and before his ascension to Heaven. Or he may have meant they would see him establish his kingdom in the lives of believers after Pentecost. And John had the visions reported in the book of Revelation where he saw Jesus returning to reign as King. [Revelation 19:11—20:6]* ➤

17

God Reveals Jesus' True Glory

1 About six days later, Jesus took just Peter, James, and John up a high mountain so they could pray by themselves. 2 While they were there, his appearance changed before their very eyes. His face started to shine like the sun, and his clothing shone with a brilliant white light. 3 Then Moses and Elijah suddenly appeared from Heaven and were speaking with him. 4 Peter said to Jesus, "Lord, it's good that we're here. If you want, I will make three shelters here, one for you, one for Moses, and one for Elijah."

5 While he was saying this, a cloud A appeared around them like a thick fog. Then they heard God saying, "This is my Son, my Chosen B One, who pleases me greatly in all he says and does. *He* is the one you should listen to and obey!" *[Isaiah 42:1; Deuteronomy 18:15-19]* ❖ *Moses was the one to whom God had given his Torah teachings and was the most revered of all their prophets. Moses represented the Torah which ruled their lives. Elijah represented the teachings of all the other prophets. Together, they represented all the writings of the Hebrew Scriptures, everything that was known about God and his will. In this context when God told them to listen to his Son, he was saying that Jesus and his teachings had more authority than Moses, Elijah, and everything written in the Hebrew Scriptures. So in this event, commonly called the "Transfiguration," God clearly said that Jesus was his Son and, therefore, also God, and that his authority exceeded every authority they had been taught to revere.* ➤ 6 When the three followers heard this voice, they were

terrified and prostrated themselves in worship. 7 Jesus came over, touched them, and said, "There's nothing to be afraid of. Get up." 8 When they raised their heads to look around, they only saw Jesus as he normally was.

9 While they were going down the mountain, Jesus commanded them, "Don't tell anyone about the vision you saw until after I, the Son of Man, have died and come back from death." 10 Since they had just seen Elijah, they asked him, "Why do the Scripture teachers say that Elijah must come before the Messiah does?" *[Malachi 3:1; 4:5-6]* 11 Jesus replied, "That prophecy is certainly true. Elijah came C and inaugurated events that will restore everything to the way it should be. 12 Elijah came, but no one recognized him. Instead, they mistreated a prophet from God any way they liked. In a similar way, they will also cause me, the Son of Man, to suffer." ❖ *John the Baptizer was not actually Elijah. [John 1:21] The Scripture is clear that there is no reincarnation. [Hebrews 9:27] But Elijah was a prefiguring "type" of John the Baptizer. [Matthew 11:14; Luke 1:17] Both were great prophets. [Matthew 11:11; Luke 7:28] Both dressed alike [2 Kings 1:8; Matthew 3:4] and lived in the wilderness. Both had an evil queen who wanted to kill them. [1 Kings 19:1-18; Matthew 14:3-5] People did recognize John as a prophet, but not that he was the herald of the Messiah. Since Elijah performed miracles, the Jews expected him to do so again when he came, but John never did any. [John 10:41] Both John's and Jesus' lives were humble, involved rejection by the religious authorities, suffering, and dying; but the Jews were expecting greatness. They refused to consider the Scriptures that predicted his rejection, suffering, and death. [Psalm 22:1-18; 69:4; 7-12; 19-21; 118:22a, Isaiah 53:1-12]* ➤ 13 Then they understood that John the Baptizer was the one who fulfilled that prophecy. ❖ *This is a clear example of fulfilled prophecy showing us that not all prophecy has a literal fulfillment.* ➤

Jesus' Followers Fail to Expel a Demon

14 When they got to the foot of the mountain, they came upon a crowd. A man came

---

A **17:5a** One of the ways God visibly manifests his presence is with a cloud. [Exodus 13:21; 40:34-38; Numbers 9:15-22; 10:11-12; Ezekiel 10:4; and possibly in: Acts 1:9; Revelation 10:1; 11:12; 14:14-16] Even today, people sometimes report the same phenomenon in connection with God's special presence.

B **17:5b** Literally it says, "beloved," but some

commentators think it was a Messianic title.

C **17:11** The present tense of Jesus' statement, in the literal text, is meant to assert the continuing truth of the prophecy, not to indicate it was happening right then. The tense of his statement in the next verse indicates it had already happened. To conform to the way English speakers expect to hear tenses used, this verse was changed to past tense.

and prostrated himself in front of Jesus and said, 15 "Sir, please have mercy and help my son who is demented **A** and suffers greatly. He often falls into fire or water. 16 I brought him to your followers but they couldn't heal him." 17 Jesus said to his followers, "You people are stubborn and faithless! How long will I have to be with you and put up with you before you learn how to use my power?" Then he said to the man, "Bring your son here." ❖ *Jesus had already trained his apostles and had given them power and authority over every demon and sickness. See Matthew 10:1; Mark 6:7, 13; and Luke 9:1. But they had failed to learn the lesson well enough. They had probably given up trying too soon. Most demons obey fairly quickly, but some strongly resist and you have to persist in prayer and commanding them before they leave. See Luke 8:28-30 where some demons did not obey even Jesus right away. ¶ As this story indicates in the following verses, their failure to expel the demon did not mean it was God's will that the boy not be delivered, as many people today would conclude under similar circumstances, particularly with regard to someone they pray for who is not quickly healed.* ➤ 18 Jesus rebuked the demon that was causing the boy to behave this way and it came out of him. He was instantly cured.

19 Later, Jesus' followers came to him in private and asked, "Why couldn't we expel that demon?" 20 He answered, "Because of your unbelief. **B** You must understand this. If you have even a small amount of genuine faith, you can overcome even seemingly impossible obstacles. Nothing that God wants you to do will be impossible for you. ❖ *The statement in the literal text about moving a mountain was a common figure of speech for something that was extremely difficult. He did not mean it literally. We are to have faith in God's power to accomplish what he wants done. Jesus had already explicitly revealed to his followers that it is God's will for them to heal people and expel demons. [Matthew 10:1; Mark 3:14-15; 6:7; Luke 9:1-2; 10:19] So they should have persisted in faith until it was accomplished, not given up*

quickly. See the note at Luke 17:6.* ➤ 21 But this kind of demon does not leave easily with just a command. You also need to fast and pray." **C**
❖ *There are different kinds of demons, some more powerful than others. [Daniel 10:12-13; Ephesians 6:12] Some demons even resisted Jesus and didn't come out the first time he commanded them. [Luke 8:28-30]* ➤

Jesus Talks a Second Time About His Coming Death

22 When Jesus was together with his close followers in Galilee, he told them, "I, the Son of Man, will soon be betrayed and handed over to men who hate me. 23 They will kill me, and on the second **D** day after my death, God will make me alive again." When they heard this, they were greatly distressed. ❖ *They evidently didn't pay attention to his telling them that he would become alive again. The IVP commentary suggests they were thinking in terms of the resurrection on the Last Day.* ➤

Jesus Miraculously Pays the Temple Tax

24 When Jesus and his close followers arrived in Capernaum, those who were collecting the annual two-drachma Temple tax came to Peter and asked, "Your rabbi pays the Temple tax, doesn't he?" ❖ *Almost all adult male Jews paid this yearly tax which was equivalent to two days wages. It helped maintain the Temple in Jerusalem. Priests and beggars did not have to pay.* ➤ 25 He said, "Yes." Later, Peter entered the house where Jesus was, but Jesus spoke to him first, "Simon, I'd like to hear your opinion on a matter. Do the kings of this world collect taxes from their own sons or from others?" 26 Peter answered, "From others." Jesus replied, "Then you agree that the king's sons are exempt. 27 But we don't want to unnecessarily offend the Temple-tax collectors who wouldn't understand that we're exempt. So go down to the lake and throw

---

A 17:15 Literally, "moonstruck," which is what the word "lunatic" means. The symptoms are similar to epilepsy but verse 18 and the other accounts make clear that they were caused by a demon.

B 17:20 Some manuscripts have "small faith" rather than "unbelief."

C 17:21 The oldest manuscripts lack verse 21. It was probably added here by some scribe to make it conform with Mark 9:29. But since it is in Mark, we know that

Jesus did say it on this occasion. A number of commentators note that the disciples had not had the opportunity to fast when Jesus arrived, and they believe that the words "fast and" were not in the original manuscript of Mark 9:29, but were added later. Yet we know fasting can aid the efficacy of prayer, so it is a valid point to remember, even if Jesus did not say it on this occasion.

D 17:23 See note at Matthew 16:21 for the reasoning behind not using the traditional phrase "the third day."

in a fishing line. Inside the mouth of the first fish you catch, you will find a shekel. ❖ *worth four drachmas* **A** ➤ Give it to the tax collector for your tax and mine."

18

How to Be Important in God's Sight

1 About that time, Jesus' close followers came and asked, "Who among us will be the greatest in God's Kingdom?" 2 Jesus called a small child and stood him in front of them. 3 He then said, "It's important you understand this. Unless you become humble and forget about your status, you will never even enter God's Kingdom. *[Mark 10:15; Luke 18:17]* 4 Those who become humble like this child will be among the greatest in God's Kingdom. 5 And those who welcome and serve a small child in order to obey me, welcome me. ❖ *We are not to consider people of status as more important than those with no status. Truly humble people will consider even children important and worth serving.* ➤

6 "But anyone who tempts one of these young believers or causes them to sin can expect a severe punishment. Such a person would be better off by far if his only punishment were to be thrown into the sea with a huge stone tied to his neck.

7 The punishment for those who tempt or cause my people to sin will be terrible! It's inevitable that people will be tempted to sin. But God will severely punish anyone who deliberately tempts or causes others to sin! 8 If your hand or foot entices you to sin, you would be better off getting rid of it and entering eternal life maimed than to end up in Hell's eternal fire. *[Matthew 5:29-30; Mark 9:43-45]* 9 Even if your eye entices you to sin, you would be better off getting rid of it than to keep it and end up in Hell. ❖ *Jesus didn't think that hands or feet or eyes are true sources of sinful temptations. He was making the point that sin is serious, and you should do whatever is necessary to avoid sinning. Nothing*

is too extreme an option if it enables you to avoid Hell. See Luke 16:22-24 and also 2 Thessalonians 1:9 with the following note about Hell. ➤

10 "Take care not to look down on any of my people as insignificant, not even small children. For their guardian angels are always in my Heavenly Father's presence and will report any way that you mistreat them. 11 For I, the Son of Man, have come to save people who are spiritually lost. None of them are insignificant to me. **B**

12 "Think about this. If a man has 100 sheep and one of them gets lost, don't you think he would leave the 99 that are grazing and go look for the lost one? 13 And if he then finds it, he will certainly be far happier about that one sheep than about the 99 that didn't get lost. 14 So in a similar way, your Heavenly Father doesn't want anyone, not even a supposedly insignificant child, to be lost. Everyone is important to him."

How to Handle Unrepented Sin Among Believers

15 Jesus told his followers, "If a fellow believer sins against you, **C** lovingly confront him in private about it. If he listens to you and repents, you have restored your relationship. 16 But if he refuses to listen, take one or two other believers along with you as witnesses to confront him again. This way, any accusation you need to make against him later will have two or three witnesses to confirm your story. *[Deuteronomy 19:15]* 17 But if he also refuses to listen to them, then bring the matter before the assembly. And if he will not listen even to the assembly, then treat him as a nonbeliever who is not part of the assembly. ❖ *The purpose of this treatment is so he might realize the seriousness of his behavior and its consequences and repent, so he can be restored to the community of believers. See an example of this in 1 Corinthians 5:1-5 and the restoration in 2 Corinthians 2:5-8.* ➤

18 "It's important to understand this. Whatever you prohibit or allow here on earth

---

A **17:27** The drachma was used as the coin equivalent to a single day's wage during Jesus' time. Later, the drachma was replaced by the denarius, which is mentioned in other places in the Gospels. The writers of some of the Gospels substituted "denarius" for "drachma" because they were roughly equivalent in value and the denarius was the coin in actual use at the time the Gospels were written, a few decades after Jesus returned to Heaven.

B **18:11** Verse 11 is not found in the oldest manuscripts and was probably added as a transition to verse 12. It comes from Luke 19:10.

C **18:15** Most manuscripts have "against you," but some do not.

with regard to order, practice, and discipline in the Assembly of Believers will correspondingly be prohibited or allowed in Heaven. **19** Furthermore, if two of you agree about anything you ask for in prayer, my Heavenly Father will do it for you. ❖ *Commentators are not agreed if verse 19 starts a new topic or continues the previous one. They are also not agreed as to the scope of the promise, i.e., if it is general in scope or confined to the context of verse 17. Whatever the scope, the assumption is that the request is within the Father's will. But also see the note after verse 21.* ➤ **20** For even if as few as two or three believers have come together to submit to me in worship or to pray, I will be there to give them my attention." ❖ *Jesus is speaking of the time after his return to Heaven. God is everywhere and is aware of everything. Even one person can pray or worship and God will hear. But these verses tell us that praying and worshipping with others is important. There is power in unity and agreement among believers.* ➤

The Consequences of Unforgiveness

21 Then Peter came to ask Jesus, "Lord, how many times should I forgive a fellow believer who sins against me? As many as seven times?" *[Luke 17:3-4]* ❖ *Verses 15-17 and 21 are all about dealing with sin. The interpretation given to verse 18 was derived from the immediately preceding context. It is likely that verses 19-20 are also about dealing with sin since that is the context before and after them. (Section headings, such as the one dividing verses 20 and 21, are helps to the reader but are not themselves Scripture.) The precise meaning that Matthew intended for these verses should be determined by the surrounding context.* ➤ **22** Jesus answered, "Not just seven times! Don't place a limit, not even seventy times seven times. A Always be willing to forgive. **23** Here's a parable that teaches how God views someone who is unwilling to forgive.

"There was a king who decided to see how his servants were handling his finances. **24** He had just started the process when one servant was brought before him who owed 10,000 talents. ❖ *A talent was a large unit of weight, and the debt was in gold or silver. We have no way of knowing exactly what a talent was worth, but 10,000 talents was a staggering amount that no individual could ever hope to repay. See the note about talents just before Matthew 25:14.* ➤

25 Since the servant could not possibly pay his debt, the king ordered him, his wife, and children to be sold as slaves, and also that all he had be sold to help repay part of the debt. **26** But the servant prostrated himself before the king and begged, 'Please have patience with me and I will find a way to repay you everything!' **27** As a result, the king felt compassion for the man and decided to cancel his debt and allow him to go free.

28 "But that same servant then went and found one of his fellow servants who owed him only a hundred days' wages. He grabbed him around the neck and started choking him and demanded, 'Pay what you owe me immediately!' **29** Then, that fellow servant prostrated himself and begged, 'Please have patience with me and I will find a way to repay you everything!' **30** But he refused to wait. Instead, he had the man arrested and put in debtors prison until the debt was paid in full. ❖ *Someone in debtors' prison would have no means of acquiring money to pay his debt. He would be at the mercy of friends and relatives who would want to pay it for him, if they could.* ➤ **31** When some of the other servants saw what had happened, the injustice distressed them. So they went to the king and told him everything. **32** Then, the king summoned the servant and said, 'You are evil! I had pity on you and canceled your entire debt just because you pleaded with me for mercy. **33** Since I granted you great mercy, you should have also been willing to grant your fellow servant mercy for a much smaller debt!' **34** The king was so angry that he had the man tortured until his debt was paid in full.

35 "That's exactly the attitude my Heavenly Father will have toward you if you refuse to sincerely and completely forgive someone who sins against you, especially a fellow believer."

19

Jesus Answers a Question About Divorce

1 When Jesus finished teaching, he and his close followers left Galilee and walked

---

A **18:22** The Greek here is ambiguous and can mean either 70 times 7, or 77.

south to Judea province along the eastern side of the Jordan River. ❖ *This was the route that most Jews took to avoid going through Samaria, since Jews and Samaritans hated each other.* ➤ 2 As usual, a large crowd followed him and he healed all who were sick among them.

3 Some Pharisees came to trap Jesus with a question they thought would make him unpopular. They asked, "Does the Torah allow a man to divorce his wife for any reason he wishes?" ❖ *This was the view of the famous Rabbi Hillel. The issue of divorce was constantly debated at that time.* ➤ 4 Jesus replied, "Haven't you read the Scriptures? ❖ *This was a rebuke, since the Pharisees considered themselves authorities on the Scriptures. They were debating an issue that the Scriptures were clear about.* ➤ They teach that in the beginning the Creator made one male and one female ❖ *This implies that God never intended for Adam or any man or Eve or any woman to have the option of divorce.* ➤ 5 and he said, 'A man will leave his parents and be united to his wife, and the two will become one.' *[Genesis 1:27; 2:24; 5:2]* 6 So they are no longer two, but have become one. Therefore, people should not separate what God has joined." 7 The Pharisees responded, "Then why did Moses command that a man give his wife a written document to divorce her?" ❖ *They were misrepresenting Deuteronomy 24:1-4. Moses did not command this. He merely allowed the custom—which had already existed prior to the Torah—and regulated it to some extent. See the note at Matthew 5:31.* ➤ 8 Jesus replied, "Moses allowed you to divorce your wives because many people are stubborn and unteachable. But when God first made mankind, he never intended divorce to happen. 9 I tell you that if someone divorces his wife for anything less than the fact that she was unfaithful to him, then he commits adultery if he marries another woman." ❖ *See the note at Matthew 5:32 and the footnote at 1 Corinthians 7:11.* ➤

10 Then Jesus' close followers said, "If the marriage relationship is this binding in God's sight, then perhaps it's better to remain single." ❖ *They knew the difficulties that marriages can get into. If God didn't allow divorce, to remain in such a situation could be miserable. But they did not take into account what God can do between two people who are fully submitted to him and are willing to forgive each other.* ➤ 11 Jesus replied, "Not everyone can be content to remain unmarried, only those whom God has called to be that way. 12 Some men are born deformed and are physically incapable of having relations with a woman. Others are celibate because they've been castrated. And some decide to be celibate so they can devote all their time and energy to serving God's Kingdom. Those who are able to live this way should do so."

Jesus' Attitude Toward Little Children

13 Then some people brought their small children and infants to Jesus so he could put his hands on them and bless them. ❖ *Laying hands on a person is a biblical pattern for conferring a blessing. See the Note at Hebrews 6:2 about laying on hands.* ➤ When his followers saw this, they rebuked the people, telling them not to bother the rabbi. 14 But Jesus said, "Don't stop them! Allow the children to come to me! These are the kind of people that God loves to have in his Kingdom, people who are humble and trusting like children." 15 After he had laid his hands on them and blessed them, he left that place.

The Stumbling Stone of Being Rich

16 One day, a man came to Jesus and asked, "Good **A** rabbi, what good thing do I need to do in order to live forever?" 17 Jesus replied, "Why are you asking me about what is good? You should know that only God is good. Think about what you say when you use that word. If you want to live forever, obey all the commandments perfectly." 18 The man asked, "But which ones?" Jesus replied, "You know the ones: Don't murder, don't commit adultery, don't steal, don't give false testimony, 19 honor your parents, love your neighbor in the same way you love yourself, and so on." *[Exodus 20:12-16; Deuteronomy 5:16-20; Leviticus 19:18]* ❖ *Jesus wasn't giving an exhaustive list of God's requirements, only a few representative ones. He knew the man was familiar with them all and by bringing them to his attention, he was trying to*

A 19:16 Many manuscripts have "good" here (and it's in the parallel accounts in Mark and Luke), but many others do not.

get the man to recognize that he was a sinner in need of God's forgiveness. ➤ 20 The young man replied, "I've kept all of those commands but I still feel it's not enough. What else do I need to do?" ❖ *He had been taught that an outward legalistic keeping of the rules was what God required. He did not know that the attitude of his mind was important too. Yet even though he believed he had kept all these rules, he knew he was lacking something and wasn't sure he was going to Heaven.* ➤ 21 When Jesus heard this, he knew the man didn't recognize his sin. He also knew that the biggest thing hindering him from whole-heartedly following God was his love for his riches. So he told him, "If you want to completely dedicate yourself to God, sell everything you have and give the money to the poor. This will gain you eternal riches in Heaven. Then come and be one of my followers." 22 But when the young man heard this, he was dejected because he was very rich. He was unwilling to surrender his wealth and put his life in Jesus' hands.

23 Jesus said to his followers, "It's very difficult for the rich to enter God's Kingdom! ❖ *Because either they depend on their riches for their security and find it difficult to trust only in God, or they love their riches and comforts more than they love God. Note that Jesus didn't try to make it easier for the man. He did not tell him that trusting God was enough, and that later he could learn to be a more committed follower, as many teach today. Jesus requires total commitment and obedience at the outset.* ➤ 24 I will reiterate the difficulty. It would be easier for a camel to go through the eye of a common sewing needle than for a rich man to enter God's Kingdom." ❖ *Some people incorrectly say that there was a gate into Jerusalem called the "eye of the needle" which was small and difficult for camels to enter, but that it was possible. There never was such a gate. This was probably a well-known saying in Jesus' time. He was simply stating that it's impossible, humanly speaking, for a rich man to enter Heaven.* ➤ 25 When his followers heard this, they were surprised and asked, "If rich people can't be saved, then who can be saved?" ❖ *A common misconception among Jews at that time was that riches were God's blessings showered upon those who merited them because of their righteous lives. In their minds, it was rich people who were the most likely to be saved. So if such "good" people—whom God obviously approved of and had blessed—can't get in, how can anyone get in? This was their question.* ➤ 26 Jesus looked at them and said, "It may be impossible for

people to enter on their own, but with God's help, anything is possible." 27 Then Peter said, "We've left our homes and everything we have to follow you. So what can we expect from God?" 28 Jesus answered, "You can be sure of this: When I, the Son of Man, sit on my throne in all my glory, then you who have followed me will also sit on twelve thrones and rule the twelve tribes of Israel. ❖ *Some commentators think the twelve tribes of Israel represent all of God's people. Dispensationalists interpret it literally to mean that the twelve tribes of Israel will be restored on earth and will remain distinct from those who are saved in this age, who are part of Jesus' assembly, his body.* ➤ 29 All who leave home or brothers or sisters or parents or children or their land in order to follow me will receive compensation many times over what he has given up *[see Mark 10:30]* and also eternal life in Heaven. ❖ *Jesus isn't talking about people who needlessly or selfishly abandon those who depend on them, like spouses and children. He's speaking of people who place more importance on God's call than on human loyalties, and who are willing to choose to follow God even if their families reject him.* ➤ 30 But many who are important in this life will be among the least important in Heaven; and many who are least important in this life will be among the most important in Heaven." *[Matthew 20:16; Mark 10:31; Luke 13:30]* ❖ *There will be rank and status in Heaven. How we live our lives in this world will affect our status there.* ➤

20

A Parable About God's Generosity

1 Jesus continued, "The reward of eternal life in God's Kingdom can be illustrated by a landowner who went at dawn to find men to work in his vineyard. 2 With those he found, he agreed to pay them each a denarius for working all day, and sent them to work. ❖ *A denarius was the common wage for a full-day's work at that time.* ➤ 3 About midmorning, he noticed some more men standing in the market waiting for someone to hire them 4 He told them, 'Go work in my vineyard for the rest of the day and I will pay you an appropriate wage for your time.' They agreed and went to work. 5 He went to the market again at midday and also midafternoon,, and did the same thing

with more men. 6 About an hour before the end of the work day, he went again and found still more men standing around. He asked them, 'Why have you been standing here all day with nothing to do?' 7 They replied, 'Only because no one has hired us.' He told them, 'You go work in my vineyard for the rest of the day.' 8 When evening came, the landowner told his foreman, 'Call all the workers in from the vineyard and pay them their wages. Start with the last group I hired and end with the first group.' ❖ *The Torah required an employer to pay his workers at the end of every day. [Leviticus 19:13; Deuteronomy 24:15]* ➤ 9 Those who worked only the last hour of the day were each paid a denarius. 10 When those hired at dawn came to be paid, they expected to receive more since they had worked much longer. But they were also each paid a single denarius, as had been agreed. 11 When they received their money, they started complaining to the landowner, 12 'Those men worked only one hour and you gave them the same wage you gave us. And we worked under the hot sun all day. It's not fair!' 13 But the landowner answered one of them, 'My friend, you agreed to work for me all day for a denarius, didn't you? I've paid you that and have done you no wrong. 14 So take it and go home. It was my desire to pay those last workers the same as you. 15 The Torah allows me to do what I want with my own money. Are you ungrateful and envious just because I'm generous to others?' " ❖ *The point of this parable is that eternal life is offered as undeserved favor, not because of merit. The landowner felt compassion on those who had less opportunity to work. A denarius per day was barely enough for a man to support his family. The Torah also encourages generosity to the poor. Some commentators compare the first and last workers to Jews and Gentiles. Others compare them to people who spend their entire lives as believers versus those who believe at the end of their lives. Other parables teach that we will be rewarded in Heaven in proportion to our good work and obedience. But entry into Heaven, the greatest prize, is entirely because of God's freely offered favor that we can never deserve.* ➤ 16 Jesus concluded, "In the same way that you find this equal treatment unexpected, you will also be surprised that many who are important in this life will be among the least important in Heaven. And many who are least important in this life will be among the most important in Heaven. *[Matthew 19:30; Mark 10:31; Luke 13:30]* {Just as it's also true that God calls *everyone* to turn to him and be saved, but only a few are chosen."} **A**

Jesus Speaks a Third Time About His Coming Death

17 While Jesus and his close followers were on their way to Jerusalem, he took the twelve apostles aside and told them, 18 "We're going up **B** to Jerusalem where someone will betray me, the Son of Man, and hand me over to the power of the chief priests and Scripture teachers. They will then condemn me to death 19 and hand me over to the Romans who will mock me, whip me, and then crucify me. But on the second **C** day after I die, God will bring me back to life again."

Kingdom Authority

20 Then Zebedee's wife **D** came to Jesus with her sons James and John. She bowed down and asked a favor from him. 21 He asked her, "What do you want me to do for you?" She said, "Promise that my two sons will sit on either side of you when you become King, the two highest positions under you." 22 Jesus replied, "You don't understand the implications of what you're asking. Are the two of you willing to endure the suffering that I'm about to go through?" ❖ *Even though the mother asked, he addressed the two men for it was their request.* ➤ They answered, "Yes, we are." 23 Jesus said, "Then you will

---

A 20:16 This last sentence is in many major Greek manuscripts but not in many others. Literally, it says, "many are called," but that is most likely a Semitic idiom meaning "all are called." Even though this gospel is written in Greek, Matthew—who was writing to fellow Jews—would most likely have expressed his thoughts using idioms common to his own language and culture.

B 20:18 People always went "up" to Jerusalem because it's the highest point in that area. But the "going up" also had a spiritual connotation.

C 20:19 See note at Matthew 16:21 for the reasoning behind not using the traditional phrase, "the third day."

D 20:20 Some think she was Miriam's sister, hence Jesus' aunt.

indeed share in my suffering, but I do not have the authority to decide who will have the top two positions under me. My Father has decided who will have them."

24 When the other ten apostles heard about this request, they were indignant with their presumption that they were above the rest of them. ❖ *Many of them probably wanted those positions for themselves.* ➤ 25 Jesus called them all together and said, "You know the way of most earthly rulers and men of authority. They use their positions to boss others around or even tyrannize them, and they make sure that their status and privileges remain clearly above those under them. 26 But that's not the way it's going to be among my people. Whoever wants God to consider them as being important, or wants to become a leader over my people, must become everyone else's servant. 27 If you want to attain the highest rank, then you must be like a slave to everyone else. *[Matthew 23:11; Mark 9:35; Luke 22:25-26]* ❖ *There are many leaders among God's people today that fail to obey this instruction. Don't be one of them.* ➤ 28 I, the Son of Man, am your example, for I came into this world to serve people and to give my life to redeem them, not to be served by them."

Jesus Heals Two Blind Men

29 As Jesus and his followers were leaving A Jericho on their way to Jerusalem, 15 miles away, a large crowd was following him. 30 There were two blind men sitting by the road and when they heard that Jesus was passing by, they began to shout, "Lord! Son of David! Have mercy and help us!" ❖ *By this time, everyone had heard about the miraculous healings Jesus could do. It's apparent that they believed Jesus was the Messiah because "Son of David" was a messianic title.* ➤ 31 Some in the crowd told them to be quiet and know their place, but they just shouted even louder, "Lord! Son of David! Have mercy and help us!" 32 When Jesus heard them, he stopped and called for them to

come. Then he asked, "What do you want me to do for you?" 33 They answered, "Lord, we want to see." 34 Jesus felt compassion for them and touched their eyes. Immediately, they could see and followed after him.

21

Jesus' Triumphal Entry into Jerusalem on Palm Sunday

1 As Jesus neared Jerusalem, they came to the village of Bethphage at Mount Olivet, about a mile from Jerusalem. He told two of his men, 2 "Go to that village. When you enter, you will see a donkey tethered next to her young colt. Untie them both and bring them here. 3 If anyone asks what you're doing, just tell them that the Lord needs them, and they will allow you to take them."

4 He did this to fulfill the prophecies that say, 5 **"Tell the people of Jerusalem that your King is coming, humbly riding on a young donkey colt."** *[Zechariah 9:9; also Isaiah 62:11]*

6 His men went to the village and did just as Jesus had told them. 7 They brought the donkey and the colt to him, put their outer robes on the colt, and then Jesus sat on the robes. ❖ *The young colt had never been ridden [Mark 11:2; Luke 19:30] so the mother donkey walked alongside to keep the colt calm.* ➤ 8 As he rode toward Jerusalem, many in the crowd spread their outer robes on the road and others cut tree branches to spread on the road. ❖ *These things were done for a triumphant king or general who had conquered his enemies and was making his procession into a city. It was also traditional for people who had already arrived for the Passover Festival to go out and welcome others just arriving from distant places by putting branches in their path to walk on. Carrying branches may have been a traditional part of Festival worship. While finally allowing the people to proclaim him as the Messiah, Jesus tried to counter their expectation of a military leader who would expel the Romans from Israel. Such would process into the city on a horse or a chariot, but a donkey is a humble mount. So he came as a peaceful king, not as a zealot. The context following Zechariah*

A 20:29 The parallel account in Mark 10:46 says they were leaving Jericho, and Luke 18:35 says they were approaching Jericho. David Stern says there were two Jericho's a few kilometers apart, one the ancient inhabited city and the other a Roman spa that was nearer to Jerusalem. So this

event could have happened between the two sites and in one view be seen as happening while leaving the populated city of Jericho, and in another view be seen as happening while approaching the Roman Jericho. So no error of fact need be read into this apparent discrepancy of detail.

9:9 *(quoted in verse 5 above) proclaims that the king comes in peace and will extend his sovereignty and peace throughout the world. The last part of Zechariah 9:10 quotes from Psalm 72:8, which in its context says that the Son of David will rule over the entire earth.* ➤ 9 The crowd ahead and behind him shouted, "**Hosanna to the Son of David! May God bless the one whom he sent with his authority!** *[Psalm 118:25-26]* **All glory and praise be to God in the highest Heaven!**" ❖ *Hosanna is a Hebrew word literally meaning "Save us!" But in Jesus' time it had become an expression of praise. They were welcoming Jesus as the long-expected Messiah who was making his triumphal entry into Jerusalem. They expected that he would now openly declare himself as God's Messiah, make himself King of Israel, and finally fulfill their expectations of freeing them from their Roman conquerors, ushering in a golden age of peace, prosperity, and greatness for their country.* ➤ 10 By the time Jesus entered Jerusalem, everyone in the city knew something was happening. When they saw Jesus on the donkey, many asked, "Who is he?" 11 The crowd that was accompanying him answered, "This is the prophet Jesus from Nazareth in Galilee."

Jesus Cleanses the Temple a Second Time

❖ *The account of the first cleansing of the Temple is in John 2:13-22. Some commentators believe there was only one cleansing, and that either John or the other three gospel writers reported it at a different time than it happened. But taking the texts at face value leads to the conclusion that Jesus did this twice, a few years apart.* ➤ 12 Then, Jesus entered the outer Court of the Gentiles in the Temple and drove out all who were doing business there. He overturned tables used by money changers and the seats of those who sold doves for sacrifices. 13 He said to them, "It's written in the Scriptures that God said, '**My house will be a house of prayer for people of all nations.**' *[Isaiah 56:7]* But you have turned it into a **den of thieves!**" *[Jeremiah 7:11]* ❖ *The merchants were providing needed services for pilgrims coming for the Passover Festival who couldn't bring sacrificial animals with them from far away. They also operated currency exchanges, since Roman coins were not acceptable for Temple offerings because they bore the emperor's image. [Exodus 20:4 prohibited images, and the emperor was worshipped as a deity by the Romans. To bring God a coin with the image of a false god as an offering would have been an abomination.] But these mundane activities defiled God's Temple. They also*

robbed Gentiles of their appointed place to worship the one true God. Jesus was righteously angry, reflecting God the Father's attitude toward what was happening. ➤ 14 After that, people who were blind and lame came to him in the Temple courtyard and he healed them. 15 The chief priests and Scripture teachers indignantly observed Jesus healing people and the children shouting, "Hosanna to the Son of David!" ❖ *Jesus had invaded their territory, driven out their businesses, and was encouraging people to consider him the Messiah, which they believed was a lie and a threat to their authority.* ➤ 16 They approached Jesus and demanded, "Do you hear what these children are saying?" Jesus replied, "Yes I do. Haven't you ever read the Scripture that says, '**You** ❖ *i.e., God* ➤ **have caused infants and children to speak words of perfect praise**'?" *[Psalm 8:2]* ❖ *Jesus quoted from the Psalm as it is phrased in the Septuagint, the Greek translation of the Hebrew Scriptures. The wording of this verse is different in the Hebrew Masoretic text, which is the source for most English translations of the Psalms today.* ➤ 17 Then he left them and spent the night in the village of Bethany.

The Relationship Between Faith and the Release of God's Power

18 The next morning on his way back to Jerusalem, Jesus was hungry. 19 Noticing a fig tree by the road, he went to it but didn't find any fruit, only leaves. So he said to the tree, "You will never again bear fruit!" Then the fig tree quickly withered. ❖ *Fig trees blossom before their leaves appear. When the leaves are fully grown, there should be young figs on the tree. This tree with its leaves promised fruit from afar but didn't have any. Such trees were called "hypocrites." The fig tree is sometimes a figure for Israel itself. [Hosea 9:10; Joel 1:7] Commentators believe Jesus cursed the fig tree as a sign that the nation of Israel could expect the same judgment if they didn't start bearing the fruit of repentance and obedience to God's will. This is brought out more clearly in Jesus' parable in Luke 13:6-9. Matthew's account of this incident differs in detail from the account in Mark 11:12-14, and 20-24 where the withering wasn't noticed by Jesus' followers until the next day. This bothers some modern readers, but ancient biographies were not required to be chronological or record accurate time sequences. Matthew shortens some incidents and reorders them in temporal sequence because he isn't concerned about all of the details, only those he reports. Such minor differences*

in detail between parallel accounts were not considered significant to people of that time. The gospel writers were more interested in reporting what Jesus said and did than to get all the other details as precise as modern readers would prefer to have them. They were not writing to meet our standards, so it's unfair to judge them by standards they were not trying to meet. ➤ 20 His followers were amazed to see this and asked him, "How could it wither so quickly?" 21 Jesus replied, "It's important you understand this. If you have faith and don't doubt, you can do even more than this. You can overcome great obstacles and accomplish the seemingly impossible, if it's within God's will. ❖ *"Moving mountains," in the literal text, was a common figure of speech for doing something nearly impossible. His original listeners would not have taken this saying literally. Yet it's still quite a fantastic promise that few believers seem to have the faith to exercise in order to see miracles.* ➤ 22 When you ask for something in prayer, you will receive it if you have faith in God and his faithfulness, and your request is within his will." ❖ *Note there is no promise about how quickly you will receive your answer. Most people today give up far too soon. You need to persist in asking while having faith in God's faithfulness to his promises. If God always responded instantly, we wouldn't need faith, and he would also give the impression that he was our servant rather than the other way around.* ➤

Jesus' Authority Is Questioned

23 Jesus went into the Temple courtyard and was teaching when the chief priests and elders came to him. They demanded, "What right do you have to do things like you did here in the Temple the other day? Who gave you this authority?" ❖ *They were not really seeking information. They believed that they could use any answer he gave against him in some way. Jesus was fully aware of their intentions and turned their question against them.* ➤ 24 Jesus replied, "I will answer that if you first answer this question. 25 When John was baptizing and preaching, was his authority from God or did he do it on his own authority?" They debated among themselves what to answer, "If we acknowledge John's authority was from God, then he will ask why we didn't believe his message and his witness that Jesus is the Messiah. 26 But if we say that his authority wasn't from God, this crowd will reject us and stone us since they are convinced John was a prophet." 27 So they finally answered, "We don't know." Jesus replied, "If you are unwilling to answer that question, then I'm not going to tell you where my authority comes from either."

Parable About the Response of Two Sons to Their Father

28 Still talking to the religious leaders, Jesus said, "But what's your opinion about this? There was a man who had two sons. He went to his firstborn and said, 'Son, I want you to work in the vineyard today.' 29 His son replied, 'No, I don't want to!' But later he repented of his rebellion and went to work as his Father had asked. ❖ *A disobedient son was a disgrace. Jews would have considered his first behavior to be very shameful, and their culture was strongly motivated by honor and shame.* ➤ 30 Then the father went to his second son and said the same thing. This son respectfully replied, 'I will, sir,' but he didn't. 31 Which of the two sons obeyed his father?" They answered, "The first one." Jesus then said, "This is something you need to understand. Tax collectors and prostitutes are entering God's Kingdom and you are not because they are repenting like that older son, but you are like the younger son whose obedience was a lie. 32 For John the Baptizer came and taught you the way God wants you to live, but you rejected him. Many tax collectors and prostitutes did believe and have repented and changed their ways, but even after seeing this good fruit from his ministry you refused to repent and believe him."

Parable About the Evil Tenants

33 Still speaking to the religious leaders, Jesus said, "Listen to another parable. There was a landowner who **planted a vineyard, built a wall around it, dug a winepress, and built a watchtower.** Then he rented it out to some tenant farmers and went on a long journey. *[Isaiah 5:1-2,`7]* ❖ *The vineyard represents Israel, the owner represents God, and the farmers represent the leaders of Israel.* ➤ 34 When harvest time arrived, the owner sent servants to collect a portion of the crop as payment for their rent. ❖ *The servants represent the prophets that God sent to his people over the years.* ➤ 35 But the farmers beat one servant, killed another, and threw stones at a third.

36 So the owner sent a larger group of servants to the farmers, and the farmers treated them just as badly. 37 Last of all, the owner sent his son to them, thinking, 'They will surely respect my son.' 38 But when the farmers saw the son, they thought, 'This is the owner's heir. If we kill him, we can keep the vineyard for ourselves!' 39 So they threw him out of the vineyard and killed him. 40 Now when the owner himself comes, what do you think he will do to those tenant farmers?" 41 The leaders answered, "He will kill those evil men and will rent the vineyard to other tenants who will give him his rightful share of the crop at harvest time." 42 Jesus said, "Certainly you must have read the Scripture that says, **'The stone the builders rejected became the cornerstone. This is Yahweh's doing, and it's a marvel to see.'** *[Psalm 118:22-23]* ❖ *Jesus was speaking of himself as that stone.* ➤ 43 So I'm telling you that God will take his Kingdom away from you leaders and give it to those who will produce the fruit he wants. 44 All who stumble over that stone will be broken into pieces, and it will crush those it falls on, into dust." *[Isaiah 8:14-15]* ❖ *This means that people who reject Jesus as God's Messiah and way of salvation "stumble" over him and harm themselves spiritually. If they continue to reject him, God will eventually judge them and they will be destroyed, just like a stone falling on pottery crushes it. The New Testament writers used this figure several times in Romans 9:31-33; 1 Corinthians 1:23; and 1 Peter 2:7-8. The Jews were very familiar with the use of Scriptural figures in argumentation and teaching, so they probably followed Jesus' meaning fairly closely. Verse 44 is in most manuscripts but is missing from a few. Yet it is also in Luke 20:18.* ➤ 45 The chief priests and Pharisees realized that Jesus was speaking about them in his parables. 46 They tried to find a way to arrest him but they didn't dare do it publicly because the people believed he was a prophet.

22

Parable of the Great Banquet in Heaven

1 Then Jesus told the leaders another parable, 2 "God's inviting people to submit to him as their King can be illustrated by a king who prepared a wedding banquet for his son. 3 When the banquet was ready, he sent his servants to the invited guests, telling them it was time to come. But they didn't want to come! 4 So he tried again, sending out different servants to the invited guests with the message, 'The banquet is ready! I've butchered fattened cattle and bulls, and everything is ready for you. Come quickly to the wedding banquet!' 5 But the invited guests ignored the summons and went to work, some to their farms, others to their businesses, 6 while others physically attacked the servants and killed them. 7 The king was outraged and sent his army to kill those murderers and burn their city. 8 Then he told his servants, 'The wedding banquet is ready but the invited guests were not worthy. 9 So go to the crossroads and invite as many people as you can.' 10 His servants went out in the streets and gathered everyone they could find, both good and bad, and finally the banquet hall was filled with guests.

11 "But when the king entered to view his guests, he saw a man who wasn't wearing the special wedding garment that he provided for everyone. 12 The king said to him, 'Sir, you are not wearing a wedding garment. Why did you refuse one?' But the man couldn't think of anything to say. 13 Then the king told his servants, 'Tie him up and throw him outside where it's dark and others like him are crying in great agony and defiant rage.' " 14 Jesus concluded, "For God calls everyone A into his Kingdom, but only a few are chosen." ❖ *The king is God and the banquet feast represents the wedding celebration of his Son, Jesus, in Heaven. The servants represent the prophets and John the Baptizer, whom God sent to his invited guests, the Israelites (later called Jews) to invite them to submit to him as King in their lives. Jesus didn't mean that all Jews would reject his invitation, only that most of them did. The good and bad people gathered from the streets are Gentiles. And the special wedding garment provided by the king for all the guests represents the righteousness (acceptability) given by Jesus to all who are his people. No one is accepted into God's presence without the Messiah's righteousness. The darkness*

A 22:14 The Greek says literally "many," but most commentators believe it's a Hebrew idiom that means "everyone."

Though Matthew wrote in Greek, he probably thought in Aramaic, which is closely related to Hebrew.

outside is Hell. The chosen ones are those who respond properly and submit to God as their King. ➤

The Question About Paying Taxes to Rome

15 Then the Pharisees went off and plotted a way to trick Jesus into saying something they could use against him. 16 They sent some of their followers to Jesus, accompanied by men loyal to King Herod. ❖ *Herod's men would be witnesses to anything Jesus said that would be against Roman law.* ➤ They tried to put him off his guard by flattering him, "Rabbi, we know that you speak with integrity and teach God's way based on the truth of his message in the Scriptures, not based on what you think people want to hear. You don't try to hedge your teaching so it won't offend certain people because you aren't trying to please any particular group. You just teach the plain truth. 17 We're looking for a clear definitive answer to this question. Is it right for Jews to pay taxes to Caesar ❖ *i.e., our conquerors, the Roman government which actively promotes the worship of false gods* ➤ or not?" 18 But Jesus knew their evil intent ❖ *possibly through a word of knowledge [1 Corinthians 12:8]* ➤ and said, "You are a bunch of lying hypocrites! Do you really think you can trap me? ❖ *He knew that if he answered "Yes," then the Jewish leaders could accuse him of being a Roman collaborator—which would destroy his popularity with the people. If he answered "No," then they could accuse him of sedition to the Roman authorities.* ➤ 19 Show me one of the coins that is used to pay the tax you are talking about." They produced a denarius. ❖ *Since they were in the Temple, they likely had to have someone fetch one, since Jews wouldn't normally carry a coin with an image of a false god on it into the Temple. The image was Caesar's, but the Romans worshipped him as a god.* ➤ 20 Then he asked them, "Whose face and name are on it?" 21 They answered, "Caesar's." Then Jesus said, "So, give to Caesar what he rightfully demands and give to God what rightfully belongs to him." 22 They were amazed at his answer and couldn't think of anything to say, so they just went away. ❖ *The Roman coin was not acceptable for any holy use, such as tithes, offerings, and Temple taxes because it bore an image on it which is forbidden in the Torah. [Deuteronomy 4:15-16, 23]* ➤

The Question About Life After Death

23 That same day, some Sadducees—who deny there will be a resurrection—came to Jesus with a question. ❖ *The Sadducees were a Jewish religious sect that held to several incorrect beliefs. Of particular relevance to this story was their belief that there is no life after death. They believed that people have no immortal souls and simply cease to exist when they die and, therefore, there will be no resurrection on the Last Day. [Acts 23:8] They posed a question that they thought would logically prove the impossibility of such a resurrection because it would mean God contradicted himself. They correctly understood that God never contradicts himself.* ➤ 24 They said, "Rabbi, Moses wrote in the Torah that **if a man's brother dies and leaves a widow with no children, he must take her to be his wife and the first son they have will be considered the son of the dead brother.** ❖ *This was so the dead man could have at least one legal heir to carry on the family name and inherit his property. This was to prevent the eventual unequal distribution of land and wealth within families. [Genesis 38:8; Deuteronomy 25:5-10; Ruth 4:5-10]* ➤ 25 Now, there were seven brothers among us. The oldest married and died with no child. So his wife was left to his next brother. 26 The exact same thing happened to the second brother, and the third, right on down to the seventh and last brother. 27 Last of all, the wife died too. 28 So on the day when God raises the dead back to life, if there is such a day, whose wife will she be since she was married to all seven brothers?" ❖ *They reasoned that God would never command people to do anything against the teachings of his Torah. But for a woman to be married to more than one man violated God's Teachings. (There is no explicit prohibition against polyandry in the Torah, but it was understood to be implicitly prohibited from other explicit prohibitions.) Therefore, there couldn't be any resurrection because God's command, requiring a brother to marry his dead brother's childless widow, would force some women to be illegally married to more than one husband after the resurrection.* ➤

29 Jesus replied, "Your understanding is faulty because you are ignorant of both the Scriptures and God's power. 30 After the resurrection, people will not marry or still be married to their former partners in this life. In this matter, they will be like the angels in Heaven. 31 And as for the resurrection, certainly you must have read what God said

to Moses, 32 'I am the God of Abraham, the God of Isaac, and the God of Jacob.' *[Exodus 3:1-6, 15]* ❖ *The Sadducees only accepted the writings of Moses as Scripture, and claimed that Moses never taught about a resurrection. So Jesus used Moses' writings to refute them. Otherwise, he could have also quoted Job 19:26; Isaiah 26:19; and Daniel 12:2.* ➤ It should be obvious that Yahweh is not the God of people who no longer exist. He is God of those having a living existence." ❖ *The souls of the dead are still alive in either Heaven or Hell.* ➤

33 When the crowd heard this, they were amazed at his teaching.

God's Most Important Command

34 But when the Pharisees heard that Jesus had answered the Sadducees so well that they had no reply, they met together to see if they could find a way to trap him. 35 One of them, an expert in the Teachings of Moses, asked him this question: 36 "Rabbi, which command in the Teachings of Moses is the most important?" ❖ *The Scripture teachers had identified 613 commands in the Torah. There was always much debate about how to rank them. They thought that no matter what Jesus answered, they would have some basis to debate him and have a chance at making him look ridiculous in the eyes of the common people.* ➤ 37 Jesus answered, " 'You must love Yahweh, your God, with your entire being, all your heart, thoughts, personality, and determination.' *[Deuteronomy 6:5]* ❖ *In quoting this passage, Jesus undoubtedly used the Aramaic equivalent of "the Lord," instead of saying the name "Yahweh." It was the practice of Jews at this time to never speak God's name aloud. However, the name is present in the Hebrew text and is included here for the benefit of the reader who doesn't know Hebrew.* ➤ 38 This is the first and most important command God has given. 39 The next most important one is similar, 'You must love all people that you come in contact with in the same tolerant accepting way that you love yourself.' *[Leviticus 19:18; Matthew 19:19; Romans 13:9; Galatians 5:14; James 2:8]* 40 All the teachings in the Torah written by Moses and in the writings of the other Prophets are based on these two commands."

A Question About the Messiah

41 While the Pharisees were still gathered there, Jesus asked them a question, 42 "Who do you think the Messiah is descended from?" They answered, "He will be a descendant of King David." 43 Jesus said, "If that's the case, then why did the Holy Spirit inspire David to call him his Lord? For David himself wrote about the Messiah in a Psalm, 44 'Yahweh said to my Lord, the Messiah, "Sit here in the place of highest honor at my right side until I've humiliated all your enemies and put them under your power." ' *[Psalm 110:1]* 45 David calls the Messiah 'Lord,' so how can also be his descendant?" ❖ *Jews of this time assumed that an ancestor was always greater than his descendants. David was one of the greatest Israelites to ever live. How could he humble himself under one of his own descendants and call him "Lord?" The Scriptures were clear on both points. The Messiah would be descended from David, and yet David called him "Lord." Jesus was trying to get them to see that the Messiah, while a descendant of David, had to be more than just a man. But none of them were willing to accept this idea.* ➤ 46 No one was able to give him an answer. And after that, none of them dared ask him any more questions because they were afraid of further public embarrassment.

23

Jesus Exposes
the Hypocrisy of the Religious Leaders

1 Then, Jesus said to the crowd and his followers there, 2 "The Scripture teachers and the Pharisees have taken it upon themselves to be the official interpreters of the Torah's teachings. 3 So you should carefully obey what they tell you to do. But don't follow the example of their own behavior because they don't follow their own teachings. 4 They require you to obey an unending list of burdensome rules, but they make no effort to help people be successful in following them. ❖ *Some commentators think the last part means they didn't follow the rules themselves. Others say that they knew many loopholes which they used themselves to avoid some of the more difficult rules, but they didn't teach them to the people. They were content to be superior and look down on common people.* ➤ 5 Everything they do is for the purpose of making sure people notice how holy they supposedly are. That's why they make their phylacteries and symbolic tassels more prominent. ❖ *The*

Torah required men to wear symbolic tassels ("tzitziyot" in Hebrew) on the corners of their clothing to remind them to obey all the commands in the Torah. Phylacteries were small boxes worn on the forehead with Scripture passages inside. They were also meant to help people remember to obey God's commands. The Pharisees mainly wore them and made them prominent to try to impress people, rather than to stay close to God. So they were hypocrites. See Exodus 13:9, 16; Deuteronomy 6:8; 11:18; 22:12; Numbers 15:38-40; and Matthew 6:1. Also see the footnote at Matthew 9:20. ➤

6 They love to sit in the seats of honor at banquets and in the most important seats in the synagogue. 7 They love to hear people greet them respectfully in public and call them, 'Rabbi.' ❖ *"Rabbi" is a transliteration of a Hebrew word that means "my great one" or "my master."* ➤

8 But I don't want you to allow others to call you 'Rabbi' because I am your only master and you are all to be on the same level as brothers and sisters to one another. 9 And don't call anyone in this world 'Father'—as someone who is your spiritual superior—for your only spiritual father is your Heavenly Father. ❖ *Commentators are agreed that this does not prohibit us from calling our biological fathers by this title. It's a prohibition against using it as an honorific to address someone of superior spiritual rank. This doesn't prohibit other titles of rank, but reserves "Father" and "Master" (Rabbi) to be used for God alone. The term "spiritual father" is used by Paul, but he did not tell his "spiritual children" to call him by that term as a title. All members of the Messiah's assembly are to be seen as peers, though some have functional roles as servant-leaders.* ➤ 10 And don't allow others to call you 'Teacher' **A** because the Messiah is your only teacher. ❖ *Again, commentators believe this is restricted to the sense of exalting a person as a spiritual teacher to a spiritual rank above other believers. Even if there are some people who are good at teaching God's truths, the truths and their ability to teach come from the Holy Spirit and could just as easily be ministered through any other believer. Given the breadth of meaning of this word in Greek, one might wonder if some people today put some spiritual leaders (e.g., pastors, Bible teachers, evangelists, and seminary professors) on a pedestal above us in a way that violates the intent of this prohibition, to the detriment of their relationship with the Lord.* ➤ 11 Those who want to be important leaders among you must become everyone else's servant. *[Matthew 20:26-27; Mark 9:35; 10:43-44; Luke 22:26]* 12 For God will oppose those who are proud, breaking their pride. But he will bring honor to those who choose to be humble. ❖ *See the note at Mark 10:44.* ➤

13 "You hypocritical Scripture teachers and Pharisees are in real trouble with God! People look up to you as teachers, yet you hide from them the key which opens the way to understanding God's truth. You yourselves refuse to submit to God and thus enter his Kingdom, and you do your best to prevent others from entering too!

14 "I pity you hypocritical Scripture teachers and Pharisees because of the punishment waiting for you! You are greedy and take advantage of helpless widows, taking their homes and lands from them, leaving them destitute. And you recite long prayers purely for show, trying to impress others with your spirituality. God isn't taken in by your pretense, and on Judgment Day your punishment will be all the greater because of your hypocrisy!

15 "God is going to punish you hypocritical Scripture teachers and Pharisees! You go to great efforts to convert a person to follow God's ways and then make him twice as deserving of Hell as yourselves!

16 "You blind guides are going to be punished harshly! You teach people that swearing an oath by the Temple means nothing but that swearing by the gold in the Temple makes them bound by their oath. ❖ *The swearing talked about in these verses is making an oath to call down a curse upon yourself if you are not telling the truth, similar to swearing to tell the truth in court. This is not about using swear words or cussing. This also taught people to be deceptive, that they could swear by the Temple and not be bound before God by their oath so that they could deceive the ignorant.* ➤ 17 You spiritually blind fools have wrong values and priorities! You should know that it's the Temple that's more important than the gold, for it is what makes the gold sacred. 18 You also teach that swearing by the altar means nothing but swearing by the offering on the altar makes them bound by their oath. 19 You are blind to what's important. It's the altar that makes

---

A 23:10 The word καθηγητής (kathēgētēs) can mean "teachers," "leaders," or "masters."

the offering sacred! 20 So in God's sight, those who swear by the altar also swear by everything on it. 21 And those who swear by the Temple also swear by God who lives in it. 22 Swearing by Heaven is to swear by God's throne and by the one who sits on it. *[Matthew 5:34]*

23 "You hypocritical Scripture teachers and Pharisees should tremble in fear! You meticulously give a tenth of all income and material increase to God, even down to a tenth of the herbs from your garden, but you totally ignore the major issues of justice, mercy, and faithfulness to God. It's these more important commands that you should be most anxious to keep, without neglecting the minor ones. *[Leviticus 27:30]* 24 You blind guides are extremely picky about minor matters in the Torah, but totally ignore the important ones!

25 "You hypocritical Scripture teachers and Pharisees deserve the punishment that awaits you! You are so concerned about externals, such as carefully washing the outside of cups and dishes. But you totally neglect internal motives and attitudes of the mind which are more important. Outwardly you are ritually clean and meticulous about keeping rules. But your minds are full of greed and self-indulgence. 26 You blind hardhearted Pharisees! You must first make your hearts and thoughts clean, then your outward actions will also be clean in God's sight.

27 "It's going to be bad for you hypocritical Scripture teachers and Pharisees on the Last Day! You are like immaculately clean tombs which look nice on the outside but are full of decay, corruption, and foul stench on the inside. 28 So outwardly you appear to others as good and holy, but inwardly God sees that you are full of hypocrisy and are actually rebellious against him.

29 "You hypocritical Scripture teachers and Pharisees, your punishment will be severe! You build memorial tombs for God's prophets whom your ancestors killed, and you decorate the graves of godly people that they also killed. 30 You sanctimoniously claim, 'If we had lived in those times, we certainly would not have helped them kill God's prophets!' 31 Your words and deeds

testify against you. You admit that you are 'sons of' those who murdered God's prophets, and you are just like them. ❖ *"Sons of," in addition to meaning "descendants of," is an idiom in Hebrew that means "just like them in character." They were like them in rejecting both John the Baptizer and Jesus whom God sent, and they were intending to kill him.* ➤ 32 So go ahead and do what you intend. Finish what your ancestors started if you have no fear of God! 33 Don't think you will escape condemnation in Hell if your ancestors didn't, you hypocritical sons of vipers! ❖ *See note on vipers at Matthew 3:7.* ➤ 34 Since it's happened this way over and over again, I will continue to send you prophets and men of wisdom and teachers of God's ways, and you will continue to kill and crucify some of them, and to flog others in your synagogues, hounding them from town to town. 35 As a result, God will hold you responsible for the murders of all of his people from the beginning of creation until now, starting with Cain killing Abel ❖ *the first murder* ➤ and ending with the murder of Zechariah who was killed between the altar and the Holy Place. *[2 Chronicles 24:20-21]* ❖ *This was the last murder mentioned in the Tanakh (i.e., the Jewish Scriptures) whose books are ordered differently than in the Bible Christians have.* ➤ 36 I guarantee that you will be held accountable for all of their deaths! ❖ *Unspoken but implied is, "unless you repent." God will always forgive the repentant sinner. Jesus wasn't upbraiding them just to let off steam. Nothing more subtle had so far worked in leading them to repentance, so here he tries dire warnings of punishment and shoving their sins in their faces in the hope that some of them will wake up and repent. Even though he is angry with them, he still loves them and wants them to repent. After his resurrection, some did repent and believe.* ➤

37 "O my people in Jerusalem! You kill the prophets and stone God's messengers! Many times I wanted to shield you from God's coming punishment. I wanted to gather you in together to protect you, as a hen gathers her chicks under her wings. But you didn't want me. 38 Take notice! God will turn his back on you and abandon you! He will no longer protect you from your enemies! 39 And you won't see me again until you say, '**Blessed is the he who comes in the name of Yahweh!**' " *[Psalm 118:26]* ❖ *Because most of the Jews rejected Jesus as God's*

Messiah, God allowed Jerusalem and the Temple to be destroyed by the Romans in AD 70, and the Jewish nation ceased to exist for nearly 1900 years. Prophecy predicted the rise of Israel again as a nation which happened in 1948; [Leviticus 26:41-45; Ezekiel 34:12-13; 37:11-13; Isaiah 49:11-20; 66:8-9; Jeremiah 32:36-37] and it also predicts that many Jews in Israel will accept Jesus as their Messiah very shortly before he returns. [Romans 11:25-26] That is most likely the timing of Jesus' prediction here when they will see him again. ➤

24

Jesus Predicts the Temple's Destruction

1 Jesus left the Temple and was walking away when his followers came and remarked on the beauty of the Temple buildings. 2 Jesus replied, "The day will come when all the things you see here are destroyed. Not even one stone will be left on top of another." ❖ *This is probably hyperbole (exaggeration to make a point—a figure of speech often employed by Rabbis) emphasizing the severity of the destruction but not to be taken literally.* ➤

Signs of Jesus' Returning

3 Later, as Jesus was sitting on Mount Olivet, his followers approached him privately and said, "Tell us when this destruction will happen and what sign we should look for in connection with your coming again and the end of the age." ❖ *Their request indicates that Jesus had taught them something about his leaving and returning again, and that they associated his return with the end of the age, even though this is not recorded in the Gospels. As is often true in biblical prophecy, Jesus' prophecy here combines predictions about events that are far apart in time so they sound like they all refer to the same time. Such prophecies in the Hebrew Scriptures confused Jewish scholars and even John the Baptizer about events connected with the Messiah's first and second comings. In this case, although Jesus' followers asked about the time of the Temple's destruction which happened about 40 years later in AD 70, Jesus starts out the talking about the last days before he returns. What these events have in common, though widely spaced in time, is their terror and calamity. Some of these signs of the last days have happened throughout the past 2000 years. But many people expect them to intensify or become more frequent shortly before he returns.* ➤ 4 Jesus answered, "Be careful that you are not deceived. 5 For many men will

come to prominence saying that they are the Messiah, and they will deceive many into following them. 6 You will hear about wars and revolutions, but don't be afraid. These things need to happen first but the end of all things doesn't follow immediately after them. 7 Ethnic groups will fight against each other and entire countries will be at war. There will be major earthquakes and famines in various places. 8 All this is just like the beginning of birth pains. They will last for a while before I return.

9 "Then, every people group will hate you because you are my followers. They will arrest you, persecute you, and kill you. 10 At that time, many professing believers will deny their faith because they fear persecution. They will betray true believers to the authorities and hate them. 11 Many false prophets will claim their messages are from God and they will deceive many people. 12 Most people will find it difficult to love God or anyone else because they will increasingly reject all rules and authority, allowing every sinful impulse to run wild. 13 But those who stand firm in their faith and obedience to the end of their lives, or until I return, will be saved. 14 The Good News message about how to be saved and become a part of God's Kingdom will be preached to every people group in the world to let them know what God has done for them, and then the end of the age will come." ❖ *It is quite possible that the Gospel will be preached to every people group in the very near future.* ➤

Jesus Predicts the Great Tribulation

15 ❖ *The events in this section clearly talk about the Final Tribulation. [Revelation chapters 5—7] But some of them may have also happened in the first century AD.* ➤ Jesus continued, "The prophet Daniel prophesied about an **'abomination that causes destruction.'** ❖ *Or: "horrible abomination" [Daniel 8:13; 9:27; 11:31; 12:11] Some commentators see this as referring to the Anti-messiah (also called the False Messiah in this interpretation) talked about in Revelation.* ➤ (The reader of this book should look carefully into the matter as prophesied by Daniel and try to understand what this means.) ❖ *This parenthetical comment is from Matthew to the reader of his gospel.* ➤ When you see it in the Temple's holy place,

then terrible things will soon happen. ❖ *Such a thing happened in the Temple before Jesus was born, in the second century BC. [1 Maccabees 1:41-61* **A** *] It might have happened again in AD 66 when zealots killed priests in the Temple. It might have happened again with Roman standards (which bore the insignia of Caesar who was worshipped as a god) when the Romans destroyed Jerusalem and the Temple in the year AD 70. And it will happen again when Jews in Israel rebuild the Temple in the last days.* ➤ 16 So those who are in Judea should flee to hide in the mountains. 17 If you are on the roof of your house, don't take the time to get your things from inside. Flee from the city. ❖ *Houses in Israel all had flat roofs with exterior stairs leading up to them. They were used as work spaces and spare rooms.* ➤ 18 And those working in their fields shouldn't try to go back to their house for any reason. They should flee to the mountains. 19 It will be terrible for pregnant women and those who are still nursing babies because it will be hard for them to run and escape to the mountains. 20 Pray that this will not occur on a Sabbath or in the winter, for that would add to your difficulties. ❖ *Winter weather would make the going harder and make it difficult to survive in the mountains.* ➤ 21 For there will be a Great Tribulation, a time of calamities with distress far worse than anything that has ever happened anywhere in the world before that time. *[Daniel 12:1]* And there will never be anything like it again. 22 God has limited the number of days that this will last. If he didn't, nobody in the world would survive. But for the sake of his elect people, he has limited the number of days. ❖ *The "elect" are those people that God has chosen to be his own and has saved.* ➤

23 "If anyone says, 'I know where the Messiah is,' or 'The Messiah is in such a place,' don't believe it. 24 For false Messiahs and false prophets will become prominent and perform such great miraculous signs to deceive people that even God's elect might be tempted to believe in them. ❖ *Many believe this verse implies that the faith of the elect will be protected so they won't be deceived. Others think it isn't clear. But Jesus thought it was worth warning about.* ➤ 25 Now you

have advance warning, so be on your guard. 26 If anyone says, 'The Messiah is in the wilderness,' don't go out looking for me. Or if they say, 'The Messiah is in a particular house,' don't believe them. ❖ *Some commentators think "in the inner rooms," in the literal text, implies he is hiding.* ➤ 27 For when I, the Son of Man, return, it will be as obvious as lightning flashing across the entire sky. Nobody will miss it. 28 Wherever there's a dead body, that's where the vultures gather." ❖ *Many commentators think this may have been a well-known proverb at that time. It probably means that just like the circling of vultures makes it obvious where something has died, it will be equally obvious at the time where Jesus can be found.* ➤

The Coming of the Son of Man

29 Jesus continued, "Immediately after those days of Tribulation, the sun will be darkened so the moon will not shine. The stars will fall from the sky and the spiritual principalities and powers of the heavens will be shaken. *[Isaiah 13:9-13; 24:21-23; 34:4; Ezekiel 32:7-8; Joel 2:10-11; 30-31; 3:15; Amos 8:9; Acts 2:19-20; Revelation 6:12-14]* ❖ *The stars falling could describe a meteor shower. Or the dimming of the sun and moon could be caused by an opaquing of the atmosphere due to volcanic eruptions which would also blank out the light of the stars. Ancient peoples thought there was a connection between the stars and spiritual beings such as angels and demonic principalities and powers. We don't know for sure what any of this means, but it should become clear enough when it happens after the Tribulation.* ➤ 30 Then the sign of the Son of Man will appear in the sky and all the unbelievers in all the people groups of the world will mourn the fate they know is coming to them for having rejected me. Then, they will see me, the Son of Man, in the sky coming on clouds with great glory and power. *[Daniel 7:13; Zechariah 12:10-14; Revelation 1:7; 19:11-16]* ❖ *We don't know what the sign will be, but it will be unmistakable. Many early believers thought it would be a cross. Many commentators think the sign is Jesus himself, and not a separate thing.* ➤ 31 Signaling with a loud trumpet call, I will send my angels to gather my elect people from everywhere on earth. *[Exodus 19:16; Isaiah 27:13; Zechariah 9:14]*

A 24:15 1 Maccabees is a historical book in the Jewish Apocrypha, a set of books not considered inspired Scripture by Jews, yet worthy of reading. The Apocrypha books are considered to be inspired Scripture by the Roman Catholic church and appear in Catholic editions of the Bible.

Learn to Observe the Signs

32 "Learn the lesson that you should watch for these signs from what you know about the fig tree. You already know that when young green shoots start growing on its branches and it starts to grow leaves, summer is near. 33 In the same way, when you see the signs I just told you about, you can know that the manifestation of God's Kingdom in all its glory is very near. 34 I assure you that all these things will happen before all the people of this generation die. ❖ *There are two likely interpretations of "this generation." First, the people of the generation listening to Jesus would not all die before the destruction of Jerusalem would happen. That is obvious in historical hindsight and some interpreters say this was the only generation Jesus was talking about. As for the signs that will occur immediately before Jesus returns, some believe he meant that "this generation" which is alive to see these later signs start, especially those described in verses 15-30, will not all die before his actual return. Others interpret "generation" with different meanings. Looking at all the Hebrew Scripture prophecies that we know have been fulfilled, one thing we can say is that it's difficult to know exactly what some prophecies mean until after they are fulfilled.* ➤ 35 Heaven and earth will end, but my words are always true and all will happen as I've said.

Always be Ready for Jesus' Return

36 "But no one knows the exact day or hour that I will return. Even I do not. **A** Only the Father knows. ❖ *No one can predict exactly when, but Jesus gave us signs so believers would know when the time was getting near.* ➤ 37 When I, the Son of Man, do return, it will be just as it was in Noah's time when most people didn't pay any attention to God's word. 38 In the days just before the flood, life went on as usual. Every day people ate, drank, and were married right up to the time Noah entered the Ark. 39 They didn't understand what was happening until the flood came and destroyed them all. ❖ *Noah's story is found in Genesis 5:28—9:29.* ➤ In the same way, when I come again, unbelievers will not understand what's happening and will be completely taken by surprise. 40 Two men will be working in a field, one will be taken and the other left behind. 41 Two women will be working together grinding flour, one will be taken and the other left behind. 42 So watch for the signs and always be prepared because you don't know when your Lord will return. 43 As an illustration, if a homeowner knew when a burglar planned to break in, he would be awake and ready for him. But nobody can anticipate such things. 44 I, the Son of Man, will also return at a time you can't anticipate. So you always have to be ready. ❖ *To be ready means to live every day in faith, doing what he wants you to be doing.* ➤

45 "While waiting for me to return, be like a faithful and wise manager who has been given the responsibilities of supervising his master's household and feeding his fellow servants. 46 You will indeed be in a good position with me if I find you faithfully doing your duties when I return. 47 As a reward, I will certainly trust you with greater responsibilities in Heaven. 48 But if you are evil and think, 'My master won't be returning for quite a while,' 49 and then start abusing your authority over your fellow servants and use your master's resources to throw drunken parties for your friends, you will be sorry. 50 For you will be completely surprised when I unexpectedly return and catch you at it. 51 I will severely punish you and throw you outside the Kingdom with other hypocrites where you will cry in great agony and defiant rage.

25

Parable of the Ten Young Bridesmaids

1 "When I return as king, some who are waiting for me will be ready and others will not. They will be like ten bridesmaids who waited at the bride's house for the groom to come. They had their torches with them to light the way for the procession to the groom's house. ❖ *The torches were sticks with rags tied to one end. They poured olive oil on the rags and lit them. Weddings were at night. While they waited, the groom was*

A 24:36 Many manuscripts lack the phrase "or the Son," in the literal text.

haggling over the bride price which was paid in gifts—not money—by the groom to the father of the bride. This often went on a long time. ➤ 2 Five of these young women were foolish and the other five were wise. 3 The foolish ones took their torches but didn't have enough oil with them. ❖ They would light their torches when the groom arrived, but they would burn out after about 15 minutes and would then need more oil poured on them to keep them burning. ➤ 4 But the wise ones took jars of oil along with their torches. 5 Now the groom was long delayed and they all became drowsy and fell asleep.

6 "At midnight, someone shouted, 'Here comes the groom! Come out to meet him!' 7 Then the bridesmaids woke up and lit their torches. 8 The foolish ones said to the others, 'Give us some of your oil or our torches will go out before we get to the groom's house.' ❖ It was their responsibility to have enough oil for their torches to burn during the procession to the groom's house and also during the ceremony and celebration. ➤ 9 But the wise bridesmaids replied, 'If we do that, there won't be enough for all of us. Go out and buy some.' ❖ If all the torches ran out before the end of the festivities, it would ruin the celebration. Despite the announcement that the groom was coming, there was still a little time before he arrived and the entire village would be awake for the wedding. So it might be possible to find some-one to sell them oil. ➤ 10 But while they were away the groom arrived, and those who were ready went with him to the wedding banquet. All the guests went in and the door was shut. 11 Later, the other bridesmaids came to the house and called out, 'Sir! Please let us in!' 12 But he answered them from the other side of the door, 'I don't have any relationship with you. My friends are already here. Go away!' " ❖ The IVP commentary says that they had missed the most important part of the wedding, which was an insult to the groom. ➤

13 Jesus concluded, "So always be ready for my return because you have no way of knowing when I will come."

Parable of the Talents

❖ This parable is very similar to the parable of the minas in Luke 19:11-27, with the same general point. But the details are considerably different, especially the ending. Jesus likely told variations of the same parables many times. A talent was the largest unit of weight used in the Hebrew system,

used for weighing metal. For money, it could be a talent of gold or silver or copper. Jesus doesn't tell us which because it's not important for his point. No one knows exactly how much a talent weighed. One source says that a talent was about 75 pounds, and another says it was about 93 pounds, and another says about 94 pounds. A Greek talent was about 84 pounds. One commentary says a talent was worth about 5000-6000 denarii (one denarius equaling a normal man's wage for one day). For an ordinary man working six days a week, that's 16-19 years worth of wages. But another commentary estimates a talent was worth about 10,000 denarii (32 years wages). Take your pick. But we can conclude that even one talent was a considerable amount of money, if in silver or gold. ➤

14 "My going to Heaven to later return as King on the Last Day can be illustrated by a man who planned to go on a journey. Before he left, he called his servants together and told them to take care of his possessions while he was gone. 15 He gave five talents to one servant, two talents to another, and one talent to a third, according to his estimate of their abilities. Then he left on his journey. 16 The man with the five talents used them for trading and eventually doubled his capital. 17 The man with the two talents did the same and doubled his capital. 18 But the man with only one talent buried it in the ground to keep it safe from theft.

19 "After a considerable length of time, the master of those men returned and called them together to find out what they had been doing on his behalf while he was away. 20 The first servant brought in ten talents and reported, 'Master, you entrusted five talents to me and I've doubled it for you.' 21 His master said, 'Well done! You are a good steward! And because you were faithful in managing this small amount, I'm going to put you in charge of much greater things. Come into my banquet and celebrate with me!' 22 Then the second servant brought in four talents and reported, 'Master, you entrusted two talents to me and I've doubled it for you.' 23 His master said, 'Well done! You are a good steward! And because you were faithful in managing this small amount, I'm going to put you in charge of much greater things. Come into my banquet and celebrate with me!' 24 Then the third servant brought in the one talent and

reported, 'Master, I knew you are a shrewd businessman and that you easily make a profit from the work of others, and reap where others have sown. 25 I was afraid of failing to earn anything with it and losing it all, so I buried it in the ground to keep it hidden and safe. Here is what belongs to you.' 26 His master said, 'You shiftless, lazy, good-for-nothing servant! You knew that I'm a shrewd businessman and easily make a profit from the work of others. 27 So you knew that I expected you to earn a profit for me. You should have at least put my money in the bank so I would get it back with interest!' 28 Speaking to other servants present, he said, 'Take the talent away from him and give it to the man who has ten. He's had his chance to make use of it. 29 For to everyone who has shown that he is responsible with what I've given him, I will give even more responsibility. But for someone who has shown no responsibility, I will take even the little he has away from him. ❖ *This is a lesson for Jesus' followers. The material wealth and resources he has given us in this life really belong to him, and he expects us to invest them in the advancement of his Kingdom. Those who do this will be rewarded with greater responsibilities in Heaven. Those who fail to use what they have in this life to further the Kingdom, will not be rewarded with wealth or responsibilities in the life to come. If the slave who kept the talent without investing it was punished, how do you think the master would have reacted to a servant who had spent it mainly on himself, as many American believers do with their wealth?* ➤ 30 Throw this worthless servant outside in the dark where he will cry in agony and defiant rage.' " *[Matthew 7:21-23]*

Jesus Judges the Righteous and the Cursed

31 Jesus continued, "When I, the Son of Man, return to this world with my angels in all my glory and majesty, I will sit on my glorious throne to judge all humanity. *[Matthew 16:27]* ❖ *What's glorious about his throne? His throne is a symbol of his right to rule and judge, and he does this according to God's holy, righteous, just, and loving character, which is his glory. (See the second note at John 1:14.) This glory is often manifested in the Scriptures by a brilliant light that symbolizes the purity and holiness of his character. It may be that the throne itself shines.* ➤ 32 All humanity from every people group of the world will be gathered in front of me, and I will separate them into two groups, like a shepherd separates sheep from goats. 33 I will put the people who are my righteous sheep in a group on my right side, and the people who are cursed goats in a group on my left. 34 Then as Sovereign King of the universe, I will say to those on my right, 'All you whom my Father has blessed, come and receive your inheritance in my Kingdom which has been prepared for you since I created this world. 35 For you fed me when I was hungry, you gave me something to drink when I was thirsty, and you offered the hospitality of your home to me, even though I was a stranger to you. 36 You gave me clothing when I needed it, you took care of me when I was sick, and visited me in prison.' 37 Then God's people will ask me, 'Lord, when did we see you hungry and feed you, or see you thirsty and give you something to drink? 38 When did we see you as a stranger and offer you hospitality in our home, or see you had need of clothes and provide them? 39 When did we see you sick or in prison and visit you?' 40 Then I will tell them, 'The truth is, whatever kindness you showed to one of those who believes in me, even those who seemed to have no status or worth, you did it to me.'

41 "Then I will say to those on my left, 'All you whom God has cursed, leave my presence and enter Hell's eternal fire that was originally prepared for Satan and his demons! 42 For you gave me nothing to eat or drink when I was hungry or thirsty. 43 When I was a stranger, you never offered me hospitality, you never gave me clothing I needed, and you never visited me when I was sick or in prison.' 44 Then they will ask me, 'Lord, when did we ever see you hungry or thirsty or a stranger or needing clothing, or sick or in prison, and did not help you?' 45 Then, I will tell them, 'The truth is, whatever kindness you failed to give to one of those who believes in me, even those who seemed to have no status or worth, you failed to give to me.' 46 And I will send those cursed people to eternal punishment in Hell, but my righteous ones will enter into eternal life."

26

The Plot to Arrest Jesus

1 When Jesus finished talking about all these things, he told his close followers, 2 "You are aware that Passover begins in two days and that I, the Son of Man, will be handed over to my enemies who will have me crucified."

3 About that time, the chief priests and Jewish elders were meeting in the palace of Caiaphas, the High Priest. 4 They were plotting how to arrest Jesus and execute him before the common people could protest. 5 They said, "It can't happen during the Passover Festival or the people might riot."

Mary Anoints Jesus

6 One day, Jesus was in Bethany as a guest in the house of a man called Simon the leper. ❖ *Jesus had probably healed Simon. According to John's gospel, Lazarus was present and Martha helped serve. Some commentator's speculate that Simon was the father of Mary, Martha, and Lazarus. But Martha could have helped serve at anyone's house in Bethany. Villages were small, and hospitality was a community obligation. Matthew doesn't identify the woman in this story, but John 12:1-3 says it was Mary—the sister of Martha and Lazarus—and that this happened six days before the Passover.* ➤ 7 While he was reclining **A** at the meal, a woman came with an alabaster jar of very expensive perfume **B** which she poured over his head. 8 But his close followers who observed this were indignant and muttered among themselves, "That was a thoughtless waste! 9 It could have been sold for a considerable amount of money to help the poor." 10 But Jesus heard them and said, "Why are you criticizing this woman for doing such a beautiful thing to me? 11 There will always be poor people around to help, but I won't always be with you. *[Deuteronomy 15:11]* 12 When she anointed my body with this perfume, she was preparing it for my burial. ❖ *It's unlikely that Mary intended this act of devotion as a*

preparation for Jesus' burial. But Jesus' interpretation of it might mean that through her love and devotion, God moved her to perform a prophetic act whose significance she didn't fully realize. ➤ 13 The truth of the matter is, her act of extreme devotion is such a good example it will be told everywhere the message of salvation is preached throughout the world." ❖ *Jesus exhorts us to extreme devotion to himself, even above all other important and good causes.* ➤

Judas Agrees to Betray Jesus

14 It was after this that Judas Iscariot, one of the twelve apostles, went to the chief priests to betray him. ❖ *There have been many speculations about Judas' motives but the only one mentioned in the Scriptures is money.* ➤ 15 He asked them, "How much will you pay me if I help you find a time and a place where you can arrest him away from public notice?" They showed him thirty silver coins. ❖ *These may have been shekels, equal to about four months wages at the time. Exodus 21:32 also says it's the amount to be paid in compensation for the accidental death of a slave. For the life of a person, it was cheap.* ➤ 16 So from then on, Judas was looking for an opportunity to betray Jesus to them.

Jesus Predicts His Betrayal

17 On the first day of the Festival of Unleavened Bread, Jesus' close followers asked him, "Where do you want us to prepare the Passover meal for you?" ❖ *The one-day Festival of Passover and the week-long Festival of Unleavened Bread (which immediately follows Passover) were one festival in the minds of the Jews. Either term was applied to the entire eight-day period. It probably also included the day of preparation for the Passover (making a total of 9 days) when all leaven was removed from the houses, the Passover lamb was killed, and the Passover meal prepared. So this "first day of the Festival of Unleavened Bread" is Thursday, the preparation day for Passover. The Jewish day started at sunset, so the Passover feast itself started at sunset Thursday, which Jews thought of as Friday night and we think of as Thursday night. He was arrested that same Jewish Friday night and crucified Friday morning, all on the same Jewish day. What is also potentially confusing is that there were two*

A 26:7a Jews of that time followed the Roman custom of eating while lying down on one's side on a low bench, propped up on one elbow. The person's head would be close to the table but his feet would be pointing away from it.

B 26:7b Mark 14:3 and John 12:3 say this was pure Nard. Nard is an expensive oil extracted from a plant that grows in India in the foothills of the Himalayas. See the note at Mark 14:3 about alabaster.

"preparation" days and two Sabbaths on this particular week-end. Thursday was the preparation day for the Passover (a high Sabbath). Friday was the preparation day for the normal Sabbath (Saturday) which began at sunset Friday. ➤ 18 He told them **A** to go into Jerusalem **B** to see a certain man he described, *[Luke 22:10]* and tell him, "The Rabbi says his appointed time is near and he wants to celebrate the Passover with his close followers at your house." 19 So his followers went and prepared the Passover meal as Jesus had directed. 20 When evening arrived, Jesus was reclining at the Passover meal with his twelve apostles. 21 During the meal, Jesus told them, "This is something you should know. One of you will betray me." 22 This upset them, and thinking that one of them might do this unintentionally, they each asked him, "Lord, it won't be me, will it?" 23 Jesus replied, "One of you here, eating with me tonight as if he were my loyal friend, will deliberately betray me. *[Psalm 41:9]* 24 I, the Son of Man, will die just as the Scriptures predict, but it will be terrible for the one who betrays me! He would have been much better off having never been born." 25 Then Judas, who had already agreed to betray him, said, "Rabbi, it won't be me, will it?" Jesus answered him, "I haven't accused you in particular. You are the one asking the question." ❖ *The interchange was subtle, and Jesus' answer was clear only to Judas at that time. But Judas realized by Jesus' response that he knew, so he felt that he would have to act quickly before Jesus exposed him to the others. John 13:30 tells us that Judas left to betray him right after this.* ➤

Jesus' Last Passover
When He Instituted the Lord's Supper

26 During the course of the meal, Jesus took some bread, thanked God for it, broke it, and handed it around to his followers. He told them, "I want you to all eat from this bread. It is my body." ❖ *Given the Jewish context in which Jesus did this, his statement that "this bread is my*

body" is certainly a metaphor meaning "this represents my body." There has been much debate and disagreement over how this is interpreted by various denominations. But the fact that Jesus used figurative language does not exclude the possibility that there is a spiritual reality behind the metaphorical image in this meal. By offering them "his body" to eat, he was inviting them to receive the benefits of his sacrificial death. See the parallel accounts in Mark 14:22-25; Luke 22:14-20; and 1 Corinthians 11:23-26. See also what he says about eating his body in John 6:27-64. While Jesus may not have been directly talking about eating the bread of the Lord's Supper in John 6, he was talking about a spiritual eating in both situations. Therefore, the meaning in both situations is probably similar. Note that Matthew does not record anything about doing this for the purpose of remembrance. Therefore in Matthew's view (and also Mark's), inspired by the Holy Spirit, remembrance was not the primary focus of Jesus' command, as many interpret this meal today. ➤ 27 Then he took a cup of wine, **C** thanked God for it, and passed it around to his followers. He told them, "I want each of you to drink from this cup. 28 For the wine in it is my blood—which I will shed in my dying—that establishes the New Covenant *[Exodus 24:8; Jeremiah 31:31-34]* so God can forgive the sins of many people. ❖ *Covenants were special life-long pacts made between two parties which were often ratified with the shedding of blood. By dying and shedding his blood, Jesus ratified the New Covenant that God was making with his people. This New Covenant says that he will forgive, save, and accept as his people all those who trust in Jesus' sacrificial death to save them and who commit their lives to obediently follow him. Some believe we are to drink the cup mainly as a reminder of what Jesus' death accomplished for us. Others believe that Jesus' offering of the wine to his followers represented his offering them participation in the New Covenant and in all the benefits that are procured by his death. Their drinking it meant that they desired to participate in this New Covenant and receive all its benefits. Many believe that partaking of the cup with faith is more than a symbolic memorial but is also a means of receiving his undeserved enabling favor, whereby they receive those New Covenant benefits that we continually need in this life (e.g. forgiveness, physical and emotional healing, comfort, spiritual strength, increased faith,*

A 26:18a Luke 22:8 says he sent Peter and John.

B 26:18b The Torah required all able adult male Jews to celebrate the Passover within the city of Jerusalem. [i.e., at the place God would choose; see Deuteronomy 16:5-7]

C 26:27 That it was wine and not unfermented grape juice is a certainty. Jews drank fermented wine at most meals and certainly during the Passover meal. Those who

believe Jews did not drink alcoholic beverages should read Numbers 28:7 and Deuteronomy 14:26. The tradition of some (mainly American) believers of abstaining from all alcoholic beverages comes from a desire to avoid drunkenness, which is prohibited in the Scriptures. But total abstinence from alcohol is never commanded in the Scriptures—only soberness.

sanctification, unity with other believers, etc.). See the notes at 1 Corinthians 10:16-17. ➤ 29 But I will not drink wine again until I drink it with you with a new meaning at the great banquet in my Father's Heavenly Kingdom." ❖ *Here the wine represents the blood of his sacrificial death and the ratification of the New Covenant between God and his people. In Heaven, it will represent the fulfillment of the New Covenant, all the benefits that God's people have obtained through it, joy, and possibly more.* ➤ 30 Then they sang a hymn, went out of the city, and made the 15-minute walk to Mount Olivet. ❖ *It was customary to sing Psalms 115—118 at the end of the Passover meal.* ➤

Jesus Predicts Peter's Denial

31 Then Jesus told them, "Tonight, you will all have a temporary lapse of faith and run away because of what will happen to me. The Scriptures prophesy, **'I will strike down the shepherd and his flock will scatter.'** [Zechariah 13:7] ❖ *Yahweh is speaking in the prophecy, and "strike down" is an idiom that means "kill." This was not originally a Messianic prophecy but Jesus applied it to this situation. God would allow evil men to "strike down" his Son that night through his arrest, and ultimately would allow them to "kill" his Son later that same Jewish day.* ➤ 32 But after my Father has raised me from death, I will go to Galilee where you will see me." 33 Peter replied, "I will never run away because of anything that happens to you, even if everyone else does." ❖ *Peter was sincere in his declaration. But he didn't realize how easy it is for any of us to succumb to temptation if we are caught off guard, or if we depend on our own strength.* ➤ 34 Jesus replied, "The truth is that before you hear a rooster crow tonight, you will three times publicly deny having any association with me." 35 But Peter asserted, "I will never deny that I'm your follower, even if it means I have to die with you!" And all the others said the same thing.

In Gethsemane

36 Then, Jesus and his followers arrived in an olive grove on Mount Olivet called Gethsemane. He told most of them, "Sit here for a while. I'm going over there a little farther to pray." 37 But he took Peter and Zebedee's two sons, James and John, with him. As he contemplated the sufferings that awaited him later that same day, **A** he was overcome with grief and distress. 38 He told his three companions, "I'm so oppressed that I feel like I'm dying. Stay here and keep me company while I pray."

39 Then, he went a short distance apart from them and prostrated himself on the ground. He prayed, "Father, if it's at all possible, don't make me go through the suffering I face. But despite my own desires, I surrender myself to follow your will." ❖ *"Cup," in the literal text, is a figure of speech referring to the suffering and crucifixion he knew was coming. [Psalm 75:8; Isaiah 51:17-23; Jeremiah 25:15-29; Ezekiel 23:31-35] It was not only physical suffering and death he faced, but also the punishment for humanity's sin. While submitted to his Heavenly Father's plan, Jesus was fully human and dreaded the suffering that he knew he would soon experience. The words that he prayed in this verse are only a summary. The "one hour," in the next verse, implies he prayed a considerable length of time.* ➤ 40 When he returned to his three companions, he found them asleep. He woke Peter and said, "Don't you three have the strength to stay awake with me for even an hour? 41 You should be praying for God's help to resist the temptation that's about to come on you! Your spirits are willing enough to do what's right, but your own ability to resist temptation is weak." ❖ *The temptation that was about to come on them that they failed to resist that night was the urge to save their own skins when Jesus was arrested and it became clear that he was not going to fight back.* ➤

42 Then, he went and prayed a second time in the same way, saying, "Father, if I cannot avoid this suffering and it's your will that I go through it, then I want to follow your will." 43 Again, when he returned to his three companions, he found them asleep. They were just unable to keep their eyes open.

44 So he left them sleeping and went to pray a third time, saying essentially the same things. ❖ *Even Jesus felt it necessary to pray three extended times for the ability to remain submitted to his*

A 26:37 Jewish days start at sunset. This was Friday night, which preceded the daylight hours of Friday when he was crucified.

Father's will before he felt he could do so. We shouldn't be surprised if it takes us even more effort in prayer to conquer temptation. ➤ 45-46 Then, he returned to them and said, "Now is not the time to be sleeping! **A** Get up and come with me! The time has finally arrived for me, the Son of Man, to be betrayed into the power of evil men. See, here comes the traitor!"

Jesus' Arrest

47 While he was still talking, a large crowd of men arrived led by Judas, one of their own group. They were armed with swords and clubs and had been sent by the chief priests and Jewish elders to arrest Jesus. 48 The traitor had told them, "Arrest the man who I greet with a kiss."

49 Going straight to Jesus, Judas said, "Greetings, **B** Rabbi!" and kissed him. ❖ *As a follower of Jesus, Judas would probably have kissed his hand. Or if he greeted him as a friend on equal terms, he would have kissed him on the cheek.* ➤ 50 Jesus replied, "My friend, what have you come for?" **C** Then, the men with Judas arrested Jesus. 51 One of Jesus' men drew a sword and struck out at the High Priest's slave, cutting off his ear. ❖ *John 18:10 tells us Peter did this and that the slave's name was Malchus. Slaves of important persons could have authority and high status. Malchus may have been representing the High Priest for this arrest. Peter was ready to defend his master and may have been attempting a more serious injury. But being a fisherman, it's unlikely he had any skill with a sword.* ➤ 52 But Jesus commanded him, "Put that sword away! All who fight with swords will just end up getting killed. 53 You should realize that if I wanted to, I could ask my Father for help and he would instantly send more than twelve legions of angels to rescue me. ❖ *Roman legions normally had about 6000 soldiers. He wasn't intending to specify an exact number, but was indicating that he could request thousands of angels to protect each one of them.* ➤ 54 But if I resisted, then how could the Scriptures be fulfilled

that say this must happen to me?" 55 Then Jesus said to the armed crowd, "Why have you come armed with swords and clubs to arrest me as if I were a violent criminal? I've been with you every day in the Temple and you could have easily arrested me there. 56 But things have happened this way to fulfill the prophecies in the Scriptures." When his close followers realized that he didn't intend to resist, they became afraid for their own lives and ran away. ❖ *Jesus had the ability to walk out of this unscathed if he chose. But this all happened according to his Father's plan and he was perfectly submitted to it. His enemies couldn't know that God planned to use their evil intentions for his own purposes. Jesus' followers were totally confused as to why their Messiah didn't resist and use his power to overcome his enemies. Jesus' predictions about his arrest, suffering, and death were still incomprehensible to them.* ➤

Jesus Before the Sanhedrin

❖ *The Sanhedrin was the council of religious leaders that ruled the religious lives of the Jews.* ➤

57 They took Jesus to the house of Caiaphas, the High Priest, where he and the Scripture teachers and elders were waiting for him. 58 But Peter returned and followed stealthily at a distance, and then entered the High Priest's courtyard and sat with the guards to see how things would go for Jesus. ❖ *John also followed. [John 18:15-16]* ➤ 59 Inside the house, the chief priests and the entire Sanhedrin were questioning witnesses—many of whom gave false testimony—to try to find sufficient evidence to have him executed. 60 But they couldn't find any, even though many witnesses came forward and told lies about him. ❖ *The court required two witnesses to agree without contradiction in order for their testimony to be accepted as fact. When two witnesses contradicted each other under questioning, their testimony was invalidated and technically someone should have been severely punished for giving false testimony.*

A **26:45** The Greek sentence is ambiguous and could either be a sarcastic command (as rendered) or the rhetorical question, "Are you still asleep?" meaning "You shouldn't be sleeping."

B **26:49** The Greek word literally means "rejoice," and was used as a friendly greeting. He would have greeted him

in Aramaic, though, not Greek.

C **26:50** The Greek sentence is ambiguous and could either be a command or a question. Literally, it says, "For what you are coming." It could mean, "(Do that) for which you have come."

Evidently, the procedure required these witnesses to testify separately so they couldn't hear each other. The Sanhedrin had to at least give the appearance of going through proper legal procedure, even though a night trial was illegal for capital cases. We know that not all the members were antagonistic toward Jesus, (e.g. Nicodemus [John 7:50-51] and Joseph of Arimathea [Mark 15:43-46; Luke 23:50-53; John 19:38-41]) so there could have been a few who kept them from abandoning all legal procedure. ➤ Finally, two men testified, 61 "This man said, 'I am able to destroy God's Temple and rebuild it in three days.' " ❖ *This was a distortion of what Jesus had said in John 2:19.* ➤ 62 Then, the High Priest stood and asked Jesus, "Aren't you going to say something? Don't you want to reply to this accusation?" 63 But Jesus remained silent. *[Isaiah 53:7]* Then, the High Priest said, "I'm putting you under oath before the Living God. Tell us whether or not you are the Messiah, God's Son." 64 Jesus answered, "Yes, if not exactly as you interpret that. **A** But it is true that you will see me, the **Son of Man, sitting in the place of highest honor at the right hand of Almighty God** *[Psalm 110:1]* and **coming to earth with the glorious clouds of Heaven.**" *[Daniel 7:13-14]* 65 Then the High Priest tore his clothes **B** and shouted, "He has blasphemed God! ❖ *According to the Mishna (written about AD 200), he could not be found guilty of blasphemy unless he actually pronounced the name of God (i.e. Yahweh). But that may have been a later definition.* ➤ We don't need any more witnesses. You have all heard his blasphemy! 66 What is your verdict?" They answered, "The death penalty!"

67 They then proceeded to spit in his face, slap him, and beat him with fists. 68 They blindfolded him and then took turns hitting him and saying, "Prophesy for us, Messiah! Tell us who hit you!" ❖ *They were mocking him based on Isaiah 11:3.* ➤

Peter Denies Knowing Jesus

69 While this was going on, Peter was sitting outside in the courtyard. A serving girl came up to him and said, "You are one of those who follow Jesus of Galilee." ❖ *Jesus was a common enough name. Specifying the famous one from Galilee clarified who she meant.* ➤ 70 But Peter publicly denied it. He said, "I have no idea what you're talking about." 71 Then he got up and went to the gate where another serving girl noticed him and said to those nearby, "This man was with Jesus of Nazareth." 72 Afraid, Peter again denied it. He vehemently said, "I swear before God that I don't even know the man!" 73 A bit later some of the men came up to Peter and said, "It's clear that you are one of those who follow him. Your Galilean accent gives you away." 74 Fearing for his life, Peter declared, "May the Lord curse **C** me if I'm telling a lie! I swear before the Lord of Heaven that I do not know that man!" Immediately after he said it, he heard a rooster crow. **D** 75 Then he remembered what Jesus had told him earlier, "Before you hear a rooster crow tonight, three separate times you will publicly deny having any association with me." He was overcome with remorse and went outside the courtyard into the darkness, weeping bitterly because of what he had done.

A 26:64 Literally, he answered, "You said it." This is understood by some commentators as affirmative, but not totally agreeing with the High Priest's assumptions about the Messiah. Others take it to be an unequivocal "yes."

B 26:65 Tearing one's clothing was a cultural gesture of extreme anger, horror, or grief. [Genesis 37:34; Numbers 14:6; Joshua 7:6; 2 Samuel 1:11; 2 Kings 18:37; 19:1; Ezra 9:3; Job 1:20; Jeremiah 36:24] Here, he was expressing horror at what he perceived as blasphemy. Leviticus 10:6 and 21:10 forbid the High Priest from tearing his official robes of office. The Greek word ἱμάτια (himatia) rendered as "clothes" is plural and refers to outer garments, such as a robe. Mark 14:63 says he tore his χιτῶνας (chitōnas) (chitōnas), an inner garment worn next to the skin, but this word is also

plural. Given the plurals, it seems likely he tore all the garments he was wearing. While the Torah forbade him from tearing his robes of office, one commentator says this only applied to expressing horror over private troubles, but when acting as a judge, Jewish tradition required him to express his horror of blasphemy in this way.

C 26:74a Literally, it says, "He began to curse and swear that..." The word ὀμνύω (omnuō), translated "swear," means "to swear an oath." Some commentators think "curse" means Peter was merely using foul language to emphasize his statement and was not calling a curse down on himself.

D 26:74b Roosters in Jerusalem are known to crow as early as 12:30-2:30 a.m.

27

The Jewish Leaders
Hand Jesus Over to Roman Authority

1 When it became light, all the chief priests and Jewish elders conferred together in an official session of the Sanhedrin and planned how they would have Jesus executed. ❖ *It was illegal to try a capital case at night, so they met officially in daylight to put a veneer of legality on their proceedings. It was also illegal to pass the death sentence on the same day as the trial, but this requirement was ignored. They didn't have authority to execute him, because the Roman government reserved that power for themselves. So they planned how to present the case to the Roman governor. Roman officials often did their business in the morning, so they had to move quickly to present their case and have Jesus executed before the general public became aware that he was under arrest and rioted in protest.* ➤ 2 Then they bound him, took him to the Roman authorities, and handed him over to be dealt with by Pilate, the governor. ❖ *Pontius Pilate was the Roman military governor over Judea, Samaria, and Idumea Provinces from AD 26–36 under Tiberius Caesar.* ➤

Judas Commits Suicide

3 When the traitor, Judas, saw that Jesus was sentenced to death, he felt remorse over what he had done. He took the money he had received for the betrayal back to the chief priests and elders who had paid him. 4 He told them, "I've sinned by betraying an innocent man to his death." They replied, "That's no concern of ours; you are responsible for your own actions." 5 Judas threw the money on the Temple floor, went outside the city, and hung himself. ❖ *Judas felt guilt and acknowledged his sin but he didn't ask God for forgiveness. The oppressive guilt which led him to commit suicide was probably induced by Satan who had entered him and influenced him to betray Jesus in the first place. [Luke 22:3; John 13:27]* ➤ 6 The chief priests picked up the coins and said, "It's against the teachings of the Torah to put money used for evil purposes into the Temple treasury." *[Deuteronomy 23:18]* ❖ *They recognized that the money wasn't fit to be used for holy purposes, but were blind to their own sin in the matter.* ➤ 7 So they discussed what to do with it and decided to purchase a potter's field A to be used as a cemetery for strangers who died while visiting Jerusalem. 8 That's why that field has been called the "Field of Blood" even to this day. *[Acts 1:18-19]* ❖ *i.e. At the time Matthew wrote his gospel, probably 2-4 decades after these events happened.* ➤ 9 This fulfilled the prophecy made by Jeremiah which says, "They took B the 30 silver coins, the price some of the men of Israel had placed on him, C 10 and they D used them to purchase a potter's field, as Yahweh commanded me." E ❖ *This quotation is actually a combination of elements from Zechariah 11:12-13 and Jeremiah 32:6-10 which talks about buying a field. Jeremiah also talks about a potter in Jeremiah 18:2 and 19:1-2. Such loose quotation—combining more than one passage—was common. The main part of what Matthew quotes in this verse comes from Zechariah's writings, but his writings were part of a larger scroll where Jeremiah's writings came first. So some commentators believe the entire scroll was sometimes referred to as "Jeremiah," even though it also contained the writings of other prophets. Part of Zechariah 11:13 says, "and Yahweh said to me, 'Throw it to the potters...'" (Hebrew text), but the Syriac translation says, "Throw it in the treasury..." The Syriac translation is older than existing Hebrew manuscripts, and "potters" and "treasury" are spelled very similarly in Hebrew. Some commentators believe the Hebrew text is defective in this word and they prefer the Syriac rendering as more likely the original. Note also in the context of the Zechariah passage that the 30 silver coins were paid to get rid of Israel's Shepherd.* ➤

Jesus Is Questioned by Pilate

11 In the meantime, Jesus was being questioned by the governor who asked him, "Do you claim to be King of the Jews?" ❖ *This was the charge made against him by the Jewish leaders, but it was not recorded by Matthew. "King of the Jews" was a Messianic title, but also one that the Romans would have considered seditious.* ➤ Jesus answered,

---

A **27:7** It's not clear in the Greek if "potter's field" is a description of the field or its name.

B **27:9a** The Greek verb λαμβάνω (lambanō) can mean either "they took" or "I took." In the Septuagint translation of Zechariah 11:13, it is "I took," but most English translations use "they took."

C **27:9b** Literally "the one having been valued (or priced)." Some commentators think it means "the precious one."

D **27:10a** Many manuscripts have "I" instead of "they" here.

E **27:10b** i.e. Zechariah the prophet

"Those are your words and meaning." ❖ *He wasn't denying the charge. Many scholars believe it was an affirmative answer. Yet it is also hedged, since he wasn't intending to be a king who was a rival to Caesar and Roman rule. Had Pilate understood his answer to mean a simple "yes," then he would have concluded that Jesus was a potential rival to Caesar and worthy of execution. Pilate's question and Jesus' answer are reported identically in the three synoptic gospels (Matthew, Mark, and Luke).* ➤ 12 But while the chief priests and Jewish elders were making accusations against him, he remained silent. 13 So Pilate demanded, "Aren't you going to respond to all these charges they're bringing against you?" 14 But Jesus amazed the governor by remaining totally silent. *[Isaiah 53:7]*

Jesus Is Sentenced to Die

15 Now the governor wanted to release Jesus and he had a custom that he would free a prisoner of the crowd's choosing during the Passover Festival. 16 At that time, he had a well-known troublemaker in custody named Barabbas. 17 So when the crowd gathered to hear Pilate's verdict, he asked them, "Do you want me to release Barabbas to you this Passover, or Jesus who is called 'Messiah?' " ❖ *Since Jesus was popular with the people and Barabbas had a bad reputation, he thought the crowd would choose Jesus. But this crowd was mostly the chief priests and Jewish elders and their supporters. The general population that liked Jesus was not yet aware of his arrest.* ➤ 18 For he knew that the Jewish leaders had handed Jesus over to him because they were jealous of his popularity.

19 While Pilate was sitting on the official judgment seat, presiding over Jesus' trial, his wife sent him a note that said, "Don't have anything to do with condemning that innocent man to death. For I had a dream about him last night that upset me a lot." ❖ *Romans thought that such dreams were warnings from their gods and took them seriously.* ➤

20 But the chief priests and Jewish elders persuaded the crowd to ask for Barabbas' release and Jesus' execution. 21 The governor asked them again, "Which of the two do you want released?" And they shouted, "Barabbas!" 22 Then Pilate asked, "And what should I do with Jesus, who is called 'Messiah?' " They all shouted, "Crucify

him!" ❖ *Crucifixion was the standard Roman method of execution, and was a prolonged torturous death.* ➤ 23 Pilate exclaimed, "But why? What crime has he committed?" But they all kept shouting, "Crucify him!" 24 When Pilate realized that he wouldn't get the crowd to listen to him and that they were on the verge of rioting, he ceremonially washed his hands in front of them and declared, "I refuse to take responsibility for killing this innocent man! The guilt will be yours!" *[Deuteronomy 21:6-7; Psalm 26:6; 73:13]* 25 The crowd answered, "We take responsibility for his death! Let any consequences come to us and our children!" ❖ *They, of course, considered themselves to be doing a righteous deed in having a blasphemer executed. They thought that God would reward them, not punish them. Some commentators say that there is no Scriptural warrant for guilt of the parents to be passed on to the children. But what about Exodus 20:5-6; 34:7; Deuteronomy 5:9; and Numbers 14:18? Yet the Torah limited such punishment to God's hand and only for a few generations. Many people have wrongly taken this verse in Matthew as justification for the persecution of Jews throughout history. Such people have chosen to ignore Genesis 12:3; 27:29; Numbers 24:9; and Romans 12:19 to their own condemnation.* ➤ 26 So Pilate reluctantly released Barabbas to them and ordered Jesus whipped in preparation for his crucifixion. ❖ *The whip used for non-Romans was a multi-stranded leather whip called a "flagellum" which had pieces of bone or metal embedded in the strands. Romans had three levels of flogging: 1) the fustigatio, the least severe of the three—given for small offenses, 2) the flagellatio, a severe flogging given to criminals for serious offenses, 3) the verberatio, the most severe scourging that was often given before crucifixion. In the verberatio, the flogging continued until the soldiers doing it grew tired. Sometimes the result of such a flogging was death or bare bones protruding from ripped flesh. Examining all the gospel accounts, it seems likely that Jesus was flogged twice. Matthew doesn't record the first whipping that Pilate ordered before this one (either the fustigatio or the flagellatio) in hopes of turning the crowd's sympathy toward him. [John 19:1] This whipping was the verberatio.* ➤

27 Then, the soldiers took Jesus into the Praetorium ❖ *which was the name of governor's palace and was also the headquarters for the Roman cohort stationed in Jerusalem* ➤ and gathered the entire Roman cohort around him. ❖ *A cohort consisted of about 600 soldiers.* ➤ 28 They stripped him and put a scarlet cloak around his shoulders.

❖ *Jews had a taboo about nudity and would leave a prisoner wearing a loin cloth. Romans would normally strip their prisoners naked. We don't know if they were sensitive to Jewish attitudes and only stripped off his outer clothing, or not. Mark and John record the color of the cloak (or robe) as "purple," a word that represents colors ranging from maroon to what we think of as purple. Purple dye was very expensive and only worn by high-ranking rulers. It's unlikely the soldiers had access to such a robe unless it was the one Herod sent with Jesus. [Luke 23:11] It may have been an old worn scarlet lictor's cloak whose faded or darkened color resembled purple at a distance.* ➤ **29** They wove some thorn branches together—making a mock wreath crown as vassal kings wore—and put it on Jesus' head. Then they put a stick in his right hand as a mockery of a scepter and made fun of him. They knelt in front of him and said, "Hail, King of the Jews!" ❖ *Note the irony. He was the rightful King.* ➤ **30** They spit in his face and took the stick and beat him on the head with it, beating in the thorns. **31** After they tired of ridiculing him, they removed the cloak and put his own clothes back on him for the march through the city, out to where they would crucify him.

The Crucifixion

32 As the soldiers were leading Jesus out of the city to the execution site, they forced a bystander named Simon—from the city of Cyrene in North Africa—to carry the crossbeam for Jesus. ❖ *They were being practical. Jesus was too weak at this point after all his beatings to carry the crossbeam, and soldiers had the legal right to force citizens to carry burdens for a certain distance.* ➤ **33** They went to a place of execution outside the city which was called "Golgotha" in Aramaic, meaning "the place of the skull." ❖ *In Latin, its name is "Calvaria" from which "Calvary" is derived. Many think it was called this because of the hill's physical resemblance to a skull, but no one knows for sure.* ➤ **34** They offered Jesus some wine mixed with gall, but after tasting it and discovering what it was, he refused to drink it. [Psalm 69:21] ❖ *Many commentators believe this was a pain-killing mixture that was customarily prepared by the women of Jerusalem. If so, the reason Jesus refused it was he wanted to remain fully conscious and sober until he died. Mark says it was myrrh*

instead of gall. The IVP commentary says that the words for myrrh and gall in Aramaic are very similar. Other commentators say the soldiers put the gall in the wine to make it bitter to further mock him. ➤ **35** After they had stripped him and nailed him to the cross, they cast lots to see who would get his clothing. [Psalm 22:18] **36** Then they sat nearby to keep guard as he hung there. ❖ *This would prevent anyone from trying to rescue him.* ➤ **37** Above his head, they fastened a written notice announcing his crime. It read,

"THIS IS JESUS, KING OF THE JEWS."

38 Two revolutionaries were crucified at the same time, one on each side of Jesus. **39** Many who passed by blasphemed [A] him and shook their heads in scorn. [Psalm 22:7] **40** They said things like, "And you were going to destroy the Temple and rebuild it in three days! If you are God's Son, come down from the cross and save yourself!"

41 The chief priests, Scripture teachers, and Jewish elders also made it a point to come and ridicule him. **42** They said, "He had the power to save others but he can't even save himself. If he is really the King of Israel, ❖ *this was a Messianic title* ➤ let's see him come down from the cross! Then we will believe in him! ❖ *He could have done so, but then God's purpose of saving humanity from eternal death would have been thwarted. So in a way, what they said was true. He could save others, but in order to do so he could not save himself.* ➤ **43** He claims that he is God's Son and trusts in God. So let God rescue him now if he really approves of him!" [Psalm 22:8]

44 Even the revolutionaries who were crucified next to him insulted him with similar sentiments.

Jesus' Death

45 Then, from about noon until mid-afternoon, the entire land—as far as could be seen—was shrouded in darkness. [Exodus 10:22; Amos 8:9] ❖ *This occurred at Passover which is always at a full moon, so it was not a solar eclipse but a supernatural event. Darkness was considered to be an evil sign and was also associated with judgment and punishment. [Isaiah 5:30; 13:10-11; Joel 3:14-15] This was the time when*

A 27:39 This word βλασφημέω (blasphēmeō) literally is "blaspheme," and is so translated in other contexts. They

were insulting him, but because of who Jesus is, they were also unknowingly blaspheming God.

God was punishing Jesus for all of humanity's sins. ➤
46 Around midafternoon, Jesus shouted, "*Eloi, eloi,* **A** *lama sabachthani!* " ❖ *This is Aramaic, the everyday language of the Jews at that time.* ➤ which means, **"My God, my God, why have you left me!"** *[Psalm 22:1; Isaiah 59:2]* ❖ *Part of the penalty for sin is complete separation from God. [Habakkuk 1:13; 2 Corinthians 5:21; Galatians 3:13]* ➤ **47** Some who were nearby heard him say this and thought, "He's calling for Elijah to help him." **48** One of them **B** ran to get a sponge. He soaked it in sour wine, ❖ *the soldiers' drink* ➤ put it on a stick, and raised it to Jesus' lips so he might drink it. **49** But the others said, "Wait! Let's see if Elijah will come to save him first!" **C** **50** Then Jesus again shouted something, voluntarily gave up his spirit, and died. *[Luke 23:46; John 19:30]* ❖ *When the spirit of a man departs from the body, the body dies. Jesus was not killed. He surrendered his spirit to his Father and died in full control of his death. [John 10:17-18]* ➤ **51** At that moment, the thick curtain in the Temple was torn in two from top to bottom. ❖ *This curtain blocked the entryway from the Holy Place in the Temple into the Holy of Holies where the omnipresent God was manifestly present with the light of the Shekinah glory. God tore open this curtain to show that the barrier of sin—which had kept people from approaching him—was now removed by his Son's death. God's people now have direct access to him because their sins have been removed and they've been made holy in his sight. The IVP commentary says the rending of the curtain more likely indicated the presence of God leaving the Temple, as in Ezekiel chapters 10—11. These two views are not necessarily mutually exclusive.* ➤ **D** There was also an earthquake so severe that rocks were split. **52** Tombs broke open and many of God's holy people buried in them were raised back to life. **53** They came out of the tombs and— after God made Jesus alive again—they

went into Jerusalem and showed themselves to many who knew them. ❖ *The sequence here is not totally clear. It's possible the tombs were cracked open when Jesus died, and the people in them became alive and came out of the tombs when Jesus became alive.* ➤

54 When the centurion and the other soldiers guarding Jesus saw the earthquake and all the other things that happened, they exclaimed in terror, "Truly this was God's Son!" ❖ *The Roman soldiers were convinced that Jesus was more than a mere man. With their pagan background, they probably meant, "He was a god's son." (The Greek phrase can be read either "a god's son" or "the God's Son." There is no definite article in the Greek text.) But Mathew meant it as a testimony to the truth, that he was the Son of the one and only living God. It's ironic that pagans should accurately recognize the signs of his divinity while most of God's own people did not.* ➤ **55** Many women who had traveled with Jesus from Galilee to help support him and his ministry observed all these things while standing some distance away. ❖ *Most of his followers—except John [John 19:26-27] and these women—were conspicuously absent, hiding in fear for their lives.* ➤ **56** Among those watching were Mary of Magdala village, and the mother of James and John (Zebedee's wife), and Miriam who was the mother of James and Joseph. **E** ❖ *Some commentators think Miriam—the mother of James and Joseph—was Jesus' mother, and that Matthew didn't refer to her as such because he was emphasizing Jesus' deity. Other commentators disagree and think that she was the wife of Clopas [John 19:25]. We don't know for sure, but Zebedee's wife may have been Salome. [Mark 15:40] Some think she may have been the sister of Miriam (the mother of Jesus). [John 19:25]* ➤

Jesus' Burial

57 As the end of the day approached, **F** Joseph—originally from the town of

---

A 27:46 Some manuscripts have "Eli, eli" which is the Hebrew form of "Eloi, eloi."

B 27:48 Some commentators think this is a soldier, and also in John 19:29.

C 27:49 Many manuscripts add, "Then another took a spear and stabbed his side, and out came water and blood." But most manuscripts don't have it here. This is recorded in John 19:34 as happening after his death.

D 27:51 David Stern's Jewish New Testament Commentary on this verse has a very interesting note about a passage in the Talmud witnessing to a change

in God's system of atonement that occurred 40 years before the Temple was destroyed (i.e., the year Jesus was crucified). The reader is encouraged to look this up.

E 27:56 Most manuscripts have "Joses" which is a shortened form of "Joseph."

F 27:57a The Greek can be interpreted as "when it was evening" or "when evening was near." In any case, evening is defined as the time before dark near the end of the day which ended at sunset. It was not defined as certain hours on a clock because clocks didn't exist. After sunset, it was always the "night" of the next Jewish day, never evening.

Arimathea **A** and a wealthy ❖ *and secret [John 19:38]* ➤ follower of Jesus ❖ *and a member of the Sanhedrin [Mark 15:43; Luke 23:50-51]* ➤ **58**—went to Pilate asking permission to remove his body from the cross for burial, and Pilate granted his request. ❖ *Permission was needed since the Romans often left the bodies of crucified men hanging for many days as warnings against other would-be lawbreakers. They were also usually buried in a common grave. In going to Pilate and showing his devotion to Jesus, Joseph was endangering his position on the Sanhedrin.* ➤ **59** So Joseph took the body down and ❖ *following the Jewish burial customs of the time* ➤ wrapped it in clean linen cloth. ❖ *John 19:39-42 tells us he was helped by Nicodemus. They undoubtedly also had servants who helped them.* ➤ **60** Then, he put it in his own unused tomb—which he had recently ordered cut out of rock in the side of a cliff *[Isaiah 53:9]*—and then had the entrance sealed with a large disk-shaped stone rolled in front of it. **61** Mary from Magdala and Miriam (the mother of James and Joseph **B**) were sitting nearby facing the tomb, observing where Joseph put Jesus' body.

62 The next day, ❖ *Saturday—the Sabbath—which started at sundown on Friday, the day he was buried* ➤ the chief priests and Pharisees went to see Pilate. ❖ *They probably went in the morning. Their Saturday Sabbath (or Passover) meal would have taken place the previous night. Commentators disagree about whether Jesus was crucified on the Passover (the traditional view) or the day before Passover. The arguments are not conclusive in either direction, but overall the traditional view seems to have the most going for it.* ➤ **63** They said to him, "Sir, we recall that charlatan Jesus claimed, 'God will make me alive again the second **C** day after my death.' **64** So we are formally requesting that you order the grave to be guarded until the end of that day, to prevent his followers from stealing the body {during the night} **D** and claiming he has come back to life. If that happened, this last fraud would be worse than the one where he claimed to be the Messiah." **65** Pilate replied, "You have a guard. Go make things as secure as you can." ❖ *Pilate's statement in Greek is*

ambiguous. It could mean he was granting their request for Roman soldiers to guard the tomb, or it could mean they had their own Temple guard and were to do the best they could with it. There are good arguments and indications on both sides of the issue and none of them are conclusive. The only thing we can be sure of is that some men were set at the tomb as a guard force, whether they were Roman soldiers or Temple guards. This interpreter believes the arguments for a Temple guard are more reasonable overall. ➤ **66** So they went and made sure the grave was securely guarded and a seal was placed on the stone covering the entrance so if the tomb was opened, they would know. ❖ *We don't know the exact procedure they used, but a wax, clay, or plaster seal with a unique emblem pressed into it, as was often used in wax seals on letters, would guarantee that they could tell if the stone had been moved. Their efforts only aided in proving that Jesus' followers could not have stolen the body, as they later claimed.* ➤

28

God Makes Jesus Alive Again

1 At dawn on Sunday morning—the first day of the week—Mary from Magdala and Miriam went to Jesus' tomb. **2** Suddenly, an angel appeared and there was a violent earthquake. The angel then rolled away the stone that sealed the tomb—in order to show that the tomb was empty—and sat on it. **3** The angel's clothes were snow white and as bright as a flash of lightning. **4** The guards trembled and fell to the ground paralyzed with fear, as if they were dead.

5 The angel said to the women, "There's no need to be afraid! I know you are looking for Jesus who was crucified. **6** But he is not here! God has made him alive again, just as he told you it would happen. Come and see the place where they put his body and see that it's gone. **7** Then hurry to tell his close followers that God has made him alive again, and that Jesus is planning to meet you all in Galilee. This is the message I've been instructed to give you." **8** So after peering in the empty tomb, the women hurried off to

---

A 27:57b Commentators think Arimathea was located about 10 miles east of Joppa, but the exact location is not known.

B 27:61 See verse 56. This is not Joseph from Arimathea.

C 27:63 See note at Matthew 16:21 for the reasoning behind not using the traditional phrase, "the third day."

D 27:64 These words are found in some manuscripts.

tell these things to Jesus' followers. They were both afraid and joyful at the same time.

9 As they were on their way, Jesus suddenly met them and said, "Rejoice!" ❖ *This was a standard greeting in Greek, though he probably spoke to them in Aramaic.* ➤ The women came up to him and knelt down at his feet, grabbing hold of them, both to be sure he was real and as an act of worship. 10 Then Jesus said, "There's no reason to be afraid! Go tell my followers to meet me in Galilee."

11 While the women were taking the message to Jesus' followers, some of the guards who had been at the tomb went into the city and reported everything that had happened to the chief priests. 12 After hearing their report, the chief priests met with the Jewish elders and agreed upon a course of action. They gave a large bribe to the soldiers 13 and told them, "You are to say that Jesus' followers came during the night and stole his body while you slept. 14 And if this story gets to the governor's ears, we will persuade him to not give you any trouble."

❖ *If these were Roman soldiers, it is unlikely they would first report to the Jewish authorities and they would have required a lot of convincing to spread this story, since it was a capital offense for a Roman soldier to sleep while on duty. They would have been placing a lot of faith in the Jewish authorities who they would tend to despise. The story would also not be credible, since Roman soldiers were known to not sleep on duty; and how would they know who stole the body if they were asleep? But the important thing to note is that the Jewish authorities never disputed the fact that the body was missing. If it wasn't, they could have produced it, but there is no record that they ever tried to do so.* ➤ 15 So the soldiers took the bribe and spread the story as they were instructed. And it's widely circulated among the Jews even to this day.

Jesus' Last Instructions to His Followers

16 Jesus' eleven close followers went to Galilee to a hill where Jesus had told them to meet him. ❖ *It's most likely that the message the angel and Jesus gave as recorded in Matthew 28:7 and 10 was just a summary leaving out this detail, or else Jesus had told them to meet him at this particular place before he was crucified.* ➤ 17 When he met them there, some of them worshipped him as God's Son but some still had doubts. ❖ *Commentators debate who was there at this time, just the eleven, or the eleven plus other followers of the 120 present later at Pentecost, [Acts 1:15] or the 500 mentioned by Paul. [1 Corinthians 15:6] Also, who were the "some" who worshipped and the others who doubted? Your guess is as good as any of the commentators'. And what was it that they doubted? Most think it was the fact that Jesus had actually physically been made alive again after dying. That he had died, there could be no doubt. Whether or not he was physical could be settled with a touch. But perhaps they weren't sure it was really Jesus. If this was the doubt, then it's unlikely that it was any of the eleven who doubted, as they knew him best.* ➤ 18 Then Jesus came closer and told them, "God the Father has given me absolute authority over everything and everyone in Heaven and on Earth. *[Daniel 7:13-14]* 19 Therefore, **A** from that position of authority, I'm commanding you to go to every people group in the world and fully train people from each group to be my faithful followers. *[Acts 1:8]* Baptize each of them in the one name of the Father and the Son and the Holy Spirit. 20 And I want you to teach each of these new followers to obey all of the commands that I gave you while I was with you. ❖ *These would include his commands to heal the sick, expel demons, raise the dead and fully train others. [Matthew 10:5-8; Mark 6:7-13; Luke 9:1-6; 10:1-9, 17; John 14, 12-14] Jesus here says that these commands and authority are for all his followers, not just for the apostles or special leaders. Some think this would also include all the teachings in the Torah that Jesus has not explicitly changed since he faithfully followed the Torah teachings himself and taught his followers to not disregard them. [Matthew 5:17-19]* ➤ Also, trust that I am always with you ❖ *and all my followers, through the Holy Spirit,* ➤ until I return again at the end of the age."

A 28:19 Many manuscripts lack "therefore."

The Good News About Jesus the Messiah

as told by

Mark

John Mark, son of Mary, [Acts 12:12] *sometimes called Mark, [Acts 12:25] a cousin of Barnabas, [Colossians 4:10] and a close associate of Peter, [1 Peter 5:13] wrote this book. He probably did this about AD 64 while he was with Peter in Rome during a severe persecution of believers by Emperor Nero. Peter was an old man and knew that his life was nearly over. Tradition says that Peter gave Mark the details he records in this gospel. [2 Peter 1:15] He wrote for Gentile readers so he explained Jewish customs and didn't quote from the Hebrew Scriptures very often. Many scholars believe that this was the first of the four gospels to be written and that both Matthew and Luke based much of their gospels on it.*

One purpose for this book was to comfort Roman believers who were suffering persecution with the fact that Jesus had predicted it would happen, that it was part of God's plan, and that Jesus expected them to endure. [Mark 8:34-38; 13:9-13] He emphasized the suffering that Jesus experienced during his earthly ministry so they could know that Jesus sympathized with them.

Matthew's gospel portrays Jesus as the long-expected Messiah and King. Luke portrays him as the "Son of Man," emphasizing his humanity, John portrays him as God's Son, and Mark portrays him as God's humble servant who heals people and who died in their place to pay for their sins. Mark doesn't include a genealogy since a humble servant needs none.

1

John the Baptizer Prepares God's People to Receive the Messiah

¹ The Good News about Jesus the Messiah—God's Son—begins with Isaiah's prophecy ² in which God said, **"Hear this! I will send my messenger who will prepare people for your** **A** **arrival.** *[Malachi 3:1]* ³ **You can hear someone in the wilderness calling out to God's people, 'Prepare for Yahweh's arrival!** **B** **Be prepared to welcome him properly.' "** *[Isaiah 40:3]* ❖ *Mark combines two quotes, one from Malachi, but he only mentions Isaiah. This was common in his day. Those who knew the Scriptures knew them very well so it wasn't necessary to accurately attribute each part to the proper author.* ➤

⁴ In fulfillment of this prophecy, John the Baptizer started to preach in the Judean wilderness. He told people to publicly confess their sins, submit to being baptized as a sign that they would turn away from their sinful ways, and then God would forgive them. ⁵ Many people from Jerusalem and the surrounding region of Judea Province came out to hear John. In response to his message, many publicly confessed their sins and then had John baptize them in the Jordan River. ❖ *Their confessions may have been a general admission that they were sinners rather than a detailed list of sins, but we don't know. Jews traditionally baptized Gentile converts but John was baptizing Jews who supposedly already had a relationship with the one true God. See the note at John 1:25. John's baptism for repentance is not the same as baptism*

A **1:2** The literal text in Malachi 3:1 says "my" instead of "your," indicating that Yahweh himself was planning to come. Mark changed the pronoun to make the claim that Jesus the Messiah is Yahweh.

B **1:3** The Greek text literally has κύριος (kurios) meaning

"Lord" here, following the Jewish practice of substituting that title in place of the name "Yahweh," which is in the Hebrew text that he quotes from Isaiah. "Yahweh" is restored in this text so the modern reader is clear about what Isaiah wrote and meant.

into the name of Jesus that Jesus commanded in Matthew 28:19. [Acts 2:38; 8:16; 10:48; 19:5] ➤

6 Like the prophet Elijah who lived nearly 900 years earlier, John wore a leather belt and coarse clothing woven from camel hair. [2 Kings 1:8] He lived in the wilderness as a poor ascetic, eating mainly locusts and wild honey. 7 Part of his message was, "The Messiah is coming after me, and his authority and power far exceed mine. He's so much greater than me that I'm not even worthy enough to serve him by untying his sandals. 8 I only baptize you in water, but he will baptize you in A the Holy Spirit."

Jesus Is Baptized and Tempted

9 While John was still ministering this way, Jesus came from Nazareth in Galilee Province and had John baptize him in the Jordan. 10 As Jesus came out of the water, he saw the heavens opened [Isaiah 64:1] and God's Spirit coming down on him in the form of a dove. ❖ This means that the Holy Spirit came upon Jesus in a way that he was not present before. Many believe it was for the purpose of empowering his ministry and was similar to the baptism of the Holy Spirit his followers later experienced at Pentecost, after his return to Heaven. [Acts 1:1-5; 2:1-4; 38-39] ➤ 11 Then God's voice thundered out of Heaven, "You are my only Son and I'm very pleased with you." [Psalm 2:7; Isaiah 42:1]

12 Immediately afterward, the Holy Spirit led him into the dangerous unpopulated highlands of the Judean wilderness. 13 He stayed there 40 days while Satan unsuccessfully tempted him to sin. [Matthew 4:1-11; Luke 4:1-13] There were also wild animals in the wilderness, but angels came to take care of him.

Jesus Starts His Public Ministry in Galilee

14 Later, after Jesus heard that the tetrarch Herod Antipas had arrested John the Baptizer, he returned to Galilee Province and began to preach God's message about how to be saved. ❖ More about John's arrest can be found in Matthew 14:3-4; Mark 6:17-18; and Luke 3:19-20. ➤ 15 He proclaimed, "Today is your appointed opportunity to turn away from sinful ways, start obeying God, and believe that he will accept you into his Kingdom!"

16 One day, as Jesus was walking along the shore of Lake Galilee, he saw two fishermen casting their net into the lake. One was Simon (later called Peter) and the other was his younger brother Andrew. 17 Jesus called out to them, "Come be my followers, and I will teach you how to catch people for God's Kingdom." 18 They immediately left behind their nets and livelihood as fishermen and became his followers.

19 A little farther on, Jesus saw two more brothers, James and John, in a boat working on their nets. 20 Right away he called them, and they didn't hesitate to leave their father, the hired workers in the boat, and their livelihood to become his followers.

Jesus Expels Demons from a Man in the Capernaum Synagogue

21 They went to the town of Capernaum on the north shore of Lake Galilee; and on the Sabbath, Jesus began to teach in the synagogue. 22 The people marveled at his teaching because, unlike the Scripture teachers who always quoted other authorities, he spoke from personal authority. [Matthew 7:29; Luke 4:31-32]

23 Then a man who was defiled with demons came into the synagogue. He yelled at Jesus, 24 "Arrrgh! Get out of here, Jesus of Nazareth! Just leave us alone! B You've come to destroy us! I know who you are! You are God's special Holy One!" ❖ In the Hebrew Scriptures, Yahweh is frequently referred to as "the Holy One" or "the Holy One of Israel." [2 Kings 19:22; Job 6:10; Psalm 16:10; 71:22; 78:41; 89:18; 106:16; Proverbs 30:3; Isaiah 1:4; 5:19, 24; 10:17, 20; 12:6; 17:7; 29:19, 23; 30:11, 12, 15; 31:1; 37:23; 40:25; 41:14, 16, 20; 43:3; 43:14, 15; 47:4; 48:17; 49:7; 54:5; 55:5; 60:9, 14; Jeremiah 50:29; 51:5; Hosea 11:9, 12; Habakkuk 1:12; 3:3] While angels are occasionally called "holy ones," this phrase is mostly used of Yahweh himself. ➤

25 But Jesus said in rebuke, "Be silent and come out of him!" 26 The demon made

---

A 1:8 The Greek preposition ἐν (en) can be translated either "in" or "with" in this context. It has a broad range of meanings that depend on context.

B 1:24 The sense of hostility that's implied by the Greek idiom is rendered here, rather than the more literal "What have you to do with us?"

the man convulse and scream, and then it came out. 27 The people were in awe and exclaimed, "This is certainly a new kind of authoritative teacher! He simply commands demons and they obey!" 28 So reports about him spread like wildfire throughout the surrounding area of Galilee.

Jesus Heals All Who Are Brought to Him

29 Right after they left the synagogue, Jesus, James, and John went with Simon and Andrew to their house.

30 When Jesus arrived, he was told that Simon's mother-in-law was sick in bed with a fever. 31 He went to her and helped her to stand. Immediately, the fever left and she started to serve them a meal.

32 When the sun set—ending the Sabbath—people brought all who suffered from sickness or demons to Jesus. 33 Everyone in town gathered outside the doorway to that house. 34 Jesus healed everyone who was sick with various ailments and he expelled many demons. But he didn't allow the demons to speak because they knew he was God's Son, and he didn't want it openly proclaimed.

Jesus Preaches Throughout Galilee

35 Long before daylight the next morning, Jesus got up and left the house to find a place outside of town where he could be alone to pray. ❖ *Even God's Son required daily time alone with his Heavenly Father. We need this even more than he did if we desire to know his will and to be used for his purposes.* ➤ 36 Later, Simon and Jesus' other followers went out searching for him. 37 When they found him, they said, "Everyone's out searching for you!"

38 But he told them, "Let's go to other towns and villages nearby so I can proclaim my message to them too, because that's my mission." 39 So he went throughout Galilee Province, preaching in the synagogues and expelling demons from the demonized.

Jesus Wants to Heal

40 One day, a man with a contagious skin disease knelt before Jesus and said, "I know you can heal me, if you want to." 41 Jesus felt deep compassion for the man. So despite the Torah's prohibition against touching such a person and the fact that he would become ritually unclean by doing so, he reached out and touched him. He said, "Of course I want to. I command you to be healed!" 42 Instantly, the man was visibly cured. 43 Then, Jesus sent him on his way with these instructions, 44 "Don't tell anyone about my part. But go immediately to a priest so he can examine you as the Torah requires. *[Leviticus 14:1-32]* Make the required sacrificial offerings so the priest can announce you are both well and ritually clean." 45 Despite the admonition not to talk about it, he spread the story everywhere. Jesus attracted so many people who wanted to be healed that he couldn't openly enter a village without being mobbed. So he tended to stay out in the unpopulated areas, but people still found out where he was and came to him from everywhere.

2

Jesus Heals a Paralyzed Man
to Prove He Can Forgive Sin

1 Sometime later, Jesus returned to Capernaum and the news that he was home again quickly spread throughout the area. ❖ *When Jesus started his preaching ministry, he moved from Nazareth, a minor village, to Capernaum—a strategically situated town on a major road—as his home base. He might have stayed at Peter and Andrew's home.* ➤ 2 One day, there were so many people packed into the house where he was teaching that there was no room for more, and a crowd was gathered around the door outside to hear him. ❖ *Houses of common people were often only a single room.* ➤ 3 Then, four men arrived carrying a man who was paralyzed. They intended to bring him to Jesus for healing. 4 But since the crowd made it impossible to get inside, they went around to the outside steps and carried him up onto the house's flat roof. ❖ *The flat roofs of houses were often used as spare rooms.* ➤ There, they made an opening in the roof and lowered the man on his stretcher right into the center of the house in front of Jesus. 5 When Jesus saw their faith in him, he said to the man, "My son, I declare that your sins are forgiven." 6 But

some Scripture teachers were observing Jesus and thought to themselves, 7 "How dare this man blaspheme God by claiming he forgives sins made against God himself? Only God can forgive sins!" ❖ *To blaspheme means to talk impiously, irreverently, or disrespectfully about God. Blasphemy was considered a serious sin, punishable by death. [Leviticus 24:16] In this instance, they thought Jesus was presumptuously speaking for God. To do so was disrespectful of God's authority, and hence blasphemous.* ➤

8 Right away, Jesus was aware in his spirit what they were thinking ❖ *probably via a "word of knowledge" from the in-dwelling Holy Spirit [1 Corinthians 12:8]* ➤ and asked, "Why are you thinking such evil about me? 9 Which do you think is less likely that I'm able to do— forgive this man's sins or enable him to stand up and walk? 10 You correctly believe that only God has the power to do either of these things. So I will demonstrate that I have power and approval from God to heal so you can know for sure that I, the Son of Man, also have his authority to forgive sins." Jesus said to the paralyzed man, 11 "I command you to get up, pick up your stretcher, and go home." ❖ *They correctly believed that God would only do a miracle through a person who had proper a relationship with God. He would never give a blasphemer the power to heal. Thus the healing proved that Jesus was not a blasphemer and what he said about forgiving sins was true. They believed that only God could heal and never attributed healings to Satan. (Although Jesus' detractors did think his power to expel demons came from Satan.)* ➤ 12 Immediately, the man got up, picked up his stretcher, and carried it out in full view of everyone. All who witnessed this were astonished and began to praise God. They said, "We've seen an incredible thing today!"

Jesus Associates with Disreputable People

13 Later, Jesus went down to walk along the shore of Lake Galilee. A large crowd followed him so he began to teach. 14 As he was going along, he saw Matthew Levi, the son of Alphaeus, sitting in his tax collector's booth. ❖ *He later wrote the gospel of Matthew. Tax collectors were social outcasts because they collaborated with their Roman conquerors, and they got rich by extorting more than the legal tax from people and then pocketed the* difference. ➤ Jesus went up to him and said, "Come be one of my followers." Matthew, having heard a lot about Jesus, immediately left behind his lucrative job and everything he owned and began to follow him.

15 Later, Jesus and his close followers dined at Matthew's house with many of his tax-collector friends and other disreputable people, for many of them were Jesus' avid followers. 16 When some Scripture teachers—who were also Pharisees—saw the company he kept, they complained indignantly to his close followers, "Why does your Rabbi pollute himself by eating and drinking with tax collectors and other such sinners?" ❖ *They believed that eating with sinners implied Jesus approved of their godless ways, and also made him ritually unclean in God's sight.* ➤

17 But when Jesus heard this, he said, "A doctor doesn't tend to people who are well. It's the sick who need his attention. In the same way, I didn't come to call righteous people to follow me but, rather, to invite those who know that they are sinners to repent and change their way of life." ❖ *The word "righteous" is used in different senses in the Bible. When referring to God, it means sinless perfection. But when used of people, it means someone God has forgiven and accepted into relationship with himself. Jesus may have meant that he didn't come to invite righteous people because there are none in the sense of being sinless. He could also mean that those who God accepts as righteous don't need to be invited since they already have a proper relationship with him. In any case, the Pharisees and Scripture teachers thought that by legalistically following all of the Torah's commands, they were automatically accepted as righteous by God and that he cared for no other kind of person. But their "self-righteousness" was, in fact, "unrighteous" in God's view because they refused to acknowledge their own sin and thus their need for his forgiveness. Such people see no need for a Savior for themselves. So ironically, it was the social outcasts who had no pride and knew they were sinners who were most open to responding to Jesus' invitation.* ➤

Jesus Answers a Question About Fasting

18 Now it was the practice of John the Baptizer's followers and the Pharisees to fast twice a week. One day, some of them came to Jesus and asked, "Why is it that you don't have your followers fast as the Pharisees and John's followers do?" ❖ *Fasting means going*

without food or without certain foods (usually meat and richer foods) and without drinks other than water for a meal or for a longer period to discipline the body, to become more sensitive to God's speaking, to show seriousness about prayer, to gain spiritual reward, [Matthew 6:17-18] or to increase the power of prayer. [Matthew 17:21; Mark 9:29] See the footnote at Matthew 6:16 on fasting. ➤

19 To explain that it wasn't appropriate for his followers to fast while he was with them, Jesus replied, "Nobody would suggest that a groom's close friends fast while he is with them at his wedding banquet. 20 But the time will come when I'm taken away from them, and then they will fast." ❖ Jesus assumed his followers will fast. Do you? ➤ 21 And to explain that the Pharisees' teachings and legalistic fasting couldn't be mixed with his teachings without ruining both, Jesus gave these illustrations, "No one sews a piece of unshrunk cloth onto an old garment to patch it since the patch would shrink in washing and rip the garment even more. 22 Also, no one puts new wine into rigid old wineskins since the pressure from the fermenting wine would burst the already-stretched skins. It would ruin the wineskins and spill the wine. New wine must be put into new wineskins, then both the wine and wineskins are preserved." ❖ Jesus' teaching about how to join God's Kingdom was incompatible with the Pharisees' emphasis on the legalistic observance of man-made rules. Their focus was on outward behavior only, while Jesus stressed humility and attitudes of the heart and mind. A person could not follow Jesus' teaching and maintain all the legalistic rules the Pharisees taught because their focus would ruin what Jesus was trying to teach. Jesus' teachings were much more than a new patch on the Old Covenant's way of approaching God. It was about an entirely New Covenant. ➤

Jesus Is Master over Sabbath Regulations

23 One Sabbath, A while Jesus and his followers were walking along a path through a grain field, his followers were picking some of the grain and eating it.

❖ The Torah allowed picking wheat in another man's field by hand while walking along, but not cutting it with a sickle. [Deuteronomy 23:25] So they were not stealing. ➤ 24 Some Pharisees who saw them do this accused them, "Your followers are disobeying God's command by working on the Sabbath!" ❖ They considered picking the grain to be the work of harvesting. See Exodus 20:8-10; 31:14-17; 35:1-3; Leviticus 23:3; Deuteronomy 5:12-14; and Jeremiah 17:21-27 about Sabbath regulations. The Pharisees were stretching the definition of work. No such details that they claimed to be work were in the Torah. ➤

25 Jesus counter argued, "Don't tell me you aren't familiar with the example David set in the Scriptures when he and his men were hungry! [1 Samuel 21:1-6] 26 He entered the Tabernacle when Abiathar was High Priest and ate consecrated bread which only priests are allowed to eat. [Leviticus 24:9] He ate it and also gave it to his men to eat." ❖ Jesus used David as an example because he knew the Pharisees thought highly of him. His point was: There's no mention or implication in the Scriptures of God condemning David or the priest B who gave the bread for disobeying this Torah command in order to meet his men's need. So God isn't going to condemn Jesus' followers for breaking the Pharisees' man-made Sabbath rules in order to satisfy their hunger. The Pharisees, who were proud of their detailed knowledge of the Scriptures, should have been able to see the implications of this story and not demand more from people than God does. Note that Jesus' argument is an argument from silence, yet it is still valid. ➤ 27 Then Jesus said, "God made the Sabbath to benefit people. It's not more important than they are, and he certainly didn't intend it to make life more difficult. 28 So I, the Son of Man, am Master of the Sabbath and its regulations."

3

Jesus Heals a Man with a Crippled Hand on a Sabbath

1 Then, Jesus entered the local synagogue to teach and a man with a

---

A 2:23 The Sabbath was a holy day of rest when no work was allowed. God instituted it to keep people from working seven days a week without rest and to provide time for their relationship with him. The Biblical Sabbath begins at sunset Friday and ends at sunset Saturday.

B 2:26 Jesus tells the story mentioning Abiathar as the priest, but the account in 1 Samuel 21:1-6 only mentions Ahimelech. 2 Samuel 8:17; 1 Chronicles 18:16; and other references say Ahimelech is the son of Abiathar. 1 Samuel 23:6 says Abiathar was the son of Ahimelech. It's likely that both father and son had both names.

crippled hand **A** was present. ² The Pharisees watched to see if Jesus would heal him, since they considered this to be work that was forbidden on the Sabbath *[Exodus 20:8-11; 31:14-17; 35:2-3; Leviticus 23:3; Deuteronomy 5:12-15; Jeremiah 17:21-27]* and they were seeking grounds to accuse him of disobeying Torah commands. ³ Jesus told the man with the crippled hand, "Come and stand here." ⁴ Then Jesus said to the Pharisees, "What do you think the Torah allows on the Sabbath? May we do good works, or must we allow harm to happen because work is forbidden? May we save a life, or must we allow life to be destroyed on Sabbath days?" ❖ *Jesus' point: The Torah teaches it is appropriate to honor God by helping people on the Sabbath. It was only Pharisaic tradition that defined many activities—which the Torah was silent about— as being work. Jesus refused to accept their traditions as having authority equal to God's Torah.* ➤ But they remained sullenly silent. ⁵ Jesus looked around at them and became angry. He was deeply upset at their self-righteous uncaring attitudes. He told the man, "Straighten out your hand." As he did so, it became completely normal {just like the other}. **B** ⁶ The Pharisees were furious because he had publicly discredited their Sabbath rules and they began plotting with some of King Herod's men how they could kill him. ❖ *They ignored the fact that Jesus only said a few words—which isn't work—and that God did the actual healing. They also ignored their own violation of God's commands by conspiring to kill him. [Genesis 9:6; Exodus 20:13; 21:12-14; 23:7; Leviticus 24:17; Deuteronomy 5:17] Their only concern was their continued status as authoritative interpreters of the Scriptures.* ➤

Large Crowds Follow Jesus Everywhere

⁷ Jesus and his close followers left there and went to the shore of Lake Galilee. A large crowd followed him. They had come from Galilee and Judea Provinces, ⁸ Jerusalem, Idumea Province (south of Judea), and also from the Gentile areas east of the Jordan River, and from around the Gentile cities of Tyre and Sidon on the Mediterranean coast, north of Galilee. They had all heard about the miracles and healings he did and came to see for themselves. ⁹ He told his followers to get a boat ready so he could sit in it a little offshore and not be crowded while he taught. ¹⁰ For he had healed so many people that the sick kept pushing their way through the crowd to be healed by touching him. ¹¹ Whenever demonized people came close, the demons would make them prostrate themselves in front of him and shout, "You are God's Son!" ¹² But Jesus always forbade them from saying that about him. ❖ *Though Mark doesn't make this clear, Jesus probably said this to the people after the demons left. See Matthew 16:20 and the following note for a possible reason why Jesus did this.* ➤

Jesus Appoints Twelve Apostles

¹³ Then, Jesus went up a hill and summoned certain men. ¹⁴ He appointed twelve of them whom he called apostles. **C** ❖ *"Apostle" means "someone sent as a messenger." Jesus gave them authority to be his representatives.* ➤ They were meant to always be with him, for he planned to train them to preach the Good News about God's way of salvation ¹⁵ and give them authority to expel demons. ¹⁶ These are the names of the twelve:

Simon, whom he also named Peter
    ❖ *In Hebrew: Kefa [Kay-fah], which is transliterated into English as Cephas.* ➤

¹⁷ James (the son of Zebedee)
John (James' younger brother), (Jesus called James and John "*Boanerges*" which in Aramaic means "sons of thunder") ❖ *This may have been for their loud voices or for their hot tempers.* ➤

¹⁸ Andrew (Simon's younger brother)
Philip
Bartholomew ❖ *who might have also been called Nathanael* ➤
Matthew (also called Levi)
Thomas
James (the son of Alpheus)

A 3:1 The Greek word χείρ (cheir), traditionally translated here as "hand," includes the wrist and forearm and can even include the entire arm. (Many languages lack separate words for "hand" and "arm.") It's possible it was more than what we would call his "hand" that was crippled or withered.

B 3:5 Most major manuscripts to not have these words. They were likely added from Matthew 12:13.

C 3:14 Many manuscripts lack "who he called apostles."

Thaddeus (also called Judas,
the son of James)

Simon (who was called the Zealot)

❖ *this was because of his association with
the left-wing Zealot group that wanted to revolt
against Roman rule* ➤ and

19 Judas Iscariot, **A** who would later
betray Jesus to his enemies.

❖ *Jesus' apostles included common uneducated
fishermen, a social outcast who collaborated with the enemy
(Matthew), a violent political fanatic (Simon the Zealot), and a
man whom he knew would betray him. Anyone can become a
follower of Jesus, although it does involve leaving behind your
former sinful ways.* ➤

Beware of Saying
that the Spirit's Work Is of Satan

20 Then, Jesus returned home to Capernaum, but such a large crowd gathered there
to be healed and to listen to his teaching that
neither he nor his close followers had time
to even eat. 21 When Jesus' family—20 miles
away in Nazareth—heard about this, they
set out to rescue him and bring him home.
From the things they heard about him, they
thought he wasn't rational.

22 Some Scripture teachers from Jerusalem had been saying, "Satan controls him!
Jesus' power to expel demons comes from
the prince of demons himself."

23 So Jesus called the people together
and began to counter this accusation with
these illustrations: "How could it profit
Satan to expel his own demons? 24 Any
kingdom divided in civil war can't last
long, 25 and a household fighting against
each other will fall apart. 26 If Satan is
fighting against his own demons, how can
his kingdom continue?" 27 Comparing
Satan to a strongman, Jesus continued,
"No one can rob a strongman of his
possessions unless he is first overpowered. If someone stronger does this and
ties him up, then he can rob the strongman's house. ❖ *Jesus' point is that he is able to
expel demons because he is mightier than Satan. The*

*strongman's "possessions" are the people he has under
the control or influence of his demons.* ➤

28 "It's important that you understand
this: God is willing to forgive every sin
people commit and every blasphemy that
they say 29 except for blasphemy against the
Holy Spirit. He will never forgive that sin."

❖ *To blaspheme means to talk impiously, irreverently, or
disrespectfully about God. God will not forgive blasphemy
against the Holy Spirit because it is the Spirit who enables
us to repent—and without repentance there is no
forgiveness. If a person rejects or offends the Holy Spirit so
that he leaves, that person will never again desire to repent.
Anyone who is worried about having committed this sin,
hasn't. Anyone who has committed this sin will never worry
about it. The Pharisees said that Jesus' power came from
Satan when it really was the Holy Spirit's power. Therefore,
they were insulting the Holy Spirit and were in danger of
committing this unforgivable sin. Some believers today are
in danger of doing the same thing when they accuse
believers who are exhibiting the Holy Spirit's power of doing
things by Satan's power. Genuine skepticism does not
justify such an accusation.* ➤ So be careful about
the accusations you make." 30 He was warning them because people were saying the
Spirit within him was demonic.

Jesus' True Relatives

31 While Jesus was still speaking to the
crowd, his mother and brothers [*Matthew
13:55*] arrived from Nazareth to see him.
But they couldn't get inside the house
where he was teaching because it was
crammed with people. So they passed a
message inside asking him to come out.
32 Someone in the crowd sitting around
him said, "Your mother and brothers are
outside wanting to see you."

33 Using this as a teaching opportunity,
Jesus asked, "Who is my mother and who
are my brothers?" 34 Looking around at all
those sitting there who wanted to learn from
him, he said, "These people are as mothers
and brothers to me! 35 Those who obey my
Heavenly Father are as close to me as my
brother and sister and mother."

A 3:19 Iscariot may be a transliteration into Greek of Aramaic
words that mean "from Kerioth" (a town 20 miles south of
Jerusalem), [Joshua 15:25; Jeremiah 48:24] but no one is
certain of its meaning. Another idea is that it's a corruption of

the Latin word "sicarius" (meaning "assassin") which was transliterated into Aramaic and then again into Greek. Others think
it means "liar" or "fraud." But in John 6:71, he is called Judas,
son of Simon Iscariot, so the pejorative meanings are unlikely.

4

Parable of the Four Soils

1 Later, Jesus again went down to the shore of Lake Galilee to teach. So many people gathered that he sat in a boat just offshore so the entire crowd could see and hear him. 2 Then he taught them many spiritual truths in parables. In one he said, 3 "Pay attention to this! A farmer went out to sow seed in his field. ❖ *He scattered the seed over the ground and later plowed it under.* ➤ 4 As he scattered the seed, some fell on a hard-packed path and birds ate them. 5 Some fell where the soil was just a thin layer over rock. These sprouted quickly because the soil was shallow. ❖ *The sun rapidly warmed the shallow soil so the seed grew faster there than in cooler deeper soil.* ➤ 6 But the sun scorched the young plants and they withered because the underlying rock blocked their roots from reaching water. 7 Some fell on ground where thorn bushes had grown and their roots still remained. These sprouted and grew for a while but the young plants couldn't compete for light and water with the thorn bushes that also grew and choked them. So they produced no grain and died. 8 And some seed fell on good soil. These sprouted, grew strong, and bore more seed in varying amounts, some 30, some 60, and others 100. 9 If your minds are attuned to God, try to understand this parable!"

Why Jesus Taught in Parables

10 Later, when only Jesus' usual followers were with him, they asked what the parables meant. 11 He told them, "You have the privilege of being the first to learn about Kingdom truths that God hasn't revealed before. But for the present, I will only teach others about them in parables. 12 This is so the prophecy may be fulfilled that says, **'Even though they look, they don't perceive. Even though they hear, they don't understand. If this wasn't true about them, they would turn away from their sinful ways and I would forgive them.' "** *[Isaiah 6:9-10]* ❖ *Jesus intended that only those whose minds were open to God's truth would be able to understand the parables. But those with hard hearts and closed minds would not understand.* ➤

Jesus Explains the Parable of the Four Soils

13 Jesus said, "Don't you understand even this simple parable? If you don't understand this one, how will you possibly understand any of my other parables? 14 The seed represents God's message about the way of salvation. The farmer is anyone who preaches that message. 15 The hard-packed path illustrates people whose minds are closed toward God's message. They may hear his truth but it can't enter their hardened hearts. Just like the birds ate the seed, Satan snatches the memory of the message away from them. 16 The layer of shallow soil over rock illustrates people who hear God's message and happily receive it at first. 17 But just like a plant in shallow soil can't develop the roots it needs to survive, God's message doesn't go deep in their hearts and minds because they aren't willing to fully surrender themselves to him. Their shallow faith lasts for only a short time until the first real testing of their faith or persecution occurs. Then it quickly dies. 18 The ground with thorn bushes illustrates people who initially accept God's message 19 but they never give it first priority. So other concerns and higher priorities, such as worries, materialism, and pleasure keep his word from producing good fruit in their lives. Eventually, their faith is smothered and dies. ❖ *Some commentators believe the plants did not die but were merely unproductive. Jesus taught elsewhere that trees producing no fruit were only fit to be burned. [Matthew 3:10; 7:19; Luke 3:9; John 15:4-6] The focus in this parable is on how the seed is received and the resulting fruit. Only good soil results in fruit and the point is that good soil is the only acceptable kind. Just as in your own garden, plants that don't produce are rejected as worthless.* ➤ 20 But the good soil illustrates people who hear God's message, recognize its worth, grab onto it, and allow it to take deep root in their hearts and minds. They surrender themselves to God and make him first priority in their lives. So their faith matures and their lives cause God's Kingdom to increase and prosper to varying degrees." ❖ *The implication is that individuals can determine what kind of "soil" their hearts are by how they respond to God's message.* ➤

God Intends to Reveal His Truth to Everyone

21 Jesus continued, "No one lights a lamp and then hides it under a bed or covers it so its light is hidden. Instead, they put it where the light can illuminate as much of the room as possible. 22 Then, the light will reveal everything that was hidden in darkness. ❖ *Jesus made his points with illustrations. Sometimes those illustrations are less than clear today because of the gap in time and culture. He meant that God fully intends for people to see and understand the illumination of the spiritual truths he taught. He would never want it hidden since that would defeat its purpose.* ➤ 23 If your minds are attuned to God, try to understand what this means!

24-25 "Pay close attention to God's teaching that I give you because God will increase your understanding if you receive it with proper regard and a desire to understand and obey it. But if you don't receive it properly, you will lose even the little understanding you have."

A Parable About How God Causes His Kingdom to Grow

26 Jesus continued, "A farmer who scatters wheat on the ground can illustrate the growth of God's Kingdom. 27 The farmer does nothing further that helps the seed grow. He goes about his daily work and sleeps but the wheat grows of its own accord without his knowing how. 28 The soil causes the wheat to grow without help. First the stalk appears, then the head of grain, then the mature grain. 29 And when the wheat ripens, it's time to harvest it." ❖ *In this parable, unique to Mark's gospel, the farmer is anyone who proclaims God's Word and the seed is the message. The growth of the plants and the production of grain represent new believers and their spiritual growth and maturity, and the harvest represents Judgment Day.* ➤

Parable of the Mustard Seed

30 Jesus said, "How can I teach you what God's Kingdom is like in this world? What can I compare it to? 31 God's Kingdom grows like a mustard seed. Even though it's one of the smallest seeds, 32 once it's planted, it grows into one of the largest garden plants and becomes a tree large enough for birds to nest in its branches." *[Psalm 104:12; Ezekiel 17:23; 31:6; Daniel 4:12]* ❖ *God's Kingdom starts small in people's hearts. But it grows and becomes quite influential, blessing those around it. Jesus may have had in mind that birds often represented Gentiles and the Kingdom would even take in Gentiles under its sway. This would have been a radical thought for the Jews of his day.* ➤ A

33-34 Jesus told many similar parables to teach truths about God's Kingdom. Since he only taught in parables, people understood only as much truth as they were ready to believe. But afterward, when he was alone with his close followers, he explained the parables to them.

Jesus Demonstrates Authority over Weather

35 Late afternoon that same day, Jesus said to the twelve, "Let's sail to the other side of the lake." 36 So they got into the boat with Jesus and set out, leaving the crowd behind—although some followed in other boats. 37 As they were crossing, a sudden storm came up. It was so severe that waves were breaking over the sides and filling the boat. ❖ *Sudden storms are common on Lake Galilee.* ➤ 38 But Jesus was asleep on a cushion in the elevated stern of the boat. His men were afraid so they woke him and said, "Rabbi, don't you care that we're about to drown?" 39 Jesus got up and commanded the wind and waves to calm down. The storm quickly dissipated and the water became calm. 40 Then he said, "Why were you so frightened? Your trust in God is too small!" 41 They were overcome with awe and fear, and asked each other, "Who is he? He even has authority over the wind and waves!" *[Psalm 65:7; 89:8-9; 93:3-4; 107:25; 28-29; Jonah 1:15-16]* ❖ *Jews believed only God controlled these things.* ➤

5

Jesus Demonstrates Authority over Demons

1 They arrived at the other side of the lake in the region of Gergesa. B 2 When Jesus went ashore, right away a demonized man

---

A **4:32** See the footnote at Matthew 13:32.
B **5:1** The name of this town varies among the different

Gospels and among manuscripts. Some say it was Gadara (8 miles from the lake). Others say it was Gerasa

met him who had come out of the tombs [3] where he lived. The demons made him supernaturally strong and no one could keep him bound, not even with chains. [4] People had chained him many times but he was able to break them, and no one was strong enough to control him. [5] People heard him yelling day and night among the tombs and the hills because the demons made him cut himself with stones.

[6] He had first seen Jesus from a distance then ran and prostrated himself in front of him. [7-8] As Jesus was commanding the demons to come out of him, the man shouted, "Arrrgh! Get out of here, Jesus, Son of the Most High God! Leave me alone! [A] I adjure you by God, do not torment me!" ❖ *Note that the demons did not obey even God's Son immediately. It's not entirely clear what the Greek word rendered as "adjure" means in this context. Some commentators think the demons were trying to control Jesus, as exorcists tried to control demons with the same formula. But it seems unlikely that demons would think they could control the Son of God. Others think they are putting Jesus under oath before God as a witness that he would not harm them.* ➤ [9] Then Jesus asked, "What's your name?" He replied, "My name is Legion, because we are many." ❖ *A Roman legion could have 4000—6000 soldiers in it, indicating the man could have had several thousand demons in him.* ➤ [10] And the demons begged Jesus to not make them leave that region.

[11] Since there was a large herd of pigs feeding on a nearby hillside, [12] they begged him, "Allow us to enter those pigs." [13] Jesus gave them permission, so they left the man and entered the pigs. Then the entire herd of about 2000 ran down the steep hillside into the lake and drowned.

[14] The herders ran to the nearby town and reported what they had seen so many came out to see for themselves what had happened. [15] When they arrived, they found Jesus with the previously demonized man sitting near him, clothed and sane. Realizing what had happened, they became afraid of Jesus and his power. [16] Eye-witnesses kept telling the newcomers exactly how Jesus had delivered the demonized man and what the pigs had done. [17] Then out of fear, the people respectfully asked Jesus to leave their district.

[18] So Jesus got in the boat to return to the other side of the lake. But the man he had delivered begged to go with him.

[19] Jesus told him, "No. I want you to go home to your people and tell them how God showed you great mercy and what he did for you." [20] So the man went throughout the entire Decapolis [B] district telling everyone he met what Jesus had done for him. All who heard it were amazed and awed.

A Woman's Faith Heals Her, and Jesus Demonstrates Power over Death

[21] When Jesus arrived at Capernaum, a large crowd gathered around him on the shore. [22] Then Jairus, a leader of the local synagogue, prostrated himself in front of Jesus. [23] He pleaded, "My little girl is dying. Please come and lay your hands on her so she will live." [24] Jesus agreed to do so and as they walked through the narrow streets, the crowd following them pressed in on every side. [25] Among them was a woman who suffered from chronic bleeding. [C] She'd had this problem for twelve years [26] and had spent all she owned on doctors whose treatments caused additional suffering with no positive results. Her condition had only become worse. [27] Since she had heard about the things Jesus could do, she came up behind him in the crowd and unobtrusively touched his robe. ❖ *Her condition made her ritually unclean. Anyone she touched in the crowd would become unclean until evening and would have to go through ritual washing. This was a terrible burden to bear and a constant embarrassment. She probably hoped no one would notice*

(about 30 miles southeast of the lake). Both were in a region called the Decapolis. Others say it was Gergesa, on the lake shore where there are cliffs in the vicinity. This one fits the story details best.

A **5:7** Literally, "What to me to you," the sense of hostility that's implied by the idiom is rendered here, rather than the more literal "What have you to do with me?"

B **5:20** The Decapolis was a district of Syria province with its own governor. Decapolis means "ten towns" and was predominantly a Gentile area, mostly east of the Jordan River and southeast of Lake Galilee.

C **5:25** Probably uterine bleeding.

her. *[Leviticus 15:19-30]* ➤ 28 She was thinking, "If I can just touch his robe, I will be healed." 29 Immediately, the bleeding stopped and she knew from the way her body felt that she was completely healed. 30 At that same instant, Jesus sensed that healing power had flowed out of him, so he abruptly stopped, turned around, and asked, "Who touched me?" 31 His close followers said, "Everyone's crowding around you; anyone could've accidentally touched you." 32 But Jesus kept looking around to find who had done it. 33 When the woman realized she hadn't gotten away unnoticed, she came forward trembling with fear and prostrated herself before him. Then she confessed what she had done and why, and how she had been immediately healed. 34 Jesus said to her gently, "My daughter, your faith in me has healed you. Go home in wholeness and be at peace."

35 While Jesus was still speaking to her, someone arrived from Jairus' house and reported, "Your daughter has died. There's no reason the Rabbi should bother to come." 36 But Jesus overheard and told him, "Don't be afraid. Just continue to trust in me." 37 Then, Jesus didn't allow anyone from the crowd to follow him any farther except Peter, James, and his brother John. 38 When they arrived at Jairus' house, Jesus saw a crowd of mourners wailing. 39 He went in and told them, "You shouldn't be crying and making all this commotion. The girl isn't dead; she is only sleeping." ❖ *Jesus is the creator who speaks into being things that are not yet. But unbelief could prevent Jesus from performing a miracle. [Matthew 13:58; Mark 6:5] He may have wanted them away from there and said what he did to minimize the unbelief present.* ➤ 40 They ridiculed him because they knew she was dead. But he made all the mourners leave. Then, with the girl's parents and his three companions, he entered the room where the girl was lying. 41 Holding her hand, he said in Aramaic, A *"Talitha koum!"* which means, "Little girl, stand up!" ❖ *Mark probably recorded the exact words he said to emphasize there was no magical incantation, only a simple command.* ➤

42 The twelve-year-old girl immediately stood and began walking around. Everyone there was astounded. 43 Then, Jesus told her parents to give her something to eat and sternly commanded them not to tell anyone what had happened.

6

People in Nazareth Reject Jesus

1 After this, Jesus and his close followers went to Nazareth where he had grown up. 2 As was his practice on Saturday—the Sabbath—he went to the local synagogue and taught. All who heard him were shocked. They indignantly asked each other, "Where did he get this wisdom and the power to do miracles? 3 He's just a carpenter, isn't he? Isn't Miriam his mother and his brothers are James, Joses, Simon, and Judas? ❖ *Though none of his brothers believed in him before his resurrection, James became the leader of the assembly in Jerusalem and Judas (a.k.a. Jude) became a missionary and wrote "Jude's Letter." We don't know anything more of Joses (a.k.a. Joseph) and Simon or his sisters. Protestants assume these were younger brothers and sisters born to Miriam (Mary) and Yoseph after Jesus' birth. Catholics believe they were Yoseph's older children from a previous marriage.* ➤ Aren't his sisters living here too? What makes him think he's a prophet?" ❖ *In many cultures, people are expected to remain in the class, station, or occupation into which they were born. To do otherwise is considered presumptuous.* ➤ They took offense and rejected him. 4 So Jesus responded, "A prophet is honored everywhere except in his hometown and among his own family and relatives." *[John 4:44]* ❖ *Here, Jesus implicitly claimed to be a prophet.* ➤ 5 And because of their unbelief, he was unable to do any miracles there except heal a few people by laying his hands on them. 6a He was astonished at their refusal to believe. *[Matthew 13:58]* ❖ *Unbelief keeps God from working miracles. Mark says he was "unable," not "unwilling." Therefore, it is not surprising that people who do not believe God works in certain ways anymore, fail to see him do so. This doesn't mean that unbelief can actually prevent God from performing a miracle, but that he has chosen to only*

---

work in response to faith. Do you have unbelief that stops God from working miracles in your life or through you? ➤

Jesus Sends His Apostles
to Evangelize and Heal

6b Jesus continued his ministry to visit and teach from village to village. 7 Then one day, he summoned his twelve apostles together, organized them in pairs to go out and minister, and gave them authority to expel demons. 8 He gave them the following instructions: "Aside from a walking stick, don't take anything with you, no bag, food, money, 9 or extra clothing, though you may wear sandals. Instead, trust that God will provide your needs through the people you minister to. 10 When you arrive in a village and are welcomed in a house, stay there as long as you minister in that village. Don't seek better accommodations or move from house to house. 11 And when people refuse to receive you or your message, as you leave, shake off the dust of that place from your feet." ❖ *This was a rebuke, implying that they were no better than pagans so even the dust of their house (or town) was defiling and offensive. It warned that they had better repent or God would judge them. [John 15:23]* ➤ 12 So the apostles set out and preached that people should turn away from their sins and submit to God's will for their lives. 13 They also expelled many demons and anointed the sick with oil so many were healed. *[James 5:14-16]* ❖ *Anointing oil symbolizes the Holy Spirit. In the New Testament, evangelism always included healing ministry. Yet this is this neglected by most believers today because of unbelief.* ➤

John the Baptizer's Death

14-15 The news about Jesus and the things he was doing spread everywhere. People said that Jesus was John the Baptizer returned from the dead, and that was why he had power to do miracles. Others said he was the prophet Elijah. ❖ *who had also performed miracles during his ministry around 850 BC* ➤ Still others thought he was a great prophet like those who had lived long ago. All this came to the notice of Herod Antipas, tetrarch over Galilee Province. 16 When he heard about it, he started saying, "This is John, the man I had beheaded come back to life!" ❖ *It's odd*

that Herod had not heard of Jesus doing miracles while John still lived, and also odd that he would think this is John since John had never done any miracles. [John 10:41] He obviously thought highly of John and felt guilt over having him beheaded. Such guilt can torment a person with irrational thoughts. ➤

17-20 This is how John died. Herod had married Herodias, who was the wife of his younger brother Philip. ❖ *Herod and Herodias had an affair and then divorced their spouses to marry each other.* ➤ John kept telling Herod that the Torah forbade such a relationship *[Leviticus 18:15-16; 20:21]* so Herodias wanted him dead. Herod imprisoned John to silence his public criticism and to protect him from Herodias. He both feared John and respected him, knowing he was a good and holy man. Herod liked John's preaching, even though it upset him every time he listened. 21 But on Herod's birthday, Herodias saw an opportunity to have John killed. Herod gave a banquet for his high-ranking military and administrative officers and important leaders in Galilee. 22 Herodias' daughter danced erotically for Herod and his guests. She pleased them all so much that Herod imprudently told the girl in front of everyone, "As a reward, ask me for anything and I will give it to you. 23 I make a solemn oath before everyone here that I will give you anything at all, up to half of my kingdom." 24 So she went to her mother and said, "What should I ask for?" Her mother said, "John the Baptizer's head." 25 The girl immediately returned to the king and said, "I want John the Baptizer's head on a platter, right now." 26 Herod then regretted his oath but would lose face in front of his guests if he refused to keep it. 27 So he immediately ordered an executioner to bring him John's head. The man did as instructed 28 and soon brought the head on a platter. It was given to the girl who took it to her mother. 29 When John's followers heard about it, they retrieved his body and buried it in a tomb.

Jesus Demonstrates Power
to Multiply Resources

30 When the apostles returned from their ministry tour, they reported to Jesus everything they had done. 31 But there were so many people coming for healing that they hardly had a chance to eat. So Jesus said,

"Let's go someplace where we can be alone and get some rest." 32 They took a boat to find an isolated place. 33 But the crowd saw them leave and many of them ran along the lake shore and reached the place where Jesus was heading before he did. 34 When Jesus arrived, he saw the large crowd waiting for him and felt compassion. They were like helpless sheep with no one to care for them. So he started to teach them many spiritual truths they needed to know. 35 Late in the afternoon, his close followers approached him and said, "This place is pretty remote and it's already getting late. 36 You should send everyone away so they have time to reach some village and find something to eat before dark." 37 But Jesus replied, "I want *you* to give them something to eat." Shocked, they replied, "Would you really expect us to go somewhere and spend two hundred denarii ❖ *about 8 months wages at 1 denarius a day, 6 days per week* ➤ on bread to give them all a little something to eat, even if we had it?" 38 Jesus asked, "How much bread do you have? Go find out." When they had looked, they told him, "We have five loaves and two cooked fish." ❖ *Five of their small flat loaves would feed about two people.* ➤ 39 He then directed everyone to recline in groups on the green spring grass 40 and they did so in groups of fifty and a hundred. 41 He took the five loaves and two fish, looked up toward Heaven, and thanked God for the food. ❖ *If Jesus followed the common form of Jewish thanksgiving, he said this: "Blessed (i.e., praised) are you, O Lord our God— King of the universe—who brings forth bread from the earth."* ➤ He then broke the bread and fish into pieces and kept giving them to his followers to distribute. 42 Everyone ate as much as they wanted and were fully satisfied. 43 When the leftover pieces were gathered, they filled twelve baskets. ❖ *Even miraculous provision is not to be wasted. This is the only miracle recorded in all four Gospels, and all four mention the twelve baskets so it must be significant. Most take it to mean that Jesus is able to supply all the needs of the twelve tribes of Israel, which symbolize all of God's people.* ➤ 44 The crowd that he fed

numbered about 5000 men, not counting women and children. ❖ *In that culture, women and children were not commonly counted. There were likely 10,000 to 20,000 people in the crowd.* ➤

Jesus Walks on Water

45 Right after that, Jesus told his close followers to get back in the boat and cross the lake ahead of him to Bethsaida while he dismissed the crowd. 46 After making his good-byes, Jesus went up the mountain by himself to pray. 47 He stayed there all alone until well after sunset. By that time, the boat with his followers was quite a ways out on the lake. 48 He was able to see them rowing hard to make headway against the wind. During the fourth watch, ❖ *i.e., between 3 and 6 a.m. before dawn* ➤ Jesus came walking toward them on the water, intending to continue past them. [Job 9:8] 49 But when they saw him on the water, they thought he was a ghost 50 and were terrified. So he called out to them, "Don't worry! It's me! There's nothing to be afraid of!" 51 Then he climbed into the boat and the wind suddenly died down. They were completely amazed and surprised at this. 52 Even though they had seen his power to multiply bread, they failed to grasp the implications for who he was because they resisted conclusions outside of their cultural expectations.

Jesus Heals in Gennesaret

53 When they finished their crossing, they landed in Gennesaret and tied the boat up there. ❖ *There was a village named Gennesaret, but this was likely the area of that name which was located on the northwest shore of Lake Galilee, southwest of Capernaum.* ➤ 54 As soon as they got out of the boat, people recognized Jesus 55 and ran to spread the news to everyone in the area that he was there. As a result, many carried sick people to him on sleeping mats. 56 Wherever he went, in towns, villages, or fields people brought the sick and laid them in the marketplaces for him to heal. The sick begged permission to just touch a tassel **A** of his robe as he passed by, and all who did so were healed.

A 6:56 The Greek word κράσπεδον (kraspedon) can also mean "fringe" or "edge," but here it probably corresponds to the Hebrew word "tzitzit," which is a special kind of tassel and the holiest part of a Jewish man's robe. The

7

What Defiles Us in God's Sight, and What Does Not

[1] One day, some Pharisees and Scripture teachers from Jerusalem approached Jesus. [2] They had noticed that Jesus' close followers didn't ritually wash their hands before eating to "purify" themselves [3] as required by the traditions of the Jewish elders. [4] They taught that when you came home from the marketplace, you must ritually wash before eating. There were many other traditions that they religiously observed, such as the proper ritual washing of cups, pitchers, copper pots, and dining couches [A] (upon which they reclined when they ate). ❖ *These were man-made rules—not found in the Torah—which had become traditions. The Pharisees and Scripture teachers taught that these traditions were as important as God's commands. Their traditions built a "hedge" around the Torah. They believed that if you kept all the traditions, then you would never disobey any actual Torah commands—for the traditions were more strict in their demands on outward behavior than the Torah was. These traditions were later written down in the Mishna about AD 200. Jesus rejected these traditions and said that they placed an unnecessary burden on people. He also rejected them because the religious leaders claimed breaking them was sin. The focus of these rules encouraged people to think that God was mainly concerned with outward behavior but not with heart attitudes. Concerning ritual washing, they taught that many of the things you touch made you ritually defiled in God's sight. So if you touch your food with ritually defiled hands, then the food will be defiled; and eating defiled food will defile your entire body.* ➤ [5] So these Pharisees and Scripture teachers indignantly complained, "You are responsible for the behavior of your followers. Why do you allow them to break the traditions that our elders established? They don't ritually wash their hands before eating!" [6] Jesus retorted, "You are a bunch of hypocrites! God was speaking about people just like you when he had Isaiah write: 'These people say they honor me and make a show of it; but in their hearts, they don't love me at all. [7] Their so-called submission in worship is worthless to me since they teach their followers that their man-made rules are my commands!' *[Isaiah 29:13]* [8] For you consider your own traditions more important than God's teachings in the Torah [9] and teach people to disobey his commands in order to follow your petty rules! [10] As an example, God said, '**Honor your parents,**' *[Exodus 20:12; Deuteronomy 5:16]* and '**Execute those who curse their parents.**' *[Exodus 21:17; Leviticus 20:9]* [11] But you teach that people can dedicate their resources to God ❖ *with the hidden motive of impressing others with their spirituality* ➤ [12] and then they don't have to use those resources to support their parents in their old age. [13] So your tradition circumvents God's clear command that people should honor and help their parents. And that's only one way among many that you avoid obeying God."

[14] Then Jesus called everyone's attention to what he was about to say, "Listen carefully and try to understand this! [15] People defile themselves by what comes out of their mouths, not by what goes in as the Pharisees teach! [16] If your minds are attuned to God, try to understand what this means!" [B]

[17] When he had left the crowd behind and gone inside [C] with his close followers, they asked him what he meant about how to become defiled. [18-19] Exasperated, Jesus replied, "Don't you understand either? What goes in your mouth goes down to your stomach then through your bowels and eventually out of your body, cleansing all food. ❖ *The Greek literally says, "cleansing all food." This is often wrongly interpreted to mean, "He declared all food clean," implying that Jesus nullified the Torah's regulations about unclean (non-kosher) food. However, the topic in this passage is "eating without ritually washed hands," **not** "eating non-kosher food"—which is never mentioned and was not even being considered by Jesus or others involved in this discussion. All the food in question is kosher. It never would have occurred to Jews in Jesus' time that non-kosher food was in the "food" category at all. Other New Testament*

---

plural of "tzitzit" is "tzitziyot." The Torah commands Jewish men to wear tzitziyot (symbolic tassels) on the corners of their outer garments. [Numbers 15:38-40]

[A] **7:4** Some manuscripts lack "dining couches."

[B] **7:16** Many manuscripts lack verse 16.

[C] **7:17** The Greek is ambiguous. He could have gone inside a house, or gone home (i.e., to Capernaum).

Scriptures address the issue of non-kosher food but Jesus was not addressing it here. ➤ Don't you see that eating something with unwashed hands doesn't affect how God views you? 20 Your words are what come out of your mouth. They originate in your heart and mind. If they are sinful, then God considers you defiled. 21 An evil mind **A** produces evil thoughts and desires, such as murder, adultery, sexual immorality, stealing, 22 evil deeds, coveting, envy, stinginess, deception, lust, indecency, slander, blasphemy, pride, arrogance, moral foolishness, and other sins. 23 These are the kinds of things that defile people in God's sight."

A Gentile Woman's Persistent Faith

24 After that, Jesus left Galilee and traveled north to the area near the Gentile port cities of Tyre and Sidon. **B** He was staying at a particular house, not wanting people to know where he was. But as usual, he was recognized and news of his location spread quickly. 25-26 A Gentile woman from that area heard about him and immediately went to find him. She prostrated herself in front of him and begged him to expel a demon that was afflicting her daughter. ❖ *Tradition says her name was Justa and her daughter's name was Bernice.* ➤ 27 Jesus told her, "God's children, the people of Israel, have first priority in my ministry. It wouldn't be right to take food that's meant for them and give it to their pet dogs."
❖ *Jesus immediately recognized her great faith. He extended the interaction so his followers could learn from her. He knew that she would persist in the face of his apparent reluctance. So she became an example for believers to follow in approaching the Lord.* ➤ 28 She replied, "Yes, Lord. But even the dogs are allowed to eat the bits of food that fall under the table." 29 Then Jesus exclaimed, "For this excellent response—demonstrating your faith—I will grant your request. The demon has left your girl." 30 When she returned home, she found her girl lying peacefully in bed because the demon was gone.

Jesus Heals a Deaf Mute

31 Then, Jesus left the area near Tyre, went south through Sidon, then southeast down to Lake Galilee, and then on to the Gentile Decapolis district. ❖ *This would have taken several days. The Greek text is ambiguous. Some commentators believe his destination was Lake Galilee via the Decapolis, but that would be a very roundabout way to get there.* ➤ 32 Some people there brought him a man who was deaf and mute **C** and begged Jesus to touch and heal him. 33 Jesus led the man a distance away out of sight from the crowd, put his fingers in the man's ears, then spit on his own fingers and touched the man's tongue with the saliva. 34 He then looked up toward Heaven in prayer and sighed **D** deeply. Then he said in Aramaic, ❖ *the everyday language of the Jews in Israel at that time* ➤ "Effatha!" which means, "Open!" ❖ *Why did Jesus do and say these particular things? We only know for sure that he was doing what his Father wanted him to do. [John 8:28; 12:49; 14:10, 31] Mark probably recorded his exact word in Aramaic (the rest of the text is in Greek) so people would know that Jesus was not using any magic words.* ➤ 35 Immediately, the man could hear and speak clearly. 36 Jesus told the man's friends not to tell anyone what he had done. But it seemed that the more strictly he forbid this, the more people spread what they knew. 37 They were astonished at this healing and said, "Everything he does turns out good! He even enables the deaf and mute to hear and speak."

8

Jesus Multiplies Resources Again to Feed 4000 Men

1 Not long after this, another large crowd gathered around Jesus that ran out of food, so Jesus summoned his close followers and

---

A 7:21 Literally, the word "heart" is here. But in the biblical cultures—and therefore in the Scriptures—the "heart" was not a figure for the center of emotions, like it is in our culture. When the Scriptures say "heart," it is usually more accurate to translate that as "mind" or, sometimes, "human spirit."

B 7:24 Some manuscripts lack "and Sidon."

C 7:32 The word μογιλάλος (mogilalos) rendered "mute" can also mean "have a speech impediment." But most deaf people at that time never learned to speak at all, unless they became deaf after early childhood.

D 7:34 The word στενάζω (stenazō) rendered "sigh" can alternatively mean "groan."

told them, 2 "I feel sorry for these people. They've been with me for three days and their food is gone. 3 I don't want to send them away without something to eat because some of them are far from home and might faint from hunger on their way." 4 His followers said, "But this crowd is so huge! Where could we find enough bread in this remote place to feed them, even if we could afford it?" 5 Jesus asked, "How many loaves of bread do you have?" They answered, "Seven." 6 Jesus told the crowd to recline on the ground. Then he took the seven loaves, thanked God for them, broke them, and kept giving them to his followers to distribute. 7 They also had a few small cooked fish. So after blessing them, he told his followers to distribute them as well. 8 Everyone ate all they desired and were full. The leftovers filled seven large baskets. 9 That crowd included about 4000 men, not counting the women and children. Then Jesus sent them all home, 10 got into a boat with his close followers, and sailed to the area of Dalmanutha. ❖ *Matthew 15:39 says they went to Magadan. These may have been two close villages or different names for the same village. But the location is unknown.* ➤

Jesus Warns About the Evil Influences of the Pharisees and King Herod

11 There, some Pharisees came and started arguing with Jesus. They wanted a clear miraculous sign proving that God had sent him. 12 Jesus sighed deeply in his spirit and said, "People living today want a sign before they will believe, but none will be given!" ❖ *Jesus refused to perform on demand. He healed out of compassion, and those many healings plus the witness of others to miracles he had done should have been sufficient. Nothing would have satisfied them, as can be seen by their refusal to believe after his resurrection. So their seeking a sign was insincere.* ➤ 13 Then he left them, got back into the boat with his followers, and crossed the lake.

14 As they were crossing, his men realized they had forgotten to buy bread. All they had with them was one loaf. 15 Jesus, still thinking about his confrontation with the Pharisees, said, "Guard yourselves against the leaven of the Pharisees and Herod." ❖ *"Leaven" was a piece of unused dough that had been set aside to leaven another batch of bread. The natural yeast in that piece multiplied as the dough sat for a few days. Leaven was often a symbol of influence, sometimes positive, and often negative. It represented impure influence when they rid their houses of it during the preparation for Passover. They should have easily understood his meaning but were focused on their own concerns.* ➤ 16 His followers started discussing his statement among themselves and concluded Jesus was concerned that they had no bread with them. 17 But Jesus was aware of their discussion and said, "Why are you talking about not having any bread? Are you so resistant to truth that you still don't understand? 18 Have you failed to understand the things you've seen and heard? Or are your memories faulty? *[Jeremiah 5:21; Ezekiel 12:2]* 19 When I fed the crowd of 5000 men with just five loaves of bread, how many baskets of leftovers did you gather?" They answered, "Twelve." 20 Jesus continued, "And when I fed the crowd of 4000 men with seven loaves of bread, how many large baskets of leftovers did you gather?" They answered, "Seven." 21 He asked them, "Don't you understand the significance of what you've seen? I can provide any food you need, so I wasn't concerned about your not bringing bread along." ❖ *See Matthew 16:11-12.* ➤

Jesus Heals a Blind Man

22 They arrived at the village of Bethsaida on the northeast shore of Lake Galilee, near where the Jordan River enters the lake. Some people brought a blind man and begged Jesus to touch him for healing. 23 Jesus took him by the hand and led him out of the village where they could be alone. He spit in the man's eyes and lay his hands on him, then asked, "Are you able to see anything now?" 24 The man looked around and said, "Yes, I can see people, but not clearly. They look like trees walking around." ❖ *This, along with the word "restored" in the next verse, suggests that the man was not born blind and knew what trees looked like, so he knew he wasn't seeing clearly.* ➤ 25 Then Jesus put his hands over the man's eyes again. Afterward, the man stared intently and his sight was restored. He saw everything clearly. ❖ *This is the only recorded*

instance where Jesus did not heal completely the first time he tried. Some commentators suggest this is symbolic of the fact that our understanding of spiritual things comes in stages. But remember that not all of Jesus' healings and miracles are recorded. [John 21:25] It's possible there were other times when full healing did not happen the first time. The Gospel writers wanted to stress his power and would naturally report the more spectacular healings. But the experience among people who pray for healing today is that most healings are gradual rather than instantaneous. Certainly people today have less anointing for healing than Jesus had. [John 3:34] But perhaps this story is included to teach us that persistence is needed since not even Jesus always healed perfectly the first time. ➤ 26 Then Jesus sent him home but said, "Don't go into the village to tell others about this."

Peter Recognizes That Jesus Is the Messiah

27 Then, Jesus and his close followers walked about 25 miles north to the villages near Caesarea Philippi. On the way, he asked them, "Who do people think I am?" ❖ *Jesus was fully human. It's clear from the question he asked the blind man in verse 23 and his question here that he did not normally know what people were thinking. When he did know this, it was a "word of knowledge" [1 Corinthians 12:8] from the Holy Spirit.* ➤ 28 They answered, "Some say you are John the Baptizer. Others say you are the prophet Elijah, and still others say you are one of the other prophets from long ago." *[2 King 2:1-12; Malachi 4:5; Matthew 14:1-2; Mark 6:14-15; Luke 9:7-8]* 29 Then Jesus asked, "And what about you? Who do you think I am?" Peter immediately answered, "You are the Messiah!" 30 But Jesus warned them not to tell this to anyone. ❖ *It wasn't his intention to force people to make a decision yet about who they believed he was. If he pressed the point at this time, some would reject him and harden their hearts against him who otherwise might respond after the evidence of the resurrection.* ➤

Jesus Predicts His Suffering and Death

31 Starting at that time, Jesus began to explain to his close followers that he, the Son of Man, must suffer many things. The elders, chief priests, and Scripture teachers would reject him and have him executed.

Then God would bring him back to life the second **A** day after he died. 32 He explained it all very plainly. But Peter took Jesus aside and rebuked him for saying these things. 33 Jesus turned away from Peter, looked at the others and said, "Get out of my way, Adversary! **B** You are tempting me to sin. Avoiding what must happen is your human response, but it's not what God wants me to do." ❖ *A person can one minute be used by God to speak revelatory truth and the next minute speak lies from the enemy. We must take care how we interpret any revelation the Lord gives us. The Father showed Peter that Jesus was the Messiah, but he interpreted what this must imply from his own cultural expectations about the Messiah, and his conclusions were wrong. The idea that the Messiah would die was inconceivable to Jews of his day.* ➤

The Price of Following Jesus

34 Then Jesus got the attention of the crowd and his close followers and told them, "Those who want to be my people must put aside their own desires. Every day, they must be willing to suffer and even die in order to follow me. 35 Those who want to retain control of their own lives and protect them will ultimately lose them. But those who are willing to give up all that they are and have—even their own lives—in order to follow me, will ultimately gain eternal life. 36 What benefit have you gained if you acquire everything you desire in this temporary world but in the process lose your chance to live in Heaven? 37 Isn't eternal life worth more than anything else, even more than saving your temporary life in this world? 38 When I, the Son of Man, return in the glory of my Father and his holy angels, I will reject those who were ashamed to be associated with me or my message because they feared persecution.

9

1 "And I assure you that some of you standing here right now will see God's Kingdom manifest in power before they

---

A 8:31 See the note at Matthew 16:21 for the reasoning behind not using the traditional phrase, "the third day."
B 8:33 The literal text says, "Satan," which means

"adversary." Jesus meant that Peter was opposing the Father's plan, which made him an adversary and an ally of Satan.

die." *[Matthew 16:28; Luke 9:27; 2 Peter 1:16]*
❖ *Jesus may have been referring to the event Mark reports next. Or he may have meant those who would be believers after his resurrection and Pentecost who would see the miraculous power of God manifest through those who had miraculous gifts of the Holy Spirit to heal and to perform miracles. Also, John had the visions reported in the book of Revelation where he saw Jesus returning to reign as king. [Revelation 19:11—20:6]* ➤

God Reveals Jesus' True Glory

2 Six days later, Jesus took Peter, James, and James' younger brother John up a high mountain to pray. While they were there, his appearance changed before their very eyes. 3 His clothing became whiter than anything man can produce and shined with a brilliant light. 4 Then Elijah and Moses suddenly appeared from Heaven and spoke with Jesus. 5 Peter said, "Rabbi, it's good that we're here. If you want, we will make three shelters, one for you, one for Moses, and one for Elijah." 6 (He didn't really know what to say, since he and his companions were terrified.) 7 While he was saying this, a cloud **A** appeared around them like a thick fog. Then they heard God say, "This is my Son, my Chosen **B** One. *He* is the one you should listen to and obey!" *[Isaiah 42:1]* ❖ *Moses had spoken to God and received the teachings that he recorded in the Torah. He was the most revered of all their prophets. Elijah represented the Torah which ruled their lives. Elijah represented the teachings of all the other prophets. Together, they represented all the writings of the Hebrew Scriptures, everything that was known about God and his will. When God told them to listen to his Son, he was saying that Jesus and his teachings had more authority than Moses, Elijah and everything written in their Scriptures. So in this event, commonly called the "Transfiguration," God proclaimed that Jesus was his Son—and therefore also God—and that his authority exceeded every authority they had been taught to revere.* ➤ 8 Suddenly, only Jesus was there with them, appearing as he normally did. 9 While they were going down the mountain, Jesus commanded them not to tell anyone about the vision they had seen until after he,

the Son of Man, had risen from the dead. 10 So they kept this as a secret among themselves, but discussed what Jesus might have meant about "rising from the dead." ❖ *The Jews of that time expected God to raise the dead on Judgment Day, [Daniel 12:2; John 11:24] so they may have thought he was talking about that still-future event. Their expectations about the Messiah kept them from understanding that he was talking about his own death and resurrection in the near future.* ➤ 11 Since they had just seen Elijah, they asked, "Why do the Scripture teachers say Elijah must come before the Messiah comes?" *[Malachi 4:5-6]* 12 Jesus replied, "That prophecy is certainly true. Elijah did come and he inaugurated events that will restore everything to be as it should be. ❖ *The prophecy was talking about Elijah restoring the hearts of people so they would be in a proper relationship with God. But the Scripture teachers thought it meant restoring the power and glory of Israel. ¶ Then, he asked them about prophecies which Jews of that time tended to ignore.* ➤

"Why do the Scriptures say that the Son of Man will suffer many things and be despised and rejected? How does this fit in with your expectations about the Messiah? *[Psalms 22:1-18; 69:8-9, 11, 20-21; 118:22a, Isaiah chapter 53]* 13 Elijah came, but they mistreated him any way they liked, just as the Scriptures say about him." ❖ *John the Baptizer was not actually Elijah. [John 1:21] The Scriptures are clear that there is no reincarnation. [Hebrews 9:27] But Elijah and his life was a "type" of John the Baptizer. [Matthew 11:14; Luke 1:17] Both were great prophets. [Matthew 11:11; Luke 7:28] Both dressed alike [2 Kings 1:8; Matthew 3:4] and lived in the wilderness. Both had an evil queen who wanted to kill them. [1 Kings 19:1-18; Matthew 14:3-5] People did recognize John as a prophet, but not that he was the herald of the Messiah. Since Elijah performed miracles, they expected him to do so again when he came, but John never did. [John 10:41] John's life was humble and involved rejection by the religious authorities, suffering, and dying. But the Jews were expecting Elijah himself to appear with power and glory. Jesus was interpreting the events in Elijah's life as predicting the kinds of things that had happened to John. This an example of a prophecy that had a figurative rather than a literal fulfillment.* ➤

A 9:7a One of the ways God visibly manifests his presence is with a cloud. [Exodus 13:21; 40:34-38; Numbers 9:15-22; 10:11-12; Ezekiel 10:4; Acts 1:9; Revelation 10:1; 11:12; 14:14-16] People today have reported seeing the same phenomenon in connection with God's special presence.

B 9:7b Literally, it says, "beloved," but some commentators think it was a Messianic title.

Jesus' Followers Fail to Expel a Demon

14 When they had descended the mountain to where they had left the rest of Jesus' close followers, they saw them surrounded by a large crowd and arguing with some Scripture teachers. 15 The people were surprised when they saw Jesus coming and they all ran to greet him. 16 Jesus asked his followers, "What are you arguing with them about?" 17 Then a man in the crowd spoke up, "Rabbi! I've brought my son to you. He has a demon that keeps him from speaking. 18 It also causes seizures. It makes him fall on the ground, foam at the mouth, grind his teeth, and become entirely rigid. I asked your followers to expel it, but they couldn't." 19 Jesus said to his apostles, "You people are stubborn and faithless! How long will I have to be with you and put up with you before you learn how to use my power?" Then he told the man, "Bring your son here." ❖ *Jesus had already trained his apostles and given them power and authority over every demon and sickness. See Matthew 10:1; Mark 6:7, 13; and Luke 9:1. But they had failed to learn the lesson well enough. They had probably given up trying too soon. Most demons obey fairly quickly, but some strongly resist and you have to persist in prayer and commanding them before they leave. See Luke 8:28-30 where some demons did not obey even Jesus right away. ¶ As this story indicates in the following verses, their failure to expel the demon did not mean it was God's will that the boy not be delivered, as many people today would conclude under similar circumstances, particularly with regard to someone they pray for who is not quickly healed.* ➤ 20 They brought the boy but when the demon saw Jesus, it immediately caused the boy to have a violent seizure. He collapsed on the ground, writhing and foaming at the mouth. 21 Jesus asked the boy's father, "How long has he been having these seizures?" He answered, "Ever since he was a child. 22 The demon makes him fall into fires and water, trying to kill him. If you can do anything at all, please have pity and help us!" 23 Jesus replied, "Why do you express doubt by saying, 'If I can?' God can do anything for the person who believes in his power and love." 24 The man immediately replied, "I do believe, but help me overcome my doubts!" 25 When Jesus noticed the crowd was quickly getting larger, he said to the demon, "You, demon of deafness A and muteness, I command you to leave him and never return!" 26 In fury, the demon made the boy scream and have one last violent seizure, then it left him. The boy lay unmoving on the ground as if he were dead, and most of the people thought he was. 27 But Jesus took his hand and helped him to stand.

❖ *He was completely well, as is clear in Matthew's and Luke's accounts. [Matthew 17:14-21; Luke 9:37-42]* ➤ 28 Later, when Jesus was alone with his close followers in a house, they asked, "Why couldn't we expel that demon?" 29 Jesus answered, "You can only expel that kind through prayer and fasting." B ❖ *This implies that some demons are more powerful than others. To expel the kind that resists, we must not only command them to leave but also pray and fast until they do so.* ➤

Jesus Talks a Second Time About His Coming Death

30 Jesus and his close followers left that place and though they were traveling through Galilee, he didn't want people to know where he was. 31 He wanted to be alone with his close followers so he could teach them and he was trying to tell them, "I, the Son of Man, will be handed over to the Roman authorities. They will kill me, and on the second C day after my death I will come back to life again." 32 But his followers were blinded by their cultural expectations regarding the Messiah so they

---

A **9:25** Jesus called it a "deaf and mute spirit." The demon itself was not deaf and mute but caused these symptoms. It's not clear if the boy was deaf as well as mute or not. Some people who have experience in deliverance ministry classify demons by what they do. A deaf and mute demon does not necessarily cause both symptoms at the same time.

B **9:29** Some early manuscripts lack "and fasting." Some commentators doubt that "and fasting" is part of the original text because the apostles had no real opportunity to fast at that time, so it was unlikely that this was why they failed. But we know that fasting does aid us in prayer so it is not a wrong conclusion, even if Jesus did not say it in this particular instance. He could also have said it here just to express a general truth about such demons and how to expel them, rather than implying that they failed to fast in this instance.

C **9:31** See the note at Matthew 16:21 for the reasoning behind not using the traditional phrase "the third day," which is in the literal text. Many manuscripts have "after three days."

didn't understand what he was talking about. They were also too timid to ask him what he meant.

How to Be Important in God's Sight

33 When they arrived in Capernaum and were with Jesus indoors, he asked them, "What were you discussing before we arrived?" 34 They were too embarrassed to answer him as they had been arguing about which of them he considered the greatest of his followers. 35 But Jesus knew what they had been talking about, so he called them all together and sat down to teach them. He said, "If one of my followers wants to be the greatest in my sight, he must serve all the others as if he were the least important among them." ❖ *See the note at Mark 10:44.* ➤ 36 Then he brought a child and had him stand in front of the men. Jesus took the child in his arms and told them, 37 "If you obey me **A** by humbly welcoming and serving others, even people as low in status as this child, I will consider you as having done it to me. And my Father who sent me will also consider you as having done it to him."

Jesus' Followers Try to Exclude Others

38 John said to Jesus, "Rabbi, we saw someone expelling demons using your name as if you had given him your authority. So we tried to stop him since he isn't associated with us." 39 But Jesus responded, "You shouldn't stop such people! Those who do miracles using my name won't be among those who slander me. 40 Anyone who isn't against us is on our side. 41 For God will certainly reward anyone who helps one of you because you are known to follow me, the Messiah, even if it's as small a thing as giving you a cup of water to quench your thirst. ❖ *Even such a small act is evidence that a person is on Jesus' side.* ➤

Jesus Teaches About Temptation and Sin

42 "And conversely, God will severely punish anyone who tempts someone to sin or leads someone to reject me, even if the person he so leads is as low in status as this child. He would be far better off if his only punishment were to have a large stone tied to his neck and he were thrown into the sea to drown. For his punishment in Hell will be much worse. 43 The consequences of sin are serious! If your hand entices you to sin, you would be better off getting rid of it and entering eternal life as a cripple than to have both hands and end up in the eternal fire of Hell, *[Matthew 5:29-30]* 44 {where **there is no relief from the torment of fire that burns but does not consume, or from the maggots that eat your decaying flesh}. B** 45 Or if your foot entices you to sin, you would be better off getting rid of it and entering eternal life as a cripple than to have both feet and end up in Hell, 46 {where **there is no relief from the torment of fire that burns but does not consume, or from the maggots that eat your decaying flesh** }. 47 Or if your eye entices you to sin, you would be better off getting rid of it and entering eternal life with only one than to have both and end up in Hell, 48 where **there is no relief from the torment of fire that burns but does not consume, or from the maggots that eat your decaying flesh.** *[Isaiah 66:24]* ❖ *Jesus didn't think that hands or feet or eyes are true sources of sinful temptations. He was making the point that sin is serious and you should do whatever is necessary to avoid sinning. Nothing is too extreme an option if it enables you to avoid Hell. See Luke 16:22-24; and also 2 Thessalonians 1:9 with the following note about Hell.* ➤

49 "Do your utmost to resist temptation, for everyone will have to endure the fires of testing that result in purification and stronger faith. **C** *[1 Peter 1:7]* ❖ *Commentators offer*

A 9:37 The clause in the literal text, "Whoever receives such a child as this in my name" (rendered above as: "If you obey me by humbly welcoming and serving others, even people as low in status as this child,") could alternatively be understood to mean, "If you welcome and serve someone belonging to me, even people as low in status as this child."

B 9:44 Verses 44 and 46 are identical with verse 48, and are not in some of the older manuscripts.

C 9:49 Many manuscripts lack the words (in the literal text), "and every sacrifice will be salted with salt (or fire)." In the Hebrew Scriptures, salt was used on sacrifices. [Leviticus 2:13; Ezekiel 43:24] We are to live self-sacrificial lives, [Romans 12:1] and the illustration in these words may mean that we are to remain faithful and obedient during the fiery tests and temptations we experience. [1 Peter 4:12, 19]

more than 15 possible explanations for the obscure statement in the literal text of this verse, indicating no one really knows what Jesus originally meant. The interpretation given is just one possibility. The word "fire" ties together verses 48 and 49, and Jesus (or Mark) is switching to a different but related point. Jewish teachers often did this, with certain words tying the discourse together, even though they were shifting topics. In the original text of this verse, "salt" ties verses 49 and 50 together, but the topic of verse 50 moves on to a different illustration and point, yet related to the overall topic of resisting temptation and avoiding sin. ➤ 50 Salt is good, but if it loses its flavor, it can't be made salty again. So don't foolishly give in to temptation and lose the ability to positively influence those around you. And strive to live in harmony with each other." ❖ *Salt was important for several reasons in Biblical times, so several different explanations for Jesus' point in this verse have been posited. Salt was used for flavoring, for preserving, for pay, and as a figure for wisdom. [Colossians 4:6] So salt was valuable. His point may have been that even though they are valuable to him, they need to resist temptation and avoid sin or they might become worthless to him for accomplishing his purposes. Jesus uses the same illustration in Matthew 5:13 and Luke 14:34. Yet the same illustration may make different points in different contexts.* ➤

10

Jesus Answers a Question About Divorce

1 Then Jesus and his close followers left Galilee and walked south along the eastern side of the Jordan River to Judea Province. **A** As usual, a large crowd gathered around him so he taught them spiritual truths, as he did at every opportunity. 2 Some Pharisees came to trap Jesus with a question that they thought he couldn't answer to anyone's satisfaction. ❖ *See the note at Matthew 19:3.* ➤ They asked, "Does the Torah allow a man to divorce his wife?" 3 Jesus responded, "What do you think that Moses commanded about divorce in the Torah?" 4 They said, "Moses allowed a man to give his wife a document indicating he had divorced her, and then he could send her away." ❖ *They were twisting Deuteronomy 24:1-4. Moses, or the Torah, did not command*

this. *It merely allowed the custom that had already existed prior to the Torah and regulated it to some extent. See the note at Matthew 5:31.* ➤ 5 Jesus said, "Moses wrote that command ❖ *which you have partially quoted and only implicitly allows divorce,* ➤ only because men are so stubborn and unteachable. 6 But God's original plan for marriage is clear, for the Scriptures say that he 'created people male and female,' [Genesis 1:27; 5:2] 7 and 'that is why a man will leave his parents and be united to his wife 8 and the two will become one.' [Genesis 2:24; Matthew 19:5; 1 Corinthians 6:16; Ephesians 5:31] So God has joined them, and they are no longer two in his sight, but a permanent unity. 9 Therefore, people should not separate what God has joined." 10 Later, when only his close followers were indoors with him, they asked about this topic again. 11 Jesus told them, "Any man that divorces his wife and marries a different woman is guilty of committing adultery against his former wife. For in God's sight, he is still married to her. 12 And if a woman divorces her husband and remarries, she is guilty of committing adultery against him." [Malachi 2:16; Matthew 5:31-32; 19:8-9] ❖ *Jewish law didn't allow women to divorce their husbands, but Roman law did and Mark was pointing out the implications for those who lived under such laws. See the note at Matthew 5:32 and the footnote at 1 Corinthians 7:11.* ➤

Jesus' Attitude Toward Little Children

13 One day, some people were bringing their small children and infants to Jesus so he would bless them. When his followers saw this, they rebuked the people, telling them not to bother the Rabbi. 14 But Jesus was displeased when he noticed them doing this and told them, "Allow the children to come to me—don't stop them! These are the kind of people that God wants in his Kingdom, people who are humble and trusting like children. 15 Remember this! Anyone who isn't humble and doesn't trust God like a child does will never enter his Kingdom." 16 Then he held the children in his arms, placed his hands on them, and blessed them.

A 10:1 The meaning of this verse is not clear because of the variants among manuscripts. Many have "he went to Judea and (then) across the Jordan." The parallel account in Matthew 19:1, which has no manuscript variants, agrees with the interpretation given. This is the route Jews took to avoid going through Samaria.

The Stumbling Stone of Being Rich

17 As Jesus and his followers were starting out on a journey to another village, a man came running up, knelt down in front of him, and asked, "Good Rabbi, what must I do to live forever?" 18 Jesus replied, "Why do you call me 'good?' No one is good except God himself. Do you realize what you are saying about me when you call me 'good?' 19 You know what God commands in the Torah, 'Don't murder, don't commit adultery, don't steal, don't lie about others , don't cheat others, honor your parents.' " *[Exodus 20:12-16; Deuteronomy 5:16-20] ❖ Jesus wasn't giving an exhaustive list of God's requirements, only a few representative ones. He knew that the man was familiar with them all and by bringing them to mind he was trying to get the man to recognize his sin and his need for God's forgiveness.* ➤ 20 The man replied, "But Rabbi, I've kept all of these commandments ever since I was young." *❖ He failed to recognize that he was a sinner. He believed that all God required was an outward legalistic obedience, and did not understand that the attitude of his heart was important too. But he knew he was lacking something so he wasn't sure he was going to Heaven.* ➤ 21 Jesus looked at him with God's pure love, wanting to bring him into a proper relationship with himself. But he knew the man didn't recognize his sin and knew that the main thing hindering him from wholeheartedly following God was his idolatrous love for his riches. So he told him, "If you want to completely dedicate yourself to God, sell everything you have, give the money to the poor, and God will give you riches in Heaven. Then come be one of my followers." 22 But when the man heard this, he became dejected. He went away sad because he was very rich and unwilling to surrender his wealth and put his life in Jesus' hands. 23 Jesus saw him go and said to all his followers there, "It's very difficult for the rich to enter God's Kingdom!" *❖ Because either they depend on their riches for their security and find it difficult to trust only in God, or they love their riches and comforts more than they love God. Note that Jesus didn't try to make it easier for the man. He didn't tell him that trusting God was enough and later he could learn to be a more committed follower, as many pastors and evangelists do today. Jesus requires total commitment and obedience at the outset.* ➤ 24 When

his followers heard this, they were astonished. But Jesus continued to emphasize his statement. "My children, it's extremely difficult for anyone to enter God's Kingdom! 25 I will reiterate the difficulty. It would be easier for a camel to go through the eye of an ordinary sewing needle than for a rich man to enter God's Kingdom." *❖ Some people incorrectly say that there was a gate into Jerusalem called the "eye of the needle" which was small and difficult for camels to enter, but that it was possible. There never was such a gate. This was probably a well-known saying at the time. Jesus was simply stating that it's impossible—humanly speaking—for a rich man to enter Heaven.* ➤ 26 His followers were even more astonished at this and asked him, "If it's so hard for rich people to be saved, then who can hope to be saved?" *❖ A common misconception among the Jews at that time was that riches were God's blessings showered upon those who merited them because of their righteous lives. In their minds, it was rich people who were most likely to be saved. So if such "good" people—whom God obviously approved of and had blessed—can't get in, how can anyone get in? This was their question.* ➤ 27 Jesus looked at them and said, "It's impossible for people to enter on their own, but with God's help, anything is possible." 28 Then Peter said, "We've left our homes and everything we have to follow you, just like you told that man. So what can we expect from God?" 29 Jesus answered, "I assure you that anyone who leaves home or brothers or sisters or parents or children or livelihood to obey me—and to proclaim the Good News about how people can be saved—30 will receive from God in this life a hundred times as much as he has given up (including homes and brothers and sisters and mothers and children and means of living), but in addition should expect to be persecuted. *[John 15:18-20; 16:33; Acts 14:22; 1 Thessalonians 3:3-4; 2 Timothy 3:12; 1 Peter 2:20-21]* And in the next age after I return, they will receive eternal life in Heaven." *❖ Jesus isn't talking about people who selfishly and needlessly abandon those dependent on them, like spouses and children. He's speaking of people who place more importance on God's call than on human loyalties and who are, therefore, willing to choose to follow God even if their families reject him.* ➤ 31 But many who are important in this life will be among the least important in Heaven; and many who are least important in this life will

be among the most important in Heaven."
[Matthew 20:16; Mark 10:31; Luke 13:30]

Jesus Speaks a Third Time
About His Coming Death

32 Now, Jesus and his followers were heading toward Jerusalem with Jesus walking quickly and determinedly in the lead. They were amazed that he was so eager to go there since they knew the Jewish leaders were plotting against him—and they feared what might happen. ❖ *This is just one opinion on why they were amazed and fearful, as it says in the literal text. Commentators don't agree on the reason Mark mentioned these feelings, or even who had them.* ➤ On the way, Jesus took the twelve apostles aside and once again told them what was going to happen to him. 33 He said, "We're going up to Jerusalem where I, the Son of Man, will be handed over to the custody of the chief priests and Scripture teachers. They will sentence me to death and hand me over to the Roman authorities for execution. 34 The Romans will mock me and spit on me and then whip and execute me. But on the second **A** day after my death, God will bring me back to life again."

Kingdom Authority

35 Then James and John, Zebedee's two sons, came to Jesus privately and said, "Rabbi, we want you to grant us a favor." 36 He asked them, "What is it you want?" 37 They replied, "Grant us the privilege of sitting on either side of you when you become King, the two highest positions under you." 38 Jesus replied, "You have no idea what the implications are of what you're asking. Are the two of you willing to endure the suffering that I'm about to go through?" 39 They answered, "Yes, we are." Jesus said, "Then you will indeed share in my suffering. 40 But I don't have the authority to decide who will have

those positions. My Father has decided who will have them."

41 When the other ten apostles heard about this request, they were indignant with James and John for their presumption that they were above the rest of them. ❖ *Many of them probably wanted those positions for themselves.* ➤ 42 Jesus called them all together and said, "You know the ways of earthly rulers and men in authority. They use their positions to order others around or even tyrannize them, and they make sure that their status and privileges remain clearly above those under them. 43 But that's not the way it's going to be among you. Whoever wants to become a leader or have God to consider them important must become everyone else's servant. 44 If you want to attain the highest rank in Heaven, then you must be a slave to everyone else in this life. [Matthew 23:11; Mark 9:35; Luke 22:25-26] ❖ *Many church and ministry leaders rule from above rather than serve in humility. And they expect the people they lead to look up to them, rather than as regarding them as equals or those whose role is to serve them, as Jesus instructs in this passage. Don't be one of them.* ➤ 45 For even I, the Son of Man, came into this world to serve people and to give my life to redeem them, not to be served by them."

Jesus Heals a Blind Man Named Bar-Timaeus

46 As Jesus and his followers were leaving **B** Jericho on their way to Jerusalem—15 miles away—with a large crowd following him, a blind man named Bar-Timaeus (meaning son of Timaeus) was begging on the roadside. 47 When he heard that Jesus from Nazareth was passing by, he started shouting, "Jesus, Son of David! Have mercy on me!" ❖ *By this time, everyone had heard about the miraculous healings he could do. It's apparent that he believed Jesus was the Messiah, descended from King David, since "Son of David" was a messianic title.* ➤ 48 Some in the crowd told him to be quiet and know his place, but he just shouted all

---

A **10:34** See the note at Matthew 16:21 for the reasoning behind not using the traditional phrase "the third day." In the literal text, most manuscripts have "after three days," but many have "on the third day."

B **10:46** The parallel account in Matthew 20:29 says they were leaving Jericho, and the one in Luke 18:35 says they were entering Jericho. David Stern says there were two Jerichos a

few kilometers apart, one the ancient inhabited city and the other a Roman spa that was nearer to Jerusalem. So this event could have happened between the two sites, and in one view be seen as happening while leaving the populated city of Jericho, and in another view be seen as happening while approaching the Roman Jericho. So no error of fact need be read into this apparent discrepancy of detail.

the louder, "Son of David! Have mercy and help me!" 49 When Jesus heard him, he stopped and commanded that the man be summoned. So those near him said, "Stand up and get yourself together. He's calling for you to go to him!" 50 Immediately, he threw aside his robe, ❖ *which had been in his lap to collect the coins tossed to him (he was still wearing his tunic)* ➤ got quickly to his feet, and went in the direction of Jesus' voice. 51 When he arrived, Jesus asked him, "What do you want me to do for you?" Bar-Timaeus said, "Rabbi, I want to see again." 52 Jesus replied, "You may go on your way, for your faith in me has saved you." ❖ *The word translated as "saved" can mean both "save" and "heal." Jesus may have only meant he was healed, but it's likely that he meant both meanings at the same time.* ➤ Immediately, he could see again and he followed Jesus as he continued on the road.

11

Jesus' Triumphal Entry into Jerusalem on Palm Sunday

1 As Jesus and his followers approached the villages of Bethany and Bethphage— near Mount Olivet and only a mile or so from Jerusalem—he sent two of his close followers ahead 2 and told them, "Go into that village just ahead. Immediately inside it, you will find a young donkey that's never been ridden. Untie it and bring it to me. 3 If anyone asks what you're doing, just tell them that the Lord needs it, and they will allow you to take it."

4 So they went and found it in the street, tied to a door. They started to untie it 5 when some people standing nearby said, "What do you think you're doing, untying that donkey? It doesn't belong to you!" 6 They gave the answer that Jesus told them to say, and the people allowed them to take it.

7 They brought the young donkey to him, put their outer robes on it, and then Jesus sat on the robes. 8 As he rode toward Jerusalem, many in the crowd spread their outer robes on the road and others cut branches in the fields and spread them on the road. ❖ *This is the kind of welcome they would extend to a triumphant King or general who had conquered his enemies and was returning to his capital city. It was also traditional for people who had already arrived for the Passover Festival to go out and welcome others just arriving from distant places by putting branches in their path to walk on. Carrying palm branches may have been a traditional part of Festival worship. While finally allowing people to proclaim him as the Messiah, Jesus tries to counter their expectation of a military leader who would expel the Romans from Israel. Such a person would process into the city on a horse or in a chariot, but a donkey was a humble mount. So he came as a peaceful king, not as a zealot.* ➤ 9 The crowd ahead of him and behind shouted, "Hosanna! **May God bless the one whom he sent with his authority!** [Psalm 118:26]* 10 May God bless the Messiah, King David's descendant, in re-establishing his Kingdom! All glory and praise be to God in the highest Heaven!" ❖ *The first part of their chant is quoted from Psalm 118:25-26a. Psalms 113—118 were regularly sung during Passover. Hosanna is a Hebrew word that literally means "save us!," but by Jesus' time it had become an expression of praise. The people expected that he would now openly declare himself to be God's Messiah, make himself King of Israel, and finally fulfill their expectations by freeing them from their Roman conquerors and ushering in a golden age of peace, prosperity, and greatness for their country.* ➤

11 Jesus entered Jerusalem with this fanfare, then went into the Temple courtyard and observed everything there. But he soon left again with his apostles to spend the night in Bethany, since it was already late in the day.

A Hypocritical Fig Tree

12 The next morning as he left Bethany on his way back to Jerusalem, Jesus was hungry. 13 Noticing a fig tree by the road some distance away that had leaves, he went to it to find some fruit. Even though it wasn't yet the season for ripe figs, he expected some young immature fruit. But when he reached it, he found nothing but leaves. 14 Then his followers heard him say to the tree, "No one will ever eat fruit from you again!" ❖ *Fig trees blossom before their leaves appear. When the leaves are fully grown near Passover when this story happened, there should be young unripe figs on the tree. [Micah 7:1b] This tree with its leaves promised fruit from afar but didn't have any. Such trees were called "hypocrites." The fig tree is sometimes a figure for Israel. [Hosea 9:10; Joel 1:7] Commentators believe Jesus cursed the fig tree as a prophetic sign that the nation of Israel*

could expect the same judgment if they didn't start bearing fruit. This is brought out more clearly in Jesus' parable in Luke 13:6-9. Matthew's account of this incident [Matthew 21:18-19] differs in detail from the account here in Mark [verses 20-21] which says that Jesus' followers didn't notice the withering until the following day. This bothers some modern readers, but ancient biographies were not required to record accurate time sequences. Matthew shortened some incidents and reordered them in temporal sequence because he wasn't concerned about all of the details, only those he reports. Such minor differences in detail between parallel accounts would have been considered insignificant to people of that time. The gospel writers were more interested in reporting what Jesus said and did than to get all the other details as precise as modern readers would prefer to have them. They were not writing to meet our standards, so it's unfair to judge them by standards they were not trying to meet. ➤

Jesus Cleanses the Temple a Second Time

❖ *The account of Jesus' first cleansing of the Temple is in John 2:13-22. Some commentators believe there was only one cleansing, and that either John or the other three gospel writers reported it at a different time than it happened. But taking the texts at face value leads to the conclusion that Jesus did this twice, a few years apart.* ➤

15 When Jesus and his followers arrived in Jerusalem, he entered the court of the Gentiles in the Temple and drove out all who were doing business there. He overturned tables used by money changers and the seats of those who sold doves for sacrifices. 16 He also stopped people from disregarding Temple sanctity who were carrying things through the courtyard as if it were an ordinary thoroughfare. 17 He told them, "God said in the Scriptures, **'My house will be a place of prayer for people of all nations.'** *[Isaiah 56:7]* But you have turned it into a **den of thieves!"** *[Jeremiah 7:11]* ❖ *The merchants provided needed services for pilgrims coming to Jerusalem who couldn't bring sacrificial animals with them from far away. They also operated currency exchanges, since Roman coins were unacceptable to give as offerings to the Temple. One problem was their turning the Temple into a market. Another was they were doing this in the Court of the Gentiles, thus robbing the Gentiles of a place to worship the one true God. Jesus' anger was righteous, reflecting his Father's attitude toward the abuses.* ➤

18 When the chief priests and Scripture teachers heard what he had done, they began to be desperate for a plan to get rid of him. They were afraid of his influence with the crowds—who were mesmerized by his teaching and miracles and believed he was the Messiah.

19 Near the end of the day, Jesus and his close followers left the city and went to spend the night in Bethany.

The Relationship Between Faith and the Release of God's Power

20 As they were returning to the city the next morning, Jesus' followers noticed that the fig tree he had cursed the morning before was withered all the way to its roots. 21 Remembering what Jesus had said to the tree, Peter exclaimed, "Rabbi, look! The fig tree you cursed yesterday is completely withered! How is this possible?"

22 Jesus replied, "You just need to have faith in God. 23 It's important that you understand this. If you trust him and don't doubt his faithfulness, you can do even more than this. You can overcome great obstacles and accomplish the seemingly impossible, if it's God's will. ❖ *"Moving mountains," in the literal text, was a common figure of speech for doing something nearly impossible. He did not intend his hearers to take him literally. But it's still a fantastic promise that few believers seem to have the faith to exercise. The added phrase "if it's God's will" is implied and was understood by his Jewish listeners who were familiar with all the Scriptures' teachings.* ➤ 24 So when you ask for something in prayer and you know that it's God's will, firmly believe that he has already said yes to your request and you will eventually receive it. ❖ *Note he did not promise you will receive your answer quickly. Most people today give up far too soon. We need to persist in faith. If he always responded instantly, we wouldn't need faith and he would give a wrong impression that he is our servant, rather than the other way around.* ➤ 25 But when you are praying, first forgive anyone you haven't yet forgiven, so your Father in Heaven will forgive you too. ❖ *This is a condition on the promise in verse 24.* ➤ 26 {But if you refuse to forgive others, then your Heavenly Father will not forgive your sins either.}" **A**

A 11:26 Many manuscripts lack verse 26, but it is 1) implied and 2) explicitly stated elsewhere. [Matthew 6:14-15; 18:21-35]

Jesus' Authority is Questioned

❖ *From 11:27—12:40, Jesus verbally spars with the Jewish religious leaders. They try to trap him into saying something they can use against him, and Jesus avoids their traps, exposes their sin, and challenges them with questions they can't answer. Their interaction involves challenge and counter challenge with Jesus always coming out on top and the large crowd of onlookers apparently enjoying the sight of Jesus putting their proud leaders in their place. [12:37b]* ➤

27 Jesus and his followers once again entered Jerusalem and went to the Temple. As he was walking in the Temple courtyard, a group of chief priests, Scripture teachers, and Jewish elders boldly approached him and 28 demanded, "What right do you have to do the things you did the other day? Who gave you this authority?" ❖ *They were not really seeking information. They believed that they could use any answer he gave against him. Jesus was fully aware of their intentions and turned their question against them.* ➤

29 Jesus replied, "I will answer that if you first answer this question. 30 When John was baptizing and preaching, was his authority from God, or did he do it on his own authority?"

31 They debated among themselves what to answer. "If we acknowledge that his authority was from God, then he will ask why we didn't believe John's message and his witness that Jesus is the Messiah. 32 But we don't dare say his authority wasn't from God or this crowd will reject us and stone us—for they're convinced John was a prophet." 33 In the end they answered, "We don't know." Jesus replied, "If you are unwilling to answer that question, then I'm not going to tell you where my authority comes from either."

12

Parable About the Evil Tenants

1 Then Jesus told this parable to the Jewish leaders and others who were there: "There was a landowner who **planted a vineyard, built a wall around it, dug a winepress, and built a watchtower.** Then he rented it out to some tenant farmers and went on a journey for a long time. *[Isaiah 5:1-2, 7]* ❖ *The vineyard represents Israel, the owner represents God, and the farmers represent the leaders of Israel.* ➤

2 When it came time for the grapes to be harvested, the owner sent a servant to collect a portion of the crop as payment for their rent, per their agreement. 3 But the farmers beat him and sent him away empty handed. ❖ *The servants represent the prophets that God sent to his people.* ➤ 4 The owner sent another servant and they beat him too, treated him shamefully, and sent him away with nothing. 5 So he sent a third servant and this one they murdered. So it went with many other servants the owner sent. Some they killed and others they beat severely.

6 "Last of all, the owner sent his son to them, thinking, 'Surely they will respect my son.'

7 "But when the farmers saw the son, they reasoned like this: 'He's the owner's heir. If we kill him, the vineyard will be ours!' 8 So they captured him, killed him, and threw his body outside the vineyard.

9 "So what will the owner of the vineyard do to them? He will come and kill them and will give the care of the vineyard to other tenants. 10 Certainly you must have read the Scripture that says, '**The stone the builders rejected became the cornerstone. 11 This is Yahweh's doing and it's a marvel to see.**' " *[Psalm 118:22-23]* ❖ *Jesus is speaking of himself as that stone.* ➤

12 The Jewish leaders understood that Jesus portrayed them as the evil tenant farmers. They wanted to arrest him but were afraid the crowd would riot in protest, so they left him for the time being.

The Question About Paying Taxes to Rome

13 Later, the Jewish leaders sent some Pharisees to Jesus accompanied by some men loyal to King Herod in an attempt to trap him into making a damaging statement they could use against him. ❖ *Herod's men would be witnesses to anything Jesus said that would be against Roman law.* ➤ 14 They tried to put him off his guard by flattering him: "Rabbi, we know you have integrity and teach God's way based on the truth of his word, not on what you think people want to hear. You don't hedge your teaching so it won't offend certain people because you aren't trying to

please any particular group. You just teach the plain truth. We are looking for a clear definitive answer to this question. Is it right for Jews to pay taxes to Caesar, ❖ *i.e., our conquerors, the Roman government which actively promotes the worship of false gods* ➤ or not?" 15 But Jesus knew their evil intent ❖ *through a word of knowledge. [1 Corinthians 12:8] He knew that if he answered "Yes," then the Jewish leaders would accuse him of being a Roman collaborator—which would destroy his popularity with the people. If he answered "No," then they could accuse him of sedition to the Roman authorities.* ➤ and said, "Do you really think you can trap me? Show me one of the coins that's used to pay the tax you are talking about." 16 They produced a denarius. ❖ *Since they were in the Temple, they likely had to fetch one, since religious Jews wouldn't normally carry a coin with a graven image of a false god on it into the Temple. The image was Caesar's, but Romans worshipped him as a god.* ➤ Then he asked them, "Whose face and name are on it?" They answered, "Caesar's." 17 Then Jesus said, "So give to Caesar what he rightfully demands, and give to God what rightfully belongs to him." They were amazed at his answer which avoided their trap. ❖ *The Roman coin was not acceptable for any holy use, such as tithes, offerings, and Temple taxes because it bore an image on it, which is forbidden in the Torah. [Deuteronomy 4:15-16, 23]* ➤

The Question About Life After Death

18 Then some Sadducees—who deny that there will be a resurrection—came to Jesus with a question. ❖ *The Sadducees were a Jewish religious sect that held several incorrect beliefs. Of particular relevance to this story was their belief that there is no life after death. They believed that people have no immortal souls and simply cease to exist when they die. Therefore, there would be no resurrection on the Last Day. [Acts 23:8] They posed a question that they thought would logically prove the impossibility of such a resurrection because it would mean God contradicted himself. They did correctly understand that God never contradicts himself.* ➤ 19 They said, "Rabbi, Moses wrote in the Torah that if a man's brother dies and leaves a widow with no children, then his brother must take her to be his wife and the first son they have will legally be the son of the dead brother. ❖ *This was so the dead man could have at least one son to carry on the family name and inherit his property. [Genesis 38:8; Deuteronomy 25:5-10; Ruth 4:5-10]* ➤ 20 Now, there

were seven brothers among us. The oldest married a woman and died with no child. 21 Then the second brother married the widow and also died childless, and then a third did the same. 22 In the same way, all seven men married her and died leaving no children. Last of all, the widow died too. 23 So on the day when God raises the dead back to life—if there is such a day—whose wife will she be, since she was married to all seven brothers?" ❖ *They reasoned that God would never command people to do anything that violated one of his other commands. But a woman married to more than one man violated the teaching of God's Torah. (There is no explicit prohibition against polyandry in the Torah, but it was understood to be implicitly prohibited from other explicit prohibitions.) Therefore, there couldn't be any resurrection because God's command requiring a man to marry his brother's childless widow would force some women to be illegally married to more than one husband after the resurrection.* ➤

24 Jesus replied, "Your understanding is faulty because you are ignorant of both the Scriptures and God's power. 25 After the resurrection, people will not marry or still be married to former spouses. In this matter, they will be like the angels in Heaven. 26 And as for the resurrection, even Moses gave you evidence for it in his account of the burning bush where he recorded that Yahweh said, **'I am the God of Abraham, the God of Isaac, and the God of Jacob.'** *[Exodus 3:1-6, 15]* ❖ *The Sadducees only accepted the writings of Moses as Scripture and claimed that Moses never taught about a resurrection. So Jesus used Moses' writings to refute them.* ➤ 27 It should be obvious that Yahweh is not the God of people who no longer exist. He is God over those having a living existence. ❖ *Those who have died still exist in either Heaven or Hell.* ➤ Your belief about there being no resurrection is entirely wrong and a serious doctrinal error."

God's Most Important Command

28 One of the Scripture teachers who heard this discussion recognized that Jesus had done well in answering the Sadducees' question from the Scriptures. So he asked Jesus, "Which command in the Torah is the most important?" ❖ *The Scripture teachers had identified 613 commands in the Torah. They often debated about how to rank them. He thought that no matter what Jesus answered, he would have some basis to debate him and have*

a chance at making him look ridiculous in the eyes of the common people. ➤ 29 Jesus answered, "God's most important command is this: **'Hear and respond, people of Israel! Yahweh is your God who created you! He's the only one that really exists,** 30 **and he is calling you to love him with all your heart, thoughts, personality, and determination!'** *[Deuteronomy 6:4-5]* 31 The next most important one is this: **'You must love all people that you come in contact with in the same tolerant accepting way that you love yourself.'** *[Leviticus 19:18; Luke 10:27; Romans 13:9; Galatians 5:14; James 2:8]* There is no other command more important than these two."

32 The Scripture teacher said, "You are right, Rabbi. You have correctly declared that there is only one God and none other like him, *[Deuteronomy 4:35; 6:4; Isaiah 45:21]* 33 and that to love him with all your heart, thoughts, personality, and determination, and to love others in the same way that you love yourself, is more important than all the commands about offerings and sacrifices."

34 When Jesus heard that man's understanding, he told him, "If you really believe that, then you are very close to having a proper relationship with God as your King." After that, the Jewish leaders realized it was futile to try to trap Jesus into saying something they could use against him, so they gave up asking him questions.

A Question About the Messiah

35 Then, while he was teaching in the Temple, Jesus asked the people, "How can it be true that the Messiah is descended from King David as the Scripture teachers say? 36 For David himself—under the inspiration of the Holy Spirit—prophetically wrote about the Messiah in a Psalm, **'Yahweh said to my Lord, the Messiah, "Sit here at my right side—the place of highest honor—until I have humiliated all your enemies and put them under your power." '** *[Psalm 110:1]* 37 David calls the Messiah 'Lord,' so how can he also be his descendant?" The crowd loved to listen to him. ❖ *The Jewish assumption was that an ancestor is always greater than his descendants. David was one of the greatest Israelites to ever live. How could he humble himself under one of his own*

descendants and call him "Lord?" The Scriptures were clear on both points: The Messiah would be descended from David, and yet David called him "Lord." Jesus wanted them to see that the Messiah—while a descendant of David—had to be more than just a man. ➤

Jesus Exposes the Hypocrisy of the Religious Leaders

38 While all the people were listening, Jesus told them, "Don't allow yourselves to have attitudes like the Scripture teachers. They like to dress in expensive long robes to impress people. They love to hear people greet them respectfully in public 39 and to sit in the most important seats in the synagogue and in seats of honor at banquets. 40 They are also greedy and take advantage of helpless widows, taking their homes and lands from them and leaving them destitute. They also recite long prayers just to impress others with their spirituality. God isn't taken in by them. On Judgment Day, their punishment will be all the greater because of their hypocrisy."

Sacrificial Giving

41 Jesus sat in the Temple facing the treasury box and observed wealthy people putting their gifts into it. People could hear the clinking of the many coins they dropped in. ❖ *Paper money did not exist in those times.* ➤ 42 Then he saw an impoverished widow put in two small copper coins. ❖ *They were the smallest coins in use at that time, each worth about 1/128 of a man's wage for one day.* ➤

43 Getting his followers attention, he told them, "I assure you that by God's standard, that poor widow contributed far more than anyone else. 44 Everyone else put in offerings out of what they could easily spare, but she put in everything she had and has nothing left to even live on."

13

Jesus Predicts the Temple's Destruction

1 As Jesus was leaving the Temple compound, one of his followers spoke to him, exclaiming about the Temple's beauty and greatness. 2 Jesus unexpectedly replied, "The day will come when all the things you

see here are destroyed. The destruction will be so complete that not even one stone will be left standing on another."

Signs of Jesus' Return

3 Later, as Jesus was sitting on Mount Olivet looking across the valley at the Temple, Peter, James, John, and Andrew approached him privately and said, 4 "Tell us when this destruction will happen and what sign will indicate it's about to happen."

5 Jesus answered, "Be careful that you are not deceived. 6 For many men will come to prominence saying they are the Messiah and they will deceive many into following them. 7 You will hear about wars happening nearby and reports of wars far away, but don't be afraid. These things need to happen first but the Last Day doesn't follow immediately after them. 8 Ethnic groups will fight against each other and entire countries will war against each other. There will be major earthquakes and famines in various places. All this is like the beginning of a woman's birth pains. They will last for a while before I return.

9 "But you need to watch out for your own safety because people will arrest you and persecute you for being my followers. They will deliver you before synagogue courts and before kings and other legal authorities and will imprison you. This will be an opportunity for you to testify about the things you have heard and seen me do. 10 Before I return, the Good News message about how to join God's Kingdom will be preached to every people group in the world. 11 When you are arrested, don't be concerned ahead of time about what you will say in your defense. When the time comes, just say whatever comes to your mind, for it will be the Holy Spirit speaking through you. The words won't be your own. 12 "Know in advance that you will be betrayed to the authorities by siblings, parents, and even your own children—and

some of you will be executed. 13 Many will hate you simply because you are my followers. But if you endure in your faithfulness to me until the end of your life, you will live with me forever in Heaven."

Jesus Predicts Times of Great Tribulation

14 ❖ *The details in this section describe the final tribulation. [Revelation chapters 5—7] But a "type" of them also happened in AD 70 when the Romans destroyed Jerusalem and the Temple.* ➤ Jesus continued, "The prophet Daniel prophesied about an "abomination that causes destruction." ❖ *Or: horrible abomination [Daniel 8:13; 9:27; 11:31; 12:11; 2 Thessalonians 2:3-4; Revelation 13:14-15] Some commentators think this refers to the Anti-messiah talked about in Revelation—called "False Messiah" in this interpretation.* ➤ (The reader should look carefully into the matter as prophesied by Daniel and try to understand what this means.) A When you see it in the Holy Place of the Temple, then terrible things will soon happen. ❖ *Such a thing happened in the Temple before Jesus was born in the second century BC. [1 Maccabees 1:41-61 B] It might have happened again in AD 66 when zealots killed priests in the Temple. It happened with Roman standards—which bore the insignia of Caesar who was worshipped as a god—when Jerusalem and the Temple was destroyed by the Romans in the year AD 70. And it will happen again when the Jews in Israel rebuild the Temple in the last days.* ➤ So those who are in Judea should flee to hide in the mountains. 15 If you are on the roof your house, don't take the time to get your things from inside. Flee from the city. ❖ *Houses in Israel all had exterior stairs leading up to flat roofs. They were used as work places and spare rooms.* ➤ 16 Those working in their fields should not return to their house for any reason. They should flee to the mountains. 17 It will be terrible for pregnant women and those who are still nursing babies because it will be hard for them to run and escape to the mountains. 18 So pray that this will not occur in the winter, for that would add to your difficulties. ❖ *Winter weather would make the going harder and make survival in the mountains more difficult.* ➤ 19 For there will be a great

---

A **13:14a** This parenthetical comment was written by Mark to his readers.

B **13:14b** 1 Maccabees is a historical book in the Jewish Apocrypha—a set of books not considered inspired

Scripture by Jews, yet worthy of reading. The Apocrypha books are considered to be inspired Scripture by the Roman Catholic church and appear in Catholic editions of the Bible.

tribulation, a time of calamities with great distress, far worse than anything that has ever happened anywhere in the world before that time. *[Daniel 12:1]* And there will never be anything like it again. 20 God has limited the number of days that this will last. If he didn't, nobody in the world would survive. But for the sake of his elect people, he has limited the number of days. ❖ *The "elect" are those people that God has chosen to be his own and has saved.* ➤ 21 During those difficult times, if anyone says, 'I know where the Messiah is,' or 'The Messiah is in such a place,' don't believe it. 22 For false Messiahs and false prophets will become prominent and perform such great miraculous signs to deceive people that even God's elect might be tempted to believe in them. ❖ *Many believe this verse implies that God will protect the faith of the elect so they won't be deceived. Others think it isn't clear. But Jesus thought it was worth warning about.* ➤ 23 Now you have advance warning, so be on your guard."

The Coming of the Son of Man

24 Jesus continued, "Immediately after those days of tribulation, **the sun will be darkened and the moon will not shine.** 25 **Stars will fall** from the sky and the spiritual principalities and powers of the heavens will be shaken. *[Isaiah 13:9-13; 24:21-23; 34:4; Ezekiel 32:7-8; Joel 2:10-11; 30-31; 3:15; Amos 8:9; Acts 2:19-20; Revelation 6:12-14]* ❖ *The falling stars could be a meteor shower. The dimming of the sun and moon could be caused by volcanic eruptions that cloud the atmosphere, which would also blank out the stars. Ancient peoples thought there was a connection between stars and spiritual beings such as angels and demonic principalities and powers. We don't know for sure what any of this means, but it will become clear when it happens after the tribulation.* ➤

26 "Then I, the Son of Man, will appear in the sky coming on clouds with great glory and power. *[Daniel 7:13]* 27 I will send my angels to gather my elect people from everywhere on earth."

Learn to Observe the Signs

28 Then, Jesus gave this illustration: "Learn a lesson from fig trees. You know that when young green leaves start growing on their branches, summer is near. 29 In the same way, when you see the signs I just described, you can know that I will return very shortly. 30 I assure you that all these things will happen before all the people of this generation die. ❖ *There are two likely interpretations of "this generation." First, the people of the generation listening to Jesus would not all die before his prophecy about the destruction of Jerusalem would happen. That is obvious in historical hindsight and some interpreters say this was the only generation Jesus meant. As for the signs that will occur immediately before Jesus returns, some believe he meant that "this generation" which is alive to see these later signs—especially those in verses 19-25—will not all die before his actual return. Others interpret "generation" with different meanings. Looking at all the Hebrew Scripture prophecies that we know have been fulfilled, one thing we can say is: it's difficult to know exactly what some prophecies mean until after they are fulfilled.* ➤ 31 Heaven and earth will end, but my words are always true and all will happen as I have said.

Always Be Ready for Jesus' Return

32 "But no one knows the exact day or hour that I will return. Even I do not. Only the Father knows. ❖ *No one can predict exactly when, but Jesus gave us signs so we would know when the time is getting near.* ➤ 33 So watch for the signs and always be prepared because you don't know when I will return. 34 As an illustration, my going and returning again is like a man who went on a trip. He left his servants in charge of his household while he was away and assigned each one specific duties. He instructed the guard at the gate to be continually on watch for his return.

35 "So you always have to be ready because you don't know when your master is returning. It could be in the evening or at midnight or in the wee hours of the morning when roosters crow or after dawn. 36 If I were to return unexpectedly, it will not be good if I catch you off guard, neglecting your duties. 37 So I exhort you to always be alert for signs of my return and to be ready." ❖ *To be ready is to live every day in faith doing what he wants you to be doing.* ➤

14

The Plot to Arrest Jesus

1 It was only two days before the start of the joint festivals of Passover and

Unleavened Bread. The chief priests and Scripture teachers were trying to find a way to arrest Jesus without the public knowing about it so they could execute him. 2 But they all agreed, "We can't do it during the festival since the people would riot if they found out." ❖ *A riot would provoke the Romans to a violent response and probably also cause them to replace Caiaphas as High Priest. So the Jewish leaders were mainly looking out for their own welfare. They didn't really care what the people thought of them.* ➤

Mary Anoints Jesus

3 One day that week, Jesus was in Bethany as a guest at the house of Simon (who at one time had a contagious skin disease). He was reclining A at the table eating when a woman entered carrying an expensive alabaster ❖ *translucent white or yellow calcite, imported from Egypt* ➤ flask of very expensive perfume, made of pure nard. ❖ *Nard was imported from India.* ➤ She broke open the neck of the flask and poured the perfume over Jesus' head. ❖ *Simon "the Leper" (in the literal text) sounds like a nickname. He had probably been cured by Jesus, or perhaps he was dead and this was just known as his house. Some think he may have been the father of Lazarus, Martha, and Mary. Mark doesn't tell us, but John 12:3 says it was Mary—the sister of Martha and Lazarus—who poured the perfume. John 12:1 also says this happened six days before the Passover. Ancient writers were not overly concerned with exact chronology and many events in the gospel accounts are probably told out of the order they occurred.* ➤

4 But some of the guests who witnessed this extravagant display of affection were indignant and considered the act wasteful and inappropriate. 5 They sharply criticized her, saying the perfume was worth more than a year's wages. She could have sold it and given the money to the poor.

6 But Jesus rebuked them: "Leave her alone! Why are you criticizing her for doing such a beautiful thing to me? 7 There will always be poor people around to help, but I won't always be here with you. *[Deuteronomy 15:11]* 8 She did the only thing she was able to do for me. By anointing my body with this perfume, she was preparing it for my burial.

❖ *It's unlikely that Mary intended this act of devotion as a preparation for Jesus' burial. But Jesus' interpretation of it leads to the conclusion that through her love and devotion, God moved her to perform a prophetic act whose full significance she didn't realize.* ➤ 9 The truth of the matter is, her act of extreme devotion is such a good example that it will be recounted everywhere the message of salvation is preached throughout the world." ❖ *Jesus exhorts us to extreme devotion to himself, even above all other important and good causes.* ➤

Judas Agrees to Betray Jesus

10 It was after this that Judas Iscariot— one of the twelve apostles—went to the chief priests to betray him. ❖ *Many speculate about his motives, but the only one mentioned in the Scriptures is money.* ➤ 11 They were glad for the opportunity and agreed to pay him if he did this. Judas consented to the arrangement and began seeking an opportunity to betray Jesus to them when no crowd was around.

Jesus Prepares to Eat the Passover

12 On the first day of the Festival of Unleavened Bread, Jesus' close followers asked him, "Where do you want us to prepare the Passover meal for you?" *[Leviticus 23:5-6; Exodus 12:12-20]* ❖ *The one-day Festival of Passover and the week-long Festival of Unleavened Bread— immediately following Passover—were combined into one festival in the minds of the Jews. Either term was applied to the entire eight-day period of the two festivals. [Matthew 26:2, 17; Mark 14:1, 12; Luke 22:1] It probably also included the day of preparation for the Passover—when all leaven was removed from their houses and the Passover lamb was killed. The Jewish day started at sunset so the Passover feast itself started at sunset of the day of preparation. By Jewish reckoning, this preparation day was a Thursday, with Friday beginning at sunset. The Passover meal was eaten Friday night, which was still Thursday night by our way of dividing days. He was arrested that night and crucified in the morning, all on the same Jewish Friday. So, the same day that the Jews ate their Passover lambs was when the Messiah—the "true Passover Lamb"—was crucified. The original Passover [Exodus chapter 12] was when God saved the Israelites in Egypt from the angel of death through their using the blood of lambs to paint their houses' door frames. That event was a*

A 14:3 Jews of this time followed the Roman custom of eating while lying down on one's side on a low bench, propped up on one elbow. The person's head would be close to the table, but his feet would be pointing away from it.

prefiguring "type" of the Messiah's blood (death) which saves those who trust in it from eternal death. Therefore, the Messiah is sometimes referred to as "our Passover Lamb," [1 Corinthians 5:7] or just "the Lamb." [1 Peter 1:19; Revelation 5:6, 8, 12-13; 6:1-6; 7:9-10, 14, 17; 12:11; 13:8; 14:1, 4-5, 10; 15:3; 17:14; 19:7, 9; 21:9, 14; 22-23; 22:1, 3] ➤

13 He told two of them **A** to enter Jerusalem and said, "You will meet a man carrying a water jar. ❖ *This would be unusual since it was women's work.* ➤ Follow him 14 until he enters a house. Then say to the owner of that house, 'The Rabbi asks, "Where is the guest room where I can eat the Passover with my followers?" ' 15 He will show you a large room upstairs, furnished with all you need. Prepare everything for us there."

16 So they went and found everything just as Jesus had described it and prepared the Passover meal.

17 As sunset was approaching when the day of Passover would begin, Jesus arrived with his twelve close followers. 18 Later, as they were all reclining at the table eating the Passover meal, Jesus said, "This is something you should know. One of you, who is eating with me tonight as if he were my loyal friend, will hand me over my enemies." *[Psalm 41:9]*

19 This upset them, and thinking that one of them might do something without intending to, they each asked him, "Lord, it won't be me, will it?" 20 Jesus replied, "It will be one of you twelve who are eating with me now. 21 I, the Son of Man, will die just as the Scriptures predict, but it will be terrible for the one who deliberately betrays me! He would have been much better off having never been born." ❖ *Many liberal Christians stress God's love to the point of denying he will punish unrepentant sinners. In order to do so, they have to ignore many verses like this one.* ➤

Jesus Institutes the Lord's Supper

22 During the course of the meal, Jesus took some bread, thanked God for it, broke it, and handed it around to his followers. He told them, "I want you to all eat from this bread. It is my body." ❖ *Given the Jewish context in which Jesus did this, his statement that "this bread is my body" is certainly a metaphor meaning "this represents my body." There has been much debate and disagreement over how this is interpreted. But figurative language doesn't mean that there is no spiritual reality behind the metaphorical image. By offering them "his body" to eat, he was inviting them to receive the benefits of his sacrificial death. See the parallel accounts in Matthew 26:26-29, Luke 22:14-20 and 1 Corinthians 11:23-26. See also what he says about eating his body in John 6:27-64. While Jesus was not talking about eating the bread of the Lord's Supper in John 6, in both situations he was talking about a spiritual partaking. Therefore, the meaning in both situations is likely to be similar. Note that Mark neglects to record anything about doing this for the purpose of "remembrance." Therefore in Mark's view—and also Matthew's—inspired by the Holy Spirit, remembrance was not the prime focus of Jesus' command, even though that is how most Protestant believers interpret it today.* ➤

23 Then he took a cup of wine, **B** thanked God for it, passed it around to his followers, and they all drank from it.

24 He told them, "This wine is my blood that I will shed in my dying, which will establish a New Covenant *[Exodus 24:8; Jeremiah 31:31-34]* for the benefit many people. ❖ *Covenants were life-long pacts that were often ratified with the shedding of blood. In dying and shedding his blood, Jesus ratified the New Covenant that God was making with his people. This New Covenant says that God will forgive, save, and accept as his people all those who trust in Jesus' sacrificial death to save them, and who commit themselves to live in obedience to him. Some believe that we are meant to drink the cup mainly as a reminder of what Jesus' death accomplished for us. Others believe that Jesus' offering of the wine to his followers represented his offering them participation in the New Covenant and in all the benefits that would be procured by his death. Their drinking it meant that they desired to participate in this New Covenant and receive all of its benefits. Many believe that partaking of the cup with faith is more than a symbolic memorial, but is also a means of receiving his undeserved favor whereby we receive those benefits of the New Covenant which we continually need in this life*

A 14:13a Luke 22:8 says he sent Peter and John.

B 14:23 It was wine, not unfermented grape juice. Those who believe that Jews did not drink alcoholic beverages should read Numbers 28:7 and Deuteronomy 14:26 (they should also talk to some religious Jews). The tradition of some believers to abstain from all alcoholic beverages comes from a desire to avoid drunkenness—which is prohibited in the Scriptures. But total abstinence is neither commanded nor expected in the Scriptures, only soberness.

(e.g. forgiveness, physical and emotional healing, comfort, spiritual strength, increased faith, sanctification, unity with other believers, etc.). See the notes at 1 Corinthians 10:16-17. ➤ **25** But I will not drink wine again until I drink it with you with new meaning in my Father's Heavenly Kingdom." ❖ *Here, the wine represents the blood of his sacrificial death and the ratification of the new covenant. In Heaven, it will represent the complete fulfillment of all that the new covenant promised, joy, and more.* ➤

26 Then they sang a hymn, went out of the city, and made the 15-minute walk to Mount Olivet. ❖ *It was customary to sing Psalms 115—118 at the end of the Passover meal.* ➤

Jesus Predicts Peter's Denial

27 Then Jesus told them, "You will all have a temporary lapse of faith and run away. The Scriptures prophesy, **'I will kill the shepherd and his flock will be scattered.'** *[Zechariah 13:7]* **28** But after my Father has made me alive again, I will go to Galilee where you will see me."

29 But Peter told him, "I will never run away, even if everyone else does." ❖ *Peter was sincere but didn't realize how easy it is for any of us to succumb to temptation if we're caught off guard, or if we depend on our own strength to resist it.* ➤

30 Jesus replied, "The truth is, that before you hear a rooster crow two times tonight, you will three times publicly deny having any association with me."

31 But Peter asserted, "I will never deny that I'm your follower, even if it means I have to die with you!" And all the others said the same thing.

In Gethsemane

32 Then, Jesus and his followers arrived at a place on Mount Olivet called Gethsemane. He told most of them, "Sit here for a while. I'm going over there a little farther to pray." **33** But he took Peter, James, and John with him. As he contemplated the sufferings that awaited him later that day, he was overcome with grief and distress. **34** He told his three companions, "I'm so oppressed that I feel like I'm dying. Stay here and keep me company while I pray."

35 Then, he went a short distance away and prostrated himself on the ground. He asked his Father if it was possible for him to avoid the tortuous suffering and death ahead of him. **36** He said, "Daddy! My Father! You can do anything! Please don't tell me to go through with this painful plan! But despite my desires, I surrender to your will." ❖ *"Cup," in the literal text, is a figure of speech referring to the suffering and crucifixion he knew was coming. [Psalm 75:8; Isaiah 51:17-23; Jeremiah 25:15-29; Ezekiel 23:31-35]It was not only physical suffering and death that he was facing, but also God's punishment for humanity's sin. While submitted to his Father's plan, Jesus was fully human and he dreaded the suffering. His words in this verse are only a summary of his prayer. The "one hour" in the next verse implies that he prayed for a considerable length of time.* ➤

37 When he returned to his three companions, he found them asleep. He woke Peter and said, "Simon, don't you have the strength to stay awake with me for even an hour? **38** You should be asking for God's help to resist the temptation that's about to overtake you! Your spirit wants to do what's right, but your ability to resist temptation is weak." ❖ *The temptation they failed to resist that night was the urge to save their own skins when Jesus was arrested and it became clear that he was not going to resist.* ➤

39 Then he went and prayed a second time, saying basically the same words. ❖ *Jesus' example teaches us that it's OK to pray the same thing repeatedly until we have a clear answer from God, or until we are fully submitted to his will.* ➤ **40** Again, when he returned to his three companions, he found them asleep. They were unable to keep their eyes open and were so embarrassed that they didn't know what to say.

41 So he went to pray a third time, then returned to them and said, "Now is not the time to be sleeping! **A** The time has finally come. I, the Son of Man, am betrayed into the power of evil men. **42** Get up and come with me! See, here comes the traitor!"

A 14:41 The Greek sentence is ambiguous and could either be a sarcastic command (as rendered), or the rhetorical question, "Are you still asleep?" meaning "You shouldn't be sleeping."

Jesus' Arrest

43 While he was still talking, a large crowd of men arrived led by Judas, one of his own apostles. The chief priests and Jewish elders had sent them to arrest Jesus and they came armed with swords and clubs.

44 The traitor had told them, "Arrest the man who I greet with a kiss. He's the one you want. Seize him and take him away." 45 Going straight to Jesus, Judas respectfully greeted him, saying, "Rabbi!," and kissed him. ❖ *As a follower of Jesus, Judas would probably have kissed his hand. Or if he greeted him as a friend on equal terms, he would have kissed him on the cheek.* ➤ 46 Then, the men with Judas grabbed Jesus and held him. 47 But one of Jesus' men drew a sword and struck out at the High Priest's slave, cutting off his ear. ❖ *John 18:10 tells us that Peter did this, and the slave's name was Malchus. Slaves of important persons could have authority and high status. Malchus may have been representing the High Priest for this arrest. Peter was ready to defend his master and may have been attempting a more serious injury. But being a fisherman, it's unlikely he had any skill with a sword.* ➤

48 Then Jesus said to the crowd, "Why have you come armed with swords and clubs to arrest me as if I were a violent criminal? 49 I've been with you every day in the Temple and you could've easily arrested me there. But things have happened this way to fulfill prophecies in the Scriptures." 50 When his followers realized that he didn't intend to resist, they became afraid for their own lives and ran away. ❖ *Jesus had the ability to walk out of this unscathed if he chose. But this was happening according to his Father's plan and he was perfectly submitted to it. Jesus' followers were confused as to why their Messiah didn't resist and use his miraculous power to assert his authority as God's Chosen One. Jesus' predictions of his arrest, suffering, and death were still incomprehensible to them.* ➤

51 A certain young man had been following Jesus and his close followers that night. The crowd that arrested Jesus tried to seize him too. But he was only wearing a linen tunic 52 and wriggled out of it leaving his captors holding it while he ran away naked into the darkness. ❖ *Many believe this was John Mark, the author of this gospel. If his identity was unknown to Mark's readers, there would be no reason to mention him. The nature of his linen garment, whether or not it was a tunic, sheet, or something else, is not clear. Linen was an expensive fabric in those days.* ➤

Jesus Before the Sanhedrin

53 They took Jesus to the High Priest's house where he and the chief priests, Scripture teachers, and elders were assembled and waiting for Jesus. 54 But Peter returned and followed behind at a distance, hidden in the dark. Then he came right into the High Priest's courtyard and sat with the guards, warming himself by the fire to see how things would go for Jesus. ❖ *John also followed. [John 18:15-16]* ➤

55 Inside the house, the chief priests and the entire Sanhedrin were questioning witnesses—many of whom gave false testimony—to try to find sufficient evidence against him that they could have him executed. But they couldn't find any, 56 even though many witnesses came forward and told lies about him—for their testimony did not agree. ❖ *The court required two witnesses to agree without contradiction in order for their testimony to be accepted as fact. When two witnesses contradicted each other under questioning, their testimony was invalidated and, technically, they should have been severely punished for giving false testimony. Evidently, procedure required these witnesses to testify separately so they couldn't hear each other. The Sanhedrin had to give at least the appearance of going through the proper legal procedure, even though a night trial was illegal for capital cases. We know that not all the members were antagonistic toward Jesus (e.g. Nicodemus [John 7:50-51] and Joseph of Arimathea [Mark 15:43-46; Luke 23:50-53; John 19:38-41]) and there could have been a few others that kept them from abandoning procedure.* ➤ 57 Finally, some men testified, 58 "We heard this man say, 'I will destroy God's Temple which was built by men and miraculously build another.' " ❖ *This was a distortion of what Jesus had said in John 2:19.* ➤ 59 But even in this matter, their testimonies did not agree in every detail.

60 Then the High Priest stood and asked Jesus, "Aren't you going to say something? Don't you want to reply to this accusation?" 61 But Jesus remained silent. [Isaiah 53:7] Then the High Priest asked, "Are you the Messiah and God's Son?" ❖ *"Blessed One," in the literal text, was a euphemism for God. The Jews of that time avoided saying the word "God" to avoid any possibility of being disrespectful.* ➤

62 Jesus answered, "I am. You will see me, the Son of Man, sitting in the place of highest honor at the right hand of God Almighty *[Psalm 110:1]* and coming with clouds in the sky." *[Daniel 7:13]*

63 Then the High Priest tore his clothes, **A** and said, "We don't need any more witnesses! 64 You are all witnesses to his blasphemy! ❖ *According to the Mishna (written about AD 200), he could not be found guilty of blasphemy unless he actually pronounced the name of God (i.e. Yahweh). But that may have been a later definition.* ➤ What is your verdict?" They unanimously condemned him to death. *[Leviticus 24:16]* ❖ *This was technically an illegal meeting of the Sanhedrin because it was at night. It's unlikely that all of them were present. Verse 55 mentioning "the entire Sanhedrin" may simply mean that there was a quorum present. We know of at least two members who did not agree with their decision (Nicodemus and Joseph of Arimathea) so they and any others who were known sympathizers with Jesus would not have voted "unanimously" for his death, and may not have been notified of this meeting.* ➤ 65 Then they proceeded to spit in his face, slap him, and beat him with fists. They blindfolded him and took turns hitting him and saying, "Prophesy for us, Messiah! Tell us who hit you!" ❖ *They were mocking him based on Isaiah 11:3.* ➤

Peter Denies Knowing Jesus

66 While this was going on inside, Peter was sitting out in the courtyard. A serving girl came by 67 and noticed him by the fire. She looked at him closely and said, "You are one of those who was with Jesus of Nazareth!"

68 But Peter denied it. He said, "I don't know such a person and have no idea what you're talking about." Then he got up and went to the area near the courtyard entrance. He heard a rooster crow but was barely aware of it.

69 The serving girl later saw him again and once more said to those nearby, "He's one of Jesus' followers!" 70 Afraid, Peter again denied it. A bit later some of the men came up to Peter and said, "It's clear that you are one of his followers. Your Galilean accent gives you away."

71 Fearing for his life, Peter declared, "May the Lord curse **B** me if I'm telling a lie! I swear before the Lord of Heaven that I do not know that man!" 72 Immediately after he said it, for the second time that night he heard a rooster crow. **C** Then he remembered what Jesus had told him earlier, "Before you hear a rooster crow two times tonight, at three separate times you will publicly deny having any association with me." He was overcome with remorse and wept bitterly because of what he had done.

15

Jesus Before Pilate

1 When it became light, all the chief priests and Jewish elders conferred together in an official session of the Sanhedrin and planned how they would have Jesus executed. ❖ *It was illegal to try a capital case at night, so they met officially in daylight to put a veneer of legality on their proceedings. It was also illegal to pass the death sentence on the same day as the trial, but this requirement was ignored. They didn't have the authority to execute him, because their Roman conquerors reserved that power for themselves. They had to plan a case to present to the Roman governor who often did his business in the morning. So they had to move*

A **14:63** Tearing one's clothing was a cultural way of indicating extreme anger, horror, or grief. [Genesis 37:29; Numbers 14:6; Joshua 7:6; 2 Samuel 1:11; 2 Kings 18:37; 19:1; Ezra 9:3; Job 1:20; Jeremiah 36:24] Here, he was expressing horror at what he perceived as blasphemy. Leviticus 10:6 and 21:10 forbid the High Priest from tearing his official robes of office. The Greek word χιτῶνας (chitōnas), rendered as "clothes," refers to an inner garment worn next to the skin, and not to an outer garment. But the word here is plural, and Matthew 26:65 has a different Greek word, ἱμάτια (himatia), also plural, which referred to outer garments, such as a robe. Given the plural, it seems likely he tore all the garments he was wearing. While the Torah forbade him from tearing his robes of office, one commentator says that this only applied to private troubles. But when acting as a judge, Jewish tradition required him to express his horror of blasphemy in this way.

B **14:71** Literally, it says, "He began to curse and swear that..." The word ὀμνύω (omnuō) translated "swear" means "to swear an oath." Some commentators think "curse" means Peter was merely using foul language to emphasize his statement, and not calling a curse down on himself.

C **14:72** Roosters in Jerusalem are known to crow as early as 12:30 to 2:30 a.m.

quickly to present their case and have Jesus executed before the general public became aware that he was under arrest and rioted in protest. ➤ Then they bound him, took him to the Roman authorities, and handed him over to be dealt with by Pilate, the governor. ❖ *Pontius Pilate was the Roman military governor over Judea, Samaria, and Idumea provinces from AD 26–36 under Tiberius Caesar.* ➤ 2 Pilate asked Jesus, "Are you making yourself out to be King of the Jews?" Jesus answered, "Those are your words and meaning." ❖ *He wasn't denying the charge. Many scholars believe it was an affirmative answer. Yet it is also hedged since he wasn't intending to be a king who was a rival to Caesar and Roman rule. Had Pilate understood his answer to mean a simple "yes," then he would likely have considered him a potential rival to Caesar and worthy of execution. But he didn't come to this conclusion. Pilate's question and Jesus' answer are reported identically in the three synoptic gospels (Matthew, Mark, and Luke).* ➤

3 Then the chief priests started shouting all sorts of accusations against him. 4 Pilate demanded, "Aren't you going to respond to all these charges they're bringing against you?"

5 But Jesus amazed the governor by remaining silent. *[Isaiah 53:7]*

Jesus Is Sentenced to Die

6 Now, the governor had a custom of freeing a prisoner of the crowd's choosing every Passover. 7 At that time, he had a well-known troublemaker in custody named Barabbas who was awaiting execution for a murder he committed during a revolt. 8 The Jewish crowd outside Pilate's palace started demanding that he release a prisoner for them, as he always did on Passover.

9 So Pilate asked them, "Do you want me to release the King of the Jews to you?" 10 He was aware that the chief priests had handed Jesus over to him because they envied Jesus' popularity. He was expecting the crowd to ask for Jesus' release, thereby relieving him of this matter. ❖ *He didn't know that the crowd was mostly the chief priests and Jewish elders and their supporters. The general population that liked Jesus was not yet aware of his arrest.* ➤ 11 But the chief priests persuaded the crowd to ask for Barabbas' release instead.

12 Then Pilate asked them, "And what should I do with Jesus, who you've said is 'King of the Jews?' "

13 They all shouted, "Crucify him!"

❖ *Crucifixion was the standard Roman method of execution and was normally a prolonged torturous death.* ➤

14 Pilate asked, "But why? What crime has he committed?" But they all just kept shouting, "Crucify him!"

15 So giving in to them, Pilate reluctantly ordered Barabbas released and had Jesus whipped in preparation for his crucifixion.

❖ *The whip used for non-Romans was a multi-stranded leather whip called a flagellum, with pieces of bone or metal embedded in the strands. Romans had three levels of flogging: 1) the fustigatio—the least severe of the three—given for small offenses, 2) the flagellatio, a severe flogging given to criminals for serious offenses, 3) the verberatio—the most severe scourging—often given before crucifixion. In the verberatio, the flogging continued until the soldiers doing it grew tired. Sometimes the result of such a flogging was death, or bare bones protruding from the ripped flesh. Examining all the gospel accounts, it seems likely that Jesus was flogged twice. Mark doesn't record the first whipping Pilate ordered before this one (which would have been either the fustigatio or the flagellatio) in hopes of turning the crowd's sympathy toward him. [John 19:1] This whipping was the verberatio.* ➤

Jesus Is Mocked

16 Then, the soldiers took Jesus into the governor's palace (called the "Praetorium") ❖ *which also served as headquarters for the Roman cohort stationed in Jerusalem which consisted of about 600 soldiers* ➤ and gathered the entire cohort around him. 17 In order to mock the claim that he was a king, they dressed him in a purple robe. ❖ *See the note at Matthew 27:28.* ➤ They also made a crown of thorn branches twisted together and put it on his head. 18-19 Then they began to bow and kneel before him in mock homage and saluted him, saying, "Hail, King of the Jews!" They also beat the thorns into his head with a stick and spit on him. 20 After they tired of ridiculing him, they removed the purple robe and put his own clothes back on him for the march through the city out to the crucifixion site.

The Crucifixion

21 As the soldiers were leading Jesus out of the city, they forced a bystander named Simon—from the city of Cyrene in North Africa (Alexander's and Rufus' father)—to carry the crossbeam for Jesus. ❖ *Jesus was too*

weak after his beatings to carry it, and soldiers had the right to force civilians to carry burdens for a certain distance. It seems likely that the people to whom Mark was writing already knew who Alexander and Rufus were. This might be the same Rufus mentioned in Romans 16:13. ➤ 22 They brought Jesus to the execution site outside the city which ins Aramaic was called *"Golgotha,"* meaning "the place of the skull." ❖ *In Latin, it is "calvaria," from which "Calvary" is derived. Many think the hill had this name because of its resemblance to a skull, but no one knows for certain.* ➤ 23 They offered Jesus some wine mixed with myrrh, but after tasting it and discovering what it was, he refused to drink it. *[Psalm 69:21]* ❖ *Many commentators believe this was a pain-killing mixture, customarily prepared by the women of Jerusalem. If so, Jesus refused it because he wanted to remain conscious and sober until he died. Matthew says it was gall instead of myrrh. The IVP commentary says that the words for myrrh and gall in Aramaic are very similar. Other commentators say the soldiers put gall in the wine to make it bitter and further mock him.* ➤ 24 After they had stripped him and nailed him to the cross, they cast lots to see who would get his clothing. *[Psalm 22:18]*

25 It was during the third hour when they crucified him. ❖ *The "third hour" was any time between 9:00 a.m. and noon. Clocks had not yet been invented and they roughly divided the daylight into four parts, the first "hour" (from sunrise to midmorning), the "third hour" (about midmorning until noon), the "sixth hour" (from noon to midafternoon) and the "ninth hour" (about midafternoon until sunset). Crucifixion was a prolonged, agonizing, and shameful death. The condemned were usually stripped naked before being crucified. Jews considered anyone who hung on a "tree"—which included a stake, post, or cross—to be under God's curse. [Deuteronomy 21:22-23; Galatians 3:13]* ➤ 26 A sign announcing his crime read,

"THE KING OF THE JEWS."

❖ *It was treason to be a king that Caesar had not appointed over a nation that was part of the Roman Empire.* ➤ 27 Two revolutionaries were crucified at the same time, one on each side of Jesus. 28 {This fulfilled the Scripture that says, **"He was considered to be just another law breaker."**} A *[Isaiah 53:12]* 29 Many who

passed by blasphemed B him and shook their heads in scorn. *[Psalm 22:7]* They said things like, "And you were going to destroy the Temple and rebuild it in three days! 30 So come down from the cross and save yourself!"

31 The chief priests and Scripture teachers also made it a point to come and ridicule him. They said, "He had the power to save others but can't even save himself! ❖ *The irony is that he could have done so, but then God's purpose of saving humanity from eternal death would have been thwarted. So in a way what they said was true. He could save others, but in order to do so he could not save himself.* ➤ 32 If he is really the Messiah, the King of Israel, ❖ *this was a Messianic title* ➤ let's see him come down from the cross! Then we will believe in him!" Even the revolutionaries who were crucified next to him insulted him with similar sentiments.

Jesus' Death

33 Then, from about noon until mid-afternoon the entire land as far as could be seen was shrouded in darkness. *[Exodus 10:22; Amos 8:9]* ❖ *This occurred at Passover—which is always at a full moon—so it was not a solar eclipse, but a supernatural event. Darkness was considered to be an evil sign and was also associated with judgment and punishment. [Isaiah 5:30; 13:10-11; Joel 3:14-15] This was the time when God was punishing Jesus for all of humanity's sins.* ➤ 34 Around midafternoon, Jesus shouted in Aramaic, *"Eloi, eloi, lama sabachthani!"* which means, **"My God, my God, why have you left me!"** *[Psalm 22:1; Isaiah 59:2]* ❖ *Part of the penalty for sin is complete separation from God. [Habakkuk 1:13; 2 Corinthians 5:21; Galatians 3:13]* ➤

35 Some who were nearby heard him and said, "Listen! He's calling for Elijah to help him." ❖ *They mistook "eloi" for Elijah's name, which in Hebrew is "Eliyahu." Elijah was a great prophet who lived about 850 years before Jesus was born and was taken up to Heaven without dying. [2 Kings 2:11] The Jews expected Elijah to return before the Messiah came. [Malachi 4:5]* ➤

36 One of them C ran to get a sponge. He soaked it in sour wine, ❖ *the soldiers' drink* ➤ put in on a stick and raised it to Jesus' lips

---

A **15:28** Most manuscripts lack verse 28.

B **15:29** This word βλασφημέω (blasphemeō) literally is "blaspheme" and is so translated in other contexts. They were insulting him, but because of who

Jesus is, they were also unknowingly blaspheming God.

C **15:36** Some commentators think this is a soldier, also in John 19:29.

so he might drink from it. *[Psalm 69:21]* He said, "Now let's see if Elijah will come to take him down and save him."

37 Then Jesus again screamed something *[Luke 23:46; John 19:30]* and died. ❖ *Normally, a crucified person would suffer for days and gradually lose consciousness before dying. His manner of death on a cross was very unusual because in the end, it wasn't due to crucifixion, but because he voluntarily surrendered his life. [John 10:17-18]* ➤

38 At that moment, the thick curtain in the Temple was torn in two from top to bottom. ❖ *It blocked the entryway from the Holy Place in the Temple into the Holy of Holies where God was present in a special way. [Exodus 26:31-33] Most commentators believe God tore this curtain open to show that the barrier of sin which had kept people from approaching him was now removed by his Son's death. [Hebrews 6:19-20; 9:1-15; 10:19-22] God's people now have direct access to him because he has removed their sins and made them holy in his sight. The IVP commentary says the rending of the curtain more likely indicates the presence of God leaving the Temple, as in Ezekiel chapters 10—11. These two views are not necessarily mutually exclusive.* ➤ **39** When the centurion who was standing right in front of Jesus saw the way he died, he said, "Truly this man was God's Son!" **A** ❖ *The Roman soldiers [plural from Matthew 27:54] were convinced that Jesus was more than a mere man. With their pagan background, they probably meant, "He was a son of a god." But Mark meant it as a testimony to the truth, that he was the Son of the one and only living God. It's ironic that pagans recognized the signs of his divinity while most of God's own people did not.* ➤

40 Some women who loved Jesus watched his crucifixion from a distance. ❖ *Most of his followers—except John [John 19:26-27] and these women—were conspicuously absent, hiding in fear for their lives.* ➤ Among them were Mary of Magdala village, and Salome, ❖ *probably Zebedee's wife, the mother of James and John* ➤ and another Mary who was the mother of James the lesser **B** and Joses. ❖ *Some commentators think Mary, the mother of James and Joses, was Jesus' mother, and that Mark didn't refer to her as such because he was emphasizing Jesus' deity in this book. Other commentators*

disagree and think that she was the wife of Clopas [John 19:25]. Some think Salome may have been the sister of Miriam (the mother of Jesus). [John 19:25] ➤ **41** These women had traveled with Jesus from Galilee to help financially support him and his ministry. There were many other women there too who had traveled to Jerusalem with him.

Jesus' Burial

42 It was Friday—the day of preparation for the Sabbath—and sunset was approaching when the Sabbath would begin. ❖ *The original text just says it was the "preparation day." Every Friday was a preparation day for the Saturday Sabbath. But the day before Passover was also a preparation day for the day of Passover which was considered a "high Sabbath" day. Commentators disagree on which preparation day was meant, but traditionally it has been interpreted as stated above.* ➤ **43** There was a prominent member of the Sanhedrin named Joseph, from the town of Arimathea. **C** He had been eagerly looking forward to the establishment of God's Kingdom as taught by Jesus. ❖ *He was a secret follower of Jesus [John 19:38] who was rich [Matthew 27:57] and opposed to the Sanhedrin's condemnation of Jesus. [Luke 23:51]* ➤ He boldly went to Pilate and asked permission to remove Jesus' body from the cross for burial. ❖ *Romans normally left crucified bodies hanging until they rotted, and then buried them in a common grave. But the Jewish leaders didn't want the bodies hanging on the Sabbath which started at sunset, so Pilate would grant Joseph's request to avoid further problems with them. By openly revealing his devotion to Jesus, Joseph was endangering his own position on the Sanhedrin.* ➤ **44** Pilate was surprised to hear that Jesus was already dead, and sent a centurion to verify it was true. ❖ *A crucified person usually took several days to die.* ➤ **45** When the centurion confirmed it, Pilate granted Joseph permission to take the body. **46** Joseph bought some linen cloth for a burial shroud and ❖ *after washing the body and anointing it with oil, following Jewish custom* ➤ wrapped the body in the cloth and put it in a tomb that had been cut out of a

---

A 15:39 The words υἱὸς θεοῦ (huios theou) in the Greek text can mean either "the Son of God" or "a son of (a) god." There is nothing in the Greek text that tells us which meaning he meant.

B 15:40 "The lesser" is ambiguous and could mean "the younger" or "the shorter." He was probably referred to in

this way to distinguish him from James, the brother of John, who was one of Jesus' close followers.

C 15:43 Commentators think Arimathea was located about 10 miles east of Joppa and about 19 miles northwest of Jerusalem, but the exact location is not known.

rock cliffside. ❖ *John 19:39-42 says that Nicodemus helped him, and they were almost certainly assisted by servants. Matthew 27:60 tells us this was Joseph's own tomb. This fulfilled the prophecy in Isaiah 53:9.* ➤ Then, he rolled a large stone to block the tomb entrance. ❖ *This protected the body from wild animals and helped keep the stench of decay inside.* ➤ **47** Mary of Magdala village and Mary the mother of Joses were nearby, observing where Joseph buried Jesus' body.

16

God Makes Jesus Alive Again

1 When the Sabbath was over ❖ *after sunset on Saturday, which is the start of Sunday for Jews,* ➤ Mary of Magdala, Salome, and Miriam **A** the mother of James bought burial spices so they could anoint Jesus' body. ❖ *The Torah did not allow them to buy or carry things on the Sabbath. Even though they knew where Joseph of Arimathea had buried Jesus, they were evidently unaware that he had already anointed the body with spices. [John 19:38-40]* ➤ **2** At dawn Sunday morning—the first day of the week—these women went to Jesus' tomb. **3** On their way there, they were discussing how they would find someone to roll the stone away from the tomb entrance. ❖ *This would normally require several men.* ➤

4 But when they arrived, they found the tomb entrance open and the stone to one side. **5** As they entered the tomb, they were shocked and frightened **B** to see a young man wearing a white robe sitting to the right of where Jesus' body had been. ❖ *This was an angel, but they didn't realize it immediately.* ➤

6 He said to them, "Don't be frightened! I know you are looking for Jesus of Nazareth who was crucified. But he is not here! God has made him alive again. Come see that the place where they put his body is empty. **7** Then tell his close followers and Peter that Jesus is planning to meet you all in Galilee, just as he told you." *[Mark 14:28]*

8 Shocked and trembling with fear, the women ran from the tomb and were too frightened to say anything to anyone they passed on the way. ❖ *Matthew 28:9-10 says that Jesus appeared to them after they left the tomb, and Luke 24:9-11 says that they did deliver the angel's message to Jesus' close followers—even though no one believed them at first. The oldest existing Greek manuscripts (of which there are only a few) end here. Others have a variety of endings. No one knows why this variation exists. Most commentators think that Mark ended his gospel here and that the shorter and longer endings, below, were added later by others.* ➤

A SHORT ENDING TO MARK'S GOSPEL

❖ *This ending is found in a few manuscripts, but not in those considered important for determining what the original text was.* ➤

{When the women reached Peter and his companions, they reported the angel's instructions. Later, Jesus himself commissioned them to go to people everywhere and share the holy message that will never be silenced, about how to be saved and live forever. Yes, may it be so!}

A LONGER ENDING TO MARK'S GOSPEL

❖ *Verses 9-20 do not occur in the two oldest existing Greek manuscripts from the fourth century, and are also not included in the oldest translations in Syriac, Old Latin, Armenian, Ethiopic, or Georgian. But they do appear in most important manuscripts of a later date. Most scholars believe they were not written by Mark—the Greek vocabulary and style of these verses is considerably different than the rest of the gospel—but think they may have been added between AD 100-140. Many people consider them to be "canonical" (i.e., authoritative Scripture, inspired by God) even if they weren't penned by Mark. The content of verses 9-20, except for some of the things in verses 17 and 18, are corroborated by the other gospels. And those few details in verses 17 and 18 not directly corroborated in the gospels are corroborated in the book of Acts and in Paul's letters—except for the sign of drinking poison without harm. So there is almost nothing in this longer ending that is not clearly part of God's word elsewhere.* ➤

Jesus Appears to Mary from Magdala

9 After Jesus became alive again early Sunday morning, he appeared first to Mary of Magdala (from whom he had expelled seven demons). ❖ *Since Mary was accompanied by*

A 16:1 This is probably Jesus' mother.
B 16:5 The word ἐκθαμβέομαι (ekthambeomai) rendered "shocked and frightened" can either mean "surprised" or "alarmed."

other women, they may also have witnessed this appearance. Gospel writers often mentioned only the people they considered most important in an event, even though there were others involved. ➤ 10 She then went and reported this to his followers who were still in grievous mourning. 11 But when they heard her say that she had seen Jesus alive, they refused to believe her. ❖ *Jewish men of this time believed that a woman's witness was essentially worthless. They still didn't expect Jesus to come back from death until Judgment Day. They dismissed her as hysterical and to be pitied.* ➤

Jesus Appears to Two Men Leaving Jerusalem

12 Later that same day, Jesus appeared to two of his followers while they were walking away from Jerusalem. But his appearance was different from how he had previously looked, so they didn't recognize him at first. 13 After they realized it was Jesus, they returned to Jerusalem and reported it to his other followers, but they didn't believe this report either.

Jesus Appears to the Eleven Apostles

14 Later that day, Jesus appeared to the remaining eleven apostles while they are eating together. He rebuked them for their stubborn refusal to accept the witness of others concerning his being alive and for their persistent unbelief—despite his having told them ahead of time that all this would happen.

15 Then he told them, "I want you to go everywhere in the world to every people group and preach the Good News about how to be saved. 16 God will save those who believe your message and are baptized. But he will condemn to Hell those who reject your message. 17 These miraculous signs will happen to verify the Gospel message shared by believers. They will expel demons from people, they will speak in unknown languages, 18 they will safely pick up poisonous snakes, *[Acts 28:3-6]* if they unknowingly drink poison it won't harm them, and when they lay their hands on the sick to pray for healing, the sick will recover." *[James 5:14-16]*

Jesus Ascends to Heaven

19 After saying these things, the Lord Jesus was taken up into Heaven where he now sits in the position of highest authority and power at the right side of God the Father. 20 Later, his followers did go and preach the message of the Good News in as many places as they could. The Lord worked in and through them and confirmed their message with the miraculous signs that he had promised. Yes, that's the way it was, and may it continue to be so! **A**

A 16:20 The final "amen" (in the literal text) is not in some manuscripts.

The Good News About Jesus the Messiah

as Told by

Luke

The Gospel of Luke and the book of Acts—which continues the story where this Gospel leaves off— were written, according to tradition, by Luke, a traveling companion of the Apostle Paul. He was with the apostle during much of Paul's travels as chronicled in Acts and also during his first imprisonment in Rome. Luke was a physician and probably a Gentile. [Colossians 4:10-14] Tradition says that he was from Syrian Antioch, never married, and died at the age of 84.

This Gospel was written while Luke was in Rome, before he wrote Acts. Since there's no mention in either book of the destruction of Jerusalem and the Temple in AD 70, and since nothing that happened after AD 62 is mentioned in Acts, both books were most likely written around AD 59–62. Luke clearly wrote for a Gentile audience since he explains many Jewish customs and substitutes Greek names for Hebrew ones.

Both Luke and Acts are dedicated to an unknown person named Theophilus, which in Greek means "friend of God" and was a common name among Jews living outside of Israel. Scholars think that Theophilus may have been a sponsor who financed the publication of Luke's writings. Luke addresses him as "most excellent" in the same way Roman governors are addressed in Acts 23:25; 24:2; and 26:25.

Matthew portrayed Jesus as the long-expected Messiah and King. Mark portrayed him as a servant. John portrayed him as God's Son. And Luke portrayed him as the "Son of Man," a title Jesus commonly used to refer to himself, and an allusion to Daniel 7:13-14. This was not understood by the Jews to be a messianic title, and Jesus probably used it because:

1) It didn't have the political overtones they associated with other Messianic titles.

2) If someone were to recognize the allusion to Daniel 7:13-14, they would realize he was claiming these things about himself: He came from Heaven, he was worthy to enter into the very presence of God, God gave him authority, glory, and power over all people and nations, he is to be submitted to in worship, and his Kingdom will never end.

While making it clear that Jesus is much more than a mere man, this Gospel emphasizes his human nature. Luke tells us more about Jesus' feelings than the other gospels, and about the way he honors women, and his concern for the poor, people of low status, sinners, and outcasts. He also tells about Jesus' prayer life and his total dependence on God the Father. While Jesus' genealogy in Matthew shows he is legally descended from King David in the line of Israel's kings, the genealogy in Luke shows his human line through his mother, Miriam, all the way back to Adam, the first man.

The theme of this gospel is summarized in chapter 15 and also in verse 19:10: "The Son of Man came to save those who are lost." Of the four gospel accounts, this one has the most complete biography of Jesus' life (half of the stories in it are not found in any other gospel) and is most like a modern historical account.

Kenneth E. Bailey outlines an interesting chiastic **A** structure to a large section of Luke, usually called "The Travel Narrative," but Bailey calls it "The Jerusalem Document" **B** (below). In such chiastic structures, the most important point is usually in the middle, or at the two ends. This chiasm shows that Luke carefully crafted the organization of his gospel. **C**

A The term "chiastic" [kī ăstĭk] comes from the name of the Greek letter χ (chi [kī] which rhymes with "sky") because of its symmetric shape. There are numerous chiasticly structured passages throughout the New Testament that are often pointed out by commentaries.

B From "Jacob & the Prodigal" by Kenneth E. Bailey, pg 47. Also in greater detail in "Poet & Peasant" by Kenneth E. Bailey, pgs 80-82.

C Many chiastic structures also exist in Luke's reporting of Jesus' parables that can only be seen in the Greek or in a very literal translation. I highly recommend Kenneth E. Bailey's excellent book, "Poet & Peasant and Through Peasant Eyes" (combined edition) which shows the chiastic structures of some of the parables in Luke in detail. He explains how recognition of chiastic structures helps to reveal the intended point of a passage. He also brings in-depth cultural knowledge and extensive scholarship to bear on interpreting them.

1

Luke's Purpose in Writing His Gospel

1-3 Most excellent Theophilus,

The following narrative is about Jesus' life and ministry from his birth until he ascended into Heaven. These accounts have been handed down in the writings and teachings of actual eyewitnesses, who themselves became guardians and reciters of the message about the Messiah. **A** Many others have tried their best to write about the Messiah's life and the things he did. So it seemed appropriate to assemble a logical and orderly account of these events for you, since I have thoroughly investigated these matters from beginning to end. 4 My aim is for you to recognize the reliability and truth of the things you have been taught.

An Angel Foretells the Birth and Significance of John the Baptizer

5 When Herod the Great was king over the Roman province of Judea in Israel, there lived a Jewish priest named Zechariah who was a member of Abijah's division of priests, eighth of the 24 divisions. **B** His wife Elizabeth was also a descendant of Aaron, being the daughter of a priest. **C** ❖ *This story begins about 7-6 BC. Due to an error when our calendar was created, the birth of Jesus took place prior to 4 BC.* ➤ 6 God considered them to be righteous because they conscientiously followed all the requirements of Yahweh's Torah teachings. **D** ❖ *"Righteous" in this context doesn't mean that they were perfect, but that God accepted them as his people because they believed what God said in the Scriptures was true, they trusted in his promises, and they were faithful in following his ways.* ➤ 7 But they

---

A 1:1-3 "Messiah" is an English transliteration of a Hebrew word meaning "Anointed One," and was the title of the Savior that God promised to send to his people. The word "Christ" is a transliteration of a Greek word that means exactly the same as Messiah. Both are titles, comparable in meaning to "God's Chosen Savior King." "Messiah" is used in this interpretation because to English speakers it sounds more like a title than "Christ," which many people today incorrectly think is a name.

B 1:5a Abijah was the name of the first leader of this priestly division. Every priest belonged to one of 24 divisions, [1 Chronicles 24:10] and each division had its appointed

week (two Sabbaths and the intervening week) to serve in turn at the Temple in Jerusalem. So each division and priest served for eight days in the Temple about every six months.

C 1:5b All priests are descended from the first High Priest, Aaron, the brother of Moses, of the tribe of Levi.

D 1:6 Yahweh is the Hebrew name of God used in the Hebrew Scriptures. He revealed this name to Moses and it means "I am." This name appears over 6000 times in the original Hebrew Scriptures, but has been removed from most English translations and replaced by "the LORD." In the past, this name has sometimes been incorrectly transliterated into English as "Jehovah."

were childless because Elizabeth was barren, and they were both quite elderly by the time of this story.

8 During one of the weeks that Zechariah was on duty in the Temple, 9 he was chosen by lot for the honor of burning incense on the altar in the Temple's "Holy Place." ❖ *A priest could be chosen for this honor only once in his life, and they believed that God directed the result of the lottery.* ➤ 10 While he was burning the incense, people were gathered outside in the Temple courtyard praying. ❖ *This was one of the regular daily prayer times.* ➤

11 Suddenly, an angel appeared to Zechariah, standing to the right of the incense altar. 12 When Zechariah saw him, he was startled and frightened. 13 But the angel said, "Don't be afraid, Zechariah! God has heard your prayer that he send the Messiah soon, and he is answering it. As part of his plan, your wife will have a son whom you must name John. 14 Many will rejoice with you because of his birth, 15 for this child is important in Yahweh's plan. You must instruct him to never drink wine or other alcoholic beverages, ❖ *This signified that his life was dedicated to serving God. See Numbers 6:3 on the vow of a Nazirite.* ➤ and he will be filled with the Holy Spirit even before he is born. 16 When he is grown, his preaching will convince many Israelites to turn away from their sins and be reconciled to Yahweh, their God. 17 John will preach with the power of the Holy Spirit like the prophet Elijah did long ago. Then, people will see Yahweh himself. ❖ *This refers to Jesus.* ➤ **He will reconcile children with their fathers,** [Malachi 4:5-6] and lead those who've been rebelling against God to repent and live righteously. He will prepare the Jews, who are chosen by God, to recognize and receive the Messiah when he comes."

18 Zechariah skeptically replied, "I don't see how that's possible, since I'm old and my wife is well past her childbearing years."

19 The angel replied, "My name is Gabriel, **A** and I've come from the very presence of God. He sent me to bring you this good news. 20 But since you don't believe it, as a sign that what I've said is true, you will be deaf and unable to speak from now until it happens. For God will bring it about in his perfect timing."

21 Meanwhile, the people were waiting **B** for Zechariah in the Temple courtyard, wondering why he was taking so long in the sanctuary. 22 When he finally came out, he was unable to speak. But they understood that he had seen a vision while burning the incense, because he communicated this with gestures. His inability to speak continued, 23 and when his week of service at the Temple was finished, he returned to his hometown in the hill country of Judea.

24 Sometime after this, his wife Elizabeth became pregnant. But for five months she stayed secluded so people wouldn't laugh at her if she said she was pregnant. ❖ *They wouldn't believe it possible because of her age, but after five months, the fact would be clear.* ➤ 25 When she finally did go out, she said, "Look what the Lord has done! He has enabled me to become pregnant! He has blessed me and removed the shame that people ascribed to me because I've been childless!" ❖ *Jews of that time commonly and inaccurately believed the inability to have children was punishment from God for some secret sin.* ➤

The Angel Gabriel Appears to Miriam

26 During the sixth month of Elizabeth's pregnancy, God sent the angel Gabriel to the village of Nazareth in Galilee. ❖ *Galilee Province is in northern Israel, to the north and west of Lake Galilee.* ➤ 27 He took a message to a virgin named Miriam **C** who was engaged to a man named Yosef, a descendant of King David. ❖ *David was Israel's second king and the father of King Solomon. They were the two most famous kings of Israel. David lived about 1000 BC and it was prophesied that the Messiah would be one of his descendants. For the story of his*

A 1:19 "Gabriel" is variously translated as meaning "God is Mighty," "strength/power of God," "strongman of God," "hero of God," "God's able-bodied one," "God is my strength." Gabriel is one of seven archangels, according to Jewish tradition, though he is not explicitly called an archangel anywhere in the Bible.

B 1:21 They were waiting for him to and bless them using the words in Numbers 6:24-26, known as the Aaronic blessing.

C 1:27 Today, she is commonly known as "Mary," the mother of Jesus. But the name she really went by was the Hebrew name "Miriam" from which "Mary" is derived.

life see 1 Samuel chapters 16—31, all of 2 Samuel, 1 Kings chapters 1—2 and 1 Chronicles chapters 10—29. ➤

28 The angel appeared to her and said, "Greetings, Miriam! Yahweh is with you and has chosen you to receive a special honor."

29 Miriam was flustered by the angel's words and wondered what this appearance might mean. 30 So the angel reassured her, "Don't be frightened, because God has chosen to favor you. 31 Listen carefully! You will become pregnant and have a son. When he is born, you must name him 'Jesus.' 32 He will be a great man and will also be God's Son. Yahweh will establish him as the rightful king and heir of his ancestor David. 33 He will reign over all of Israel forever, and his Kingdom will never come to an end." [2 Samuel 7:12-13, 16; Isaiah 9:7]

34 Miriam replied, "I'm not married and I'm still a virgin. So how will this happen?"

35 The angel answered, "The Holy Spirit will come on you and God's power will cover you, making you pregnant. Therefore, the baby will be holy and will be God's Son. 36 As a sign that what I say is true, your relative Elizabeth is now six months pregnant, even though she is elderly and has been barren all her life. 37 For nothing is impossible for God, and everything I've told you will happen."

38 Miriam replied, "I'm the Lord's willing servant and submit to his will as you've revealed it." Then the angel left. ❖ *No one would believe Miriam's story about how she became pregnant. By humbly accepting this role, she was willing to accept public disgrace and rejection for the sake of God's purposes. Gossip about Jesus being illegitimate followed him his entire life. Illegitimacy was not a minor matter in that time and place, as it is in America today. The burden of shame she and her child would carry would be hard to bear. For more details about Jesus' birth not contained in Luke's Gospel, read Matthew 1:18-25 at this point.* ➤

Miriam Visits Elizabeth

39 Soon afterward, Miriam got ready and hurried to the village in the hill country of Judea where Elizabeth lived. 40 When she arrived, she entered Zechariah's house and greeted Elizabeth. 41 When Elizabeth heard Miriam's greeting, the baby in her womb kicked hard because the Holy Spirit in the baby recognized the Messiah's presence in Miriam. Then, Elizabeth too was filled with the Holy Spirit 42 who moved her to prophetically exclaim, "God has blessed you more than any other woman in the world! And His blessing will be upon your son! 43 I'm amazed that the mother of my Lord should come to visit someone as unimportant as me! 44 The moment I heard you speak, the baby in my womb jumped for joy. 45 The Lord has greatly blessed you because you believed what his angel told you."

Miriam's Song of Praise

46 Then Miriam said, "I praise the Lord for his greatness. [Psalm 34:2] 47 In my spirit, I rejoice that he is my Savior. [Psalm 35:9] 48 For he has shown me great kindness even though I am no more than a servant. From now until the end of time, people will know that I've been blessed 49 because Almighty God has done this wonderful thing for me. He is holy! 50 **He has compassion on those who fear and worship him in every generation!** [Psalm 103:17] 51 He has demonstrated his power, [Psalm 98:1] scattering the proud and haughty. [Psalm 68:1] 52 He overthrows evil rulers and exalts those who humble themselves before him. [Job 5:11; 12:19; Psalm 136:18] 53 **He satisfies the hungry and needy with all they need,** but strips the wicked of their wealth. [Psalm 68:6; 107:9] 54-55 He has come to help his chosen people, Israel, fulfilling his promise to our ancestors that he would demonstrate his mercy to Abraham and all his descendants forever." ❖ *See Genesis 17:7 about the promise God gave Abraham. Also Psalm 89:19-29; 132:10-12, 1/-18.* ➤

56 Miriam stayed with Elizabeth about three months until John was born, and then returned to Nazareth.

The Birth of John the Baptizer

57 Now, Elizabeth's due date arrived and her son was born. 58 Her neighbors and relatives heard how Yahweh had finally blessed her with a child and they all celebrated with her.

59 When the baby was a week old, their relatives and friends came for the circumcision ceremony required by the Teachings of

Moses to mark him as belonging to God. ❖ See Leviticus 12:3 about circumcision on the 8th day. ➤ They intended to name him Zechariah after his father, 60 but his mother said, "No. His name will be John." ❖ In Hebrew, his name was "Yochanan." ➤

61 They protested, "But you don't have any relatives named John!" 62 So they made gestures asking Zechariah what he wanted the boy's name to be.

63 Zechariah motioned for something to write with and wrote, "His name is John," surprising everyone. 64 As soon as he wrote this, he was able to speak and hear again and began to praise and thank God. 65 A sense of awe and fear came upon all the neighbors, and news of these events spread throughout the hill country of Judea. 66 Everyone who heard about it wondered, "What will this child become?" For it was evident that Yahweh's favor, direction, and power was with him.

Zechariah's Prophecy

67 Then, Zechariah was filled with the Holy Spirit and began to prophesy about the Messiah and his son John. He said, 68 "We must praise the Lord God of Israel! For he is coming to set his people free from the power of their enemies. 69 He is raising up a mighty Savior among the descendants of his exalted servant King David. 70 God promised through his holy prophets long ago 71 that he would save us from the power of those who hate us. [Psalm 106:10] 72 He did this to demonstrate his compassion to our ancestors, just as he promised in his Holy Covenant. ❖ A covenant is a special binding agreement between two parties. The covenant referred to here is the Abrahamic covenant. [Genesis 12:1-3; 15:1-5, 7, 13-16, 18-21; 17:1-16; 22:16-18] ➤ 73 He made this oath to our ancestor Abraham 74 that we, his descendants, would be rescued from the power of our enemies so we would be able to worship and serve him without fear of persecution, 75 and so we might live righteously and holy in God's presence our entire lives."

76 Then, Zechariah prophesied about the infant John, "My son, you will be God's prophet, and you will go ahead of the Lord God, telling people that they must prepare themselves for his coming. [Malachi 3:1; Isaiah 40:3; Luke 1:17] 77 You will tell his people that they can be saved from his judgment through their sins being forgiven 78 because our God is tender and compassionate. He is sending the Messiah to us, who will be like a sunrise from Heaven that dispels the spiritual darkness. The Messiah comes 79 to shine on those who are living in the darkness of their sin, under the threat of eternal death. He will reveal the way to be saved and how to live in peace with God." [Isaiah 9:2]

80 So the child John grew spiritually strong, and when he became a man, he went to live in the wilderness areas of Judea until the day he appeared in public as a prophet, about 30 years after his birth.

2

The Birth of Jesus

1 Around the time John was born, the Roman emperor, Caesar Augustus, decreed that everyone in the empire was to be registered in a census for tax purposes. 2 This was the first such census ordered by Rome and happened while Quirinius was governor of the Roman province of Syria. 3 Every man had to go to his ancestral hometown in order to register.

4 So Yosef set out from his home in Nazareth in Galilee and traveled south to the town of Bethlehem in Judea. ❖ Bethlehem is 63 miles south of Nazareth, near Jerusalem, but the trip was probably longer since Jews usually went around Samaria Province which is between Galilee and Judea. They did this because Jews and Samaritans hated each other. It would be a long and difficult trip for a woman near the end of her pregnancy. ➤ Bethlehem, called "David's town," had been King David's home ❖ about a thousand years previously ➤ and Yosef was his direct descendant. 5 He took Miriam with him to be registered because she was his legal wife and was pregnant. ❖ But their marriage was not yet consummated. [Matthew 1:25] 6 While they were in Bethlehem, 7 her first child, a son, was born. They wrapped him in strips of cloth ❖ as was the custom ➤ but his cradle was only a feeding tough for animals. They were staying in a stable behind a relative's house because there was no space

for them in the guest room. ❖ *The word κατάλυμα [kataluma] traditionally translated here as "inn" can alternatively mean "guest room." (The word usually used for a public "inn" is πανδοχεῖον [pandocheion] as in Luke 10:34. Some scholars think Bethlehem was too small to have a commercial inn.) Since Bethlehem was Joseph's ancestral home, the natural place for him to seek lodging would be with relatives. Typical first-century Jewish homes were one-room buildings with a "guest room" on the flat roof. Animals often slept inside the house or in an attached stable, which a second-century tradition says, in this case, was a cave behind a private house.* ➤

Angels Announce the Messiah's Birth

8 That same night, there were shepherds looking after their sheep in the fields outside Bethlehem. ❖ *Despite the traditional celebration of Christmas on the 25th of December—which was probably started sometime in the 4th century—it was generally too cold for shepherds to have their flocks out at night from November through March. There are many opinions about what month Jesus was born, but there is no way to know for sure.* ➤ **9** An angel suddenly appeared to them, and the glorious light of Yahweh's presence that was shining all around the angel terrified them. **10** But the angel said, "Don't be afraid! I've come to bring you wonderful news that will cause all Israelites to rejoice. **11** Today, a Savior was born in David's town. This baby is the long-promised Messiah who is also Yahweh himself. **12** This is how you can recognize him and be sure that I'm telling the truth. You will find the baby wrapped in strips of cloth, lying in an animals' feeding trough in a stable."

13 Then suddenly. a huge army of angels appeared with the first one and they all praised God, saying, **14** "All honor and glory belong to God who lives in the highest Heaven! Let there be shalom here on earth among all those whom God chooses to favor!" ❖ *Shalom means peace, calmness, success, comfort, contentment, safety, health, wholeness, prosperity, integrity, well-being, and good relationships with God and people.* ➤

15 Then the angels left, returning to Heaven. The shepherds said to each other, "Let's go to Bethlehem right away to find this newborn Messiah that the Lord has told us about through his angel."

16 So they went as quickly as they could and found Miriam and Yosef in a stable, with the baby lying in a feeding trough just as the angel had described it. **17** When the shepherds saw the baby, they told Yosef and Miriam and others in Bethlehem what the angel had said about him. **18** Everyone who heard their story was amazed by it. ❖ *God announced his Son's birth to shepherds, who were extremely low on the social scale and were considered to be unreliable witnesses in court.* ➤ **19** Later, Miriam often recalled their story and her own angelic encounter and thought about them. **20** The shepherds returned to their sheep, praising God because of all the things they had heard from the angels and had confirmed with their eyes.

The Baby Messiah Is Named

21 When the baby was a week old, it was time for him to be circumcised according to the Torah's requirement, thus marking him as an heir of God's promise to Abraham. At that time, they named him "Jesus," which means "Yahweh saves," following the instructions the angel gave Miriam before he was conceived. **A**

Baby Jesus Is Dedicated in the Temple

22 Forty days after Jesus' birth, it was time for Miriam to undergo the ceremony for "ritual purification after childbirth" according to the requirements in the Torah. So at the same time, they took the infant to the Temple in Jerusalem to dedicate him to serve Yahweh. **23** In doing this, they were obeying the command which says, **"Every firstborn child that is male must be dedicated to serve Yahweh."** [Exodus 13:2, 12, 15] **24** They also offered the sacrifice for ritual purification after childbirth required by the

---

A 2:21 "Yeshua" [Yeh-SHOO-uh] is his name in Hebrew. The New Testament was written in Greek, and in that language his name is Ἰησοῦς (Iēsous) [YAY-soos], which written in the Roman alphabet was "Jesus" but was still pronounced [YAY-soos]. Centuries later, the sounds of the letters "j," "e" and "u" changed among English speakers so that in modern English his name came to be pronounced [JEE-zuhz].

Torah, which says, "If a woman can't afford a lamb, she may bring two doves or two pigeons—one for a burnt offering and one for a sin offering." **A** *[Leviticus 12:8]*

25 At that time, an old man named Simeon lived in Jerusalem. He was righteous in God's sight and very devout. He was waiting expectantly for the coming of the Messiah to save the people of Israel, because the Holy Spirit was on him and 26 had told him that he would live to see Yahweh's Messiah with his own eyes. 27 Now the same day that his parents brought Jesus to the Temple to pay for his redemption, the Holy Spirit prompted Simeon to go there too. ❖ *This fulfilled the prophecy in Malachi 3:1 which says, "The Lord, who you seek, will suddenly come to his Temple." ¶ Read Exodus 13:15. Since—according to the Torah—every firstborn male (human son or animal) belonged to Yahweh and was to be sacrificed to him, firstborn sons were presented and dedicated to serve him and then their lives were "redeemed" or "bought back" with an offering of five shekels.* ➤ 28 When Simeon saw the baby, he took him in his arms and praised God, saying, 29 "Lord, you may now allow your servant to die. I'm content because you have fulfilled your promise to me. 30 I've finally seen with my own eyes the Savior you promised, 31 whom you will reveal to all the peoples in this world. 32 He is **a light that will show your way of salvation to Gentiles.** *[Isaiah 42:6; 49:6; 52:10; Acts 13:47]* ❖ *Gentiles are all those who are not Jews.* ➤ He will also bring honor to your chosen people, the descendants of Israel."

33 Jesus' parents were astonished at Simeon's prayer. 34 Then, he prayed that God would bless them and prophesied to Miriam, "This child has been chosen by God. Because of his life, many Israelites will come under God's judgment and many others will be saved. He will be a sign from God that many will oppose and reject. 35 What people really believe about him will be seen in their actions. And what some will do to him will bring you grief as painful as a sword piercing your heart."

36 There was also an old woman there, a prophetess named Anna. ❖ *There had been no major prophets in Israel for the previous 400 years who were sent to the nation as a whole or who wrote Scripture. But during this time, even before Pentecost, God's Holy Spirit caused some people to prophesy on occasion, such as Elizabeth, Zechariah, and Simeon and there was also Anna who was recognized as a prophetess. There may have been others too who were not recorded in the Scriptures.* ➤ Her father was Phanuel of the tribe of Asher. She had been married for seven years when she was young, 37 but had now been a widow for 84 years. ❖ *Or, she was now 84 years old.* ➤ She was almost always in the Temple worshiping with fasting and prayer, both night and day. 38 While Simeon was there with Yosef and Miriam, Anna came up to them and gave thanks to God for sending his Messiah. Later, she continued to speak about the infant Jesus to anyone who was still waiting for the Messiah to save the people of Jerusalem and all of Israel.

Miriam and Yosef Return to Nazareth

39 When Miriam and Yosef had done everything required of them by Yahweh's Torah with regard to their son's birth, they returned to their home village of Nazareth in Galilee. 40 There, the boy grew up and became strong. He also became very wise, and God greatly blessed him.

❖ *For more details of the events that happened while Jesus was an infant that are not contained in Luke's Gospel, read Matthew chapter 2.* ➤

The Boy Jesus in the Temple

41 Jesus' parents traveled together to Jerusalem every year to observe the feast of Passover. ❖ *This begins on the 15th of Nisan on the Jewish calendar, which occurs in March or April and varies because the Jewish calendar is based on the lunar cycle. The Torah required all men who were able to come to Jerusalem for the Passover. See Exodus chapters 12—13 about the first Passover.* ➤ 42 When Jesus was twelve years old, he was old enough to go with them so

---

A 2:24 Contrary to popular tradition, the visit of the wise men (recorded in Mathew chapter 2) didn't occur until much later. This is deduced from the fact that Miriam and Yosef were still poor 40 days after Jesus' birth. When the wise men came, one of the gifts they brought was gold, which would have enabled them to afford a lamb to sacrifice.

the three of them made the pilgrimage to Jerusalem for the feast. 43 Now, when the eight days of the back-to-back Festivals of Passover and Unleavened Bread were over, his parents set out on the journey back to their home in Nazareth. But young Jesus stayed behind in Jerusalem without telling his parents. 44 They were traveling with others from their area and assumed that he was somewhere among the group of travelers. So they walked an entire day before starting to search for him among their relatives and acquaintances in the group. 45 When they didn't find him, they returned to Jerusalem spending the entire next day searching for him. 46 On the following day, they found him in the Temple sitting with Scripture teachers. He was listening to their teaching and asking questions. ❖ *The teachers would also question their students to find out how much they understood about what they had been taught.* ➤ 47 All who heard the answers he gave to the teachers' questions were amazed at his understanding. 48 When his parents saw him there, they were astonished. His mother said, "My son, why did you do this to us? Your father and I have been searching and worrying about you!"

49 Jesus answered, "Why didn't you know where I'd be? Didn't you know that I had to be involved in my Father's affairs?" 50 But they didn't understand what he was talking about. ❖ *Even at the age of 12, Jesus recognized that his true Father was God and there was a special calling on his life. These are his first quoted words and they reveal that even before adulthood he was focused on pursuing his heavenly Father's will. He was fully human and didn't know everything, so he had to learn the way we all do. But because he was sinless, he had a special relationship with God and was in communication with him, for his human spirit was not "dead." Both of his parents knew the angel's message about who he was and heard Simeon's and Anna's prophecies. But time dims memory, even of miraculous events and angelic visitations.* ➤ 51 Then, he went back with them to their home in Nazareth and always obeyed

them. But his mother remembered all the unusual things connected with his birth and childhood and often thought about them. 52 As the years passed, Jesus grew, continued to increase in wisdom, and gained favor with God and the people who knew him. ❖ *There is no further mention of Yosef, and it is presumed by many that he died sometime between Jesus' 12th year and when he began his ministry in his early 30s. Note that even Jesus progressively gained in favor with God as he increased in wisdom (i.e., knowing what God wanted him to do and doing it).* ➤

3

John the Baptizer Prepares God's People to Receive the Messiah

1 After Jesus was an adult, in the 15th year of the reign of the Roman Emperor Tiberius, ❖ *Tiberius became Emperor after Augustus, who is mentioned in Luke 2:1.* ➤ Pontius Pilate was the Roman governor of Judea, Herod Antipas, son of Herod the Great—who was king when Jesus was born *[Matthew 2:1-23]*—ruled the Roman province of Galilee, Herod's brother Philip ruled the Roman provinces of Iturea and Trachonitis northeast of Galilee, and Lysanias ruled the province of Abilene northwest of Damascus. A 2 And Caiaphas was High Priest, although he effectively shared his authority with his father-in-law Annas. ❖ *Annas had been High Priest but was forced out of office by Roman authority. According to the Torah, a High Priest held his position for life. So in the eyes of the Jews, Annas was still the legitimate High Priest.* ➤

It was at this time that God's word of commission came to Zechariah's son, John, while he was living in the wilderness just north of the Dead Sea. 3 In obedience to God's command, John preached all around the area near the Jordan River. He exhorted people to publicly confess their sins and be baptized as a sign of their decision to turn away from their sinful way of life, and then

---

A 3:1 The exact year in our calendar of the 15th year of the reign of Tiberius is not known for certain, but it was in the range of AD 26–29. The titles of Herod Antipas, Philip, and Lysanias were "tetrarch." A tetrarch was a lesser king ruling a partial kingdom under the Roman emperor. King Herod the Great's kingdom was divided after his death and ruled by Roman-appointed tetrarchs. Even though Augustus Caesar had allowed Herod the Great to retain the title of king, Tiberius Caesar was paranoid and refused that title to anyone.

God would forgive them. 4 As he was doing this, he was fulfilling the prophecy that says, "A voice can be heard of someone in the wilderness calling out to God's people, 'Prepare your hearts for the coming of Yahweh. 5 Every sinful valley in your heart must be filled in and every mountain and hill of pride must be leveled. The crooked ways in your life must be made straight and the rough areas made smooth to receive him with proper humility and submission. 6 Then all humanity will see the Messiah who is God's way of salvation.' " [Isaiah 40:3-5]

7 Large crowds came from the cities to see John and to be baptized. But he reproved many of them, saying, "You hypocritical sons of vipers! ❖ *See the notes at Matthew 3:7, which also says this was directed at Pharisees and Sadducees.* ➤ I find it hard to believe you are finally admitting that you, like everyone else, need to repent and turn from your sins in order to escape God's righteous wrath and judgment! 8 Well, don't think that getting baptized without genuinely repenting will do you any good at all! True repentance will be demonstrated in the way you live. So don't deceive yourselves by thinking, 'We're saved because Abraham is our ancestor, so we are automatically God's favored people.' ❖ *This was the common assumption of many Jews.* ➤ I assure you, God could make righteous descendants for Abraham from these stones. He doesn't need you to fulfill his plans and promises! 9 God's judgment ax is poised at the roots of his trees ❖ *i.e., the Jews* ➤ and every tree that doesn't bear good fruit as a result of true repentance he will cut down and throw in Hell's fire!" [Matthew 3:10; 7:19] ❖ *See the note at Matthew 3:10.* ➤

10 So the crowds asked him, "What should we do to show that we've repented?"

11 He answered, "Live unselfishly like this: Whoever has two coats must share with someone who has none. And whoever has food must share it too." ❖ *This verse has major implications for all but the poorest of American believers. Yet very few perceive their own failure to follow it, and of the few who do understand the implications, even fewer are obedient. And most leaders do not teach on this topic for fear of becoming very unpopular. See also Luke 12:48b; 16:9-13; the note at 19:26; and 1 Timothy 6:6-10, especially verse 8, and the note at verse 9.* ➤

12 Some tax collectors—the very dregs of Jewish society—also came to be baptized. They asked, "Rabbi, what should we do to show our repentance?"

13 John answered, "Don't steal by collecting more than your Roman masters require."

14 Some Jewish soldiers also asked, "And what about us? What should we do?"

John answered, "Don't use your authority to threaten people with violence or false accusations in order to extort money. Instead, be content with your legitimate pay."

15 Now, the Jews had been waiting for the Messiah to come and John's preaching had raised their expectations. Many wondered if he was the Messiah himself. 16 John realized what people were saying and addressed the issue by declaring, "I only baptize you with water. But the Messiah—whose authority and power far exceeds mine—is coming soon. He is so much greater than me that I'm not even worthy to be a servant who would untie his sandals. He will baptize **A** you in the Holy Spirit—who will purify you like fire purifies silver. ❖ *See the note at Matthew 3:11.* ➤ 17 The Messiah will come with his winnowing pitchfork **B** of judgment, separating the righteous from the wicked just like people separate wheat from worthless chaff, and will clear the threshing floor of this world of all worthless chaff. He will gather the righteous 'wheat' in his barn in Heaven, but the wicked 'chaff' he will burn in Hell's eternal fire." ❖ *John prophesied this about Jesus but didn't understand that it described his second coming. So when Jesus failed to fulfill this part of his prophecy, John started to wonder if Jesus really was the Messiah. [Luke 7:18-23] ¶ John and Jesus both taught that there is a real Hell and that many will be condemned to eternal punishment there. People who say that God would never send anyone to Hell are contradicting the clear teaching of Scripture. Their claim is mere wishful thinking.* ➤

A 3:16 The word "baptize" is an English transliteration of βαπτίζω (baptizō) which means "to wash" or "to immerse."
B 3:17 A winnowing pitchfork was used to toss wheat into the air where the wind would blow the inedible dry outer shell of "chaff" away and the heavier grains of wheat would fall to the ground.

18 And in many other ways he warned and exhorted the people as he preached the Good News about God's way of salvation and the coming Messiah. **A**

Herod Imprisons John

19 John also rebuked Herod Antipas, tetrarch over Galilee Province, exhorting him to repent of his adulterous marriage to his brother's wife, Herodias—while his brother still lived—and to repent of other evils he had done. 20 But Herod refused and compounded his sins by having John arrested.

Jesus Is Baptized and Empowered by the Holy Spirit

21 Now one day before John was arrested, Jesus also came to him and was baptized after everyone else. Afterward, while Jesus was praying, the sky appeared to open [Isaiah 64:1] 22 and the Holy Spirit flew down in the visible bodily form of a dove and alighted on him. Then, God's voice thundered out of Heaven, "You are my only Son and I'm very pleased with you."

Jesus' Genealogy

23 When Jesus started his public ministry, he was about thirty years old. He was the legal son of Yosef, and it was assumed that he was also his natural son.

Now this is Jesus' line of descent going back in time:

Heli
24 Matthat
Levi
Melchi
Jannai
Joseph
25 Mattathias
Amos
Nahum
Esli
Naggai
26 Maath
Mattathias
Semein

Josech
Joda
27 Joanan
Rhesa
Zerubbabel
Shealtial
Neri
28 Melchi
Addi
Cosam
Elmadam
Er
29 Joshua
Eliezer
Jorim
Matthat
Levi
30 Simeon
Judah
Joseph
Jonam
Eliakim
31 Melea
Menna
Mattatha
Nathan
King David ❖ *who lived about 1000 BC.* ➤
32 Jesse
Obed
Boaz ❖ *See Ruth chapters 2—4 for the story of Boaz.* ➤
Salmon
Nahshon
33 Amminadab
Ram
Hezron
Perez
Judah ❖ *4th of the twelve sons of Jacob whose descendants became the tribes of Israel* ➤
34 Jacob ❖ *whom God renamed "Israel."* ➤
Isaac ❖ *See Genesis 17:19-21 and 21:1—28:9 for the story of Isaac.* ➤
Abraham ❖ *See Genesis 11:26—25:11 for the story of Abraham who lived about 2000 BC.* ➤
Terah
Nahor
35 Serug

A 3:18 The word "Gospel," in the literal text, simply means "good news." But in the New Testament, it particularly means "the Good News about God's way of saving people by their believing and following Jesus." In this interpretation, "Gospel" is usually rendered as "Good News" with capital letters.

Reu
Peleg
Eber
Shelah
36 Cainan
Arphaxad
Shem
Noah ❖ *See Genesis 5:28—9:28*
for the story of Noah. ➤
Lamech
37 Methuselah
Enoch
Jared
Mahalaleel
Cainan
38 Enos
Seth
Adam ❖ *See Genesis 1:26—5:5*
for the story of Adam. ➤
and Adam was the son of God,
   created in his image.

❖ *In genealogies of this time, not every person in the line was mentioned. To say a person was the "son of" someone merely meant he was a descendant, and only the more prominent people in the line would normally be mentioned. Jewish genealogical records were kept in the Temple in Jerusalem and could be inspected there before its destruction in AD 70. After that, no Jew was able to officially prove his ancestry. Since the Messiah was prophesied to be a descendant of King David, he had to make his claim before the Temple's destruction to be able to prove his ancestry. Some scholars believe the genealogy in Luke shows his biological descent through his mother Miriam's line. This genealogy deviates from the one recorded by Matthew in the generations after King David, which shows him descended from David's son Nathan. The genealogy in Matthew shows his legal descent as the son of Yosef, descended through Solomon in the royal line of David, demonstrating his legitimate claim to David's throne.* ➤

4

Jesus Undergoes a Trial of Temptation

1 Now from his baptism onward, Jesus was filled with the Holy Spirit. And the Spirit led him away from the Jordan River into the unpopulated and dangerous Judean Desert 2 to be tempted by Satan. He remained there 40 days, all that time being tempted by Satan but never succumbing to sin. He ate nothing during that time, so at the end of that period he was hungry.

3 Then, Satan appeared to him and said, "Since **A** you are God's Son, why don't you simply command this stone to become bread?" ❖ *This temptation was to use God's power for his own needs apart from any direction from his Father. Jesus only did what his Father told him to do. [John 5:19]* ➤

4 Jesus answered, "No, I won't. God's word says, '**The way for a person to have true life is not by eating food, but by obeying Yahweh's every command.**' " *[Deuteronomy 8:3]*

5 Then Satan transported him up to a high place and showed him all the kingdoms of the world in an instant of time. 6 He said, "I can give you the glory of having complete authority over all these kingdoms. For they were all handed over to me by Adam through his disobedience, and I can give them to whomever I wish. ❖ *Satan wasn't lying in saying this. God originally gave humanity authority over this world. But when Adam and Eve sinned, they put themselves under Satan's power, thus giving effective control of this world to him. He was offering Jesus a shortcut to power over the world. Later, when Jesus defeated Satan on the cross by allowing himself to be executed, he restored that authority to redeemed humanity.* ➤ 7 If you will only bow down and submit to me in worship, they will be yours to rule." ❖ *It was Satan's pride and desire to be like God that caused him to rebel in the first place. To have God's Son bow down and submit to him in worship would enable him to claim victory over God.* ➤

8 But Jesus answered, "No, I won't. God's word commands, '**You must only submit yourself in worship and service to Yahweh, who is your God.**' " *[Deuteronomy 6:13]* ❖ *"No, I won't," is not in the actual text of Jesus' replies, but it is clearly implied.* ➤

9 Then Satan transported him to Jerusalem onto the highest place of the Temple, overlooking the Kidron valley 450 feet below. He said, "Since you are God's Son,

---

A 4:3 The word εἰ (ei) is a conjunction that has a range of meanings. It's often translated here as "if," but since common demons clearly knew he was God's Son (e.g., Luke 4:34) it's highly unlikely that Satan didn't know this fact or was suggesting that it wasn't true. So translating this word as "since" makes more sense.

prove it to the people by jumping down from here. 10 The Scriptures say that you won't be harmed because 'God will command his angels to take care of you and guard you from harm. 11 They will carry you in their arms to prevent even your foot from scraping against a stone.' " *[Psalm 91:11-12]* ❖ *Satan easily quotes and twists Scripture for his own purposes.* ➤

12 Jesus said, "No, I won't. God's word also commands, 'Do not deliberately test the patience and promises of Yahweh, your God.' " *[Deuteronomy 6:16]*

13 After Satan finished trying every kind of temptation on Jesus without success, he went away, waiting for an opportune time to try again.

Jesus Starts His Public Ministry in Galilee

14 Then Jesus returned to Galilee, empowered for ministry by the Holy Spirit. He began doing miracles, and news about him spread throughout the region. 15 He also began his teaching ministry in the synagogues and was praised by all who heard him.

Jesus Is Rejected in Nazareth

16 Now in the course of his itinerant ministry, Jesus came to Nazareth where he had been raised as a child. As was his practice on the Sabbath, ❖ *i.e., Saturday* ➤ he went to the local synagogue. He stood in front to read from the Scriptures 17 and was handed the scroll of the prophet Isaiah which he had requested. He opened it and read from the place where it says, 18 "The Spirit of Yahweh is upon me, for he has anointed me to preach the Good News of God's way of salvation to the poor. He has sent me to proclaim the way of freedom for all who are bound as slaves to sin, to enable those who are spiritually blind to see God's truth, to

free those who are oppressed by the physical and emotional consequences of sin, 19 and to announce that the time has arrived when Yahweh will show undeserved favor to his people and save them." *[Isaiah 61:1-2]*

20 After reading that, Jesus rolled up the scroll, handed it back to the assistant, and sat down to teach. Everyone had their eyes fixed on him to listen to his commentary. 21 He began by saying, "The prophecy in the Scripture you just heard was fulfilled in me today while I was reading it." 22 The people were amazed at his elegant manner of speaking, yet they all were indignant **A** at what they thought was his presumption. They said to each other, "Who does he think he is? He's only Yosef's boy! We've known him all his life!" ❖ *In many cultures, people are expected to remain in the class, station, or occupation into which they were born. Jesus was known to them as the son of the local carpenter. They considered his claim to being the fulfillment of prophecy to be presumptuous and offensive.* ➤

23 So Jesus said to them, "I expect you would like to quote the proverb, 'Doctor, prove your ability by healing yourself!' and then say, 'Demonstrate the kinds of things we've heard you supposedly did in Capernaum. If you want us to believe you, do the same kinds of things here, where you belong.'

24 "But instead, I will quote you the saying, 'No prophet is accepted as such in his hometown.' ❖ *Jesus implicitly claimed to be a prophet.* ➤

25 "And so I tell you, in the prophet Elijah's time, there was no rain for three and a half years—resulting in severe famine everywhere in Israel. But even though there were many needy widows in Israel, 26 God didn't send him to any of them. Rather, he sent him to a pagan widow in the

---

A 4:22 The word μαρτυρέω (martureō) translated "indignant" literally means "to bear witness to." It can be understood in the sense "to praise," and is usually translated this way in this verse to indicate that they spoke well of him. But it can also mean "to bear witness against." The reaction of the people was uniformly either positive or negative (since they "all" spoke of him in whichever way it was). The accounts in Matthew 13:53-58 and Mark 6:1-6 report a uniformly negative reaction, but the occasion reported in those two gospels is likely at a much later time than the one reported by Luke (though we can't be sure). Since the reaction of the people in the later part of Luke's account is negative, and they are questioning the appropriateness of what he said because he is only the carpenter's son, and since Jesus responds to their reaction with reproof (verses 23-27), it seems the negative sense fits better. Also, if their reaction is interpreted as positive (as it's traditionally translated), then it appears that Jesus was deliberately trying to provoke them—which seems unlikely—rather than responding to their rejection of him.

Phoenician town of Zarephath on the coast near the city of Sidon. *[1 Kings. 17:8-16]* 27 Again, in the prophet Elisha's time, there were many lepers in Israel but he didn't heal any of them. He only healed Naaman, a pagan from Syria." *[2 Kings. 5:1-14]* ❖ *By these examples, Jesus was saying that their unbelief and rejection of him made them unworthy, so they would be passed over from receiving miraculous help in favor of pagan Gentiles, just like their ancestors had been passed over in the times of Elijah and Elisha because of their unbelief and unfaithfulness. They fully understood what he implied as is seen by their reaction.* ➤

28 When the people heard this, they were furious. 29 They became a mob and drove him outside of town to the edge of a cliff on the hill where the town was built, intending to push him over the edge. 30 But because it wasn't yet his appointed time to die, Jesus calmly turned and walked through the middle of the crowd and went on his way.

Jesus Expels Demons from a Man in the Capernaum Synagogue

31 Jesus traveled down to Capernaum on the north shore of Lake Galilee. On the Sabbath, he taught in the synagogue there 32 and they marveled at his teaching because—unlike the Scripture teachers who always quoted other authorities—he spoke from personal authority. *[Matthew 7:29; Mark 1:22]* 33 While he was there, a man entered the synagogue who was defiled with demons. He yelled at Jesus, 34 "Arrrgh! Get out of here, Jesus of Nazareth! Just leave us alone! **A** You've come to destroy us! I know who you are! You are God's special Holy One!"

35 But Jesus rebuked the demons, "Be silent and come out of him!" They made the man convulse on the floor in front of every-one, then came out without injuring him.

36 The people were awed and exclaimed, "His words have power! He simply commanded the demons and they left!" ❖ *Luke often uses direct quotes in his narrative to highlight people's responses to Jesus.* ➤ 37 So reports about him spread throughout the area.

Jesus Heals Simon's Mother-In-Law

38 Afterward, Jesus left the synagogue and went to Simon's house for the Sabbath meal. When he arrived, he learned that Simon's mother-in-law had a high fever, and her family asked him to heal her. 39 So he went to where she was lying, stood over her, and rebuked the fever. It left, and she immediately got up and began to serve them the meal.

40 When the Sabbath was over at sunset, everyone in town who was sick with any kind of ailment was brought to him. ❖ *Work, such as carrying the sick, wasn't allowed on the Sabbath.* ➤ He laid his hands on them and healed every one of them. 41 He also expelled demons from many. They would start to yell, "You are God's Son!" But he rebuked them and didn't allow them to speak, because they knew he was the Messiah and he didn't want it openly proclaimed. ❖ *Jesus would not want the testimony of demons to be the basis of people viewing him as the Messiah. Also, he knew that if he openly and unambiguously claimed to be the Messiah at that time, many people and most of the religious leaders would immediately reject him and actively oppose him— because their expectations about the Messiah did not line up with what he intended to do. But if he did not precipitate an immediate decision from people, after his resurrection many more of them would be open to believing he was the Messiah than if he proclaimed it beforehand.* ➤

Jesus Preaches Throughout Judea

42 At dawn, Jesus left Capernaum and went to find a place where he could be alone to pray. When they discovered that he was gone, a crowd went searching for him. When they found him, they tried to keep him from leaving their village. 43 But he told them, "I have to proclaim the Good News about God's Kingdom in other towns too because that's what he sent me to do."

44 So he traveled throughout the prov-inces of Galilee and Judea preaching in the synagogues.

A 4:34 Literally, "What to me to you," the sense of hostility that's implied by this Greek idiom is rendered here, rather than the more literal "What have you to do with us?"

5

Jesus Calls His First Followers

1 One day, when Jesus stood on the shore of Lake Galilee, throngs of people were crowding in close to hear him teach God's message. 2 He noticed two empty fishing boats pulled up on the shore and the fishermen who owned them were washing their nets. 3 So Jesus got into the boat belonging to Simon and asked him to put the boat out a little from shore so people could see and hear him more easily. He did so, and Jesus sat down and taught the crowd from the boat.

4 When he finished teaching, he told Simon, "Move the boat out into deep water and let your nets down to catch some fish."

5 Simon replied, "Master, we worked hard all night and caught nothing. But since you command it, we will let the nets down." ❖ *Most effective net fishing is done at night.* ➤ 6 When they did, they caught a huge number of fish. They were so heavy that the nets started to break, 7 so they signaled to their partners in another boat for help. They came out and together filled the boats with so many fish that both started to sink. 8 When Simon saw this, he recognized that Jesus was a prophet. Prostrating himself before Jesus, he exclaimed, "You should leave me sir! For I'm a sinful man and not worthy to be in your presence!"

9-10 For he, along with his fishing partners, James and John—the sons of Zebedee—and all their other companions were astounded at the huge number of fish they had caught. Then Jesus said to him, "Don't be afraid! From now on you will be 'catching' people and bringing them to me, instead of catching fish."

11 After they had pulled their boats up on shore, Simon, James, and John left their old profession and became followers of Jesus. ❖ *"Followers" is usually translated "disciples." It means they were students and apprentices. Jesus eventually had many disciples, not just twelve. Anyone today who believes that Jesus is the Messiah and follows his teachings is his disciple.* ➤

Jesus Wants to Heal

12 One day, a man covered with leprous sores was in the same town as Jesus. When he saw Jesus, he prostrated himself before him and begged, "Sir, I know you can heal me if you want to."

13 Jesus reached out and touched him, saying, "Of course I want to. I command you to be healed!" Instantly his leprosy was gone. ❖ *Touching a leper made Jesus ritually unclean and would require him to go through purification rituals before he could worship. But affirming the leper—who was an "untouchable"—was more important to Jesus than the inconvenience.* ➤ 14 Jesus ordered him not to tell anyone about the healing, and then said, "Go immediately to a priest so he can examine you as the Torah requires. [Leviticus 14:1-32] Make all the required sacrificial offerings so the priest will be able to publicly announce that you have been healed and are ritually clean." ❖ *Jesus often commanded people not to talk about his healing them. He healed out of compassion, but the notoriety associated with his healing miracles made it difficult to lead any kind of normal life.* ➤

15 Despite the admonition not to talk about it, news about Jesus spread even more, and large crowds were always gathering to hear him teach and to be healed. 16 But even though he had these constant demands placed on him, Jesus frequently made it a priority to slip away by himself into the wilderness to pray. ❖ *Even God's Son required daily time alone with his Heavenly Father. It should be clear that if we desire to know God's will and be used for his purposes, we need such alone time with God even more than Jesus did.* ➤

Jesus Heals a Paralyzed Man
to Prove He Has Authority to Forgive Sin

17 One day, when Jesus was teaching in Galilee, some Pharisees and Scripture teachers were present who had come from Jerusalem and nearly every other town in Judea and Galilee. And Yahweh's power was with Jesus, enabling him to heal. ❖ *This implies that Jesus didn't heal from his own power as God's Son, but from the power of the Holy Spirit.* ➤

18 While he was teaching, some men came carrying a paralyzed man on a stretcher. They wanted to carry him into the

house to set him in front of Jesus to be healed. [19] But because of the crowd in and around the house, they couldn't get inside. So they went around to the outside steps and carried him up onto the house's flat roof. ❖ *The flat roofs of houses in Israel were often used as spare rooms.* ➤

Then they opened a hole in the roof tiles and lowered the man on his stretcher into the center of the house right in front of Jesus. [20] Jesus saw that they had faith in him, so he said to the paralyzed man, "My friend, I declare that your sins are forgiven."

[21] Then the Scripture teachers and the Pharisees said to each other, "How dare this man blaspheme God by claiming he forgives sins made against God himself? Only God can forgive sins!" ❖ *To blaspheme means to talk impiously, irreverently, or disrespectfully about God. Blasphemy was considered a serious sin, punishable by death. [Leviticus 24:16] In this instance, they thought Jesus was presumptuously speaking for God, which was disrespectful of his authority.* ➤

[22] Knowing they thought that only God could forgive sin or heal, Jesus said, "Why are you thinking these things? [23] Which do you think is less likely that I'm able to do— forgive this man's sins or enable him to stand up and walk? You correctly believe that only God has the power to do either of these things. [24] So I will demonstrate that I have power and approval from God to heal in order that you may know for sure that I, the Son of Man, also have his authority to forgive people's sins." Jesus said to the paralyzed man, "I command you to get up, pick up your stretcher, and go home."

[25] Immediately, the man got up, picked up his stretcher, and went home praising God. [26] All the people who witnessed this were astonished and also began to praise God. They were filled with awe and said, "We've seen an incredible thing today!

Jesus Associates with Disreputable People

[27] After this, Jesus went out and noticed a tax collector named Matthew Levi sitting in his tax booth. Jesus said to him, "Come and be my follower." ❖ *Tax collectors were social outcasts because they collaborated with their Roman conquerors, and they also got rich by extorting more than the legal tax from people and pocketing the difference.* ➤ [28] Levi—having heard a lot about Jesus—immediately left behind his lucrative job and everything he owned and began to follow him.

[29] Later, he gave a big party for Jesus and invited all his friends. So there was a large crowd of tax collectors and other disreputable people dining with them. [30] Now, some Pharisees and Scripture teachers who were also Pharisees saw this and complained indignantly to Jesus' other followers, "Why are you polluting yourselves by eating and drinking with tax collectors and other such sinners?" ❖ *They believed that eating with sinners implied approval of their godless way of life and made a person ritually unclean in God's sight.* ➤

[31] But Jesus heard and answered, "A doctor doesn't tend to people who are well. It's the sick who need his attention. [32] In the same way, I didn't come to call righteous people to follow me, but to invite those who know that they are sinners to repent and change their way of life." ❖ *The word "righteous" is used with different senses in the Scriptures. When referring to God, it means sinless perfection. But when used of people, it means someone God has forgiven and accepted into a close relationship with himself. Jesus may have meant that He didn't come to invite righteous people because there are none in the sense of being sinless. He could also mean that those who God accepts as righteous don't need to be invited since they already have a good relationship with him. In any case, the Pharisees and Scripture teachers thought that by legalistically following all of the Torah's teachings they were automatically accepted as righteous by God and that he cared for no other kind of person. But their kind of "self-righteousness" was in fact "unrighteous" in God's view, because they refused to acknowledge their own sin and thus their need for his forgiveness. Such people saw no need of a Savior for themselves. So ironically, it was the social outcasts who had no pride and knew they were sinners who were the most open to responding to Jesus' invitation to repent and follow him.* ➤

Jesus Answers a Question About Fasting

[33] Then they said to Jesus, "The followers of John the Baptizer often fast and pray, as do the Pharisees' followers. But your followers are always eating and drinking and never fast." ❖ *Fasting means going without any food, or without certain foods (usually meat and richer foods), and drinks other than water for a meal or for a longer period of*

time. Its purpose is to discipline the body, to become more sensitive to hearing God, to show seriousness about prayer, to gain spiritual reward [Matthew 6:17-18], or to increase the power released as a result of prayer. See the footnote at Matthew 6:16. [Matthew 17:21; Mark 9:29] ➤

34 To explain that it wasn't appropriate for his followers to fast while he was with them, Jesus replied, "Nobody would suggest that a grooms' friends fast while he is with them at his wedding banquet. **35** But the time will come when I'm taken away from them, and then they will fast." ❖ *Jesus assumed his followers will fast. Do you?* ➤

36 And to explain that the Pharisees' teachings and legalistic fasting couldn't be mixed with his teachings without ruining both, Jesus gave these illustrations, "No one rips a piece of cloth out of a new garment and uses it as a patch on an old one, since that would needlessly ruin the new one and the patch wouldn't even match the old garment's pattern. **37** Also, no one puts new wine into rigid old wineskins since the pressure from the fermenting wine would burst the already-stretched skins. It would ruin the wineskins and spill the wine. **38** New wine must be put into new wineskins. ❖ *Jesus' teaching about how to join God's Kingdom was incompatible with the Pharisees' emphasis on legalistically observing many man-made rules. Their focus was on outward behavior only, while Jesus stressed humility and attitudes of the heart. A person could not follow Jesus' teaching and maintain all the rules the Pharisees taught because their focus would ruin what Jesus was trying to teach. Jesus' teachings were much more than a new patch on the Old Covenant's way of approaching God. It was about an entirely New Covenant.* ➤ **39** It's also hard for someone who has tasted aged wine to desire to drink un-aged new wine because he will think, 'The old wine is better.' " ❖ *Similarly, it was natural that those who followed the Pharisees' teachings and were comfortable with them wouldn't be open to following Jesus' new ways.* ➤

6

Jesus is Master over Sabbath Regulations

1 One Sabbath, **A** while Jesus and his followers were walking through some grain fields, his followers were picking grain, rubbing it in their hands to remove the chaff, and eating it. ❖ *The Torah allowed picking wheat in another man's field by hand while walking along, but not cutting it with a sickle. [Deuteronomy 23:25] So they were not stealing.* ➤ **2** Some Pharisees who saw them do this, accused them, "Why are you disobeying the Torah's command by working on the Sabbath?" ❖ *They considered picking the grain to be the work of harvesting and rubbing them in their hands the work of threshing. See Exodus 20:8-10; 31:14-17; 35:1-3; Leviticus 23:3, 25; Deuteronomy 5:12-14; and Jeremiah 17:21-27 about Sabbath regulations. The Pharisees were stretching the definition of work. No such details that they claimed to be work were in the Torah.* ➤

3 Jesus counter-argued, "Surely you are familiar with the example David set in the Scriptures when he and his men were hungry! [1 Samuel 21:1-6] **4** He entered the Tabernacle and took consecrated bread which only priests are allowed to eat. [Leviticus 24:9] He ate it and also gave it to his men to eat." ❖ *Jesus used David as an example because he knew the Pharisees thought highly of him. His point was: There's no mention or implication in the Scriptures of God condemning David or the priest who gave the bread to him for disobeying this Torah command in order to meet the needs of David's men. So God isn't going to condemn Jesus' followers for breaking the Pharisees' man-made Sabbath rules in order to satisfy their hunger. The Pharisees, who were proud of their detailed knowledge of the Scriptures, should have been able to see the implications of this story and not demand more from people than God does.* **B** ➤

5 Then he added, "I, the Son of Man, am Master of the Sabbath and its regulations."

A 6:1 The Sabbath was a holy day of rest when no work was allowed. It was instituted by God to keep people from working seven days a week without rest, and to provide a time to devote to their relationship with him. The Biblical Sabbath begins at sunset Friday and ends at sunset on Saturday.

B 6:4 For Scripture exegetes: Here is an example of how Jesus exegeted Scripture. Note that he implicitly used an argument from silence (which many exegetes claim is not a legitimate way to exegete Scripture) and implied that the Pharisees should also have been able to derive the same conclusion from the silence of the Scriptural record.

Jesus Heals a Man with a Crippled Hand on a Sabbath

6 On another Sabbath, Jesus entered a synagogue to teach, and a man with a crippled right hand **A** was present. **7** Some Pharisees and Scripture teachers wanted to find grounds for accusing Jesus of disobeying Torah commands. So they watched him carefully to see if he might heal him, since they considered this to be work that was forbidden on the Sabbath. **8** But Jesus knew what they were thinking and told the man with the crippled hand, "Come and stand here." The man got up and stood with Jesus. **9** Then Jesus said to those present, "I ask you, what does the Torah allow us to do on the Sabbath? Are we allowed to do good works, or should we allow harm to come through our inaction? Does it allow us to save life, or does it command us to allow life to be destroyed through inaction?" ❖ *Jesus' point: It was very clear that according to the Torah it was acceptable and appropriate to honor God by helping people on the Sabbath. It was Pharisaical tradition that added detailed rules defining many activities as work which were not specified as such in the Torah. Jesus refused to accept their man-made rules as having authority equal to God's commands.* ➤ **10** Jesus looked around at all of them, waiting for a response. When none was given, he told the man, "Straighten out your hand." The man did so and his hand became completely normal.

11 The Pharisees and the Scripture teachers were furious because he had publicly discredited their Sabbath rules, and they began plotting how they could get rid of him. ❖ *They ignored the fact that Jesus only said a few words, which isn't work by any definition, and that it was God's power that healed the man—so they were really angry about something they believed only God could do. They were also blind to their own violation of God's commands by their conspiring to kill him. Their only real concern was their continued status as interpreters of the Scriptures.* ➤

Jesus Appoints Twelve Apostles

12 It was about that time, early in his ministry, that Jesus went up a mountain by himself to pray. He spent the entire night praying to God the Father for guidance. **13** In the morning, he summoned all of his followers to him and selected twelve of them to be appointed as his apostles. ❖ *"Apostle" means "someone who is sent as a messenger." He intended to train them and give them authority as his representatives after he returned to Heaven.* ➤ **14** They were:

Simon, to whom he also gave the name
  Peter, ❖ *In Hebrew, Peter is Kefa [Kay-fah], which has been transliterated into English as Cephas.* ➤
Andrew, Simon's younger brother,
James (the son of Zebedee),
John (James' younger brother),
Philip,
Bartholomew, ❖ *who might have also been called Nathanael [John 1:45-49; 21:2]* ➤
15 Matthew (also called Levi),
Thomas,
James (the son of Alpheus),
Simon (who was called the Zealot),
  ❖ *because of his association with the left-wing Zealot group that wanted to free Israel from Roman rule by revolution* ➤
16 Judas (the son of James—also called
  Thaddeus), and
Judas Iscariot—who would later betray
  Jesus to his enemies.

❖ *Jesus' choice for his apostles included common uneducated fishermen, a social outcast who collaborated with the enemy (Matthew), a violent political fanatic (Simon the Zealot), and a man who he knew would betray him. Anyone can become a follower of Jesus, although it does involve leaving behind your former sinful ways.* ➤

Jesus Teaches and Heals Many

17 Jesus came partway down the mountain with his chosen apostles to a large level area where they stood with a large group of his other followers and a huge crowd of people. The people had come from Jerusalem and all other parts of Judea and even as far as the Mediterranean coastal area around the Gentile cities of Tyre and Sidon. **18** They came to hear Jesus teach and to be healed. People also came who were afflicted by demons, and they were freed from their

---

A **6:6** The Greek word χείρ (cheir), commonly translated "hand," can include the wrist and forearm. It's possible it was more than what we would call his "hand" that was crippled or "withered."

affliction. [19] Everyone crowded around to touch him because power was going out from him, healing all who did so. ❖ *God's healing power is often transferred via touch.* ➤

Jesus Teaches About
God's Blessings and Judgments

[20] Jesus looked at his followers and taught them, "Those of you who recognize your own spiritual poverty and have renounced all desire for riches in this world in order to seek God and his help are indeed in his good favor. You are already members of his Kingdom.

[21] "Those of you who hunger after God's approval are in his good favor, and he will certainly satisfy your craving.

"Those of you who weep in repentance over your sins in this life are in God's good favor **A** because in the life to come, he will make you laugh with joy. *[Matthew 5:4; James 4:9]*

[22] "Those of you who experience that people hate you, exclude you, insult you, or slander you because you follow me—the Son of Man—are in very good favor with God. [23] When that happens, you should be thrilled and jump for joy because you can rest assured that he has a great reward for you in Heaven. Their persecution proves that you are his servant because all true servants of God are persecuted, just like the ancestors of these people persecuted the prophets long ago. *[2 Chronicles 36:16]*

[24] "But how terrible it will be for you who are rich or want to be rich, and believe that possessions are able to make you happy and give you satisfaction and meaning in life. In this life, you are enjoying all the comfort you will ever have—for you will have no comfort in Hell!

[25] "How terrible it will be for you who are well fed and content with your sinful life, and have no desire to change it by submitting to God's will. For when you are in Hell, you will hunger for contentment that you can't have!

"How terrible it will be for you who laugh and only think about enjoying life in the present—having no concern about your sins. For when you are in Hell, you will mourn and weep forever!

[26] "How terrible it will be for you who seek fame and praise in this life. Praise from people is not to be equated with God's approval. On the contrary, it was the false prophets who were always praised by your rebellious ancestors!"

We Must Love Even Our Enemies

[27] Jesus continued, "If you are willing to hear God's will for your life, I'm saying that you must love everyone—even including your enemies. You must also do good to everyone—including those who hate you. [28] You are to ask God to bless those who curse you, and you must pray for those who mistreat you. [29] If someone slaps you on the cheek as an insult, don't retaliate. Instead, offer your other cheek to him to show your love and forbearance. ❖ *See the note at Matthew 5:39.* ➤ If someone steals your only coat, offer him your shirt too to win him for the Kingdom by showing him love. [30] If someone in need asks you for something, give it to him. If someone steals from you, don't necessarily seek to get it back. [31] And the kind and loving things you would like people to do for you, you should do for others first—even for those who aren't nice to you or are hostile.

A 6:21 The Greek word μακάριος (makarios) is usually translated "blessed" mainly because many translators think a single word in the Greek must be translated by a single word in English, so "blessed" is the best choice. Some recent translators insist that this word usually means "happy," but they ignore the fact that context always determines the precise meaning that a word is intended to have. Another meaning assigned to this word is "fortunate." It's not the point of this passage that God has already actively blessed people who have these attitudes (which is why some translators want to move away from translating it as "blessed"). And it should be obvious that people who are poor (in spirit or otherwise), or are hungry (whether physically or spiritually), or are mourning, or who are being hated—are probably not "happy." "Fortunate," on its own, can be misinterpreted to mean "lucky" which implies chance—ignoring the fact that God is in control of everything. So "in God's good favor" (i.e., their attitudes or situation put them in a position where God favors them and wants to bless them) is an attempt to clarify in what sense such people are "blessed."

32 "Do you think that God will bless you for only showing love to those who are likely to love you back? Certainly not! That's the way unbelievers live. 33 Do you think that God counts it in your favor if you only do good for those who will likely respond in kind? Certainly not! Even selfish sinners do that! ❖ *These verses imply we will be blessed and rewarded for acts of kindness done for the undeserving.* ➤ 34 And do you really think that God approves if you are only willing to lend to people who you are sure will return what they borrow? Most certainly not! Even the worst kind of sinners are willing to lend with the expectation that they will get back what they lend. 35 You are to live differently! You must demonstrate God's love to your enemies and do good to them. Lend and give generously to all in need while expecting to get nothing back. If you live like this, your reward in Heaven will be great and you will be known as God's true sons and daughters who reflect his character. For he is always kind—even to ungrateful and evil people—and he expects his children to do the same. 36 You are to show mercy to the undeserving in the same way your Heavenly Father does to you."

Jesus Forbids Us to Criticize or Condemn Others

37 Jesus continued, "If you condemn others, God will condemn you. If you criticize others, God will hold you accountable for all your faults. If you want God to forgive you, not executing his just punishment on you for the wrongs you've done, then you must also forgive everyone who wrongs you. 38 Help people who are in need, and in return, you will receive your reward from God in Heaven. The generous way he will pay you back is like a basket of grain that's been filled with a full measure, then tightly packed, pressed down, and shaken to settle the contents, and yet even more heaped on top to overflowing. The same standard of generosity—or lack of it—that you use in giving to people in need is the standard that God will use in rewarding you."

39 Then Jesus told a parable to say that we shouldn't criticize others because there are many times when we don't recognize our own faults. He said, "A person who is blind to his own sin can't lead others away from their sins. If he tries, they will all fall into a sinful trap. 40 It should be obvious that a student can't become better than his teacher. But a student who is fully trained can hope to be just like his teacher. ❖ *He means that if we aspire to be like Jesus, we mustn't criticize others.* ➤

41 "Why are you fixated on the tiny speck of sin in your brother's life, but don't notice the major sin in your own? 42 How can you dare to critically say, 'My brother, allow me to point out the small sin I see in your life and help you get rid of it,' when you refuse to recognize your own major sins! You self-righteous hypocrite! First, remove the major sins and pride from your own life and then you will have the humility and sensitivity to help others with the small sins in their lives."

❖ *Jesus' original picture was of a speck of dirt in your brother's eye and a log in your own. The eye is the most sensitive part of our body. When we do correct others, we need to be sure that we aren't being self-righteous and failing to recognize our own faults. We also need to be extremely careful not to hurt the person we are trying to help, just as you would take great care in removing something from an eye. Our attitude must be one of love, not superiority.* ➤

Trees and People Can Be Reliably Identified by the Fruit They Bear

43 Jesus said, "It's self-evident that a tree in good health won't produce bad fruit, and a tree in bad health can't produce good fruit. 44 It's also obvious that every kind of tree is identified by the fruit it bears. Figs aren't gathered from bramble bushes and grapes aren't picked from thorn bushes. 45 In the same way, from the abundance of goodness that fills the heart and mind of a righteous person proceeds the fruit of good words and actions. And from the evil that fills the heart and mind of an evil person proceeds the fruit of evil words and deeds. What a person speaks and does reflects the character of his innermost being. That's how righteous and evil people can be identified." ❖ *We are forbidden to criticize and condemn, but we are commanded to discern sin and evil so we can pray for the lost and avoid being influenced by them. We are also forbidden from allowing our discernment to influence us to treat such people in an unloving manner. But there are times when we*

must make decisions based on the character we see in people. And the way we can know the right people to trust and follow is given by Jesus here. ➤

Wise and Foolish Living

46 Jesus said, "Why do some of you call me 'Lord and Master,' but ignore my commands concerning the way you are to live? 47 I will tell you what someone's like who comes to me, hears my teaching, and lives by it. 48 That person is like a man who digs down to bedrock for a firm foundation on which to build his house. ❖ *In this illustration, a person's house represents his life. All that a person does in this life contributes to building his "house."* ➤ Later, when the flood of death comes and smashes against that house, it isn't even shaken because it was firmly built on a proper foundation. ❖ *If our lives are built on obedience to Jesus' teaching, then all the good things we do will have lasting value beyond our deaths, and God will reward us for them in Heaven.* ➤ 49 But those who hear my teaching and refuse to live by it are like a man that builds his house on top of the ground without any foundation at all. When the flood of death smashes against it, that house will immediately collapse and be completely destroyed!" ❖ *Even though people do good works in this life, if their lives aren't based on the foundation of obedience to Jesus, ultimately all those good works will count for nothing after their deaths.* ➤

7

Jesus Heals a Roman Centurion's Slave

1 When Jesus finished preaching these things, he went to Capernaum. 2 Stationed there was a Roman centurion who had heard about Jesus. His slave, of whom he thought highly, was dying from a sickness. 3 So when he found out that Jesus was in town, he sent a message to him with some friends who were Jewish elders, asking him to come and heal his slave. 4 When these elders came to Jesus, they urged him, "Even though he's a Gentile, he's a good and worthy person, and we beg you to grant his request. 5 For he loves our people and practically built our synagogue by himself with his contributions."

6 So Jesus went with them and as he was nearing the house, the centurion saw him and sent some other friends out to meet him with a message. They said on his behalf, "Sir, don't trouble yourself to come any further, for I'm not a Jew and therefore, not worthy to have you enter my house. I don't want you to ritually defile yourself by doing so. 7 That's why I didn't presume to come to you in person. But I ask you to command my slave to be healed and I know it will happen. 8 For I'm a man under authority and I understand how authority works. I have soldiers under my command and when I tell one, 'Go!' he goes, and to another, 'Come!' and he comes, and to my slave, 'Do this!' and he does it." ❖ *He recognized that Jesus had divine authority to make a healing command work.* ➤ 9 When Jesus heard this, he was amazed at his faith and understanding since he was a Gentile who didn't have the benefit of growing up learning about the one true God. He turned and said to those following him, "I tell you, I haven't encountered such great faith even among God's chosen people!"

10 So Jesus commanded that the slave be healed, and when the messengers returned to the centurion's house, they found the slave completely well.

Jesus Resurrects a Widow's Son

11 Soon after this, Jesus made the nine-hour walk to the town of Nain, southwest of Capernaum. His followers and a large crowd went with him. 12 As he approached the town entrance, a large funeral procession was coming out of the gate. They were carrying the body of a man who had been the only son of a widow, who would now have no male relative to take care of her. ❖ *A Jewish woman couldn't own land, so if she had no male relative to take care of her, she had no legal rights or property.* ➤ 13 When the Lord saw the woman, he felt compassion. Approaching her, he said, "You don't need to cry anymore." 14 Then, ignoring the fact that it would make him ritually unclean, he touched the bier and the bearers came to a halt. He said, "Young man, I command you to get up!" ❖ *According to the Torah, [Numbers 19:11-12] after touching a dead body or the bier, Jesus would be ritually unclean for seven days and be required to go through ritual washing on the third and seventh day before he could again join in*

worship at the Temple. ➤ 15 The man who had been dead sat up and started talking. Jesus then presented him to his mother.

16 Those who witnessed this were filled with fear and awe. They began to praise God and exclaim, "After so long a time, God has sent us a great prophet!" and "God has come to help his people through this prophet!" ❖ *It had been over 400 years since had God sent a major prophet to Israel.* ➤

17 The news about this incident spread throughout Galilee, Judea, and the surrounding areas.

John the Baptizer Sends Messengers to Jesus

18 Now, John the Baptizer was in prison, and his followers reported all these things about Jesus to him. 19 But since Jesus was not initiating the end-time judgment that John had prophesied, *[Luke 3:17]* he summoned two of his followers and sent them to the Lord.

20 When they came to Jesus, they said, "John the Baptizer sent us to ask you if you really are the long-awaited Messiah, or if we should be looking for someone else."

21 Just as they were arriving, Jesus had been healing many who were sick and suffering from various afflictions, casting out demons, and restoring sight to the blind. 22 He answered, "Go and tell John what you have seen and heard me do. ❖ *He was fulfilling the prophecies in Isaiah 35:5-6; 26:19; 29:18-19; and 61:1; concerning what the Messiah would do:* ➤ Those who were blind can see; those who were crippled can walk; those who were lepers are cured; those who were deaf can hear; some who have died now live again; and the poor are hearing the Good News about God inviting them into his Kingdom. 23 May God bless anyone who doesn't reject me for not fulfilling their preconceived ideas of what the Messiah will do."

24 After the messengers had gone, Jesus spoke to the crowds about John. "When you went out to John in the wilderness, what did you expect to see? A man who goes with the flow of popular opinion—like a reed that bends with the wind in any direction? Hardly. Who would listen to such a man? 25 So why did you go out to see him? To see a man who knows how to ingratiate himself with the king so as to be rewarded with royal favors and soft clothing? Those who wear rich apparel and live in luxury are found in palaces, not in the wilderness. 26 So tell me, what did you hope to find? A prophet sent by God? Yes, you went to hear God's prophet. But I tell you that he is more than just a prophet for his work surpasses that of all previous prophets. 27 John is the messenger who proclaimed the coming of the Messiah. This Scripture was written about him: 'I will send my messenger in advance to prepare the way for you to be accepted by my people.' *[Malachi 3:1]* 28 I tell you, from the beginning of creation until now no one has had a more important role than John. Yet, even the lowest-ranking person in God's Kingdom is greater than he is. ❖ *As great as John was, he lived in the time of promise, before Jesus' resurrection and before the Holy Spirit came to dwell in all of God's people. Those who enter God's Kingdom and are indwelt by the Holy Spirit and are adopted as God's children achieve a higher status than John ever did in his life on earth. Of course after his death, he joined God's people in glory and certainly has high status there.* ➤

29 "When all the people heard him preach, many believed God's message that they were sinners and needed to repent. They demonstrated this by having John baptize them. Even tax collectors responded. 30 But the Pharisees and Scripture teachers refused to acknowledge their need for repentance or their need for John to baptize them, and thus they rejected God's will for themselves.

31 "How can I characterize the leaders and many of the people of this generation? Do you know what they are like? 32 They are never satisfied with God's messengers. They are like children sitting in the market who complain to one another, 'We played a happy tune, but you wouldn't dance. Then we sang a song of mourning, but you wouldn't cry.'

33 "For John came as an ascetic and didn't eat bread or drink wine like most people, so they rejected him and claimed he was demonized.

34 "Then I, the Son of Man, came and was willing to dine and drink as a guest in people's homes, and they say, 'Look at that

glutton and drunkard, hanging around with tax collectors and other sinful outcasts!' ❖ *The Jewish leaders were unwilling to accept anyone who disturbed the status quo. They were interested in their own power more than God's truth. It didn't matter what kind of prophet God sent. If a prophet criticized them, they would reject him.* ➤ 35 But as the proverb says, 'Wisdom is vindicated by all her children.' **A** So we will be vindicated by the good fruit that God produces in the lives of those who follow our teaching."

Jesus at the House of Simon the Pharisee

36 One day, a Pharisee named Simon invited Jesus to dine with him. So Jesus went into the Pharisee's house and—as was the custom—reclined on a couch at the table. 37 Now, a woman who lived in the city and was known to have lived an immoral life heard that he was a guest there. Much to the indignation of the Pharisees present, she barged in with an alabaster flask of expensive perfume. 38 She stood behind him at the end of the couch near his feet, crying out of gratitude for his message of God's love and forgiveness. Her tears fell and wet his feet and, in her anxious state, she forgot propriety—further shocking the guests—and let down her hair ❖ *which was considered immodest and never done in public* ➤ and dried his feet with it. She also kissed his feet in reverence and gratitude and then broke the flask and poured the perfume on them. 39 When Simon saw this, he despised her as a worthless sinner, refusing to believe that she had repented. He was thinking, "If this man were really a prophet, he would know what kind of a person is touching and defiling him and he wouldn't allow it." ❖ *Pharisees considered themselves ritually defiled if even their clothes came in contact with common sinners.* ➤

40 Addressing these thoughts, Jesus bluntly said, "Simon, I would say something to you." ❖ *Knowledge of a person's thoughts or attitude can come via the "gift of knowledge" from the Holy Spirit. [1 Corinthians 12:8]* With insincere politeness and apparent reluctance, he replied, "Go ahead, Rabbi."

41 Jesus said, "A certain money lender was owed money by two men, one who owed five-hundred-days wages and the other who owed fifty. 42 When he learned that they were unable to repay their debts, he graciously canceled both of them. Now tell me, which of the two would be more grateful?"

43 Simon answered, "I suppose the one who had the larger debt."

Jesus said, "You've come to the correct conclusion." 44 ❖ *Jesus wanted to vindicate the repentant woman to the self-righteous Pharisees who he knew would continue to reject her. So he added to the tension and astonishment in the room by breaking a strong middle-eastern taboo that prohibited a guest from criticizing his host.* ➤ Turning to face the woman—dignifying her presence—he said to Simon, "Do you see this woman? I entered your house as a guest, and you failed to offer me the common courtesy of water—normally offered to all guests—so I could wash my feet. But she wet my feet with her tears and dried them with her hair. 45 Everyone here witnessed your insult when you didn't welcome me with a kiss of greeting. ❖ *Custom dictated that he welcome Jesus with a kiss on the hand to show respect, or on the cheek as one would with a peer. To not do so was a deliberate insult, like you offering to shake a person's hand, but they pointedly refuse to touch it.* ➤ But ever since I came in, she hasn't stopped kissing my feet. 46 You didn't even offer the hospitality of anointing my head with inexpensive olive oil, but she has anointed my feet with costly perfume. ❖ *Far from being inappropriate, her actions were very appropriate. She may have witnessed the ways Simon insulted Jesus, which would have been additional incentive for her tears and actions. Such insults show that Simon didn't invite Jesus to honor him or to learn from him. He probably expected Jesus to turn around and leave when he was snubbed so they could have a good laugh at his expense. But Jesus didn't receive these insults or acknowledge them on his own behalf. He only brought them up in defense of the woman.* ➤

47 "Therefore I must tell you, her great love clearly reveals that she has repented, and her many sins have already been forgiven. But he who has been forgiven little—because he hasn't recognized his own sinfulness—shows little love."

---

48 Then Jesus said to the woman, "Your sins really have been forgiven."

49 The people at the table with him were indignant and said, "Who does he think he is to claim that he forgives sin?" ❖ *They knew that only God can forgive sin.* ➤

50 But ignoring them, Jesus said to the woman, "Your faith has saved you. Go in peace." **A**

8

Women Who Helped Jesus

1 Not long after this, Jesus went around to many towns and villages preaching the Good News that God was wanting a new relationship with people who would submit to him as king. His twelve apostles went with him 2 and also some women he had healed, or from whom he had expelled demons. Among them were Mary of Magdala village (from whom he had expelled seven demons), 3 Joanna, (whose husband, Chuza, was an administrator for tetrarch Herod Antipas), Susanna, and many other women. They supported Jesus and his followers financially from their own resources.

Parable of the Four Soils

4 One day, when a large crowd from many towns had gathered to hear Jesus, he told them this parable, 5 "A farmer went out to sow seed in his field. ❖ *This was done by scattering the seed over the ground and then later plowing it under.* ➤ As he scattered the seed, some fell on a hard-packed path where people walked on them and birds ate them. 6 Some fell where there was just a thin layer of soil over rock. These seeds sprouted, but the plants withered quickly because the underlying rock blocked their roots from reaching water. 7 Some fell on ground containing the roots of thorn bushes. Those also sprouted and were able to grow for a while, but the young plants weren't able to compete for light and water with the thorn bushes that also grew and choked them. So they produced no grain and died. 8 But some seed

fell on good soil. These sprouted, grew strong, and bore more seed, each producing about 100 grains."

Then Jesus said with emphasis, "If your minds are attuned to God, try to understand what this parable means!"

Why Jesus Taught in Parables

9 Later, when only Jesus' usual followers were with him, they asked about the meaning of the parable. 10 He said, "You have the privilege of being the first to learn about Kingdom truths that God hasn't revealed before. But for the present, I will only teach others about them in parables. This is to fulfill Isaiah's prophecy that says, '**Even though they look, they don't perceive. Even though they hear, they don't understand.**' "
[Isaiah 6:9] ❖ *Jesus intended that only those whose minds were open to hearing God's truth would be able to understand the parables. But those with hard hearts and closed minds would not understand. God never forces truth on anyone in this life. His hiding truth in parables actually protected the disinterested because God holds people responsible for things they know. They will be punished for rejecting Jesus, but will not receive additional punishment for rejecting truth because they did not understand it.* ➤

Jesus Explains the Parable of the Four Soils

11 Jesus said, "This is what the parable means. The seed represents God's message about the way of salvation that is preached to people. 12 The hard-packed path illustrates people whose hearts are hard and whose minds are closed toward God's message. They may hear his truth, but it can't enter their hardened hearts. And just like the birds ate the seed, Satan snatches the memory of it away from them. 13 The layer of shallow soil over rock illustrates people who hear God's message and happily receive it at first. But just like a plant in shallow soil can't develop the roots it needs to survive, God's message doesn't go deep in their hearts because they aren't willing to fully surrender themselves to him. Their shallow faith lasts for only a short time until the first real testing of it occurs. Then it

---

A 7:50 Commentary for the story in verses 36-50 comes from Kenneth E. Bailey's book "Through Peasant Eyes," pp. 1-21.

quickly dies. 14 The ground with thorn bushes illustrates people who initially accept God's message into their lives, but they never give it first priority. So other concerns and higher priorities, such as worries, materialism, and pleasure don't allow his word to produce good fruit in their lives. Eventually, their faith is smothered and dies.

❖ Some commentators believe that the plants did not die, but were merely unproductive. Jesus taught elsewhere that trees producing no fruit were only fit to be burned. [Matthew 3:10; 7:19; Luke 3:9; John 15:4-6] The focus in this parable is on how the seed is received and the resulting fruit. Only the good soil results in fruit, and the point is that the good soil is the only acceptable kind. Just as in your own garden, plants that don't produce are rejected as worthless. ➤ 15 But the good soil illustrates people who hear God's message, grab onto it, recognize its worth, and allow it to take deep root in their hearts and minds. They surrender themselves to God and make him first priority in their lives. So their faith matures and their lives cause God's Kingdom to increase."

❖ The implication is that individuals can determine what kind of "soil" their hearts are by how they respond to God's message. ➤

God Intends to Reveal His Truth to Everyone

16 Jesus continued, "No one lights a lamp and then hides it under a bed or covers it so its light can't be seen. Instead, they put it where the light can illuminate as much of the room as possible. 17 Then, everything that was hidden in darkness will be clearly seen in its light. ❖ Jesus followed the practice of teachers in his time, making points with clear graphic illustrations. Sometimes those illustrations are less than clear today because of the gap in time and culture. He meant that God fully intends for the light of the spiritual truths he taught to be seen and understood by people. He would never want it hidden because that would defeat its purpose. ➤

18 "Therefore, you should be cautious about how you receive the revelatory light of God's teaching because God will increase the understanding of those who receive it with proper regard and a desire to understand and obey it. But those who don't receive it properly, even the understanding they think they have will be taken away from them."

Jesus' True Relatives

19 One day, Jesus' mother and brothers came from Nazareth to see him, but they couldn't get in the house where he was teaching because it was crammed with people. 20 So they passed a message inside saying, "Your mother and brothers are outside wanting to see you." 21 Using this as a teaching opportunity, Jesus said, "People whom I consider as close to me as a mother or a brother are those who accept God's word and obey it."

Jesus Demonstrates Authority over Weather

22 One day, Jesus and his close followers got into a boat on Lake Galilee and he said, "Let's sail to the other side." So they started out. 23 Jesus fell asleep while they were sailing, and a little later a sudden storm came up. ❖ This is common on Lake Galilee. ➤ It became so rough that the boat took on water and was in danger of being swamped. 24 So they woke Jesus and said, "Master! Master! We're going to sink!" Jesus got up and rebuked the wind and waves. The storm quickly dissipated and the water became calm. 25 Then he asked, "Why didn't you trust God to protect you?" They were utterly amazed and awed, and asked each other, "Who is he? He even has authority over the wind and waves!" [Psalm 65:7; 89:8-9; 107:25; 28-29; Jonah 1:15-16] ❖ Jews believed that only God controlled these things. ➤

Jesus Demonstrates Authority over Demons

26 They arrived on the eastern shore in the region of Gergesa, A across from Galilee Province. 27 When Jesus went ashore, he was met by a man from the city who was

---

A 8:26 The name of this town varies among the different gospels. Some manuscripts and other gospels say it was the region of Gadara (8 miles from the lake). Others say it was the region of Gerasa (about 30 miles southeast of the lake). Both were in the same general region in the area of the Decapolis, a predominantly Gentile area. Others say it was the region of Gergesa on the lake shore where there are cliffs in the vicinity, and this one seems to fit the story best.

severely demonized. He had been living naked in the nearby tombs for a long time. 28-29 Demons had taken control of him many times. Authorities had tried keeping him chained under guard, but he always broke free, and the demons drove him into the wilderness. When he saw Jesus, he screamed and fell to the ground in front of him. As Jesus was commanding the demons to come out of him, the man shouted, "Arrrgh! Get out of here, Jesus, Son of God Most High! Just leave me alone! **A** I beg you not to torment me!" ❖ *Note that Jesus was commanding the demons to leave, but they did not obey even God's Son immediately.* ➤ 30 Jesus asked, "What's your name?" He replied, "My name is Legion." (Because there were many demons in him.) ❖ *A Roman legion consisted of 4000–6000 soldiers, indicating that the man could have had several thousand demons in him.* ➤ 31 Then, the demons begged Jesus not to send them to the abyss in Hell.

32 A large herd of pigs was feeding on the hillside nearby and the demons begged him to let them enter the pigs. Jesus gave them permission, 33 so they came out of the man and entered the pigs. Then, the herd ran down the steep hillside into the lake and drowned.

34 When the herders saw what happened, they ran away and reported what they'd seen to others in the city and all around the countryside. ❖ *This was clearly a Gentile area since the Torah categorized pigs as "unclean," and Jews never raised them.* ➤ 35 Many who heard the news came out to see for themselves what had happened. When they arrived, they found Jesus with the previously demonized man sitting near him, clothed and sane. When they realized what had happened, they became afraid of Jesus for he obviously had great power. 36 Eyewitnesses kept telling the newcomers exactly how the demonized man had been delivered. 37 Then, because they feared him, the people of that district respectfully asked Jesus to leave. So Jesus got in the boat to return to the other side of the lake. 38 But the man he had delivered begged to go with

him. Jesus told him, 39 "No. I want you to go home to your family and tell them what God has done for you." So the man went throughout the entire city, telling everyone he met what Jesus had done.

A Woman's Faith Heals Her and Jesus Demonstrates Power over Death

40 When Jesus arrived on the Capernaum side of the lake, a crowd met him because they had all been waiting for him to return. 41 Then, a man named Jairus came and prostrated himself at Jesus' feet. He was the leader of the local synagogue. ❖ *Synagogues are Jewish gathering places for worship and religious instruction.* ➤ He implored Jesus to come to his house 42 because his only daughter—age twelve—was dying. Jesus agreed, and as they walked through the narrow streets, the crowd pressed in on every side.

43 In the crowd was a woman who suffered from chronic bleeding. She had had this problem for twelve years and had spent all she owned on doctors, but no one could cure her. 44 She came up behind Jesus and touched a symbolic tassel **B** hanging from his robe, and the bleeding immediately stopped. ❖ *Her condition made her ritually unclean so anyone she touched would become unclean until evening and would have to go through ritual washing. This was a terrible burden to bear and a constant embarrassment. She probably hoped no one would notice her. [Leviticus 15:19-30] ¶ Healing comes from God. Note that God allowed his healing power to be available to her because of her faith and expectation, even without Jesus consciously willing it to be released. Also note that God does not change, and consider that fact when you wonder if God is willing to heal you.* ➤ 45 Jesus abruptly stopped and asked, "Who touched me?" Everyone nearby denied it and Peter said, "Master, everyone's crowding around you; anyone could've accidentally touched you." 46 But Jesus said, "I know someone deliberately touched me because I felt power go out from me." 47 When the woman realized that she hadn't gotten away unnoticed, she came forward—trembling with fear—and prostrated herself before him. Then, in front

---

A 8:28 Literally, "What to me to you," the sense of hostility that's implied by this Greek idiom is rendered here, rather than the more literal "What have you to do with me?"

B 8:44 This word can also mean "fringe" or "edge." Jewish men wore tassels on their outer garments. [Numbers 15:38-40] See the footnote at Matthew 9:20.

of everyone, she confessed what she had done and why, and how she had immediately been healed. 48 Jesus gently said to her, "My daughter, your faith in me has healed you. Go in peace and wholeness and don't be afraid."

49 While Jesus was still speaking to her, someone arrived from Jairus' house and reported, "Jairus, your daughter has died. There's no reason that the Rabbi should bother to come." 50 But Jesus overheard and told him, "Don't be afraid. Continue to trust in me, and she will be OK."

51 When they reached the house, Jesus didn't allow anyone to go in with him except the parents, Peter, John, and James. 52 The house was surrounded by people wailing over the girl's death. Since Jesus knew he was going to wake her back to life, he told them, "Stop crying! She isn't dead, but merely sleeping!" ❖ *Jesus is the creator who speaks into being things that are not yet.* ➤ 53 But they ridiculed him because they knew she was dead.

54 Jesus went in and holding her hand, said, "My child, wake up!" 55 Her life returned and she immediately sat up. Then, Jesus told her parents to give her something to eat. 56 They were amazed, but Jesus told them not to tell anyone what had happened.

9

Jesus Sends the Twelve to Evangelize and Heal

1 Jesus summoned his twelve apostles together and gave them power and authority over every demon and sickness. 2 Then he sent them out to proclaim the Good News that God is seeking people to become part of his Kingdom, and told them to heal those who were sick. 3 He instructed them, "Don't take anything with you, no walking stick, bag, food, money, not even spare clothing. You are to trust that God will provide what you need. 4 When you arrive in a town and are welcomed in a house, stay there as long as you are ministering in that town. 5 Where people refuse to receive you or your message, as you leave, shake off the dust of that town from your feet." ❖ *This was a symbolic rebuke, implying that even the dust of their house or town was defiling and offensive because they were no better than*

pagans. It also warned that they had better repent or they would face God's judgment. [John 15:23] ➤

6 So the apostles set out and went through many Jewish towns and villages proclaiming God's Good News and healing those who were sick in every place. *[James 5:14-16]* ❖ *Evangelism in the New Testament always included healing ministry. Why is this almost totally neglected by believers today? Could it be due to unbelief?* ➤

News About Jesus Reaches Herod

7 When Herod Antipas, tetrarch over Galilee Province, heard news about the things Jesus and his followers were doing, he was confused and troubled. Not long before, he had ordered John the Baptizer killed, but people were saying that John had come back to life and it was he who was doing these things. 8 Others reported that the prophet Elijah had come back. ❖ *Elijah was a prophet who had lived about 900 years previously and who had also performed miracles. The story of Elijah starts in 1 Kings 17.* ➤ And some said that it was a different prophet who had come back to life. 9 Herod said, "I myself had John beheaded. So who is this man who's doing all these things?" And he made unsuccessful efforts to see Jesus.

Jesus Demonstrates Power to Multiply Resources

10 When the apostles returned from their tour of ministry, they reported to Jesus all that they had done. Jesus led them away toward the town of Bethsaida so they could have some time to themselves. 11 But the crowds found out and followed. When they caught up, he welcomed them and began teaching about God's Kingdom and healed all who were sick.

12 Late in the afternoon, the twelve apostles approached him and said, "Master, send these people away so they can reach villages and farms to find food and lodging for the night because there's nothing nearby." 13 But Jesus told them, "I want you to give them something to eat." They protested, "We only have five rolls of bread and two fish! Unless you expect us to go buy food for all these people, that's all we have." 14 They were incredulous at Jesus' command

because there were about 5000 men in the crowd. ❖ *In that culture, women and children were not commonly counted. There were easily 10,000 to 20,000 people in the crowd.* ➤ Jesus replied, "Tell the people to sit down in groups of about 50."

15 They did so, and the people sat as Jesus instructed. 16 He then took the five rolls and the two fish, looked up toward Heaven in an attitude of prayer, and thanked God for the food. Then he broke them into small pieces and kept giving them to his followers to distribute to the people. 17 All the people ate and had enough to be satisfied, and the leftovers filled twelve baskets.

Peter Recognizes that Jesus is the Messiah

18 One day when Jesus was alone with his followers praying, he asked them, "Who do people think I am?" 19 They answered, "Some say you are John the Baptizer come back to life, and some say you are the prophet Elijah. Others say that you are another prophet from long ago who has returned." 20 Then he asked, "And what about you? Who do you think I am?" Peter replied, "You are God's Anointed One, the Messiah." 21 But Jesus warned them not to tell this to anyone, because it wasn't his intention to force people into making a decision at this time about who they believed he was.

Jesus Predicts His Suffering and Death

22 Jesus said, "I, the Son of Man, must suffer many things and be rejected by the elders and the chief priests and Scripture teachers. They will kill me, but God will bring me back to life on the second **A** day after my death."

23 Later, he said to all of his followers, "Those who really want to be my people must put aside their own desires and every day be willing to suffer and even die in order to follow me. 24 Those who want to retain control of their own lives and protect them will ultimately lose them. But those who are willing to give up all that they are and have—even their own lives—in order to follow me, will ultimately gain their true lives. 25 What benefit have you gained if you acquire everything you desire in this temporary world but in the process lose your chance at eternal life in Heaven? 26 Those who are ashamed to be associated with me and my message because they fear persecution, I, the Son of Man, will reject when I return in my glory and the glory of my Father and his holy angels. 27 I assure you that some of you standing here right now will see the glory of God's Kingdom before they die." *[Matthew 16:28; Mark 9:1; 2 Peter 1:16]* ❖ *Jesus may have been referring to the event that Luke reports next. Or he may have meant that those who would be believers after his resurrection and Pentecost would see the miraculous power of God manifest through those who had miraculous gifts of the Holy Spirit to heal and to perform miracles. Also, John had the visions reported in the book of Revelation where he saw Jesus returning in glory to reign as king. [Revelation 19:11—20:6]* ➤

God Reveals Jesus' True Glory

28 About eight days later, Jesus took Peter, John, and James up a mountain to pray. 29 While he was praying, his appearance changed and his clothing shone with a brilliant white light. 30 Then Moses and Elijah appeared from Heaven and spoke with him. 31 They too shone with the light of God's glory and they spoke with Jesus about his upcoming departure and what would soon happen to him in Jerusalem. 32 Peter and his friends had fallen asleep while Jesus was praying. But now they woke up and saw Jesus' glory and the two men standing with him, whom they somehow recognized. 33 As Moses and Elijah were about to leave, Peter blurted out (without really knowing what he was saying), "Master, it's good that we're here. Allow us to make three shelters, one for you, one for Moses and one for Elijah."

34 While he was saying this, a cloud appeared around them like a thick fog, making everything look shadowy and frightening them. 35 Then they heard God say, "This is my Son, my Chosen One. *He* is the one you should listen to and obey!" *[Isaiah 42:1]*

A 9:22 See the note at Matthew 16:21 for the reasoning behind not using the traditional phrase, "the third day."

❖ Moses was the one to whom God had given the Torah and was the most revered of all their prophets. Moses represented the Torah, which ruled their lives. Elijah represented the teachings of all the other prophets. Together, they represented all the writings of the Hebrew Scriptures, everything that was known about God and his will. In this context, when God told them to listen to his Son, he was saying that Jesus and his teachings had more authority than Moses, Elijah, and everything written in the Scriptures. So in this event—commonly called the "Transfiguration"—God audibly said that Jesus was his Son, and therefore also God, and that Jesus' authority exceeded every authority they had been taught to revere. ➤

36 When the voice stopped, Jesus stood there alone. And Peter, James, and John didn't tell anyone what they had experienced until after Jesus' resurrection.

Jesus' Followers Fail to Expel a Demon

37 In the morning, they went down the mountain to where a large crowd met Jesus. 38 A man shouted to him from out of the crowd, "Rabbi! I beg you to look at my only son. 39 A demon keeps seizing control of him. It makes him scream and convulse so he foams at the mouth. It hardly ever leaves him alone and it's continually injuring him. 40 I begged your followers to expel it, but they couldn't."

41 Jesus said to his followers, "You people are stubborn and faithless! How long will I have to be with you and put up with you before you learn how to use my power?" Then he said to the man, "Bring your son here." *❖ Jesus had already trained his apostles and given them power and authority over every demon. (See Matthew 10:1; Mark 6:7, 13; and Luke 9:1) But they had failed to learn the lesson well enough. They had probably given up trying too soon. Most demons obey fairly quickly, but some strongly resist and you have to persist in prayer and commanding them before they leave. See Luke 8:29 where some demons did not obey even Jesus right away. ¶ As this story indicates in the following verses, their failure to expel the demon did not mean it was God's will that the boy not be delivered, as many people today would conclude under similar circumstances, particularly with regard to someone they pray for who is not quickly healed. ➤*

42 As the boy was coming, the demon made him fall to the ground and violently convulse. But Jesus rebuked the demon, making it leave. Then he healed the boy

and presented him back to his father. 43 All who saw it were awed by this display of God's power.

Jesus Talks About His Death a Second Time

While the people were standing there in amazement, Jesus said to his followers, 44 "Listen carefully to what I tell you and remember it. I, the Son of Man, will soon be betrayed and handed over to men who hate me." 45 But they didn't understand what he was talking about because God prevented them and they were afraid to ask what he meant. *❖ Everything that was to happen to Jesus was part of God's plan and he would not allow anything to interfere. Jesus' words were meant to help them understand later that all this happened according to God's plan. ➤*

How to Be Important in God's Sight

46 One day, Jesus' followers were arguing about which of them was most important. 47 Jesus knew what they were thinking so he brought a small child to his side 48 and said, "Whoever welcomes this child in order to obey me, welcomes me. And whoever welcomes me, also welcomes my Father who sent me. For whoever is the most humble in serving others, he has the highest status in God's sight."

49 John spoke up, "Master, we saw someone expelling demons using your name as if you had given him your authority, so we tried to stop him because he isn't associated with us." *❖ This incident shows that authority over demons in Jesus' name is not just for the apostles. It is for any believer. ➤* 50 But Jesus responded, "You shouldn't stop him! Anyone who isn't against us is on our side!"

A Samaritan Village Refuses Jesus Hospitality

51 Jesus knew the time was approaching when he would have to die and then be taken up to Heaven. So he resolutely started out toward Jerusalem to face his time of trial. 52 He sent messengers ahead to make arrangements for him and his traveling companions to spend the night in a village in Samaria. *❖ Most Jews traveling from Galilee to Jerusalem would avoid going through Samaria, taking the longer route around it because Jews and Samaritans hated each other. ➤* 53 But the Samaritans there

refused to take him in because it was clear that they were Jews who were headed toward Jerusalem for the Passover Festival. 54 When James and John heard this, they were furious and said, "Master, do you want us to command fire to come down from Heaven to destroy them?" 55 But Jesus turned and rebuked them, {"You don't realize that a demon's influencing you to say this. I didn't come to destroy people, I came to save them!"} A ❖ *Even though the words in brackets may not be part of the original text, this kind of attitude is most likely caused by demonic influence. Demons can tempt even relatively mature believers to give in to their emotions and thereby influence them to make rash and even evil decisions. Note this as a warning to be on your guard when emotions of hurt, offense, and anger are strong.* ➤ 56 So they went on to a different village.

The Cost of Following Jesus

57 As they were going along, a man came to Jesus and said, "I will follow you wherever you go."

58 But Jesus replied, "Do you really realize what that involves? Foxes have their dens and birds have their nests. But I, the Son of Man, am rejected by the leaders of this nation. If you follow me, they will also reject you. Are you sure you want to follow me?" ❖ *Jesus called Herod—who was a half-foreign ruler—a fox, [Luke 13:32] and birds sometimes represented Gentiles, [Ezekiel 31:5-6] which could refer to the Romans. Both Herod and the Romans were foreigners and in power, but Israel's own Messiah was rejected by the Jewish leaders. Jesus demands that potential followers consider the consequences of following him and to expect rejection by society if they choose to do so.* ➤

59 Jesus said to a different man, "Come and be my follower." But he replied, "Sir, I must first fulfill my duty to serve my father as long as he lives—as tradition demands and society expects. After my father dies, I will be free to follow you." 60 Jesus replied, "Let those who are spiritually dead take care of themselves. I'm calling you to go and proclaim the Good News about God's Kingdom." ❖ *Jesus demands loyalty from his followers*

that is above loyalty to tradition, cultural norms, or the expectations of others. ➤

61 Another man said, "I'd like to follow you, sir. But first, I must ask permission from my family." 62 Jesus replied, "A man who starts plowing a field and keeps looking back isn't fit for God's Kingdom." ❖ *The task of plowing required exacting focus ahead to do the job properly, lest adjacent furrows be damaged by a crooked course and the job made harder. Jesus demands absolute loyalty from his followers, even over that of their own family. This illustration means that anyone who sets his mind to follow Jesus and then has second thoughts and keeps looking back to his former life, or can't resolve the tension of conflicting loyalties, isn't fully committed and is judged as useless for the purposes of God's Kingdom.* ➤ B

10

Jesus Sends Out 72 as Evangelists

1 Later, just like he had sent out the twelve apostles to preach before, Jesus now chose 72 C more men from among his followers and sent them out in pairs. He sent them ahead of him to minister in all the Jewish towns and villages that he was planning to pass through on his way to Jerusalem. 2 He told them, "Many people are ready to enter God's Kingdom. They are like a field that promises a plentiful harvest. But the number of harvesters are few so ask God to send out more workers. 3 Get ready to go, but be aware that there are people who will attack you. You are as helpless as lambs among wolves, but trust God to take care of you. 4 Don't take any money with you, or a bag, or extra footwear. God will provide what you need. Go quickly and don't allow people you meet on the way to delay you. ❖ *These instructions were for a short-term mission. After his resurrection, Jesus give quite different instructions for people going out to minister long term. [Luke 22:35-36]* ➤ 5 Whatever house you enter, greet them with a blessing, saying, 'May God bless you with shalom.' ❖ *The Jewish greeting and blessing of "shalom"—which Jesus undoubtedly used here—is a word full of meaning. It is a single-word blessing and prayer for peace,*

A 9:55 The part in { } isn't in the oldest manuscripts.
B 9:62 Commentary for verses 57-62 comes from Kenneth E. Bailey's book "Through Peasant Eyes," pp. 22-32.

C 10:1 Some manuscripts have 72 and others have 70. Either number could be correct.

calmness, success, comfort, contentment, safety, health, wholeness, prosperity, integrity, well-being, and good relationships with God and people. ➤ 6 If they are worthy and accept your blessing, it will remain on them. Otherwise, your blessing will not be effective. 7 If they accept you, stay in their house as long as you are in that town, instead of moving from house to house. Don't hesitate to accept whatever they offer you to eat and drink because you are working for God, and a worker should be compensated. 8 Whenever you enter a town and they welcome you, be content to eat whatever they set before you. 9 Heal those who are sick in that town and tell them, 'God's Kingdom has touched you, and you may join it if you are willing to submit to him as your King.' 10 But if you go to a town and they refuse to welcome you, go out in the streets and warn them that God is displeased with them and that they are the same as pagans in his sight. 11 Say, 'We are wiping off even the dust of your town from our feet as a sign of God's rejecting you because you have rejected us, his messengers. God's Kingdom was offered to you today, but you rejected it.' " 12 Jesus said to the 72, "I assure you that on Judgment Day, God will show more mercy to the citizens of Sodom than the citizens of that town."
❖ *Sodom was infamous for its immorality, but Jesus considers rejecting his messengers to be a worse offense.* ➤

Jesus Laments for Towns That Rejected Him

13 Jesus continued, "O how terrible it will be for you Jews of Chorazin and Bethsaida! ❖ *These were Jewish towns just north of Lake Galilee, near Capernaum. Many Jews of that time believed they were automatically saved just because they were Jews.* ➤ God will punish you because you refused to repent in spite of the miracles you have seen. If the miracles which were done for you had been done for the pagan citizens of Tyre and Sidon, they would've repented long ago and demonstrated their sorrow by wearing sackcloth and ashes. *[Isaiah 23:1-18; Ezekiel 26:1—28:26; Joel 3:4-8; Amos 1:9-10; Zechariah 9:2-4]* 14 On Judgment Day, the wicked pagans of Tyre and Sidon will be better off than you because you saw God's miracles and heard his Good News, but

rejected it. 15 And you people of Capernaum! You think you will be honored in Heaven? No, you will be cast down to the world of the dead!" *[Isaiah 14:13-15]*

16 Then Jesus said to the 72, "Anyone who accepts your message is accepting me. Anyone who rejects you is rejecting me. And anyone who rejects me is rejecting God who sent me." Then, they went on their way.

The Return of the 72

17 Later, the 72 returned from their mission and joyfully reported to Jesus, "Lord, even the demons obeyed us when we commanded them in your name!"

18 Jesus said, "Yes, while you were ministering, I saw Satan fall from the heights of power like a flash of lightning. Your work was defeating him. 19 I gave you authority so you can trample on demonic serpents and scorpions with impunity and overcome all the power of Satan. There's nothing they can do to harm you. ❖ *Serpents and scorpions are figures representing demons. But don't mistake having authority for automatic protection. Believers have to verbally exercise that authority in Jesus' name for it to be effective.* ➤ 20 But don't center your joy on the fact that demons obey you. Rather, focus your joy on the fact that your names are written in the 'Book of Life' in Heaven." ❖ *All whose names are written there will live forever in Heaven.* ➤

Jesus Rejoices

21 Then, Jesus was filled with the Holy Spirit and exulted, "Yes, my Father! Lord of Heaven and earth! I praise and thank you for hiding your truths from those who think much of themselves and for revealing them to the humble! Yes, Father, I know this is what pleases you!"

22 To his followers, he said, "My Father has given me power and authority over everything. No one really knows me, God's Son, except my Father in Heaven. And no one knows the Father except me, his Son, and those to whom I choose to reveal him."

23 When they were in private, Jesus turned to his followers and said, "You really are fortunate to be seeing the things you see! 24 For many prophets and kings longed to

see the things you see and hear what you hear, but they didn't happen in their time."

Parable of the Good Samaritan

25 One day, a Scripture teacher stood up and asked a question to see what kind of answer Jesus would give. He asked, "Rabbi, what must I do to gain eternal life?"

26 Jesus answered, "What do the Teachings of Moses say? What's your understanding of their requirements?"

27 He answered, "**You must love Yahweh, your God, with your entire being, all your heart, thoughts, personality, and determination. You must also love your neighbor in the same tolerant accepting way that you love yourself.**" *[Leviticus 19:18; Deuteronomy 6:5; Matthew 22:34-40; Mark 12:28-33; Romans 13:9; Galatians 5:14; James 2:8]*

28 Jesus said, "You have answered correctly. If you really love God and your neighbor in this way, you will gain eternal life." ❖ *It's not legalistic obedience to any set of rules that gives life, but a proper whole-hearted love relationship with God. From that will proceed the proper trust and dependence on him and his words, and also love for our neighbors and obedience to his will. Only this kind of heart attitude toward God will bring eternal life. The teacher may not have properly understood the answer he gave, but it was correct.* ➤

29 But the teacher wanted to justify himself, so he asked, "Who exactly is my neighbor?" ❖ *He either wanted to justify asking the first question—which he ended up answering himself—or he wanted to justify his own life by having Jesus confirm what he thought the answer would be. It's not clear what his intention was, but it's likely that he was surprised by Jesus' answer.* ➤

30 Jesus replied by telling this story, "A man was walking down the road from Jerusalem to Jericho when he was attacked by robbers. They beat him up, stripped him of his clothes and possessions, and left him half dead. **31** It happened that a priest came down that same road from Jerusalem. When he saw the man, he passed by on the other side of the road. ❖ *Had the man been clothed, it would have indicated if he was Jewish or not, but he was probably left with only a loin cloth and might have been a Gentile. There was also the possibility that the man was already dead or would die in the course of helping him if the priest tried to help. If he touched a Gentile or a dead man, it* would make him ritually unclean. To become clean again so he could perform his priestly duties was expensive and would have taken a week of his time. Thus helping the man risked significant inconvenience. The Torah says it was important for a priest to remain ritually clean. So he thought that he had adequate justification to avoid getting involved. Of course, a proper love for God would have given him compassion that outweighed all these considerations. ➤ **32** In the same way, a Levite also came by, saw the man, and passed by on the other side of the road.
❖ *A Levite is a man from the tribe of Levi whose job was to assist the priests in Temple duties. He also had concerns about ritual purity for his job, even though his would have been of less consequence than the priest's.* ➤ **33** But then a Samaritan came along on his journey, and when he saw the man, he felt compassion for him. ❖ *Samaritans were descended from Jews who had intermarried with Gentiles. Jews and Samaritans hated and avoided each other. Jesus shocked his Jewish audience by introducing a despised Samaritan as a hero. The Samaritan was in Jewish territory and knew the man was most likely a Jew. If he helped the man, he risked the man's rejection when he woke; and if he took him to the nearest Jewish town, he risked being blamed for the attack. But his actions were based on compassion, despite the fact that the man he helped would probably consider him an enemy.* ➤ **34** He went to him and poured wine and oil on his wounds and then bandaged him. ❖ *Wine and olive oil were the standard medicinal treatment at the time, the wine used as a disinfectant and the oil as a dressing.* ➤ Then, he put the man on his donkey, took him to an inn, and cared for him there. **35** In the morning, he gave the innkeeper money equivalent to two-day's wages and said, 'Continue to look after him, and when I return, I will reimburse you for any additional cost.'" ❖ *He didn't leave him in the hands of other Jews with the minimum of decent help. He stayed and took care of him for the rest of the day and night, then arranged for his room, board, and care until he should recover—with a pledge to cover all expenses. By any human standard, this was beyond the call of duty for a stranger.* ➤

36 Addressing the teacher, Jesus asked, "Which of these three men acted as a neighbor to the man who was attacked by robbers?"

37 Not even able to utter the word "Samaritan," he answered, "The one who showed him mercy."

Then Jesus told him, "Go and demonstrate love to others in the same way."

Jesus Visits Martha and Mary

38 As Jesus and his followers traveled along, they entered Bethany village just outside of Jerusalem, and a woman named Martha offered them hospitality in her home. 39 While she was working, her sister Mary sat on the floor near Jesus, listening to him teach—hanging on his every word. 40 But Martha was mainly concerned with all the preparations needed to feed her guests. She came to Jesus and said, "Lord, don't you care that my sister has left me to do all the work myself? Please tell her to come and help me!"

41 But he told her, "My dear Martha, you worry too much about too many things. 42 There's only one thing you should really be concerned about, and Mary has chosen it by sitting here listening to me. I will not make her give it up."

11

Jesus Teaches How to Pray

1 One day, Jesus had been praying in a certain place. When he finished, one of his followers came to him and said, "Lord, teach us how to pray, just like John the Baptizer taught his followers."

2 Jesus said, "When you pray, pray simply like this and for these kinds of things: 'Father, cause people to honor your name and submit to your kingship. 3 Provide us with the food and anything else we need today. 4 Forgive our sins in the same way that we forgive those who wrong us. And help us so we won't yield to temptation.' "

5-7 Then he said, "Imagine this situation: A friend of yours has been traveling and just arrived at your home at midnight for a visit and you have no food in the house to offer him. So you go to a friend's house and wake him. You say, 'A friend has just arrived for a visit and I've nothing to feed him. Would you please loan me three loaves of bread?' Can you imagine him answering like this? 'Don't bother me! I've already locked the

door and my children are in bed with me. I can't get up to give you anything!' Of course he would never refuse! ❖ *Middle-eastern culture considered hospitality to be one of the highest obligations—with the entire village's honor at stake. A neighbor would never refuse such a request, and the bread was the least important part of the meal.* ➤ 8 I tell you, the man might not want to get up and give you something for the sake of friendship, but to avoid spoiling his good reputation in the village he will get up and give you everything you want, not just the bread you asked for." ❖ *Jesus' point was: If a mere man will do this for the sake of his integrity and reputation, you can be certain that your Heavenly Father who loves you is even more willing to give you what you ask for in prayer.* ➤ A

9 Jesus continued, "When you ask God for something that you need, keep on asking, and at the proper time he will give it. Keep on seeking him and you will find him. Keep on knocking on his door in prayer and he will open it to you. 10 Everyone who asks will receive. Everyone who seeks will find what he is seeking. And the door will open to everyone who knocks. 11 You fathers, if your son asked you for a fish, would you give him a snake? 12 Or if he asked for an egg, would you give him a scorpion? 13 If you know how to give good things to your children—even though you are sinners—certainly your Heavenly Father is even more willing to give the Holy Spirit to those who ask him!" ❖ *We can always ask to be filled with the Holy Spirit. This will never be denied us. It's as basic and necessary for our spiritual life as food is for our bodies.* ➤

People Accuse Jesus of Working with the Prince of Demons

14 One day, Jesus expelled a demon that had made a man mute. When it left, he could talk, and the crowd was amazed. 15 But some said, "He can only expel them with the help of Beelzebul B who rules over all demons."

16 Others wanted to test Jesus to make him prove that his power came from God and not from Satan; so they demanded he perform some miraculous sign that was clearly from God. 17 But Jesus knew their

---

A 11:8 Insight for interpreting this parable comes from Kenneth E. Bailey's book "Poet & Peasant," pp. 119-141.

B 11:15 Beelzebul was a Jewish name for Satan.

thoughts and said, "Any Kingdom divided in civil war won't last long, and a divided household will fall apart. 18 You think that I'm expelling demons with Beelzebul's help. But if Satan is fighting against his own demons, how can his Kingdom continue? 19 And if I'm expelling them with Beelzebul's power, then what about your own followers? They expel demons too. Whose power do they use? They will judge the reasonableness of your accusation! 20 But if I'm expelling demons by God's power, then this proves that the Kingdom of God has come among you."

21 Jesus then compared Satan to a strongman, "When a strongman is fully armed and guarding his house, his possessions are safe. 22 But when a stronger man attacks and defeats him, he will first disarm him and then divide the spoils. ❖ *Jesus' point was that he was able to expel demons because he is mightier than Satan. The spoils that belonged to the strongman are the people he had under the control or influence of his demons.* ➤

23 "You have to choose sides. Those who aren't helping me are against me. And those who don't help me lead people to God are helping to drive them away."

Expelled Demons Will Try to Return

24 Jesus continued, "When a demon is expelled from a person, it travels through arid places looking for a new place to rest in someone's body. If it doesn't find such a place, it says to itself, 'I will return to my former residence.' 25 When it returns, it finds the residence clean, vacant of any demons, and in order. 26 Then it goes and brings seven worse demons and they all enter to live there so the person is worse off than before." ❖ *He is warning people who have had demons expelled that they must repent, allow the Holy Spirit to enter their lives, and submit to God if they don't want the demons to return and bring others too.* ➤

True Blessing

27 When Jesus had said this, a woman in the crowd called out, "God blessed your mother who bore and nursed you!" 28 But Jesus replied, "Those who are really blessed by God are people who hear his word and obey it."

Jesus Refuses to Do Miracles on Demand

29 As the crowd grew larger, Jesus continued to say, "Many people living today are evil. They want me to perform spectacular signs to prove that my power comes from God, but I won't. The only sign I will give is similar to the sign that happened to the prophet Jonah. 30 Jonah's reprieve from death after three days in the stomach of a large fish was a sign to the people of Nineveh long ago. *[Jonah chapters 1—2]* And what will happen to me, the Son of Man, will be the same kind of sign to people living today. ❖ *Jesus was speaking cryptically about his future resurrection after being in the grave parts of three days. This would be all the proof they needed that he had been sent by God.* ➤

31 "On Judgment Day, the Queen of Sheba who visited Solomon *[1 Kings 10:1-10]* will stand and condemn those living today, because she traveled from a distant land just to listen to Solomon's wisdom. But you refuse to recognize that someone greater than Solomon is here. ❖ *i.e., Jesus the Messiah* ➤ You refuse to believe the signs you have already seen me do—or my message. 32 On Judgment Day, the people of Nineveh will also stand up and condemn you because they listened to Jonah's message and repented. And now someone greater than Jonah is here, yet you refuse to repent."

33 Jesus continued, "No one lights a lamp and then hides it or covers it up. Instead, he puts it on a stand so all who enter the room can see by the light. ❖ *This is a figure where light stands for God's truth that Jesus had been proclaiming. His point is, he hasn't at all hidden the truth about where his power comes from. Rather, his teaching and miracles have all been in the open so everyone could see them and recognize the obvious fact that he was sent by God and has God's approval and power. They were wanting yet another sign to prove that he came from God, but he refused to perform on demand. He healed out of compassion and did miracles in obedience to his Father's direction. But he had no intention of forcing people to choose to believe in him. He only wants people coming to him who really desire to know God. The same people demanding signs said that he expelled demons using Satan's power. They would say the same about any other sign if they didn't want to believe. So he refused to cater to their demands.* ➤ 34 The eye of spiritual discernment is the window

to your mind. If your discerning eye is clear, your mind will be filled with the light of truth. If your discerning eye is bad, your mind will be filled with the darkness of error. **35** Be sure that what you think is spiritual light isn't actually the deception of darkness! **36** If your mind is filled with truth, then you won't be deceived by error and will have proper understanding." ❖ *In even clearer terms:* **34** *If your mind is open, then you will clearly perceive what's true. If your mind is closed, then your perceptions will be wrong.* **35** *Be sure that you are really perceiving truth and aren't deceiving yourself!* **36** *If you have comprehended the truth from what you've seen, then it's obvious that God has sent me and no further miracles as proof are necessary. (Also see the note at Matthew 6:23.)* ➤

Jesus Condemns
the Pharisees and Scripture Teachers

37 When Jesus finished speaking, a Pharisee invited him to lunch. So Jesus went with him, entered his house, and reclined at the table. **38** His host was surprised that Jesus didn't ritually wash his hands first before reclining for the meal, following Jewish custom. ❖ *This custom was not a command from God but was added by Jewish elders, and the Pharisees followed it religiously. They believed that contact with the outside world made them ritually unclean and that the washing ritual made them clean again and thus acceptable to God. But they had elevated this rule to a status as important as the commands which God gave Moses in the Torah; and they condemned anyone who didn't follow it, just as if they had sinned against God's Torah. Jesus pointedly refused to follow this custom because he didn't approve of man-made rules being taught as if they were equally important as God's commands. He considered their rules—which they insisted that people follow—as unnecessary burdens that hid the true significance of what God was trying to teach in the Torah.* ➤ **39** Since Jesus knew what the Pharisee was thinking, ❖ *via a "word of knowledge" [1 Corinthians 12:8]* ➤ he said, "You Pharisees are so concerned about externals such as carefully washing the outside of cups and dishes. But you totally neglect internal motives and attitudes which are more important. Outwardly, you are ritually clean and meticulous about keeping rules. But your hearts and minds are full of greed and evil. **40** You are morally depraved! Didn't God make the inside as well as the outside?

41 If you really want to be 'clean' in God's sight, then motivated by love for him, give what you have to the poor. If you do this, he will count everything about you as 'clean.'

42 "You Pharisees are in real trouble with God! You meticulously give a tenth of all your income, crops, animals, and material increase to God, even a tenth of the herbs from your garden, but you totally ignore the major issues of justice and loving God. It's these more important commands that you should be most anxious to keep, without neglecting the minor ones. ❖ *Jesus clearly expected people to still follow all the Torah's commands. He did not teach that they were unnecessary. Obeying them doesn't earn salvation or God's favor. But they are indicative of God's will that he wants his people to follow. Only those commands that God has clearly changed—as recorded in the New Testament Scriptures—are no longer in effect. i.e., the commands to make sacrifices for sin (since Jesus' sacrifice replaces them), [Hebrews chapters 9–10] and the commands about ritual cleanness. [Mark 7:19; Luke 11:41; Acts 10:15, 28; Romans 14:14, 20; Ephesians 2:13-16; Titus 1:15] Jesus told his apostles to teach their followers to obey everything he had commanded them, [Matthew 28:20] and the gospel accounts are clear that Jesus expected his apostles to continue to follow the Torah's commands in the way that he clarified they should be followed (e.g., in the Sermon on the Mount and other places). An argument on the other side of this issue is that the Council of Jerusalem made minimum demands on Gentile believers, [Acts 15:1-30] so some believe that the commands in the Torah are only binding on Jewish believers.* ➤ **43** It's going to be bad for you Pharisees on the Last Day! Because your main desires are to sit in the seats of honor in the synagogue and for people to kowtow to you in public. **44** You will be judged harshly! You are like unmarked graves in a field that people walk over without being aware of it." ❖ *To touch a grave, even unknowingly, made a Jew ritually unclean. Jesus was saying that outwardly people couldn't see anything wrong with them, but by associating too closely with the Pharisees, they would be corrupted and made unacceptable to God by the inner rot and decay of their moral influence.* ➤

45 A Scripture teacher said, "Rabbi, what you are saying insults us too!"

46 Jesus replied, "Yes, God's judgment of you Scripture teachers is going to be terrible as well! Your man-made rules and regulations crush people under a burden that they can't and shouldn't have to carry, and you don't lift a finger to help them. You yourselves don't even follow all those rules! 47 Your punishment will be severe! You build monuments on the tombs of prophets murdered by your ancestors. 48 But you are no different than your ancestors were. You reject God's prophets just like they did. This shows that you approve of what they did and are as guilty as they are. ❖ *Two prophets they rejected were John the Baptizer and Jesus.* ➤ 49 This is what God in his wisdom said, 'I will send prophets and apostles to them. They will kill some and persecute others.' 50 Therefore, you will be held responsible for the murders of all of God's prophets from the beginning of creation until now, 51 starting with Cain's killing Abel ❖ *the first murder* ➤ and ending with the murder of Zechariah who was killed between the altar and the Holy Place. *[2 Chronicles 24:20-21]* ❖ *This was the last murder mentioned in the Tanakh (i.e., the Jewish Scriptures) whose books are ordered differently than in Christian Bibles.* ➤ I guarantee that you will be held accountable for all of their deaths! ❖ *Unspoken but implied is, "unless you repent." God will always forgive the repentant sinner. Jesus wasn't upbraiding them just to let off steam. Nothing more subtle had so far worked in leading them to repentance, so here he tries dire warnings of punishment and shoving their sins in their faces in the hope that some of them will wake up and repent. Even though he is angry with them, he still loves them and wants them to repent. After his resurrection, some did repent and believe.* ➤

52 "I pity you Scripture teachers because of the punishment waiting for you! People look up to you as teachers, yet you hide from them the key which opens the way to understand God's truth. You yourselves refuse to submit to God and so enter his Kingdom, and you do your best to prevent others from entering too!"

53 When Jesus left there, the Pharisees and Scripture teachers hated him. After this, they often interrogated him in public on many subjects 54 and plotted to trap him into saying something they could use against him in court.

12

Jesus Warns About Hypocrisy

1 In the meantime, thousands of people had gathered around Jesus to hear him, to the point that they were stepping on each other's feet. Jesus first addressed his followers, "Beware of the infectious influence of the Pharisees, particularly their hypocritical pretense of holiness. Don't think that any pretense will ultimately succeed. 2 Remember that Judgment Day will come when God will publicly reveal all hidden thoughts, attitudes, motives, and deeds. 3 Whatever you have said in darkness will be heard in broad daylight. Whatever you have whispered in secret will be shouted from the housetops for all to hear. All your secret sins will be exposed."

Fear God Rather Than People

4 Jesus continued, "My friends, don't be afraid of those who might kill you. They can only kill your body, but after that they can't touch you. 5 But my warning to you is that you should have a healthy fear of God. He not only has power over your life in this world, but after you die, he decides if you will be sent to Hell or not. If you have any sense at all, you should realize that he is the one to be afraid of—not people.

6 "You know that sparrows are so common they are nearly worthless. Five of them can be bought for next to nothing. But God notices even creatures as unimportant as sparrows. He's aware of each and every one of them and what happens to them. 7 I assure you, you are far more important to him than mere sparrows! God's awareness and care for you is so great that he even knows how many hairs are on your head every moment. Nothing takes him by surprise and nothing can defeat his power so there is no reason for any of his children to ever fear what people can do to them. ❖ *Jesus taught that people are much more important than animals, contrary to the attitude of many people today. He also implies here that nothing happens to his people except what he allows to happen. God is in control of our lives. If bad things happen to us, he has allowed them for his reasons and purposes. See Romans 8:28.* ➤

8 "So don't be afraid to proclaim your allegiance to me from fear of persecution or death. I want you to know that all who are willing to publicly declare that they are my followers—regardless of the consequences— will find out on Judgment Day that I, the

Son of Man, will declare before God and his angels that they belong to me. 9 But those who deny that they belong to me, even if it's only because they fear persecution or death, will find that I too will deny before God and his angels that they belong to me.

10 "Yet know that God can forgive everyone who in any way speaks against me, the Son of Man—if they repent. But God will not forgive anyone who blasphemes against the Holy Spirit. ❖ *This is because it is the Spirit who enables us to repent; and without repentance, there is no forgiveness. If the Spirit is rejected and leaves, that person will never again desire to repent. So anyone who is worried about having committed this sin, hasn't. Anyone who has committed this sin will never worry about it.* ➤

11 "When you are brought to trial in synagogues or before rulers or other authorities because of your allegiance to me, don't worry ahead of time about how to defend yourself or what you will say. 12 Because the Holy Spirit will give you the words to say right when you need them."

Parable About the Rich Fool

13 A man in the crowd said to him, "Rabbi, please tell my brother to fairly divide the inheritance with me that he got from our father."

14 Jesus replied, "I wasn't sent to be an arbiter or judge between you."

15 Then, using this request as a topic to teach on, he said to the crowd, "Be careful to guard against every kind of greed in your life. Quality of life is not determined by what you have, not even when you are wealthy."

16 Then he told them this parable, "There was a rich farmer whose land was very productive. 17 He began to reason with himself like this, 'I don't have enough storage capacity for my crops. What should I do?'

❖ *Jesus' listeners would immediately realize that while this man is materially rich, he has no friends or family for he doesn't discuss his problem with others. He can only interact with himself about it. He is so selfish that it doesn't even occur to him to give some of his surplus to the poor.* ➤ **A** 18 Then he said to himself, 'This is what I'll do. I'll tear down my old barns and build new ones big

enough to store everything I have. 19 Then I'll say to myself, "Take it easy and enjoy life! Eat, drink, and be merry! You've got enough stored up to last for years!" ' 20 But God said to him, 'You are a fool because tonight you will die and you've made no preparations at all for that event. So what good will all this wealth you've accumulated do you?' " 21 Jesus concluded, "That is the fate of those who are mainly interested in acquiring wealth for themselves in this life, but haven't used it to serve God."

The Proper Attitude Toward Possessions

22 Then, Jesus told his followers, "So what I'm telling you is this: Don't worry about having enough to eat or having decent clothes to wear 23 because there are much more important things than food and clothing in this life. 24 Consider birds. They don't plant crops or harvest them or even store food. Yet God sees to it that they eat what they need. And you are much more valuable to God than birds. He will certainly take care of your needs. 25 All the worrying in the world can't add a single moment to your life. **B** 26 If your worrying can't even accomplish a small thing like that, why worry about anything at all? 27 Think about how the wildflowers grow. They don't have to work or make their beautiful petals. But not even King Solomon in all his splendor looked as good as they do. 28 Think about it. If God so beautifully clothes field grass with wildflowers—grass that grows for only a short time before it is cut and burned—he will be even more concerned to provide you with clothing! Your faith in God's provision is too small! 29 Don't worry about what you will eat and drink today or tomorrow. 30 Those who don't know God worry about such things. But you have a Father in Heaven who knows that you need them. 31 So submit to him and mainly be concerned about the affairs of his Kingdom. Then he will take care of providing you with the necessities. 32 Don't be afraid, my children. Your Father is happy to give you all that's in his Kingdom."

A 12:17 Insight for this interpretation is from Kenneth E. Bailey's book, "Through Peasant Eyes," pp 64-66.

B 12:25 In fact, we know that worry harms our emotional and physical health, reducing our quality of life.

How to Acquire Wealth for Yourself in Heaven

33 "This is how to store up treasure in Heaven that you will have forever: Sell what you own and give the money to those in need. ❖ *Did you just gloss over this instruction? Have you really taken it to heart and acted upon it?* ➤ Treasure stored in Heaven is safe from theft and decay.

34 "And unlike accumulating earthly wealth, it's good for you to accumulate the eternal kind. For if this is your focus, your heart and mind will be in the right place."

Always Be Ready for Jesus' Return

35 "Always be ready for my return on the Last Day, like servants who are dressed and alert and keeping their oil lamps lit 36 while they wait for their master to return from a wedding feast. They will want to be ready to open the door for him the moment he returns. 37 There will be special rewards for those he finds alert when he arrives. I assure you, he will prepare himself to serve, have them sit down to dine, and wait on them. 38 They will indeed be in his good favor if he finds them ready, even if he returns late at night or in the wee hours of the morning.

39 "To use another illustration, if a homeowner knew when a burglar planned to break in, he would be awake and ready when the burglar came. But of course, nobody can anticipate such things. 40 I, the Son of Man, will also return at a time you can't anticipate. So you always have to be ready." ❖ *To be ready is to live every day having faith in his promises, doing what he wants you to be doing, and not wasting your life and resources on things other than Kingdom business.* ➤ 41 Peter asked, "Lord, does this illustration only apply to us, or is it for everyone?"

42 The Lord answered, "I'm talking to anyone who wants to be a faithful and wise manager whom God has given the responsibilities of supervising the master's household and feeding his other servants. ❖ *Jesus is talking about the leaders he puts over his followers.* ➤ 43 Such a manager will indeed be in a good position with his master if he finds him faithfully doing his duties when he returns. 44 As a reward, the master will put him in charge of everything he owns.

45 "But what if such a manager thinks to himself, 'My master won't be returning for quite a while,' and then starts to beat the other servants and to party and get drunk? 46 He will find the time of His master's return totally unexpected. The master will severely punish him and throw him outside the Kingdom with others who aren't faithful, and the disobedient.

47 "The servant who knows what his master wants him to do but doesn't do it will be severely punished. 48 But the servant who doesn't know what his master expects will be punished lightly for doing wrong. God requires a lot from those he has blessed with much in this life. If he has entrusted you with many resources, he expects proportionally more from you." ❖ *This applies to knowledge, material wealth, resources, authority, influence, ability, and time. All we are and have God gave us to use for his purposes. This also indicates that there will be degrees of punishment in Hell, depending on how much a person knows about the truth and the degree of his or her unfaithfulness to it.* ➤

Loyalty to Jesus
Will Cause People to Reject You

49 Jesus continued, "I've come to ignite a fire in this world and I wish it were already burning. ❖ *He means the heat of division between those who choose to follow him and those who reject him. Fire also often represents purification, and he may also have been thinking about the purification of those who choose to follow him. His whole purpose in coming into this world was to save those who are willing to enter into a close relationship with him and willing to allow him to purify them. He yearns for this to be accomplished.* ➤ 50 But first, I have to undergo a baptism of suffering, and it's a difficult thing for me to contemplate until it's finally over. ❖ *Baptism, in this sense, means "complete immersion." Jesus knew the suffering that awaited him in Jerusalem and was not looking forward to it. Yet he was determined to go through with it.* ➤ 51 Did you think that I came to bring peace to this world? Not at all! I came to bring division between those who follow me and those who reject me. 52 Families will divide, three who reject me against two who follow me, and all other possible combinations. 53 They will divide father against son, mother against daughter,

mother-in-law against daughter-in-law, and every other possible relationship." ❖ *Jesus doesn't desire division, but because his purpose is to draw those who want to enter into a love relationship with him, and since he wants people to choose this of their own free will, he won't coerce anyone. Thus the inevitable conflict is, in his eyes, totally due to those who reject him since he is their creator and rightful master.* ➤

Interpreting the Signs of the Times

54 Jesus also said, "When you see a rain cloud coming out of the west from the Mediterranean Sea, you say, 'It's going to rain,' and you are right. 55 And when you notice a wind out of the south from the desert, you say, 'It's going to be hot,' and that's exactly how it turns out. 56 You hypocrites! If you are able to interpret the weather signs, you should be able to interpret the signs that are happening during these times." ❖ *They were hypocrites because they claimed to know God and to understand his ways, yet they refused to understand that Jesus was the Messiah sent by God, and they refused to accept his teaching despite the clear miraculous signs he did. The meaning of the signs and the message he preached were as obvious as the weather signs.* ➤

Make Peace with God Before It's Too Late

57 "Why don't you judge for yourselves what's right? ❖ *i.e., Why don't you recognize your need to repent and get right with God instead of ignoring what he is saying to you?* ➤ 58 If someone brings a legitimate lawsuit against you, it's in your own best interest to make peace with him before it gets to court. If you are convicted, the judge will hand you over to an officer and he will throw you into debtors prison. 59 If that happens, I guarantee you won't get out until you've paid the last penny you owe." ❖ *Jesus' picture and point may seem obscure because we no longer have debtors prisons. The judge represents God. The one who brings the lawsuit against you is also God. He will play two roles in our lives, accuser and judge. The point is, we need to make peace with God before we die or before Judgment Day, whichever comes first. Because if we don't, when we stand before him as judge, it will be too late to do anything about our fate. The picture of paying the last penny of your debt has no parallel with our lives since it's impossible for us to pay off our debt of sin to God. The point of that part of the story is that you will never get out.*

Your punishment will be forever. Jesus offers us the way to be at peace with God before it's too late. ➤

13

A Call to Repentance and a Warning

1 At that time, some people told Jesus about Pilate ordering some Galileans killed while they were offering sacrifices. ❖ *It's known from historical sources that Pilate was a heavy-handed and harsh ruler, and Galileans had a reputation for rebelliousness. This event most likely occurred during a Passover Festival, the only time when people offered their own sacrifices, and may have been Roman retaliation for someone else's act of rebellion. It was common for Jews of that time to think that a disaster or an apparently unjust punishment was really God's punishment for some unknown sin. This understanding of how God supposedly works is wrong.* ➤ 2 Jesus said to them, "Do you think these Galileans were worse sinners than others because this happened to them? 3 Not at all! But I warn you, unless you repent of your sin and turn to God, you too will suffer violent destruction. 4 And what about those eighteen men who died when the tower of Siloam fell on them? Do you think they were the worst sinners living in Jerusalem? 5 I say they were not! But if you don't repent, you too will suffer violent ruin." ❖ *Jesus emphasizes his point with a second story of identical meaning. Those people who died were not particularly bad sinners and their deaths had nothing to do with God's punishment. But if you don't repent of your sins, you will experience God's punishment on Judgment Day. See 2 Thessalonians 1:9 and the following note about what it means to experience ruin in Hell.* ➤

Parable of the Barren Fig Tree

6 Then Jesus told this parable, "A man had a fig tree in his vineyard and he kept coming around to look for fruit on it but never found any. 7 So he told his gardener, 'For three years now, I've waited for this tree to bear fruit and I haven't seen any yet. Chop it down; it's wasting good space.' 8 But the gardener said, 'Sir, let it stay for one more year. I will loosen the soil and fertilize it. 9 If it bears fruit next year, you can keep it. If not, then you can have it chopped down.' " ❖ *The fig tree sometimes symbolizes the people of Israel in the Scriptures. [Hosea 9:10; Joel 1:7] Jesus' parable was a*

warning. God found no fruit in their lives. i.e., They weren't living the way he meant for them to live. They are under threat of destruction if they don't repent and start producing the fruit of obedience. They've been given a short reprieve to see if they will respond to special attention and feeding. Jesus' ministry would be that season of special attention. Unfortunately, most of the nation of Israel did not repent and accept Jesus as God's Messiah (though several tens of thousands did, possibly as much as 10% of the population in Israel). [Acts 21:20] ➤

Jesus Heals a Crippled Woman on a Sabbath

10 One Sabbath, Jesus was teaching in a synagogue. **11** A woman was present who had been sick for eighteen years because of an afflicting demon. She was bent over and unable to stand up straight. **12** When Jesus saw her, he called her forward and said, "You are free from your sickness!" **13** Then he placed his hands on her and she immediately straighten up normally and started praising God.

14 But the leader of the synagogue was angry that Jesus had healed her on the Sabbath. So he took it out on the people, saying, "There are six work days in a week! Come on one of those days to be healed, but not on the Sabbath!"

15 The Lord replied to him and others who agreed with him, "You self-righteous hypocrites! Every one of you work on the Sabbath when you untie your ox or donkey and lead them out to drink. You know it's necessary to take care of them this way and that the teachings in the Torah allow it. **16** Isn't a human being much more important than a dumb animal? ❖ *This is an incidental point, but this verse clearly shows that in God's sight, humans are much more important than animals, contrary to the view of many today.* ➤ And she's a descendant of Abraham, thus a rightful heir to the blessings that God promised him! Satan has held her in bondage for eighteen years and you are saying it isn't right that she be set free from this bondage today, even if it is the Sabbath?" ❖ *Not to mention that it was God's power doing the healing, so they were criticizing God.* ➤ **17** When he said this, those who had opposed him were humiliated because it was clear he

was right. And all the people were thrilled at the wonderful things he did.

Parable of the Mustard Seed

18 Then Jesus said, "How can I teach you what God's Kingdom is like? What can I compare it to? **19** It's like a mustard seed that a man planted in his garden. It grew into a tree and many birds nested in its branches." *[Psalm 104:12; Ezekiel 17:23; 31:6; Daniel 4:12]* ❖ *God's Kingdom starts in a small way in people's hearts. But it grows in influence, eventually becoming quite large and a blessing to those around it. Jesus may also have had in mind the fact that birds often represented Gentiles, and the Kingdom would even take in Gentiles under its sway, which was a radical thought for the Jews of his day.* ➤ **A**

Parable of the Yeast

20 Again, Jesus said, "How can I teach you what God's Kingdom is like? What can I compare it to? **21** It's like a little yeast that a woman mixes with a large amount of flour until it's worked through the whole lump of dough." ❖ *That little bit of yeast affects all of the dough. In the same way, God's people may be few, but their quiet slow influence in the world can be far reaching and have large effects.* ➤ **B**

The Narrow Door to Heaven

22 Afterward, Jesus traveled through villages and towns on his way to Jerusalem and taught as he went. **23** Someone asked him, "Lord, is it true that only a few people will be saved and go to Heaven?" ❖ *As in this case, Jesus often didn't answer questions directly, but instead led the person to focus on what he considered more important. He may also have implied, "Yes, therefore..."* ➤

Jesus replied, **24** "Try hard to enter Heaven through the narrow door now, because many will try to enter when it's too late ❖ *i.e., after death, or after he returns* ➤ and not succeed because the door will be shut. **25** The time will come when the master of the house ❖ *i.e., Jesus* ➤ will shut the door to Heaven. Then, they will stand outside knocking and pleading, 'Lord, open the door for us!' But he will answer, 'I don't know you, so I won't.' **26** Then they will say, 'But we ate and drank with you, and you taught in our village!'

A 13:19 See the footnote at Matthew 13:32.

B 13:21 See the footnote at Matthew 13:33.

27 But he will reply, 'I don't know you. Go away and don't come back! You are not welcome because you are evil!' *[Psalm 6:8]* 28 Then they will wail with grief and grind their teeth in anger when they see Abraham, Isaac, Jacob, ❖ *their Jewish ancestors* ➤ and all the prophets present in God's Kingdom, with themselves banished! 29 But Gentiles will have come from every nation in the world to take their places at the feast in God's Kingdom. 30 And note this, some who are the lowliest in this world will be the most important in the Kingdom. And some who are the most important in this world will be the lowliest in Heaven." *[Matthew 19:30; 20:16; Mark 10:31]* ❖ *The picture of a narrow door to Heaven implies that it's difficult to enter. Elsewhere, Jesus says that he is the only entryway to eternal life. [John 14:6] But following him isn't easy because it requires total commitment. Most people are looking for an easier way, and so they bypass the narrow door and difficult way until it's too late. The difficult way starts with faith and repentance and continues with obedience to God, but few people are willing to go that way. Instead, many prefer to believe Satan's lies that, "Obedience isn't important since we are saved because of his undeserved favor," or that "Everyone will be saved."* ➤

Jesus' Love for the People of Jerusalem

31 At that time, some Pharisees came to Jesus and told him, "You should leave here and go elsewhere because Herod Antipas says he is going to kill you!" ❖ *Whether this was true or just a ploy by the Pharisees, we don't know. But Jesus' reply shows that he had no fear of Herod.* ➤

32 Jesus replied, "You go and tell that vicious and destructive fox **A** that I will continue to expel demons and heal people today and tomorrow ❖ *meaning for the near future,* ➤ and on the third day ❖ *some special day not too far off, or perhaps the day of his resurrection* ➤ I will finish my work. 33 Regardless of what Herod intends, I must continue on to Jerusalem for now. It just wouldn't do for a prophet to be killed anywhere but in Jerusalem! ❖ *In the history of Israel, the leaders of Jerusalem had killed so many prophets that it could have been nicknamed, "the city that kills*

God's prophets." Jesus was speaking sarcastically, for he knew he would be killed in Jerusalem too. ➤

34 "O my people in Jerusalem! You kill the prophets and stone God's messengers! Many times I wanted to shield you from God's coming punishment. I wanted to gather you in together to protect you, as a hen gathers her chicks under her wings. But you didn't want me. 35 Take notice! God will turn his back on you and leave you. He will no longer protect you from your enemies. And you won't see me again until you say, **'Blessed is the he who comes in the name of Yahweh.'** " *[Psalm 118:26]* ❖ *Because most Jews rejected Jesus as God's Messiah, he allowed the Romans to destroy Jerusalem and the Temple in AD 70, and the Jewish nation ceased to exist for nearly 1900 years. Prophecy predicted the rise of Israel again as a nation, which happened in 1948; [Deuteronomy 30:3-5; Isaiah 66:7-8; Jeremiah 16:14-15; 31:10; Ezekiel 34:13; 37:10-14; 21-22; Amos 9:14-15] and it also predicts that many Jews in Israel will accept Jesus as their Messiah very shortly before he returns. [Romans 11:25-26] That is most likely the timing of Jesus' prediction here when they will see him again.* ➤

14

Jesus Heals on a Sabbath

1 One Sabbath, Jesus accepted an invitation to eat with a prominent Pharisee, but they were actually watching him closely to see if they could catch him in some violation of the Torah's commands that they could use against him. 2 A man with a serious illness that caused swelling in his arms and legs came to Jesus. 3 So Jesus said to the Pharisees and Scripture teachers present, "Do the Teachings of Moses allow healing on the Sabbath, or not?"

4 But they sat in stony silence. ❖ *They were reluctant to admit that God's Torah didn't forbid it, because their traditions did forbid it unless a person was about to die.* ➤ So Jesus touched the man, healed him, and sent him away. 5 Then he said, "Is there anyone here who would even hesitate to help his son or ox if one fell into a well on the Sabbath?"

A 13:32 In the Hebrew mind, a fox is both weak and a destroyer. [There is a mild hint of this in Nehemiah 4:3] The connotation of sly and crafty is an English and American idea, and not likely to have been the point Jesus was making about Herod.

6 There was nothing they could say to refute this, nevertheless, they hated him for justifying this public violation of their Sabbath rule.

Jesus Teaches on Humility

7 Jesus noticed that many of the guests had maneuvered to sit in seats of honor, so he began to teach them, 8 "When you are invited to a wedding reception, don't presume to sit in the seat of honor. It might be reserved for someone else 9 and then your host would be forced to embarrass you by asking you to move. You could end up in whatever seat is still available, possibly the worst one in the house. 10 So when you are invited, take the worst seat in the house and your host is likely to honor you by asking you to move to a more prominent position. 11 This is the way God rules in his Kingdom. Those who try to exalt themselves will be humbled, and those who humble themselves will be honored."

12 Then Jesus said to his host, ❖ *Note that middle-eastern cultures have a strong taboo against criticizing a host.* ➤ "If you invite people to a meal and want God's approval, don't invite only—or mainly—your friends, brothers, relatives, or rich neighbors. For they will just invite you back and their return invitation will be your only reward. 13 Instead, invite those who are poor, crippled, and blind. ❖ *We are to generously bless the poor, beggars, and the homeless with our abundance.* ➤ 14 As a consequence, God will bless you in this life and also reward you when he raises his people from death on the Last Day because you have unselfishly blessed those he loves who are unable to pay you back."

Parable of the Great Banquet in Heaven

15 When one of the men sitting at the table heard this, he said to Jesus, "Those who will feast in God's Kingdom are in a good position indeed!"

16 So Jesus told this parable to say that—contrary to their expectations—many Gentiles will feast in God's Kingdom while many Jews will not. "A man planned a big banquet and sent out many invitations. 17 When the banquet was ready, he sent out his servant to tell all the invited guests, 'Everything is ready, so come right now!' 18 But one after another—in grave insult and offense to their host—they all made extremely lame excuses why they couldn't come. The first guest said, 'I just bought some land that I haven't seen yet so I have to go inspect it. I ask that you excuse me.' 19 Another one said, 'I just bought five pair of oxen and need to try them out to see how well they plow. I ask that you excuse me.' 20 Another said, 'I just got married last week so I can't come.'

21 "The servant returned and reported this to his master who became very angry. So he told his servant, 'Hurry and go down all the streets and alleys in town and bring back those who are poor, crippled, and blind to attend my banquet.' 22 After doing as he was told, he reported, 'Master, I've done as you ordered, but there's still room for more people.' 23 The master said, 'Go and search the country roads and paths for more people and urge them all to come. I want my house to be filled. 24 But I can guarantee you that none of the invited guests will get even a taste of my banquet!' " ❖ *Note that Jesus' use of "all" and "none" in his parable is typical hyperbole (exaggeration to make a strong point) used by Jewish rabbis in teaching. It doesn't mean that "all" Jews will be excluded from his Kingdom, only those who reject his invitation.* ➤

The Price of Being Jesus' True Follower

25 Now, large crowds were traveling with Jesus on the way to Jerusalem for the upcoming Passover Festival. He turned to them and said, 26 "If you want to be one of my followers but can't place your loyalty and obedience to me above your loyalty to your parents, spouse, siblings, children, and even your own desires for your life, then I won't accept you. A 27 If you aren't willing

---

A 14:26 Jesus actually said, "If anyone wants to follow me and does not hate his own father and mother and wife and children and brothers and sisters and even his own life, he cannot be my follower." The people listening to him were Jews, and Jewish teachers (rabbis) often used hyperbole (exaggeration to make a strong point). They knew that the Torah commands us to respect and love all these people and that Jesus was not advocating going

to give up your own plans and desires in order to obey my will for you—even if it means you must suffer or die for me—then you can't be one of my true followers.

28 "If you wanted to build a tower, you would, of course, carefully plan it out first, determine how much it would cost, and make sure that you had enough resources to finish the project. 29 If you didn't, you might only get the foundation laid, run out of funds, and become the laughing stock of everyone who found out. 30 You would become known as someone who doesn't finish what he starts.

31 "Or suppose a king decides to wage war against another king. If he is smart, he will carefully evaluate whether his 10,000 men are really able to defeat his enemy's 20,000 men. 32 If he decides that he can't, then he had better send ambassadors to negotiate a peace treaty before it's too late. 33 The point of all this is, if you want to be one of my true followers, you need to consider what it will cost you and whether or not you can go through with it to the very end of your life. For you have to be willing to give up everything in your life that will hinder you from following and obeying me."

Worthless Salt

34 Jesus continued, "Salt is good, but if it loses its flavor, it can't be made salty again. 35 It's not fit for anything—not even for the ground or a pile of manure. It will be thrown away. If you have your ears attuned to God, try to understand what I'm saying!" ❖ *The exact meaning of each part of this illustration isn't clear to us today, but the overall point is. Salt was a valuable commodity in Jesus' time. But even something good and valuable can become worthless. His point is that people who start out following him are valuable to him. But if they lose their commitment, they become worthless to his Kingdom. They will be rejected and cast out and nothing will be able to restore them. It's a final warning in his teaching about counting the cost of following him. You must be 100% committed and never turn back, or all your efforts will become worthless and you will be rejected and thrown out of the Kingdom.* ➤

15

The Good Shepherd and the Lost Sheep

1 Many tax collectors and other notorious sinners were regularly coming to listen to Jesus. 2 But the Pharisees and Scripture teachers complained, "This man always welcomes habitual sinners and even eats with them!" ❖ *According to middle-eastern custom, hosting someone at a meal signifies that the host accepts and approves of his guest, and is honoring him. The Pharisees thought that Jesus' eating with habitual sinners meant that he approved of their sinful lifestyles, and that eating with sinners ritually defiled him. But Jesus neither approved of sin nor was he defiled by eating with sinners.* ➤ 3 So Jesus told this parable to show that God is concerned about people who are "lost" and can't find the way to have a proper relationship with him. ❖ *He tells three stories but Luke calls them "this (one) parable,"—emphasizing that together they make one point which Jesus was trying to get across to the Pharisees and Scripture teachers. In these stories, the good shepherd, the good woman, and the good father all represent Jesus. He moves from a story about a valuable sheep to one about a valuable coin, both of which his audience would have no problem agreeing were worth searching for. The third story about people brings home the difference between his audience who despised "lost" sinners, and himself who searches them out. The main characters in his stories also represent God the Father, but ultimately, Jesus is the one who goes out searching—which is why he eats with sinners.* ➤

4 Jesus began, "Which of you, if you had a hundred sheep and had lost one of them, wouldn't leave the 99 grazing in the pasture and search for the lost one until you found it? ❖ *This is a rhetorical question. Sheep were valuable property and anyone would search for a lost sheep. Yet the religious leaders had less regard for "lost" people—those they called sinners. Jesus' illustration is typical of his teaching in that it's deeper than it first appears. This simple illustration has at least three levels of meaning. On one level he portrays the religious leaders as shepherds. This would be offensive to them because they considered shepherds to be disreputable and the lowest of occupations. But he also implies that the shepherd—representing the leaders—was responsible for losing the sheep in the first place. He's saying that the leaders have a responsibility to bring the lost sheep—those same*

---

against God's Torah. They would have properly understood this Semitic idiom and the point he was making

about the relative degree of loyalty he was requiring, as has been expressed in the interpreted translation above.

sinners they despise—back into the fold of God's people. On a second level, Jesus' illustration shows God's attitude toward those who are "lost" in sin. He actively seeks them out to bring them to repentance and back into a proper relationship with himself. See the note after verse 7 for the third level of meaning. ➤ 5 When you found the lost sheep, you would put it on your shoulders and carry it back again, rejoicing. ❖ This is no trivial task and represents the price of redemption. Though there is a burden in restoring the lost, it results in great joy. ➤ 6 When you got home, you would call your friends and neighbors together and say, 'Celebrate with me, because I've found my lost sheep!' ❖ The community of the redeemed also rejoices in the restoration of one who was lost. ➤ 7 I'm telling you, it's the same way in Heaven. God rejoices more over one sinner who repents and turns back to him than over 99 godly people who have no need to repent."

❖ In this illustration, Jesus equates "accepting being found" with "repentance." The sheep cannot save itself, but the shepherd (God) must come and find it. There can be no repentance without God reaching out to find the lost one. This is his undeserved enabling favor toward us. There's a third level of meaning in his conclusion which expresses irony. All people need to repent and turn to God, but not all realize it. Many of the religious leaders were self-righteous and oblivious to their own sins and the sinfulness of their judgmental attitudes. Jesus was probably implying that there was no special rejoicing over the 99 sheep out in the pasture who hadn't yet been brought "home"—because they didn't realize that they weren't yet "home"—and thus in a sense were also still "lost." [Isaiah 53:6; Ecclesiastes 7:20] This first story would have brought to his listeners' minds Psalm 23; Jeremiah 23:1-8; and Ezekiel 34:1-31 on which Jesus bases his story. In Jeremiah and Ezekiel, God himself promises to come to restore his lost sheep. Jesus is the fulfillment of these prophecies. ➤

The Good Woman and the Lost Coin

8 Then, Jesus told a second story with the same point. He said, "Or what woman who has ten silver coins—each worth a day's wage—and loses one, wouldn't light a lamp and thoroughly sweep the dirt floor of her house, searching until she finds it? 9 When she found it, she would call her friends and neighbors and say, 'Celebrate with me, for I've found the coin I lost!' 10 I'm telling you, it's just like that in Heaven. God rejoices in front of his angels over even one sinner who repents." ❖ Note that at the end of each story there's a celebration which includes eating, demonstrating the reason why Jesus eats with sinners. Kenneth E. Bailey brings out several fascinating reasons why Jesus includes this second story with a woman protagonist in his book "Jacob & the Prodigal." (See the Bibliography.) ➤

The Good Father and His Two Lost Sons

11 Then Jesus told a third story meant to contrast God's welcoming attitude toward repentant sinners versus the unforgiving attitude of those who are self-righteous. He said, "There was a man who had two sons. 12 The younger one grievously insulted his father by saying, 'Father, right now I want the share of your estate that I will get when you die.' ❖ His request implied that he would just as soon his father were dead. Such a request was culturally unprecedented, and Jesus' audience expected the father to angrily refuse. A son's duty was to stay with his father, care for him until he died, and submit to him while he lived. ➤ So the man divided his life ❖ Literally, his life— i.e., his land, which was his livelihood and identity ➤ between his two sons. ❖ Despite the pain of rejection, the father wanted to show his son that he loved him. Neither anger nor force would restore the relationship. Note that the older brother made no attempt to mend the rift, even though it was his cultural obligation to do so. Had he loved his father, he would have refused his share at that time. Even though the father divided the estate, it would have been assumed by all that he would still use the land as his own while alive. It was unthinkable to sell part of it; and it would be impossible to do so without his cooperation. No buyer would have touched it. And normally, such a sale would take months to negotiate. But... ➤ 13 Within a few days, the younger son sold his share of the estate and left home with the money. ❖ Selling the land publicly announced the betrayal that had occurred, violating the family honor (which in middle-eastern Jewish culture is very important). ➤ He went to a distant country where he squandered it all on wasteful living. 14 When all his money was gone, a severe famine spread throughout the region and he had nothing to live on. 15 So in desperation, he got a job from one of the citizens of that country feeding pigs in the fields. ❖ Jesus' audience would assume that this was a Jewish boy. Since pigs are ritually unclean, to work with them was the lowest degradation he could come to. A famine implies more than one year of bad harvests, so a few years have passed. ➤ 16 Because of the famine, food was scarce and no one would feed him. He

was so hungry that he would have gladly eaten the carob pods he fed to the pigs, but these are not digestible by people. 17 Finally, he came to his senses and said to himself, 'My father's hired workers have more than enough to eat—and here I am starving to death! 18 I will go back to my father and—playing on his soft heart—say, "Father, I've sinned against both God and you. 19 I'm not worthy to be treated as a son, but please hire me as one of your employees." ' ❖ *The Pharisees would have recognized the first part of this plan as quoting Pharaoh, king of Egypt [Exodus 10:16] who was trying manipulate Moses—and thus they would have understood it as insincere and manipulative. He was not repentant since he did not intend to ask for forgiveness. He intended to earn money to replace what he had lost, thereby earning the right to return by his own efforts. Being a hired hand, he wouldn't have to be reconciled with his brother. He is only doing this because he is starving and sees no alternative.* ➤ 20 So he went to his father. But while he was still a long way off, his father—who had already planned what he would do if his son returned and had been looking for him every day—saw him and was filled with compassion. He ran to his son, embraced him, and repeatedly kissed him. ❖ *If the son's returning represented repentance—as many teach—Jesus would be saying that the lost son could take the initiative and repent on his own. But in fact, it's the father who takes the initiative to restore the relationship. A middle-eastern father would never run or go out to meet a son who had humiliated him. He was behaving the way a mother might, but as a father, he was publicly sacrificing his dignity because of his great love. He had to reach his son and publicly welcome him back before others officially banned him from the community for his disgraceful behavior—as he knew they would. Jesus' audience would be shocked at the father's actions. The father was freely offering undeserved forgiveness.* ➤ 21 The son contritely said, 'Father, I've sinned against both God and you. I'm not worthy to be treated as a son.' ❖ *Many think he was interrupted, but a better explanation is that his father's behavior—his public self-humiliation in order to help him and restore the relationship—shocked the son and touched his heart. He became ashamed of what he had put his father through so he didn't finish his planned speech, but instead, genuinely confessed his sin. To go through with his plan would imply that he didn't believe in—or accept—his father's forgiveness.* ➤ 22 But the father said to his slaves, 'Hurry! Bring out my best robe and

put it on him. ❖ *He gives the son the best of his own, sharing his wealth and glory. This represents a state of righteousness that is conferred on repentant sinners which is called "imputed righteousness."* ➤ And put my signet ring on his finger as a sign of his authority to transact business in my name; and put sandals on his feet to show that he is neither a slave nor a servant, but my son. 23 And slaughter a calf that's been specially fattened for feasting. Then let's have a party to celebrate 24 because it was like my son was dead to me, but now he is alive again; he was lost to me, but now I've found him!' ❖ *The father "found" him in restoring him to his position as a son. The son was restored when he "accepted being found," i.e., when he accepted his father's undeserved favor and forgiveness.* ➤ Then they began to celebrate. ❖ *A slaughtered calf would feed a couple hundred people. A party of that size was a rare occasion. The community, which had been outraged by the son's behavior, was being restrained and mollified by the father's extreme actions. For his sake, they wouldn't embarrass him further and would reluctantly re-admit his son into their community. They rejoiced with the Father because they were happy for him.* ➤

25 "Now, the older son had been working in the fields. When he approached the house, he heard music and dancing. 26 So he summoned one of the young boys and asked him what was happening. 27 He answered, 'Your brother has returned, and your father had a fat calf slaughtered for a party to celebrate because he has welcomed him in shalom and restored their relationship.' ❖ *ὑγιαίνω (hugiainō), here translated "shalom," means "being in good health." "Shalom" also means "good health" and also carries the further meaning of peace, calmness, success, comfort, contentment, safety, health, wholeness, prosperity, integrity, well-being, and good relationships with God and people. Jesus' focus was not on the fact that the son came back healthy—he was, in fact, starving—but that the father received him back into good relationship. He was forgiven and restored as a son.* ➤

28 "The older son became angry; and in a display of rebellion and deliberate public insult to his father, refused to enter the house. ❖ *The younger son had insulted his father in private when requesting his inheritance. But the older son's insult was much graver because it was done in front of the whole community. For a son to publicly rebel against his father caused a great loss of face. The community would have expected the father to have his servants drag the son off and*

shut him up somewhere until he could deal with him severely in private. But instead... ➤ His father—again publicly sacrificing his own dignity because of his love for his son—came out and pleaded with him to come in and join the celebration. 29 But further humiliating his father in front of everyone, the son loudly protested, 'Look! All these years I served you like a slave and never disobeyed a single one of your commands. And you've never given me even so much as a young goat so I could have a party and celebrate with my friends—let alone a calf! ❖ *i.e., You are unjust and play favorites! It's clear that the older son hasn't had a good relationship with his father either. His attitude of service was that of a slave, not of a loving son. And since the younger brother had already taken all of his own inheritance, all of the older brother's hard work was going to eventually benefit himself since he would inherit all the remaining property. Yet he resented working for his father and also resented the way his father used the property that he would inherit, even though it still belonged to his father. He didn't love his father any more than the younger son had and was willing to shame his father in front of the entire community. Such public shaming was a much more serious matter in that culture than it would be in our own, even though the community would realize that the older son's accusations were not justified.* ➤ 30 But this son of yours comes home after wasting your money on prostitutes, and you honor him by killing a calf and having a party for him!' ❖ *Note that he calls him "this son of yours." He has totally rejected his brother and is unwilling to forgive him. He accuses him of sexual immorality—without basis. Had the younger son been guilty of this, the news of it would have made it back to the community and he would have been an outcast. All the father's efforts to restore him to the community would not have succeeded. The older brother attempts to portray the younger as a "rebellious son" for which the penalty was death by stoning. [Deuteronomy 21:18-21] Yet it is he himself who is a rebellious son. He also falsely accuses his father of honoring the younger son with the party. Had that been the point, no one would've come. Rather, it was to celebrate the father's success in restoring his relationship with his son.* ➤ 31 His father—who chose to ignore the display of rebellion and the resulting public shame to himself because of his great love for his son—appealed to him, 'My son, you have

always been with me and everything I now own is your inheritance. ❖ *i.e., My being reconciled with your brother does not violate your rights or threaten your inheritance. Therefore, you have no basis for this rejection.* ➤ 32 But we had to celebrate and rejoice because your brother was dead to me, but now he is alive; he was lost to me, but now I've found him again!' " ❖ *Jesus doesn't disclose the final response of the older brother—who represents the self-righteous religious leaders—in the hope of urging a response from them. In telling this parable, Jesus was pleading with them to forgive sinners and join him in celebrating the restoration of their brothers. His parable was meant to show them God's response to repentant sinners and to show them that their unforgiveness was as shameful as the older son's actions. ¶ Further observations: Jesus defines sin in this parable as a broken relationship with the Father. Deep down, sinners want God dead and out of their lives. Some sinners are lawbreakers (like the younger son) and some are law keepers (like the older son)—but all have a broken relationship with the Father. Jesus portrays the Father as compassionate and self-giving, whose great love makes him willing to pay the price of his own humiliation in order to restore sinners to a proper relationship with himself. The sinner cannot restore this relationship on his own, nor can he initiate it. The initiation of restoration lies with the Father. [John 6:44] The younger son was still estranged on the edge of the village; and nothing he planned to do—or could do—would have restored the relationship. Repentance is portrayed as "accepting the undeserved favor offered." It was offered before the prodigal gave his confession; and his planned "confession" was not going to be genuine until the favor was offered—which then transformed his attitude and made it genuine. The Father represents God, but in the end it's clear that he also represents Jesus—who welcomes repentant sinners and eats with them in celebration of their restored relationship.* ➤ A

16

The Dishonest Manager's Shrewdness

1 Jesus said to his followers, "A rich man had a general manager that looked after his estate and all his business. It was reported to him that his manager was wasting his resources. 2 So he summoned him and said, 'What's the truth about what I've

---

A 15:32 Insights for interpreting the three parables in this chapter come from Kenneth E. Bailey's books: "Finding The Lost – Cultural Keys to Luke 15," and "Jacob & the Prodigal – How Jesus retold Israel's story." Bailey brings out many more insights than are included here.

been hearing? Have you been mismanaging my estate? Prepare me a report accounting for all your transactions and actions on my behalf. If what I've heard is true, you will no longer be working for me!' 3 The manager said to himself, 'My employer is going to fire me! What will I do for a living? No one will hire me for such a job again. I'm not strong enough to do manual labor and would be too ashamed to become a beggar. 4 I know what I will do! By the time I'm fired, I will have plenty of friends indebted to me who will help me out.'

5 "Then, before the rumor got out that he was about to lose his job, he summoned all the people who owed his employer. He asked the first one, 'How much do you owe my master?' 6 He said, '800 gallons of olive oil.'

"The manager said, 'Here's the original bill. Let's write out a new one for only 400.'

❖ *Since he was still the rich man's general manager, those who owed him would assume that he was doing this with his master's knowledge and blessing. He may also have insinuated that he had convinced his master to display such generosity, which would make both the rich man and the manager very popular among those who were indebted to him.* ➤ 7 He asked another, 'And how much do you owe?'

"He replied, 'A thousand bags of wheat.' The manager said, 'Here's the original bill. Let's write out a new one for only 800.'

8 "When the rich man found out about this, he praised the dishonest manager for his shrewdness." ❖ *The rich man was unlikely to want to undo what his manager had done and so destroy the good reputation of generosity that his manager had given him in the community. He admired the shrewdness of the manager's actions in knowing how to get ahead, even though he had been dishonest. Jesus doesn't say if he ended up firing him or not. He wasn't saying that the manager's actions were right or good, but that he was shrewd—and his point was: It's good to be shrewd.* ➤

Jesus continued, "I tell this story because unbelievers often surpass believers in their shrewdness in getting ahead, each toward their respective goals. ❖ *Unbelievers know how to use money to get ahead and make themselves rich and powerful in this world, which is their goal. But most believers are not nearly as shrewd in getting ahead in God's Kingdom, which should be their goal.* ➤ **A**

9 "I'm saying that you should be using your resources to help people in this life. That way, you earn their friendship and also have God's favor. So when you are broke, they will help you; and when your life in this world is ended, they will welcome you into their homes in Heaven. 10 God knows that a person who is faithful in minor responsibilities will also be faithful in larger ones. And the person who is dishonest in minor matters will also be dishonest in major things. 11 So if he doesn't find you being faithful in your use of such minor things as money in this world, he certainly isn't going to trust you to administer greater riches in Heaven. 12 So if you haven't been responsible to use the resources he has put into your hands for his purposes and to advance his Kingdom, then don't expect to be given much in the way of your own resources in Heaven.

13 "No one can serve two masters at the same time. You will either hate the first and love the second, or the other way around. In the same way, you have to choose between loving God and serving him with your money, or loving money and trying to acquire it for your own purposes. You can't do both."

14 Some Pharisees heard all this and made fun of Jesus because they loved money. They believed that riches were a sign of God's blessing for their being righteous and were theirs to do with as they pleased. 15 Jesus admonished them, "You want to look good in the eyes of others, but God knows what's in your hearts. Many things that are highly esteemed and admired by people are despised by God. ❖ *e.g. To list just a few: wealth displayed to impress people, the acquisition of wealth and luxury to spend on yourself, rubbing elbows with the rich and powerful for personal prestige and gain, to rise in station so that you are able to avoid associating with the poor and powerless, to have the power to be "above the law," to be famous for the sake of your own pride and influence, the freedom to easily divorce, and much more.* ➤

A 16:8 The interpretation of this parable follows the analysis of Kenneth E. Bailey in "Poet & Peasant," pp. 86–118.

16 "God's word and will was proclaimed in the Torah and the writings of the prophets ❖ *i.e., the Hebrew Scriptures* ➤ until John the Baptizer came. Since then, the Good News about how to enter God's Kingdom has been openly preached, and many people are exerting their utmost to enter it. 17 But the Torah and the writings of the prophets are still God's holy word and remain in force. It would be easier to destroy Heaven and Earth than for a single letter in the Torah or the other Scriptures to be made invalid. ❖ *Some people teach that God's commands in the Torah have been abolished or are no longer pertinent to believers. This verse negates that possibility. It's the penalty of eternal death for sinners—as taught in the Torah—that no longer applies to believers. But God's will and standards remain the same. See the last note at Matthew 5:17 for clarification.* ➤

18 "Any man that divorces his wife and marries a different woman is guilty of adultery. And a man who marries a divorced woman is also guilty of adultery." *[Malachi 2:16; Matthew 5:31-32; 19:8-9; Mark 10:11-12]* ❖ *Also relevant to the topic of God's view of divorce is the command in Leviticus 21:7 directed to priests, which prohibits them from marrying a divorced woman. See the note at Matthew 5:32 and the footnote at 1 Corinthians 7:11.* ➤

The Rich Man and Lazarus

19 To conclude his teaching on the proper use of money, Jesus told the following story—which also indicates that the purpose of the Scriptures is to warn people that they need to repent and change their way of living. He said, "There was a certain rich man who wore only the best clothing and daily indulged himself in every luxury. ❖ *Like many Americans who say they are believers.* ➤ 20 There was also a poor man named Lazarus, whose body was covered with sores from lack of proper nutrition and treatment. Every day, those who cared about him carried him to the rich man's gate, 21 for he was hoping to be fed scraps that the rich man's servants would throw away. But he was consistently ignored by the rich man and was a pathetic sight, with dogs licking his sores as the only relief he received in his suffering.

22 "So it came about that the poor man died, and angels carried his spirit to Paradise to be with Abraham and others rewarded by God. And the rich man too eventually died and was buried. 23 But he ended up in Hell, the place of eternal torment for all who have rejected God. There, he was able to look up and see Abraham far away and Lazarus with him. 24 So he called out, 'Father Abraham! Grant me a small mercy. Send Lazarus to dip his finger in some water to cool my tongue because I'm in agony in this fire!'

25 "But Abraham answered, 'Remember, my son, that during your life on earth, God gave you plenty of good things, but Lazarus only experienced hunger and suffering. Now he is being comforted here and you are suffering in agony as you deserve. 26 Anyway, it's impossible for us to help you because there's a great chasm between us that no one can cross.' 27 The rich man said, 'Then I beg of you, Father Abraham, that you send Lazarus to my father's household. ❖ *Implied by this plea in Jesus' story is that even in Hell people can care about others but will be tormented by their inability to help them.* ➤ 28 For I have five brothers and I want him to warn them to repent and change their ways so they don't end up in this place of torment too.'

29 "But Abraham said, 'Your brothers have the writings of Moses and the other prophets in the Scriptures to warn them. They must listen to them and heed their warnings.' 30 The rich man answered, 'That's not enough, Father Abraham! They have heard the Scriptures but haven't believed them. But if someone from the dead were to go to them, then they would believe and repent!' 31 Abraham replied, 'If they won't heed the warnings of Moses and the prophets in the Scriptures, then they won't believe even if someone were to rise from the dead.' " ❖ *Don't miss Jesus' irony. He would later rise from the dead, but many people still don't believe in him or the message of the Scriptures. Do you? This story is the clearest picture in the Scriptures of what eternal punishment awaits those who go to Hell. Jesus taught there is a Hell. It would be foolish to ignore his teaching just because it's distasteful to you.* ➤

17

Jesus Teaches About
Temptation, Sin, and Forgiveness

1 Jesus said to his followers, "It's inevitable that people will be tempted to sin. But

God will severely punish anyone who deliberately tempts others to sin! 2 If someone were to tempt one of these children to sin, he would be better off by far if his only punishment were to have a huge stone tied around his neck and he were thrown into the sea to drown.

3 "So be on your guard against temptation! If fellow believers sin, rebuke them. ❖ *Many believers think that it's wrong to rebuke those who sin. Yet this is what Jesus commands us to do. From other Scriptures, it's clear that we are normally to do this in private and gently, motivated by love. [Matthew 18:15-17; Luke 6:42]* ➤ And if they repent, forgive them. 4 Even if someone sins against you the same way seven times in a day, and every time comes to you saying that he is sorry and will try to change, then you must forgive him." ❖ *Jesus didn't mean that forgiveness ends after the eighth offense in a single day. In the Bible, the number seven is often symbolic of completeness. Jesus meant that we should always forgive, no matter how many times someone sins against us.* ➤

The Relationship Between Faith and the Release of God's Power

5 The apostles recognized that they would find it difficult to forgive in this way, so they said, "Lord, help us to increase our faith."

6 The Lord answered, "If you have faith ❖ *i.e., in God and his word and promises* ➤ that's only as large as a mustard seed, it's enough that you could say to this mulberry tree, 'Be uprooted and planted in the sea,' and God would make it obey you." ❖ *Jesus isn't saying that God will be our magic genie doing anything we wish, if we have faith. He was again using hyperbole to make a point. The particular point he made here is that it's God's power that works mighty miracles, not our great faith. In fact, only a little faith on our part is needed before God will release his power to do great things. What needs to be understood, is that this only happens when what we request or command is in alignment with God's will. In this context, Jesus said it is God's will for us to forgive—no matter how hard it may seem to do so. All we need is a little faith and he will give us all the power we need to forgive. (See the Appendix—About Salvation in this book, Section 3.F. Forgiving Other People.) This is also true of other things that God wants us to do. Once we know his will, only a little faith is needed to release his power which will enable us to do what he wants us to do.* ➤

The Proper Attitude to Have in Serving Jesus

7 Jesus said, "Suppose one of you has a slave who is hoeing a garden, or perhaps looking after sheep. When he comes in from his work, would you say, 'Sit down and eat, you deserve a break.'? 8 You would not because it's his job to serve you your meal before his work for the day is finished. You would tell him, 'Prepare my evening meal, then get out of your outdoor work clothes and dress for serving. Wait on me until I've finished eating, and then you may be dismissed to eat your own meal.' ❖ *Jesus isn't advocating slavery or the mistreatment of servants. He is simply stating what was the common expectations of a slave in that culture. If you were rich and had a butler and hired servants, your expectations would be similar.* ➤ 9 And you don't go out of your way to praise a slave just for adequately doing his normal duties, do you? Of course not. 10 So you ought to have a similar attitude in serving God. When you have done everything that you are commanded to do, don't think that you have earned some big reward for just doing what you ought. Instead, have the attitude, 'We are unworthy slaves. We have only done our duty.' " ❖ *In fact, Jesus and other Scriptures teach that God will reward us for our obedience and faithfulness. But that is due to his generosity, not due to our merit. While looking forward to those rewards, our attitude is to be as Jesus taught here. [Psalm 62:12; Proverbs 24:12; Isaiah 40:10; 59:18; 62:11; Jeremiah 17:10; Matthew 5:12; 6:6, 17-18; 10:41-42; 16:27; 25:31-46; Mark 9:41; Luke 6:23, 35; Romans 2:6; 1 Corinthians 3:8, 14; 2 Corinthians 5:10; Galatians 6:7-8; 2 Timothy 4:14; Revelation 2:23; 20:13; 22:12]* ➤

Jesus Heals Ten Men with Leprosy

11 On his way to Jerusalem, Jesus traveled along the border between Galilee and Samaria. 12 As he was entering a certain village, ten men with leprosy came to meet him but kept their distance. ❖ *They were required to do this by law and custom, lest their disease spread to others.* ➤ 13 They shouted to him, "Jesus! Master! Have mercy on us and heal us!"

14 When Jesus saw they were lepers, he told them, "Go and show yourselves to the priests." ❖ *This was what the Torah required them to do if they were healed. [Leviticus 14:1-32] The priests had to*

examine them and officially declare them healed before they would be allowed to reenter society. Jesus always followed the Torah's teachings. ➤ As they were on their way to see a priest, God completely healed them. 15 Now one of them—when he saw that he was healed—returned to Jesus and loudly praised God on the way. 16 When he found him, he prostrated himself at Jesus' feet and thanked him profusely. That man was a Samaritan. ❖ *Who were despised by Jews.* ➤ 17 Jesus said to those around him, "Weren't there ten who were healed? Where are the other nine? 18 Was this foreigner the only one who was thankful and thought to turn back and give praise to God?" 19 Then Jesus said to the man, "Stand up and go where I told you to go. Your faith has healed you."

The Coming of God's Kingdom

20 Some Pharisees asked Jesus just when the Kingdom of God was coming. He answered, "You can't observe it by looking for outward signs. 21 And you can't rely on people that say, 'Look, here it is!' or, 'There it is!' For the Kingdom of God—where he rules—is in the hearts and minds of those who are submitted to him."

22 Then he said to his followers, "The time will come when you will long to see me, the Son of Man, return in power as king, but you will not see it because it isn't yet time. 23 People will be saying, 'Look, the Messiah is over there!' or 'He is here!' But don't believe them and go looking for me 24 because my coming will be seen by all—as obvious as lightning flashing across the sky. 25 But first, I must suffer many things and be rejected by most of those living today. 26 When I do return, it will be just as it was in Noah's time when most people didn't pay any attention to God's word. 27 Life went on as usual. Every day, people ate, drank, and were married right up to the time that Noah entered the Ark and the flood came and destroyed them all. ❖ *Noah's story is in Genesis 5:28—9:29.* ➤ 28 The same thing happened in Lot's time. Life went on as usual with nobody listening to God's warnings to repent. They ate and drank and bought and sold and planted and built. 29 On the day that God's angels led Lot out of Sodom, fire and brimstone rained down on them from the sky and destroyed them all. ❖ *Lot's story is in Genesis chapter 19.* ➤ 30 It will be just like that on the day that I, the Son of Man, return in glory.

31 "On that day, if a man is outside his house, he mustn't take the time to go inside to get anything to take with him. And someone working in the field mustn't take time to go to his house. They must go immediately. ❖ *Given the example in the next verse, Jesus may be saying that we need to exactly follow whatever instructions we are given by angels at that time, without delay.* ➤ 32 Remember Lot's wife who failed to listen to the instructions given to her by the angels who were trying to help her. She looked back and died. 33 Whoever tries to keep control over his own life will ultimately lose it forever. But whoever is willing to lose his life for my sake, will—in the end—preserve it forever. 34 On the night that I return, it will be like this: Two people will be sleeping in the same bed; one will be taken to be with me, the other will be left behind. 35 Two women will be working together; one will be taken and the other left behind. 36 Two men will be working in a field; one will be taken and the other left behind."

37 His followers asked, "Where will you be, Lord?" Jesus answered, "Wherever there's a dead body, that's where the vultures gather." ❖ *Many scholars think this may have been a well-known proverb at that time. It probably means that just like the circling of vultures makes it obvious where something has died, it will be equally obvious at that time where he can be found.* ➤

18

Parable of the Widow and the Corrupt Judge

1 Then Jesus told them a parable to teach that we need to persist in prayer until God answers. ❖ *An implied condition from other Scriptures is that you are praying for something in line with God's will. [James 4:3]* ➤ 2 He said, "There was a judge in a certain town who didn't believe in God and didn't care what people thought about him. 3 But a widow living in that town was constantly begging him to help her. She would say, 'Please grant me justice against my adversary!' ❖ *A widow with no living male relative*

had no legal rights in that culture. Someone was probably trying to take away her property after her husband had died—which would have left her destitute. ➤ **4** For a long time he refused, but eventually he said to himself, 'Even though I don't believe in God and don't care what people think about me, **5** I will do what she asks because her constant begging is getting on my nerves. I will do it just to have some peace and quiet.' "

6 Jesus continued, "Note what the corrupt judge said. **7** If even a corrupt judge like that will grant justice just to stop a woman from bothering him, you can be sure that God—who loves his people—is even more willing to help them when they cry out to him in prayer day and night! He will not delay long in helping them. **8** I assure you that he will bring about justice for them quickly. ❖ *Some commentators believe this means: When he finally acts, he will act quickly. It's certainly true that to people today—who are used to everything happening almost instantly—it sometimes seems like God's answers are slow in coming. But his timing is perfect; and we need to understand that while he will answer our prayer—and by his standards, his answers are quick and perfectly timed—to us it will sometimes appear unreasonably long. We need to have faith that he does love us and will help us in his own way when the time is right.* ➤ But when I—the Son of Man—return, will I find people who still believe in me?"

Parable of the Pharisee and the Tax Collector

9 Jesus also told this parable to those who think they are better than others, or who believe that God thinks more highly of them than others, **10** "Two men went up to the Temple to pray. One was a Pharisee and the other a tax collector. ❖ *Pharisees were considered upright model citizens and moral leaders in Jesus' time, while tax collectors were social outcasts because they collaborated with their Roman conquerors—and they were also greedy and corrupt. Jesus' audience would have initially assumed that God approved of the Pharisee and that he would reject the tax collector.* ➤

11 "The Pharisee stood ❖ *this was a common posture for praying* ➤ and prayed to himself. ❖ *Commentators interpret this in various ways, but most think that Jesus meant he was really just speaking to himself because God was not listening. [Job 35:13; Proverbs 3:34; John 9:31; James 4:6; 1 Peter 5:5] Praying aloud was also normal.* ➤ He said, 'Thank you, God, that I'm

not evil like others who are greedy and rob people, or who are unjust or adulterers, or like that tax collector over there. ❖ *He assumed that he had no sins to confess.* ➤ **12** I fast twice a week ❖ *which was much more than required by the Torah, and he thought it made him more holy* ➤ and I give you a tenth of everything I get.' ❖ *Which again was more than the Torah required. He assumed that God was very pleased with him.* ➤

13 "But the tax collector stood some distance away and didn't even look up toward Heaven ❖ *as Jewish men normally did when they prayed* ➤ because he was ashamed. Instead, he beat his chest ❖ *a cultural gesture of sorrow and distress* ➤ and said, 'God, have mercy on me, for I'm a sinner!' " ❖ *His statement was a confession of his sin, and his attitude was that he was sorry and wanted to change. Otherwise, he wouldn't have come to pray for mercy and forgiveness.* ➤ **14** Jesus said, "I tell you, this man went back to his home accepted by God, but not the Pharisee; because God will humble anyone who exalts himself, but he exalts those who humble themselves before him."

Jesus' Attitude Toward Little Children

15 One day, people were bringing their small children and infants to Jesus so he would lay his hands on them and bless them. ❖ *Laying hands on a person is a biblical pattern for conferring a blessing. [Genesis 48:13-20; Hebrews 6:2]* ➤ When his followers saw this, they rebuked the people, telling them not to bother the Rabbi. **16** But Jesus called the children to come to him and told his followers, "Allow the children to come to me; don't stop them! These are the kind of people that God loves to have in his Kingdom, people who are humble and trusting like children. **17** Remember this! Anyone who isn't humble and trusting like a child will never enter God's Kingdom at all."

The Stumbling Stone of being Rich

18 One day, a Jewish religious leader asked Jesus, "Rabbi, I recognize that you are a good man. What do I need to do to obtain eternal life?"

19 Jesus replied, "Why do you call me 'good?' No one is good except God himself. So do you realize what you are saying about me when you call me good? 20 You know the commands in the Torah, 'Don't commit adultery, don't murder, don't steal, don't lie about others, honor your parents.' " *[Exodus 20:12-16; Deuteronomy 5:16-20]* ❖ *Jesus wasn't giving an exhaustive list of God's requirements, only a few representative ones. He knew that the man was familiar with them all, and by bringing them to mind he was trying to get the man to recognize that he was a sinner in need of God's forgiveness.* ➤

21 But the man said, "I've kept all of these commands ever since I was young." ❖ *He failed to recognize that he was a sinner. He believed that an outward legalistic keeping of the rules was what God wanted, and did not understand that the attitude of his heart was important too. Yet even though he believed that he had kept all these rules, he knew he was lacking something. He wasn't sure that he was going to Heaven and that's why he asked Jesus about this.* ➤

22 When Jesus heard this, he knew that the man didn't recognize his sin. He also knew that the biggest thing hindering him from wholeheartedly following God was his idolatrous love for his riches. So he told him, "There's one main thing that you still need to do. Sell everything you have and give the money to the poor so you will have riches in Heaven. Then come and be one of my followers." 23 But when the man heard this, he became dejected because he was very rich and unwilling to surrender his wealth and put his life in Jesus' hands.

24 Jesus saw him go and said, "It's very difficult for the rich to enter God's Kingdom! ❖ *Because either they depend on their riches for their security and find it difficult to trust only in God, or they love their riches and comforts more than they love God. Note that Jesus didn't try to make it easier for the man. He didn't call him back and say that trusting God was enough, and that he could later learn to be a more committed follower, as many preach today. Jesus requires total commitment and obedience at the outset.* ➤ 25 It would be easier for a camel to go through the eye of a sewing needle than for a rich man to enter God's Kingdom." ❖ *Some people incorrectly say that there was a gate into Jerusalem called the "eye of the needle" which was small and difficult for camels to enter, but that it was possible. There never was such a gate. This was probably a well-known saying at the time. Jesus was simply stating that it's impossible—humanly speaking—for a rich man to enter Heaven.* ➤

26 The people who heard this said, "If rich people can't be saved, then who can be saved?" ❖ *A common misconception among the Jews of that time was that riches were God's blessings showered upon those who merited them because of their righteous lives. In their minds, it was rich people who were the most likely to be saved. So if such "good" people—whom God obviously approved of and had blessed—can't get in, how can anyone get in? This was their question.* ➤

27 Jesus replied, "It may be impossible for people to enter on their own, but with God's help, anything is possible."

28 Then Peter said, "We've left our homes to follow you. So what can we expect from God?"

29 Jesus answered, "I assure you that anyone who leaves home or wife or brothers or parents or children to serve in God's Kingdom, 30 will in this life receive compensation many times over what he has given up, and in the coming age, he will have eternal life in Heaven." ❖ *Jesus isn't talking about people who irresponsibly abandon those who depend on them, like spouses and children. He is speaking of people who place more importance on God's call than on human loyalties, who are willing to choose to follow God even if their families reject God.* ➤

Jesus Speaks About His Death a Third Time

31 Then Jesus took the twelve apostles aside and said, "We are going up to Jerusalem and when we get there, all the things that the prophets wrote about the Son of Man in the Scriptures will happen to me. 32 I will be handed over to the Roman authorities who will mock me and abuse me and spit on me. 33 After whipping me, I will be executed. But on the second **A** day after I die, I will rise and live again."

34 But his followers didn't understand any of what he was trying to tell them because their expectations for the Messiah were entirely different and they couldn't see beyond them. So they completely failed to understand what he was saying. ❖ *The*

A 18:33 See the note at Matthew 16:21 for the reasoning behind not using the traditional phrase, "the third day."

common expectation which the Jews had about the Messiah was that he would be a political savior who would become King over Israel, kick the Romans out of their country, and usher in a golden age for Israel even greater than when Solomon was king. A Messiah who would suffer humiliation and die was incomprehensible to them. Both pictures of the Messiah are found in the Hebrew Scripture prophecies because they speak about the two different times the Messiah would come. But they were expecting the prophecies concerning his coming in glory to be fulfilled very shortly; and the Jews had tended to totally ignore the prophecies about the Messiah that pertained to his suffering and dying since they didn't fit in with their hopes or desires. ➤

Jesus Heals a Blind Man

35 As Jesus was approaching **A** Jericho, there was a blind man sitting on the side of the road begging. 36 When he heard the crowd passing, he asked what was happening. 37 They told him that Jesus of Nazareth was passing by.

38 So he started shouting, "Jesus! Son of David! Have mercy on me!" ❖ *By this time, everyone had heard about the miraculous healings he could do. It's apparent that he considered Jesus to be the Messiah because the Messiah would be a descendant of King David, and "Son of David" was a messianic title.* ➤

39 Those in the front of the crowd were telling him to be quiet, but he kept calling out even louder, "Son of David! Have mercy on me!"

40 When Jesus heard him, he stopped and commanded that the man be brought to him. When he arrived, Jesus asked, 41 "What do you want me to do for you?" He answered, "Lord, I want to see again." 42 Jesus said, "Receive your sight. Your faith in me has saved you." ❖ *The word translated "saved" can mean both "save" and "heal." Jesus may have only meant he was healed, but it's likely that he meant both meanings.* ➤

43 Immediately, he could see again, and he began following Jesus and praising God. When the people in the crowd saw what had happened, they too praised God. ❖ *In the minds*

of the common people of Jesus' day, there was no doubt that the power to heal came from God. Jesus may have been the person God used to heal, but it was appropriate to give thanks and praise to God, whose power did the healing. ➤

19

Zaccheus

1 Jesus entered Jericho with the crowd following behind him and was passing through the town. 2 A man lived there named Zaccheus, who was the chief tax collector and, therefore, quite rich. 3 He had heard about Jesus and desperately wanted to see him, but he was short and unable to see above the heads of the crowd. 4 So he ran ahead of the crowd and climbed a Sycamore tree to see Jesus as he passed by on the road. 5 But when Jesus reached that spot, he stopped, looked up, and said, "Zaccheus, hurry down because I must stay at your house today." ❖ *There's no evidence that Jesus previously knew about Zaccheus. Yet he knew his name and said that he "must" stay at his house. Evidently this was a "divine appointment" planned by God the Father who knew that Zaccheus was ready to repent. Jesus said that everything he did and said was directed by his Father. [John 5:19; 8:28; 14:10]* ➤

6 Zaccheus came down quickly and was happy to host him at his house. 7 The people in the crowd who saw this grumbled because Jesus was honoring a collaborator with their Roman conquerors who had gotten rich by abusing his office. They said, "He's gone to be the guest of a sinner!" ❖ *In this sense, they didn't mean he was an ordinary sinner—because they knew all people sin. They meant a man who chose a lifestyle of sin and immorality and had shown no signs of being repentant.* ➤

8 While Jesus stayed with him, Zaccheus' heart attitude changed and he repented. He stood up and publicly announced, "Lord, I'm going to give half of all my possessions to the poor. And those whom I've defrauded, I will pay back four times as much." ❖ *This*

A 18:35 The parallel accounts in Matthew 20:29 and Mark 10:46 say that this happened as they were leaving Jericho, not approaching it. David Stern says there were two Jericho's a few kilometers apart, one the ancient inhabited city and the other a Roman spa that was nearer to Jerusalem. So this event could have happened between the two sites and in one view be seen as happening while leaving the populated city Jericho, and in another view be seen as happening while approaching the Roman Jericho. So no error of fact need be read into this apparent discrepancy of detail.

was double the typical rate of restitution as commanded in the Torah. [Exodus 22:1, 4, 7, 9] ➤

9 Jesus said to those listening, "It's clear that God has saved this man because he has given his life to God in faith, just like his ancestor Abraham did. 10 It was for this very reason that I, the Son of Man, came to this world—to look for and save people like him who are lost in sin and have turned their backs on God."

Parable of the 10 Minas

❖ *This parable is very similar to the parable of the talents in Matthew 25:14-30, with the same general point. But the details are considerably different, especially the ending. Jesus likely told variations of the same parables many times. A mina was a gold coin worth about 100 days' wages.* ➤

11 While the people were listening to this, Jesus went on to tell a parable. He was nearing Jerusalem in his journey and he knew that they were expecting him to visibly establish God's Kingdom there very shortly. ❖ *So this parable was intended to prepare them for events that would be contrary to their expectations. He was not going to make himself king right away, but instead, was going away to Heaven for a while and would later return as king. This parable gives his people instructions on what he expects them to be doing with their lives while waiting for his return.* ➤ 12 He said, "A certain nobleman went to a distant country intending to receive authority to become a king, and he planned to return to his home country to rule. 13 But before he left, he summoned ten of his slaves and gave each of them a mina. He instructed them, 'Invest this and see what profit you can make for me while I'm gone.' Then, he left on his journey. 14 Some of the citizens in that country hated him and sent a delegation to the high king, where the nobleman was headed, to tell him, 'We don't want this man to become our king.'

15 "But eventually, the nobleman did return as their rightful king and he sent for his slaves to whom he had entrusted his money. He summoned them in one at a time to find out what they had accomplished with it. 16 The first one entered and reported, 'Master, I've earned 10 additional minas from the one you left in my charge.' 17 The king said, 'Well done. You are a good slave! Because you were faithful in this small

matter, I'm placing you in authority over ten of my cities.' 18 The second slave entered and reported, 'Master, I've earned five additional minas from the one you left in my charge.' 19 The king told him, 'And I'm placing you in authority over five of my cities.'

20 "Then, another slave entered and reported, 'Master, here is your mina which I kept hidden in a cloth. 21 I was afraid of failing to earn anything with it and risk losing it all because I know you are a strict businessman. You easily make a profit from the work of others and reap where others have sown.' 22 His master replied, 'You are a worthless slave! By your own words, you are condemned because you didn't obey my command to invest it. You didn't even try. You know that I'm a strict businessman and that I make a profit from the work of others and reap where others have sown. 23 So why didn't you at least put my money in a bank so I could've collected interest on it?'

24 "Then he told the people gathered there, 'Take the mina away from him and give it to the slave who earned ten minas.' 25 They said, 'But Master, he already has ten minas!' 26 He replied, 'I promise you that everyone who has shown he is responsible with what I've given him, will be given even more responsibility. But someone who has shown no responsibility will have even what little he has taken away from him. ❖ *This is a lesson for Jesus' followers. The material wealth and resources that he has given us in this life really belong to him, and he expects us to invest them in the advancement of his Kingdom. Those who do this will be rewarded with greater responsibilities in Heaven. Those who fail to use what they have in this life to further the Kingdom will not be rewarded with wealth or responsibilities in Heaven. If the slave who kept the mina without investing it was punished, how do you think the king would have reacted to a slave who had spent it mainly on himself, as many believers do with their wealth?* ➤ 27 Now as for my enemies who didn't want me to be their king, bring them here and kill them in my presence!' " ❖ *Many people today like to only think about God's love. However, the Scriptures clearly portray him as a God of justice who hates sin and will severely punish his enemies and those who reject him. Wishful thinking on our part will not change who God is or how he will act when he returns. If you ignore the clear warnings of*

passages such as this one, you will have no excuse and find no mercy on Judgment Day. ➤

Jesus' Triumphal Entry into Jerusalem on Palm Sunday

28 After saying these things, Jesus continued on his journey up to Jerusalem, leading the crowd. ❖ *Jerusalem is about 17 miles from Jericho and about 2600 feet higher in elevation.* ➤ 29 When he came near to Bethphage and Bethany, two villages near Mount Olivet, ❖ *Bethany is less than two miles from Jerusalem.* ➤ he sent ahead two of his followers, 30 telling them, "Go to that village. When you enter, you will see a young donkey tethered that has never been ridden. Untie it and bring it here. 31 If someone asks, 'Why are you untying it?' tell them, 'The Lord needs to use it.' "

32 So they went and found it just as Jesus had described. 33 As they were untying the young donkey, the owners asked, "Why are you untying it?" 34 They replied, "The Lord needs to use it," and they were allowed to take it. 35 They brought it to Jesus and spread their outer garments on its back as a kind of saddle, and helped Jesus onto it. 36 As he rode, the crowd spread their outer garments on the road in front of him. ❖ *This was commonly done to honor a triumphant King or general who had conquered his enemies and was making his procession into a city.* ➤

37 As he approached the place where the road descends Mount Olivet toward Jerusalem, the entire crowd started rejoicing and loudly praising God for all the miracles they had seen Jesus do. 38 They shouted, **"Praise to the one who comes representing the Lord!** *[Psalm 118:26]* ❖ *"Lord" in this Psalm in Hebrew is God's name, "Yahweh." But Jews in Jesus' time avoided saying his name and substituted, "Adonai" which is translated into English as "LORD" with small caps for the "ORD" in many translations, indicating this is being substituted for God's actual name.* ➤ May there be peace between God and his people! All glory and praise be to God in the highest Heaven!" ❖ *The people were hailing Jesus as God's Messiah, making his triumphal entry into Jerusalem. They expected that he would now openly declare himself as the Messiah, make himself King of Israel, and finally fulfill their expectations of freeing them from their Roman conquerors and usher in a golden age of peace, prosperity, and greatness for their country.* ➤

39 Some Pharisees in the crowd were angry because the people were proclaiming him to be the Messiah and they didn't believe it. They admonished Jesus, "Rabbi, rebuke your followers!" ❖ *This kind of demonstration would create a disturbance in the city that could possibly cause the Romans to violently punish the people. Riots and uprisings caused by self-proclaimed Messiahs had happened several times before, and the Romans had a dim view of charismatic leaders who might lead the people in revolt against Roman authority. This was probably on their minds as they urged Jesus to restrain his followers.* ➤

40 But Jesus replied, "I assure you, if they were quiet, then the stones themselves would cry out!" ❖ *This was the appointed time in God's plan for Jesus to be publicly proclaimed as the Messiah. Nothing would prevent that proclamation from happening, not even if they managed to quiet the people. But God's plan was not that Jesus would be crowned king at this time; rather, it would lead to his death.* ➤

Jesus Cries for the People of Jerusalem

41 As he approached Jerusalem, Jesus cried because he loved God's people who lived there but he knew that most of them and the city would be destroyed as a result of their rejecting him. ❖ *This would happen about 40 years later in AD 70 when the Roman army destroyed the Temple and the city, killing most of the people in it.* ➤ 42 He said, "If even today you would realize how you could repent and be at peace with God, it wouldn't be too late to escape his judgment. But because of your stubbornness, it's hidden from you. 43 The day will come when your enemies will surround you and build an embankment to breach your walls. You will be hemmed in on every side with no chance of escape. 44 The city will be leveled. Not a single stone will remain on top of another. ❖ *This is hyperbole, indicating the destruction would be extreme.* ➤ Everyone inside will be destroyed, all because you didn't recognize your own God when he visited you." ❖ *Literally, they didn't recognize their "visitation." Many commentators and modern translations interpret this as referring to a visitation by God. The verb "visitation" means "to look upon" them for the purpose of blessing them or judging them, depending on their response. See Isaiah 23:17 and 1 Peter 2:12. Jesus' claim to be God is only implied here, but would have been understood in that cultural context.* ➤

Jesus Cleanses the Temple a Second Time

❖ *The account of the first cleansing of the Temple is in John 2:13-22. Some commentators believe there was only one cleansing and that either John or the other three gospel writers reported it at a different time than it happened. But taking the texts at face value leads to the conclusion that Jesus did this twice, a few years apart.* ➤

45 Later, Jesus entered the Temple and drove out those who were selling animals for sacrifices within the area set aside for worship. 46 He said to them, "It's written in the Scriptures that God said, '**My house will be a house of prayer for people of all ethnicities.**' *[Isaiah 56:7]* But you've turned it into **a den of thieves!** " *[Jeremiah 7:11]* ❖ *The merchants were providing needed services for pilgrims coming to Jerusalem for the Passover Festival—who couldn't bring sacrificial animals with them from far away. They also operated currency exchanges. One problem was that they were turning the Temple into a marketplace. But even more significant is that they were doing this in the "Court of the Gentiles," thus robbing Gentiles of a place to worship the one true God. Jesus was righteously angry, reflecting God the Father's attitude toward what was happening.* ➤

47 Then, for the next several days, Jesus taught in the Temple while the chief priests and Scripture teachers and other leaders of the people were seeking a way to have him killed. 48 But they could never find an opportunity because there were always crowds around him, hanging on his every word. Any attempt to arrest him in public would have caused a riot.

20

Jesus' Authority Is Questioned

1 On one of those days while he was teaching in the Temple and preaching the Good News of God's Kingdom, some of the chief priests and the Scripture teachers and elders confronted him. 2 They demanded, "What right do you have to do things like you did here in the Temple the other day? Who gave you this authority?" ❖ *They were not really seeking information. They believed that they could use any answer he gave against him in some way. Jesus was fully aware of their intentions and turned their question against them.* ➤

3 Jesus replied, "I will answer that if you first answer this question. 4 When John was baptizing and preaching, was his authority from God or did he do this on his own authority?"

5 They debated among themselves what to answer: "If we acknowledge that John's authority was from God, then he will ask why we didn't believe John's message and his witness that Jesus is the Messiah. 6 But if we say that his authority wasn't from God, this crowd will reject us and stone us since they're convinced John was a prophet." 7 So in the end, they said they didn't know where John's authority came from.

8 So Jesus said, "If you are unwilling to answer that question, then I'm not going to tell you where my authority comes from either."

Parable About the Evil Tenants

9 Then Jesus told the people this parable. "A man planted a vineyard, rented it out to some tenant farmers, and went on a journey for a long time. *[Isaiah 5:1-2, 7]* ❖ *The vineyard represents Israel, the owner represents God, and the farmers represent the leaders of Israel.* ➤ 10 When it came time for the grapes to be harvested, the owner sent a servant to collect a portion of the crop as the agreed-upon payment for their rent. But the farmers beat him and sent him away empty handed. ❖ *The servants represent the prophets that God sent to his people over the years.* ➤ 11 The owner sent another servant and they beat him too—treating him shamefully—and sent him away with nothing. 12 So he sent a third servant and this one they wounded and threw out of the vineyard. 13 Now the owner said to himself, 'What should I do? I will send my son whom I love. Perhaps they will respect him and pay what they owe me.' 14 But when the farmers saw the son, they reasoned, 'This is the owner's heir. If we kill him, we can keep the vineyard for ourselves!' 15 So they threw him out of the vineyard and killed him. Now, what will the owner of the vineyard do to them? 16 He will come and kill them and give the vineyard to other tenants."

The people fully recognized what Jesus' parable meant, that their leaders would kill the Messiah and that God would take the Kingdom away from the Jews and give it to Gentiles. Both ideas were abhorrent to them and they exclaimed, "May it never be!"

17 Jesus looked at them and asked, "Then what do you think this Scripture means, '**The stone the builders rejected became the cornerstone**'? *[Psalm 118:22]* ❖ *Jesus was speaking of himself as that stone.* ➤ 18 All who stumble over that stone will be broken into pieces, and it will crush to dust those it falls on." *[Isaiah 8:14-15]* ❖ *This means that people who reject Jesus as the-Messiah and the way of salvation "stumble" over him and harm themselves spiritually. If they continue to reject him, God will eventually judge and destroy them, just like a stone falling on pottery crushes it. The New Testament writers used this figure several times in Romans 9:31-33; 1 Corinthians 1:23; and 1 Peter 2:8. Jews were very familiar with the use of Scriptural figures in argumentation and teaching, so they probably followed Jesus' meaning fairly closely.* ➤ 19 The Scripture teachers and the chief priests wanted to arrest Jesus immediately because they fully understood that his parable was aimed against them. But they didn't because they feared the reaction of the people.

The Question About Paying Taxes to Rome

20 The Jewish leaders watched him carefully and they sent men to him who pretended sincerity in an attempt to trap him into some damaging statement that they could use against him. They wanted something the Romans would consider unlawful 21 and approached him like this: "Rabbi, we know that you speak with integrity and teach God's way based on the truth of his word, not on what you think people want to hear. 22 So tell us, is it right for us to pay taxes to Caesar, ❖ *i.e., our conquerors, the Roman government which actively promotes the worship of false gods* ➤ or not?"

23 But Jesus saw their trap. ❖ *If he answered "Yes," then the Jewish leaders could accuse him of being a Roman collaborator—which would destroy his popularity with the people. If he answered "No," then they could accuse him of sedition to the Roman authorities.* ➤ He said, 24 "Show me a denarius." ❖ *This was the Roman coin used to pay the head tax that they were talking about. Since they were in the Temple, they likely had to have someone fetch one because Jews wouldn't normally carry a coin with a graven image of a false god on it into the Temple. The image was Caesar's, but the Romans worshipped him as a god.* ➤ They produced one, and he asked, "Whose face and name are on it?" They answered, "Caesar's." 25 Then Jesus said, "So give to Caesar what he rightfully demands, and give to God what rightfully belongs to him."

26 They were stunned by his answer and were speechless because they weren't able to catch him saying anything in public that they could use against him. ❖ *The Roman coin was not acceptable for any holy use—such as tithes, offerings, and temple taxes—because it bore an image on it, which is forbidden in the Torah. [Deuteronomy 4:15-16, 23]* ➤

The Question About Life After Death

27 Then some Sadducees—who deny that there will be a resurrection—came to Jesus with a question. ❖ *The Sadducees were a Jewish religious sect that held to several incorrect beliefs. Of particular relevance to this story was their belief that there is no life after death. They believed that people have no immortal souls and simply cease to exist when they die and therefore, there would be no resurrection on the Last Day. [Acts 23:8] They posed a question that they thought would logically prove the impossibility of such a resurrection because it would mean that God contradicted himself. They did correctly understand that God never contradicts himself.* ➤ 28 They said, "Rabbi, Moses wrote in the Torah that **if a man's brother dies and leaves a widow with no children, his brother must take her to be his wife, and the first son they have is to be considered the son of the dead man.** *[Genesis 38:8; Deuteronomy 25:5-6; Ruth 4:5-10]* ❖ *This was so the dead man could have at least one legal heir to carry on the family name and inherit his property. This was meant to preserve the relatively equal distribution of land among extended families, so that some families did not end up acquiring significantly more land and wealth than others.* ➤ 29 Now, there were seven brothers. The oldest married and died with no child. 30 Then, the second brother married her and also died childless. 31 And then a third did the same, and in the same way, all seven men married her and died leaving no children. 32 Last of all, the wife died too. 33 So on the day when God raises the dead back to life—if there is such a day—whose wife will she be since she was married to all seven brothers?" ❖ *They reasoned that God would never command people to do anything that violated one of his*

other commands. But for a woman to be married to more than one man violated the teaching of God's Torah. (There is no explicit prohibition against polyandry in the Torah, but it was understood to be implicitly prohibited from other explicit prohibitions.) Therefore, there couldn't be any resurrection because God's command requiring a brother to marry his brother's childless widow would force some women to be illegally married to more than one husband after the resurrection. ➤

³⁴ Jesus said, "People who live in this age before the day of resurrection get married. ³⁵ But it won't be like that in the age to come. Those whom God judges worthy to participate in the resurrection and live with him in Heaven will neither be married nor get married. ³⁶ And they will never die again. They will be like the angels who never marry nor procreate, and they will be God's children because they will have risen from death to live forever. ³⁷ Even Moses gave you evidence for the resurrection in his account of the burning bush, where he recorded that Yahweh said, 'I am the God of Abraham, the God of Isaac, and the God of Jacob.' [Exodus 3:1-6, 15] ❖ The Sadducees only accepted the writings of Moses as Scripture and claimed that Moses never taught about a resurrection. So Jesus used Moses' writings to refute them. ➤ ³⁸ It should be obvious that Yahweh is not the God of people who no longer exist. He's God of the living, and everyone is alive to him." ❖ The souls of the dead are still alive in either Heaven or Hell. ➤

³⁹ Some Scripture teachers spoke up and said, "Rabbi, that was well argued!" ⁴⁰ After that, they were all afraid to ask him any more questions to try to trap him lest he publicly shame them again.

A Question About the Messiah

⁴¹ Then Jesus asked them, "How can it be true that the Messiah is a descendant of King David, as people believe? ⁴² For David himself wrote about the Messiah in a Psalm, 'Yahweh said to my Lord, the Messiah, "Sit here at my right side—the place of highest honor—⁴³ until I have humiliated all your enemies and put them under your power." ' [Psalm 110:1]

⁴⁴ "David called the Messiah, 'Lord,' so how can he also be his descendant?" ❖ The Jewish assumption was that an ancestor is always greater

than his descendants. David was one of the greatest Israelites to ever live. How could he humble himself under one of his own descendants and call him "Lord?" The Scriptures were clear on both points. The Messiah would be descended from David, and yet David called him "Lord." Jesus was trying to get them to see that the Messiah—while a descendant of David—had to be more than just a man. But none of them were willing or able to accept this idea so no one could give him an answer. ➤

Jesus Warns His Followers to Guard Against Greed, Pride, and Hypocrisy

⁴⁵ While all the people were listening, Jesus told his followers, ⁴⁶ "Don't allow yourselves to have attitudes like the Scripture teachers. They like to dress in expensive long robes to impress people. They love to hear people greet them respectfully in public and to sit in the most-important seats in the synagogue and in seats of honor at banquets. ⁴⁷ They are also greedy and take advantage of helpless widows, taking their homes and lands from them, leaving them destitute. Purely for show, they recite long prayers to impress others with their spirituality. God isn't taken in by them and on Judgment Day, their punishment will be all the greater because of their hypocrisy." ❖ Note that Jesus clearly implies here that some people in Hell will be punished more severely than others because their sins are worse. It is true that all sin is the same in the sense that any sin makes you unworthy of Heaven. But on the other hand, some sins have worse consequences and God will punish people with greater or lesser severity according to the severity of their sins. To do wrong is one thing, but hypocrisy—pretending they are better than others while they do wrong—is even worse in God's eyes. The fact that punishments in Hell differ in severity is also implied in Job 34:11; Psalm 28:4; 62:12; Jeremiah 17:10; Matthew 7:2; 16:27; 23:14; Mark 12:40; Luke 12:47-48; 20:47; Romans 2:6; James 3:1; Revelation 2:23; and 22:12. ➤

21

Sacrificial Giving

¹ Jesus was looking around the Temple and observed wealthy people putting their gifts into the treasury box. ² Then he saw an obviously poor widow put in two small copper coins. ❖ They were the smallest coins in use at that time, each worth about 1/128 of a man's wage for one

day. ➤ **3** He said to those listening, "I assure you that by God's standard, that poor widow contributed far more than anyone else because she made the bigger sacrifice. **4** They all put in offerings out of what they could easily spare, but she put in everything she had and has nothing left to even live on."

Jesus Predicts the Destruction of the Temple

5 Some of his followers were talking about the Temple, how beautiful the stones were and the adornments of intricate goldwork that had been given as special offerings. Jesus broke in and said, **6** "The day will come when all the things you see here are destroyed. Not even one stone will be left standing on another."

Signs of Jesus' Returning

7 Shocked, they asked him, "Rabbi, when will this happen? And what signs should we look for that will tell us when it's about to take place?" ❖ *As is often true in biblical prophecy, Jesus' prophecy here combines predictions about events that are far apart in time so they sound like they all refer to the same time. Such prophecies in the Hebrew Scriptures confused Jewish scholars—and even John the Baptizer— about events connected with the Messiah's first and second comings. In this case, although Jesus' followers asked about the time of the destruction of the Temple which was to happen only about 40 years later in AD 70, Jesus starts out in the next verse talking about the last days before he returns. What these events have in common, though widely spaced in time, is their terror and calamity. Some of these signs of the last days have happened throughout the past 2000 years. But many people expect them to intensify or become more frequent, shortly before he returns.* ➤

8 Jesus said, "Be careful that you are not deceived, for many men will come to prominence claiming that they are the Messiah and that the time of judgment is almost here. Don't be misled by them. **9** When you hear about wars and revolutions, don't be afraid. These things need to happen first, but the end of all things doesn't follow immediately after them.

10 "Ethnic groups will fight against each other, and entire countries will war against each other. **11** There will be major earthquakes, plagues, and famines in various places. There will be terrifying things happening and great signs in the sky. ❖ *Now he switches to talking about events in their near future, before the destruction of the Temple, but which have also been true for the past 2000 years.* ➤ **12** But before all these things happen, people will arrest you and persecute you because you are my followers. They will deliver you before courts in synagogues and before Kings and other legal authorities and imprison you. **13** This will be an opportunity for you to testify about the things you've heard and seen me do. **14** But decide that you will not prepare your defense ahead of time. **15** When you need the words to speak, I will put words of wisdom in your mouth that none of your opponents will be able to contradict or refute. **16** Know that many of you will be betrayed to the authorities by parents, siblings, relatives, and friends and some of you will be executed. **17** Many people will hate you simply because you are my followers. **18** But they can't really harm you as far as eternity is concerned, not even slightly. Their power is only over your physical bodies—and even that is in God's hands. **19** If you endure in your faithfulness to me until the end of your lives, you will live forever with me in Heaven."

Jesus Predicts the Destruction of Jerusalem

20 ❖ *Now he talks about the time of the destruction of the Temple. We can interpret this part confidently because it is recorded history.* ➤ Jesus continued, "When you see Jerusalem surrounded by armies, then you can be sure that her destruction is imminent. **21** When you see that army coming, those who are in Judea should flee to hide in the mountains. Those in the city should escape. And those in the country shouldn't try to enter the city for any reason **22** because that will be the time of God's vengeance against the people of Jerusalem for their rejection of his Messiah. That time fulfills all the prophecies in the Scriptures about God's vengeance on those who rebel against him. **23** It will be terrible for pregnant women and those who are still nursing babies because it will be hard for them to run and escape to the mountains. The people will experience disaster, panic, grief, and horror because of God's judgment. **24** Many will be killed and others will be captured and taken into exile as slaves, scattered all over the Gentile world. Jerusalem will be oppressed under the power of Gentiles until the time God has set for their control over it to end." ❖ *Some people believe that when Israel obtained full control of Jerusalem in 1967, this prophecy was fulfilled.* ➤

The Coming of the Son of Man

25 ❖ *Then again, he switches to talking about the last days before he returns.* ➤ Jesus continued, "There will be unusual signs in the sun and moon and stars. There will also be great dread among countries of the world at the roaring and tossing of the sea. ❖ *Nobody knows what this means. Events physically affecting the sun and moon could affect tides and storms. It could refer to tsunamis or to global warming (e.g. from increased solar activity) and rising sea levels. Prophetically, the sea often refers to large numbers of people and this could predict millions of people out of control destroying and looting. Or, it could refer to something we haven't thought of.* ➤ 26 People will lose heart, faint, and even die from terror when they think about the things happening in the world because the very powers of the heavens will be shaken. ❖ *This has been interpreted as referring to the sun, moon, and stars or alternately, to powerful spiritual beings.* ➤ 27 Then, everyone will see me, the Son of Man, coming in a cloud with power and dazzling glory. [Daniel 7:13; Revelation 1:7; 19:11-16] 28 When these last things start to happen, ❖ *as described in verses 25 and 26, not the sight of his actual coming* ➤ rejoice and look up expectantly because the time of your complete redemption and transformation is extremely near."

Learn to Observe the Signs

29 Then, Jesus gave this illustration. "Think about the fig tree and all other trees. 30 When the leaves bud, you know that summer is just around the corner. 31 In the same way, when you see the signs I just told you about, you can know that the manifestation of God's Kingdom in all its glory is very near.

32 "I assure you that all these things will happen before all the people of this generation die. ❖ *There are two likely interpretations of "this*

generation." First, the people of the generation listening to Jesus would not all die before those portions of his prophecy about the destruction of Jerusalem would happen. That is obvious in historical hindsight, and some interpreters say this was the only generation Jesus was talking about. As for the signs that will occur immediately before Jesus returns, some believe he meant that "this generation" which is alive to see these later signs start, especially those described in verses 25 and 26, will not all die before his actual return. Others interpret "generation" with different meanings. Looking at all the Hebrew Scripture prophecies that we know have been fulfilled, one thing we can say about them is that it's difficult to know exactly what some prophecies mean until after they are fulfilled. ➤ 33 Heaven and earth will end, but my words are always true and all will happen as I've said."

Jesus Warns His Followers to Always be Ready for His Return

34 Jesus concluded his discussion of these things with this warning, "Take care! Do not allow yourselves to be distracted from prayer and preparation for my return. And do not allow your emotions to be weighed down with worry, which could lead to your seeking escape in drunkenness and various kinds of intoxication that cloud your thinking. If you do, you will not be ready for me on the day I return. It will spring on you as suddenly as a trap and you will be caught in your folly. 35 For it will happen at the same time—without warning—to everyone living in the world. 36 So keep spiritually alert. Pray that your faith will endure all the things that are about to happen so you can escape condemnation at the judgment and stand before me, the Son of Man, as one whom I approve."

37 Now, for those last few days before his arrest, Jesus was teaching in the Temple during the day, but in the evening he went out of the city and spent the night on Mount Olivet. 38 Early each morning, all the people would get up and go to the Temple to listen to his teaching.

22

The Plot to Arrest Jesus

1 The Passover Festival was approaching—which was immediately followed by

the week-long Festival of Unleavened Bread. ❖ *Read about the first Passover which this feast commemorated in Exodus 12:1-27.* ➤ 2 The chief priests and Scripture teachers were trying to find a way that they could secretly have Jesus executed because they were afraid the people would riot if they found out he had been arrested and was still alive.

Judas Agrees to Betray Jesus

3 Judas, also called Iscariot, was one of Jesus' twelve apostles. Satan entered his heart to influence him. ❖ *He could only do this if Judas gave him opportunity through unrepented sin in his life. [Ephesians 4:27]* ➤ 4 So Judas went to the chief priests and Temple guards and discussed how he might hand Jesus over to them when there would be no crowd around to see it. 5 They were glad for the opportunity and agreed to pay him if he did this. 6 Judas consented to the arrangement and began seeking an opportunity to betray Jesus to them when no crowd was around.

Jesus Prepares to Eat the Passover

7 The first day of the festival arrived, the preparation day when the Passover lambs were sacrificed. ❖ *Then just after sunset, the actual day of Passover would begin and the Passover meal would be eaten. The Jewish day begins at sunset.* ➤ 8 Jesus sent Peter and John with these instructions, "Go prepare the Passover meal for us." 9 They asked, "Where do you want us to prepare it?" 10 He said, "When you enter Jerusalem, you will meet a man carrying a pitcher of water. ❖ *This would be an unusual sight since it was women's work.* ➤ Follow him into the house he enters. 11 Then say to the owner of that house, 'The Rabbi asks you, "Where is the guest room where I can eat the Passover with my followers?" ' 12 He will show you a large furnished room upstairs. Prepare everything there."

13 So they went and found everything just as Jesus had described it, and they prepared the meal.

Jesus' Last Passover
When He Instituted the Lord's Supper

14 When the sun had set, Jesus reclined at the table with his apostles to eat the Passover meal. 15 He said, "I've been looking forward to eating this Passover with you before I suffer and die. 16 I will not eat it again until what it represents has been completely fulfilled in God's Kingdom."

❖ *The Passover commemorated God's saving the firstborn sons of Israel from the angel of death by means of the blood of the sacrificed Passover lamb. It also celebrated their ancestor's freedom from slavery in Egypt. The Passover is full of imagery that was meant to illustrate the true salvation from eternal death and slavery to sin that Jesus—God's sacrificial lamb [John 1:29, 36]—gained us through the shedding of his blood unto death on the cross. When all those who are saved are glorified with Jesus at the great wedding feast in Heaven, then everything that the Passover represented will be fulfilled.* ➤

17 Then Jesus took a cup of wine, thanked God for it, and said, "Take this cup and all of you drink from it. 18 I will not drink wine again until the Kingdom of God comes in its fullness."

19 Then, he took a piece of bread, thanked God for it, broke it, and gave it to them, saying, "This is my body that I'm offering up as a sacrifice for you. From now on, the main way I want you to remember my death is by eating bread together like this." 20 After they had eaten, he took the cup and said, "The wine in this cup represents a New Covenant between God and his people that I will establish with my blood, which I will pour out for you in my dying. ❖ *"Blood" is a biblical figure meaning "death." Covenants were special life-long pacts made between two parties that were often ratified with the shedding of blood. In dying and shedding his blood, Jesus ratified the New Covenant that God was making with his people. This New Covenant says he will forgive, save, and accept as his people all those who trust in Jesus' sacrificial death to save them, and who commit their lives to follow him in obedience. To drink from the contents of this cup means that you desire to participate in this Covenant and receive the benefits procured by Jesus' death. Some believe we are meant to drink the cup mainly as a reminder of what Jesus' death accomplished for us. Others believe that in drinking the cup, we participate in his death (blood) [1 Corinthians 10:16] and receive some of the spiritual benefits of the New Covenant as we drink it in faith.* ➤

21 "But the one who will betray me is with us at this table. 22 It's true that I, the Son of Man, am going to die according to

God's plan. But it will be terrible for the one who betrays me!"

23 Then, the apostles started to discuss among themselves which of them it might be who would betray him.

How to Be Among the Greatest in God's Kingdom

24 While they were dining, the apostles began to dispute among themselves who of them would be the greatest in God's Kingdom. 25 Jesus admonished them, "The kings in this world exercise power over their people. And those in authority often force those under them to call them 'Benefactors of the people' when they are actually oppressors. 26 But this isn't how I intend it to be among you. You—who consider yourselves among the most important—should act as if you are the least important, being willing to do the lowliest things. And if you want to lead, you should do so by serving others.

27 "Who is greater, the one who dines or the waiter? In human society, it's the one who dines. But I've set an example for you as a leader who serves rather than one who makes demands. ❖ *See the note at Mark 10:44.* ➤

28 "You are the ones who have stood by me through thick and thin; 29 so just as my Father has given me authority to rule, I too will give you 30 the privilege of dining at my table in the Kingdom and will make you rulers over the twelve tribes of Israel."
❖ *The reference to the twelve tribes of Israel probably means all of God's people who are saved. [Romans 10:12; Ephesians 2:11-15]* ➤

Jesus Predicts Peter's Denial

31 Jesus said to Peter, "Simon, my friend! You must know this: Satan has demanded permission from God to severely test all of you. He will try to destroy your faith, and God has granted him permission. ❖ *It's likely that the apostles' sin of pride—when they were arguing about who was the greatest—gave Satan the legal right to tempt them in this area. He would show them just how great and loyal to Jesus they really were. See the footnote at Ephesians 4:27.* ➤ 32 But I've prayed especially for you, Simon, that your faith won't be destroyed. When you have composed

yourself, help to comfort and strengthen the faith of your brothers here."

33 Peter protested, "But Lord, I'm prepared to be imprisoned with you and to even die with you!" ❖ *Peter was certainly sincere in his declaration. But he didn't realize how easy it is for any of us to succumb to temptation if we are caught off guard or if we depend on our own strength.* ➤

34 Jesus prophesied, "Peter, you won't hear a rooster crow today ❖ *the day that started at sundown* ➤ until you have three times publicly denied having any association with me."

Jesus Warns That Difficult Times Are Coming

35 Jesus asked them, "When I first sent you out to minister without money or spare clothes, did you ever lack for anything you needed?" They replied, "No."

36 Jesus said, "But from now on, things will be different. If you have money or extra clothing and a bag, take them along when you travel to minister. And if you don't own a sword, you should sell your cloak and buy one ❖ *Jesus may have been speaking figuratively concerning the sword, meaning that they should be prepared for hardship and persecution. Or, if he meant it literally, it would likely have been for defense against bandits. Commentators are divided on interpreting this, but the latter interpretation seems unlikely since there is nowhere else in Jesus' teaching to encourage his followers to use armed resistance at any time. Nor is there any example in the book of Acts of his followers defending themselves with weapons.* ➤ 37 because the Scripture about me must be fulfilled that says, 'He was considered a criminal.' " *[Isaiah 53:12]* ❖ *It is also possible that their possessing swords that night would aid in the authorities justifying their arrest of Jesus as a potentially dangerous criminal.* ➤

38 They said, "Look, Lord, here are two swords." He replied, "That's enough." ❖ *If he was speaking figuratively in verse 36, then this reply could simply be the equivalent of saying, "That's enough talk about swords for now, you just don't seem to understand."* ➤

In Gethsemane

39 After the Passover meal was finished, Jesus and his followers left Jerusalem and went up Mount Olivet to a garden called Gethsemane where he often went. 40 When they arrived, he said to them, "Pray so you

will be able to resist the temptation that will shortly come to you."

41 Then, he withdrew about a stone's throw away from them and knelt in prayer. 42 He said, "Father, if it's within your will, don't make me drink from this cup of suffering. But I want to follow your will and not my own desires." ❖ *"Cup of suffering" is a figure of speech referring to the suffering and crucifixion that he knew was coming. While fully submitted to his Heavenly Father's plan, Jesus was fully human and dreaded the suffering he knew he would soon experience.* ➤ 43 While he was praying, God sent an angel to minister to him and strengthen him. 44 He was in great emotional distress over the suffering and torture he faced, and he struggled to remain submitted to his Father's will that he go through it. He was praying so intensely and was in so much distress that he sweated profusely and the sweat fell from him like drops of blood on the ground. ❖ *Some scholars believe his stress was so extreme that capillaries broke in his skin and blood actually mixed with his sweat. Some early manuscripts do not contain verses 43 and 44.* ➤

45 When he finally got up from praying, he went over to his followers and found them sleeping. Their own sadness had drained them and made them tired. ❖ *We know there was a lot of emotional tension over Jesus' prediction that one of them would betray him. And from John's Gospel, we know that Jesus told them other emotionally disturbing things that night during the meal.* ➤ 46 He woke them and admonished them, "Why are you sleeping? You should be praying for God's help to resist the temptation that's about to come on you!"

Jesus' Arrest

47 While he was still speaking, a large crowd arrived—led by Judas, one of Jesus' apostles. He approached Jesus and greeted him with a kiss. ❖ *A kiss of greeting was as customary then as a handshake is in our culture. Because Jesus was his master, he probably kissed him on the hand. A kiss on the cheek would have indicated that they were equals. From the accounts in Matthew and Mark, we know that this kiss was a prearranged sign to identify Jesus as the person the guards were to arrest.* ➤ 48 But Jesus said, "Judas, are you betraying me with a kiss?"

49 When Jesus' followers saw that he was going to be arrested, they asked, "Lord, should we fight with our swords?" 50 And one of them struck the High Priest's slave with his sword, cutting off his right ear. ❖ *John 18:10 tells us that Peter did this, and the slave's name was Malchus. Slaves of important persons could have authority and high status. Malchus may have been representing the High Priest for this arrest. Peter was ready to fight to defend his master and may have been attempting a more serious injury. But being a fisherman, it's unlikely that he had any skill with a sword.* ➤

51 But Jesus commanded, "Stop! No more of this!" Then he touched the man's ear and healed it.

52 Jesus confronted the chief priests and Temple officers and elders who had come to arrest him, "Why have you come armed with swords and clubs to arrest me as if I were a violent criminal? 53 I've been with you every day in the Temple and you could have easily arrested me there. But now is the time that God has appointed for this to happen and for the forces of darkness to have a free hand." ❖ *Jesus had the ability to walk out of this unscathed if he chose. But this was all happening according to his Father's plan, and he was perfectly submitted to it. His enemies couldn't know that God would use their evil intentions for his own purposes.* ➤

Peter Denies Knowing Jesus

54 Having arrested Jesus, they took him to the house of the High Priest. But Peter followed behind at a distance, hidden in the dark. ❖ *The other apostles had fled—fearing arrest—except for John. [John 18:15-16] They had all boasted of their willingness to be arrested and even die with Jesus, but Satan's temptation of fear overcame their proud boasts. He attacked them in the area of their sin of pride. They were also probably confused as to why Jesus, their Messiah, didn't resist and use his power to assert his authority as God's Chosen One. Jesus' predictions of his arrest, suffering, and death were still incomprehensible to them.* ➤ 55 The guards lit a fire in the middle of the house's courtyard to keep warm, and Peter slipped in to join those sitting around it. 56 A certain serving girl noticed his face in the firelight and staring at him, said to the others there, "This man was with Jesus too!" 57 But Peter denied it, "Woman, I don't even know the man!"

58 A while later, another person recognized him and said, "You are one Jesus'

followers!" But Peter protested, "I most certainly am not!"

59 After about an hour passed, another man began to insist, "I'm certain this man was with him! It's clear from his accent that he's a Galilean too!"

60 But Peter declared, "I don't know what you're talking about! It simply isn't true!" And while he was still saying this, he heard a rooster crow. 61 The Lord—who was visible inside the house from the court-yard—turned and looked straight at Peter. Then, Peter remembered the Lord's predic-tion, "You won't hear a rooster crow today until you have publicly denied having any association with me—three separate times." 62 Peter was overcome with remorse and went outside the courtyard weeping bitterly because of what he had done.

Jesus Is Mocked and Beaten

63 Those in charge of guarding Jesus mocked and beat him. 64 They blindfolded him and then would hit him and taunt, "Since you are a prophet, prophesy and tell us who hit you." 65 They also ridiculed and insulted him in many other ways. ❖ *They were mocking him based on Isaiah 11:3.* ➤

Jesus Before the Sanhedrin

66 When dawn came, the Sanhedrin ❖ *the council of religious leaders that ruled the religious lives of the Jews* ➤ assembled, including the chief priests and Scripture teachers. They led Jesus into their council chamber and demanded, 67 "If you are the Messiah, tell us plainly!"

He answered, "If I do tell you, you won't believe me. 68 And if I ask you questions, you will refuse to answer me. We've been over this before. 69 But I will say this: From now on, **I, the Son of Man, will be seated at the right hand of Almighty God.**" *[Psalm 110:1]*

70 They all asked, "Then, are you claim-ing to be God's Son?" ❖ *They probably didn't believe God had a Son, for God's Son would also be a deity and equal to God and the Scriptures clearly taught that there was only one God. But some commentators think the Jews were expecting the Messiah to be God's Son. [Psalm 2:6-7; Matthew 26:63] Even if they had accepted the possibility of God having a Son, they believed that Jesus was a sinner who*

violated God's Sabbath command and who refused to recog-nize their authority. ➤ He answered, "Yes, I am."

71 Then, they exclaimed among them-selves, "Why do we need any more witnesses against him? We've heard him confess his blasphemy with his own mouth!" ❖ *While they were determined to find a reason to kill him, Jewish law required evidence of guilt from at least two eyewitnesses. They preferred to stick to the formalities so they could later justify their actions to the people. But Jesus confessed what they considered was blasphemy in front of them all, making them all witnesses of his guilt. According to the Torah, blasphemy was punishable by death. Unfortunately for them, ever since they had been conquered by Rome, only Roman authorities could legally sentence anyone to die and execute them, except for Temple violations. So now they had to find some basis for convincing the Roman governor that Jesus was worthy of execution.* ➤

23

Jesus before Pilate

1 Then the entire council escorted Jesus to Pilate, the Roman governor over Judea. 2 When they were brought into Pilate's presence, they started making accusations against Jesus, saying, "We've found this man guilty of stirring up trouble and encouraging people not to pay their taxes. He also calls himself 'the Messiah,' which means he intends to set himself up as a king." ❖ *From the Roman point of view, all of these were serious charges. Together, they portrayed him as a leader who was trying to foment revolt against Roman rule. It's interesting that these religious leaders, who considered themselves so much more in God's favor, didn't have any problem telling lies to Pilate. The only part of their accusations that was true was about his claim to be the Messiah.* ➤

3 Pilate asked Jesus, "Are you making yourself out to be a king of the Jews?" Jesus answered, "Those are your words and meaning." ❖ *He wasn't denying the charge. Many scholars believe it was an affirmative answer. Yet it is also hedged since he wasn't intending to be a king who was a rival to Caesar and Roman rule. Had Pilate under-stood his answer to mean a simple "yes," then he would likely have considered him a rival to Caesar and worthy of execution. But he didn't come to this conclusion. Pilate's question and Jesus' answer are reported identically in the three synoptic gospels (Matthew, Mark, and Luke).* ➤

4 Then Pilate said to the chief priests and the crowd that had come with them, "I don't find this man guilty of breaking any Roman law." ❖ *There was more interrogation than is reported in this account. It's unlikely Pilate would find him innocent on the basis of one question unless he already knew that the charges were trumped up and he wanted to irritate the Jewish leaders. From historical sources, it's known that Pilate and the Jewish leaders did not get on well at all.* ➤

5 But they kept insisting, "He is always stirring up the people, all the way from Galilee down through Judea." 6 When Pilate heard this, he asked, "Is this man from Galilee?" 7 When he found out that Jesus came from Herod's jurisdiction, he sent him off to Herod who happened to be in Jerusalem for the festival.

Jesus before Herod

8 Now, Herod was thrilled to see Jesus because he had been hearing about his miracles and popularity for a long time and wanted to see him perform a miracle. 9 Herod questioned him at length, but Jesus just stood there silently. ❖ *According to Jewish tradition, the accused was not required to answer any questions put to him—not even if they came from a king.* ➤ 10 When given the opportunity, the chief priests and Scripture teachers angrily accused him of many crimes. 11 Since he got neither miracles nor answers from him, Herod and his soldiers got their entertainment by mocking and humiliating Jesus. Then they put a fancy robe on him and sent him back to Pilate. 12 It was because of that occasion—when Pilate and Herod deferred to each other with regard to judging Jesus—that they became friends, even though prior to this they had been unfriendly rivals.

Jesus Is Sentenced to Die

13 After receiving Jesus into his custody again, Pilate summoned together the chief priests and Jewish leaders 14 and said, "You've accused this man of inciting the people to rebel against Rome. But I've interrogated him in your presence and I find no basis for the charges you've brought against him. 15 Neither did Herod, since he sent him back to me. He has certainly broken no Roman law deserving the death penalty. 16 But he has obviously caused trouble for you, so I will have him whipped as a warning against making any further trouble and let him go."

17 Now, it was a tradition that every Passover the Roman governor would release one Jewish prisoner as a gift to the people. 18 But the Jewish leaders all yelled, "Execute that man and release Barabbas for us!" 19 (Barabbas was awaiting execution for a murder he committed during a revolt.)

20 Pilate wanted to release Jesus, not kill him. So he appealed to the crowd again, trying to change their minds. 21 But they refused to listen to him and kept shouting. "Crucify him! Crucify him!" ❖ *Crucifixion was the standard Roman method of execution and was a prolonged torturous death.* ➤

22 For the third time, Pilate asked, "But why? What evil has he done? I haven't been able to find any reason according to Roman law that he should be executed. So I will only punish him and then release him."

23 But they were insistent and kept shouting demands that he be crucified. And their determination prevailed. ❖ *Pilate normally didn't care what the Jewish leaders thought or demanded. But there had been enough incidents that complaints about him to Caesar could have proved harmful to his career. John 19:12 tells us that the Jewish leaders made such threats, and that's probably why Pilate gave in to them. The crowd demanding Jesus' execution was made up almost entirely of Jewish leaders opposed to him and their loyal followers. At this point, very few of the common people knew that Jesus had been arrested.* ➤ 24 So Pilate decreed that Jesus would be crucified to satisfy their demands. 25 He released Barabbas—a murderer and revolutionary—but handed Jesus over to be executed.

The Crucifixion

26 As the soldiers were leading Jesus out of the city to the execution site, they forced a bystander named Simon—from the city of Cyrene in North Africa—to carry the crossbeam for Jesus. ❖ *The Roman soldiers were being practical. Jesus was too weak after all his beatings to carry the crossbeam, and soldiers had the legal right to force citizens to carry burdens for a certain distance.* ➤

27 A large crowd was following this procession through the narrow streets of

Jerusalem and many were wailing in mourning for him, especially the women. ❖ *This crowd was a different one from that which demanded his crucifixion. It was mostly the common people who loved him.* ➤ 28 But Jesus turned to them and said, "Women of Jerusalem, don't cry for me but cry for yourselves and your children because of God's judgment that will come upon this city. 29 The time will come when people in Jerusalem say, 'Normally barren women are pitied, but now they are the lucky ones because they don't have to see their children suffering.' 30 Things will be so terrible that people will wish for an earthquake to bury them under landslides and put them out of their misery. *[Isaiah 2:19-20; Hosea 10:8; Revelation 6:16]* 31 For if men do these things with a green tree, what will happen to one that is dry?" ❖ *Scholars think this was a proverb in use in Jesus' time, but he gives it a new twist. Its meaning is something like this: If the people of Jerusalem are able to punish a righteous man, which is like throwing a green branch (difficult to burn) into a fire, then it's even more certain that God will punish the guilty, which is like throwing a dry branch (easy to burn) into a fire. Even though the people were not involved in Jesus' arrest and trial, they had often rioted for less reason than this. He was very popular as a teacher and prophet, he obviously had been sent from God as was attested by his miracles and healings, and less than a week prior to this they had hailed him as God's promised Messiah. Yet they wouldn't raise a hand or voice in protest to stop this injustice. Even though their guilt was much less than that of their leaders, they were in their own way rejecting God's Messiah—and Jesus was predicting that God's judgment would come upon them because of it. This happened about 40 years later in AD 70. While that may seem like a long time for God to wait to hand out his punishment, he was also giving them time to repent and accept Jesus as their Messiah after his resurrection. Tens of thousands did, yet the great majority of them did not.* ➤ 32 There were also two criminals being led out to be executed with Jesus at the same time. 33 They took them out to a hill called the "skull" outside the city wall. ❖ *It may have resembled a skull. [John 19:17]* ➤ That's where they crucified Jesus and the two criminals, one on each side of him. 34 While he was hanging on the cross, {Jesus prayed, "Father, forgive them. They don't really know what they are doing."} A ❖ *Jesus was praying for those who crucified him, both the Romans and the Jewish leaders. They didn't realize that they were executing God's Son, and he was willing to forgive them. But when they continued to refuse to recognize who he was after his resurrection, forgiveness was not available to them because they refused it.* ➤

The soldiers who carried out the executions cast lots to see who would get to keep Jesus' clothes. ❖ *That the soldiers got to keep the clothes of the person executed was a common practice, and their casing lots to decide who kept them fulfilled a prophecy in Psalm 22:18. [John 19:23-24]* ➤ 35 People stood nearby watching his suffering while Jewish leaders mocked him. They said, "He had the power to save others. If he really is God's Messiah, let him save himself!" ❖ *The irony is that he could have done so, but then God's purpose of saving humanity from eternal death would have been thwarted. So in a way, what they said was true. He could save others, but in order to do so he could not save himself.* ➤

36-37 The soldiers also made fun of him. They said, "If you are the king of the Jews, save yourself! Come on down and we will share our wine with you!"

38 There was an inscription hanging above him that said,

"THIS IS THE KING OF THE JEWS"

❖ *Such inscriptions stated the crime the person had committed as a warning to anyone else who might think of doing the same thing. [John 19:19-22] And putting oneself forward as a king in rival to Caesar was a capital crime.* ➤

39 One of the criminals hanging next to him also mocked him, "Aren't you supposed to be the Messiah? Then save yourself and us too!"

40 But the other criminal rebuked the mocker. He said, "Have you no fear of God since you too are about to die and meet your maker? 41 We deserve what we are getting, but this man has done nothing wrong. By mocking a righteous man you are only adding to your list of sins and to the punishment that God will give you." 42 Then he said, "Jesus, when you do become king, please remember me and have mercy!"

43 Jesus replied, "I promise you, today you will join me in Paradise!" ❖ *Paradise was*

---

the place where the souls of righteous people went after they died. Some people believe it's just another name for Heaven. Others believe it was like Heaven but separate from Heaven until the Messiah paid for the sins of all humanity through his self-sacrificial death. Then, Paradise was moved to the true Heaven where the righteous could live in the presence of God. This criminal was declared righteous, i.e., declared acceptable to God and all his sins forgiven, merely for recognizing that Jesus was the Messiah and asking for his mercy. The plea for mercy is only implied in the original text, but it was real enough. ➤

Jesus' Death

44 By this time, it was about noon, but the sun was obscured so it was dark over the entire country until midafternoon. *[Exodus 10:22; Amos 8:9]* ❖ *This occurred at Passover which is always at a full moon, so it was not a solar eclipse but a supernatural event. Darkness was considered to be an evil sign and was also associated with judgment and punishment. [Isaiah 5:30; 13:10-11; Joel 3:14-15] This was the time when God was punishing Jesus for all of humanity's sins.* ➤ **45-46** Then, Jesus called out in a loud voice, "Father! **I give my spirit into your hands!**" *[Psalm 31:5]* And he died. At that moment, the thick curtain in the Temple was torn in two from top to bottom. ❖ *This curtain blocked the entryway from the Holy Place in the Temple into the Holy of Holies where God was present in a special way. God tore open this curtain to show that the barrier of sin which had kept people from approaching him was now removed by his Son's death. God's people now have direct access to him because their sins have been removed and they have been made holy and acceptable in his sight.* ➤ **47** The centurion in charge of the execution saw what had happened while Jesus hung on the cross ❖ *i.e., his prayer to forgive those who were killing and mocking him, the darkness, his unusually quick death, and other events that are recorded in the other Gospels* ➤ and he began praising God. He said, "I'm certain this man was innocent of any wrong!"

48 Then, all who had gathered to watch the spectacle began to return home, beating their chests in sorrow after having seen all that had happened, and believing that an innocent man had died. **49** Many who knew Jesus—plus the women who had followed him from Galilee—observed all these things while standing some distance away. ❖ *Most of his followers—except John and these women—were conspicuously absent, hiding in fear for their lives.* ➤

Jesus' Burial

50-51 There was a member of the Jewish Council named Joseph, from the town of Arimathea. He was a good man who was eagerly looking forward to the establishment of God's Kingdom as taught by Jesus, and he had not agreed with the Council's plans or their actions. **52** He went to Pilate and asked permission to remove Jesus' body from the cross so he could bury it. ❖ *Permission was needed since the Romans often left the bodies of crucified men hanging for many days as warnings against other would-be lawbreakers. In going to Pilate and showing his devotion to Jesus, he was endangering his position on the Council.* ➤ **53** When permission was granted, Joseph took the body down and wrapped it in a linen cloth ❖ *following the usual Jewish burial custom* ➤ and laid it in an unused tomb cut out from rock. ❖ *It was common for more than one body to be buried in a single tomb, but this one had not yet been used.* ➤ **54** He buried it quickly because the Sabbath was about to begin at sunset. ❖ *It was late Friday afternoon. No work could be done once the Sabbath started at sunset, and Jewish tradition preferred that bodies not hang on a cross on a Sabbath.* ➤

55 The women who had come with Jesus from Galilee followed after Joseph and saw the tomb and where he laid Jesus' body to rest. **56** Then they returned to where they were staying and prepared burial spices and perfumes to pack in the burial cloth around his body. ❖ *Again, following the Jewish burial custom.* ➤ But they had to rest on the Sabbath—as the Torah required—before they could return to finish the details of Jesus' burial.

24

God Makes Jesus Alive Again

1 Before dawn on Sunday, the women returned to the tomb with the spices they had prepared for Jesus' body. **2** But when they arrived, they found the entrance to the tomb open, with the stone that had blocked the entrance rolled to one side. **3** When they went in, they saw that Jesus' body was gone. **4** While they were standing there confused, two angels suddenly appeared near them. They looked like men but their clothes radiated a brilliant light. [5] Terrified, the women crouched down with their faces touching the ground, and the angels said, "Why are you looking in a tomb for someone who is alive? [6] He's not here, but alive again. Don't you remember that he told you all this would happen when he was still teaching in Galilee? [7] He said that the Son of Man would be handed over to sinful men, he would be crucified, and on the second day after his death he would come back to life again."

❖ *Many are confused about the statement that he would rise on the third day (in the literal text) even though he was probably dead less than 40 hours. Today, we would say that he rose the second day "after" his death. They said he rose the third day "of" his death, or "on the third day." It was quite common among Jews of that time to count even a small part of a day when counting days. The first day of his death was Friday, even though he died just a few hours before the end of that day. He died around midafternoon and the day ended at sunset. The second day of his death was Saturday, the Sabbath. The third day of his death was Sunday, which started at sunset on Saturday. Most of Sunday night (we would call it Saturday night because the night of a 24-hour Jewish day comes before the day portion) he was still in the tomb. Then, sometime early in the morning of Sunday, the third day of his death, he was raised to life.* ➤

[8] Then the women remembered what he had said [9] and immediately went back into the city to where the eleven apostles and others of Jesus' followers were staying, and reported what they had seen and heard. [10] Among the group of women that reported these things were Mary of Magdala, Joanna, Miriam the mother of James, as well as some other women. [11] But the men considered their report to be hysterical nonsense and wouldn't believe them. ❖ *In that culture, the testimony of women was not considered trustworthy. If this was a false story concocted by Jesus' followers sometime later, as some have contended, they never would have included women as the first witnesses in their tale. The idea would never have occurred to them because it would have weakened their story, not strengthened it.* ➤ [12] But Peter got up and ran to the tomb anyway to see for himself. When he got there, he stooped over, looked through the entryway, and only saw the burial cloths. He returned to his lodgings wondering what was going on. **A**

Jesus Appears on the Road to Emmaus

[13] Later that same day, two of Jesus' followers were walking from Jerusalem to the village of Emmaus, about seven miles away. [14] They were talking about all the things that had happened to Jesus—and now the confusion about what had happened to his body. [15] While they were walking and discussing this, Jesus approached them from behind. When he had caught up to them, he started walking along with them—[16] but they were prevented from recognizing him. ❖ *We don't know if Jesus changed his appearance and voice or how this was done.* ➤

[17] Jesus asked them, "What have you two been talking about as you've been walking?" They stopped and stared at him with very sad expressions on their faces. [18] The one named Cleopas exclaimed, "Are you the only person that has been in Jerusalem who doesn't know what's been happening there these past few days?" [19] Jesus asked, "What things do you mean?" They said, "The things that have happened to Jesus of Nazareth. He was a mighty prophet of God who performed miracles and taught God's message and was popular with most of the people. [20] But the chief priests and other rulers delivered him over to the Romans and got him sentenced to death—and they crucified him on Friday. [21] We were hoping that he was the Messiah who was going to save Israel. Today is the second **B** day after he died and we've all been depressed. [22-23] And now, some of the women in our group went to his tomb early this morning and came back with a crazy story of seeing angels and that his body was gone and that he is alive again. [24] So some of the men went to the tomb and confirmed it was empty, but they didn't see Jesus or any angels."

A 24:12 Some ancient copies of this Gospel don't include verse 12. (The addition of chapter and verse numbers came hundreds of years after the gospels were written.)

B 24:21 See the note at Matthew 16:21 for the reasoning behind not using the traditional phrase, "the third day."

25 Then Jesus said, "Why are you so muddle headed and slow to believe the things written by the prophets in the Scriptures? 26 Didn't they clearly write that the Messiah had to suffer these things before entering into his glory?" ❖ *See especially Isaiah 52:13—53:12 for one of these prophecies. See also the list of prophecies after 2 Peter in this book.* ➤ 27 Then he began to explain to them all the predictions about the Messiah in the Scriptures, starting with the writings of Moses and continuing through the writings of all the other prophets.

28 As they approached the village where they were going, Jesus acted like he was going to continue farther on the road. 29 But they begged him, "Please stay with us for the night. After all, it will be dark soon." So he went with them to their lodging. 30 While they were reclining at the table, ready to eat, Jesus took some bread, thanked God for it, and broke it. As he was passing it to them, 31 it was like their eyes were newly opened and they recognized who he was. But then he vanished before their very eyes. 32 They exclaimed to each other, "While he was explaining the Scriptures to us on the road, didn't your heart burn with joy? How could we not have recognized him!"

33 They were so excited that they left within the hour to hurry back to Jerusalem to tell the eleven apostles and the others. 34 When they arrived, even before they could tell their story the others said, "The Lord really is alive again! He appeared to Simon!"

35 Then they started to tell their story about Jesus' walking with them on the road and how they didn't recognize him until he broke the bread.

Jesus Appears to All His Followers

36 While they were telling their story, Jesus suddenly appeared among them {and said, "I bless you with shalom."} **A** ❖ *See the note at John 20:19.* ➤ 37 But they were startled and frightened and thought they were seeing a ghost. 38 Jesus said, "Why are you afraid? And why do you continue to doubt that I'm really alive, or who I am? 39 Look at the nail scars in my arms and feet from my crucifixion. It's really me! Touch me and confirm for yourselves that I'm a living human being, not an insubstantial apparition." ❖ *The Greek text says "hands" rather than "arms," but the meaning of the Greek word for "hand" includes the hand, wrist, and forearm (as it does in many languages). Nails in the palm of a hand or in a wrist wouldn't support much weight, and most scholars believe the nails were put through his arms near his wrists.* ➤

40 When he had said this, he showed all of them his arms and his feet. **B** 41 They were thrilled, stunned, and so overwhelmed that it was still difficult for them to fully believe he was alive. ❖ *If your loved one came back from the dead, you too would be experiencing both joy and fear that you were having a delusion.* ➤ So Jesus asked, "Do you have anything here to eat?" 42 They gave him a piece of broiled fish, 43 and he ate it while they watched to prove that he wasn't a ghost.

44 Then he said, "I want to go over with you again the things I taught you while we were together before all this happened. I told you that all the things written about me in the Teachings of Moses ❖ *the first five books of the Hebrew Scriptures* ➤ and in the writings of the prophets and in the Psalms had to be fulfilled."

45 Then, he enabled them to clearly understand how all the different prophecies about him had come true. 46 In conclusion, he said, "And so it was written that the Messiah would suffer and die and rise from death the second day after he died. 47 And the message about how a person can receive forgiveness for his sins by repenting must be proclaimed on the basis of the authority I've given you to represent me. You will proclaim this message starting here in Jerusalem and continuing on until people in every nation and ethnic group have heard it, 48 because you are eyewitnesses of all these things. 49 And I will send the Holy Spirit to come upon you, just as my Father promised. But you are to wait here in Jerusalem until he comes and fills you with his power."

A 24:36 The words in { } are in some manuscripts. They may have been added to conform to John 20:19.

B 24:40 Some ancient copies of this Gospel do not include verse 40.

Jesus Ascends to Heaven

❖ *The scene shifts to 40 days later.* ➤

⁵⁰ After that, he led them out of Jerusalem until they approached Bethany. There, he raised up his hands *[Leviticus 9:22]* and blessed them. ❖ *Hebrews chapter five tells us that Jesus is our High Priest. In Numbers 6:24-26, God gave Aaron—the first High Priest—the words to say when blessing his people. Jesus likely said those words here. Every day in the Temple, the priest who offered up the incense pronounced this blessing over God's people. At the beginning of Luke's account in 1:22, Zechariah was unable to give this blessing. Here at the end of his account, Jesus finally gives it.* ➤ ⁵¹ And while he was blessing them, he left them {and returned to Heaven}. **A** ⁵² They {worshipped him and} **B** then returned to Jerusalem full of joy ⁵³ and every day after that, they met together in the Temple to worship and praise God.

❖ *Luke continues this story in the book of Acts. In Acts chapter 1, there are more details about Jesus' departure to Heaven.* ➤

A 24:51 The words in { } are in some manuscripts.

B 24:52 The words in { } are in some manuscripts.

The Good News About Jesus the Messiah

as Told by

John

This gospel was written by the Apostle John. He was "the disciple whom Jesus loved," [John 13:23] the brother of the Apostle James, and a son of Zebedee. [Matthew 4:21] After Jesus' ascension to Heaven, he was one of the main leaders of the believers in Jerusalem, [Galatians 2:9] along with Peter and James (the brother of Jesus). He took care of Jesus' mother, Miriam, after Jesus' death. [John 19:25-27] Tradition says that before Jerusalem was destroyed in AD 70, he moved to Ephesus. Later, he was exiled by the Romans for a time on the island of Patmos. [Revelation 1:9] He was also the author of John's First, Second, and Third Letters, and the book of Revelation, which were written after this gospel.

Tradition says that John wrote this gospel while in Ephesus, probably about AD 85–90. But more recently, some scholars think it was written as early as the 50s and no later than AD 70. John tells us clearly why he wrote this gospel in John 20:30-31: "Jesus' followers saw him perform many other miraculous signs that aren't recorded in this book. But I've recorded these so you may come to believe that Jesus really is the Messiah—God's Son—and gain eternal life by trusting in him."

Matthew's gospel portrays Jesus as the long-expected Messiah and King of the Jews. Mark portrays him as a servant. Luke portrays him as the "Son of Man," emphasizing his human nature. And John presents Jesus as God's Son. The Jews correctly understood that any claim to be "God's Son" was a claim to be equal with God the Father. John's gospel is significantly different from the other three and is ordered topically rather than chronologically. It centers around eight signs that point to his deity—and seven "I Am" statements.

The Eight Signs:

Water changed into wine. 2:1-12
Cleansing the Temple. 2:13-22
Healing at a distance. 4:43-54
Healing a paralyzed man on a Sabbath (at the pool of Bethesda). 5:2-16
Feeding 5,000 men. 6:1-15
Walking on water. 6:16-21
Healing a man born blind. 9:1-41
Raising Lazarus from the dead. 11:1-44

The Seven "I AM" Statements:

I am the Bread of Life. 6:35, 48
I am the Light of the world. 8:12; 9:5
I am the Gate. 10:7, 9
I am the Good Shepherd. 10:11, 14
I am the Resurrection and the Life. 11:25
I am the Way, the Truth, and the Life. 14:6
I am the True Vine. 15:1-5

Jesus' Other "I AM" Claims:

I am he (the Messiah). 4:25-26
I am the One (the Messiah and God's Son). 13:19; 18:5-6, 8
I am (Yahweh). 8:24, 28; 8:58
Jesus claims to be one with the Father. 10:30; 14:9
Other affirmations of Jesus' deity. 1:1, 34; 20:281

1

Jesus Is the Creator

¹ Before God created anything, the "Word of God" existed as a person. This person—the Word or Expression of God—has always existed in unity of essence with God the Father, and so is himself also God. ❖ *The "Word of God" or "the Word of Yahweh (i.e., the Lord)" is mentioned a number of times in the Hebrew Scriptures as an active agent who speaks God's message to people. [Genesis 15:1, 4; 1 Samuel 3:7, 21; 15:10; 1 Kings 12:22; 1 Chronicles 17:3; 22:8; 2 Chronicles 11:2; Psalm 33:6; Isaiah 38:4; Jeremiah 1:4] So the "Word of God" was perceived as a person by the Jews long before John wrote his gospel. Yet his nature was not well defined in their thinking.* ➤ ² Since he was already with God when time was created, he himself is not a created being. ³ In fact, it was the Word of God who created all that was created, including everything that lives. *[Acts 17:28; Romans 11:36; 1 Corinthians 8:6; Colossians 1:16-17; Hebrews 1:3; 2 Peter 3:7]* ❖ *Psalm 33:6 says: The heavens were made by the Word of Yahweh. Proverbs 8:12, 22-30 speaks of "Wisdom" being with God and creating everything with him. Genesis 1 says, "And God said,..." meaning that he created things by speaking them into being. Later Scriptures show that it came to be understood that God's "Word" was a person. John isn't introducing a new idea here. What is new, is his identifying Jesus as the "Word of God." Colossians 1:17 and Hebrews 1:3 teach that he also maintains the existence of all things by his "Word of Power."* ➤ ⁴ Eternal self-existing life is part of his essence, and he is the source of all life for every living thing. He is also the person who reveals eternal truths about God and the way to obtain eternal life. So he is a spiritual "Light" to ⁵ those who live in the darkness of sin under the threat of eternal death; and the demonic powers of darkness have never overcome this Light. ❖ *The last statement is ambiguous in Greek. It could mean that "darkness has not understood it." In this sense, darkness is personified as evil and means Satan, his demons, and those who are still lost have never understood God's Truth. John may have intended both meanings. We know that darkness is* the absence of light and not a physical thing at all. Thus darkness can never conquer light. It's important that people who have been influenced by Eastern religious ideas understand that the Bible does not teach the equality of spiritual Light and darkness, for the smallest amount of Light banishes darkness. ¶ *In the Scriptures, "light" is often a symbol of purity, or a metaphor for spiritual enlightenment. But sometimes it is a metaphor for God as the source of life, health, victory, and blessings, and the darkness which opposes it is a metaphor for death, sin, and sickness which weaken people. [Psalms 18:28,; 27:1; 36:9; 37:6; 97:11; 112:4]* ➤

⁶ God commissioned a prophet named John the Baptizer as a messenger to the Jews, his chosen people. ⁷ John's mission was to tell what God had shown him about this divine Light so that as a result of his testimony, many would be open to listening to and trusting the Light when he was introduced to them. ⁸ John wasn't the Light, as some thought. But he did come to tell people what God wanted them to know about the Light—who was yet to be introduced.

⁹ Now, the genuine Light of God came into this world where all humanity was in rebellion against their creator. He came to reveal the truth about spiritual realities to all who were willing to listen. ❖ *John's use of "world" in his writings almost always has a negative connotation.* ➤ ¹⁰ He came and lived in this sinful world as a man, but those in rebellion against God didn't recognize him as their creator. ¹¹ He was born among the Jews—whom God had chosen to be his own people—but most of them rejected him and his message. ¹² Yet to those who believed his claims and put their confidence in him, he gave the right and ability to enter into a new relationship with God as his spiritual children. ¹³ They were spiritually born into this new relationship by God's power, not because they had a particular human ancestry, ❖ *as many Jews thought* ➤ and not as a result of human-initiated decision or desire.

¹⁴ That person—who is the Word of God and an eternal spirit—became flesh and blood by being born as a human being **A** and

---

A 1:14 The "Word of God" is the "Son of God" who was born as a human being and grew up to be the man Jesus. He is called "the second person of the Trinity," the Father being the first person and the Holy Spirit being the third person in the one "Godhead." The event of the eternal spirit—who is the Son of God—becoming man is called the "Incarnation." Traditional Christian teaching says that Jesus was and remains both fully God and fully human. He didn't

lived among us for a time. ❖ *John literally wrote: "He tabernacled among us," which brought to the Jewish mind the remembrance of God living in the midst of his people in the Tabernacle during their time in the desert wilderness. [Exodus 25:8-9] This foreshadowed later realities when God lived among his people as a man, and even further as he now lives in his people through the Holy Spirit.* ➤ We apostles have seen his divine glory which is uniquely his as the one and only eternal divine Son of God. He came to us from God the Father; and his glory—reflected in his character—is full of both truth and a desire to give people undeserved divine favor and enabling power so they can have a proper relationship with God. ❖ *The word "glory" often means a brilliant light which is a visible manifestation of God's presence, as in the light of the "shekinah glory" which was occasionally seen in the Tabernacle. [Exodus 40:34-35; Leviticus 9:23; Numbers 14:10; 16:19, 42; 20:6; 1 Kings 8:11; 2 Chronicles 5:14; 7:1-3] "Shekinah" is a Hebrew word that doesn't appear in the Scriptures but refers to a visible manifestation of God's presence. Thus John implies that the "Word made flesh" (i.e., Jesus) is the ultimate manifestation of God's presence among his people. In saying "we have seen his glory," John may be referring to the transfiguration [Matthew 17:1-8; Mark 9:2-8; Luke 9:28-36] when he saw Jesus glorified and contrasted with the glorified Moses and Elijah—who are probably among the most glorious humans in Heaven. But it's more likely that he refers to those who had the spiritual insight to recognize that Jesus had the character and glory of God. Many people saw Jesus, but relatively few recognized his divine glory. ¶ The words "grace and truth" (at the end of verse 14 in the literal text) brought Exodus 33:18-23 and 34:5-7 to the minds of John's readers. In Exodus 33:19 and 22, God refers to his "glory" as his "goodness"—referring to his character. In 34:6 he describes his character as "compassionate and gracious, slow to anger, abounding in gracious love and truth." (The Hebrew word translated "truth" can also mean "faithfulness.") This passage in Exodus also shows that God identifies his character with his "Name" (compare what he "proclaims" in Exodus 33:19 and 34:6). Thus John the apostle claims here that Jesus' glory—"full of grace and truth"—is the same as Yahweh's, the God of Israel.* ➤ 15 When the Word came to John the Baptizer, John pointed to him and said, "This is the person I was talking about when I said, 'The one who comes after me is greater than I am

because he existed long before I did.'" ❖ *The Jews regarded those who were older as having inherently higher status. John the Baptizer was born before Jesus, but he was referring to the Son of God's eternal existence before John's birth.* ➤ 16 All of us who believe in him have also received a never-ending flow of blessings from the fullness of his favor and truth. 17 Through Moses, God gave favor and truth to the nation of Israel in his Torah teachings which enabled them to have a relationship with him. But a superior expression of God's favor and truth is offered to all humanity through Jesus the Messiah. 18 No human living in this world has ever seen God as he really is. But God's only Son has revealed to us what he is like. For his eternal divine nature comes from his eternal divine Father, and he has the most intimate relationship possible with God the Father. ❖ *No sinner can see God and live. [Exodus 33:20] But the Word of God who became incarnate as Jesus said that if we've seen him, then in a real sense we have seen the Father. [John 14:9] Everything that Jesus said and did was what his Father told him to say and do, and was done to reveal the Father's character and ways to us. [John 8:28-29; 12:50; 15:15; 17:6, 26] Thus those aspects which God considered most important for his people to know about him in this life were revealed and modeled by Jesus. His words and deeds were the Father's words and deeds.* ➤

John the Baptizer Prepares God's People to Receive the Messiah

19 After John the Baptizer had gained some public recognition, the Jewish leaders in Jerusalem sent priests and Levites to ask him, "What claims do you make about yourself?" ❖ *The leaders who sent them were probably members of the Sanhedrin (the Jewish council that ruled the Jews) since they controlled the priesthood, and Levites were Temple assistants to the priests.* ➤ This is what he said about himself. 20 He didn't refuse to answer but openly declared, "I'm not claiming to be the Messiah, if that's what you're thinking." 21 Then they asked, "Then are you the prophet Elijah whom God promised to send back from Heaven before the Messiah comes?" *[Malachi 4:5]* ❖ *According to Jesus, this*

---

temporarily take on the form of a man and then later give it up. He now exists for all eternity as human—as well as God. But his body is "glorified" and does not have the limitations

of our present human bodies. After the resurrection at the end of this age, God's people will have immortal glorified bodies like Jesus'—which will still be real physical bodies.

prophecy did refer to John, of whom Elijah was a prefiguring 'type' who preached in the power of the Holy Spirit. [Matthew 11:14; 17:12; Mark 9:13; Luke 1:17] But John himself was not literally Elijah, and evidently did not understand that prophecy as referring figuratively to himself. ➤ He said, "No, I'm not." They asked again, "Are you the prophet whom Moses said God would send, who will be like Moses?" [Deuteronomy 18:15-18] ❖ Moses' prophecy referred to the Messiah, but this was not clear to the Jews at that time. ➤ He answered, "No." 22 Then they said, "We have to take some answer back to our superiors. So what claims do you make about yourself and your ministry?" 23 John replied by quoting the prophet Isaiah, "I am **the person in the wilderness whose voice can be heard calling out to God's people, 'Prepare the way for the coming of Yahweh!'** " A [Isaiah 40:3]

24 Now, some of those in this group who had been sent to John were Pharisees. ❖ Most priests and Levites were Sadducees. There were very few Pharisees among them. ➤ 25 They asked John, "If you aren't the Messiah or Elijah or the prophet that Moses spoke about, then where do you get your authority to baptize people?" ❖ They assumed that only certain end-time figures would have special authority to institute something new like John's baptism. If he wasn't one of the main three they were expecting, then where did his authority come from? The meaning and purpose of John's baptism was different from the baptism that Jews used for converts. Any change in their traditions—such as John was doing—would require authority from God. They didn't know how to deal with him until they knew his claim to authority. "Baptize" is a transliteration of a Greek word meaning "to wash, dip, or immerse." As a rite of initiation, people were immersed in water to symbolize the death and burial of their old way of life, and coming out of the

water symbolized their entering a new pure way of life. The IVP commentary says that the point of John's baptism was that all people, including Jews, had to approach God in the same way, via repentance. Most Jews of that time assumed that they were saved if they didn't reject God's Torah teachings. ➤ 26 John's reply was, "I only baptize people in water to prepare them to welcome the Messiah—who is living among you right now. You don't know who he is yet, but he is the one you should be asking about. ❖ John's authority came from God, but aside from quoting the passage in Isaiah above, he apparently made no other claim to authority. Instead of directly answering their question and thus focusing on himself, he fulfills his mission to point them to the Messiah. John either continued to evade their question or they refused to accept his answer if he gave it later, because the Jewish leaders refused to acknowledge him as a prophet. The common people easily believed this of John. But from the other gospel accounts, we know that John was harsh in his criticism of the Pharisees and other Jewish leaders— which turned them against him. ➤ 27 He's the one who comes after me but is my superior. Compared to him, I'm not even worthy to be the slave who unties his sandals." 28 These events happened near Bethany on the eastern bank of the Jordan River where John was baptizing people. ❖ This Bethany is not the village near Jerusalem, but another one with the same name. ➤

John Proclaims Jesus to be God's Sacrificial Lamb

29 The next day, John saw Jesus coming and said to those present, "That man is God's chosen sacrificial Lamb. His death will take away humanity's sin and it's penalty. ❖ The sacrifices for sin required by the Teachings of Moses prepared

---

A 1:23 John the Baptizer was quoting from the Septuagint, the Greek translation of the Hebrew Scriptures. This is known because its wording is slightly different from the Hebrew text. The Septuagint and John's gospel in Greek translated "Yahweh" as "Kurios" meaning "Lord," but in the original Hebrew, the name "Yahweh" is written in Isaiah's prophecy. This quote is further testimony from John that the coming Messiah was himself God, but that fact is hidden behind the Greek translation "Kurios." Kurios has a wide range of meaning that could apply to mere humans as well as God. Its traditional preservation as "Lord" in most English translations also obscures this fact from English readers. Of course, even if John the Baptizer was speaking in Greek (unlikely since Aramaic was used among the Jews in Israel

at that time), he and his listeners and the Apostle John who wrote this book and the early readers of this gospel all knew that the original Hebrew text referred to Yahweh himself. At some point in the period between the writing of the Hebrew Scriptures and the New Testament, it had become a Jewish tradition to refrain from saying God's name and to refer to him indirectly, probably to avoid using his name in vain. But the name "Yahweh" was seen in the Hebrew scrolls every time they were read, even though they substituted the Hebrew word "Adonai" for his name (which means "Lord") when they read it aloud. This interpretation restores the original "Yahweh" in the quote to let the modern reader also know what all the people at that time knew the quote said, even though they avoided saying the name themselves.

God's people to understand the significance of this statement and Jesus' sacrifice. This is explained more fully in the Letter to the Hebrew Believers. ➤ 30 This is the person I was speaking about when I said, 'Someone is coming after me who is greater than I am because he existed long before I did.' 31 At first, I didn't realize that he was the Messiah. But God sent me to baptize people in water so they would be prepared for his coming, and so I could point him out to the people of Israel. 32-33 God told me, 'You will see the Holy Spirit come down from Heaven and remain on a man. That man is the one who will baptize people in the Holy Spirit.' And I've seen the Spirit come down from Heaven in the form of a dove and remain on this man. *[Matthew 3:16; Mark 1:10; Luke 3:22]* Otherwise, I wouldn't have recognized him as the Messiah. 34 So I'm declaring to you, I've seen this happen and this man is God's Son."

❖ *John is repeating what he heard God say about Jesus at his baptism. [Matthew 3:17; Mark 1:11; Luke 3:22]* ➤

Jesus' First Followers

35 The next day, John was in the same place with two of his followers. 36 When Jesus walked by, John said to them, "Look, that man is God's chosen sacrificial Lamb!" 37 When they heard this, they went to catch up with him. 38 Jesus turned around and saw them coming, so he asked, "What do you want?" They said, "Rabbi (a respectful title given to Jewish religious teachers), where are you staying?" 39 He answered, "Come and see for yourselves." So they went with him, saw where he was staying, and spent the rest of the day with him, since it was already about four in the afternoon. ❖ *The Jewish day ended at sunset.* ➤

40-41 One of the two men was Andrew, the brother of Simon Peter. ❖ *Many think the second was John, the author of this gospel.* ➤ The first thing Andrew did after leaving Jesus was to find his brother Simon and tell him, "We've found the Messiah!" (Messiah means, "anointed one.") ❖ *"Messiah" is an English transliteration of "meshiach," a title in Hebrew. An anointed person was someone chosen by God for a special office, usually a prophet, priest, or king. Jesus is all three. Messiah is the title for the Savior that God promised to send to his people. His main purpose was to save people from the power of sin and the fate of Hell. But in Jesus' time, the Jews were looking for a political savior who would drive the Romans out of their country and set up a powerful kingdom similar to Solomon's of 1,000 years earlier, when Israel's political and economic power was at its peak. The Greek word for "anointed one" is "kristos," which has been transliterated into English as "Christ."* ➤ 42 Then Andrew took Simon to meet Jesus, who looked at him and said, "You are Simon, son of John. But I will call you 'Rock.' " ❖ *Jesus spoke in Aramaic, a Semitic language related to Hebrew. The name "Rock" that he gave Simon was "Kefa" [kay-fah], which transliterated into English became "Cephas," [kay-fahs] today often pronounced [SEE-fuhs]. In Greek, this same name "Rock" is rendered as "Petros," which is transliterated into English as "Peter." Hence he is commonly known as "Simon Peter." But Jesus was focusing on the meaning of his name, "Simon, the Rock," with the common positive metaphorical meanings attached to "rock," such as "reliable" and "strong." Throughout Scripture, certain people were given new names when they entered into a new relationship with God, and the new name signified a change that God intended to make in them. [Genesis 17:5, 15; 32:28; Isaiah 62:2, 4 (this refers to Jerusalem); Revelation 2:17] Rabbis also commonly gave their disciples nicknames.* ➤

Jesus Calls Philip to Follow Him

43 The next day, Jesus decided to go into Galilee Province. There he found Philip and said, "Come be one of my followers!" So he did. 44 Philip was from Bethsaida, the same village as Andrew and Peter (Rock). **A** 45 Then Philip went and found Nathanael, **B** and told him, "We've found the Messiah who Moses wrote about in the Torah,

---

A 1:44 Mark 1:21 and 29 say Peter's house is in Capernaum. Some see this as a contradiction. But Jesus' home village was Nazareth and during his ministry, he made Capernaum his home and base. Both places were "home" to him. Capernaum and Bethsaida were close and both on the shore of Lake Galilee. Andrew and Peter could have been raised in Bethsaida and later moved to Capernaum. If this were the case, Bethsaida would still be known as their home village.

B 1:45 Nathanael may also have been known as "Bartholomew," which might be a patronymic. "Bar" means "son of" and "Bartholomew" could mean "son of Tholomaeus." In the lists of the apostles in Matthew 10:3; Mark 3:18; and Luke 6:14; (but not in Acts 1:13) Bartholomew is linked with Philip. Or, Nathanael may have been a follower who was not an apostle. He was from the village of Cana. [John 21:2]

[Deuteronomy 18:15] and who's also written about in the Prophets. [Isaiah chapters 9; 11; 53; and other places] He's Jesus from Nazareth, the son of Yosef." 46 Nathanael replied, "How can anyone of significance come from Nazareth?" A Philip said, "Come and find out." 47 When Jesus saw Nathanael approaching, he said, "Now here comes an Israelite who is honest and has pure motives!" 48 Nathanael asked, "How do you know about me?" Jesus replied, "Even before Philip called you to come, I saw you under the fig tree." ❖ Jesus was saying that his knowledge of Nathanael's character was given to him by God, just as his seeing where Nathanael had been was clearly a vision from God. There would have been no other way for him to know these things. Jesus probably knew about Nathanael's character through the spiritual gift called a "word of knowledge." [1 Corinthians 12:8; 13:2, 8; 14:6] ➤ 49 Nathanael said, "Rabbi, you are God's Son! You are the King of Israel!" 50 Jesus said, "You believe that just because I said I saw you under the fig tree? You will see greater evidence than this! 51 I solemnly assure all of you that you will have clear revelation from God that he has appointed me to be the Son of Man." ❖ "Son of Man" was an obscure Messianic title that avoided the political overtones of other Messianic titles in use at that time. He didn't want to encourage false expectations. It was an allusion to Daniel 7:13-14 and not understood by the Jews to be a messianic title at all. But if someone were to recognize the allusion to the description of the "Son of Man" in Daniel 7:13-14, they would realize he was claiming these things about himself: he came from Heaven, he was worthy to enter into the very presence of God, God gave him authority, glory and power over all people and nations, he is to be submitted to in worship, and his kingdom will never end. ¶ In the literal text of verse 51, Jesus referred to a vision that Jacob had which is recorded in Genesis 28:12. Jesus' intended meaning is given above instead of his actual words. ➤

2

Jesus' First Miraculous Sign

1 Two days later, there was a wedding in the village of Cana in Galilee Province. Jesus' mother was there 2 and he and his followers were also invited. 3 When the wine ran out (sometime during the seven-day feast following the wedding), Jesus' mother told him, "They're out of wine." 4 Jesus replied, "What business is that of ours? It isn't my time yet." ❖ The phrase "my time" in John's gospel, refers to his death and exaltation. [John 13:1; 17:1] It's unlikely that his mother was asking for anything beyond money to help buy more wine, as up to this point Jesus had never done a miracle. But Jesus often answered questions beyond what people were asking. He may have seen the wedding feast as symbolic of the wedding feast in Heaven when wine will be abundant [Jeremiah 31:12; Amos 9:13-14; Matthew 22:1-14; 25:1-13] and he was saying that the time when he will be glorified and will provide wine and joy, hasn't yet come. ➤ 5 But his mother told the servants, "Do whatever he tells you to do." ❖ Jews would understand her refusal to take "no" for an answer as showing strong faith that her son would do something. In other places, Jesus initially refuses or resists a request and then responds to persistent faith—which he may have been trying to evoke here as well. [Matthew 15:21-28; John 4:47-50; 11:21-44] ➤ 6 There were six stone containers there to hold water for Jewish ritual washing. Each one could hold about 20-30 gallons. 7 Jesus told the servants, "Fill the containers with clean water." So they filled them all to the brim. 8 Then he told them, "Now draw some out and take it to the man in charge." 9 When the man in charge tasted it, it had already become wine. He didn't know where it came from, but the servants knew. He called the groom 10 and said, "Everyone else serves his best wine first, and after people have been drinking awhile, then they bring out the cheap stuff. But you have kept the best until now!" ❖ The Hebrew Scriptures disapprove of drunkenness, [Deuteronomy 21:20; 1 Samuel 1:13-14; Proverbs 23:19-21; Isaiah 63:6] and wine was normally served diluted to a third or a quarter strength. The man in charge would have been responsible for diluting the wine and making sure that no one became drunk. But after days of feasting, people's sense of taste would become less discerning and cheaper wine wouldn't be noticed. The Torah does allow drinking fermented drink. [See Deuteronomy 14:26] ➤

11 So Jesus' first miraculous sign was performed in the village of Cana in Galilee. This sign revealed his glory to those who

---

A 1:46 Nazareth was a small insignificant village with a bad reputation. To say someone was from Nazareth was an insult, similar to our saying someone is a "hick" or a "redneck."

had eyes of faith, [John 1:14; 20:30-31] and his followers believed that he was the Messiah. 12 After this, Jesus, his mother and brothers and his followers made the one-day journey down from the hill country of Cana to Capernaum and stayed there a few days. ❖ *Capernaum was about 16 miles east-northeast of Cana, on the northwest shore of Lake Galilee (which is nearly 700 feet below sea level). It became Jesus' home base during his years of ministry.* ➤

The Passover at the Start of Jesus' Ministry When He First Cleansed the Temple

❖ *The second cleansing of the Temple was on Palm Sunday, the week of his crucifixion. [Matthew 21:12-13; Mark 11:15-17; Luke 19:45-46] Some commentators believe there was only one cleansing and that either John or the other three gospel writers reported it at a different time than it happened. But taking the texts at face value leads to the conclusion that Jesus did this twice, a few years apart.* ➤

13 When the time for the Passover Festival approached, Jesus went up to Jerusalem. ❖ *All Jewish men who were capable were required to make the pilgrimage to Jerusalem for the Passover every year. [Deuteronomy 16:5-6] Passover is celebrated on Nisan 14 (the full moon at the end of March or beginning of April). The first Passover is described in Exodus 12:1-17. Jerusalem is at an elevation of about 2400 feet so all roads lead "up" to it. The distance from Capernaum to Jerusalem is about 75 miles, but his actual route would have been longer. On foot, the trip would take four to six or more days.* ➤

14 When he arrived in the outer courtyard of the Temple (the Court of the Gentiles), he saw people selling cattle, sheep, and doves for sacrifices, and money changers doing business at tables. ❖ *The money changers exchanged foreign coins for those acceptable for paying the Temple tax. These people were all providing needed services, but it was where they were doing it that was inappropriate. In the accounts in Matthew 21:12-13; Mark 11:15-17; and Luke 19:45-46, when Jesus cleansed the Temple the second time, he quoted Isaiah 56:7. This implied one reason why he was upset. By making the Court of the Gentiles a marketplace, they were robbing Gentiles of a place to worship the one true God, when God had specifically intended the Temple to be a place of prayer for people of all nations.* ➤

15 So he made a multi-stranded whip of cords and drove them all out of the Temple court, along with their sheep and cattle. He overturned the money changers' tables, scattering their coins. 16 To those who were selling doves, he commanded, "Take these birds out of here! Stop making my Father's house a place of business!" 17 And his followers remembered the Scripture that says, **"Zeal for the purity of your house will consume me."** [Psalm 69:9 in the Septuagint] 18 Then, the Jewish leaders demanded, "Can you show us a miraculous sign to prove that you have God's authority to do these things in his Temple?" 19 Jesus replied, "Destroy this Temple and I will raise it up again within three days." 20 They exclaimed incredulously, "It took forty-six years to build this Temple! You're going to rebuild it in three days?" ❖ *The Temple was under construction from 20-19 BC until AD 64. Specifying forty-six years places this incident in approximately AD 27 or 28.* ➤ 21 But he had been speaking cryptically about the Temple of his body. ❖ *Jesus' body and all believers' bodies are temples (i.e., dwelling places) of God through the indwelling Holy Spirit. Jesus was probably indicating that the Jewish Temple—where sacrifices for sin were offered and where God met his people—was a "type" of his body, which became the ultimate sacrifice for sin and where believers truly meet and are united with God. When the Jewish authorities later "destroyed" the living Temple of his body by executing him, on the third day A God "raised it up" from death, providing the sign they had demanded.* ➤ 22 Some three years later—when he was alive again after having died—his followers remembered that he had said this, and they believed the things the Scriptures said about the Messiah, and also this statement that he would "raise it up again within three days."

23 During that Passover festival in Jerusalem, Jesus performed some miraculous signs, and many who saw them believed that he was the Messiah. 24 But Jesus understood what people are like, so he didn't trust them to continue to believe in him. 25 No one had to tell him about human motivations and ways since he knew what went on inside them. [Jeremiah 17:9]

A 2:21 See the notes at Matthew 16:21 and Matthew 12:40 about the expression "the third day" with regard to Jesus' death and resurrection.

3

Nicodemus and the New Birth

1 Now there was a Pharisee named Nicodemus who was a member of the Sanhedrin. ❖ *The Sanhedrin was the Jewish council headed by the High Priest that ruled the religious lives of the Jews. Pharisees were a sect of laymen devoted to the strict keeping of the Scriptures and Jewish traditions. Most Pharisees rejected Jesus because he didn't respect their traditions—which they promoted as being as important as the Teachings of Moses.* ➤ **2** Coming to see Jesus one night, he said, "Rabbi, we know that God has sent you to teach us since no one can do the miraculous signs you do unless God enables him." **3** Going straight to Nicodemus' unrecognized need, Jesus said, "I'm going to tell you a very important fact. No one can be part of God's Kingdom without being born again." ❖ *The word ἄνωθεν (anōthen) translated "again" can alternatively mean "from above," which would mean "from God" (Jews of that time avoided saying "God"). It may be that John intended both meanings. (But Jesus would have conversed with Nicodemus in Aramaic, not Greek.) But from his response in verse 4 about entering his mother's womb a second time, it's clear that Nicodemus understood Jesus to mean "again."* ➤ **4** Nicodemus said, "How can an old man be born again? He can't enter his mother's womb a second time to be born, can he?" ❖ *Commentators differ as to whether Nicodemus knew what Jesus was talking about and was answering in figurative language, or whether he really misunderstood. Since he was a Jewish elder and was used to speaking, teaching, and debating in figures and he focuses on an "old" man being reborn (whereas it's equally impossible for anyone to be physically reborn, regardless of age), it seems more likely that he understood Jesus and was saying that it would be very difficult for an old person, set in his ways, to start all over again on a new spiritual journey.* ➤ **5** Jesus replied, "I'm telling you the way it is. Unless you are born of water and spirit you can't enter God's Kingdom. ❖ *"Born of water and spirit" has been interpreted three main ways. Many say "water" means the normal human birth process and "spirit" means either spiritual birth or the Holy Spirit. But it seems unlikely that Jesus would specify natural birth as a requirement since everyone is already born in this way. Another interpretation says "water" refers to baptism. Nicodemus would have been familiar with Jewish proselyte baptism and John's baptism and could have understood the reference. The third interpretation*

says that "water and spirit" both refer to spiritual rebirth, and together substitute for "again" in verse 3 as a clarification. These words would have brought Ezekiel 36:25-27 to Nicodemus' mind (about being made pure with water and receiving a new heart and spirit). ➤ **6** The physical gives birth to a physical body, but the Holy Spirit gives birth to a new spirit in a person. **7** You shouldn't be surprised at my saying, 'People must be born again.' **8** You can hear the wind blowing and observe its effects, but where it blows is unpredictable and you can't control it. It's the same with the Holy Spirit. You can observe his effect on those in whom he births new spirits, but you can neither control him nor predict how or in whom he will work." ❖ *Both Hebrew and Greek have one word that can mean either "wind," "spirit," or "breath" depending on context. (The Hebrew word is רוּחַ "ruach" and the Greek word is πνεῦμα "pneuma.") Jesus' words would bring Ezekiel 37:1-14 to Nicodemus' mind (about the valley of dry bones into which life was breathed).* ➤ **9** Nicodemus asked, "How can people be born of the Spirit?" **10** Jesus exclaimed, "You are one of the most respected rabbis in Israel, yet you don't understand these things! ❖ *Nicodemus knew the Hebrew Scriptures inside and out. All of Jesus' teaching was grounded in truth revealed in the Hebrew Scriptures, but Nicodemus didn't understand them properly.* ➤ **11** I'm telling you the truth. We're only able to talk about and confirm what we've seen and known, and that is what I'm doing. Yet you and many like you refuse to accept what we say. ❖ *"We" in this verse refers to Jesus and probably John the Baptizer.* ➤ **12** If you don't believe me about basic truths that happen here on earth, like the new birth, how can you believe me if I tell you about Heaven? **13** No one has ascended into Heaven and returned to tell about it except me, the Son of Man, [Daniel 7:13] for I have come from Heaven and am able to do so. **14** Just as Moses lifted up the bronze snake in the wilderness to save people's lives, [Numbers 21:4-9] in a similar way I, the Son of Man, must be lifted up to die on a cross **15** so that anyone who believes in me can have eternal life. ❖ *The original Greek text has no punctuation, so it isn't clear where Jesus' quote ends. Many end it here, interpreting verses 16-21 as a commentary by John. Others think Jesus' words continue to the end of verse 21. This interpretation is written as if Jesus continued to speak about* *himself. Jesus often spoke about himself in the third person (at least as recorded in the Greek translation of what he said), but since this isn't natural in English, this interpretation has been modified to a first-person expression to sound more natural.* ➤

16 "Since God loves people despite their sin and rebellion, he sent me—his only eternal divine Son—into this world to die for them so that everyone who really believes in me will not perish in Hell, but instead have eternal life. 17 God didn't send me into this world to condemn people, but to save them through what I will do. ❖ *All people are born under the sentence of rejection by God and eternal isolation from him in Hell (i.e., damnation) because all are, by nature, self-oriented and rebellious against him.* ➤ 18 All who believe in me are saved from condemnation. But all who refuse to believe in me remain under God's condemnation because they have rejected his only eternal divine Son. ❖ *Belief is more than intellectual assent. Other passages teach that true belief results in repentance from sin, obedience to God's will, and trust in God's word. Belief that doesn't result in repentance is, therefore, not genuine.* ➤ 19 People are condemned on this basis: I came into this world as God's spiritual Light to enable people to know him and to give them eternal life. But many people love the darkness of spiritual ignorance because their ways are evil and they don't want to change. 20 Everyone whose way is evil hates me because I am the spiritual Light that reveals God's truth. They avoid his Light because they're afraid that their evil ways will be exposed. 21 But those whose ways are good are attracted to me—God's Light—thus everyone can see that their good ways have come about by God's power."

John the Baptizer's Testimony About Jesus

22 After this, Jesus and his followers left Jerusalem and went out into the rural areas of Judea where he spent some time with them and had them baptize people. 23 At the same time, John was also baptizing at Aenon—near Salim, because of the many springs there—and people were constantly coming to him to be baptized. 24 (This was before John's imprisonment.) 25 One day, John's followers had an argument with a certain Jew about ritual washing for purification. ❖ *This may have been about differences between John's baptism and Jesus'.* ➤ 26 Afterward, they went to John and said, "Rabbi, you know the man you testified about who was with you when you were baptizing on the other side of the Jordan river? Well, now he is baptizing people too and it seems like everyone is going to him instead!"

27 John replied, "Everything good that a man has, even success, comes from God. 28 You heard me declare that I'm not the Messiah and have only been sent ahead of him to prepare his way. *[John 1:20]* 29 "I'm like a groom's best man. I rejoice to hear the groom's voice, and when I see the bride go to him, my joy is complete. 30 His prominence must increase and mine must decrease. ❖ *In the Hebrew Scriptures, God refers to his people as his bride. [Isaiah 62:4-5; Jeremiah 2:2; Hosea 2:16-20] In the New Testament, those who believe in him are the Messiah's bride [Ephesians 5:23-32; Revelation 19:7; 21:2, 9; 22:17]* ¶ *Many commentators believe that John the Baptizer's quote continues through verse 36, and it's marked that way in this interpretation. But we don't know for sure. It could be the Apostle John's commentary.* ➤

31 "People of this world can only speak authoritatively about the things of this world. But Jesus—who comes from Heaven—is greater than any other human being. 32 He authoritatively tells us about what he has seen and heard in Heaven, yet almost no one believes what he says. 33 But those who do believe him are only acknowledging that God's words are always true 34 because it is God who sent him, and his message comes from God. We can be sure of this because God gave him his Holy Spirit without limit. ❖ *Other prophets had the Holy Spirit in limited measure, according to their task. Jesus had the Spirit without limit, as was seen in the unlimited power of his miracles and healing ministry and in his unlimited wisdom.* ➤ 35 God the Father loves his Son Jesus and has given him power and authority over everything that exists. *[Matthew 11:27; Luke 10:22]* 36 Those who really believe in the Son have eternal life. But those who don't obey **A** the Son will not

---

A 3:36 ἀπειθέω (apeitheō), means "to disobey," or "to reject belief." These basically mean the same thing. In Greek, "belief" and "obedience" are not separable concepts like they are in English. There are other languages in the world in which this is also true.

experience eternal life, for they remain under God's sentence of punishment for sin and end up in Hell." ❖ *Note in verse 36 that the opposite of believing in Jesus is "not obeying him." This makes it clear that true belief involves obedience.* ➤

4

Crossing Cultural & Social Barriers to Evangelize (The Woman at the Well)

1-2 The news went around that Jesus was baptizing more people and had more followers than John the Baptizer, though it was Jesus' followers who did the actual baptizing. When Jesus learned that the Pharisees had heard this, **3-4** he and some of his followers left Judea and made the three-day journey to Galilee Province, passing through Samaria. ❖ *He may have left to avoid damaging John's ministry and to avoid confrontation with the Pharisees. Baptizing Jews was considered divisive since they normally only baptized Gentile converts. ¶ The Samaritans were descended from Jewish men who had married pagan Gentile wives. They worshipped Yahweh but had also mixed pagan elements into their faith. The Jews hated and avoided Samaritans, and the Samaritans reciprocated. However, the shortest route between Judea and Galilee was through Samaria, so many Jews went that way. The original text says that Jesus "had" to go through Samaria. Since this was not true geographically, nor required by Jewish Law or tradition, many think it implies that God required it in order for Jesus to meet a particular woman.* ➤ **5-6** On their journey, they arrived at the Samaritan town of Sychar around noon. Jesus was tired and sat down by the famous well Jacob had dug, for this was near the plot of land that Jacob had given to his son Joseph more than 1500 years earlier. *[Genesis 48:22; 33:19]* ❖ *The land was later inherited by Joseph's descendants. [Joshua 24:32]* ➤

7-8 Jesus' followers went into the village to buy food, so he was alone when a Samaritan woman came to draw water from the well. ❖ *Women would usually come to the well together in the cooler parts of the day. That she came alone in the heat of the day indicates that she was probably socially ostracized and avoiding other women.* ➤ Jesus asked her, "Would you give me a drink?" **9** Now normally, a Jew wouldn't even use the same cup as a Samaritan. ❖ *And a Jewish man wouldn't normally speak to a female stranger.* ➤ So the woman asked incredulously, "Now why would a

Jew ask me, a woman and a Samaritan, for water?" **10** Jesus said, "If you knew who I was and what gift God is offering you, you would be asking me for life-giving water and I would give it to you." *[Jeremiah 2:13; 17:13; Zechariah 14:8]* **11** She replied, "Sir, the well is more than 100 feet deep and you have nothing to draw with. So just where would you get this life-giving water? **12** Do you think you are greater than our ancestor Jacob who dug this well? Do you offer better water than this which he and his sons and their cattle drank?" ❖ *Samaritans did share Jacob as a common ancestor with the Jews, but her referring to him as such was probably intended to be an affront to Jesus—as it would have been to most Jews at that time. She clearly thought he did consider himself greater than Jacob and was not impressed by this idea. Her response was skeptical and probably derisive.* ➤ **13** Jesus answered, "Everyone who drinks water from this well gets thirsty again. **14** But once people drink the water I give, they never thirst again. For the water I give becomes a spring within them, out of which flows life-giving water, giving them eternal life." *[Numbers 24:7; Isaiah 12:3; 44:3; 49:10; 55:1-3; Revelation 7:16-17]* ❖ *He was speaking of the Holy Spirit, who is often symbolized in the Scriptures by water. But she takes him literally.* ➤ **15** The woman replied, "Sir, then give me this kind of water so I will never be thirsty or need to come all the way here from town for water."

16 Jesus told her, "Go get your husband and bring him here." ❖ *She has failed to understand what Jesus was talking about so he takes a different approach to enable her to know who he is, by showing that he has supernatural knowledge about her.* ➤ **17** She replied, "I don't have a husband." ❖ *Given the ambiguity of the situation for her, since Jesus was flaunting social norms in speaking to her, she could have thought he was flirting and she might have been flirting back, saying she was "available." Or, she could just have been trying to hide her shame by not elaborating.* ➤ Jesus said, "You answered truthfully when you said that you don't have a husband. **18** You have had five husbands and are not married to the man you are currently living with. So you've at least told the truth." ❖ *Having had more than three husbands was a scandal, and living with a man without being married was not socially acceptable in that culture.* ➤ **19** Taken aback, the woman said, "Sir, it's apparent you are a prophet. ❖ *She knew that* *only God could have revealed those facts to him.* ➤ 20 My Samaritan ancestors worshipped here on Mount Gerizim, but you Jews claim Jerusalem is the proper place to worship." ❖ *Jews and Samaritans disputed the location of the site mentioned in Deuteronomy 12:5 which God chose as the appropriate place to worship. Her statement implied a question as to Jesus' view on the subject, since he was clearly a prophet. Her question was also an attempt to deflect the conversation from her shame.* ➤ 21-22 Jesus answered her, "You Samaritans don't really know the God you worship. ❖ *The Samaritans only accepted the five books of Moses as Scripture, known as the "Torah" or the "Pentateuch." So they lacked the further revelation about God and his will given in the rest of the Hebrew Scriptures.* ➤ We Jews have a much better understanding of the God we worship because he decided to use the Jews to bring salvation to this world. *[Genesis 18:18]* But the truth is that in just a short time, you Samaritans will no longer worship the Father on this mountain nor even in Jerusalem. 23 For the time is coming—and in fact has already started for some—when true worshipers will worship the Father in spirit and truth. ❖ *True worship is focused on the true God as he has revealed himself in the Scriptures. This is worship "in truth." False worshipers focus on concepts of God that deviate from reality. For example, a god who would never punish people in Hell is not the true God of the Scriptures. It's the wishful thinking of some—and such a god does not exist. Another aspect of true worship is that the worshipper means what he or she says. Their worship is genuine. Believers in Jesus are indwelt by the Holy Spirit who enables and moves them to genuinely worship God as he really is. Their worship, while it may have ritual form, is not based on formalism or location. It is based on the spiritual unity they have with Jesus and the Father through the Holy Spirit, and it can occur without ceremony in any location. This is worship "in spirit." Romans 12:1 similarly says, "Offer yourselves and bodies and everything you do to serve God, following his holy will in all things, as your sacrificial offering to him. This is the essence of true spiritual worship and what pleases him."* ➤ The Father is seeking people who will truly worship him in this way. 24 God is an infinite spiritual being, not confined to one place, and those who would really worship him must worship him by means of the Holy Spirit and worship him for who he really is." 25 The woman said, "I know that God's Anointed One is coming, who is called the 'Messiah.' When he comes,

he will make things clear to us." 26 Jesus replied, "I am the Messiah and I'm making them clear to you right now."

27 Just then, his followers returned from town and were shocked to find him speaking with a woman. But none of them dared ask him what he wanted from her or why he was speaking with her. ❖ *Jesus was never bound by cultural expectations. He did exactly what the Father wanted him to do. [John 5:19; 8:28; 12:49; 14:10, 31]* ➤ 28 Then, the woman left her water jar and hurried back to town. She told people there, 29 "Come and see a man who told me everything I've ever done! He might even be the Messiah!" 30 When they heard that, many of them headed out to see him.

31 Meanwhile, after the woman had left, Jesus' followers were urging him to eat. 32 But he told them, "I have food that you don't know about." ❖ *Food is sometimes used as a metaphor for spiritual food. [Deuteronomy 8:3; Jeremiah 15:16]* ➤ 33 So they started asking each other, "Did someone else bring him something to eat?" 34 Jesus explained, "My sustenance comes from doing my Father's will and finishing the work he has given me. ❖ *Jesus wasn't saying that he had no need of physical food, but that there was more satisfaction and spiritual sustenance from doing his Father's work than from what food could provide.* ➤ 35 Just after planting, don't you commonly say, 'There are four months until harvest.'? ❖ *This probably meant: "Now there's no urgency to do anything. We can relax."* ➤ But take a look at the people coming this way. I've just planted today and already they are like a field that's ready for harvesting. 36 Those who are gathering a harvest of souls into eternal life are already earning eternal rewards. The time has come when those who plant God's word as seed and those who harvest souls can work and rejoice together. ❖ *Jesus was trying to create a sense of urgency with regard to bringing people into God's kingdom. Unlike agricultural harvests, there isn't necessarily a significant delay between planting God's Word and seeing the fruit of new lives born into God's kingdom. The days of Amos 9:13 had arrived.* ➤ 37 The saying, 'One person plants and another harvests,' is true. 38 I've commissioned you to harvest souls where you didn't plant. Others have planted and labored before you, and now

you join in their work to finish it and benefit from it."

39 Many of the Samaritans in that town believed in Jesus as the Messiah merely on the basis of the woman's testimony that, "He told me everything I've ever done." **40** So when they came to him at the well, they begged him to stay with them, and he ended up staying there two days. ❖ *Jesus' staying with Samaritans would have produced shock, disapproval, and possibly hostility from both Jews and Samaritans. His willingness to go against cultural and social conventions in order to bring people into God's kingdom shows us that we shouldn't be restricted by similar prohibitions, such as "Don't push your faith on others!" or "Religion is a private matter!" because the need to evangelize is urgent and God has prepared many people to respond. But they have to hear first.* ➤ **41** During his time with them, many more believed in him because of the things he said. **42** Then they told the woman, "It's no longer just because of your testimony that we believe in him. For now we've heard him ourselves and know for sure that he is the Savior of the world."

Jesus Heals an Official's Son at a Distance

43 After two days in the town of Sychar, Jesus and his followers continued north into Galilee. **44** Unlike the Samaritans who believed in him without seeing miracles, Jesus knew it would be difficult for his fellow Jews to believe in him. For he himself said that a prophet is not honored in his own country. **45** Therefore, when he arrived in Galilee, the people welcomed him mainly because they had been at the Passover Festival in Jerusalem and had seen all the miraculous signs he had done there.

46 While he was in Galilee, Jesus returned to Cana—where he had turned water into wine. *[John 2:1-11]* While in Cana, the son of a royal official in Capernaum was sick. ❖ *Capernaum and Cana are about 16 miles apart which is about a day's journey. He was probably an official of Tetrarch Herod Antipas who ruled over the Roman province of Galilee from 4 BC to AD 39.* ➤ **47** When the man heard that Jesus had returned to Galilee

from Judea Province, he went to him in Cana and begged Jesus to come down to Capernaum to heal his son who was near death. **48** Jesus said, "Unless you people see miraculous signs and wonders, you refuse to believe in me." ❖ *Jesus considered his teaching to be clear and sufficient evidence that he was the Messiah, and he knew that faith prompted only by miracles is often shallow. [John 2:23-25]* ➤ **49** The man pleaded, "Sir, please come quickly before my child dies." **50** Jesus replied, "You can go home. Your son will live." He believed what Jesus told him and left. **51** On his way home the next day, the man's servants met him on the road and told him that his son was alive and well. **52-53** The father knew it was at one o'clock that Jesus had said to him, "Your son will live." So he asked them when he had begun to get better and they said, "The fever broke at one o'clock yesterday afternoon." As a result of this, he and his whole household came to believe that Jesus was the Messiah.

54 This was the second miraculous sign that Jesus performed in Galilee, which he did after returning from Judea. ❖ *The first sign in Galilee was at the wedding in Cana. John didn't report any details of the signs he did in Jerusalem in between these two in Galilee, nor does he count them. Healing at a distance was a sign of great power since such a thing was virtually unknown.* ➤

5

The Healing at Bethesda

1 Sometime after these events, Jesus and his followers went up to Jerusalem for one of the Jewish festivals. ❖ *The three festivals when all able Jewish men were required to travel to Jerusalem were Passover, Pentecost (knows to Jews as "Shavuot") and Shelters (a.k.a. Tabernacles, or in Hebrew, "Sukkot"), so it was probably one of these.* ➤ **2** Now, there was a pool in Jerusalem near the Sheep Gate, which in Aramaic was called "*Bethesda*" and means "house of mercy." It had five pillared pavilions. **A** ❖ *There was a pavilion on each side of the pool and one divided the pool into two parts.* ➤ **3-4** Large crowds of sick people used to lie in these

---

A 5:2 There are a couple of textual problems in this verse: e.g., a missing word and different spellings of the name among manuscripts. Also, the word Ἑβραΐς (Hebrais) can mean either "Hebrew" or "Aramaic." Hence the variations among translations are greater than for most verses. Yet nothing important depends on them.

pavilions. ❖ *"Used to lie" probably means before the destruction of Jerusalem in AD 70.* ➤ They included the blind, lame, and paralyzed {who were waiting for an angel that occasionally came to stir up the water. After that happened, the first person to step into the water was healed.} **A** 5 At that time, one of the men there had been an invalid for 38 years. 6 When Jesus saw him lying there and knew that he had been this way for a long time, he asked him, "Do you want to be well?" 7 The man said, "Sir, I don't have anyone here to help me get me into the pool quickly when the water is stirred. While I'm trying to get in, someone else always gets in ahead of me." 8 So Jesus told him, "Stand up! Pick up your sleeping mat and walk!" 9 Immediately the man was completely healed. He picked up his mat and began to walk normally.

Now, this incident took place on a Sabbath. ❖ *The weekly Jewish Sabbath was from sunset Friday until sunset Saturday. There were also one or more High Sabbaths associated with the festival that they were attending.* ➤ 10 So when some Jewish leaders saw the man as he was going, they said, "Today is a Sabbath and you are not allowed to carry your mat!" ❖ *The Teachings of Moses forbade work on a Sabbath, but Jewish elders had made their interpretation of the Torah significantly more stringent than God originally intended by stretching the definition of "work." There were also some exceptions explicitly allowed. [Exodus 20:8-10; 31:14-15; 35:2-3; Leviticus 16:29-31; 23:3; Deuteronomy 5:12-14; Jeremiah 17:21-24] It appears that the originally intended meaning of "work" in the Torah was that of performing one's usual work of occupation or employment on that day.* ➤ 11 He replied, "The man who healed me told me to pick up my mat and walk." ❖ *Some commentators say that he was blaming Jesus. But it's just as reasonable to assume he was appealing to the authority of the man of God who healed him.* ➤ 12 So they asked, "Who is this man who told you to carry your mat?" 13 But he didn't know Jesus by name and was unable to point him out because Jesus had slipped away into the crowd.

14 Later, Jesus saw him in the Temple and said, "You are healthy now, so stop sinning lest something worse happens to you." ❖ *Commentators disagree on whether or not this implies the man's sickness was due to sin. In the Scriptures, some sicknesses or deaths are attributed to sin, [1 Kings 13:14-24; 1 Corinthians 11:29-30; 1 John 5:16] and others are explicitly not. [2 Samuel 4:4; John 9:2-3]* ➤ 15 Then, the man went and told the Jewish leaders that Jesus was the man who had healed him. 16 So because Jesus was healing on a Sabbath, the Jewish leaders started persecuting him. ❖ *Since the healing was not needed to save the man's life, it was within their man-made definition of forbidden work.* ➤

Jesus Claims to be Equal with God

17 But Jesus' reply to their accusation was, "My Father is always working, and so must I." ❖ *The Jews acknowledged that God was always working, even on the Sabbath.* ➤ 18 The Jewish leaders recognized that Jesus was calling God his Father, thus implying that he was deity and equal with God. So they became even more intent on killing him since this crime of blasphemy was more serious than breaking the Sabbath rules. ❖ *Blasphemy means showing disrespect to or denigrating God, and was punishable by death. If a mere man claimed equality to God, this comparison diminished God's uniqueness and greatness. Many people today say that Jesus never claimed to be God. But his claims are clear in several places. And this is one place where he clearly does make this claim, given the cultural context. The Jews understood that "like begets like," so if a person is God's Son, he must be of the same divine eternal nature as God. Jesus' words were a clear claim to deity, as can be seen by the fact that he doesn't try to "correct" their conclusion. While believers in Jesus are now called God's children, they are not deity. They are like adopted children who have a special relationship with him, but are not in the same category as the eternally existing Son of God.* ➤

19 Jesus said, "I will tell you this important truth. As God's Son, I can do nothing on my own initiative. I can only do what I see my Father doing. Whatever the

---

A 5:3-4 The oldest and best Greek manuscripts lack the part in curly braces { }. Most scholars think it was a later addition by a scribe to explain the popular belief of people at that time and to clarify verse 7. If this is the case, then the information about an angel may not be factual. Such healing shrines were common in ancient times. John may have included this incident to show that Jesus' power is greater than that of healing shrines.

Father does, I must also do. ❖ *Jesus clarifies his relationship with God the Father. He isn't an independent or competitive deity, but in total subservience to his Father's will. John called him "the Word" or "expression" of God. [John 1:1] Since the Hebrew Scriptures clearly teach that there is only one God, followers of Jesus have concluded that the Son of God is not a separate independent being, but only a separate "person" within the one "Godhead," equal in many respects to the Father, since they are both one being, having one will, yet in role the Son is submissive to the person of the Father.* ➤ 20 I can do these things because my Father loves me and shows me everything he is doing. And he will show me even greater miraculous works for me to do than those you've seen, such that you will be astonished. ❖ *The Father shows his love for the Son by showing him all that he does and wants done. The Son shows his love for the Father by his perfect obedience. Therefore, by his obedience, the Son reveals the Father to us. [John 14:9] So God the Father's revelation to us of his character and will is a direct result of his love for his Son and of his Son's love for him.* ➤ 21 For I can give life to anyone I wish, just like my Father brings dead people back to life. ❖ *This is no contradiction to what he said in verse 19 since the will and desires of the Father and Son are never in conflict.* ➤ 22 Contrary to what you believe, my Father doesn't judge anyone in this world, but has delegated all authority for judging people to me, his Son, ❖ *In Genesis 18:25, God is "Judge of all the earth." Thus Jesus is again implicitly claiming deity, yet acknowledging that his authority is delegated.* ➤ 23 so that all will honor me equally with my Father. Those who refuse to honor me are in fact refusing to honor my Father who sent me. ❖ *This is another claim to deity and equality with God the Father. [Isaiah 42:8; 48:11] Jesus might sound egotistical to some, but given the fact that the Father intends for him to be honored equally, how would we know this unless he or some other prophet explicitly told us? Since God is totally self-sufficient, he has no egotistical need to be honored by people. But since it's appropriate to honor that which is most honorable, it would be wrong not to point out that Jesus, God's Son, is worthy of equal honor with the Father. All honor and glory rightly belong to the creator. It's only wrong for a created being to claim honor for himself. As C. S. Lewis pointed out, given the fact that Jesus made these claims about himself, if he isn't who he claims to be, he is either an evil deceiver or to be pitied as deluded. Therefore, it's illogical to say that he isn't God but is still a great moral teacher, as many people like to do.* ➤

24 "I'm going to tell you an important truth. Those who hear and obey my words (which I get from my Father) and believe in my Father who sent me (and therefore, believe in me), have eternal life right now and will not be condemned on Judgment Day. ❖ *Judgment Day is when Jesus will judge everyone who has ever lived and will assign them their eternal fate. [Matthew 25:31-46]* ➤ For they have already crossed over from being spiritually dead and under the sentence of eternal death into a state of being spiritually alive and possessing eternal life. ❖ *For believers, the death of the body is not death at all, but merely a transition to a fuller experience of the eternal life they already possess.* ➤ 25 I want to emphasize this truth. The time has been long in coming and has finally arrived when many who are spiritually dead will hear and respond to the voice of God's Son, and thereby become spiritually alive. 26 For just as my Father is the self-existing source of all life, in my relationship to him as his Son, I too am this self-existing source of all life and am able to give life to others. 27 And because I've also become human as the Son of Man, *[Daniel 7:13-14]* he has given me all authority to pass judgment on humanity. 28 Don't be surprised at these things. ❖ *It isn't clear if "these things" refers to what he said before, or what he says next. Perhaps it refers to both.* ➤ The time is coming when all who have died will hear my voice *[Daniel 12:2]* 29 and they will become alive again with physical bodies. Those who have done what is good will be made alive to live forever. Those who have done evil will be made alive to be eternally condemned. ❖ *Before the resurrection, those who have died on earth are "alive" in either Heaven or Hades (the place of torment for the condemned). But at the resurrection, they become alive again in this world with new physical bodies. The saved will live forever in their glorified physical bodies. The condemned will live forever in Hell. To do "good" means to choose to obey God, since only he and his will are "good." What sinful humanity calls "good" may or may not be good according to God's will. Since God is the judge, he determines what is "good" and what is "evil." These terms are not defined by us, but their definitions are clearly spelled out in the Scriptures. It's also clear that true belief results in obedience to God, i.e., "doing good." Any belief that doesn't result in obedience is not true belief, since we will be judged by what we do, not just by what we intellectually acknowledge.* ➤

30 "I can do nothing on my own authority. I only judge according to what I hear from my Father. So my judgment is fair and just because I'm not following my own will but my Father's will, just as he sent me to do.

31 "If my testimony about myself is the only testimony backing up my claims, then it's not true. ❖ *Jewish law required two witnesses to prove something was true. [Deuteronomy 19:15] If there were no supporting testimony from any source, then it would be clear that his claims are false. But there is supporting testimony.* ➤ 32 But someone else does testify about me and I know that his testimony about me is true. ❖ *Most commentators believe he is referring to God the Father here. But he explicitly refers to the Father a few verses later and some see this verse as leading naturally into the next verse where he talks about John the Baptizer. John was Jesus' first witness, and it seems to more naturally refer to him.* ➤ 33 You sent many people to John the Baptizer, and he told the truth about me. *[Matthew 3:11-12; Mark 1:7-8; Luke 3:16-17; John 1:26-27; 29-34, 36]* 34 Now, the testimony that I accept is directly from God and not from a man. But I remind you of John's testimony so you might believe what he said about me and thereby be saved. 35 John was like a lamp that gave out the prophetic light of God's message, and for a while, you all enjoyed his message. ❖ *His message of the coming Messiah was exciting for a while. But ultimately, the Jewish leaders and most Jews didn't believe his testimony about Jesus. Since Jesus speaks of John in the past tense, he was probably already dead by this time, or his ministry was cut off because of his being in prison. [Matthew 14:3-12; Mark 6:17-29; Luke 3:19-20; 9:7-9]* ➤

36 "But I have much more authoritative testimony than John's, which are the words, deeds, and miraculous signs my Father has given me to do. These all demonstrate that God the Father sent me, approves of me, and is working through me.

37 "Through these things, he has testified to you, revealing the truth about who I am, ❖ *The Father also audibly testified about Jesus. [Mathew 3:17; Mark 1:11; Luke 3:22]* ➤ and he is still testifying about me. But you have never heard him or seen him, ❖ *Jesus is implying that they should have been able to hear and see the Father through the Son, like the Israelites heard him through Moses. It was their stubbornness and unbelief that prevented them from doing so.* ➤ 38 and in your hearts you reject his words and message because you refuse to believe me, whom he sent to you.

39 "You diligently study the Scriptures because you think that by knowing them and legalistically following their commands you will gain eternal life. But these very Scriptures point to me as being the source of the life you seek. ❖ *Even though they knew the Scriptures thoroughly, they failed to understand their purpose and true meaning.* ➤ 40 Yet you refuse to come and learn from me so I can give you eternal life. ❖ *They were proud of their obedience to the Teachings of Moses, yet were rejecting the person those Teachings pointed to. So they were, in effect, rejecting what Moses said about God. To understand a little about how the Torah itself pointed to Jesus, particularly the sacrificial system, read the Letter to the Jewish followers of Jesus (i.e., the book of Hebrews).* ➤

41 "I'm not seeking approval or honor from people, for I only care about what my Father thinks of me. 42 But I know that you really have no love for God at all in your hearts. 43 I've come representing my Father with his authority—as he attests to by the miracles he does through me—and yet you refuse to accept me. But if someone else comes having no authority at all backing him, you will readily accept him as the Messiah. ❖ *The Jewish historian Josephus reports that there were a string of people who claimed to be the Messiah in the years before AD 70, many of whom gained followings. People who reject the truth will always be susceptible to accepting lies.* ➤ 44 It's no wonder you reject me and will accept those who aren't from God, because you are clearly much more concerned with flattery and praise from people than approval from the only one who counts—God himself.

45 "On Judgment Day, I won't be the one standing before the Father accusing you of rejecting his Messiah. You've set your hopes on obeying the Teachings of Moses to gain favor with God, rather than by believing in the one he wrote about. But you will be surprised to hear Moses using the teachings of the Torah to accuse you of rejecting me. 46 For if you really believed what Moses wrote in the Torah, then you would believe me too because he wrote about me. ❖ *In addition to the many "types" pertaining to him (e.g. Abraham willing to sacrifice his only son Isaac, [Genesis 22:1-18] the*

Passover lamb, [Exodus chapter 12] the brass serpent, [Numbers 21:6-9] the High Priest making atonement, [Leviticus chapter 16] the sacrificial system, the scapegoat, [Leviticus 16:7-10] manna, [Exodus 16:4-21] the rock with the water coming out, [Exodus 17:1-7] etc.), one passage in particular that Jesus may be thinking about is Deuteronomy 18:15. Less clear to modern readers—but not so to serious students of the Hebrew Scriptures—are passages like Genesis 3:15; 12:3; 18:18; 22:18; 26:4; 28:14; and 49:10 among others. The way Moses wrote about the Messiah was mainly in figurative types, but interpreting such figures was something Jewish teachers did all the time. It was only because they were unwilling to accept Jesus as the Messiah that they refused to see the obvious. ➤ 47 But since you don't correctly understand and believe what Moses wrote about, of course you won't believe me either." ❖ It's clear that sincerity is not all that matters in faith, because the Pharisees were sincere in their misguided interpretation of Scripture, and Jesus said their sincere beliefs would not get them into Heaven. Sincerity of belief is important, but a correct understanding of what God intended to say in the Scriptures is also important. He will give people a correct understanding of the Scriptures if they really desire to please him and not themselves. But people who believe what they want to believe, even if they supposedly base it on God's word, will not be accepted by God if their belief rejects what God actually meant in his word. ➤

6

Jesus Demonstrates Power
to Multiply Resources

1-4 Sometime after this, near the time for the Passover Festival, Jesus and his close followers went to the eastern shore of Lake Galilee—which was also known as Lake Tiberius. ❖ Around AD 20–26 Herod Antipas built a city on the west shore of Lake Galilee called "Tiberius," named after the emperor Tiberius Caesar. By the time John wrote this gospel in the later part of the first century, Lake Galilee was commonly called Lake Tiberius. In the Hebrew Scriptures, it had been called Lake Kinnereth (meaning "lyre" because of its shape). ¶ This is the second Passover mentioned in John's gospel, unless the feast in 5:1 was also a Passover. If the feast in 5:1 was the feast of Shelters (Tabernacles), half a year had passed between the end of chapter five and the start of chapter six. If the feast in 5:1 was a Passover feast, a year had passed. The uncertainty about the feast in 5:1 is one factor in the uncertainty of the length of Jesus' ministry, for which estimates vary

from two and a half to three and a half years. The reason John mentions the Passover is because it prefigures and points to the Messiah's sacrificial death as a substitute to save God's people. Each time John explicitly mentions the Passover, he brings out some teaching or act by Jesus that shows how Passover really points to the Messiah. During the first Passover of Jesus' ministry [2:13-22] he prophesied that the Temple of his body would be "destroyed" and within three days he would raise it up again. John the Baptizer pointed out that Jesus is the sacrificial lamb that God provided to save us, and the body of the Passover lamb prefigures the Messiah's body. Near this second explicitly mentioned Passover of his ministry, Jesus gives his "bread of life" teaching. [6:22-58] That teaching ties him to the unleavened bread of the Passover and the manna in the wilderness [Exodus chapter 16]—which is tied to the Festival of Unleavened Bread that immediately follows Passover—showing how both of these festivals point to him. In the third and last-mentioned Passover of his ministry, [John chapters 13—21] he instituted the Lord's Supper (a.k.a. Holy Communion, or the Eucharist, or Mass) which is another figure of his sacrificial death. [Matthew 26:26-28; Mark 14:22-26; Luke 22:14-20] Then shortly thereafter he was crucified, which is the event that Passover itself prefigures. ➤ A large crowd kept following him all the way there because they had seen the signs he had done in healing the sick. Jesus went up a hill and sat down with his close followers, intending to be alone with them. [Mark 6:32-33] ❖ Today, this area is called the Golan Heights. ➤

5 When Jesus saw a large crowd coming toward him, he asked Philip, "Where can we buy enough bread to feed all these people?" 6 But he knew what he was going to do and was simply testing Philip's faith. 7 Philip replied, "Even two hundred denarii ❖ about eight months wages at one denarius per day, six days per week ➤ wouldn't be enough to feed everyone just a little!" 8 Then another of his followers—Simon Peter's brother Andrew—said, 9 "There's a boy here with five small loaves of barley bread [2 Kings 4:42-44] and two small fish, but they are nothing for so many." ❖ Barley bread was cheaper than wheat bread and was the ordinary food of the poor. ➤ 10 Jesus said, "Tell the people to sit down." There was plenty of grass there, so they all sat and the number of men in the crowd was about 5000. ❖ Counting women and children—which they didn't do in that culture—the total

number could easily have been 10,000–20,000 people. ➤
11 Jesus took the loaves, thanked God for them, and distributed them to all who were seated. He did the same with the fish, and everyone ate all they wanted. ❖ *If Jesus followed the common form of Jewish thanksgiving, he looked up toward Heaven and said something like this: "You are blessed (i.e., praised), O Lord our God, King of the universe, who brings forth bread from the earth."* ➤
12 When everyone was full, he told his followers, "Gather up the leftovers so nothing will be wasted." 13 So they gathered all the leftovers and filled twelve baskets with bread. ❖ *This miracle is the only one recorded in all four Gospels, and all four accounts record the twelve baskets so it must be significant. Most take it to mean that he is able to supply all the needs of the twelve tribes of Israel—which are symbolic of all of God's people. Others say it was one basket per apostle, to assure them that Jesus would also meet the needs of each one of them.* ➤
14 When the people saw the miraculous sign Jesus had done, they said to each other, "He must be the Prophet that Moses promised would come!" *[Deuteronomy 18:15-18]* 15 But Jesus perceived ❖ *probably via a "word of knowledge" from the Holy Spirit* ➤ that they intended to come and force him to be a king to rally behind who would overcome the Romans—so he withdrew by himself higher up into the hills. ❖ *The Jews were looking for a political messiah to free them from Roman domination. Jesus' ability to miraculously provide convinced them that he was the person they needed.* ➤

Jesus Walks on Water

16 When it was evening, his followers went down to the lake to wait for him. 17 But when it got dark and Jesus still hadn't returned, they got in the boat and started out across the lake toward Capernaum. 18-20 They had reached the midpoint of the lake—about three miles out—when the lake became very rough because of a strong wind. Then, they saw something coming toward them and they were terrified because they thought it was a ghost. *[Mark 6:49]* But it was Jesus walking on the water, *[Job 9:8]* and he shouted to them, "It's me! Don't be afraid!" 21 So they gladly took him on board and discovered that they had immediately reached the shore at Capernaum. *[See Psalm 107:23-32; especially verse 30]*

Jesus' Discourse on "The Bread of Life"

22 The next day, the crowd that had stayed on the other side of the lake were waiting to see Jesus because they knew there had only been one boat and that his followers had left in it without him. 23 Then some boats from Tiberius came to shore near the place where the Lord had given thanks for the bread they had eaten the day before. 24 So when the crowd realized that neither Jesus nor his followers were there, they got into the boats and went looking for him in Capernaum. 25 When they found him there, they asked him, "Rabbi, when and how did you get here?"

26 Jesus replied, "The truth is, you are only following me because you know that I have the power to feed you, not because you understand the significance of that miraculous sign. 27 You shouldn't be nearly as concerned about obtaining food that sustains this temporary life as you should be about obtaining spiritual food that results in eternal life. I, the Son of Man, am the one who gives this spiritual food and eternal life. This should be clear because God the Father has put his sign of approval on me." ❖ *This sign of approval may have been the visible appearance of his Holy Spirit as a dove and the audible voice from Heaven at his baptism. [Matthew 3:16-17; Mark 1:9-11; Luke 3:21-22] It may also have been the miraculous signs he was doing, which the people knew were done by God's power and therefore, with his approval.* ➤ 28 So they asked him, "What work does God want us to do to obtain eternal life?" ❖ *Just as many Jews misunderstood the Teachings of Moses, thinking that by "doing works" or "obeying rules" they could earn eternal life, so here they think that Jesus is talking about legalistic works and following rules.* ➤ 29 Jesus replied, "The only work God requires of you to gain eternal life is to believe in ❖ *and obey—which is implicit in belief* ➤ me, whom he sent to you." 30 They demanded, "What miraculous sign will you do to convince us that he sent you, so we can believe in you? 31 Moses gave our ancestors manna in the wilderness, *[Exodus 16:4; 14-15]* just as it's written, 'He gave them bread from Heaven to eat.' " ❖ *This is not an exact quote from*

anywhere in Scripture but is similar to Exodus 16:15; Psalm 78:24; and Psalm 105:40. They were demanding signs similar to those that Moses had done. They didn't accept all the signs and healings he had done already, so they weren't really willing to believe. If he accommodated them, they just would have expected him to fulfill their expectations of a political savior. They weren't focused on the things that God was concerned about. ➤ 32 Jesus replied, "The truth is, it was my Father—not Moses—who gave them the bread from Heaven called 'manna.' It's also my Father who offers you the 'True Bread from Heaven' that gives eternal life. 33 For God's 'Bread' comes down from Heaven and gives eternal life to the people of this world." ❖ The masculine ending on the Greek verb καταβαίνων (katabainōn) translated "comes down," can mean either "bread that comes down" or "he who comes down." Jesus probably was speaking Aramaic, but since they misunderstood him, this interpretation reflects the ambiguity of the Greek as a possible reason for their misunderstanding. ➤ 34 They said, "Sir, give us that bread every day!"

35 Jesus told them, "I am the 'Bread from Heaven' that gives eternal life. Those who believe in me and follow me will never again have spiritual hunger or thirst, for they will be satisfied with eternal life. 36 But as I've said before, you have seen me and the signs that I've done, yet you refuse to believe that God sent me. 37 However, the people my Father gives me will believe in me, and I will always keep them close to me. 38 For I came from Heaven to do his will, not my own, 39 and his will is that of all the people he gives me to be my true followers, none will be lost. They will all persevere in faith, and I will give them eternal life on the Last Day. ❖ This doesn't contradict the fact that we can have eternal life right now. He is referring to giving believers on the Last Day the full experience of all the blessings of eternal life that we will have in Heaven. Our eternal life starts when we believe, but we don't yet enjoy the fullness of the blessings that we will eventually have. ➤ 40 For my Father's will is that all who look to me—his Son—for eternal life and believe in me, will gain eternal life. And on the Last Day, I will raise them up and usher them into that new life."

41 Then the people started to grumble and complain against Jesus because he said, "I am the Bread from Heaven that gives eternal life." 42 They were saying, "How can

he claim to have come down from Heaven? We know who his parents are. He's just the son of Yosef!" 43 Jesus told them, "Stop grumbling about what I said. 44 No one can believe in me unless my Father who sent me first draws them and enables them to believe. And that's who I will indeed raise up on the Last Day. 45 As it's written in 'the Prophets' about those who come to God, **'They will all be taught by Yahweh.'** [Isaiah 54:13] ❖ The Jewish Bible—the Hebrew Scriptures, called the Tanakh—is divided into three sections, the Torah, the Writings, and the Prophets. ➤ So everyone who listens to the Father and learns from him will come to believe in me. 46 Not that anyone has ever seen the Father except me, whom he sent. I've seen him, and you can only get to know him through me. 47 I'm telling you an important truth. Those who believe in me have eternal life. 48 I am the Bread that gives eternal life. 49 Your ancestors ate manna in the wilderness—a miraculous bread from Heaven—but they still died. ❖ They died physically, but the entire generation that came out of Egypt—with a few exceptions—did not enter the promised land, and many commentators believe they also failed to gain eternal life because of their unbelief. ➤ 50 But those who eat the Bread that I'm talking about—which comes down from Heaven—won't die. ❖ He's referring to spiritual death, also called the "second death"—which is damnation in Hell. [John 11:25-26; Revelation 2:11; 20:6; 14-15; 21:8] Physical death for a believer is a transition from this life to a better life. ➤ 51 I am that eternal-life-giving Bread that came down from Heaven. Those who eat this Bread will live forever. And the Bread that I offer up in sacrifice for the lives of everyone in this world, is my flesh." ❖ Jesus' teaching was often heavily laced with metaphors and other figures of speech. Bread, the staple food of the Jews, was necessary for physical life. Jesus was claiming to be spiritual Bread, necessary for spiritual and eternal life. Bread was also offered as a sacrifice under the Mosaic covenant, [e.g. Exodus 29:23-25; Leviticus 7:12-15; 8:26-28; 23:10-13] and the bread of sacrifice that he offers is his body, through his allowing himself to be executed. Bread is often a symbol of life, and his life is offered in sacrifice so that sinful people in this world might obtain eternal life. His "flesh" is also the incarnate Word of God. [John 1:14] "Eating" this spiritual Bread means believing in and following Jesus, the incarnate Word of God. But the people didn't understand what he meant. ➤

52 These words offended the people and made them angry. They began to argue about what he meant. They asked each other, "How can he give us his flesh to eat?" 53 So Jesus said, "This is an important truth. I am the Son of Man, *[Psalm 80:17; Daniel 7:13]* and you can't have eternal life unless you eat my flesh and drink my blood. ❖ *Drinking blood was forbidden by the Torah, and the idea was exceedingly offensive to Jews. [Genesis 9:4; Leviticus 17:10-14; Deuteronomy 12:23-25] "Flesh and blood" together often symbolized the whole person. To "eat his flesh and drink his blood" means—among other things—to receive all that Jesus is.* ➤ 54 But those who eat my flesh and drink my blood have eternal life. And on the Last Day, I myself will raise them up and usher them into that new life. ❖ *Note the parallel with verse 40. Eating his flesh and drinking his blood clearly corresponds to looking to the Son as the source of eternal life and believing in him. It's a spiritual eating and drinking in order to receive the eternal spiritual benefits—especially eternal life—procured by Jesus' self-sacrificial death. This is also parallel with the Lord's Supper, where eating his body and drinking his blood also refers to a spiritual eating and drinking for the purpose of receiving spiritual benefits.* ➤ 55 Food and drink are necessary for physical life, but my flesh and blood are the true food and drink that are necessary for eternal life. 56 Those who eat my flesh and drink my blood are spiritually united with me; I live in them and they live in spiritual union with me. 57 Just as the Father who sent me is the source of all life, I too am the source of life because of my unity with him. So those who feed on me will live forever because I am the source of eternal life. ❖ *Here Jesus substitutes "me" for "my flesh and blood."* ➤ 58 So I am the Bread that came down from Heaven. Your ancestors ate manna from Heaven and died. But those who feed on me will live forever." 59 Jesus said these things while teaching in the synagogue in Capernaum.

60 When many who had been following him heard this, they said, "This teaching is offensive! Who can accept it?" ❖ *These were people who followed Jesus because of his healing ministry and miracles and their hope for a political messiah. They didn't really believe in him and submit themselves to him. These may have been some of the same people referred to in John 2:23-24 and 4:45, or were the same kind of people.* ➤ 61 But Jesus was aware that his followers were grumbling about this, so he said, "Do my words offend you and cause you to reject me? 62 Then what would your reaction be if you were to see me, the Son of Man, ascend back up into Heaven? ❖ *Some commentators think Jesus was saying they would take even greater offense at the idea of a suffering Messiah being crucified as a means to his glorification and return to Heaven.* ➤ 63 It's God's Holy Spirit who gives eternal life. Physical efforts cannot produce it. The things I've been saying to you have been about spiritual truths and come from him, and they will impart eternal life to those who receive them. *[Deuteronomy 8:3; Jeremiah 15:16]* 64 But some of you don't believe me." Jesus knew right from the beginning when they started following him, which of them didn't believe in him and who would betray him. 65 Then he added, "That's why I told you nobody can believe in me unless my Father who sent me first draws them and enables them to believe." 66 As a result of this teaching, many of his followers left him and no longer desired to associate with him.

67 So Jesus challenged his twelve closest followers, "You are not going to leave me too, are you?" 68 Simon Peter answered, "Lord, who else could we go to? You are the one with God's message about eternal life. 69 We believe in you and are convinced that you are the Holy One sent by God." ❖ *"The Holy One sent by God" was probably a Messianic title. [Mark 1:24; Luke 4:34; also Matthew 16:16; Mark 8:29; Luke 9:20]* ➤ 70 Jesus replied, "Each of you twelve was handpicked by me, yet one of you is Satan's henchman!" 71 He was referring to Judas, son of Simon Iscariot, because even though he was one of Jesus' twelve closest followers, later he would betray him.

7

Jesus at the Festival of Shelters

1 After this, Jesus ministered in the villages of Galilee. He didn't want to go to Judea because the Jewish leaders there wanted to kill him. 2 But the time for the Jewish Festival of Shelters was approaching. ❖ *The Festival of Shelters (or "Tabernacles" or "Booths" or "Tents", or in Hebrew, "Sukkot" [sue-coat]) was the most popular of the three great pilgrim festivals of the Jewish year*

celebrated in Jerusalem. It originally lasted for seven days in September or October. [Leviticus 23:33-44; Deuteronomy 16:13-17] By Jesus' time, an eighth day was added. It took place about six months after the Passover mentioned in verse 6:4. During the festival, everyone lived in temporary shelters to remind them of how God had been faithful to his people when they lived in tents in the wilderness, about 1400 years prior to that time. ➤ 3-5 So Jesus' brothers, [Matthew 13:55] who didn't believe in him, sarcastically told him, "If you want to be known, you can't remain here working in obscurity. Leave Galilee and go to Judea so people can see you do your miracles publicly and become your followers. Since you are doing these things, why not let everyone see them?" ❖ Jesus' brothers knew he did miracles, but they lacked faith that he was the Messiah. After all, he was their brother. ➤ 6-7 Jesus replied, "The time God has appointed for me to go there hasn't come yet. But you can go any time you want because the sinful people of this world don't hate you. They hate me because I tell them what they do is evil. 8 So go up to the festival without me, for it's not yet the right time for me to go." ❖ Normally, Jesus would have traveled with his extended family to the festival. His comment that they "could go any time" implied that their steps weren't ordered by God, as his were. The Father would tell him when he was to go. ➤ 9 So he remained in Galilee awhile longer.

10 But after his brothers had left for the festival, he and his close followers also went quietly, without letting others know about it. ❖ Though many people would recognize him if they saw him, most of those in Jerusalem would not. Therefore, his unannounced arrival in Jerusalem would most likely go unnoticed. ➤ 11 Now the Jewish leaders were watching for him at the festival. They kept asking around if anyone had seen him. 12 There was a lot of whispering about him among the crowds. Some said he was a good man. Others said he led people astray from following the Torah and traditions of the elders. 13 But no one would openly support him because they were afraid of persecution from the Jewish leaders.

14 In the middle of the week-long festival, Jesus went up to the Temple and openly taught in the courtyard there. 15 The leaders were astonished by the quality of his teaching and asked, "How did this man become so knowledgeable, since he has no formal rabbinical education?" 16 Jesus told them, "The things I teach aren't based on my own knowledge. They come straight from God, who sent me. 17 Those who are committed to following the will of God will know whether what I say comes from God, or if I'm speaking from my own authority. 18 Someone who speaks from his own authority will say things to gain the praise of others. But someone who only seeks honor for the one who sent him has pure motives and speaks the truth. 19 I know you would agree with me that Moses gave you God's Torah. Yet none of you obey all of the commands in those teachings. If you did, you wouldn't want to kill me." ❖ The fifth commandment is, "Do not murder." [Exodus 20:13; Deuteronomy 5:17] ➤ 20 The crowd replied, "You must have a demon deluding you! Who do you think wants to kill you?" 21 Jesus said, "I did one particular miracle on a Sabbath, [John 5:8-16] and you were all shocked that I disobeyed your Sabbath traditions. 22 But you disobey the Sabbath command too. Moses commanded you [Leviticus 12:1-3] to circumcise your sons a week A after their birth—though the command really started with Abraham, not Moses. [Genesis 17:9-14] So you routinely circumcise boys on the Sabbath. 23 But if you can circumcise on the Sabbath in order to obey the Teachings of Moses and it takes precedence over your own Sabbath traditions, why are you angry with me for healing a man on the Sabbath? ❖ Since circumcision was established before the Torah was given, circumcision was given precedence in any conflict with commands given later. Circumcision was a mark of redemption. Jesus' healing ministry was a partial fulfillment of the intention of circumcision, which was the person's redemption, including the body. It was commonly argued at that time that any act of mercy could be lawfully done on the Sabbath. Jesus

---

A 7:22 Literally, the Torah says "on the eighth day" [Leviticus 12:3] but the Jews of that time inclusively counted the day of birth as day one. So "the eighth day" as we would normally express it is a week after the birth, or one-week old, or seven days after being born.

had done nothing wrong, yet he was perceived as a threat to their authority as interpreters of the Torah and hence their power to rule. That was the real source of their animosity. ➤ 24 Stop judging by superficial legalistic criteria and judge correctly."

25 Some of the people who lived in Jerusalem were saying, "This is the man our leaders wanted to kill, isn't he? 26 And here he is teaching in public and they're not opposing him! Could they have decided that he really is the Messiah? 27 But we know where Jesus comes from, and when the Messiah comes, nobody will know where he came from." ❖ This was a popular misconception based on non-Scriptural teaching that said he would "appear." ➤ 28 Then, while Jesus was still teaching in the Temple, he called out, "So you think you know me and where I'm from? ❖ This sentence in Greek could either be a statement or a question. Since they didn't really know where he was from (they presumed Nazareth and Capernaum, when he really came from Heaven and Bethlehem) it's unlikely that it was a statement, unless made sarcastically. ➤ I'm not here on my own authority. I was really sent by God, but you don't know him. 29 I know him because I came from him, and he sent me to you." ❖ The Jewish leaders believed they knew God through the Torah. But if they had really known him, they wouldn't have rejected his Son. ➤

30 Then some of the people tried to seize him for saying he had come from God, but no one could lay a hand on him because it was not yet God's time for him to be arrested. 31 But many in the crowd believed in him and said, "He must be the Messiah! Surely no one could perform more miraculous signs than he has!" 32 When some Pharisees heard these whisperings in the crowd, they went to the chief priests and had them send some Temple guards to arrest him. 33 Jesus said, "I will only be with you for a little while longer, then I will return to my Father who sent me. ❖ He probably meant that he would be with them for several months, until the next Passover when he would be crucified. ➤ 34 At that time, you will search for me, but you won't find me because I'm going where you can't go." ❖ He was referring to his returning to Heaven and the

fact that they would continue to look for the Messiah, but they wouldn't find the Messiah because they thought he would be someone other than Jesus. ➤ 35 The Jewish leaders were puzzled and asked each other, "Where does he plan to go that we won't be able to find him? Certainly he isn't intending to go live among our people in Gentile countries and teach Gentiles! 36 And what does he mean by, 'We will search for him and not find him because he is going where we can't go?' "

❖ At some point between verses 14 (the middle of the week-long Festival) and 37 (the last day of the Festival), several days passed. And John's account isn't entirely chronological with regard to when the guards were sent to arrest him (verse 32) and when they reported back (verse 45). ➤

37 Now, on the climactic last day of the Festival, Jesus stood up and shouted to the crowds, "All who are spiritually thirsty should come to me and drink. [Isaiah 55:1] 38 Those who believe in me will discover that, 'From out of his innermost being will flow rivers of living water,' just as the Scriptures say." A ❖ The last day probably means the eighth day. On the previous seven, priests carried water in a gold pitcher from the Pool of Siloam to the Temple, and at the time of the morning sacrifice, the High Priest poured it out at the base of the altar. This was symbolic of Yahweh's provision of water for their ancestors in the wilderness, [Exodus 17:1-7; Numbers 20:7-13; Psalm 78:16] and his provision of adequate rain for them. [Zechariah 14:16-19] It was also symbolic of Yahweh's pouring out his Spirit in the last days, [Joel 2:28-32] and of the expected Messianic Age when a river would flow out from the foundation of the Temple over all the earth. [Ezekiel 47:1-9; Zechariah 14:8; Isaiah 44:3; Revelation 22:1-2] Jesus' bold words at that particular time, in the midst of this symbolism, was clearly a public declaration that he was the fulfillment of all that the Festival of Shelters promised. He was claiming to be the promised Messiah who could provide them with the river of living water, which symbolized God's Holy Spirit. ➤ 39 Jesus meant that those who believed in him would later receive the Holy Spirit to live in them. [Ezekiel 36:24-27] But at that time, the Spirit had not yet been given because Jesus was not yet glorified. [John 12:23-24; 17:1] ❖ John's reference to being glorified probably means his being "lifted up" on the cross, as well as

---

A 7:38 This is not a direct quote of any single Scripture verse. But it is similar in parts to these passages: Zechariah 13:1; 14:8; Isaiah 12:3; 44:3; 58:11; Ezekiel 47:1-9.

his glorification at his ascension. Jesus gave the indwelling Holy Spirit to his close followers before he ascended to Heaven. [John 20:22] But the "pouring out" of the Spirit at Pentecost came after his ascension. ➤

40 When the people heard this, some of them said, "Surely he is the 'Prophet like Moses.' " *[Deuteronomy 18:15-19]* ❖ *They probably thought this because it was Moses who produced water from a rock. They were right, but they thought the predicted Prophet would be a different person from the Messiah. It was probably followers of Jesus who first recognized that he fulfilled the prophecies concerning both the Messiah and the Prophet.* ➤ 41 Others said, "He is the Messiah." But others responded to this, "But the Messiah isn't going to be from Galilee! 42 The Scriptures say that the Messiah will be a descendant of King David and be born in Bethlehem where David lived!" *[2 Samuel 7:11b-13; Psalm 89:4; Micah 5:2]* ❖ *They assumed that Jesus was born in Nazareth in Galilee since in that culture people rarely grew up in a different place from where they were born.* ➤ 43 So public opinion was divided about who he really was. 44 There were also some who wanted to arrest him, but no one laid a hand on him.

45 Then, the Temple guards returned to the chief priests and Pharisees who had sent them to arrest Jesus. Their superiors demanded, "Why haven't you arrested him?" 46 The guards replied, "No one has ever spoken the way he speaks." ❖ *The guards were Levites, trained in the Scriptures. They were not blindly obedient soldiers and they had heard a lot of teachers in the Temple over the years. They, like the crowds, would have been divided their opinions and they may have been influenced by the fact that many people clearly thought Jesus was the Prophet or the Messiah.* ➤ 47 The Pharisees sneered, "Are you so credulous to be deceived too? 48 Have you heard of even one of the ruling council or of the Pharisees who has believed in him? 49 Of course not! But those uneducated rabble know nothing of the Torah! They are under God's curse for listening to him!" 50 Then Nicodemus, who had met with Jesus before, spoke up. ❖ *He was both a Pharisee and a member of the ruling council. [John 3:1]* ➤ He said, 51 "You know that our law doesn't allow us to condemn a man without first listening to him and investigating what he has done." 52 They retorted contemptuously, "Are you a Galilean sympathizer now

too? Go back and search the Scriptures and you will see that no prophet ever comes from Galilee!" ❖ *They were wrong, and later rabbis admitted that prophets had come from every Israelite tribe, Jonah and Nahum among those from Galilee. One reliable ancient manuscript says, "you will see that the Prophet doesn't come from Galilee," but the majority of manuscripts and translations back the more general statement.* ➤ 53 After that, they all went home.

8

The Woman Caught in Adultery

1 Jesus spent the night on Mount Olivet, which overlooks the city. 2 Early in the morning, he again returned to the Temple courtyard. Many people came to listen to him, and he sat down to teach.

3 While he was teaching, some Scripture teachers and Pharisees brought in a woman who had been caught committing adultery. They made her stand in the middle of the crowd 4 and then said to Jesus, "Rabbi, this woman was caught in the act of adultery. 5 The Teachings of Moses say an adulteress must be stoned to death. *[Deuteronomy 22:22-24; Leviticus 20:10]* What do you think we should do?" 6 The question was intended to trap him into saying something they could use against him. ❖ *One might wonder how they caught her in the act, why they didn't also bring the man, and why they would defile the Temple by illegally bringing a ritually unclean person into it. But they were more concerned with trying to trap Jesus than with justice or purity. ¶ If Jesus advocated stoning her, they could report him to the Roman authorities who didn't allow the Jewish leaders to execute anyone except for Temple violations. If he said to let her go, he would be disobeying God's command, which would prove that he had no regard for God or his law, thus making him unpopular with the people.* ➤ But Jesus stooped down and wrote with his finger in the dust on the ground. ❖ *No one knows what he wrote, but it may have been something to prick their consciences, e.g. to remind them that lusting for a married woman was also disobeying the command about coveting, [Matthew 5:28] so they were as guilty in God's sight as this woman.* ➤ 7 But they kept on questioning him about this, so he stood up and said, "The one to throw the first stone must be someone

who's not guilty of the same **A** sin." *[Leviticus 24:14]* **8** Then he stooped down and wrote on the ground again.

9 When her accusers heard this, they began to leave, one by one, the older ones first, until only Jesus and the woman were left in the middle of the crowd. ❖ *The older men would have been guilty of this sin more often and were less likely to be self-righteous.* ➤ **10** Jesus stood up and spoke gently to her, "Miss, where are those who accused you? Didn't anyone remain to condemn you?" **11** She answered, "No, sir." Then Jesus said, "And I don't condemn you either. So you may go, but keep yourself from sin." ❖ *Jesus loves sinners, but never condones sin. He also never condemns anyone in this life. It is only when we die, or when he returns (for those still alive at that time) that the sentence of condemnation will be given to those who have never turned to him with repentance. Until then, he always offers us his undeserved favor and mercy and urges us to turn away from sin. ¶ Note that most of the oldest Greek manuscripts don't include John 7:53—8:11. Most scholars agree that it wasn't originally a part of John's gospel, but also that the story is typical of many stories widely circulated among the first-century believers, and that it probably really happened.* ➤

Jesus Claims to be God's Light Sent to the Sinners of this World

12 Later, Jesus taught the people again. He said, "I am God's Light, sent into this sinful world to illuminate his path to salvation. Those who follow me won't walk in the spiritual darkness of sin and death, but will possess the Light that reveals the way to true life." ❖ *Assuming this still took place during the Festival of Shelters, one of the celebrations during that time involved torches that lit up the city. Light symbolism is frequent in the Hebrew Scriptures and such things would have been on the minds of Jews during this festival. [Psalm 27:1; 119:105; Isaiah 49:6; 60:19-22; Zechariah 14:5b-7] In this context, his claim would have had great impact.* ➤ **13** The Pharisees objected, "You are simply making claims about yourself. Without someone to back you up, your claims are insufficient grounds for us to accept them." ❖ *See the note at John 5:31.* ➤

14 Jesus replied, "You are wrong that my claims are unsupported. And even though I'm making claims about myself, they are still true because I know where I came from and where I'm going. But you don't know these things about me. **15** You are judging based on limited human understanding without insight from God, but I don't judge anyone that way. **16** If I do judge people, my judgment is true because I don't make judgments on my own, but I do it with the help of my Father who sent me. **17** Your Torah states that the testimony of two men is to be accepted as fact if their testimonies agree. *[Deuteronomy 17:6; 19:15]* **18** I am one witness who tells you about myself and my Father who sent me is the other who testifies about me."

19 Then they asked, "Where is your father?" Jesus replied, "It's clear that you don't know me or my Father, since if you really knew me, you would also know him." ❖ *If they really knew God, they would recognize his Son and would know without a doubt who his Father was. Given previous interactions, they knew he claimed that God was his Father. They were in effect saying, "Produce your father so we can hear his testimony about you."* ➤ **20** This interaction took place in the Temple near the treasury where he had been teaching. But he wasn't arrested because the time God had set for it to happen hadn't yet arrived.

21 Once more, Jesus told them, "I'm going away and you will look for me and you will die without your sins being forgiven. You won't be able to come where I'm going." ❖ *Their sin of rejecting the Messiah is particularly in focus, and because they lack forgiveness, they will never reach Heaven.* ➤ **22** So they were asking each other, "What does he mean that we can't go where he is going? He can't be thinking of killing himself, can he?" **23** Jesus said, "You are from this world which is below. I'm not from this world but from above. **24** If you don't believe that I AM, ❖ *Many translations add "he" or "the one" here, but these are not in the Greek. The two interpretations are: 1) "He" or "the one" is implied after the verb, meaning "I am who I claim to be" or "I am the Messiah." 2) Jesus was claiming to be Yahweh, who called himself,*

A 8:7 Some commentators interpret the text this way; others say it means someone who is not guilty of any sin. But if Jesus was interpreting the law from Leviticus 24:14 as requiring a sinless person to start the stoning, his interpretation would have been rejected by the Jewish leaders as impossible nonsense.

"I AM." [Exodus 3:14; Isaiah 43:10] See also John 8:58. ➤ you will die with your sins unforgiven."

25 They asked him, "Who do you say that you are?" Jesus replied, "Just who I've been claiming to be all along. 26 I have much I could say to you and there's much for which I could condemn you, but I don't. I only represent the one who sent me. His words are entirely trustworthy and true, so I only tell people what I hear from him." 27 They still didn't catch on that he was speaking about God the Father as the one who sent him. 28 So Jesus said, "After you have lifted up the Son of Man, *[Isaiah 52:13]* then you will know that I AM. ❖ *See the note at 8:24.* ➤ I do nothing from my own initiative. I only say what my Father instructs me to say. 29 And he who sent me hasn't left me on my own. He's always with me because I only do what pleases him." 30 While Jesus was saying these things, many of those listening started to believe in him.

31 Jesus said to those who believed in him, "If you continue to faithfully obey my teaching, then you are my true followers. 32 And as such, you will know God's thinking about what's really true, and that truth will set you free." ❖ *Genuine faith in Jesus results in perseverance in obeying him.* ➤ 33 They replied, "We are descendants of Abraham and have never been in spiritual slavery. So what do you mean we will be 'set free'?"

34 Jesus said, "I'm telling you an important truth. Everyone who sins is enslaved by sin. 35 A slave has no permanent place in a family, but a son is part of the family forever. ❖ *The discussion is most likely on the plane of spiritual slavery, as they knew that they were currently under Rome's domination and as a nation they had been enslaved several times. The Jewish leaders believed that because they had the Torah's teachings and outwardly followed them, the compulsion to sin which made Gentiles so sinful and in "spiritual slavery" couldn't dominate them. Sin is rebellion against God and enslavement to sin is enslavement to a state of rebellion against God. The Jews considered themselves sons of Abraham and heirs of the promises that God made to him and therefore, part of God's family. But Jesus was saying that they didn't have the rights of sons in God's family because they were slaves of sin.* ➤ 36 So if God's Son sets you free, you will really be free. ❖ *He's speaking of freedom from sin, with the result that*

they are adopted as sons into God's family. ➤ 37 I know you are Abraham's physical descendants, but you want to kill me because you can't accept my teaching. ❖ *They were not Abraham's spiritual heirs, because physical descent is not sufficient. Ishmael too was a physical descendant, but received no inheritance. Physical descent and circumcision are not enough. Circumcision of the heart (i.e., repentance) is also necessary. [Jeremiah 9:25-26]* ➤ 38 The things I'm telling you are what my Father has revealed to me. In the same way, you are also doing the things that you learned from your father."

39 They replied, "Abraham is our forefather!" ❖ *They were claiming that since they were descended from Abraham, they were like him, they measured up to Abraham's standards and were favored by God.* ➤ Jesus said, "If you were true spiritual descendants of Abraham, then you would do the righteous things he did. 40 But instead, you want to kill me when all I've done is tell you truths I've heard from God. Abraham's way was to listen to God, so you aren't imitating him. 41 You are following the example of your true father." They replied, "We're not illegitimate!" ❖ *They may have been implying that Jesus was illegitimate.* ➤ The only father we have is God!" *[Exodus 4:22; Deuteronomy 14:1-2; Jeremiah 31:9]*

42 Jesus said, "If God were your true Father then you would love me, for I came from him into this world. I didn't come on my own authority. He is the one who sent me. 43 Why aren't you getting what I'm saying? It's simply because you are not willing to accept my message. 44 It's clear that you belong to Satan. He is your true father because you have the same desires he does. He was a murderer from the beginning of this world and he completely rejects God's truth, so there's no truth in him. Thus lying is his native language and reflects his true nature. He is both a liar and the originator of all lies. 45 Since you embrace Satan's lies, you don't believe me because what I tell you is true and comes from God. 46 Can anyone prove that I have sinned in any way? ❖ *Jesus here implicitly claimed to be sinless.* ➤ If not, then what I say must be true. So why don't you believe me? 47 Those who really belong to God listen to what he says. The reason you don't accept

his message given through me is because you are not really his children."

48 The Jews replied, "We were right all along to say that you are a demonized Samaritan!" ❖ *It isn't clear if "the Jews" here refers to the whole crowd present or primarily to the leaders. The leaders were almost uniformly opposed to him, but some of the common people did believe him. Their calling him a Samaritan was just intended as a strong insult.* ➤ 49 Jesus replied, "I don't have a demon. I'm simply honoring my Father in what I say, and you are dishonoring me. ❖ *And by implication, they were dishonoring the Father who sent him.* ➤ 50 I'm not seeking honor for myself. But there is one who honors me and he is the one who judges between us. ❖ *i.e., God the Father* ➤

51 "This is most certainly true: Those who obey my teaching will never die." ❖ *He was referring to the "second death" in Hell.* ➤ 52 They said, "Now we know you are demonized! Abraham died and so did the prophets. It's clear that no one is exempt from dying. Yet you say if people obey your teaching they won't die! 53 Who do you think you are? Do you think you are greater than our patriarch Abraham or God's prophets?"

54 Jesus replied, "If I honored myself, it would be meaningless. But it's my Father who honors me. He is the one whom you call your God, 55 even though you don't really know him. But I do know him. If I said I didn't, I would be a liar like you are. But I do know him and I obey his instructions.

56 "Even your ancestor Abraham rejoiced when he foresaw the day when I would come to this world." 57 They scornfully retorted, "You aren't even fifty years old and you claim to have seen Abraham!" ❖ *Abraham lived about 2000 years before Jesus did. It's possible they meant that since he was less than 50—the age when a man could be a public leader—he didn't have the maturity or wisdom to claim to understand and teach about Abraham.* ➤ 58 Jesus replied, "The truth is, I existed before Abraham was even born because I AM." ❖ *Jesus here overtly claimed to be Yahweh, the God of Abraham and Moses. [Exodus 3:14; Isaiah 41:4; 43:10, 13]* ➤ 59 They assumed that

he was blaspheming, so they picked up stones to stone him, but Jesus hid and slipped out of the Temple. ❖ *The Temple was still under construction at that time, so there would have been loose stones around.* ➤

9

Jesus Gives Sight to a Man Born Blind

1 As Jesus and his followers were walking along, they saw a man who had been born blind. 2 His followers asked him, "Rabbi, what caused this man to be born blind? Was it his sin or his parents sin?" ❖ *It was a common belief that sickness and physical deformities were God's punishment in this life for specific sins. Some rabbis taught that it was possible for a baby to sin while still in the womb. The Scriptures teach that sickness or suffering can be a direct result of sin, (e.g. Miriam's revolt in Numbers chapter 12; John 5:14; 1 Corinthians 11:30) but they also teach that it's not necessarily so, (mainly the book of Job and John 9:3).* ➤ 3 Jesus answered, "His blindness is not due to any sin, neither his nor his parents'. He was born this way so God's power could be clearly demonstrated in his life. 4 As long as it's still daytime, we A must do the work of my Father, who sent me. Night is coming, when no one can work. ❖ *Some commentators believe the "day" refers to the period before Jesus' death and "night" refers to the period immediately after his death and before his resurrection. Jesus' comment clearly implies an urgency to do the Father's work now, while there is opportunity. However, "night" could refer to any period of time when spiritual darkness rules and it's difficult to openly do the Father's work, and the phrase "when no one can work" is probably hyperbole. God is always at work and so are his people. Yet there are times of persecution when it's much more difficult than at other times. Others have suggested that "night" refers to death. After we leave this life, we will no longer have opportunity to do the Father's work in this world and have an impact on the lives of others.* ➤ 5 While I'm on earth, *I am* the Light that enables sinners to see the truth about God." [John 1:9; 8:12] ❖ *After Jesus' ascension to Heaven, he started to live in his people through the Holy Spirit, and now his people are the "Light of the world." [Matthew 5:14]* ➤

A 9:4 There are some Greek manuscripts that have "I" as the subject instead of "we." Both "I" and "we" are well supported options.

6 Having made this point, Jesus spat on the ground, making some mud which he smeared on the man's eyelids. ❖ *Jesus proceeded to literally bring light to the blind man, as a picture of his mission to bring spiritual illumination to the spiritually blind. There have been many speculations about why Jesus used saliva, and no one is sure. But the mud, applied to the eyes, might be symbolic of the sin that blinds us to the Light of God's truth.* ➤ 7 Then he sent the man, saying, "Go to the Pool of Siloam and wash off your eyes." (In Hebrew, "Siloam" means "sent.") So he went where he was sent, washed, and went home able to see. ❖ *The Pool of Siloam is in Jerusalem and is where the water was drawn from for the ceremonies during the Festival of Shelters. It received its water through a channel which "sent" it from the spring of Gihon in the Kidron valley (between Mt. Olivet and the Temple Mount). Isaiah 8:6 refers to the water of Shiloah, which is the same water source. (Siloam comes from the Greek transliteration of the Hebrew name. Shiloah is a direct English transliteration of that same Hebrew name.) In Isaiah 8:6, the Israelites rejected the water of Shiloah, which means "sent." Jesus is the one who is "sent" by God and they reject him too. So the pool of Siloam (Shiloah) is a symbol of the Messiah, who was "sent" by God, and to whom believers go to be cleansed of sin, but whom many reject.* ➤ 8 His neighbors and others who had always seen him when he was begging asked, "Isn't this the man who used to sit on the side of the street and beg?" 9 Some said that he was, but others claimed he only looked like the beggar. But he kept telling them, "Yes, I'm that beggar!" 10 So they asked him, "What happened that enabled you to see?" 11 He replied, "The man people call 'Jesus' made some mud and put it on my eyelids. He told me to go wash it off in Siloam. So I went there and washed and then I was able to see." 12 They asked, "Where is he now?" He replied, "I don't know."

13 Then some of his neighbors took him to the Pharisees. ❖ *The miracle of a man born blind being able to see was previously unknown. It was natural that they would want to bring it to the attention of their local synagogue leaders.* ➤ 14 Now the day that Jesus made the mud and enabled the man to see was a Sabbath. 15 So the Pharisees questioned the man about how he received the ability to see. He told them, "He put mud on my eyelids, I washed it off, and I was able to see." 16 Then some of the Pharisees said, "The man who did this is not God's

messenger because he breaks the rule about working on the Sabbath." ❖ *They considered making the mud and causing the miracle to be doing work.* ➤ But other Pharisees said, "It wouldn't be possible for a sinner do so such miraculous signs as these." So they were divided in their opinion of Jesus. ❖ *Their assumption was that only God could do such a miracle and God would never use someone whom he didn't approve of to do miracles. Therefore, God must approve of him, which means he can't be a "sinner." The meaning of "sinner" in this context is someone whose way of life is ungodly and in rebellion against God and his Torah teachings. Some of the Pharisees ignored the fact that it had to be God's power that healed the man. They were so concerned about their legalisms and Jesus' threat to their own status that they were blind to the obvious. This is a general truth. People who arrogantly reject anything contrary to their way of thinking will be totally blind to the most obvious facts that contradict their own viewpoint—even miracles.* ➤ 17 Then they asked the man again, "Since he enabled you to see, what do you think about him?" He said, "I believe he is a genuine prophet from God." 18 The Jewish leaders were unwilling to believe that he had been born blind and was now able to see for the first time. So they summoned his parents 19 and asked them, "Is this your son? Is it true that he was born blind? If so, then how did it come about that he can now see?" 20 His parents answered, "We know that he's our son and that he was born blind. 21 But we don't have any idea who enabled him to see or how it was done. He's of legal age to testify, so ask him." 22 Now, the Jewish leaders had already threatened to expel anyone from the synagogue who said that Jesus was the Messiah. So they were afraid to say anything that would make the leaders expel them. ❖ *To be expelled from the synagogue was to be made a social outcast. All other Jews would avoid them. It was a severe threat.* ➤ 23 That's why they said, "He's of legal age to testify, so ask him."

24 So the man who had been blind was summoned again and they told him, "Glorify God by telling us the truth about what happened. For we know that this man Jesus— who you claimed healed you—is a sinner." 25 He replied, "As to whether or not he is a sinner as you claim, I don't know. But one thing I do know: I was blind, but now I can

see because of him!" 26 So they asked him again, "What did he do to you? How did he make you able to see?" 27 He sarcastically retorted, "I've already told you, but you apparently didn't listen! Why do you want to hear it again? Do you want to become his followers too?" 28 They responded to this with anger and insults, "You are clearly one of his followers! But we follow the teachings of Moses! ❖ *They meant that they adhered to the Teachings of Moses in the Torah and to the oral traditions handed down from their elders which interpreted the Torah teachings. Jesus rejected these oral traditions as having no authority, while they held them as the authoritative interpretation of the Torah. That's why they accused Jesus of not keeping all the commands in the Torah.* ➤ 29 We know that God spoke to Moses, but as for that Jesus, we don't even know where he comes from, let alone whether he has authority from God." 30 The man exclaimed, "That's incredible! He enabled me to see, yet you are unsure of his credentials! 31 We all know that God doesn't listen to unrepentant sinners. He only answers the prayers of those who are properly in awe of him and do his will. 32 Since the beginning of time, no one has ever heard of anyone that could enable a person to see who was born blind. 33 He wouldn't be able to do miracles like this if he didn't have God's authority!" ❖ *Modern medicine might sometimes be able to give sight to a person born blind, but that person's brain would not be able to immediately interpret what he "saw," as this man did.* ➤

34 The leaders blasted him, "Who do you think you are, trying to lecture us! You were born in such sin that God caused you to be born blind!" Then they expelled him from the synagogue and thus from fellowship with the Jewish community.

35 When Jesus heard that the man had been expelled, he went and found him and asked, "Do you put your trust in the Son of Man?" A 36 He replied, "Sir, tell me who he is, so I can." 37 Jesus answered, "You've already seen him and have been talking with him. I am he." 38 The man declared, "Lord, I believe you are the Messiah!" Then he bowed down in submissive worship to Jesus.

❖ *He also recognized Jesus' deity, since no religious Jew of that time would bow down to worship anyone other than the one true God.* ➤

39 Then Jesus said, "I came into this sinful world to expose sin and to precipitate decisions that will determine the way people will be judged. I came to enable the spiritually blind to see God's truth and his way of salvation, and to show those who think they have spiritual sight that they are blind to the truth." 40 Some Pharisees overheard him and said, "Are you saying that we are spiritually blind?" 41 Jesus replied, "If you were blind in the sense of being genuinely ignorant of God's truth but were seeking it, then he wouldn't hold you accountable. But since you claim to have spiritual sight and knowledge of God's truth, you will be judged guilty for rejecting it."

10

The Good Shepherd

1 Jesus continued, "Let me talk about a self-evident truth to make a point. Someone who enters a sheep pen by climbing over the wall instead of going through the gate is clearly a thief and a vandal. 2 But the shepherd enters through the gate, and 3 the watchman recognizes him and lets him in. The sheep respond to his voice as he calls them by name and leads them out to pasture. 4 When he has called out all of his own sheep, ❖ *Since there are sheep belonging to others in the same pen.* ➤ he walks ahead of them and they follow him because they recognize his voice. ❖ *The details concerning shepherding in this chapter accurately reflect the way shepherding is done in the Middle East.* ➤ 5 But they would never follow a stranger. Instead, they would run away from him because they didn't recognize his voice."

6 Jesus used this image to make his point, but they didn't understand what he was getting at. ❖ *Jesus was speaking in terms of a common image in the Hebrew Scriptures where sheep represent God's people and the shepherd is either God or the leaders of Israel, depending on context. [God as shepherd:*

A 9:35 Some later manuscripts have "Son of God," But none of the earliest manuscripts do.

*Genesis 48:15; 49:24; Psalm 23:1; 28:9; 77:20; 78:71; Isaiah 40:11; Ezekiel 34:11-31. **Israel as God's sheep:** Psalm 74:1; 78:52; 79:13; 100:3; **Leaders as shepherds:** Numbers 27:15-18 (Joshua—who was a type of Jesus—their names are the same in Hebrew), 2 Samuel 5:2 (King Saul), Psalm 78:71-72 (David), Jeremiah 3:15 (general), 23:1-4 (general), Ezekiel chapter 34; Micah 5:4 (the Messiah)] The most important of these passages for understanding Jesus' point are Numbers 27:15-18 and Ezekiel chapter 34.* ➤ 7 So Jesus spoke again to clarify, "This is an important truth for you to understand. I am the gate for the sheep. ❖ *Jesus is the gate—or entrance—to Heaven.* ➤ 8 All false teachers and messianic pretenders who came before me are thieves and vandals. But my sheep didn't respond to them. ❖ *Jesus considered most Pharisees and Sadducees in the thief and vandal category.* ➤ 9 I am the gate. Those who come in through me will be saved. They will come in and go out and find good pasture. *[John 14:6]* 10 Thieves come to steal and destroy the sheep. But I come so they may obtain eternal life and enjoy all it has to offer.

11 "I am also the Good Shepherd who is so dedicated to taking care of the sheep that he willingly sacrifices his life to save them. 12-13 A hired hand will abandon them and run away when he sees a wolf coming, allowing the wolf to attack and scatter them. He isn't concerned about the sheep because they don't belong to him. ❖ *Those taking care of another person's animals weren't held responsible if they were killed by wild animals. [Exodus 22:10-13] Jesus was probably also thinking about Jeremiah 23:1-4 and Ezekiel 34:6-16.* ➤ 14-15 But I am the Good Shepherd and owner of the sheep. In the same way that my Father knows me and I know my Father, I know which sheep belong to me and they also know me. So I'm willing to sacrifice my own life for the sake of my sheep. ❖ *In the Hebrew Scriptures, "knowing" God refers to having a close relationship with him and obeying him. [e.g. Jeremiah 4:22; 9:3; 22:15-16; 24:7; 31:34; Hosea 4:1; 6:6]* ➤ 16 I also have other sheep which aren't part of this fold. I must bring them in too. They will respond to my voice and when that happens, there will be only one flock under one shepherd. ❖ *Jesus was referring to gathering in believers among those Jews living in Gentile countries—called the Diaspora [Ezekiel 27:21-24; Micah 2:12]—and also believers from among*

the Gentiles. *[Isaiah 42:6; 49:6, 22; Galatians 3:28-29; Ephesians 2:11-22]* ➤

17 "My Father loves me because I always obey him even to the point of sacrificing my life, and I do that so I can afterward take it back again. ❖ *He will take back his life after saving his people through his sacrifice. Taking it back refers to his resurrection, and doing so does not undo what he accomplishes through his sacrificial death.* ➤ 18 Following my Father's plan and command I will lay down my life of my own free will. No one can take it from me without my consent. I have the authority to lay it down in sacrifice, and I have the authority to take it up again." ❖ *Jesus' death was under his own control. If he didn't allow it, nothing the Jewish leaders or the Romans could do could have taken his life from him.* ➤

19 The people were again divided in their opinions about Jesus as a result of what he said. 20 Many of them exclaimed, "He has a demon which has made him insane. Why bother listening to him?" 21 But some countered, "Demonized people don't talk like this! And you certainly don't believe that a demon has the power to give sight to a man born blind, do you?"

Jesus Again Claims to Be God so the Jewish Leaders Attempt to Stone Him

22-23 A couple of months later it was winter and time for the eight-day Festival of Dedication in Jerusalem. This festival is also called Hanukkah or the Festival of Lights. Jesus was walking in the roofed area in the Temple courtyard called Solomon's Portico. ❖ *This was on the East side of the Temple courtyard.* ➤ 24 Many Jewish leaders gathered around him and said, "How long are you going to keep us in suspense? If you are the Messiah, then tell us clearly." ❖ *Jesus didn't speak plainly because: 1) even though he was the Messiah, his true role and what the Jews expected of the Messiah were quite different, and 2) they weren't asking so they could submit to him if he claimed to be the Messiah, but so they could denounce him to the Roman authorities as a self-proclaimed revolutionary.* ➤ 25 Jesus answered, "I've already in effect told you, but you refuse to believe me. The miracles I've done using my Father's authority and power are sufficiently clear testimony about who I am. 26 But you don't believe me because you are not my sheep. *[John 6:44]* **27** I know my own sheep. They respond to my voice and follow me. **28** I give them eternal life and they will never die because no one has the power to snatch them away from me. **29** My Father is the one who gave them to me and his power is greater than everything. No one can snatch them away from him. **A** **30** My Father and I are a unity." ❖ *The Father and the Son are one in essence, will, and action, but not one person nor one in role. In person and role they are distinct.* ➤

31 They immediately picked up stones to execute him. ❖ *They had no right to stone him without a trial—according to the Teachings of Moses—and Roman law prohibited their executing anyone, but they were overcome with rage.* ➤ **32** But Jesus said to them, "You've seen me do many good works that my Father told me to do. For which of these are you intending to kill me?" **33** They replied, "We don't execute you for doing good works, but for blaspheming by claiming you, a mere man, are God." **34** Jesus retorted, "Isn't it written in your own Torah that God said to the people of Israel, 'You are gods'? *[Psalm 82:6]* ❖ *The "Torah" (Law) in the New Testament sometimes refers to all the Hebrew Scriptures, of which the Torah (Pentateuch) was the most important part. Rabbis said this verse in Psalm 82:6 was addressed to the people of Israel when they received the Torah at Mount Sinai. The Hebrew word translated "god" is "el," and "gods" is "elohim." The range of meaning of this word is broad. It usually refers to God himself but is also used in the Hebrew Scriptures to refer to false gods, angels, and even men in authority. So the meaning of the word is determined by context. Jesus uses this ambiguity to his advantage. The verse he quotes also says "you are all sons of the Most High." The relationship described as "sons" also has broad meaning that is defined by context.* ➤ **35** Since he called the people who received his Torah teachings 'gods'—and Scripture is always true—**36** it must be even more true of me whom the Father set apart and sent into this world for his purposes. So how can you accuse me of blaspheming him just because I said that I'm God's Son? **37** If the works I do are not clearly from my Father, then don't believe me. **38** But if I'm doing works that clearly originate with my

Father, even though you don't accept my witness that I'm God's Son, at least accept the witness of my Father through these works. Then you will recognize that the Father is in me and I am in the Father."

❖ *This expression indicates the unity of the Father and the Son. In Deuteronomy 6:4 is the great declaration of the oneness of God, known by Jews as "the Shema:" "Listen and note, people of Israel: Yahweh is our God, and Yahweh is one." The Hebrew word translated as "one" is not the number one, but a word that indicates a unity and singleness of a plurality. It would be appropriate to use in the statements: The 50 states of our country are one nation. The United States is one. These indicate a unity and singleness of a plurality. In this verse, Jesus' expression of the Father being in him and he is in the Father expresses this same concept of a unity and singleness of a plurality. Jesus and his Father (God the Father) are one. Not one as the number one. They are not the same person. They are distinct, yet together have a singleness and unity of nature (omnipotent deity), essence (a single infinite spirit), and will. When Jesus says this about his relationship with his followers in John 6:56; 15:4; 17:11 and 21-23, he is speaking about his spiritual unity and singleness of identity with them as children of God, who have a unity in nature (their intimate relationship to the Father as his children), essence (they are united in spirit to the Father through the Holy Spirit), and will (they are submitted to the Father's will).* ➤

39 But they weren't convinced and so once again tried to seize him. But he eluded them.

40 He and his close followers went outside of the jurisdiction of the Jerusalem leaders to the east side of the Jordan River where John had first baptized people. *[John 1:28]* **41** Many people came to hear him teach. They were saying to each other, "Even though John the Baptizer never did any miraculous signs, everything he said about Jesus is true." **42** So many there believed that Jesus was the Messiah.

11

The Story of Lazarus

1-2 Jesus had friends who lived in Bethany. ❖ *less than two miles from Jerusalem on the east side of Mt. Olivet* ➤ They were Lazarus and his sisters, Mary and Martha. *[Luke 10:38-42]*

A **10:29** There are textual problems with the first part of this verse. An alternate possible rendering would be: "What my Father has given me is greater than all." This reading would go along with passages like Ephesians 1:11 and 1:18, if the less popular interpretations of them are taken.

Mary was the one who anointed the Lord with expensive perfume and wiped his feet with her hair. *[John 12:1-8]* ❖ *John assumes his readers are already familiar with this story, which is told later in this gospel.* ➤ Now Lazarus became very sick, 3 so the sisters sent a messenger to Jesus with this message, "Lord, your close friend is very sick."

4 But when Jesus heard this, he said, "This sickness will not result in his death. It's been allowed to reveal God's glory and so I, his Son, may receive glory through what happens." 5 Now Jesus loved Martha and her sister and Lazarus. 6 Yet when he heard Lazarus was sick, he stayed where he was for two more days.

7 Then after the two days, he said to his followers, "Let's return to Judea." 8 His followers said, "Rabbi, our leaders tried to kill you and you want to risk going back there?" 9 Jesus replied, "Every day has twelve hours of light. Those who walk during the day won't stumble because they can see by the light. 10 But those who walk at night stumble because they don't have light." ❖ *Jews of that time divided the daylight period of the day into twelve equal hours, even if the length of an hour varied through the year. To "walk" represents what we do in our lives. The "light" represents the guidance of the Father. That every day has twelve hours means the day isn't over yet, so we should keep following the Father's will as long as he is showing it to us. But those who try to "walk" or "live" without the Father's guiding light, will stumble. Jesus was saying that his Father was still guiding him and the "day" of his life was not yet over. He needs to walk in the light his Father is giving him regardless of the consequences, since to do otherwise is to reject the light and live in darkness and stumble in sin.* ➤

11 Then he went on to say, "Our friend Lazarus has fallen asleep. I'm going there to wake him up." 12 His followers said, "Lord, if he's sleeping, it's a good sign that he will recover." 13 Jesus had been speaking euphemistically and meant that Lazarus was dead, but his followers had taken him literally. 14 So he told them plainly, "What I meant was, Lazarus is dead. 15 But I'm glad for your sakes that I wasn't there to heal him so your faith in me may increase. Let's go to him now." 16 Then Thomas—whose nickname was "Twin"—said to the others, "Let's go too so we can die with him." ❖ *Thomas' name is derived from the Hebrew word meaning "twin," and his Greek nickname "Didymus" has the same meaning. He thought it was inevitable that Jesus would be killed if he returned to the vicinity of Jerusalem.* ➤

17 When they approached Bethany, they heard that Lazarus had already been entombed for four days. ❖ *They had evidently been staying in a place that was a few-days walk from Bethany.* ➤ 18 Since Bethany was less than two miles from Jerusalem, 19 many of the Jewish leaders had come to Martha and Mary's house to console them over their brother's death. ❖ *This suggests that their family had some prominence.* ➤ 20 When Martha heard that Jesus was approaching, she went out to meet him but Mary stayed home. ❖ *Her meeting him away from the house might have been intended to prevent the leaders from knowing that he was there.* ➤ 21 Martha said to Jesus, "Lord, if only you had been here, my brother wouldn't have died! 22 But even now I know that God will grant you whatever you ask of him." 23 Jesus replied, "Your brother will come back to life again." 24 Martha said, "Yes, I know that will happen on the Last Day when everyone is resurrected from death." 25 Jesus said, "I am the source of resurrection power and eternal life. Those who believe in me will live forever, even if their bodies die. 26 And those who believe in me and thereby have eternal life, will never experience death. Do you believe me?" ❖ *He could mean that they will never experience eternal spiritual death in Hell, a.k.a. "the second death." Or he could mean that even though their bodies will die, they will not consciously experience the reality of death, but only a transition from this life to a better life in Heaven. Or he could mean both.* ➤ 27 Martha answered, "Yes Lord. I believe that you are the Messiah who was prophesied would come, and are also God's Son." 28 After she said this, she went back to the house and called her sister Mary aside. She told her secretly, "The Rabbi is nearby and he wants you to go to him." 29 When Mary heard it, she quickly got up and went out to meet him. 30 Now, Jesus hadn't yet entered the village but was still where Martha had met him. 31 When the Jewish leaders who had been trying to console Mary saw her leave so quickly, they followed her, thinking that she was going to cry at the tomb. 32 When Mary

reached Jesus, she fell at his feet and cried, "Lord, if only you had been here, I know my brother wouldn't have died!" 33 When Jesus saw her grief and the grief of those who followed her, he was deeply moved and angered. ❖ *There are several speculations about the source of his anger. Whatever it was, was triggered by his seeing their grief. Some think he was angry at sin, sickness, and death, (and perhaps Satan who initiated it all) and all the grief it causes. Some think he was angered by the hopelessness and unbelief reflected in their grief. It's possible both are true. Other speculations that have been made seem less likely.* ➤ 34 Then he asked, "Where have you put him?" They answered, "Lord, come and we will show you." 35 Then, Jesus expressed his grief and mourned with them. 36 People noticed this and said to each other, "See how much he loved him!" 37 But some of them said, "He had the power to give sight to a blind man. Why couldn't he have kept this man from dying?"

38 Jesus arrived at the tomb and was deeply moved again. The tomb was a cave with a large stone covering the entrance. 39 He said, "Remove the stone!" Martha replied, "Lord, he has been in there for four days. There will be a terrible stench." 40 Jesus responded, "Didn't I tell you that you would see God's glory if you believed?" 41 So they removed the stone from the entrance. Then Jesus looked up to Heaven in an attitude of prayer and said, "Father, I thank you that you listen to my prayers and answer them. 42 I know you always do this, but I'm saying this for the benefit of those listening so they will be able to believe that you really sent me with your authority." 43 Then he shouted into the tomb, "Lazarus! Come out!" 44 The dead man came out of the tomb, his hands and feet still bound with strips of linen and his face still wrapped with a cloth. ❖ *He couldn't have walked. John doesn't tell us if he hopped out or floated out.* ➤ Jesus said, "Unbind him and let him go."

45 Many of the people who had come to comfort Mary saw what Jesus did and believed in him. 46 But some of them returned to Jerusalem to tell the Pharisees the latest thing that Jesus had done.

Jewish Leaders Plot to Kill Jesus

47 In response to this latest report about Jesus, the Pharisees and the chief priests convened a session of the Sanhedrin. ❖ *This was the highest judicial and legislative council for the Jews, having 70 members plus the High Priest who presided over it. Most members were priests who were also Sadducees and aristocrats. Pharisees were a minority on the council, but influential because of their popularity with the people.* ➤ The question was brought up, "What are we accomplishing in our efforts to quash the popularity of Jesus? He keeps performing all these miraculous signs! 48 If we allow him to go on like this, everyone will believe that he is the Messiah, there will be a revolt, the Romans will destroy our Temple, and we will lose our positions as rulers over the nation!" ❖ *Their fears were well founded. The people expected the Messiah to overthrow the Romans and many were just waiting for a chance to revolt. Roman authority always responded harshly in response to such revolts.* ➤ 49 Then Caiaphas—who was High Priest at that time—spoke up, "You don't know what you're talking about! ❖ *Caiaphas was High Priest from AD 18 until he was deposed by the Romans in AD 36, the same year Pilate also lost his office.* ➤ 50 You should realize it is expedient for us that this one man die for the people, so the whole nation won't be destroyed."

51 He didn't realize it, but these words weren't his own. As High Priest, God caused him to prophesy that Jesus was going to die for the nation. 52 And not only for that nation, but for all of God's people all over the world, to make them one in spiritual union with him. 53 So from that day on, they were resolved to kill Jesus. 54 Therefore, he no longer traveled publicly, but he and his close followers left the vicinity of Jerusalem to stay in the village of Ephraim—near the wilderness. ❖ *This is probably the present-day village of Et-Taiybeth, about twelve miles from Jerusalem and four miles northeast of Bethel.* ➤ 55 When it was nearly time for the Passover Festival, many people came to Jerusalem from the hill country to go through the week-long purification rites before the Passover, using the purification pools in the Temple courts. ❖ *This is the third explicit Passover mentioned by John. If the first Passover was*

in AD 28 (see the note at John 2:20) then this final Passover and year of his death would have been AD 30. The estimate of this year varies among commentators from AD 27–33, depending on a number of assumptions. ➤ 56 People kept looking for Jesus while they were in the Temple courtyard, asking each other, "Do you think he will show up for the festival or not?" ❖ *The Torah teachings required all adult males to attend the Passover in Jerusalem if they were able. Yet they knew the authorities wanted to arrest him.* ➤ 57 Because they wanted to arrest him, the chief priests and Pharisees had announced that anyone who knew where Jesus was, had to report it to them.

12

Mary Anoints Jesus

1 Six days before the Passover, Jesus and his close followers arrived in Bethany, the village where Lazarus lived—whom he had brought back to life. 2 A dinner was prepared in his honor, and Martha helped serve while Lazarus reclined at the table with Jesus and the other guests. ❖ *According to Matthew and Mark's gospels, this meal took place at the house of Simon the leper. Lazarus would have been a celebrity and a guest. In a large banquet, it was common for women from other families to help out with the serving. There's nothing in John's account to indicate this took place at Lazarus' house.* ➤ 3 Mary brought in a bottle of extremely expensive perfume of pure nard. She anointed Jesus' feet with it and then wiped his feet with her hair. The entire house was filled with the fragrance. ❖ *The amount she used was extravagant. Normally, an honored guest would have his head oiled or perfumed, but the feet would only be washed with water. Since they were reclining at the table, Jesus was lying on his side on a low couch with his feet away from the table, making them easily accessible. Mary's use of her hair to wipe Jesus' feet was a bit risqué and it would have been quite unacceptable for her to let down her hair in public if she was married. Even if she was unmarried, it would probably have raised some eyebrows. Her actions demonstrated extravagant love and devotion without regard to what others might think about her.* ➤ 4 Then Judas Iscariot—one of Jesus' close followers who later betrayed him—protested, 5 "Why didn't she sell this perfume and give the money to the poor? It's worth nearly a year's wages!" 6 But he didn't say this because he was overly concerned

about helping the poor. In reality, he was a thief and often helped himself from the funds that the group held in common, since he was their treasurer. ❖ *In Matthew and Mark's account, it's clear that many of Jesus' followers and others who were there agreed with Judas.* ➤ 7 Jesus responded, "Leave her alone! Allow her to remember and not regret what she has done for me in preparation for the day of my burial. ❖ *The meaning of the Greek in this verse can be taken several different ways, which explains the noticeable variation among translations. Many try to make it reflect what is more clearly recorded in Matthew's and Mark's accounts. It's unlikely that Mary intended the act as a preparation for Jesus' burial. But Jesus' interpretation of it might lead to the conclusion that through her love and devotion, God moved her to perform a prophetic act whose significance even she didn't realize.* ➤ 8 There will always be poor people among you to help, but I will not always be with you." [Deuteronomy 15:11]

9 When people heard that Jesus was in Bethany, a large crowd came to see him and Lazarus. 10 So the chief priests decided to kill Lazarus as well as Jesus 11 because many people had started to believe in Jesus as the Messiah as a result of Lazarus' resurrection.

Jesus' Triumphal Entry into Jerusalem on Palm Sunday

12 The next day, the large crowd that had come to Jerusalem for the Passover Festival heard that Jesus was approaching the city. 13 They took palm branches and went out to meet him. ❖ *It was traditional for people who had already arrived for the festival to go out and welcome others just arriving from distant places by putting branches in their path to walk on. Carrying branches may have been a traditional part of festival worship. Waving branches was also a way of honoring rulers.* ➤ When they saw him, they started shouting, **"Hosanna! May God bless the one whom he sent with his authority! May God bless the King of Israel!"** ❖ *The first part of their chant is a direct quote from Psalm 118:25-26a. Psalms 113-118 were regularly sung during the Passover Festival. "Hosanna" is a Hebrew word literally meaning "Save us!" But by Jesus' time, it had become an expression of praise. Their calling him "king" shows that they were welcoming Jesus as the long-expected Messiah.* ➤ 14 Jesus found a young donkey and rode it in fulfillment of the Scriptures that say, 15 **"Have no fear** [Zephaniah 3:16a] **people of**

Jerusalem, for your King is coming, riding on a young donkey." *[Zechariah 9:9]* ❖ *While finally allowing the people to proclaim him as the Messiah, Jesus tries to counter their expectation of a military leader who will expel the Romans from Israel. Such a ruler would process into the city on a horse or a chariot, but a donkey was a humble mount. So he comes as a peaceful king, not as a conquering zealot. The context following Zechariah 9:9 proclaims that the king comes in peace and will extend his sovereignty and peace throughout the world. The last part of Zechariah 9:10 quotes from Psalm 72:8, which in its context says that the Son of David will rule over the entire earth.* ➤ 16 At that time, his followers didn't realize this event was a fulfillment of prophecy. But after Jesus' resurrection, they remembered the prophecies written about the Messiah and realized that they themselves had been a part of their fulfillment. 17 The people who had come with him from Bethany and who had also been with him when he called Lazarus out of the tomb and raised him back to life, started telling this story to everyone they met. 18 As a result of hearing about this miraculous sign, many others flocked to Jesus. 19 So the Pharisees exclaimed in frustration to each other, "Our efforts have been useless! The whole world is following him now!"

Jesus Talks About His Death Again

20 Now, there were some God-fearing Gentiles among those who came to Jerusalem to worship during the festival. 21 They came to Philip—who was from Bethsaida in Galilee—and said, "Sir, we would like to meet Jesus." ❖ *They may have approached Philip because his name was Greek and he may have had Gentile contacts back home.* ➤ 22 Philip went and told Andrew, and together they went and told Jesus. 23 Jesus replied, "The time has come for me, the Son of Man, to be glorified. ❖ *Jesus doesn't directly respond to the request of the Gentiles, and John doesn't tell us if he met with them or not because it was of no theological significance, and John's gospel is focused on the spiritual significance of all that Jesus said and did. Spiritually speaking, Gentiles could not yet "see" Jesus because they didn't yet belong to God's people. But Jesus was responding indirectly to their request by saying that the time had come for him to be glorified—when he would institute the New Covenant that would include Gentiles so that they could "see" him.* ➤ 24 This is an important truth for you to understand: Unless a grain of wheat is put in the ground and dies, it remains just a single grain. But if it dies, it will produce many grains. ❖ *Seeds that germinate do not biologically die. But the common way of referring to a seed germinating and having a plant grow was that the seed "died." It was a common metaphor that made sense in an agricultural society. Jesus is here figuratively speaking of his death and the many new lives that would result.* ➤ 25 Those who love their lives in this world more than they love me will end up losing them. But those who consider their lives in this world less important than living in obedience to God, will end up exchanging them for eternal life. ❖ *The original text contrasts "love" and "hate" which is a Semitic idiom contrasting the relative importance of two things. Literal hatred was not intended. This saying parallels the figure in verse 24 of a grain dying (i.e., hating life) or remaining an unplanted grain (i.e., loving life). [Matthew 10:39; 16:25; Luke 9:24; 17:33]* ➤ 26 Those who want to serve me must obey me and follow my leading. If they do this, then they will remain with me wherever I am. ❖ *Including Heaven.* ➤ My Father will honor all those who serve me. ❖ *Some commentators think verses 23-26 were given as an answer to the Gentiles who wanted to see him in verse 21.* ➤

27 "But now, my emotions are rebelling loudly within me. Yet is it right for me to ask my Father to allow me to escape the suffering that's almost upon me? ❖ *He knew about the beatings, humiliation, and crucifixion that he faced.* ➤ Not at all, since the very reason I came into this world was to suffer and die! ❖ *As a substitute for sinful humanity.* ➤ 28 Father, I ask that you enable me to go through with what you sent me to endure, and so bring you great glory!" Then, God spoke audibly from Heaven, "I've already revealed my glorious character through your work, and I will do so again." 29 The crowd standing nearby heard the voice. Some—not discerning the words—said it was thunder. But others said, "It was an angel speaking to him!" 30 Jesus told them, "The voice wasn't so much for my benefit as for yours—to let you know that God sent me. ❖ *Different people heard it more or less clearly, probably depending on how open their hearts were to God.* ➤ 31 The time for God's judgment has come, and the prince of this world will be overthrown. ❖ *Jesus is speaking of God's judging and*

punishing all of humanity's sin in himself when he was crucified. [Isaiah 53:4-6; 1 Peter 2:24] All future judgment and condemnation will be based on a person's acceptance or rejection of God's judgment of humanity's sin in Jesus as our substitute. By suffering our punishment in our place, he defeated the power that sin, death, and Satan (the prince of this world) had over people. ➤ 32 And when I'm lifted up from the earth, [Isaiah 52:13] ❖ on the cross, and also later after his resurrection in his exaltation in Heaven as Lord over everything, ➤ I will draw all people to myself." ❖ He doesn't mean he will draw all people without exception to himself (the error of universal salvation), but all kinds of people (including Gentiles) from every people group (tribe, language, and ethnicity) without distinction. [Revelation 5:9; 7:9; 11:9] One way of interpreting this is that he "attracts" all people, but not all people respond and follow him. Calvinists interpret it to mean that he sovereignly draws all those—and only those—whom he has chosen. ➤ 33 He talked about being "lifted up" to indicate that the way he would die was on a cross. 34 The crowd asked him, "We have heard that the Torah ❖ (in this context, Torah must mean all the Hebrew Scriptures) ➤ teaches the Messiah will stay here forever. So how can you say that the Son of Man must be 'lifted up?' What kind of Son of Man are you talking about?" ❖ They evidently understood being "lifted up" to refer to death (or possibly leaving to be in Heaven), but this idea was irreconcilable with their conception of the Messiah. The Jews of Jesus' time focused on the Scriptures that we now realize predict Jesus' second coming in glory and power when he will reign forever. [2 Samuel 7:16; Psalm 72:17; 89:35-37; 110:4; Isaiah 9:6-7; Daniel 7:13-14; Ezekiel 37:25] They didn't associate the Scriptures that talked about his suffering and death as applying to the Messiah. [Psalm 22:1-18; 69:8, 11; 20-21; 118:22; Isaiah 52:13—53:12] ➤ 35 Jesus responded, "My Light will be with you for just a short time. Walk in the spiritual Light that I give while it's here to guide you, so that spiritual darkness won't conquer you. Those who walk in spiritual darkness have no idea where they're going. ❖ The metaphors of "light," meaning "good, righteous, and truth," and "darkness," meaning "evil, sin, and deception" were commonly used, and the people easily understood what Jesus was saying. ➤ 36 While I'm still with you, put your trust in me so you can become heirs who follow the Light." ❖ Jesus didn't directly answer their question in verse 34 because he had already done so. Instead, he urged them to trust him while they had the opportunity. ➤ After saying this, Jesus left them and secluded himself from the public.

Most Jews Refused to Believe in Jesus

37 Despite the many miraculous signs he had done by the Father's power, most of the people didn't believe he was the Messiah. ❖ Even though they had recently hailed him as the Messiah when he entered Jerusalem, they later rejected him because he didn't meet their expectations. He refused to become a king and political savior and he kept talking about dying. Everyone "knew" the Messiah would never die. ➤ 38 This fulfilled the prophecy of Isaiah which says, "Yahweh, who among those who have seen your mighty power ❖ i.e., his miraculous signs done through Jesus ➤ have believed our message?" ❖ i.e., about the suffering Messiah. [Isaiah 53:1] This question in Isaiah's prophecy reflects the astonishment of the Gentile nations at the Messiah's rejection by his own people, even though God demonstrated his mighty power through him. ➤ 39 But the people couldn't believe in him, as Isaiah also predicted, 40 "God has blinded them to truth and closed their minds so they have no spiritual insight and no understanding. Hence they don't turn to me for spiritual healing." ❖ This is quoted from Isaiah 6:10, yet isn't an exact quote of either the Hebrew or the Septuagint. Jewish teachers often made their arguments by quoting Scriptures loosely and combining them together. Some commentators interpret this important text to mean that God's people first hardened their hearts to his truth, so he chose to punish them by further hardening them. He did this by sending his message anyway which he knew they would find offensive and reject, so they would be even more guilty and have even less excuse. Calvinist commentators interpret this hardening as a sovereign choice of God for his purposes, yet not relieving the people of responsibility for the choice they made. Spiritual healing (literally just "healing") refers to salvation. ➤ 41 Isaiah wrote this because of the vision he had of Jesus' glory. ❖ That vision is recorded in Isaiah 6:1-13. John here tells us that "the King, Almighty Yahweh" [Isaiah 6:5] whom Isaiah saw was the pre-incarnate Son of God (i.e., before he was born as a human). ➤ 42 Even though most of the people rejected him, there were quite a few who did believe in him, even many who were leaders. ❖ Some commentators

interpret "leaders" as synagogue leaders, and others interpret it as meaning members of the Sanhedrin (who were mostly priests and Sadducees)—Nicodemus and Joseph of Arimathea among them. ➤ But they were unwilling to profess their belief publicly because they were afraid that the Pharisees would expel them from the synagogue and community. 43 For even though they believed Jesus was the Messiah, they still valued public acceptance more than God's. ❖ *Their "belief" was intellectual. They were convinced that Jesus was the Messiah, but they lacked true commitment to follow him regardless of the cost. Hence they were not yet saved, but many of them became saved after Pentecost.* ➤

People Will Be Condemned
for Rejecting Jesus' Teaching

44 At another public appearance before the Passover, Jesus shouted out to the crowd, "Those who believe in me aren't only believing in me, but also in God who sent me. *[Matthew 10:40; Mark 9:37; Luke 10:16]* 45 When you look at me, you are also looking at the one who sent me. *[John 14:6-11]* 46 I've come as a spiritual Light shining in this sinful world, revealing the way of salvation so that all who believe in me will not remain in the spiritual darkness of sin and death. *[John 8:12]* 47 I don't condemn those who hear my teaching but choose not to follow it because I didn't come to judge people—I came to save them. ❖ *Jesus is speaking of his first coming—during which he provided a way of salvation. When he comes a second time on the Last Day, he will come to judge. [John 5:26-30]* ➤ 48 But there is a judge who will—on the Last Day—condemn those who reject me and my teaching. Their rejection of the words I've said will condemn them. 49 This is because the words I've spoken aren't my own but come from my Father who always tells me exactly what to say. 50 I know that his words and commands lead those who receive them to eternal life—so I always say exactly what my Father tells me to say."
❖ *Jesus was proclaiming his words to be equal to God's Torah teachings—since the Jews believed that God would judge people on the last day by the standard of his Torah. Since Jesus' teaching and also all the teachings in the New Testament came from God, all these teachings are now part of God's amended Torah (i.e., teaching).* ➤

Jesus Models the Role of a Servant Leader

1 Now it was just before sunset when the Passover would begin. Jesus knew the time had come when he would be leaving this sinful world and return to his Father in Heaven. His followers had always been very dear to him and now he demonstrated the full extent of his love for them. ❖ *There are some difficulties reconciling the timing of this meal between John's gospel and the other gospels. But this difficulty is largely eliminated if the event of Jesus washing his followers' feet that occurred "just before the Passover" is interpreted as happening "just before sunset when the Passover would begin" rather than "a whole day before Passover." The biblical and Jewish reckoning of the start of a new day was at sunset.* ➤ 2 The evening Passover meal was being set out before them, and Satan had already tempted Judas Iscariot to betray Jesus. 3 But Jesus was fully aware that his Father had given him complete authority and power over everything, and that he had originally come from God and would soon return to him. 4 So he got up from the table, took off his outer garment ❖ *now dressed like a low-level slave* ➤ and wrapped a towel around himself. 5 Then he poured some water in a basin and began to wash his followers' feet and drying them with the towel. ❖ *They would have been reclining on low couches with their feet away from the table, making their feet easily accessible. A host would provide water for a guest to wash his own feet, or the lowliest of slaves might do it for them, but it would have been inconceivable for a rabbi to wash his followers' feet. Even peers would never wash one another's feet, except very rarely as a sign of extraordinary love. Jews of that time were very status conscious. Even people who were otherwise quite humble would not lower themselves to do something below their status. So Jesus' followers were quite shocked at his actions and would have considered it unacceptable for even one of them to do such a task, let alone their master, and especially the Messiah.* ➤ 6 When he came to Simon Peter, Peter asked him, "Lord, do you intend to wash my feet?" 7 Jesus answered, "You don't have to understand right now what I'm doing. Just submit and later you will understand." 8 Peter objected, "No, it isn't fitting! I will never have you wash my feet!" Jesus replied, "If you don't allow me to wash you, then you

can't have anything to do with me." ❖ *Washing their feet was symbolic of his humbling himself to die to purify them from their sins. This is the main reason he came to this world. If they won't allow him to do this for them, then they can't have any inheritance of eternal life with him. But Peter's main objection here is his Lord's loss of dignity.* ➤ ⁹ With that at stake, Peter capitulated and said, "Lord, if washing me enables me to remain with you, don't just wash my feet, but my hands and head too!" ¹⁰ Jesus replied, "A person who has bathed is completely clean {except for his feet}. **A** And all but one of you are clean." ¹¹ He said one of them wasn't clean because he knew Judas was going to betray him. ❖ *Jesus is probably overtly referring to the ritual bathing they performed in the pools in the Temple court before the Passover. Their bodies were clean except for their feet since they afterward had to walk through the dusty streets. On a spiritual level, Jesus was saying that they were spiritually clean (i.e., their sins were forgiven), all except for Judas who was unrepentant and planning to betray him. They had previously been purified before God—because of their faith in Jesus—and only the daily sins in their lives need to be dealt with, as represented by the dirty feet. The symbolism changes as the story unfolds as it does elsewhere in John's gospel. (e.g. In chapter 10, Jesus is first the gate and then the shepherd.) Initially, the washing of feet symbolizes Jesus' cleansing them from sin. But when Peter objects and then wants more than his feet washed, Jesus takes the opportunity to make two further points—that there are two levels of cleansing, and a person can go through the motions of being washed and still not be spiritually clean.* ➤ ¹² When he finished washing their feet, he put on his outer garment again and resumed his place at the table. Then, he asked them, "Do you understand what I was doing for you? ¹³ You appropriately call me your Rabbi and Lord, for that is what I am to you. ¹⁴ So since your Lord and Rabbi has washed your feet, you should follow my example and be humble enough to wash each other's feet. *[Luke 22:27]* ¹⁵ I've given you an example of a leader humbly serving those who follow him, so you must be willing to be just as humble with those who will follow you. ¹⁶ This is an important truth: A slave

can't be greater than his master, nor is a messenger greater than the one who sent him. *[Matthew 10:24; 20:25-28; Mark 10:42-45; Luke 6:40; 22:25-27; John 15:20]* ❖ *The point of this saying is: Since their master is willing to humble himself and serve his followers in such a way, they dare not consider themselves above doing the same kind of thing because then they would be claiming they are greater than their master. Also implied is that the master would take a dim view of such a follower because he isn't really submitted to his master's instructions.* ➤ ¹⁷ Now that you know this, God will bless you if you put it into practice! ❖ *Few people mistake this command to mean we must literally wash other people's feet, which is not a common need in our culture. The focus is on humbly serving others regardless of your status and regardless of the lack of dignity involved in the task. Yet some groups of believers have a rite of foot washing in their services to serve as a reminder of this lesson which is often forgotten, particularly by leaders.* ➤

Jesus Predicts His Betrayal

¹⁸ "But I'm not including all of you in the things I've been saying. I knew the hearts of each of you when I chose you to be my close followers. *[John 6:70]* But I made my choice to fulfill the prophecy in Scripture that says, **'My close friend that I trusted who ate with me has turned against me.'** *[Psalm 41:9]* ❖ *Jesus didn't quote the first part of Psalm 41:9 that says, "My close friend that I trusted." But his followers would have known the context and its meaning is implied even by what Jesus did quote. In Jewish culture, eating a meal with someone implied a level of intimacy, trust, and approval—and eating with a superior implied a pledge of loyalty. The implication is that Judas' betrayal was far more wicked since he pretended loyalty and friendship.* ➤ ¹⁹ I'm telling you about this beforehand so when it does happen, you may believe even more that I am the One. *[Exodus 3:14; Isaiah 43:10]* ❖ *Again, Jesus is hinting at his being Yahweh, but it could also simply mean he is the Messiah. Having supernatural insight to future events clearly indicated that he was—at the very least—a prophet sent by God, and he has already made clearer and bolder claims. This is just one more piece of confirming evidence.* ➤ ²⁰ It's important to understand this: Those who welcome you as those I have

---

A 13:10 Many modern exegetes are convinced that the phrase {except for his feet} was not in the original text because of its absence in important early manuscripts. If this is true, then the point in the commentary about

dealing with daily sins is not addressed in this passage. Jesus' reply would then mean that his washing their feet was symbolic of their complete spiritual cleansing, so it was unnecessary wash anything else.

sent to represent me are also—in effect—welcoming me. Consequently, they also—in effect—welcome God who sent me." *[Matthew 10:40; 25:40; Mark 9:37; Luke 9:48; 10:16]*

21 After this, Jesus felt anguish over what he knew was about to happen and exclaimed, "I know for a fact that one of you is going to betray me!" 22 They started looking at each other, wondering who he meant. 23 Reclining just in front of Jesus was his closest friend. ❖ *John is referring to himself. Jesus' inner circle of friends were Peter, James, and John who was closest to him. By writing the gospel in the third person (i.e., using "they" and "he" rather than "us" and "I") John was being humble by his cultural standards. Those reclining on Jesus' right and left (or in front and behind since they were reclining on their left sides, propped up by their left elbow and using their right hands to eat, with their heads close to the table and the foot of the dining couches angled out away from the table) were in the positions of honor at the meal.* ➤ 24 Simon Peter caught that man's eye, nodded toward Jesus and mouthed the message, "Ask him who it is." 25 So he leaned back until his head was touching Jesus' chest and he could see him eye to eye, and quietly asked, "Lord, who is it?" 26 Jesus quietly answered, "After I dip this piece of bread in the sauce, I will give it to him." Then he dipped the bread and—as an indication of his love—gave it to Judas, son of Simon Iscariot. ❖ *This action was the way a host honored one of his guests. Some commentators think that Judas was reclining to Jesus' left (i.e., leftward if they all sat up and turned to face the table.)* ➤ 27 As soon as Judas ate the bread, Satan entered him. Aware of this, Jesus told him, "Be quick about what you are going to do." ❖ *We know from Matthew 26:14-16; Mark 14:10-11; and Luke 22:3-6 that Judas had agreed to betray Jesus to the chief priests before the Passover started, but he still had the option of not following through. Despite Jesus' act of love and friendship, Judas strengthened his resolve, thus surrendering control of his actions to Satan's influence—even though he may have been unaware of Satan's presence within him.* ➤ 28 But no one else at the table knew why he said this to him. 29 Since Judas was their treasurer, some of them thought Jesus was telling him to buy what they needed for the Feast of Unleavened Bread, which would begin at sundown the next day, or to go out and give money to the poor. 30 Then Judas immediately left, heading out into the darkness. *[Luke 22:53]* ❖ *"Darkness" here refers to spiritual darkness. It wasn't merely the darkness of night, it was the time appointed by God when Satan would have free reign over Jesus.* ➤

Jesus Predicts Peter's Denial

31 When Judas was gone, Jesus said, "The time has come for my glory as the Son of Man to be revealed, and through me, God's glory too. ❖ *Jesus is speaking mainly about his sacrificial death, but also of his resurrection. Through this sacrificial act, God's glorious character—namely his holiness and righteousness in punishing sin, and his love, mercy, and undeserved favor in redeeming sinful humanity—would be revealed to all who heard about it and understood it. This is probably the main aspect of the glory that Jesus was talking about. As a result of understanding this about God, people will turn to him and acknowledge his glorious character with praise.* ➤ 32 And {since God's glory will be revealed through me,} **A** God will also very soon reveal the glory that belongs to me as the Son of Man because I am one with God. ❖ *The main aspect of the glory spoken of in this verse is probably his identity as the eternal Son of God, his role as creator, and his corresponding greatness, power, majesty, and sovereignty over all creation. These aspects of his glory are revealed through his resurrection, his ascension, and the witness of the Holy Spirit after Pentecost.* ➤ 33 My sons, I will only be with you for a little while longer. ❖ *He was referring either to his death or to his ascension.* ➤ You will still seek me out, but as I told the leaders, you won't be able to go where I'm going—at least not right away. *[John 7:34; 8:21]* ❖ *Jesus probably meant that they will seek him out in prayer, or that they will long for his physical presence. They certainly won't be searching for him, as they will know he is in Heaven.* ➤ 34 And now I'm giving you a new command: Love each other as deeply and fully as I have loved you. *[John 15:12, 17; 1 John 3:23; 2 John 5]* ❖ *Jesus' command was new in the sense that the standard he gave was explicitly greater than previous commands to love found in the Torah, and it was also new in that it was based on the New Covenant established by Jesus' self-sacrificial death that sprang from his love for them.* ➤ 35 This is what will prove to

---

A 13:32 The words in { } are not in the oldest and best Greek manuscripts, but they are merely a transition and don't affect the meaning.

outsiders that you are my true followers—they see your great love for each other."

❖ *"Each other" includes all who are followers of Jesus. Many believers unfortunately ignore the universality of this command and only love those in their own group or denomination, showing less than love to other followers of Jesus who don't agree with them in every particular.* ➤

36 Simon Peter asked, "Lord, where are you going?" Jesus replied, "You won't be able to follow me where I'm going right away, but only later." 37 Peter asked, "Lord, why can't I follow you right away? I'm willing to go anywhere with you—even if it costs me my life!" 38 Jesus replied sadly, "Are you really willing to die in order to follow me? The truth is, tonight—before you hear a rooster crow—you will three times deny that you know me just to save your own life." ❖ *Roosters in Jerusalem would crow any time between about 12:30 a.m. and sunrise. Peter was sincere, but didn't realize how weak he was in the face of danger and Satan's temptation. See Ephesians 4:27 and the footnote at the end of that verse.* ➤

14

Jesus Is the Only Way to the Father

1 Jesus said to all of them, "Don't start worrying. Just trust God to take care of you, and trust me too. 2 There are many dwelling places in Heaven where my Father lives, and I'm going there to prepare a permanent place for each of you. If it were otherwise, I would tell you. 3 And since I'm going away to prepare your places, I will return to receive you into spiritual union with myself so you can always be with me. ❖ *Jesus was mainly referring to his self-sacrificial death to prepare their places in Heaven by redeeming them, and his returning to them via the Holy Spirit so they could always be spiritually one with him, and thus be continually in his presence in the spiritual realm. This also refers to his coming to receive them into Heaven when they die, or to his second coming for those who are still alive at that time.* ➤

4 "And you know the way to where I'm going." 5 Thomas spoke up, "Lord, since we don't know where you are going, how can we know the way?" 6 Jesus answered, "I'm going to my Father in Heaven, and I am the only for anyone to get there. For I am God's ultimate revelation of and I am the only

source of eternal .7 "Since you have known me, you now know my Father too. Starting now, you can realize that you know him and have seen him." 8 Philip said, "Lord, show us God the Father and we will be content." 9 Jesus replied, "Philip! Don't you know who I am by now? How can you ask me to show you God the Father? I've been with you all for so long and you still don't understand! Anyone who sees me sees the Father too! 10 Don't you believe that I and my Father are one being and that he reveals himself through me? None of the words I've said were my own, but they came from the Father who lives in spiritual union with me and does his work through me. 11 Please believe me when I say that my existence is tied to the Father's existence and the Father's existence is tied to my existence, for we are one being, and that he reveals himself to you and others through me. Or at least believe it's true because of the miraculous works you have seen, which only the Father could do. 12 I will tell you an important truth. Those who believe in me will do the same kinds of miraculous works I have been doing. And by means of their spiritual union with me, they will do even greater ones than these because I'm going to my Father to be glorified. 13 Anything you ask me to do that's in line with my will, I will do so I can reveal the greatness of my Father's character and bring him praise. 14 Ask me to do anything at all that's in line with my will and I will do it for you!" ❖ *Note that he made no promise as to the timing of his doing what you ask. The original text says "ask in my name." To ask in someone's name is to ask with their authority. But one can only have authority to ask for something that's in line with the will of the person who grants that authority.* ➤

Jesus Promises the Holy Spirit

15 Jesus continued to say, "If you start by loving me, then out of that love will naturally flow your desire and ability to obey my commands. [Exodus 20:6; Deuteronomy 11:1, 13; 13:3-4; 30:6] 16 I'm going to ask my Father to send you another person who will be to you what I have been to you, who will always be in and with you. ❖ *The Holy Spirit will be their master, teacher, revealer of the*

Father's will, counselor, comforter, and empowerer. ➤ 17 He is the Holy Spirit who will lead you to understand all the spiritual truth that my Father wants you to know. Those who follow the sinful ways of this world can't submit to the Holy Spirit because they are unable to spiritually perceive him, or understand him. But you know him because he lives *with* you now, and later he will be *in* you. ❖ *Later, after the resurrection. [John 20:22]* ➤ 18 I will not abandon you and leave you helpless like orphans. Through the Spirit, I will come back to be with you. 19 In a short time, those who follow the ways of this sinful world will no longer see me. But through the spiritual insight given by the Holy Spirit, you will see me. And because I live eternally, you too will live eternally with me. 20 When the Spirit lives in you, then you will know without a doubt that I exist in unity with the Father, and that you exist in spiritual unity with me, and that I'm living in you and revealing myself to others through you. 21 Those who understand my commands and obey them are the ones who really love me. ❖ *See verse 15 again. It's not that we prove our love by obeying, but that our obeying spontaneously springs from our love.* ➤ My Father and I will love them, and I will reveal myself to each of them." 22 Then Judas Thaddeus (not Iscariot, who had already left) *[John 13:30]* said, "But Lord, what has happened to change what the Scriptures say about the Messiah such that now you are only going to reveal yourself to your followers and not to the rest of the world?" ❖ *Luke refers to him as Judas, son of James, [Luke 6:16; Acts 1:13] who may be the person referred to as Thaddeus in Matthew 10:3 and Mark 3:18. The disciples were still focused on their expectations of the Messiah as detailed in Scriptures that speak about his second coming in glory when all people will see him.* ➤ 23 Jesus answered, "I'm speaking of a special revelation that's only given to those who love me and live in obedience to my teachings. They are the ones my Father will love, and we will both come to them and live with them. ❖ *Some believe that the Father and Son only live in believers through the Holy Spirit. Others, including St. Augustine, have taken this to mean that all three persons of the Trinity indwell believers.* ➤ 24 But those

who don't love me won't live in obedience to my teachings. My teachings didn't originate with me, but they are my Father's, and he sent me to give them to you.

25 "I'm telling you all this while I'm still physically with you. 26 But my Father will send the Holy Spirit to you as my emissary to help you. The Spirit will teach you everything you need to know and will also remind you of all the things I've taught you.

27 "I'm leaving you with shalom, real well-being that comes from me, not the superficial peace this world offers. So don't be afraid or worried about what will happen. ❖ *The Greek word εἰρήνη (eirēnē), usually translated "peace," reflects the depth of the Hebrew word "shalom," which means: peace, calmness, success, comfort, contentment, safety, health, wholeness, prosperity, integrity, well-being, and good relationships with God and people. It was used as a greeting and as a farewell, indicating the good wishes on the part of the speaker. Jesus provides the substance and reality of shalom to his followers.* ➤ 28 You heard me say that I'm leaving and will later return to you spiritually through the Holy Spirit. If your love for me was less selfish, you would rejoice that I'm returning to my Father to again share in his glory, for his glory is greater than mine while I'm here. *[John 17:5]* 29 I'm telling you these things before they happen, so when they do happen, you will continue to believe in me. 30 I won't be able to speak with you much longer, for Satan—the prince of this sinful world—is coming to kill me. He has no legal hold or power over me. 31 But I will do exactly what my Father has told me to do so the world can know that I love my Father. So come, let's be on our way." ❖ *Even though he said this, it's apparent that they didn't leave at this time. Or else the events aren't told chronologically.* ➤

15

Jesus' Followers Relate to Him
Like Branches to a Vine

1 Jesus continued, "*I am* the True Vine and my Father is the gardener. ❖ *In the Hebrew Scriptures, a grapevine is a common symbol for God's people, Israel. [Psalm 80:8-16; Isaiah 27:2-6; Jeremiah 2:21; 12:10; Ezekiel 15:1-8; 17:1-10; 19:10-14; Hosea 10:1-2; but*

especially Isaiah 5:1-7] Whenever this figure has been used for Israel, the focus is on their failure to produce good fruit (good fruit is a picture of obedience) and God threatens to judge them for it. Now, Jesus is claiming to be the True Vine, the only one that will produce good fruit which is pleasing to the Father. The only way God's people, the branches, can expect to bear good fruit is by being in a vital living relationship with the True Vine, which is the source of their spiritual life and power. [Galatians 2:20] ➤ 2 He cuts off **A** any of my branches that don't bear fruit. *[James 2:17]* He also prunes **B** ❖ *i.e., disciplines* ➤ every branch that does bear fruit, so it will be even more fruitful. 3 You are like already-pruned branches who will produce much fruit because you have believed my message. 4 Stay spiritually joined to me and I will continue to live in and through you as your source of life. Just as a branch can't produce fruit unless it's attached to the vine, you can't bear the spiritual fruit that comes from obedience unless you stay joined to me in a vital living relationship and allow me to live through you.

5 "I am the source of spiritual life, and you relate to me as branches do to a vine. Only those who stay in vital relationship with me will produce abundant spiritual fruit, because separated from me you can accomplish nothing of eternal value. 6 Those who don't continue in a vital relationship with me are rejected and cut off as useless unproductive branches. They dry up and die and are only fit to be burned. *[Ezekiel 15:1-8]* 7 But those who continue in a vital relationship with me and live according to the truths I've taught, may ask God for anything they wish and he will grant it. ❖ *The implication is clearly that those who live according to Jesus' teaching will only be asking for things in line with God's will. These answered prayers are fruit that the branches bear.* ➤ 8 When you bear abundant fruit in this way, my Father's glorious character and power is revealed and praised, and this proves that you belong to me.

9 "I love you in the same way my Father loves me. So continue to live in relationship with me and receive my love. 10 You do this by living in obedience to things I've told you to do. This is the same way I continue in relationship with my Father and receive his love, by doing what he wants me to do. 11 I've told you this so you will experience the same joy I have, and that you may be entirely filled with this perfect joy. ❖ *True obedience to Jesus produces genuine joy, with no regrets. [John 17:13]* ➤

12 "The most important command I give you is to demonstrate love to each other in the same selfless self-sacrificial way that I've loved you. *[John 13:34; 15:17; 1 John 3:23; 2 John 5]* 13 This is the standard of my love for you—and there is no greater love than this—that a person is willing to sacrifice his life for his friends. 14 And the main characteristic of my friends is that they obey me. 15 I will no longer call you servants because a servant isn't taken into his master's confidence. You are my friends, so I've told you everything that I've heard from my Father. ❖ *A person may be a friend to an absolute ruler, but the obligations of that friendship are not totally reciprocal. The ruler's friend is still under the authority of the ruler, but he has the ruler's confidence and the privilege of knowing his plans and thinking. This is our relationship to Jesus.* ➤ 16 I was the one who took the initiative in choosing you. Your choice was only a response. And I've chosen you for the task of producing fruitful results that will last eternally. ❖ *This fruit most likely refers to bringing other people into his kingdom.* ➤ To enable you to accomplish this, my Father will grant you anything that you ask of him with my authorization. ❖ *Literally, using "his name," but this means "from his authority," which clearly implies that the requests are in line with Jesus' will.* ➤ 17 So remember to obey my command to demonstrate your love for each other."

A **15:2a** αἴρω (airō) has several meanings, depending on context. Because of the context of the picture Jesus is making and because of verse 6, most commentators believe this word was intended to mean "he takes away, removes, cuts off." But a few commentators interpret it to mean "he lifts up" in this context. The NET Bible has an extensive and helpful footnote on this word in this verse that I recommend you read.

B **15:2b** καθαίρω (kathairō) in this context clearly means "he prunes," but the word also means "he cleans," which applies on the spiritual level.

Those Who Reject Jesus
Will Also Hate His Followers

18 Jesus continued, "Don't be shocked when people of this sinful world hate and reject you. Remember that they hated and rejected me first. *[Mark 10:30; John 16:33; Acts 14:22; 1 Thessalonians 3:3-4; 2 Timothy 3:12; 1 Peter 2:20-21]* 19 The people of this world live in rebellion against God. If you were still like them, they would accept you as their own. But you are no longer like them because I chose you to be mine, and that's why they will hate you. 20 Remember I told you, 'A slave can't be greater than his master.' *[John 13:16]* So don't expect them to treat you any better than they treated me. If they persecute me, they will persecute you too. But those who follow my teaching will also follow you. 21 The people of this world don't know God who sent me, so they reject me. And they will persecute you because you follow me. 22 If I hadn't come and revealed God's truth to them, they wouldn't be held accountable for not following it because they would still be ignorant. But now they have no excuse for not living the way God wants them to. ❖ *The more knowledge people have of God's will, the more God will hold them accountable. And there will be severe punishment for rejecting revelation that's clearly given to them.* ➤ 23 Since my words and deeds come from my Father, he considers their hating and rejecting me the same as hating and rejecting him. 24 If I hadn't performed miraculous signs among them—unlike any ever done before—they wouldn't be held accountable for not recognizing that the Father sent me. But they have seen these things and yet they still reject me and my Father. So they will be held accountable. 25 Their doing this fulfills the prophecies written in the Hebrew Scriptures **A** that say, '**They hated me without valid cause.**' *[Psalm 35:19; 69:4]*

26 "But I will send the Spirit of Truth to help you. He will come from my Father and will tell you things from me. 27 Then, you will tell others about me and also tell them things I've said because you have been with me from the beginning of my ministry."

16

1 "I'm giving you advance warning about the persecution you will face so when it happens, you won't lose faith due to surprise and discouragement. 2 They will expel you from synagogues, making you outcasts from Jewish society. It will come to the point where some fellow Jews will think they are serving God by killing you. 3 But they will do these things because they've never really known my Father or me, despite their show of religious fervor. 4 I'm warning you now in advance so when that time comes, you will remember that I told you it would happen and you can take comfort knowing that all these things are still in God's control. I didn't tell you about these things earlier because they were mainly attacking me while I was with you. But now they will attack you.

Jesus Talks About Leaving Them

5 "Soon, I'm going back to God who sent me here—yet none of you are asking me where I'm going, or how it will affect our relationship. 6 Instead, you are feeling sorry for yourselves because of the things I've been saying. 7 But the truth is, it will be better for you when I leave because I will send the Holy Spirit to help you. If I stayed, you wouldn't have the benefit of his help. 8 When he comes, he will continue my work of convicting people of their *sin*, of the imperfection and inadequacy of their self-*righteousness*, and of God's coming *judgment* in order to bring them to repentance. 9 He will convict them of their primary sin which is not believing in me. 10 Since I'm returning to my Father and I will no longer be seen, he will be the one who will continue my work of convicting people of their inadequate righteousness—through the witness of your righteous lives. 11 And because Satan—the prince of this sinful world—will have been judged and defeated, the Spirit will convict people of their wrong judgment concerning me and convince them that God will execute his judgment on all who reject me. **B** 12 There

---

A 15:25 Literally this is "Law," but this word is sometimes used to refer to the entire Hebrew Scriptures, not just the

Torah (Pentateuch).

B 16:11 It's very difficult to determine *[Continued next page]*

are many more things that I have to tell you which you aren't able to bear hearing yet. 13 But when the Spirit of Truth comes, he will help you understand all of God's truth that he desires for you to know. He won't tell you things on his own authority, but will tell you what he hears from the Father, just as I have. He will also tell you about some events before they happen. 14 He will bring me praise and honor by revealing to you knowledge that I have. 15 Everything my Father has also belongs to me. That's why I said the Spirit will reveal to you knowledge that I have, because it all comes from my Father.

16 "In just a very short time, you won't see me. Then, a short time after that, you *will* see me again." ❖ *Given the context of verse 20, this clearly refers to his death and resurrection, as opposed to his ascension and second coming.* ➤ 17 Some of his followers asked each other, "What does he mean by, 'In just a very short time, you won't see me. Then, a short time after that, you will see me again,' and that he won't be seen 'because I'm returning to my Father?' *[John 16:10]* 18 What does 'a short time' mean? What's he talking about?" 19 Jesus knew they wanted to ask him some questions, so he said, "Are you trying to figure out the meaning of what I've just said? 20 This is very important. You will cry and grieve over what's about to happen, but others will rejoice. You will grieve for a time, but then your grief will be transformed into great joy. *[Psalm 30:11]*

21 "Your experience will be like a woman going through childbirth. During her labor she suffers great pain. But immediately after giving birth, the pain is forgotten because of her joy in seeing her new child. 22 In a similar way, you are experiencing emotional pain right now. But later, when you see me again, you will rejoice and no one will be able to steal that new-found joy from you. 23 When that time comes, you won't need to ask me about anything or for anything. But it's important for you to understand that if you ask my Father for anything with my authorization, he will give it to you. ❖ *"With my authorization" is literally "in my name." It implies that we ask on the basis of our unity with Jesus and the authority he has given his followers—and that we ask for something in line with his will. What we ask for may include information. Note that no promise is given regarding the timing of the answer.* ➤ 24 Until now, you haven't asked my Father for anything with my authorization. Go ahead and start asking for things in this way. Then, you will receive and be filled with joy. *[Matthew 7:7-8, 11; 21:22; Luke 11:9-10; John 14:13]*

25 "I've been speaking to you in somewhat cryptic terms, but the time is coming when I will be able to explain things about my Father more clearly. 26 Then, I won't need to ask my Father to help you. For he wants you to ask him directly using my authorization 27 because he loves you. And he loves you because you love me and believe that he sent me. 28 It's true that I came from my Father into this sinful world, but now I'm going to leave it and return to him."

29 Then, his followers overconfidently said, "Finally, you are speaking clearly without obscure figures! 30 Now we realize that you know everything, even what we're about to ask. This helps us believe that you came from God." 31 Jesus replied, "Yes, you think you believe this. 32 You say it, but your belief is weak. And this very night you will all be frightened for your lives and scatter, leaving me alone. *[Zechariah 13:7; Matthew 26:31]* But I won't really be alone since my Father is always with me. 33 I've been telling you all these things that will happen so that later, you can have peace knowing you are united with me. While you live in this sinful world, you will experience trials and persecution. *[Mark 10:30; John 15:18-20; Acts 14:22; 1 Thessalonians 3:3-4; 2 Timothy 3:12; 1 Peter 2:20-21]* But take courage because I've defeated every evil power, and you will experience my power sustaining you through those times because of your relationship with me."

---

the originally intended meaning of verses 8-11, and several interpretations have been proposed. This one takes a simple grammatical interpretation and adds explanations of ways in which the Spirit convicts people regarding their sin, righteousness, and judgment.

17

Jesus Prays for His Followers

1 After he was done saying these things, Jesus looked up toward Heaven in an attitude of prayer and said, "Father, the time has finally come for me to suffer and die. I ask you to reveal your glorious character of self-sacrificial love, holiness, and righteousness through me—your Son—as I carry out your will so that I will bring you great praise and honor. 2 I ask you to do this since according to your plan in eternity past, you gave me authority over all humanity so I could give eternal life to those you enable to be my people. 3 For eternal life comes from entering into a vital intimate relationship with you and with me—the Messiah you sent to them. This relationship with us happens through their belief in the revelatory knowledge we've given them, and through their response of loving obedience. 4 I've revealed the glory of your character here on earth in doing everything you have given me to do, and so I've brought you great praise. 5 Now, Father, I ask you to accomplish your plan and then bring me into your presence, restoring to me the fullness of the glory I had with you from eternity past—which I temporarily laid aside in coming to this world. [Hebrews 2:9] ❖ Inherent in Jesus' thinking is that the path back into the Father's presence and the full restoration of his glory as the eternal Son of God is through his death and resurrection. ➤

6 "I've revealed your true character to those you separated from the unbelievers in this sinful world and then gave to me. They were your people and you have given them to me. ❖ The Father "gives" believers to his Son in the sense that they are to become his eternal human companions. They also still belong to the Father as his children. ➤ And they've responded to your message with obedience. 7 Now they've come to realize that everything I say, do, and have comes directly from you. 8 I passed on your teachings to them and they've welcomed them. They really believe that I come from you, and that it was you who sent me to earth.

9 "Now, it's for them that I'm making my requests. I'm not asking on behalf of the unbelievers in this world, but on behalf of those you have given to me because they are your own people. 10 For everything I have belongs to you and everything that is yours belongs to me too. And the glory of my character has been revealed through them to others as well. 11 I'm going to be returning to you and will no longer be in this world, but they will remain here for a while. So, Holy Father, I'm asking you to keep them united with your holy and loving character ❖ literally: keep them in your name ➤—the same character you have given me—so they may be united as one just as we are one. ❖ The other possible interpretation of "in your name" is given in most translations as "safe by the power of your name." ➤ 12 While I've been with them, I've kept them united with your character which you've given me and guarded their faith. None of them have fallen into unbelief except Judas, the one destined to experience eternal ruin in Hell so the prophecy in Scripture about him would be fulfilled. [Psalm 41:9; John 13:18] ❖ The particular phrase Jesus used to refer to Judas, literally, the "son of perdition" (or destruction), seems to indicate he is a type of the Anti-messiah. [2 Thessalonians 2:3; 1 John 2:18, 22; 4:3; 2 John 7] In Revelation, the Anti-messiah is called "the beast." [Revelation chapters 13, 17; 19:19-20] ➤

13 "But now I'm returning to you and I've said these things to my followers this evening so they may be filled with the same joy that I have in serving you. [John 15:11] 14 I've passed on your message to them and they've believed it. So now the unbelievers of this world hate them, for my followers are no longer any more a part of this sinful world than I am. ❖ To believe God's message involves presenting the truth about Jesus, exposing evil, and requiring surrender and obedience to him. Unbelievers who continue to reject the truth hate and rage at this message and at its messengers. ➤ 15 I'm not asking that you to take them out of this world yet, but that you keep their faith safe from destruction by the Evil One. ❖ Many commentators interpret this as a request to keep them safe from Satan's power. Yet other Scriptures clearly indicate that believers will be persecuted and even die at the hands of Satan's agents. [Matthew 5:10-11, 44; 10:22-23; 24:9; Mark 10:30; Luke 21:12; John 15:20; Acts 5:41; 8:1-3; 9:16; Romans 5:3-4; 8:17-18; 35-36; 12:14; 1 Corinthians 4:12-13; 2 Corinthians 1:5-10; 4:8-11;

11:23-27; 12:9-10; Philippians 1:29; 3:10; 1 Thessalonians 1:6; 2:14; 3:3-4; 2 Thessalonians 1:4-5; 2 Timothy 1:8; 3:12; Hebrews 10:32-33; James 1:2-3, 12; 1 Peter 1:6; 2:19-21; 4:1; 12-19; 5:9-10; Revelation 1:9; 2:10; 3:10] His request is most likely for the protection of their faith, to keep them from apostasy (i.e., denying their faith). ➤ **16** For like me, they don't belong to this world or to the one who rules it. *[John 12:31; 14:30; 16:11]* **17** Set them apart and consecrate them to serve you exclusively. Purify them and equip them for this service by transforming them to think and live in conformity to your truth and revelation—which is the truth of your Word. ❖ *The "Word" here is the Scriptures [Psalm 119:142] and Jesus himself—the "Word of God." [John 1:1-4, 14] Jesus and his teachings are the clearest and most complete revelation of God's truth. [John 1:18; 14:6-7; Colossians 2:9; Hebrews 1:2] The Word sanctifies (makes us holy) and transforms us through our minds as we meditate upon it and believe it and live by it. [Romans 12:1-2]* ➤ **18** Just as you sent me into this sinful world to reveal your truth about sin, death, the only way to be saved, and to bring people into your Kingdom, in the same way, I'm sending them out with the same message and mission. **19** I'm consecrating myself to do your will and thereby redeem them, so that they will be able to consecrate themselves to do your will, through the transforming power of your truth.

20 "And I'm not asking these things just for these men with me right now, but also for all those who will later come to believe in me through the message they will preach. **21** Father, I ask that you would make them all united in faith, purpose, love, and action, just like you and I are united. I ask that they may be joined spiritually as one, in union with us, so that we may be seen in their lives, and the people of this world will be convinced that you really sent me and that we live in them. **22** Your glorious loving and righteous character which you've given me, I've also given to them so they can be united just like we are. **23** I live in them and you live in me, so they can be brought into perfect unity with us. As a result of that unity, the people of this world will have to realize that you sent me and that you love my followers just like you love me. **24** Father, it's my desire that the people you've given me will

eventually be with me in Heaven, so they can see the glorious splendor you've given me because you loved me, even before anything was created. *[John 17:5; 1 John 3:2]*

25 "Righteous Father, even though the unbelievers in this world don't know you, I know you and my people know that you sent me. **26** So I've enabled them to know you and your loving character too; and I will continue to enable others to know you, that is, those who will believe in me later. Because I want them all to experience the great love you have for me—as it lives in them. And I want to live in them too." *[John 14:23; Galatians 2:20; Colossians 1:27]*

18

Jesus Is Arrested

1 When Jesus finished praying, he and his followers left Jerusalem going east, crossed the Kidron Valley and went up Mount Olivet into a grove of olive trees. ❖ *This place is commonly known as the Garden of Gethsemane.* ➤ **2** Now Judas—who had left to betray Jesus—was familiar with that place, for Jesus often met there with his followers. **3** So Judas went to the grove, leading part of a cohort of soldiers and officials from the chief priests and Pharisees. They came with lanterns, torches, and weapons. ❖ *Many commentators interpret "cohort" to indicate a cohort of Roman soldiers. However, the same term was used for Jewish soldiers of the Temple guard. It's unlikely that they were Roman troops since they were under the command of Jewish leaders and took Jesus to the High Priest.* ➤ **4** Jesus already knew everything that was going to happen to him. So he went up to them and asked, "Who are you looking for?" **5** Judas, who had betrayed him, was standing there with them. They replied, "Jesus of Nazareth." He said, "*I am* he." ❖ *Jesus literally answered, "I am," which in Greek means "I am he" but is also God's name "Yahweh" which he revealed to Moses in Exodus 3:14.* ➤ **6** When he said this, they all stepped back and fell to the ground. ❖ *Jesus was clearly in charge of the situation. [Matthew 26:53]* ➤ **7** Jesus asked them again, "Who are you looking for?" Again they replied, "Jesus of Nazareth." **8** Jesus said, "I've told you that I am he. So if it's me you want, let these others go free." ❖ *Even though John doesn't mention it, this request is granted and none of his followers are arrested.* ➤ 9 He said this to fulfill the prophecy he had made in his prayer that none of his people would be lost. *[John 17:12]* ❖ *The literal phrasing of Jesus' statement in 17:12 was that none of his people would "be lost." The emphasis in 17:12 was on their eternal salvation, but here John focuses on a different aspect of its meaning. Their being saved from arrest and possible death is a picture of their spiritual salvation.* ➤ 10 Now Simon Peter had a sword, so he drew it and struck at Malchus—the High Priest's slave—cutting off his right ear. ❖ *A slave of Malchus' position had considerable status and authority.* ➤ 11 But Jesus said to Peter, "Put away your sword! I must go through with this because it's my Father's will for me." *[Matthew 26:52-54]* ❖ *Literally, he said, "Shall I not drink the cup which my Father has given me?" To drink a cup implied receiving blessings [1 Corinthians 10:16] or suffering. He knew this was a cup of suffering. [Matthew 26:39; Mark 14:36; Luke 22:42] From Luke 22:49-51 we know that he also healed Malchus' ear. When his followers realized that Jesus did not intend to resist, most of them ran away, but Peter and John followed. [Matthew 26:56-58; Mark 14:50-54; Luke 22:54; John 18:15]* ➤

12 Then, the soldiers and the commander and Jewish officers arrested Jesus and tied him so he couldn't escape. 13 They took him to Annas, the father-in-law of Caiaphas who was High Priest that year. ❖ *Annas had been High Priest previously but had been deposed by Pilate's predecessor in AD 15. Yet he continued to wield a lot of influence and power in Jewish religious politics and appears to take precedence over Caiaphas. According to the Teachings of Moses, a High Priest was appointed for life so most Jews still considered him to be the true High Priest, even though the Romans did not.* ➤ 14 It was Caiaphas who had advised the Jewish leaders that it would be expedient for one man to die for the people so the whole nation wouldn't be destroyed. *[John 11:50]*

Peter Denies Knowing Jesus

15 Peter and John followed at a distance behind those who had arrested Jesus. John knew Annas—the former High Priest—so he was allowed to enter the courtyard of his house along with Jesus, ❖ *John modestly never mentions himself by name in his gospel, yet tradition says he was writing about himself in this way. Some modern commentators have disputed this on the basis that a fisherman* wouldn't have connections with a High Priest. But there's no conclusive reason to reject this interpretation. ➤ 16 but Peter waited outside the gate. So John—who was known in the household—came back and spoke to the woman in charge of the gate, and she allowed Peter in too. 17 The woman who was the gatekeeper said to Peter, "Aren't you one of Jesus' followers too?" Peter replied, "No, I'm not." 18 Now, it was cold and the servants and guards were warming themselves around a charcoal fire, so Peter joined them.

Jesus Is Questioned by Annas

19 Inside the house, Annas—the former High Priest—questioned Jesus about his followers and what he had taught them. ❖ *He was concerned about the likelihood—in his mind—that Jesus' followers would revolt against the Romans and also about Jesus' theology, out of concern that he was leading Jews astray.* ➤ 20 Jesus answered him, "I've always spoken publicly for all to hear and I've said nothing in private that's different from what I've taught openly. All my teachings have been presented in synagogues and in the Temple court. 21 Why are you questioning me? Ask those who have listened to me. They know what I've said." ❖ *Even though this interview was not yet a formal trial, it was the normal legal practice of the time to question witnesses rather than the accused. And witnesses in defense were heard before witnesses against the accused. So Jesus may have been asking for a proper trial or questioning the propriety of his being questioned.* ➤ 22 When he said this, one of the guards standing near him backhanded him across the face saying, "Is that the proper way to answer the High Priest?" ❖ *It was against Jewish Law to strike a prisoner.* ➤ 23 Jesus replied, "If I've said anything wrong, tell us what it was. But if I've spoken the truth, why do you strike me?" ❖ *Some commentators think Jesus' reply was to the High Priest, and that the guard wouldn't have struck him without the High Priest's prompting.* ➤ 24 Then Annas sent him to Caiaphas—the official High Priest—still bound.

Peter's Second and Third Denials

25 While Peter was warming himself by the fire, some of the people there asked him, "Aren't you one of Jesus' followers too?" But again he said, "No, I am not!"

26 Then, one of the High Priest's servants—a relative of Malchus whose ear Peter had cut off—said, "Didn't I see you in the olive grove with Jesus?" 27 But Peter again denied it, and immediately he heard a rooster crow. [John 13:38]

Jesus Is Taken Before Pilate

28 Very early in the morning, after the Sanhedrin had met, they took him from Caiaphas to the palace being used by the Roman governor in Jerusalem. They didn't enter the palace proper so they wouldn't be ritually defiled and could continue to participate in all the Passover feasts. ❖ *Jews who entered the house of a Gentile would be ritually unclean and unable to participate in religious observances for at least a day, possibly for a week. Jesus had already eaten the main Passover meal the evening before—which by Jewish reckoning, was the same day because Jewish days begin at sundown. Some see a discrepancy here with John's referring to the Jewish leaders wanting to eat the Passover. There are several possible solutions to this apparent discrepancy. One is that different Jewish groups calculated the beginning of the month differently and ate the Passover on different days. Another is in how you interpret John's phrase. Since the Passover was the beginning of an eight-day festival, "eat the Passover" could simply be a general way of referring to another feast to be eaten later that same day and to the other feasts during the festival, rather than referring exclusively to the primary first meal that took place in the evening at the beginning of the "day" when Jesus ate it. Other solutions are possible too. There's no need to assume that a discrepancy of historical detail exists in the text.* ➤ 29 So Pilate—the Roman governor—went outside to meet them and asked, "What are the charges you are bringing against this man?" ❖ *Pilate was Prefect of Judea from AD 26–37 and had been appointed by the Roman Emperor, Tiberius Caesar. From non-biblical sources, historians say that he was morally weak and exhibited stubbornness and savage brutality in dealing with the Jews. The Jews loathed him. Pilate asked this question since formal charges were required for the Roman governor to hear a case.* ➤ 30 The Jewish leaders replied, "If he weren't a criminal, we wouldn't have brought him to you." ❖ *Frank Morison—in his book "Who Moved The Stone"—convincingly argues that this interaction implies there had been a prior arrangement between the Jewish leaders and Pilate to execute Jesus without a formal trial, since the leaders seem annoyed that Pilate doesn't just take him without their stating charges. Since Pilate* *didn't get along with the Jewish authorities and was known to change his mind, this is entirely possible.* ➤ 31 Pilate replied, "Then, take him and try him according to your own laws." The Jewish leaders answered, "But we're not allowed to put him to death." ❖ *Jewish law allowed death by stoning, but the Romans didn't allow subservient governments to issue death sentences. Only a Roman court could try capital cases. Pilate undoubtedly knew what they wanted, but was giving them a hard time.* ➤ 32 This happened in fulfillment of Jesus' prophecy about how he would die. [Matthew 20:19; John 12:32-34] ❖ *Being "lifted up" in Jesus' prophecy in John 12:32-34 referred to crucifixion—the Roman method of execution.* ➤

33 Pilate went back inside the palace and summoned Jesus for questioning. He asked, "Are you King of the Jews?" ❖ *Luke records in Luke 23:1-2 that the Jewish leaders formally accused Jesus of claiming to be the Messiah—who is a king. They knew that Roman law wasn't interested in their religious disputes, but the accusation of his claiming kingship was an accusation of treason against the Roman emperor.* ➤ 34 Jesus replied, "Did others accuse me of this, or are you asking for reasons of your own?" ❖ *The way he would answer Pilate would depend on why he asked the question. Was he asking if Jesus was a political rival to the emperor, or was he asking about the nature of Jesus' spiritual authority as the Messiah?* ➤ 35 Pilate retorted, "Do you think I'm a Jew and know or care about these things? It's your own people who've handed you over to me and brought this charge! What have you done that they want to kill you?" ❖ *Pilate suspected the motives of Jewish leaders who handed over a Jew they claimed was a rival to the emperor, since he knew they hated being under Roman rule.* ➤ 36 Jesus answered, "My Kingdom is not someplace in this world in rival to the emperor. If I were such a king, then my followers would have fought to prevent my arrest. But my authority doesn't originate in this world." 37 Pilate said, "So you are a king, then." Jesus replied, "You are the one calling me a king. Yes, I'm a king, but not in the way you think. I came into this world for one purpose—which is to reveal what is absolutely true. Those who really want to know about absolute truth are the ones who listen to me and follow me." 38 Pilate cynically retorted, "What is truth?" ❖ *Jesus' reply in verse 37 probably classified him as a harmless philosopher in Pilate's mind. He wasn't interested in hearing*

about truth and was convinced that the charge against him was false—by Roman standards. ➤ Then, he went outside again and told the Jewish leaders, "I find him innocent of the charge. 39 There's a tradition that at Passover I should release one prisoner to you. Shall I release 'the King of the Jews?' " ❖ *If Pilate had any moral integrity, he would have released Jesus after finding him innocent. His question was designed to taunt the Jewish leaders, yet not antagonize them too much.* ➤ 40 The Jewish leaders shouted their reply, "Not him, but Barabbas!" Now Barabbas was an insurrectionist. ❖ *Pilate would have noted the irony of their reply. They falsely accused Jesus of being a threat to Rome, then demand the release of a known enemy of Rome. It may have been their way of sneering back at Pilate without risk of reprisal.* ➤

19

1 Then Pilate ordered that Jesus be whipped. ❖ *The whip used for non-Romans was a multi-stranded leather whip called a flagellum—with pieces of bone or metal embedded in the strands. Romans had three levels of flogging: 1) the fustigatio—the least severe of the three—given for small offenses, 2) the flagellatio—a severe flogging given to criminals for serious offenses, 3) the verberatio—the most severe scourging—often given before crucifixion. In the verberatio, the flogging continued until the soldiers doing it grew tired. Sometimes the result of such a flogging was death or bare bones protruding from the ripped flesh. Examining all the gospel accounts, it seems likely that Jesus was flogged twice. This one was likely either the fustigatio or the flagellatio, designed to appease the Jewish leaders without the death penalty. Later, after he was sentenced to death, (as in Matthew and Mark's gospels) he was also subjected to the verberatio before being crucified.* ➤ 2 The soldiers wove some thorn branches together, making a mock wreath crown as vassal kings wore. They put it on Jesus' head and also put a purple robe on him. ❖ *Matthew's gospel says the robe was scarlet. Purple dye was very expensive and only worn by high-ranking rulers. It's unlikely the soldiers had access to such a robe, unless it was the one sent with Jesus from Herod. [Luke 23:11] It may have been an old worn scarlet lictor's cloak whose faded or darkened color resembled purple at a distance.* ➤ 3 Then they mocked him by saying, "Hail, King of the Jews!" and then striking him in the face. ❖ *Note the irony. He was the rightful King.* ➤

4 Pilate went outside to the crowd again and said, "Look, I'm bringing him out to you but I haven't found him guilty of any capital crime!" 5 When Jesus was brought out—wearing the crown of thorns and the purple robe—Pilate announced, "Here's the man!" ❖ *He was presenting him as an apparently harmless and pathetic figure, hoping the crowd would take pity on him. But he was indeed "The Man" sent from God, displaying the glory of God's self-sacrificial loving character in the midst of this humiliation.* ➤ 6 But when the chief priests and Jewish officials saw him, they yelled, "Crucify him! Crucify him!" Pilate taunted them, "You take him and crucify him yourselves! You brought him to me, and I find him innocent!" ❖ *Pilate knew that they dared not take him and kill him themselves.* ➤ 7 Expressing their frustration, the Jewish leaders replied, "According to the teachings in our Torah he must die because he claims to be God's Son!" *[Leviticus 24:16]* 8 When Pilate heard this, he became afraid. ❖ *Most Romans believed in many gods, and he had just ordered Jesus whipped. He would be even more reluctant to execute him if Jesus was possibly divine.* ➤ 9 He went back inside the palace and ask Jesus, "Where do you really come from?" But Jesus didn't answer. 10 In irritation, Pilate exclaimed, "Why won't you answer me? Don't you see I have the power to release you or crucify you?" 11 Jesus replied, "Your having the power to make that decision about me wouldn't have arisen if God hadn't allowed it. That's why Caiaphas—who decided to hand me over to you for execution—is guilty of a greater sin than you are."

12 When Pilate heard this, he tried to find a way to set him free. But the Jewish leaders shouted, "If you release this man, you are no friend of Caesar! Anyone who claims to be a king is Caesar's enemy!" ❖ *This was a serious threat. If Pilate refused to crucify Jesus, he knew they would send a delegation to the emperor complaining about him—as they had done in the past—to accuse him of protecting a rival king. Tiberius Caesar was paranoid about rivals and would certainly have Pilate executed.* ➤ 13 When Pilate heard their threat, he had Jesus brought outside and then sat on the judgment seat to pass sentence. This was in a place called the "Stone Pavement"—or *"Gabbatha"* in Aramaic. 14 It was about midday on Friday—

the day of preparation for the Sabbath.
❖ *The text literally says "the preparation day," and to specify "for the Sabbath" or "for Passover" is interpretation. Specifying Friday preserves the usual use of the term "preparation day" and doesn't conflict with the day of crucifixion as told in the synoptic gospels. ¶ John specifies the time of sentencing as "about the sixth hour" and Mark 15:25 specifies the time of crucifixion as "the third hour." One commentary says the Jews of that time divided the day into four "hours" and the night into four "watches." The "third hour" meant the period from midmorning till noon. The "sixth hour" meant the period from noon till midafternoon. If it was a little before noon, it could legitimately be said to still be "the third hour" or "about the sixth hour." Luke 23:44 also places the start of the crucifixion at "about the sixth hour." Understand that no clocks existed, and if the sky was overcast, any estimation of the time would be an imprecise guess. It was likely late in the morning given all the events that took place, including Jesus' side trip to see King Herod as related in Luke's account.* ➤ Pilate taunted the Jewish leaders by proclaiming, "Here is your king!" 15 But they shouted, "Away with him! Crucify him!" Pilate responded, "You want me to crucify your king?" The chief priests replied, "The only king we have is Caesar!" ❖ *Jews of that time prayed daily for the Messiah to come and be their king and overthrow Roman rule. Pilate knew their claim was an expedient lie. But it was also blasphemy because it was an explicit rejection of God as their king. The Hebrew Scriptures clearly proclaimed that God was the only true King of Israel. [e.g. Judges 8:23; 1 Samuel 8:7]* ➤ 16 Then, Pilate gave in and handed Jesus over to be subject to their will by sentencing him to be crucified.

The Crucifixion

17 Some soldiers took charge of Jesus and he was led out of the city carrying on his back the crossbeam of the cross on which he would be executed. ❖ *The synoptic gospels (i.e., Matthew, Mark, and Luke) record that Simon of Cyrene was forced to carry the crossbeam from the city gate to the execution site because Jesus was too weak from his beatings. While scholars are sure this happened, the incident doesn't fit with John's main themes so he omitted it. The gospel writers each had specific messages they were trying to communicate and chose the details they included accordingly. The kind of detailed chronological historical account most modern readers would like to see was not their goal. To read a more complete account of Jesus' arrest, trial, execution and resurrection which combines all of the details from all the Gospels, read the Gospel Harmony sections 217-236.* ➤ They went to

the place of execution called the "skull"—which in Aramaic is *"Golgotha."* ❖ *In Latin, it is "calvaria" from which "Calvary" is derived. Many think the name was because of the hill's physical resemblance to a skull, but no one knows for certain.* ➤ 18 There, they crucified him and two other men with him—one on each side and Jesus in the middle. ❖ *Crucifixion was a prolonged, agonizing, and shameful death. Usually, people were stripped naked before being crucified. And Jews considered anyone who hung on a "tree"—which includes a stake, post, or cross—to be under God's curse. [Deuteronomy 21:22-23; Galatians 3:13]* ➤ 19 As was the custom, Pilate had a sign made and hung over Jesus which publicly proclaimed his crime. Jesus' read,

"Jesus of Nazareth, King of the Jews."

20 The place of execution was near the city so many people could see and read the sign which was written in three languages: Aramaic—the common language of Judea; Latin—the language of Rome and the army; and Greek—the language of wider communication throughout the Roman empire. ❖ *Any literate person in Jerusalem could read at least one of these languages.* ➤ 21 The chief priests protested to Pilate, "Don't allow it to say, 'King of the Jews,' but that he claimed to be King of the Jews!" ❖ *Pilate phrased the accusation as if Jesus were King of the Jews and therefore a traitor to the emperor. He did this mainly to humiliate the Jewish leaders by proclaiming the Jewish King—and hence Jewish sovereignty—to be powerless under Roman rule. But in doing so, he publicly proclaimed the truth of Jesus' kingship without realizing its truth.* ➤ 22 But Pilate—enjoying their frustration—said, "What I've already written, stands!"

23 After the soldiers had crucified Jesus, they divided his outer clothing among the four of them. ❖ *Roman law gave the clothing of those executed to the executioners.* ➤ But his long tunic undergarment was woven in one piece without any seams. 24 So they said, "Let's not tear it, but cast lots to determine who gets it." ❖ *Casting lots was a means of gambling, similar to casting dice, but probably used small stones or broken pieces of pottery.* ➤ This fulfilled the prophecy in Scripture that reads, **"They divided my garments among them, casting lots for my clothing."** [Psalm 22:18]

25 Standing near Jesus' cross were four women—his mother, his mother's sister, Mary the wife of Clopas, and Mary of Magdala village. ❖ *Comparing the list of names in the four gospels, it's traditionally concluded that Jesus' aunt was Salome—the wife of Zebedee and the mother of James and John. There are good reasons for thinking this identification is probably correct, but it can't be known for certain since Mark's gospel says there were many other women who had come up to Jerusalem with him that were there too.* ➤ 26 When Jesus saw his mother and John—his close friend ❖ *who was probably also his cousin* ➤—standing there, he said to his mother, "Mother, he will be as a son to you." 27 Then he said to John, "She is to be as a mother to you." So from that day on, John took her care of her in his own home.

Jesus' Death

28 After this, when Jesus knew that he had accomplished everything his Father had sent him to do, he fulfilled one last prophecy from Scripture by saying, "I'm thirsty." *[Psalm 69:21; 22:15]* 29 The soldiers had a jar of cheap wine there, ❖ *their own drink* ➤ so they put a sponge soaked with the cheap wine on a hyssop stalk and elevated it to Jesus' mouth. ❖ *This "act of mercy" would—under normal circumstances—actually prolong his life and suffering, hence their willingness to give it.* ➤ 30 When he had sucked some of the wine, Jesus said, "It is finished!" ❖ *This refers to his accomplishing the work of redemption assigned to him by his Father.* ➤ Then he bowed his head, handed over his spirit to his Father, and died. ❖ *When the spirit of a man is separated from the body, the body dies. Jesus was not killed. He surrendered his spirit to his Father and died, in full control of the situation. [John 10:17-18]*

31 Since it was Friday—the preparation day for the Sabbath during the Passover festival—the Jewish leaders didn't want bodies left hanging on the crosses when the Sabbath began at sunset. So they asked Pilate to have the legs of the men on the crosses broken to speed their deaths. They wanted the bodies removed and buried before sunset. *[Deuteronomy 21:23]* ❖ *Normally, a person crucified would suffer agony on the cross for several days, but with his legs broken, he would quickly suffocate since it was only possible to breathe by painfully elevating the body with the legs.* ➤ 32 Pilate gave the order, and soldiers went to break the legs of the two men crucified on both sides of Jesus. 33 But when they reached Jesus, they saw that he was already dead so they didn't bother to break his legs. 34 But to be sure he was dead, one of the soldiers stabbed a spear into Jesus' side, and immediately blood and water flowed out. ❖ *The water would be the clear blood plasma that results when the red blood cells settle and separate from it after death. If Jesus had still been alive, then normal red blood without the clear plasma would have flowed out.* ➤ 35 I, John, was an eyewitness to these things and report them to you so you can believe they are true. 36 It happened this way to fulfill the prophecy in Scripture that says, "**None of his bones will be broken.**" *[Psalm 34:20]* ❖ *The Passover lamb was a "type" of the Messiah, and in preparing the Passover lamb, none of its bones were allowed to be broken. [Exodus 12:46; Numbers 9:12; Psalm 34:20]* ➤ 37 And another prophecy says, "**They will look at me—at him whom they pierced.**" *[Zechariah 12:10; Revelation 1:7]*

Jesus' Burial

38 Joseph from Arimathea village—a member of the Sanhedrin *[Mark 15:43]*—believed Jesus was the Messiah but had kept his belief secret out of fear of the other leaders. However, after Jesus' death, he daringly asked Pilate for permission to take Jesus' body down from the cross to bury it—and Pilate granted his request. ❖ *Crucified criminals were usually buried in a common grave. Asking for permission to bury Jesus was effectively a public declaration of his love for Jesus that the Jewish leaders would resent. This act would endanger his standing as a Sanhedrin member.* ➤ So Joseph went and took the body, 39 aided by Nicodemus—the same one who had visited Jesus at night. *[John 3:1]* Nicodemus and his servants brought about 75 pounds of burial spices—a mixture of myrrh and aloes. ❖ *This was to pack around the body to cover the stench of decay. The amount was lavish and expensive. Myrrh was an aromatic resin used in powdered form, and aloes was a powder made from aromatic sandalwood.* ➤ 40 They wrapped Jesus' body with the spices in wide strips of linen, following Jewish burial custom. 41 Near the place of crucifixion was a new unused tomb in a garden. ❖ *Tombs were often used for more than one burial.* ➤ 42 Since it was nearly sunset when the Sabbath would begin, they were in a hurry and put Jesus' body in this tomb because it was so close. ❖ *The tomb belonged to Joseph. [Matthew 27:59-60]* ➤

20

God Makes Jesus Alive Again

1 Shortly before sunrise on Sunday morning, Mary of Magdala village went out to the tomb with some other women and discovered that the stone which sealed the entrance had already been rolled away. ❖ *It would be natural that Mary didn't come alone, even though the text doesn't say this explicitly. It is inferred from the "we" in the next verse and from the other gospel accounts. [Matthew 27:61; Mark 15:47—16:1; Luke 23:55—24:1] From the other accounts, we learn that they had seen where Jesus was buried but evidently didn't know that Joseph and Nicodemus had already wrapped the body with spices, since this was their purpose in going to the tomb. The other accounts also say it was at dawn when they were on their way and arrived at the tomb. It is likely that they set out before dawn, and dawn happened while they were on their way.* ➤ 2 So she ran ahead of the other women ❖ *being younger than the others* ➤ to Simon Peter and John and told them, "Someone has removed the Lord's body from the tomb where it was buried, and we don't know where they've taken it!" 3 So Peter and John hurried to the tomb to see for themselves. 4 They both ran, but John got there first. 5 He bent over to look inside the tomb and saw the linen cloths lying there that had been wrapped around the body. But he didn't go in. 6 Then Peter arrived and ducked inside the entrance. He also saw the linen cloths lying there 7 and the cloth that had been around his head which was rolled up and lying separately from the linen strips. 8 Then John went inside too and saw these same things and believed that Jesus had risen from death. ❖ *Thieves would not have left the linen wrappings with the spices, as they were valuable. The same would be true of someone merely moving the body. There could be no logical reason for removing the wrappings from a corpse and leaving them behind.* ➤ 9 But even then, they didn't understand that the Scriptures said it was necessary for the Messiah to die and rise again. 10 Then they returned to where they were staying in the city.

Jesus Appears to Mary of Magdala

11 But Mary—who had returned to the tomb—stood outside it crying. While she was crying, she bent over to look inside 12 and saw two angels clothed in white, one sitting at the head and one at the foot of where Jesus' body had been. 13 They asked her, "Miss, why are you crying?" She replied, "Someone has taken my Lord's body and I don't know what they've done with it!" 14 Turning around, she saw a man standing there but didn't recognize him as Jesus. 15 Jesus asked her, "Miss, why are you crying? Are you looking for someone?" Mary assumed that he was a gardener and said, "Sir, if you took him away, please tell me where you've put him and I will go take him to be properly buried!" 16 Jesus said, "Mary!" *[John 10:3-4]* She turned, and realizing it was Jesus, said in Aramaic, *"Rabboni!"*—which means "my teacher." 17 Jesus told her, "You don't need to keep clinging to me because I'm not returning to my Father yet. But go to my brothers ❖ *i.e., his followers* ➤ and tell them I said, 'I'm ascending to my Father and God, who is also your Father and God.' " ❖ *There are many interpretations offered for verse 17. One explanation for his telling Mary not to cling to him is presented, i.e., it isn't necessary to hold onto him because he isn't about to permanently disappear yet. He will be around for a while. It is debated as to whether or not his "ascending" meant that he was ascending that very day, to later return, or whether he meant he was in the process of ascending during the 40 days after the resurrection. To find out about all the interpretations offered, you will need to consult various commentaries.* ➤ 18 So Mary went to his followers and said, "I've seen the Lord, and he is alive!" Then she told them what he said to her.

Jesus Appears to His Followers

19 Late in the afternoon A of that same Sunday, many of Jesus' close followers were in a house behind locked doors because they were afraid the Jewish leaders might still be searching to arrest them. Suddenly, Jesus

---

A 20:19 The text literally says that it was "evening of that day, the first day of the week." Jewish days begin at sundown, so sundown would have been Monday, the second day of the week. Hence the interpretation that it was "late afternoon"—which is how we would express it.

appeared standing among them and said, "I bless you with shalom!" ❖ *This was the standard Jewish greeting and undoubtedly given in Aramaic using the word "shalom." See the note at John 14:27 about its meaning.* ➤ 20 Then, he showed them the scars of the wounds in his arms and side and his followers rejoiced at the confirmation that he was their Lord. ❖ *The location of the scars in his "hands" was most likely in his arms near his wrists. The human hand or wrist with a nail through it couldn't support much weight. The Greek and Aramaic words for "hand" (as in many languages) include the wrist and forearm.* ➤ 21 Then Jesus said to them, "Peace be with you! I'm sending you to minister to the people of this world in the same way that my Father sent me to minister to them." ❖ *Jesus' ministry of preaching, teaching, healing, concern for the poor, dependency on his Father, etc., was a model for his followers to follow in their ministry.* ➤ 22 Then he breathed on them and said, "Receive the Holy Spirit. *[Genesis 2:7; Ezekiel 37:9]* ❖ *There are many interpretations of this verse. You can consult various commentaries for them. A Pentecostal and Charismatic interpretation (which I give because it's not commonly found in commentaries) is that this was when Jesus' followers were "born again" [John 3:3] and received the indwelling Holy Spirit. On Pentecost, what they received was the "gift of the Holy Spirit"—also called the "baptism in the Holy Spirit"—which is his empowering for ministry and is different from his indwelling ministry. However, many believe there is no separate "baptism of the Holy Spirit" that is distinct from the indwelling of the Spirit received at the time of conversion.* ➤ 23 If you forgive someone, then God has forgiven their sins too. If you withhold forgiveness from someone, then God also withholds his forgiveness." ❖ *This verse also has many interpretations, which you can investigate in commentaries. Some denominations restrict this authority to ordained clergy. This assumes—as with all other promises made concerning the exercise of Jesus' authority and power—that everything is being done in line with God's will. No major denominational group has ever interpreted this verse to mean that we can forgive anyone and thus save them, even if they reject Jesus and refuse to admit or repent of their sin. The interpretation of this verse is often tied to Matthew 16:19 and 18:18.* ➤

Thomas' Response to the Resurrection

24 Now Thomas—one of the original twelve apostles who was nicknamed "Twin"—was not with the other followers when Jesus appeared to them on that first Sunday. 25 When the others told him, "We've seen the Lord and he is alive!" he said, "I refuse to believe it! The only thing that could convince me is to see the scars of the nail prints in his arms and actually feel them with my finger and to put my hand into the wound in his side to feel its reality." ❖ *He believed it was possible to see a non-material apparition or hallucination that was deceiving the others, but that such things could not be touched and handled.* ➤

26 On the next Sunday, Jesus' followers were again together in the same house behind locked doors—as they had been when Jesus first appeared to them—and this time Thomas was with them. Once again, Jesus suddenly appeared standing among them and said, "I bless you with shalom!" 27 Then speaking to Thomas, he said, "See my arms. Come and touch the scars with your fingers. Come and feel the wound in my side. Then stop exercising your unbelief and believe that I really have physically come back to life!" 28 Thomas, in awe, exclaimed, "You are my Lord, and now I know that you are also my God!" 29 Jesus said, "You believe I'm alive because you've seen me. But God will accept and bless all those who believe the same, even though they haven't seen me."

John's Purpose in Writing This Gospel

30 Jesus' followers saw him perform many other miraculous signs that aren't recorded in this book. *[John 21:25]* 31 But I've recorded these so you may come to believe that Jesus really is the Messiah—God's Son—and gain eternal life by trusting in him.

21

Jesus Appears to His Followers at Lake Galilee

1 Some days later, Jesus once again appeared to some of his followers on the shore of Lake Tiberius. *[Mark 14:28; 16:7]* Here's the story. ❖ *See the note at John 6:1 about Lake Tiberius.* ➤ 2 Simon Peter, Thomas (known as the "Twin"), Nathanael from Cana in Galilee, ❖ *See the footnote at John 1:45.* ➤ James and John (the sons of Zebedee), and two other followers were together.

3 Peter said to the others, "I'm going fishing." They all replied, "We'll come with you."

So they went out in a boat to do some net fishing that night but didn't catch a single fish. *[Luke 5:5]* 4 At daybreak, Jesus was standing on the shore but his followers didn't recognize who he was. 5 He called out to them, "Hey guys! Haven't you caught anything?" They called back, "Nothing!" 6 Then he said, "Cast your net on the right side of the boat and you will get some!" So they did, and the net became so heavy with fish that they couldn't haul it into the boat. *[Luke 5:6]*

7 Then John said to Peter, "It's the Lord!" When Peter heard this, he wrapped his outer garment around his waist—for he didn't wear it while he worked—dove into the water and swam to Jesus. 8 The others followed in the boat, dragging the net full of fish. They were only about 100 yards from shore. 9 When they came ashore, they saw a charcoal fire with some fish already cooking and some bread. 10 Jesus told them, "Bring some of your catch." 11 Peter went back up into the boat to help drag the net ashore. It wasn't torn, even though it contained 153 large fish. ❖ *Many commentators speculate on possible symbolic meanings of this number, but none is necessary.* ➤ 12 Then Jesus said, "Come and have some breakfast." None of the men dared ask him who he was because they knew he was their Lord. 13 Then Jesus took the bread and divided it among them and did the same with the fish he had cooked. 14 This was the third time that Jesus appeared to a group of his followers after his resurrection.

15 When they had finished eating, Jesus said, "Simon, son of John, do you love me more than these other followers do?" Peter replied, "Yes Lord, you know that I love you." Jesus then said, "Then take care of my lambs." ❖ *Lambs and sheep are figures representing Jesus' followers.* ➤ 16 Then, Jesus asked him a second time, "Simon, son of John, do you love me?" Peter replied, "Yes Lord, you know that I love you." Jesus said, "Then watch over my sheep." 17 A third time Jesus asked, "Simon, son of John, do you love me?" Peter was grieved because he asked the same thing a third time. He said, "Lord, you know everything, so you must know that I love you!" Jesus told him a third time, "Then take care of my sheep. ❖ *Some*

commentators have speculated that there's a difference in meaning between the two different Greek words for "love" used in these verses. But there are good arguments that John simply used them for stylistic variation with no difference in meaning. It's also unlikely that Jesus conversed with Peter in Greek. They probably used Aramaic among themselves. Jesus asked Peter the same question three times because of Peter's three denials [John 18:15-18; 18:25-27] to help him understand that he forgave and accepted Peter and still considered him a leader of his people. ➤

18 "This truth is for you: When you were younger, you dressed yourself and went wherever you wanted. But when you are old, you will stretch out your hands. Others will dress you and take you where you don't want to go." ❖ *The phrase "stretch out your hands" was a widely used euphemism that referred to crucifixion, and this is how tradition says that Peter eventually died.* ➤ 19 Jesus said this to indicate how Peter would die and bring glory to God. Then Jesus told him, "Follow in my footsteps." ❖ *Jesus was calling Peter to live a life of ministry and then die just like his master had.* ➤

20 Peter turned and saw John following them—Jesus' special friend who had leaned back against his chest at the last supper and asked who would betray him. *[John 13:25]* ❖ *John's gospel is written in the third person and he never mentions his own name, but it's been added for clarification.* ➤ 21 When he saw John, he asked Jesus, "Lord, what will happen to him?" 22 Jesus answered, "If I want him to live until I return again, that should be of no concern to you. You are only to concern yourself with following me!" 23 So a rumor spread among the believers that John wouldn't die. But that isn't what Jesus said. He meant that whether or not John died before Jesus returned was not Peter's business. ❖ *According to tradition, John lived to old age—dying a natural death around the year AD 100—while most or all of the other apostles died as martyrs.* ➤

John's Closing Words

24 I—who am an eyewitness of the events I've recorded in this gospel—am that John, Jesus' close friend. And we know that this account is true. ❖ *Just who the "we" in the last sentence refers to is debated. It may mean just John himself, or other leaders, or it may mean "it's well-known."* ➤ 25 Jesus did many other things not recorded here.

If all of them were written down, I would guess that even the entire world couldn't contain all the books that would be written.

❖ *This is clearly hyperbole but accentuates the fact that what is recorded in this gospel is only a small sample of the things Jesus did.* ➤

The Ministry of the Holy Spirit

Also Known as 'The Acts of the Apostles'

This book was written by the same Luke who wrote 'The Good News about Jesus the Messiah as told by Luke.' See the introduction to his gospel to find out more about him. He was a traveling companion of the Apostle Paul, and this book continues the story where his gospel left off. In fact, chapter 13 to the end largely documents the ministry of Paul, and Luke was with him much of that time. Wherever Luke was present in this account, he writes in the first person using 'we.' But when he was not present, he narrates the events in the third person, saying 'they.' He probably finished this book around the year AD 62 since, in it, he records nothing that happened after that date.

Luke's Purpose in Writing This Book:

1) to record important things that happened to believers after Jesus ascended into Heaven
2) to show how believers fulfilled Jesus' command in Acts 1:8 to be his witnesses in Jerusalem, Judea, Samaria, and to the ends of the earth
3) to show that Jesus saves both Jews and Gentiles
4) to show how the apostles applied Scriptural principles to specific problems
5) to show how the Holy Spirit guides God's people
6) to show that the body of believers continues to grow even when it is persecuted

Important Events Recorded in This Book:

Believers witness in Jerusalem. [chapters 1—7] circa AD 30–35
    Jesus ascends into Heaven [chapter 1]
    Pentecost (Shavuot) [chapter 2]
    Ananias and Sapphira are punished [chapter 5]
    Deacons are appointed [6:1-8]
    The death of Stephen [6:9—7:60]

Believers witness in Judea and Samaria [chapters 8—12] circa AD 35–48
    Saul persecutes followers of Jesus [chapter 8]
    Saul is converted [chapter 9]
    The Good News is for Gentiles too [chapters 10—11]
    The Apostle James is killed. [chapter 12]

Believers witness to the ends of the earth. [chapters 13—28] circa AD 48–62
    Paul's first missionary journey with Barnabas. [chapters 13—14]
    The Council in Jerusalem. [chapter 15]
    Paul's second missionary journey with Silas. [15:36—18:22]
    Paul's third missionary journey. [18:23—21:16]
    Paul is arrested in Jerusalem. [21:17-26]
    Paul's journey as a prisoner to Rome. [chapters 27—28]

1

Jesus Promises to Send the Holy Spirit with Enabling Power

1 Dear Theophilus, in my first book
❖ *i.e., The Good News about Jesus the Messiah as told*

by Luke ➤ I wrote about all the things that Jesus did and taught from the beginning of his ministry 2 until the day God took him up to Heaven. *[Luke 24:33-53]* But before he ascended, he gave instructions to his apostles—under the leading of the Holy Spirit—{to proclaim the Good News about him to others.} **A** 3 After his suffering, death, and resurrection, he frequently appeared to these men during a 40-day period and proved to them in many convincing ways that he was indeed physically alive. He also spoke to them about matters pertaining to God's Kingdom. 4 One of those times while he was eating **B** with them, he said, "Don't leave Jerusalem yet, but wait for the gift of the Holy Spirit that my Father promised to give you. I've told you about him before. *[Luke 24:49; John 14:15-17, 26; 15:26; 16:7-8; 13-15]* 5 For John baptized people with water, but in just a few days you will be baptized with **C** the Holy Spirit." ❖ *"Baptize" means to "wash" for the purpose of ritual cleansing, sometimes by dipping. Some understand "be baptized in the Holy Spirit" to be an immersion in him. Several water figures are used in the Scriptures to represent the Spirit. In the Hebrew Scriptures, God promised to "pour out" the Holy Spirit on his people, [Isaiah 44:3; Ezekiel 39:29; Joel 2:28-29; Zechariah 12:10] and to "put his Spirit" in his people. [Ezekiel 36:25-27] Charismatics and Pentecostals understand the "baptism in the Holy Spirit" to be an empowering for service that is different from the indwelling Spirit that all believers receive when they are saved. [Acts 8:5-17] They cite John 20:22 as evidence that the apostles had already received the indwelling Holy Spirit. Others say that believers receive the indwelling Holy Spirit at conversion and that this indwelling is the same as the baptism in the Holy Spirit.* ➤

6 When they met together with Jesus on the 40th day after his resurrection, they asked him, "Lord, are you now going to restore the glory of the Kingdom of Israel and get rid of the Romans?" ❖ *The Jews of Jesus' day were expecting the Messiah to be a political savior who would defeat their Roman conquerors and make Israel a powerful kingdom like it had been during its golden age when David and Solomon were kings—1,000 years earlier.* ➤ 7 He answered, "The time for such things has been set by my Father and he doesn't want you to know when it will happen. 8 But what you should be expecting is that the Holy Spirit will come on you, ❖ *this is the same as the "baptism"* ➤ and give you

access to his enabling power for ministry. Then you will tell everyone what you know about me—what I've done and taught. You will start here in Jerusalem, move out to all of Judea and Samaria, and some of you will even go to remote parts of the world."

Jesus Returns to Heaven

9 After he told them these things—and while they were still watching—he rose high into the air until finally, a cloud hid him from their sight. ❖ *The cloud could have been a natural one or a special sign of God's presence, as in Exodus 13:21; 40:34; 1 Kings 8:10-11; and Luke 9:34-36.* ➤ 10 As he was going—and while they were still staring up in the sky—two angels suddenly appeared standing there with them in the form of men, dressed in white. 11 They said, "Men of Galilee, why are you just standing there staring into the sky? Jesus has been taken up into Heaven, and he will someday return on a cloud in exactly the same manner you saw him leave." [Mark 13:26; Luke 21:27] ❖ *There were also two angels at Jesus' empty tomb. [Luke 24:4] This is probably because the Torah said that two witnesses were required to establish the truth of what they say. [Deuteronomy 19:15] ¶ This happened 40 days after his resurrection and 10 days before the Pentecost Festival—known as Shavuot among Jews.* ➤

Matthias is Chosen to Replace Judas Iscariot

12 After the angels departed, the believers left Mount Olivet and returned to Jerusalem—less than a mile away. ❖ *Mt. Olivet overlooks Jerusalem—200 feet above the city across the Kidron valley. But the peak is about 2,675 feet above sea level.* ➤ 13 When they arrived in the city, they went to the upstairs room where they were staying. Those in the group were Simon Peter (also called Kefa [kay-fah]), John, James (John's brother), Andrew, Philip, Thomas, Bartholomew, ❖ *who might have also been called Nathanael [John 1:43-49]* ➤ Matthew Levi, James (the son of Alphaeus), ❖ *It's*

A **1:2** There are a few Greek manuscripts that include the phrase "to proclaim the Good News" at the end of this verse.

B **1:4** The word συναλίζομαι (sunalizomai) here rendered "was eating with" is ambiguous in this context and could mean "was gathered together with" or "was lodging with."

C **1:5** The Greek preposition ἐν (en) before "the Holy Spirit" could legitimately be translated "in," "by," or "with." John's water baptism could also be either "in" or "with" water.

possible that this Alphaeus is the also the father of Mathew, [Mark 2:14] so this James and Matthew may have been brothers. ➤ Simon the Zealot, and Thaddeus Judas (the son of James). ❖ *This third James— the father of Thaddeus Judas—is different from James the brother of John and different from James the son of Alphaeus. Thaddeus Judas is also a different man than Judas Iscariot. [Matthew 10:2-4; Luke 6:13-16; Mark 3:16-19]* ➤ 14 These men were all together, along with the women who had followed Jesus and his mother Miriam and his brothers James and Jude. Their common purpose was to wait for the promised Holy Spirit. So they devoted themselves to prayer while they waited.

15 One day during this period, there were about 120 men **A** gathered there who believed in Jesus. ❖ *The women were never counted.* ➤ Peter stood and spoke to everyone there. ❖ *The followers of Jesus—while all still Jewish—would want to form their own recognized community within Judaism. Jewish Law required such a community to have a minimum of 120 men.* ➤ 16 He said, "My brothers and sisters in the Lord, the prophecy about Judas in the Scriptures had to be fulfilled. The Holy Spirit moved King David to prophecy about this man— who betrayed Jesus by guiding those who arrested him. ❖ *[Psalm 41:9] which says: But now my friend who ate with me and had my trust has turned against me.* ➤ 17 Jesus chose him to be one of us twelve—to be an apostle. 18 ❖ *It's not clear if verses 18-19 are part of Peter's speech or a parenthetical comment by Luke.* ➤ With the money he got for his evil betrayal, he obtain a field. ❖ *Matthew 27:3-10 tells us that Judas returned the money and then hanged himself. The chief priests took his money and bought a field in his name, since it was his money. They apparently bought the field where he hanged himself.* ➤ It was there that he fell face downward from a height, his body hit the rocks and burst open, spilling out his intestines. ❖ *He evidently hanged himself from a height, possibly over a cliff. At some point the rope broke, or perhaps the branch he tied the rope to broke, and his body fell to the rocks below.* ➤ 19 Everyone in Jerusalem heard about it, so they called it the 'Field of Blood'—which in their language (Aramaic) was *'Hakeldama.'* 20 As David wrote in the Psalms, '**May his place become deserted, may no one live in it,**' *[Psalm 69:25]* and "**Let another take his position.**" *[Psalm 109:8]* ❖ *Peter adapts the curses in these Psalms—which originally applied to David's enemies—by changing a few words in the first quote. Jewish teachers of that time considered this a legitimate application of Scripture.* ➤ 21 We need to choose a man to take his place, someone who has been with us the entire time the Lord Jesus was among us—22 from the very beginning when John baptized him ❖ *or: when John first started baptizing people* ➤ until he was taken up to Heaven. Such a person must join us to complete our number as we tell others about his resurrection."

23 They nominated two men, Joseph Bar-Sabbas—who was also called Justus— and Matthias. ❖ *Bar-Sabbas can mean either "son of Sabbas," or "son of the Sabbath"—which would mean he was born on a Sabbath day. Early traditions say that Matthias was one of the 70 who Jesus sent out in Luke 10:1, and that he later became a missionary to Ethiopia.* ➤ 24 Then they all prayed, ❖ *probably following Peter* ➤ "Lord, you know everyone's thoughts. So show us which of these two you have chosen 25 to take this position of apostolic ministry which Judas abandoned to go to his own place **B** in Hell." ❖ *The text in verse 24 literally says "heart" instead of "thoughts," but Jews of that time considered the heart to be the source of their thoughts.* ➤ 26 Then they ❖ *probably one of the apostles, representing the others* ➤ cast lots to make the choice, and Matthias was chosen. He became an apostle with the other eleven. ❖ *Names or marks for each man were put on stones, and the stones were shaken in a cup until one fell out. The name on the one that came out was chosen. Based on Proverbs 16:33, they believed that God intervened to choose the person he desired. This practice was common in the Hebrew Scriptures, but is not mentioned again after Pentecost because after that, believers received guidance directly from the Holy Spirit. Twelve apostles were needed to represent the twelve tribes of Israel. This number is symbolic of the totality of God's people. [Matthew 19:28; Revelation 21:12-14]* ➤

A 1:15 A few major Greek manuscripts have "120 disciples." But most have "120 brothers."
B 1:25 Most major Greek manuscripts have "his own place," but many have "his own part." The meaning in both cases is likely a euphemism for his damnation.

2

The Holy Spirit Comes on Pentecost

1 On Pentecost—10 days after Jesus' ascension—they were all together in one place in Jerusalem. ❖ *We don't know if "they" are the twelve or the 120. Many commentators think it was the larger group. In the Hebrew Scriptures, Pentecost was called the Harvest Festival, [Exodus 23:16; Leviticus 23:15-21] or the Festival of Weeks—which in Hebrew is "Shavuot.". [Exodus 34:22] After the destruction of Jerusalem in AD 70, it became a celebration about God giving the Torah. Pentecost means "fiftieth" and occurs 50 days after the Passover.* ➤ 2 Suddenly, from out of the sky ❖ *or Heaven* ➤ there was a loud sound—like a strong wind blowing ❖ *but it wasn't a wind* ➤—and the sound filled the whole house A where they were gathered. 3 Then, what looked like small flames of fire appeared and separated and one rested on each of them. ❖ *Fire is symbolic of God's presence. [Genesis 15:17; Exodus 3:2-5; 13:21-22; 19:18; 40:38]* ➤ 4 They were all filled with the Holy Spirit ❖ *this is the "gift" of the Holy Spirit—also called the " baptism" in the Holy Spirit* ➤ and they began to speak in other languages as a result of the Holy Spirit giving them this ability.

5 Now, at the time of this festival, there were Jews visiting Jerusalem from everywhere in the known world, and all of them were people who tried hard to obey God. 6 When they heard the loud sound, a crowd gathered where the followers of Jesus were. Then, the crowd was surprised and didn't know what to think because each person in the crowd heard Jesus' followers speak in his or her own language. ❖ *There are two possibilities. One is that Jesus' followers were each speaking in a different language such that each foreigner could find one follower speaking his own language. (This would have been quite a babble and is what is generally assumed to have happened by commentators.) It is also possible that Jesus' followers were speaking "in unknown languages (a.k.a. tongues)," and every foreigner miraculously heard only his own language being spoken.* ➤ 7 The crowd was amazed and some were exclaiming, "Aren't

all B these men who are speaking from Galilee? ❖ *Residents of Jerusalem considered Galileans to be ignorant hicks.* ➤ 8 So how is it that each of us hear them speaking in our own native language from the different countries where we were born? 9-11 We represent:

"Parthia, Media, and Mesopotamia in
    the far east,
"also the Roman provinces of
    Cappadocia, Pontus, Pamphylia,
    Asia, and Phrygia in Asia Minor,
"Elam, Egypt, and Libya around the
    city of Cyrene in North Africa,
"visitors from Rome and Judea,
"both those born Jewish and also
    some who are converts to Judaism,
"and people from Crete and Arabia.
    ❖ *16 areas are listed* ➤

"We each hear them in our own language, telling about the wonders God has done!" 12 The people in the crowd were amazed and puzzled about how this could happen, and many asked each other, "What does this miraculous sign mean?" 13 But some mocked Jesus' followers by saying, "They're just drunk!"

Peter Explains the Significance of What Just Happened

14 Then, Peter stood up with the other eleven apostles and—guided by the Spirit—boldly addressed the crowd in a loud voice, "Men of Judea and all of you who are visiting Jerusalem at this time, listen carefully and let me explain this sign for you. 15 These people aren't drunk, as some of you seem to think. It's only nine o'clock in the morning, after all! ❖ *Jews of that time only drank wine when they ate meat. They ate bread in the morning and meat in the evening. [Exodus 16:8; 1 Thessalonians 5:7]* ➤ 16 No, this is a sign that was predicted by the prophet Joel:

17 'God says: In the last days, ❖ *before Judgment Day and the end of the world* ➤ I will pour out my Spirit on all my people. Your sons and daughters will prophesy my words, and I will give your young men visions, and

---

A 2:2 The word οἶκος (oikos) here rendered as "house" can alternatively mean "temple." Commentators are divided on if they were in a house near the Temple, or in the Temple itself.

B 2:7 Most major Greek manuscripts have "all," but many do not have it.

communicate to your old men in dreams. **18** In those days, I will even pour my Spirit on my people who are slaves, both men and women, and they will prophesy my words. *[Joel 2:28-29]* **19** I will do amazing things in the sky and perform signs on the earth. There will be blood and fire and smoke. **20** The sun will be darkened and the moon will look blood red. All this will happen before that great and glorious day of the Lord arrives when he will judge the world. *[Isaiah 13:9-10; 24:21-23; 34:4; Ezekiel 32:7-8; Joel 2:10-11; 30-31; 3:15; Amos 8:9]* **21** And everyone who calls on Yahweh to save them, will be saved.' " *[Joel 2:32]* ❖ *This prophecy is interpreted in many ways. But one common view is that this speaks of the entire age since the Pentecost festival recorded here until Jesus returns, [Hebrews 1:2; 9:26; 1 Peter 1:20 and 1 John 2:18] and that verse 20 will happen shortly before he returns. Verse 21 is true for the whole period. Verses 17-18 clearly came true in the first century. People disagree on whether they remained true for the rest of the period. Charismatics and Pentecostals believe they hold true for the entire period. But they believe that starting around 1900 (when the Pentecostal movement first started) until Jesus returns (which many think will be in the near future), these signs are increasing in frequency and effectiveness, in preparation for the end.* ➤

22 Peter continued, "Men of Israel, listen carefully to me! God sent and approved of the man Jesus from Nazareth. And he demonstrated his approval by performing miracles and signs and wonders through him. You all know this is true since many of you saw them yourselves. ❖ *The Jews generally believed that only God could do such miracles as Jesus had done.* ➤ **23** It was God's plan from the beginning that Jesus be handed over into your power so that you would have him executed by crucifixion at the hands of the Romans— who neither know nor obey the one true God. **24** But God brought him back to life —having destroyed the agony of death— because it was impossible for death to hold him. ❖ *Many interpret "having destroyed the agony of death" as "freeing him from the agony of death," but it could also mean at the same time that he destroyed death's power for all, especially for those who are united with him. Jesus*

is—in his essence—eternal life. He could not remain dead. [John 1:4; 5:21] ➤ **25** King David prophesied that the Messiah would say, 'I always see Yahweh with me. Since he is at my right side defending me, I cannot be frightened. **26** Therefore, I'm jubilant and joyfully exult! I have every expectation that you will raise my body, **27** for I know that you, God, won't leave me—your Holy One—in the world of the dead or allow my body to rot in the grave. **28** You have revealed to me the way of eternal life, and in your presence, I will know complete joy.' *[Psalm 16:8-11]* ❖ *Most commentators think "the paths of life" (in the literal text) refer to the resurrection, not to another mortal life, but to eternal life.* ➤

29 "My Jewish brothers and sisters, I can tell you without a doubt that our ancestor, King David, was clearly not prophesying about himself not remaining dead and his body not rotting because he died, was buried, and his tomb is still here with his remains in it. ❖ *David's tomb is just outside the old city of Jerusalem.* ➤ **30** But he was a prophet and knew that God had sworn an oath to him that one of his descendants would reign as king over Israel forever. **A** *[2 Samuel 7:12-13; Psalm 132:11-12]* **31** David prophetically saw the future and spoke about the Messiah's resurrection when he said that God wouldn't leave the Messiah in the world of the dead, and would also not allow his body to decay. *[Psalm 16:10]* **32** Now, God has raised Jesus from the dead, and we twelve—who are his apostles—are all witnesses to this fact. ❖ *The clear implication is that Jesus is the Messiah. The Torah only required two witnesses to establish their testimony as being true. The people he was speaking to certainly knew about the rumors of the resurrection happening—less than two months previously. Jews of that time had not interpreted the prophecies about the Messiah's death as pertaining to the Messiah. Until this prophecy was pointed out to them, Jesus' death was—in their minds—proof that he was not the Messiah. Even Jesus' followers initially had this view after his death, prior to when he appeared to them alive again. [Luke 24:18-21]* ➤ **33** God has exalted him to the place of highest honor and authority at

---

A 2:30 Some major Greek manuscripts have a different wording: "God had sworn an oath to him that from his descendants, he would raise up the Messiah to reign as king over Israel." Most manuscripts do not read like this, but the implication is the same since Peter is clearly saying that this prophecy is about the Messiah.

his right hand. ❖ *A few commentators think it means "exalted him **by means of** his right hand of power."* ➤ And having received the Holy Spirit from God the Father—the same Spirit that the Father promised to give his people—Jesus has caused the Spirit to be poured out on us. That is the real explanation for what you have seen and heard today. 34 For again, it's clear that David wasn't talking about himself because he didn't ascend to Heaven as Jesus did. But David did write the following about the Messiah, 'Yahweh said to my Lord, ❖ *i.e., the Messiah* ➤ "Sit at my right hand 35 while I bring your enemies into submission under you." ' *[Psalm 110:1]*

36 "Therefore, every Israelite should clearly understand this: God has made this man Jesus—whom you crucified—Messiah and Lord." ❖ *"Lord" in this context implies his deity and hence his equality with God the Father. They commonly addressed God as "Lord". See the note at Romans 10:9.* ➤

37 When the people heard all this, they were deeply convicted and asked Peter and the other apostles, "Brothers, what should we do so God will forgive us?"

38 Peter replied, "Repent ❖ *this means turning away from their sin of rejecting Jesus as the Messiah* ➤ and be baptized in the name of Jesus the Messiah. ❖ *To be baptized in his name implies that they are willing to become his obedient followers.* ➤ Do this, and he will forgive your sins. You will also receive from him the gift of the Holy Spirit living in you, just as we have. 39 For the Lord, our God, promised to give his Spirit to all those he calls to be his own people, including you and your descendants and even the Gentiles." ❖ *To be called to be one of his people implies the call to obedience and submission to his will—in addition to all the blessings his people receive.* ➤

40 Peter kept on exhorting and warning them for some time and he pleaded, "Allow God to save you from the punishment that he intends to execute on those who have rebelled against him by rejecting his Messiah!" 41 About 3,000 people were convinced by his message that day, so they were baptized and became a part of the assembly of those who accepted Jesus as their Messiah.

The Lifestyle of the Early Believers

42 Those belonging to the assembly were continually diligent to listen to the apostles' teaching, and they changed their ways to live in obedience to the instruction they received. They were diligent to meet together for worship, to encourage each other, ❖ *i.e., fellowship* ➤ to eat with each other, and to celebrate the Lord's Supper at those meals, ❖ *i.e., break bread* ➤ and to pray. ❖ *Most commentators believe this is a description of their corporate worship.* ➤ 43 Everyone in Jerusalem was awestruck because of the many miraculous signs and wonders that God did through the apostles. 44 All the believers were united in thought and action and frequently met together. They also freely shared what they had with each other. 45 Whenever there was a need, someone would sell some land or other possession and share the money with those who needed it. 46 Every day they did these same things: They continued to meet together in the Temple courts, and then taking turns as hosts, they joyfully ate together in different homes—humbly and generously sharing what food they had with each other—and celebrating the Lord's Supper at those meals. 47 They were continually praising God, and the entire Jewish community thought well of them for a time. Every day, the Lord Jesus was saving more people who then joined with the community of believers.

3

Jesus Heals a Crippled Beggar Through Peter

1 One day, Peter and John went up to the Temple, as usual, for the regular public prayer time at three in the afternoon. ❖ *There were public sacrifices and prayer at the Temple at nine in the morning, three in the afternoon, and at sunset every day.* ➤ 2 One of the Temple entrances was called the "Beautiful Gate," and a man who was crippled from birth was taken there every day so he could beg from those going into the inner Temple. ❖ *Most commentators think this entrance was also called the Nicanor Gate, which was a very ornate bronze gate. It separated the outer Temple courtyard of the Gentiles from the next innermost court—called the*

women's court—where any Jew could enter. ➤ 3 When the crippled man saw Peter and John entering, he begged them for money. ❖ *This was a socially acceptable way for the disabled to earn a living. God promised to bless those who gave money to the poor, blind, and crippled.* ➤ 4 But Peter and John stopped and looked at him intently. Then Peter politely said, "Look at us!" 5 So the man gave them his full attention, expecting to receive a special donation from them. 6 But Peter said, "I don't have any money, but I will give you what I do have. I tell you by the authority of Jesus the Messiah from Nazareth to stand up and walk!" 7 He then grabbed the man's right hand and pulled him to his feet. Instantly, the man's feet and ankles became strong. 8 He was so excited that he leaped into the air several times and then began to walk. He entered the Temple court with them, walking and leaping for joy and all the while praising God. 9 When all the people inside saw him walking and heard him praising God, 10 they recognized him as the one who was always begging outside the Beautiful Gate and were astounded that he was walking.

Peter Uses the Healing as an Opportunity to Preach

11 While the man clung to Peter and John, a crowd quickly gathered around them in Solomon's Pavilion and all who saw him were amazed. ❖ *The Temple courtyard was bounded on two sides by roofed areas variously called porches, porticos, colonnades, or pavilions. The roofs were held up by rows of 40-foot-high stone pillars. Scholars think that Solomon's Pavilion formed the east side of the Temple courtyard.* ➤ 12 When Peter saw this, he said to the crowd, "My fellow Israelites, why does this healing surprise you? And why do you stare at us as if we made this man walk by our own power, or think that God healed him because we are especially holy? 13 Our God—whom our revered ancestors Abraham, Isaac, and Jacob worshipped—has greatly honored his servant, A Jesus the Messiah, by raising him from death and taking him to Heaven.

❖ *The Messiah is called God's servant in Isaiah 42:41; 9:6; 52:13; 53:11.* ➤ He is the man you handed over to the Romans to execute. In Pilate's hearing, you rejected him as your king and insisted that he be put to death—even though Pilate knew he was innocent of any crime and wanted to release him. 14 You completely rejected the one whom God regards as holy and righteous, and asked to have a murderer released instead. *[Matthew 27:16-26; Mark 15:6-15; Luke 23:18-25; John 18:38-40]* 15 You had the Origin and Source of all Life put to death, but God showed his opinion of him by raising him back to life. John, here, and I are witnesses to this fact. ❖ *The Torah required them to accept the testimony of two witnesses as being true.* ➤ 16 And now, because we have faith in the authority of Jesus' name, it is Jesus himself who made this man's legs strong. You know who this man is and what he was. God's power was released to heal him completely as you can see. But it only happened based on our faith that Jesus is the Messiah and that he has given us authority to heal in his name. ❖ *Some commentators say the man's faith healed him. There is nothing in the text to indicated that, but clearly Peter and John had faith.* ➤

17 "Now my friends, I know that you and your leaders didn't realize you were rejecting and executing the true Messiah. *[Luke 23:34]* ❖ *The Jews believed only God could miraculously heal people and that he would only do it through people who pleased him. Since he healed the man in Jesus' name, through Peter, this was a powerful testimony that God considered Jesus righteous. And if that is true, then everything that Jesus said must have been true, and also everything Peter was saying. The facts of the resurrection and the healing in Jesus' name left no excuse for not recognizing that Jesus is the Messiah.* ➤ 18 God allowed this to happen to fulfill what his prophets said about the suffering of the Messiah. *[Psalm 22; 41:9; 69:4, 21; 118:22; Isaiah 8:14; 50:6; 53:3-11; Micah 5:1; Zechariah 12:10; 13:7]* 19-20 But now you must recognize the truth, repent of what you did, turn to God, and accept his Messiah so your sins may be forgiven. If you do,

---

A 3:13 The word παῖς (pais) translated as "servant" can alternatively mean "child," or in this context, "son."

then I trust that God will later send Jesus—the appointed Messiah—back to you so you may have times of spiritual refreshing. ❖ *Jesus always was the Messiah. His "appointment" refers to the revelation of that fact. Jews associated "times of refreshment and joy" with the coming of the Messiah. And his return, therefore, is connected with the restoration of Israel when all or most of Israel will believe in Jesus as the Messiah. So their turning to believe in him can only hasten his return and the coming of the expected times of refreshing. [Isaiah 40:9-11; Jeremiah 32:42-44; Ezekiel 37:21-28; Hosea 11:9-11; 14:4-7; Amos 9:11-15]* ➤ 21 But for now, he must remain in Heaven until the long-ago-prophesied time comes for God to restore everything to perfection for his people. *[Psalm 110:1; Matthew 19:28]* ❖ *The restoration is the same as the times of refreshing referred to in the previous verse.* ➤ 22 Remember that Moses said this about the Messiah, '**Our God, Yahweh, will cause one from among us Israelites to be a prophet like me. You must listen carefully to everything he tells you.** 23 Those who don't listen to him and obey him will no longer be his people, and he will destroy them.' *[Deuteronomy 18:15-19; Leviticus 23:29]* ❖ *How will he be like Moses? See Numbers 12:8. This destruction refers to punishment in Hell. See 2 Thessalonians 1:9 and the following note about what it means to experience eternal ruin in Hell.* ➤

24 "All the prophets after Moses—from Samuel on—also prophesied about what the Messiah has recently done and what he will do when he returns. 25 You were privileged to see the fulfillment of the things the prophets foretold about the Messiah, and you are the inheritors of the covenant promise that God made with your ancestors which is being fulfilled in this time. God promised Abraham, '**I will bless people from every country in the world through your descendant,**' and he was talking about the Messiah. *[Genesis 12:3; 18:18; 22:18; 26:4]* 26 When God sent his servant ❖ *or: Son* ➤ Jesus to this world, he first sent him to bless us Jews. His intention was and is for each of you to turn to the Messiah and abandon your evil ways."

4

Peter and John Are Brought Before the Sanhedrin

1 While Peter and John were still preaching to the people, some priests and Sadducees and the captain of the Temple guard approached them. ❖ *The captain of the Temple guard was one of the chief priests and next in authority after the High Priest.* ➤ 2 They were quite agitated that the apostles were teaching the people that Jesus—whom they had put to death—was the promised Messiah, and that someday God would raise other people from death just like he did Jesus. ❖ *Most of the chief priests were Sadducees who believed that when people die, they cease to exist, and that God would never raise anyone from death.* ➤ 3 So they ordered the guards to arrest them. Since it was already evening, they put them in jail until they could be tried the next day. ❖ *Jewish Law forbade trials at night.* ➤ 4 But many of the people who had heard Peter's message believed in Jesus, and the number of believing men—not counting women and children—grew to about 5,000.

5 The next day, the High Priest summoned the chief priests, elders, Scripture teachers, and other members of the Sanhedrin and they gathered together in Jerusalem. ❖ *The Sanhedrin was the Jewish council that governed the religious lives of the Jews. It consisted of the High Priest, who was the chairman, 24 other priests, 24 elders, and 22 Scripture teachers for a total of 71 members. During this time, most of the priestly members were Sadducees and most of the Scripture teachers were Pharisees.* ➤ 6 Annas—the High Priest—was there, as well as Caiaphas and John A and Alexander and all the other priests of Annas' family. ❖ *Annas was High Priest from AD 6–14 but had been deposed by the Romans and replaced by Caiaphas, his son-in-law. But since the Torah said that the High Priest kept his position for life, the Jews considered Annas to still be the true High Priest. John and Alexander were members of Annas' family, and this John may be the Jonathan who succeeded Caiaphas as High Priest.* ➤ 7 They had Peter and John brought in and began to question them. They asked, "By what power or whose authority did *you* heal that man?" ❖ *The*

A **4:6** Jonathan in some manuscripts.

pronoun "you" in the Greek is emphatic and shows that they felt contempt toward the apostles. ➤

8 Then, Peter was filled with the Holy Spirit who empowered and directed him to boldly address them, saying, "Rulers and leaders of the people of Israel. 9 Since you require us to account for the act of kindness done for a crippled man and want to know how he was saved, ❖ *the word σώζω (sōzō) here can mean saved and/or healed* ➤ 10 then I most certainly want you and all the rest of Israel to know that this man—who stands here in your presence in good health—was healed by God when we commanded it to happen by the authority that the Messiah, Jesus of Nazareth, gave to us. He is the one you crucified as a blasphemer, but God showed his regard for him by bringing him back to life and also by healing this man in his name. 11 In fulfillment of the prophecy about the Messiah, Jesus is the 'stone that you builders rejected which has become the Chief Foundation Stone in God's plan.' *[Psalm 118:22]* 12 There is, in fact, no one else who can save us. For God has given Jesus—and no one else—for people to call on to be saved."

13 The members of the Sanhedrin were amazed at Peter and John's confidence, considering they had no formal rabbinical education. They took note of the fact that they had been with Jesus for some time and the obvious influence he had had on their lives. ❖ *Jesus told the apostles to expect this in Luke 12:11-12 and 21:12-15.* ➤ 14 But since they could see the man—whom God had healed through the apostles—standing in front of them verifying their claims, there was nothing they could say against them. 15 So they ordered the guards to take the apostles outside the room while they discussed the situation with each other. 16 Frustrated, they said, "There's really nothing we can do to punish these men. Everybody in Jerusalem knows they performed this amazing miraculous sign, so we can hardly deny it. 17 But we need to stop this idea about Jesus being the Messiah from spreading among the people, so let's threaten them with punishment if they ever claim to speak with Jesus'

authority again." 18 Then they had the apostles brought back in and commanded them never to speak about Jesus or claim to teach with his authority. 19 But Peter and John replied, "If we obey you, then we would be disobeying God who wants us to tell others about Jesus. You certainly can't think it would be right for us to have a higher allegiance to you than we do to him! 20 It is impossible for us to stop telling others about what we've seen and heard because it's critical for everyone to know these things." 21 Ultimately, all the Sanhedrin could do was threaten them again and let them go because there was no legal basis for punishing them—and the all the people were praising God for what had happened through them. ❖ *The people might very well have rioted had they punished the apostles for performing a miracle.* ➤ 22 What made this healing so amazing was the fact that the man had been crippled for his entire 40-plus years, so clearly only God could have done this.

The Believers Pray for Boldness

23 Immediately after their release, Peter and John went to the other apostles and believers and reported to them everything that the chief priests and elders of the Sanhedrin had told them. 24 After they heard it, they were in agreement as they joined together in praying aloud to God. They prayed, "Master, you are the one **A** who made the heavens, Earth, sea, and everything that exists. *[Psalm 146:6]* 25 Your faithful servant—our ancestor King David—prophesied under the prompting of the Holy Spirit, **B** saying that you said, 'It's futile for the Gentiles to arrogantly rage against me and for the people to plot against me. 26 The kings and rulers of this world prepared to fight against Yahweh and his Messiah.' *[Psalm 2:1-2]* ❖ *The Greek word "rulers," used here when the apostles quoted Psalm 2, is the same word that Luke used earlier in Acts 4:5 that is rendered as "chief priests."* ➤ 27 That has been fulfilled in this city. For the tetrarch Herod Antipas and Pontius Pilate, together with Gentiles ❖ *i.e., Roman soldiers* ➤ and Israelites here in Jerusalem, plotted against your holy servant Jesus whom you

---

A 4:24 Some manuscripts say "God."   **B** 4:25 Some manuscripts lack "by means of the Holy Spirit."

anointed. ❖ *For God to anoint someone means that he placed his Holy Spirit upon him and chose him for a special office, such as prophet, priest, or king. Jesus was all three, and this particularly means that he was anointed to be the Messiah—which literally means "anointed one."* ➤ 28 But they were only able to do what you had sovereignly predestined would happen. 29 So now, Lord, notice their threats against us and if it's your will, protect us from them. But enable us—your willing slaves—to keep on boldly proclaiming your message, unintimidated by their threats. 30 And while we are doing this, release your power to heal and perform miraculous signs and wonders through us by the authority that your holy servant Jesus gave us to confirm to all that we represent you." 31 When they were finished praying, the place where they were meeting shook because of God's presence and the power he was releasing. They were all filled with the Holy Spirit, and from that time on, continued to boldly proclaim God's message in the face of possible arrest and punishment. ❖ *Sometimes God's presence in a place causes it to shake. [Exodus 19:18; Isaiah 6:4]* ➤

The Believers Shared Their Possessions with Those in Need

32 All the believers were united in love and purpose. None of them considered their personal property as something to horde to themselves, but they were willing to share everything they had with other believers who had a need. 33 By the Spirit's empowering, the apostles continued to tell others what they knew about the resurrection of the Lord Jesus, and their testimonies and accompanying healings and signs and wonders had a large impact on those who heard. God's great favor and blessing rested on all the believers 34 for there wasn't a single person among them who had unmet needs. Whenever a need arose, someone with land or other property they could spare would sell it and bring the money from the sale 35 as an offering to the apostles, who would distribute it to those who had need of it.

36-37 As an example, Joseph **A**—a Levite from the island of Cyprus—did this. He sold a field that he owned and brought the money to the apostles for those in need. The apostles nicknamed him "Barnabas"—which means "son of encouragement"—because he was an encourager. ❖ *This is the same Barnabas who later partnered with Saul, a.k.a. Paul. [Acts 11:25-26; 13:2-3] Since Levites could not own land in Israel, [Numbers 18:20, 24; Deuteronomy 18:1-2] the land was either on Cyprus, or belonged to his wife, or this particular teaching was no longer followed by that time.* ➤

5

God Clarifies the Seriousness of Hypocrisy

1 But in contrast to Barnabas, also among the believers was a man named Ananias who, with his wife Sapphira, sold a piece of land that he owned. 2 With the full knowledge and agreement of his wife, he presented only part of the money to the apostles while claiming it was the full amount from the sale. He held back some of it for their own use and they expected to gain a reputation for being more generous than they really were. 3 Then Peter said to him, "Ananias, how is it that you have allowed Satan so much influence in your life that you would lie to us and to the Holy Spirit about what you've done? You've held back some of the money for yourself while claiming it is the full amount you received from the sale. ❖ *Peter knew this through a word of knowledge. [1 Corinthians 12:8]* ➤ 4 Before you sold the land, it was entirely yours. And after you sold it, all the money still belonged to you to do with as you wished. You were under no compulsion from us to give anything to anyone. Why would you do such a thing as lie about your gift to make yourself look good in the eyes of others? By doing so, you didn't just lie to people, but you also lied to God." ❖ *What we do to believers is the same as doing it to Jesus. [Matthew 10:40; 25:40]* ➤ 5 When Ananias heard these words, he immediately dropped dead. ❖ *This was God's disciplinary punishment for hypocrisy and was intended as a warning to other believers.* ➤ Everyone who heard about this was terrified. ❖ *As we all would be if we thought God might strike us dead at any time for lying or being hypocrites.* ➤ 6 Then,

---

A 4:36-37 Some manuscripts have "Joses."

some young men wrapped Ananias' body in linen, carried it out of the city, and buried him. ❖ *Jewish custom required the burial to happen within 24 hours.* ➤

7 About three hours later, unaware of what had happened to her husband, Sapphira came to Peter. 8 He showed her the money her husband had brought and asked her, "Tell me truthfully, is this the full amount that your husband got for the land he sold?" She answered, "Yes, that was the amount." 9 So Peter said to her, "You shouldn't have agreed together with your husband to a deception that would test the tolerance of the Lord's Spirit! I can hear those approaching who just finished burying your husband. They will carry you out for burial too." 10 She too immediately fell down in front of him and died. When the young men entered, they found she was dead too and carried her out to be buried beside her husband. 11 All the believers and everyone else who heard about this became very afraid, wondering if God would also punish them for some sin. ❖ *We are all blessed that God doesn't routinely discipline his people so severely. Yet this is a clear indication of his attitude toward a heart full of sin. Those who forget about God's holy character and think a loving God would never punish anyone should think about the implications of this story.* ➤

The Apostles' Ministry Is Characterized by Healings and Miraculous Signs

12 The apostles continued to demonstrate God's backing of their message with many miraculous signs and wonders done among the people, and the believers would frequently meet together in Solomon's Pavilion **A** in the Temple courtyard. ❖ *See the note at 3:11. The miracles were an answer to the prayer in 4:24-30.* ➤ 13 But even though the Jews who didn't accept Jesus as the Messiah thought highly of the believers, after the deaths of Ananias and Sapphira they didn't dare join in meeting with them. 14 Yet, even so, large numbers of men and women were constantly becoming believers in Jesus as Lord and joined with the other believers.

15 Because of the healings that were done by the apostles, people brought sick people out and laid them on mats or stretchers in the street so that when Peter walked by, if he didn't have time to lay hands on them, at least his shadow would pass over some of them and they would be healed. ❖ *The streets of Jerusalem were very narrow. Luke would not have mentioned this if the passing of his shadow had no beneficial effect on the sick.* ➤ 16 There were also large groups of people from the towns around Jerusalem who brought their sick to the apostles, as well as those afflicted by demons. God enabled the apostles to heal all of them. ❖ *The word "demons" is literally "unclean spirits." Someone afflicted by such a demonic spirit was ritually unclean and not allowed to worship in the Temple until the demon was gone and they went through ritual purification. Anyone who touched them became unclean as well.* ➤

The Apostles
Are Persecuted for Their Obedience

17 Now, the High Priest and his associates—who were all Sadducees—were extremely jealous of the popularity and influence of the apostles, 18 so they had them arrested and put in prison. 19 But during the night—without the guards being aware of it—an angel from the Lord opened the prison doors and brought them out. He then instructed them, 20 "Go and stand in the Temple courtyard and tell all the people there the complete message about obtaining eternal life by trusting in Jesus the Messiah." 21 So about dawn, they entered the Temple courtyard as instructed and began to teach all the people there. Meanwhile, when the High Priest and his associates arrived where the Sanhedrin met, they summoned all the members of the Sanhedrin to come for a meeting. At the same time, they sent orders that the apostles were to be brought to them from prison. 22 But when the Temple guards arrived at the prison, they discovered the apostles were missing so they returned to report it. 23 They said, "We found the prison securely locked with guards properly stationed at all

---

A 5:12 The Greek literally says they "were with one mind" in Solomon's Pavilion. Scholars think that by the time

Luke wrote this book, the meaning of the phrase had changed and meant that they "were meeting together."

the doors. But when we had them opened, there was no one inside." 24 When the High Priest, **A** the captain of the guard, and the chief priests heard this, they were quite perplexed and wondered what kind of strange thing would happen next. 25 Eventually, someone came from the Temple courtyard and told them, "Listen! The men you put in prison are back in the Temple courtyard teaching people about Jesus again, right now!"

26 So the captain of the Temple guard and some of his men went to bring them back, but this time without using force— for they were afraid the people might stone them if they treated the apostles roughly. 27 When they had brought them, they stood in front of the assembled Sanhedrin, and the High Priest rebuked them, 28 "We strictly prohibited you from teaching about *that man*, but everyone in Jerusalem has heard what you've been claiming about him and that you are trying to blame us for his death!" ❖ *The High Priest's avoidance of saying Jesus' name showed his hatred and contempt of him.* ➤ 29 But Peter—replying for himself and the other apostles—said, "When God's command conflicts with commands from human authority, we have to obey God instead of men. 30 You had Jesus executed by crucifixion, but the God whom we and our ancestors worshipped brought him back to life. ❖ *The Jews believed that anyone executed this way was cursed by God. [Deuteronomy 21:22-23; Galatians 3:13] They were right—in that he was cursed for our sins—but wrong in thinking that God was pleased with their condemning him.* ➤ 31 Then he exalted him to the place of highest honor and authority at his right hand in Heaven, making him both coruler with him and Savior, so that we—his people in Israel— might repent and receive forgiveness. 32 We apostles are witnesses to these events and have been commanded to proclaim what we have seen and heard. The Holy Spirit is also a witness, and God has given him to those who obey him." ❖ *Peter has strongly implied in verse 30 and here that the leaders are not obeying God, but are working against him.* ➤

33 When the members of the Sanhedrin heard Peter's reply, they were furious and wanted to have them put to death. 34 But one of the members of the Sanhedrin was a Pharisee named Gamaliel. He was a noted Scripture teacher and was respected by everyone. He stood up and ordered that the apostles be taken outside the room for a while. ❖ *Gamaliel was the greatest rabbi of his time and trained the Apostle Paul. [Acts 22:3]* ➤ 35 When they were gone, he addressed the rest of the Sanhedrin. "Men of Israel, I think you should be careful about what you do with these men. 36 Some years ago, a man named Theudas rebelled against Rome— claiming to be important—and gained a following of about 400 men. But he was killed and his followers dispersed, and they and their cause came to nothing. 37 After him, a man named Judas from Galilee rebelled against Rome during the census and he led some in revolt. He too was killed and all those who followed him were scattered. ❖ *This probably happened in the AD 6 census, taken by the Roman government for the purpose of taxing their subjects. The Jews considered God to be their only rightful King and so considered it treason to pay taxes to the Roman Emperor—a pagan who was worshipped as a god. That's why it was easy for someone like this Judas—mentioned by Gamaliel—to incite other Jews to revolt. After their defeat, the Zealot party carried on the movement to organize people to fight Roman domination. The census mentioned in Luke 2:2 was done in about 6 BC.* ➤ 38 So in this situation, I advise you not to interfere with these men, but to let them go. For if their actions are merely the plans of men, they will fail. 39 But if God has commanded them to do what they are doing, you won't be able to stop them and you would find yourselves fighting against God." ❖ *Gamaliel's warning would bring 2 Chronicles 13:12 to their minds.* ➤ 40 The members of the Sanhedrin decided to take his advice. So they had the apostles brought in again. They had them all flogged, ordered them once again not to speak about Jesus, and let them go. ❖ *Jewish Temple guards used a whip made from strips of leather. They were probably each given 39 lashes, one third*

A 5:24 Most manuscripts lack "the High Priest," but he was there.

on the chest and two thirds on the back. The scars marked them as criminals and were intended to disgrace them. A limit of 40 lashes was set in Deuteronomy 25:2-3, but they only did 39 in case they miscounted—so they would not accidentally disobey the command in the Torah. ➤

41 The apostles left the Sanhedrin openly rejoicing because God had considered them worthy to suffer public disgrace for following Jesus. ❖ *Would you have the same attitude? Has God considered you worthy of this honor? All you have to do to be worthy is to be fully obedient and not compromise.* ➤ **42** Despite what happened to them and the risk of further punishment, every day the apostles continued to go to the Temple and from house to house, teaching people and proclaiming that Jesus is the Messiah.

6

The First Seven Deacons Are Chosen

1 In those early days when the number of Jewish followers of Jesus was rapidly increasing, those Jewish believers who were from other countries and only spoke Greek complained to the apostles about the Aramaic-speaking Jewish believers who had always lived in Israel. They said that those who daily distributed food or money to the needy were repeatedly discriminating against the minority of Greek-speaking widows. ❖ *These women had probably moved to Jerusalem to die there. The Jews believed that the resurrection and final Judgment would happen in the Valley of Jehoshaphat, just outside of Jerusalem. [Joel 3:2, 12]* ➤ **2** So the twelve apostles summoned the entire assembly of believers and said, "It would not be right for us to spend all our time distributing food and money instead of teaching God's word—which Jesus commanded us to do. **3** So, brothers and sisters, you choose seven men from among you that everyone respects, who you know are always filled with the Spirit because they continually submit to his leading, and who you know are wise. We will give them the responsibility to oversee the distribution. **4** But we apostles will spend our time in

prayer and in teaching and proclaiming God's word." **5** All the believers liked this idea. They chose Stephen, whose faith was strong and who was filled with the Holy Spirit, and also Philip, Prochorus, Nicanor, Timon, Parmenas, and Nicolas—a Gentile from Antioch who had gone through the requirements to become a Jewish convert before he followed Jesus. ❖ *All seven men had Greek names.* ➤ **6** The believers brought these seven men to the apostles who prayed and then laid their hands on them to bless them and confer on them the authority and spiritual abilities they would need to carry out their assigned work. ❖ *Today, this is commonly called "ordination."* ➤ **7** So God's message continued to be spread by the believers, and the total number of those following Jesus in Jerusalem continued to grow rapidly, and a large number of priests began to obey God by believing in Jesus. ❖ *There were about 20,000 priests living in Israel at that time and they took one-week turns serving in the Temple in Jerusalem.* ➤

Stephen Is Arrested

8 Now, God favored Stephen and enabled him to exhibit great power. **A** He performed great miraculous signs and wonders among the people. ❖ *Stephen was not an apostle, so the miraculous signs and wonders were not restricted to the apostles.* ➤ **9** But there were some Jewish men who opposed Stephen and argued with him. They were members of the Synagogue of Freedmen and were from Cyrene and Alexandria in North Africa, and also from Cilicia and Asia Provinces in Asia Minor. ❖ *Some commentators think those Jews mentioned from North Africa and Asia Minor were not members of the Synagogue of Freedmen, but that the Freedmen were a separate group. A synagogue is a place where Jews gather to worship, pray, study God's word, and conduct local court cases. It was the center of Jewish life, and each town with a sufficient number of Jewish men in it had one. The Synagogue of Freedmen were descendants of Jews who had been taken prisoners of war by the Romans in 63 BC, sold as slaves, and later set free.* ➤ **10** They disputed what he taught, but were unable to refute

---

A 6:8 The literal text says Stephen was full of grace and power, but a few manuscripts have "faith" instead of "power."

what he said because the Holy Spirit in him gave him wisdom and guidance. 11 Since they were thwarted in refuting him, they secretly convinced some men to say, "We heard Stephen blaspheming Moses and God!" ❖ *To blaspheme means to say something that dishonors someone. Blaspheming Moses would make Jews reject him, and blaspheming God carried the penalty of death by stoning. [Leviticus 24:16] This implies that their dispute was regarding Moses and the Torah teachings and probably also regarding God.* ➤ 12 In this way they incited many Jews and elders and Scripture teachers against him. They seized Stephen and forcibly brought him before the Sanhedrin. 13 Then they brought in false witnesses to testify against him, who said, "This man is always speaking blasphemy against the Temple and the teachings in the Torah. ❖ *According to the Torah, witnesses found to be giving false testimony were punished for the crime that they falsely accused someone of doing. [Deuteronomy 19:16-21]* ➤ 14 We've heard him say that this Jesus of his from Nazareth will destroy this Temple and make us change to follow ways different than those handed down to us from Moses." ❖ *Jesus predicted the destruction of the Temple but didn't say he would destroy it. [Luke 21:5-6]* ➤ 15 While the members of the Sanhedrin were staring at Stephen, they saw his face shine like that of an angel's. ❖ *This is what happened to Moses in Exodus 34:29, 35, indicating God's presence with him.* ➤

7

Stephen's Answer to the Charges

1 Then the High Priest ❖ *probably Caiaphas* ➤ who presided over the Sanhedrin, asked him, "Are these accusations against you true?" 2 Stephen answered, "My Jewish brothers and respected leaders, please listen to me for these accusations against me are not true. ❖ *While the text does not have Stephen overtly saying the accusations are not true, this is implied in his argument—in which he shows that he respects both God and Moses.* ➤ The great and glorious God first appeared to our ancestor Abraham while he was still in Mesopotamia before he lived in Haran. ❖ *The meaning of the literal "God of glory" is not certain. Some commentators think it means "God, the source*

of glory" and others "God, who deserves all honor and praise." The same phrase is used in Psalm 29:3 and similar ones are used in Ephesians 1:17 and 1 Corinthians 2:8. Stephen's point in this verse is that God can be met and worshipped anywhere, not just in the Temple in Jerusalem as these Jewish leaders thought. Mesopotamia is hundreds of miles to the east of Israel in modern-day Iraq. ➤ 3 God told him, 'Leave your country where your relatives live and come follow me to the land where I will lead you.' *[Genesis 11:32—12:5]* 4 So he left the land of the Kaldeans ❖ *This is another name for Mesopotamia. Specifically, he left the city of Ur.* ➤ and settled in the city of Haran. ❖ *in northern Mesopotamia, far to the northwest of Ur* ➤ He took his father with him. After his father died, God directed him to move to this land ❖ *Israel* ➤ where we are now living. 5 But when he got here, God didn't give him so much as a square yard of land to own. Instead, he promised him that **he would give it to him and his descendants and that they would always own it thereafter,** even though Abraham was childless at that time. *[Genesis 12:7; 17:8; 48:4]* 6 Later, God told him, '**Your descendants will be foreigners in another country where they will be slaves and mistreated for 400 years. 7 But I will punish that nation where they are enslaved. Then they will leave that country and come to this land and worship me here.'** *[Genesis 15:13-14; Exodus 3:12]* 8 God made a covenant agreement with Abraham, promising to take care of him if he and his descendants would obey their God. The sign of that covenant was circumcision. ❖ *which showed that he belonged to God [Genesis chapter 17]* ➤ Later, Abraham had a son, Isaac, whom he circumcised when he was a week old, *[Genesis 21:1-4]* and Isaac had a son, Jacob, whom he circumcised, *[Genesis 25:19-26]* and Jacob had twelve sons who became our revered tribal ancestors, whom he also circumcised. *[Genesis 29:31-35; 35:16-18]* ❖ *Circumcision was done on the eighth day after birth, counting the day of birth as day one. The way we count days, it would be one week after birth. The circumcision of Jacob and his 12 sons is not mentioned by Stephen in this verse or in Genesis. It is all implied and was understood to be true.* ➤

9 "But ten of Jacob's sons became jealous of their younger brother Joseph and sold him to merchants who took him to Egypt and sold him as a slave. *[Genesis chapter 37]* But

God cared for him and helped him continuously, 10 and repeatedly caused good to result from the bad things people did to him. *[Genesis chapters 39—40]* God made him wise and caused Pharaoh, the king of Egypt, to greatly favor him and make him governor ❖ *second in command* ➤ over of all Egypt and over all the king owned. *[Genesis 41:1-45]* ❖ *Pharaoh is what the king of Egypt was called. It's a title, not a name.* ➤ 11 While he was governor, there was famine in all of Egypt and Canaan, and people in Canaan were starving. Our ancestors couldn't find enough to eat. ❖ *Canaan is the name of the land that later was called Israel.* ➤ 12 But when Jacob heard a report that there was wheat for sale in Egypt, he sent ten of his sons—our ancestors—there on their first trip to buy food. *[Genesis chapter 42]* ❖ *Even though there was famine in Egypt, they had plenty of wheat stored because God had warned them of the coming famine.* ➤ 13 On their second trip to Egypt to buy food, Joseph told his brothers who he was (since they didn't recognize him) and he told Pharaoh about his family in Canaan. *[Genesis chapters 43—45]* 14 Then, Joseph sent a message with his brothers to invite his father Jacob and all his relatives to come to live with him in Egypt—at Pharaoh's invitation. There were 75 of them in all. ❖ *Stephen is quoting from the Septuagint—the Greek translation of the Hebrew Scriptures in common use during Jesus' time—which says 75 (not including Jacob and Joseph, but including all nine descendants of Joseph born in Egypt). The Masoretic Hebrew Scriptures say 70 (including Jacob, Joseph, and Joseph's two sons). [Genesis 46:26-27] The Septuagint mentions four grandsons of Joseph and one great-grandson, in Genesis 46:20, that are not mentioned in the Hebrew text. The reason the discrepancy exists in our English Bibles is because most modern scholars consider the Hebrew text to be more accurate, while the writers of the New Testament quoted from the Septuagint. (The Hebrew text in the Dead Sea Scrolls agrees with the Septuagint account.) Despite minor discrepancies like this one, none of them affect a teaching or doctrine that has to do with our relationship to the Messiah and God.* ➤ 15 So Jacob and his family all went to live in Egypt, and he and all his sons—our tribal ancestors—died there. 16 Hundreds of years later, their descendants brought their remains *[Exodus 13:19; Joshua 24:32]* ❖ *actually only Joseph's bones are mentioned* ➤ back to the town of Shechem in Canaan and put them in a tomb that Abraham had bought there from the tribe of Hamor. ❖ *Actually, it was Jacob who bought land in Shechem. [Genesis 33:19] Abraham bought a field and a burial cave from Ephron the Hittite. [Genesis 23:15-18] Stephen's listeners all knew these stories intimately and that he was condensing and combining these two stories for brevity. The discrepancies were not intended to deceive, nor were they really errors of fact. Such condensing and combining was common, even though it appears inaccurate by our standards. He was simply repeating enough information to bring all the facts to the minds of his listeners. They knew that Joseph buried Jacob's body in the cave that Abraham had bought, [Genesis 50:13] and that Joseph was buried at Shechem. [Joshua 24:32]* ➤

17 "As the time came closer to when God was going to fulfill his promise to Abraham, ❖ *verses 5-7 above* ➤ the number of Israelites living in Egypt greatly increased. ❖ *It's estimated there were around 1.5 million Israelites when Moses led them out of Egypt. But we have no idea how many there were at this point in the story, starting in the next verse, which one source says happened only about 60 years after Joseph died. Stephen is following the account in Exodus 1:6-22. It appears that the story is highly condensed somewhere in those verses. The Israelites lived in Egypt 400 years and were probably only slaves toward the end of that time, assuming the Pharaoh in Exodus 1:8 is the same one in Exodus 1:22. But the exact sequence of events is not clear. Exodus 1:7 (and this verse) says that the Israelites multiplied and filled the land and seems to imply that this was before they were enslaved. Genesis 15:13 says they will be enslaved for 400 years. Exodus 12:40 says they were in Egypt 430 years, which may indicate that the 400 years prophesied in Genesis and quoted by Stephen in Acts 7:7 above, was merely a round number. The prophecy might be interpreted to say they would be in Egypt 400 years, where they would be enslaved. We can't be sure from the Scriptural accounts when the slavery started.* ➤ 18 Then **there was another king over Egypt who knew nothing of Joseph** and the favor he had had with another Pharaoh generations earlier. *[Exodus 1:8]* 19 He took advantage of our ancestors and mistreated them. He forced them to throw their infants in the Nile river so they would die. *[Exodus 1:22]* 20 At that time, Moses was born and he was pleasing to God. ❖ *Commentators debate what this means. It could mean that God had chosen him for a task and knew that in the course of his life he would fulfill that task and please him.* ➤ In violation of Pharaoh's command, his parents secretly took care of him for three months in his

father's house. 21 When he had to be placed outside to avoid discovery, Pharaoh's daughter found him in the place they had hidden him and adopted him, raising him as her own son. *[Exodus 2:1-10]* 22 He was taught everything that the Egyptian culture knew and became a powerful and influential man who spoke with authority. ❖ *In Exodus 4:10, Moses says he has never been eloquent, but this was after spending 40 years as a shepherd. He may also have been exaggerating his lack of ability to avoid the task the Lord was calling him to do.* ➤

23 "But when he was about forty years old, he decided to visit his fellow Israelites. ❖ *Though raised as royalty, he evidently knew of his origins from his adopted mother and possibly from his own mother who was hired to nurse him as an infant. [Exodus 2:7-10]* ➤ 24 He saw one of them being abused by an Egyptian, so went to defend him and took revenge by striking the Egyptian down, killing him. 25 He thought that his own people, the Israelites, might understand that God was going to use him to free them from slavery, but they didn't. 26 The next day, he saw two Israelites fighting and tried to make peace between them. He said, 'Men, you are fellow Israelites. You shouldn't be hurting each other!' 27 But the one who was beating up on his neighbor gave Moses the brush off and sarcastically retorted, **'And who appointed you as a ruler and judge over us? 28 I hope you don't intend to kill me like you killed that Egyptian yesterday.'** 29 When Moses heard this, he realized that many people probably knew what he had done and that he would soon be wanted for murder. So he ran away about 100 miles east to the country of Midian. He lived there as a foreigner and eventually married and had two sons. *[Exodus 2:11-21]* 30 Forty years later, **an angel appeared to Moses in a burning bush in the desert near Mount Sinai.** ❖ *It's not clear in the Exodus account, or in Stephen's, if God himself appeared in the form of an angel, or an angel appeared and spoke for God. Exodus 3:1 says this happened at Mount Horeb but this is just another name for Mount Sinai.* ➤ 31 When Moses saw it, he was

amazed that the bush wasn't consumed. As he went nearer to investigate, he heard the Lord say to him, 32 **'I am the God that your ancestors Abraham, Isaac, and Jacob worship.'** Moses trembled with fear and didn't dare to look at the bush. 33 **Then the Lord told him, 'Take off your sandals, for you are standing on holy ground.** ❖ *Removing the sandals showed reverence and humility. Holy ground means it was set apart and dedicated for God's special use.* ➤ 34 **I am aware of how my people are oppressed in Egypt. I've seen their suffering and heard their groaning, so I've come down to appoint you to set them free. Now come, I'm sending you to Egypt.'** *[Exodus 3:1-10]*

35 "This Moses was the same man who tried to help the Israelites years earlier, but whom they rejected, saying, **'And who appointed you as a ruler and judge over us?'** *[Exodus 2:14]* He is the one God sent—through the angel who appeared to him in the burning bush—both to rule over them and to ransom them from slavery. ❖ *Moses didn't pay any kind of ransom, but Stephen was amplifying the parallels between Moses and Jesus. Just as the Israelites rejected Moses as their savior from slavery, their descendants rejected Jesus as their Savior from slavery to sin.* ➤ 36 This man led them out of Egypt and performed miraculous signs and wonders in Egypt and at the Red Sea and during the 40 years they wandered in the wilderness. *[Exodus chapters 5—17]* ❖ *Stephen gives another parallel with Jesus: The miraculous signs and wonders demonstrated that God was behind both Moses and Jesus.* ➤ 37 This Moses is the one who spoke about the Messiah when he told our ancestors, the Israelites, **'Our God, Yahweh, will cause one from among us Israelites to be a prophet like me. You must listen carefully to everything he tells you.'** A *[Deuteronomy 18:15]* ❖ *Stephen is implying that Jesus is that prophet and that they have not obeyed Moses' command about him.* ➤ 38 This is the man who was the leader of our people when they assembled in the wilderness. God's angel spoke to him on Mount Sinai, giving him the Torah, and through him God spoke to our ancestors. Moses

---

A **7:37** The last sentence in this quote is included in Deuteronomy 18:15 and is in this verse in some Greek manuscripts. Even if Stephen didn't quote it,

it would have come immediately to the minds of his listeners after hearing the first part of the quote.

received—from God—words that told us how to live in God's presence, and Moses passed them on to us. 39 But our ancestors were unwilling to obey Moses. They rejected him as a leader and yearned to return to Egypt. [Exodus 14:12; 16:3; 17:3] They wanted to worship gods like the Egyptians had. [Exodus chapter 32] 40 They told Aaron, ❖ Moses' brother ➤ 'Make us idols that will be gods who will lead us back to Egypt and protect us. For we don't know what's happened to that guy Moses who led us here!' [Exodus 32:1, 23] ❖ Yahweh had led them out of Egypt, going before them in the visible forms of a cloud and a pillar of fire, and he had protected them. Now they were rejecting Yahweh and replacing him with an idol, and they were rejecting Moses— Yahweh's chosen leader. ➤ 41 So they made a gold idol in the form of a calf and offered sacrifices to it and celebrated in honor of the god they had made with their own hands. [Exodus 32:2-8] ❖ Yahweh had just forbidden them from making or worshipping idols. [Exodus 20:4-5, 23] Jews in Stephen's time considered this event to be their ancestors' worst sin. ➤ 42 Therefore, God was angry and rejected them, removing his blessing and protection from them, and allowed them to devote themselves to worshipping the sun, moon, and stars as their gods and thus earn more of his wrath and punishment. ❖ This happened later, after they settled in the land of Canaan and started worshipping the same gods as the Canaanites. [Deuteronomy 4:19] ➤ This is what Yahweh said about them in the book of the prophets, 'You people of Israel, during those 40 years you wandered in the wilderness you gave offerings and sacrifices, but you were really worshipping other gods and not me! 43 It was the tabernacle ❖ i.e., tent, containing a statue ➤ of the god Molech that you carried and worshipped. You also carried an image of the star god Rephan. These were idols that you made to worship instead of me. Therefore, I will send you to exile beyond Babylon.' [Amos 5:25-27] ❖ Molech was the planet Venus, worshipped by the Canaanites and Phoenicians as the sky and sun god. It's worship involved child sacrifice. Rephan is the planet Saturn, which was an Egyptian god. Stephen

combines the Assyrian and Babylonian captivities by quoting from Amos, which predicted the Assyrian captivity, and by substituting "Babylon" for "Damascus." He is also combining the rebellion of the Israelites during their 40 years in the wilderness with the repeated idolatry of the Israelites over a period of nearly 1,000 years as recorded throughout the Hebrew Scriptures. Stephen is driving home the repeated pattern of the Israelites rejecting their own God. ➤

44 "Our ancestors had the Tabernacle of the testimony ❖ i.e., the tent that contained the ark A of the covenant ➤ with them in the wilderness as a reminder of Yahweh's presence with them. They had constructed it exactly as God directed Moses to make it, following the model he had seen while he was on the mountain. ❖ The two stone tablets on which God wrote the ten commandments were referred to as "the testimony." They were kept in the ark inside the Tabernacle, which is why it was called the "Tabernacle of the testimony." [Exodus 25:16, 21] ➤ 45 Later, under the leadership of Joshua, those ancestors who received the Tabernacle from their parents brought it with them when they forcibly took this land from the nations that God drove out of it. And the Tabernacle remained through the time when David was King. 46 God was pleased with David, so David asked if he might build a permanent dwelling place for the God of Israel B to replace the Tabernacle. ❖ Jacob's name was changed to Israel [Genesis 32:28] and often the name Jacob was used to refer to the entire nation of Israel. Stephen may have been implying that if the Temple was as important as the Jewish leaders thought, then God would have let the man who pleased him build it. Instead, it was Solomon—who did not please God as his father David did—who built it. ➤ 47 But it was Solomon who built it for him. 48 However, God, the Most High, is not confined to living in buildings made by humans. As the prophet Isaiah recorded Yahweh as saying, 49 'Heaven ❖ or: the sky ➤ is the place from which I rule, and Earth is nothing more than my footstool. What kind of house could you possibly build that would adequately express my greatness or be a fitting place for me to live in? 50 Didn't I make Heaven and Earth myself?' " [Isaiah 66:1-2] ❖ Stephen's point is that God

---

A **7:44** This is not a boat, as was Noah's ark. See Exodus 25:10-15 for a description of the ark of the covenant, which was a special box where God manifested his presence and promised to live among his people, the Israelites.

B **7:46** Some manuscripts have "house of Jacob" rather than "God of Jacob."

is everywhere and can be worshipped anywhere, just like their ancestors did with the transportable Tabernacle. The Jews of his day put too much emphasis on worship in the Temple, almost making it an idol. The Temple did not even exist until Solomon's time, so it wasn't essential. For hundreds of years, the Tabernacle had been adequate. ➤

51 Stephen then concluded his argument, spelling out the implications of all he had related up to this point. He said, "You are just like your rebellious ancestors! You are proud of your circumcision, but your ears are uncircumcised because you don't listen to God, and your hearts are uncircumcised because you don't obey him! [Deuteronomy 10:16; 30:6; Jeremiah 4:4] You are stubborn and always resist the leading of the Holy Spirit, whether he speaks through the writings of the prophets or through Jesus' words. ❖ Implied: People accuse me of speaking against the Torah teachings and Moses, but you oppose God himself and are no better than pagans! ➤ 52 Your ancestors persecuted every one of God's prophets, including Moses. They even killed those who prophesied about the coming of the Righteous One. ❖ i.e., the Messiah [Isaiah 53:11; Jeremiah 23:5; 33:15] ➤ And like them, you handed him over to our enemies and had him killed. You betrayed and murdered God's Messiah! 53 You have had the privilege of having God's Torah, which was delivered to Moses by angels, but in spite of the supernatural revelation God has given you, you have not obeyed it."

Stephen Dies for His Witness to the Truth

54 When the members of the Sanhedrin and the other Jews there heard this, they were so furious that they gnashed their teeth at him. ❖ One commentator says "gnash their teeth" is an idiom meaning "they shouted angrily." ➤ 55 But Stephen, still filled with the Holy Spirit, calmly gazed into Heaven and saw the brilliant light of God's glory and Jesus standing at the place of highest authority and power at his right hand. ❖ Note the mention of all three persons of the Trinity in this verse. ➤ 56 He said, "Look, I can see into Heaven and I see the Son of Man standing at God's right hand." ❖ See the note about the title "son of Man" in the introduction to the gospel of Luke. ➤ 57 But when the members of the Sanhedrin and other Jews there heard him say this, they yelled at the

top of their lungs and covered their ears so they wouldn't hear anything else he said about Jesus that they considered blasphemous. Then, they all rushed at him 58 and drove him outside the city and began to stone him to death. ❖ Blasphemy was punishable by stoning, but they were so angry that they didn't bother making a formal judgment. They were also breaking Roman law, which forbid them from executing anyone. Some commentators think the Romans allowed a few exceptions that concerned the Temple and that this fell within those bounds. Others think that at this time, (AD 35–36) Pilate was losing control over Judea and they had nothing to fear from him. Pilate was removed in AD 36 because he wasn't able to maintain peace among the Jews. ➤ The witnesses took off their outer garments—so they could more easily throw stones—and put them at the feet of a young man named Saul, for him to keep them from being stolen. ❖ The witnesses threw the first stones. [Leviticus 24:14; Deuteronomy 17:7] It's not clear if the witnesses are just those who accused him in 6:13, or if it was the entire Sanhedrin since they were all witnesses to his supposed "blasphemy." This Saul (a Hebrew name) later became the Apostle Paul (the Greek version of his name) and he was probably in his early 30s at this time. ➤ 59 While they were stoning him, Stephen prayed, "Lord Jesus, I entrust my spirit to you." ❖ His words were similar to Jesus' on the cross. [Luke 23:46] ➤ 60 Then, he fell to his knees and prayed loudly, "Lord, forgive them for killing me." [Luke 23:34] And he died.

8

2 Some godly men buried Stephen and publicly mourned his death. ❖ It was illegal for Jews to mourn the death of a condemned criminal, so their public mourning indicated that they believed their leaders had killed an innocent man. ➤

The Holy Spirit Uses Persecution to Spread the Believers Outside of Jerusalem

1,3 But Saul was in full agreement that Stephen deserved to be killed. From that very day, people started to persecute the believers in Jerusalem to try to get them to renounce their faith in Jesus. ❖ Since the believers had enjoyed the favor of most of their fellow Jews up to this point, this persecution was likely instigated mainly by the unbelieving Jewish leaders. ➤ Saul went about trying to destroy this movement of people who followed Jesus. He went from house to house searching for believers and dragged them off to prison, both men and women. Most of the believers in Jerusalem fled to the countryside throughout Judea and Samaria, except for the apostles who remained in the city. ❖ *It's estimated that there were about 20,000 believers in Jerusalem before the persecution started.* ➤ 4 Wherever those believers went, they told others the message about Jesus.

Philip the Deacon
Ministers to Gentiles in Samaria

5 One of them was Philip, *[Acts 6:5]* who went down from Jerusalem, north to a city **A** in Samaria, and began to proclaim the message about the Messiah there. ❖ *We know this Philip is not the apostle Philip, because all the apostles stayed in Jerusalem.* ➤ 6 When the crowds in that city heard him speak and saw the miraculous signs that God did through him, they all paid close attention to what he said. 7 For example, when Philip commanded demons to leave people in Jesus' name, they screamed and left. There were many who were delivered this way. He also healed many who were paralyzed or lame. 8 As a result, there was a lot of rejoicing in that city.

9 Now, a Samaritan named Simon lived in that city who practiced sorcery and had amazed all the people in that region. ❖ *God forbids his people from practicing magic, sorcery, witchcraft, divination, etc. [Leviticus 19:26, 31; 20:6; Deuteronomy 18:9-14; 1 Samuel 15:23; 2 Kings 17:16-17; 21:6; 2 Chronicles 33:6; Micah 5:12; Galatians 5:20]* ➤ He frequently boasted that he was someone great, 10 and all the people in that city from all classes and every status paid attention to what he said. Everyone believed he was empowered by God and called him "the Great One." 11 He had such great influence because he had astonished them for a long time with his magic arts. ❖ *The Scripture doesn't claim that there is no power in magic and sorcery. It forbids it because it is empowered by demons, who are God's enemies.* ➤ 12 But when Philip preached the Good News about Jesus the Messiah and how to have

God live in them as they submit to him, many men and women believed his message and were baptized. 13 Even Simon believed the message and was baptized. He was astonished by the signs and great miracles he saw Philip do, and followed him everywhere.

14 When the apostles in Jerusalem heard that many Samaritans were believing God's message about Jesus, they sent Peter and John there. 15 When they arrived, they prayed for the Samaritan believers to receive the Holy Spirit, 16 for the Spirit had not yet come upon any of them. Philip had only baptized them in the name of Jesus. **B** ❖ *Many commentators think these new believers did not yet have the Holy Spirit at all and that they received the indwelling Holy Spirit when Peter and John laid hands on them. They think this was a special one-time occasion when the Lord was waiting for the apostles to come to make official that he was accepting Samaritans as his people. On the other side, Pentecostals and Charismatics say they were professing belief and had been baptized in the name of Jesus, so there was no way for the apostles to know that Holy Spirit had not yet "come upon them" unless there was some outward manifestation that they were looking for which signified the presence of the Spirit—other than profession of belief. God did not need the apostles' confirmation that he was accepting Samaritans. He had already clearly stated that he would include Gentiles in his Kingdom, and in Acts 10, when Cornelius is converted, he did not wait for Peter to lay hands on the Gentiles before giving his Spirit to them. What this whole passage is about is the "baptism" or "gift" of the Holy Spirit which empowered them with outwardly visible signs, such as prophesying, speaking in tongues, or the ability to heal, etc. This passage is evidence that the indwelling of the Spirit and the baptism of the Spirit are separate events, which may take place at the same time as conversion, or at separate times.* ➤ 17 So Peter and John put their hands on the heads of those they were praying for, and they received the Holy Spirit. ❖ *One of the elementary teachings of the faith [Hebrews 6:1-2] is that one purpose of laying hands on people is so that they will receive the gift—a.k.a. baptism—of the Holy Spirit.* ➤

18 Now, when Simon the magician saw that God gave the Holy Spirit to people when the apostles laid hands on them, he offered the apostles money, 19 saying, "Give

---

A 8:5 Most manuscripts have "a city of Samaria," some have "the city of Samaria," and a few have "the city of Caesarea." Many commentators think it was Neopolis,

the main city in Samaria, next to Mount Gerizim.
B 8:16 Some manuscripts say "the Lord Jesus" and a few have "Jesus the Messiah."

me this authority so everyone that I lay my hands on will also receive the Holy Spirit."

❖ *Simon was not envying the ability for people to receive the indwelling Holy Spirit so they could have faith. He was seeing supernatural manifestations from the baptism in the Holy Spirit that was given through the laying on of hands. It's clear from the next verses that he had improper motives, which would have been for more power, not to enable people to believe. He probably wanted to be able to charge people for the opportunity to receive this kind of supernatural power, even though they didn't have it because they didn't believe.* ➤

20 But Peter rebuked him, "May you and your money go to Hell because you think you can obtain with money God's free gift which is only offered to those who believe in Jesus! 21 God has not authorized you to have any part in this ministry or in the giving of the Holy Spirit because you are not in a proper relationship with him. 22 So turn away from your evil scheming and decide to submit to the Lord's will. Then beg him to forgive you for having such thoughts, if that's possible. ❖ *Either Peter's rebuke is a severe warning and there is no doubt that the Lord would be willing to forgive Simon if he repented, or there was a genuine question in Peter's mind if this offense might have constituted blaspheming the Holy Spirit, which can't be forgiven. If the latter were the case, Simon would have no desire to repent. [Matthew 12:31-32; Mark 3:28-29; Luke 12:10; 1 John 5:16]* ➤ 23 For I perceive that you are full of bitter envy of us apostles, and are enslaved to your sinful ways." ❖ *Peter could perceive this about Simon from a "word of knowledge." [1 Corinthians 12:8]* 24 Simon answered, "Both of you, please beg the Lord for me so none of those bad things will happen to me!" ❖ *Unfortunately, Luke doesn't tell us what happened to Simon, perhaps because the result was well-known.* ➤ 25 After Peter and John had testified to what they had seen and heard in the life of Jesus and had proclaimed the Lord's message about how to be saved, they returned to Jerusalem. On the way, they preached the Good News in many Samaritan villages.

Philip Baptizes an Ethiopian Eunuch

26 One day, the Lord sent an angel to Philip, who told him, "Get ready and go south ❖ *or: go at noon* ➤ to ❖ *or: along* ➤ the road that goes from Jerusalem down to the city of Gaza on the Mediterranean coast."

This is a desert. ❖ *We don't know where the quote ends. Many commentators think the last sentence was added as commentary by Luke. It could mean that the road went through an uninhabited area, or that the Gaza referred to was an old abandoned city that had become desert, i.e., not the inhabited one in Philip's time.* ➤ 27 So he started out and encountered a eunuch who was an official in the court of Queen Candace of Ethiopia and was in charge of all her treasure. ❖ *This is not modern-day Ethiopia but was a country that is now the southern part of Egypt and the northern part of Sudan. Candace was the title given to the king's mother, and she was the default ruler of the country because the king was considered to be the son of the sun god and too holy to do any work. This man was probably identifiable as a eunuch by his lack of a beard—the result of having been castrated as a youth.* ➤ He had been to Jerusalem to worship, but because of his mutilation, he was not allowed to become a full Jew. *[Deuteronomy 23:1]* ❖ *He could only enter the court of the Gentiles at the Temple.* ➤ 28 While he was returning home sitting in his chariot, he was reading aloud from the book written by the prophet Isaiah. ❖ *Reading silently is a relatively recent innovation. Everyone who read, did so aloud.* ➤ 29 The Holy Spirit told Philip, "Go up to that chariot and stay near it." 30 So he ran up to the chariot and heard the man reading from Isaiah. He asked him, "Do you understand the meaning of what you are reading?" ❖ *Many prophesies in the Hebrew Scriptures are difficult to understand.* ➤ 31 The man answered, "How can I, unless someone explains it to me?" So he urged Philip to ride with him and explain it. 32 He was reading from this passage of Scripture: **"He was led like a sheep to be slaughtered. Just as a lamb is silent while being sheared of its wool, he didn't even open his mouth in protest. 33 He was humiliated and deprived of justice. He had no descendants because his life was cut short."** *[Isaiah 53:7-8]* ❖ *This prophecy was written in the past tense—even though it was predicting the future—to indicate that it was certain to happen.* ➤ 34 The eunuch asked Philip, "Who is the prophet talking about, himself or someone else?" 35 Then Philip started to explain that the passage was about Jesus. He told him the Good News and the eunuch believed. 36 As they continued along the road, they came to some water and the eunuch said, "Look, water! Is there anything that would prevent me from being baptized?" ❖ *This was a real question. As a eunuch, he was not allowed to become a full Jew. He was wondering if there was any similar restriction against his being baptized and becoming a full follower of Jesus. Also, note the parallels between the eunuch and the Messiah from the prophecy. They both were humiliated (the eunuch, by his being a eunuch) and both could not have descendants. These were probably facts that caused the eunuch to identify with the Messiah.* ➤ 37 Philip answered, "If you believe in Jesus with all your heart, you may." The eunuch replied, "I believe that Jesus the Messiah is God's Son." **A** 38 Then, he ordered the driver to stop the chariot, and both Philip and the eunuch went down into the water, and Philip baptized him. 39 When they came up out of the water, the Spirit of the Lord suddenly took Philip away, miraculously transporting him elsewhere. The eunuch no longer saw him but continued on his journey home rejoicing because of his salvation. 40 Meanwhile, Philip suddenly found himself in the city of Azotus and traveled around that region preaching the Good News about Jesus in every place he came to, all the way to the city of Caesarea. ❖ *Azotus was called Ashdod in the Hebrew Scriptures when it was one of five major Philistine cities. [Joshua 13:3] It was located about 22 miles north of the city of Gaza and about 56 miles south of Caesarea. Gaza, Azotus, and Caesarea are all on the Mediterranean coast, and Caesarea was a major seaport. It may have been Philip's hometown or where he settled. [Acts 21:8]* ➤

9

Saul Becomes a Follower of Jesus

1 All during this time, Saul was threatening to kill those who followed the Lord Jesus. He went to the High Priest 2 and asked him for letters of introduction that he could

to take to the leaders of the synagogues in Damascus, authorizing him to act with the authority of the Sanhedrin. ❖ *The Roman government had given the Sanhedrin authority over all Jews living outside of Israel. The High Priest was the head of the Sanhedrin, so his authorization was as good as law.* ➤ Saul intended to go there and—with the cooperation of the local Jewish authorities—arrest any men or women who belonged to "The Way" movement, that is, those who believed Jesus was the Messiah. He would then bring them back to Jerusalem for trial. ❖ *Jesus called himself "The Way" in John 14:6. During this time, most believers in Jesus still worshipped at their local Jewish synagogue. Damascus was a major city where thousands of Jews lived—about 150 miles north of Jerusalem.* ➤

3 The High Priest gave him the letters, and Saul and his traveling companions set out for Damascus. As they were approaching that city, suddenly, a brilliant light from Heaven ❖ *or: the sky* ➤ dazzled him. [Acts 22:6; 26:12-13] 4 He fell to the ground and then heard a voice say to him, "Saul, Saul, why are you persecuting me? ❖ *The repetition of his name expresses disappointment, but not anger. Jesus considers anything done to his followers as being done to himself. [Matthew 25:40, 45; Luke 9:48; 10:16; Romans 12:4-5; 1 Corinthians 12:12; 26-27; Ephesians 1:22-23]* ➤ 5 Saul replied, "Who are you, sir?" The voice answered, "I am Jesus, the one you are persecuting. {You are just hurting yourself by fighting against me.}" **B** 6 But instead of continuing in your rebellion, get up and go into Damascus where you will be told what you have to do." 7 Saul's traveling companions stood there speechless. They heard the voice as a sound, but unlike Saul, they didn't see anyone. **C** ❖ *Saul—later called Paul—tells this story again in 22:9. There, he says the men saw the light, and here he says they didn't see anyone.*

A 8:37 Most major Greek manuscripts do not have verse 37. Only a very few and the Textus Receptus have it.

B 9:5 The expression in { }—"kick against the goads" in the literal text of the KJV, other translations based on the Textus Receptus, and in Latin translations—is found in no Greek manuscripts of this verse. But it is in Paul's account in 26:14. It was a Greek proverb about fighting a god.

C 9:7 This says they heard/understood ἀκούω (akouō) the voice/sound φωνή (phōnē), but 22:9 says they did not hear/understand the voice/sound. The word in 22:9 for

"understand" is the same Greek word in 9:7 that means "hear." It can have either meaning depending on context. I have translated it as "heard" in 9:7 and as "understand" in 22:9 to make the two accounts consistent. The word in this verse and in 22:9 for "voice" can also mean "sound." If one assumes that Paul told basically the same story both times, it's easy and legitimate to translate them with no contradiction. But it is also easy to translate them to appear contradictory, as some translations do.

Paul saw the Messiah despite the light. The text doesn't explicitly say so here, but it does in 9:27; 22:14; and 26:16. In the next verse, he is blind, but that doesn't mean he didn't see Jesus first. ➤

8 Afterward, when Saul got up from the ground, he was blind. So his companions led him by the hand into Damascus. 9 He was blind for three days and neither ate nor drank anything. ❖ *He was in shock and was re-evaluating his understanding of who Jesus was. He may also have been fasting for the purpose of prayer.* ➤

10 Now, there was a follower of Jesus in Damascus named Ananias. The Lord appeared to him in a vision and said, "Ananias!" He replied, "Here I am, Lord." ❖ *His answer implied that he was listening and waiting to obey.* ➤ 11 The Lord commanded him, "Go to the house of Judas on Straight Street and ask for a man who is staying there. He is originally from the city of Tarsus and his name is Saul. He is praying right now. 12 I've sent him a vision in which he has seen a man named Ananias come and lay hands on him so he can see again." *[Hebrews 6:1-2]* ❖ *This is another part of the elementary teaching about laying on of hands, which is for the purpose of healing.* ➤ 13 But in fear, Ananias answered, "Lord, I've heard many reports about this man. He has done much harm to your people in Jerusalem. 14 And the chief priests have given him authority to arrest all who say they are your followers." ❖ *To "call on your name" (in the literal text) means to worship him, pray to him, and to depend and call on him for help and salvation.* ➤ 15 But the Lord told him, "Go and do what I've told you to do! For I've chosen this man to serve me by telling Gentiles and their kings and also fellow Jews about me. 16 I myself will show him how much I'm requiring him to suffer in the course of his telling people about me." ❖ *Saul—later called Paul—lists some of the things he suffered for serving the Messiah in 2 Corinthians 11:23-33. Once he started following Jesus, he considered it a great privilege to suffer for him. [Philippians 1:29]* ➤

17 So Ananias went, found the house, and entered. He laid his hands on Saul and said, "My brother in the Lord, Saul, the Lord Jesus who appeared to you on the road on your way here has sent me to you so you can regain your sight and be filled with the Holy Spirit." 18 Immediately, something like scales fell out of Saul's eyes and he could see again. He got up and Ananias baptized him. 19a After this, he ate some food and regained his strength.

Saul Begins to Preach About the Messiah

19b Saul spent several days learning from the believers in Damascus 20 and right away began to preach about Jesus **A** in the synagogues there. He proclaimed, "Jesus is God's Son." ❖ *Some commentators think the Jews were expecting the Messiah to be God's Son. [Psalm 2:6-7; Matthew 26:63]* ➤ 21 All who heard him preach were astonished at his attitude toward Jesus. They were saying, "Isn't this the same man who was killing Jesus' followers in Jerusalem? Didn't he come here in order to arrest them and take them to trial before the chief priests?" 22 But God made Saul's preaching even more compelling and convincing. The Jews in Damascus were unable to find anything to say against his Scripturally based arguments which demonstrated that Jesus was the Messiah.

23 After more than a year in Damascus, some Jews plotted to kill Saul. ❖ *Galatians 1:17-18 says it was a period of three years, but Jews of that time counted partial years so it could have been as short as one full year and a partial year on either side.* ➤ 24 But someone told him about the plot and that some Jews were watching the city gates both night and day to catch him as he left so they could kill him. *[2 Corinthians 11:32]* 25 So one night, his followers helped him escape by lowering him to the ground in a basket from an opening in the city wall.

26 When Saul returned to Jerusalem, he tried to meet with other believers but most of them were afraid of him and didn't believe he was a true follower of Jesus. 27 But Barnabas took him to the apostles and told them how Saul had seen the Lord Jesus on the road to Damascus, and that Jesus had spoken to him, and that afterward he had stayed there and boldly proclaimed Jesus as

---

A 9:20 A very few manuscripts have "the Messiah" instead of "Jesus."

the Messiah and God's Son. ❖ *Barnabas is also mentioned in Acts 4:36-37; 11:25-26; and 13:2.* ➤ 28 So Saul stayed with the apostles and other believers and moved freely throughout Jerusalem, boldly proclaiming that Jesus was the Messiah. 29 He also talked about Jesus with Jews who were there from other countries who only spoke Greek. He argued with them that Jesus was the Messiah, but they responded by repeatedly trying to kill him. 30 When the other believers found out about this, they took him down to the port at Caesarea, 62 miles northwest of Jerusalem, and sent him safely off on a ship to his home city of Tarsus in Cilicia Province.

31 So then for a while, the believers living in Judea, Galilee, and Samaria enjoyed a time of peace because no one was actively persecuting them. During this time, the Holy Spirit encouraged them. He strengthened their faith and ability to obey; he caused many more people to become believers; and he caused them all to live their lives in fear and reverence of the Lord.

Peter Heals and Raises the Dead

32 As Peter was traveling around these provinces, he visited the believers in a town called Lydda. ❖ *Lydda was about 21 miles northwest of Jerusalem and about 10 miles southeast of the port of Joppa, on the coastal plain called "Sharon."* ➤ 33 There, he met a paralyzed man named Aeneas who had been bedridden for eight years. 34 Peter said to him, "Aeneas, Jesus the Messiah is healing you right now. Stand up and make your bed!" A Immediately, he was healed and stood up. 35 And when they saw Aeneas healed, most of the people who lived in Lydda and in the region of the plain of Sharon began to believe in the Lord Jesus. ❖ *The plain of Sharon is a fertile strip of land about 10 by 50 miles along the Mediterranean coast, with Lydda on the southeast edge of the plain.* ➤

36 Now, in the nearby city of Joppa there was a woman named *Tabitha* (her Aramaic name) who was a follower of Jesus. In Greek, her name was Dorcas. ❖ *Both Tabitha and Dorcas mean "gazelle."* ➤ She was always

doing good works and helping the poor. 37 While Peter was in Lydda, she became sick and died. Following Jewish custom, some women washed her body for burial, then wrapped it with a cloth and put it in an upstairs room. 38 When the believers in Joppa heard that Peter was only 10 miles away in Lydda, they sent two men to beg him to come to Joppa immediately. ❖ *People were normally buried the same day. A 20-mile round trip would take 6-8 hours, so they would have to hurry.* ➤ 39 Peter went with them immediately and when they arrived, they took him to the room where Dorcas' body was laid out. All the widows she had helped stood around him mourning and showed him all the clothing they were wearing that she had made for them while she was still alive. ❖ *The crying of mourning in that culture, as in many cultures, was loud wailing.* ➤ 40 But Peter chased them all out of the room because they didn't want to leave, then he knelt and prayed. Then, he turned to the dead woman and said, "Tabitha, get up!" She opened her eyes, saw Peter, and sat up. 41 He took her by the hand and helped her to her feet. Then he called the widows and other believers to come in and presented Tabitha to them alive. 42 Soon, everyone in Joppa had heard about the miracle and as a result, many believed in the Lord Jesus. 43 Afterward, Peter stayed on in Joppa for quite a few days as a guest at the house of a tanner named Simon. ❖ *Tanners made leather from animal skins, but touching dead animals made them ritually unclean. [Leviticus 11:39-40] The fact that Peter stayed with Simon shows that he was open to separating himself from a rigid legalistic following of the Torah's commands.* ➤

10

Cornelius' Vision

1 In the city of Caesarea, there lived a Roman centurion named Cornelius who belonged to the Italian Cohort. ❖ *A Roman legion had about 6000 men divided into 10 cohorts of 600 men each—each cohort commanded by a tribune. Each cohort was divided into 6 centuries of 100 men each, each century commanded by a centurion.* ➤ 2 He and all his

---

A 9:34 The Greek literally says, "spread for yourself." Some think it might mean to "get something to eat."

family and servants—though Gentiles—were devout and submitted themselves in worship to the one true God. He gave generously to poor Jews and prayed regularly. 3 One day, while praying at about three in the afternoon during a regular Jewish prayer time, he had a vision. An angel came into the room and said, "Cornelius!" 4 Cornelius stared at him in fear and asked, "What do you want, sir?" ❖ *Literally, he called him "lord" but that was the same common form of respectful address he would have used with any man, and does not imply that he considered the angel to be God.* ➤ The angel replied, "Your prayers and gifts to the poor are like pleasing offerings in God's sight. ❖ *Literally "a memorial offering." [Leviticus 2:2]* ➤ 5 Now, send some men to Joppa and have them ask a man named Simon Peter to come back here with them. 6 He is staying at the house of Simon the tanner, near the sea." 7 When the angel had left, Cornelius called in two of his trusted servants and a soldier who was one of his personal attendants that also worshipped God. 8 He told them about the angel and everything he had said and sent them he 33 miles south to Joppa to get Peter.

Peter's Vision

9 About noon the next day—as the three men were approaching Joppa—Peter went up to the flat roof of the house where he was staying to pray. ❖ *All the houses had flat roofs which were used as spare rooms. There were stairs leading up to the roof—which had a short wall around the edge—and it was used for a place to visit or rest or to have privacy.* ➤ 10 He became very hungry and wanted to eat, but while he was waiting for the food to be prepared, he fell into a trance and had a vision. ❖ *A person who is in a trance is not sleeping but is not aware of his surroundings. In the vision Cornelius had, he was awake and aware of his surroundings at the same time as seeing the angel.* ➤ 11 He saw the sky open and something like a large sheet being lowered to the earth by its four corners. ❖ *Greek has one word οὐρανός (ouranos) that means either "sky" or "Heaven."* ➤ 12 It contained all kinds of four-legged animals {and wild animals} A and reptiles and birds, including those the Torah forbids people to eat. *[Leviticus chapter 11]*

13 Then a voice told him, "Peter, get up and kill some of these animals to eat!" 14 But Peter answered, "Lord, you can't be serious! I've never eaten anything that the Torah says is impure or ritually unclean." 15 The voice spoke to him again, "Don't call things unclean that God has declared clean." 16 The same words were spoken to Peter three consecutive times for emphasis, and then the sheet was quickly taken back up into the sky out of sight.

17 While Peter was wondering what the vision meant, the men sent by Cornelius had found out where Simon the tanner's house was and had arrived at the gate. ❖ *You may wonder why Peter didn't immediately conclude that the vision was to be taken literally, to mean that all animals are "clean" and fit to eat. He didn't come to that conclusion and neither should we immediately jump to it. It is a traditional view, but it may not be correct.* ➤ 18 They called out, asking if this was the place where Simon Peter was staying. 19 While Peter was still thinking about the vision, the Holy Spirit said to him, "Listen, three men are looking for you. 20 So get up, go downstairs, and don't hesitate to go with them just because they are Gentiles, for I was the one who sent them to you." 21 So Peter went down and told the men, "I'm the one you are looking for. But tell me, why have you come?" 22 They answered, "We were sent by Cornelius, a centurion who is also a God-fearing and good man, respected by all the Jews who know him. An angel told him to have you come to his house to hear a message from you." 23a So Peter agreed to return with them and invited them in to spend the night. ❖ *The Torah forbade Jews to associate with Gentiles, so Peter was choosing to obey the Holy Spirit rather than this command in the Torah. God had already taught Peter that Jesus' teaching—and that of the Holy Spirit whom Jesus sent to teach them—superseded the teachings of the Torah and other Hebrew Scriptures. [Matthew 17:5; Mark 9:7; Luke 9:35]* ➤

Peter Preaches to Gentiles

23b The next day, he went with them—accompanied by some of the believers from Joppa. 24 They spent the night somewhere en route, and the following day they arrived

---

A 10:12 Most manuscripts don't have "and wild animals."

at Caesarea. Cornelius—knowing how long the trip would take—was waiting for them together with all his relatives and close friends whom he had invited to also listen to Peter. 25 When Peter entered the house, Cornelius met him and bowed low in an attitude of submissive worship. ❖ *Even though he worshipped the one true God, as a Gentile, Cornelius may have still had some pagan ideas about what was appropriate to do for a messenger from God. He was used to doing this same thing before high officials and may only have meant a high degree of respect.* ➤ 26 But Peter made him stand up, saying, "Stand up, for I'm just an ordinary man like you." ❖ *We are only to submit ourselves in worship to God. [Exodus 20:3-5; Deuteronomy 5:7-9; 6:13; 10:20; Luke 4:5-8; Revelation 19:10; 22:8-9]* ➤ 27 As Peter talked with Cornelius, they went inside to where many people were waiting. 28 After introductions, Peter said to everyone there, "You are all aware that it's against the teachings of our Torah for Jews to visit or associate with you Gentiles, because it would make us ritually unclean. But God has recently shown me that I should not consider any person ritually unclean. ❖ *Note that this was Peter's interpretation of the meaning of his vision. He makes no statement or hint that he thought it meant that all animals were now considered "clean" and therefore, fit to eat. Dreams and visions are rarely interpreted literally, for the images have figurative meanings. I am not implying that Gentile believers must follow the Jewish dietary laws found in the Torah. I am only saying that this vision did not address that issue.* ➤ 29 So when you sent for me, I did not object to coming. Now, would you please tell me why you sent for me?" 30 Cornelius answered, "Three days ago, **A** about this same time in the afternoon, I was {fasting and} **B** praying in my house, and suddenly a man dressed in shining clothes stood in front of me. 31 He said, 'Cornelius, God has heard your prayers and favorably noticed your gifts to the poor. 32 Now send some men to Joppa and invite Simon Peter to come to you. He's staying at the house of Simon the tanner, near the sea. {When he comes he will speak

to you.}' **C** 33 So I sent for you immediately and I thank you for coming. We are all here in God's presence waiting to listen to everything the Lord has told you to tell us."

34 Then Peter began to speak, "Now at last, I understand that God really treats all people the same, not favoring Jews over Gentiles. 35 He accepts those from every people group who reverently fear and obey him. 36 I believe you already know the message that God sent to the descendants of Israel, telling how anyone can have peace and a good relationship with God through believing in Jesus as the Messiah—who is Lord over everyone, not just over us Jews. 37 You know the events concerning Jesus that happened in Judea, starting in Galilee after John the Baptizer started preaching. ❖ *In this context, Judea probably refers to all of Israel, not just the Roman province of Judea—which excluded Galilee.* ➤ 38 You've heard how God anointed Jesus from Nazareth with the Holy Spirit and the Spirit's power to perform miracles, and how he traveled to many places doing good and healing all who were suffering as a result of Satan's affliction. ❖ *This included sicknesses as well as oppression by demons.* ➤ He was able to do these things because God was helping him. 39 We apostles are eyewitnesses of all the things he did in Jerusalem and the rest of the country. The Jewish leaders convinced the Romans to put him to death by crucifixion, 40 but God brought him back to life on the second **D** day after his death and granted certain people the privilege of seeing him alive again as proof that it had really happened. 41 All Jews didn't get to see him, but only those whom God chose ahead of time to be eyewitnesses who would testify to the fact. Specifically, he chose us apostles and those others who ate and drank with him after he rose from the dead. 42 Jesus commanded us to preach the Good News about him to people and testify that God has appointed him to be the judge of

---

A 10:30a The Greek says "four days" ago, but they commonly counted the current day in recounting such passage of time. Also, if you count the days accounted for in the text, according to the way we would say it today, it was "three days ago."

B 10:30b Most Greek manuscripts don't have the part in { }.
C 10:32 Most Greek manuscripts don't have the part in { }.
D 10:40 See the note at Matthew 16:21 for the reasoning behind not using the phrase "the third day"—which is in the literal text.

all humanity—both those still living and all who have died—when he returns on Judgment Day. ❖ *He will reveal those who are God's people—who therefore will live with him forever—and also those who are not.* ➤ 43 The writings of the prophets in the ❖ *Hebrew* ➤ Scriptures continue to testify that everyone who trusts in the Messiah will be forgiven by means of what he accomplished through his death and resurrection." *[Isaiah 33:24; 53:4-12; Jeremiah 31:34; 33:8; 50:20; Micah 7:18-19]*

Gentiles Are Baptized with the Holy Spirit

44 While Peter was still speaking, the Holy Spirit came upon all who were listening to his message. 45 The Jewish believers who had come with Peter from Joppa were amazed that God had clearly given the gift of the Holy Spirit to Gentiles. 46 For they were hearing them speaking in unknown languages and also spontaneously praising God as they were overcome with joy. So, Peter asked the other Jewish believers there, 47 "Surely none of you would object to baptizing these people with water since they have received the Holy Spirit just like we did?" 48 When no one objected, he told the Gentile believers that they needed to be baptized into union with Jesus the Messiah. A *[Romans 6:3-4; 1 Corinthians 12:12-13; Galatians 3:27]* ❖ *according to Jesus' instructions [Matthew 28:19]* ➤ After the baptisms, they asked him to stay with them for a few days to give them more teaching about Jesus.

11

Peter Explains What Happened at Cornelius' House to the Jewish Believers in Jerusalem

1 It wasn't long before the news about Gentiles ❖ *Cornelius and his household* ➤ receiving God's word spread throughout Judea and reached the ears of the other apostles. 2 When Peter arrived back in Jerusalem, many of the Jewish believers criticized him for 3 associating with Gentiles and eating with them.

4 So Peter began explaining to them everything that had happened. He said, 5 "I was staying in Joppa and praying when I went into a trance and had a vision. I saw something like a large sheet being lowered from the sky to earth by its four corners, right in front of me. 6 I looked into it and saw all kinds of four-legged animals, wild animals, reptiles, and birds, including those the Torah forbids us to eat. 7 Then I heard a voice telling me, 'Peter, get up and kill some of these animals to eat!' 8 I answered, 'Lord, you can't be serious! I've never eaten anything that the Torah says is impure or ritually unclean.' 9 But the voice from Heaven said to me, 'Don't call things unclean that God has declared clean.' 10 The voice told me the same thing three consecutive times and then everything was pulled back up into the sky.

11 "Right then, three men arrived at the house where I was staying. They had been sent from Caesarea to find me. 12 The Holy Spirit clearly told me to have no hesitation about going with them. These six Joppan brothers in the Lord here went with me to Caesarea and together we entered Cornelius' house. 13 Cornelius told us how he had seen an angel standing in his house, who told him, 'Send some men to Joppa and invite Simon Peter here. 14 He will bring a message through which you and all the people in your household will be saved.'

15 "Then, after I had spoken to them only briefly, the Holy Spirit came upon them just as he did upon us at the beginning. *[Acts 2:4]* 16 I remembered what the Lord Jesus told us, that John baptized with water, but that we would be baptized with the Holy Spirit. *[Acts 1:5; Luke 3:16]* 17 So since God gave them the same gift of the Holy Spirit as he gave those of us who believe in Lord Jesus the Messiah, who was I that I should try to oppose what he was doing?" 18 When the Jewish believers in Jerusalem heard this, they ceased their criticism and praised God, saying, "Clearly then, God has granted even Gentiles the privilege of repenting from their sins so they can obtain eternal life too." ❖ *Notice how the*

A 10:48 Most manuscripts have "Jesus the Messiah" but a few have "the Lord," and a few have "the Lord Jesus" or "Lord Jesus the Messiah."

apostles and early believers were willing to accept an idea that was totally foreign to their sense of rightness, based on the subjective visions of Peter and Cornelius and the experience of the Holy Spirit coming upon Gentiles. They fully trusted the leading of the Holy Spirit. ➤

Gentiles Become Believers in Antioch

19 After Stephen's death, many of the believers had left Jerusalem because of the persecution. [Acts 8:1] Some traveled as far as Phoenicia, ❖ an area of the Mediterranean coast 15 miles wide by 120 miles long, which included the cities of Tyre and Sidon ➤ the island of Cyprus, and the city of Antioch in Syria Province, over 300 miles north of Jerusalem. Most of them told the message about Jesus only to fellow Jews. 20 But some Jewish believers from the island of Cyprus and from the city of Cyrene in North Africa—who spoke Greek and were not natives of Judea—went to Antioch and started spreading the message about the Lord Jesus to Gentiles. 21 The Lord's power helped them, so a large number of Gentiles believed their message and also became followers of the Lord Jesus.

22 When the news about this reached the believers in Jerusalem, the leaders sent Barnabas to Antioch to help instruct them. [Acts 4:36; 9:27] 23 When he arrived there, he saw clear evidence that God was working in the lives of Gentile believers. He was glad and encouraged them to continue believing and obeying the Lord Jesus. 24 Barnabas was a good man, strong in his faith and fully dependent on the Holy Spirit, and as a result, he was able to lead a great number of people to trust in Jesus.

25 Sometime later, he went to the city of Tarsus in Cilicia Province to find Saul. ❖ About ten years had passed since Saul went to Tarsus in Acts 9:30. ➤ 26 When he found him, he brought Saul back to Antioch to help instruct the new believers. For an entire year, they met regularly with the assembly of believers there and taught large numbers of people about Jesus and how to live as his people. The believers in Antioch were the first ones to be called "Messianics." ❖ "Messianic" in the Greek text is literally "Christian" and means "one who follows Christ" or possibly "Christ's slaves." "Christ" is a transliteration into

English of the Greek word "Kristos" which means "Anointed One." "Messiah" is a transliteration into English of the Hebrew word "Meshiach" which also means "Anointed One." Many commentators think the term "Christian" was originally a derogatory term, but no one knows for sure. ➤

27 During that year, some believers who were prophets came to Antioch from Jerusalem. 28 One of them—named Agabus—prophesied by the prompting of the Holy Spirit that there would be a severe famine all over the inhabited world. ❖ The people of this time were not aware of the extent of the entire world. This phrase might refer to the Roman Empire, which was most of what they knew of the world. But for Jews, it might very well have referred only to Judea—which was their "world." ➤ This famine happened while Claudius was the Roman emperor. ❖ Claudius reigned from AD 41–54 and there was a severe famine in Judea Province around AD 46. There were also several famines scattered throughout the Roman Empire during Claudius' reign. But since the believers in Antioch decided to send money to Judea, it's likely that the area around Antioch was not expected to suffer from the famine. ➤ 29 So the believers in Antioch decided to help the believers in Judea. Each of them contributed what they were able to give. 30 After doing this, they sent Barnabas and Saul with their gift to give it to the elders of the assembly in Jerusalem. ❖ This may be the trip to Jerusalem that Paul mentions in Galatians 2:1-10. Even though his account in Galatians doesn't mention bringing famine relief, the timing was about right and it was in response to a revelation—which could have been about the famine. Most commentators assume the gift was money since it would have been difficult to transport large amounts of food. During a famine, food would be available but at greatly increased prices since it would be imported from a distance. ➤

12

King Herod Agrippa I Persecutes the Apostles

1 About the time Barnabas and Saul were in Antioch, King Herod Agrippa the first had some of the leaders of the assembly in Jerusalem arrested, intending to persecute them. ❖ Agrippa the first reigned from AD 41–44 over the Roman provinces of Judea, Samaria, Galilee, Perea, Iturea, Trachonitis, and Abilene, having been granted the title "king" by Claudius Caesar. His father was Aristobulus—the half-brother of Herod Antipas—who were both sons of Herod the

Great. ➤ [2] He ordered the Apostle James— who was the brother of the Apostle John and the son of Zebedee—to be beheaded. ❖ *Some people confuse this James—the apostle— with James the brother of Jesus (not one of the 12 apostles) who later became the main leader of the assembly in Jerusalem.* ➤ [3] When Herod saw that this pleased the Jewish leaders, he ordered Peter arrested during the Festival of Unleavened Bread, intending to kill him too. ❖ *Herod was from Idumea—the country to the south of Israel which is called Edom in the Hebrew Scriptures—was only partly Jewish by blood, and was appointed to his position by the Romans so he was not considered Jewish by most Jews. The Festival of Unleavened Bread began immediately after the Passover and the two feasts together were often referred to as the Passover Festival.* ➤ [4] After they seized Peter, they put him in prison under continuous guard by four soldiers. There were four groups of four soldiers, each taking a three-hour shift during the day to guard him, and another three-hour shift at night. Herod intended to bring him out for a public trial after the festival was over. [5] So they closely guarded Peter in prison for several days, but at the same time the assembly of believers in Jerusalem was praying earnestly for his protection.

An Angel Miraculously Frees Peter

[6] The night before the day when Herod planned to put him on trial, Peter was sleeping between two soldiers to whom he was chained—with the other two guards at the entrance to his cell. [7] Suddenly, an angel appeared and there was light in the cell. He nudged Peter in the side to wake him and said, "Get up! Quickly!" The chains that bound him to his guards fell off his wrists. ❖ *The guards were apparently put to sleep and kept asleep by the angel.* ➤ [8] Then the angel told him, "Tie your sash around your waist and put on your sandals. Now wrap your outer robe around you and follow me." ❖ *He probably had been using the robe like a blanket while he slept.* ➤ [9] Peter followed the angel out of the prison but didn't know it was real. He thought he was having a vision or a dream. [10] They passed two different sets of guards but were not seen. When they came to the main iron gate that led outside the prison to the city, it opened by itself. They passed through and walked the entire length of a street outside when the angel suddenly disappeared. [11] Only then did Peter realize it was all real and thought to himself, "Now I know for sure it's not a dream. The Lord really did send his angel to save me from Herod's power and the plans that the Jewish leaders had for my harm."

[12] When this fully sank in, he went to the house of Mary—the mother of John Mark. He knew there would be many people gathered there praying. ❖ *This Mark is probably the same one who wrote the Gospel, and his mother's house was probably one of the regular meeting places for believers.* ➤ [13] He knocked on the gate to the courtyard, and Rhoda—a servant—came to see who it was. [14] When she recognized Peter's voice, she was so excited that she forgot to open the gate and ran in to announce to everyone that Peter was standing outside. [15] They told her, "You must be imagining things!" But when she continued to insist it was so, they said, "It must be his guardian angel." ❖ *They believed that a person's guardian angel could take on the appearance of the person he guarded, and they may have thought he came to tell them that Peter had died. [Psalm 91:11; Matthew 18:10; Hebrews 1:14]* ➤ [16] Meanwhile, they could hear Peter's continued knocking and when they finally opened the gate, they were stunned to see him. [17] Peter motioned for silence and then reported how the Lord had set him free from prison. Then he said, "Tell James ❖ *the Lord's brother* ➤ and the others about what happened." After this, he left to find a safe place. ❖ *Some commentators believe he left Jerusalem.* ➤ [18] In the morning, there was considerable consternation, shouting, and finger pointing going on among the guards over Peter's disappearance. [19] Herod ordered a thorough search of the city for Peter, but he wasn't found. He questioned the guards himself and then ordered their execution. ❖ *According to Roman law, guards who allowed a prisoner to escape were punished with the same punishment the prisoner was to be given.* ➤ Then Herod went from Jerusalem to stay in Caesarea for a while.

❖ *Caesarea was the capital of the Roman province of Judea. In the text, Luke says he left "Judea," which would have to mean the Judea as defined by the land given to the tribe of Judah, not the Roman province.* ➤

God Kills King Herod Agrippa I

20 Now, Herod had been disputing for some time with the people of the cities of Tyre and Sidon which are north of Caesarea in Syria Province. Representatives from those cities came together and asked for an audience with him. They had somehow ❖ *probably through a bribe* ➤ secured the support of Blastus—one of Herod's most-trusted and highest-level officials—in their petition for a peaceful settlement. They needed a settlement because they depended on the area under the king's control for food which he had prohibited his people from exporting to them. **21** On the day that Herod had appointed for their audience, he wore his royal robes and delivered a public speech from his throne, addressed to the representatives. ❖ *The Jewish historian Josephus said Herod chose a day when there was a celebration for the Roman Emperor. He described Herod's robes as woven from silver.* ➤ **22** Those gathered, favorably impressed with his speech, were shouting, "He speaks like a god, not a man!" ❖ *The Romans had many gods and believed that some rulers could become deity, but this was most likely just flattery.* ➤ **23** But even though he knew such praise should only be rendered to the one true God, he did not refuse it. Therefore, the Lord immediately sent an angel to strike him so that later, he was afflicted by intestinal worms and died. ❖ *According to Josephus, Herod experienced a sudden pain in his stomach and died five days later in AD 44.* ➤

24 But God's message about Jesus continued to spread and the number of believers continued to increase.

25 Meanwhile, after Barnabas and Saul took the money to Jerusalem, *[Acts 11:29-30]* they returned to Antioch, taking John Mark ❖ *Barnabas' cousin [Acts 12:12; Colossians 4:10]* ➤ with them. ❖ *Jerusalem is more than 300 miles from Antioch.* ➤

13

Paul's First Missionary Journey

1 Among the believers in Antioch there were the following men who were both prophets and teachers of the Word: Barnabas (the same one already mentioned), Simeon (called, "the black"), Lucius from the city of Cyrene in North Africa, *[Romans 16:21]* Manaen (foster brother **A** of Herod Antipas) and Saul. **2** One day, while these men were fasting and worshipping the Lord, the Holy Spirit said to them, "Appoint Barnabas and Saul to the special work that I've already put in their minds and called them to do, and release them from other responsibilities so they can do it." **3** So after further fasting and praying for the two of them, the others placed their hands on them and commissioned Barnabas and Saul for the work. ❖ *One function of laying on hands is to set a person into a new office or ministry and confer God's enabling power and blessing for that work.* ➤

The Confrontation with Elymas on Cyprus

4 Directed by the Holy Spirit, the two of them went down to Port Seleucia—16 miles to the west of Antioch—and boarded a ship bound for the island of Cyprus, about 100 miles southwest of Seleucia. ❖ *Barnabas was from Cyprus. [Acts 4:36]* ➤ **5** After they reached Salamis—the main city of Cyprus on its east coast—they started their ministry by proclaiming God's message about Jesus in the Jewish synagogues there. John Mark had gone along with them as their helper. *[Acts 12:25]* **6** Then, they went through the whole island proclaiming the message until they came to the city of Paphos—the capital of Cyprus on the west end of the island— about 90 miles southwest of Salamis. There, they met a Jew named Bar-Jesus Elymas. ❖ *"Bar" means "son of" and "Jesus" was a common name among Jews at that time. Elymas was his Greek name.* ➤ He was a sorcerer and a false prophet. ❖ *That means he claimed to speak prophecies from God, but in fact, his prophecies did not come from God. A sorcerer's power*

A 13:1 The word σύντροφος (suntrophos) can mean either "foster brother" or "close friend from childhood."

comes from demons. ➤ 7 He was a friend of Sergius Paulus—the proconsul—a man of considerable intelligence. ❖ *Proconsul was the title of the governor of a Roman senatorial province, in this case, the province of Cyprus. Sergius Paulus was proconsul of Cyprus around AD 45–46.* ➤ The proconsul had heard about Barnabas and Saul and sent for them because he wanted to hear the message they brought from God. 8 But the sorcerer Elymas opposed them and repeatedly tried to dissuade the proconsul from believing their message. 9 Saul—whose Greek name was Paul—empowered and directed by the Holy Spirit, looked intently at him and with righteous anger said, 10 "You servant of Satan and enemy of everything God approves! You are a treacherous fraud who is always trying to twist and pervert what the Lord says. 11 Observe the Lord's judgment against you! You are going to be blind and not even able to see the sun for a period of time." Immediately, it seemed to Elymas as if a misty darkness surrounded him, and groping about, he searched for someone to lead him by the hand. 12 When the proconsul saw this happen, he believed in the Lord Jesus and was amazed at what Barnabas and Paul taught him.

How Paul Presented the Message About Jesus to Fellow Jews

13 From Paphos on Cyprus, Paul and his companions—Barnabas and John Mark—took passage on a ship going a little over 200 miles northwest to the city of Perga on the coast of Asia Minor in Pamphylia Province. ❖ *Notice that prior to this, Barnabas was the senior member of the team, but from now on, Paul is.* ➤ While they were there, John Mark left them to return to his home in Jerusalem. ❖ *Luke doesn't go into any details, but from Acts 15:38 it's clear that Paul considered it a desertion and dereliction of duty.* ➤ 14 From Perga, Paul and Barnabas traveled by land about

110 miles north to another city named Antioch in the region of Pisidia, inside Galatia Province. ❖ *Luke calls this "Antioch of Pisidia," to distinguish it from Antioch in Syria Province where they started their missionary journey.* ➤ On the Sabbath, they went to the local synagogue and sat to worship with their fellow Jews who had gathered there. 15 After the public reading of selections from the Torah and the writings of the prophets, the leaders of the synagogue sent someone over to Paul and Barnabas with an invitation, "Brothers, if you have a message of encouragement or exhortation to share with the people, please feel free to do so." 16 Standing up, Paul motioned for quiet and said, "Fellow Israelites and God-fearing Gentiles, may I please have your attention. ❖ *There were many Gentiles who believed in the one true God but refused to be circumcised as a full Jewish convert was required to be. They were called "God fearers."* ➤ 17 The God that we Israelites worship chose our ancestors to be his special people, and while they lived in Egypt, he caused them to become very numerous. With great demonstrations of his miraculous power, he led them out of Egypt. *[Exodus 6:1, 6; Psalm 136:10-12]* 18 He took care of them A in the wilderness for 40 years. 19 Then, he enabled them to conquer seven ethnic groups who lived in the land of Canaan and gave them that land as their own. ❖ *These seven groups are listed in Deuteronomy 7:1.* ➤ 20 All this took about 450 years. B Afterward, God gave them judges to rule over them until the time of the prophet Samuel. *[1 Samuel 3:19-21; 7:15-17]* 21 Then, the Israelites demanded a king, and God chose Saul—the son of Kish—of the tribe of Benjamin. He ruled as king for 40 years. 22 After removing Saul, God made David king and said about him, 'I have found in David—the son of Jesse—a man who always pleases me and submits to my will.' *[1 Samuel 13:14; Psalm 89:20]* 23 Just as he

---

A 13:18 Most manuscripts say "he endured their conduct." But from other manuscripts, most commentators think "he took care of them" is most likely the original text, which follows Deuteronomy 1:31 in the Septuagint. Both statements are true, but Paul's purpose in this narrative is not to criticize his ancestors, but to give a brief historical overview. Since there are no other critical comments in his account, it's unlikely that he said "he endured their conduct."

B 13:20 Most commentators think this refers to the 400 years they were in Egypt, plus the 40 years in the wilderness and about 10 years to actually conquer Canaan. Others think it refers to the period when the judges ruled them. Some manuscripts have a different word order which says, "And after that, for about 450 years God gave them judges." See the book of Judges.

promised David he would do, God caused one of David's descendants to be a Savior for his people. *[2 Samuel 7:11-16; Psalm 89:2-37; 132:10-12]* ²⁴ Before this Savior began his work, John the Baptizer preached to all the people of Israel that they needed to turn away from their sinful ways of living and be baptized as a sign of their repentance. ²⁵ Near the end of John's ministry, he frequently said, 'I'm not the One who is coming! ❖ *Jews often referred to the Messiah as "the One who is coming." [Matthew 11:3]* ➤ He will come after me and he is so much greater than I am that I'm not even worthy to serve him by untying his sandals.'

²⁶ "My friends, both you who are descended from Abraham and you God-fearing Gentiles, God has sent this message to you A about how to be saved! ²⁷ For most of the people living in Jerusalem and their rulers did not recognize that Jesus was the Messiah, or that he is the one the prophets wrote about, even though they read their prophecies every Sabbath. Yet when they condemned him to death, they fulfilled those same prophecies. ❖ *See many of these prophecies listed in this book after Peter's second letter.* ➤ ²⁸ Even though they had no valid basis for a death sentence, they insisted that Pilate have him crucified. ²⁹ When they had fulfilled everything written about him by the prophets, his body was taken down from the cross and put in a tomb. ³⁰ But God demonstrated his approval of him by raising him from death back to life. ³¹ And for many days afterward, he appeared to his followers who had traveled with him to Jerusalem from Galilee. These people are now witnessing to their fellow Jews about what they've seen. ³² And now the two of us ❖ *Paul and Barnabas* ➤ are here to proclaim this Good News to you: The promise God made to our Jewish ancestors that one of David's descendants would be a Savior for his people, ³³ he has now finally fulfilled for us—their descendants—by raising Jesus from death to life. As King David wrote in the second Psalm—in which God addressed the Messiah, 'I am your Father. Today I am

publicly revealing that you are my Son.' *[Psalm 2:7]* ❖ *See the footnote on this verse at Hebrews 5:5.* ➤ ³⁴ The fact that God intended to raise the Messiah from death to life—never again to die—is stated in the Scripture where God says, 'I will surely help you, my people Israel, just as I promised David that I would.' *[Isaiah 55:3]* ❖ *Paul used this passage to clarify that verse 35, below, refers to the Messiah and not to David himself.* ➤ ³⁵ Elsewhere, David prophesied about the Messiah saying to God, 'I know that you, God, won't leave me—your Holy One—in the world of the dead, or my body to rot in the grave.' *[Psalm 16:10]* ❖ *Peter interpreted this quote from the Psalms the same way in Acts 2:27, 31.* ➤ ³⁶ That David was not referring to himself is clear, for after he had fulfilled what God wanted him to do in his life, he died and was buried—just as all his ancestors had been—and his body decayed. ³⁷ But Jesus, the One whom God raised from death to life, did not experience decay. This clearly indicates that the prophecy was about him and that he is the Messiah. ³⁸ Therefore, my friends, I want you to realize we are proclaiming that God will forgive your sins if you accept Jesus as the Messiah. ❖ *There are many implications to this statement, but to accept him as the Messiah means that a person believes all he said about himself was true, and will therefore submit to living according to his will.* ➤ ³⁹ God declares that everyone who believes in him is righteous in his sight and is thereby freed from all the condemnation that you cannot be freed from by following the Teachings of Moses. *[Romans 3:9-12, 23, 28; 5:12; 2 Corinthians 5:21; Galatians 2:16]* ⁴⁰ Therefore, take care that these words from the book of the prophets don't apply to you: ⁴¹ 'God says, "Pay attention, you who ridicule my Word! I will do something to astonish you and then destroy you. I'm going to do something so terrible in your time that you would never believe it if someone predicted it would happen to you." ' " *[Habakkuk 1:5]* ❖ *This prophecy was originally about God's judgment and the impending invasion of Israel by the Babylonians, and Paul's Jewish listeners would have been quite familiar with it. But he applies it to the punishment awaiting those who displease God by rejecting his Messiah.*

A **13:26** Some manuscripts have "to us."

Verses 16-41 are probably typical of the message Paul preached in the synagogues in every new place he went. Of course, if they responded favorably, he would tell them much more. ➤

42 When Paul had finished speaking, and he and Barnabas were leaving the synagogue, the people who had heard him begged A that they return the following Sabbath to tell them more about these things. 43 After the meeting was over and the people had left, many Jews—and also some who were converts to Judaism—followed Paul and Barnabas who urged the people to continue trusting God to favor them and to help them understand. ❖ *They urged them to literally "continue in the grace of God." It's not clear what Paul and Barnabas were urging them to do. It's possible that they were urging them to trust in God's freely offered undeserved favor which he grants to those who trust in Jesus.* ➤

When His Fellow Jews Rejected the Good News Paul Proclaimed It to Gentiles

44 On the next Sabbath, it seemed that nearly everyone in the city had gathered at the synagogue to hear Paul and Barnabas proclaim the message about the Lord. 45 But when the Jewish leaders saw the crowds of Gentiles, they became extremely jealous of the attention Paul and Barnabas attracted, and contradicted everything Paul said with insults and blasphemy against Jesus and them. 46 So Paul and Barnabas told them boldly, "God required us to proclaim his message to you—our fellow Jews—first. But since you reject it and have thereby revealed you aren't worthy of receiving eternal life, we will now proclaim his message to Gentiles. ❖ *Not all of the Jews there rejected the message.* ➤ 47 For God commanded us to do so when he said, 'I'm sending you to reveal the way of salvation to the Gentiles so people all over the world can be saved.'" [Isaiah 49:6] ❖ *In this prophecy, God was speaking to the Messiah, but Paul applies it to himself and all of the Messiah's people.* ➤ 48 When the Gentiles heard this, they rejoiced and exclaimed how wonderful the Lord's message of salvation was. So all of those among them whom God had chosen to receive eternal life, believed in the Lord Jesus. ❖ *Literally, it says, "as many believed as had been appointed to eternal life," with it not stated as to who did the appointing. Most commentators believe this is speaking about God's predestining some people to be saved. But some think it means "those who were open to receiving eternal life." It's clear that Paul practiced this procedure everywhere he went, and this was not the first time. First, he presented the Good News to Jews in their synagogues in a city. If they received it, he would continue to use that venue to preach to both Jews and Gentiles. But if the Jews rejected the message, he would start proclaiming it directly to the Gentiles in that area.* ➤

49 Thus, the message about salvation through believing in the Lord Jesus was being spread throughout the region around Antioch in Phrygia and Galatia Provinces. 50 But the Jewish leaders convinced some prominent God-fearing Gentile women and men in the city to oppose Paul and Barnabas and to harass them. And they, in turn, incited others to drive them out of the region. 51 But before they left, Paul and Barnabas symbolically shook the dust off their feet. ❖ *This was a gesture that Jews understood to be a rebuke, implying that God had rejected them and would punish them like they were heathens if they didn't repent.* ➤ Then they moved on to the city of Iconium—about 80 miles to the east of Antioch. ❖ *Overland, they would travel about 20 miles or less per day.* ➤ 52 Meanwhile, the new believers in Jesus in Antioch continued to be filled with joy and were empowered and directed by the Holy Spirit.

14

Paul and Barnabas in the City of Iconium

1 The same sort of thing happened in Iconium that had happened in Antioch. Paul and Barnabas went to the synagogue and were so convincing that a large number of Jews and Gentiles believed in Jesus. 2 But those Jews who refused to accept their message convinced the unbelieving Gentiles of the city to resent them and to be antagonistic toward the believers. 3 However, because of the positive response of so many, Paul and Barnabas

---

A 13:42 Some manuscripts have "when the Jewish leaders were leaving the synagogue, the Gentiles were begging…"

stayed there a long time, relying on **A** the Lord as they spoke boldly. And the Lord confirmed that their message about his saving people who trust in Jesus was true by performing miraculous signs and wonders through them.

4 But the people of that city remained divided, some siding with those Jews who rejected their message and some siding with the apostles. ❖ *Luke clearly regarded Barnabas as an apostle in the same sense that Paul was.* ➤ 5 Some of the antagonistic group plotted to attack the apostles and stone them to death. ❖ *Stoning was a Jewish form of execution.* ➤ 6 But Paul and Barnabas heard about it, so they fled. *[Matthew 10:23]* They went to the city of Lystra first and later, to the city of Derbe—both in the Lycaonia region of Galatia Province— and also spent time in the regions surrounding those cities. ❖ *Lystra was about 18 miles southwest of Iconium and Derbe was about 60 miles east of Lystra.* ➤ 7 In all those places they continued to proclaim the message of the Good News.

The Lystrans Mistake the Apostles for Greek Gods, and Later Stone Paul

8 In Lystra, there was a man who was lame from birth and had never walked. 9 He was listening to Paul's preaching when Paul looked at him and discerned that he had faith to be saved and healed. ❖ *The Greek word σῴζω (sōzō) can refer to either physical salvation (healing) or spiritual salvation, or both. The same faith that will save a person will enable a person to be healed.* ➤ 10 So Paul, looking directly at him, called out, "Stand up!" Immediately the man jumped up and was able to walk. 11 When the people saw what Paul had done, they started shouting in the Lycaonian language, "These men are gods in human form!" ❖ *Paul was probably speaking to them in Greek, and he and Barnabas did not understand what they were saying until someone translated for them.* ➤ 12 They called Barnabas, "Zeus," who was king of the Greek gods, and they called Paul, "Hermes," who was the son of Zeus and acted as a spokesman for the gods—

because he was the main speaker. 13 There was a temple to Zeus just outside the city and one of the priests from there brought bulls and wreaths to the city gates so the people could offer them as sacrifices to the apostles. ❖ *Since there was time for the news of the healing to spread outside the city and for the priest to come in response, it's evident that some time passed while the apostles didn't realize what was happening.* ➤ 14 But when Barnabas and Paul finally realized what was going on, they tore their robes to symbolize their horror at the blasphemy that was happening, and rushed into the crowd shouting, 15 "You shouldn't be doing this! We are only mortal men like you, not gods! We came to proclaim Good News to you about turning away from these worthless idols to the one God who really exists and who made the entire world and everything in it. *[Exodus 20:11; Psalm 146:6]* 16 In the past, he let you Gentiles to do whatever you wanted. 17 Though you don't know him, he left evidence of his existence for you to see by showing you kindness in providing rain, seasonal crops, plenty of food, and joy." 18 Even after saying they were not gods, they had great difficulty convincing the people not to offer them sacrifices.

19 Sometime after that, some Jews came from Antioch in Pisidia and from Iconium and turned the people against the apostles. They stoned Paul, dragged him outside the city, and left him for dead. ❖ *Lystra and Antioch in Pisidia were about 100 miles apart. This was probably the stoning Paul mentions in 2 Corinthians 11:25.* ➤ 20 But when the new believers of Lystra gathered around him, he stood up and went back to the city. ❖ *This was a miracle. No one who is presumed dead after stoning would normally be capable of getting up and walking. ¶ Since they had the opportunity to convert some people to the faith—and those Jews from Antioch and Iconium probably came because they had heard news about Paul and Barnabas in Lystra—it's apparent that a significant amount of time elapsed between verses 18 and 19.* ➤ The next day, he and Barnabas left for the city of Derbe—60 miles to the east.

A 14:3 Literally "speaking boldly upon the Lord," some commentators think it means they "spoke boldly for the Lord."

Paul and Barnabas Return to Antioch in Syria, Finishing their First Missionary Journey

21 After they had spent some time proclaiming the Good News in Derbe and brought many people to faith in Jesus, they retraced their journey, going back through Lystra, Iconium, and Antioch in Pisidia. 22 In each place, they met with the believers, teaching and encouraging them, strengthening their faith, and warning them that, "Believers must faithfully endure many hardships and persecutions in this life before they enter God's Kingdom in Heaven." *[Mark 10:30; John 15:18-20; 16:33; 1 Thessalonians 3:3-4; 2 Timothy 3:12; 1 Peter 2:20-21]* 23 Paul and Barnabas appointed leaders over each assembly of believers. Then, meeting with them for a time of prayer and fasting, they blessed these new leaders and entrusted them to the care of the Lord Jesus in whom they believed.

24 From Antioch in Pisidia within Galatia Province, they traveled south through the region of Pisidia and went to the city of Perga in Pamphylia Province. *[Acts 13:13-14]* ❖ *They probably exactly retraced their journey, stopping in any place where they had left new believers.* ➤ 25 After they had again preached in Perga, they went down to the port city of Attalia 26 where they boarded a ship heading for Antioch in Syria Province. For that's where the assembly leaders had first commissioned them for this work and had entrusted them to God's care and sent them off. And now they had completed that work. ❖ *They didn't return through the island of Cyprus which had been their first stop. The entire trip took about one and a half years and was directed by the Holy Spirit. He told them where to go and when it was time to return.* ➤

27 When they arrived in Antioch, they called all the believers to meet together and reported all the things that God had done through them and how he had enabled many Gentiles to believe. ❖ *What would the Apostles have thought if the assembly leaders in Antioch had given them only 5 minutes to share about what the Lord had done during their one and a half years of mission work? Yet, this is what happens to missionaries in many assemblies today, reflecting the true attitude of those leaders toward mission work—that it is not nearly as important as their own ministry.* ➤ 28 After that, they stayed with the believers in Antioch for a long time. ❖ *Many commentators think that Paul wrote his letter to the believers in Galatia Province during this time.* ➤

15

The Council of Believers in Jerusalem

1 While Paul and Barnabas were in Antioch, some Jewish followers of Jesus arrived there from Judea and began teaching the Gentile believers, "Even though you believe in Jesus, you can't be saved unless you are also circumcised as required by the Teachings of Moses." *[Genesis 17:9-14; Exodus 12:48-49]* 2 Paul and Barnabas heatedly disputed this teaching with those men, and it was finally decided that Paul, Barnabas, and some other local believers would go to Jerusalem and consult with the apostles and assembly leaders there to seek their authoritative view on this matter. 3 The assembly of believers in Antioch gave them provisions and sent them on their way. As they traveled south through Phoenicia and Samaria Provinces, Paul and Barnabas reported to the believers in various places about their missionary journey and that many Gentiles had been converted. This news brought much joy to all the believers who heard it.

4 When Paul, Barnabas, and their companions arrived in Jerusalem, they were welcomed by the apostles, assembly elders, and other believers and they reported all the things God had done through them among the Gentiles during their missionary journey. 5 But some of the Pharisees who had become followers of Jesus stood up and said, "Gentile believers must be required to be circumcised and to obey the Teachings of Moses if they are to be a part of us and be saved." ❖ *In Jerusalem at this time, the Jewish followers of Jesus still worshipped in the synagogues and Temple and were part of the Jewish community. The only difference between them was that they believed Jesus was the Messiah and they followed his teachings. But they had not given up any of their Jewish customs. Most of them still expected Gentile followers of Jesus to go through the process that converts to Judaism went through to become fully Jewish. After all, Jesus was a Jewish Messiah and the first believers were Jewish.* ➤ 6 Then, the apostles who were in Jerusalem met together with the assembly

elders to try to reach consensus on this issue. ❖ *Verse 22 indicates that there were also many other believers in attendance listening. This council happened about AD 49–50.* ➤ 7 After days of discussion and debate, Peter stood up to address the council. "My fellow believers, you all know that about 10 years ago God chose me from among all of Jesus' followers to be the one to share the message of the Good News with Gentiles so they might believe. *[Acts 10:1—11:18]* 8 God knows exactly what people think, not just what they do. He knows who loves him and who does not. And he clearly demonstrated that he accepted those Gentiles as his own people by giving them the Holy Spirit, just as he did to us. 9 God himself made absolutely no distinction between us Jewish believers and those Gentiles. He forgave them and made them righteous in his sight because they believed his message. 10 This issue has already been settled by God, so why do you test his tolerance by questioning what he has already made clear? That's not the way to please him. You are trying to place a burdensome requirement of obeying the Torah's teachings on these Gentile believers, when neither we nor our Jewish ancestors were ever able to successfully bear it. ❖ *The Teachings of Moses contains 613 commands and Jewish elders had added hundreds of others that they considered just as important. To keep them all was difficult and no one could do it perfectly.* ➤ 11 That's not right, because we Jewish followers of Jesus believe we are saved through accepting the undeserved favor offered to us by the Lord Jesus, not because we obey all of the Torah's teachings. ❖ *Even though he strove to obey the commands in the Torah, he did not believe that had anything to do with his being saved.* ➤ And these Gentile believers are saved in exactly the same way." *[Galatians 2:16; Ephesians 2:8]*

12 There was silence after Peter's statement, and then they all listened as Barnabas and Paul supported Peter's view by reporting all the miraculous signs and wonders God had done through them while they were proclaiming the message of the Good News to Gentiles.

13 When they had finished, James—the brother of Jesus who had become the main leader of the assembly in Jerusalem—said,

"My fellow believers, please listen to me. 14 Simon Peter has explained to us how God first demonstrated his desire to bring out from among the heathen Gentiles a group of people who would be his own. ❖ *James is referring to the events with Cornelius and his household and was not implying that the Gentile believers would be separate from the Jewish believers.* ➤ 15 This is consistent with what is written in the book of the prophets where God said, ❖ *The book of the prophets was a scroll containing the writings of the twelve "minor" prophets and is a part of the Hebrew Scriptures.* ➤ 16 'After this time of punishment, ❖ *i.e., the Assyrian and Babylonian captivities* ➤ I will once again look favorably on my people and will establish a descendant of David ❖ *i.e., the Messiah* ➤ as king over my people 17 so that all the people I call to be my own—from the survivors of my people in Israel and also from among the Gentiles —may seek to know me. I, Yahweh, will accomplish this plan 18 which I made known long ago.' " *[Amos 9:11-12 in the Septuagint]*

19 James continued, "Therefore, it is my conclusion that we Jewish believers shouldn't make things difficult for Gentiles who are changing their lives to follow God by requiring them to become Jewish and to obey all the Teachings of Moses—since it's apparent that God is calling them to be his people even while they remain Gentiles. 20 But instead, we should write them a letter stating that in order for us Jewish followers of Jesus to have fellowship with them, they need follow these four rules: 1) refrain from sexual sin, 2) don't eat any food that's been offered to false gods or is in any way associated with such, 3) do not consume blood, 4) and don't eat animals that have been strangled and prepared for eating leaving the blood still in them. *[Genesis 9:4; Leviticus 17:10-14]* 21 They should do this because Jews have for generations spread to every city in the empire and have established synagogues where the Teachings of Moses are read every Sabbath." ❖ *It's not certain why James added this last statement. One view is that he was mollifying them that these Gentile believers would have plenty of opportunity to learn more about the Teachings of Moses. Another view is that the Gentile believers should abstain from these things because they would have Jewish contacts wherever they lived.* ➤

22 James' proposal was accepted. So the council—composed of the apostles and assembly elders plus all those believers present—decided to choose two men from among them as representatives to accompany Paul and Barnabas back to Antioch to verify their decision. They chose Judas Bar-Sabbas and Silas—who were recognized leaders ❖ *Judas Bar-Sabbas is nowhere else mentioned in the New Testament, but some commentators think he may be the brother of Joseph Bar-Sabbas in Acts 1:23. Most commentators think this Silas is the same one mentioned in Paul's letters.* ➤—23 and sent the following letter with them:

"This letter is from the apostles and assembly elders in Jerusalem, who consider you Gentile followers of Jesus to be our brothers and sisters in the Lord. We are writing to you Gentile believers in the city of Antioch and others believers in the rest of Syria and Cilicia Provinces. ❖ *Antioch was the capital of the united provinces of Syria and Cilicia.* ➤

24 We have heard that some individuals from the assembly here came to you without official authorization and have caused controversy by saying that you have to be circumcised and obey the Teachings of Moses to be saved. 25 Since we have come to a consensus on this issue, we decided to send some men to you along with our colleagues Barnabas and Paul—who are loved by both you and us 26 and who are dedicated to serving our Lord Jesus the Messiah even at the risk of their own lives. 27 We are sending Judas and Silas who will verbally confirm that what you read in this letter is indeed what we have decided in this matter. ❖ *Troublemakers could otherwise accuse Paul and Barnabas of forging the letter.* ➤

28 The Holy Spirit has made clear to us that we are not to burden you with any requirements from the Teachings of Moses beyond the following rules: ❖ *It's worth noting that the entire council of apostles and assembly elders were conscious that they were being led by the Holy Spirit in their conclusions. They considered this directive to be from the Spirit, not just their idea.* ➤

29 1) refrain from sexual sin, 2) don't eat any food that's been offered to false gods or is in any way associated with such, 3) do not consume blood, 4) and don't eat animals that have been strangled and prepared for eating leaving the blood still in them. If you avoid these things, you will be doing what is right and will prosper in your relationship with us. ❖ *Jesus considered these rules as his will in Revelation 2:14, 20. They were still observed in the late second century by assemblies of the Rhone valley in France and in Africa. And they were still observed in the late ninth century in England. This decision—directed by the Holy Spirit—means that no Gentile believers today need feel pressure to observe the remaining ceremonial details of the Teachings of Moses (i.e., those that have not been explicitly changed by New Testament teaching). They are free to do so if they desire, or out of respect when fellowshipping with Jewish believers, or in order to gain spiritual insight and blessings, or because they are so led by the Holy Spirit. But many Jewish believers today do feel an obligation to keep them, not in a legalistic manner, nor to earn God's favor, but out of obedience under the freedom of grace since many of them believe that they have not been given general permission in Scripture to ignore them. Hence Gentile believers should not judge Jewish believers as being legalistic or in error for observing the Torah teachings. We all must do what we believe the Spirit leads us to do and we will all give an account to Jesus on the Last Day for our obedience or disobedience to the Holy Spirit's leading.* ➤

30 So the four men were sent on their way and arrived in Antioch where they delivered the letter to the gathered assembly of believers. 31 When the believers there read it, they rejoiced because it was an encouragement in that it relieved them of the burden of following all the Jewish laws. 32 Judas and Silas were also prophets like Paul and Barnabas, and they encouraged the believers there with many prophetic messages from God. ❖ *The Greek literally says, "with many words" (from the Greek root "logos") which some interpret as a long message.* ➤ 33 After being there

for some time, the believers in Antioch sent them home with a blessing of shalom to be conveyed to the leaders and believers in Jerusalem who had sent them. **A** ❖ *See the note at Matthew 10:12 about "shalom." ¶ We don't know how long they stayed, but since it was about 300 miles from Jerusalem—and if they walked it would be more than a two-week trip—it's likely that they spent several weeks there.* ➤ 34 {But at the last minute, Silas decided to remain there so Judas returned to Jerusalem alone.} **B** 35 Paul and Barnabas remained in Antioch to help teach new believers and proclaim the message about the Lord Jesus, along with many other believers who were ministering in this way too.

Paul and Barnabas Split Up, and Paul Starts His Second Missionary Journey

36 Sometime after this, Paul said to Barnabas, "Let's go back and visit the believers in all the cities where we proclaimed the Lord's message during our missionary journey and see how they are progressing spiritually." 37 Barnabas agreed it was a good idea and wanted to take John Mark along with them. 38 But Paul didn't like the idea since he had deserted them in Pamphylia Province during their first journey and not seen the task through to the end. *[Acts 13:13]* 39 They disagreed about this so strongly that they decided they couldn't work together, and they separated. Instead, Barnabas took his cousin John Mark to the island of Cyprus. ❖ *Barnabas had been born on Cyprus, and he and Paul had started their first missionary journey there but did not visit it on their way back to Antioch. Luke is careful not to take sides in reporting this split. Clearly, Barnabas saw potential in John Mark which turns out to have been justified since Paul is later reconciled with him and considered him a valuable coworker. [Colossians 4:10; Philemon 24; 2 Timothy 4:11] We don't hear anything further about Barnabas or John Mark in the book of Acts.* ➤ 40 But Paul chose Silas as a coworker for his second missionary journey. The believers in Antioch prayed for the Lord to bless them with his favor and care, and sent them off. 41 This time, Paul and Silas traveled north by land through Syria and Cilicia Provinces, helping to strengthen the faith of believers in assemblies they encountered on the way.

16

Paul Chooses Timothy to Accompany Him and Silas

1 On their journey, they reached the city of Derbe in Lycaonia Province, and then went on to Lystra. *[Acts 14:6]* A believer named Timothy lived there whose mother, Eunice, *[2 Timothy 1:5; 3:15]* was a Jew, but whose father was a Gentile. 2 The other believers in Lystra, and also those in Iconium, spoke well of him. 3 Paul wanted to take Timothy along with him on the missionary journey, but all the Jews in that area knew his deceased father was a Gentile. Therefore, Paul had Timothy circumcised so they would accept him as fully Jewish, thus increasing his effectiveness in ministry among his fellow Jews. ❖ *Timothy was legally a Jew since his mother was Jewish, but he was considered apostate since he wasn't circumcised. In other circumstances, Paul argued that Titus—a Gentile—did not need to be circumcised. [Galatians 2:3-5] But Timothy's case was different. If Paul took him as an associate who was technically apostate, he would lose credibility among Jews. This measure was simply for his social acceptance in the Jewish community as a Jew in good standing.* ➤ 4 Thus Timothy joined Paul and Silas as they visited the assemblies in various cities and made known the decisions of the apostles and assembly elders in Jerusalem which Gentile believers should follow. 5 So through this letter from Jerusalem, they helped to strengthen the faith of the assemblies of Gentile believers, and every day more people were coming to the faith.

The Holy Spirit Guides Paul Through a Vision

6 The Holy Spirit had prevented Paul, Silas, and Timothy from entering Asia Province, so they traveled through the Phrygian section of Galatia Province. ❖ *Paul later went to Asia Province in Acts 19:1-10. Had they ignored the Spirit's leading, they might have had less success in their*

A 15:33 Most manuscripts have "to those who had sent them" but some have "to the apostles."

B 15:34 This verse is not in most manuscripts and it seems to contradict verse 33. On the other hand, it is supported by verse 40, unless Silas returned to Jerusalem with Judas and then came back to Antioch again.

work or possibly had something bad happen to them. When we blunder on our own in ministry, following our own ideas rather than being clearly led by the Spirit, can we be sure that we are "in the Lord's will?" ➤ 7 Having come to the border between Mysia and Bithynia Provinces, the Spirit of Jesus A would not allow them to enter Bithynia. ❖ It's interesting that the Spirit sometimes treats geopolitical entities, like provinces, as wholes. Some people believe that high-level demonic beings can hold influence over such geopolitical entities. Alternatively, the Spirit might simply have had a much higher priority assignment for them elsewhere, but was only gradually leading them to it step by step. ➤ 8 So they passed through Mysia Province and went down to the port city of Alexandria Troas. ❖ Troas is located near the ancient city of Troy. ➤ 9 One night while they were there, Paul had a vision. In it, he saw a man pleading with him, "Cover over to Macedonia Province ❖ northern Greece, just across the Aegean Sea from where they were ➤ and help us!" 10 I, Luke, ❖ the author of this book ➤ had joined them in Troas, and as soon as Paul told us about the vision, all four of us concluded that God had called us to proclaim the message of the Good News in Macedonia. So we got ready to leave.

The Conversion of Lydia

11 We boarded a ship and sailed from Troas on a straight course northwest about 38 miles to the island of Samothrace, and the following day we arrived in the port city of Neapolis in Macedonia Province. 12 From there, we traveled inland 10 miles northwest to the city of Philippi—which is a Roman colony and a prominent city in Macedonia—where we spent several days. 13 Since there was no synagogue there, on the Sabbath we went outside the city gate to a river where we expected B to find a place of prayer. When we arrived, we sat and began to speak to the Jewish women who had gathered there. ❖ Had there been even 10 Jewish men in the city, they would have constituted a legal synagogue. Where there was no regular synagogue, Jews preferred to meet in a place near water because it would be ritually pure and they could ritually wash in it before

praying. ➤ 14 One of them was Lydia, a Gentile convert to Judaism from the city of Thyatira in Asia Province. Her trade was selling purple fabric. ❖ She was probably wealthy since purple cloth was very expensive. Her name and trade indicates that she was a former slave who was now a free woman. Under Roman law, a freed woman with four children could make legal transactions on her own. ➤ The Lord made her receptive to what Paul was saying. 15 After she and her family and household dependents had been baptized, she said to us, "If you are convinced that I'm a true believer in the Lord, come and stay at my house while you minister in this city." And we were persuaded to do so.

Paul and Silas Are Imprisoned in Philippi

16 One day, as we were on our way to the place of prayer by the river, we encountered a slave girl who was demonized by a Pythonian spirit which enabled her to predict the future. ❖ Pytho is an area in Achaia Province where the Greek god Apollo—the god of prophecy—was worshipped. Any spirit that enabled someone to do this was called a Pythonian spirit. ➤ Her owners earned a lot of money through her fortune telling. 17 From that first encounter, she kept following Paul and the rest of us and loudly announced everywhere we went, "These men serve the Most High God and are proclaiming the way you C can be saved!" 18 She did this for many days until finally, Paul became so annoyed that he turned to her and said to the spirit, "By the authority that Jesus the Messiah gives me as one of his followers, I command you to come out of her!" And it immediately left her. ❖ Why didn't he do this sooner? Probably because it isn't always helpful to deliver someone who is not a believer. [Matthew 12:43-45] ➤

19 But when her owners realized that her usefulness for making money by fortune telling was ended, they seized Paul and Silas and dragged them to the center of the city to see the Roman authorities. 20 When they came before the chief magistrates, they said, "These men are Jews and are causing trouble in our city. 21 They are teaching

---

A 16:7 Some manuscripts have "Holy Spirit" instead of "Spirit of Jesus."

B 16:13 Some manuscripts have "where it was customary" rather than "where we expected."

C 16:17 Some manuscripts have "we" rather than "you."

people to follow customs that are against the law for Roman citizens to accept or practice." ❖ *Not long before this, Claudius Caesar had expelled all Jews from Rome in AD 49 for causing a religious disturbance. Since Philippi was a Roman colony, it may have done the same thing, accounting for the few Jewish men there. Paul and Silas were noticeably Jewish (probably by their beards and clothing), whereas Luke was a Gentile, and Timothy—a half Gentile—may have shaved and dressed more "normally." Many Romans were unaware that it was possible to be Jewish and also a Roman citizen like Paul was, so they assumed he had no rights. There was considerable anti-Semitic feeling among Roman citizens.* ➤ 22 A gathering crowd was quickly aroused to join in the attack on Paul and Silas. The magistrates ordered them to be stripped of their clothing down to their loin cloths and beaten with wooden rods. ❖ *It was common for accused criminals to be physically beaten before a trial unless they were Roman citizens. The crowd and magistrates assumed that they were not.* ➤ 23 After Paul and Silas had been severely beaten, they were dragged into prison and the jailer was instructed to guard them carefully. 24 So the jailer put them in an inner cell and locked their feet in stocks.

25 Now around midnight, Paul and Silas were praying aloud and singing hymns to God while the other prisoners were listening. 26 Suddenly, there was a violent earthquake that shook the prison even down in the depths of the dungeons. All the doors were sprung open and the chains holding the prisoners came loose. ❖ *The text is not clear if the chains became unattached to the walls (the likely natural effect of an earthquake) or if they miraculously came off the prisoners. Given the severity of the quake, it was a miracle that the walls and ceilings were not destroyed, burying the prisoners.* ➤ 27 When the jailer woke up, he saw the doors to the prison all open and assumed the prisoners had escaped. So he drew his sword and was about to kill himself to avoid a more painful and prolonged death by the authorities for having let them escape. 28 But Paul ❖ *apparently prompted by the Spirit* ➤ shouted out to him, "Don't harm yourself! We are all still here!" 29 The jailer called for torches and rushed into the jail.

❖ *It's implied that he and his men would now make sure none of the prisoners escaped.* ➤ Trembling from fear, he knelt in front of Paul and Silas. 30 A He brought them out and asked them, "Sirs, what must I do to be saved?" ❖ *The jailer, like most people in the city, undoubtedly had heard about Paul and the slave girl and the fact that they were proclaiming a message of salvation.* ➤ 31 Paul and Silas answered him, "Trust in the Lord Jesus, and you and your entire household will be saved." ❖ *A household would include wife, children, servants, and slaves and their children. While not negating the importance of each individual believing, it is quite common in many cultures for mass conversions to happen when the head of a group believes. If he believes, it is the responsibility of the others to believe too.* ➤ 32 Then they proclaimed the Lord's message about how to be saved both to him and to all who lived in his house. 33 The jailer took them right then, in the middle of the night, to a place where he could wash their wounds. Then, he and all his family were baptized. ❖ *The text does not tell us, but in view of the baptism, it seems likely he took them to a river.* ➤ 34 Then the jailer brought them to his house and fed them. He was filled with joy because he and his whole household had come to believe in the one true God.

35 When daylight came, the chief magistrates sent their officers to the jailer with the message, "You can release those men now." 36 So the jailer happily reported to Paul, "The chief magistrates have ordered me to release both of you, so you can leave. May God grant you peace." ❖ *It's not entirely clear what the jailer meant by "go in peace," in the literal text.* ➤ 37 But Paul had the jailer tell the officers, "We are Roman citizens, and these magistrates have violated our rights by having us severely beaten without trial and thrown into prison. Now they want to get rid of us quietly? I don't think so. If they don't want us to file an official complaint, they can come here themselves and escort us out with the courtesy they should have granted us yesterday!" ❖ *It was a capital offense to falsely claim Roman citizenship. We don't know how easy or difficult it would be for Paul to produce proof, but he had the magistrates in a difficult situation. It was against Roman law to*

A 16:30 One manuscript adds here: "after securing the rest (of the prisoners)."

punish or jail citizens without a proper trial. If he made an official complaint, they could lose their jobs and be severely punished themselves. Paul was unlikely to be vindictive, but he wanted to ensure that these officials would be less likely to do the same thing in the future to other traveling Jews, or to the assembly of believers. This incident could later be prosecuted if they harmed the assembly of believers there. Paul would not have to make explicit threats. The fact that he was making this protest over his violated rights would imply the potential threat. Thus the Lord was able to use this incident to protect his people in this city. Paul and Silas probably thought it was worth the pain they had suffered for the protection they "purchased." ➤ **38** The officers reported Paul's words to the chief magistrates who became afraid when they heard that Paul and Silas were Roman citizens. **39** So they came to the prison apologizing and begged Paul and Silas not to prosecute them. They also kept begging them to leave the city because their presence might cause another riot and they would be unable to protect them. ❖ Since they were citizens and not convicted of any crime, they could not be expelled from the city. ➤ **40** After Paul and Silas left the prison, they returned to Lydia's house. There, they met with the new believers and encouraged them before leaving the city. ❖ Starting in the next verse, Luke reverts to saying "they"—which implies he remained in Philippi to teach the new believers and perhaps do medical work. He seems to have stayed behind frequently and then caught up to Paul and company later. Paul meets up with Luke again on his return to Philippi in Acts 20:5-6. Timothy probably was among the people who left with Paul and Silas since in 17:14, Paul leaves Silas and Timothy behind in Berea when he has to escape quickly. ➤

17

Paul and Silas in the City of Thessalonica

1 Paul, Silas, and their companions followed the Roman highway called the "Via Egnatia" from Philippi though the cities of Amphipolis ❖ 30 miles southwest of Philippi ➤ and Apollonia ❖ 27 miles southwest of Amphipolis ➤ and on to the port city of Thessalonica, the capital of Macedonia Province ❖ 38 miles west of Apollonia ➤ where there was a synagogue. ❖ There may not have been synagogues in the other two cities, and Paul almost always chose to first proclaim the Good News to the Jews in a city before moving on to Gentiles. At a synagogue, there would be many people open to receiving and easily understanding God's message, so it made an ideal starting point. After he had a number of converts, they would be contacts to others who did not attend the synagogue. In addition to fulfilling God's promise to first offer salvation to his chosen people in this world, i.e., the Jews, it was a sound strategy to reach the maximum number of people in a short time. Thessalonica was a major seaport and commercial center of over 200,000 people. An assembly of believers founded in such a center could strategically spread the message to many connecting ports and cities. ➤ **2** As was Paul's usual practice, he went to the synagogue services on the Sabbath three weeks in a row and explained to those present **3** that the Scriptures predicted the Messiah had to suffer and die and rise again from death. ❖ One of the main reason Jews rejected Jesus as the Messiah was that they didn't believe the Messiah would suffer and die. ➤ Then, he would announce to them, "This Jesus, whom I'm talking about, is the Messiah." **4** Some of the Jews who listened to him were persuaded that Jesus was the Messiah, and joined with Paul and Silas. There were also a large number of God-fearing Gentiles who believed and also a number of leading women in the city. ❖ It's not clear if these women were prominent in their own right or were the wives of important men. Either way, they would have influence. From 1 Thessalonians 2:9; 2 Thessalonians 3:7-10; and especially Philippians 4:16 it's apparent that Paul and Silas stayed in Thessalonica for several months before the events in the next verse happened. After those first three weeks in the synagogue, they must have concentrated on preaching to Gentiles. ➤

5 But some of the Jewish leaders became jealous of Paul and Silas' popularity and gathered some lowlifes from the market area to form a mob and start a riot. They broke down the doors and searched Jason's house where Paul and Silas were staying, wanting to bring them out for mob justice. **6** But when they couldn't find who they were looking for, they dragged Jason and some other believers before the city authorities and shouted their accusation, "The men we are looking for have caused trouble everywhere they've traveled in the empire, and now they've come here to do the same! **7** Jason has taken them in his house as guests so he is supporting their subversion. They are all guilty of treason against the emperor since they claim someone named Jesus is their king." [8] They were successful in stirring up the crowd and the city authorities with these accusations. [9] But after the authorities made them post bail, they released Jason and the other believers who had been seized. ❖ *The bail was probably contingent on no further trouble happening, which would inevitably occur if Paul and Silas remained. That's probably why Paul could not return to Thessalonica despite his desire to do so. [1 Thessalonians 2:18]* ➤

[10a] So that night, the believers in Thessalonica helped Paul and Silas leave the city unseen, and they set out for the city of Berea, 148 miles to the west.

Paul and Silas in Berea

[10b] After Paul and Silas arrived in Berea, on the Sabbath they went to the synagogue there. [11] Now the Berean Jews were more open-minded and virtuous than those in Thessalonica. They eagerly received the message about Jesus, and every day they searched and studied the Scriptures to see if they supported Paul's teaching. [12] As a result, many of the Jews in that city believed, as well as a good number of prominent Gentiles—both women and men.

[13] But when the Jews in Thessalonica found out that Paul was proclaiming God's message about Jesus in Berea, they went there and started agitating people into a mob to attack Paul. [14] So the believers in Berea quickly sent Paul—along with some companions to escort him safely—to the coast. But Silas and Timothy stayed behind in Berea to continue to instruct the new believers. ❖ *Timothy hasn't been mentioned since 16:6 and the last place we knew that he was with Paul was in Philippi. See the note at 16:40. Some commentators think he came from Philippi and joined Paul and Silas while they were in Berea.* ➤ [15] Those who accompanied Paul saw him safely all the way to Athens, and then Paul sent them back with instructions for Silas and Timothy to join him there as soon as possible. ❖ *It's possible to read the text in verses 14-15 two ways. Either they went to the coast to port Methone or port Dium and boarded a ship to Athens, or they pretended to go toward the coast and went by land to Athens.* ➤

Paul Preaches in Athens

[16] Now, while Paul was waiting for Silas and Timothy to join him in Athens, his spirit was very upset to see that the city was full of idols, robbing the one true God of the honor due him. [17] So on the Sabbaths, he went to the that city's synagogue to proclaim and debate the message about Jesus with the Jews and God-fearing Gentiles who were there. Other days, he went to the marketplace and did the same thing there. ❖ *The market was where many people went to talk and debate, as well as to shop.* ➤ [18] He had some discussions with Epicurean and Stoic philosophers. ❖ *These were the two main schools of Greek philosophy at that time. Epicureans believed the main purpose in life was to attain happiness. Hence they were materialistic and pursued pleasure, very similar to many Americans today. They believed that the gods were not interested in humanity. The Stoics, on the other hand, opposed pleasure and taught that people should live in harmony with nature, suppress their desires, develop their ability to reason, and be self-sufficient. They were pantheistic, fatalistic, and proud. In opposition to the Epicureans, Paul taught that God is very interested in people, and in rebuttal to the Stoics, he said that we are dependent on God and should obey his will.* ➤ Some spoke about Paul disparagingly, "What is this ignorant show-off trying to say?" Others said, "He seems to be advocating we worship some foreign gods, one called 'Yesus' ❖ *i.e., Jesus* ➤ and a female called 'Anastasis.' " ❖ *meaning "Resurrector," a female name* ➤ They said that because Paul was preaching about Jesus and the resurrection, but they had so little in common with the monotheistic Jewish worldview that they didn't understand what he was talking about. [19] In any case, they invited Paul to speak to the Areopagus, their council of twelve philosophical and religious experts. ❖ *The council was not going to judge him on a legal basis but was a forum for public debate and discussion.* ➤ They said, "Come and tell us more about this new teaching you are proclaiming. [20] For we're hearing some amazing things from you and want to know what they mean." [21] (It was an Athenian passion, also indulged in by their visitors, to be fascinated with new and unusual ideas.)

[22] So Paul stood before the Areopagus and addressed them, "People of Athens, I observe from the many shrines dedicated to the gods in your city that Athenians are very religious. ❖ *The word rendered "religious" was probably*

neutral, although in other contexts it could mean "superstitious." It's unlikely he would want to insult them, but neither would open flattery go over well with this audience. ➤ 23 As I was walking around and looking carefully at your shrines, temples, and altars, I noticed one altar with this inscription carved onto it,

'TO AN UNKNOWN GOD'

Since you acknowledge that there is a god that you worship but don't know about, I am going to tell you about him. 24 He is the God who made the cosmos and everything in it. He is ruler over everything in the heavens and on Earth. He doesn't live in temples made by human hands. 25 Nor can mere human beings really serve him or minister to him, as if he had needs like we do; for he himself is the life-giver and need-supplier of all people and for everything that lives. 26 From the first man A ❖ i.e., Adam ➤ he created, he has made every human in every people group in this world. And he is the one who determined where they would live, their physical boundaries, and even the seasons of their lives, when they would die. ❖ The reference to "seasons" has also been interpreted as referring to seasons of nations, their rise and fall, and also as referring to the seasons of the year. ➤ 27 He created humanity so they would seek and find him, though in fact he is not far from any of us and is easily found by those who genuinely seek him. 28 Just as some of your own poets have said, 'He is the one who causes us to live and move and exist,' [Job 12:10; Daniel 5:23; John 1:3; Romans 11:36; 1 Corinthians 8:6; Colossians 1:16-17; Hebrews 1:3; 2 Peter 3:7] and elsewhere, 'We are his created children.' ❖ The first quotation is attributed to Epimenides of Crete (c. 600 BC) and the second to Aratus of Cilicia (born 310 BC). In Greek thought, both of these quotes were about Zeus, their chief god. Paul is not claiming that Zeus is the one true God, but is using these commonalities as a basis for presenting his arguments because Paul's hearers would have been familiar with them. ➤

29 "So I tell you, since we are God's created children, we shouldn't think that his divine nature can be characterized by an image made from stone, silver, or even gold—a mere image made by the limitations of human thought and skill. 30 In the past,

God chose to overlook humanity's ignorance of his nature and their failure to seek him. But now he is commanding that all people, everywhere, repent of their evil ways and former ignorance, and turn to him. 31 He has set a date when he will judge everyone in this world and render justice, giving out punishments and rewards for how people have lived. He has also chosen a particular man whom he has appointed to be the judge. And he has given us all proof of who this man is, by raising him from death to life." ❖ Paul was simply giving an introductory lesson for pagans that they must turn away from worshipping lifeless idols to worshipping the one true God. Some of their own philosophers had speculated about the same things. But these Greeks had no conception of a Judgment Day or end of the world as we know it. They believed that the world would continue on forever as it was. The idea of the resurrection was also totally new to them, and not one they were particularly open to. ➤

32 When they heard Paul talk about someone who died being raised back to life, some began to mock him, but others said, "We would like to hear you speak about this again sometime." ❖ Epicureans denied the immortality of the soul. Other Greeks believed in a shadowy afterlife in the underworld, and some of them believed in reincarnation. Stoics believed that the soul lived in this world after death until it was eventually absorbed back into their pantheistic god. Most of them would have had the view attributed to their god Apollo, who was to have said, "Once a man dies and the earth drinks up his blood, there is no resurrection." ➤ 33 So it was to this response that Paul left the council. 34 But some who heard him identified themselves with Paul and became believers. Among them were Dionysius—a member of the Areopagus—a woman named Damaris, and some others. ❖ Neither Dionysius nor Damaris is mentioned again in the New Testament. A later Dionysius—bishop of Corinth in about AD 170—said that the Dionysius mentioned in this verse became the first bishop of Athens. ➤

18

Paul Goes to Corinth

1 Not long afterward, Paul left Athens and traveled the 50 miles to Corinth. ❖ Silas

---

A 17:26 Some manuscripts say "blood" rather than "man."

and Timothy had not yet rejoined him. Corinth was the capital of Achaia Province, with a population of about 500,000 of which 300,000 were slaves. It had a reputation for the sexual immorality of its citizens. ➤ 2 He met a Jewish couple there—Aquila and Priscilla—who had recently come from Italy when the emperor Claudius had expelled all Jews from Rome. Aquila was originally from Pontus Province—in Asia Minor, along the southern shore of the Black Sea. ❖ This expelling of Jews happened more than once but is known to have happened in AD 49. ¶ Luke uses the familiar name, Priscilla, while Paul, in his letters, calls her by her formal name, Prisca. It's not certain that Priscilla was born Jewish. ➤ Paul went to visit them 3 and ended up staying and working with them because they were tent-makers like he was. ❖ It was not considered proper for Jewish rabbis to accept payment for teaching so they supported themselves with a trade, usually learned from their fathers. ➤ 4 Every Sabbath, he would go to the synagogue and use the Scriptures to try to convince the Jews and God-fearing Gentiles that Jesus was the Messiah.

5 Then, Silas and Timothy arrived from Macedonia with a financial gift from the assemblies there, [2 Corinthians 11:9; Philippians 4:14-15] so Paul gave up tent making and spent all of his time preaching the Word and testifying to fellow Jews that Jesus was the Messiah. 6 But when some of the Jews started to oppose him and blasphemed Jesus, he ritually shook off the dust from his clothing to indicate he would have nothing further to do with them and considered them to be unclean pagans. He said, "If you end up in Hell, it's your own fault for I've told you the truth. From now on in this city, I will preach God's message to the Gentiles since you reject it." 7 Then he left the synagogue and went next door to the house of Gaius Titius Justus A—a God-fearing Roman who offered his house as a place to meet with those interested in Paul's message and a place to worship with new believers. 8 But Crispus—the synagogue leader—and all the people in his household believed that Jesus was the Messiah, and many others in Corinth also believed and were baptized.

9 One night, the Lord told Paul in a vision, "Don't be afraid of your opponents, [1 Corinthians 2:3] but keep on speaking my message and refuse to be silenced. 10 For I am with you to protect you and I won't allow anyone to attack you or harm you like they have in other places. For I have many people in this city that I've chosen to be saved." 11 So Paul stayed in Corinth for 18 months teaching God's message. ❖ This was probably from about the fall of AD 50 to the spring of AD 52. Paul wrote 1 & 2 Thessalonians during this time in Corinth. ➤

12 But during the time that Gallio was proconsul of Achaia Province, ❖ This was from AD 51–52, according to historical sources. See the note about proconsuls at Acts 13:7. ➤ some Jews got together and seized Paul and brought him before the proconsul to make the accusation, 13 "This man persuades people to worship God in a way that is contrary to Jewish Law." ❖ Jewish beliefs were protected by Roman law, but new religions were not. It's apparent that the proconsul considered the situation to be an internal matter among Jews, not about a new religion. ➤ 14 Just as Paul was about to defend himself, Gallio said to the Jews, "If this were a criminal matter or a clear violation of Roman law, it would be reasonable for me to put up with you Jews and hear you out. 15 But since this is a dispute over words and names in your own religious Law, settle the matter yourselves. I'm not willing to judge such things." 16 And he had them ejected from his court. 17 Then a group of Gentile Corinthians grabbed Sosthenes—Crispus' replacement as leader of the synagogue—and beat him up in front of the court, but Gallio pretended he didn't notice. ❖ Many manuscripts say Greeks grabbed Sosthenes, but most do not and it's possible that it was the other Jews who turned on him out of frustration that his plan failed. Assuming it was unbelieving Gentiles who did this, it may have been the case that they considered Jews to be undesirables and looked for any excuse to accuse them of stirring up trouble so they could persecute them. If this is the same Sosthenes mentioned in 1 Corinthians 1:1, he later became a believer. ➤

A 18:7 No manuscript has "Gaius," but most commentators believe this is the man Paul calls "Gaius" in Romans 16:23 and 1 Corinthians 1:14. Most manuscripts have only "Justus" here. And some have "Titus Justus" instead of "Titius Justus."

Paul Returns to Antioch

18 Paul stayed in Corinth for quite a while longer, but finally said his good-byes to the believers there and went with Priscilla and Aquila to Port Cenchrea—seven miles east of Corinth. While he was in Cenchrea, he had his head shaved to show that he had fulfilled his vow as a Nazirite. ❖ *He probably took a Nazirite vow that he would continue to preach in Corinth as long as God wanted him to do so. After completing his vow, he shaved his head in accordance with the teaching in Numbers 6:1-21. He would later take his hair to the Temple in Jerusalem to offer it and sacrifices to complete his obligation. [Acts 21:24]* ➤ From there, they boarded a ship headed for Syria Province via Ephesus and Caesarea. ❖ *No mention is made of Silas and Timothy, who apparently remained in Corinth to minister.* ➤ 19-21 When they arrived at Ephesus in Asia Province, Paul went to the synagogue there and used the Scriptures to try to convince his fellow Jews that Jesus was the Messiah. ❖ *The Holy Spirit had previously prevented Paul from entering Asia Province. [Acts 16:6]* ➤ The Jews there asked him to stay with them, but he declined because he was on his way to Antioch in Syria Province. But while he was saying good-bye to them, he said, "{I must definitely be in Jerusalem for the Passover Festival.} A I will come back to visit you again if God allows it." So he left Priscilla and Aquila there and reboarded the ship to continue the remaining 600 miles to Caesarea in Judea Province.

22 When he arrived in Caesarea, he traveled the 62 miles up to Jerusalem to visit the assembly of believers there and to celebrate the Passover. Afterward, he traveled 300 miles north to Antioch in Syria Province to visit the church that had sent him out. ❖ *The Council in Jerusalem—just before Paul started his second missionary journey—was in AD 49–50. Paul left Corinth in the Spring of AD 52. Therefore, his second missionary journey probably lasted between two and three years, ending sometime in mid-to-late AD 52.* ➤

Paul Begins His Third Missionary Journey

23 After spending some time with the believers in Antioch, Paul departed on his third missionary journey, going from place to place through Galatia Province and the Phrygia area in Galatia Province, encouraging the believers and strengthening their faith. ❖ *Among other places, he probably revisited the cities of Derbe, Lystra, Iconium, and Antioch in Pisidia.* ➤

Priscilla and Aquila Instruct Apollos

24 About this time, a Jew from the city of Alexandria in Egypt—named Apollos—came to Ephesus. He was an eloquent speaker and knew the ❖ *Hebrew* ➤ Scriptures thoroughly. 25 He had been taught about "The Way" movement, the Lord Jesus, his teachings, and how to be saved and taught others about him quite accurately and with great zeal. But he only knew about John's baptism for repentance and not about baptism in the name of Jesus or the baptism in the Holy Spirit. 26 Priscilla and Aquila heard him speak boldly in the synagogue in Ephesus and then invited him to their home. There, they filled in the gaps of his knowledge, explaining God's way of salvation more completely.

27 When Apollos wanted to go across the sea to Corinth in Achaia Province to minister, the believers in Ephesus encouraged him and wrote him a letter of commendation which encouraged believers he met en route to welcome him and provide him with hospitality. When he finally arrived in Achaia, he greatly helped those who had believed in Jesus as a result of God's favor toward them. 28 For he clearly demonstrated from the Scriptures that Jesus was the Messiah, and powerfully refuted any Jewish teachers who opposed him in public.

19

Paul in Ephesus

1 While Apollos was at Corinth, Paul traveled through the Phrygian area of Galatia Province along the more-direct high road into Asia Province and arrived at Ephesus. There he met some followers of Jesus. ❖ *It's unlikely that they were followers of John the Baptizer. If that had been the case, Luke would have said so. The literal text just says "disciples" but doesn't say who they*

A 18:19-21 Most manuscripts do not have the part in { }.

were disciples of. ➤ 2 He asked them, "Did you receive the gift of the Holy Spirit when you became his followers?" They replied, "No. We didn't even hear about a Holy Spirit."

❖ *These are clearly Gentiles with no knowledge of the Hebrew Scriptures. Paul somehow discerned there was something lacking in their lives.* ➤ 3 So he asked, "Into what name where you baptized?" They replied, "Into the baptism of John."

❖ *John's baptism was an outward sign of repentance. Baptism into Jesus joins them spiritually to him in his death and resurrection. [Romans 6:3-4] Receiving the gift of the Holy Spirit is also tied to baptism into the name of Jesus. [Acts 2:38]* ➤ 4 Paul said, "John's baptism was a sign of repentance. But John also taught that people should believe in the Messiah who was coming after him—and that is Jesus."

❖ *Paul probably also told them that John said Jesus would baptize people with the Holy Spirit and taught them about the Holy Spirit himself. [Matthew 3:11; Mark 1:8; Luke 3:16; John 1:32-34] We should not assume that Luke has recorded the full extent of their conversation.* ➤ 5 When they heard this, they allowed Paul to baptize them in the name of the Lord Jesus. 6 Then Paul laid hands on them ❖ *probably on their heads* ➤ to impart the gift of the Holy Spirit, and the Spirit came upon them, causing them to speak in unknown languages and to speak messages directly from God. ❖ *It may be that some of them spoke in unknown languages and some of them prophesied.* ➤ 7 There were twelve men in that group. ❖ *There may have been women too, who were not normally mentioned or counted.* ➤

8 Then for the next three months, Paul went to the synagogue in Ephesus every week and boldly proclaimed God's message, trying to convince them from the Scriptures that what he was saying about God's Kingdom and the Messiah was true. 9 But some of the Jews refused to believe and became antagonistic toward his message. They would openly slander the teachings and followers of "The Way Movement." ❖ *"The Way" was a movement of people within Judaism that believed Jesus was the Messiah and followed his teachings. It might have been short for "The Way of Salvation." Jesus also called himself*

"the Way." [John 14:6] ➤ So Paul took the believers to meet every day {from 11:00 a.m. to 4:00 p.m.} **A** in Tyrannus' lecture hall where he could teach them and have unhindered discussions. 10 This continued for the next two years so that nearly every Jew and Gentile in Asia Province heard the message about Jesus. ❖ *Paul himself stayed and taught in Ephesus, but many of those he taught spread the message throughout the province. It was during this period that assemblies were started in the cities of Colosse, Laodicea, and Hierapolis, [Colossians 4:13] and possibly also the rest of the seven assemblies mentioned in Revelation 1:11; chapters 2—3, which were: Smyrna, Pergamum, Thyatira, Sardis, and Philadelphia.* ➤

11 During this time, God also enabled Paul to perform miracles different from the ones he usually did. 12 Even head cloths and work aprons that were touched by him and carried to those who were sick were effective in healing diseases and expelling demons from people. *[2 Kings 13:21; Mark 5:27-34; 6:56; Acts 5:15-16]* ❖ *The text literally reads, "handkerchiefs or aprons to be taken away from his skin." Some commentators think these were sweatbands and aprons that Paul used in his work and that the spiritual power in him was automatically transferred to what he touched. But he would have had a very limited supply of such cloths and aprons, so they were probably items brought to him by the people who wanted to help their sick loved ones. It should be evident from the Scriptures cited at the beginning of this note that spiritual power can be transferred via inert physical objects. It's likely Paul laid hands on and prayed over these cloths and aprons before sending them off to those who needed him. Physical impossibility and his busy preaching ministry prevented a personal visit to minister healing to everyone in the area who needed it.* ➤

13 There were also some Jews who normally traveled around expelling demons from people. They observed that demons responded quickly to the authority of the name of Jesus, so they tried to increase their effectiveness by using his name to expel demons. They would say, "I command you to leave this person by the name of Jesus, whom Paul preaches about!" ❖ *Before this, they*

---

probably used the name "Yahweh." They thought that the name itself had magic power, which is a wrong understanding. ➤ **14** There was a Jewish chief **A** priest named Sceva, whose seven sons were doing this. **15** But once when they tried to do this a demon responded, "I know who Jesus is and I know about Paul, but who do you think you are that you can order me around!" **16** Then the man with the demon attacked all seven of them so violently that they all ran out of the house wounded and naked. ❖ *Jesus gives authority over demons to his true followers who are in spiritual union with himself, but those who are not true believers and lack that spiritual union do not have that authority. [Matthew 10:1; 28:20; Mark 3:15; 6:7; 16:17; Luke 10:17-20]* ➤ **17** Everyone in Ephesus—both Jew and Gentile—heard about this story. As a result, everyone had a much greater respect for the Lord Jesus and were careful about speaking his name.

18 Many of the new believers now confessed that they had been involved with sorcery and the occult, and they weakened the power of these practices by exposing the occult secrets that they knew. **19** They also brought their occult-related books together for a public burning to demonstrate their rejection of such practices. The estimated value of these books was about 50,000 silver coins. ❖ *Ephesus was a center for the practice of magic and the occult. The practitioners believed that the power of their spells depended on secrecy. So by revealing their secret spells, they rendered them ineffective. They were not teaching others the secrets of how to do magic. God forbids his people from participating in any kind of sorcery. [Deuteronomy 18:10-14] This does not mean magic tricks for the purpose of entertainment, where everyone knows they are merely illusions. But it refers to any spiritual, supernatural, psychic, or magical means used to gain power or knowledge apart from submission to the one true God as its source. The silver coins mentioned probably were Greek drachmas, which were each worth about one day's wage. So the books burned were worth a year's wages for more than 130 men.* ➤ **20** So the message about the Lord Jesus spread widely and had a powerful impact on people, transforming their lives.

21 After all this had happened, Paul made plans to travel overland through Macedonia and Achaia Provinces to visit the assemblies he had established as far as Corinth, and from there he would go by sea to Jerusalem. From Jerusalem, he intended to go on to Rome. **22** So he sent two men who had served the Lord with him on ahead to prepare his way. These were Timothy and Erastus. But Paul stayed on in Asia Province awhile longer. ❖ *While he was in Ephesus this time, many commentators believe he wrote the letter of First Corinthians, because he mentions these travel plans in 1 Corinthians 16:1-11.* ➤

23 About that time, there was a major riot in Ephesus because people were upset with those who belonged to "The Way" movement. **24** A silversmith named Demetrius—who made silver miniatures of the temple of the Greek goddess Artemis ❖ *the Romans called her "Diana"* ➤—had a huge business that brought his workers much income. **25** He gathered all the workmen from similar trades together and said, "Men, you know that we make a good living from our business. **26** But you've seen and heard for yourselves that this Paul has convinced many people here in Ephesus and throughout the rest of Asia Province that man-made gods are not gods at all. So none of these people buy from us anymore. **27** Not only is our trade and means of living in danger, but if he is allowed to continue, the great goddess Artemis—who is worshipped by everyone in Asia Province and the known world—will be robbed of her glory, and her temple will be left destitute and without influence. Our whole way of life is threatened!" ❖ *The temple of Artemis—one of the seven wonders of the ancient world—was in Ephesus, and worshippers came from all over the empire to worship her there. Many years later—according to non-biblical sources—the Apostle John fulfilled what they dreaded. He prayed against Artemis and her temple, and it was destroyed in an earthquake. Within the 50 years following that event, her following dwindled to almost nothing.* ➤

28 When they heard this, they were enraged and started shouting over and over, "Great is our goddess Artemis!" ❖ *Demetrius and his workers may be the people Paul refers to as "wild*

A 19:14 The word ἀρχιερεύς (archiereus) can mean either "chief priest," or "High Priest." He clearly was not a true High Priest, but he might have called himself one for business purposes.

beasts" in 1 Corinthians 15:32. ➤ 29 Soon the entire city was in an uproar. A mob seized Gaius and Aristarchus—who had traveled with Paul from Macedonia Province—and dragged them into the amphitheater. ❖ *This great semi-circular open-air theater—carved out of the slope of a mountain—could seat nearly 25,000 people.* ➤ 30 Paul wanted to go speak to the crowd there himself, but the other believers would not let him. 31 Even some of the leading citizens of the city with the title "Asiarch" sent him a message pleading that he not to risk his life by going to the amphitheater.

32 The mob at the amphitheater was in total confusion. Some people were shouting one thing and others something else, while the majority of the people didn't even know why they were there. 33 The Jews there—fearing that the worshippers of Artemis would think they were behind Paul's work—pushed Alexander forward on the stage to speak to the crowd to say that Paul was their enemy too. Seeing him, some in the crowd prompted A him to speak. Alexander motioned for silence so he could speak, 34 but when they realized that he was a Jew ❖ *probably by his clothing and beard* ➤ and thus someone who refused to worship Artemis, they all started shouting again, "Great is our goddess Artemis!" and kept it up for two hours. ❖ *The worshippers of Artemis probably saw no difference between Jews and followers of Jesus.* ➤

35 Later, after quieting the crowd, the city clerk ❖ *one of the most important officials in the city* ➤ said, "People of Ephesus! Everyone knows that the city of Ephesus and its citizens are the guardians of the temple of the great goddess Artemis and of the sacred stone in her image that fell from the sky. ❖ *They thought that Zeus—their chief god—had thrown down the image of Artemis to them. Most scholars think they worshipped a meteorite having the shape of a woman with many breasts.* ➤ 36 Since no one can deny these facts, you need to calm down and not do anything without considering the consequences. 37 The men you've brought here are not temple thieves and they have

not insulted our goddess. 38 So if Demetrius and the other craftsmen with him have a legal complaint against anyone, the courts are available, along with the proconsuls who act as judges. They can bring their charges and go through the proper channels. 39 If there are other things you want to bring up, it should be done before a lawfully congregated assembly—which this is not. 40 We are in danger of being accused of rioting today since there is no valid cause for what has happened. If the Roman authorities I report to require an explanation, I will be hard pressed to give one that would satisfy them." ❖ *The city clerk represented the city assembly to the Roman authorities. If they were found guilty of rioting, the city would lose some of the privileges of self-rule that they had enjoyed.* ➤ 41 After saying this, he dismissed them.

20

Paul Returns
to Macedonia and Achaia Provinces

1 Sometime after the disturbance was over, Paul called together the believers in Ephesus. After exhorting and encouraging them, he made his farewells and left for Macedonia Province. ❖ *2 Corinthians 2:12-13 and 7:5-7 give a few more details of what happened between verses 1 and 2.* ➤ 2 He traveled through Macedonia and met with the assemblies of believers he had established in Philippi, Berea, and Thessalonica and spent time exhorting and encouraging them, and finally arrived in Corinth in Achaia Province 3 where he spent three months during the winter of AD 56–57. ❖ *Paul wrote 2 Corinthians while in Macedonia and it was delivered before he arrived in Corinth. During his time in Macedonia, he was also collecting money to help the poor Jewish believers in Jerusalem. While he was in Corinth, he wrote his letter to the Romans.* ➤ Paul had planned to leave Corinth by sailing to Antioch in Syria Province. But when he was ready to depart, he learned that some Jews who opposed his work were planning to kill him. ❖ *possibly on the way to the port, or on*

A 19:33 The word συμβιβάζω (sumbibazo) can mean "prompt," "instruct," "conclude," "decide," and several other meanings depending on context. Most manuscripts are ambiguous here. But a few manuscripts specifically say, "urged Alexander to speak."

board ship ➤ So he decided to go north into Macedonia Province first. 4 He was to be accompanied **A** by Sopater, who was the son of Pyrrhusa from Berea in Macedonia, ❖ *probably the same as Sosipater in Romans 16:21* ➤ Aristarchus and Secundus from Thessalonica in Macedonia, Gaius from Derbe in the Lycaonia region of Galatia Province, Tychicus and Trophimus from Asia Province, and Timothy of Lystra in Galatia Province. ❖ *These men were likely accompanying Paul to watch over the money he had collected and was taking to Jerusalem. [Romans 15:25-28; 1 Corinthians 16:1-4; 2 Corinthians chapters 8—9]* ➤

5 But due to the change in plan, they went on ahead and sailed from port Cenchreae ❖ *the port closest to Corinth* ➤ to Troas, where they waited for us. ❖ *The "us" indicates that Luke is traveling with Paul again and possibly some others. Luke was last with them in Acts 16:17 in Philippi, and it is likely that when Paul reached Philippi again, Luke joined him there.* ➤ 6 After we celebrated the Feast of Unleavened Bread in Philippi, ❖ *which in that year of AD 57, was April 7-14* ➤ we sailed from Neapolis—the port city of Philippi—and five days later met the other men in Troas ❖ *a 150-mile trip* ➤ where we stayed seven days.

Paul Raises a Young Man from Death

7 After sundown Saturday evening, ❖ *at the start of Sunday, the first day of the week for Jews* ➤ we gathered together with other believers in Troas to celebrate the Lord's Supper. Then Paul began to preach, and since he was intending to leave the next morning and had much he wanted to say, he kept on talking until midnight. 8 There were many lamps lit in that third-floor room where we were meeting, and the fumes and heat made people drowsy. 9 A young man named Eutychus was sitting in the window for the fresh air, but as Paul continued to talk for hours, he eventually fell asleep and fell out of the window to the ground, more than two stories below. When they picked him up, it was clear that he was dead. 10 But Paul went down and stretched himself over the boy's body and wrapped his arms around him. ❖ *This is a biblical pattern. [1 Kings 17:21-22; 2 Kings 4:34-35; Matthew 10:8]* ➤ Then, the boy's life returned and Paul said, "Stop your mourning, because he is alive!" 11 He then went back upstairs, along with Eutychus and everyone else, led them in a celebration of the Lord's Supper, and then continued to teach them until dawn when it was time for him to leave. 12 Then, the believers took the young man home alive and well and were considerably encouraged.

The Trip from Troas to Miletus

13 Paul wanted to travel by land the 20 miles to the city of Assos, but he told the rest of us to go by ship and said he would meet us there. ❖ *The trip by ship was 50 miles.* ➤ 14 When he met us in Assos, he came aboard with us and we sailed to the city of Mitylene on the island of Lesbos. 15 Sailing on from there, the next day we passed by the island of Chios and the day after that, we passed Ephesus and stayed in the town of Trogyllium **B** on the mainland opposite Samos island. Then the next day, we arrived in the city of Miletus, about 36 miles south of Ephesus. 16 Paul was in a hurry to get to Jerusalem before Pentecost, ❖ *May 29, AD 57* ➤ if at all possible. He had decided to sail past Ephesus so he wouldn't have to stay long in Asia Province. ❖ *Miletus was also in Asia Province, but Luke's reference to it referred to being in Ephesus and it's immediate area. Paul wanted to deliver the financial gift to the poor believers in Jerusalem during the festival when many people would be there to witness it, and thereby make more of an impact to promote the unity between Jewish and Gentile believers.* ➤

Paul's Farewell Message to the Assembly Leaders from Ephesus

17 Paul sent a messenger to the assembly leaders in Ephesus, asking them to come see him in Miletus. ❖ *His ship must have planned to stay in Miletus several days. It would take a minimum of three days for a messenger to get to Ephesus and the assembly leaders*

A 20:4 Many manuscripts have "as far as Asia province" here and many do not. It seems likely that these men were accompanying Paul as representatives of churches that had contributed to the gift for the poor in Jerusalem. If this is the case, it makes no sense that they were only planning to go as far as Asia province.

B 20:15 Most manuscripts do not have "stayed in the town of Trogyllium on the mainland opposite."

to get to Miletus. He sent for the leaders rather than stopping in Ephesus itself because he knew he would have had a difficult time leaving there quickly in order to arrive in Jerusalem in time for Pentecost. It would be easier to have only a short meeting with the leaders and say good-bye to them. ➤

18 After they arrived and were meeting together, he gave this speech, "You know that I stayed in your city the entire time I was in Asia Province before. 19 You saw me humbly do the Lord's work, often sad because of my concern over people's sin and their difficulties, and persevering in spite of persecution from Jews who reject Jesus. 20 I never let fear of my opponents or rejection keep me from telling you anything that might help your spiritual lives. Everything I taught was done openly in public, or in the houses where you met together. Nothing was done in secret. 21 I have been faithful to give clear and forceful warnings to both Jews and Gentiles that they need to turn away from their sin, submit to God in obedience, and believe in our Lord Jesus the Messiah. **A**

22 "And now the Holy Spirit is directing me to go to Jerusalem, but I'm not sure exactly what I will have to face. 23 For the Spirit speaks to me through his prophets in every city I'm in, that I will be bound and suffer there. 24 But I consider the work I've been assigned to do by the Lord Jesus to be so important that it's worth risking my life in order to joyfully **B** complete it. For that work is nothing less than proclaiming the message of Good News about the undeserved enabling favor that God offers everyone.

25 "I have fully proclaimed the message of God's Kingdom to you, but now I don't expect I will ever get to see any of you again. ❖ *At the end of Acts, Paul is in prison in Rome. It's not 100% certain what happened to him, but tradition says that he was released, spent several years in ministry, was imprisoned in Rome again a second time, and was then executed. Some commentators believe he may have had an opportunity to reach Ephesus again.* ➤ 26 So I want you to clearly understand that if any of you are eternally lost, I am not responsible

27 because I have never hesitated to tell you everything you need to know about God's will and his way of salvation.

28 "The Holy Spirit has raised you up as assembly leaders so you will take care of the Lord's people whom he rescued with his death. So you are responsible to guard yourselves and your people against the attacks and lies of the enemy who will attempt to deceive you and lead you away from the truth. 29 I know that after I leave, false teachers will come and decimate the assembly of true believers by leading people away from the truth, like savage wolves ravage a flock. ❖ *There is evidence that this did happen from references in his letters to Timothy, [1 Timothy 1:19-20; 4:1-3; 2 Timothy 2:17-18; 3:1-9] and Jesus' letter to the church in Revelation 2:2, 20. Ignatius' letter to the Ephesians, written in the early second century, indicates the believers in Ephesus did respond to Jesus' warning in Revelation.* ➤ 30 Even members of your own assemblies will gain prominence by corrupting the truth in order to lead some of your people away to follow them. 31 So be on guard to prevent it from happening! Remember how I spent my time for three years **C** teaching and warning everyone, often with tears of concern. That is an example for you to follow in taking care of your people.

32 "So now I'm trusting God **D** to take care of you, and I'm believing that the message I've taught you about the undeserved favor he freely offers through Jesus will cause you to grow in spiritual maturity, and will lead you to the full inheritance of eternal life in Heaven that he gives to all his holy people. 33 I've never wanted anyone's money or clothing. No one can accuse me of preaching for material gain. 34 You yourselves know that while I was with you, I always worked to earn my own money to meet my own needs and those of my coworkers. 35 My entire lifestyle while I lived among you was an example for you, to demonstrate that believers should work hard to earn their

---

A 20:21 A few manuscripts do not have "Messiah."
B 20:24 Most manuscripts lack "with joy."
C 20:31 Acts 19:8, 10 only mention two years and three months,

but Jews often counted part years (and days) as full ones.
D 20:32 A few manuscripts have "the Lord" instead of "God."

own way and also earn enough to be able to help those unable to work. Remember that the Lord Jesus said, 'You experience more satisfaction and blessing when you give to others than when you receive from them.' " ❖ *These words are not recorded in the Gospel accounts, which reminds us that much that Jesus did and said was never recorded. [John 20:30-31; 21:25]* ➤

36 When Paul finished speaking, he knelt down with them for a time of prayer. 37 Then, as they said their farewells, they all cried as they embraced him and expressed their deep affection for him, 38 for they were particularly distressed over the possibility they might not see him again in this life. Then they went down to see him off on the ship.

21

From Miletus to Jerusalem

1 When we ❖ *i.e., Paul, Luke, and the seven men mentioned in Acts 20:4* ➤ had torn ourselves away from the Ephesian assembly leaders we had met in Miletus, we sailed straight to the city of Cos on Cos island, and the next day to the city of Rhodes on Rhodes island, and then to the city of Patara on the coast of Lycia Province. 2 There, we boarded a ship that was bound for the city of Tyre in Phoenicia—the coastal region of Syria Province. ❖ *northwest of Galilee, a 400-mile five-day trip from Patara* ➤ 3 About halfway to Tyre, we sighted the island of Cyprus off the port side of the ship as we sailed by to the south of it, and finally landed in Tyre where we had to wait for the ship to offload its cargo. 4 We sought out some believers in that city and ended up staying with them for seven days until the ship was ready to continue its voyage. Some prophets among these believers kept urging Paul not to go to Jerusalem. ❖ *The Holy Spirit had already directed Paul to go to Jerusalem and had given him a warning that he might suffer. [Acts 20:22-24] The Holy Spirit never contradicts himself. He probably revealed to these prophets that Paul would suffer in Jerusalem and then they added the interpretation that he should not go.* ➤ 5 When the ship was ready to sail, all the assembly members—along with wives and children—accompanied us out of the city to the beach where we knelt and prayed and made our farewells. 6 Then, we boarded the ship and they returned home.

7 We sailed from Tyre, going 27 miles south to the city of Ptolemais. We greeted the believers there and stayed with them for a day. 8 The next day, we sailed another 35 miles south to the city of Caesarea, and while there, we stayed at the house of Philip the evangelist—one of the seven original deacons. *[Acts 6:1-7; 8:5-7]* 9 Philip had four unmarried daughters who regularly prophesied. 10 After we had been there for a few days, the prophet Agabus came down to Caesarea from Judea. *[Acts 11:27-29]* 11 When he came to us, he took Paul's cloth belt and tied up his own hands and feet with it. He said, "The Holy Spirit says this, 'Jewish leaders in Jerusalem will bind the owner of this belt and hand him over to the Gentile authorities for trial.' "

12 When we heard this, those of us traveling with Paul—as well as the believers in Caesarea—begged him not to go up to Jerusalem. 13 Then Paul replied, "Please stop making me feel so guilty with your crying! You cannot deter me, for I'm not only willing to be arrested and imprisoned for the Lord Jesus in Jerusalem, but also to die for him if that's his will for me." 14 When we saw that he could not be persuaded to change his mind, we stopped trying and said, "May the Lord's perfect will be accomplished in your life!" 15 After some days in Caesarea, we got ready and started on the road up to Jerusalem. ❖ *This was a three-day trip of about 62 miles to the south-southeast of Caesarea.* ➤ 16 Some of the believers from Caesarea accompanied us and guided us to the house of Mnason where we were to spend the night. He was originally from the island of Cyprus and was one of the early believers. ❖ *This was in AD 57—about 27 years after Jesus ascended into Heaven. He may have become a believer around AD 30, on or shortly after the Pentecost described in Acts chapter 2. In Jerusalem, Paul was soon arrested, thus ending his third missionary journey which had lasted nearly five years.* ➤

Paul's Time in Jerusalem

17 When we arrived in Jerusalem, the believers there warmly welcomed us. 18 The

day after we arrived, Paul and all of us who had accompanied him went to see the Lord's brother—James ❖ *who was the head of the assembly of believers in Jerusalem* ➤—and all the assembly leaders were also present. ❖ *About seven to eight years had passed since the last time Paul was in Jerusalem. [Acts chapter 15]* ➤ 19 Paul greeted everyone and then began to report all the things that God had done through his ministry among the Gentiles over the past several years since they had last met. 20 When he finished his report, all the leaders there praised God for what he had done. But then they told Paul, "You must understand the situation here. Several tens of thousands of fellow Jews have become believers in Jesus as the Messiah, but they are still committed to following the requirements of the Teachings of Moses. ❖ *Jewish nationalism was on the rise at this time, and sticking to their cultural practices was very important to the Jews. James literally said, "how many ten-thousands." Ten thousand was the largest number they had a word for. This would have meant a minimum of 50,000 Jewish believers in the Messiah—which would be about a tenth of the estimated population of Judea and Galilee at that time and eight times the estimated number of Pharisees.* ➤ 21 Unfortunately, some of your enemies have spread the false accusation that you exhort all Jews who live outside of Judea to abandon the Teachings of Moses and to not circumcise their boys and to not keep our Jewish customs. ❖ *What Paul actually taught was that Gentiles should not be forced to follow Jewish customs and that following the Torah teachings did not save people. But he was not against Jewish believers continuing to follow the Torah and Jewish customs as long as they had a proper understanding that the basis of salvation was through faith in the Messiah alone and not based on circumcision or obedience to the Torah.* ➤ 22 People will hear that you've returned to Jerusalem and a crowd will gather A to attack you. Something needs to be done to convince them that these accusations against you are false. 23 This is what we suggest: There are four men here who have made a Nazirite vow to God. *[Numbers 6:1-21]* 24 Associate yourself with these men and go through the purification

ceremony with them and pay their expenses to have their heads shaved. ❖ *Paying their expenses was considered a pious and charitable act.* ➤ Then, everyone will see that you still follow the Torah's teachings and our customs and that these accusations against you are false. ❖ *Paul had come from Gentile areas, so was ritually unclean and needed to go through a purification ceremony himself anyway.* ➤ 25 But as for Gentile believers, we still hold to the decision we wrote about that the only requirements laid upon them in order to have fellowship with Jewish believers are: they should not eat any food that's been offered to false gods or is in any way associated with such, they should not consume blood, they should not eat animals that have been strangled and prepared for eating leaving the blood still in them, and they should refrain from sexual sin." *[Acts 15:20]*

26 So the next day, Paul went with the four men and they started the purification process which would take seven days. Then he went into the Temple courtyard to post a notice announcing the date that the days of purification would end and when a sacrifice would be made for each of them. ❖ *The notice would probably also have indicated that Paul was paying the expenses of the other four men. In Acts 18:18, it seems that Paul shaved his head at the end of a Nazirite vow, so he may have been going through the identical process as these men to complete the requirements of that vow—which he could not complete outside of Jerusalem.* ➤

Paul is Arrested

27-29 When the seven days of purification were nearly over, some Jews from Asia Province—who had come from Ephesus for Pentecost—recognized Paul in the Temple. They had rejected Paul's message about Jesus and hated him. Earlier, they had seen him in the city with Trophimus—a Gentile believer from Ephesus—and they assumed that Paul had brought him into the inner courtyard of the Temple which was forbidden to Gentiles. ❖ *The penalty for such a violation was death.* ➤ So they seized him and started yelling to stir up the crowd, "Men of

---

A 21:22 Most manuscripts have "a crowd will gather, because," but the older manuscripts don't have these words, even though they are implied.

Jerusalem, help us! This the man travels all over the empire teaching everyone to despise and reject our Torah, this Temple, and our people! And now he has illegally brought Gentiles into the Temple area, defiling this holy place!"

30 A mob in the Temple courts grabbed Paul and dragged him out of the Court of Women into the Court of the Gentiles, and immediately the Temple guard closed the gates to the inner courtyards. ❖ *He had probably been in the chamber of the Nazirites in the southwest corner of the Court of Women. The gates separated the Court of the Gentiles from the Court of Women, and the Levite guards were protecting the inner courts of the Temple from being defiled by violence and bloodshed.* ➤ Soon the entire city was in an uproar and on the verge of rioting. 31 As the mob was trying to kill Paul, news reached Claudius Lysias—the tribune in charge of the Roman troops stationed in Jerusalem—that the entire city was rioting. ❖ *"Tribune" literally means "commander of 1,000," but in reality, he commanded a cohort of 600 men stationed in Antonia fortress, just above the Court of the Gentiles* ➤ 32 He immediately he took some soldiers and centurions and ran down the steps from the fortress to the Court of the Gentiles. When the mob saw the tribune and the soldiers, they stopped beating Paul. ❖ *Centurions—plural, each commanding 100 men—means that at least 200 soldiers were with the tribune.* ➤ 33 The tribune arrested Paul and ordered him to be bound between two soldiers with chains. Then he tried to find out from the crowd who Paul was and what he had done to upset everyone. 34 But some in the crowd were shouting one thing and others shouting something different. In the commotion, the tribune couldn't find out any facts so he ordered the soldiers to take Paul up into the barracks of the fortress for questioning. 35 When they got Paul as far as the stairs going up to the fortress, the mob became so violent that the soldiers had to carry him in order to keep him out of the mob's reach. 36 All the while, the mob following them kept shouting to each other, "Kill him!" ❖ *Literally, "away with him," but it meant "let's kill him."* ➤

Paul Speaks to the Mob

37 As he was about to be taken into the barracks, Paul asked the tribune, "May I have permission to speak with you?" The tribune replied, "You speak fluent educated Greek! 38 So you are not the Egyptian who led a revolt a few years back and then led 4,000 men of the fanatical group 'the Dagger Men' out into the wilderness?" ❖ *This was a Jewish group that had planned to take over Jerusalem. They had killed Jews who accommodated the Romans. They would kill an enemy in the middle of a large crowd with a dagger, then slip away.* ➤ 39 Paul replied, "No, I'm not that man. I'm a Jew and a citizen of an important city, Tarsus in Cilicia Province. Please allow me to try to speak to the people." 40 When the tribune gave him permission, Paul stood on the stairs and motioned for the crowd to be silent. ❖ *Such a gesture was usually obeyed by a crowd if they had any desire to hear what the person had to say.* ➤ When they were quiet enough for him to be heard, he started speaking to them in Aramaic, the common language of the Jews in Judea. ❖ *The word Ἑβραΐς (Hebrais) can mean either "Hebrew" or "Aramaic," but only the most educated Jews of that time understood Hebrew.* ➤

22

1 "My Jewish brothers and elders, please listen to what I have to say in my defense!" 2 When the mob heard that he was speaking to them in Aramaic, they became very quiet. Then he said, 3 "I am a Jew. I was born in the city of Tarsus in Cilicia Province, but was raised here in Jerusalem and became a disciple of Gamaliel, who trained me to strictly follow the Torah teachings of our ancestors. ❖ *Gamaliel was a Pharisee, a member of the Sanhedrin, and one of the most respected rabbis of the time. [Acts 5:34]* ➤ I am as zealous to serve God today as you are. 4 I persecuted followers of 'The Way' movement, arresting both men and woman, putting them in prison, and seeing to it that some of them were executed. 5 The High Priest and the Sanhedrin can testify that what I say is true. I even asked them for letters of authority addressed to the Jewish leaders in Damascus so I could go there and bring people who followed 'The Way' back to Jerusalem for punishment."

Paul Tells About His Conversion

6 "But on my journey, at about noon of the day I was nearing Damascus, a brilliant light from Heaven [Acts 9:1-19; 26:12-18] ❖ or: the sky ➤ glared all around me. 7 I fell to the ground and heard a voice saying, 'Saul, Saul, why are you persecuting me?' 8 I answered, 'Sir, who are you?' And the voice said, 'I am Jesus from Nazareth, the one you are persecuting.' 9 Those who were traveling with me saw the light but didn't understand the voice of the person speaking to me. ❖ See the footnote at Acts 9:7. ➤ 10 I asked, 'Sir, what do you want of me?' He replied, 'Get up and continue on into Damascus. When you are there, you will be told everything that God has appointed you to do.' 11 But since the light had blinded me, my companions had to lead me by the hand into Damascus.

12 "A Jew named Ananias lived in Damascus. He was devout and followed the Torah's teachings and had a good reputation among all his fellow Jews there. 13 He came to me and said, 'Brother Saul, receive your sight back!' And immediately, I could see him. 14 Then he said, 'The God of our ancestors has chosen you to know his will and to see his Righteous One and to hear him speak to you. ❖ The "Righteous One" was a title for the Messiah. ➤ 15 For you are to be his witness, to tell all people about what you have seen and heard. 16 So what are you waiting for? Get going! Be baptized and have your sins forgiven by calling on him to save you.'

17 "Later, one day after I had returned to Jerusalem and was praying in the Temple, I went into a trance. 18 I saw Jesus again and he said to me, 'You must hurry and leave Jerusalem because the people here won't believe your testimony about me.' 19 I said, 'Lord, these people know that I persecuted, imprisoned, and beat those from every synagogue who believed in you. 20 And when your witness, Stephen, was executed, I was there with the executioners, approving of his death and guarding their outer garments.' ❖ Paul was assuming that since people knew how zealous he was for the Torah's teachings and his past persecution of "The Way" movement, that they would

assume he had a good reason for changing his mind. ➤ 21 Then, the Lord told me, 'Go now! For I'm sending you far away to witness to the Gentiles.' "

22 The crowd had been patiently listening until this point, but they abruptly started shouting, "Kill him! He's not fit to live in this world!" ❖ What angered them was the statement that the Lord (whether they were interpreting this as God or the Messiah) told him to go preach to the Gentiles. This implied that God considered Gentiles as important as his chosen people, the Jews. They would not tolerate such an idea. ➤ 23 They shouted and in their rage, waved ❖ or: tore off ➤ their outer garments and threw dust in the air. ❖ No one is sure what these actions meant, aside from expressing their rage. They may have torn off their outer garments as a protest against blasphemy. Throwing dust may have been an expression of horror, or may have been the only thing at hand to throw at Paul. ➤ 24 The tribune ordered that Paul be brought into the barracks and then flogged and interrogated to find out why the people were so agitated. ❖ The tribune had not understood what Paul was saying in Aramaic and probably wouldn't have understood the reasoning of the Jews even if he had understood Paul's words. See the note at John 19:1 about the flogging. The intent was interrogation under torture. It was legal to flog slaves and non-Roman citizens with the flagellum to extort confessions. Paul had been beaten with rods three times and had received the Jewish 39 lashes with a whip five separate times, [2 Corinthians 11:24-25] but this flogging, if it didn't kill him, could leave him a cripple for life. ➤ 25 As the soldiers stretched him out and tied him with leather thongs to flog him, Paul asked the centurion standing there, "Is it legal for you to flog a Roman citizen who hasn't been tried and found guilty?" ❖ Roman law forbade flogging or beating Roman citizens without a proper trial. See the note at Acts 16:37. ➤ 26 When the centurion heard this, he immediately went to the tribune and said, "What are you doing? This man is a Roman citizen!" 27 The tribune went to Paul and said, "Tell me the truth. Are you a Roman citizen?" Paul answered, "Yes." 28 The tribune said, "I acquired citizenship by paying a large amount of money." Paul answered, "But I was born a citizen." ❖ This meant that his father was also a citizen. Roman citizenship could be obtained through a bribe or given as a reward for service to the empire. Or one could be born the son of a Roman citizen. Paul's natural citizenship gave him

higher social status than the tribune. ➤ 29 The soldiers who were about to flog him immediately loosed him from his bonds and withdrew. The tribune was afraid of possible repercussions for his chaining a Roman citizen. ❖ Paul had probably waited until they were about to flog him before letting his citizenship be known because it gave him some leverage over the tribune. ➤

Paul Speaks to the Sanhedrin

30 The tribune wanted to find out exactly what crime the Jewish leaders were accusing Paul of, so he had him released from prison ❖ though still under guard ➤ and ordered the chief priests and the Sanhedrin to meet. He then brought Paul before them. ❖ In the absence of the procurator (i.e., the Roman governor), the tribune had absolute military authority over the Jews and could order the Sanhedrin to meet. ➤

23

1 Paul looked boldly at the members of the Sanhedrin and said, "My Jewish brothers, I have always lived in such a way that I believed was pleasing to God." 2 Ananias, the High Priest, ordered those standing close to Paul to strike him across the face. ❖ This Ananias (different from those mentioned in previous chapters)—son of Nedebaeus—was put into this office by Herod of Chalcis (the younger brother of Herod Agrippa I) in AD 47. He was removed from office by Herod Agrippa II about two years after this trial in AD 59 and was killed by zealots in AD 66. History records details of his greed, evil, and violence. This action showed that Ananias had already assumed Paul was guilty, and such an assumption before he was properly tried violated Jewish law. [Leviticus 19:15; John 18:23] ➤ 3 Then Paul said, "God will strike you for that, you hypocrite of a judge! You sit there pretending to try me according to the teachings of the Torah, but you yourself disobey those commands by ordering these men to strike me!" 4 Those standing near Paul exclaimed, "You've slandered God's High Priest!" 5 Paul humbly replied, "My Jewish brothers, I did not realize he was the High Priest or I wouldn't have said that, for the Torah says, 'Do not curse a leader of your

people.' " [Exodus 22:28] ❖ Evidently the High Priest was not wearing his robes of office, which would have identified him as the High Priest. ➤

6 Paul knew that the Sanhedrin was made up of Sadducees and Pharisees. Seeking to gain some support, he called out, "My Jewish brothers, I am a Pharisee and the son of a Pharisee. Basically, I'm on trial here because I believe God will raise people from death!" ❖ At that time it was possible for a Pharisee to become a follower of Jesus and still remain a Pharisee, although such a person might be persecuted. There was no fundamental conflict in their beliefs. ➤ 7 Immediately, the Pharisees and Sadducees in the Sanhedrin began to renew their long-standing dispute over this very issue. 8 For the Sadducees don't believe in angels or spirits of any kind, or that God raises people from death, while the Pharisees believe in all these things. [Matthew 22:23-32; Mark 12:18-27; Luke 20:27-38; Acts 4:1-2]

9 Their dispute became a shouting match and some of the Scripture teachers who were Pharisees stood up and strongly protested the charges against Paul. They said, "We don't see that this man has done anything wrong at all. It's quite possible that a spirit or an angel really spoke to him as he claims! {Let's not fight against God here!}" A 10 Their disagreement became so great and violent that the tribune feared Paul might be torn apart, so he ordered the soldiers to go down and forcibly remove Paul from the fight and take him back to the barracks.

11 That night, the Lord Jesus appeared standing next to Paul and said, "Cheer up and be brave! For it's my will that you go to Rome to tell others about me, just as you've done here in Jerusalem."

Paul's Enemies Plot to Kill Him

12 The next morning, some Jews conspired together to kill Paul. They vowed to God that they would neither eat or drink again until they killed him. ❖ These men were not able to fulfill their vow, but it's not necessarily true that any of them died. The Torah allowed them to make a sacrifice to atone for not fulfilling their vow. ➤ 13 More than 40 men took this vow. 14 They went to the chief

---

A 23:9 Most manuscripts don't have this sentence { }.

priests and leaders and informed them, "We have vowed to eat and drink nothing until we've killed Paul. 15 So we're asking you and the Sanhedrin to ask the tribune to bring him down to stand before you tomorrow, **A** as though you were going to interrogate him further. We will be ready to kill him before he reaches here." ❖ *They were willing to risk their lives to kill Paul since they would be attacking Roman soldiers to get to him, and could, therefore, expect that many of them would die in the attempt.* ➤

16 But Paul's nephew—his sister's son—heard about their plan and went to the barracks to tell Paul. 17 So Paul asked to speak to one of the centurions and told him, "Please take this young man to the tribune, for he has something important to report." 18 The centurion took him to the tribune and explained, "The prisoner Paul asked to speak to me and then asked me to bring this young man to you because he has something important to report." 19 The tribune took the young man by the hand and led him to a place they could talk in private. Then he asked, "What is it you have to say?" 20 The boy replied, "The Jewish leaders have agreed to ask you to bring Paul down to stand before the Sanhedrin tomorrow, as if they wanted to interrogate him further. 21 But please don't listen to them because more than 40 men will be ready to ambush him on the way. They've vowed not to eat or drink until they kill him. They are all ready and waiting for you to agree to their request." 22 The tribune warned him, "Don't mention to anyone that you've told me about this." Then he dismissed the boy.

Paul Is Sent to Caesarea for Safety

23 The tribune summoned two centurions and ordered, "By 9:00 o'clock tonight, I want 200 infantry, 70 cavalry, and 200 spearmen ready to travel to Caesarea. ❖ *Caesarea was the Roman capital of Judea Province and their military headquarters.* ➤ 24 Also bring some horses for Paul and get him safely to Governor Felix." ❖ *Felix was appointed procurator (i.e., governor) over Judea by Claudius Caesar in AD 52 and* held the position until AD 59-60. ➤ 25 The tribune wrote the following letter to the governor:

26 "From Tribune Claudius Lysias to his Excellency, Governor Felix, "Greetings!

27 "The Jews seized this man, Paul, and were about to kill him, so I went with my troops and rescued him. I learned he is a Roman citizen. 28 I wanted to find out what they were accusing him of, so I brought him before their Sanhedrin. 29 I found out that his 'crime' had something to do with disputes over their own Law, but there was no charge made that would justify imprisonment or death by Roman law. 30 When I was informed of a plot to kill him, I sent him to you immediately and I've also ordered his accusers to appear before you to present their charges against him. Farewell." **B**

31 So the soldiers carried out their orders and that night, they took Paul as far as the Roman military base in the city of Antipatris. ❖ *35 miles northwest of Jerusalem* ➤ 32 The next day, while the 400 foot soldiers returned to their barracks in Jerusalem, Paul was taken by the cavalry the remaining 27 miles to Caesarea. 33 When they arrived, they delivered Paul and the tribune's letter to the governor. 34 He read it and asked Paul which province he was from and learned that he was from Cilicia Province. ❖ *Felix could have sent Paul to the city of Tarsus in Cilicia for trial, but knowing that would anger the Jewish leaders, he decided to judge the case in Caesarea.* ➤ 35 He then told Paul, "I will convene a hearing when your accusers arrive." He ordered that Paul be kept under guard in the palace built by Herod the Great, which was now his own residence. ❖ *Herod the Great had died about 60 years previously.* ➤

24

Paul Speaks Before Governor Felix

1 Five days later, a delegation arrived in Caesarea from Jerusalem to appear in court before the governor and bring

---

A 23:15 Most manuscripts don't have "tomorrow."

B 23:30 Many manuscripts don't have "farewell."

formal charges against Paul. They included the High Priest Ananias, some elders, and an expert in Roman law named Tertullus. 2-3 When Paul had been brought into the courtroom, Tertullus began to present the case against him to governor Felix. He said, "Your Excellency, we Jewish leaders acknowledge with great gratitude that by your wise foresight, you've instituted reforms that benefit our people and you've brought us a time of peace. ❖ *Felix's administration was actually oppressive and corrupt, resulting in increasing rebellion among the people such that Emperor Nero removed him from office two years after this trial.* ➤ 4 But I don't want to make you weary with recounting the many wonderful things you know that you've done, so I beg your kind attention for a brief hearing of our case against this man.

5 "Our leaders have found him to be guilty of being a troublemaker who stirs up riots among Jews all over the empire. He is a main leader of the illegal sect of people who follow a man from Nazareth. ❖ *Tertullus is trying to portray the followers of Jesus as members of an illegal sect. Roman law did not allow people to practice a religion not officially recognized by the government. Those who did could be executed. Judaism was a legally recognized religion, and Paul argues in verses 14-16 that this "sect" is part of Judaism.* ➤ 6 He was attempting to defile our Temple in Jerusalem when we arrested him. {We wanted to try him by our own Law, 7 but tribune Lysias came and forcefully removed him from our custody. 8 Then, he ordered that this man's accusers had to appear before you.} **A** By questioning this man yourself, you should be able to learn that all these accusations we make against him are true." 9 Then the Jewish leaders vocally supported these accusations and asserted they were true.

10 When the governor motioned that it was his turn to speak, Paul said, "Your Excellency, I know that you have been a judge over this nation for several years and are familiar with our ways. So I gladly present my defense before you. 11 You can easily ascertain that I arrived in Jerusalem to worship in the Temple there no more than twelve days ago. ❖ *Since he had been in custody for about 6 days, he would not have had much time to organize any rebellion.* ➤ 12 There is nobody who can claim they found me arguing or stirring up a crowd in a synagogue, or in the Temple, or anywhere else in that city. 13 And they are unable to provide evidence—such as witnesses—to substantiate the charges they are making against me. ❖ *They could only say that Paul "tried" to defile the Temple, as they had no proof that he did so.* ➤ 14 I will admit to being part of 'The Way' movement, which they are trying to brand as an illegal sect. But I serve the same God that all our Jewish ancestors worshipped, and believe all the holy writings in the Teachings of Moses and the writings of the Prophets ❖ *i.e., all the Hebrew Scriptures* ➤ just as my accusers claim to do. 15 I have the same expectation that some of these men here do, that our God will one day raise all who have died back to life—both those who have been good and those who have been evil—in order to judge them. 16 With this in mind, I always do my best to live in such a way that neither God nor people can accuse me of doing wrong.

17 "After having been away from Judea Province for several years, ❖ *It had been five years since his visit in Acts 18:22 and ten years since his visit in Acts 15:4.* ➤ I came to Jerusalem to bring my people a financial gift for the poor and to offer sacrifices to God. ❖ *The financial gift is the one he collected from the assemblies in Galatia, Macedonia, and Achaia Provinces. [Acts 11:27-30; Romans 15:25-28; 1 Corinthians 16:1-4; 2 Corinthians chapters 8—9]* ➤ 18 I had gone through the necessary purification ceremonies and so was ritually clean when these accusers saw me in the Temple courtyard for the purpose of making those sacrifices. There was no crowd around me and I was not making any disturbance. 19 The disturbance was started by some Jews from Asia Province. They ought to be here before you if they have accusations they can prove. ❖ *The absence of these men to accuse Paul greatly weakened the case of the Jewish leaders.* ➤ 20 Or ask these men what crime

---

A 24:8 The end of verse 6 through this part of verse 8 in { } does not appear in most manuscripts.

they found me guilty of when I was made to stand before the Sanhedrin. 21 The only thing they could possibly have against me is the one thing I shouted in their presence, which was, 'Basically, I'm on trial here because I believe that God will raise people from death!' " *[Acts 23:6]*

22 Then Felix, who was well informed about "The Way" movement, adjourned the hearing and told the Jewish leaders, "When Tribune Lysias arrives and I can consult with him, I will decide your case."

❖ *Felix's wife was Jewish, so he probably had an interest in the Jews and their different factions. Since Paul was a Roman citizen and had clearly not broken any Roman law, he should have been allowed to go free.* ➤ 23 He then ordered the centurion in charge of Paul to keep him under guard, but to allow him some freedom and to let his friends come to provide for his needs.

24 Some days later, Felix came to the courtroom with his Jewish wife, Drusilla. He summoned Paul and they listened to him speak about trusting in Jesus as the Messiah.

❖ *Drusilla was the daughter of Herod Agrippa I and sister of Herod Agrippa II. Felix had her divorce her first husband, and she became his third wife. According to manuscripts called "the western text," it was Drusilla who really wanted to meet Paul.* ➤ 25 But as Paul was teaching about the need to live in a way that pleased God, about exercising self-control over the body's sexual desires, and about Judgment Day when people will be judged by their actions, Felix became afraid and dismissed him, saying, "When I find some time, I will summon you again." 26 In addition to being interested in Paul's teaching, he was hoping Paul would offer him a bribe to let him go free, so he sent for him quite frequently and had numerous discussions with him.

27 But after two years of this, the emperor replaced Felix with Porcius Festus. Since Felix wished to do something to gain the Jewish leaders' favor, he left Paul in prison. ❖ *Festus was procurator of Judea Province from about AD 58–59 to 62. Roman law said that a person was to be released if not prosecuted within two years. But when Felix was ousted from office because of Jewish*

unrest, he didn't want to further turn them against him and have them make an additional complaint, since he would soon face them in court. ➤

25

Paul on Trial Before Festus

1 Three days after Festus arrived in Caesarea to take over from Felix as governor of Judea Province, he went up to Jerusalem. 2 There he met with the chief priests **A** and other Jewish leaders who presented him with charges against Paul, and urged him 3 to have Paul brought to Jerusalem as a favor to them. They had plans to kill Paul while he was on the way. 4 Festus said that since Paul was in custody in Caesarea and he was going there himself soon, 5 it would be best if the appropriate authorities among them would come with him and present their charges against Paul there.

6 About eight to ten days later, **B** he went to Caesarea, and the day after he arrived there, he summoned Paul to stand before him in court. 7 When Paul arrived in the courtroom, the Jewish leaders who had come from Jerusalem stood around him and made many serious accusations against him, none of which they were able to prove with supporting witnesses. 8 In his own defense, Paul said, "I haven't broken any Jewish Law, or committed any crime against the Temple, or broken any Roman law."

9 But Festus wanted to curry favor with the Jewish leaders, so he asked Paul, "Are you willing to stand trial before me in Jerusalem with regard to these charges?"

10 Paul replied, "No I am not. I'm already standing before the emperor's court where—as a Roman citizen—I should be tried. You yourself know that I've done nothing wrong, even against Jewish Law. 11 If I had done something that deserves capital punishment, then I wouldn't resist that penalty. But since I'm not guilty of any of the things these men accuse me of doing, no one has the right to turn me over to them—as you seem inclined to do. Therefore, I exercise my legal right as

---

A 25:2 A few manuscripts have "High Priest" instead of "chief priests."

B 25:6 A few manuscripts say "more than ten days."

a Roman citizen and formally appeal that the emperor hear my case!" ❖ *Festus could not deny Paul the right of appeal to the emperor. Nero was emperor from AD 54-68, but at this time in AD 59, he had not yet given any hint of the kind of animosity he would later show toward the followers of Jesus in AD 64 and afterward. The first five years of his reign were seen as a mini golden age. Since Paul had already spent two years in prison under Felix, and Festus was inexperienced in dealing with the Jewish leadership and seemed prone to try to please them, Paul was taking no chances. He would certainly have suspected another plot to kill him and knew that he would get no justice from the Sanhedrin. So he had little practical choice to do otherwise.* ➤

12 After conferring with his advisors, he told Paul, "Since you have appealed to the emperor, that is where we will send you!"

Paul Speaks Before King Agrippa and Bernice

13 A few days later, King Herod Agrippa II and his sister Bernice visited Caesarea to pay their respects to the new governor. **A** 14 Since **B** they were staying there several days, Festus explained Paul's case to the king. He said, "Felix left a case for me to deal with—a man who has been a prisoner for the past two years. 15 When I was in Jerusalem, the chief priests and other Jewish leaders brought charges against him and asked **C** me to find him guilty and condemn him to death.

16 "I told them that Roman law does not allow me to convict a man and hand him over for execution before he has faced his accusers in court and had an opportunity to defend himself against the charges. 17 So when they came here with me, I didn't delay but heard the case the next day. 18 When his accusers brought their charges, they weren't at all what I expected. 19 They were simply some insignificant points they disagreed with him about that concerned their own religion and a man named Jesus who had died, but Paul claimed is alive. 20 Since I had

no idea how to investigate such things, I asked Paul if he was willing to stand trial before me in Jerusalem with regard to these charges. 21 But then he appealed to have the emperor try his case, so I ordered him held in custody until I send him to the emperor."

22 King Agrippa told Festus, "I'd be interested in hearing what this Paul has to say." Festus replied, "Then you may see him tomorrow."

23 The next day, King Agrippa and Bernice entered the audience hall with great pomp, accompanied by tribunes and other prominent men of the city. Then Festus commanded that Paul be brought in. 24 Festus said, "King Agrippa and honored guests, I present to you this man whom the entire Jewish leadership would like to see dead. Both here and in Jerusalem they stridently shouted that he is not fit to live. 25 Yet as far as I can determine, he has done nothing to deserve the death penalty. Since he himself formally appealed that the emperor hear his case, I've decided to send him to Rome. 26 But I have no valid charges to make against him in the official documents I will have to send to my divine Lord Nero concerning his case. ❖ *Roman emperors were considered to be gods, and the title "Lord" that Festus used here has that connotation.* ➤ Therefore, I've brought him before all of you and especially you, King Agrippa, so that after you have investigated this matter, I might have something to write about his case that will make sense to the emperor. 27 It wouldn't be wise for me to waste the emperor's time by sending him a prisoner without specifying reasonable charges against him."

26

1 Then Agrippa said to Paul, "You now have permission to present your case." So

---

A 25:13 Herod Agrippa II governed Galilee, Itruea, and Trachonitis provinces from AD 53 until his death around AD 100. He had the power to appoint the High Priest. Bernice later became the mistress of the Roman general Titus, who destroyed Jerusalem in AD 70 and later became emperor.

B 25:14 The conjunction ὡς (hōs), translated "since," has a wide range of meaning and could just as likely mean "after" in this context.

C 25:15 The word αἰτέω (aiteō), translated "asked," can alternatively mean "demanded."

Paul stretched out his hand—in the style of accomplished orators to gain everyone's attention—and began to speak.

2 "King Agrippa, I am indeed fortunate to be able to present my case to you regarding the charges that the Jewish leaders have made against me, 3 because I know you are an expert on all Jewish customs and points of controversy. So I ask you to please listen patiently.

4 "The Jewish leaders who have accused me are well aware of my dedication to the Teachings of Moses since I was a child, from the beginning of my life in Cilicia Province and my youth in Jerusalem to adulthood. 5 If they are willing to testify honestly, they will verify that they've known me a long time and that I was a Pharisee, which you know is the strictest sect of Judaism with regard to keeping the teachings of the Torah. ❖ *Since Agrippa knew all about Pharisees, Paul did not need to say that all Pharisees had a strong belief in God's promises that he would send the Messiah to save them, and would raise dead people back to life to restore the twelve tribes of Israel.* ➤ 6 But strangely enough, I'm standing here on trial because I believe God has fulfilled the promise he made to our ancestors, the same promise all the Pharisees believe in. 7 This is the same promise that all of Israel expects God to fulfill as they earnestly worship him day and night. And yet, your Majesty, the Jewish leaders are accusing me as if having this expectation is a crime! 8 Since this is Israel's expectation and hope, why should any Jew consider it so unlikely that God really does raise people from death to life?

9 "Actually, I too held the same viewpoint the Jewish leaders do and did everything I could to stop people from believing in Jesus of Nazareth's resurrection. 10 I did this right in Jerusalem, acquiring authority from the chief priests and then imprisoning many of Jesus' followers. And I agreed with the leaders when they condemned and executed them. ❖ *Paul was probably not a member of the Sanhedrin, being too young at the time. His "vote" (in the literal text) may have* been unofficial or a figure of speech. In relating this, Paul is implying an accusation against the Jewish leaders (and himself) that they repeatedly broke Roman law by executing these people. Rome only allowed the Sanhedrin to do this in cases where people violated the Temple.* ➤ 11 I went to all the synagogues, threatening and physically punishing his followers, trying to force them to repudiate and curse Jesus. I was so furious that I even went to foreign cities to persecute them.

12 "I was on my way to Damascus with the assignment and authority from the chief priests to arrest Jesus' followers there. 13 While I was on the road, your Majesty, about midday I saw a brilliant light from Heaven *[Acts 9:1-19; 22:6-16]* ❖ *or: the sky* ➤ blazing all around me and my companions, brighter than the sun. 14 We all fell to the ground and I heard a voice speaking to me in Aramaic, 'Saul, Saul, why are you persecuting me? You are just hurting yourself by fighting against me.' ❖ *See the note at 9:4.* ➤ 15 I asked, 'Sir, who are you?' The Lord A answered, 'I am Jesus, the one you are persecuting. 16 Stand up and get ready to go. I've appeared here to commission you to serve me and tell others about having seen me, and about other things that I will show you later. 17 I'm sending you to testify about these things both to your own people—the Jews—and to Gentiles, and I will protect you from those who will oppose you. 18 You are to open their eyes to understand the truth, *[Isaiah 42:7]* and help them turn from living in the darkness of sin under Satan's domination, to living in obedience to the spiritual light of the message that shows how to be saved and how to become members of God's Kingdom. *[Isaiah 42:16]* Then, through faith in me, I will forgive their sins and give them an eternal reward in Heaven, along with all the others who have become my holy people.'

19 "So then, King Agrippa, I did not disobey the orders Jesus gave me in that vision from Heaven. 20 I started preaching that people needed to repent of their sins and demonstrate it by obeying God's

---

A 26:15 A few manuscripts have "the voice" or "the person" instead of "Lord."

message that he gave through Jesus. I first started preaching in Damascus, and then I went and did the same in Jerusalem. News of my preaching spread to all of Judea, and then I also preached the same message to the Gentiles. *[Romans 15:15-16; Galatians 2:8]* 21 And it is mainly because I preach this message to Gentiles that some Jews seized me while I was in the Temple and tried to kill me. *[Acts 22:21-22]* 22 But God has, even to this day, protected me so that I'm able to stand here and give my testimony about the Messiah to everyone—regardless of rank. In all this, I am only claiming that what Moses and the prophets predicted would happen, has indeed happened. 23 That the Messiah would come and suffer and die and be the first to be permanently raised from death to never die again, and that he would reveal the way of salvation to his own people, as well as to Gentiles." ❖ *These things are all prophesied in the Hebrew Scriptures. His suffering and death were predicted in Psalm 22 and Isaiah 53:3-11, among other places, but the Jews of that day did not interpret these passages as referring to the Messiah—though some older Jewish commentators had. Their expectations made it difficult to accept that their Messiah would suffer and die. There are also many prophecies about God including the Gentiles among his people, [Genesis 12:3; 17:4-16; 18:17-18; 22:18; 26:4; Psalm 22:27-28; 67:2-4; 72:11, 17; 86:9; Isaiah 2:2-4; 42:1-7; 49:6; 60:3; Jeremiah 4:2; 16:19-21; Daniel 7:13-14; Amos 9:12; Micah 4:2; Zechariah 2:10-11; 8:22-23] but the political climate and attitudes of that time made it difficult for most Jews to accept that idea too.* ➤

24 At this point, Festus interrupted and shouted, "Paul, you are out of your mind! Too much learning has totally confused you!" ❖ *The idea of people being resurrected from death was totally foreign to most Gentiles and was viewed as nonsense.* ➤

25 Paul replied, "There's nothing wrong with my mind, your Excellency! The things I've been saying are actually quite reasonable and true. 26 The king is familiar with these issues and events, so I'm speaking freely to him as one who understands what I'm talking about. I'm sure that he has heard about all these things ❖ *i.e., Jesus' ministry, miracles, death, and resurrection* ➤ because nothing was done in secret or in some out of the way place where no one would hear about them.

27 King Agrippa, do you believe the writings of the prophets? I know that you do!" 28 Agrippa replied, "Do you think you can persuade me to become a follower of Jesus as the Messiah in such a short time?" ❖ *The phrase translated, "in such a short time" is ambiguous and could alternatively be translated, "with so little effort," or "with so few words." Commentators are not agreed on whether Agrippa's reply was serious, sarcastic, or intended as a ploy to avoid giving an answer.* ➤ 29 Paul said, "Whether it takes only a short time or a long time, I pray that every one of you listening to me would become a follower of Jesus like I am, except, of course, I have no desire for you to become prisoners."

30 Then the king, the governor, Bernice, and all the others with them got up and left the hall. 31 As they were walking, they said to each other, "Whatever he has done, it isn't anything that deserves imprisonment, let alone the death penalty." 32 Agrippa agreed with Festus, *[Acts 25:25-26]* "If he hadn't appealed his case to the emperor, he could have been set free."

27

Paul Is Sent to Rome for Trial

1 When all the arrangements were made for our voyage, Paul and some other prisoners were put in the custody of a centurion named Julius who belonged to one of the Imperial cohorts. ❖ *See the note at Acts 10:1 on cohorts. There was more than one called the "Augustan" cohort (in the literal text), which means "His Imperial Majesty's cohort." The "we" indicates that Luke was accompanying Paul on this voyage, along with Aristarchus mentioned in verse 2 and possibly other companions too. The last time Luke referred to himself was in Acts 21:18, when they had just arrived in Jerusalem—not long before Paul's arrest. It's likely that Luke and some of Paul's friends visited him frequently during his two-year imprisonment at Caesarea.* ➤ 2 In Caesarea, we boarded a ship from the city of Adramyttium in Mysia Province (opposite the island of Lesbos) which was northbound for ports along the coast of Asia Province. We were accompanied by Aristarchus—a believer from Thessalonica in Macedonia Province. *[Acts 19:29; 20:4; Colossians 4:10; Philemon 24]* ❖ *Aristarchus is not mentioned again by Luke, but if Paul's letters to the Colossians and Philemon were written*

while he was a prisoner in Rome—as many commentators believe—then it's likely that he was with Paul and Luke on the entire trip to Rome, for he is mentioned in them as being with Paul. ➤

3 We sailed about 70 miles north along the coast, and the next day landed at the city of Sidon. Julius kindly allowed Paul to go into the city to visit friends who would provide him with any things he might need for the long voyage. ❖ *Paul was probably still under guard, but this was a remarkable kindness to show toward a prisoner.* ➤ 4 From Sidon, we sailed north and around the northern side of Cyprus island to be protected from the prevailing westerly winds ❖ *typical of the summer months* ➤ that were against us. 5 Then we sailed west—well-off the coast of Cilicia and Pamphylia Provinces—until we landed at the city of Myra in Lycia Province. ❖ *With the help of land winds and a westerly current, the trip from Sidon to Myra probably took 10-15 days.* ➤ A 6 There, the centurion found a ship from Alexandria Egypt bound for Italy, and he arranged passage for all of us. ❖ *This was a grain ship (see Acts 27:38), as Egypt was the main source of grain for Rome. Such ships were about 180 feet long, 45 feet wide, over 40 feet deep (at their deepest) and could carry several hundred passengers in addition to the cargo. Ships took this long route because the prevailing winds made it very difficult to sail directly from Egypt to Rome. The trip from Alexandria to Rome could take 50-60 days, while the return trip would take only 9-12 days.* ➤ 7 Because of headwinds, we sailed slowly for many days and, with difficulty, arrived off of the city Cnidus in Asia Province, ❖ *probably another 10-15 days after leaving Myra* ➤ but we were unable to enter the port. Since the wind wouldn't allow us to sail further west, we headed south, passing Cape Salmone off the eastern side of Crete island, to gain the sheltered south side of the island. ❖ *There were very few ports on the north coast of Crete because strong northerly winds from the Aegean Sea threatened to wreck ships along the north coast. The southern coast had more harbors and gentler winds.* ➤ 8 With difficulty, we continued to sail westward about halfway along the length of Crete's southern coast to a small harbor called Fair Haven—about

five miles from the city of Lasea—where we put in to wait for more favorable winds. ❖ *Shortly beyond Fair Haven, the coast turns sharply north and there is no further protection from the northwesterly winds.* ➤

9 Much time had been lost with the unfavorable winds. The Jewish fast on the Day of Atonement ❖ *Yom Kippur on Tishri 10—which in AD 59 was on October 5th by our calendar* ➤ had passed, and it was now the dangerous time of year to sail in the Mediterranean Sea. ❖ *The "dangerous" season was from about September 14th until about November 11th. After that, no one risked sailing on the open sea again until early March.* ➤ So Paul began to urge those in charge of the ship and voyage, 10 "Men, it's my opinion that if we leave Fair Haven and continue our voyage this year, it's almost certain the ship will be damaged—with loss of cargo and lives." 11 But the centurion—who as a Roman official was in ultimate command of the voyage—was more persuaded by the ship's pilot and captain-owner than by Paul. 12 Since they considered the harbor at Fair Haven unsuitable to winter in, the majority decided to sail on and hoped to reach a more suitable harbor at the city of Phoenix—about 40 miles further along the coast of Crete. That harbor was more sheltered and had entrances facing both southwest and northwest.

Two Weeks in a Storm

13 When a light southerly wind came, they thought they had what they needed to reach Phoenix. ❖ *Had the wind stayed in this direction, they would have made their intended destination in several hours. But the wind in this region often changes suddenly from south to north.* ➤ So they weighed anchor and sailed west, hugging the coast. 14 But shortly after they set out, a hurricane-like storm called a "Euraquilo" ❖ *which means "northeast wind"* ➤ swept down from the center of the island. 15 It was impossible for the ship to sail into the wind toward Crete, and there was nothing we could do but let the ship be driven along by the storm. 16 As we passed

---

A 27:5 If you are looking at a map and are trying to make sense of the directions given, wind directions indicate the direction the wind blows "from." So a west or westerly wind blows out of the west toward the east. But the direction of a water current flows toward the direction specified. So a westerly current flows toward the west, the opposite direction of a westerly wind.

on the relatively sheltered side of the small island of Clauda, **A** ❖ *about 23 miles south of the coast of Crete* ➤ it was still so rough that we were barely able to secure the ship's dinghy—which is normally towed—on board the ship. 17 After they had pulled the dinghy aboard, the crew passed ropes under the hull of the ship and tied them tight to help hold the ship together. They were afraid that the storm would drive them south all the way to the bars of quicksand off the north coast of Africa at the bay of Syrtis. So to slow themselves down, they lowered the "instrument." ❖ *No one knows for sure what this is. Some commentators think it was the sail and others that it was a sea anchor, which is a sail mounted on a frame which is dragged behind the ship in the water to slow it down. This latter seems more likely as the sails would be the first thing they lowered in such a storm.* ➤ 18 On the second day, as we continued to be violently tossed about by the storm, the crew began to lighten the ship by throwing some cargo overboard. ❖ *A lighter ship floats higher, meaning fewer waves would splash on board and they would be less likely to run aground in shallow water.* ➤ 19 On the third day, the crew threw part of the ship's tackle overboard. ❖ *They didn't throw everything overboard. Verse 29 mentions four anchors and verse 40 mentions a sail. They probably got rid of the main spar—which was as long as the ship and very heavy. They were clearly fighting for their lives.* ➤ 20 When the storm had raged for many days ❖ *but less than 14, see verse 27* ➤ with no glimpse of the sun or stars, we had no idea where we were, and we finally gave up all hope of surviving.

21 After they had gone a long time without eating, ❖ *due to sea sickness, difficulty in preparing anything, and most of it was probably spoiled by sea water* ➤ Paul stood up and addressed everyone, "Men you should have listened to my advice and not left Crete. We could have avoided this damage and loss. 22 But I'm urging you now to keep up your courage, for I know that none of us will die, even though the ship will be destroyed. 23 Last night, the God I serve and belong to sent an angel who appeared right next to me. ❖ *Most of the men on the ship were pagans who believed in many gods.* ➤ 24 He said, 'Paul, don't be afraid! God has determined that you will live to stand trial before the emperor, and in response to your prayers, he has generously decided to spare the lives of all who are on this ship.' 25 So be brave and don't despair, men, for I trust my God and believe it will happen just as he said. 26 But it will be necessary for us to run aground on an island."

27 About midnight on the 14th night of the storm, we were still being driven across the Adriatic Sea when the sailors detected signs that we were near land. ❖ *The section of the Mediterranean Sea between the islands of Crete and Malta was considered part of the Adriatic sea in ancient times. Signs of land were probably the sound of breakers on a beach, and perhaps drifting branches.* ➤ 28 They took soundings of the depth with a weight attached to a rope, and the depth was 20 fathoms. ❖ *120 feet* ➤ And sailing a little further, the depth was 15 fathoms. ❖ *90 feet. Today a fathom is exactly 6 feet. Then, it may have been less precisely measured as the distance between the middle finger tips of a man with outstretched hands.* ➤ 29 Fearing that the ship might soon be dashed to pieces on rocks in the shallows, the crew threw out four anchors from the stern and prayed to their gods for daybreak so they could see their situation. 30 Then, the sailors were lowering the dingy into the water and claimed that they were going to anchor the bow, but they were really planning to abandon the ship. ❖ *The dinghy had a better chance of reaching shore, or at least getting closer to shore without running aground, but would only offer this opportunity to a few people and would leave the ship without a skilled crew.* ➤ 31 But Paul told the centurion and the soldiers, "If the sailors don't remain on board, none of you will survive." 32 So the soldiers cut the ropes that held the dingy and let it drop away.

33 Just before dawn, Paul urged everyone to eat something for strength. He said, "You've gone 14 days without eating. 34 But I'm exhorting you to eat something now, to help you survive. You will survive without harm. None of you will so much as lose a hair from your head." 35 Then, he took some bread and thanked God for it in front of everyone. After that, he broke off a piece,

---

A 27:16 A few manuscripts have "Cauda" instead of "Clauda."

passed it on, and began to eat. ❖ *Assuming that they had no way of cooking bread during a violent storm, and no one had wanted to eat for 14 days—so it's unlikely that anyone tried to do so—the bread was probably rather hard and dry, like hard tack. The cold October weather would have kept it from spoiling.* ➤ 36 Everyone began to feel more hopeful, and so had something to eat. 37 There were 276 **A** of us on board. 38 When they had eaten as much as they wanted, they lightened the ship further by throwing the rest of the cargo of wheat in the sea.

39 When it became light, they couldn't tell where they were because the land they could see was unfamiliar. But they did see a bay with a beach where they decided they would try to run the ship aground. 40 The crew cut loose the anchors and lowered the steering oars on either side of the rear of the ship. Then they raised a small sail in the bow and steered for the beach. 41 But at a place where the entrance to the bay met another channel leading out to the sea, the bow of the ship ran aground and wouldn't budge, while the stern of the ship was being broken up by the pounding of the waves.

42 The soldiers planned to kill all the prisoners so none of them could swim away and escape. ❖ *They would have been executed if their prisoners escaped, and killing them eliminated that risk.* ➤ 43 But the centurion wanted Paul to live, so he prevented them from carrying out their plan by ordering those who could swim to jump overboard and make their way to shore. 44 He ordered the others to follow, holding onto planks or anything from the ship that would float, and this is how everyone safely reached land.

28

Three Months on Malta

1 After everyone was safely on shore, we found out from local people that we were on the island of Malta, 560 miles from Fair Haven. 2 The people of the island—most of whom didn't speak Greek ❖ *and therefore would have been considered barbarians by Greeks and Romans* ➤—demonstrated unusually generous hospitality to us. They built a big fire

because of the rain and cold and invited all of us to warm ourselves around it. 3 Paul had gathered an armload of branches and put them on the fire when a poisonous snake came out of them and sank its fangs in his hand. 4 When the local people saw the snake hanging from his hand, they began saying to each other, "He must be a murderer! Even though he survived drowning in the storm, Diké ❖ *dee-kay* ➤—the goddess of Justice— won't allow him to live." 5 But Paul shook it off into the fire and failed to develop any signs of being poisoned. *[Mark 16:18; Luke 10:19]* 6 The locals were watching him, waiting for his hand to swell or to see him drop dead. But when nothing unusual happened to him after a long while, they revised their conclusion and said he was a god.

7 After that, the governor of the island— Publius, whose estate was nearby— welcomed us as guests in his home for three days. 8 While we were there, we found out that his father was bedridden with a fever and dysentery. So Paul went in to see him, prayed, then laid hands on him and healed him. *[Matthew 10:1, 8; Mark 16:17-18; Luke 9:1-2; 10:9; James 5:14-15]* 9 After that, during our stay every sick person on the island came to Paul, and all who came were healed. 10 As a result of Paul's healing ministry, they honored us in many ways, and when we were ready to resume our journey, they generously gave us everything we needed.

11 After a three-month stay, when the weather allowed, we resumed our voyage on another ship from Alexandria that had spent the winter on the island. It was named after the ship's patron gods that were carved on its figurehead, "the Twins." ❖ *These twin gods, whose names were Castor and Pollux, were sons of Zeus and were considered special protectors of ships. Their constellation is Gemini.* ➤ 12 We arrived in the port of Syracuse—the main city of the island of Sicily which is located on its east coast—and stayed there three days. 13 From Syracuse, we sailed north and arrived at the city of Rhegium on the toe of Italy. The next day, a southerly wind came up, and on the second day out of Rhegium, we reached the harbor

---

A 27:37 A very few manuscripts have "about 76" instead of "276."

of Puteoli. ❖ *Puteoli is in the bay of Naples—125 miles from Rome—and at that time, Rome's only port.* ➤ 14 In Puteoli, we met some followers of Jesus who invited us to stay with them for seven days. ❖ *The centurion probably had business in Puteoli during that time.* ➤ After that, we headed northwest, overland to Rome. 15 When the believers in Rome heard we were coming, ❖ *obviously someone in Puteoli had gone ahead of them* ➤ some of them traveled southeast on the Appian Way as far as the 33 miles to the Three Taverns, and some of them the 43 miles to the Market of Appius, in order to meet us. When Paul saw them, he was encouraged by their obvious love and concern and thanked God for them. ❖ *Paul had sent his letter to the believers in Rome about three years earlier, so they knew as much about him as was in that letter, and more from people in Rome who knew him.* ➤

Paul Under House Arrest in Rome

16 When we arrived in Rome, {the centurion handed the prisoners over to the tribune there, but} **A** Paul was allowed to rent a house and live there by himself, chained to a soldier who guarded him. 17 After settling in for three days, Paul invited the leaders of the Jewish synagogues in Rome to visit him, and when they arrived, he addressed them, "My Jewish brothers, I was arrested in Jerusalem and handed over to the Roman authorities in Caesarea, even though I've done nothing against our people or the customs of our ancestors. ❖ *At this time, there were at least ten major synagogues in Rome, and it is estimated that there were more than 40,000 Jews in the city. Notice that Paul minimizes his criticism of the Jewish authorities.* ➤ 18 When the Roman authorities finished examining me, they wanted to release me, because they determined I was not guilty of any crime deserving the death sentence. 19 But when some of the Jewish leaders objected to my release, I was forced to appeal to the emperor to hear my case in order to establish my innocence. I assure you, though, that I have no charge to bring

against our own people. ❖ *Roman law was strict against those who accused people of wrong and then could not prove their case. So Paul doesn't want to imply that he came to Rome to seek revenge against the Jewish leaders who accused him.* ➤ 20 I invited you to come so I could explain why I'm here as a prisoner. I'm chained to this soldier because of my belief in the Messiah, the 'Hope of Israel.' "

21 They replied, "We haven't received any letters about you from our Jewish brothers in Judea, nor have any of those who have come from there said anything bad about you. 22 But we are interested in hearing what your views are about this sect of people who say that Jesus is the Messiah. We do know that people are speaking against them everywhere."

23 They set a date when Paul would speak to them on this subject, and on that day, a large number of Jews came to his house. Paul spent from morning until evening explaining his message to them about God's Kingdom under Jesus, and trying to persuade them that Jesus was the Messiah by quoting and arguing from the Teachings of Moses and the writings of the Prophets. ❖ *The "Law of Moses and the Prophets" (in the literal text) typically refer to all the Hebrew Scriptures taken together, even though the Jews divided them into three parts: the Torah, the writings, and the prophets.* ➤ 24 Some of them were convinced by what he said, but others refused to believe his message. 25 The Jews were disagreeing among themselves and just before they left, Paul made this final statement to them, "The Holy Spirit really spoke the truth through the prophet to your **B** ancestors when he told Isaiah, 26 'Go to my people and say, "Even though you see the truth, you don't perceive it. Even though you hear the truth, you don't understand it. 27 For my people's minds have become closed to my truth; they are unwilling to listen to it and even refuse the evidence they can see. Otherwise **C** they would have seen the evidence, listened to the truth and understood it, and then they would have

---

A 28:16 Most manuscripts do not have the section in { }.
B 28:25 A few manuscripts have "our" instead of "your."
C 28:27 The word μήτοτε (mēpote) is ambiguous in this context. It could mean "otherwise," with the interpretation

given, but some commentators take it to mean "lest," implying that God didn't allow his people to repent and be forgiven.

turned to me in repentance and I would
have spiritually healed and saved them." '
[Isaiah 6:9-10; Matthew 13:14-15]

28 "Therefore, I want you to realize that
since most Jews have rejected this message
about how to be saved, God is offering it to
the Gentiles, and many of them will accept
it." 29 {When he finished saying this, the
Jews left, still disputing among themselves
about Paul's message.} A

30 Then, for two full years, Paul
remained under guard in the house he
rented. He welcomed everyone who came
to see him, 31 and without any hindrance,
he boldly preached the message about
God's Kingdom and taught people about
Lord Jesus—the Messiah. ❖ *During this period
of his first imprisonment (AD 60–62), he wrote his "letters
from prison" to the believers in Ephesus, Colosse, and
Philippi and also his letter to Philemon. Many commentators
believe that he was eventually exonerated and released
from prison, traveled to Spain and other places, Romans
15:23-29] and was then arrested and imprisoned a second
time in Rome. These commentators think he wrote his first
letter to Timothy and his letter to Titus during his second time
in prison, and wrote his second letter to Timothy just before
his execution. Tradition says that Emperor Nero had him
beheaded sometime in the period AD 66–68.* ➤

A 28:29 Most manuscripts do not have this verse.

Paul's Letter to Jesus' Followers in Rome

The Apostle Paul wrote this letter to the believers in Rome, probably while he was in Corinth [Romans 15:26; 16:1-2] sometime during the years AD 55–58 near the end of his third missionary journey. [Acts 18:23—21:14] The assemblies in Rome were made up of both Jewish and Gentile believers.

Paul had never visited Rome but had heard about the believers there and knew some of them whom he had met elsewhere in his travels. He believed that he had finished his missionary work in Greece and Asia Minor and wanted to go where no one had yet heard the Good News. So he was planning to go to Spain and wanted to make Rome his new base, like Antioch had been previously. He hoped the believers in Rome would help support him in this new mission venture. Thus he wanted to clearly lay out for them the message that he preached so they would be able to endorse and support his ministry. Since he was writing to people to whom he had never preached before, Paul's basic salvation message is spelled out very clearly, making this one of the most important books in the New Testament for understanding the doctrine of salvation.

Key passages in this letter are: Romans 1:16-17 and 3:21

Outline

Paul's purpose in writing to them. [1:1-17]
All people are born condemned to Hell. [1:18—3:20]
God's provision of a way to be saved. [3:21-31]
Abraham's story shows that people are saved by trusting in God. [chapter 4]
How righteousness benefits us. [5:1-11]
Sin and death came because of Adam's sin, but the Messiah's death conquers sin and death. [5:12-21]
Accepting the undeserved favor that God freely offers us does not lead people to sin. [chapter 6]
The Torah's teachings can no longer condemn believers because we have died with the Messiah. [7:1-13]
The power of sin within us fights against our good desires. [7:14-25]
God's true children follow the Holy Spirit. [chapter 8]
God's favor toward Gentiles does not change his promises to Israel. [chapters 9—11]
How believers are to live. [chapters 12—15]
Closing personal greetings. [chapter 16]

1

Opening Greetings

¹ I, Paul, am a willing slave of Messiah Jesus. ❖ *Paul is not debasing himself by calling himself a slave. He is declaring his total loyalty and voluntary service to Jesus, but at the same time he is claiming a high position. In Roman culture, the slave of a powerful person who was trusted to represent his master had high status and considerable power himself. He willingly offers his life as a slave to serve the Messiah to whom he is indebted for being saved. It's a devotion motivated by love and gratitude, and is an attitude that all committed believers should have.* ➤ God called me to be an apostle and commissioned me to proclaim his message about how to be saved. ² Long ago through the writings of his prophets, God promised that he would send the Messiah to save his people. ³ This Messiah was to be a descendant of King David, but now we know that he is also God's eternal Son who came into this world by being born as a human being. ⁴ God confirmed that Jesus the Messiah—in his eternal spiritual nature—is in fact God's Son and our Lord, when he raised him back to life from death. ❖ *It's debated what the phrase "according to the spirit of holiness" (in the literal text), rendered here as "in his eternal spiritual nature," means. A minority view says it means "by the Holy Spirit," but Paul doesn't use this phrase anywhere else to refer to the Holy Spirit. Other commentators interpret it as above.* ➤ ⁵ And through what the Messiah did for me, ❖ *i.e., by his death and also his appearing to Paul [Acts 9:1-20]* ➤ God showed me great favor that I could never deserve and made me an apostle. He told me to preach his message to people from every people group about what he has done to

save them through Jesus the Messiah. My goal is that they will respond with belief and obedience and give God the honor and praise he deserves.

6 You believers in Rome are also among those whom God called to belong to Jesus the Messiah—7 and that's why I'm writing to you. For God loves you and called you to be his own people who are fully dedicated to him. I pray that God—who is our Father—and our Lord Jesus the Messiah will look upon you with great favor far beyond anything you could deserve and bless you with peace and well-being. ❖ *The idea behind Paul's greeting of "peace" is the Hebrew word "shalom" which means "peace, calmness, success, comfort, contentment, safety, health, wholeness, prosperity, integrity, well-being, and good relationships with God and people."* ➤

Paul Tells of His Desire to Come to Rome

8 I want to tell you at the outset that through my spiritual union with Jesus the Messiah, I thank God for all of you believers in Rome because people all over the empire are hearing about the quality of your faith and obedience. 9 God—whom I serve in my spirit by proclaiming the Good News about his Son—knows I'm telling the truth when I say that I speak to him about you nearly every time I pray. ❖ *The meaning of the phrase "in my spirit" is debated. The preposition ἐν (en) in this prepositional phrase can legitimately be translated as "in," "with," or "by means of." Also in question is the meaning of "spirit." Is he talking about the human spirit, as in "body, soul, and spirit," [1 Thessalonians 5:23] or does it mean "with all my heart," as it's rendered in some translations?* ➤ 10 For I am always asking if he might, at long last, allow me to come and visit you 11 as I've longed to do. I want to impart some spiritual blessing to you as a gift to help strengthen your faith. 12 By that, I mean that we could encourage each other—I by your faith and you by mine. 13 My brothers and sisters in the Lord, I want you to know that I've actually planned to come visit you many times but something always comes up to prevent me. My desire is to preach the message of the Good News in Rome and see you grow in your faith, and even see some new people come to faith there just as I've done in many other places. 14 I want to do this because

God has given me the responsibility to preach the Good News to as many people as I can, everywhere I can, especially if they are Gentiles. This includes those who live in civilized lands and those who live beyond, the educated and wise, and even the uneducated and foolish. 15 I've never yet been to Rome so that's why I want come and preach to you too.

The Core of Paul's Message

16 I am never ashamed to proclaim the Good News about what Jesus has done for us since this message always fulfills my expectations. It's the way God has chosen to release his power in people's hearts and minds to save them. It saves everyone who trusts in the Messiah as a result of hearing the message. All who receive salvation are saved the exact same way, whether they are Jews—to whom the Good News was first proclaimed because they have a special priority with God—or whether they are Gentiles. 17 It's the Good News that tells us how God makes people righteous in his sight. From start to finish, it's by trusting in the Messiah. This is what the prophet meant when he wrote, **"Those who are righteous in God's sight because of their faith in his promises will continue to live by faith."** [Habakkuk 2:4; Galatians 3:11; Hebrews 10:38] ❖ *They will continue to trust in everything God has said and promised in the Scriptures.* ➤

God Hates Sin
and Punishes Those Who Reject Him

18 From his vantage point in Heaven, God expresses his hatred of the sin and evil done by those who refuse to acknowledge the truth about who he is and what he requires. He does this by causing them to suffer the consequences of their actions. But such people always attempt to suppress the truth so they can continue in their rebellion and sin—19 even though deep down they know there is a God and that what they do is evil. For he has made it clear enough to them that they won't be able to deny it when they stand before him to be judged. 20 Ever since he created the universe, people have been able to see the Earth, the night sky, and

everything he made. From the things they observe, they can understand things about God whom they can't see—such as the fact that there really is a God who made everything and that he has power to do anything. So they have no excuse to say they don't know these things about him. 21 Even though they know he exists and created them, they refuse to honor him or thank him for the good things he provides them through his creation. They reject the truth about him and make up their own foolish ideas of what they want him to be like. So their thoughts concerning him become confused and full of error. 22 They claim to be wise, but are in fact self-deceived fools. 23 The false gods they worship are images of mortal things like people, birds, animals, or reptiles. ❖ *More "sophisticated" today, they submit and dedicate themselves to (i.e., they worship) false ideas about people (such as: "everyone is god," or "people can make their own truth"), or animals (which some regard as having value equal to that of people), or they worship false conceptions of a god they have made up to suit themselves.* ➤ They stoop to worship these worthless things instead of the true God who is holy, immortal, and infinitely superior in beauty, worth, and character to anything he has created. 24 Therefore, God punishes them by leaving them alone and by allowing them to be totally dominated by their urges and passions. As a result, they become enslaved to all sorts of forbidden activities that are shameful, disgusting, degrading, and self-destructive. 25 They have deliberately chosen to believe lies instead of what they know is true about him. So they are reduced to worshipping and serving mere things he has made that are even inferior to themselves—who were made in God's image—instead of worshipping and serving their Creator who deserves our praise and honor forever. 26-27 Some women among them have exchanged natural sexual relations with men for unnatural relations with other women. Some men among them have abandoned natural sexual relations with women, and instead burn with desire to have sex with other men—and so engage in indecent activities with them. That's why God leaves them to be consumed by their shameful yearnings. They bring upon themselves the penalty of permanently twisted unnatural desires that they can't escape unless they turn to God in repentance. ❖ *The basis for Paul's assertion that homosexual relations are unnatural comes from the Torah's teachings. See all of Leviticus chapter 18—especially verse 22. Some have claimed that Paul is here talking about promiscuous homosexual relationships only. Yet given the wording in Leviticus, such a conclusion is clearly wrong.* ➤ 28 Since those who reject the truth about God haven't seen fit to acknowledge or obey him, he allows their thought processes to become fully twisted. As a result, they continue to do what is indecent ❖ *storing up for themselves greater punishment in Hell [Romans 2:5]* ➤ because they think what they are doing is acceptable or even good. 29 Consequently, their lives become filled with all sorts of sin and evil such as envy, greed, murder, animosity, quarreling, fighting, lies and deceit, vicious gossip, 30 slander, hatred of God and of those who follow him, insolence, arrogance, boastfulness, ever-new depths of evil, and rebellion against parents and other authority. 31 They refuse to believe that the things they do are evil, they can't be trusted, and they show no love or compassion to others. ❖ *Paul doesn't mean that every person who rejects God will exhibit all of these evil qualities, but that some of these qualities—and often several of them—will be obviously evident in their lives because indulging in one kind of sin always leads to doing other kinds.* ➤ 32 Deep down they are aware that God forbids these things and will punish those who live that way with eternal death in Hell, but they push these thoughts out of their minds and continue to do them. Worse than this, they approve of others who do the same things they do and encourage them to do so.

2

God Will Judge All People

1 If some of you Jewish believers think it's acceptable for you to judge Gentiles, you are wrong! When you judge them, you also condemn yourselves because you too are guilty of sin and often of the same sins—though their outward manifestation may be different. 2 We all know that when God

judges people and declares them guilty, he is being fair and accurate. 3 But who do you think you are that you have the right to judge others? Do you really think that God will condemn them for their sins and let you off the hook for doing essentially the same things? 4 Take care not to despise the great kindness, patience, and tolerance he shows you and all people! Don't you realize that the only reason he hasn't punished you yet is because he is giving you plenty of opportunity to repent and change your ways?

5 But when you are stubborn and refuse to change, you just accumulate more punishment for yourselves. On Judgment Day, God will judge everyone fairly and his wrath toward sin will be released in proportion to your sin. 6 The Scriptures say that God will give the appropriate reward or punishment to everyone for what they've done in this life. *[Psalm 62:12; Proverbs 24:12]* ❖ *Since the sins of believers have already been punished in the Messiah's death and are forgiven, they will not receive punishment. But they will be rewarded for good that they've done, and rewards will be withheld for evil they have done.* ➤ 7 He will give eternal life to believers who consistently try to do good in this life, who seek to be conformed to God's glorious holy and loving character, and seek to be honored by him for their obedience while looking forward to the immortality he has promised them. 8 But his wrath and punishment will be released upon unbelievers who have focused on pleasing themselves instead of God in this life—for they have consciously rejected the truth. 9 God will bring great distress and suffering on all those who do evil, whether they are Jews—whom he will judge first since they are his special people—or Gentiles. ❖ *Evil here—and good in the next verse—is defined by God's standards, not by human ideas. Many who—humanly speaking—live "good" lives but have ignored God are living in evil rebellion against his standards. God's definitions of good and evil are clearly spelled out in the Scriptures.* ➤ 10 But he will give great honor, glory, and shalom to believers whose lives he judges as "good," whether they are Jews—whom he will judge first— or Gentiles. ❖ *Paul emphasizes that God will judge Jews because many them at that time thought they were automatically saved and exempt from judgment.* ➤ 11 For

God is totally impartial and his judgment is entirely fair.

12 He will punish Gentiles for doing evil—even though they are ignorant of his Torah's teachings—and he will punish Jews who sin against the Torah which they know well. 13 For righteousness is not a matter of knowing or possessing the Torah ❖ *as some thought* ➤ but is a matter of obeying its teachings. God will judge those who do right as being righteous in his sight. ❖ *No one will be judged righteous because they have done right in their own ability—because nobody is able to do so. Their doing right will be a result of his making them righteous by spiritually joining them to Jesus, and a result of their allowing him to live his righteous life through them, as Paul explains in Romans 3:10-20.* ➤

God Will Judge Gentiles

14 Some Gentiles instinctively do what the Torah commands because they know these things are good—even if they've never heard about the Torah. 15 This shows that deep down they know, for the most part, what is good and what is evil, and their consciences let them know which is which. God has put this knowledge within every person. 16 And when Judgment Day comes, on God's behalf, Jesus the Messiah will even judge everyone's innermost thoughts, comparing what they have done to what they know. This is part of the message I preach.

God Will Also Judge Jews

17 Those of you with Jewish backgrounds should pay attention to this. Some of you think that knowing the teachings in God's Torah automatically makes you his child. So you boast that you are righteous in his sight. 18 From the Torah, you have been taught his will and know how he wants his people to live. You know right from wrong. 19 Some of you are confident that you are able to guide the spiritually blind and reveal God's truth to the ignorant. 20 You consider yourselves superior to Gentiles—whom you look down upon as morally foolish—and you think that you are competent to teach those who know nothing about God's way because you know his Torah. You think that in it, you have all truth and everything anyone needs to know.

21 You are bold to teach these things to others, but some of you don't follow your own instructions! You tell others not to steal, but you yourselves steal! 22 You tell others not to commit adultery—all the while being guilty of this same sin yourselves! You detest those who worship false gods, but you yourselves vandalize and steal from pagan temples! 23 You boast about knowing the Torah, but you diminish our God in the sight of pagans by breaking it yourselves! 24 Some of you fulfill the Scripture that says, **"Gentiles speak evil of Yahweh because you—who are his own people—don't follow your own teachings that he gave you."** [Isaiah 52:5; Ezekiel 36:20-21]

25 You boast that your circumcision is a sign that you are God's child. But this sign is only valid if you also obey the Torah's teachings. If you don't, you are exactly the same in his sight as an uncircumcised pagan. 26 As for uncircumcised Gentiles, if they obey God's teachings then he considers them his children just the same as he does circumcised Jews who obey them. 27 So some Jews have this sign on their bodies and know and read God's Torah, but don't obey it. And some Gentiles obey God's Torah even though they lack circumcision. God sees all this, and because of the obedience of those Gentiles, he will have to judge that they deserve better than the Jews who don't obey—so the latter will be condemned.

28 For as far as God is concerned, a person isn't truly Jewish just because his parents are Jewish. And a man isn't God's child just because he is circumcised. These are only superficial things that can be negated by disobeying his teachings. 29 People are truly Jewish and God's children if they love him and obey him. The true sign that a person is God's child is found in the heart—and that sign is the presence of the Holy Spirit there. True circumcision is marked invisibly on a person's spirit, not merely the outward mark cut on a man's body as required by the Torah. Those who have this true sign in their hearts might not be praised by people, but they will be praised by God.

3

Everyone Deserves Damnation

1 Since being Jewish doesn't guarantee that we are righteous in God's sight, what advantage do we have over Gentiles? And what value does the sign of circumcision have? 2 Actually, Jews have many advantages over Gentiles. The most important of these is that God made them the caretakers of his Word as recorded in the Scriptures—which contain the promises he made in his covenant agreements with them. 3 It's true that some Jews have not believed God or obeyed him. But does that mean God will be unfaithful and break the promises he made in the Scriptures to the Jews as a people group? 4 A curse on such thinking! God will always be true to his promises even if every human being is unfaithful. King David said something that pertains to this in a Psalm addressed to God, which says, **"You will always demonstrate that your words and judgment are true."** [Psalm 51:4]

5 A "devil's advocate" might ask, "If our sinfulness highlights—by contrast—God's holiness and righteousness, then isn't he wrong to be angry and punish us for our sin?" 6 That's absurd! If God were not righteous and didn't hate sin then he wouldn't have the right to judge those who sin. 7 A "devil's advocate" will ask again, "But if my unfaithfulness and falseness enhances—by contrast—people's ability to recognize God's faithfulness and truth— which causes them to honor and praise him even more—then I'm actually helping his image. So why should he punish me?" 8 That kind of thinking is twisted and absurd! If you accept it, you might as well conclude that it's good to do evil because it brings praise to God. Some people actually slander me by saying that's the kind of thing I teach! But God will punish them as they deserve.

9 Going back to the differences between Jews and Gentiles, does God consider Jews better than Gentiles? Not at all. I've already said that both Jews and Gentiles are under the power of sin. 10 This is what the Scriptures say,

"No one is righteous in God's sight—not even one. 11 No one is wise. No one tries to find God. 12 Everyone has turned away from God and they are all useless to him. No one does what is right—not even one. *[Psalm 14:1-3; 53:1-3; Ecclesiastes 7:20]* 13 Their words are foul like the stench of an opened grave, ❖ *OR: like an open grave waits to swallow the dead, their words are murderous in intent or effect* ➤ they are treacherous with flattery. *[Psalm 5:9]* Their words injure others as surely as the bite of poisonous snakes. *[Psalm 140:3]* 14 They habitually inflict curses and say hateful things. *[Psalm 10:7]* 15 They kill with little provocation—16 causing misery and destruction wherever they go. 17 And they never contribute toward making peaceful relationships. *[Isaiah 59:7-8; Proverbs 1:16]* 18 They have no fear, reverence, or regard for God." *[Psalm 36:1]* ❖ *Verses 10-18 are loose partial quotes from the Scriptures noted in the cross references, and summarize what the Scriptures say is characteristic of all people without God's influence in their lives.* ➤

19 We know that everything God's teachings say—including what I just quoted—applies to the Israelites who received the Torah and their descendants, the Jews who still live under its authority. ❖ *Usually "the Law" (in the literal text) refers mainly to the Torah (a.k.a. the Pentateuch—i.e., the first five books of the Bible). But sometimes Paul also uses this term to refer to the entire Hebrew Scriptures. The above quotes are all from the Hebrew Scriptures but not from the Torah itself.* ➤ Thus it's clear that in God's sight, everyone—Jewish and Gentile—deserves to be condemned. No one can claim to be innately righteous before God. *[Psalm 143:2]* 20 Therefore, no one can become righteous in God's sight by legalistically and self-righteously keeping the Torah commands in order to merit righteousness—as many try to do. ❖ *David Stern rightly points out that God intended for his people to keep his Torah commands, that they were not too hard to keep [Deuteronomy 30:11-14], and that they provided for a sacrificial means to be forgiven when they failed to keep them. Therefore, Paul could not be meaning that no one could be declared righteous in God's sight because they could not keep his commands properly. No one can keep them "perfectly" in the sense of not sinning, but they can keep them "properly" in the sense of humble obedience and repentance along with the prescribed sacrifices for sins committed. In fact, the proper keeping of the Torah's commands—including the*

proper attitude of humility and repentance—did make them acceptable to God because he did forgive their sins. And that forgiveness was based on their practical faith in his promises worked out in obedience to the sacrificial laws, and—from God's view—the Messiah's future sacrifice. But a legalistic self-righteous keeping of the commands in order to try to merit righteousness—without humbly recognizing one's sin and need for forgiveness—achieves nothing. ➤ In fact, God never gave the Torah so people could try to merit righteousness by keeping it's commands. He gave it to show people that they are sinners and deserve to be condemned.

The Only Way
to Become Righteous in God's Sight

21 But now—since the Messiah's coming—God has more completely revealed to us a different way for people to become righteous in his sight. This way is not by keeping commands or rules, but by the way he promised in the Scriptures long ago. 22 That way is this: by granting us great favor we can't deserve, God declares people righteous when they trust in the finished work that Jesus the Messiah accomplished on the cross through his self-sacrificial death to take away their sins. It doesn't matter whether you are Jewish or Gentile ❖ *or whether you think you are a good or evil person* ➤—this is now the only way anyone can become righteous in God's sight. ❖ *Traditionally, this is stated: "We are saved by grace through faith in the Messiah." Faith—by itself—would be powerless except for God's promise in which we place our faith. God saves people purely because he wants to for his own purposes—and he promises to save those who fulfill his condition of having faith in his Son, the Messiah. The ability to have true saving faith is also God's gift because sinful people are—in their own power—incapable of producing that kind of faith. [Ephesians 2:8] This genuine faith in the Messiah—which results in God spiritually joining us to the Messiah and putting his own spiritual life in us—also results in our having a desire to obey him, which leads to our obeying his commands. Anyone who doesn't have this desire does not have true faith from God—no matter what they profess. [James 2:14-17]* ➤ 23 Since all people have sinned and have failed to live righteous lives that reflect God's holy and loving character, they are—therefore—condemned by his teachings in the Torah. 24 But God offers everyone righteousness and salvation

as a free gift because Messiah Jesus paid the price to save all people—and that price was to die in their place. ❖ *The penalty for sin is eternal damnation—not just physical death. The price Jesus paid involved more than mere physical death but also rejection by his Father. In some way that we can't fully understand, he suffered on the cross the same or equivalent punishment that a person does who is damned for eternity. The price he paid through his death is sufficient—by whatever theory you choose to explain it—to save all humanity. But all are not automatically saved—only those relative few who have genuine faith. [Isaiah 10:22; Matthew 7:13-14; 21-23; Luke 13:23-28; 1 Timothy 2:6; 4:10]* ➤ 25 God offers the Messiah to humanity as a sacrificial substitute **A** who can take away both our sins and God's righteous anger toward us. *[Genesis 22:8]* ❖ *God's holiness requires that he punish sinners with eternal separation from himself (often called eternal death, or Hell). If he were to forgive without punishment, he would violate his own nature. So his solution was to send the Messiah to suffer the punishment that all people deserve—as their substitute. While Jesus was on the cross, God in some way identified him with all sinners [2 Corinthians 5:21] and punished him for their sins [1 Timothy 2:6; 4:10] by abandoning him [Matthew 27:46; Mark 15:34] and causing him to die.* ➤ And now, for those who trust in Jesus' blood, ❖ *"Blood" is a figure of speech meaning his death. [Leviticus 17:11]* ➤ God joins them spiritually to Jesus, counts his death as theirs so they have already been punished, and declares them righteous in his sight since they are united to Jesus who is righteous. In doing this, he demonstrated that he is righteous and consistent with his holiness. Prior to the Messiah's death on a cross, God patiently refrained from punishing people for their sins. But for those who believed in his promise to send the Messiah to save them, he temporarily set their sins aside to be ultimately dealt with by the Messiah's sacrifice. But now that he has punished all of humanity's sins, it's clear that he really is righteous

and does what his holiness requires. 26 So God demonstrated that he is righteous and just, both by punishing sin and also by declaring people righteous who believe in Jesus and trust in his sacrifice to save them.

27 Therefore, no one can validly boast that they are inherently good or righteous. For God's way of declaring people righteous does not depend on what they can do but only depends on their trust in his promise. 28 For we apostles and others who know the truth hold the position that people can now be declared righteous only through faith in God's promise and never by keeping the Torah's commands. ❖ *To be declared "righteous" is the same as being "justified," "saved," and receiving eternal life. To "trust" means the same as believing and having faith. What is faith in God's promise? God promised to forgive and save all those who believe the following: 1) Jesus is the Messiah and God's Son—therefore, everything he taught was directly from God. 2) Jesus' death on the cross is effective for removing our sins. 3) God spiritually joins those who believe to the Messiah. 4) Such people will receive the gift of the Holy Spirit living in them. 5) And those who persevere in believing and obeying him until they die will live with him forever in Heaven. "Faith" means that one believes this is all true and therefore acts upon that belief in obedience. For part of what Jesus taught was that only people who obey God will go to Heaven—even though obedience doesn't earn our place there. [Matthew 7:21; 12:50]* ➤ 29-30 You Jews had better not think that God will only declare Jews to be righteous. As you know, there is only one God and he created all that exists—so he must be God of the Gentiles too. He only declares people righteous who trust in the Messiah. This is true for both Jews and Gentiles. 31 Some might want to ask: Since people are declared righteous for trusting the Messiah, are the Torah's teachings now worthless and to be ignored? A curse on such thinking! The Torah itself teaches that people are saved by believing, and true

---

A **3:25** Literally ἱλαστήριον (hilastērion)—this word is often translated into English as "propitiation." It means—in this context—a "means by which sins are forgiven." It can also mean a "place where sins are forgiven" [Hebrews 9:5] and is one of the Greek words used in the Septuagint (the Greek translation of the Hebrew Scriptures) to translate the Hebrew word כפרת (kapporet) that refers to the "mercy seat," i.e., the cover to the Ark of the Covenant. [Exodus 25:17-22; 31:7; 35:12;

Leviticus 16:2; 13-15; Numbers 7:89] כפרת (kapporet) means "atonement cover." So Jesus' dying on the cross is God's means and place of atonement—which was foreshadowed by the sprinkling of blood on the mercy seat (atonement cover) of the Ark. Paul deliberately implied that tie by using this word. The mercy seat was a "seat" in the sense of being the central place from which God's mercy was dispensed. This sense of "seat" is also used in the phrase "seat of government."

belief enables people to live in obedience the way that God really wants them to live.

4

Even Abraham Was Declared Righteous Because of His Faith in God's Promise

[1] Now consider Abraham—the revered ancestor of the Jews. What does his story tell us about being righteous in God's sight? [2] If Abraham was declared righteous for what he did, then he would have had something to boast about. But from God's view, he had no basis for pride. [3] The Scriptures tell us, **"Abraham believed God's promise, therefore, God declared that he was righteous."** *[Genesis 15:6; Galatians 3:6; Hebrews 11:8-12; James 2:23]* ❖ *Actually—at that time, Abraham's name was still "Abram."* ➤

[4] Now, when people work, their wages are earned so they are not a gift. So if God declared people righteous because of the good things they did, then they would have earned this status—it would not be a gift. [5] But if people don't try to earn God's favor by what they do and instead trust him—knowing that he considers sinners who believe in his promises to be righteous—then God sees their faith and declares them to be righteous. This is clearly a gift—not something earned. [6] King David said something about such people in the Psalms. He wrote, [7] **"Those people whose disobedience has been forgiven and whose sins have been permanently covered and forgotten are indeed in God's good favor. [8] Because Yahweh no longer regards them as having sinned at all."** *[Psalm 32:1-2]*

Abraham Was Declared Righteous While Still a Gentile

[9] Is this blessing of unearned forgiveness only available to Jews because of their circumcision—which is the sign of God's covenant agreement with them? No! It's also for uncircumcised Gentiles. For as I quoted before, **"Abraham believed God's promise, therefore, God declared that he was righteous."** [10] When did this happen? Was it before or after Abraham was circumcised? It was when he was still an uncircumcised Gentile! *[Genesis 15:6]* [11] Later, God commanded Abraham to be circumcised as a sign to show that he already believed God's promise and that God had already declared him righteous. *[Genesis 17:9-14]* So before Abraham was circumcised, he was a Gentile. And at that time, God declared him righteous because of his faith. Therefore, Abraham is the spiritual father of all Gentiles who believe in God—even if they aren't circumcised. God declares them righteous because of their faith. [12] Of course, Abraham is also the spiritual father of the Jews who do have the sign of circumcision. But only if they trust in God's promises just like Abraham did before he was circumcised.

The Benefits of God's Promises Are Received by Trusting That He Will Fulfill Them

[13] God promised Abraham that he would give the whole world to him and his descendants. *[Genesis 12:3; 13:14-17; 15:4-5; 17:2-8, 16, 19; 22:15-18; Galatians 3:29]* He promised this because Abraham believed him—and so God considered him righteous. Abraham didn't earn this by following the Torah's teachings since God did not give the Torah until hundreds of years later. *[Galatians 3:17]* ❖ *God's promise to Abraham—known as the Abrahamic Covenant—has these four parts: 1) Abraham would have a son and—through him—many descendants who would become a mighty nation. [Genesis 12:2-3] This was fulfilled when Isaac was born—whose descendants became the Israelites who today are the Jews. 2) Abraham's descendants would be so many that they would be uncountable. He would also be the father of many people in many people groups. And his "seed"—which Paul interprets as referring to the Messiah—would be a source of blessing to every people group. This is fulfilled by all believers in the Messiah being his spiritual descendants. 3) Abraham and his descendants—through Isaac—would inherit the land of Israel and ultimately the whole world. Their inheriting the land of Israel was initially fulfilled after their deliverance from slavery in Egypt [See the book of Exodus.] and their conquering of the land of Canaan. [See the book of Joshua.] Ultimately, this will be fulfilled when Jesus returns and the only people in the Renewed Earth will be those who believed as Abraham did. All unbelievers will be in Hell. 4) God blesses those who bless Israel—which is both the nation of Israel and the Jewish descendants of Jacob, a.k.a. Israel—and curses those who curse Israel.*

[Genesis 12:3] ➤ 14 If God only fulfills his promise to those who follow his commands perfectly, then faith in God is worthless and his promises to us are worthless because no one can qualify. 15 God didn't make his promise to Abraham because he was following any law. The Torah clearly states that God is angry with those who violate its commands and he will punish them. But everyone violates it. The only way there could be no violation is if there were no Torah. Therefore, if perfect obedience to the Torah is a requirement for God to consider people righteous and for them to receive his promise, no one qualifies!

16 That's why God fulfills his promises only to those who believe he will do so. He does this in order that his declaring them righteous is clearly seen to be a free gift. If we—like Abraham—trust that God will fulfill his word, we can be sure that we will eventually receive what he promised— whether we follow the Torah's teachings or not. For Abraham is the spiritual father of all who trust God like he did, and God will treat all who believe like Abraham did just like he treated Abraham. 17 This is what the Scriptures mean where God told Abraham, **"I have made you the father of many people in many people groups."** *[Genesis 17:5]* This was fulfilled because God considers Abraham to be the spiritual father of all believers. For Abraham fully trusted in God— whom he knew is able to give life to the dead and to create anything out of nothing. 18 When God promised Abraham that he would become the father of people in many people groups, God also told him that his descendants would be as numerous as the stars in the night sky. *[Genesis 15:5]* And Abraham believed him—even though he had no idea how God would do this and it seemed impossible. 19 Furthermore, Abraham's faith in God's promise never wavered even though his 100-year-old body was as good

as dead as far as its ability to produce offspring, and his wife was barren and far beyond childbearing age. *[Genesis 17:17]* 20 He never doubted that God would give him a son and—through that son—many descendants just as he promised. Actually, Abraham's faith became stronger as he thanked and praised God over the years for what he was going to do. ❖ *Some commentators think it was his body that became stronger as a result of his faith. Both are possible, but Paul's argument focuses on his faith.* ➤ 21 He was completely confident that God was able to do what he promised—and that he would do it. 22 That's why **God declared him righteous in his sight, because Abraham trusted him so absolutely.** *[Genesis 15:6]* 23 Now, these words in the Scriptures about God declaring Abraham righteous because of his faith were not written just to document his story. 24 They were also written so that we could benefit from them. They assure us that God—who raised our Lord Jesus to life from death—also declares us righteous if we trust him to fulfill his promises to us. 25 For God allowed Jesus to be handed over to evil men to be executed for our sins. Then he gave him life again to show that he accepted Jesus' death as the basis for being able to declare us righteous in his sight.

5

Believers Now Have
Close Relationships With God

1 Now, since God has declared us righteous because of what our Lord Jesus the Messiah did for us, and because we have trusted in his death to save us, we have a close peaceful relationship with God. **A** 2 We can come close to God in prayer because of our faith, and he will always treat us with great favor because we are spiritually joined to the Messiah. And we rejoice because we look forward with anticipation to the day

---

A 5:1 Most commentators translate the Greek as saying "we have peace with God"—even though most manuscripts have this as an exhortation, i.e., "we should continue to have peace with God." The difference between these in Greek is a single letter, and spoken Greek of the first century didn't differentiate between the pronunciation of the two different letters found in this position in different manuscripts. Their reasons for going against the weight of manuscript evidence are most likely sound.

the Messiah will return when we will be completely transformed and share God's glory and character. 3 We are even able to rejoice in the midst of difficult circumstances because we know that our enduring them while trusting God will result in an increased ability to persevere in trusting him in the midst of even more difficult circumstances. 4 And when we have learned to persevere in difficulties, we will have the strength of proven character that God approves of. When we are sure of his approval, we will be completely confident—never doubting that we will receive our full salvation when the Messiah returns. [James 1:2-3; 2 Peter 1:5-8] 5 And when we patiently wait with this kind of expectation, God will not disappoint us. We know that he will do what he promised because he has given us the Holy Spirit to live within us who helps us experience God's great love for us—and this kindles his kind of love in us for others.

6 Think about this. The time that God chose to save humanity was while we were under the threat of damnation and unable to save ourselves. The Messiah died to save a rebellious humanity—not one of whom was seeking to please him. 7 There are very few who would be willing to die to save someone unrelated to themselves—even if the person to be saved was good and admirable. Although there might be someone who would have the courage to do so for such a person. 8 But the Messiah died to save us while we were still rebellious sinners! This demonstrates how great God's love for us really is. 9 Since he has already declared us righteous because of the Messiah's death in our place, we can be certain that the Messiah will see to it on Judgment Day that we won't experience God's righteous wrath and punishment—which he *will* loose on those who reject his sacrifice on their behalf. 10 For if God wanted so much to be reconciled with people who were his enemies that he was willing for his Son to die to accomplish it, it's obvious that he will do even more for those who are already reconciled and in close relationship with him. Therefore, we

can be sure that the living Son of God will save us from any punishment on Judgment Day. 11 But there's even more. Now we experience joy in having this close relationship with God through our spiritual union with our Lord Jesus the Messiah—who made it all possible.

Adam's Sin Brought Death but the Messiah's Obedience Brings Life

12 When Adam sinned, sin entered humanity. Adam's spirit died—separating him from God—and his body eventually died. [Genesis 2:17; 3:19; 5:5] These two kinds of death were passed on to all humanity since everyone is descended from Adam, and this is clear because everyone sins. [Ezekiel 18:4] 13 Yes, people sinned even though it wasn't until later that God gave his teachings in the Torah. When there are no commands, then it's not possible to sin by disobeying a command. 14 But it's still clear that they sinned because they died. From the time of Adam until Moses when the Torah was given (around 2500 years later), people sinned and died even though they weren't disobeying a clear command like Adam did.

Now, it's good if you realize that Adam was a "type" of the Messiah who would come later. ❖ *A "type" is a historical person or event that is a pattern, image, or shadow of a later person or event. There are many "types" in the Hebrew Scriptures that reflect truths and realities in the New Testament. Adam was a type of the Messiah in the sense that their lives each started a race of humanity that was patterned after them. Adam was the progenitor of sinful humanity, and the Messiah is the progenitor of redeemed humanity.* ➤ 15 There are similarities between them, but there are also opposites because God's free gift of forgiveness is not like Adam's sin. It's true that all people die because of Adam's sin. But Jesus the Messiah brought the free gift of forgiveness and eternal life to many— merely because God decided to grant us his favor which we could never deserve. 16 There's another difference between God's gift and Adam's sin. After the one sin, Adam and all his descendants were condemned to the fate of eternal punishment. But God's free gift of forgiveness results in many being declared righteous—even though they are guilty of many sins. 17 It's true that Adam's sin brought all humanity under the power of death—even though he was only one man. But another man, Jesus the Messiah, accomplished something much greater. All who receive and embrace God's abundant favor—and his gift of being declared righteous—will triumphantly conquer death and the power of sin through their spiritual union with Messiah Jesus. ❖ Or: All who receive and embrace God's abundant favor—and his gift of being declared righteous—will share the Messiah's power and rule over all things in Heaven. ➤ 18 Therefore, just as Adam's one sin brought death to all people and the expectation that God will punish them on Judgment Day, in contrast, the Messiah's one act of dying out of obedience to God caused all people to have the opportunity to be declared righteous and to receive eternal life—if they believe. 19 Just as all people became sinners as a result of Adam's disobedience to God, in contrast, many will be declared righteous as a result of the Messiah's obedience to God. 20 God gave his teachings in the Torah so we could clearly recognize that everyone is—by nature—evil in his sight. But while the Torah helps us realize that sin is much worse than we first thought, we also realize that God's undeserved favor toward us—his willingness to forgive our sins—is much greater than our sinfulness. 21 So all of humanity was under the power of sin and death before the Messiah came. But now we can be under God's favor and be declared righteous. Thus we can live forever because of what our Lord Jesus the Messiah did for us.

6

We Are No Longer Enslaved
to Our Former Sinful Nature
but Instead Serve God

1 A "devil's advocate" might say that since God has granted us great favor in forgiving us because we sinned, perhaps we should continue to sin so he will show us even greater favor. 2 My answer to that is, "A curse on such thinking!" God caused us to die with the Messiah so that we would no longer be slaves of sinful desires. ❖ Just as a corpse no longer responds to temptations, we are to consider ourselves dead to all sinful desires and not respond to them. ➤ 3 It's important for you to understand that when we were baptized we were spiritually joined to Messiah Jesus. We are—through that union—also in union with his death. Therefore, as far as God and the Torah are concerned, we too have died. [Galatians 2:20; 2 Timothy 2:11] 4 Through our baptism, we were also buried with him. [Colossians 2:12] And the purpose of our spiritual union and identification with the Messiah in his death and burial is so we would also be united with him in his resurrection and share his new resurrected life and power. [Ephesians 2:5; Colossians 2:13] Through a wondrous manifestation of God the Father's power, the Messiah was given life—the same supernatural life that he now shares with us. This is a taste of God's eternal life and holy nature—which enables us to reject temptations and live holy lives.

5 Since we are united with the Messiah in his death, we are also united with his resurrection—which is manifested by his sinless life now being lived in and through us, and which will be fully manifested when we receive our glorified bodies. 6 We know that our old sinful nature was crucified with him for the purpose of setting us free from slavery to always committing sin. 7 For people that God considers as having died—because they are in union with the Messiah—are set completely free from their former bondage to sinful desires. 8 Since we know that we have died with him, we believe that we also live in union with him both now and forever in Heaven. 9 We also know that the Messiah—who was given back his life again after he died—will never die again. So death no longer has any power over him. 10 And when he—the representative of humanity—died, he ended redeemed humanity's slavery to sinful desires forever. And the new life that he lives—to which we are united—he lives only to serve God. 11 Therefore, you must believe that you are dead and unresponsive to the temptation of sinful desires and that you have Messiah Jesus living his life in you—and this enables you to serve God. 12 No longer allow

yourselves to follow sinful desires. ❖ *This clearly indicates that we have the ability to choose either way. We still have sinful desires, but they no longer have power to force us to submit to them. Our new spiritual nature—united to the Messiah—gives us his desire and ability to reject them and to choose to obey God instead.* ➤ 13 Don't allow any part of your body to be engaged in acts of sin. Instead, give yourself completely to God because he gave you a new life. Surrender yourself and your entire body to him to be a means **A** for him to accomplish good. 14 The teachings in the Torah can no longer condemn you. But you are still expected to live as a recipient of God's undeserved favor and enabling power, and to let that help you live in a way that pleases him. You must not allow sinful desires to control you.

We Can Choose to Submit to God

15 Again, a "devil's advocate" might say, "It doesn't matter if we sin because we are not required to keep the Torah's teachings in order to be saved—and it no longer has the power to condemn us. After all, God favors and forgives us." A curse on such thinking! 16 It's important for you to realize that when you choose to serve someone or something, then they become your master and they have power over you. Either your sinful desires are your master or God is. You cannot serve both—and these are the only choices. You can choose to submit to your sinful desires—but that way leads to eternal death. Or you can choose to submit to God's will and receive his eternal approval. 17 At one time, you were all slaves to your sinful nature. But I thank God that now you are sincerely obeying the things you were taught when you first believed. 18 You were set free from slavery to your sinful nature and all sinful desires, and now you have submitted to God and committed yourselves to live within his will. 19 I'm trying to speak in a way that's easy to understand because your sinful desires make it harder to understand spiritual truths. Before you believed, you were enslaved to impurity and evil which led you into ever-increasing evil

deeds. But now that you are saved, you must choose to surrender the use of your bodies and lives to God's will—which will result in your becoming more and more like the Messiah. 20 When you were a slave to your sinful nature, you felt under no obligation to obey God. 21 And what benefit did you obtain as a result of living that way? Nothing good! And now you are ashamed of those things! Living that way leads to eternal death. 22 But now, sinful desires have no real power over you. And by continually submitting to God's will, you will gain the experience of becoming like the Messiah and living with him forever. 23 Submitting to sinful desires pays you back with eternal death. But to those who submit to him, God offers the free gift of eternal life in union with Messiah Jesus our Lord. ❖ *This means that even if you consider yourself a believer and think you are saved, if your normal lifestyle is to submit to your sinful desires—without repenting (i.e., without turning away from those sinful ways)—then you are on the road to eternal death.* ➤

7

Our Relationship to God's Teachings in the Torah

1 My brothers and sisters in the Lord, I'm writing to you with the assumption that you are familiar with the teachings in the Torah. Do you realize that people are only under the Torah's authority while they're alive? **B** 2 For example, a wife is legally bound to her husband as long as he lives. But if he dies, she is free from the law that bound her to him and is no longer under the prohibition to marry another. 3 If she were to marry another man while her husband was still alive, she would commit adultery. But if her husband dies, then she is free to remarry and in doing so does not commit adultery. 4 My brothers and sisters in the Lord, in a similar way God caused you to die so you are no longer under the jurisdiction of the Torah's teachings. He did this by spiritually joining you to the Messiah's body and identifying you with him when he died on the cross.

A 6:13 or: weapon, instrument, tool. The primary meaning of the word ὅπλον (hoplon) is usually "weapon."

B 7:1 This is because judgment about your eternal fate is executed at the time you die.

❖ *The Torah teaches that people must either keep all of God's commands perfectly or die eternally as sinners. And we did die in our spiritual union with the Messiah—so now we have fulfilled the Torah's requirement that we must die eternally.* ➤ God did this so you can now belong to the Messiah whom he raised from death. The intended result of belonging to him is that you will do the good things he wants you to do for his purposes while you are alive. ❖ *We have died to the authority of the Torah in three ways: 1) It can no longer stir up the desire to sin in us [Romans 7:5] because we are no longer under the power of our previous sinful nature. 2) It can no longer make us feel guilty and separated from God because we know that we have been forgiven. 3) The death penalty for sin has already been executed upon Jesus and also us through our spiritual union with him, therefore it no longer has jurisdiction over us. However, now that we have a close relationship with God and have the Holy Spirit living in us, we will want to follow the Spirit's leading and submit to God's will. There are many specific commands in the Torah as it was given to Moses that we no longer follow (e.g. commands regarding being ceremonially clean and unclean, the regulations pertaining to the priesthood and sacrificial system, the specific punishments meant for the nation of Israel's government, and the requirement to be separated from Gentiles). This is because God has clearly changed some of the Torah's requirements since Jesus has come. [e.g., Hebrews 7:12] He notified us about these changes through Jesus' teachings and through the New Testament writers' teachings that were given by the Holy Spirit. But God's Torah teachings (as amended by the New Testament) remain a clear revelation of his will for his people. We don't attempt to keep them to gain God's favor or to merit salvation—because that can't be achieved by obeying commands. Instead, moment by moment we choose to allow the Messiah to live his perfect life through us, choosing to follow what we know to be God's will—both from a knowledge of the requirements in the amended Torah and from the leading of the Holy Spirit. The two are never in conflict. We do this because we love God—and it is his power and life in us that enables us to do so. Jesus also said that if we love God with our whole being and love others in the same way we love ourselves, we will, in fact, be following the Torah's moral requirements. [Matthew 22:37-40]* ➤ 5 When we lived in submission to the desires of our sinful nature, knowing about the prohibitions of God's laws in the Torah actually made those desires stronger. From God's perspective, everything we did resulted in evil and led to eternal death. 6 But now we are free from the Torah's condemnation. And as far as the Torah is concerned, we have already been properly executed so it no longer has legal jurisdiction over us. So now we are finally free to serve God in a new way by following the leading of the Holy Spirit—who enables us to do so by his power—rather than striving unsuccessfully in our own power to keep the commands in the Torah.

The Relationship Between the Torah's Teachings and Sin

7 Please don't think I'm implying that God's teachings in the Torah are in any way evil! Not at all! The truth is, I never would have recognized my actions as sinful if the Torah didn't clearly state that they were. For if the Torah had not said, "You must not covet things that belong to others," *[Exodus 20:17; Deuteronomy 5:21]* then I wouldn't have known that coveting was a sin. 8 But when I was still an unbeliever and I heard that command, my sinful nature tempted me to covet many things. Only if there were no divine commands would there then be no action that could be called "sin." ❖ *But even before God gave his written commands, he had standards that he required of humanity in order for us to have a relationship with him. Those standards were an "unwritten Law," so any action that violated those standards were sinful, even if humanity was unaware of them.* ➤ So God gave his teachings in the Torah in order to reveal to us what sin is—not in order to provide a way to be saved. 9 At one time, I didn't know the Torah said certain actions were sinful and I thought I had a good relationship with God. But when I became aware of specific commands, I suddenly realized that I was a sinner and separated from him. ❖ *Separation from God is the same thing as spiritual death.* ➤ 10 The commands in the Torah—which I thought would enable me to live forever if I obeyed them—made me realize that in reality I was spiritually dead. 11 My sinful nature found an opportunity to deceive me when I first heard the Torah's commands. I was tricked into believing that I could obey the Torah and thereby be righteous in God's sight. But because of my sinful nature, I was a sinner and therefore separated from him. 12 But God's Torah is itself holy and the commands I disobeyed are holy, righteous, and good.

13 Does this mean that something good caused me to be separated from God? Absolutely not! It was my corrupted sinful nature that caused me to sin. But the commands stirred up sinful desires that already existed in me so that my hidden sinful ways would be revealed when I sinned—with the purpose of making me recognize how bad my sinful nature really is. ❖ *A non-Scriptural analogy: A swimming pool has a layer of mud settled on the bottom, leaving the water clear. The pool is not really clean, it's defiled with dirt. But the pool seems clean until a stick stirs up the mud and distributes it through the water, revealing how much dirt there really is in the pool. We are the pool, the Torah's teachings are like that stick, and our sinful nature is like that mud. The stick isn't bad just because it revealed that the pool was defiled with dirt. ¶ Note that a clear detailed understanding most of chapter 7 is difficult, and godly people disagree on many specific details. The rest of the commentary in this chapter reflects my own conclusions, but despite how they may come across, I don't hold to them dogmatically. Other views exist, but discussing them would take too much space, so serious Bible students will need to investigate them for themselves. I advise looking at the passage as a whole and in the light of the rest of Scripture. An overly literal interpretation based only on words, phrases, and sentences taken out of the overall context of Scripture could lead you to conclusions that will be difficult or impossible to reconcile with other Scriptures. ¶ "Sin" is talked about in the Scriptures as if it's an active agent and personality. How are we to understand this, since "sin" is either wrong thoughts or actions—or the state of having done them—and not actually a living agent? Here is an attempt to unravel it. We inherited from our parents (ultimately from Adam) a nature that was intrinsically self-oriented instead of God-oriented. This is called "original sin" or the "sinful nature," and for believers it is also called the "old self." This orientation makes us unacceptable to God and worthy of damnation. It also causes us to think and act in sinful ways once we are old enough or have the ability to do so. When we commit specific acts of sin, we come under Satan's jurisdiction and he and his demons have a legal right to afflict us in that area of sin. If we repent, God forgives us and that legal right is removed. Before we are saved, we sin in many areas and have no forgiveness, so the enemy has relatively free reign to tempt, deceive, and afflict us. So our "sinful nature," in effect, invited the living agents of sin (i.e., Satan and his demons) to be active influences in our lives. When the Scriptures talk about sin as if it were a person, I believe this is what is meant— i.e., both our sinful nature and the active sin agents that tempt us. But after salvation, we were freed from our slavery to that sinful nature. We were spiritually united to a new, perfect,* sinless nature which is God's own life and nature. [Romans 6:2-6] Our dead sinful human spirits were made new and alive and are indwelt by the Holy Spirit. But our bodies are not yet redeemed and we have formed in our brains certain ingrained sinful thought patterns and habits that incline us to automatically behave in the same sinful patterns that we did before we were saved (or, sadly, in patterns of sinful behavior we recognize but freely choose to persist in after salvation). External sin agents are also able to inflame urges that come from our physical bodies and so increase the level of temptation, but they can no longer force us to sin because they cannot rule our new spiritual nature. I believe that these remaining ingrained sinful habit patterns in our brains, together with the urges of our physical bodies that can be satisfied in sinful ways, are what Paul means by σάρξ (sarx) or "the flesh" or "the sinful nature" as it's commonly translated. In this interpretation, I'm rendering "sarx" as "the remaining influence of ingrained sin habits and physical urges after we have been saved" (or portions of that long phrase as appropriate). Yet the influence of these remaining sin habits are not empowered by the enemy, and our new spiritual nature only desires to submit to God. Therefore, the sinful nature which resides in our physical bodies no longer has the power to control us, and the remaining external sin agents no longer have the power to enslave us. They can no longer force us to submit to those habits or to any sinful desire. We can, in fact, choose to do what is right if we pay attention to, and rely on, the Spirit within us—who will give us his enabling power to resist the influence of sin as we consciously decide to submit to his leading.* ➤

The Conflict Within Believers

❖ *There is much debate as to whether this section refers to believers or to unbelievers. But since unbelievers have no desire to do what God wants, I conclude it is talking about believers. This is supported by the fact that unlike the previous passages which are written in the past tense, this section is written in the present tense, implying it was true of Paul at the time he was writing.* ➤

14 We know that God's teachings in the Torah are good and "spiritual." ❖ *Paul uses "spiritual" in contrast to "carnal" (in the literal text). "Spiritual" in this context means it reflects God's character. "Carnal" refers to those who still experience the remaining influence of ingrained sin habits after being saved and frequently choose to submit to them. In terms of the tripartite model of a human being (spirit, soul, and body), our spirit is perfect and holy, has God's own nature and life, and only desires his will. Our soul (mind, will, and emotions) is redeemed. Our redeemed will is capable of making the choice to not sin, but is free to choose either way (like Adam's sinless will was able to choose to obey—before he sinned—or to sin). Our redeemed mind only*

originates good thoughts and it desires God's will. **A** *But our body has not yet experienced redemption. Jesus has paid the price for it but we will not experience the fullness of that physical redemption and freedom from the body's sinful influences until Jesus returns and we gain our glorified bodies. Our brains are a part of our body and sin habits remain ingrained in them. They and our body's urges influence our mind and emotions which pressure our will to give in to them and commit sin. (Our body's natural urges are not in themselves sinful—it's the desire to satisfy those urges in forbidden ways that is sinful.) External sin agents (i.e., demons) can also place sinful thoughts in our minds and try to trick us into accepting them as if they are our own. (It is not a sin for an evil thought to have entered our mind, but it becomes sin if we don't immediately reject it and, instead, welcome it and dwell on it.) If we commit sin and don't repent, those external sin agents have God's legal permission to greatly magnify the further temptations we experience, making them harder to resist.* ➤ But as long as I live in this body I will experience its physical urges and the remaining influences of ingrained sin habits. 15 Often, I do things but don't understand why I do them. I don't do some of the good things I want to do, but instead, I sin in ways that I hate. 16 I recognize that those actions are sinful and my mind and spirit agree with the Torah that they are sin. This demonstrates that I believe the Torah's teachings are good. ❖ *And it demonstrates that my mind is redeemed.* ➤ 17 Therefore, it's not the case that my true self (spirit and soul) is sinning or desires to sin, but I sin because remaining ingrained sin habits and physical urges tempt me, and in my own strength I often fail to reject them. 18 I agree that the desires that come from my remaining ingrained sin habits are entirely evil because it's my true desire and will to do only what is good. But at the same time, I am unable to do it in my own strength. 19 Often, when I want to do good, I don't. And when I try to reject the temptation to sin, I do it anyway. 20 But when I do evil that I don't want to do, my

true self is not wanting to do it. So the "redeemed me" is not the one originating it. It's the remaining influence of habitual sin in my brain and body that's originating it. But I'm still held accountable for choosing to do that sin.

21 In conclusion, I observe that this is what is happening within me: Whenever I want to do good, there is an ingrained sin influence present that pulls in the opposite direction. 22 In my spirit and my mind, my true self joyfully agrees with what God wants me to do. 23 But I recognize that an evil influence is working in my body and brain which opposes the good things my redeemed mind wants to do. And I find I can still be subject to the influence of sin patterns from my past which are still resident in my body and brain. 24 Thus I am truly miserable! Who will set me free from my body's sinful desires that try to lead me to eternal death? 25 I thank God that our Lord Jesus the Messiah is the one who sets me free when I allow him to live his life through me. *[Galatians 2:20]* So this is the way I am: My mind and spirit desire to obey God's will, but my physical brain is still subject to the influence of sin habits established in it.

8

Living in Submission to the Holy Spirit

1 In view of all that I've told you in this letter so far, it's clear that those who are spiritually united with Messiah Jesus are neither condemned nor punished. 2 We know this is true because the power of the Holy Spirit—who causes us to live in spiritual union with Messiah Jesus—has set us completely free from slavery to our former sinful nature, from slavery to external sin agents, and even from slavery to those remaining ingrained sin habits and physical urges that lead us to eternal death.

A 7:14 Some argue that our minds are not redeemed because we have evil thoughts. The Scriptures teach that something that is pure cannot produce evil, and something evil cannot produce good. [Matthew 7:16-18; 12:33-35; Luke 6:43-45] Evil thoughts can be introduced by the remaining sin habits ingrained in our brain or by external sin agents like demons or people. We can choose to entertain such thoughts or reject them. Evil thoughts can influence or tempt a pure mind. If not, then how could Jesus be tempted? But since we also clearly originate many good thoughts and desires in our minds, in particular, our desires to obey God, this demonstrates that our minds are redeemed. [Romans 7:25; 1 Corinthians 2:16] That our brains are not identical with our minds is clear from the fact that after our bodies and brains die, we will still be able to think and remember.

3 The commands in the Torah were power-less to make us righteous because our former sinful nature was weak in its ability to obey God's commands. So God made us righteous by sending his Son to become human just like us, having desires just like us—except that sin had no power over him. He sent him to suffer the penalty of condemnation as a substitute for us—so that we could be spirit-ually united with him for the purpose of becoming one in identity with him in God's sight. Thus our sins have already been punished in his Son's death. ❖ *When God sees us, he sees that we are totally united and one with Jesus on the spiritual level—which is the most important level. His suffering the punishment for our sins is counted as if we suffered the punishment for our sins—so there is nothing left to punish and condemn. And Jesus' righteousness is counted as our righteousness—so we are acceptable to God.* ➤ 4 God did this so that in our union with the Messiah we can now be free from slavery to all sinful influences and instead, choose to follow the leading of the Holy Spirit by continually choosing to allow the Messiah to live his life through us. By living this way, we also fulfill what the Torah requires.

5 Those unbelievers who continually choose to submit to the influences of their ingrained sin habits and physical urges will have their minds dominated by those inclinations. But those who continually choose to submit to the Holy Spirit will try to only think about what he desires. 6 Those whose minds are dominated by evil influ-ences in their bodies are following the road to eternal death. But those whose minds are focused on the thoughts of the Spirit have eternal life and peace with God. 7 Those whose minds are controlled by the desire to sin are hostile toward God and his ways—for they refuse to submit to him and, in fact, they cannot do so. 8 Such people can never please God. 9 But if the Spirit of God really lives in you, then you will not continually choose to submit to any evil desires you experience, but will, instead, continually choose to submit to his leading. ❖ *You will not always submit perfectly, but it will be your desire to do so and, for the most part, you will do so. And when you fail, you will repent and return to submitting to God.* ➤ Those who don't have the Spirit of the Messiah living

in them do not belong to him. 10 Your human spirit is alive and righteous in God's sight because the Messiah lives in your spirit through the agency of the Holy Spirit—even though your body will die because of sin. 11 But God—who made Jesus the Messiah alive again—will one day make your body alive with the same kind of glorified body Jesus has, through the power of the Holy Spirit who lives in you.

12 Therefore, my brothers and sisters, we are indebted to the Holy Spirit and must live as he leads us. We have no reason to submit to physical urges or to the remaining influences of ingrained sin habits. 13 If you normally choose to submit to such sinful desires and influences without repenting, you will experience eternal death in Hell. But if you allow the power of the Holy Spirit to enable you to reject those desires and influences, then you will live forever. *[Galatians 5:13, 19-21; 1 Peter 2:11]* ❖ *These things will help you reject sinful desires: 1) Recognize they are not part of your "true self" because: (a) our "old self" was crucified with the Messiah[Romans 6:6], and (b) you are a "new creation" [2 Corinthians 5:17] and are already "sanctified" [1 Corinthi-ans 1:2] and are seated with the Messiah in Heaven. [Ephesians 2:6] 2) When sinful desires come: (a) immedi-ately reject them—rejecting them verbally can help, (b) ask the Lord Jesus to live his life through you, (c) trust that he is doing so, (d) then act in obedience. [Galatians 2:20] 3) Set your mind on pure and good things. [Philippians 4:8] It is important that you not dwell on the temptation. 4) Recognize that temptation is a spiritual attack against you and that "offense is the best defense," even against Satan. Have on hand a list of people to pray for and their needs, and when you are tempted, start interceding on behalf of those people for salvation, healing, restored relationships, provision, etc. Wage spiritual warfare against the enemy on behalf of your family, friends, colleagues, and acquaintances. Do this out loud if possible. This will distract you from the temptation and will have you actively focusing on God's word, standing on his promises, exercising your faith, strengthening your resolve to oppose the enemy, his temptations, and ways, while actively depending on God's power to overcome on behalf of those for whom you are praying. You will be resist-ing and opposing Satan, and as a result he will cease attacking you with temptation, flee, [James 4:7] and leave you alone, at least for a while. [Luke 4:13] 5) If you have established habits of sin over many years, expect that it might take a few years of persistence to fully establish new thought*

and behavior habits, such as automatically doing steps 1 through 4. ➤ 14 Realize that it's those who actively submit to the leading of God's Spirit who are really his children. 15 For the Spirit—whom God gave you—does not force you to obey him or cause you to fear him. But in giving you his Spirit he has adopted you as his children; and the Spirit causes us to call out to our Heavenly Father—with whom we have a close relationship—"Daddy!"

16 The Spirit himself speaks to our human spirits to assure us that we really are God's children. 17 And since we are his children, we are also his heirs. Everything God has he gives to his Son, the Messiah, and he also gives to us. If we suffer in this life to obey him [1 Peter 4:1-2]—as the Messiah did in the course of obeying God's will—then we will also share his glory and honor in Heaven. ❖ If you obey God's will, then you will suffer and fulfill this condition. You need not worry about it or seek suffering. Merely live in obedience and be willing to suffer in order to obey. ➤

We Long for Our Glory

18 For even though we must suffer in this life in the course of obeying the Messiah, in my opinion, the price of enduring these temporary sufferings is negligible compared to the value of the eternal glory that God will give us in Heaven for enduring them. 19 In a sense, all of creation waits in anticipation for God to reveal who his heirs truly are and what their glory and status will be. 20 For God subjected all of creation to a curse of decay as a result of Adam's sin— just as Adam was under a curse. [Genesis 3:17-18] 21 So all of creation looks forward to the day when God will reveal his true children and completely set them free from death and share his glory with them— because he will then also free everything in creation from the curse of decay, and everything will share in his children's glory. 22 We know that from the time of that curse until now, the entire creation has experienced decay and death. The pains of its decay have been like labor pains—in anticipation of something much better. 23 And not just the rest of creation, but we too—who have

the Holy Spirit as the down payment of what we will inherit—experience longing for the labor pains to cease and for our birth into our redeemed and glorified bodies to finally happen when we will receive the full inheritance that is promised us as God's adopted heirs. 24 Ever since God saved us, we've been eagerly looking forward to receiving these things from him. If we had already received them then we wouldn't still be waiting. Nobody waits expectantly for something they already have. 25 But we are waiting expectantly for something that we haven't yet seen. And we patiently wait with confidence that we will indeed receive it.

The Spirit Helps Us Pray

26 In the same way that our confident expectation helps us to endure the waiting, the Spirit helps us when our faith is weak. When we don't know what to say to God in prayer and inwardly we groan because we have feelings that we don't know how to express—then the Spirit prays for us. 27 God knows what's in our hearts and minds [1 Samuel 16:7; 1 Kings 8:39; 1 Chronicles 20.9; Psalm 7:9; Proverbs 15:11; Jeremiah 17:9-10; Acts 1:24; 1 Thessalonians 2:4; Revelation 2:23] ❖ The last reference in Revelation identifies Jesus as one who does this, as well as the Father. ➤ and he also understands the Spirit's prayers for us because the Spirit always prays for God's holy people in line with the Father's will.

God's Plan for Us

28 According to his own plan and for his own purposes, God called us to be his people—and so we love him. We know for certain that God uses everything that happens to us for our own good—even if it seems bad at the time. He does this for everyone who loves him. ❖ Therefore, we can thank and praise him in all circumstances. [1 Thessalonians 5:18] ➤ 29 Even before God made this world, he knew who would believe in his Son. So he predestined that we would become just like his Son in character and glory (but not in his deity). Therefore, the Messiah is his firstborn son and we—who are his children—are like the Messiah's

many younger brothers and sisters. ❖ *Some teach that God's foreknowledge is the same as predestination. Others make a clear distinction between them.* ➤ 30 He predestined us to be like his Son, then he called us to be his children, declared us righteous in his sight, and has given us great glory. ❖ *That glory is already given, but is currently hidden. [Colossians 3:3-4]* ➤

God Is on Our Side

31 In view of all these things that God does for us, it's clear that nothing and no one can ultimately defeat us because God is on our side. 32 God did everything he could to help us—even to the point of sending his Son to die as our substitute. So it should be obvious that he will also freely give us everything he has promised. 33 No one can accuse God's chosen people of doing wrong—because he himself has declared them righteous. ❖ *Sometimes, we allow our sins to make us feel bad because we think it's hard for God to love us. But this is the Enemy trying to destroy our faith. If we have repented and want to obey God, then we can be sure that we are righteous in his sight. We need to ignore those feelings of condemnation and choose to praise and thank God for his love and forgiveness. Focus on God—not on your sin. That is how we will find our victory over our feelings and over our sin.* ➤ 34 No one can condemn us because Messiah Jesus—who has the place of highest honor at the right side of his Father—tells him that we belong to him. The Father clearly accepts what Jesus says because Jesus died for us. And the Father showed his approval of Jesus' sacrifice on our behalf by raising him back to life. 35 Therefore, nothing can stop the Messiah from loving us or stop his love from reaching us, not tribulation, suffering, hunger, poverty, danger, or even death. 36 These things are in agreement with what David wrote to God in the Scriptures, **"Because we are your people, others are always trying to kill us. To them, we are like sheep that are fit to be slaughtered."** *[Psalm 44:22]* 37 But even if all these bad things happen to us, we are still victorious over Satan's temptation to despair, sin, and unbelief during them because of our union with the Messiah who loves us and helps us. 38-39 God showed that he loves us through what Messiah Jesus, our

Lord, did for us. I'm sure that nothing can stop him from loving us and nothing can stop his love from reaching us—not death or anything in this life, not angels or powerful demons, not anything that can happen to us today or in the future, no power, nothing in Heaven or Hell or anything in all of creation, nothing and no one at all can do it.

9

What About Jews Who Don't Believe That Jesus Is the Messiah?

1-2 Now I want to discuss the fact that most Jews have rejected Jesus as the Messiah. My heart is continually filled with great sadness about the Jews—who are my own people. I say this as one who belongs to the Messiah and I'm telling you the truth. Both the Holy Spirit and my conscience confirm to me that I am not lying. 3 I'm sad because most of them don't believe that Jesus is the Messiah. I want to help them believe. But aside from preaching the Good News and praying for them, nothing I can do will make them change. Not even if I were to offer myself as a sacrifice to God to take the curse they live under onto myself so that I was separated from God. *[Exodus 32:32]* I think I would be willing to do this if it would help them. 4 They are the Israelites—God's special people whom he adopted as his heirs. He revealed his glory to them in the wilderness and made his covenant agreements with them. *[Genesis 9:9; 17:2; Exodus 24:8; Joshua 8:33; 2 Samuel 23:5]* On Mount Sinai, he gave them his teachings in the Torah and instructions on how to worship him in his Temple. He gave special promises to them about the Messiah. 5 Their ancestors Abraham, Isaac, and Jacob were great men of God and the Messiah himself is descended from them in his human nature. But most of them have rejected the Messiah—who is over everything. May God be praised forever for choosing the Israelites, for giving them these advantages, and for bringing the Messiah to us from among them. Yes, let it be so! ❖ *The phrase "God blessed to the ages" in the literal text is in the form of a standard Jewish blessing, so it has been translated "May God be praised..." It's unlikely that*

Paul intended this phrase to focus on the deity of the Messiah with such a brief mention, as is done in some translations (e.g., the NIV). ➤ **6** But don't think that God has broken his promise to them. ❖ *God promised Abraham, Isaac, and Jacob that their descendants would be his people and receive his blessing.* ➤ Because not everyone who is physically descended from Israel really belongs to God **7** or is Abraham's child according to God's promise. God told Abraham, **"Your descendants through Isaac's line** ❖ *and not from any other son of yours* ➤ **will be the descendants that I promised to give you."** *[Genesis 21:12]* **8** This means that God doesn't automatically make every descendant of Abraham one of his children, but only those who—as a result of God's promise—trust God like Abraham did. ❖ *Many Jews in Paul's day thought they automatically had God's favor because of their physical descent.* ➤ **9** These are the words of God's promise to Abraham, **"By this same time next year I will return and Sarah will have a son."** *[Genesis 18:10]* ❖ *Paul's point is that only Sarah's son, Isaac, was promised—not Ishmael. See Genesis chapters 15—18 and 21.* ➤ **10** And yet again, God showed that his true children are not chosen based on physical descent for the same thing happened to Rebekah. She had twin boys, both the sons of Isaac in the line of promise. **11-12** Before they had done anything good or bad, even before they were born, God said to Rebekah, **"The firstborn will serve the second born."** *[Genesis 25:23]* He said this so it would be clear that his choice in people is not based on what they do but on his own plans. ❖ *The firstborn had special rights and privileges, so God's declaration violated the cultural norms of that time and place.* ➤ **13** This is just as God said in the Scriptures, **"I loved Jacob but I rejected Esau."** *[Malachi 1:2-3]* ❖ *Esau was the firstborn and Jacob was his younger twin. Literally, it says, "I hated Esau." There are many clear cases in the Scriptures where "hate" is a Semitic idiom meaning "love less." [e.g., Genesis 29:31, 33; Deuteronomy 21:15; Matthew 6:24; Luke 14:26; and John 12:25] And many interpret it that way here. But it's more likely that here it means he rejected him and did not choose him for special service while Jacob was chosen for that purpose. In the prophecy in Malachi, these names not only refer to the two brothers but also to the nations descended from them, Israel from Jacob, and Edom from Esau.* ➤

14 Can we conclude that God was not fair in doing this? Never! God is always fair. **15** God said this to Moses about his ways, **"I will show mercy to any undeserving person that I want to. And I will have compassion on anyone I want to."** *[Exodus 33:19]* **16** Therefore, it is God who chooses those who will receive his promises and it doesn't depend on people's desires or what they do—but only on his mercy. ❖ *If God is fair and all people are undeserving, how can he choose one over another? God's knowledge, purposes, and choices are beyond our comprehension. We only see the smallest tip of the choices he makes, and have only the smallest glimpse of his ultimate purposes. We have to trust that by his standards— which are much higher than our own—he is always fair and impartial. The verses in this chapter are strong support for the Calvinist view of election. There are clear Scriptures that God is in complete control and can make people do what he wants—as in Deuteronomy 29:4. But at the same time, it's clear that God wants people to voluntarily turn to him so he can bless them—as in Deuteronomy 5:29. Some non-Calvinists hypothesize that even before they are born, God knows which people will choose to seek him and that he chooses to bless them based on his foreknowledge of that choice.* ➤ **17** Another example of his sovereign choice is Pharaoh, the king of Egypt at the time of Moses. The Scriptures say that God told Pharaoh, **"I made you king so that I could demonstrate my power by opposing you, and in this way make my name known everywhere in the world."** *[Exodus 9:16]* ❖ *God hardened Pharaoh's heart (i.e., made him stubborn) [Exodus 9:12, 35; 10:27; 11:10], but only after he had hardened his own heart several times. [Exodus 7:22; 8:15, 32]* ➤ **18** So it's clear that God shows mercy to some people just because he wants to, and he chooses to make some people stubborn if he wants to.

19 A "devil's advocate" will ask, "Why does God blame people for not listening to him if they only do what he makes them do?" **20** But my answer is this: Do you think that lowly mortals have the right to protest the way their Creator uses them? That would be as absurd as a clay pot protesting to the potter, "Why did you make me like this?" **21** A potter has the right to make whatever he wants to make. He can make a special pot for special occasions or one for ordinary use. ❖ *Some will still protest that this isn't fair, but keep in mind that the two kinds of pot are made from the* *same kind of clay. God created humanity perfect, for high purposes, but humanity sinned. Now, he still uses us for his purposes—but from his perspective we have no rights because sinners are all deserving of damnation. If you think you will be able to stand before God and protest what he has done with you or others, you have no proper conception of who God is. And you need to realize that for a sinner to demand strict justice is to demand damnation. The Scriptures teach that God never tempts us to sin and is only a source of good. [James 1:13-14] Therefore, he never causes anyone to sin. He also promises to never reject those who seek him.* ➤ 22 God is like the potter. He has the right to execute his anger and demonstrate his power against sinners at any time. But he also has the right to be patient and allow people to continue living who will later be punished in Hell because of his anger over their sins. 23 He chooses not to end this world quickly and start executing his punishment because he also has the right to reveal the exceeding greatness of his goodness and mercy on people not yet born—whom he chose to be his own even before he created the world. ❖ *In Exodus 33:19-22, God equates his glory with his goodness, hence the translation here of "glory" (in the literal text) as "goodness," which is an easier idea to grasp.* ➤ 24 This is what he did for us whom he called—whether we are Jews or Gentiles. 25 Just as God says about the Gentiles in the book written by the prophet Hosea, "People who were not my people before, I now declare that they are my people. And people to whom I did not show my love before, now I say that I love them." *[Hosea 2:23; 1 Peter 2:10]* 26 And in another place, this is written, "In that place where they were told, 'You are not my people,' now he will say, 'You are the heirs of God—the life giver.' " *[Hosea 1:10]* 27 But the prophet Isaiah wrote this about the Israelites, "Even though the number of Israel's descendants are as uncountable as the grains of sand on a beach, only a small number of them will be saved. 28 Because Yahweh will soon execute his punishment on the unbelievers in this world—completely and quickly—just as he said he would do." *[Isaiah 10:22-23; 28:22]* 29 And Isaiah predicted in another place, "If Almighty Yahweh had not left us a few descendants alive, we Israelites would have been completely wiped out—

just like the people of Sodom and Gomorrah." *[Isaiah 1:9]* ❖ *The story of Sodom and Gomorrah is in Genesis chapter 19.* ➤

30 So what can we conclude about these things? Only this—that Gentiles were declared righteous in God's sight because they believed in the Messiah, even though previously they had not been trying to live righteous lives to please him. 31 But the descendants of Israel ❖ *the Jews* ➤—who tried to become righteous in God's sight by keeping his commands in the Torah—did not attain their goal. 32 Why not? Because they didn't try to attain that status by trusting God's promises, as Abraham had done. Instead, they tried to attain it in their own strength by outwardly obeying the Torah's commands without proper faith. They didn't expect the Messiah to die—so when they hear the message about him dying for them, they reject it. The Messiah's death became a stumbling block to them. 33 This is what God said about the Messiah in the Scriptures, **"Recognize this, I am placing the Messiah in Zion as a Stone which will cause people to stumble, and he will be a Rock that offends them. But in the end, those who believe in him will not be disappointed."** *[Isaiah 8:14; 28:16; Acts 4:8-11; 1 Peter 2:7-8]* ❖ *Zion is the mountain on which Jerusalem is built, and the name Zion often stands for Jerusalem itself, or the nation of Israel, or sometimes the location of the Temple. Isaiah 8:14 says he (the Messiah, who in the prophecy is clearly Yahweh) will be a sanctuary, and the passage in Isaiah 28:16 says the Stone in Zion will be a cornerstone—giving a hint that it (the Messiah) would replace the Temple which was located there.* ➤

10

1 Brothers and sisters in the Lord, my greatest desire is that the Jews be saved, and this is what I'm always asking God to do for them. 2 I can say this about them: They genuinely try to follow God's will, but they lack a proper understanding of it. 3 They don't understand the way that God has now provided to be declared righteous in his sight. Instead, they try to find their own righteousness by obeying the Torah's commands. They don't submit to believing that Jesus is the Messiah whom God sent to

save them. ❖ *This indicates that sincerity and good intentions are not enough to establish a relationship with God—as many people falsely believe. He requires a person to respond correctly—with faith in his Son.* ➤ 4 The goal of God's teachings in the Torah is to lead people to trust in the Messiah—who has fulfilled the Torah's requirements perfectly. And God bestows his righteousness on all who trust in what the Messiah has already done. This was God's plan from the beginning. ❖ *Another interpretation of this verse says that the Messiah ends the validity of the teachings in the Torah. But Jesus himself said that the Torah's teachings would not pass away until Heaven and Earth pass away. [Matthew 5:17-18] The writer to the Hebrews talks about a change in the Torah—which implies that it still is in force, but as amended. [Hebrews 7:12]* ➤

What Many Jews Misunderstand

5 Moses said this about righteousness based on keeping the Torah's teachings, "The person who obeys all these commands perfectly will live forever." *[Leviticus 18:5]* 6 Moreover, the Scriptures say this about receiving righteousness by faith, "Don't think A that you have to go up to Heaven," (to bring the Messiah down with the message of salvation). *[Deuteronomy 30:12]* ❖ *Paul is arguing that the Torah teaches salvation by faith—not by keeping the all of the Torah's commands. He is **not** saying that there are two kinds of righteousness, one by obeying the commands in the Torah—which has been abolished—and one by faith. (This idea of two kinds of righteousness is an incorrect understanding of Paul's teaching).* ➤ 7 And "You don't have to descend into the abyss" (to bring the Messiah up from the dead). *[Deuteronomy 30:13]* ❖ *The entire passage that Paul is loosely quoting from says, "This command (Paul is reinterpreting this as a command to believe in the Messiah) that I'm giving you today is not too hard or beyond your reach. It's not in Heaven, so you have to ask, 'Who will go up to Heaven and bring it down so we can hear and obey it?' And it's not across the (Red) sea, so you have to ask, 'Who will descend into the sea to bring it back so we may hear it and obey it?' For the word is very near to you, it is in your mouth and mind so you can obey it." He is making a Jewish midrash argument in which he shapes the text he is quoting for the purpose of his analogy. This type of argumentation was very common among Jewish teachers, but is not well understood by most Gentile*

believers today. *Originally, this text applied to the Torah's teachings. Paul substituted "abyss," which means "place of the dead," for "sea," to make his reference to the Messiah's resurrection clearer, and he uses this passage to say that according to the Torah, people don't have to do difficult things to be saved because God does them for us. He sent the Messiah down from Heaven with the Good News and raised him from the dead. He has given us the way to be saved and made it as easy as believing in our hearts and announcing the truth.* ➤ 8 It also says, "The message is near and familiar to you, it is in your heart and you speak it." *[Deuteronomy 30:14]* This is the message that we preach about believing in the Messiah. 9 If you publicly announce that you submit to Jesus as Lord, and believe in your heart that God the Father made him alive again after he died, then you will be saved. ❖ *To a Jew of his time, saying "Jesus is Lord" was equivalent to saying "Jesus is God." This is because they had a tradition to not say God's actual name (i.e. Yahweh) but to instead always refer to him as, "Adonai," which means, "Lord." In the Septuagint—the Greek translation of the Hebrew Scriptures that was in common use by Jews in Jesus' day—it substituted "Adonai" for every occurrence of "Yahweh" in the original Hebrew text (over 6000 times). In English translations, this tradition has been continued with the substitution of "the Lord" in the place of "Yahweh."* ➤ 10 For when you believe in your heart and publicly announce this to others, then God declares you to be righteous, and you are saved. ❖ *These are not two separate events. Being "declared righteous" and being "saved" are two ways of saying the same thing.* ➤ 11 Just as the Scriptures say about the Messiah, "Whoever believes in him will not be disappointed on Judgment Day." *[Isaiah 28:16 in the Septuagint]* 12 This is true for both Jews and Gentiles. They all have the same Lord who generously blesses everyone who prays to him for help. 13 As the prophet Joel said, "Everyone who prays to Yahweh for help will be saved." *[Joel 2:32]* 14 But how can they pray to him for help if they don't believe in him? And how can they believe if they've not heard the Good News about him? And how can they hear the Good News if nobody proclaims it to them? ❖ *Paul is speaking of Jews here, but the application is universal.* ➤ 15 And how can there be people proclaiming it if they aren't sent out? Just as the Scriptures say,

---

A 10:6 Literally: "Don't say in your heart," from Deuteronomy 9:4.

"The arrival of those bringing Good News is greatly welcomed." *[Isaiah 52:7]* **16** But not all Jews accepted the Good News. As the prophet Isaiah wrote, "Lord, no one has believed our message!" *[Isaiah 53:1; John 12:38]* **17** So believing comes from hearing the Good News, and the opportunity to hear happens when people proclaim the message about the Messiah. **18** But what about the Jews? Have they really heard the Good News? Yes they have. Just as the Scriptures say, "Their message has gone out to all the earth, even to the most distant places." *[Psalm 19:4]* **19** But did the Jews really understand the message? They should have, because even Gentiles can understand it. In Moses' day, God said to the Israelites, "I will make you jealous of insignificant Gentiles. I will make you angry by blessing people who never understood about me before." *[Deuteronomy 32:21]* **20** And Isaiah boldly wrote what God said about Gentiles, "Those who did not search for me, found me. I revealed myself to those who didn't even ask me to come to them." *[Isaiah 65:1]* **21** But he says this about the Israelites, "For a long time I've held out my hands to invite them to return to me, but they continued to disobey me and rebel against me." *[Isaiah 65:2]*

11

God Has Not Given Up on the Jews

1 So, has God rejected the Jews as his own special people? A curse on such thinking! For example, I too am a Jew, and God hasn't rejected me. I am descended from Abraham in the line of Benjamin. ❖ *Benjamin was one of the twelve tribes of Israel, the twelfth son of Jacob.* ➤ **2** God has *not* entirely rejected his people, the Jews, whom he chose before the creation of the world! You know what the Scriptures say about this when the prophet Elijah complained to God about the Israelites, **3** **"Yahweh, they have killed all your prophets and have torn down your altars. I'm the only one left who believes in you—and they are trying to kill me too!"** *[1 Kings 19:10, 14]* **4** What was God's answer? **"I've preserved for myself 7000 men who haven't bowed in worship to the false god Baal."**

[1 Kings 19:18] **5** In the same way, at this time there is still—and always will be—at least some remnant, a number of Jews whom God has chosen to be saved because of his freely granting them undeserved favor. **6** His choosing is based on his undeserved favor—not on what they've done. For if he chose based on what they did, his favor would not be free and unmerited—as it actually is.

7 So here's the situation: Many Jews tried hard to be righteous, but most of them were unsuccessful. Only those whom God chose obtained righteousness. As for the others, their hearts were hardened. ❖ *The passive construction of the last sentence is ambiguous in the Greek. It could mean they, themselves, hardened their hearts, or that God did it. The next verse clearly says the latter is true. Yet in historical context, it can be claimed that it was only after they had already hardened their own hearts that he punished them by adding to it.* ➤ **8** As the Scriptures say, **"God gave them a spirit of stupor so that even today it's like they are blind and deaf to his truth."** *[Deuteronomy 29:4; Isaiah 6:9-10; 29:10]* ❖ *The spirit of stupor could be a deadness toward spiritual things, or a literal demonic spirit that causes that state, or both.* ➤ **9** King David asked God to make his enemies blind to truth like that. He said, **"Let their feasts become a trap for them—giving them false security. Let them stumble and be destroyed. 10 Make them blind and burden them like slaves."** *[Psalm 69:22-23]*

11 When the majority of the Jews stumbled by rejecting the Messiah, did that permanently separate all Jews from God? A curse on such thinking! By saving Gentiles, God wants to make Jews jealous so they will want to believe too. **12** If the fact that most Jews rejected the Messiah has resulted in God turning to greatly bless Gentiles—as he had planned to do all along through Abraham's descendants—then we can expect even greater blessings for everyone when the complete number of Jews that he has chosen have been saved. ❖ *The Messianic Jewish movement is rapidly growing. More Jews have accepted Jesus as their Messiah in the past few decades than have done so since Gentiles started dominating the number of believers in the first century AD.* ➤

13 I'm saying all this particularly to you Gentiles. I boast about my work because

God sent me as an apostle to the Gentiles. [14] And I hope my Jewish brothers and sisters will become envious of your salvation so that God will be able to save some of them as an indirect result of my work among you. [15] The result of most Jews rejecting Jesus as the Messiah was that God offered salvation to the rest of the world. So what will be the greater result of God's accepting them when they someday trust in Jesus? It will be like a resurrection for the entire world.

The Jews Are Still God's Chosen People

[16] If the first part of the flour that is ground from your grain harvest is offered to God, then he causes all that you make from that flour to also be holy. *[Numbers 15:17-21]* And if the roots of a tree are holy, then the branches will be holy too. In the same way, the Jews will belong to God because their ancestors belonged to him. [17] ❖ *In the following illustration, the olive tree is symbolic of Israel.* ➤ God has broken off some of the branches from his olive tree—which are like the Jews who don't believe. And you Gentiles are like branches of wild olive trees that grow outside of God's garden. But now, by your believing, he has grafted you onto the tree of his people. So now you share in the blessings of his promises to them. [18] Therefore, do not despise those branches that were broken off. Remember that it is the roots that are causing you to grow, and not the other way around. ❖ *In other words: God's blessings that you now enjoy came to you because God first gave them to the Jews. But the blessings that the Jews have did not come from Gentiles.* ➤ [19] Some of you will be tempted to boast, "God broke off branches so I could be grafted onto the tree." [20] That is correct. But they were broken off because of their unbelief, and you remain grafted on because you continue to believe. So don't think too highly of yourselves, but have a healthy fear of what could happen to you, too, if you cease to believe. [21] Since God didn't hesitate to get rid of some of the natural branches because of their unbelief, he would also not hesitate to do the same to you. [22] Recognize that God shows both kindness and strictness. He punished those who didn't believe, but shows kindness to you—as long as you continue to trust in his kindness for your salvation. Otherwise, you too will be cut off. [23] And if the Jews repent of their unbelief, they too will be grafted back onto his tree without displacing Gentile believers. God is perfectly capable of doing this. [24] Since God is able to cut you off from a wild tree and graft you onto his holy tree—which is the opposite of what is usually done—then it will be even easier for him to graft branches that originally came from his tree back into their proper place. ❖ *Grafting is usually done to put branches from productive cultivated trees, onto unproductive wild trees.* ➤

Someday Most Jews Will Believe in Jesus as the Messiah

[25] My brothers and sisters, I want you to know about this truth that has been a secret until now—so you won't be conceited. God has hardened the hearts of many of Jews, but only until the fullness of Gentiles he has chosen have been saved. ❖ *The "fullness of Gentiles" probably doesn't mean the full number of Gentiles who will eventually be saved, but the full scope of Gentiles from every people group and language in the world. [Revelation 5:6; 7:9]* ➤ [26] Then, most of the Jews living at that time will also believe and be saved. Just as the Scriptures say, **"The Savior will come from Israel and he will remove all godlessness from the Israelites."** *[Isaiah 59:20]* [27] God also says about them, **"I will make this covenant agreement with them when I take away their sins."** *[Isaiah 59:21a, 27:9]* ❖ *See also Jeremiah 31:33-34.* ➤ [28] Many Jews are now enemies of the Good News. And this has benefited you Gentiles because God has given his gifts to you. But the Jews are still God's chosen people and he loves them because he is bound to keep his promises to their ancestors Abraham, Isaac, and Jacob. [29] You should understand that God never takes back the gifts that he gives, nor does he change his mind about the ones he chooses. [30] At one time, you Gentiles disobeyed God. But since the Jews refused his mercy and favor, he gave it to you instead. [31] And now, the Jews are disobedient so that later, God can also show them the same mercy and undeserved favor that he showed you. [32] For he declares that all

people are under the power of sin and are it's prisoners. Thus he can offer his mercy and undeserved favor to them all.

A Song of Praise to God

❖ *Commonly called a "doxology"* ➤

33 I'm amazed at the depth of God's wisdom and the height of his knowledge! No one can fully understand his decisions or his ways. 34 As the Scriptures say, "Who can know what Yahweh thinks? Who knows enough to give him advice?" *[Isaiah 40:13-14]* 35 Who could ever give anything to God—making God indebted to him? *[Job 41:11]* 36 For he is the one who made everything for his own purposes. And it only continues to exist because he wills it. *[John 1:3; Acts 17:28; 1 Corinthians 8:6; Colossians 1:16-17; Hebrews 1:3; 2 Peter 3:7]* May all people praise and honor him forever! Yes, may it be so!

12

The Way God Wants You to Live

1 My brothers and sisters, God has shown us that he is merciful to us and grants us favor we can never deserve. Therefore, I exhort you to live in this way: *[1 Corinthians 13:1-7; Galatians 5:16—6:10; Ephesians 4:1—6:9; Colossians 3:12—4:6; 1 Thessalonians 4:1-12; 5:6-22; James 1:19—2:12; 3:13—4:17; 1 Peter 4:1-11]* Offer yourselves, your bodies, and everything you do to serve God—following his holy will in all things. Do this as your sacrificial offering to him. For this is the essence of true spiritual worship which pleases him. *[John 4:23-24]* 2 But don't allow yourselves to conform to the ethical, moral, and social standards of nonbelievers. Instead, allow God to completely change the way you think about things so it conforms to his view of truth and reality. Do this by pondering his words in the Scriptures. If you do this, then you will always know what his will for you is and what is good, pleasing, and perfect in his sight. 3 As God's apostle, I admonish each of you to be realistic about your self-image and not be conceited. Recognize the abilities that God has given you because you believe in the Messiah, but evaluate yourself with honesty and humility. 4 For example, you have one body but it has many parts which don't all have the same function. 5 In a similar way, even though individuals are joined to the Messiah, all of us together constitute one spiritual body. We are all parts of his body and are spiritually connected to each other. 6 And God has decided to shower us with his enabling favor—giving each of us different spiritual gifts and abilities that enable us to bless each other. The Holy Spirit within us gives us his power to do these things. Therefore, each of us must utilize the gift that God has given us. If he gave you the ability to prophesy, then speak out God's message when you believe he wants you to do so. 7 If he gave you the ability to serve others, then do this to the best of your ability. If he has given you the ability to teach, then teach his truth as well as you can. 8 If he gave you the ability to exhort others, then do it as he leads. If he gave you the ability to share your wealth, be generous and give without ulterior motives. If he gave you the ability to lead, work hard at being a godly leader. If he gave you the ability to show others mercy and kindness, do it cheerfully.

9 Love each other without pretense, but despise evil deeds. Always do what you know is good in God's sight. 10 Be loving and affectionate with each other as if you are all members of one family. Honor everyone else more highly than you do yourself. ❖ *Or: Be eager to honor each other.* ➤ 11 In serving your Lord, don't be lazy, but be industrious, enthusiastic, and always do your best. 12 Always rejoice too because of the wonderful things God has promised you. Persevere in trusting him during difficult times and don't neglect your prayer life. 13 Whenever you are aware of a need among God's people, share what you have with them. Cheerfully welcome traveling believers into your home—offering them every hospitality.

14 Ask God to bless those who make life difficult for you. You must bless them and never curse them. *[Luke 6:28]* 15 Rejoice and be happy for others who have reason to rejoice ❖ *instead of being envious* ➤ and when someone is mourning, be sympathetic and grieve with them. 16 Live together in harmony. Be

humble—not conceited or arrogant. Be willing to associate with the most ordinary and lowly people and don't think that you are above doing the same kind of menial tasks they do. Don't consider yourself smarter or wiser than others.

17 Never retaliate when someone does you wrong. *[Matthew 5:39-41]* But always do what everyone in the community of believers would agree is proper—even if that is more restrictive for you than exercising the freedom you think you should have. 18 As much as it's within your ability and within God's will, be on amiable terms with everyone. 19 My friends, never take revenge! Instead, allow God to execute his holy anger to punish those who do wrong to you. For Yahweh says in the Scriptures, **"Only I have the right to take revenge—and you can trust that I will do so."** *[Deuteronomy 32:35]* 20 Your duty is to do just as the Scriptures command, **"If your enemy is hungry, feed him. If he is thirsty, give him water to drink. In this way, you make him ashamed for wronging you."** *[Proverbs 25:21-22]* ❖ *It's possible that the expression in the literal text, "heap burning coals on his head"—in this context of taking revenge—means that God will punish him even more severely on Judgment Day. In the Dead Sea Scrolls, the Essene community viewed non-retaliation as increasing your enemy's ultimate punishment. It could mean both: causing him to feel ashamed and increasing his punishment if he doesn't repent.* ➤ 21 Don't allow the evil others do to you to ruin your relationship with God or make you want to take revenge. Instead, overcome the power of their evil intentions by paying them back with good deeds and words.

13

Respect Government Authority

1 Every believer must submit to governing authorities. For every authority ultimately comes from God, so those people who have power in government were put there by God. ❖ *Realize that Paul is saying this to believers who lived under a dictatorial Roman emperor. God's way for believers never involves rebellion against legitimate authority—even if it is oppressive.* ➤ 2 Therefore, those who disobey the government are disobeying what God has established—and

they will be punished. 3 Those who do what is right should have no cause to fear legitimate authorities for they were established to restrain those who do wrong. If you want to live without fear of them, do what is right and they will commend you. 4 For they are God's servants who are appointed to help you. But if you do wrong, then you ought to be afraid of them for they have the legitimate power to punish people—even with death. They are appointed by God to execute his anger on those who do wrong. 5 Therefore, it's important for you to submit to them, not only to avoid punishment, but also because you know it's the right thing to do.

6 That is why it's also appropriate for you to pay taxes—for government authorities are God's servants, doing the work he gave them to do. 7 So pay everyone what you owe them. Pay every kind of tax you owe and also every debt. Also, show respect to authorities on the basis of the position they hold, and honor those who should be honored.

How to Live in These Last Days Before the Messiah Returns

8 Pay off all your debts, but recognize that you are always indebted to God to love one another. If you always demonstrate love to one another, then you are fulfilling everything the Torah requires. 9 For the commands to not commit adultery, not murder, not steal, not covet, and every other command is contained in this one: Love other people in the same way you love and take care of yourself. *[Exodus 20:13-17; Deuteronomy 5:17-21; Leviticus 19:18; Matthew 19:19; 22:39; Mark 12:31; Luke 10:27; Galatians 5:14]* 10 If you love other people, you will never do wrong to them; therefore, showing love fulfills all the requirements in the Torah.

11 You should be living this way because you recognize that we are living in the last days. The time when the Messiah will return and we will receive the fullness of our salvation is nearer than when we first believed. So be spiritually alert and do the work your Lord has given you to do—12 for the time of evil's dominance in this world is

nearly over. The time of the Messiah's return is almost here. So stop participating in evil deeds of darkness and start living like a soldier whose armor and weapons are the light of God's truth. ❖ *Light is a figurative expression that refers to the illuminating truths contained in the Scriptures and also the expression of God's character in us. We are to be seen by others as displaying God's character in all that we say and do (which corresponds to being enveloped in his armor of light). And we are to use his truth in the Scriptures to defend ourselves and oppose evil. These are the armor and weapons of light used in our spiritual warfare. See Ephesians 6:11-18 for further clarification.* ➤ 13 We should always conduct ourselves decently in ways that we would not be ashamed to be seen doing publicly in broad daylight. Shun drunken carousing and wild parties, sexual promiscuity and unrestrained lust, fights and jealousy, and the like. 14 You are spiritually joined to our Lord Jesus the Messiah, so you must conform yourselves to his character—allowing people to see him in you more than they see you. And don't even allow yourselves to think about doing the things your sinful desires tempt you to do.

14

Accept Believers who Have Differing Opinions and Live in Harmony

1 Welcome people into your fellowship who have scruples about what sorts of things are acceptable or not for a believer to do. ❖ *This likely applied to converts who associated certain activities with their previous sinful lifestyles and were afraid that doing them might be sinful, or might drag them back into their previous lifestyles. This would also apply to Jewish converts who didn't realize the freedom from legalisms that believers have in their spiritual union with Jesus. The issues he addresses in this section are vegetarianism (verses 2 and 21), drinking wine (verse 21) (neither of which has anything to do with Jewish laws or practices since Jews eat meat and drink wine with no problems of conscience),* A *and observing special holy days (verses*

5-6). ➤ Don't argue with them or condemn them for their opinions. 2 Some people think that God allows us to eat anything. But some—whose consciences are weak—are not yet convinced that it's acceptable for them to eat meat. ❖ *Because the one group eats only vegetables, it seems that meat is the issue. But it could as easily be meat offered to idols. The principle is the same.* ➤ 3 Those who eat meat should not look down on those who don't. And vegetarians should not condemn those that do because God accepts people with both convictions. 4 Who gave you the right to criticize God's servants? They are not accountable to you! The Lord will decide if his servants have done right or wrong and he will accept them—regardless of their eating or not eating meat—for he is able to keep them believing in himself. 5 Similarly, some people think certain days are more important than others and some think every day is the same. Each person must be convinced of what they believe about this issue and then live accordingly. 6 Those who follow special observances for certain days do that to honor the Lord. Those who eat meat honor the Lord because they thank him for it. Those who are vegetarians also honor the Lord and thank him for their food. Therefore, any of these customs are acceptable to God. 7 It is clear that none of us believers lives to honor and serve ourselves, nor do we die to honor ourselves. 8 But while we live, we live to bring honor to our Lord; and when we die, we hope to die in such a way as to also bring him honor. So whether in life or death, we belong to him. 9 It was for this very purpose that the Messiah died and was brought back to life—that he would become Lord over those who live and also of those who have died. 10 So why do you criticize and look down on believers who live differently from you? You have no right to do so! We will all stand before God to be judged on

---

A 14:1 I highly recommend that Gentile believers read David Stern's commentary on this passage in his "Jewish New Testament Commentary" (see the Bibliography) which gives a very different interpretation from that expressed by most Gentile commentators, and one that should be seriously considered. However you interpret this section, it should be compatible with Jesus' teaching in Matthew 5:19—which many interpretations are not. Also see the last note at Matthew 5:17.

Judgment Day, and *he* is the one who will decide if we've done right or wrong. 11 As our Lord said in the Scriptures, "As certainly as I live, *[Isaiah 49:18]* every person will kneel before me and recognize that I am Lord, and they will also praise God." *[Isaiah 45:23; Philippians 2:10-11]* 12 Thus we will all have to give an account of our lives to God for everything we've done.

13 So cease criticizing each other! Instead, firmly decide you won't do anything that will cause other believers to doubt or be tempted to sin. 14 I know—from my being joined with the Lord Jesus—that he doesn't consider any food as unclean or unfit to eat. But if other believers think something is unacceptable to God, then to them it *is* unacceptable. It would be wrong for you to tempt them to go against their consciences. 15 If what you eat causes other believers to sin against their consciences, then you are not loving them. Don't be so selfish as to destroy their faith just so you can eat what you want! The Messiah died to save them too! *[1 Corinthians 8:7-13]* 16 Therefore, restrain yourself from doing something that you consider good if it will lead others to sin or cause them to think you are evil. 17 For as far as God's Kingdom is concerned, what you eat and drink is not particularly important. What is important is that you live in a way that pleases God, that you live together in harmony with other believers, and that you are all filled with joy from the Holy Spirit. 18 If you serve the Messiah by living this way, then God will accept you and people will respect you.

19 So then, we should strive to do things that enable us to live together in peace and harmony and that also help strengthen each other's faith. 20 Don't ruin what God has done in the lives of fellow believers over petty disagreements about food. God has said that it's alright to eat any kind of food, but it's wrong to exercise your freedom to do so if it tempts others to sin against their consciences. 21 If it's something that might cause your brother or sister to follow your example and sin by violating their conscience, then it's wrong for you to eat meat or drink wine or do anything else they

think is wrong. 22 Aside from that possibility, whatever you believe about these matters is between you and God and not to be forced on others. God approves of those who do what they believe is right and, as a result, have no reason to feel guilty because they have not violated their conscience. 23 If you do anything that you believe is wrong, then you have sinned. So if your conscience bothers you about eating something but you do so anyway, then you have sinned. Only do what you firmly believe is right and what is pleasing to God.

15

1 We know that these things don't really matter to God, but it's wrong to just do anything we want. We must also think about the doubts of other believers who think these things are wrong. 2 When we are with them, we must do what they think is good and thus help them to strengthen their faith. 3 The Messiah is our model. He lived to please God the Father instead of himself—even when others insulted him. So we should do the same. In the Scriptures, the Messiah said to God, **"When people insulted you, it's like they were also insulting me."** *[Psalm 69:9]* 4 Everything written in the Scriptures was written to teach us *[2 Timothy 3:16-17]* so that in our thinking about what it says, we would be encouraged in our faith and be willing to persevere in our obedience—despite interpersonal difficulties—as we look forward to receiving what God has promised us. 5 And I ask God—who encourages us and helps us to persevere in trusting him—to enable you to live in harmony with each other—following the will ❖ *or: example* ➤ of Messiah Jesus. 6 Then all of you can join together in perfect unity as you praise God— who is the Father of our Lord Jesus the Messiah. ❖ *The last part could mean: praise God—who is both God and Father of our Lord Jesus the Messiah.* ➤

7 Therefore, accept each other despite your faults just as the Messiah accepted you, for your unity will cause people to praise God. 8 Remember that the Messiah became a servant to us Jews to show that God is faithful and that he fulfills the promises he

gave to our ancestors—especially the one that he would send the Messiah. 9 He also came so that Gentiles will praise God because of his granting them his great mercy and enabling favor. This fulfills what King David said to God in the Scriptures, "Therefore, I will praise you while I'm among the Gentiles and I will exalt your name in song." *[2 Samuel 22:50; Psalm 18:49]* 10 In another place it says, "Rejoice, you Gentiles, along with God's people!" *[Deuteronomy 32:43]* 11 And in yet another place it says, "Praise Yahweh, all you Gentiles, and let everyone in this world praise him with enthusiasm." *[Psalm 117:1]* 12 Also, the prophet Isaiah said, "A descendant of Jesse will become king over the Gentiles. They will put their trust in him." *[Isaiah 11:10]* ❖ *Jesse was the father of King David, and Jesus the Messiah was descended from him.* ➤

13 So, I pray that God—who gives us hope—will fill you all with joy and peace through your faith in him. Then the Holy Spirit will strengthen your trust so that your hope and expectation of receiving what God has promised will overflow, giving you great joy.

Paul's Plans to Visit the Believers in Rome

14 My brothers and sisters, I know that you always do good to others, that you know everything God wants you to know, and that you are able to admonish each other about these things. 15 But I've written rather boldly about some issues in order to remind you of their importance. I'm doing this because God—by granting me his undeserved favor—sent me 16 to you Gentiles as a special servant of Messiah Jesus. I serve as a priest who helps people come to God. I do this by preaching his Good News so that Gentiles who believe in the Messiah may become accepted by him, and their lives will be offered to him—having been made holy by the Holy Spirit.

17 Therefore, in my union with Messiah Jesus, I am proud of serving God in this way. 18-19 But I will only talk about what the Messiah has done through me to lead Gentiles to obey God. He accomplished this by empowering my preaching with his Spirit and enabling me to perform miraculous signs and wonders. So I have proclaimed the complete message of the Good News about the Messiah from Jerusalem all the way to Illyricum Province. ❖ *Illyricum Province was in the area of modern-day Yugoslavia and Albania. It's not clear if Paul meant that he had preached in that province or only as far west as the eastern border of that province.* ➤ 20 It has always been my goal to preach the Good News in places where people have not yet heard about the Messiah. I don't want to work where others have already preached and there are already believers. 21 Rather, my mission in life is to fulfill what the Scriptures say about the Messiah, **"Those who never heard about him will perceive the truth and understand his message."** *[Isaiah 52:15]* 22 Therefore, I have many times been prevented from visiting you because you were already believers and I was busy preaching to those who hadn't yet heard.

23 But now I plan to visit you because I've longed to do so for many years and there is nowhere else in this region where the Good News has not yet been preached. 24 I'm planning to go to Spain and hope to visit you on my way there. We can fellowship together for a time, and I hope you will then help support me as I start on my new mission. 25 But first, I'm going to Jerusalem to deliver a financial gift to God's people there. 26 For it pleased the mostly Gentile assemblies in Macedonia and Achaia Provinces to raise money to help the poor among God's people in Jerusalem—who are mostly Jews—to demonstrate their ties of fellowship with them. *[2 Corinthians chapters 8—9]* 27 They were very happy to do this, as they should be since they are indebted to them spiritually. This is because the Jewish believers have shared with pagan Gentiles the many spiritual blessings that God gives those who believe in the Messiah. Thus Gentiles have an obligation to reciprocate by sharing their material wealth with Jews who have none. 28 Therefore, when I've safely handed over to them all the money that was raised and have finished this task, I will leave for Spain and stop on the way to visit with you. 29 I know that when I arrive in Rome, the

Messiah will bless us both in many ways. ❖ *Or: will enable me to bless you in many ways.* ➤

30 My brothers and sisters, I urge you to pray for me because we are spiritually joined together with our Lord Jesus the Messiah and because the Holy Spirit moves us to love each other. Join me in praying fervently that 31 God will protect me from the animosity of unbelieving Jews in Judea. Also pray that God's people in Jerusalem will accept the gift I bring them. 32 Then, if it's God's will, I will be able to come to you filled with joy and be spiritually refreshed and encouraged by your fellowship. 33 I pray that God—the source of all well-being—will be with all of you and bless you. Yes, may it be so!

16

Paul Greets Those he Knows in Rome

1 With this letter, I introduce you to our sister in the Lord, Phoebe, who brought this letter to you from me. She holds the position of deacon among God's people in Cenchrae city. ❖ *Cenchrae was the seaport for Corinth on the eastern side of the isthmus. The Greek word διάκονος (diakonos), translated "deacon," is masculine, not feminine (but this is an artifact of grammar and does not necessarily conform to the gender of the person described). The term "deaconess" did not come into use until much later. The word "deacon" can mean "servant," "helper," or "minister," and commentators debate what her role was. But many believe Paul would not have used this term unless she held some recognized office. She probably would not have been able to do so if she were among Jews, but it's possible that in Greek culture a woman could have held an official position for ministry among women.* ➤ 2 I'm asking that you warmly welcome her as a servant of the Lord in a manner worthy of God's people. And I want you to help her in every way that you are able because she has also helped many— including me. 3 Warmly greet Prisca and her husband Aquila for me, for they are my coworkers in serving Messiah Jesus. ❖ *Prisca is the diminutive form of Priscilla and may express familiarity and affection. Husbands would normally be mentioned first, but four out of six times that she's mentioned in the New Testament her, name comes first. [Acts 18:1-3; 18-19, 26; 1 Corinthians 16:19; 2 Timothy 4:19] Commentators*

speculate that she may have had higher social status or higher status as a leader among the believers. ➤ 4 They have risked their lives to save my own and I owe them a debt of thanks—as do all the Gentile assemblies. 5 Also greet for me all the members of the assembly that meet in their house. And convey my warm greetings to my dear friend Epaenetus—who was the first in Asia Province to believe in the Messiah. 6 Greet Mary for me—who has worked very hard for the Messiah in order to help you. 7 Also greet Andronicus and his wife Junia for me. They are fellow Jewish believers and were in prison with me before. They are respected apostles and also believed in the Messiah before I did.

❖ *Commentators debate whether they were "respected apostles" or "respected by the apostles," but the grammar of the Greek naturally means the former. St. John Chrysostom— who became Bishop of Constantinople in AD 398—clearly refers to Junia as a woman and as an apostle. He wrote: "Oh! How great is the devotion of this woman that she should be even counted worthy of the appellation of apostle!" Even so, modern commentators still debate it. But the name is definitely a female name and the tradition of the early church bears witness to the fact that Junia was a female apostle. It's only the assumption that a woman could not be an apostle that has led exegetes to find other ways to interpret it. Several commentators say Junia is a diminutive of the male name Junianus (or Junias), but this male name has never been found in Greek literature whereas the female name Junia is found over 250 times. Certainly these were not apostles in the same class as the twelve and Paul. But this is evidence that there were other apostles, leading to the conclusion that there could be apostles today. [Acts 14:4; 1 Corinthians 12:28-29; Ephesians 4:11] This is also an important fact to consider when teaching on the valid roles of women among believers. See the note on 1 Corinthians 14:34-35.* ➤ 8 Warmly greet my dear friend Ampliatus whom I love because of his service to the Lord. ❖ *Ampliatus and Urbanus (next verse) were common slave names.* ➤ 9 Greet Urbanus, our coworker for the Messiah, and my dear friend Stachys. 10 Greet Apelles for me. God has tested him in difficult circumstances and he has clearly shown the strength of his faith. Greet the believers who live in Aristobulus' house. 11 Greet Herodion, my fellow Jew. Greet those believers who live in Narcissus' house. 12 Greet Tryphaena ❖ *which means "delicate"* ➤ and her sister Tryphosa

❖ *which means "dainty"* ➤ for me. Those women work hard for the Lord. Also greet my dear sister in the Lord, Persis, who has also worked hard for the Lord. 13 Greet Rufus— an outstanding believer—for me, and also his mother who has been like a mother to me. ❖ *Rufus ("red") was also a common slave name. He may be the same Rufus mentioned in Mark 15:21.* ➤ 14 And greet Asyncritus, Phlegon, Hermes, Patrobas, Hermas, and the other believers who meet with them. ❖ *It's likely that these men were all part of one household, possibly some were slaves.* ➤ 15 Also greet Philologus and Julia, Nereus and his sister, and Olympas, and all of God's people who meet with them. ❖ *Julia was one of the most common female slave names. These are likely members of one assembly.* ➤ 16 When you gather together, greet each other warmly as fellow family members would. ❖ *In that culture, this was with a kiss on the cheek.* ➤ All the people in the assemblies of the Messiah send you their greetings too. ❖ *These greetings may have been from the delegates who were with him from all the churches that contributed to the financial gift he was carrying to Jerusalem.* ➤

Paul's Closing Exhortation

17 My brothers and sisters, I urge you to beware of those who create divisions among you and ruin people's faith by teaching doctrines that contradict what you learned about the Good News. Have nothing to do with such people. 18 For they are not serving the Messiah, our Lord, but are following their own sinful desires. They flatter people and have a way with words, but they deceive those who are not watching out for false teaching. 19 Your reputation for your obedience to the Lord has traveled widely, so knowing about you fills me with joy. But I want you to clearly understand what is good and remain innocent of doing evil, and be wary of those who would lead you astray. 20 God— the source of all peace and well-being— will soon destroy Satan's power and make you triumphant over him, enabling you to resist people who try to cause divisions among you. I pray that our Lord Jesus the Messiah will look upon you with great favor far beyond anything you can deserve, and bless you.

21 Timothy—who works with me—also sends his greetings to you. And so do Lucius, Jason, and Sosipater, my fellow Jews. ❖ *Lucius may be the same Lucius mentioned in Acts 13:1. Jason may have been Paul's host in Thessalonica. [Acts 17:5-9] And Sosipater may be the Sopater in Acts 20:4. Sopater is a shortened form, and Luke often used such shorter forms.* ➤ 22 I, Tertius—who am writing down Paul's words in this letter—also greet you as a brother in the Lord. 23 Gaius—my host here—and the whole assembly who meets here in his house send you their greetings. Erastus—the city treasurer here—sends his greetings and so does Quartus, our brother in the Messiah. ❖ *Paul was probably writing this letter from Corinth. Gaius is probably the same Gaius mentioned in 1 Corinthians 1:14.* ➤

24 {I pray that our Lord Jesus will continue to grant you undeserved favor and bless you. Yes, may it be so!} **A**

Paul's Closing Prayer of Praise
❖ *Commonly called a "doxology"* ➤

25 We should praise God—who is able to strengthen your faith by my preaching the Good News about Jesus the Messiah. He does this by my revealing the mystery— hidden from the beginning of the world— which is God's plan to save everyone who trusts in the Messiah, including Gentiles. *[Ephesians 1:9-10; 3:2-9; 6:19; Colossians 1:25-27; 2:2-3]* ❖ *Some commentators believe the mystery is the message of the Good News itself.* ➤ 26 But now this mystery has been clearly revealed to Gentiles everywhere—just like the prophets foretold in the Scriptures and as God commanded—so that people from every people group in the world will believe and follow the Messiah. 27 We—who are joined to Jesus the Messiah—must praise the only true God, who alone is wise. We will praise him forever! Yes, may it be so!

A 16:24 This verse is left out of most modern translations, because it is a repeat of what's in verse 20 and is found in only a few Greek manuscripts, though it is included in the King James version.

Paul's First Letter
to Jesus' Followers in Corinth

Paul wrote this letter from Ephesus during his third missionary journey—around AD 54–55. Three men—Stephanas, Fortunatus, and Achaicus—had carried a letter to him in Ephesus from the believers in Corinth and he wrote this letter in reply.

Corinth was a major city and commercial center with about 600,000 inhabitants—about a third of whom were slaves. It was the capital of the Roman Province of Achaia and culturally very diverse. It's inhabitants were widely known for their drunkenness and sexual immorality.

Paul founded the assembly of believers there, as recorded in Acts 18:1-8, during his second missionary journey—about three years prior to his writing this letter. The community of believers in Corinth was mostly Gentile from the lower economic classes, although there were a few who were wealthy. Raised in a pagan society, they retained much of their pagan worldview when they became believers. They were divided over various social issues and were exhibiting immature and immoral behavior. Yet because of the spiritual manifestations that were common during their worship services and their ability to "speak in tongues," they proudly thought that they had "arrived" at the peak of spiritual knowledge and maturity.

There is evidence that Paul had written a letter to them prior to this one—dealing with various problems—probably some of the same ones addressed in this letter. [5:9] It seems likely that the letter they sent to Paul via Stephanas, Fortunatus, and Achaicus was a response to Paul's first letter. If this is the case, it appears that many of the Corinthian believers rejected Paul's directions in his first letter and were leading others to question his authority. Before this letter arrived, Paul had also received some verbal reports about the situation there. [1:11]

Apparently, a majority of the Corinthians were interpreting their new faith in terms of a pagan Greek worldview which valued certain kinds of "wisdom." From their viewpoint, Paul's teaching lacked eloquence and his manner of supporting himself with manual labor didn't conform to what they expected of someone with "wisdom and true spiritual authority." They also considered the content of Paul's teaching and the basic gospel message as something inferior—fit for the immature—but thought that they had moved on to greater heights of revelation, wisdom, and knowledge. When they compared his lack of eloquence with Apollos' polished speaking style, they found him lacking in the qualities that they admired or expected in a moral teacher. Their Hellenistic worldview also led them to regard the physical world as unimportant—which resulted in the attitude that behavior involving the body (such as sexual immorality) wasn't all that important. It also led to erroneous views of sex, marriage, and the resurrection.

In This Letter, Paul Asserts His Apostolic Authority over Them and Argues That:

Their ideas about wisdom and knowledge are wrong.
Their pride is sinful and something that God opposes.
Their divisiveness is a clear sign of their spiritual immaturity.
Their attitude toward leadership is off base.
Their tolerance of immorality is shameful.
They were flirting with idolatry.
Their ideas about what constitutes true spirituality are totally wrong.
In fact, they are not the spiritually mature people they think they are.
And their view of the resurrection is absurd—among other issues.

The majority (but not all) of the exegetical insights and viewpoints expressed in the interpretation of this letter and its accompanying commentary are derived from Gordon D. Fee's commentary. In giving him the credit he deserves, I only hope any errors of my own will not reflect negatively on his work.

1

Opening Greetings

[1] Greetings from Paul—who was called by God to be an apostle of Messiah Jesus. Also, greetings from Sosthenes. ❖ *Sosthenes may have been a leader of the assembly of believers in Ephesus who was known to the Corinthian believers. [Acts 18:17]* ➤ [2] I'm writing to all of you in the community of God's people at Corinth, whom he set apart to serve him through your spiritual union with Jesus, and whom he called to be his holy ones—just as he did with all others everywhere who also worship our Lord Jesus the Messiah. [3] I pray that God our Father and our Lord Jesus will look upon you with great favor far beyond anything you can deserve—and therefore, grant you every spiritual blessing, peace, and well-being.

[4] I often thank God for you and for his showering you with spiritual abilities because of his great favor toward you as a result of your relationship with Messiah Jesus. [5] For through that relationship, he has equipped you in every area of ministry with various kinds of spiritual abilities related to speaking and knowledge. [6] These abilities demonstrate that what I preached to you about him and what he would do for you is true. [7] As a community, he has supplied you with every grace-enabled ability needed to accomplish his work while you wait with anticipation for his return. [8] And he will help you to remain strong in faith and obedience until he returns or until the end of your lives. So when he does return to judge all people, he will declare you "forgiven" and "righteous in his sight"—and therefore, "not guilty" of sin and rebellion. [9] God will accomplish this in you since he is faithful to fulfill his promises. After all, he was the one who called you to enter into the intimate relationship you have with his Son—our Lord Jesus the Messiah.

Don't Cause Divisions Among God's People

[10] My brothers and sisters in the Lord, as a representative of our Lord the Messiah, I urge you stop arguing with each other and come to a true consensus so there will no longer be anything that divides you. You should be bound together in loving unity—having one mind and one purpose. [11] I know about your quarreling since some brothers from Chloe's household came and told me about it. [12] I'm referring to the situation where some of you claim to be followers of the teachings of Paul, and others of Apollos, or Peter, or the Messiah—as if our teachings were not the same. [13] You are all spiritually joined to the Messiah! Do you think he is divided into factions? Why do some of you claim to follow me? Did I die on a cross to save you? Were you baptized in my name so as to be joined to me? What are you thinking! [14] This makes me thankful that I didn't baptize any of you myself—except Crispus and Gaius—[15] so no one can say I baptized you in my name and made you my followers! [16] (Oh, I do remember also baptizing Stephanas and the people of his household. I don't remember if I baptized anyone else. But if I did, it wasn't many.) [17] For the Messiah mainly commissioned and sent me to proclaim the Good News about how to be saved—not to baptize. When I proclaim his message, I don't depend on a dynamic style of speaking or logical arguments to convince people it's true because I don't want to win them over on a merely intellectual basis. It's the simple message about the Messiah's death on a cross that has the real power to change people's lives. I don't want to get in the way of its working in people's hearts.

God's "Foolishness" Is Greater than Human "Wisdom"

[18] The message about the cross may seem to be foolish nonsense to those who are on the road to Hell. But to those of us who are on the road to Heaven, it's the means through which God's power was channeled to save us. [19] This agrees with what God said in the Scriptures, "I will show those who think they are wise and intelligent that they really know nothing. I will violate their brilliant theories and thwart their plans." *[Isaiah 29:14]* [20] Since we now know what God has done through the Messiah's death on the cross, all the reasoning of philosophers, all

the knowledge of experts on God's Torah, and all the arguments of the skilled rhetoricians of this age prior to the Messiah's return—are seen to have been futile. Their attempts to know about God and his way of salvation through human wisdom and knowledge were vain. God has clearly demonstrated that human wisdom put forth by those who don't know him is foolish nonsense. ❖ *This is not generally apparent to unbelievers yet, but will become clear on the Last Day.* ➤

21 For in his divine wisdom, he made it impossible for people to come to know him or his ways through human reasoning and wisdom. Instead, he decided to save those who believe in the message we apostles preach about the Messiah—which many regard as foolish. 22 Jews typically regard it as nonsense and demand confirming miraculous signs to prove that the message is true before they will accept it. And Gentiles typically reject it because they only believe ideas that go along with their own brand of philosophical wisdom. 23 But we don't cater to their desires. Instead, we preach that the Messiah was crucified to save people. Jews find the idea of a dying Messiah offensive, and Gentiles think the resurrection [Acts 17:32] and the idea of a crucified Savior are nonsense. ❖ *A person who was crucified was under God's curse. [Deuteronomy 21:23] In Jewish thought, the idea of the Messiah undergoing a cursed death was absurd and offensive. They knew that the Messiah would live forever. For Gentiles, a God who was crucified was weak, defeated, and humiliated. Criminals and slaves were crucified. These ideas in the Good News about Jesus seemed crazy to them.* ➤ 24 But to the contrary, the crucified Messiah is actually a display of God's great wisdom and saving power—and this is clear to those he has called to be his people, whether they are Jewish or Gentile. 25 For the message of the cross—which appears to many to be God's foolishness—is in reality far wiser than any human wisdom. And what seems to be God's weakness in allowing his Son to die is, in fact, a display of saving power far greater than any humanity possesses.

26 My brothers and sisters in the Lord, consider the fact that before you were saved, when God first called you to become his own, very few of you were considered wise by human standards, nor did many of you have any real influence or social status. ❖ *Most of the first believers in Corinth were uneducated and poor, or slaves.* ➤ 27 But God chose many who are uneducated—whom the proud and educated despise as fools—to show that human wisdom gives no help or advantage for having a relationship with him. And he chose many who are "nobodies" in this world to show that human power and status also offer people no advantage in his estimation. 28 Yes, he chose many from the despised lower classes who have no status—the worthless "nobodies" of this world who are sometimes considered subhuman. He chose such to be his own to demonstrate that the world's values are worthless in his sight. 29 He did this so no one can boast before God that they are better than anyone else or that they have in some way merited his favor. 30 It is only because of God's plan and initiative that you are joined to Messiah Jesus—it has nothing to do with what you've done or who you are. In God's wisdom, he planned that Jesus would save us—making it possible for us to become righteous in his sight. ❖ *i.e., justified* ➤ He did this by freeing us from the power of sin so we can become his holy people ❖ *i.e., sanctified* ➤ and by ushering us into his eternal Kingdom in Heaven to receive our promised inheritance. ❖ *i.e., our final redemption. There are other possible interpretations of "redemption" (in the literal text), but the order suggests a past work (justification), a current work (sanctification) and a future work (final redemption).* ➤ 31 Therefore, our response should be the one commanded in the Scriptures, "Whoever wants to boast should only do so about what Yahweh has done for them." [Jeremiah 9:24]

2

1 As an example of this, when I came to Corinth to preach God's message, I didn't try to make my preaching eloquent or present myself as an intellectual possessing superior wisdom. 2 I decided that while I was with you, I would only speak plainly about Jesus the Messiah and the fact that he died on a cross to save you. 3 While I was with you, my

health was weak and I was afraid. ❖ *Many commentators believe his weakness was a sense of inadequacy to the task set before him, and that he was afraid he would fail in the responsibility the Lord gave him in Corinth. But Acts 18:9-11 suggests he was afraid of being physically attacked.* ➤ **4** My message was simple and my style of preaching was plain—unadorned with eloquent oratory or impressive-sounding argumentation. Instead, my message was accompanied by demonstrations of the Holy Spirit's power. ❖ *This refers to conversions, spiritual gifts received by believers, healings, deliverance from demons, and other miraculous signs and wonders. [2 Corinthians 12:12; Romans 15:18-19; Mark 16:17-18]* ➤ **5** I didn't want your faith to be based on your estimate of my wisdom or my speaking ability, but only on your witnessing the reality of God's power—which was his confirmation that what I said was true.

God's Secret Wisdom

6 Yet among spiritually mature believers, I do teach a kind of wisdom. But it is not human wisdom invented during this age before the Messiah's return, nor is it wisdom that comes from rulers and leaders whose power will evaporate at the end of this age. **7** Instead, it is God's wisdom, which is a plan he made for our benefit before he created this world, but which he never revealed to anyone until the Messiah came. In his plan, he determined to spiritually join us to the Messiah so we will later share in his glory. *[Ephesians 1:9-14; 3:3-6; Colossians 1:26-27]* **8** None of the rulers of this world were aware of this wisdom. If they had known about it, they wouldn't have crucified the Lord of all glory. **9** This is just as it's written, "All the wonderful things that God has prepared for those who love him *[Sirach 1:8 a non-Scriptural apocryphal book]* are things that no human eye has seen, nor ear has heard, *[Isaiah 64:4]* and no mind **A** has ever imagined." *[Isaiah 65:17 in the Septuagint]* ❖ *This composite quote may have been a fixed form from an unknown Jewish apocalyptic source since it appears in "The Ascension of Isaiah"—an apocryphal book. The phrase "as it's written" indicates that Paul considers the quote to be inspired Scripture.* ➤ **10** But God sent the Holy Spirit to reveal this secret plan to his apostles. For the Spirit knows all things—even God's most secret thoughts. **11** Even in the case of people, no one knows a person's thoughts except that person's own spirit. In a similar way, no one can know God's thoughts except the Holy Spirit. ❖ *Despite the analogy, the relationship between the Holy Spirit and God, and the relationship between the human spirit and a person, are not identical. However, this verse does imply that neither demons nor so-called psychics can actually know another person's thoughts.* ➤ **B** **12** But we apostles and

---

A 2:9 This is literally "heart," but in the Hebrew Scriptures the "heart" was the center of thought and corresponds more to what we think of as the "mind" than to emotions.

B 2:11 Verse 2:11 may support idea of the tripartite nature of man, i.e., that a person has a body, a soul, and a spirit. The word "spirit"—in both Hebrew and Greek—has a broad range of meaning. It can literally mean "breath," "wind," or "spirit." It can mean "spirit" as opposed to "physical," as a type of substance. It can mean a "spiritual being" like an angel or a demon. It can mean the Holy Spirit. Its specific intended meaning is often clear from context. It can also refer to a person's mind or emotions. It can be used abstractly in the sense of "disposition" or "attitude"—as in the English expressions "a spirit of levity" and "a spirit of seriousness." And many people believe that it can refer to a human spirit which is part of the human makeup and is distinct from a person's soul (i.e., mind, emotions and will). Unfortunately, in many places the precise meaning intended is not clear. But the following references—especially those underlined—may refer to a human spirit that is part of a person, yet distinct from the soul (You will need to look in a very literal translation to see the word "spirit" in some of these references since many translators have interpreted it to mean something else.): [Ecclesiastes 12:7; Isaiah 26:9; Ezekiel 11:19; 13:3; 36:26; Malachi 2:16; Matthew 26:41; 27:50; Mark 2:8; 8:12; 14:38; Luke 1:46-47; 8:55; 23:46; John 19:30; Acts 17:16; Romans 1:9; 8:10, 16; 1 Corinthians 5:5; 6:17; 7:34; 14:2, 14-15; 2 Corinthians 2:13; Galatians 6:18; Philippians 4:23; 1 Thessalonians 5:23; 2 Timothy 4:22; Philemon 1:25; Hebrews 4:12; James 2:26] Many of these are ambiguous—and many more such references could have been included—but 1 Thessalonians 5:23 explicitly refers to the human spirit, soul, and body as three distinct things, and Hebrews 4:12 distinguishes soul and spirit. If these verses are accepted as clear and definitive, then they will affect one's interpretation of the more ambiguous verses listed. ¶ The other view is that man is bipartite, having a body and a soul—and that the word "spirit" is essentially equivalent to "soul" or else variously refers to a person's mind, or heart (seat of emotions). Many Christians today hold to the tripartite view. Traditionally and historically, most Christians have

other mature believers do know about the gifts that God has freely given to all of us, because we have received the Spirit he sent who reveals them to us. Thus our understanding is different from those who don't love God. 13 When we tell others about these wonderful things, we use words that the Spirit tells us to use—not depending at all on human wisdom or knowledge. So we explain these spiritual truths with spiritual words given by the Spirit of God himself. A 14 But unbelievers reject spiritual truths that come from God's Spirit since they think such revelations are nonsense. They can't properly understand such truths because their value can only be discerned with the enlightenment that comes to a believer from the indwelling Spirit. 15 Since believers have the Spirit, they are able to discern the true value of all these truths concerning God's secret plan. But unbelievers—lacking the Spirit—are not able to understand the faith of those who believe, nor can they properly judge them concerning spiritual matters. ❖ A literal rendering of this verse—as in some translations—taken out of context, yields a very different and erroneous meaning. It's meaning should be interpreted within the context of Paul's argument. ➤

16 This agrees with what is written, "No one knows Yahweh's thoughts. No one is fit to give him advice." [Isaiah 40:13] ❖ If, therefore, an unbeliever doesn't know God's thinking, he is unable to correctly judge those who believe with regard to spiritual matters. ➤ But we who have the Spirit can understand these things because he guides us to think the Messiah's thoughts. ❖ In this verse, Paul clearly identifies the Messiah with Yahweh. ➤

3

Division Is a Sign of Immaturity

1 My brothers and sisters in the Lord, when I was staying with you, I couldn't speak to you as if you were spiritually mature. I had to talk to you as I would to unbelievers or to spiritual infants newly joined to the Messiah. 2 Just as young infants are only able to feed on milk and aren't able to take in solid food, in a similar way I had to feed you with only the simplest spiritual truths because you weren't ready to hear the more difficult things which mature believers can understand. Even now, you are not ready for them 3 because you are still following your sinful desires instead of submitting to the Spirit's leading. It's obvious that you are still living like those who don't know the Lord since jealousy, envy, resentment, and quarreling are present among you. 4 When some of you arrogantly say, "I follow Paul," and others say, "I follow Apollos," you are behaving like unbelievers.

5 Who do you think Apollos and I are, anyway, that we are worth dividing the assembly of believers over? We are only God's servants who helped lead you to faith. Each of us only did the task that the Lord gave him to do. 6 I planted the word of God in your hearts and Apollos watered it with his teaching, but it was God who caused it to grow—not us. 7 It doesn't really matter who plants or who waters. It is God who matters since only he can produce spiritual growth in your lives. 8 Both the planter and the waterer have the same goal. They aren't competing with each other. And God will reward each of them according to the way they did the work he gave them to do.

9 Apollos and I are just servants doing the work that God gives us. You belong to God—not us. You are like his "field" in which he wants to grow good things.

Moving to a different comparison, all of you together are also like a building that he is constructing for himself. 10 Using the gift of apostleship that God gave me, I started God's "building" in Corinth ❖ i.e., he started the assembly of believers there ➤ as a master builder would do—by laying a proper foundation. Since then, others have come and built on that foundation by their teaching and ministry. But they should take care to build wisely

---

held to the bipartite view. The choice of view can have practical and theological implications.

A 2:13 The meaning of the last sentence is ambiguous in Greek. This interpretation is used by some translations, but it could alternatively and validly be translated, "We are explaining spiritual truths to spiritual people," as in other translations. It could also be validly translated, "We are comparing spiritual things with spiritual (words)," as in the KJV.

and build only on that foundation. [11] For God has set "salvation through Messiah Jesus alone" as the foundation for his building, so let no one dare try to replace it with something else. [12] Each builder ❖ *i.e., believer who works for the Lord—meaning every believer* ➤ chooses the materials he will build with. Some do God's work while allowing the Messiah to live and work through them *[Galatians 2:20]*—which is like choosing to build with valuable materials that won't burn, such as gold, silver, and precious stones. Others do God's work while depending on their own strength and ability—which is like building with worthless materials that won't last, such as wood, hay, and straw. [13] On Judgment Day—when the Messiah returns as judge—he will reveal the quality of each builder's work through the "fire" of his judgment. This fire will test the durability of every work. [14] If what a builder built on the foundation survives the judgment fire, he will receive an eternal reward for his work. [15] But if the judgment fire destroys what was built on the foundation, that builder will receive no special reward. He will still be saved, but just like a person who barely escapes from a burning building loses all his possessions, he will have lost any further reward. ❖ *Our status and treasure in Heaven will depend on our faithfulness in allowing the Messiah to live and work through us in this life.* ➤

[16] Don't you realize that all of you together are the inner sanctuary of God's Temple where he lives? Don't you know his Spirit lives in and among you? ❖ *Together, all true believers constitute the restored Temple of Ezekiel's vision (Ezekiel chapters 40—48). See especially Ezekiel 43:9-12 and 47:1-12.* ➤ Don't you realize that divisions among you destroy God's Temple? [17] Be warned that anyone who fosters divisions or teaches lies—and thereby destroys God's Temple—will in turn be destroyed by him, for all of you jointly are his Temple and are holy to him!

[18] Don't deceive yourselves by thinking you are wiser than others! You think you are wise by human standards, but you would be much better off to be seen as foolish in the eyes of worldly people so you can gain God's wisdom. [19] For God considers this sinful world's wisdom to be worthless. As the Scriptures say, **"God uses the wise man's own cleverness to make him fail."** *[Job 5:13]* [20] And in another place, **"Yahweh knows that the thoughts of the wise are worthless."** *[Psalm 94:11]* [21] So then, don't boast about being wiser than others just because you follow a particular human leader. For it's God who has made every spiritual blessing available to you by joining you to the Messiah—and he causes everyone and everything that comes into your life to be a blessing to you. [22] He has given you Apollos, Peter, and me as your teachers. He has made everything in this world for your benefit. If you live or die, it will be for your best eternal good. And whatever happens now or in the future, God will use it for your ultimate benefit. All things are yours and for your benefit. *[2 Corinthians 4:15]* [23] But never forget that you belong to the Messiah. He alone is your leader. And he belongs to God.

4

The Right Attitude Toward Spiritual Leaders

[1] Given what I just said, you should consider me and other spiritual leaders as merely servants of the Messiah who have been given the responsibility of explaining God's secret plan concerning his way of salvation. [2] Now, a master expects a servant who has been given such a responsibility to faithfully carry out his duty. [3] Some of you haven't been very impressed with my teaching. But I'm not at all concerned if you or anyone else criticizes my performance. Actually, I don't even consider myself competent to judge my own performance. [4] I'm not conscious of being deficient in any way in fulfilling my responsibility. But just because my conscience is clear, doesn't mean my work has been satisfactory. Only the Lord can validly judge my performance because he is the one I serve. [5] So it's not your place to be criticizing the Lord's servants—nor is it the proper time. The judgment will take place when the Lord returns. He will expose all the inner motives and thoughts that we've kept hidden—both yours and

mine—and he will praise or criticize each of us according to his standards.

6 Now I've been using Apollos and myself as examples to help you learn how you should think about teachers of the faith, so that you properly understand how the saying, "Don't be more demanding than the Scriptures require," applies to this situation. To avoid falling into the prideful trap of siding with one particular teacher and considering him superior to others, you must not apply non-Scriptural standards in judging them. 7 Who do you think you are? Who made you superior to other believers? What abilities do you have that you didn't receive as undeserved gifts from God? And if every ability you have was a gift, why do you boast as if you acquired them by your own effort or merit?

8 Do you think you have "arrived"—that you are so spiritually mature and rich in grace-enabled abilities that you have no need of anything more? Have you become so spiritually self-sufficient and exalted that you think you no longer need apostolic leadership? How I wish that your inflated self-image was accurate! If it were, we would be able to enjoy exalted status with you. 9 As it is, God allows people to treat his apostles as though we were condemned prisoners. We are a public spectacle and objects of scorn. Our lack of respect is seen by everyone—even angels. And because you view us through worldly eyes, you are embarrassed by us. 10 As far as you and the world are concerned, we seem foolish for preaching about a crucified Messiah—and we seem to lack power and authority in our service to him. But you consider yourselves wise in your faith and think that you are spiritually strong. While you accept honor from others, you still think it's acceptable for us to be belittled. 11 Unlike you, we often lack enough food, drink, and adequate clothing—even right now. We are often treated harshly and have no place we can call home. 12 We work hard to earn our own food. ❖ *The Corinthians thought this was beneath a true leader and was another reason they didn't respect him. But Paul wanted to identify with the common man and not be indebted to the wealthy.* ➤ When people speak rudely to us, we bless them in return. When they persecute us, we patiently endure it. 13 When people impugn our reputations, we respond with kind words. Even now, we are considered by most to be worthless outcasts.

14 My purpose in writing this way isn't to shame you, but to lovingly correct you as my spiritual children. 15 I can treat you this way for no matter how many other spiritual leaders you have, I am your spiritual father. I was the one who led you into your relationship with Messiah Jesus by being the first one to present you with the message of salvation. 16 So I plead with you to follow Jesus the same way I do. 17 To help you do this, I'm sending you Timothy. He's my spiritual son whom I love dearly, and I can depend on him to be faithful to the Lord. He will remind you of the things I've taught and how I live my life in union with the Messiah—the very things I teach in every assembly of believers that I visit.

18 Some of you have become arrogant as if you thought I was afraid to visit you again. 19 But if the Lord allows, I intend to visit you soon. Then I will see for myself if these arrogant bigmouths really display God's power in their lives—or if they're just talk. 20 For being in God's Kingdom isn't a matter of what you say, but a matter of living by God's power which changes your life and enables you to do his work. 21 Your attitudes will determine how I will deal with you when I come. Will I need to use my authority to rebuke and punish you? Or will you repent so I can minister to you in gentleness and love?

5

Discipline in the Assembly of Believers

1 I'm astonished to hear that you accept a believer in your fellowship who engages in a form of sexual immorality that even unbelievers abhor! I hear he is sleeping with his stepmother! *[Leviticus 20:11]* 2 And in spite of this, you are still arrogant about your spiritual maturity! You should be so ashamed and grieved over discovering this gross sin among you that you will have nothing to do with him until he repents

! 3 Even though I'm not with you physically, we are all joined to the Holy Spirit—and on a spiritual level, I am with you. So I'm exercising my apostolic authority as if I were actually there and I've decided that you must punish this man. 4 When you are assembled together and I am with you in spirit, by the authority and power our Lord Jesus gave us, 5 you are to have nothing to do with him and are to remove God's protection from his life—handing him over to Satan's power. Perhaps through experiencing physical affliction without the support of fellowship with other believers he will repent and be saved from spiritual death on Judgment Day.

6 Your boasting about your spiritual maturity while such sin is among you is disgraceful! Don't you know that the defiling influence of sin will spread among you if it's tolerated—just like a little yeast affects all of the dough? 7 Among the Jews, yeast is symbolic of impurity. So before the Passover Festival, they remove every trace of it from their homes. You should do this in reality by removing this sinner from your fellowship so your fellowship can be "pure"—without the defiling influence of sin among you. It is fitting to do this since the Messiah—who was sacrificed as our "Passover Lamb" to save us—has made you pure. ❖ *The first Passover [Exodus chapter 12] is rich in symbolism and was a Hebrew Scriptural "type" foreshadowing the Messiah's sacrificial death on our behalf. In light of this Passover "type"— where a lamb was sacrificed and its blood saved God's people from death—Jesus is often referred to as "the Passover Lamb" and "the Lamb of God."* ➤ 8 So let's properly celebrate our Messiah's "Passover"— through which he freed us from sin—by always living as God's holy people. Just like the Jews rid their houses of yeast in preparation for this celebration, we should rid our lives of all remnants of our former way of living—every malicious and evil intent. The unleavened bread of Passover symbolizes the pure lives that we should lead in genuine submission to the Messiah's will—not allowing those who live in blatant sin to influence and defile us by tolerating their presence in our fellowship. ❖ *Paul would have the same harsh words for many assemblies today, who—in the name of*

"love"—accept people as part of their fellowship that live unrepentantly in blatant sin. ➤

9 In a previous letter, I told you to avoid close association or fellowship with people who clearly indulge in sexual sin. 10 But I wasn't referring to unbelievers—whose lifestyles include sexual immorality, greed, swindling, and worshipping false gods. You can't avoid all such people in this life. 11 I meant that you shouldn't have anything to do with people who claim that they follow Jesus, yet continue to indulge in blatant sin such as sexual immorality of any kind, or greed, worshipping false gods, insulting and slandering others, getting drunk, or cheating people, and other such things which God has forbidden in his Torah. Don't let them think that you tolerate such behavior in a professing believer— even by sharing a meal with them. 12 God hasn't given us the right to judge or condemn unbelievers for such sins. But he certainly does expect us to judge and discipline those who claim to be believers— for the Messiah's reputation is at stake. 13 God will take care of judging those who don't claim to be believers. But God's Torah commands us to, **"Remove the person who practices evil from among your fellowship."** *[Deuteronomy 17:7]* ❖ *This does not mean the use of physical force.* ➤

6

Disputes Among Believers Are to Be Settled by Believers

1 If any of you has a dispute with another believer, don't even think of taking the matter to a secular court where it will be aired before unbelievers and judged by ungodly standards. The problem should be handled by God's people. 2 Don't you remember that when the Messiah returns, we believers will judge the rest of the world? Since that is our future, shouldn't you be able to settle these relatively unimportant cases between believers now? 3 Don't you remember that we will even judge angels? ❖ *This probably refers to when we will reign and rule with the Messiah in Heaven, or possibly in the Millennial Kingdom. [Psalm 149:9; Revelation 20:6]* ➤ So you should

certainly be competent to judge the everyday problems in your lives. 4 If there are such disputes, even the least regarded among you should be capable of settling them properly. ❖ *An equally possible interpretation of this verse is: If you have such disputes, why do you go to unbelievers—whose standards you despise—to settle them?* ➤ 5 You should be ashamed! I find it hard to believe you can't find anyone among you who has the wisdom to settle such things! 6 You actually have fellow believers suing each other. And to make matters worse, they make their accusations in front of unbelievers!

7 The very fact that you have lawsuits against fellow believers tarnishes the reputation of Jesus' followers and demonstrates that you have failed to live the way God wants you to live. Isn't it clear that it's better for your relationship with Jesus, for the reputation of all believers, and for the eventual restoration of the offender to not insist on legal retribution when someone wrongs or cheats you? *[Romans 12:17; 1 Thessalonians 5:15; 1 Peter 2:19-21]* ❖ *Instead, we should pray for the offender to repent.* ➤ 8 But far from quietly enduring it when fellow believers wrong you, some of you act just like the unbelievers living around you and actually cheat and wrong other believers! 9 Surely you realize that those who live in rebellion against God's commands will not live with him in Heaven! Don't let anyone deceive you into thinking that you can rebel against him and still be one of his people. He will reject people who unrepentantly indulge in blatant sin, such as sexual immorality of any kind, *[Leviticus 18:6-23; 20:11-21]* or worshipping false gods, *[Exodus 20:3-4; Leviticus 19:4; Deuteronomy 4:15-31; 5:7-8]* adultery, *[Exodus 20:14; Leviticus 20:10; Deuteronomy 5:18]* a man having sexual relationships with another man, *[Leviticus 18:22; 20:13; Romans 1:26-27]* 10 stealing, *[Exodus 20:15; Leviticus 19:11,13; Deuteronomy 5:19]* greed, *[Exodus 20:17; Deuteronomy 5:21; Isaiah 57:17; Jeremiah 6:13-15; Luke 12:15]* drunkenness, *[Deuteronomy 21:20-21; Romans 13:13; Ephesians 5:18]* insulting and slandering others, *[Exodus 20:16; Leviticus 19:16; Deuteronomy 5:20; Proverbs 10:11; 1 Timothy 5:13; Titus 3:2; James 4:11; 1 Peter 2:1]* cheating people, *[Leviticus 19:13]* and other such things which he has forbidden in his word. *[Matthew 15:19; Mark 7:20-22; Romans 1:28-32; 2 Corinthians 12:20-21; Galatians 5:19-21; Ephesians 4:31; Colossians 3:8; 1 Peter 4:3]* No one who does these things will enter Heaven. ❖ *This is not an exhaustive list of sins that disqualify a person from eternal life, but lists some sins common among the Corinthians. Willfully indulging in any unrepented sin will disqualify you. Repentance doesn't mean you won't stumble again, but it does mean that with conscious dependence on God's help, you actively try to avoid sin and obey him.* ➤ 11 Some of you lived lives like that before you believed. But such evil should no longer be present in your lives because God has forgiven you and washed away all the filth of your sins. Through the work of the Holy Spirit, he has joined you spiritually with Jesus the Messiah. And for his sake, he has declared you acceptable in his sight and made you his special holy people.

Your Bodies Belong to God

12 Some of you are saying, "Since we are no longer condemned by God's teachings in the Torah, we can do anything we desire that he hasn't explicitly forbidden." Your conclusion is too broad because not all things help me remain close to my Lord. Yes, in my union with the Messiah, I am not condemned by any Torah command and I do have a degree of freedom—but I will avoid anything that would enslave me to sin. 13 Some of you say, "When our bodies desire food, it's good to feed them," as an argument by analogy for indulging in sex when your bodies desire it. It's true that our bodies need food, but someday we will die and God will deliver us from their sinful desires. Therefore, we shouldn't be controlled by such desires. Your conclusion about sex is wrong because our bodies are not meant to be used in sexually immoral ways. They exist to do what the Lord Jesus wants us to do with them—and he is the one who died to redeem them so they are his to rule. 14 Our bodies are important to God. He not only raised the Lord Jesus' body from death, but he will also one day use his power to raise our bodies from death. 15 Don't you know that your bodies are part of the Messiah's body? Since our bodies are part of his, it can't be right to defile part of his body by having sex with a

prostitute! The very idea is abhorrent! 16 Or didn't you realize that when a person joins his body sexually with a prostitute that a union is forged which goes beyond the physical. The Scripture says that in sexual union, "The two shall become as one." *[Genesis 2:24; Matthew 19:5; Mark 10:8; Ephesians 5:31]* ❖ *Thus when you join with a prostitute, you are joining both yourself and the Messiah to one who is not saved, thus defiling yourself and sinning against him.* ➤ 17 But you are already spiritually joined to the Lord and are spiritually one with him. ❖ *Thus it is unthinkable to also join yourself and the Lord to a prostitute. It is also wrong to join yourself to any unbeliever (except your spouse if you were married before you became a believer), but a prostitute is more extremely defiled. It is also wrong to join yourself to anyone who is not your spouse, even if that person is a believer, but Paul's argument here does not address that situation.* ➤

18 Do all within your power to avoid sex with anyone other than your spouse. No other kind of sin harms your body in the same way that sexual sin does. ❖ *Another interpretation is: You say that sin has nothing to do with what the body does, but you are wrong.* ➤ When you indulge in sexual sin, you sin against your own body and harm your spiritual union with the Lord. 19 Don't you know that the Holy Spirit lives in your body as a gift from God? It is his home and belongs to him. By rights, it doesn't really belong to you 20 because God saved both you and your body at a huge cost to himself. Therefore, you now belong to him—so you should use your body to bring him honor.

7

1 Now I will address the issues you wrote to me about. You think that if a man desires to please God, it is better if he doesn't have sex at all—even if he is married. I would say that it's better if a man can remain unmarried and celibate, but not for the reason you are thinking. 2 For even though I think there are advantages to being single, it's still better for men and women to marry if they are tempted to sexual sin because of the prevalence of so much sexual temptation and immorality. That way, they can satisfy their sexual desires within a marriage

relationship as God intended. 3 It's the duty of every husband and wife to satisfy their spouse's sexual needs so they will not be tempted to satisfy them outside of marriage. ❖ *Thus the idea of abstaining from sex while married in order to please God is wrong.* ➤ 4 A wife no longer has sole authority over her own body because she has given her husband certain sexual rights in marrying him. ❖ *This does not imply that rape is acceptable.* ➤ In the same way, a husband no longer has sole authority over his own body because his wife also has sexual rights. 5 So it's wrong to deprive your spouse of sexual relations unless you both agree to do so for a short period in order to spend special time in prayer. ❖ *Sexual abstinence often accompanied periods of prayer and fasting.* ➤ But after that agreed upon period ends, you must resume normal sexual relations so that you and your spouse are not tempted to adultery from lack of self-control. 6 But I want it to be clear that such a mutual agreement is permission for occasional abstinence and is not a requirement. ❖ *Paul was countering the ascetic view of some of the Corinthians that in God's sight, it's better to abstain from sex within marriage than to indulge. He didn't want them to make this possibility a requirement.* ➤

7 I have reasons to wish that everyone were able to be content remaining single and living in celibacy, as I am. But God clearly doesn't intend this. He gives different gifts to different people. ❖ *To some he gives the ability to remain single, celibate, and content—and to others he gives marriage.* ➤

8 You asked me what widowers and widows should do. I think it's better if they remain unmarried like me. 9 But if they can't control their sexual desires, it's perfectly all right for them to marry again. It's better to marry than to allow uncontrolled sexual passions to lead them into sin.

10 For the situation where a believer is married to another believer, I have this command which was given by the Lord Jesus when he was still on earth: Those who are married should not get divorced. 11 But if they do, they must remain unmarried or else be reconciled with their former spouse. They are not allowed to

marry anyone else. **A** *[Deuteronomy 24:1-4; Jeremiah 3:1; Malachi 2:16; Matthew 5:31-32; 19:8-9; Mark 10:2-12; Luke 16:18]* **12-13** For the situation where a believer is married to an unbeliever, the Lord left no command, but my own is this: If the unbeliever is willing to continue living with the believer, the believer must not divorce the unbelieving spouse. **14** This kind of marriage is not defiled, as some think—because for the sake of the believing spouse, God has made the marriage holy and his covenant blessing is upon it and also upon the children issuing from it. If such a marriage were defiled, then the children would be outside of his covenant, but in fact, they are accepted by him and receive his blessings. ❖ *The unbeliever is not saved by being married to a believer, but God blesses the marriage for the sake of the believing spouse.* ➤ **15** But if the unbelieving partner desires a divorce, you are to allow it. Under such circumstances, a believer is no longer bound in marriage to the unbelieving partner. ❖ *Paul implies that such a person is allowed to remarry* ➤ But if possible, it's better to remain married because God wants us to live in peace with others. **16** And you never know, there's always the possibility that your spouse might become saved through your relationship.

17 Everywhere I go, I teach this general principle to God's people: Be content to remain in the same situation or status that you found yourself in when you became a believer—for God put you there. ❖ *This applies to the question of marital status as well as other situations. Apparently, someone was teaching the Corinthians that they had to change certain things in their lives to be able to live a life pleasing to God—like getting divorced or not having sex or getting circumcised—because their current situations were supposedly not in line with God's will.* ➤ **18** For instance, were you already circumcised when you became a believer? Then don't attempt to remove the mark of circumcision. ❖ *There was a medical procedure that some Jewish men underwent to appear uncircumcised, since circumcision was considered mutilation by Romans and Greeks and they were often ridiculed if they tried to socialize in Gentile society. Nudity was common for exercise and sports among Greeks.* ➤ And if you were uncircumcised when God called you to believe, be content to remain that way. **19** It makes no difference to God whether or not you've been circumcised. What matters is whether or not you obey his commands. ❖ *This clearly doesn't include all of the Torah's original ritual commands, of which circumcision was a part. It refers to God's commands in the Torah as amended by the New Testament, and to the Spirit's guidance. Paul was writing this instruction in verses 18b-19 to uncircumcised Gentile believers only, not to Jewish believers.* ➤ **20** Everyone should remain as they were when they first responded to God's call and believed. **21** Or, for another example, were you a slave when God called you? Don't let your status trouble you because you can still serve the Messiah as a slave. But if your master allows you your freedom, you may take it. **B** **22** You can serve and please the Lord whether you are free or a slave. For those who were slaves when the Lord called them into relationship with himself have been set free from slavery to sin. And those who were free when he called them are voluntarily his slaves. **23** God paid a high price to save you—the death of his own Son. ❖ *See the note at 1 Peter 2:18.* ➤ Since you now belong to him, don't be slaves to other people's ideas of what you must do to please God. **24** So, my brothers and sisters in the Lord, as I said before, remain in the same situation or status in which you found yourselves when you first believed and trust that God is available to help you live in a way that is pleasing to him within your particular situation.

25 You asked me what people who have never yet married should do. I have no

---

A 7:11 If a divorced person remarries and his or her previous spouse is a believer who has not committed adultery, then such a person commits adultery which is a serious sin. Conservative believers disagree on whether the adultery committed by remarrying is a one-time sin or a continuing state of sin. The present tense of the verbs (committing adultery) in Matthew 5:32; 19:9; Mark 10:12; and Luke 16:18 could mean a continuous state. But this argument is not conclusive since other present state verbs in Greek clearly indicate one-time events and not a continuous state. So this issue cannot be resolved by grammatical arguments.

B 7:21 Some scholars think the last sentence means: Even if you have the opportunity to become free, don't take it, but make use of your life as a slave. But the aorist tense of the verb translated "take it" makes this unlikely, as well as all logic.

command from the Lord for you on this subject, but I offer my own opinion as one whom the Lord has, by his mercy, changed and made worthy of your trust. 26 In view of the persecution believers are experiencing at this time, I think it would be better for them to remain single. 27 Now, if a man is married, he shouldn't seek to be free from that marriage. But if he is not currently married, it would be better to remain single at this time. 28 Yet if you do get married, it's certainly not a sin! And if a girl marries, she isn't sinning either. But those who marry will find greater difficulties during these times of persecution, and I would like to spare you from them.

29 But remember this: Our time left in this world to do the Lord's work is short— so if you are married, you shouldn't live as if your marriage was your primary focus. ❖ This does not mean that married people should neglect their responsibilities to love and care for their spouses. But their main focus should be on serving the Lord—not each other. ➤ 30 And while you may mourn, continue to serve the Lord and don't make mourning the focus of your life. And when you are rejoicing, don't let that sidetrack you from your proper focus either. And when you buy something, don't be obsessed with it for it's only temporary. 31 In other words, don't be overly focused on the things of this life for they are temporary and our lives will soon end.

32 I want you to be able to be free from all worries related to this life and particularly from the concerns that married people have. A single man can be totally focused on the Lord's work and on pleasing only him.

33 But a husband has other legitimate concerns and responsibilities and also wants to please his wife. 34 So his interests are necessarily divided between two legitimate responsibilities. A single woman can totally focus on the Lord's work and be completely dedicated to him in body and spirit. But a wife has other legitimate concerns and responsibilities and also wants to please her husband. 35 I'm pointing these things out to help you decide for yourselves what you should do—not to give you a universal command that you must remain single. I encourage you to determine what is best for you so that you can serve the Lord with minimal distractions.

36 Now, concerning the situation you brought up in your letter about the man with a virgin daughter whom he has restrained from marrying. If he now thinks this wasn't the best thing to do and that she should really be married—especially if she will soon be considered too old to marry—he should do what he thinks is right. He is not sinning by allowing her to marry. 37 But if he has reached a firm decision that it's still best for her to remain unmarried—and he is under no outside constraints such as a previous agreement or his daughter's behavior or an inability to support her himself, and he has full control of the situation—then he is free to act as he desires and there is nothing wrong with that decision. 38 So either decision is fine, but in my opinion—given the present circumstances—it is better to keep her unmarried. A

39 Going back to the situation of widows, a woman is legally and morally bound to her

---

A 7:38 The Greek in these verses is vague and ambiguous and has been interpreted three different ways, of which two are equally possible and likely to be correct. But there is now no way of knowing which situation Paul was addressing. One has been given above. The other is as follows: 36 "Now concerning the situation you brought up in your letter about the man who was engaged, but then decided not to get married—thinking it was more holy. If he now thinks that this isn't treating his girl properly and he has passions he can't control (or: if she is getting beyond marriageable age) and thinks it would be better if they go ahead with the marriage, then he should do as he wants. It's not a sin for them to marry—and no one should oppose it. 37 But if he has reached a firm decision that he will not marry and has no external pressures to do so and is in full control of his own passions, then he has made a good decision. 38 So either decision is fine. But in my opinion—given the present circumstances—it is better not to marry." ¶ The interpretation given in this footnote is the one usually chosen by translators, probably because this situation is much more frequent and understandable in our culture than the one given above. Yet this situation has already been covered by Paul's instructions in the immediately preceding verses, and the interpretation given in the text above was much more likely to happen in that culture than a fiancé backing out of his marriage.

husband as long as he lives—whether or not they are estranged. But if her husband dies, then she is no longer married and may marry anyone she wishes—as long as it's another believer. ❖ *Paul only explicitly addresses widows here, but the same would be true of a widower as he said earlier in verses 8 and 9 of this chapter. Paul implies that believers should never marry unbelievers. And if they do, they should come under discipline by the assembly of God's people.* ➤ 40 But in my opinion—given the current circumstances—her life will have less heartache if she remains unmarried. And I believe I received this wisdom from the Holy Spirit.

8

Concerning Eating Food Offered to False Gods

We are to sacrifice personal freedoms and rights for the sake of a weak believer's conscience

1 Now, concerning your question about whether or not it's allowed to eat food that others have sacrificed to false gods. As you say, we all have special knowledge given to us by the Spirit. But possessing knowledge can lead to pride and arrogance if it isn't tempered with unselfish love. Having this kind of love for the welfare of others is what really helps the community of believers to grow together in maturity. 2 Those who are sure that they know everything they need to know on an issue—have, in fact, not learned to have the correct attitude about possessing knowledge. Their understanding is not mature. 3 Rather, it is those who temper their knowledge with unselfish love for others who have true understanding. **A**

4 So, as this pertains to the topic of eating food that others have sacrificed to false gods, yes, we know that there are no real gods behind the idols that pagans worship. We know that there is only one real God— 5 even though people do indeed acknowledge

many so-called gods and lords who they believe live in Heaven and some on Earth. ❖ *There are spiritual beings called demons who interact with people and pretend to be deities. They were created to be servants of the one true God, but they rebelled against him and are now his enemies. They have been defeated and—on Judgment Day—will be confined to Hell forever.* ➤ 6 But we acknowledge only one deity who is also our Lord—God the Father—who willed all things to be created for his own purposes, and our one Lord—Jesus the Messiah—who was the means through which all things were made and through whom we now live in relationship with God. *[John 1:3; Acts 17:28; Romans 11:36; Colossians 1:16-17; Hebrews 1:3; 2 Peter 3:7]* ❖ *The emphasis of this verse is not Trinitarian or the deity of the Messiah, as I have made somewhat more explicit than Paul did originally—but certainly the deity of Jesus and his unity with the Father are assumed.* ➤

7 But not all believers in Jesus have this clarity of knowledge about the non-reality of other gods. They still have the habit of thinking that these gods are real. So if they eat food that has been offered to a pagan deity, they believe that they are in some manner honoring these deities—and therefore, do what their consciences say is sin. For them it is sin because they know it's forbidden to honor other gods—and their consequent shame hinders their seeking to remain close to Jesus. 8 We may know that what we eat doesn't affect our relationship with God—if our hearts and minds are in the right place. For our relationship with him is neither harmed by what we eat nor helped by what we don't eat if our actions are done to honor him.

9 But those who are loving will be considerate of fellow believers in the way that they exercise their freedom in this matter. It would be wrong for you to inadvertently influence other believers to sin against their consciences when they are not sure if God approves of such behavior or not. 10 For if

---

A 8:3 Most translations read as follows: "But if anyone loves God, this person has been known by him." Two early Greek manuscripts omit "God" and omit "by him." Fee notes it is likely that their appearance in later manuscripts were early scribal additions in an attempt to clarify the text. It is easier to understand why an addition was made rather than why an omission might have been made. While the addition creates a verse which—in itself—expresses truth, it doesn't fit nearly as well in the logic of Paul's argument. Without those words, the Greek literally means: "But if anyone loves, this person knows."

such believers see you—who know there are no other gods—eating in a pagan temple, they may be influenced to do the same thing and thereby sin against their own consciences. 11 Then you will have had a part in ruining the weak faith of someone for whom the Messiah died because you were proud of your knowledge. 12 But when you sin against other believers this way—weakening their resolve to do what they believe is right—you also sin against the Messiah. [Matthew 25:45] 13 Therefore, if my eating certain foods might lead immature believers to stumble in sin, I will never eat that food again so as to avoid harming the faith of others.

As an example that believers should give up their rights in order to help others, Paul points out that he hasn't insisted on his rights as an apostle

❖ *Paul isn't finished with his arguments about why they should not eat food offered to false gods. He started off in chapter 8 with the argument that even if their knowledge would allow them that freedom, they need to give up their rights for the benefit of those who might be tempted to sin by observing their freedom. Then in chapter 9, he gives himself as an example of one who has given up his rights as an apostle in order to help others. But the Corinthians had questioned the authenticity of his apostleship. So he also defends his apostleship in order to assert that he has rights as an apostle which he has voluntarily given up. Then in chapter 10, he gives further arguments why they should not eat food sacrificed to false gods.* ➤

9

1 Don't I also have rights and freedoms that I have given up for the sake of others? I am an apostle—though some of you question my authority. I certainly meet the qualifications. I've seen our Lord Jesus in the flesh. And the fact that you are believers is a direct result of my obeying the commission he gave me to preach the Good News to Gentiles. 2 Even if others don't recognize that I'm an apostle—you should! Your faith in the Lord is proof that I am an apostle to you. ❖ *Paul was the first believer to go to Corinth and preach the Good News—bringing them to a saving faith—and he taught them the basics of that faith. He was the one who established the assembly of believers in Corinth and therefore, had spiritual authority over it.* ➤

3 This is my defense for not accepting support while I worked among you—which has caused some of you to question the authenticity of my apostleship. ❖ *It was precisely because Paul did not exercise some of his rights as an apostle that some of the Corinthians doubted his authority. They expected a teacher and leader to be supported by others—not work for his own living. Then other teachers came after him who did use their rights to be supported by others and that added to their doubts about Paul. These same rights and privileges were often associated with Greek philosophers, and Paul may have decided not to allow others to support him so as not to become identified with preconceptions they had of pagan philosophers.* ➤ 4 Apostles certainly have the right to have the necessities of life provided by those they minister to. 5 We also have the right to be accompanied by a believing wife as a coworker who should also be provided for. Peter, the other apostles, and the Lord's brothers all do this. 6 Or do you think that Barnabas and I are the only exceptions to this principle and lack the right to be supported by you? ❖ *This does not imply that Barnabas visited Corinth, but it was probably well-known that both Paul and Barnabas worked to provide for their own living.* ➤ 7 The principle that a worker is provided sustenance from his main labor is obvious. Aren't soldiers paid? Don't farmers eat some of the grapes from their own vineyards? Doesn't a shepherd drink some of the milk from the sheep he tends?

8 But I don't really base my right to your support from these examples. For God's Torah teaches the same thing. 9 Moses wrote in the Torah, **"Never prevent an ox from eating some of the grain he is threshing by muzzling him."** [Deuteronomy 25:4] Do you think God is only concerned in this way about oxen? 10 If he is concerned that a mere ox not be prohibited from benefiting from his own labor, certainly he is also concerned for his apostles in the same way. Just as the one who plows and the one who threshes should expect some share of the harvest, spiritual leaders should be supported by those they serve. 11 If we work to bring you eternal spiritual benefits, is it too much to expect that you provide us with some basic material needs? 12 If others who ministered to you spiritually received support from you—as was their right—don't I and my companions

❖ *Silas and Timothy* ➤ have an even greater right to expect this since I am your apostle and spiritual father? But we decided not to accept support from you—even though it is our right. Instead, we would rather endure any hardship than to risk hindering people from accepting our message about the Messiah. ❖ *By preaching the Good News without pay, Paul was able to demonstrate the "free" nature of Jesus' salvation. He also avoided the accusation that his motive for preaching was to obtain easy support from others for no physical labor. He may have had other reasons as well.* ➤ 13 Even-more-pertinent examples showing we have such a right are those who work in the Temple. ❖ *What he says here was equally true of the Jewish Temple and pagan temples.* ➤ Those who work in the Temple—by right—take some of the food brought there for their own needs, and those who offer the sacrifices receive a share from those sacrifices. 14 More importantly, our Lord himself commanded that those who proclaim the Good News should be supported by those they minister to. *[Matthew 10:10; Luke 10:7]* ❖ *Paul says the same thing again in Galatians 6:6, 2 Thessalonians 3:9, and 1 Timothy 5:18.* ➤

15 So I do have the right as an apostle to have you support me, but I chose not to make use of that right. And I'm not making this long argument just so you will start supporting me now. I would rather die than allow anyone to deprive me of the privilege of boasting that I preach the Good News without pay. 16 I can't boast about the fact that I preach the Good News because God commanded me to do so. I don't like to think what would happen to me if I didn't obey that command. 17 If I had freely chosen to do this work, then I would have earned a reward. But as it is, God committed this work to me as his steward ❖ *A steward was usually a slave.* ➤ and I gain no merit for simply doing my duty. 18 So how can I merit reward and do something worth boasting about? Only by proclaiming the Good News freely, by not making full use of my right to receive support from those to whom I minister—lest anyone think I was abusing that right—so I won't hinder anyone from believing my message.

19 This also gives me the advantage of not being obligated to others for their generosity and removes the potential for manipulation. But even though I'm free of such obligations, for the sake of leading as many people to believe in Jesus as I can, I humble myself to accommodate everyone—even as a slave does. ❖ *He did this as far as he could without compromising the truth.* ➤ 20 When I live among Jews, I follow their religious rules as much as I can—particularly in regard to food—so that they will listen to me, and I might lead them to believe in Jesus as the Messiah. When among those who live under the Torah's teachings, I also live as they do—even though I know that God doesn't require this of me for salvation and, therefore, I'm "free" to live without those restrictions. I do it to gain a hearing for the Good News among those who try to earn their salvation by obeying the Torah. I want to lead them to, instead, depend on Jesus alone for their salvation. 21 But when living among Gentiles who know nothing of the Torah's teachings, I live as they do without following the constraints of the Torah's ritual commands—but within the constraints of God's moral commands because I am submitted to obeying the Messiah. ❖ *Paul meant that he didn't follow the Jewish regulations regarding kosher food and matters of ritual purity.* ➤ 22 When I live among those who are weak in their understanding of the truth who might be easily led into sinning against their own consciences, I live as they think is right so that I might have opportunity to help them mature in their understanding and faith. I attempt to accommodate every group of people I live among so as not to offend or tempt them—in order that I might lead them to a saving faith in Jesus as the Messiah. 23 I will do anything within God's will to further the spread of the Good News, so that I may also ultimately share in God's eternal blessings with those who believe and who persevere to receive them. ❖ *To receive all the blessings God has promised, we have to persevere in obedience to the end of our lives. Part of Paul's obedience required him to proclaim the Good News.* ➤

24 Our perseverance to the end can be compared to a race. Don't you realize that

not everyone who runs in the race gets the prize? Only those who win get the prize. So live in such a way that you qualify to receive the prize of eternal life. ❖ *Paul's focus in this metaphor is not that "only one can win," but that people should run in such a way that they are not disqualified from winning. Salvation is a free gift that no one can merit. Yet perseverance in obedience until the end of our lives is required and is always characteristic of those who have truly repented and possess true faith. All who persevere in obedience will "win" the prize of eternal life, though none can say they have in any way "earned" it.* ➤ 25 Everyone who intends to compete in the Olympic games is required to undergo strict training and to exercise self-control. ❖ *Greek Olympic athletes had to swear to ten months of strict training beforehand, and were disqualified if they didn't fulfill it.* ➤ They do all this to win a perishable wreath as their victor's crown—signifying a short-lived glory. But we strive to win an eternal crown of glory. 26 This, then, explains my own behavior. I live the way I do—often giving up my rights and privileges—with a purpose in view. Continuing with sport metaphors, in order to win the race, I focus on the finish line. To win the boxing match, I make sure my punches don't miss. I am focused and self-controlled—27 disciplining my body to make it my obedient slave so I can win the prize. After having exhorted others not to be self-indulgent, I don't want to end up being disqualified myself.

10

Eating in pagan temples is participating in idolatry

1 For it *is* possible for us to become disqualified! For example, remember that when the Israelites fled from Egypt, they were under divine favor—being protected and led by the cloud which represented God's presence. And God saved them—allowing them to escape from their enemies by walking through the middle of the Red Sea on dry land. *[Exodus 13:17—14:31]* 2 In the same way that Jesus delivered us and we were baptized into union with him *[Romans 6:3; Galatians 3:27]*—resulting in our submission to him—our spiritual ancestors were all "baptized" through the Red Sea experience, bringing them under the leadership of Moses, their deliverer. 3 And in a way that is similar to how we all partake of spiritual food and drink in the Lord's Supper, they all ate food that was provided miraculously ❖ *i.e., manna [Exodus 16:4-30]* ➤ 4 and they all drank water provided miraculously from a rock. *[Exodus 17:1-7; Numbers 20:2-13; Deuteronomy 8:15-16; Nehemiah 9:15, 20; Psalm 78:15-31; 105:40-41]* This rock symbolized the Messiah who was present with them to help them in their travels. *[Deuteronomy 32:4, 15, 18, 30, 31]* Just as the Messiah provided them with physical sustenance, he provides us with spiritual sustenance. 5 But despite all the advantages they had, most of them later made God angry because of their idolatry—so he slaughtered **A** them in the wilderness. ❖ *By drawing these analogies, Paul was warning the members of the Corinthian assembly that their baptism and all their spiritual knowledge and blessings would not necessarily prevent them from being disqualified for the prize of eternal life. By eating food offered to false gods, some of them were in danger of idolatry.* ➤

6 These historical events are recorded as a warning to us that we shouldn't desire evil things as they did—lest we suffer the same consequences. 7 The Scriptures say, "**The people feasted and danced before the idol.**" *[Exodus 32:6]* ❖ *Many commentators believe that the dancing involved sexual immorality and worship—which was common in many forms of pagan worship. Fee notes that every other mention of food offered to idols is accompanied by a reference to sexual immorality. [Acts 15:29; Revelation 2:14, 20]* ➤ So don't allow feasting in temples on food offered to false gods to lead you into worshipping them 8 or into indulging in sexual immorality—like some of the

---

A 10:5 This last phrase Paul took directly from Numbers 14:16 in the Septuagint where it says "scattered" rather than "slaughtered"—which is in the Hebrew text and also in the rendering above. The quote is from Moses' appeal to God to **not** slaughter the Israelites. But God promised to "destroy" them rather than allow them to enter the promised land. [Numbers 14:35] In modern English, the word "scatter" usually doesn't include the idea of killing people off—as he actually did. He prevented all but two—Joshua and Caleb—from receiving the "prize" of entering the promised land because of their rebellion. [Numbers 14:30] This rebellion was a form of idolatry, since idolatry is putting anything—including our own desires—before the true God.

Israelites did. The fact that 23,000 of them died in one day is a warning to you. *[Numbers 25:1-9]* ❖ *There is a discrepancy, as the passage in Numbers says 24,000 died. One commentator suggests both could be true—that 23,000 could have died in one day and the other thousand died a bit later. No one knows the source of this discrepancy, but it doesn't affect the point Paul is making.* ➤ 9 Don't test the Messiah **A** to see how far you can go before he allows you to be destroyed. Some Israelites did this and died from snake bites. *[Numbers 21:4-7]* 10 Don't grumble and complain against me like some Israelites did against Moses. For God sent the destroyer to kill them in order to remove their evil influence from among his people. ❖ *See Numbers 14:1-38 and all of chapter 16. Paul might have meant either of these two events.* ➤

11 All these events that happened to God's people were recorded in the Scriptures to be examples and warnings about the consequences of rebelling against God. They were written for our benefit—who are privileged to live in the time when all of God's plans are reaching their fulfillment in the Messiah. 12 So those of you who think you are so strong in your faith and knowledge that you are in no danger when you participate in pagan feasts—you should take care lest you be tempted and fall into the sin of idolatry. For those who do will not be exempt from the consequences and may fail to "win the prize" of eternal life. ❖ *See note at 1 Corinthians 9:24.* ➤ 13 You will not experience any temptation or testing of your faith other than those which all people experience. And God is faithful to help you in all such times. He will not allow you to be tempted beyond what you are able to resist if you depend on his help. He always provides a way to escape the snare of temptation so you can endure it without sinning. ❖ *Yet you have to actively depend on his help and choose the way of escape that he offers. Fee suggests that Paul might be warning them that God will help believers endure ordinary testings, but not if they "test" the Messiah by flirting with idolatry.* ➤

14 Therefore, my dear friends for whom I am very concerned, stay as far away from idolatry as you can! You shouldn't even be found in a pagan temple—let alone be eating food sacrificed to their false gods! 15 I know you are reasonable people so you should be able to see that the following argument is valid. 16 You would all agree that when we thank the Lord for the "cup of blessing" and drink from it in the Lord's Supper, we are desiring to have fellowship with the Messiah and receive from him the benefits procured by his death. ❖ *"Cup of blessing" was a technical term used for the cup of wine which was blessed and drunk at the end of Jewish meals, and also the third cup of the Passover meal. The term came to be used for the cup at the Lord's Supper. The "blood of the Messiah" in the literal text is a figure of his death. To "share in his blood," means to have fellowship with him and to receive the benefits procured by his death. The symbolism of the cup is undeniable, but the presence of symbolism doesn't necessarily preclude the existence of other spiritual realities also being present.* ➤ And you would also agree that when we break the bread and eat it in the Lord's Supper, we are fellowshipping together as the body of the Messiah and therefore, are identifying ourselves as part of him. ❖ *Another interpretation is: When we break the bread...we receive the body of our Lord and all the benefits procured by his suffering.* ➤ 17 Since there is only one loaf—which is the Messiah, the bread of life *[John 6:32-58]*—when all of us eat it, we proclaim that we are all part of one body which is the Messiah's. ❖ *Paul's point is that participating in the Lord's Supper is clearly—at the very least—a form of submissive worship and identification with our Lord. Thus participating in a pagan feast in the presence of an idol is a form of worship and identification with that false god and with those who worship it. Therefore, eating a pagan feast in a pagan temple is—in itself—idolatry. Even if they didn't believe the god was real, they are identifying with the pagans who believe it is real and are implicitly honoring their pagan worship. Worship does not have to be centered on a real deity to be worship.* ➤

18 Consider the Israelites. When they eat part of their sacrifices, it's clear that they are fellowshipping with God to whom they offered the sacrifice, and are bound together with that sacrifice as an offering or act of worship. *[Deuteronomy 14:22-27]* ❖ *The implication is*

A 10:9 Some manuscripts say "Lord" and some say "God," but the best opinion is that the original said "Messiah."

No difference in meaning results with any choice.

that when they eat food sacrificed to false gods—they are in fact worshipping those false gods. ➤ 19 I am not saying that the realities of celebrating the Lord's Supper and it's benefits in our relationship to our Lord imply that food sacrificed to idols is of any value, or that idols represent real deities. 20 What is sacrificed on pagan alters is not offered to real deities since—aside from Yahweh—there are none. They are sacrificed to demons who pretend to be gods. But I don't want you to identify yourselves with demons and worship them—which you would be doing if you partook of their sacred feasts. 21 You cannot participate in the covenant relationship signified by drinking the cup of the Lord and also drink to honor demons! You cannot eat at the Lord's table in fellowship with him and do the same thing with demons! ❖ *Table fellowship—with people or deities—implied close relationships.* ➤ 22 If you do, you will provoke the Lord to jealous anger and not get away with it. He will reject you. *[Deuteronomy 32:21-26]*

23 Some of you say, "Since we are no long condemned by God's teachings in the Torah, we can do anything we desire that he hasn't explicitly forbidden." *[1 Corinthians 6:12]* Your conclusion is too sweeping because not everything we do helps our fellow believer. Yes, in our spiritual union with the Messiah we are not condemned by any Torah command and we do have a degree of freedom—but not everything we could do helps the body of the Messiah grow together in unity and maturity. 24 The constraint on your freedom is that you should be using it to do things that help other believers—not only things that benefit yourself.

25 As an example of that freedom, you may eat any meat that is sold in the market without asking whether or not it has been offered to a false god because that is irrelevant and not a matter that your conscience should be bothered about. ❖ *Some meat in the market was left over from sacrifices and some was not. (This is implicitly addressed to the wealthy, as most people couldn't afford to buy meat.) Since the meat would not be eaten in a temple or to honor a false god, and a believer would in fact bless it and thank God for it, it was not the same as eating it at a pagan feast. Unless one specifically asked about the source of the meat, no one could know or be tempted to sin by* *observing a believer eating it.* ➤ 26 For it is written in the Scriptures, **"This world belongs to Yahweh and also everything in it."** *[Psalm 24:1]* Therefore, you can eat anything with thanksgiving because it belongs to your God who has given it to you.

27 And if you are invited to the home of an unbeliever for a meal and want to attend, eat whatever is served without asking whether or not it has been offered to a false god. That should be irrelevant to your conscience since such meals do not have the intent of honoring a false god. 28 But if anyone ❖ *Paul most likely has a pagan in mind who is a fellow guest at the meal.* ➤—out of consideration for you—tells you that the meat being served was sacrificed to a false god—thinking that followers of Jesus, like Jews, would not want to eat such food—then don't eat it. You do this for the sake of not offending the moral conscience of the person who told you because he expects that it would be wrong for you to do so. 29 It's not a matter that bothers your own conscience, but it does bother his.

So why should I restrain my freedom in this matter because of someone else's conscience? ❖ *What Paul means in verses 29b-30 is not clear, so the interpretations are quite varied.* ➤ 30 If I can thank God for the meat and eat it in good conscience, why should I be blamed for doing wrong if I were to eat it? 31 The reason is, when we eat or drink or do anything else, it should always be done in a way that will bring praise to God—even if it means limiting our personal freedoms. 32 Never deliberately do anything that would unnecessarily offend Jews or pagans and therefore make it less likely that they would listen to the Good News. Also never deliberately do anything that would alienate fellow believers. 33 I try to accommodate everyone in everything that I say and do as much as is possible within God's will, so they will be willing to listen to the Good News and might be led to trust in Jesus as their Savior. When it comes to a choice, I always try to do things that will help or please others, rather than make things more convenient or pleasant for myself. ❖ *Paul is not advocating being a "people pleaser," [1 Thessalonians 2:4; Galatians 1:10] because many of the things God says are often found to be offensive to unbelievers—and even to believers who have compromised God's word. We are never to compromise the truth. Yet as much as is possible, we are to be considerate of how others view things and not offend them unnecessarily [Romans 15:1-3]—as long as we can do so and remain in God's will.* ➤

11

¹ So you should follow my example in this, just as I try to follow the example of the Messiah.

On Women Covering Their Heads When They Pray Aloud or Prophesy in Worship Services

❖ *Many possible interpretations have been proposed for this very problematic section (11:2-16). I avoid mentioning most of them to avoid confusion, but recommend Gordon D. Fee's commentary for his excellent discussion of this passage. Many of Fee's views are represented in the interpretation presented here. Given the way Paul argues in this section, it's clear that he doesn't consider this issue as serious as most of the others he addresses in this letter. It was most likely an issue of what was culturally appropriate, and he gives no clear command. The principle of not unnecessarily offending cultural norms is one possible application of this section for modern readers.* ➤

² You say that you remember all of my teaching and the example of my lifestyle and are faithfully following most of the apostolic traditions that I passed on to you. In this I commend you. ³ But I want you to understand the following: The Messiah is the source of life for every believing man. Man ❖ *in Adam* ➤ is the source of life for women, ❖ *For Eve was made from Adam.* ➤ and God is the source of the incarnate Messiah. ❖ *The word "head," that Paul used in the literal text, rarely had the sense of "authority" in Greek, as it does in Hebrew and English. It is much more likely that his Greek audience would have understood it to mean "source of life." We don't know exactly what the situation was in Corinth that Paul was addressing. The interpretation given here assumes the following situation: Corinthian women believers were exercising their freedom to be equal with men. Paul did teach that in our spiritual union with the Messiah there is no distinction between male and female. [Galatians 3:28] But in exercising their freedom, they were violating cultural standards and were trying to blur the distinctions between men and women. Paul's focus here is not*

on the authority of men—which he never mentions (unless he meant that in referring to headship)—but on relationships. He argues that because these relationships exist, it is not appropriate to try to obscure them. In Heaven, more of the distinctions between men and women will be removed since we will be like the angels, [Matthew 22:30; Mark 12:25; Luke 20:34-36] but that is not yet the case in this life. ➤ ⁴ So, if a man completely covers his head—thus veiling his face—while praying aloud or prophesying in public worship, he dishonors the Messiah who is his source of life. ❖ *Literally, the Greek says, "...or prophesying having (something) down over his head." No Gentile commentator knows why Paul thought such a head covering on a man would dishonor the Messiah—although he obviously expected the Corinthians to agree with him. One guess is that covering one's head was a sign of mourning, which would be inappropriate. Another speculation is that since a prophet in the Isis cult wore a head covering, it would be inappropriate to imitate such a false prophet. Since there are no prohibitions or teachings on this in the Hebrew Scriptures or elsewhere in the New Testament, it likely concerns a cultural norm. Messianic Jewish commentators say this does not refer to a head covering like a cap or a prayer shawl, but refers to a head covering that veils the face—as rendered above—and that this was appropriate for women, who wore veils, but not men. The idea that it was inappropriate for a man to be veiled in worship might come from Exodus 34:33-35—following Moses' practice to remove the veil he wore when he entered Yahweh's presence. That the Torah allows a man to wear a covering on top of his head during worship is inferred from God's command for the High Priest to wear a turban [Exodus 28:4] as part of his priestly garments. See also Exodus 28:36-38.* ➤ ⁵ But if a woman prays aloud or prophesies in public worship with her head uncovered, ❖ *possibly meaning having her face unveiled* ➤ she dishonors men by trying to eliminate the distinctions between the sexes. To do this is as shameful as if she were to shave her head. ❖ *We don't know for sure why a bald woman was shameful, but it was likely a cultural value. In our culture, it would merely be embarrassing. As for having her head uncovered, Messianic author David Stern speculates that the covering was something that held her hair up. It was considered indecent (at least in Jewish culture) for a woman to have her hair down in public. Only her husband was allowed to see her that way. Or, it might be the lack of a veil over her face that was meant, which may have been considered indecent in that culture. ¶ This verse clearly shows that Corinthian women believers participated verbally in public worship by praying aloud and exercised the gift of prophecy—and Paul does not prohibit them from doing so.*

Hence the interpretation of 1 Corinthians 14:34 needs to be considered in this light. ➤ 6 If a woman refuses to cover her head, she might as well cut her hair like a man does. But since it's shameful for her to have her hair shaved off or cut short like a man's, then she ought to preserve this distinction between the sexes and also cover her head. 7 A man shouldn't completely cover his head with a veil while praying and prophesying because he was made in God's image and was made to praise and honor him. But women were made to complement and glorify men. ❖ Without women, men would be incomplete and less praiseworthy in many ways. Women were also created in the image of God, [Genesis 1:27] but Paul is focusing here on the fact that God first created the man for the purpose of glorifying himself. He does not deny this is equally true of women, but wants to make the point why a woman should not try to be like a man. Man was made for God, but woman was made for man, to complement and complete him. [Genesis 2:18-24] This in no way implies that women are subordinate to men, only that there is a divinely intended distinction. What Paul fails to explicitly say—because his original readers already understood it—is why this truth implies that men should not cover (or veil) their heads. ➤ 8 For Adam didn't come from a woman, but Eve came from the man. 9 And Adam was not created for the woman's benefit, but the woman was created for his sake. 10 Therefore, a woman ought to have authority over her own head, ❖ i.e., to cover it or not as she wishes ➤ because of the angels. ❖ The meaning of this verse is obscure and difficult. Fee thinks the verse says the opposite of what we would expect (with the interpretation that she should have "authority over" her head). Other interpreters translate what they think it should mean in the context. Following Fee, I have chosen to try to make sense of what it does say. The Greek preposition ἐπί (epi) can mean "on," so most translations add words [ ] that are not in the text to say: "a woman should [have a symbol of] authority **on** her head." But Fee says this preposition usually means "over" in the New Testament when following ἐξουσία (exousia), meaning "authority." ¶ What have the angels to do with this matter? No one knows. Maybe because believers—including believing women—will someday judge angels [1 Corinthians 6:3] or eventually be like the angels, they should have authority over such insignificant matters as covering their head or not. ¶ With respect to the traditional interpretation of this verse—that a woman should have a covering on her head (or a veil over her face) as a sign of her being under authority because of the angels—David

Stern suggests that it might have to do with Isaiah 6:2, where the angels cover their face with their wings, perhaps as a sign that they are under God as a higher authority. Another suggestion he makes is that if the women don't care about shocking the men with their unveiled faces, perhaps they would care about shocking the angels—who are also present at their worship services. ➤ 11 However, in our life in union with the Lord, men and women are interdependent on one another. ❖ This implies that women should exercise their freedom in such a way as not to violate cultural norms or shame men. i.e., In the Corinthian context, they should wear a head covering (or veil) when praying aloud or prophesying. ➤ 12 Even though in the beginning Eve came from Adam, since that time, men are born of women. So neither can be seen to be subordinate to the other, but all are subordinate to God who brought us into existence.

13 I think most of you will agree with me that it isn't proper for a woman to pray to God aloud in public worship without a head covering. 14 We feel it's unnatural for a man to have long hair—and consider it disgraceful. ❖ Paul isn't arguing from natural law, but from cultural norms that dictate what "seems" natural. That this is a cultural norm (i.e., not a universal norm) should be clear from the fact that God created ethnic groups where people have kinky hair (like some Africans) that doesn't hang down—and in those groups, male and female hair lengths are often not contrastive. They have no cultural norm that women should have long hair and men should not. ➤ 15 But for a woman, long hair is beautiful. In fact, it's a kind of natural covering for her. ❖ Paul implies that since God has indicated in this way that it's good for a woman's head to be covered with long hair, she should also wear an external covering over her head when she prays or prophesies in public. ➤ 16 As for those women who want to make an issue of this, they should submit to the common custom of using a head covering, which all of the assemblies of believers ❖ in the relative uniformity of culture in the Roman empire ➤ follow and which we followed when I was among you. ❖ Paul makes it clear that this is a "practice," or "custom"—not a doctrine. He quotes no Scriptural command. They are to submit for the sake of cultural sensitivities, but he did not intend this to be made into a universal law where other standards are the norm—as long as they don't conflict with Scriptural teaching on moral matters. Even if someone disagrees that this is a matter of a cultural norm, it is only explicitly pertinent to women when they pray aloud or prophesy in public worship, and not a requirement for

any other purpose such as singing or participating in the liturgy. Normally, the men and women in that time and culture were segregated and the men would not look at or focus on the women unless one of them were praying aloud or prophesying. ➤

Abuse of the Lord's Supper

17 I am able to commend you for following some of the apostolic traditions that I passed on to you, but not in the way you celebrate the Lord's Supper together. What you are doing causes people more harm than good. 18 For what I've heard is that there are divisions among you when you meet together as God's people. And I believe the report is basically true, although my sources may not be totally impartial in their reporting. 19 I suppose it's inevitable that there be some divisions among you—if only so those whom God has tested and approved of will stand out. 20 But the class distinctions that you—who are well-off—enforce when you meet together with poorer believers indicate that you are not really eating the meal in a way that honors our Lord, as you intend. Instead, it's a selfish mockery of it. ❖ *The Corinthian believers met in the large homes of rich believers. In normal society, the rich would separate guests by seating their own higher social class in the best room with the best food, and those of a lower social class would be seated in a larger room and served inferior food and drink. The poorer guests could easily see the other guests and their better food in the next room. Those who hosted worship meetings in their homes carried this social discrimination over into these meetings, which created discontent among the poorer believers.* ➤ 21 Instead of eating a communal meal together in honor of our Lord, you are each eating your own separate meals. Some of you have so much food and drink that you get drunk while others remain hungry. ❖ *It was still the custom at this time that the Lord's Supper was celebrated at a full meal, just as the Passover was. It's likely that the meal was started with a leader breaking the bread and blessing it, following the tradition started by Jesus. It probably concluded with the leader giving a final blessing over the cup of wine. It's possible that the poor believers only received a portion of bread and wine, while the rich feasted on rich food in front of them.* ➤ 22 If you are unwilling to share what you have with those among you who are poor, you should eat and drink your fill in your own homes before meeting

together. Your actions humiliate some of God's people and reveal that you despise them. ❖ *They abused this meal which is meant to unite God's people and instead, created disunity with it.* ➤ Do you expect me to praise you for this? Rather, you should be ashamed! ❖ *There's nothing wrong with the idea of eating a meal together to celebrate the Lord's Supper. But we should only do what promotes unity among God's people.* ➤

23 This is the tradition I received from our Lord and taught to you: On the same night one of his own followers betrayed him, our Lord Jesus took some bread. 24 He thanked God the Father for it, broke it, and said to his followers, "This bread is my body which I will offer up in death as a sacrifice to take away your sin. *[Isaiah 53:12]* Do *this,* frequently, as a memorial of what I have done for you." ❖ *Given the Jewish context in which Jesus initially did this, his statement that "this bread is my body" is certainly a metaphor meaning "this represents my body." There has been much debate and disagreement over how this is interpreted by various denominations. But the fact that Jesus used figurative language does not exclude the possibility that there is also a spiritual reality behind the metaphorical image in this meal. By offering them "his body" to eat, he was inviting them to receive the benefits of his sacrificial death. See the parallel accounts in Matthew 26:26-29; Mark 14:22-25; and Luke 22:14-20.* ➤ 25 After they had eaten the main part of the Passover meal, he took the cup ❖ *See the note at 1 Corinthians 10:16.* ➤ and said to his followers, "The wine in this cup is the New Covenant *[Jeremiah 31:31-34]* which will be established by the shedding of my blood unto death. *[Exodus 24:8]* Whenever you drink from this cup to observe this meal, remember what I have done for you." ❖ *Jesus' offering of the wine to his followers represented his offering them participation in the New Covenant and in all the benefits that would be procured by his death. Their drinking it meant that they desired to participate in this New Covenant and receive all its benefits. Many followers of Jesus believe that partaking of the cup with faith is not only a symbolic memorial, but is also a means of receiving his undeserved favor whereby we receive those benefits of the New Covenant which we continually need in this life (e.g. forgiveness, physical and emotional healing, comfort, spiritual strength, increased faith, sanctification, unity with other believers, etc.).* ➤ 26 This means that whenever you eat the bread and drink from the cup in this meal, you should be honoring

the Lord by proclaiming what he has done for all of us equally through his death and resurrection. And we should continue to do this frequently until he returns. ❖ *Rich and poor were equally unworthy and equally saved because of his undeserved favor—through their response of faith in his promises. But their manner of celebrating this meal did not proclaim their common salvation or their spiritual equality in union with the Lord—as it was intended to do.* ➤

27 So when you celebrate this meal in a way that dishonors the Lord, ❖ *by dishonoring the poor whom he died to save, and dishonoring the Lord by not properly remembering what he has done for you* ➤ he will hold you accountable for his death. ❖ *Verses 27-29 are often interpreted apart from the context of Paul's argument, leading to interpretations that do not fit the abuse that Paul was trying to correct. Their manner of observing this meal as individual selfish celebrations—not expressing love and unity by sharing their food with the poor— was how they ate and drank unworthily. Instead, they considered the poor as less important and thereby did not remember that the Lord died to save all of them and made them all equally his people and united all of them to himself. They were essentially rejecting some of Jesus' people, and Jesus takes that as a rejection of himself. To be "guilty of the body and blood of the Lord" (in the literal text) means that instead of benefiting from his death, they will be held accountable for his death—like those who actually crucified him.* ➤ 28 That is why you should examine yourselves before you eat to be sure that you have the proper attitude toward your fellow believers and that your actions are consistent with what this meal is intended to proclaim. 29 For those who partake of this holy meal without recognizing and embracing the fact that all participating are part of the Messiah's body [1 Corinthians 10:17]—and that they themselves are equally undeserving recipients of his favor and so are required to extend the same undeserved favor to others—bring about God's judgment and discipline on themselves. ❖ *The main concern of Paul's argument in this passage is that they are considerate of the poor members of the assembly of believers—which is the Messiah's body. But*

this does not necessarily exclude other possible abuses of wrong discernment when participating in the Lord's Supper— as many have interpreted from this verse. ➤ 30 This is why many in your community are weak and sick and why some have died. ❖ *This was Paul's "word of knowledge" discerning the cause of sickness and death in the Corinthian community. It does not imply that all sickness and death among believers is related to God's discipline—as it was in this case. It's also not necessarily true that sickness or death came upon every individual who abused the Lord's Supper. It may have been a general discipline on the rich community, where many of those guilty became sick and some died.* ➤ 31 If we first judge our own attitudes and then submit ourselves to the Messiah's will before eating this meal, then we will not come under his judgment and discipline. 32 But when the Lord judges that we have dishonored him in this meal, he disciplines us so we might repent and not ultimately be condemned along with unbelievers.

33 Therefore, my brothers and sisters in the Messiah, when you assemble to eat this meal together, fully welcome one another as equals. **A** 34 If any of the rich want to satisfy their hunger with the kind of meal they are accustomed to, let them do it in their own homes so they will not humiliate the poor when you come together to eat the Lord's Supper. This way, you will avoid coming under the Lord's judgment and discipline. The other matters you mentioned in your letter I will deal with when I visit you.

12

Discerning What Comes from the Holy Spirit

1 And now, my brothers and sisters in the Lord, with regard to the comments in your letter about things that are truly of the Holy Spirit and hence "spiritual," I want to correct your understanding. **B** ❖ *In chapters 12—14, Paul is correcting the Corinthian believers' understanding regarding which gifts and "spiritual" behaviors come*

A 11:33 The verb ἐκδέχομαι (ekdechomai)—commonly translated "wait for" (but here translated as "welcome")— has a broad range of meanings and it's precise intended meaning must be determined from the context. It's primary meaning is "to receive." In view of his instructions in verse 34, it seems unlikely that he meant

for the rich to wait for the poor to arrive before eating.
B 12:1 The word for "gifts"—inserted in some translations—is not actually used in this verse, although most commentators believe those are the specific "spiritual things" Paul was implying. Some believe he was referring to "spiritual people."

from the Holy Spirit and which do not. Chapters 12—13 are background arguments leading to his correction in chapter 14—which deals primarily with their abuse of the "gift of tongues." But in the course of his correcting them, we learn much about spiritual gifts in general and their intended purpose. As a corrective to their over-emphasis on "speaking in tongues," Paul emphasized the need for many different spiritual gifts to be exercised—and for all to be done with love. ➤ 2 Before you became believers, you spoke under the influence of evil spirits who led you to worship lifeless idols. 3 Therefore, you should realize that speaking under the influence of a spirit doesn't necessarily mean it's the Holy Spirit. Anyone speaking under the influence of the Holy Spirit would never say, "Jesus is cursed," or anything else against him—and only someone under the Holy Spirit's influence would be led to confess that, "Jesus is Lord over all creation." ❖ *We don't know if some Corinthians under the influence of evil spirits were making a pronouncement about Jesus being cursed, or if this was an example of what could be heard in pagan temples, or if Paul was giving a hypothetical example.* ➤

4 You are overly focused on one particular spiritual manifestation. But the one Holy Spirit gives us a variety of grace-enabled abilities. ❖ *A "grace-enabled ability" is a supernatural ability that God gives his people—through the Holy spirit who lives in them—in order to accomplish his will and to show his favor toward them.* ➤ 5 There are a variety of grace-enabled abilities, just as there are a variety of ways to serve our one Lord, Jesus, 6 and just as there are various levels of ability among those who serve him. But all those abilities come from one God who is their source in each of us. 7 The reason that the Spirit shows his power through us in these diverse ways is so each of us can help the entire believing community. 8 For example, God will give a message to one person—through the Spirit—about what is wise to do in a situation, and through the same Spirit, he reveals knowledge to someone else that they could not otherwise have known. ❖ *There is considerable debate as to what Paul meant by "wisdom" and "knowledge" in the literal text of this verse. The interpretation given is typical of Charismatic and Pentecostal understanding.* ➤ 9 To yet another person—through the same Spirit—he gives special faith to overcome obstacles, and to others he

gives various abilities for healing sickness—all from the one Holy Spirit. 10 He will give power to do miracles to one person, to another the ability to hear and speak messages directly from God, to another the ability to discern if a spiritual manifestation is from God or from an evil spirit, and to another various kinds of gifts related to speaking unknown languages, and yet to others the ability to express the meaning of what is spoken in those unknown languages.

❖ *There is considerable controversy as to what each of these spiritual gifts is and is not. But Paul's focus here is not to explain what these gifts are, but that the Spirit gives a diversity of gifts. Many commentators believe this list of spiritual gifts is not exhaustive, but illustrative of their diversity, and ends with "tongues" and "interpretation of tongues" because these were the focus of the Corinthian believers. It's unlikely that the order they are mentioned implies a corresponding ranking of the gifts.* ➤ 11 The one Holy Spirit empowers all these diverse abilities and he is the one who determines which ability each believer receives.

Diversity in Unity Is Necessary

12 As an illustration of the value of this diversity, consider the human body. Even though it's a single unit with one purpose, yet it's made up of many different parts with many different—but essential—functions. This is the way it is with the diversity of believers who together make up the Messiah's one "body." 13 All of us were indeed made part of that "one body" at the time of our conversion because we have all been immersed in the one Holy Spirit. Jewish believers, Gentiles, slaves, and non-slaves are all part of the same body. This is evident because God has given the same Holy Spirit to each of us. ❖ *In our spiritual unity with the Messiah, all social, cultural, racial, and economic reasons for division and separation are obliterated. ¶ The meaning of "baptize" in the literal text of this verse (rendered "immerse" above) is debated. Many say this verse teaches that the Spirit unites us spiritually to the Messiah through the rite of water baptism. The Greek preposition ἐν (en) can mean "in," "by," "with," or "in union with." Fee claims the focus of this verse is that Paul considered the reception of the Holy Spirit to be the common experience that joins believers into one body. When we receive the Spirit, we are joined to him—and also to Jesus through the Spirit's being joined to him. Thus we are all*

joined to Jesus on a spiritual level. These two views are not necessarily mutually exclusive. In the Scriptures, water is often symbolic of the Holy Spirit. Our "baptism" or "immersion" in water is symbolic of our "immersion" in the Holy Spirit, and may be the sacramental means whereby this spiritual immersion is sometimes accomplished. ➤

14 The necessity for diversity in unity is demonstrated in the human body. The parts of one body are not identical in form and function, but are diverse. **15** If a foot said, "Since I'm not a hand, I'm not part of the body," it has come to an absurd conclusion. **16** And if an ear said, "Since I'm not an eye, I'm not part of the body," its declaration would not make it true. **17** A body made up entirely of eyes, couldn't hear. And one made up entirely of ears, wouldn't sense odors. ❖ *Thus diversity of function among the members is clearly a necessity, both in a human body and in the Messiah's body.* ➤ **18** In fact, it is God who places every believer in the Messiah's body—each with their various functions and abilities—precisely where he wants them to be. *[1 Corinthians 12:11]* **19** If every believer had the same function and ability, the "body" would lack many essential functions. It wouldn't be a body at all. **20** Thus it's necessary that there be a diversity of functions and abilities among the people who make up the Messiah's body—while at the same time, they together comprise only one body.

21 It would be absurd for an eye to think that it had no need of a hand, or for a head to think it had no need for the feet. ❖ *From chapter 11, it's apparent that some of the rich Corinthian believers despised poor believers, and Paul continues to address that situation here.* ➤ **22** The reality is that some body parts which seem weaker—such as the internal organs—are in fact essential. **23** And some parts which we think of as less honorable, we cover with clothing—in effect honoring them with our attention. And those parts considered shameful to display, we take particular care to cover so the body as a whole is presentable. **24** But the more

presentable parts—such as our face and hands—have no need of such attention. In the same way, God's plan for the Messiah's body is that more honor should be given to those parts that lack it. **25** He did this so there would be no division in the body, but that all who are part of it should care for the others the same way they care for themselves. **26** If one part of the body suffers, all the other parts should suffer with it and support it with love and prayer; and if one part is honored, all the other parts should rejoice with it.

27 Together, you are the Messiah's body—and each of you is a vital part of it. **28** Among the diversity of people and ministries God has placed in his Assembly of Jesus' followers, he has ranked apostles first; prophets who regularly and accurately hear and speak messages directly from God are second; teachers of Scripture, doctrine, and how to apply it to daily life are third; then others with grace-enabled abilities such as the power to do miracles, various abilities for healing sickness, special abilities to help others, the ability to give wise advice and guidance to the local assembly, and various kinds of grace-enabled abilities for speaking unknown languages. ❖ *Many people believe there were only 13 apostles (the original twelve, minus Judas, plus Matthias and Paul). Others believe Barnabas (Acts 14:3-4, 23; 1 Corinthians 9:5-6), Silas, Timothy (1 Corinthians 16:10), Andronicus and Junias (Romans 16:7),* **A** *and probably others were also called apostles. Apostles usually had authority over the local assemblies they founded. People with the ministries listed (aside from apostles), were generally members of local assemblies. Most commentators believe that the gifts listed after the first three are not in any particular order or rank. Compare the order of gifts listed in 1 Corinthians 12:8-10 (wisdom, knowledge, faith, healing, miracles, prophecy, distinguishing of spirits, tongues), with the list in 1 Corinthians 12:28 (apostles, prophets, teachers, miracles, healing, helps, administration, tongues), the list which occurs in question form in 1 Corinthians 12:29-30 (apostles, prophets, teachers, miracles, healing, tongues, interpretation),*

A 12:28 See the footnote at Romans 16:7 about Junias being a woman. Paul, Barnabas, and Silas are explicitly called prophets (Acts 13:1; 15:32). Barnabas is referred to as an apostle by Luke in Acts 14:4. Some infer from their association with Paul and their authority over

churches that they were functioning as apostles. Many believe that apostles were only appointed by God in the first century. Pentecostal, Charismatic, and apostolic churches teach this office and gift is still given today—although not with the authority to write Scripture.

the list in Ephesians 4:11 (apostles, prophets, evangelists, pastors, teachers), the list in Romans 12:6-8 (prophecy, serving, teaching, encouraging, giving, leading, mercy) and the list in 1 Peter 4:10-11 (speaking gifts, serving). Paul is emphasizing the diversity of gifts and ministry in the assembly of all followers of Jesus, not presenting an exhaustive list. When he repeats this list in verses 29-30, he leaves out "helps" and "guidance" (commonly called "administration") and adds "interpretation of tongues." ➤ 29 It certainly is clear that not every believer is an apostle, nor is everyone a prophet, or a teacher, and not everyone has the power to do miracles, 30 not everyone has the ability to heal sicknesses, not everyone speaks in unknown languages, and not everyone has the ability to interpret or explain what is said in those unknown languages. ❖ Paul is saying to the Corinthians: God has clearly given a diversity of spiritual gifts and ministries to his people. So why are you so focused on everyone speaking in unknown languages in your services—as if everybody should have the same grace-enabled ability? ➤

Spiritual Gifts Must Be Exercised with the Purpose of Loving Others

31 You should be setting your hearts on receiving those grace-enabled abilities that have the greatest potential to benefit the entire community of believers, A instead of using them to exalt yourselves the way you have been. Let me tell you about a higher and more noble way to live and use those abilities for the benefit of others.

13

1 I may be able to speak in unknown—or even angelic—languages, but unless I also show Messiah-like self-sacrificial love in helping others, then such speaking is as worthless in God's sight as the meaningless, harsh, hollow, clanging noises made by pagans in their worship. ❖ This first verse of Paul's digression on "agape" love reveals the main point of this chapter. The Corinthians were focused on speaking in tongues as a sign of spirituality. He does not say that love is a spiritual gift that is "better" than tongues or other gifts. He says that unselfish love for others is the necessary context for exercising the spiritual gifts—including tongues—if they are to be of any value or benefit to anyone. Paul's point that showing unselfish love for others is true spirituality goes beyond the topic of spiritual gifts and challenges the Corinthians in every area of their claims regarding being spiritual and having wisdom and knowledge. ➤ 2 I may have the grace-enabled ability to hear and speak messages directly from God, I may know all of God's mysteries hidden from humanity and know all about the future and I may have miracle-working faith that can accomplish the impossible. [Matthew 17:20; 21:21; Mark 11:23] But unless I also show love for others, in God's sight I am worthless for accomplishing his purposes. 3 I may sell all that I own and distribute the money to the needy, [Matthew 6:2; 19:21; Luke 12:33] and sell my body into slavery to ransom or feed others D so I could boast C to God about my sacrifices. [1 Corinthians 1:9-31; 9:15; 2 Corinthians 1:14; 11:23-30; 12:9-10] But if I'm just doing this out of pride and not out of love for those I help, then God will not reward me for these otherwise good deeds.

4 The characteristics of unselfish love manifested toward others by all who have the Spirit in them are: extreme patience with the shortcomings of others, kindness and mercy, ❖ which is characteristic of God's attitude toward us ➤ and a total lack of: ❖ the things the Corinthians were guilty of ➤ jealousy, envy, rivalry, prideful bragging, conceit,

---

A **12:31** The first sentence of this verse is ambiguous in Greek. Most commentators and translations interpret the first sentence as a command, "you should set your hearts on," but it could mean, "you are setting your hearts on." Some manuscripts have "better gifts," rather than "greater gifts."

B **13:3a** From a letter by Clement of Rome to the church in Corinth written near the end of the first century, we know that some first-century Christians did this.

C **13:3b** Some manuscripts have καυχήσωμαι (kauchēsōmai), "I may boast," some have καυθήσωμαι (kauthēsōmai), "I may be burned," and some καυθήσομαι (kauthēsomai), "I will be burned." Fee says that the external

evidence and transcriptional probability favors "boast." Most translations have chosen "burned" because it's easier to make sense of it. But Christian martyrdom by fire didn't happen until a decade after Paul wrote this letter (and though it was known among Jews, the Gentile Corinthians would have been unaware of this). It would also be much more natural to say, "I give over my body so it may be burned," rather than, "so I may be burned," so it's more likely he was saying, "so I may boast." The difficulty then is to understand Paul "boasting" in some positive sense. The rendering above suggests that Paul meant boasting to God, rather than to people.

arrogance, 5 acting in an improper or disgraceful manner, or selfishly thinking your needs are more important than others. ❖ *Moving beyond problems among the Corinthian believers:* ➤ Those who demonstrate unselfish love in their lives are not easily irritated, offended, or provoked to anger; they hold no grudges or resentments, 6 they grieve over injustice and evil acts, and rejoice over all good, kind, merciful, and just deeds that reflect God's character. 7 They patiently endure all difficulties, hardships, and suffering, and also forgivingly put up with all offenses and persecution in silence, without retaliation. *[Proverbs 10:12; 17:9; 1 Peter 4:8]* They persevere in: trusting God and his promises, in being confident that he will make things work out for the best, and in loving others in every situation. ❖ *Some commentators say the "faith and hope" (in the literal text) are directed toward others, not God.* ➤

8 Having unselfish love in the center of our lives is important because it's an aspect of our spirituality that is eternal. But the grace-enabled abilities such as hearing and speaking messages from God, speaking in unknown languages, and divinely revealed knowledge are only useful in this present life. And along with this age, they will cease at the second coming of Jesus. 9 For the knowledge that the Spirit reveals to us in this life is incomplete, and our grace-enabled ability to hear and speak messages from God is partial and imperfect. 10 But when the completion and perfection of all things is established with the coming of Jesus in glory, then these incomplete and partial abilities won't be needed any longer and will disappear.

11 As an analogy, when I was a child, I spoke, thought, and reasoned like children do—and this was appropriate for that time of my life. But when I became an adult, my childish ways were displaced by abilities and behavior appropriate for adults. ❖ *Similarly, spiritual gifts—which are appropriate to the needs of God's people in this life—will be inadequate and inappropriate in the next age when Jesus returns.* ➤ 12 In this age, we perceive spiritual truths and realities indirectly and figuratively, just as in a mirror you can only see a reflection of someone's image. ❖ *According to Fee, since Corinth produced the finest bronze mirrors in antiquity, it's unlikely they thought that a mirror's image was in any way poor or distorted. But it was indirect and not as accurate in color.* ➤ But when the Messiah returns in glory, we will see him face to face and perceive spiritual truths and realities directly and accurately. In this life, my knowledge of God and spiritual realities is partial. But in the next life, my knowledge of these things will be completely accurate, similar to the completely accurate way God knows me. ❖ *Paul doesn't mean that we will know everything about the infinite God and all realities exactly like God knows all things about us. He is focusing on the relative incompleteness of our knowledge and the quality of spiritual gifts in this life compared to what we will possess in the next life.* ➤

13 For now, the three most important spiritual virtues are: faith in God, a confident expectation that he will fulfill his promises, and demonstrating unselfish love to others. But love is greatest of these because it's nature never changes and it lasts for eternity. ❖ *So spiritual gifts are not signs of spirituality, virtue, or maturity as the Corinthians thought. Romans 8:24; 2 Corinthians 5:7; and Hebrews 11:1 show us either that faith and hope are not eternal or that they will change in eternity from what they are now.* ➤

14

Spiritual Gifts
Are Meant to Encourage God's People

1 So strive to always love others and—in that context—you should also earnestly desire to manifest abilities from the Spirit so you can use them to encourage God's people. Through prayer, you should especially seek to hear and speak messages directly from God. This is much more desirable than speaking in unknown languages in public worship. 2 People who speak in unknown languages are speaking to God, not to his people. Their human spirits are speaking *[1 Corinthians 14:14]* secret truths under the prompting of the Holy Spirit, but no one understands what is being said. ❖ *Paul writes about "various kinds of tongues" in 1 Corinthians 12:10. This has been interpreted by some to mean "different kinds of languages." But given what the Scriptures say, it is more likely that he meant "different kinds of gifts of speaking in*

languages." *In Acts 2:4-8, the kind of gift of tongues that was given enabled people from many countries to hear them speak in their own languages. Here, in 1 Corinthians 14, Paul talks about speaking in tongues that no one understands, which are spoken to God and not to people. Clearly, these are two different kinds of gifts of speaking in tongues. Many Charismatics and Pentecostals teach that the kind of tongues Paul teaches about in this chapter can be further divided into two, three, or more different kinds: one where the speaker speaks to God in prayer privately (the kind Paul does more than anyone else [verse 18]), the kind where someone speaks in public worship to praise and thank God (verse 16), and the kind where the speaker sings to God in public worship (verse 15). The kinds of tongues exercised in public must be interpreted, but what is spoken in private does not need to be. Many also claim another kind of tongues is that of prophesying in tongues in public worship. There is no explicit support for this in Scripture, but it could be a combination of the gift of prophecy and the gift of tongues. This verse may also support the tripartite view of humans that we are composed of spirit, soul, and body. If it is accepted that this verse refers to the human spirit, it is seen that a person's spirit can control the faculty of speaking without the conscious mind (part of the soul) determining what is said. This is consistent with verse 14 below. But some commentators believe the word "spirit" in the literal text of verses 14 and 15 refers to the Holy Spirit, not a human spirit.* ➤ **3** But those who hear and speak messages directly from God are speaking to his people to strengthen, encourage, exhort, and comfort them. ❖ *These are the purposes of the spiritual gift of prophecy. Prophetic utterances are not new revelation on equal par with Scripture. And since it is God's message, it will never contradict what he has already spoken in the Scriptures. In practice, prophetic messages are aimed at specific groups of people and specific circumstances. They are never pronouncements for all of God's people for all time as the Scriptures generally are. As 1 Corinthians 13:9 says, these prophecies are also "in part." See the note at Acts 21:4 and the urgings given to Paul by prophets—which he ignored. See also the note at 1 Corinthians 14:29.* ➤ **4** Those who speak unknown languages are only edifying themselves. But those who hear and speak messages directly from God, edify all who hear them. ❖ *It is good to edify yourself, since you are one of God's people. But in a public gathering, it is much better to edify others too. Prophecies may be directed at individuals at times, yet all who hear of God's concern to speak to individuals are also encouraged and edified.* ➤ **5** I wish it were possible for all of you to speak unknown languages in order to edify yourselves in private. But I wish even more

that all of you would hear and speak messages from God to others. Those who have the ability to do this have been entrusted with a more important ability than those who speak in unknown languages— unless they can also interpret or explain what they've said so that everyone can be encouraged by the Spirit's words. ❖ *The important thing in public worship is that what is ministered be intelligible. Those who can both speak in tongues and interpret them have gifts that together are equivalent to the gift of prophesy in value, if not in function. Paul's wish that all spoke in tongues does not clearly specify if this is an unfulfillable wish or not, but in the context, it is clear that he wishes this were true for their private edification, not for use in public services.* ➤ **6** So, my brothers and sisters, if I came to you and only spoke in unknown languages—which I know you would like me to do to affirm your view of spiritual- ity—how would that help you? It would be a waste of time as far as you are concerned. The only way I can edify you spiritually is to speak to you intelligibly about what God has revealed to me, or give a word of knowledge, or speak a message directly from God, or teach you about some truth.

7 As an illustration, consider musical instruments. If they don't play different notes clearly, how can anyone tell what tune is being played? The playing communicates nothing. **8** Or if a trumpeter doesn't clearly play the correct call to battle, who will recognize what his signal means and get ready to fight? **9** It's the same in your services. If you don't speak intelligible words, how will anyone know what you are saying? As far as the listeners are concerned, you are speaking nonsense to the air. They get nothing from it. **10** There are probably a large number of languages in the world and each of them is meaningful to the people who speak them. **11** But if I don't understand a particular language being spoken by some- one, we are like foreigners to each other who are incapable of communicating. ❖ *The whole purpose of speaking is to communicate. It never makes sense to speak in the presence of others in a way that they cannot comprehend.* ➤ **12** So you should apply this to yourselves. Since you earnestly desire to be spiritual, you should be seeking the frequent exercise of those grace-enabled abilities that are intelligible and therefore help God's people to grow in maturity. ❖ *This desire was seen in their eagerness for everyone to speak in tongues in the mistaken belief that this was the ultimate sign of true spirituality.* ➤

13 Thus the normal practice for those who speak in unknown languages in public worship should be that they also pray for the ability to interpret or explain the general meaning of what they have said. 14 For when I pray in a language that I don't understand, my human spirit is praying by the prompting of the Holy Spirit and is being edified, but my mind isn't participating or benefiting from it—and neither are the minds or spirits of anyone else. 15 So here's what have I concluded from this. First, I will pray and sing with my spirit in unknown languages by the prompting of the Holy Spirit when I worship in private. Second, I will pray and sing with my mind in an intelligible language when I worship with others. And you should mostly do the same. ❖ *Paul didn't forbid speaking in tongues in public worship, but he did limit it to two or three speakers per meeting, and only if someone with the gift of interpretation was present. [1 Corinthians 14:27-28]* ➤ 16 For if you are praising and thanking God in an unknown language, all the others are unable to join with you and agree with what you are praying since they don't understand it. 17 You are expressing genuine thanks to God, but no one else gains spiritual benefit from it. 18 I thank God that he has given me the grace-enabled ability to speak in unknown languages, and I can honestly say before him that in private, I probably pray this way more than any of you ever do. So I'm not denigrating this grace-enabled ability. 19 However, during a gathering of believers, I would much rather speak only five words I understand in order to instruct others than to speak ten thousand words in an unknown language that they can't understand.

20 My brothers and sisters in the Messiah, with regard to these spiritual abilities, don't be self-oriented and overly fascinated with novelty as children are. Your understanding needs to be mature and based on what's important. The only thing in which you should emulate immature infants is their inexperience in practicing evil. 21 It says in the Scriptures, " 'I will speak judgment to my people through foreigners who speak in languages they don't understand …and they still won't listen to me,' says Yahweh." A *[Isaiah 28:11-12]* ❖ *The context of this verse is that God had spoken through his prophets to his people in Israel in words they could understand—but they refused to obey him. Then he communicated his judgment and condemnation to them through the invasion of the Assyrians who spoke languages the Israelites didn't understand. But still they refused to listen to God's message to them. The unknown languages were a sign of God's judgment on unbelievers.* ➤ 22 Thus speaking in unknown languages is not a sign of true spirituality for believers—as you thought. In fact, when these unintelligible languages remain uninterpreted, this ability functions as a sign that brings about judgment for unbelievers who visit your meetings—since they will reject it and your witness and remain condemned. ❖ *It is not, however, a sign from God of what he wants for those unbelievers. It is a sign the tongues speakers themselves produce which acts to the detriment of unbelievers by driving them away.* ➤ But the grace-enabled ability to hear and speak messages directly from God is a sign of true spirituality for believers—which shows his approval. And it doesn't function as a sign that brings about judgment for unbelievers.

23 So if the entire group of believers in Corinth met together and everyone spoke in unknown languages, ❖ *probably at the same time, but the phrase is not clear on this, it could be in turn* ➤ any unbelievers or people ignorant about this ability who were present would think you were all crazy or possessed. B 24 But if everyone spoke—in turn—messages directly from God, any unbelievers who are present would

---

A **14:21** This is not an exact quotation from either the Hebrew text or the Septuagint (the Greek translation of the Hebrew Scriptures). He may have adapted it for his purposes (this was a common practice among Jewish teachers) or he may have been quoting from a different Greek translation. B **14:23** Fee says that prophecy was known and respected by pagans in the Roman empire (oracles spoke messages from the pagan gods), but tongues

realize they are guilty of sin and are worthy of God's condemnation by the content of all the messages they hear. 25 The Holy Spirit would reveal their hidden sins and attitudes to them so they would repent, prostrate themselves in humble submission, worship God, and be saved. They would openly acknowledge that God was really among you. ❖ *Thus prophecy would be recognized by the former unbelievers as a sign of God's genuine presence and his working in the lives of the believers—and would also be a sign of true spirituality such as the Corinthians were seeking.* ➤

Regulate Your Worship so Everyone Can Be Edified

26 So my brothers and sisters, how should this affect your worship meetings? When you meet together, each person may have something to contribute, whether a psalm, or a lesson to teach, or a revelation from the Holy Spirit, or a prayer in an unknown language, or an interpretation for such a prayer, and so forth. Whatever is done at the worship meetings should spiritually strengthen and encourage all those present. 27 If people want to speak in unknown languages, only two, or at most three, should be allowed per meeting, and each must speak in turn—not at the same time. And someone must interpret each such utterance. 28 But if speakers of an unknown language do not themselves have the ability to interpret and don't know of anyone else present who is able to do this, they must remain silent in the meeting. They may pray in an unknown language quietly, heard only by themselves and God. ❖ *Or, they may pray in this way privately, when only God and themselves will hear. The type of meeting where everyone had opportunity to contribute was likely small, probably fewer than 50 people. In such a group, everyone would get to know who among them had the ability to interpret. Or a leader could ask before the meeting began if someone present had that ability so those who spoke in tongues would know if it was permitted to exercise their gift.* ➤ 29 Allow two or three to speak who have messages that they have heard directly from God, then the assembly should discuss if what has been said conforms to the ❖ *Hebrew* ➤ Scriptural revelation and to the

teachings of the apostles that have been handed down to you. ❖ *i.e., the New Testament Scriptures, which were not yet fully written or codified at the time Paul wrote this. In light of verse 31 below, this verse cannot mean that only two or three prophecies may be spoken in a meeting, like tongues. It also implies that not all prophecies will be found to be from the Holy Spirit, or entirely from the Spirit. Yet Paul gives no instruction to denounce a person who speaks a prophecy that is found in error as a false prophet (fit to be executed following the command in Deuteronomy 18:20). In 1 Corinthians 13:9, Paul has already explained that the prophecies given through the spiritual gift of prophecy are "in part," hence not always complete and not always completely from God because of the prophet's imperfect ability to hear from God with 100% accuracy.* ➤ 30 But if one person is standing and speaking a message he received from God, and then another receives such a message and stands up, the first one should stop and allow the second person to speak. ❖ *There is a tendency for less mature prophets to continue speaking beyond the message given to them by the Spirit. If another prophet rises to speak, the one speaking should assume that the Spirit has prompted him to do so and humbly give way. The assembly will later discern whether the second message (and the first) was from the Spirit or not.* ➤ 31 That way, everyone present who receives such a message directly from the Spirit will have the opportunity to speak in turn, so that all may learn and be encouraged. 32 This is possible since those who have the ability to receive and speak messages from God have full control of themselves and can speak or be silent as they decide. ❖ *The Holy Spirit never "possesses" a believer—taking away a person's voluntary control. This is true for all the spiritual gifts, including tongues. Thus the view that speaking in tongues is an ecstatic experience beyond the control of the speaker is erroneous.* ➤ 33 For confusion and disorder are not part of God's character, but peace and harmony are. And this is meant to be reflected in the worship of all the assemblies of God's people. ❖ *Note that Paul doesn't say the opposite of confusion and disorder is quietness, somberness, or rigid regimentation. Spirit-led spontaneity is to be allowed. From other Scriptures, we know that an important characteristic of God's people and their worship is supposed to be joy.* ➤

34 But some of you are going way too far in saying, "Women are not permitted to

---

was either unknown or relatively rare.

speak during worship meetings. They are to be submissive to the assembly ❖ *or to their husbands* ➤ in this—just as the Torah says. 35 If they want to ask about something, they are to wait and ask their own husbands about it at home. It is shameful for a woman to speak in a worship meeting." ❖ *The interpretation of verses 34-35 is difficult (though the text is clear) and commentators offer many solutions.* **A** *That Paul may be quoting something the Corinthians wrote—as he seems to do in 6:12 and in 10:23—is a very attractive possibility because it may be true and it very simply solves all the problems. Most commentators assume that these verses are an authentic part of this letter.* **B** *But if he is not quoting the Corinthians and is giving this as a command, then there are several difficulties.*

First, it contradicts what Paul said in 1 Corinthians 11:5 and 13 where he assumes that women pray aloud and prophesy in their worship meetings, and also 1 Corinthians 14:26 and 31 where he says "everyone has a hymn or lesson or revelation or a tongue or interpretation," and "all can prophesy." Second, the Torah nowhere states that women are not permitted to speak in worship meetings. The only specific references commentators offer that this might possibly be referring to are Genesis 1:26; 2:18-24; and 3:16—none of which seem pertinent. Third, no Scriptural quote is given in support of this prohibition—as Paul always does elsewhere.

In attempting to reconcile these problems with the text, only one commentator (that I found) believes Paul meant to say exactly what the text says and that he simply changed his mind from what he wrote earlier in the same letter. But if one accepts that Scripture is inspired, this assumption means that God changed his mind and is inconsistent. Since most commentators don't believe that of God or of Paul, they almost uniformly interpret it to mean something other than what it says—because it is inconsistent with what Paul says elsewhere, even in this same letter, and is an absolute legalism which is very uncharacteristic of him.

One common interpretation is that this prohibition is not as absolute as it sounds, but prohibits women from teaching, [1 Timothy 2:12] or evaluating prophecies, or publicly challenging things that their husbands have said. Some commentators interpret the reference to the Torah as referring to women submitting to men (which the Torah doesn't say explicitly either, but this conclusion has been argued from

general principles in the Hebrew Scriptures and it was the practice among Jews) rather than to their being silent. In that case, it would seem that if the men didn't insist on their being silent, then the Torah would not prohibit them from speaking.

Most commentators explain these verses by positing that this was a particular cultural problem in Corinth, or that the speaking referred to was excessive and disruptive. However, the declaration on the surface is absolute with no qualification and appeals to the Torah as it's basis—yet there is no such clear prohibition in the entire Hebrew Scriptures, let alone the Torah (Pentateuch). I find the interpretation that Paul was quoting the Corinthians in these verses—rather than giving a command in them—as the simplest explanation. Verses 36-38 also make more sense in light of the interpretation that Paul is quoting the Corinthians in verses 34-35. But whichever interpretation you accept, no commentator that I've read (aside from the one I mentioned above) believes Paul meant to give a blanket command prohibiting women from speaking in meetings of believers. So take care in what you conclude from these verses. ➤

36 Who do you think you are that you can follow your own way and deviate from what is accepted by all other assemblies of believers? Do you think God's message about the Good News originated among you—so you have the right to interpret it any way you like? Or do you think you are the only people who have heard his message and know the truth? ❖ *If Paul was quoting the Corinthians in verse 34-35, then here he is soundly rebuking them for making such a prohibition.* ➤ 37 If any of you think they are prophets ❖ *Paul probably means those with the office or rank of prophet, not just those who have the spiritual gift of prophecy.* ➤ or think they are spiritual, they need to acknowledge that what I've written to you about the practice of these grace-enabled abilities is a direct command from our Lord Jesus the Messiah. ❖ *Paul is speaking from his authority as an apostle, which is a higher authority than that of prophets, [1 Corinthians 12:28] and from the fact that he is also a prophet—having received this direct command from the Lord. Paul was recognized as a prophet early in his ministry. [Acts 13:1, when he was still known as Saul.]* ➤ 38 But if anyone

---

A 14:35a Exegetical support for the interpretation I've used is found in Daniel Arichea's article in The Bible Translator. See the Exegetical Bibliography for the reference.

B 14:35b It's impossible to reproduce Fee's lengthy arguments here, but the interested reader is encouraged to read his commentary on verses 34-35, where he argues strongly that these two verses were not authored

by Paul but were added by some other author at a later, but still very early, date. The main argument against his theory is that there is no existing manuscript that lacks these verses. But Fee's arguments, refuting the idea that these verses are Paul's sentiments, do go along with the interpretation given here that Paul was just quoting the Corinthians.

refuses to acknowledge the Lord's authority behind my command, then the Lord will also refuse to acknowledge that person as his own. ❖ *Or, Paul will not recognize that person's authority, or, the Corinthian believers are not to recognize that person's authority.* ➤

39 So in summary, my brothers and sisters in the Lord, earnestly desire the grace-enabled ability to hear and speak messages directly from God. And don't absolutely forbid people from speaking in unknown languages as long they are always interpreted in your meetings or are used in private. 40 But the overriding principle in conducting your worship meetings is that everything be done properly and without confusion or disorder.

15

Jesus Really Did Rise from Death in a Physical Body

1 ❖ *It seems from what Paul writes in this chapter that the Corinthians started out believing in the resurrection of the Messiah, yet were now teaching that there would be no physical resurrection for believers. They may have had the idea that after death they lived on like angels—without physical bodies. Some of them may have even doubted that Jesus' resurrection was a physical one—as many liberal scholars say today.* ➤ And now, my fellow believers, I will remind you of the message of Good News that I originally preached to you, which you received with faith, which you currently claim you believe, 2 and which will bring you to the full experience of salvation if you continue to firmly trust in the body of teaching I passed on to you (unless some of you want to conclude that everything they have believed in is a lie). 3 The creedal teaching that I received from the other apostles is exactly what I passed on to you. It contains the most important declarations of our faith, namely that: 1) The Messiah died to provide forgiveness for our sins—just as it was prophesied in the Hebrew Scriptures, *[Isaiah chapter 53; Matthew 26:28]* 4 2) He was buried, 3) God brought him back to life on the second **A** day after his

death—just as it was prophesied in the Scriptures, ❖ *While there is no single clear Hebrew Scripture that predicts the Messiah's resurrection on the "third day" (in the literal text), it is likely referring to the witness of the Hebrew Scriptures as a whole. Psalm 16:8-11 implies a resurrection. Peter's sermon in Acts 2:25-36 quotes Psalm 16:8-11 as prophetic evidence that the resurrection was to be expected. Some texts might cryptically refer to the "third day," such as 2 Kings 20:5; Hosea 6:2; and Jonah 1:17; i.e., the "sign of Jonah." [Matthew 12:40] In Luke 24:46, Jesus himself claims that the Hebrew Scriptures predicted his resurrection on the third day. While this prediction is not as clear as some modern readers might like, it was evidently clear enough to the early believers once it was pointed out to them by Jesus himself.* ➤ 5 4) He appeared to Kefa, ❖ *pronounced Kay-fah, i.e., Simon Peter* ➤ and later to the inner group of his close followers—known collectively as "the Twelve." ❖ *"The Twelve" referred to the group of apostles, even though at the time of his resurrection appearances, Judas was dead and Matthias had not yet been chosen to replace him. Most scholars believe verses 3-5 are a very early creed which was recited by Jesus' early followers, and it shows that standard Messianic theology was well developed even before Paul started preaching. While he received his message of the Good News directly from the Messiah himself, this creed was formulated by the early community of Jewish believers.* ➤

6 After that, he appeared to more than five hundred believers at once—and most of those eyewitnesses are still alive at the time of my writing, ❖ *about 23-26 years after Jesus' resurrection* ➤ even though some have died. ❖ *Paul implied that these witnesses were avail-able to be interviewed. The Torah required two witnesses to verify something as fact. [Deuteronomy 17:6] The witness of over 500 people is put forth as overwhelming proof. The fact that this event is not recorded in the gospels, or in Acts, reminds us that the written documentation we have of Jesus' life and events among the first-century believers covers only a small fraction of what occurred.* ➤ 7 Then he appeared to his brother James ❖ *who became the head of the assembly of believers in Jerusalem* ➤ and then to all the apostles. ❖ *Many think this implies there was a group of apostles that was larger than the twelve plus Paul. Paul is not including himself in the group he mentions here, as he lists himself separately in the next verse. Galatians 1:19 implies that James (a brother of Jesus) was considered an apostle. See the note at 1 Corinthians 12:18 about others who*

A 15:4 See the note at Matthew 16:21 for the reasoning behind not using the traditional phrase, "the third day."

may have been apostles. ➤ 8 Finally—long after his ascension—he also appeared to me. *[Acts 9:1-19]* In the eyes of some, my apostleship is as grotesque as an aborted fetus. ❖ *Some commentators think it likely that the Corinthian believers had referred to Paul in this way.* ➤ 9 For I am the least worthy of all the apostles and certainly don't deserve to be one because I persecuted God's people. *[Acts 8:1-3; 9:1-2]* 10 It is only because of God's enabling favor toward me—which I could never do anything to deserve—that I am a believer and an apostle. ❖ *Despite his unworthiness to be an apostle, God chose him to be one. The Corinthian believers had no authority to judge his fitness to be an apostle as they had been doing.* ➤ And the effect of his generous favor in revealing himself to me and calling me to be an apostle has been to produce significant results. For I responded to his favor and have done more to spread the Good News and bring people into his Kingdom than any other apostle. Your faith is a direct result of my work. But I get no credit for that since it was only because God graciously decided to work in and through me that I have done anything. 11 But it doesn't matter if I or other apostles preached the message of the Messiah's resurrection to you; the facts above are the message that we all continue to preach, and the one that you yourselves believed when it was preached to you.

Since the Messiah Rose from Death, So Will All People

12 Now, if you really believe what we preach—that the Messiah has been raised to life from among those who are dead—how can certain leaders among you claim that those who are dead will not be raised back to life? 13 Assuming for the moment it is true that those who have died cannot be made alive gain, then logically, it couldn't have happened to the Messiah. 14 If this is the case and the Messiah is still dead, then our preaching has no basis in fact and your faith is also not based on reality and is therefore worthless. 15 Another implication is that we are false witnesses who have lied about God since we said he brought the Messiah back to life when he didn't (assuming it's true that he doesn't bring anyone who is dead back to

life). 16 For the inevitable logic is that if God doesn't bring the dead back to life, then he didn't bring the Messiah back either. 17 If this is true, then your faith in the Messiah gains you nothing—for your sins are unforgiven and you remain under the sentence of eternal damnation in Hell. ❖ *Since the Corinthian believers had subjectively experienced the reality of their sins being forgiven, they are forced to recognize the absurdity of their premise in verse 14.* ➤ 18 And all those who were believers in the Messiah but have died are condemned just like unbelievers. ❖ *Those who taught that there was no physical resurrection probably thought that believers lived on in a spiritual existence in Heaven—without bodies. Paul counters by saying, if there is no bodily resurrection, then the Messiah didn't rise and the Gospel message is a sham. No resurrection means there is no forgiveness of sin and no salvation in Heaven of any kind for anyone.* ➤ 19 If it's true that our expectant hope for salvation from the Messiah only gives us comfort in this life but has no future reality, then we are the most pathetic people in the world. ❖ *For we strive to live holy lives for no purpose. We give up worldly pleasures for no gain. We have wasted our lives following a delusion, and have also deceived others.* ➤

20 But the fact is, the Messiah *has* been raised to life from among those who are dead. He is the "first fruits" of all who have died and will later be raised to life. ❖ *Paul's argument in these verses focuses on believers who have died—not unbelievers. Other Scriptures teach that unbelievers will be raised for the judgment, but he does not address that situation in this argument.* ➤ 21 Just as death came to humanity through a man, so also resurrection from death comes to a new humanity through a man. ❖ *Paul's point is that the Messiah's resurrection was not a special case, based on his deity. The Messiah is the first member of a new redeemed humanity, and what happens to him must inevitably happen to all who are spiritually joined to him through faith.* ➤ 22 Just as we all die because we are descended from Adam and inherit his mortality, in the same way, we who believe in the Messiah will also be made alive again as he was because we are spiritually joined to him and inherit his immortality. 23 But there is a proper sequence to all this. First, the Messiah was raised as the "first fruits." Then when he returns, he will raise all who belong to him. 24 Then, comes the end of this world as we

know it, when the Messiah vanquishes every demonic ruler, authority, and power. Finally, he will hand over control of the Kingdom to God the Father—25 because Jesus must reign as king until the Father has subjugated all of Jesus' enemies, 26 the last of which to be destroyed will be death itself. 27 The Scriptures say that God the Father has put all things under the authority of the Messiah. [Psalm 8:6; 110:1] (But clearly "all things" doesn't include God the Father himself.) 28 When God the Father finally brings about the complete subjugation of everything under the Messiah's rule, then the Son will subject himself to the Father so once again—as in eternity past—all that exists will be subject to the Father's will. ❖ *Paul's point is that when God raised the Messiah from death, he set in motion a plan that leads to the complete destruction of death, so everything will once again be subject to his perfect will. If death is destroyed and all the work of the enemy is undone, then death must also be undone. Thus we can be confident that there will be a physical resurrection.* ➤

29 But if there won't be any resurrection from death, then what do those people hope to accomplish by being baptized for those who have died? ❖ *No one knows what this practice was that Paul refers to. The only thing that's clear is that their practice assumed there would be a resurrection. Paul neither affirms nor criticizes this practice, but is using it to show that their actions are absurd if they don't believe in a resurrection. In most of this letter—even when only some of the Corinthian believers are doing something—Paul addresses the issue to them as a whole. Here (in the Greek text), he uses the pronoun "they." This might imply that it was the practice of a very small minority. There is no historical record of such a practice among believers, nor among pagans, so it remains a mystery. Commentators have posed at least 40 different possible explanations—which indicates that no one knows for sure what Paul was referring to here.* ➤ 30 And if the message about the Messiah's resurrection isn't true, then why do we apostles continually risk our lives to preach it? 31 My brothers and sisters in the Lord, I face persecution and the possibility of martyrdom every day in order to preach it! And I swear it's worth it because I am proud of what Messiah Jesus our Lord has done in your lives as a result of my work. 32 If everything I've preached is a lie and I've been struggling with those demonically inspired men of Ephesus—who oppose my work and threaten my life—on only a human level, then my ministry there hasn't accomplished anything of eternal value! If there will be no physical resurrection for those who have died, then we might as well forget about God and follow the adage, **"Eat, drink, and enjoy life while we can—for all too soon we will die,"** since we have no future existence to look forward to or to prepare for. ❖ *The quote is from Isaiah 22:13 and expresses an attitude toward life that Yahweh condemns in that passage.* ➤

33 Don't allow others to deceive you! If you continue to listen to those who deny the resurrection, they will corrupt your character! 34 So wake up and start thinking clearly as you should! Cease doing those shameful sins of yours! You are living as though you don't have any relationship with God—and it's clear that those who have been leading you into these errors don't know him at all. ❖ *One important implication of this section is that our expectations of what is in store for us in the future—regarding the resurrection, final judgment, and rewards in Heaven—will affect the way we live. Many believers are complacent about sin in their lives because they lack a proper focus on what is to come.* ➤

35 But I know what your real objection is. You are thinking, "How can a corpse be reanimated? What kind of disgusting body will it be?" 36 That's the question of a fool who doesn't know what God can do! You should know better from examples in the world around you! Seeds can't become what they are meant to be unless they are first planted in the earth and "die." ❖ *Even though we know a germinating seed doesn't "die," it ceases to exist as a seed. This is an illustration, not a botany lesson.* ➤ 37 And the body of the seed of wheat (or any kind of seed) that you plant bears no resemblance to the body of the plant it will produce. ❖ *This illustration shows the continuity (the plant is genetically identical to the seed) and also the transformation (from seed to plant) that is characteristic of resurrected bodies. They will be the same and yet transformed.* ➤ 38 Rather, it produces a body that God has designed, and he has designed each kind of seed body to produce a different kind of plant body.

39 Not all bodies have the same construction and characteristics. There is one design

for humans, another for four-legged animals, another for birds, and another for fish, each suited to its environment and needs. 40 There is also a difference between terrestrial bodies (e.g. plants, animals, and humans) and the celestial bodies we see in the night sky. The splendor of celestial bodies is different from the splendor of terrestrial bodies. ❖ *The reference to celestial or "heavenly" bodies could also be hinting at the bodies of spirit beings. Jews in Paul's time associated the stars with angels.* ➤ 41 The sun, moon, and stars have different splendors, and even stars differ from one another in their splendor. ❖ *e.g., color and brightness* ➤

42 And so it will be when God raises those who are dead. The body that is planted in the ground is mortal—but will be raised having immortality. 43 The body that is planted is an embarrassment—but will be raised having God-like glory. The body that is planted is weak—but will be raised having power. 44 The body that is planted is a natural "soulish" body—but will be raised as a supernatural "spiritual" body, empowered by the Spirit and designed for eternal life such as the glorified Messiah possesses. Since you know about natural bodies, you should understand that they are merely "types" or "shadows" of the supernatural bodies we will have after the resurrection. ❖ *Paul literally compared "soulish" bodies and "spiritual" bodies. Since physical bodies are not made of "soul" substance, it is equally clear that the "spiritual" body isn't composed of "spirit" substance. Rather, the words refer to the two contrasting natures and the sources of direction and empowering that they have. He used the same word, "spiritual," that the Corinthians had used of themselves, thinking that with the gifts of the Spirit and especially the gift of tongues, they had entered into the "spiritual" existence that was their future in Heaven. The only thing they thought they lacked was the shedding of their mortal bodies. All of this letter has been aimed at countering their view of what constitutes true "spirituality," and correcting their inflated understanding of*

their progress along that road. ➤ 45 For the Scripture says, "The first man, Adam, received life and became a living 'soul,' " *[Genesis 2:7b]* and because of his sin, he was the progenitor of a humanity that is subject to decay and death. But the "last-days Adam"—the Messiah—through his perfect obedience and resurrection became the spiritual-life-giving progenitor of a new redeemed humanity which will live forever. **A** 46 But we cannot yet fully experience our true "spiritual" life which is to be our inheritance. First, we must continue to live out this natural "soulish" life, then later, only at the resurrection will we enter fully into our supernatural "spiritual" existence. 47 The life and nature of the first man (i.e., Adam, who represents fallen humanity) was temporary and subject to decay— as is characteristic of this world. The life and nature of the second man (i.e., the resurrected Messiah, who represents the new redeemed humanity) is eternal and imperishable—as is characteristic of Heaven. 48 The progeny of the first man share his fallen "earthly" nature and are subject to decay and death. The progeny of the second man ❖ *i.e., those who are spiritually joined to the Messiah* ➤ share his nature as he is in Heaven. ❖ *Hence, just as he was raised to life in a new glorified supernatural physical body, we who share his nature will also be raised to life in the same kind of body.* ➤ 49 We have inherited mortal bodies from Adam, and in the past, our lives reflected his fallen nature. Since we hope to inherit glorified Heavenly bodies like the Messiah's at the resurrection, our lives should also be reflecting his perfect nature. **B** ❖ *Paul implies that the Corinthians have not yet "arrived" as "spiritual" people, and that they never will unless they start reflecting the Messiah's character of holiness, humility, and love in this life.* ➤

50 Now, my brothers and sisters in the Lord, I will explain something. Mortal

---

A 15:45 Paul was quoting from the Septuagint, the Greek translation of the Hebrew Scriptures. He added the words "first" and "Adam" to his quotation in order to make his comparison clearer. Jewish teachers commonly quoted Scripture "loosely" by our standards. As long as the same general meaning was conveyed, they didn't quibble over quoting the exact words. In Hebrew, the

name "Adam" is identical to the word for "man" used in the sense of "mankind" or "humanity."

B 15:49 It seems likely that the final verb in the original text was "let us bear" (aorist subjunctive), translated "should also be reflecting," rather than "we will bear" (future indicative), as in many translations.

bodies such as we now possess—which are subject to decay—cannot enter into an eternal existence in God's Kingdom in Heaven.

51 God has revealed that at the time the Messiah returns, not all believers will have died, but all of us (both those living and those who have died) *will* be transformed. 52 When the last trumpet is blown, *[1 Thessalonians 4:15-17; Revelation 10:7; 11:15]* within a split second, those who have died will be raised to life having immortal glorified bodies, and in the same instant, the bodies of those still living will also be transformed. 53 For it is necessary that our perishable mortal bodies be changed into imperishable immortal bodies in order to live in Heaven. 54 When this takes place, the Scripture will have come true that says, **"He will have complete victory over Death—destroying it forever."**

❖ *Paul loosely quotes Isaiah 25:8a from the Septuagint, where a Greek word can literally mean "in victory," or idiomatically can mean "forever." Despite this superficial discrepancy with the Hebrew text—which has "forever"—the meaning is the same.* ➤ 55 Thus in view of the Messiah's resurrection and our hope of the resurrection to come, we can say, **"So, Death, what's happened to your victory over humanity? Where's your power to eternally destroy?"**

[Hosea 13:14] ❖ *This taunts Death as if it were a person. It might be construed to be a taunt of Satan—the originator of sin and death. Death, here, includes not only physical death but also eternal death, i.e., eternal separation from God in Hell. While believers still die physically, death's power to keep us dead and separate from God has been defeated by the Messiah's resurrection, and even that small power will be destroyed forever at our resurrection.* ➤ 56 For it's our sin that causes us to die, since God's Torah requires the punishment of death for all who sin. **A** *[Romans 5:12; and all of Romans chapter 7]* 57 But we can thank God for the victory he gives us over sin, death, and the Torah's condemnation through spiritual union with our Lord Jesus the Messiah—who was victorious over them by his perfect obedience and his resurrection.

58 So then, my dear brothers and sisters in the Lord, don't allow any teaching or person to move you away from the foundation of your faith—which is the message about the Messiah's death and resurrection that you believed at the start. And you should always be investing your lives in the Lord's work since you know your efforts for him in his life are not without eternal value—as they would be if there were no resurrection.

16

Guidelines for Their Charity Drive

1 Now, your letter asked for guidelines for the charity drive for the poor believers in Jerusalem. I want you to follow the same guidelines that I gave the assemblies of believers in Galatia Province: 2 Every Sunday, each of you in his own home should put aside something for the drive from what the Lord has blessed you with that week. ❖ *Many of these people were poor or slaves and had no regular income. There is no hint of a tithe or proportional amount suggested in Paul's directions. Since the amount was put aside by each individual, no external coercion or manipulation is possible. The gift and motive was between the individual believer and his Lord.* ➤ That way, everything will already be accumulated when I come, and the sum will be greater than if you took up one collection at that time. 3 When I arrive, I will write out letters of introduction for those you choose to take your contributions to Jerusalem. ❖ *The letters of introduction would provide credibility for them when requesting hospitality from other believers along the journey. Perhaps letters of introduction to the leaders in Jerusalem would also include the amount being sent, so they would know if it all arrived, and then they could send letters back to the senders assuring them that it all arrived safely. The fact that their own people would carry the contributions would provide them with assurance that the money would reach those it was intended to help. Paul probably also hoped that the personal interaction between the Corinthian believers and those in Jerusalem would promote unity between Jewish and Gentile believers.* ➤ 4 And if it seems appropriate given the circumstances of the situation when I arrive, I may accompany them.

A **15:56** This may not be taught in a general way in the Torah, but it is derived from many specific examples where the punishment for specific sins are death. A few examples are: Genesis 2:17; 3:3; Exodus 21:14; 28:42-43; Leviticus 8:35; 22:9; Numbers 18:22, 32; Deuteronomy 17:12-13; 22:22; 24:7; and especially 28:15-68.

Paul's Itinerary
and Instructions Regarding Timothy

5 I plan on revisiting the local assemblies of believers in Macedonia Province first ❖ *in Northern Greece* ➤ on my way to visit you. ❖ *Paul is writing from Ephesus, and intended to take the overland route to Corinth.* ➤ 6 When I arrive, I will probably stay with you for a while, perhaps the entire winter. ❖ *During the winter, no one normally traveled by ship on the Mediterranean Sea for the weather was too dangerous. Since his next destination was likely to be Jerusalem or Rome, the most direct route to either would be by sea.* ➤ Then, when my visit with you is finished, you can help send me on my way to my next destination—wherever that may be. ❖ *In the past, he hadn't allowed the Corinthians to support him so he could preach the gospel to them for free. But now he was willing to allow them the privilege of helping him on his way (perhaps as a concession to them) with money, provisions, and traveling companions to ensure his safety. Paul's plans weren't definite, as circumstances or the Lord's leading could change them.* ➤ 7 I would like to have an extended visit with you—if the Lord allows it—instead of just briefly passing through, which is what I would have to do if I came to see you first. 8 But for now, I will remain here in Ephesus until the Pentecost Festival. ❖ *This occurred 50 days after Passover. We don't know if it had already become an annual day of celebration for the Gentile believers at this time or not.* ➤ 9 Right now, there's a huge opportunity to preach the Good News here. Many are open to receiving it but there are also many who oppose my preaching. ❖ *We can't know the timing for certain, but this could refer to the time recorded in Acts 19, just before Acts 19:23-41.* ➤

10 When Timothy arrives in Corinth, ❖ *In 1 Corinthians 4:17, Paul said he sent him to them.* ➤ be sure that you provide him with proper hospitality and make him feel welcome—for he is doing the same kind of work for the Lord as I am, and he is representing me to you. Therefore, he is just as worthy of your respect and support as I am. ❖ *Timothy helped Paul establish the assembly of believers in Corinth and was sent to remind them of Paul's teaching and standards. Given the animosity some of the Corinthians had toward Paul, he was concerned that their feelings toward him would be carried over to Timothy. Timothy was—at the very least—an apostolic representative, if not an apostle in his own right.* ➤ 11 So don't allow anyone to treat him with disrespect because of his youth. But when his visit is completed, I expect you to send him and those who accompany him back to me with your blessing and material support for their journey. For I will be waiting here for their return.

12 As for your request that our brother Apollos be sent to minister to you, I did strongly urge him to accompany the brothers who brought your letter to me on their journey back to you. But he was unwilling to do so at this time, although he said he will come when he has the opportunity. ❖ *The fact that Paul urged Apollos to go showed that he had no sense of rivalry with him, and the problem among the Corinthian believers had nothing to do with Apollos' teaching. The Greek is ambiguous as to who was unwilling for Apollos to go. It could mean God's will or Apollos' will. Since there is no one specified, it is more natural to assume from the context that it refers to Apollos. If so, this also likely showed that he shared Paul's view concerning the divisions among the Corinthian believers and wanted nothing to do with encouraging such division.* ➤

Paul's Closing Exhortations

13 Be on guard against the enemy's attempts to lead you into error. Hold on firmly to the purity of the message of salvation that I preached to you. Be courageous in your stand in the face of opposition and the conflict surrounding you. 14 In all matters and in all relationships, do everything with the motive of unselfish love.

15 Now, my brothers and sisters in the Lord, you all know Stephanas and his household who were the first believers in Achaia Province. ❖ *Corinth was the capital of Achaia Province. Stephanas was clearly a leader among the Corinthians and someone who was faithful to Paul. He and Fortunatus and Achaicus (mentioned in verse 17 below) brought the letter from the Corinthian believers to Paul, and would be the ones to take this letter back to them.* ➤ They have done much to serve God's people and they minister to them through teaching and proclaiming the Good News. Therefore, I strongly exhort all of you 16 to submit to their leadership, and also to the leadership of anyone who joins in the work of proclaiming the Good News and ministering to others. ❖ *True leaders are identifiable through their love*

and ministry. *Those who are divisive and in error are not as often found among those who lovingly serve others and minister the Gospel message.* ➤

17 The arrival here of Stephanas, Fortunatus, and Achaicus as your representatives made me very happy because my absence from you creates a void in my life and they have helped to fill it with their fellowship and news from you. ❖ *There is no way to know for sure, but the names Fortunatus and Achaicus were common among slaves and former slaves (freedmen) and they may have been a part of Stephanas' household.* ➤ 18 Their visit has been very refreshing and has lifted my spirits, just as I know they have often done for you. You should give appropriate recognition to such people.

Closing Greetings

19 The believers here in Asia Province send their warm regards to you. Aquila and his wife Priscilla and the believers who meet in their home also send their love in the Lord. ❖ *Aquila and Priscilla were known to the Corinthian believers because they had lived in Corinth and first met Paul there. [Acts 10.1-3]* ➤ 20 All my fellow workers and traveling companions also send you their warm greetings. Always greet one another with genuine Messiah-like love. ❖ *The "holy kiss," in the literal text, was the customary form of greeting among believers, and was probably a kiss on the cheek.* ➤

21 And I, Paul, write my own warm greeting to you with my own hand. ❖ *Most of the letter was being written down by a scribe, possibly Sosthenes, [1 Corinthians 1:1] as Paul dictated. But from here to the end of the letter, he takes the pen in his own hand to authenticate it with his own handwriting and signature.* ➤

22 If anyone does not love the Lord, then that person will be cursed with damnation! ❖ *Most of the issues and errors addressed in this letter indicated a lack of love for their Lord and Savior, Jesus. If they are not willing to submit to Paul's instructions in these matters as the Lord's apostle, then they don't really love the Lord and are under the curse of eternal death—unless they repent before the Lord returns.* ➤ O Lord Jesus, come quickly! ❖ *"Come quickly" translates "marana tha" in the original text. This is an Aramaic prayer that the Lord would come. [Revelation 22:20] It was borrowed from Aramaic-speaking d this context, Paul was probably emphasizing that the Lord—whom many of them were rejecting—was indeed returning, and those who were in rebellion were in danger of being rejected by the Lord.* ➤

23 I pray that our Lord Jesus will look upon you with great favor, far beyond anything you can deserve. ❖ *The literal text of Paul's letter begins and ends with "grace to you," for this expresses all that God has done and will do for his people through Jesus the Messiah.* ➤

24 I send my love to all of you because we are joined together in Messiah Jesus. ❖ *The final "Amen" found in some translations was probably not in the original letter, but added by scribes when the letter was later read in worship services.* ➤

Paul's Second Letter
to Jesus' Followers in Corinth

The historical circumstances behind 1 & 2 Corinthians are as follows: Paul's first visit to Corinth during his second missionary journey in AD 51–52 (recorded in Acts 18) is when he established the local assembly of believers there. Sometime after that, he wrote a letter to them (no longer in existence) that he refers to in 1 Corinthians 5:9-13. This is sometimes referred to as Letter A. Then the Corinthians sent three men to Paul in Ephesus with a letter containing a number of questions (see 1 Corinthians 16:17). Paul then wrote 1 Corinthians in reply, which was his second letter to them (that we know of) and is sometimes referred to as Letter B.

From here on, the sequence is not certain. There are two main reconstructions of what happened. Paul either sent 1 Corinthians to them with the same three men that brought their letter to Paul, or with Titus. Timothy was already on his way to Corinth, [1 Corinthians 4:17] but Paul expected his letter B (1 Corinthians) to reach them first. So Timothy was probably going by land and letter B—with its courier(s)—went more directly by sea. Then, either Timothy or Titus brought back a report to Paul that some false apostles had convinced the believers in Corinth that Paul was not a true apostle. So Paul changed his plans from what he had stated in 1 Corinthians 16:5-7 and made a quick trip directly to Corinth (his second visit) that was very brief and a painful experience for all. [2 Corinthians 2:1; 12:14; 13:1-2]

Reconstruction Alpha postulates that he returned to Ephesus and then sent Titus to Corinth to help the believers straighten things out, since they trusted Titus.

Reconstruction Beta postulates that when he returned to Ephesus, he wrote a harsh letter urging the Corinthian believers to punish the leader of the faction that was opposing Paul. This is sometimes referred to as Letter C, but if it ever existed, it too no longer exists and we don't know what was said in it. He sent Titus to carry the letter to them.

In both reconstructions of the events, when Paul was finished with his work in Ephesus, he didn't wait there for Titus' return. Instead, he went by land to Troas and then on to Macedonia to intercept Titus on his return journey. [2 Corinthians 2:12-13; 7:5-16] Paul was greatly relieved when he finally met up with Titus and heard his report that the majority of the Corinthian believers had repented of their rebellion against Paul's authority as an apostle. But a minority group, led by some Jewish believers, still opposed Paul. [2 Corinthians chapters 10—13] So while Paul was in Macedonia, probably in the town of Philippi, he wrote this letter, 2 Corinthians (called letter D by those who hold to Reconstruction Beta) and sent it with Titus to the believers in Corinth. [2 Corinthians 8:16-24] Then Paul made his third trip to Corinth [2 Corinthians 12:14; 13:1-2; Acts 20:1-3] and while he was there, he wrote his letter to the believers in Rome. A variation of reconstruction Alpha says that Paul wrote chapters 1—9 of 2 Corinthians based on Titus' good report, and then received further negative news about the remaining rebellious faction, so he added chapters 10—13 to it. This accounts for the abrupt change in tone beginning with chapter 10. Some scholars believe chapters 10—13 are part of another letter entirely. However, there is not even one existing manuscript to support that belief, in which those chapters are not a part of this letter.

Reconstruction Alpha also assumes that the person mentioned in 2 Corinthians 2:5-11 and 7:12 is the same person mentioned in 1 Corinthians chapter 5.

The translation of some verses in this letter depends on the assumptions one makes about whether or not there was a letter C (I assume Reconstruction Alpha in which there was no letter C) and whether one assumes that 2 Corinthians was originally only one letter (I do), or contains parts of two or more separate letters.

Another matter of difficulty is that Paul sometimes writes with an "epistolary we" (similar to the royal "we"), so it's often not clear when "we" is referring to other people and when he just means "I." It is also often not clear when "we" includes the Corinthians he is writing to (i.e., we believers) and when he is only talking about himself and his fellow workers (i.e., we leaders). Therefore, considerable variation exists among translations as to how these pronouns are translated. Fortunately, the main thrust of Paul's teaching and arguments does not depend on our knowing for sure which decisions concerning the pronouns are correct.

One of the great values of this letter is Paul's clear description of the characteristics of dedicated spiritual leadership and the proper exercise of spiritual authority, which include: complete humility, desiring only the best in others and glory for the Lord, great patience and gentleness in appealing to the wayward, willingness to suffer, and unassailable integrity.

Other Important Points Covered in This Letter Are:

1) God comforts his people when they are in difficult circumstances. [1:3-11]

2) Instructions about accepting repentant sinners. [2:5-13]

3) In union with the Messiah, believers are always victorious over Satan. [2:14-17]

4) The excellence of the New Covenant in comparison with the Old Covenant. [3:7-18]

5) The ministry of bringing others to know the Messiah. [5:11—6:10]

6) Believers are not to partner with unbelievers. [6:14—7:4]

7) Principles concerning the use of our money, integrity in handling other people's money given for ministry, and joy in giving. [chapters 8—9]

1

Opening Greetings

1 Greetings from Paul, who was called by God to be an apostle of Messiah Jesus. And also greetings from Timothy, your brother in the Lord. I'm writing particularly to the community of God's people in Corinth and also to all of God's people in the rest of Achaia Province. ❖ *The Roman province of Achaia covered the peninsula that today is southern Greece, and Corinth was its capital.* ➤ 2 I pray that God our Father and our Lord Jesus will look upon you with great favor far beyond anything you can deserve and therefore, grant you every spiritual blessing, peace, and well-being.

God Is the Source of All Comfort During Suffering

3 We should thank and praise God—the Father of our Lord Jesus the Messiah. For he is the source of all compassion and mercy, and he is the one who comforts, consoles, 4 encourages, revives, and strengthens us whenever we experience difficult circumstances. As a result of experiencing his help under such circumstances, we are in turn able to offer the same support to others when they experience difficult times. For we are able to pass on to them what we ourselves have received from God. ❖ *Commentators differ as to who Paul is referring to by "we" or "us." Some think he is referring only to himself and Timothy, others think it includes other colleagues in the ministry and*

missionaries, and others that it also refers to the Corinthians and any believer who suffers. He may have been primarily referring to his own experiences, yet he was expressing a truth applicable to all believers, hence I've expressed the broader interpretation. ➤ 5 We know that the Messiah suffered many things, and those of us who are spiritually joined to him also experience many of the same kinds of sufferings and persecutions in this life because we are identified with him. So we also realize that God helps us—because we are joined to Jesus—with the same comfort, encouragement, and strength that he gave the Messiah. 6 Whenever we apostles suffer persecution, you should realize that it's for the spiritual benefit of the people we teach and serve—like you. Through it, we learn how to comfort and encourage you when you suffer, and we also set an example of endurance and dependence on the Lord for you to follow. ❖ *There's a wide range of interpretations for the first half of this verse, and this interpretation encompasses three of them.* ➤ Whenever God comforts and encourages us apostles, his secondary purpose is that you might see his faithfulness and learn to endure similar suffering and persecutions with patience while trusting in God. 7 Our hope that you will patiently endure suffering while still holding strong to your faith is based on the knowledge that you will experience the same comfort and encouragement from God that we did, just as you will also experience the same kind of sufferings that we have.

8 My brothers and sisters in the Messiah, we want you to understand the severity of

the persecution and suffering we experienced in Asia Province. ❖ *Probably in Ephesus* ➤ It was so great that it was beyond our own ability to cope with it or endure it—and we didn't expect to come out alive. ❖ *Evidently, the Corinthians knew basically what had happened, but weren't aware of the extremity of the danger and suffering that Paul and his companions had experienced. We don't know with any confidence what circumstances Paul was referring to, though there have been many speculations.* ➤ 9 In fact, we felt like our immediate death was a certainty. But God allowed us to come to this point so that when we finally gave up hope that anything *we* could do would save us, we would learn to entrust ourselves to God and to his ability to help and take care of us. After all, he can even raise the dead back to life so what does it matter if we die? 10 In the end, he did rescue us from certain death. We have placed all our confident expectations in him and know that he will rescue us again in any future troubles that come our way—11 especially since you are asking him in your prayers to help us. I want you to be doing this since if many are praying for us, then when God answers and shows us his favor by rescuing us from danger, those many will also recognize his greatness and mercy and therefore thank and praise him as they should. *[2 Corinthians 4:15]*

Paul Defends His Integrity

12 I feel free to ask you to pray for us because my conscience is clear with regard to the way I've dealt with you. ❖ *Paul knew that some in Corinth were accusing him of insincerity and of taking advantage of them.* ➤ I take pride in the fact that I have never conducted myself toward you or anyone else in ways that many unbelievers would have in order to take advantage of you. Nor have I only depended on my own wisdom to know the best way to deal with you. But with God's gracious help, my dealings with you and all others have always been honest, sincere, and in accordance with his will. ❖ *since he became a follower of Jesus.* ➤ A 13-14 I say this because I want to assure you

that everything I've written to you in my letters has been straightforward—without ambiguity or hidden meaning. I write exactly what I mean and make sure my points are clear enough that you can easily understand what I intend. I hope that even though you have, to date, only partially understood my actions, motives, intentions, integrity, and authority, that soon you will come to fully understand me and retain that understanding until the day our Lord Jesus returns in glory. For on that day, I want you to be as proud of me as I am of you. B ❖ *Our basis for boasting before the Lord on Judgment Day will only be in the excellence of the lives of those in whom we have invested our lives—through our witness, teaching, resources, and prayers. For they are the "spiritual fruit" that we bear. [John 15:8]* ➤

15-16 It was because I was confident that you thought highly of me that I originally told you I planned to make my first stop to visit you on my way to Macedonia Province, ❖ *northern Greece* ➤ and then visit you again on my way back from there so you could help me on my way to Judea Province. That way, you would have had two chances to bless me and thereby receive a double blessing. ❖ *The word translated "blessing" is χαρά (chara) in some Greek manuscripts, meaning "joy," and in others χάρις (charis) meaning "grace." These two words, as they are inflected in the Greek text (χαρᾶς, χάρις), differ by only one letter. Paul implied that God would bless them for helping him.* ➤ 17 But when I changed my plan after I had already told you about it, it was for a very good reason and not because I'm unreliable or inconsistent—as some are saying. I do not make my decisions the way unbelievers do—just following some whim. Rather, my decisions are made after discerning God's will. I never say I will do something while secretly intending to do otherwise. 18 As surely as you know that God always does what he promises, you can be sure that I—whom he chose to be his apostle—will never say one thing to you and really mean something else. 19 Jesus the Messiah, God's Son, would never do such a

---

A 1:12 In verses 12-14, the Greek has "we" in the literal text instead of "I," which is in the rendition above. Paul may have been using an "epistolary we," meaning only himself, or he may have been speaking for Timothy too.

B 1:13 ἕως τέλους ἐπιγνώσεσθε (heōs telous epignōsesthe) is literally, "to the end you will know fully," and can mean, "you will understand to the end," or "you will understand fully," or "you will understand fully to the end."

thing. Therefore, I would never do this either because Silvanus, ❖ *a.k.a. Silas* ➤ Timothy, and I told you about him and we represent him. We also know that if we discredit ourselves by lying, we discredit the one we represent. And Jesus' life and death demonstrate that God always says what is true and always keeps his promises. 20 For Jesus has already fulfilled—or will fulfill—all of God's promises. He is God's unequivocal message to us that says, "Yes, I keep my promises." Therefore, our response to God—through the agency of our Lord Jesus the Messiah—is "Amen!" ❖ *i.e., Yes, we believe it will be as you have said.* ➤ Thus we exalt him by expressing our trust in him for all to see—just as it should be. ❖ *Many commentators believe the phrase "through him" (Jesus) refers to the means by which we say "Amen" and offer our worship, i.e., via our spiritual union with him. This is certainly always true.* ➤ 21 Now it is God himself who has joined you and us in an intimate relationship with the Anointed One ❖ *i.e., the Messiah* ➤ and he continues to maintain and strengthen that relationship. He has also anointed us with the Holy Spirit ❖ *In the Hebrew Scriptures, people were anointed as a sign that they were chosen by God to be a prophet, priest, or king. The Anointed One (Jesus) is all three, and all believers share in all three offices too. [John 20:21] We are a holy priesthood, [1 Peter 2:5] a royal priesthood that will reign with Jesus, [2 Timothy 2:12; 1 Peter 2:9; Revelation 1:6; 5:10; 20:6] and as witnesses of the Gospel message we are also—in some sense—prophets who proclaim God's message. [Acts 1:8]* ➤ 22 who is God's seal of ownership on us, and who also lives in us as a down payment—guaranteeing that God will give us all that he has promised us in the Scriptures. *[Romans 8:23; 2 Corinthians 5:5; Ephesians 1:13-14; 1 John 3:24]* ❖ *Paul is implying that his integrity as an apostle rests on the same kind of calling and anointing that they all share in common. If God has made them stand firm in their faith, why can't they assume that God is making Paul stand firm in his calling too?* ➤

23 Now let me tell you why I changed my plan and didn't visit you as I originally intended. I call on God to witness the fact that I'm telling the truth. ❖ *The implication is that if he is not telling the truth, God will justly punish him and such a punishment was to be feared. Since both he and the Corinthians believed God would do this, such an oath was a convincing argument that he was telling the truth. It is only* when the person saying the oath or the people hearing it don't believe in its effects that such an oath becomes meaningless. ➤ I didn't come to Corinth when I originally planned so I wouldn't have to rebuke you harshly in person, thus sparing you greater shame and also the greater strain such a meeting would have put on our relationship. For since my last communication, I heard about the evil you have done. 24 I don't want you to think that I desire to control your lives and make you believe only what I say. ❖ *Some were accusing Paul of this very thing.* ➤ My goal and that of my coworkers is that we would work together with you so you will experience joy. I am sure you are standing firm in your faith.

2

1 So, after careful consideration, I decided it would be better if I didn't come to see you as I had originally planned, lest it be an emotionally distressing time. 2 If I came and rebuked you, making you upset and remorseful, then I would also be in the dumps. How could I experience joy if you did not? For your joy is my joy, and that is what I want for you. 3 Instead, I wrote the way I did in my last letter so that you might repent and change your ways before I come again. I was confident that you would respond correctly so I could experience relief and rejoice in your behavior. That way, when I finally do come, you will bring me joy rather than distress, and my joy in your faithfulness will also result in your joy. ❖ *Some commentators believe the harsh letter of rebuke that Paul is referring to is a lost letter, written after First Corinthians and before this letter. Others believe that First Corinthians itself was that harsh letter of rebuke. The arguments for both views are reasonable. But in the end, which view is correct doesn't affect the lessons we can learn from these letters.* ➤ 4 I cried a lot as I wrote that letter for I was very distressed and disturbed about your sinful attitudes and ways. I wrote it so you would know that I deeply care about you, your attitudes, and your relationship with the Lord. I wrote those things because I love you. If I didn't care about your spiritual well-being, I wouldn't have bothered. And

even though I knew it would upset you, that wasn't my purpose.

How to Treat Repentant Sinners

5 Here are my instructions concerning the man I wrote about in my last letter, the one who caused much of this distress. He caused more harm to you than to me. But I don't want to imply that the harm done was greater than it actually was. 6 Now, since he has repented, the punishment he has received from most of you has gone on long enough. ❖ *If this is the man mentioned in 1 Corinthians chapter 5, his punishment would likely have involved being a social outcast among the believers, not welcome or else ignored at their meetings, forbidden from joining in the Lord's Supper, ostracized as a friend, and removed from prayers for physical protection from attacks by Satan, such as sickness. The purpose of such punishment is to cause the sinner to realize the consequences of his sin so he will repent and be rejoined to the community in love and holiness.* ➤ 7 Instead, you should be extending him forgiveness and comfort lest he despair that you will ever accept him again and he completely forsakes the community of believers and the faith. 8 Therefore, I exhort you to publicly reassure him of your love and restore him to fellowship in your community. 9 Another reason I wrote to you the way I did was to see how willing you were to submit to all that I asked you to do as your apostle for your own spiritual well-being. 10 And since you obeyed me in punishing him, I know you will also obey me in forgiving him. When you forgive this man, he also has my forgiveness. For I have already forgiven him for anything he did against me, and I solemnly did so before the Messiah so there would be nothing to hinder your being reconciled with him. ❖ *If the Corinthian believers were to remain submitted to Paul's authority, they could not in good conscience extend forgiveness to the man if their apostle refused to forgive him. Paul's forgiving him enabled them to extend forgiveness to him in unity with Paul as the Messiah's representative.* ➤ 11 This is necessary lest Satan take advantage of our unforgiveness, for we are constantly aware of the ways he tries to gain influence in our lives. ❖ *We are commanded to extend forgiveness when a person has repented. [Matthew 18:21-35; Luke 17:3-4] Not doing so is sin, which gives Satan a foothold in our lives, enabling him to tempt us further. [Ephesians 4:27]* ➤

12 After I sent my coworker Titus to you with my letter, I left Ephesus and went to the port city of Troas—hoping to meet him there on his way back to report to me. When I came to Troas to preach the Good News about Jesus and the way of salvation, the Lord provided great opportunities for me to preach, for the people there were very receptive. 13 But despite the great opportunities, I still lacked peace due to my concern for news about you because Titus didn't show up when I expected. So after a relatively short time there, I said good-bye to the new believers and continued on to Macedonia Province—hoping to meet him on his return journey from seeing you.

The Victory Believers Have Because of Their Union with the Messiah

❖ *From here until 7:5—where Paul again takes up the account of his journey to Macedonia and his meeting with Titus—he makes a long digression that clarifies his emotional state as he searched for Titus and awaited news of the Corinthian believers. Though a digression from the preceding thread of thought, it is in harmony with the overall theme of this letter about the inevitable triumph of God's undeserved favor which successfully works in believers despite human weakness.* ➤

14 But before I say more about that, I thank and praise God for all that happens in my life. Because in our spiritual union with the Messiah, we are always part of his victory parade—celebrating his triumph over sin, death, and Satan. ❖ *The picture is of a Roman general leading his captives in a parade, proclaiming his victory over them. But as captives of the Messiah—who are spiritually united with him—we are not humiliated prisoners but captives released from the enemy who share in the victory and honor of our triumphant liberator. Paul's point is that we share in the Messiahs' victory no matter what circumstances may be afflicting us in this life. In particular, Paul was conscious of this victory despite his concern about Titus and the Corinthians. Paul's illustration also alludes to the pleasant-smelling incense that was burned during such processions—which in verse 14 is a figure for "knowing Jesus and his victory" and in verse 15 is a figure for those who preach the Gospel message.* ➤ And the pleasant fragrance of his victory spreads as we bring others into intimate relationship with him

by proclaiming his message everywhere we go. 15 We—who preach the Good News—are like a sweet fragrance to God, the pleasantness of the Messiah himself, because he is the one who really does this through us. We and our message are also perceived as fragrances to those who are being saved and to those who are on their way to Hell. 16 The Hell-bound react to us as they do to the stench of death and decay—and their rejection results in their eternal death. But to those who will soon be saved, we are a pleasant fragrance that draws them to eternal life. In view of this great responsibility then, who is adequate in themselves to fulfill the task of telling others about the Messiah? 17 My coworkers and I are always conscious that God sees everything we do, and we draw on the ability he gives us in our spiritual union with the Messiah to teach his message exactly as it came from him—without corruption. Unlike many teachers that lack God-given authority—who peddle a message designed to bring them personal gain—we are sent by God. ❖ *Paul is comparing himself with the false apostles who have been influencing the Corinthian believers.* ➤

3

The Changed Lives of the Corinthian Believers Are Proof of Paul's Credentials

1 Now, don't think I'm saying these things about my coworkers and myself to boast or to try to convince you that God sent us—which some among you have accused us of doing. We certainly don't need letters of commendation from leaders of other assemblies to establish our credentials with you—as others do. Nor do we need letters of commendation from you to establish our credentials for other assemblies. 2 For your transformed lives in response to our preaching the Good News among you are the only credentials we should need. Our love and concern for you is written in our hearts, **A** and all who know us recognize the genuineness of our love for you and the fact that we are proud of your faith. 3 Your lives

were transformed by the Messiah himself as a result of our ministry. So now, your holy lives are like letters that establish our credentials—letters that the Messiah wrote and which all who know about you can read. The ink he used was the Holy Spirit who gave you eternal life, and he wrote the message on your hearts instead of stone tablets. *[Jeremiah 31:33; Ezekiel 11:19-20; 36:26-27]*

4 My coworkers and I are confident that you are indeed such letters of commendation for us because we know what God has done in your lives and ours through the Messiah.

5 Now, we acknowledge that we—in ourselves—lack the ability to transform lives, and we recognize that any effectiveness we have in ministry comes from God working through us. 6 He is the one who called my coworkers and me to invite others to enter into the new and superior covenant agreement that he offers people. ❖ *In it, he offers to save those who trust Jesus the Messiah and commit their lives to follow him.* ➤ This is not merely about following a written agreement—such as the Teachings of Moses which condemn those who are unable to keep them perfectly and which are unable to help us keep them. Instead, it's an agreement about following Jesus through the leading of the Holy Spirit who lives within us and gives us eternal life. For he helps and enables us to keep the New Covenant through our faith in his promises.

The New Covenant Is Far Greater Than the Mosaic Covenant

7 God gave his holy commands in the Torah to Moses—engraved in stone ❖ *in contrast to the New Covenant commands written on our hearts* ➤—and God's glory caused Moses' face to shine, signifying that the Torah's glory reflected God's character. His face shone so brightly that the Israelites were afraid to look directly at it for any length of time. But even though the Torah is holy and good, it had no power to enable God's people to keep it perfectly—hence it condemned them and, in effect, ministered eternal death. So the brilliant light of Moses'

A 3:2 Some manuscripts say "written on your hearts."

face slowly faded—indicating that the ministry of the Torah was to be temporary, even though the requirements of the Torah are eternal. ❖ *The account in Exodus 34:29-35 never mentions that the glory faded. This is a revelation that Paul gives us in this letter. It may have been an oral tradition. Note that God's "glory" in the Scriptures is often represented by a brilliant light. But such light is also symbolic of the purity, holiness, goodness, love, splendor, and other attributes of his glorious and wonderful character. Aspects of God's glorious character are seen in the Torah's teachings and in the New Covenant that he gave his people—and this is the "glory" that Paul is talking about.* ➤ 8 Now if the temporary ministry of the Torah came with such glory, we should expect the permanent ministry of the New Covenant by the Holy Spirit to be much more glorious. ❖ *This glory is seen in the transformed lives of those who accept the message of the Good News and have the Holy Spirit living in them.* ➤ 9 Since the ministry of the Torah which condemns sinners to eternal death is glorious—reflecting God's holy character—it should be obvious that the ministry of the New Covenant which enables sinners to become righteous in union with the Messiah is supremely glorious—reflecting not only God's holiness but also his great mercy and love. 10 The ministry of the Torah had glory except in its inability to bring about righteousness in God's people. But for that reason, in comparison with the supreme glory of the ministry of New Covenant—which *can* bring about righteousness—it's glory is negligible. 11 Since the temporary ministry of the Torah revealed God's glory, certainly the glory of the ministry of the New Covenant is vastly superior because it is eternal.

12 Since we are confident that the ministry of the New Covenant is eternal, my coworkers and I preach about it openly and boldly. 13 We do not need to hide the glory of the New Covenant message like Moses hid the fading glory of his face from the Israelites with a veil. We know that it will not fade away like the ministry of the Torah has. Moses veiled his shining face because the Israelites were afraid of it and didn't want a close encounter with God or his glory. [Exodus 34:29-35] ❖ *Also see Exodus 20:19-21.* ➤ Even though they had seen a

visible manifestation of God's glory in his Torah as Moses read it to them, they didn't receive it and were not worthy to continue to gaze on the glory. So after reading the Torah to them, Moses veiled his face so they wouldn't continue to gaze on the glory until it faded away. ❖ *The veil, then, was a symbol of their rebellion and unbelief which separated them from God.* ➤ 14 The Israelites saw God's glory, but they didn't respond properly to him. So he gave them over to their stubbornness and allowed their understanding to be veiled. Even to this very day, that veil remains over their minds when they read the Old Covenant ❖ *i.e., the Hebrew Scriptures, especially the Torah (a.k.a. Pentateuch)* ➤ —preventing them from perceiving the truth. That veil—or hindrance to understanding the truth—can only be removed when they are spiritually joined to the Messiah. ❖ *Moses didn't wear the veil when he met with God because he had no barrier of rebellion or unbelief, but had an intimate relationship with him. Thus he could gaze on God's glory and understand his truth.* ➤ 15 Indeed, even today when Jews or unbelievers read Moses' writings, ❖ *i.e., the Torah* ➤ they fail to apprehend the full glory in the Torah's teachings because their rebellion and unbelief still veil their hearts and minds—preventing them from hearing or seeing the truth. 16 But whenever people turn to the Lord, then God removes the veil from their hearts and minds. 17 Now this Lord—who people turn to and who works in those who believe—is the Holy Spirit. When the Holy Spirit lives in people, they are set free. ❖ *There are many thoughts as to what freedom this refers to. We are free from following the requirements of the Torah as a means of obtaining an intimate relationship with God. We are also free from the power of sin, free from judgment and eternal death, free from the veil, and free to be bold in ministering the Good News.* ➤ 18 And all of us believers boldly gaze upon the Lord's glory—by faith—as we contemplate the revelation of the Messiah in the mirror of the Scriptures. As we do this, the Spirit transforms us—making us more and more like the Messiah in every way so we ever increasingly reflect his glorious character. ❖ *From a Semitic viewpoint, "unveiled face" (in the literal text) means having freedom, boldness, and confidence.* ➤

4

The Manifestation of God's Glory in Us

1 Therefore, since God has been so merciful to us by enabling us to teach his message to others, we never get so discouraged that we stop doing it. 2 In all our work, we never do anything that we might be ashamed of. Everything we say and do is straightforward and above board. We don't resort to deception to get people to listen to us or to help us, and we don't pollute the purity of God's message by adding to it, subtracting from it, or changing it in any way. Instead, we merely proclaim the simple truth about the Messiah—knowing that God sees all we do. And we trust that honest people will recognize the truth and purity of what we teach. 3 If—as some of you say—there are people who aren't able to understand the Good News we preach about the Messiah, then it's not because we don't speak plainly, but because those people are still on their way to Hell. Their understanding is veiled because they don't want to believe it. 4 For Satan—the temporary ruler of this world—has blinded their minds so they can't comprehend that the Good News about the Messiah and his glorious character is true. They are unable to recognize that he is the exact image of God and that he came so we could know God. 5 For the Good News we preach is about Jesus the Messiah being Lord of all. We don't preach or boast about ourselves—as some people have insinuated. All we claim is that we are here to serve you on behalf of Jesus because of what he has done for us. 6 The reason we are his servants is because the same God—who at creation said, "Let light shine in the darkness," [Genesis 1:3]—has in effect said to all of us, "Let revelatory light shine in their minds"—and this has enabled us to comprehend his truth. So now we understand that when we look at the Messiah and his character, we see the glory ❖ i.e., character ➤ of God himself.

7 But this precious treasure—which is the light of the revelation of God's glorious character in the Good News and the commission to proclaim it to others—has been given to very ordinary frail human beings. He did this so it will be clear to everyone that the power of the message to change people's lives is his—not our own. 8 That is why he allows us to be inundated with problems, but because of his power, we are not defeated. We are frustrated, but don't despair and give up. 9 We are persecuted, but God never leaves us. We are severely wounded, but not killed. 10 In all these ways and wherever we go, in union with Jesus we share the same kind of sufferings he endured and we ignore our desires for self-preservation and reject any desire to sin [Matthew 16:24-25; Mark 8:34-35; Luke 9:23-24; Romans 8:17; 2 Corinthians 1:5; Philippians 3:10; 1 Peter 4:13] so that others can see Jesus' life and power in our lives without us getting in the way. ❖ The way the Lord manifests himself and his power in our lives—through our endurance and joy despite all that afflicts us—enables people to know that our ability to endure is not a product of our own character and strength, but is a result of our faith in him. ➤ 11 Throughout our lives, God allows us to suffer and be in danger of death in the course of serving Jesus, so that people can see the sustaining power of his immortal life manifested through our weak mortal bodies. [2 Corinthians 12:10] 12 So even though the suffering that comes with our being ministers of the Good News leads us toward death, yet it results in your gaining eternal life. ❖ Paul has been talking mainly about his sufferings as an apostle and those of his coworkers. But this suffering comes to all believers who commit themselves to following Jesus for the same purposes that God allowed his apostles to suffer. ➤

13 The reason we continue to preach is that we are like the psalmist who said, "I trusted in Yahweh, therefore, I spoke…" Since we also trust God to take care of us, we continue to speak his message. ❖ At first glance, it seems that Paul gives the quote from Psalm 116:10 a different slant. But in the original context, the psalmist was speaking what he said while trusting in Yahweh to take care of him and help him. ➤ 14 We do this—even though we might be killed—because we know that through our union with Jesus, God will raise us to eternal life along with you and usher us into his presence just as certainly as he raised Jesus the Messiah from death. 15 We endure all these sufferings so that you and

the others we minister to will benefit spiritually. [2 Corinthians 1:3-6] And we want as many people as possible to accept the undeserved favor and blessing that God offers through the message of the Good News—thus maximizing the praise and thanksgiving offered in return to God, who is supremely worthy of such praise. [2 Corinthians 1:11]

16 Knowing that God will be honored as a result of our trials, we never get so discouraged that we are tempted to give up our work. Even though we are physically wearing out and grow tired, yet God makes us spiritually fresh and strong every day. 17 These troubles—as burdensome as they seem—are temporary and insignificant compared to the incomprehensible magnitude of his eternal glorious character which God will produce in our lives through them. 18 That is why we don't focus on the temporary things of this world such as our troubles, but instead, we concentrate on the unseen eternal realities in the spiritual realm—such as the rewards that God has promised.

5

1 Even if the mortal bodies we have during our temporary sojourn in this world die before the Messiah returns, we look forward to the eternal glorified bodies that God will provide for our permanent residence in Heaven. These will be totally unlike the frail bodies humanity reproduces in this world. 2 In fact, during our temporary sojourn in this world, troubles and suffering cause us to groan and yearn to have the glorified immortal bodies that we will have in Heaven. 3 For when we finally have our new bodies, we will not have to live as disembodied souls. ❖ *Commentators agree that the nakedness (in the literal text) that Paul was referring to is a soul not having a body. Many believe that at death, our souls go to Heaven and we live there without physical bodies until the resurrection. During this time, we would be "soul naked." Hence they interpret Paul's longing here to be that his mortal body would be transformed, so he would not have to experience being without a body. In other words, Paul still hoped that the Messiah would return before he died. Others believe that a soul without a body is not fully*

human and that when we die and go to Heaven, we have some sort of temporary glorified body there until the resurrection. The support for this might be the pictures we have of Heaven in the book of Revelation where people seem to have bodies, [Revelation 4:10; 5:8; 6:9-11; 7:9-10, 13-17; 15:2] and the appearance of Moses and Elijah at the transfiguration, [Matthew 17:3-4; Mark 9:4-5; Luke 9:30, 33] and Jesus' depiction of the rich man physically suffering in Hades. [Luke 16:23-25] Yet such evidence is not sufficiently clear that we can be certain. ➤ 4 While we live in these mortal bodies, we groan because of their imperfections, pains, and limitations. We don't want to die, but we do want to be transformed so that our limited mortal bodies might be replaced by eternal immortal ones. 5 God himself has given us these desires, for it was always his plan for us to eventually possess such bodies. To reassure us that it will really happen, he has made his Holy Spirit live within us as a down payment on the things he has promised and as a sign that he will also fulfill his other promises to us as detailed in the Scriptures. [Romans 8:23; 2 Corinthians 1:22; Ephesians 1:13-14; 1 John 3:24]

6-8 Since we have the Spirit living in us, we are confident that we will eventually obtain those glorified bodies. We go through this life firmly believing that God will deliver on all the promises he has made—and we make decisions based on that belief. We don't assume ultimate reality is defined only by what we can see. We realize that while we live in our mortal bodies we are missing out on the greater experience of being home with the Lord. Therefore, we aren't afraid to die, but in fact, we are looking forward to leaving behind our mortal bodies and being with the Lord in Heaven—which is our true home. 9 Our greatest desire is to please him in all that we do, both now in our mortal bodies and when we leave them behind to be with him in Heaven. 10 For all believers will stand before the Messiah to be judged, and all that we have done will be revealed. He will give each of us what we deserve for what we have done in this life. Good deeds will be rewarded. But rewards will be withheld from those who don't deserve them.

11 Since we know that we are accountable to God—and we have a healthy regard for his judgment [Job 28:28; Psalm 111:10; Proverbs 1:7; 9:10; 15:33]—we are trying to convince you of our personal integrity and the authenticity of my apostleship so you will accept the message we preach. God knows the genuineness of our claims and that he has appointed us to this ministry—and I hope that deep down you recognize this too. 12 In saying this, we aren't trying to boast about ourselves, but we are giving you a basis for defending us against our detractors among you. So now you can commend us for being concerned about our character and our standing in God's sight, and for not bragging about superficial appearances—the exact opposite of what our detractors do. 13 Our detractors say we are crazy and that I'm different in my writing from when I'm with you. But if—in our zeal or witness of our ecstatic experiences—we seem crazy to people, that's really between us and God. If we seem sane when we are with you because we only speak in a plain and ordinary manner—it's for your benefit. 14 You need to realize that all we do is motivated and controlled by the Messiah's love for us and by our love in response to him. A We firmly believe that he died as a substitute for all humanity to pay the penalty of their sins and therefore—in some real sense—all of humanity died with him. ❖ Some say that Paul is speaking only of believers here. Others say that all died, but that the benefits of that death are only available to believers. [Galatians 2:20; 1 Timothy 2:6; 4:10; Romans 6:3-4] ➤ 15 The Messiah died for humanity, and God raised him back to life for our benefit. He did this because he wanted everyone to have the opportunity to believe in him and receive eternal life. His desire is that all who receive eternal life will no longer live following their own desires, but will live in obedience to him.

16 Because I realize that the Messiah loves everyone this much, ever since my conversion I've ceased to appraise and value

people following the superficial and sinful standards of this world. Even though I once thought about the Messiah that way, I don't any longer. ❖ It is thought that some of Paul's detractors in Corinth claimed to have seen or known the Messiah before his death and resurrection. [1 Corinthians 1:12] They may have challenged Paul's authority as an apostle because he wasn't a follower of Jesus during his earthly ministry. But great numbers of people had followed Jesus and "had known him," had appraised him by superficial standards, and later deserted him. Such knowledge of Jesus "in the flesh" (in the literal text) was of no value to them. Paul's comments may have been addressing such claims. ➤ 17 Therefore, we recognize that all who are joined to the Messiah have been spiritually recreated as completely new people. Their old life—with its self-centered and sinful orientation—has been done away with. They have been given an entirely new sinless and eternal life—which is Jesus in them. 18 Now, this complete change in the lives of believers is something God accomplishes. He brought us—who were condemned to eternal death because of his intolerance of sin—into repentance and into a loving intimate relationship with himself by means of the Messiah's death as our substitute. He has assigned my coworkers and me the task of bringing others into relationship with him too. 19 This is the message of reconciliation that he sent us to proclaim: God wants to bring people into intimate relationship with himself. He made this possible through the Messiah's self-sacrificial death as a substitute for them. So he will no longer hold sins against those who repent and who trust in Jesus' death to save them.

20 Therefore, my coworkers and I are sent as the Messiah's ambassadors in this world. We are his spokesmen. He has told us to urge you to repent so you can come into a loving intimate relationship with God. 21 The Messiah had no sin. [John 8:46; Hebrews 4:15; 7:26; 1 Peter 2:22; 1 John 3:5] Yet God identified him with our sin and punished him for our sin so it would be justly punished, and so we could be joined to him

---

A 5:14 ἡ ἀγάπη τοῦ Χριστοῦ (hē agapē tou Christou), "the love of Christ" (in the literal text) is ambiguous in Greek. It can mean "Christ's love for us" as most translations and commentators choose, or it can mean "our love for Christ." It's possible that it means both at the same time.

and thereby be identified with God's own righteousness.

6

¹ So now that you have already received his unmerited favor, we—as God's coworkers—urge you to live out the faith that you profess, allowing his power to transform you. Don't fail to produce his fruit in your lives. ² As God has said, "**At the time of my choosing, I heard your call to me for help, and on the day I appointed for saving, I helped you.**" *[Isaiah 49:8 Septuagint]* So realize this: Since God has already sent his Messiah, the time he has chosen is right now. Today is when he wants to save you. ❖ *Later may be too late because people die unexpectedly.* ➤

The Characteristics of Those Who Minister for God

³ My coworkers and I strive to never do anything that would discredit our ministry and so hinder people from listening to the Lord's message. ⁴ As is fitting for God's servants, we patiently endure everything that happens to us—including troubles, hardships, distressing situations, ⁵ beatings, imprisonment and attacks by mobs, as well as working to exhaustion, going without sleep, and doing without food. ⁶ As is also fitting for his servants, our lives are characterized by pure motives, high moral standards, understanding of God's ways, patience with others, kindness, manifestations of the Holy Spirit, and genuine unselfish love. ⁷ In our ministry, we exhibit God's Word of truth ❖ *i.e., the Good News* ➤ proclaimed with his power, and we possess his righteousness as a weapon for spiritual attack and defense. ⁸ We continue to serve him, whether people praise us or reject us, and whether our reputations are good or slandered. Even though we are honest, some regard us as liars. ❖ *This last sentence may refer to Paul's claim to apostleship.* ➤ ⁹ Even though God knows us and has appointed us, many do not recognize our spiritual authority. We constantly face the threat of death, yet we continue to live. Through the hands of those who persecute us, God disciplines us, yet he

doesn't allow them to kill us. ¹⁰ Even though we experience grief and sadness, his abiding joy remains in us. Even though we live in material poverty, we enable many to gain spiritual wealth. ❖ *This refers to salvation and eternal spiritual blessings.* ➤ In short, we have nothing that people in this world usually want, yet we are content to have every spiritual blessing.

¹¹ My dear friends in Corinth, we have expressed ourselves openly and frankly to you because we love you very much. ¹² We aren't holding back on our love for you, even though your love for us has been restrained. ¹³ I love you as if you were my own children and that is why I'm speaking to you this way. Since we love you so much, won't you open your hearts and love us in return?

Do Not Partner with Unbelievers

¹⁴ Do not partner with unbelievers! It is no more possible for those who seek the righteousness of the Messiah to partner with those who follow the lawlessness of Satan, than it is for light and darkness to coexist in the same place. *[Deuteronomy 22:10]* ❖ *The partnering referred to is broad in scope. It would include participating in pagan ceremonies or worship, marriage, business partnership, or any close relationship. This does not mean that we don't have any relationships with unbelievers, but that we should avoid those kinds of relationships and commitments that could tempt us or lead us to compromise our faith and obedience—especially when others can make commitments and decisions on our behalf.* ➤ ¹⁵ There is no common ground of any kind between the Messiah and Satan. Thus, believers can have no common values with unbelievers. ¹⁶ Just as it's unthinkable for idols to be placed in God's Temple, it's unthinkable for us to partner with unbelievers because together, believers are the Temple ❖ *i.e., the holy dwelling place* ➤ of the one true God. For God himself said, "**I will live within them and among them. I will be their loving God and they will be my obedient people.**" *[Leviticus 26:12; Jeremiah 32:38; Ezekiel 37:27]* ¹⁷ That's why the Lord also said, "**Come out and separate yourselves from participating in the defilements of unbelievers.**" *[Isaiah 52:11]* "**Do this and I will welcome you.**" *[Ezekiel 20:34]* ❖ *This does not teach total separation from*

unbelievers, but separation from their sins and influence. ➤ **18** "I will be your loving Father *[2 Samuel 7:14; 1 Chronicles 17:13]* and you will be my sons and daughters with all the rights and privileges that entails." *[Isaiah 43:6-7; Hosea 1:10; John 1:12]*

7

1 My beloved friends, since God promised us this wonderful relationship with himself, our appropriate response is to get rid of all sinful thoughts and behavior. Motivated by reverence, fear, and awe, we should strive to perfect our daily dedication by setting ourselves apart from any focus other than God, and determining to serve him in every aspect of our lives.

2 I plead with you to respond to us with love. We have never wronged anyone, we have never led anyone astray from truth and purity, and we have never taken advantage of anyone as those false apostles among you have accused us of doing. ❖ *Or, as those false apostles among you have done.* ➤ **3** I'm not bringing up these things to accuse you of doing wrong. I've already said that I love you very much and I believe that our bond of friendship will endure forever. **4** I have such great confidence in you that I know I can speak to you frankly, and I'm proud of what the Lord has done in your lives. You have encouraged me by your response to my previous letter—as reported to me by Titus—and you fill me with joy despite the troubles we are experiencing.

Titus' Report

5 That brings me back to my story about our search for Titus. ❖ *See the note at the section heading before 2:14.* ➤ Even after we arrived here in Macedonia, we had no peace because we still hadn't found Titus. Instead, we experienced a sense of oppression because there were conflicts with people around us and the ever-present concern for Titus, and the desire for good news about your response to my letter. **6** But God—who always ministers encouragement to those who need it—finally granted us great relief when Titus arrived. **7** Not only were we relieved to see him, but I was thrilled when I heard his report about his time with you. He told us how you long for me to visit, how grieved you were over your former attitudes and that you've renewed your zeal and loyalty to me as your apostle—all of which greatly encouraged him. **8** Now, even though it upset you, I no longer regret writing that letter to you—as I did for a time. I do regret having to hurt your feelings by what I said, but I'm relieved that the hurt only lasted a short time. **9** Now I'm rejoicing—not about the grief my letter caused you—but because it led you to repent and change. For in your grief you turned to God, with the result that you benefited from my letter rather than allowing it to push you further from him—which would have been to your loss. **10** Sadness and regret over sin that is humbly directed toward God produces repentance and no lasting regret—for it leads to salvation and joy. But sadness and regret focused only on the negative consequences of sin—without repentance—leads away from God and toward eternal death. ❖ *This is what happened to Judas Iscariot.* ➤ **11** Notice what your grief and regret over your sin—once it was directed toward God—has produced in your lives! You acted quickly to eliminate any complicity you had in wrong doing and became indignant over your own behavior. You showed proper respect toward my spiritual authority, you now long to be reunited with me, are zealous for my apostolic authority, and you executed fitting punishment for the one who did wrong. In all these ways, you have done all that you could to put things right and have now shown yourselves to be no longer guilty of these sins.

12 Even though I wrote that severe letter to you, the main reason was not to correct the one who opposed me or because I was the one offended. But rather, it was to stimulate you to realize how much love and loyalty to me you really do have so you might wake up and demonstrate it before God. **13** Since you have responded properly to all that I exhorted you, we are greatly encouraged. In addition to that, we are even more thrilled about Titus' enthusiasm over his visit. The way you all responded and welcomed him totally erased his anxiety concerning the situation and filled him with joy. [14] I had told him that I was proud of the genuineness of your faith and zeal—and you didn't let me down. Just as I have always spoken only the truth to you, even my boasting about you to Titus has been proven true. [15] As he thinks back on how you received him as my representative—with great respect and concern to properly submit to his authority—his great love for you continues to increase. [16] As for me, I am thrilled to know that I can depend on you to do what you know is right.

8

The Charity Drive for Believers in Jerusalem

[1] So now, my brother and sisters in the Lord, we want to make you aware of the situation among God's people in Macedonia Province. God has graciously been working in their lives so they would know joy in being generous. ❖ *Paul is boasting about the Macedonian believers, just as he has boasted about the Corinthians in 7:4,14; and 8:24. But his boasting is about what God is doing in their lives through the Messiah—rather than in the people themselves.* ➤ [2] Their extreme generosity in raising money for the poor in Jerusalem was accompanied by great joy—even though they themselves are extremely poor and are also suffering intense persecution. ❖ *God measures our giving based on the amount of sacrifice involved—not the absolute amount given. Even though the Macedonian believers were extremely poor, they gave generously and joyfully to those who were poorer still. One does not need to be well-off to give generously and sacrificially.* ➤ [3] I vouch for the fact that they gave not only what they could spare, but sacrificially beyond that. They decided to do this without any prompting from me. [4] For I wasn't going to ask them to contribute toward the needs of God's people in Jerusalem because of their own deep poverty. But they repeatedly begged for the privilege of participating because it would bring them great joy. [5] And they didn't just give money, as we expected. They first dedicated themselves fully to doing the Lord's will in this matter as he would make it known to them through us!

[6] Because of their enthusiasm and joy in giving, and since Titus was the one who first organized this charitable venture among you, ❖ *at sometime prior to the writing of 1 Corinthians* ➤ we have urged him to return and help you to complete this special ministry of expressing God's favor to others. ❖ *Evidently the Corinthian's collection of funds for the poor of Jerusalem had lapsed in the previous few months. Earlier, they had asked Paul for instructions on how to proceed, which he answered in 1 Corinthians 16:1-4. But Titus had learned of their lapse during his most recent visit and had reported it to Paul.* ➤ [7] You are doing well in so many areas. The grace-enabled abilities of great faith, utterance, ❖ *i.e., prophecy, word of wisdom, etc.* ➤ and knowledge ❖ *word of knowledge* ➤ abound among you. And you are zealous to help us and others out of the love we sparked to life in you. So now, you should also make the effort to excel in the grace-enabled ability to give generously with joy. ❖ *Unlike the previously mentioned grace-enabled abilities which are given to each as the Spirit chooses, all believers can choose to exercise the grace-enabled ability to give generously. Joy is a byproduct of giving. A "grace-enabled ability" is a supernatural ability that God gives his people—through the Holy spirit who lives in them—in order to accomplish his will and show his favor toward them.* ➤

[8] I'm not exercising my authority as an apostle to command you to do this. But given the zeal of the Macedonian believers in this matter, this is a test of the genuineness of your love for other believers. [9] For you should continually be conscious of the undeserved love our Lord Jesus the Messiah showed you by sacrificially giving up all his wealth, glory, and power in Heaven to become a poor human being—just to benefit you. He sacrificially embraced poverty to bring you eternal wealth in Heaven—as well as spiritual riches in this life.

[10] Here is my view concerning your role in this charity drive. Since you were the first group to begin this drive last year—and at that time you really wanted to do it—[11] you should finish what you've started. It's appropriate that you complete this drive with as much enthusiasm as you began by giving all that you are able. [12] If you really desire to give, God judges the acceptability of your gift by the amount you have. It's not the absolute amount that counts. He doesn't expect you to give what you don't have. ❖ *In*

the Hebrew Scriptures, a sacrificial offering was only accepta-
ble if it was the best you had. See Leviticus 1:3; 22:19-21;
Deuteronomy 15:21; and 17:1. Someone who gives a huge
amount, but without sacrifice, has not given the "best" or
according to his means. Someone who gives a small amount,
yet it was a sacrifice to do so, has given according to what he
has. The measure is the amount of sacrifice it is to the giver.
See Mark 12:41-44; Luke 21:1-4. A proper view of posses-
sions is that all things belong to God and we are merely
stewards of what he has given us—which is to be used mainly
for his purposes such as furthering his Kingdom and helping
others. See Luke 19:11-26. ➤

13 I'm not at all saying that others should be relieved at the price of your having less than you need. Both you and those in need equally require enough to live on. 14 So right now, it's fitting that out of your abundance you help provide for their basic needs. In turn—if in the future your situations are reversed—their abundance should be used to help provide for your basic needs. Thus you are equally responsible for helping meet each other's needs. 15 The Scripture says, "Those who gathered a lot of manna didn't have more than they needed; and those who gathered only a little manna still had enough." *[Exodus 16:18]* ❖ *Paul uses this quote to demonstrate it is God's intention that everyone have enough for their needs and no one should have excess. This does not necessarily mean there should be total equality in everything, but it does imply that hoarding excess wealth for yourself while other believers are suffering lack is outside of God's will. This should lead many American believers to consider whether their lifestyles are in excess of what God intends.* ➤

16 I thank God that he has inspired Titus to want to help you in this matter as much as I do. 17 We urged him to go help you, and he agreed because he was actually so eager to do so that he had already made up his own mind to go before we asked. 18 We've sent another coworker with Titus who is quite well-known and respected among many assemblies for his ministering the Good News. ❖ *Many names have been posited for this person, but there is no way to know for sure who it was. A traditional favorite guess has been Luke. Had the Corinthians known him, Paul would have mentioned his name.* ➤

19 But it's not just us sending him. He was chosen and appointed by leaders of many local assemblies as someone trustworthy to travel with us, who would ensure the integrity of this ministry of demonstrating God's favor as we carry the contributions to Jerusalem. We are administering this drive in order to honor the Lord himself and to demonstrate our desire to help you and the other contributors to accomplish your ministry to those in need.

20 Titus, whom you love and trust, and this man who is trusted by the other assemblies, will supervise the collection and will accompany us as we take your generous gifts to the intended recipients— to avoid any ground for accusation against us or suspicion of dishonesty. 21 For while the Lord knows we are trustworthy, we also want all the contributors to know that we are handling their money in an honorable manner.

22 We have also sent another coworker whom you don't know with Titus. But he has repeatedly proven himself in many ways to be a diligent and faithful worker. Since he heard Titus' good report about you, he desires to help you in this ministry even more than before he heard it. 23 If anyone questions the qualifications of this delegation, Titus is my close associate and coworker in my ministry among you. As for the other two men, they are fellow believers, emissaries ❖ *literally, "apostles"* ➤ of the assemblies whose characters and lives bring honor to the Messiah. 24 So welcome these men and demonstrate the quality of your love for me by loving them, so that all the assemblies of believers will hear about it and recognize that all my boasting to them about you is legitimate.

9

1 I know it's unnecessary to say anything more about the importance of helping the believers in Jerusalem 2 because you've been more than willing to do this since last year. In fact, I've boasted about your enthusiasm to the Macedonian believers and your example was a great inspiration for most of them. ❖ *See the note at 8:1 about Paul's boasting.* ➤ 3-5 But I'm sending Titus and the other two ahead to help you finish collecting what you've already promised to give so that everything

will be fully prepared when I arrive. Since some Macedonian believers will be accompanying me, it would be embarrassing for us and for you to find that you weren't yet read—especially after all the boasting I've done. But if it's all collected when we arrive, then it will be clear that it's a generous and freely offered gift from you—and not look like I had to come and apply pressure before you would give it.

⁶ Remember the saying, "Those who plant only a little will gather only a small harvest. But those who plant generously will gather in a generous harvest." ❖ *Giving to the poor is like planting in God's Kingdom. We are promised a harvest of spiritual benefits, both for the Kingdom and for ourselves. See Proverbs 11:18; 19:17; Hosea 10:12; Matthew 10:42; 25:34-36; Luke 6:38 and Galatians 6:7 about sowing and reaping.* ➤ ⁷ Each person should contribute what he or she has carefully decided after consulting with the Lord. For God approves of those who give voluntarily with joy—without regret or a sense of compulsion. ⁸ He desires and is able to give you an abundance of all things materially, emotionally, and spiritually—even though none of us can deserve it. He wants you to have what you need in every area of your life, and even more than you need so you will have plenty to share with others who lack. ❖ *What we have in excess of our needs is not intended to be selfishly kept so we can enjoy luxury and riches, but should be used to help others. How does your lifestyle measure up? See Leviticus 25:35; Deuteronomy 15:7-11; Ephesians 4:28; Philippians 4:19; and 1 Timothy 6:6-10.* ➤ ⁹ As the Scriptures say about the cheerful giver, "**He distributes his wealth freely to the poor, and a poor man's good deeds will bring him eternal rewards.**" *[Psalm 112:9 Septuagint]* ¹⁰ Our God, who provides "**seed to the planter and bread to eat,**" *[Isaiah 55:10]* will also always supply you with the surplus needed so you can give to others, and he will even multiply it so you are able to multiply your giving and thus increase the spiritual harvest you will gather from your good deeds. ¹¹ If you give generously, God will enrich you in every area of your life—materially, emotionally, and spiritually—so you can be generous in giving away what he provides. With regard to your part in the collection that we will

carry to Jerusalem, it will certainly produce praise and thanksgiving to God for your generosity from those who receive it. ¹² So not only does your giving meet the material needs of God's people, but it will also produce spiritual benefits in their lives as they overflow with thanksgiving to God. ¹³ As a result of your giving, the Jewish believers in Jerusalem will praise God for this clear proof that Gentiles—who they've heard claim to believe the Good News about the Messiah—really are devoted to obeying him as demonstrated in your generous sharing of your surplus with them and others. ¹⁴ They will also pray for you with great love because of the great undeserved favor God has extended to them through you. ¹⁵ Let's thank God for giving the indescribably wonderful gift of his Son—for this act inspires all further giving!

Paul Defends His Apostolic Authority

❖ *Some commentators believe that the following chapters were a separate letter, later joined to this one. But there is no documentary evidence for this view. Others say that at this point, he may have received more news about the situation in Corinth—which prompted the sternness of the following chapters. In any case, it's evident that while the majority of Corinthian believers were repentant over their past attitudes toward Paul's authority, there still remained a group—led by false apostles—that opposed Paul and rejected his authority as an apostle. It's to this group that he now writes.* ➤

10

¹ Now I, Paul, have an appeal to make of you which I make with the humility and gentleness of the Messiah. *[Zechariah 9:9; Matthew 5:5; 11:29; 12:19-21]* Some among you have accused me of being a false apostle—saying I'm inconsistent and therefore unreliable, that I'm a wimp when I'm with you and harsh when I write to you. ² But when I come to visit you, please don't make it necessary for me be harsh, as I expect I will need to be to deal with those who regard us as false teachers that are motivated by worldly self-interest. ³ We do live in this self-seeking world, but we do not fight our opponents by means that self-seekers use.

4 We don't depend on the weapons of human knowledge and philosophy that are used by our worldly opponents, but we rely on the weapons of truth that God provides us. For his truth has the power to demolish the demonically inspired philosophical strongholds of wrong thinking that keep people from believing the truth. 5 We tear down ideas and every lofty argument that rises up to resist the truth about God. We take every rebellious thought captive and make them submissive to the Messiah. 6 So when we arrive and most of you are completely submitted to the Messiah, then we will be ready to punish any who remain in rebellion against him and our authority.

7 You are looking at things from a superficial viewpoint. ❖ Or: Look at the facts! ➤ If our opponents are confident that they belong to the Messiah, they should realize that—at the very least—we belong to him too. 8 Even if I do seem to boast too much about our authority which the Lord himself gave us, I am not embarrassed by my boasting. For the authority he gave us was to strengthen you in the true faith—not to humiliate or destroy you. 9 It's certainly not my intention to "terrify" you with what I say in my letters. ❖ Paul was being ironic. His opponents had charged him with being harsh in his letters and a wimp in person—which was a serious charge of inconsistency from their cultural viewpoint—leading to the conclusion that he was unreliable. Paul counters this charge by pointing out to them that the idea he is trying to terrorize them from afar with his apostolic authority is absurd. The Corinthians who knew him would see this image as ridiculous. ➤ 10 My opponents say, "In his letters he seems powerful and persuasive, but in person he is unimpressive and his speech is far from eloquent." 11 Those who say this had better realize now that when we arrive, we will do exactly the things we said we would do in our letters.

12 But we wouldn't dream of considering ourselves in the same category as our detractors, or of comparing ourselves with those whose only claim to fame is what they say about themselves. They evaluate themselves by standards that they—themselves—made up. They compare themselves—again—only with themselves. This doesn't say much for their wisdom. 13 Unlike them, we will not boast beyond the truth or outside the area of authority that God assigned us. But our area of authority certainly does include you. 14 We are not going beyond our proper area of authority when we boast or write to you—as we would be if we had never preached the Good News about the Messiah to you. But in fact, we were the first to do so—which establishes our unique right to apostolic authority over you. 15 Also unlike our detractors, we do not boast about the work of others as if it were our own. But we do hope that as your faith matures, we will be able to enlarge the area where we do pioneering work—with your help. 16 We want to preach the Good News about the Messiah to areas far beyond you where it has never been heard. But we will not be found boasting about work already done in an area by someone else. ❖ We know from his letter to the Romans—which he later wrote from Corinth—that he hoped to travel to Spain. ➤

17 But in all boasting, it should only be done as the Scriptures teach: Anyone who wants to boast should only boast about what Yahweh has done. [Jeremiah 9:23-24] 18 For the Lord approves of those who work to get their commendation from him, but not those who try to commend themselves. Only his approval and his commendation count for anything.

❖ Paul has just clearly stated that all boasting should be about what God has done and that self-praise is foolishness. But his detractors are claiming that the Messiah sent them to be apostles over the Corinthian believers—and not Paul. So he is forced to compare himself with them to show the believers that even by the standards put forth by the false apostles, they are in no way superior to Paul. He finds this kind of self-glorification distasteful, and takes pains in verses 1-4 of chapter 11 to explain why he indulges in this foolishness. ➤

11

1 I hope and trust that you will bear with me as I stoop to their foolish level for a bit. 2 I'm willing to do so because I am righteously jealous for you. This is not for my own sake, but as your spiritual father, I've introduced you to the Messiah and promised you in marriage to him. So I want your love and devotion to be pure and centered on

only one man—the true Messiah. ❖ *Together, all believers are the "bride of the Messiah." [Matthew 22:1-2; John 3:29; Ephesians 5:22-32; Revelation 19:7-8; 21:2, 9] This figure conveys truths about the eternal intimate relationship we are to have with him (and has nothing to do with sexuality).* ➤ 3 But I'm afraid that just as Satan deceived Eve with his cunning, he may also succeed in corrupting your thinking through these false apostles and lead you away from simple pure devotion to the Messiah. *[Genesis 3:1-6, 13]* ❖ *Note that the Apostle Paul—under the inspiration of the Holy Spirit—believed that the account of the fall of mankind into sin in Genesis is historical fact.* ➤ 4 I say that because strangers come to you and preach a different message about Jesus than we did, and they want you to receive a spirit that is not at all the Holy Spirit. In fact, they have a message about how to be saved that is altogether different from the one you first accepted—and you swallow their falsehoods like gullible fools.

5 Well, I don't think your self-proclaimed "super apostles" are in any way superior to me. You put up with their foolish boasting, so you ought to be able to put up with a bit of mine. 6 I may lack their flamboyant polished rhetorical style, but I do have invaluable knowledge directly from God. We've made this clear enough in all we've said and done among you. So which is more important? ❖ *And Paul is certainly eloquent and persuasive enough in his writing.* ➤

7 Do you think I did you a "grave injustice" to be humble like the Messiah and preach his Good News to you without demanding pay so that you could be exalted in righteousness before God? ❖ *Greek culture and social conventions expected teachers with a message worth receiving to behave in certain ways and demand pay for their valuable message. They also viewed humility as humiliation. Paul consciously violated these expectations for good reasons—but certainly the Corinthians should have realized that in doing so he could hardly be accused of taking advantage of them, as his detractors would have them think. See 1 Corinthians 4:12; 9:3, 12, 15-19.* ➤ 8 When I was serving you, I was accepting monetary support from other assemblies who viewed me as their spiritual father. Are my detractors now going to accuse me of robbing those believers? 9 When I was living among you and didn't have enough to live on,

I purposely didn't become a burden to any of you—in stark contrast to your self-proclaimed apostles. Fellow believers came from Macedonia and provided me with what I needed. So I've never asked for money from any of you and that is the way I will continue our relationship. That way, no one can accuse me of wanting to take advantage of you. 10 I'm telling the truth here, just as surely as what the Messiah says is true. I will not start accepting support from anyone in Achaia Province and so let them rob me of my boast that I serve you without pay. ❖ *This fact was an embarrassment to Paul's detractors who did, indeed, preach to receive a living—thus rightly suggesting that their motives were not pure. To counter this, they insinuated that Paul didn't accept their support because he didn't love them.* ➤ 11 Some ask why I would refuse your support. Do you really believe it's because I don't love you? God knows that I do, and it should be quite clear to you, too! 12 I will continue to minister for free so I can undercut my detractors' boast that they are our equals because they work among you the same way we do—for I know their motive is to take advantage of you. 13 Those men are false apostles, deceivers, falsely claiming to be sent by the Messiah. 14 It's no mystery why they do this. Since Satan often tries to pass himself off as something he is not—such as a messenger from God bearing his truth—15 it shouldn't be at all surprising that his servants also try to present themselves as God's chosen leaders with the true message of how to be right before God. At the final judgment, they will get what they deserve.

16 Again, I don't want you to conclude that I'm really a fool when I start engaging in a little boasting. I've told you why I'm forced to lower myself to this level. But even if you do conclude I'm a fool, at least grant me the courtesy of listening to me as you have already listened to the boasting of my detractors. 17 In the things I'm about to say, my manner of speaking is not Messiah-like—it is the kind of self-praise only a fool indulges in. 18 But since you seem to entertain this kind of self-aggrandizement, let's see how well I stack up against my detractors on their terms. 19 For people who

consider themselves to be wise, I don't know why you tolerate such fools. 20 You seem to like it when they treat you like slaves, living off your wealth like parasites, taking every advantage of you, lording themselves over you, even slapping you. 21 Oh, I'm "so ashamed" to admit that we were "too weak" to mistreat you like that! But since they dare to boast about themselves and you seem to like that, here I go—speaking as foolishly as they do: Anything they boast about, I can do better! 22 They proudly claim to be of Hebrew stock. I too am of pure Hebrew parentage on both sides—and even speak the ancient language. They claim to be faithful Israelites, descended from Abraham. So am I. 23 They claim to work for the Messiah. (This kind of boasting is going over the top, but here goes:) Well I've done much more for him than they have. For the Messiah's sake, I've been frequently imprisoned, beaten and flogged innumerable times, and often been faced with death just for the privilege of doing what he told me to do. 24 On five different occasions, Jewish authorities have sentenced me to be whipped with 39 strokes of the lash. 25 On three different occasions, Roman authorities had me beaten with wooden rods. Once, people tried to stone me to death; three times I've been shipwrecked and one of those times I spent 24 hours adrift at sea. 26 I've made many long journeys while serving the Messiah. During them, I was frequently in danger on rivers from robbers, from attacks by my fellow Jews, and from attacks by Gentiles. There were dangers everywhere I went—in cities, in the remote areas, on the sea, even from people who claimed to be fellow believers. 27 I've worked hard and have often gone without sleep. I've often been hungry and continued to work without food or even water. I've been cold in the winter—sometimes without shelter or adequate clothing. 28 In addition to these external stresses, I'm also constantly burdened with concern for the spiritual well-being of all the people in the assemblies that I've started. 29 I feel it when they experience every kind of weakness—both spiritual and physical. And I burn with anger against those who have caused a believer to stumble in sin.

30 But enough of this foolishness. If I have to go on boasting—unlike my detractors, I will boast about my weaknesses. 31 I'm telling you the truth and God knows it. May he—the Father of our Lord Jesus— be forever praised! 32 One time when I was in the city of Damascus, the deputy governor over the Jews—under King Aretas—put guards at the city gates to arrest me. [Acts 9:23-25] 33 So I was reduced to being lowered in a basket from a window in the city wall— and that's how I escaped. ❖ *Commentators are not sure why Paul includes this incident—which occurred early in his ministry and probably was not widely known. It's likely that he was emphasizing his own helplessness and weakness as the context for the following incident about the vision. He wanted to make it clear that there was nothing great in himself, but he could really only boast about what the Messiah chose to do in and through him.* ➤

12

1 Circumstances require that I continue to boast—even though I know it doesn't prove anything. So now I will boast about visions and revelations from the Lord. ❖ *In verses 2-5, Paul speaks in the third person, as if about someone else. Yet because of verse 7—where he talks about a "thorn in the flesh" given to keep him from becoming too proud by all of his revelations—almost all commentators believe he is talking about himself. Even though he is telling about his own experiences, he wanted to downplay them and make them as little like boasting as possible. This is probably the reason he wrote this way. For the sake of conforming to current conventions, his narrative has been put in the first person.* ➤ 2-3 Fourteen years ago, I was abruptly taken up to the third Heaven. ❖ *There is no explicit Scriptural explanation of what the third Heaven is, though in verse 4 it seems to be synonymous with "Paradise." These two places are said to be the same in the apocryphal book "Revelation of Moses," and also in some of the rabbinical literature. The Jews of his time had various concepts of a number of levels of Heaven—some models having three and some having seven. The Scriptures do often refer to "the heavens" in the plural. One common interpretation is that the first Heaven is the visible sky, the second Heaven is the invisible spiritual realm where angels and demons live, and the third Heaven is what we normally call Heaven—the dwelling place of God himself where believers who die go to*

live. Commentators differ on whether Paul was telling about two experiences, one to the third Heaven and one to a different place called Paradise, or if it was just one. All interpretation on this point is conjecture, and this interpretation assumes he is talking about only one experience. ➤ Whether I was taken up there physically or if it was merely a vision, I could not tell because it was so real. Only God himself knows which it was. The only thing I'm sure of is that 4 I found myself in Paradise *[Luke 23:43; Revelation 2:7]* and heard things that I'm incapable of expressing in words. Even if I could try, the Lord doesn't permit me to speak about them. 5 I will boast about having that experience, yet I cannot boast that I caused or merited it—so I'm still only boasting about how helpless I am in myself. 6 If I were to boast more about such things, I wouldn't be speaking foolishly because I would be speaking the truth about things that God caused to happen to me. But I won't say any more about them since I don't want people to be tempted to think more highly of me for having those experiences—since they weren't anything I did. I only want people to base their view of me on what they've seen me do and heard me say.

7 In order to keep me from falling into the trap of spiritual pride as a result of having so many similar revelations, God has been allowing people to persecute me to keep me aware of how helpless and dependent on him I really am. They are like a constant "thorn in my side" **A** sent by Satan as his personal agents to torment me. 8 On three occasions, I spent time earnestly praying to the Lord that he would no longer allow these people to oppose me. 9 His answer was, "It is enough and best that you rely on the power of my enabling favor to endure these trials. For my power in your life operates best when you are weak and helpless and therefore, fully dependent on me." Since I know this is true, I welcome, embrace, and even boast about my own weakness and helplessness so that the Messiah's power will be present and manifest in my life. 10 So when I suffer helplessness, insults, hardships, persecution, and difficulties because of my obedience to the Messiah, I now welcome them and remain content. For it is only in my helplessness that I can rely on his power to give me the strength to endure.

11 I've become foolish to boast like this, yet you have—in effect—pushed me to it. You should be the ones defending me and commending me. Those self-proclaimed "super apostles" say I am "nothing," but you yourselves know that I am not inferior to them in any way. 12 While I was living among you, God patiently performed all kinds of signs, wonders, and miracles through me to prove that I was his apostle. 13 So in what ways have I treated you as inferior to the other assemblies of believers that I've started in other places? Is it that I didn't allow myself to become a financial burden to you, like these false apostles have? Is this what I've done wrong? I hope

---

A **12:7** The debate over what Paul's "thorn in the flesh" was (in the literal text) is considerable and has been going on for nearly 1900 years. Many people believe or assume that it was some sort of physical illness or pain. Many people **want** it to be interpreted that way because it's convenient for their theology that Paul had an illness which God would not heal—even though the weight of evidence points in a different direction. Commentators often rely on word studies to determine the sense a word or phrase usually carries as used elsewhere in the Scriptures or in non-biblical documents—but many seem to have ignored them in this case. Such a study reveals that the only three other places in the Scriptures where a similar expression is used, it refers to persecution by enemies. See Numbers 33:55; Joshua 23:13; and Judges 2:3. It seems unlikely that Paul—a Hebrew Scripture scholar—would have used this phrase in a very different sense than he had already learned it meant in the Scriptures. Also, the word ἄγγελος (angelos)—translated "personal agents" above—appears over 180 times in the New Testament. Most of the time it is translated "angel" and the rest of the time it is translated "messenger" in most translations. In **every** instance—except this one, some would argue—it refers to a person. The interpretation put forth here was also held by the early church fathers Chrysostom and Augustine, as well as several other lesser-known names. This view holds that Alexander, [2 Timothy 4:14] Hymeneus, [1 Timothy 1:20] Philetas, [2 Timothy 2:17] and those who opposed Paul's preaching, the circumcision party, those who put him in prison, beat him, etc., were the ones who were Paul's "thorn in the flesh." This interpretation also meshes well with verse 10, where he doesn't mention illness, but mainly external persecutions.

you can find it within yourselves to forgive me for such a terrible thing! ❖ *The rich believers among the Corinthians wanted Paul to become indebted to them as a "client" while they were his "patrons." This is not the kind of relationship Paul wanted. They needed to understand that their true roles were reversed. They were dependent upon him as their spiritual father. Even though he didn't submit to their desires, there was no way they could have thought he had done "wrong" against them, hence his asking forgiveness was sarcasm.* ➤

14 I'm ready now to come for my third visit with you and—again—I will not allow you to be burdened with paying for my expenses. I don't want to your money. I want your love, respect, and obedience to the Messiah's will. You are my spiritual children and it's not appropriate for children to provide for their parents. But as a parent, I want to supply spiritual help for my children. 15 So I will happily spend all my resources, time, energy, and love on you. Since I love you so much, will you continue to restrain your love for me?

16 Even though I have never been a financial burden on you, some still claim that I've been clever and have been trying to win your trust so that I could trick you into giving large donations for the poor and then take it for myself. 17 But have any of the men I've sent to you representing me ever taken advantage of you in any way? 18 When I previously urged Titus to go to you and sent our coworker with him, did he exploit you in any way? You know he didn't! Don't you see that we both walk in obedience to the same Holy Spirit and keep the same high standards of conduct and integrity? ❖ *From the way Paul speaks about Titus in this letter, we can infer that the Corinthian believers trusted him and held him in high esteem.* ➤

19 You've probably been thinking all this time that we are trying to defend ourselves against our detractors in such a way that you will judge in our favor. But in fact, everything we've written has been what the Messiah wants us to say to you. We know that God is watching, and so everything we do and say is done to help you to stand strong in the true faith because we love you very much. 20 I've written the way I have because I dread the possibility that I will

arrive and find that there is quarreling, jealousy, anger, people formed into opposing groups, slander, defamation of character, malicious rumors, arrogance and pride, or various other kinds of disorder among you. ❖ *These are the kinds of issues that existed among them when Paul wrote the letter 1 Corinthians to them.* ➤ If that happens, I know you won't be happy at the way I will respond to such behavior. 21 I dread the possibility that when I come, God will again cause me to be ashamed in your presence—for I've boasted about you and am your spiritual father. ❖ *The first time he was ashamed of them was mentioned in 2:1-4.* ➤ I may have to mourn over expelling those from your assembly who have been living in sin and have not repented of the sexual impurity, immorality, and indecent public behavior that they've been indulging in.

13

Paul's Final Warning to Those Who Oppose Him

1 This next visit will be my third. I will follow Scriptural rules. **"All accusations of sin against people will be verified by two or three witnesses"** before I punish them. [Deuteronomy 17:6; 19:15; Matthew 18:16; 1 Timothy 5:19] ❖ *Some commentators believe that Paul meant that his letter 1 Corinthians (in which he confronted them with their sin) was his first witness, his second visit (during which he personally confronted them with their sin) was his second witness, and his third visit will be his third witness. But this would be a non-traditional application of the Scripture he quoted.* ➤ 2 When I made my second visit to you, ❖ *During his first visit he founded the local assembly of believers there.* ➤ I warned those who were living in sin and rebellion that they needed to repent. Right now—before I come again—I'm warning any who have not yet repented that this is their last chance to do so. For when I arrive, any who have not repented will be dealt with harshly. 3 Those rebels have demanded proof that I speak with the Messiah's authority. Well, if they haven't repented and are still waiting for proof—they will have it. They will be surprised to find that the Messiah is not at all weak or timid toward those in rebellion, but that his power to discipline them will be evident in

their lives. ❖ *The Scriptures clearly teach that rebellion against God-appointed authority is the same as rebellion against God himself. See Numbers 16:1-35.* ➤ 4 It's true that in apparent weakness the Messiah was crucified to help us. But now he lives while clearly possessing God's mighty power. In a similar way, we are united with him and minister in apparent weakness to help you. But when we arrive in Corinth, you will find that we are also united to him in his power which we will exercise in dealing with those who remain unrepentant.

5-6 You who want proof that the Messiah sent me, I'm asking you to look within yourselves to see whether or not you really believe Jesus died to save you, and whether or not he really lives in you. If he does, you should recognize it was through our ministry that you received him. That is the proof you sought regarding our authority. I'm sure that many of you will see this is true—unless you fail the test. 7 It's our prayer that when we arrive, we will find that none of you are doing anything wrong—not because we want our authority to be acknowledged—but because our main concern is that you do what is right for your own well-being—even if it means we don't end up having to "prove" our authority by exercising the Messiah's power to punish people. 8 For we are unable to demonstrate his disciplinary power against those who follow the truth. We can only do so in defense of the truth against those who reject it. 9 We are thrilled when we are ministering among you without being overbearing—inapparent weakness—as long as you are standing strong in the true faith. For it is our main desire and prayer that you become mature

in faith and obedience. 10 That is why I'm writing these things to you in this letter before I arrive. It's my hope that I will not have to use my authority to be harsh with some of you. For the Lord gave me authority for the purpose of strengthening you in the true faith—not to humiliate or destroy you.

Closing Words

11 Finally, my brothers and sisters in union with the Messiah, I urge you to rejoice A in him, *[Galatians 5:22; Philippians 3:1]* pursue maturity, heed my exhortations in this letter, B come to loving consensus on the essentials, ❖ *with the understanding that you are to conform to the teaching of the Scriptures* ➤ and live in harmony together. As you live this way, God—who is love and who brings peace and well-being—will live in and among you. 12 When you come together, greet each other with warm affection as fellow members of God's family.

13 And know that all of God's holy people here send you their warm greetings. ❖ *In New-Testament usage, every true believer is a "saint" (found in the literal text) which literally means "holy one." And "holy one" means "one who is dedicated to serve God."* ➤

14 I pray that our Lord Jesus the Messiah will look upon you with great favor far beyond anything you can deserve, and that you will also experience the great love God the Father has for you, and also experience the Holy Spirit uniting you to himself and to each other in holy friendship. ❖ *From a letter by Clement—Bishop of Rome—written near the end of the first century to the Corinthian church, we know that the assembly in Corinth had an excellent reputation until further problems developed late in the first century. We can infer from this that Paul's letter and visit had positive results which lasted for nearly 40 years.* ➤

A 13:11 χαίρετε (chairete) can mean "greetings" or "rejoice." But there is no evidence it was ever used at the end of a letter to mean "farewell"—as in some translations.

B 13:11 παρακαλεῖσθε (parakaleisthe)—translated "heed my exhortations"—can mean "be encouraged (comforted)" or "be admonished."

Paul's Letter to Jesus' Followers in Galatia

This letter was written by the Apostle Paul sometime in the period AD 48–58 to believers residing in the Roman province of Galatia—which is part of the modern-day country named Turkey.

Paul had heard that some Jewish believers were requiring Gentile believers to become circumcised— teaching them that if they didn't follow all of the Torah's teachings that they couldn't be saved. They also claimed that Paul wasn't a true apostle and that he had changed the message of the Good News by removing the requirement that believers must follow the Torah. ("The Torah" refers to the first five books in the Hebrew Scriptures, also called "the Pentateuch." These books contain all the requirements that God gave to the Israelites through Moses, and the covenant agreement that he made with them.)

Paul's purpose in this letter is to assert that he is a true apostle and that the other apostles agree with his message about the way of salvation. He explains why being circumcised and following the other commands in the Torah will not save them, and emphasizes that we are only saved by trusting in the Messiah. Believers in Jesus should not to try to keep the Torah commands in order to be saved, but are to follow the leading of the Holy Spirit.

Paul does not say that it is wrong for Jewish believers to obey the commands in the Torah. It is only wrong for them to trust in such obedience to save them. It is also wrong for them to insist that Gentile believers obey them in order to be saved.

Key passages in this letter are 2:20-21 and all of chapter 5.

Outline:

Why Paul wrote this letter. [1:1-9]
Paul received his message about the Good News from the Messiah himself. [1:10-24]
The other apostles agreed that the message Paul preached is correct. [2:1-10]
Requiring believers to obey commands to be saved negates the message of the Good News. [2:11-21]
We receive eternal life by trusting in the Messiah—not by obeying the Torah [3:1-14]
The Torah's requirements don't affect God's promise of salvation, which preceded the Torah. [3:15-22]
Believers are God's children, but those using the Torah to obtain righteousness are its slaves. [3:23—4:31]
Don't submit to people who say you must follow all of the Torah's commands to be saved. [5:1-12]
We are to follow the leading of the Holy Spirit who lives in us. [5:13-26]
The Holy Spirit will lead us to serve others. [chapter 6]

1

Opening Greetings

1-2 I, Paul, and all the believers here with me are writing to you, the assemblies of believers in the Roman province of Galatia. I'm writing to you as an apostle— appointed by Jesus the Messiah and by God the Father who raised him from death. It is their authority that I bear because I was chosen by them—not by any human authority. 3 I pray that God our Father and our Lord Jesus the Messiah will look upon you with great favor far beyond anything you can deserve and bless you with peace and well-being. 4 They can do this because the Messiah submitted to his Father's will— allowing himself to die to take away our sins. He thus freed us from being enslaved to the evil ways that dominate people who belong to this present world. 5 So it is fitting for us to praise and honor God the Father forever. Yes, may it be so!

There Is Only One Way to Be Saved from Hell

6 I am dumbfounded that you are so quickly turning away from God who called you to live forever. The way you obtained eternal life was by accepting his undeserved favor and enabling power—which he freely gives those who trust in the Messiah to save

them. **A** But now you are turning toward a different way of salvation—7 which is futile since there is no other way to be saved. Somebody is deceiving you by changing the message about how the Messiah saves us. 8 Your attitude should be this: Anyone who preaches a way to be saved that is different from what we first preached to you—even if it's one of us or an angel who says he comes from God—should be eternally damned in Hell! 9 Barnabas and I told you this before and I repeat it again for emphasis: May God eternally damn anyone who preaches a way to be saved that is different from what we first preached to you!

10 It should be apparent from what I've just said that I'm not trying to tell you only what you want to hear—like some people claim I do. No, the truth is that my aim is to please God in what I say. If it were my habit to flatter people, then I wouldn't be serving the Messiah.

The Message Paul Preaches
Was Given to Him by Jesus Himself

11 My brothers and sisters in the Lord, I want you to know that the message I preach was not invented by any mere human. 12 I received it by divine revelation from Jesus the Messiah himself. Nobody taught it to me.

13 You already know about the way I lived before I knew the Messiah—how I zealously followed all the commands in the Torah and the oral traditions of the Jewish elders. You also know how I arrested the Messiah's followers and tried to terrorize them into abandoning their faith. 14 Of those in my own generation, I was advancing the most quickly in prominence and favor in the eyes of the Jewish establishment, for I was extremely devoted to following all the traditions of our ancestors.

15 I was unaware of it, but even before I was born, God had called me to be an apostle to proclaim the Good News about Jesus to Gentiles. He granted me his enabling favor and chose me—even though I didn't deserve the honor. 16 Then, at the time of his choosing, he revealed to me that Jesus was the Messiah and his Son so I could start proclaiming the Good News about him to Gentiles. When this happened, I didn't consult with anyone to find out what I should do or to obtain any more details about Jesus. 17 I didn't go to Jerusalem to learn from those who were apostles before I was. No, I instead went immediately to an uninhabited area in Arabia to think and pray about what God had shown me. ❖ *We don't know exactly what area Paul meant by Arabia. Some commentators think it means the area around Damascus in Syria.* ➤ After some time passed, I returned to Damascus and started preaching the Good News. 18 It was three years after I became a believer that I finally went up to Jerusalem to get to know Peter. But I only stayed with him for fifteen days. 19 During that time, I also visited with James—our Lord's brother—because he was the leader of the assembly of believers there. But I didn't meet with any of the other apostles. 20 I assure you—before God as my witness—that everything I've written here is true. ❖ *Paul says this because he wants his readers to understand that he didn't spend a lot of time with other apostles in Jerusalem to receive teaching about the Good News—as some people were saying. His visit was a short one and he received his message directly from Jesus himself. He only learned a few anecdotes from Peter and James about things Jesus had done that he hadn't known before. But he had his message about how to be saved by trusting in Jesus before he visited them. Therefore, he is not subordinate or inferior to the other apostles.* ➤ 21 After my visit in Jerusalem, I went to preach in the Roman provinces of Syria and Cilicia where there aren't many Jews. ❖ *Paul's hometown of Tarsus was the capital of Cilicia Province, and Antioch was the capital of Syria Province. His point is that he remained separated from the other apostles by hundreds of miles and could not have received teaching from them while he was in these provinces.* ➤ 22 At that time, the Messiah's people in Judea Province didn't even know me, since we had never met. 23 But they kept hearing reports that the man who used to persecute believers was now preaching the same

---

A 1:6 Most early manuscripts literally say: "I am amazed at how quickly you have moved away from the one who called you in grace (of Christ)," but some leave out "of Christ." Scholars aren't sure if it was included in the original or not.

message about the Messiah that he had previously tried to destroy. 24 So they praised God for how he had changed me.

2

Years Later at the Council in Jerusalem the Other Apostles Endorsed Paul's Message

1 Then fourteen years after my first visit, I again went up to Jerusalem, this time with Barnabas and Titus. *[Acts chapter 15]* ❖ *This may have occurred around AD 48. Paul isn't completely clear. He could mean 14 years after his conversion, but most commentators interpret it as above.* ➤ 2 I only went because of a revelation from God. And when I arrived, I met alone with the apostles and other leaders of the Messiah's people there. I explained to them all about the message I had been preaching for many years to Gentiles so that they could endorse it, and so no one could later truthfully say that the leaders in Jerusalem opposed my ministry. 3-6 Some false believers joined this meeting and presented their view that those who want to be saved must be circumcised— following the requirement of the Torah. They said Titus had to be circumcised to be saved, and they pretended to be followers of Jesus just so they could join the assembly and subvert the truth about how people are saved by believing in Jesus. They insisted that people must also obey all the commands in the Torah to be saved. But my companions and I stuck to the truth and didn't allow them to pervert it. We argued strongly to keep the message pure so that you could know the truth and not become confused by false teaching. We argued our case to those whom everyone accepts as leaders among the Messiah's people. Many think these leaders are important, but it doesn't matter to me what people think about them—nor does it matter to God. What is important is whether or not their teaching is true. As I said, we argued our case and found that they agreed with us. Since Titus was a Gentile, they agreed it wasn't appropriate for him to be circumcised. They completely endorsed all of my message and didn't ask me to change anything I had been preaching. 7-9 You know

that James, Peter, and John are the three whom the Messiah's people in Jerusalem consider to be their main leaders. When these three heard about my ministry, they recognized that God's blessing was upon it to reach Gentiles. They recognized that my ministry had the same kind of anointing on it as Peter's did to reach Jews. Thus it was clear to them that God had chosen me to minister to Gentiles in the same way he had chosen Peter to minister to fellow Jews. So they shook hands with Barnabas and me as a sign that we were all partners in the Messiah's work—preaching the same message. And we all agreed that Barnabas and I would continue to work among Gentiles while they would continue to work among Jews. 10 The only thing they asked us to do was to continue to help raise money for food for the poor in Jerusalem—which I had already been planning to do.

Paul Defends the Purity of the Message When Peter and Barnabas Slip into Legalism

11-13 This issue about following all the commands in the Torah to be saved came up another time, when Peter visited the Messiah's people in Antioch. ❖ *Paul is not necessarily relating events chronologically. Some commentators believe this event took place prior to the council in Jerusalem that he just talked about.* ➤ Initially, he joined with Gentile believers and ate with them—even though the teachings of the Jewish elders forbid it. But later when some Jewish believers came from James in Jerusalem, Peter separated himself from the Gentile believers because he was afraid of offending those who belonged to the circumcision party. ❖ *This doctrinal party consisted of Jewish followers of Jesus who believed that all believers must first become Jewish converts and be circumcised and follow all the requirements of the Torah before they could be saved. To separate themselves from Gentile believers implied that Gentiles were second-class members of God's kingdom. It was a violation of unity in the body of the Messiah and an insult to the Messiah who was spiritually united with them. Some think that Peter would have been eating "unclean" food with the Gentile believers, but there is no reason to believe this is true. It was more likely the simple fact that eating with Gentiles was not allowed by Jewish tradition in order to avoid becoming ritually unclean. A major change made in the Torah (God's teaching) since Jesus' resurrection—expressed in the teachings of the apostles in the New Testament—is that their union with the Messiah purifies Gentile believers so that association with them is no longer forbidden. [Acts 10:34-35; 15:7-9; Ephesians 2:11-22]* ➤ Then, all the other Jewish believers in Antioch were seduced into legalism and also separated themselves from their Gentile brothers. Even Barnabas was influenced into pretending that he always followed all of the Torah's teachings and the Jewish traditions. Everyone was following Peter's lead, so I publicly confronted him— since he was clearly in the wrong. 14 Their behavior contradicted the truth in the message of the Good News, so in front of everyone, I said to Peter, "You are a Jew, but even you don't follow everything the Torah commands anymore—so why do you want to force Gentiles to do so?" **A**

15 We—who were born Jewish and have known the Torah all our lives—are different from Gentiles who don't know it. We have the advantage of knowing from the Torah what is good in God's sight and what is evil, and in the past we looked down on Gentiles and called them "sinners." 16 But now, we know that people do not become righteous in God's sight by following the requirements of the Torah. We know that the only way to become righteous is to trust in Messiah Jesus. Only he can save people. Since we know this, we Jewish believers have trusted in the Messiah and trust that God counts us righteous in his sight for doing so. We no longer try to follow all of the Torah's requirements in order to become righteous. We now know that no one can be saved by legalistically following the Torah because trying to obey the Torah doesn't make anyone righteous. 17 Those who still attempt to obey all the commands in the Torah—in order to become righteous—will say things like: "You've trusted in the Messiah to make you righteous, but you still sin! So the Messiah must be leading you wrongly." But this conclusion is not valid! 18 The truth is, if I—who trust in the Messiah to make me righteous—now try to make myself

righteous by following the Torah, then I would be going back to the old way that I rejected. If I do that, then I'm really going the wrong way. Let me explain.

19 When I trusted in the Messiah, God joined my spirit to the Messiah's Holy Spirit. So when the Messiah died and was punished for everyone's sin, in God's sight it was as if I had died with him because we are spiritually joined and now we are a spiritual unity with him. As far as the Torah is concerned, I have already died and have been punished as it requires. So now I am no longer under the Torah's legal jurisdiction and I don't try to obey it in order to become righteous— because it can't require anything of those who have died. So as a result of my union with the Messiah, I no longer follow the Torah in order to be saved, but I follow the Messiah who saved me. 20 Now I am righteous in God's sight because the Messiah died and I'm joined to him. I no longer live in my old sinful ways, but now I allow the Messiah to live his life in and through me by means of the enabling power and guidance of his Holy Spirit who lives in my human spirit. ❖ *which sometimes is expressed metaphorically as the "heart." See Galatians 4:6.* ➤ My new way of living is to trust and obey God's Son who loves me and died to save me. 21 So clearly, I can't now turn back to obeying the commands in the Torah as a means to become righteous and be saved. If I were to do that, I would be rejecting what the Messiah did for me. For if I try to be saved by keeping the Torah, then I'm saying that the Messiah's death was worthless. And if people could attain righteousness by keeping the Torah, then the Messiah's death was unnecessary.

3

We Gain Eternal Life by Trusting the Messiah Not by Keeping the Torah

1 Now this same problem has come up among you believers in Galatia. You are misguided and acting dense, you know! It's like someone has cast a spell that blinds you

---

A 2:14 We don't know where the quote ends. Some commentators think it ends here and others that it goes to the end of verse 21.

to the truth! How can you believe this lie? When we were there, we clearly taught you how Jesus the Messiah was crucified and died so we can be saved. Now you are turning away from this truth! 2 Do I have to explain it again? I want you to remember how you first received the Holy Spirit. You know that God gave him to you when you believed the message we preached. And you certainly know that you didn't receive him by keeping the commands in the Torah!

❖ *They were mostly Gentiles, so they had never kept the Torah before.* ➤ 3 How can you be so muddled as to think you must keep the Torah to be saved? It's clear that you began your new life by receiving the Spirit who helped you to trust the Messiah to save you and made you righteous in God's sight. So now do you really want to reach your goal of becoming Messiah-like through trying to keep the Torah? You must realize it can't be done! 4 All the difficult times you have endured by standing strong in your faith will now count for nothing if you start to depend on your own efforts to save yourselves instead of trusting in the Messiah's finished work on the cross. I hope it doesn't come to that. 5 You know that God gives you the Holy Spirit and is working miracles among you even now. Tell me the truth. Does he do these things because you keep the Torah or because you believed the message we preached? It's clear that when we were there, you Gentiles were not following the Torah and yet God did these things.

6 Let me remind you of something that shows my point. The Scriptures say that God considered Abraham ❖ *who was initially an uncircumcised Gentile* ➤ righteous in his sight because he trusted in God's promises. *[Genesis 15:6]* ❖ *This happened before Ishmael was born [Genesis 16:16] and before Abraham was 86 years old. God did not command Abraham to be circumcised until he was 99 years old. [Genesis 17:1-14]* ➤ 7 You should conclude from this that those who trust God's promises the same way Abraham did are the ones who are God's people and the ones who will receive what he promised to Abraham. 8 In the Scriptures—long before it happened— God made it clear that he would make people from every people group righteous in

his sight when they trusted in Abraham's descendant—the Messiah. This is clear in his promise to Abraham, **"I will bless people from every people group through your descendant."** *[Genesis 12:3; 18:18; 22:18]* 9 Therefore, only those who trust in God's promises like Abraham did will receive the blessing that God promised him. That is—being counted as righteous in his sight and living forever in Heaven.

10 But on the other hand, the Torah itself teaches that all who depend on keeping all the commands in the Torah in order to gain God's favor are under his curse and will go to Hell. For it clearly says, **"God curses everyone who fails to follow everything in the Torah."** *[Deuteronomy 27:26]* ❖ *Paul was saying that the Torah's message was not that keeping it made you righteous, but that here are God's righteous standards which no one can keep perfectly—so all people are sinners and are under a curse. It was through trusting in God's promises that Jews were counted as righteous—just as Abraham was. Jewish teachers taught that nobody could obey God perfectly, so God could not require perfection as a condition for salvation. But God did demand perfection as a goal, and Paul uses a literal interpretation of this verse to his rhetorical advantage in making his point.* ➤ 11 Clearly, no one can make themselves righteous in God's sight by keeping the Torah because we all sin. That's not the way to obtain eternal life. We know this is true because in another place the Scriptures say, **"Those who are righteous in God's sight because of their faith in his promises, will continue to live by faith."** *[Habakkuk 2:4; Romans 1:17; Hebrews 10:38]* 12 You must realize that those who hope to gain eternal life by keeping the Torah's commands are not trusting in God's promises. They are trusting in their own ability to live without sinning. The Scriptures teach that to obtain righteousness this way, they must keep the Torah perfectly. If they can, they are righteous. If not, then they are under God's curse. *[Leviticus 18:5; Deuteronomy 28:15-68]* 13 But we are all born as sinners so we are all born under the curse of the Torah. That is why we needed the Messiah to release us from that curse— which he did by taking the curse on himself when he died on the cross. We know that he was cursed because the Scriptures say,

"Anyone who hangs on a wood post after he has been executed for his crime, has been cursed." *[Deuteronomy 21:23]* ❖ *The Hebrew word often translated "tree" in this verse has a broader range of meaning than the English word "tree" does, and it can mean a post or an execution cross.* ➤ 14 The Messiah saved us so that the blessing of eternal life—which God gave to Abraham—could also be given to all who trust in the Messiah—regardless of whether they are Jewish or Gentile. He died in our place so we might receive the Holy Spirit whom he promised to those who trust in his promises. *[Joel 2:28-29]*

The Torah Can't Cancel God's Promise Which He Gave Long Before He Gave the Torah

15 My brothers and sisters in the Lord, let me give an example that shows God's promise to Abraham can't be changed. You know that when a man writes out a legally valid will, no one can change it. It must be executed just as it's written. It's the same with God's promise to Abraham. 16 God made his promise to Abraham and to one particular descendant of his. The Scriptures do not say he made the promise to all, or many, descendants. He said to Abraham, "to your descendant," and by that he meant the Messiah. *[Genesis 12:7; 13:15; 24:7]* ❖ *Paul used Rabbinical style argumentation. The Hebrew word "seed" (here translated "descendant"), as in English, can mean either one or many. Jewish teachers interpreted Abraham's "seed"—in the verse Paul is quoting—to refer to either Isaac or to Israel as a whole. But Paul knew that God intended it to refer to the Messiah.* ➤ 17 Now, God gave the Torah to Moses for the people of Israel 430 years after he gave the promise. But that cannot cancel his promise to Abraham and to his descendant, the Messiah. In fact, the Torah and God's promise have nothing to do with each other. One does not affect the other—they are completely separate. 18 God promised to Abraham and his descendant—the Messiah—all the blessings that he gives through the Messiah—such as the Holy Spirit and eternal life. God promised to give them as a free gift, and we receive them through being spiritually united to the Messiah. If we must keep the Torah's commands in order to receive these things, then they are no longer a free gift, but

something we must earn. But God did freely give Abraham the things he promised him. Abraham did not earn them by keeping the Torah—which did not yet even exist. 19 So why did God give Moses the Torah? He gave it to help control the sinful behavior of his people until the Messiah came. ❖ *Or: He gave it to show what sin really is—until the Messiah came.* ➤ God told his angels to give the Torah to Moses who—as a mediator between God and his people—wrote it down and gave it to the Israelites. When the Messiah came, he received the promise that God had made to him and to Abraham. All of you who are spiritually joined to him by faith also receive that same promise. 20 So the Torah is an agreement between God and his people that required a mediator. It promises blessings if the people keep it, and curses if they don't. *[Deuteronomy chapter 28]* The blessings depend on what people do. But God's promise depends only on God alone—not on what people do—and he didn't use a mediator in giving the promise. ❖ *Since he spoke the promise directly—without a mediator—this implies that it had a higher level of authority than the Torah.* ➤

21 So do you think that God's giving of the Torah made his promise void? Certainly not! For it's not possible for any command or system of laws to make sinners righteous in God's sight and thereby provide them with eternal life. No command has the power to enable people to follow it. 22 No—the Scriptures teach that everyone sins and no one is able to keep the Torah perfectly. No one is able to earn eternal life. And that is why God gave the promise of eternal life to those who trust in Jesus the Messiah.

23 Before the time came for us to know how to be saved by trusting in the Messiah, we Jews lived under the guardianship and protection of the Torah. 24 As our guardian, it taught us our need for God's undeserved favor so that when the Messiah came, we would recognize him for who he is and be ready to be made righteous by trusting in him. ❖ *Another interpretation doesn't say that the Torah's purpose was to lead us to recognize the Messiah, but that it was simply to be our guardian until he came. But Jesus himself claimed that the Torah points to him. [John 5:39, 45-46]* ➤ 25 So now that we trust in him to

make us righteous, we are no longer under the Torah's legal guardianship.

Believers Are Adopted as God's Children

26 So now, all of you are also God's children because you trust the Messiah to save you. It doesn't matter if you are Jews or Gentiles. 27 You were all spiritually joined to the Messiah when you believed and were baptized and now—because of your union with him—you are becoming more and more like him in every way. 28 It no longer matters if you are Jewish or Gentile, slave or free, male or female—because we are all made righteous in God's sight by trusting in the Messiah, and we have all been united with Jesus by means of the Holy Spirit. So the Messiah lives in each of us. And when God looks at us, he sees him. No one is more important than anyone else because God sees the same Messiah in each of us. 29 Since you are joined to him, you have received the blessing that God promised to Abraham and to his descendant—the Messiah.

4

Don't Try to Gain Righteousness by Obeying the Torah, Because That Is Like Being a Slave

1 When we Jews lived under the requirements of the Torah, it was like we were young children. Even though a child might someday own land and everything his father has, while he is still a child he is like a slave. 2 For he has no power over his own life or possessions and must obey his teachers and guardians until the time his father set, when he will gain control over his inheritance. 3 It was the same with us before the Messiah saved us. We were like slaves, understanding only that we had to follow all the commands and customs taught by our leaders. ❖ The interpretation of this verse is difficult. Literally, the second part says: "We had been enslaved under the στοιχεῖα (stoicheia) of the world. στοιχεῖα means "elements" or "basic principles" or "elemental spirits." Commentators have interpreted this several ways: 1) the fundamental way things are done in this world, as opposed to how they are done in the God's Kingdom, 2) spiritual forces behind systems of beliefs in this world, 3) basic knowledge that everyone knows, 4) the basic beliefs of the Jewish faith. The same word is used in 4:9 and the same idea is mentioned in 4:8. ➤ 4 But when God considered the time was right, he sent his Son to leave behind the power and glory he had as God in order to be born as an ordinary human being. He was born as a Jew and was, therefore, required to obey the Torah—and he kept it without sinning. 5 He came to this world to save us Jews who lived under requirements of the Torah, and to free us from its power to condemn so we could become God's adopted children and legal heirs. As such, we receive everything that belongs to his Son, the Messiah. 6 You too are now God's true children, so he has sent the Spirit of his Son to live in the hearts ❖ in this context, "heart" means "human spirit." ➤ of each one of us as the sign that we belong to him. The Spirit causes each of us to intimately call out in prayer to our Father God—calling him, "Daddy!" 7 This shows we are no longer slaves under the Torah but have become God's children—so he will give us every blessing that he promised to Abraham.

Keeping Commands and Traditions Won't Save you

8 Before you heard the Good News, you Gentiles didn't know the one true God. You were under the power of demons and their traditions. You submitted to them in worship and served them. 9 So now that God has caused you to know him and accepts you as his children, why do you want to go back and serve those despised demons and traditions that have no power to save you? 10 When you say that people must observe certain traditions and keep certain holy days and months and years and seasons in order to gain righteousness and salvation, you are serving and worshipping things that are not the Messiah! When you do these things, you are actually turning away from the Messiah and the one true God. ❖ It's not the actual observance that's wrong—assuming there is no aspect of idolatry involved—it's the motive and idea that it's possible for you to earn God's favor by keeping the observance. ➤ 11 I'm afraid that if you continue to move away from trusting only in the Messiah to save you, all my work to teach you the truth

will become worthless and you will go to Hell because you reject the truth. 12a My brothers and sisters in the Lord, I beg you to follow my example and keep trusting the Messiah alone for salvation. I showed you my love by living as a Gentile while I was among you. ❖ *Paul is stressing their equality and friendship here.* ➤

Paul Speaks of his Love and Concern

12b Even though I'm rebuking you, I do this because I love you and want you to remain united to the Messiah. I hope you still love me as you did previously. Before now, you never did anything wrong to me. 13 You surely remember that I first stayed with you because of an illness, and that's when I preached the Good News to you. 14 Even though you had to work hard to take care of me, you didn't despise or reject me. Instead, you welcomed me as you might an angel from God or as you would Messiah Jesus himself. 15 You were so happy that I was with you preaching the Good News. Why have you changed your attitude about me? I'm telling the truth when I say that you loved me so much you would have given me your own eyes to help me, if that were possible. ❖ *Traditionally, it has been thought that Paul suffered from some sort of eye disease at the time. The IVP commentary says that "sacrificing one's eyes" for someone is merely a figure of speech, indicating a willingness to endure great personal sacrifice to help someone. In Greek culture, sacrifice was the way that one showed friendship.* ➤ 16 So how has it come about that you now think I'm your enemy because I told you the truth about how to be saved?

17 Those people who say that salvation comes from keeping the Torah are eager to have you join them, but not because they really want what's good for you. They want you to be estranged from us and brought under their influence. 18 Now, it's fine for others to be eager to teach you and take you under their wing if what they teach is good and true. For you should always want to hear the truth and follow it—and not just when I'm there. ❖ *This is a rebuke, as they had been zealous for the truth while Paul was with them, but had abandoned it since he left them.* ➤ 19 My dear children in the faith, I love you and will be

anxious about you until it's clear that you trust the Messiah alone for salvation and you become mature with his life clearly evident in yours. I'm as anxious as a woman in labor is until she sees that her new child is healthy. 20 I wish I could be there with you now and speak to you more gently. It's hard for me to know what to write to convince you.

God Rejects Those Who Try to Gain Righteousness by Obeying the Torah, Like He Rejected Hagar and Ishmael

21 You people of Galatia who want to gain salvation by living under the Torah, I don't think you realize what the Torah really teaches. 22 In it is recorded the fact that Abraham had two sons. The first was Ishmael, born to Hagar—his wife's slave. The second was Isaac, born to his wife Sarah who was free. [Genesis chapters 16—18 and 21] 23 Hagar's son was born as a result of Abraham trying to make God's promise of a son happen through his own efforts. But Sarah's son was born because God himself fulfilled his promise and miraculously caused it to happen.

24-25 These historical events are an illustration of two covenants that God has made with his people. ❖ *A covenant is a special kind of binding agreement in which two parties pledge all of their resources to the other's benefit. It was ratified with the shedding of blood. The first of these covenants is about keeping the commands in the Torah—which God gave to Moses. The second is about accepting undeserved favor from God— which he freely bestows on those who trust in his promises. [Jeremiah 31:31; Luke 22:20; 1 Corinthians 11:25] This second covenant is illustrated by Isaac being born in fulfillment of God's promise to Abraham. [Genesis 12:2; 15:4-6; 17:1-8; 21:1-5] Isaac's birth was a foreshadowing of the ultimate fulfillment of God's promise—many years later—in the birth of the Messiah.* ➤ Hagar represents the covenant that God made with Moses on Mount Sinai in Arabia. That is where God first bound the Israelites to the Torah. Hagar also represents Jerusalem—the heart of Israel—where Jews still try in vain to earn God's favor by keeping the Torah. They have made the Torah their legalistic master so they are it's slaves—just like Hagar and her son were slaves. 26 But Sarah represents God's covenant of undeserved favor and his keeping of his promises. She also represents the new Jerusalem which will come down from Heaven. For in that city will live all who trust the Messiah to make them righteous in God's sight. They are like Isaac—who was born in fulfillment of God's promise. So we—who are born into God's family by believing in his promise—are also Sarah's children and are, therefore, free from a legalistic slavery to the Torah.

❖ *The concept of a new Jerusalem that would come down from Heaven was common in Jewish writings.* ➤ 27 It was Sarah that the prophet Isaiah spoke about when he wrote, "Barren woman, you who have no children, rejoice! Shout out your joy, you who have never experienced labor! For you—who never before had a child—will have more descendants than the woman who has had many children by her husband." *[Isaiah 54:1]* ❖ *Paul saw in this prophecy a picture of how Gentiles who believe in Jesus will be greater in number than Jews who follow the Torah.* ➤

28 So, my brothers and sisters in the Lord, we are like Isaac—the son of Sarah. Just as he was born in fulfillment of God's promise and not because Abraham obeyed any command, in the same way, God made us his children because we believe in his promise to save those who trust in the Messiah. 29 Just as in the past, Ishmael persecuted Isaac whom the Holy Spirit caused to be born, in the same way those who want to be saved by keeping the Torah are now persecuting those who trust in the Messiah what alone to save them. 30 But notice the Scriptures say happened. Sarah told Abraham to chase Hagar and her son away because they would not inherit anything from Abraham. All would go to her son Isaac. And God told Abraham to do what Sarah said. *[Genesis 21:9-12]* So just as Ishmael inherited nothing from Abraham, those who live under the Torah—trusting in their legalistic obedience to it to save them—will not be saved. 31 Therefore, my brothers and sisters in the Lord, remember that we are not Hagar's children and we don't want to be because they are under the Torah's curse. *[Deuteronomy 28:15-68]* But we are Sarah's children because we trust the Messiah alone to save us—and we are thereby free from the Torah's curse.

5

Don't Submit to Those Who Teach That You Must Keep the Torah to Be Saved

1 The Messiah freed us from following the requirements of the Torah for salvation—and he wants us to stay free. Therefore, you must stand firm in your faith—trusting in the Messiah alone to save you—and not enslave yourselves to legalistically following the Torah.

2 Listen to me! I, Paul, your apostle, tell you Gentiles that if you allow yourselves to be circumcised for the purpose of trusting in it to save you—then the Messiah's death will no longer save you. 3 I warn you again, if you think to become righteous in God's sight by allowing yourselves to be circumcised, then you are obligated to keep all the commands in the Torah—without failure—in order to be saved. But beware! No one can do this! 4 Those who desire to keep the Torah in order to attain righteousness have severed themselves from the Messiah—for they have rejected God's freely offered unmeritable favor and his free gift of salvation. They will go to Hell. 5 But we—who live by following the Holy Spirit—are eagerly waiting to receive all that God has promised. He will give it to those who are righteous through their trusting in the Messiah alone to save them. 6 Since we are spiritually joined to him, it makes no difference whether or not we are circumcised. The important thing is trusting in him and demonstrating that trust by showing love to others.

7 You were following the Messiah so well before. So who has now stopped you from following the truth? 8 That kind of persuasion doesn't come from God who called you to be his children. 9 Just as a small amount of yeast spreads throughout a batch of dough, so a small amount of false teaching can spread to all of you and ruin your faith. 10 But I'm trusting our Lord Jesus to lead you to correct belief—just as I taught you. And I know that God will punish the person who is confusing you with this false teaching, whoever he is.

11 My brothers and sisters in the Lord, please do not believe those who say I teach that you must be circumcised in order to be righteous in God's sight. This is clearly not true since you know that many Jews still persecute me. If I taught that circumcision was necessary—instead of my message that only the Messiah's death on the cross saves us—then they wouldn't be bothering me. 12 As for those agitators who are troubling you about circumcision, I wish they would go all the way and mutilate themselves! ❖ *In addition to expressing his animosity toward those insisting on circumcision, such an act would make them outcasts among Jews. Paul isn't explicit here, and a few commentators think he means, "cut themselves off from you." But most commentators interpret it as above.* ➤

Since We Can't Become Righteous by Obeying the Torah, We Must Follow the Holy Spirit

13 My brothers and sisters, God has set you free from the curse of the Torah and from the necessity of legalistically obeying all its commands. But don't think this means that you are free to follow desires that lead to sin. Instead, show your love for God and each other by helping each other remain pure. ❖ *We are free from the penalty of the Torah and are not to think of it as a means to attain righteousness. However, the Torah does show us God's will. We can't keep it in our own strength. But we can allow the Messiah to live his life through us, [Galatians 2:20] and the Torah can serve as a reference to help us know God's will in certain matters. The Holy Spirit will never lead us to do something contrary to God's Torah, although some teachings in the Torah have been changed. e.g., Matthew 5:21-22, 27-28; Acts 10:28; 15:9-10; and Hebrews 7:12. In fact, the entire New Testament together with the rest of the Hebrew Scriptures is now part of God's amended "Torah." Anything that God has declared since giving the original Torah has already been added to it and amended it. Torah means "teaching," and everything he has said in the Scriptures is part of his "teaching."* ➤ 14 If you do this, you will actually be following God's will and doing everything the Torah requires, since everything the Torah teaches means, **"Love other people in the same way that you love and take care of yourself."** [Leviticus 19:18; Matthew 19:19; 22:39; Mark 12:31; Luke 10:27; Romans 13:9; Galatians 5:14; James 2:8] 15 But if you keep on being vicious with each other

like wild animals—watch out—or you will end up completely destroying your fellowship, your assembly, and even your own relationship with the Messiah.

16 So I exhort you to choose—moment by moment—to follow the leading of the Holy Spirit who lives in you. If you do this, then you won't follow evil desires that lead you to sin. [Ezekiel 36:27] 17 For these evil desires fight against the will of the Spirit whose leading opposes those desires. They are always in conflict, and the Spirit's goal is to lead you so that you won't follow your evil impulses. 18 If you allow yourselves to be led by the Spirit, then you are no longer under the Torah's condemnation. ❖ *Unlike the Torah—which is unable to help you keep it—the Spirit helps you want to obey him. Implicit in the idea of being led by the Spirit is that you are trusting in the Messiah to make you righteous and not trusting in what you can do. Also implicit is the idea that the Spirit not only leads but enables you to follow. There is no dependence on your own ability—like there is in being "under the Torah."* ➤

19 The kinds of things people do when they follow their evil desires are clear to everyone, such as: sexual immorality, impure thoughts, following after vices, unrestrained sexuality, a shameless disregard for public decency, 20 the worship of false gods, witchcraft and involvement in the occult, hatred and hostility, quarreling and strife, jealousy and wanting what belongs to others, fits of uncontrolled anger, ruthless striving to attain social position or power by stepping on or destroying others, fomenting division, promoting your own faction, 21 destroying others to obtain from them what you want, habitual drunkenness, drunken orgies, and many similar things. I warn you now—just as I did when I was with you—that people who live like this are not God's people. If they do not repent and change their ways, they will not get to Heaven.

22 But the good characteristics that the Holy Spirit produces in the lives of those who follow him are these: unselfish love, undisturbable joy and peace, peaceful relationships with others, patience, kindness, honesty and goodness, trustworthiness in all things, 23 humility and gentle

consideration of others, and self-control. When you follow the leading of the Holy Spirit and live this way, you can be sure that you will not be breaking any law. ❖ *i.e., You will also be keeping the amended Torah (i.e., all the teachings in the Hebrew Scriptures as interpreted in light of the New Testament Scriptures) in the way that God wants you to—but not in your own strength and not in order to obtain righteousness.* ➤ 24 Those who really belong to Messiah Jesus have crucified their evil desires and passions—which means that they always firmly reject them and refuse to follow them while depending on the power of the Spirit to enable them to obey his will. ❖ *See the note at 1 Peter 2:11 about how to depend on the Spirit's power to enable you to obey.* ➤ 25 Since the Holy Spirit made us spiritually alive and lives in us, we should always submit to his leading. 26 Never allow yourselves to become proud and think that you are better than others. If you are like that, then you will provoke each other and want to ruin each other's reputations.

6

We Must Be Humble

1 My brothers and sisters in the Lord, if a believer stumbles in sin, then let those who are known to be mature—because they always follow the Spirit—humbly and gently lead the stumbler to repent. But the mature helper must be careful that he himself doesn't give in to temptation. ❖ *Some commentators think the helper might be tempted to the same sin as the person he is helping. Others think this is a more general caution and that the helper might be tempted to pride—which would also lead to other sins.* ➤ 2 If you are aware of other believers having difficulties—whether temptations or other problems—then help them. This is part of what it means to love each other as the Messiah commanded. 3 If you start thinking that you are someone special or better than others, you are deceiving yourself and are guilty of pride. ❖ *You may be someone special in this world, but in God's sight you become just another rebel—useless as far as his purposes are concerned.* ➤ 4 Therefore, you should evaluate your own motives and actions to see if they are in line with the Spirit's will. If you judge that they are, you

can be satisfied with yourself. But don't go comparing yourself with others. You do not have the knowledge, wisdom, or permission to judge others. 5 Each person is responsible for his own attitudes and actions in relation to God's commands and guidance.

6 It's also appropriate that those who are taught God's word should share every good thing they have with those who teach them.

We Will Eventually See the Results of What We Do

7 Don't deceive yourselves—as so many do. No one can ignore God and get away with it. Just as the farmer inevitably harvests what he plants, God will present each person with the harvest of fair consequences based on how they have lived. 8 Those who live following their own evil impulses will obtain the results of spiritual corruption—which is eternity in Hell. But those who live following the Spirit of life will obtain eternal life in Heaven. 9 So don't give up because you become weary of doing good—even if it appears your efforts are in vain. If you continue to do what is right, then at God's chosen time you will finally gain the benefit of your obedience. ❖ *This does not imply that our obedience merits anything. But obedience is required and will be graciously and generously rewarded—even though the reward is in no sense earned.* ➤ 10 Therefore, we must continue to do good for all people whenever we have the opportunity—and especially for other believers.

Paul's Final Warning About Circumcision

11 Notice the large letters I'm using to write this section. I'm writing this with my own hand so you can recognize my writing and be sure who it is who is saying these things to you. This is very important. ❖ *It's likely that Paul had someone else transcribing most of the letter, but some commentators think he did it all himself and is here merely emphasizing what he says in this last section.* ➤ 12 Those who are trying hard to convince you to be circumcised are only doing so because they want to look good in the eyes of their fellow Jews who try to obtain righteousness by keeping the Torah. They are afraid they will be persecuted if they proclaim the truth that people can only

be saved by trusting in the Messiah's death on the cross. 13 But these same people who want to circumcise you don't keep every part of the Torah either. They just want to boast to fellow Jews that they convinced you to be circumcised. 14 But as for me, I will only boast about the death of our Lord Jesus the Messiah on the cross. Because of his death, I have died with him—and the pleasures, honors, and values of this world can no longer tempt me. People belonging to this world cannot understand what is dear to me. ❖ *Paul is implying that the Galatian believers had not adequately separated themselves from the world. If they are still trying to please worldly people, then they are still under their influence. Paul boasts in the crucifixion of the Messiah—which to unbelievers was a repulsive and shameful event.* ➤ 15 Since the Messiah has died, it no longer matters to God whether or not you are circumcised. The important thing is whether or not God has created a new life within you and placed his Holy Spirit there. 16 God will be merciful to all who follow my teaching in this matter, and he will bless them with peace and well-being because they are the ones who are truly his people.

17 So from now on, don't accuse me of wrong teaching, for I have the scars of stoning and whippings on my body that prove I have always been faithful to serve my Lord Jesus—no matter what the cost. ❖ *A person who was peddling false teaching for personal gain would never endure such punishment to maintain his lies. So it was proof that he fully believed everything he taught and said in this letter was true. Implied is: Would those who want you to be circumcised be willing to go through the same persecutions for their beliefs?* ➤ 18 My brothers and sisters in the Lord, I pray that our Lord Jesus the Messiah will look upon you with great favor far beyond anything you can deserve and spiritually bless you. Yes, may it be so!

Paul's Letter to Jesus' Followers in Ephesus

Paul wrote this letter during his first imprisonment in Rome [Acts 28:30-31]—estimated to be in the period AD 60–62. His letters to the Colossians, Philemon, and the Philippians were also written during this time and together are called the "prison letters."

This letter was apparently not written to correct any specific problem, but was addressed mainly to Gentile believers in the Roman province of Asia (present-day Turkey) in the general area of the cities of Ephesus, Colosse, and Laodicea. "Gentile" is a term used by Jews to refer to anyone who is not Jewish. Since most believers today are Gentiles, the message of this letter should be of particular interest to most modern-day believers.

Paul's main theme is seen in his repetition of the phrase "in the Messiah"—which appears more than 30 times in the original text and in this interpretation is often rendered "in your being joined to Jesus" or "in your union with Jesus." All that God has done for us and in us and all he has made available to us is through our being spiritually joined to his Son.

The Messiah lives in us through his Holy Spirit. Yet Paul's emphasis in this letter is that we also live in him. Jesus is in Heaven at the right hand of the Father in the position of highest authority under the Father. And we are spiritually there in and with him because of our spiritual union with him. Therefore, we have access to every power, resource, and authority that Jesus has. Of course, it's only ours to draw on as we remain obedient to his will. Yet those resources are unlimited and we need to be aware of our access to them or we will live in unnecessary weakness and spiritual poverty. But if we are aware of our access, we can live the way he wants us to live and have victory over sin and Satan.

In the first part of this letter, Paul emphasizes the spiritual blessings and power that are available to all believers because of their spiritual union with Jesus. In the second part starting at 2:11, he emphasizes the unity that exists between all believers— whether they are Jews or Gentiles—because of their being spiritually joined to Jesus and, therefore, also to each other. In both of the first two parts, he stresses what God has done for Gentiles and his ultimate purpose for them. The third part starts at chapter four, where he exhorts believers to respond properly to the great undeserved enabling favor that God has granted them, and to live in a way that's fitting for God's people—leading to spiritual maturity and good interpersonal relationships. Finally, in the fourth part which starts at 6:10, he exhorts them to wage spiritual warfare against the spiritual forces that are trying to destroy their faith.

Paul Gives Three Prominent Figures to Help Believers Understand Their Relationship with Jesus.

Those are:
1) All believers together form his body—with Jesus as our head.[1:22-23; 4:15-16]
2) All believers together form a Temple where God lives—and Jesus is its cornerstone. [2:21-22]
3) Marriage is a picture of the relationship between Jesus and all believers. [5:23-32]

1

Opening Greetings

1 Dear holy ones of God in Ephesus, **A** I am Paul—whom God chose to be an apostle of Messiah Jesus—and I'm writing to you who faithfully follow him. 2 My prayer is that God our Father and our Lord Jesus will continue to look upon you with great favor far beyond anything you can deserve and grant you peace and well-being.

Our Blessings
Through Being Spiritually Joined to Jesus

3 We should thank and praise God—the Father of our Lord Jesus the Messiah—for he has given us access to every spiritual

---

A 1:1 The earliest manuscripts do not have "in Ephesus." This was likely a circular letter sent first to believers in Ephesus and probably also to Laodicea and Colosse.

blessing that exists in the spiritual realm by means of our spiritual union with Jesus.

❖ *These blessings can help us have a close relationship with Jesus, to follow his will, and to become like him. The spiritual realm is the unseen world around us which is inhabited by spirit beings. God is an infinite spirit, [John 4:24] and angels and demons are finite spirits. Our union with Jesus is effected through the Holy Spirit who resides within our human spirits. [1 Corinthians 6:17-19 and 2 Timothy 1:14] Humans have three parts: body, soul, and spirit [1 Thessalonians 5:23] and our human spirit is that part of us which can interact with the spiritual realm. As a result of this union, we have access to blessings and authority that aid us in our interaction with God. For God never gives spiritual blessings as presents separate from himself. We only have access to these blessings because we are united to him as their source.* ➤

4 Even before God created this world, he chose us and intended us to be spiritually united with Jesus so he could see us and interact with us as holy and sinless. 5 Because he loves us, it was his plan to predestine us to be his adopted heirs—which he made possible through Jesus' sacrifice. ❖ *God's love for us is not based on anything worthy about us. It is his character and desire to love us as if we were already the perfect creatures into which he wants to transform us.* ➤ 6 His purpose in all this is to cause every created being to recognize, appreciate, and praise the supreme excellence of his character and his generosity in freely offering us undeserved enabling favor—which he showers on us through our spiritual union with his beloved Son. ❖ *God's loving, gracious, and holy character is supremely good. Hence it is for our benefit and pleasure that he wants us to recognize its worth. It is not because he needs our adulation, but because there exists nothing better that we could contemplate, appreciate, or emulate.* ➤ 7 Because of Jesus' sacrificial death in our place and our spiritual union with him, all our sins—past and future—have been completely forgiven and we

have been set free from the power of sin and death. This was all accomplished by means of his inexhaustible undeserved favor—8 which he lavished on us because in his great wisdom and understanding he foresaw the result.

9 It was also his pleasure to reveal his previously hidden plan to us which he made even before he created this world. ❖ *It remained a secret from all created beings until the Holy Spirit revealed it to the apostles. [1 Corinthians 2:7-9; Ephesians 3:3-6; Colossians 1:26-27]* ➤ 10 God's plan centers entirely on his Son, the Messiah. He intends that at the culmination of time, everything and everyone in Heaven and on earth will be visibly brought under the authority and power of the Messiah. 11 As part of this plan, he also chose us—in our union with Jesus— to be his valued possession. A And he sovereignly ensures that everything happens the way he planned. 12 So it was part of his plan that we Jewish believers—who trusted in the Messiah first—would make it possible for all people to see and acknowledge the excellence of God's character through our telling about the life, death, and resurrection of Jesus—the desired result being that they would give him appropriate praise. 13 You Gentiles were also joined to the Messiah and saved from the fate of eternal punishment in Hell when you heard the Good News about how Jesus died to save you—and you believed it was true. When you trusted in Jesus, God marked you with a seal of ownership by giving you his Holy Spirit— just as he promised to do long ago. *[Joel 2:28-29]* 14 The experiential fact of the Holy Spirit living in you is God's pledge that you will receive the full inheritance of eternal life with him in Heaven which he promised his people. *[Romans 8:23; 2 Corinthians 1:22; 5:5; Ephesians 1:13-14; 1 John 3:24]* ❖ *It's clear that Paul expects us to be able to experientially perceive the presence of the Holy Spirit*

A **1:11** The word ἐκληρώθημεν (eklērōthēmen), translated as "chose us… to be his valued possession," literally means "we were chosen as inheritance." I've represented a minority view that interprets this to mean believers are God's chosen and prized inheritance, because it fits well with the ideas in this passage—namely that God delighted to make us his people and has done everything so we will recognize and praise the supreme excellence of his character. Throughout

the Hebrew Scriptures, God's people are called his "treasured possession" [Exodus 19:5; Deuteronomy 7:6; 14:2; 26:18; Psalm 135:4; Malachi 3:17] and his "inheritance." [Exodus 34:9; Deuteronomy 4:20; 9:26, 29; 1 Samuel 10:1; 2 Samuel 20:19; 21:3; 1 Kings 8:51, 53; 2 Kings 21:14; Psalm 2:8; 28:9; 33:12; 68:9; 74:2; 78:62, 71; 82:8; 94:5, 14; 106:5, 40; Isaiah 19:25; 47:6; 63:17; Jeremiah 2:7; 10:16; 12:7-9; 16:18; 50:11; 51:19; Joel 2:17; 3:2; Micah 7:14]

in our lives. See the note in 1 John 3:24. ➤ That will happen when you physically die and he completes your redemption—freeing you entirely from all influence of sin. The evidence of Holy Spirit in your life as God's pledge here and now will also result in God's character being recognized in you and being praised by others.

Paul's Prayer for Believers

15-16 It is precisely because you have been so richly blessed by God that I'm praying you will recognize your access to these blessings and begin to experience their reality. I've prayed for you ever since I first heard how you firmly trust in Jesus our Lord, and how you show his love to all of God's people without discrimination. I also thank God for you and your example whenever I pray. **17** I always ask God—the glorious Father of Jesus our Lord—to give you wisdom from the Holy Spirit and to reveal himself to you so you can know him better. ❖ *The Holy Spirit is sometimes referred to as "the Spirit of Wisdom." [Deuteronomy 34:9; Exodus 28:3; 31:3; 35:31; and Isaiah 11:2]* ➤ **18** Since you are among those he has called to be his holy ones, I also pray that he will enable you to fully understand the wonderful things he has in store for you, and that you will realize that he considers you to be his great and glorious possession. **A** **19** I also pray that you will know and experience his infinite power—which he makes available through the Holy Spirit to those of us who trust and obey him. *[2 Peter 1:3]* ❖ *His infinite power and resources are available to help us: 1) meet our needs, 2) grow spiritually, 3) minister to others and 4) do everything he desires us to do.* ➤ I'm talking about the same mighty power **20** that God used to bring Jesus to life again after he died, and which Jesus now exercises sitting in his position of greatest authority, honor, and power in the spiritual realm at the right hand of the Father in Heaven. **21** His position is far superior in

title, authority, and power to all spiritual or earthly rulers, authorities, powers, or nations—both now and continuing in the age to come. ❖ *Paul literally wrote: "rule, authority, power, and lordship." These terms were used to refer to demonic and angelic beings who work behind the scenes to influence and effectively control rulers and nations. Daniel 4:35 and 10:13 support this idea.* ➤ **22** For God subjected everything in creation to the Messiah's power and authority and gave him—who is over all things—as the benefactor and head for all believers. **23** So now, all believers together are functionally his body in relation to Jesus as our head. And just as a wife completes her husband, so his people make Jesus complete—while he himself completes all things. ❖ *Paul's meaning in this verse is debated. This view says the Assembly of all Believers in some way completes or complements God's Son—who himself is totally self-sufficient. This is an apparent paradox, yet no more so than the one inherent in the Father desiring to create a bride for his self-sufficient Son.* ➤

2

We Were Spiritually Dead, but Now We Live in Union with Jesus

1 Before you trusted in Jesus to save you, you were spiritually dead because you were sinners. **2** At that time, you lived like the rest of the spiritually lost who live in sin and follow the ways of the prince of the demonic powers that inhabit the air around us. ❖ *First-century Jews considered the air—or atmosphere— to be the lowest Heaven, or the spiritual realm where demons lived.* ➤ He is the spirit that influences the hearts and minds of people who refuse to obey God. ❖ *Satan is the prince of demons—who were angels that rebelled against God. Most references to the work of Satan are equally true of demons, since he is a finite being who can only be in one place at a time. Demons are pleased if we believe that they don't exist so they can put thoughts in our minds and trick us into believing that they are our own thoughts. Their most common strategy is to deceive us into believing lies that they've planted in our thoughts.* ➤ **3** We

---

A 1:18 The text literally says, "that you will know the riches of the glory of his inheritance in the saints." This is usually interpreted as knowing "the great inheritance that he has in store for the saints," but alternatively, it could mean they would know that they are considered by him to be his rich and glorious inheritance or possession. A minority interpretation has been given here and as noted in verse 11 because the grammar of the Greek leans in this direction and it better fits the overall context.

all used to live the same way—following our bodies' desires and urges, doing whatever we wanted. Like all people, we were born with the selfish inclination to do evil and were, therefore, under God's sentence of eternal damnation. ❖ *God is holy and just and cannot tolerate evil. For him to do so would be as inconceivable as our tolerating the torture and murder of a loved one. All humanity is under the sentence of damnation—which is the just penalty for sin according to God's standards. And since he is the omnipotent creator of everything—only his standards count. Humanity's sinful inclination is passed on from parent to child, is universal among humans, and is theologically referred to as "original sin."* ➤

4 But God is extremely merciful to all people because he loves us very much. ❖ *God created humanity in order to have an intimate love relationship with us. But the first humans—Adam and Eve—sinned after being tempted by Satan. [Genesis chapters 1—3] Since God loves humanity and will not allow his ultimate purpose to be thwarted, he provided a means to be saved from the fate of damnation for those who voluntarily choose to have a love relationship with him—on his terms. Those who reject his provision for salvation remain under that sentence of eternal damnation.* ➤ 5 When we were born, our human spirits were dead to God because of our sinful nature. ❖ *A person's "spirit" was designed to interact with the spiritual realm. But since we are born with spirits corrupted by a nature inclined to sin, God—who is holy—refuses to interact directly with them. To him, they are "dead." Sinful human spirits do function though, and are perfectly capable of interacting with demonic spirits—as is practiced by those involved in the occult.* ➤ But by giving believers new sinless spirits, he made us spiritually "alive" and joined our spirits with Jesus the Messiah—thus saving us from the fate of damnation. God did this purely because he chose to favor us, not because of anything we did to earn his favor. ❖ *Nothing that spiritually "dead" people do can earn his favor—for even their best deeds are tainted with sin.* ➤ 6 Now, since Jesus has been resurrected from the dead,

we have also been spiritually resurrected because we are spiritually joined to him. And since he is seated in the place of highest honor and authority under God the Father in Heaven, we are spiritually there with him. 7 God did this for us so that after Jesus returns and in the ages to come, he can clearly show to all rational creatures the incomparable magnitude of his undeserved favor by pointing to the kindness that he showed to us when he spiritually joined us to Messiah Jesus, his Son. A 8 For it's by God's freely given enabling favor that you were saved—through your trusting in God's promise to save you. ❖ *a.k.a. "faith"* ➤ But even your ability to respond to God's promise with trust was God's free gift to you—having nothing to do with your own character, abilities, or efforts. 9 You didn't earn his help by anything you did. God did it this way so no one can validly boast that their own efforts had anything at all to do with their being saved. 10 For it was God who did the work in making us his holy people. He gave us a new life in union with Messiah Jesus and has planned and prepared for each of us certain good works that he wants us to accomplish in this life. ❖ *This means that God has a plan for your life—so you are not meant to merely follow your own inclinations, doing whatever seems "good." But you are to seek out his specific will for you and follow it. Many places in the Scriptures tell us that we will be rewarded in Heaven for doing his will in this life. [e.g. Matthew 16:27]* ➤

All Believers Are Spiritually United Because They Are All Joined to Jesus

11 Don't forget that before you Gentiles trusted in Jesus, Jews called you "uncircumcised pagans," but considered themselves to be God's people because their bodies bore the man-made mark of circumcision. ❖ *The Teachings of Moses require all Jewish males to take the*

A 2:7 Some commentators speculate that the reason God did not punish Satan and the other rebellious angels immediately and start over again with a new humanity—was to prove a point to them. We get hints of what this point might have been in the first two chapters of Job and also in this verse. They hint that God's purpose might have been: a) that some people would recognize the desirability of God's love and glory and voluntarily deny their own sinful desires in order to have an intimate relationship with him—

even without being able to directly perceive the greatness of his glory as the angels do, or b) that nothing Satan can do can defeat God's plan to make a righteous bride for his Son, c) or it might have been to prove the excellence of God's character—which Satan had rejected, but even fallen humanity can recognize. Or it may be something else. However, God's point will somehow be made by pointing to his great grace, love, and justice in what he accomplishes through our spiritual union with Jesus.

mark of circumcision as a sign that they belong to God's chosen people—and to remind them of their covenant relationship with him. However, circumcision didn't have the power to change a person's heart to make him desire to obey God. Thus many who were circumcised didn't have a proper relationship with him. ➤ 12 Don't forget that you Gentiles had no faith in the Messiah and didn't belong to the nation of Israel—God's chosen people. You weren't included in God's Covenant agreements with his people in which he promised to save them. You had no basis to hope for eternal salvation and you didn't know the one true God. 13 But now you are spiritually joined to Messiah Jesus. Even though at one time you were far from knowing God, now he has brought you into an intimate relationship with himself by means of the Messiah's blood. ❖ The Scriptures teach that the life of a person (or animal) is contained in their blood. [Leviticus 17:10-14; Deuteronomy 12:22-24] Under the Old (Mosaic) Covenant, when a person offered an animal to be killed as a sacrifice to take away his sins, the priest sprinkled the blood from the sacrifice on the altar. (See Leviticus chapter 1 about burnt offerings, chapter 4 about sin offerings, and chapter 16 about the Day of Atonement.) This showed that the death of the animal was substituted for the person's death in payment for his or her sins, since the punishment for sin is eternal death. (Damnation, or eternal separation from God in Hell, is called the "second death.") Sacrificial blood thus became a symbol of the death of a sacrificial substitute. In the New Testament, the Scriptures often talk about the "blood" of Jesus saving us or washing our sins away or having power. This is figurative language. The "blood" represents Jesus' death as a substitute for us to pay the penalty of our sins so that we don't have to suffer eternal death. See Ezekiel 3:18 and 22:4-6 for specific passages that clearly equate "blood" with "death." This is the predominant sense of the word "blood" in most Scripture passages. ➤ 14 Jesus himself has established peace between Jewish and Gentile believers—making us one people by joining us all to himself. As a consequence, he has demolished all ritual barriers and hostility between us. 15 When he died and made it possible for any believer to be spiritually

joined to him, Jesus abolished certain parts of the Torah's teachings that required division between Jews and Gentiles and which often produced hostility between these groups. He did this so he could establish peace between them and make one new "saved humanity." 16 By spiritually joining both groups together in himself, he also made them acceptable to God. And by means of his death on the cross, he also destroyed the hostility and division between all believers and God. **A** ❖ Since Jesus suffered God's required punishment for sin, when God sees us joined to Jesus, he sees in that unity that our sins have already been punished and his justice satisfied—so he is able to accept us. ➤

17 So in fulfillment of prophecy, the Messiah came and preached **"peace to you Gentiles who were spiritually far away from God, and also peace to the Jews who were near to him."** [Isaiah 57:19] 18 Now, both Jews and Gentiles are joined to the same Holy Spirit and have access to direct communication with God the Father because of what Jesus the Messiah did for us. 19 Therefore, you Gentile believers in Jesus are no longer strangers and foreigners to God's people. You have become fellow citizens of Heaven along with the rest of the holy ones, and now you are also members of God's own family. 20-22 God the Holy Spirit also lives in you—making all of us together his living Holy Temple. Each of us is like a living stone that's a part of that Temple. The apostles and prophets—who first worked to establish this Temple—are its foundation. Messiah Jesus is the cornerstone—the most important stone in the entire structure. And we are all joined to each other because we are all joined to him. God is causing us to be fitted closely together like stones in its walls, and together we are becoming a Holy Temple in union with our Lord Jesus—a place where God will reside through his Holy Spirit.

A 2:16 Some commentators believe that the hostility referred to in this verse was between Jews and Gentiles, and others that it was both between Jews and Gentiles and also between humanity and God. But since he has already stated in the previous verse that the hostility between Jews and Gentiles has been dealt with—and in this verse he introduces the topic of their reconciliation with God—it seems likely that the relationship of humanity with God is in focus.

3

God Sent Paul
to Preach the Good News to Gentiles

¹ God has done so much for you, and it is because of his desire to save Gentiles that I pray for you and am here in prison in Rome. For Messiah Jesus appointed me to preach the Good News about how to be saved to Gentiles like yourselves, so as to bring many into his Kingdom. And as a result of my preaching, I am a prisoner. ² You have already heard about God giving me the responsibility for telling Gentiles about his freely offered favor, ³ and that He revealed his previously hidden plan to me—as I mentioned earlier in this letter. ⁴ In reading this, you will come to understand the insight that God gave me to share with you about his plan concerning the Messiah—and the fact that it includes saving Gentiles. ⁵ God never revealed this plan to past generations, but now—since the Messiah has come—the Holy Spirit has revealed it to God's holy apostles and prophets.

⁶ God plans for both Gentile and Jewish believers to equally share the blessings that he will give his children in Heaven. People from both groups have believed God's Good News and so have been joined to Jesus. They are all members of his body and will share together the same blessings that God promised—because they are joined to him. *[1 Corinthians 2:7-9; Ephesians 1:9-14; Colossians 1:26-27]*

⁷ As a gift I could never deserve, God sovereignly exerted his power in my life to make me his servant and commissioned me to preach his Good News. ⁸ Even to someone as unworthy as I am—the least deserving of all his people (since at one time I persecuted his followers)—he chose to favor me with the privilege of proclaiming to Gentiles the unimaginable spiritual riches available to them in union with Jesus the Messiah.

⁹ He wants me to unveil his previously hidden plan to them and explain how it works. This plan is ancient—made even before he created this world—and he was the only one who knew about it until the Assembly of all Believers was established

and he revealed it to them. ¹⁰ His intention now is that all his people together will declare and demonstrate to the rulers and authorities in the spiritual realm his infinite wisdom—as seen in his plan to join both Jewish believers and Gentiles to himself. ¹¹ From eternity past, this has been his purpose and it has now been accomplished in and through Messiah Jesus our Lord. ¹² Now we can come to him in prayer without fear and know that he welcomes us into his presence because we trust in Jesus and are spiritually one with him. ¹³ Therefore, I ask you to not be discouraged by the things I'm suffering for preaching to Gentiles. Instead, you should feel grateful and encouraged because these things are bringing many to glory in union with Jesus.

Paul's Prayer for God's People

¹⁴ Because of God's plan and all the wonderful things Jesus has done for you, I kneel in prayer before God—the Father ¹⁵ and creator of every family in Heaven and on earth. ¹⁶ He has so many wonderful spiritual blessings available for his people. So I ask him to send his Holy Spirit to empower and strengthen each of you in your inner being—¹⁷ that your trust will remain firm and the Messiah will continue to live in your hearts. ❖ *In this context, the "inner being" and "heart" seem to be synonymous with the "human spirit."* ➤ I pray that your way of living will be rooted and based in Jesus' love for you and in your love for him and each other, ¹⁸ so that you and all his people will come to comprehend the infinite dimensions of his never-ending love for you. ¹⁹ And I pray that you will experience Jesus' love and perceive its vastness—which we can never fully understand—so you will be filled with his love and become just like God in his loving character.

²⁰ For the Spirit lives and works in us to transform our characters—making us like Jesus. Through his power, God is able to do transforming work in us that far surpasses what we can even think of asking him to do. ²¹ Therefore, may the glory of God's holy and loving character be seen clearly in Messiah Jesus and in the things he has done—and may it also be seen in his people,

the Assembly of all Believers, so that generation after generation people will praise him forever. Yes, may it be so!

4

The Unity of All Believers in the Body of the Messiah

1 Consider all the blessings that God has freely given you from his favor—and respond to him accordingly. As someone who is in prison because I love and obey our Lord, I urge you to live in a way that is worthy and appropriate for people whom God has called and chosen to be his own. [Romans 12:1—15:7; 1 Corinthians 13:1-7; Galatians 5:16—6:10; Colossians 3:12—4:6; 1 Thessalonians 4:1-12; 5:6-22; James 1:19—2:12; 3:13—4:17; 1 Peter 4:1-11] 2 He wants you to be humble in your own estimation, loving and gentle in dealing with others, and patient with their shortcomings. 3 Try hard to preserve the unity you have with each other because of your union with the Spirit. Do this by getting along and helping each other. 4 Do it because you are spiritually joined to each other in the same body of the Messiah via our union with the same Holy Spirit. God called all of you to be his people, and you all have the same expectation of receiving the same blessings from him in Heaven. 5 You all have the same Lord and you all trust in the same person to save you. You were all initiated into the same Kingdom through the same baptism. ❖ This refers to water baptism in the name of the Father and of the Son and of the Holy Spirit—not the specific form or theology. ➤ 6 We all worship the same God who is the same Heavenly Father of all, who reigns sovereignly over all creation, lives in all believers, and works through all to accomplish his will.

7 But even though we are the same in these ways, from the freely given enabling favor that the Messiah grants us he has given each of us different spiritual gifts and abilities to do his work—as he sees fit. 8 That's why the Scriptures say, "When he ascended on high, he led many captives and gave gifts to men." A [Psalm 68:18] 9 Now the words "he ascended on high" must mean that he first came down to the lower parts of the earth. ❖ This has been variously interpreted as 1) the place of the dead where Jesus went after his death and before his resurrection, 2) the earth itself—in reference to the incarnation when Jesus was born, 3) the descent of Jesus through the Holy Spirit at Pentecost. ➤ 10 And the person who came down is the same one who went up to the place of highest honor in order to make all things perfect. ❖ i.e., Jesus ➤ 11 It is he who distributes spiritual gifts to his people. He made some apostles, some prophets, some evangelists, some pastors, and some teachers of his word. ❖ Spiritual gifts come through the Spirit who Jesus sends to us [John 15:26]—so these gifts indirectly come from Jesus. The spiritual gifts mentioned here are "offices"—also commonly called the five-fold ministry gifts. For example, many believe that the gift of prophecy and the office of prophet are two different things, as is the gift of evangelism and the office of evangelist. We are all to evangelize, but not all have the recognized status that someone having an "office" or official calling to a particular ministry—does. This list of spiritual gifts is not exhaustive, but is representative of the diversity that he gives. See also 1 Corinthians chapter 12. ➤ 12 He gave these gifts so leaders among his people would train and prepare the rest of God's people to serve him by ministering to each other and reaching out to the lost—so the members of his body will grow in number and become mature in character and faith. ❖ Thus the main role of leaders among God's people is to train believers to do God's work of ministry to others in this world—not to do all the work of ministry themselves. ➤ 13 For his goal is that we all come to recognize that we are united in our common faith and also in our intimately knowing him as God's Son. He wants us to

---

A 4:8 As ancient Jewish teachers of the Scriptures often did, Paul adapts the text of this Psalm to make his point. In Hebrew and the Septuagint, it says, "he received gifts from men." But Paul sees this as a picture of the Messiah ascending to Heaven and giving spiritual gifts to his people. We must assume that the Holy Spirit led Paul in his interpretation. He may have thought along these lines: It was customary for a war chief to take tribute from his captives and give them to his men as rewards. Jewish commentator David Stern notes that the Peshitta—the Aramaic translation of the Bible dating from the 1st-4th century—has in this Psalm, "and gave gifts to the sons of men." Hence there was an Aramaic tradition that may have influenced Paul's interpretation. There were also Hebrew paraphrases (called Targums) in existence, and he may have used one of those.

become spiritually mature and like him in every aspect of our character. 14 When this has been achieved, we will no longer act like immature children who change their minds about what they think is true whenever they hear different teachings. We won't be deceived or led astray from his truth by clever lies and schemes. 15 Instead, as we lovingly teach and remind each other about the truth God has revealed, we will mature spiritually—becoming more and more like Jesus—and learn to submit to him in perfect cooperation like a body submits to the direction of its head. ❖ *The image of Jesus as the head of the body emphasizes the living, intimate, and inseparable relationship he has with his people.* ➤ 16 In relating to him, all the members of his body are being fitted together to support each other—like ligaments join and support a body's frame. If we demonstrate love to each other and each of us does what he tells us, then the whole body will become mature and grow strong in every way.

The Way God Wants His People to Live

17 So on the basis of the apostolic authority that our Lord gave to me, I exhort you to stop living like unbelievers. Their thinking is confused. Their judgments about what is right and wrong or true and false are totally subjective and worthless because they have no knowledge of spiritual realities. 18 They can't understand spiritual truth because their minds have never been enlightened by God's revelation in the Scriptures. Their stubborn refusal to hear and embrace God's word has left them ignorant of spiritual

realities—and they have thereby excluded themselves from the eternal life he offers. 19 They have lost all sense of shame for their immoral behavior because they have indulged in it so often that it seems normal. They freely indulge every sinful bodily impulse; they practice every kind of sexual indecency; and they are driven by addiction to their lusts.

20 But when you first learned about the Messiah, that is not the way you were taught to live. 21 Since you are believers, I'm sure that you've heard him speak to you in your hearts and have been taught the truth by Jesus himself. **A** 22 You were taught that—in effect—you had to reject your old ways and the self-identity you had when you didn't yet know Jesus. For in God's eyes, your old identity and lifestyle were thoroughly corrupted by sinful desires which deceived you and led you into wrong behavior. 23 You were taught to allow God to change you and renew your attitudes and patterns of thinking 24 and to outwardly display the new person you really are—the one God has newly created within you. That new you is holy and righteous—without even the inclination to sin—and was made with God's character built right in.

25 So don't tell lies anymore, but always tell each other the truth *[Zechariah 8:16]* since we are all spiritually joined to one another in Jesus. ❖ *Thus if we deceive another believer, we are spiritually harming ourselves and all other believers.* ➤ 26 Take care when you are angry so that you don't sin, *[Psalm 4:4]* since it's very easy to allow your emotions to carry you in the wrong direction. And don't allow your anger

---

A 4:21 Literally, this verse says, "if indeed you heard him and were taught ἐν him as truth is ἐν Jesus," where "him" refers to the Messiah—from the previous sentence. The preposition ἐν (en) has a wide range of meaning depending on context. Sometimes its meaning is clear from the context, other times it can be interpreted two or more different ways in English. Most translations translate this as the preposition "in" and the wording of the entire phrase varies a lot. Most of them also add "about" or "of" to the phrase, "if indeed you heard (about/of) him," even though no such word is explicit in the Greek—or is necessarily implied. It is, though, a valid possible interpretation. A few translations such as the Amplified Bible, J.B. Phillips translation, and the Living Bible translate the proposition ἐν as meaning "by," saying, "if indeed you heard him and were taught by him." This is also an entirely legitimate interpretation—even though some theological systems deny that God gives direct revelation to his people outside of the Scriptures. But even the rendering in this interpretation need not be understood in that light. All Christians agree that Jesus speaks to us and teaches us through his Holy Spirit by illuminating the Scriptures; and some believe that he also speaks to us directly for personal guidance—sometimes apart from the Scriptures—but never in contradiction to them. The lack of personal revelation—or at least illumination and guidance from the Holy Spirit—is a sign of a hardened (i.e., stubborn) or unregenerate (i.e., unsaved) heart (i.e., spirit).

to continue past the end of the day lest it turn into a grudge or bitterness. *[Hosea 7:6]* 27 Don't give the devil an opportunity to gain a foothold in your life **A** by nursing anger or any other sin. ❖ *Holding onto any sin—i.e., delaying repentance—only gives demons the legal right to attack or tempt us in that area of sin.* ➤

28 Believers who were formerly thieves must never steal again. Instead, they must work diligently at some useful occupation to earn enough to support themselves and their dependents—and also have enough extra to share with those in need. ❖ *This directive applies to all believers—even if they were never thieves. But here, Paul is contrasting old ways with the new way by which Jesus expects his followers to live.* ➤

29 Never allow yourselves to use vulgar language or say anything that would criticize or hurt someone else. Only say things that are appropriate to the circumstances and that encourage people and help them in their faith. 30 Take care not to say or do anything that would grieve the Holy Spirit because you need his help every day. ❖ *Isaiah 63:10 says: "Yet they rebelled and grieved his Holy Spirit. So he (Yahweh) turned and became their enemy and he himself fought against them." The particular sin referred to in this verse from Isaiah is persistent rebellion against God and his ways. So serious persistent disobedience will grieve (or vex or offend) the Holy Spirit. The implied risk is that he will stop helping you or will leave you (although Calvinism teaches the latter is impossible). Given the context, Paul implies that* saying things that harm other believers contributes to grieving the Holy Spirit—who lives in them. ➤ He is God's seal on you showing that you belong to him, and he is God's guarantee that God will completely free you from the power and influence of sin on the day of your complete redemption. ❖ *The day you die or the day Jesus returns—whichever comes first.* ➤

31 You must also purge your lives of all bitterness and resentment, inwardly felt rage, outwardly expressed anger, quarreling, disputes, slander, insults, and every other form of evil and hateful behavior toward others. 32 Instead, be kind and merciful to one another, readily forgiving all offenses the same way God has freely forgiven you of even greater sins—through your union with Jesus the Messiah.

5

1 Since you are God's beloved children and are spiritually renewed with his character, you should always imitate his ways as taught by command and example in the Scriptures. 2 Just as Jesus demonstrated his love by dying for you, show your love for others every day knowing that his self-sacrifice was a fragrant offering and pleasing to God. ❖ *This means that any self-sacrifice you make demonstrating love to others also pleases God.* ➤

A 4:27 An example of this is found in Luke 22:24 where the disciples argued about which of them was the greatest. They stumbled in the sin of pride, and by not repenting immediately, they gave Satan the legal right to attack them. Jesus informs them of this in Luke 22:31, saying that Satan demanded the right to "sift them like wheat"—which is a figurative expression meaning to severely tempt and test them—in the area of their pride. Presumably, Satan demanded this of God the Father much as he spoke to him regarding Job. *[Job 1:6-12]* But Jesus prayed for Simon in particular that his faith would not be destroyed in this test—for his testing would be the most severe. Jesus didn't ask that Satan not be allowed to attack them because he knew that they had given Satan a legal foothold through their unrepented sin. The severe temptation came when Jesus was arrested in Gethsemane and refused to resist—as the disciples expected their Messiah to do. Satan made the disciples afraid of arrest and possible execution—wounding their pride—even though they had earlier proudly claimed they would follow Jesus even to death. *[Luke 22:33; Matthew 26:33-35; Mark 14:31]* Before his arrest, Jesus again warns them of the coming temptation *[Matthew 26:41; Mark 14:27-30; Luke 22:46]* and tells them to pray for strength to resist it. After Jesus' arrest, all the disciples ran off. *[Matthew 26:56; Mark 14:50]* John and Peter followed behind at a distance—hidden in the darkness. *[John 18:15; Matthew 26:58; Mark 14:54; Luke 22:54]* But when confronted in the High Priest's courtyard, Peter was so afraid that he claimed three separate times that he didn't even know Jesus. *[Matthew 26:69-75; Mark 14:66-72; Luke 22:54-60; John 18:15-17; 25-27]* So their unrepented sin of pride gave Satan an opportunity and a foothold—which some people call "legal ground"—that the disciples were not able to resist in their own power. This is the kind of opportunity or foothold that Paul is warning about in verse 27. The case of the testing of Job was different. Satan could not demand to attack Job or even touch him because he had not given Satan any opportunity through sinning. Yet God allowed the testing for other reasons.

³ Because you are God's holy people, there should never be even the slightest cause for an accusation of sexual sin, impurity, or greed among you. For such sins are entirely out of character for believers. ⁴ It is also totally inappropriate for any of you to tell dirty stories, vulgar jokes, anything obscene, or to use profanity, or to utter foolish or shameful talk of any kind. Instead, make it your habit to express gratitude to God for all things. *[Ephesians 5:20; Philippians 4:6; Colossians 2:7; 3:15, 17; 4:2; 1 Thessalonians 5:18; 1 Timothy 2:1; Hebrews 12:28]* ⁵ For you can be certain of this: No one whose lifestyle includes sexual immorality, impurity, or greed—as defined by God's standards in the Scriptures—has any part in his Kingdom and his Messiah. ❖ *i.e., Such a person is not truly saved. Paul is not speaking of someone who might occasionally stumble in such sins and who repents and struggles against them. He means those who normally and habitually commit such sins without repentance.* ➤ Such people are guilty of idolatry. ❖ *Idolatry is the sin of worshiping a false god—which God sees as a personal rejection of himself. Commentators are divided on whether Paul intended to say that only those who are greedy are idolaters—or that immoral and impure people are also idolaters. A majority hold the former view and cite Colossians 3:5 as a parallel verse which clearly states that a greedy person is an idolater. The minority view says the grammar of this verse hints that all three kinds of people are idolaters. Putting anything before obedience to the true God is a form of idolatry—and all three kinds of people are unsaved.* ➤ ⁶ Don't allow anyone to use baseless arguments to deceive you into thinking that God will spare those who live this way. The Scriptures clearly teach that God's anger and eternal punishment will come on those who refuse to obey him. ⁷ Therefore, don't participate with them or even indirectly support people who do these sins or allow them to think you might approve. ❖ *This doesn't mean that we punish them or refuse to help them if they are in genuine need. But it should be clear that we will have nothing to do with such activities.* ➤

⁸ At one time you lived just like them in the darkness of sin and rebellion against God. But now you have been enlightened—having been joined to the Lord Jesus—and are meant to display the Light of God's truth to those still living in spiritual darkness. So live as God's children should live—as people who intimately know and love the Lord of Light. ⁹ For those who live following the Light of God's Word will always live in a way that he affirms as good, morally upright, and honest. ¹⁰ So try hard to learn from the Scriptures what pleases the Lord—and then live that way. ¹¹ Don't participate in activities that belong to the darkness of rebellion against God. Such things have no value. But instead, you should help others to realize how evil and harmful such activities really are. ¹² It would be wrong and shameful to even mention the things some unbelievers do in private. ¹³ But when these things are viewed in the Light of God's Word, then their true nature is revealed as evil. This makes it possible for the Light of God's truth to banish the darkness of sin from people's lives and transform them into children of Light. **A** ¹⁴ That's why it **B** says, "Wake up sleeper! Rise from death and the Messiah's Light will shine in your heart!"

¹⁵ Given all that, take care about the way you live. Don't live like immoral fools who will be condemned, but rather, like those who have wisdom, who are responsible, who know how God wants them to live, who can anticipate the consequences of their actions and are able to live accordingly. ¹⁶ Such people make use of every opportunity to do good since there are so many others who are doing evil these days. ❖ *This is one way wise believers "shine their Light." They do it by witnessing to God's truth and ways, by helping others, by making this world a better place, and to gain eternal rewards.* ➤ ¹⁷ So don't be morally foolish, but try to understand what the Lord wants you to do—and then do it.

A 5:13 This is a difficult verse with various interpretations. This rendering combines two of those interpretations—both of which fit the context well. ¶ In some translations, the second part of verse 13 is put in verse 14.

B 5:14 This may be a quote from a hymn—which may be a composite quote from the following Scriptures: Isaiah 26:19; 51:17; 52:1; 60:1. It contains three metaphors that each mean turning to God: 1) waking from sleep, 2) rising from death, and 3) going from darkness into light. See also Romans 13:11.

18 Don't get drunk on wine or any other intoxicant that affects your judgment, because doing so leads to poor decisions and uncontrolled behavior that can ruin your life. ❖ *We all experience demonic temptations and suggestions that they put into our minds—although many do not recognize them as such. When we are sober, we are able to judge which thoughts and impulses are good and which are evil. When we are intoxicated, our ability to judge correctly is impaired, and we easily succumb to demonic suggestions or temptations or to our own evil impulses.* ➤ Instead, strive to always be submitted to the Holy Spirit and allow him to lead you in everything you do. ❖ *You can be filled with the Spirit simply by submitting yourself to obey him and asking him to lead you. This is something you need to do continuously.* ➤ 19 He will lead you to speak to each other with words of encouragement and exhortation from the Psalms and from hymns and other spiritual songs, and to express your joy by singing and praising the Lord with all your heart. [Colossians 3:16] 20 He will help you to always thank God the Father for everything you have and for everything that comes your way—in the name of Jesus our Lord and Messiah—21 and to voluntarily submit to other believers because you want to honor the Messiah who lives in them.

The Marriage Relationship
[Colossians 3:18-19; 1 Peter 3:1-7]

22 Wives, voluntarily submit yourselves to the final decision-making authority of your husbands in the same way that you submit to the Lord Jesus. 23 For God has given the husband authority over his wife, A just as the Messiah has authority over the assembly of his people which is his body—for whom he died in order to save them. 24 So just as the assembly of all God's people submits to Jesus' authority, wives should submit to their husbands' authority in all matters.

25 Husbands, demonstrate self-sacrificial love to your wives, just like the Messiah loved his followers and selflessly sacrificed his life for them. ❖ *If you love your wife in this self-sacrificing manner—considering her needs and desires as more important than your own—then it will be a lot easier for her to submit to your authority. But this submission is voluntary on her part—motivated by love for her Lord and for her husband. If she does not submit, a loving husband will go to great lengths to woo her with his love, just like Yahweh was long suffering and reached out to his rebellious people—the Israelites—who he considered to be his wayward wife. There is no instruction in the Scriptures that God approves of husbands forcing their wives into submission. Instead, they are exhorted to exhibit self-sacrificial love and give up their lives for their wives—which would include their own desires.* ➤ 26 Jesus died to make his people holy and he made them pure through the spiritual washing that is brought about by the water of baptism and his word. B ❖ *"His word," refers to the Gospel message of salvation.* ➤ 27 He did this so he could make his people holy—without fault, weakness, or imperfection of any kind—and have his glorious character shine out from them and so present them together to himself as a perfect bride to be his eternal companion. 28 That is how husbands should love their wives—loving and caring for them as they do their own bodies. For a man who loves his wife is simply loving himself. 29 No one ever hates his own body, but instead, takes care of it, protects it from harm and pain, and feeds it. Jesus takes care of his people in the same way 30 because we are all part of his body. 31 God said, **"When a man is grown, he leaves his father and mother and joins in a relationship with his wife, and the two of them become a unity."** [Genesis 2:24; Matthew 19:5; Mark 10:7-8; 1 Corinthians 6:16] ❖ *They become one physically through the act of marriage, and become effectively one—holding everything in common and having one purpose. In a sense, they become one person, neither*

A **5:23** This does not imply that husbands should make all decisions without consulting their wives, nor that wives should submit to anything outside of God's will—like physical abuse. It means that God has ordained the husband to be the spiritual head of the family and holds him responsible for decisions that are made, so he is meant to have the final say when they are not able to reach an agreement.

B **5:26** The interpretation of this verse is as controversial as the doctrine of baptism. The two basic views (with several variations of each) are 1) "water" refers to baptism, and 2) "water" does not refer to baptism but to something else. There is commentary support for both views, although about 2 out of 3 (among over 50 commentators consulted) go with the interpretation I've given. Opinions are even more divided over the interpretation of "the word."

losing their individuality in the relationship, but each gaining from it. Marriage thus becomes the primary human relationship—second only to a person's relationship with God. Marriage is also a holy relationship instituted by God at creation for his purposes according to the pattern of one man and one woman. ➤ **32** The marriage relationship as described in these words is a profound mystery that has significance beyond human marriage, because it is also speaking of the relationship between the Messiah and his people who together are his bride.

❖ *Marriage—as God intends it to be—is a living illustration of the relationship Jesus desires with us.* ➤ **33** However, these words still pertain to you. So each husband must love his wife and be considerate of her in the same way that he loves himself—realizing that he is one with her. And each wife must respect her husband and his authority.

6

The Parent–Child Relationship
[Colossians 3:20-21]

1 Children, honor your parents and obey them as long as you live under their provision because you are joined to the Lord Jesus and this is what God wants you to do. **2** Also do this because the first command to which God added a promise says, **"Honor and respectfully obey your father and mother 3 so that God will make things go well for you and bless you with a long life in this world."** *[Exodus 20:12; Deuteronomy 5:16]* ❖ *Dishonoring your parents dishonors God.* ➤

4 Fathers, take care not to unjustly anger your children lest they resent you. Yet teach them to understand how the Lord Jesus wants them to live, and gently correct and lovingly discipline them when needed.

The Relationship Between Master and Slave (or Employer and Employee)
[Colossians 3:22—4:1]

5 Slaves, obey your masters in this world. Take care to sincerely respect, honor, and obey them as if you were obeying the Messiah. **6** Obey them all the time—not just when they are observing. Obey them as if you were Jesus' slave—whose only desire is to do what God wants you to do. **7** Do your assigned work well—as though you were doing it for the Lord Jesus and not merely for a human master. **8** And be conscious of the fact that the Lord will reward you for every good thing you do—whether you are a slave or free.

9 You slave owners and masters who are believers are to treat your slaves with respect and not threaten them. Keep in mind that the Lord Jesus in Heaven is their true Master—and also yours—and he never shows partiality. Slaves are as valuable to him as their masters are. **A**

A 6:9 Christianity has been accused of supporting slavery and oppression. This is ironic since it was mainly Christians who pushed for the abolition of slavery everywhere it has been legally abolished, and slave traders are explicitly condemned in 1 Timothy 1:10. At the time Paul wrote this letter, there was no possibility of changing the institution of slavery. Most Christians in the Roman empire were poor or slaves themselves. It would not have been loving to incite a bloody rebellion that couldn't possibly have succeeded. God's way of solving problems has never included rebellion against legal authority. One has to keep in mind the perspective that this life is relatively short and is but a preparation for the eternal life to come. God has promised to right all wrongs and balance all injustice at the final judgment. While lacking opportunity to be free, Christian slaves lacked no opportunity to earn riches and status in Heaven through humble service in this life. Jesus explicitly came to set people free, but his first focus was freeing people from their slavery to sin. The four gospels show his special compassion for the poor and oppressed and his identification with them. In his own time and in his own way he has mostly abolished legal slavery in this world. While many slave owners in the US claimed to be Christians, many were not obedient to God's word as contained in this and other passages. It's illogical to blame Jesus and the Christian faith for atrocities done by people who didn't follow his teachings. Jesus will judge everyone when he returns. The person who wants God to eliminate and punish all injustice NOW should consider that God is totally impartial. Once he starts punishing all injustice, there won't be a single human in this world who won't be judged guilty. It's folly to judge the one who will judge you. See the footnote at 1 Peter 2:18 about the conditions of slaves at that time.

We Are All Involved in a Spiritual War

10 My last exhortation is to remain in close relationship to the Lord Jesus so you have access to his power within you to make you spiritually strong. 11 We are engaged in a spiritual war with Satan and his demons. So put on the full spiritual armor which God has provided to protect you against all of the enemy's schemes for destroying your faith. ❖ *The extended metaphor of armor has obscured Paul's message for some modern readers. This armor consists of six principles concerning spiritual truth revealed in the Scriptures. Each principle is related to consciously knowing, believing, and acting upon Scriptural truths. In doing this, we will be thoroughly protected from all demonic attacks and stand firm in our faith.* ➤ 12 Our warfare in this life is not against people, but against a hierarchy of demonic spirits called "rulers, powers, and princes of darkness" and their demonic armies in the spiritual realm. 13 Therefore, take up the complete spiritual armor which God has provided for your protection so that when they attack, you won't give up being faithful, but will be able to defend yourselves and victoriously stand firm in your faith. 14 So stand firm—ready to fight against them. Put on the Belt of "the Truth contained in God's word" and the Breastplate of "Jesus' Righteousness." ❖ *[Isaiah 59:17] Recognizing that this is "God's armor"—not our own—eliminates interpretations based on things we do (e.g., always telling the truth or living righteously). Putting on the "Belt of Truth" is literally, "gird your loins with truth." The picture is of a belt that holds up a Roman soldier's tunic so his legs are not restricted by a long garment and he is ready to move quickly. The belt also supports the breastplate. This means we are to learn the spiritual truths taught in the Scriptures and recognize that they are all true—despite any apparent contradictions with what our senses, feelings, experience, reason, other people, or demons try to tell us. This protects us from deception, enables us to know how God wants us to live, and makes us ready to respond to every situation without uncertainty or delay. Putting on the "Breastplate of Righteousness" is to remember and trust the particular truth that God has declared you righteous in his sight. This protects against demonic accusations that you are not good enough to be God's child or to be loved by him. If you doubt this critical truth, Satan can make you despair, damage or destroy your faith, and also convince you to give up the* struggle to remain obedient. ➤ 15 Put on the Sandals of "being prepared with the Good News about how we can have Peace with God." ❖ *Putting on the "sandals of the preparation of the Gospel of Peace" is to a) know and believe the Gospel message so you are sure that you are at peace with God, and b) to be prepared to share this message with others. Being sure of your relationship with God and that he loves you provides you with emotional stability and keeps you from "slipping and falling" in fear or doubt concerning his love—particularly when demons attack you through difficult circumstances. The picture is of footwear that give a soldier firm footing—to keep him from slipping while fighting and while advancing on the enemy. By sharing the Gospel with others, God's army can advance—setting captives of the enemy free by saving them. So this principle is both defensive and offensive. Seeing others believe when we share the Gospel also strengthens our own faith. While we are responsible to be prepared, it is still God's Gospel that enables us to advance and free the captives—not our own power. Hence it's still armor that he provides.* ➤ 16 In addition to all this, take up the Shield of "Faith in Jesus and his faithfulness" which will protect you and will extinguish the flaming arrows of lies, doubt, and temptation that the Evil One shoots at you. ❖ *Taking up the "shield of Faith" is to remember and trust that Jesus has promised to be with you and help you in all circumstances. His word also promises that you will never be tempted beyond your ability to resist. [1 Corinthians 10:13] Faith in Jesus and his promise of help will deflect the enemy's attacks that try to set your mind on fire with lies, doubts, and temptations in order to destroy your confidence and faith.* ➤ 17 Put on the Helmet of "knowing you have Salvation" and take up the Sword of the Holy Spirit—which is God's Word in the Scriptures. ❖ *[Isaiah 59:17] Putting on the "Helmet of Salvation " is to remember that Jesus has defeated Satan and has saved you from the power of sin and death. Jesus' power is in you to help you overcome sin—and you can be sure that in the end you will win in your struggle to defeat sin because he has already won the victory for you. So keep on fighting and don't become discouraged or give up hope of victory or of seeing Heaven. Taking up the "Sword of the Spirit" means we can fight the enemy and defeat his lies and temptations by speaking the truth—found in the Scriptures—against him. Jesus showed us how to do this in the accounts of his temptation in the wilderness where he quoted Scripture to counter Satan's lies, temptations, and twisting of Scripture. [Matthew 4:1-11; Luke 4:1-13] The Greek for "word" in this verse is*

ῥῆμα (rhēma) which means a spoken word or statement. It is necessary to speak God's word aloud for it to become the Sword of the Spirit that is able to defeat demonic attacks. God's word contains truth to counter every demonic lie and the power to defeat every temptation. We should speak it aloud when we are attacked or tempted—exactly as Jesus did. When we speak God's Word in faith (i.e., believing it is true), it has the same power as if Jesus himself were speaking it since we are spiritually united with him. ¶ All six principles of spiritual warfare—God's spiritual armor—depend on a thorough knowledge of the Scriptures and a firm trust in their truthfulness and reliability. Such an understanding of God's word also prevents us from deception by Satan's twisting of the Scriptures. While a Roman soldier wasn't constantly in battle and didn't always wear every piece of his armor, every moment of our entire lives we are engaged in spiritual battle and need to have our "armor" in place. We should "put on God's armor" by daily studying and meditating on the Scriptures, learning about and reminding ourselves of the truths that are necessary for fighting the enemy's lies, affirming our trust in those truths, and seeking God's help in prayer. This is the "armor" that God has provided for the protection of our faith. ➤

18 As you conduct your warfare, always allow the Holy Spirit to lead you in the way to pray about every concern and situation. ❖ *This implies that you should ask the Holy Spirit to bring to mind what he wants you to pray about and how he wants you to pray.* ➤ To be effective, you must continually be alert for opportunities to pray to help others—and alert to the Holy Spirit's promptings. Persevere in praying for all of God's people everywhere.

19 Also pray for me that God would give me his words when I speak so I can speak boldly about God's previously hidden plan to also save Gentiles through his message of salvation—**20** because Jesus made me an ambassador to the Gentiles. My faithfulness to his command is why I am now in prison, so pray that I will continue to speak boldly as I should and not be overcome by fear.

Paul's Closing Greetings

21 I'm sending Tychicus to you with this letter. He is our dear brother in the Lord and serves him well. He will tell you all the news about what I've been doing and my present circumstances. **22** I'm sending him for the express purpose of informing you about what is happening to all of us here so you can be encouraged.

23 I pray that God our Father—and Jesus our Lord and Messiah—will grant you peace with each other and strengthen your faith so you will love each other even more. **24** I also pray that God will continue to pour out his enabling favor to all those who never stop loving our Lord Jesus—the Messiah.

Paul's Letter to Jesus' Followers in Philippi

This letter was written by the Apostle Paul to believers in the city of Philippi in the Roman Province of Macedonia—which today is part of northern Greece. No Philippians had become believers until Paul preached to them during his second missionary journey. On that tour, he, Silas, Timothy, and Luke reached there about the year AD 51. [Acts 16:6-40] He also visited them again later. Most of the believers there were Gentiles.

He wrote this letter during his first time in prison in Rome—sometime in the period AD 60–62. [Acts 28:30-31] Also during that time, he wrote his letters to Philemon, the Ephesians, and the Colossians. These letters as a group are sometimes called the "prison letters." In this letter, he thanks the Philippians because they sent Epaphroditus with money to help him.

One important theme in this letter is that we must rejoice when we suffer for obeying Jesus because he will bless us for sharing in the same kind of sufferings that he had. Paul also instructs them that God's people should be of one mind and should beware of false teachers.

Outline:

Paul thanks the Philippians and prays for them. [1:1-11]
Even though he is in prison, he rejoices because he wants people to praise the Messiah. [1:12-26]
He tells them to stand firm in their faith and live in a way appropriate for God's people. [1:27—3:1]
He tells them to humble themselves—just as the Messiah did. [2:1-11]
He says they should follow his example and Jesus' teaching until they die. [chapter 3]
He exhorts: be of one mind, rejoice in the Messiah, and be content with what God gives. [chapter 4]

1

Opening Greetings

1 I, Paul, along with Timothy—as voluntary slaves of Messiah Jesus—greet you. I'm sending this letter to all who are God's people in Philippi because of their belief in Jesus—and especially to the assembly leaders and deacons. ❖ *Even though the letter is, in some sense, also from Timothy, it's clear that Paul is the main author since he uses "I" throughout the letter.* ➤ 2 I pray that God our Father and our Lord Jesus the Messiah will look upon you with great favor far beyond anything you can deserve and therefore, grant you every spiritual blessing, peace, and well-being.

Paul's Prayer for the Philippians

3 Every time I think of you, I thank God for you. 4 And whenever I pray for all of you, I am always filled with joy. 5 I'm thankful and joyful because you have continually been my partners in the ministry of proclaiming the Good News ever since the first day you yourselves believed. ❖ *They were partners by supporting him with money, prayers, and encouragement, and also by proclaiming the Good News to others themselves.* ➤ 6 I'm quite confident that God—who started you on this journey of transforming your lives and making you people who trust in Jesus—will continue to transform and perfect you until the process is completed on the day Messiah Jesus returns. Jesus has caused you to have new life in union with himself and has already transformed you into people who thankfully respond with obedience and ministry for his Kingdom. 7 I love you all very much, so it's not surprising that I feel this way about you. And it doesn't matter if I'm in prison or out while proclaiming and defending the message of the Good News—for in either situation we continue to be partners in God's work and we both experience his undeserved favor and blessing which enables us to serve and suffer for him. 8 God knows that I'm telling the truth when I tell you how much I long to see you again—for I love you all with the same deep affection that Messiah Jesus does.

9 My prayer for you is that through ever-increasing knowledge of God and his will, he will grant you more and more love for him

and for each other, and through ever-increasing wisdom, he will teach you to spiritually discern how to love each other more appropriately in every situation. 10 For I want you to be able to discern the very best way to live and love until the day the Messiah returns—so you may live with pure motives and without causing others to take offense at anything you do. 11 Through your union with Jesus, I want you to live righteous lives characterized by demonstrated love and good deeds—which will result in people honoring and praising the God you serve.

All Circumstances
Work Together for Paul's Good

12 My brothers and sisters in the Lord, I want you to understand that the "bad" things that have happened to me—such as my imprisonment—have actually turned out to have been advantageous to my ministry of proclaiming the Good News. [Romans 8:28] 13 For one thing, the fact that I'm a prisoner because I follow the Messiah has become widely known among the Roman emperor's guards and everyone else here in Rome. 14 For another, because I'm in prison, most of our brothers and sisters in the Lord are proclaiming God's word without fear and more boldly than before—so the proclamation of the Good News has been multiplied. As they have seen the Lord help me during my imprisonment, they are trusting him more to help them too. 15 It's true that some of them are preaching about the Messiah from jealousy and wanting people to follow them. But the rest have a proper attitude and just want more people to hear the Good News. 16 These people are doing the work because they love me—and they understand the reason I'm in prison is because God brought me here in order to defend the message of the Good News. Therefore, they don't think less of me for being a prisoner, but are motivated by my example of willingly suffering for the Messiah. 17 But the others preach about the Messiah from motives of selfish ambition. They think that by doing this, they can cause me distress while I'm imprisoned because I would be jealous of their freedom to preach. 18 But that doesn't matter to me at all. The only important thing is that people are proclaiming the correct message about the Messiah—and the fact that some do it from wrong motives doesn't detract from the effectiveness of their work. Since the Good News is being proclaimed, I rejoice! 19 I can do this because I know that all these difficult circumstances I'm facing will result in spiritual victory and growth in my life through your prayers for me and through the help of the Spirit of Messiah Jesus in me. ❖ *Some commentators think "my deliverance," in the literal text (rendered "spiritual victory" above), means his freedom from prison. But since in the next verses he indicates it doesn't matter if he lives or dies, it's unlikely that he was thinking about his release here.* ➤ 20 It's my strong expectation and hope that I will never do anything to disgrace myself, but rather, will always have the courage to boldly proclaim the message about the Messiah as I am doing now—and that he will always be honored by the way I live for him and also by the way I die for him. 21 For my only motive is to honor the Messiah and to be united with him. So if I die, it will be better for me because I will be more completely united with him. 22 On the other hand, if I continue to live, that means I can do useful work for him. As a result, I don't know if I really prefer to live or die! 23 I'm torn between these two desires for I do want to leave this difficult life behind and be with the Messiah in Heaven. This is certainly much better as far as I'm concerned. 24 But since you still need my advice and encouragement, I know it's more important overall if I remain in this life for a time. 25 Since I'm convinced this is true, I'm sure the Lord will allow me to remain alive and be with all of you to help you grow in your trusting him and grow in experiencing joy because of your relationship with him. 26 Then, when I come to see you again, you will have even more reason to rejoice in your being united with Messiah Jesus and to praise him because he will have enabled my release so I can be present with you.

Stand Firm in Your Faith Despite Persecution

27 No matter what happens to me, I want you all to live in a manner that's appropriate for those who believe and proclaim the Good News about the Messiah. Do this so that regardless of whether I can come to see you myself or only hear about you from afar, I will know that you are holding firmly to your faith—working together in perfect unity to promote belief in the Good News 28 and not letting yourselves be intimidated by those who oppose your work. Your fearlessness will be a sign to your opponents that God is with you to make you brave and that he will destroy them, but save you. 29 Be fearless because God has granted you two great privileges. Not only has he given you faith to trust in the Messiah, but he has also given you the great privilege of suffering persecution because of your allegiance and obedience to him. ❖ *Jews traditionally praised those who chose to die rather than disobey God, but Gentiles with pagan backgrounds—and probably many people today—would find this idea frightening. Paul was preparing the Philippian believers to understand why they are suffering, that it is a great privilege to do so and—by implication—that it will be greatly rewarded in Heaven.* ➤ 30 As a consequence of God granting you this privilege, you are experiencing the same kind of opposition and conflict that you saw me face when I was with you in Philippi and that you hear I am having here.

2

The Path to Exultation
Is Humility and Obedience

1 Therefore, since you are
 a) encouraged through your union
   with the Messiah,
 b) are comforted by his love,
 c) have fellowship with the Holy Spirit
   and the Messiah has only shown
   you kindness and compassion,
2 I exhort you to increase my joy by
 a') being united in attitude and
   purpose,
 b') genuinely loving each other,
 c') getting along well with each other
   and agreeing with each other.

3 Don't be motivated by a desire to make yourself more important or to make yourself look good. Instead, be humble and consider others as more important than yourself. 4 Don't only think about what's best for you and your own interests and priorities, but also be concerned about what's best for others.

5 Have the same attitude that Messiah Jesus had: ❖ *Verses 6-11 may have been a hymn.* ➤ 6 Even though by nature he is God, he didn't insist on his right to keep all the power and privileges he had as God. 7 Instead, he willingly left all the power of deity behind and took upon himself the nature of an ordinary—but sinless—mortal human being who was totally subservient to God. 8 By becoming a man, he humbled himself even further and obeyed God's will—even when it included a shameful death on a cross as a convicted criminal! 9 Therefore—after having raised him back to life—God gave him the position of highest authority over all creation and gave him the rank that's above every other rank. 10 Therefore, every being in Heaven, on Earth, or in Hell must bow before Jesus in complete submission and worship *[Isaiah 45:23]* 11 and publicly acknowledge that Jesus the Messiah is God and absolute Lord over all creation. In doing this, they will also be honoring God the Father—who alone is over Jesus and who desires every creature to honor his Son in this way. *[John 5:22-23]*

Live Sacrificial Lives
That Shine in the Darkness Around You

12 So, my dear brothers and sisters in the Lord, in view of all this, just as you have always obeyed the Messiah it's important that you keep doing those things that are appropriate and acceptable for people whom God has saved. You should revere him so highly that you are afraid to disobey and displease him. You did this while I was with you, but now that I'm not, it's even more important that you live this way. 13 You are capable of living like this because God himself lives within you and is at work giving you both the desire and the ability to obey him. ❖ *Yet we still have the free choice of whether to respond in obedience or not.* ➤

14 Never grumble, complain, or argue about anything with anyone. ❖ *Since God is in control of your external circumstances—having allowed inconvenient or bad circumstances to happen to you for his purpose of shaping your character—you are in fact complaining about the way he runs the world and your life. To understand his reaction to such complaining, see Exodus 16:6-8; Numbers 11:1, 4-34; 14:26-29; 21:4-6.* ➤ 15 For God wants you to be people who have no intention of doing evil and who live such good lives that no one can criticize you. You are to be his perfect children—while at the same time living in a society that is evil and morally corrupt. Your good lives will contrast with those around you like stars against the black sky. 16 Also, faithfully proclaim the message that brings people eternal life. ❖ *Or: cling to the message that brings you eternal life.* ➤ If you live this way, then on the day that the Messiah returns I will be able to triumphantly rejoice because your lives will prove that my work among you was not wasted.

17 Your faith in the Messiah has led you to sacrificially serve him despite persecution. This is a pleasing sacrifice to God. And it may happen that I am to be executed for my faith. If so, my death will be like a drink offering added to your sacrifice. ❖ *According to the Torah, [Numbers 15:1-12] freewill offerings of animal sacrifices were accompanied by wine poured out on the ground as a drink offering. Paul is comparing their obedience to a freewill offering—and if he dies, his death will be like the accompanying drink offering that completes their sacrifice.* ➤ I will offer it gladly and rejoice with all of you for the privilege of suffering for the Messiah. 18 In the same way, you too should be rejoicing in your circumstances and rejoicing with me over mine.

Paul's Plan to Send Timothy to Philippi

19 If the Lord Jesus allows it, I hope to send Timothy to you soon so he can find out what's happening to you and return to encourage me with news about you. 20 There is no one else with me here who is as genuinely concerned about how you are doing as he and I are. 21 It seems like everyone else here that I could send mainly thinks about their own needs and desires rather than what's important to Jesus the Messiah.

22 But you already know how Timothy has proven his faithfulness to God and his people. He has worked with me proclaiming the Good News as a son would work with his own father. 23 So I hope to send him to you as soon as I find out what's going to happen to me here. ❖ *Paul is speaking about his trial before the Roman Emperor Nero and the resulting judgment. [Acts 25:8-12]* ➤ 24 But in my union with the Lord, he has given me confidence that I will most likely be coming to see you soon myself.

Paul Sends Epaphroditus Home with a Commendation

25 But I thought it necessary to send Epaphroditus back to you first. ❖ *Epaphroditus probably carried this letter to the Philippian believers. They had sent him to help Paul, and he also brought money from them to help with Paul's expenses. But Epaphroditus became sick and almost died—and his friends in Philippi had heard about it and were worried about him. So Paul was sending him home and here writes a commendation for him, lest they think he is being sent back because he wasn't useful.* ➤ He is my brother in the Lord, he has helped me proclaim the message about the Messiah, and also helped me in the spiritual struggle against those who oppose it. You sent him to look after my needs as your representative. 26 I'm sending him back because he longs to see you and he is also distressed that you heard of his illness and knows you are worried about him. 27 He certainly was sick; he almost died! But God was merciful to him and healed him—which was also a mercy to me, sparing me from going through the sorrow of his death on top of his sickness and all the other things pressing on me. 28 I wanted to send him back to thank you for your gift, but now I am all the more eager to send him back to you so you can rejoice in seeing him healthy. And I will also be relieved about you. For when you see him, your anxiety for his health will cease—thus delivering you from one stress among the many difficulties that I know you face. 29 So welcome him back warmly as a brother in the Lord and celebrate. You should appropriately honor Epaphroditus and others like him 30 because he risked his life and nearly died as a result of serving the Messiah and helping me as

your representative—doing for me what you couldn't because of the distance.

3

The Basis for Obtaining Righteousness and a Relationship with the Messiah

[1] Now, my brothers and sisters in the Lord, the last thought I want to leave with you is this: Because of your union with the Lord Jesus and all the things he has done for you—rejoice!

It doesn't bother me at all to write the same things to you repeatedly because if you remember them, they will protect you against false teachers. ❖ *Some commentators think this sentence refers to his exhortation to rejoice. But in view of his statement that it was for the purpose of protecting them, it would seem to go more with what follows.* ➤ [2] Don't allow yourselves to be deceived by those unclean dogs of men who insist that you must be circumcised to be saved. Their teaching is evil. ❖ *Jews considered dogs to be unclean (like pigs) and insultingly referred to Gentiles as dogs. Paul here turns this around and uses the same figure to refer to Jews who claimed to be followers of Jesus, but who polluted the message of the Good News with their legalistic requirements of keeping the commands in the Torah to be saved. ¶ Circumcision was a sign for Jewish men that they were in covenant agreement with God and belonged to him.* ➤ [3] But it is we—who submit to God in worship with the help of the Holy Spirit in us, who boast of Messiah Jesus as our Savior, and who refuse to depend on anything we can do in our own power to save us—it is we who are truly God's people and bear the covenant sign of true circumcision in our hearts. This sign is the Spirit himself. [4] If I believed there was anything people could do in their own power that would help them be saved, I certainly would have many reasons to think that who I am and what I've done would make me more eligible than most for God's favor. [5] I was circumcised on the eighth day after I was born ❖ *counting the birth day as day one* ➤ as the Torah requires. **A** *[Leviticus 12:3]* I'm an Israelite and can trace my ancestry back to the tribe of Benjamin. I'm a pure Hebrew with Hebrew parents. I speak the Hebrew language and have followed all the customs of our ancestors. ❖ *Many first-century Jews believed that such an ancestry automatically secured them a place in Heaven.* ➤ As far as obeying the Torah is concerned, I was a Pharisee—and there is no one stricter about keeping the Torah's commands than a Pharisee. [6] As far as having zeal to please God—I actively persecuted the followers of Jesus because I thought they were worshipping a false Messiah. As far as being righteous by means of obeying the commands in the Torah—I outwardly obeyed them so well that nobody could find fault with me.

[7] But whatever these things were that I once considered to be an advantage for gaining favor with God—I now consider them all worthless as far as their ability to help me have a relationship with the Messiah. [8] Even more than that, I realize that all I am or could do to try to merit God's favor is worthless compared to having an intimate personal relationship with Messiah Jesus as my Lord and depending on what he has done to procure that favor for me. In order to have this relationship with the Messiah—which is available only by trusting in him alone—I have renounced all other ways of trying to gain it and I consider them as useless for obtaining it as it would be to offer him dung. [9] For I want to be united with the Messiah, not futilely trying to attain righteousness by obeying the Torah, but gaining his righteousness which God gives only on the basis of faith in his Son. [10] My aim is to know the Messiah more and more intimately and thereby experience in my life the same power that he had after his resurrection, ❖ *or: the same power that caused him to be resurrected* ➤ and experience the special fellowship and identification with him that comes from obeying him and being persecuted for that obedience. I want to become completely like him—even to the point of being willing to die in order to obey God's will. ❖ *Or: I want to die to sinning—just as he died to take away my sin.* ➤ [11] I say this because it

---

A 3:5 We would more naturally say this today as "when I was one-week old" instead of "on the eighth day."

is my expectation that he will cause me to live again after I die. ❖ *Paul is not implying here that he doubts he will be raised, nor that any of the things he mentions in verse 10 are things he does to merit or attain resurrection. Rather, the sense of verses 10 and 11 are that he is striving with expectancy to accomplish the Messiah's purposes in his life. His part is to obey and cooperate. The Messiah's part is to accomplish the rest.* ➤

Strive Toward a Deeper Relationship with the Messiah

12 I'm not claiming that I have already reached the level of intimacy with the Messiah that I want, or that God has already made me perfect. But I'm trying hard—depending on his power to become the person Messiah Jesus wants me to be—since he chose me to be one of his own people for the express purpose of making me become like himself. 13 Brothers and sisters in the Lord, I certainly know that I haven't yet attained the complete character of the Messiah. But the important thing is that I don't focus on my past mistakes or successes. Instead, I focus on the future. 14 In the present, I expend all my time, energy, and effort to attain those goals for which I will receive a future reward. For in my union with Messiah Jesus, God is calling me up to Heaven for just that purpose. ❖ *This reward is not salvation—which he already possesses in his spiritual union with the Messiah—but pertains to status and rewards in Heaven.* ➤

15 So let all of us who are spiritually mature have this same attitude toward our lives and goals. If some of you think differently, I am confident that God will eventually show you this is the right attitude to have. 16 At the very least, we all must continue to obey him in the areas he has already revealed his will to us.

Live as Citizens of Heaven Should

17 Brothers and sisters, all of you should follow the same way of living that I and my coworkers modeled for you while we were with you. Also notice anyone else who already lives this way and imitate them too. 18 I've told you this many times before, but will repeat it here again—even though it makes me cry to think about it. There are many people who live in such a way that it's clear they are against the message about the Messiah and what he did for us by dying on the cross. ❖ *We don't know specifically who Paul meant. Some ideas are: the circumcision party among the Jews who professed to be believers, or professing believers who thought they didn't need to obey God's moral commands, or Jews who did not accept Jesus as the Messiah.* ➤

19 They submit to the desires of their bodies as their god which rules them. ❖ *Literally: "Their god is their stomach." This may be an idiom whose meaning has been rendered, or if not an idiom, it's a metonym meaning they were mostly interested in their food and drink.* ➤ They boast about what they ought to be ashamed of. They only think about what affects their temporary life in this world. Therefore, their end will be ruin in Hell. ❖ *See 2 Thessalonians 1:9 and the following note about what it means to experience ruin in Hell.* ➤ 20 But we must live differently for our ultimate citizenship is in Heaven—not in this temporary world. We are eagerly waiting for our Lord Jesus the Messiah to return here from Heaven because he is the one who will finally usher us into the fullness of our salvation. 21 When he returns, he will use the power he has—which enables him to control everything—to transform our weak mortal bodies into powerful, immortal, glorified bodies like his own.

4

Paul's Closing Exhortations

1 My dear brothers and sisters in the Lord, I long to see you again for you are my pride and joy! ❖ *The "crown" in the literal text—rendered "pride and joy" above—is symbolic of the eternal reward he will get in Heaven for his work among the Philippians.* ➤ So, dear friends, on the basis of all I've just told you—stand firm in your relationship to the Lord.

2 Euodia and Syntyche, I beg you to stop arguing and instead, live together in harmony since you are both united with the Lord. 3 Suzugos, I want you to help these women to live together in peace. ❖ *Suzugos means "partner." Most commentators think it isn't a name because it isn't found elsewhere in Greek literature as a name. But if it isn't, we have no idea who Paul was referring to since the letter is addressed to the entire assembly. It was common*

enough for people to have names that meant something—like "Onesimus" in Paul's letter to Philemon. ➤ For they have worked hard together with me in proclaiming the Good News, and so have Clement and the others who have worked with me whose names are all in the Book of Life. ❖ The Book of Life is the official list in Heaven of people who are saved and will live there forever. ➤

4 Always rejoice because of your union with the Lord Jesus—no matter what your circumstances. I will exhort you again because it's important—Rejoice!

5 Be so considerate and patient with everyone that all will notice it. Remember, the Lord is returning soon. ❖ Or: The Lord is always close by. ➤ 6 Don't be anxious or worry about anything because that shows a lack of faith in God who promises to take care of you. But in every situation, go to God with your prayer requests—thanking him for his care, promises, and perfect will. [Ephesians 5:4, 20; Colossians 2:7; 3:15, 17; 4:2; 1 Thessalonians 5:18; 1 Timothy 2:1; Hebrews 12:28] 7 As a result, God will grant you his shalom which is far greater than we can comprehend. Through your union with Messiah Jesus, his shalom will protect you from anxiety, fear, and doubt—no matter what your circumstances. ❖ Shalom is a Hebrew word meaning peace, calmness, success, comfort, contentment, safety, health, wholeness, prosperity, integrity, well-being, and good relationships with God and people. Even though Paul wrote this letter in Greek, he had the Hebrew concept of shalom in mind here. Usually, this word is translated as "peace," but the English word lacks the depth of meaning that Paul intended. ➤

8 Finally, my brothers and sisters, your thoughts should always be solely focused on things that are true and genuine—especially God's revelation of truth—things that are honorable and worthy of respect, things that God considers right and approves of, thoughts that are pure and free of sin, things that are good, morally excellent, admirable, and worthy of praise. ❖ These are the kinds of thoughts that will keep you on the right path. What you think about forms your character and responses. If you fill your mind with garbage, don't be surprised when garbage comes out in your thoughts, words, and actions. ➤ 9 Put into practice what you've learned from me through my letters—and imitate what you heard and saw me do when I was with you. For by

doing these things, you will experience God's presence with you—giving you his shalom. ❖ He is always with all believers, but we don't usually experience his presence and shalom when we live in unrepentant disobedience. ➤

Paul Thanks the Philippian Believers for Their Gift

10 I greatly rejoiced in my union with the Lord when at long last you were able to demonstrate your concern for me by sending Epaphroditus with your gift. I know you have always been concerned, but you had no way of acting upon it before. 11 Now, I don't say this because I was worried about any unmet need. For I've reached the point in my relationship with the Lord where I've learned to be content no matter what the circumstances are around me—and no matter what I have or seemingly lack. 12 I've learned the secret of how to depend on the Lord for my contentment in any and every circumstance. I'm content when I'm poor as well as when I'm well-off. I'm content when I have plenty to eat and even when I have to go hungry. 13 I'm able to be content in any circumstance that the Lord wants me to experience by depending on Jesus—who lives in me and gives me his strength. ❖ Literally, this verse says, "I can do all things through him who strengthens me." This is often quoted out of context and given a broader meaning that Paul intended in this letter. To some extent that is valid, as long as it is understood to be limited to things within the Lord's will. ➤

14 Yet you did well by helping me in these difficult circumstances, and I thank you. 15 As you know, when you were still new believers and I left you behind in Macedonia Province to go to Athens and Corinth, your assembly was the only one that supported me financially. 16 Even when I had only gone as far as Thessalonica, ❖ which is relatively close to Philippi and within Macedonia Province ➤ you sent me money more than once. ❖ The Greek says: "both once and twice." Commentators aren't sure if it means twice, more than once (but not exactly how many), or repeatedly. ➤ 17 Now, I don't want you to think that I'm seeking financial gifts from you mainly for the sake of my benefiting from

them. What I do want to see, though, is your continued service to God's Kingdom in such a way that he will reward you for what you do. 18 I do want you to know that I've received everything you sent with Epaphroditus for me, and now I have more than enough for my needs. Your sacrifice in helping me pleases God. It's like a sweet-smelling sacrifice to him. 19 And through your union with Messiah Jesus, God will provide for your every need from his inexhaustible riches.

❖ *The Greek says, "the wealth of him in glory," and commentators differ on what this means. Some think "in glory" modifies "wealth," and means "abundant riches." Others say that "in glory" relates to "will fill every need," meaning "he will abundantly meet every need." Yet others say "in glory" means that the riches are located "in glory"—which might mean "in Heaven."* ➤

20 May all people praise and honor God our Father forever! Yes, may it be so!

Paul's Closing Greetings

21 Convey my warm greetings to all of God's people there who belong to Messiah Jesus. My coworkers here also send all of you their greetings. 22 And all the rest of God's people here in Rome send you their greetings—especially those who work in the emperor's palace.

23 I pray that our Lord Jesus the Messiah will look on you with great favor far beyond anything you can deserve and spiritually bless you. Yes, may it be so!

Paul's Letter To Jesus' Followers In Colosse

This letter was written by the Apostle Paul to the believers in the cities of Colosse and Laodicea in the Roman province then called Asia—which is in present-day Turkey. He wrote it during his first imprisonment in Rome [Acts 28:30-31] sometime in the period from AD 60–62. During that same imprisonment, he also wrote his letters to Philemon, the Ephesians, and the Philippians, which together are called "the prison letters."

Even though Paul had not yet visited Colosse himself, the assembly of believers there had been founded by people he had taught. So he considered them under his authority and wrote to correct some wrong teachings that he had heard were going around among the Colossian believers. They had probably been influenced by the Jewish circumcision party who claimed to follow Jesus yet insisted on Gentile believers following the requirements of the Torah to be saved. From this letter, it's clear that the Colossian believers felt salvation for Gentile believers depended on celebrating certain holy days, worshipping angels, following the Jewish dietary regulations, and circumcising male believers. The Colossians thought they were suffering because God was punishing them, and they desired to know the 'secret wisdom.' These were all wrong ideas that Paul wanted to correct

Outline:

The Messiah is more important than all that the Colossians thought was important. [chapter 1]
The supremacy of the Messiah. [1:15-20]
Paul warns them not to be deceived by false teachings. [chapter 2]
The things that are really important in following the Messiah. [3:1—4:6]
Closing [4:7-18]

1

Opening Greetings

[1] Greetings from Paul, who was called by God to be an apostle of Messiah Jesus. And greetings from our brother in the Lord, Timothy.

[2] I'm writing to the community of God's people in Colosse, all of whom he set apart to serve him in union with the Messiah and are called to be his holy ones. My prayer is that God our Father will continue to look upon you with great favor far beyond anything you can deserve and grant you peace and well-being.

Paul's Prayer for the Colossian Believers

[3] When we pray for you, Timothy and I always thank God—the Father of our Lord Jesus the Messiah—for all of you. [4] We do this because we have heard from Epaphras and others about your strong faith in Jesus and how much you show love to all of God's people. [5] We know you have this faith and are able to love people this way because you look forward with anticipation to eternal life and the rewards that God has waiting for you in Heaven. You have already heard about these things in the message about God's truth that's contained in the Good News about Jesus. [6] This same message which came to you is being spread all over the world. We know it has been transforming your lives—making you live in a way that pleases God. And it has been doing so ever since you first heard it and understood how generous God is with his undeserved favor and enabling power. In the same way, more and more people around the world are believing this message and being transformed. [7] Epaphras is our dear fellow worker and voluntary slave for the Messiah. He faithfully serves Jesus among you as our representative [A] [8] and it was he who told us about your great love for others—which is inspired by the Holy Spirit in you.

[A] 1:7 Some Greek manuscripts have "servant of the Messiah on our behalf," and others have "servant of the Messiah on your behalf." Even if the "on your behalf" version is taken as the original, most commentators interpret it as meaning that Epaphras is still working among them to help them. The difference in meaning from the interpretation given is that he is not representing Paul and Timothy.

9 Ever since he told us this about you, we've been frequently praying for you. We ask God to give you a clear understanding of his will for your lives and how he wants you to live. We ask him to give you his wisdom and insight into spiritual truths. 10 We pray this way because we want you to live in a manner that is fitting for God's people that pleases him in every way. We want you to continually know God better and more intimately—continually doing good works that produce positive benefits for his Kingdom. 11 With the goal in mind that you might always live this way, we ask God to strengthen your faith and your spirits with his limitless power to help you patiently endure suffering while remaining faithful to him. And through it all, we want you to experience joy 12 and to give thanks to God our Father—remembering that he has qualified you through your union with the Messiah to participate in the blessings he has promised to give his chosen people in Heaven. ❖ *"In Heaven" in the Greek is literally, "in the light." Another possible interpretation is: "who live in the light of God's truth"—which means submitting to the sin-exposing light of his Word, shunning sin, and seeking to be holy and pure just as he is. [1 John 1:7]* ➤ 13 We have great reason to thank him. For God our Father rescued us from the power that Satan has over those in his kingdom of spiritual darkness, and then he brought us under the benevolent rule of his beloved Son—Jesus our King. 14 He accomplished this through what his Son—the Messiah—did on the cross to forgive our sins. ❖ *A fuller explanation of this is in Romans 3:21-28.* ➤

Who Is God's Son and What Has He Done?

15 The Messiah—God's Son—is the visible representation of the character of God the Father who we can't see. *[John 14:9-10]* He has the authority of an oldest son, but his authority extends over everything that was created. *[Psalm 89:27]* ❖ *The figure of "firstborn"—in the literal text—does not mean that he was in some way born of God before his birth as a human. This passage is speaking of his eternal existence before he became the man Jesus.* ➤ 16 It was in the Messiah that all things were created, ❖ *Literally, "in him," there are three main interpretations and all three may be true: 1) God created all*

things via the Messiah—who is the eternal Son of God—as the agent of creation (see "by him" later in this verse), 2) it indicates location—all things were created "in the Messiah" (or: it was his power, or his ideas), 3) all things were created to be in association with the Messiah as their pattern and point of reference. ➤ including everything in Heaven and on Earth, everything visible or invisible, even every power and authority—both spiritual and earthly—everything was created by him and for him to rule, for his purposes. ❖ *The "rulers or authorities" in the literal text refer to the hierarchy of demonic spirits. The exact same words are used in 2:10 and 2:15 where their identity is clear.* ➤ 17 He existed before anything was created, and everything continues to exist and work together the way God planned— only because of him. *[John 1:3; Acts 17:28; Romans 11:36; 1 Corinthians 8:6; Hebrews 1:3; 2 Peter 3:7]* 18 He is the head of the Assembly of all Believers— which is under his direction—because together all believers constitute his body. He is its source and beginning and he gave it eternal life. He was the first human to be permanently raised from death to eternal life as a pattern for all others who will also be raised, so that he will have preeminence over everything in the new eternal order. 19 For it was God the Father's desire that the complete nature and power of deity would continue to live in the Messiah for all eternity when he became the man Jesus. ❖ *After becoming a man—but before his resurrection— Jesus did not have his full power and glory that he previously had as the eternal Son of God in Heaven. [John 17:5, 24; Philippians 2:6-11] He worked miracles by the power of the Holy Spirit—not by his own power. Then his power and glory were restored to him after his resurrection.* ➤ 20 It was also God the Father's desire that the Messiah be the agent through whom he brings the entire universe into a proper relationship with himself. This was accomplished through the Messiah's death on the cross— which enabled him to establish peace with all things on Earth and in Heaven. ❖ *A few commentators even say there will be reconciliation with the rebellious angels (demons). But most of them explain that it will be in the form of their enforced obedience and condemna-tion. All of creation was placed under a curse of decay when mankind sinned. [Genesis 3:14-19] But when Jesus returns, all of the physical and spiritual creation will be put back to its proper relationship with God. [Romans 8:19-22] The curse will* be removed—along with rebellious humans and demons who will be confined to Hell. [Galatians 3:13-14; Revelation 19:20-21; 20:10-15; 22:3] ➤

21 But as for you, before you became believers you were separated from God—both because of your evil way of living and because of the hostile attitude you had toward him. 22 But now—through your union with the death of the Messiah's physical body—God has reconciled you with himself. He did this so you can come into his presence completely holy, pure, and innocent. ❖ Commentators differ as to whether this refers to our coming into his presence now or in Heaven. But it's true both ways. In the literal text, "holy" means "dedicated to God" and "morally pure;" "blameless" means, "pure, perfect, without accusation;" and "beyond reproach" means, "innocent and blameless." All three are synonyms which Paul used to strengthen his statement. ➤ 23 This is true of you if you continue to firmly trust the Messiah and obey him—without allowing anyone to shake your faith or your expectation that in Heaven you will receive everything God has promised his people in the Good News. This is the very same message that God told me to preach, the same one you have already heard, and the one that has been proclaimed to people all over the world.

God's Plan for Gentiles

24 Even though I'm in prison and have suffered as a result of proclaiming the Good News to Gentiles, I rejoice because of the salvation you have received as a result. I willingly suffer all that the Messiah requires of me for the sake of helping complete the task of winning people to him and helping them grow in their faith. ❖ There are many interpretations of what the literal text, "fill up what is lacking in the Messiahs sufferings" means. But they all agree that these are not referring to the sufferings the Messiah went through on the cross to redeem humanity—for those were entirely sufficient for that purpose. It likely means that we are all called to obey him, and in the course of obeying him we will all suffer to some extent as a result. Since he lives in us and experiences all that we do, when we suffer—he does too. So our sufferings are his, and those that happen from obeying him are those that are not yet completed and hence "lacking" in what must be suffered before

he returns and eliminates all suffering. ➤ 25 For God called me to serve his people—including you—by teaching them his complete message and explaining it all clearly. 26 This message is about the plan for humanity which he made in eternity past. Until the Messiah came, he only hinted about it and no one fully understood it. But now he has fully revealed to all his people 27 that this wonderful plan includes Gentiles. His plan is that the Messiah will live in Gentile believers too—so you can confidently expect to share his glory and the abundant riches that God has promised to give his people in Heaven. [1 Corinthians 2:7; Ephesians 1:9-14; 3:3-6] 28 Therefore, we tell the message about the Messiah to everyone we can—wisely warning them what they shouldn't be doing and teaching them what they should believe and do. For our goal is that everyone we tell about him will believe and grow in their faith—so we can later present them to God as spiritually mature people in their union with the Messiah. 29 This is the end toward which I work so hard—depending not on my own abilities, but relying solely on the power provided by the Messiah living in me. [Galatians 2:20; Ephesians 1.19-20]

2

Paul Doesn't Want Them to Be Led Astray by Wrong Teaching

1 I want you to be aware of how much I struggle for all of you in prayer and in writing letters to those for whom I am responsible. I want to help all of you—the believers in Laodicea and all other believers in your area whom I've not met in person—to remain strong in your faith and not be led astray by wrong teaching. ❖ Paul had not yet visited Colosse or Laodicea, but felt responsible for them as the apostle to the Gentiles—and it's also likely that the leaders in those places were people he had trained. ➤ 2 My purpose is that you and those I just mentioned would be spiritually strengthened A and united by your love for one another. I want you all to experience

---

A 2:2 "spiritually strengthened" is literally, "strengthened in heart" and commentators interpret the phrase many

different ways. The Greek word translated "strengthened" can also mean "encourage" or [Continued next page]

the full blessings and benefits that result when you completely understand God's message and are fully convinced that it's true and reliable. For that is the way to intimately know the Messiah himself. ❖ *i.e., The way to intimately know the Messiah is to fully understand God's truth, to fully believe it, and to be united with other believers* ➤ The Messiah is the center of God's eternal plan for humanity and creation which he kept hidden until Jesus came. ³ All of God's valuable wisdom and knowledge are possessed by the Messiah—and only by being in union with him and knowing him well do you have access to them.

⁴ I'm telling you how to obtain God's wisdom and knowledge so that false teachers will not be able to mislead you with their arguments—no matter how good they sound. ⁵ Even though I'm far away from you physically, we are tied together spiritually and I think of you continually. I rejoice to know how unified you are ❖ *i.e., undivided by false teachings* ➤ and how strong your faith in the Messiah is.

⁶ So then, since you have acknowledged, trusted, and submitted to Messiah Jesus as your Lord and Master, continue to live in spiritual union with him and in submission to his will. ⁷ While firmly trusting him, continue to strengthen your relationship with him. Become more familiar with all the things you were taught about our common faith—and become more convinced that they are true so you won't be deceived by false teachings. And always express your great thankfulness to God for everything that he has done in your life. *[Ephesians 5:4, 20; Philippians 4:6; Colossians 3:15, 17; 4:2; 1 Thessalonians 5:18; 1 Timothy 2:1; Hebrews 12:28]*

⁸ Take care that no one leads you astray from the truth with fine-sounding—but worthless—philosophies that are based on human traditions, values, and principles that conflict with the true teachings about the Messiah and his will. ❖ *For some modern examples: 1) Religion is a private thing—so keep it to yourself. 2) What is true for you is not necessarily true for me. 3) A loving God would never send anyone to Hell. 4) All religions lead to God. ¶ An alternate interpretation of the "elementary principles of the world" in the literal text (rendered above as "values and principles that conflict with the true teachings about the Messiah and his will"), is the spirits that the Greeks believed ruled the sun, moon, and stars and thus controlled their fates. ¶ Some reasons why you should not believe false teachers are:* ➤ ⁹ For even though the Messiah is a man, he also has the complete nature and power of deity. ¹⁰ In your union with him, you have all you need for healthy spiritual lives for he rules over every other spiritual being who has power and authority. ❖ *These spiritual beings are the hierarchy of demonic spirits—as is made clear in 2:15 where they are literally referred to by the same words.* ➤

¹¹ In your union with him, you were also "circumcised," but this was not something done physically. It was done spiritually by the Messiah who marked you as God's people with the seal of the Holy Spirit and removed your sin nature. ❖ *[Deuteronomy 30:6; Ezekiel 11:19; 36:26; Romans 2:28-29; 6:6] Jewish circumcision was a physical sign of God's ownership. But Paul is talking about a spiritual circumcision of the heart (or spirit), which is the Holy Spirit himself residing in our new perfect spirits. "Seal" means "mark of ownership."* ➤

¹² Because of your faith in God's power to raise Jesus from the dead, you were spiritually united with his death, burial, and resurrection when you were baptized. ❖ *Some commentators believe that baptism is merely a representation of what happened to us spiritually. Others believe that faith—together with obedience to the command to be baptized—is what brings about that spiritual union. In the Hebrew Scriptures, believers were commanded to offer sacrifices in order to receive forgiveness for sin. We know that those sacrifices were only representations of the Messiah's sacrifice. Yet, they would not have been forgiven if they had not performed the sacrifices out of obedience.*

"comfort." "Heart" can refer to the center of emotions, or the mind, personality, will, or human spirit, or it can be taken as a synecdoche (a kind of figure of speech) in which "heart" represents the whole person. Keeping in mind Paul's concern in this letter that the Colossian believers not be led astray by false teachers may help to narrow the choices. To translate "encouraged" (as opposed to strengthened) implies they were discouraged—and we have no indication that this was the case. He is wanting them to be strong in their faith and unity to withstand the divisions that false teachers would try to instigate among them.

Therefore, the sacrifices were more than mere representative ceremonies, but were in some sense effective—in connection with the Messiah's sacrifice—for taking away sin. Therefore, just because a ceremony is a figurative expression of something else does not mean it is necessarily limited to merely being a figure. ➤ 13 You Gentiles were spiritually dead and separated from God because of your sins and your sin nature. You were uncircumcised both physically and spiritually. But while you were still in this state, God made you spiritually alive and united you with the Messiah. He has forgiven all of us—both Jews and Gentiles—14 by canceling the written legal record of sins that condemned us. He took it away by assigning it to Jesus as he was nailed to the cross—so that he would undergo the required penalty for our sins.
❖ *The phrase "canceling the written legal record of sins that condemned us"—which is literally, "having canceled the written code"—is interpreted two ways. One is that it refers to the Teachings of Moses, but this seems unlikely since Jesus said he came to fulfill the Torah—not abolish it—and that it would not pass away until both Earth and Heaven disappear. [Matthew 5:17-18] The interpretation represented here comes from the fact that "the written code" was a common term used in Greek courts for the written statement of charges against a defendant, and the Greek word often translated "regulations" or "decrees" in this verse referred to the official proclamation of the charges against the defendant.* ➤ 15 He also nullified the power of spiritual rulers and authorities—humiliating them in a public display of his triumph over them through the Messiah's death and resurrection. ❖ *The rulers and authorities in this verse are the exact same words used in 1:16 and 2:10. The "public display" may have been in the spiritual world of demons, and it could refer to the fact that the resurrection clearly demonstrated that their power was broken.* ➤

16 So on the basis of all this, don't pay attention to Jews who say that you are not saved because of what you eat or drink, or for not participating in Jewish festivals, new moon festivals, or certain Sabbath days, or not doing things the way they think is proper. 17 As a shadow shows only the outlines of an object, these dietary rules, festivals, and holy days commanded in the Torah are prophetic shadows of the Messiah himself and the blessings he brings. But since we are now in union with him, these shadows are not necessary for salvation. 18 And don't listen to people who insist you must portray a false humility ❖ *This could mean self-abasement, self-humiliation, or asceticism.* ➤ or submit to angels in worship to be saved because if you do those things, they will disqualify you for the prize of eternal life.
❖ *Many commentators interpret this sentence as meaning, "Don't let those who insist on false humility and worshipping angels condemn you for not following their rules." There is, of course, no way you can prevent others from condemning you. All you can do is refuse to listen to them. But if you do listen to them and follow them, you are 1) submitting to a false god (i.e., angels) in worship, and 2) depending on a legalistic following of rules to save you. This means you don't have true saving faith in the Messiah.* ➤ Such people make their claims based on visions they have seen—and their unspiritual minds make them proud for no valid reason. 19 Such people are not holding firmly to the true teachings about the Messiah who is head of his body. For it is only by holding onto him that believers can grow spiritually and be held together as one body—just as a physical body is held together by its joints and ligaments.

20 Since you died spiritually with the Messiah and can no longer be condemned by elementary regulations of this world that are concerned only with externals, why do you keep on submitting to them as if you were still under their influence? ❖ *The phrase, "elementary principles of the world" is the same as in 2:8 and would have the same meaning in both verses. That he is talking about rules rather than spiritual beings seems clear from the next verse.* ➤ 21 These rules ❖ *and false teachers* ➤ forbid handling some things, even tasting certain foods and touching certain things. 22 But you don't need to obey these rules because they don't help you grow spiritually. They are only focused on temporary things for they are rules invented by men, not God. 23 Even though these rules seem to have some wisdom by forcing people to do difficult things to demonstrate their devotion to God and their outward humility ❖ *See the note on false humility in 2:18.* ➤ and their harsh asceticism, yet in reality, none of these things can actually help you control your sinful desires.

3

Focus on Heavenly Things

¹ Since you have been united with the Messiah and have been spiritually raised from death to a new eternal life, strongly desire the rewards and blessings associated with that new life in Heaven—where the Messiah has the position of highest honor and authority at the right hand of God the Father. ² Focus your thoughts on Heavenly values and concerns—not on the evil things of this world. ³ For in union with the Messiah, your sinful nature died—so you should no longer have any interest in evil. *[Romans 6:6]* You now live your new life in union with the Messiah in God's presence, though people are not yet able to see this new spiritual life you possess. ⁴ But when the Messiah—who is the source of your new life—openly returns, then you will also be clearly revealed as his perfect holy people who share his glory and have glorified bodies like his. ❖ *The false teachers were saying that the only way to be perfect was to follow all the rules they taught. Paul counters this by saying they already possess sinless perfection in union with the Messiah—which will be revealed when he returns. Therefore, they don't need to follow the false teachers.* ➤

The Way Believers Are Meant to Live

⁵ You are united with the Messiah and your sinful nature is dead, and you are, in fact, no longer slaves to the power of sin. Therefore, do not allow yourselves to follow the evil desires of your body. ❖ *The literal "put to death" in the Greek is a figure of speech meaning "have nothing to do with," "do not associate with," "refuse to do," or "completely eliminate."* ➤ Reject all thoughts of sexual relations forbidden by God, all indecency, lust, evil desires and impulses, and greed—which in God's sight is the same as worshipping a false god of wealth. ❖ *Even though we are free from the power of sin—meaning it cannot force us to sin—we can still be tempted and we can still choose to sin, as well as choose to obey. In order to choose to resist temptation and obey God, we must moment by*

moment rely on the help of the Holy Spirit. For against strong temptations, we are often not able to resist without his help. See the note at 1 Peter 2:11 about how to rely on God's help to resist temptation. ➤ ⁶ God will reveal his holy anger on Judgment Day against people who do these evil things by punishing those who refuse to obey him. **A** ⁷ And you Gentiles used to habitually do these kinds of things before you believed in the Messiah.

⁸ But now, you must eliminate such behavior from your life: inward indignation, resentment, smoldering anger, outward expressions of temper and angry frustration, meanness and evil intentions, insults, slander and abusive language, and vulgar, obscene, or offensive language. ⁹ Don't lie to each other—since you are no longer the people you used to be. *[Colossians 2:20]* ¹⁰ You have become entirely new people in union with the Messiah, *[2 Corinthians 5:17; Galatians 2:20]* and God is continually changing you to become more and more like your creator ❖ *i.e., the Messiah* ➤ so you can know him intimately. ¹¹ Because of this, it no longer matters if you are a circumcised Jew, an uncircumcised Gentile, an uncultured foreigner, a fierce and savage Scythian, a slave, or a free person. The only thing that matters is that the Messiah—who is supreme over everyone and everything—lives in all believers, making them all equally worthy and valuable.

¹² Therefore, since you now have this new nature as the people God chose, loves, and has set apart as dedicated to himself, this is the way you should live in relationship with all others: *[Romans 12:1—15:7; 1 Corinthians 13:1-7; Galatians 5:16—6:10; Ephesians 4:1—6:9; 1 Thessalonians 4:1-12; 5:6-22; James 1:19—2:12; 3:13—4:17; 1 Peter 4:1-11]* Be sympathetic, compassionate, merciful, helpful, kind, humble, and gentle. Consider all others more important than yourselves, be patient with their shortcomings, and be willing to suffer inconvenience for them. ¹³ Be tolerant of their faults, differences, habits, and views, and be quick to completely forgive each other for any offense or complaint—just as

---

A 3:6 Some Greek manuscripts to not contain the words— in the literal text—"on the sons of disobedience."

the Lord forgave you and holds nothing against you. 14 Most important of all, demonstrate love to each other—since this will bind you all together in perfect unity and harmony. ❖ *Some commentators think love binds the other virtues together, rather than the people.* ➤ 15 Allow the peace that the Messiah gives his people—which enables you to live in harmony with one another—to be the controlling factor in the decisions you make in relation to others. Do this because God has made you all parts of one body and has called you to live and work together in peace as one body. And don't forget to continually thank God for all his blessings. *[Ephesians 5:4, 20; Philippians 4:6; Colossians 2:7; 3:15, 17; 4:2; 1 Thessalonians 5:18; 1 Timothy 2:1; Hebrews 12:28]* 16 Always ponder the message about the Messiah and the things he taught so they influence all that you think and do. Relying on wisdom from God, always teach, exhort, counsel, and remind each other about the things he taught and—when necessary—correct and warn each other. Also remind yourselves and others of these truths by frequently singing psalms, songs of praise, hymns, and other kinds of spiritual songs out of genuine gratitude to God for his blessings and promises. 17 Let everything you say or do be done in such a way that it will not shame the Lord Jesus—because you belong to him and represent him. Always let what you say and do come from an attitude of thankfulness to God the Father—expressed through your obedience in union with the Messiah.

Relationships in the Household
[Ephesians 5:22—6:9; 1 Peter 3:1-7]

18 Wives, continually submit yourselves to the authority of your husbands—because this is the Lord's will for you.

19 Husbands, it is the Lord's will for you to love your wives and clearly demonstrate it by exercising your authority with humble consideration. Never abuse your authority by being petty tyrants who are angry, unkind, or harsh with them.

20 You children who are still under the authority and care of your parents, always obey them in every way for this is the Lord's will for you and it pleases him.

21 Fathers and mothers, do not make your children resentful or bitter against you by being unreasonable or harsh in your demands or attitude—or they will become discouraged from trying to please you.

22 You who are slaves, always obey your earthly masters—keeping in mind that this pleases your Heavenly master. Do what they want you to do at all times—not just when they are watching so as to create a hypocritical good impression. Do your best and be completely honest with them in order to honor the Lord. That way, your earthly master will not think poorly of the Heavenly Master that he knows you also serve. 23 Do all your work cheerfully and wholeheartedly as if you were doing it because the Lord himself asked you to do it—not a mere man—and you want to please him. 24 Do this because you know that when you obey your master, you are really serving the Lord and he will give you the eternal reward and blessings he has promised his people. 25 But remember that the Lord will punish anyone who does wrong—for he shows no partiality in his judging. ❖ *See the footnotes at Ephesians 6:9 and 1 Peter 2:18 about slavery.* ➤

4

1 You believers who own slaves, remember that you too have a Master in Heaven who is watching you. So take good care of your slaves and treat them fairly.

More Instructions for All Believers

2 All of you should spend time in prayer daily—persisting in your requests until you see results, keeping alert to the Spirit's leading, always being thankful for what God has done for you and expressing your thankfulness to him. 3 Also pray for Timothy and me that while I'm here in prison, God will give us opportunities to proclaim the Good News about the Messiah and his previously hidden plan to save Gentiles. For I'm in prison precisely because I've been faithful to do this work. ❖ *While this specific instruction to pray for Paul is no longer applicable, the principle to pray for pastors, spiritual leaders, and missionaries is a valid application and exhortation to take from these verses.* ➤ 4 So pray that I won't

be afraid to continue to proclaim the Good News publicly, because I am obligated to do so by the Lord's command.

5 Be wise in the way that you behave toward non-believers—keeping in mind that everything you say and do reflects on your Lord Jesus. Make full use of the opportunities that come your way to do them good and to lead them to the Lord. 6 When you speak with unbelievers, take care to never create a bad impression or offend them—always being wise, pleasant, kind, winsome, and gracious. If you establish this manner of speaking as a habit, then you will know how to wisely answer anyone who asks you about the Good News and do so in a way that will attract them. ❖ *The original text says "seasoned with salt" and salt is sometimes a figure for wisdom in Jewish writings. [Matthew 5:13]* ➤

Closing Greetings

7 Tychicus is a dear brother in the Lord who has faithfully served alongside of me. I've sent him to you along with this letter to tell you my news 8 so you can know what is going on in our lives and ministry, and so he can encourage you and strengthen your faith. 9 With him is Onesimus, your fellow Colossian. He is also a dear brother in the Lord and is faithful in his work. He and Tychicus will tell you all that's going on here.

10 Aristarchus—who is in prison with me—sends his warm greetings, as does Mark—Barnabas' cousin. You've already received instructions about Mark. Warmly welcome him and provide him with hospitality if he visits you. ❖ *This is the only source for our knowing that John Mark was Barnabas' cousin. About 12-14 years earlier, Mark had left Paul and Barnabas at Perga in Pamphylia [Acts 13:13] and later Paul and Barnabas split up because Paul refused to work with Mark anymore. [Acts 15:36-40] It's evident that by this time, Mark had demonstrated reliability and had been restored to a good relationship with Paul.* ➤ 11 Jesus Justus also sends his greetings. These are the only Jewish believers among my coworkers who work to extend God's Kingdom. ❖ *Most commentators*

think "these" refer to Aristarchus, Mark, and Jesus Justus, though some leave out Aristarchus. ➤ They have been a great comfort to me here.

12 Epaphras—a genuine servant of Messiah Jesus who is also your fellow Colossian—sends you his warm greetings too. I want you to know that he cares deeply for you—so he always prays with great intensity for you to be spiritually mature and confident in your discernment of God's will. ❖ *Epaphras was probably a convert of Paul's who was the first one to preach the Good News in Colosse, and therefore he felt a special responsibility for them.* ➤ 13 I can vouch for the fact that he is working hard in prayer for you and for the believers in Laodicea and Hierapolis. ❖ *Colosse, Laodicea, and Hierapolis were all in the same valley along the same river. It's likely that Epaphras preached in these two cities too.* ➤ 14 Our dear friend Luke—the doctor—sends you his greetings, as does Demas. ❖ *This is the only place that tells us Luke was a doctor.* ➤

15 Convey my warm greetings to the brothers and sisters in Laodicea, and also to Nympha and the assembly that meets in her house. A 16 After this letter has been read to the believers in Colosse, make sure it is also read to the assembly in Laodicea. ❖ *In the first century, many people didn't know how to read so they couldn't all read it for themselves.* ➤ Also make sure that the letter I wrote to the assembly in Laodicea is read to all of you. ❖ *Literally, Paul refers to the letter "from" Laodicea. It's possible he means a letter from the believers in Laodicea that he knew they were going to send the believers in Colosse, but most commentators take the view represented in this interpretation. No copy of this letter is known to exist.* ➤ 17 Tell Archippus for me, "Make sure you complete the ministry task that the Lord gave you to do." ❖ *Archippus was a member of the assembly of believers in Colosse and may have been a leader.* ➤

18 I, Paul, am writing this final greeting to you by my own hand. ❖ *He dictated most of the letter to a scribe. His taking the pen and writing in his own identifiable handwriting would enable the Colossians to be sure the letter was really from Paul.* ➤ Remember that I'm a prisoner and pray for me! I pray that our Lord will look upon you with great favor far beyond anything you can deserve.

A 4:15 The name Νύμφαν (Numphan) could be either feminine or masculine. Some manuscripts have "her" house, some have "his" house and some have "their" house.

Paul's First Letter
to Jesus' Followers in Thessalonica

The Apostle Paul wrote this letter to the believers in the city of Thessalonica in the Roman province of Macedonia—which is the northern part of modern-day Greece. Thessalonica was a major city of about 200,000 people. His first visit there was when he preached the Good News to them on his second missionary journey—resulting in the conversion of many Gentiles and some Jews. [Acts 17:1-15] But Jews who rejected his message were jealous and caused a riot. So the believers sent Paul, Timothy, and Silas to the city of Berea. Then Paul sent Timothy and Silas back to teach the Thessalonian believers. After a time, Paul wrote this letter from Corinth in about AD 50–51 to answer some things that Timothy had reported to him from his recent visit with them. This is probably the first letter that Paul wrote among those included in the New Testament.

Outline:

Paul thanks God for the Thessalonian believers' good ways. [chapter 1]
He answers criticisms. [2:1-16]
His concern about the Thessalonians who were experiencing persecution. [2:17—3:13]
How believers should live. [4:1-12]
Paul answers concerns about Jesus' return. [4:13—5:11]
More on how believers should live. [5:12-22]
Closing blessings. [5:23-28]

1

Opening Greetings

1 Greetings from Paul, Silas, **A** and Timothy. We are writing to the assembly of believers in the city of Thessalonica who are united with God the Father and our Lord Jesus the Messiah. I pray that God **B** will continue to look upon you with great favor far beyond anything you can deserve and grant you peace and well-being.

Why Paul Thanks God
for the Thessalonian Believers

2 Every time we pray for you, we thank God for all of you. 3 In particular, we thank him for these three things: that you are living out your faith by doing God's work, that you are demonstrating your love for others by helping them, and that you are enduring persecution by firmly looking forward to the return of our Lord Jesus the Messiah.

4 Dear brothers and sisters in the Lord, we also thank God because we know that he dearly loves you and has chosen you to be his own people. 5 We know you are among those he has chosen because of the powerful way God caused his message to come to you and your response to it. When we proclaimed the Good News, it wasn't with mere words, but we were empowered by the Holy Spirit and were fully convinced of the truth of the message we were sharing. ❖ *Most commentators think "power" in this context (in the literal text) refers to the empowering of the message and messengers to convince—and not demonstrations of miraculous power.* ➤ You yourselves know the way we lived and how we helped you while we were there and how that also convinced you. 6 You not only believed our message, but you have followed in our footsteps and in the Lord's by receiving his message with

---

A **1:1a** "Silas" is the Hebrew form of his name and "Silvanus" is the Latin form. Luke used "Silas" when he wrote Acts, and it is the more familiar form for many people today—hence it is used here, even though literally the Greek text reads "Silvanus."

B **1:1b** Some manuscripts have "Grace and peace from God our Father *and* Lord Jesus the Messiah."

Holy-Spirit-inspired joy—in spite of the persecution and suffering that went along with it. 7 As a result, you became a model for all believers in the rest of Macedonia Province and also those in Achaia Province. ❖ *Achaia Province was the southern half of modern Greece.* ➤ 8 For the message about our Lord has gone out from you far and wide, not only in Macedonia and Achaia, but in many other places as well where people have heard about your strong trust in God. We never have to tell others about your great faith because they already know about it. 9 People are always telling us what they've heard about how we started our work among you, and how you responded by turning away from worshipping lifeless idols to serving the one true and living God. 10 They tell how you now patiently wait for his Son Jesus—whom he raised from death to life—to return from Heaven, and how you are trusting him to rescue all of us believers from God's anger against sinners on Judgment Day.

2

Paul Answers Criticism About His Work

❖ *From what he writes in 2:1-16, it's evident that Paul had heard criticisms of his behavior. To counter that, he reminds the Thessalonian believers of things they themselves observed.* ➤

1 My brothers and sisters in the Lord, you are quite aware that our visit to you was a great success A in bringing many people to believe in the Lord Jesus. 2 Even though just prior to our visit with you we had been insulted and persecuted in the city of Philippi, God gave us the courage to come to Thessalonica and proclaim the Good News in the face of strong opposition. 3 One reason we can be so bold is that our motives for urging people to believe the message of the Good News are pure—and not for personal

gain. We aren't trying to deceive anyone, but to help them—for we know our message is entirely true. 4 We are constantly aware that God appointed us to proclaim this message and that he examines our thoughts and motives. It should be apparent that we aren't trying to be people pleasers in what we say, but only want to please him and have his continuing approval. 5 You yourselves know that we never resorted to flattery to influence people, and God knows we were never secretly motivated by greed. 6 We never wanted you or anyone else to put us on a pedestal—even though the Messiah sent us as his apostles and we could have insisted that you respect our authority. B ❖ *This is a clear indication that Paul considered Timothy and Silas to be apostles—although the word actually occurs in verse 7 in the original text. The part of this verse rendered, "we could have insisted that you respect our authority" is literally, "we could have been with weight." Another interpretation of this is that as apostles they could have made demands that the believers provide them with food and other necessities.* ➤ 7 But we were gentle C in the way we exercised our authority over you—like a nursing mother is with her child. 8 We came to love you all so much that D we were continually delighted to use our time and energy to help you in every way that we could—as well as share the Good News with you. 9 Dear brothers and sisters, I'm sure you remember the hard and exhausting work we did to earn our own living—working long hours both day and night so we wouldn't be a financial burden on any of you while we taught about God's Good News. ❖ *Paul made tents for a living. He could have taught while he worked. They probably worked part of the night so they could spend some part of the day preaching in public places to the unconverted.* ➤

10 In everything we said and did while we were among you, no one could honestly find fault with us. We were always pure and fair—as you and God can testify. 11 You know that we treated each of you as

---

A 2:1 Literally, "not a failure" (in the original Greek text), this is a figure of speech called "litotes" where the opposite of what is intended is negated for the purpose of emphasizing the statement. In English though, the original wording sounds like an understatement—which was not Paul's intent.

B 2:6 In some manuscripts, the second half of this sentence goes with the next sentence rather than with this one.

C 2:7 Some manuscripts have "we were babies among you" rather than "we were gentle among you."

D 2:8 οὕτως (houtōs)—here rendered—"so much that," has several meanings and commentators are not agreed on its meaning in this context. Another reasonable meaning for it here could be "therefore."

lovingly as if you were our own children. 12 We were constantly encouraging and comforting you and also urging you to live in a way that pleases God as befits members of his Kingdom—to which he is calling you in order that you may share his greatness and character.

13 Another reason we frequently thank God for you is because when you listened to the message we proclaimed, you had the spiritual perception to recognize it was not something made up by mere men, but was a genuine message from God that you accepted as such. Now, through that message, he is working to change those of you who believe in the Messiah. 14 It's clear that you have received our message and that God is changing you because in order to obey him, you were willing to suffer persecution at the hands of your own countrymen who reject the Messiah. In this, you have become just like the assemblies of Jewish believers in Judea who are united to Messiah Jesus. For they are also persecuted by their own people who reject him. 15 In centuries past, it was Jewish leaders who killed some of God's prophets; and some 20 years ago, it was the Jewish leaders in Jerusalem who insisted that the Romans kill the Lord Jesus; and more recently, it was other Jewish leaders who drove Silas, Timothy, and me out of Thessalonica. [Acts 17:1-10] Such people are extremely displeasing to God and are hostile to everyone except other Jews who share their views. 16 This leads them to try to prevent us from preaching God's message to Gentiles about how to be saved. By doing so, they are greatly adding to their sins—to the point that God will tolerate it no longer. For God's wrath is ready to come upon them. ❖ The last sentence is in the past tense in Greek and some commentators believe this means that their judgment is certain. Many believe this refers to the final judgment, but some think it also means the judgment on Judaism at that point in history—which in a few years would result in the destruction of Jerusalem and the temple in AD 70. ➤

Paul's Concern for the Thessalonian Believers

17 My dear brothers and sisters, even though such people forced us to leave you for a while, they could not stop us from thinking about you. Our longing for you caused us to try very hard to return 18 for we really wanted to see you. I tried several times, but Satan prevented us through the people he influences. 19 We want to see and encourage you because when we stand before the Lord Jesus at his return, we expect to joyfully and proudly present you to him as proof of our faithfulness to his command to preach the Good News—and so be rewarded for our success. 20 We are, indeed, proud of you—and you are the reason we have joy in our work.

3

1 So when we felt that we just had to know how you were doing, we thought it best if Silas and I would remain where we were in Athens 2-3 while we sent our brother Timothy—who is one of God's ministers in proclaiming the Good News about the Messiah—to see how you were enduring the persecution. We sent him to encourage you and help strengthen your trust—so that no one would be shaken from their faith by such troubles. You should know that it's part of God's plan for his people to suffer persecution for their faith. [Mark 10:30; John 15:18-20; 16:33; Acts 14:22; 2 Timothy 3:12; 1 Peter 2:20-21] 4 For while we were with you, we kept telling you in advance that all true believers will be persecuted—and you have seen we were right. 5 So as I told you, when I could no longer endure not knowing how you were doing, I sent Timothy to find out whether you were still trusting Jesus or not. For I was afraid that Satan might have tempted you to take the easy way out and renounce your faith—and then all our work among you would have been for nothing.

6 But Timothy has just returned to us here in Corinth and brought us welcome news of your continuing faith and practical love for others. He also let us know that you remember us affectionately and long to see us as much as we long to see you. 7 So, my brothers and sisters in the Lord, this news about you greatly encouraged us at a time when we are experiencing persecution and

distress. 8 We have a new sense of joy and enthusiasm since we know that your trust in the Lord is still strong. 9 When we come into God's presence in prayer, we can never thank him enough for you because you've given us so much joy. 10 So both night and day when we pray, we earnestly ask God to allow us to see you again. We want to finish teaching you the things we didn't have time to cover before we were forced to leave.

11 We ask our Father God and our Lord Jesus to remove any obstacles that would prevent us from coming. 12 We also ask the Lord Jesus to continue to increase the expressions of your love for each other and for all people to overflowing—just as our love does for you. 13 We pray that he will strengthen you spiritually, so that when our Lord Jesus returns with all his holy people, and you stand before him and God our Father, he will see that you are perfectly dedicated to him.

4

How Believers Should Live

1 Therefore, my brothers and sisters in the Lord, in view of all that I've written up to this point, I have some important matters to tell you. While we were with you, we taught you to live in a manner that pleases God—and we know you've been doing this. A Yet we want to strongly exhort you to never be content with doing the minimum you can get away with, but to strive to please him all the time because of your spiritual union with the Lord Jesus. ❖ *Or: we exhort you based on our authority from the Lord Jesus.* ➤ 2 You already know the instructions for living that we gave you—which came from the Lord Jesus himself. 3 It's God's will that you should live holy lives entirely dedicated to him—and in particular that you should avoid all sexual sin as defined in his Word. ❖ *In brief, this means no sexual relationships except between a husband and a wife.* ➤ 4 He wants each of you to learn how to control your own body in a way that is holy and considered

honorable. ❖ *The Greek literally says, "each of you to know how to control (or: respect, or: possess) his own vessel." This has been interpreted in two ways—most commentators interpreting it as is rendered above. The other interpretation is: Each husband should respect his wife (or: each unmarried man obtain his own wife), in a way that is holy and is considered honorable.* ➤ 5 Don't allow yourselves to be controlled by passionate sexual desires like people who don't know God. ❖ *Believers are to make decisions based on what they know is right—not based on what they feel.* ➤ 6 No one should wrong a brother or sister in the Lord or cheat them by having sex with their spouse—because the Lord will take vengeance against all who do such things. We have already strongly warned you about this. ❖ *While most commentators take the view presented, the Greek says, "no man should do wrong and cheat his brother in this matter." A few commentators interpret "in this matter" as referring to a new topic of business dealings, because the verbs are ones used in business contexts.* ➤ 7 For God called us to be his people so that we would live holy lives—not so we could live in ways that violate his sense of purity. 8 Therefore, those who reject this command are rejecting God himself—not mere human authority. He is the one who gave you his Holy Spirit to live within you for the purpose of enabling you to live holy lives.

9 Now, as for the area of living that has to do with demonstrating your love for fellow believers, we have no need to say anything to you about it because it's clear that God himself has taught you to do this. ❖ *When God "teaches" you to obey him in some area, you do it well with no struggle.* ➤ 10 We know you are demonstrating your love to all your brothers and sisters in the Lord throughout the rest of Macedonia. Our only exhortation is to continue to look for every possible opportunity and for new ways to do so. 11 Just as we told you when we were with you, make one of your goals in life to be industrious enough to earn your own living—not thinking yourselves above doing manual labor—while minding your own business, not being troublesome to others, and living at peace with everyone. 12 Live this way so you won't

---

A 4:1 The last phrase, which literally is "as indeed you do walk," is not in some manuscripts.

be dependent on others for your physical needs and so your daily manner of life will earn the respect of non-believers who observe you. ❖ *Your lifestyle reflects on your Lord.* ➤

About the Return of Jesus

13 Now, brothers and sisters in the Lord, we want you to understand what the situation is with those believers who have died. We don't want you to mourn hopelessly for them—like unbelievers mourn over their loved ones because they have no expectation of a resurrection and being with them in eternal life. ❖ *These early believers expected Jesus' return very soon and some of them may have thought that those believers who died before he came back would miss out on the great events when he did so. In the following discussion, Paul seems to take the resurrection of believers who have died for granted, not placing any great emphasis on it, so it was not likely a major concern of the Thessalonian believers.* ➤ 14 We believe that Jesus died and came back to life again as a pattern. Therefore, God will cause those who have died believing in Jesus to return with him when he comes back.

15 The Lord Jesus himself taught his people what we are telling you now. When he returns, those of us believers who are still alive will not be the first to meet him—leaving those who have died to miss out on anything. Nor will we have any advantage over them. 16 In fact, this is what will happen. The Lord Jesus himself will come down from Heaven and will shout a command. ❖ *Possibly ordering the resurrection of those who have died.* ➤ The voice of an archangel will also be heard and an angel will blow God's trumpet call. *[Revelation 11:15]* ❖ *Possibly summoning the dead to life or announcing Jesus' return.* ➤ Those who have died believing in the Messiah will first be raised from death to life. 17 Then those believers who are still alive—together with those who were just resurrected—will be taken up A to meet the Lord in the sky among the clouds. And forever after we will never really be separated from him. 18 So continue to comfort and encourage each other with this knowledge.

5

1 Now, my brothers and sisters, as for when this will all happen I don't need to explain anything—2 because you already understand that the day the Lord returns will arrive as unexpectedly and unpredictably as a thief does some night. *[Matthew 24:42-44]* 3 While unbelievers are saying, "We are safe and at peace"—thinking everything is going well for them—then their world will suddenly be turned upside down and they will not escape God's judgment. It will come as abruptly and certainly as labor pains come on a woman about to deliver. *[Jeremiah 6:14; Ezekiel 13:10; 2 Thessalonians 1:9]* 4 But you, my brothers and sisters, have not been left in the dark about this—so the arrival of Judgment Day will not take you by surprise, like a thief does. ❖ *We may not know exactly when it will arrive, but it's arrival is expected and we are prepared for it. Judgment Day—a.k.a. the Day of the Lord—is the day when Jesus will return in glory to judge all humanity.* ➤ 5 For you are all people who live in the Light of God's revelatory truth and belong to his Kingdom of Light and righteousness—not Satan's kingdom of evil, hidden in darkness. ❖ *Those who live as people of the "day" live in a way that they will not be ashamed of when all their thoughts and actions are revealed. Those who belong to the "night" live lives that they will be ashamed of when their thoughts and actions are revealed at the judgment.* ➤ 6 So let's not be caught unaware of what's happening around us like someone sound asleep—for that is the way unbelievers live. But instead, be alert to spiritual realities and impending events in the spiritual realm and be in full control of our thoughts, words, and actions. *[Matthew 25:13; Mark 13:35-37]* ❖ *We remain alert by keeping close to the Lord in prayer and hearing from him.* ➤ 7 For it is those who are experiencing night that are sound asleep or who get drunk and lose control. ❖ *In the spiritual analogy, it's those who live in the darkness of Satan's kingdom that are unaware of the coming judgment—and so live shameful uncontrolled lives.* ➤ 8 But since we belong to the Kingdom of Light, let's be in full control of

---

A 4:17 In Greek, ἁρπαγησόμεθα (harpagēsometha) means "will be caught up." In the Latin Vulgate, this was translated as "rapturo" from which the term "rapture" is derived.

ourselves in all we do. This is accomplished by firmly trusting in Jesus for all we need, always demonstrating our love for our fellow believers, and continuing to hold strongly to the confidence and expectation that we will receive our full salvation when Jesus returns. Living this way protects us from Satan's attacks and from the pull of those remaining ingrained sin habits in us and physical urges that tempt us to sin. Living this way protects us—like armor protects a soldier. 9 We must live this way because God did not choose us to be his people so that we would suffer the consequences of his anger against sin—like unbelievers will. ❖ *It is implied that we could also experience these undesirable consequences if we choose to live in evil—as unbelievers do.* ➤ Rather, he chose us for the purpose of receiving all the blessings of salvation through our union with Lord Jesus the Messiah. 10 He died to save us so we can live with him forever—both those who are alive when he returns and those who have already died. 11 So continue to comfort and encourage each other and help each other grow strong in faith—just as you have been doing.

More on How Believers Should Live

12 Now, my brothers and sisters, we urge you to respect and appreciate your local spiritual leaders. For the Lord is the one who has placed them over you, and they work hard to instruct and admonish you in the way you should live. 13 Show them the greatest respect you are capable of—based in genuine love because of the important work they do for you. And all of you should live together in peace—without disputes.

14 Brothers and sisters in the Lord, we exhort you to admonish those who are lazy, undisciplined, or not doing what they should. Also encourage those who are discouraged or worried, help those who are weak in their faith and so are easily tempted or afraid of persecution. Always be patient with everyone. 15 Make sure that no one among you takes revenge or retaliates for evil done to them. Always make every effort to do what is kind and good for each other and for everyone else as well.

16 No matter what your circumstances are, always rejoice because of your union with the Messiah. 17 Make it your habit to be in constant communication with the Lord. ❖ *This may not seem possible at first, but we can learn to moment by moment be aware of the Lord's presence and of our dependence on him—turning to him for help in every decision and action and allowing him to live through us. [Galatians 2:20]* ➤ 18 No matter what your circumstances are, make it your habit to thank God in the midst of them. Thank him for causing them to work toward your ultimate good and for the fact that he is with you. Do these things ❖ *i.e., the commands in verses 16-18* ➤ during adversity—because this is what God wants you to learn to do in this life in your union with Messiah Jesus.

19 Don't try to stop the Holy Spirit from doing what he wants to do in your life and in the lives of others. 20 In particular, don't reject out of hand the messages that people claim they have directly from God. 21 But do examine them carefully in the light of God's word—as you should do with everything, not just prophecies—and if you judge something to be consistent with his word, accept it as from God. 22 But avoid anything tainted with evil—whether it's a message someone claims comes from God or anything else.

Closing Blessings

23 Now I pray that God—the maker and provider of shalom **A**—will purify you in every area of your being and bring you to complete consecration in his service. I pray that he will keep every part of you—your spirit, soul, and body—free of sin from now until the return of our Lord Jesus the Messiah. ❖ *Commentators disagree on whether or not spirit and soul are distinct parts of a person. Clearly, Paul was not intending to explicitly teach that in this verse, but this is the only verse in the New Testament that uses all three terms together. Commentators agree his emphasis was on the complete person. On the other hand, since Paul mentions them separately, it's quite likely that he understood them to*

A 5:23 Shalom means: peace, calmness, success, comfort, contentment, safety, health, wholeness, prosperity, integrity, well-being, and good relationships with God and people.

be distinct. ➤ ²⁴ Since it was God himself who called you to be completely pure and holy, he will accomplish this in you—for he always keeps his promises.

²⁵ Brothers and sisters in the Lord, we need you to pray for us too.

²⁶ Greet each other on our behalf with holy affection—as you would members of your own family. ²⁷ I command you to solemnly promise the Lord Jesus that you will have this letter read to all the believers there.

²⁸ And I pray that our Lord Jesus the Messiah will always be with you and continue to look upon you with great favor—far beyond anything you can deserve.

Paul's Second Letter
to Jesus' Followers in Thessalonica

The Apostle Paul wrote this letter to the believers in the city of Thessalonica. See the introduction to his first letter to the Thessalonians for more details. He wrote this second letter some months after the first because the person who took the first letter returned and reported to Paul some news about the Thessalonians. He told Paul that they were standing firm in their faith even though they suffered persecution, but some people were teaching that the Messiah had already returned—taking people back to Heaven—and the Thessalonian believers had been left behind. As a result, some believers were refusing to work. So Paul wrote this letter to encourage them and to correct their understanding about the Messiah's return.

Outline:

Paul encourages them in the midst of their being persecuted. [chapter 1]
What must happen before the Messiah returns. [2:1-12]
More encouragement—from knowing that God chose them. [2:13-17]
An exhortation to work and how to deal with those who are lazy. [chapter 3]

1

Opening Greetings

¹ Greetings from Paul, Silas, and Timothy. We are writing to the assembly of believers in the city of Thessalonica who are united with God the Father and Lord Jesus the Messiah.

² We pray that God our Father and Lord Jesus the Messiah will continue to look upon you with great favor far beyond anything you can deserve—and grant you peace and well-being.

Prayer and Thanksgiving
for the Thessalonian Believers

³ Dear brothers and sisters in the Lord, it's not only appropriate for us to always thank God for you, but it's also our obligation—because he is causing your faith to grow and flourish, as well as the love you show to each other. ⁴ That's why we boast about you to other assemblies of believers—telling them about your patient endurance in faith and good works despite all the persecutions and hardships you are experiencing.

⁵ Your patient endurance and faithfulness in the midst of persecution is evidence that God is making you worthy of his Kingdom—which also benefits from your faithfulness in spreading his message. It also shows that when he judges humanity, he will be fair and righteous in judging you worthy. For it is he who has made you worthy. ❖ *It's somewhat difficult to follow Paul's reasoning in this verse and there are many different views on what he meant.* ➤ ⁶ And since God is just, he will certainly punish those who persecute you because of your obedience to him; ⁷ and he will also eventually give both you and us complete relief from all suffering forever. But this won't happen until God openly reveals Jesus the Messiah as Lord when he returns from Heaven. He will come accompanied by his angels—through whom he will exercise his power. He will be surrounded by brilliant blazing fire—as a symbol of God's presence, his holiness, glory, and impending judgment. ⁸ He will punish all those who reject God, who refuse to accept the message about our Lord Jesus, and who refuse to submit to him in obedience. ⁹ Their punishment will be complete and eternal separation from the presence of the Lord—who is the source of all good—as well as separation from all the benefits of his loving character which are manifested by his power—some of which they've experienced in this world. Instead, they will experience an eternal existence of ruin—totally devoid

of all that's worthwhile. ❖ *This is what is meant by being "destroyed" in Hell. It's not a destruction in the sense of "ceasing to exist," but an eternal existence of ruin—devoid of all good and pleasure.* ➤ 10 This judgment will happen on the day he returns to be honored and praised for what he has done for the people he has made holy. He is making them like himself, and he will be marveled at by all who believe in the Messiah. You will be among them because you believed the message we brought you. ❖ *The phrase "to be honored and praised for what he has done for the people he has made holy" in the Greek is, literally, "to be glorified in his saints." Other possible interpretations of "in his saints" are 1) by his holy people, or 2) among his holy people.* ➤

11 With these things in mind, we pray for you constantly that you will live your lives in obedience to him. We pray that on Judgment Day, God will consider you as having responded to his mercy in a manner that is worthy of people whom he has called to be his own. ❖ *Commentators are divided on what Paul meant in the literal text by "count you worthy of his calling"—which is rendered above as "consider you as having responded to his mercy in a manner that is worthy of people he has called to be his own." A minority think he meant "make you worthy of his calling."* ➤ We also pray that his power in you will enable you to accomplish all the good things that you want to do and that your faith prompts you to do. 12 For it is our desire that our Lord Jesus the Messiah be honored and praised for having caused his character to be manifest in and through you—and that you will share in his honor through your union with him. We expect all this to happen because our God and Lord Jesus the Messiah will greatly favor you far beyond what you can possibly deserve—and will bring it about.

2

The Man of Lawlessness Must Appear Before Jesus Returns

1 Now, brothers and sisters, we want to talk to you about the return of our Lord Jesus and the gathering together of all believers to meet him. 2 Don't be confused or disturbed if you hear that the Lord Jesus has already returned—even if the source was a prophecy or a vision or a letter or message supposedly from us. You won't need anyone to tell you it has happened because you will have experienced it. 3 Don't allow people to deceive you, for he will not return until the prophesied great rebellion against God actually happens *[1 Timothy 4:1; 2 Peter 3:3; Jude 18]* and the Man of Lawlessness **A**—who is doomed to eternal destruction in Hell—comes to prominence and power. ❖ *Elsewhere, this "man of lawlessness" is called the "Anti-messiah" [1 John 2:18, 22] and "the beast" (though in this interpretation he is called the "False Messiah"). [Revelation 11:7; 13:1-18; 14:9-11; 15:2; 16:2, 10, 13; 17:3-17; 19:19-20; 20:4, 10]* ➤ 4 He will prohibit people from worshipping Jesus, Yahweh, or any other god and will sit in God's Temple in Jerusalem—exalting himself as the only supreme deity that all humanity must submit to in worship. ❖ *Commentators are not agreed on what Paul referred to by "God's Temple." One common view is that Jews in Israel will rebuild the Temple in Jerusalem before these events happen.* ➤

5 You should remember that I often told you all about this when I was with you—and you accepted it at that time. 6 You yourselves know what **B** restrains him from coming until the time God has appointed for it to happen. ❖ *There are many speculations about what this restraint is—beyond God himself who is in ultimate control. We don't know for sure what Paul may have taught them. Some—who say that believers will be taken to Heaven in the "Rapture" (see the footnote at 1 Thessalonians 4:17) before the Tribulation [Revelation 7:14]—say that the Holy Spirit in the body of believers in this world is what restrains the Man of Lawlessness, and when the Rapture happens, that restraint will be removed.* ➤ 7 By that I mean the spiritual power of lawlessness that causes people to reject God is already secretly working behind the scenes—and it will remain under cover until that which is restraining the Man of Lawlessness is removed. 8 Then the Man of Lawlessness will come to prominence and power. But the

---

A 2:3 Some manuscripts say "man of sin."

B 2:6 The Greek word here, tò (to), indicates "something" is doing the restraining, but gives no clue as to what. In verse 7, the restrainer is referred to by a masculine determiner which some commentators interpret to refer to a person.

Lord Jesus **A** will destroy his power simply by returning—and will do away with him by a simple command. 9 The Man of Lawlessness will rise to prominence—displaying all kinds of miraculous signs and wonders that will be accomplished by Satan's power, not God's. 10 He will use every kind of deception to delude those who are on their way to Hell, that is, those who will perish eternally because they refuse to accept the true message about Jesus and so be saved. 11 And since they reject Jesus, God will allow them to fall under a strong delusion so they will believe the lies and miracles of the Man of Lawlessness. ❖ *God often punishes people by giving them over fully to the sin they have already chosen and to the consequences of it—rather than violating their wills to bring them out of their sin and rebellion.* ➤ 12 His purpose is for it to be clearly seen that all who refused to believe the truth of his message—but instead, consciously enjoyed doing evil—have been righteously condemned.

An Encouragement to Believers

13 My dear brothers and sisters whom the Lord Jesus loves, it is fitting that we always thank God for you because he chose you from the very beginning **B** of his plan to be among those he saves. He saves you through your trust in the truth that he has revealed to you—and by the work of the Holy Spirit who transformed you into his holy people. 14 He called you to be saved through our proclamation of the message of the Good News—and his purpose is that you would share the glorious character and honor of our Lord Jesus the Messiah in your union with him. 15 So then, brothers and sisters, continue to firmly trust in the Lord and to believe all the things we have taught you—whether in person or by letter.

16 We pray that our Lord Jesus the Messiah and God our Father—who have already loved and favored us by giving us the comfort and expectation of eternal life—17 will spiritually encourage and strengthen

you to continue to accomplish good in everything you say and do.

3

Instructions

1 Finally, brothers and sisters, pray for us and our work that the message about the Lord will continue to spread quickly and be received and obeyed elsewhere—just as it was among you. 2 Also pray that God will save us from the harm intended by perverse and evil people—since not everyone accepts our message and there are many who oppose it.

3 But our Lord Jesus is faithful to keep his promises, so he will strengthen your faith and protect you such that Satan can't harm your faith. *[1 John 5:18]* ❖ *There is no blanket promise of protection from suffering or physical harm in this life. On the contrary, we are promised we will experience such. [Mark 10:29-30; Philippians 1:29] The promise of protection is for our spiritual lives and faith.* ➤ 4 We are confident **C** that the Lord is enabling you and will continue to enable you to obey all the instructions we gave you before, and also those that we've given you in this letter. 5 We pray that the Lord Jesus will enable you to understand how much God loves you and how to persevere under persecution—just as he did.

An Exhortation for Those Who Are Lazy

6 By the authority given to us as apostles of our Lord Jesus the Messiah, we command you to not associate or socialize with any person who professes to be a follower of Jesus yet refuses to work ❖ *"refuses to work" in the Greek is ἀτάκτως περιπατοῦντος (ataktōs peripatountos), which is literally, "walking/living idly/lazily," and it often means "rebellious against authority"—but the meaning "being idle" or "refusing to work" seems to fit the context of verses 6-12.* ➤ or who does not live in obedience to the instructions you received from us about how all believers are to live.

A 2:8 Some manuscripts don't have "Jesus" here.

B 2:13 Some manuscripts have "as his first fruits" instead of "in the beginning." These two phrases differ by one letter in Greek.

C 3:4 Literally, "we have confidence in the Lord," which could alternatively mean, "the Lord has given us confidence that...," or, "we are confident that because you are united to the Lord..."

[1 Corinthians 5:11-13] 7 While we were with you, you saw us model how believers ought to live. We were never lazy and dependent on others. 8 We paid for our own food, instead of requiring you to support us. We worked hard—days and even nights—to earn money so we would not be a financial burden on any of you. 9 We had the right to expect you to support us for teaching you, *[Matthew 10:10; Luke 10:7; 1 Corinthians 9:1-12; Galatians 6:6; 1 Timothy 5:18]* but we didn't exercise that right and chose, instead, to live as examples for you to follow. 10 Even when we were with you, we taught you this rule: If able-bodied people refuse to do useful work, then others should not feed them.

11 We've heard that there are some among you who are idle. They are not busy working, but are busybodies—interfering in what's none of their business. 12 Those of you who are guilty of this, we command you with the authority we have from Lord Jesus the Messiah—and we also plead with you—to quietly and properly work to earn your own living and to support those you are responsible for.

13 But as for the rest of you brothers and sisters, don't allow yourselves to become discouraged or to think that there's no reason to continue doing what is right in God's sight. 14 If anyone refuses to obey our instruction to work in this letter, take note of who they are and do not associate with them or socialize with them—so they might become ashamed and repent. 15 Don't be overly harsh or treat them as enemies, but admonish them as you would a brother or sister in your family—hoping they will reform.

Closing Blessings

16 Now, I pray that the Lord who gives shalom to his people will cause you to experience his shalom A in every circumstance. And I pray that you will all experience the Lord's presence with you and his support at all times.

17 I, Paul, am writing these final words of greeting with my own hand—which I do in all my letters so you can know it's from me. ❖ *Paul always dictated his letters to a scribe (which commentators call an "amanuensis") and signed it near the end. This was a common practice in that time.* ➤

18 I pray that our Lord Jesus the Messiah will continue to look upon you all with great favor far—beyond anything you can deserve.

A 3:16 Shalom means: peace, calmness, success, comfort, contentment, safety, health, wholeness, prosperity, integrity, well-being, and good relationships with God and people.

Paul's First Letter to Timothy

The Apostle Paul wrote this letter to his colleague Timothy—who was like a son to him. Timothy was representing Paul in Ephesus in Asia Province.

At the end of the book of Acts, Paul is in prison in Rome. Some scholars think he was released from prison and was free for a few years to continue his work. One extra-biblical source says that he did reach Spain as he had planned. In AD 64, a fire destroyed a large section of Rome and the Emperor Nero blamed the followers of Jesus. Sometime in AD 65–67, Paul was again imprisoned in Rome and later executed. This letter is thought to have been written between Paul's two imprisonments—sometime in the period AD 62–63.

Timothy had traveled extensively with Paul prior to this and was a recognized leader in his own right. [Acts 16:1-3; 17:14-15; 18:5; 19:22; 20:4-5; Romans 16:21; 1 Corinthians 4:17; 16:10; 2 Corinthians 1:1, 19; Philippians 1:1; 2:19-23; Colossians 1:1; 1 Thessalonians 1:1; 3:1-2, 6; 2 Thessalonians 1:1; Philemon 1:1; Hebrews 13:23] *At the very least, he was an apostolic representative of Paul. Some think he may have been called an apostle too.* [1 Thessalonians 2:6-7] *He had oversight over many assemblies and had the authority to appoint leaders in them.*

In this letter—as in Paul's Second letter to Timothy and his letter to Titus—he gives instructions for those who lead God's people.

Outline:

1

Opening Greetings

¹ I, Paul, am an apostle of Messiah Jesus because I was commanded to do this work by God who saves us, and by Jesus who gives us confidence we will see that salvation. ² I'm writing to Timothy—my spiritual son whom I love. I pray that God the Father and Messiah Jesus our Lord will show you great favor and mercy far beyond anything you can deserve—and will bless you with peace and well-being.

Stop People from Teaching False Doctrine

³ Timothy, just as I urged you when I was leaving for Macedonia Province, I'm asking you again to remain at Ephesus— representing me there so you can stop the men who are teaching things that do not conform to truth. ⁴ Stop them from continuing to teach speculations that are derived from long complex genealogical myths. Show them and their listeners that such teachings only produce controversies and divisions. They do nothing that would further God's purposes among his people— such as encouraging them to trust him and his word in all things.

⁵ For the goal of all proper instruction in the faith is to lead God's people to unselfishly love and help each other— based on the pure motive of wanting to do what is right and genuinely wanting to please the Lord. ⁶ But those teachers of false doctrine have wandered away from this goal and these motives. They've become

enamored with their own futile arguments. [7] They want to be respected as experts in the Teachings of Moses, but they don't have a proper understanding of the things they so boldly talk about—nor do they see the false implications of what they say. [8] We know that God's Torah is good and worth teaching if it's used the way God intended it to be used. [9] But it was not given for the purpose of teaching myths and speculations to people who already love and obey God. Rather, it was given to such people as these: those who rebel against God and his ways, those who live as if he doesn't exist and so continually indulge in sin, those who hold nothing as sacred or honorable, those who murder or even kill their own parents, [10] those who live in sexual immorality, those who engage in homosexual activity, and those who are slave traders, liars, and perjurers. In summary, it's for all those who oppose God's truth about how we are to live—[11] which is contained in the message of the Good News about the gracious loving character of God, who is worthy of all praise. And this is the message God has commissioned me to proclaim.

God's Mercy and Kindness
Is Offered to Even the Worst Sinners

[12] I'm very thankful to Messiah Jesus—our Lord—because he has always given me the ability to proclaim the message of the Good News and has enabled me to faithfully do his work. He appointed me to serve him in this ministry and treated me as if I were already faithful to him—[13] even though I had spoken evil of Jesus, saying he wasn't the Messiah, and I had cruelly and violently persecuted his people. He didn't punish me as I deserved, but was merciful to me because I didn't know who Jesus really was. I thought I was serving God by opposing an imposter. [14] Our Lord was extremely kind and greatly favored me by uniting me with Messiah Jesus—enabling me to believe in him, and filling me with a love for him, and giving me his love for all people. [15] Believers are commonly heard to express this truth, "Messiah Jesus came into this world to save sinners from the fate of damnation in Hell."

This summary statement is entirely true and everyone should trust it without doubting. For I am one of the foremost examples of a sinner who was completely worthy of damnation—yet who has been forgiven and saved. [16] Messiah Jesus did this for me for the express purpose of making me a clear example to all people of how he is willing to show extreme patience and mercy to even the very worst of sinners—so they can realize he is willing to forgive them no matter how evil they have been, and then turn to him with trust and submission and receive eternal life. [17] So let us forever praise and honor the unseen King who has always existed, will never die, and is the only true God! Yes, may it be so!

Spiritual Warfare and Assembly Discipline

[18] Timothy, my dear son in the Lord, when you were commissioned for ministry, others prophesied over you—telling you what God was calling you to do for him. In line with that calling, I'm exhorting you to continue to wage spiritual warfare against the Lord's enemies in order to advance his Kingdom—no matter how difficult it gets. ✶ *This warfare is mostly done through prayer and by proclaiming and teaching the truth—motivated by love.* ➤ [19] As you do this, continue to trust in Jesus and do what you know is right. Some people—who have not listened to their consciences—chose to do what they know is wrong and have ended up destroying their faith. ❖ *People living in deliberate sin without repentance will not be forgiven. This doesn't mean that each sin has to be individually confessed and repented of—although that is good when possible—but there has to be an attitude of repentance. [Hebrews 6:4-8; 10:26-31] As long as there is a desire or willingness to repent, the relationship can be restored. If all desire for repentance has left, so has the Holy Spirit. [Matthew 12:32; Mark 3:28 29; Luke 12:10]* ➤ [20] Two such people there in Ephesus are Hymenaeus and Alexander. *[2 Timothy 2:18; 4:14-15]* I have expelled them from fellowship with members of the assembly, removed the Lord's protection over their lives, and handed them over to Satan's power so they might realize that God doesn't approve of their teaching and that it dishonors him. *[1 Corinthians 5:5, 13; 2 Thessalonians 3:14]* ❖ *The goal of*

this severe treatment was so they might come to their senses and repent. Paul is implying that Timothy might have to resort to similar measures with others who do not respond to correction. ➤

2

Instructions About Worship

¹ So in view of all these things I've written, it is most important that you urge the believers under your care to pray for all people—thanking God for what he has done, asking him to meet the urgent needs of believers, and interceding on behalf of unbelievers for their needs—especially for their salvation. ² Also urge them to pray for kings and everyone in authority that the Lord would work through them to rule in such a way that we believers may live quiet peaceful lives without persecution—so we can freely worship him and do what he wants us to do. ³ It's good to pray like this because it pleases God who saves us. ⁴ It's his desire that everyone would come to know and believe his message of truth and be saved. ❖ *This does not say that everyone will be saved—only that God desires it to be so. This implies that on some level people have the ability to choose—if only after the Holy Spirit enables them to do so—and that he respects the right of people to reject him.* ➤ ⁵ We know this is true, for we know there is only one God who is over everyone—both Jews and Gentiles—and there is also only one mediator between God and humanity who can bring them together—the man Jesus who is the Messiah. ⁶ He willingly offered his life as a sacrificial substitute to suffer the penalty of humanity's sins—which was eternal death—so they would not have to suffer it themselves. This message about his death in our place is the one that God has given us to proclaim right now. ⁷ It was for this very purpose that God appointed me to be his apostle—to proclaim his message and to teach Gentiles about truth and what it means to believe and obey him. I'm telling the truth about my calling as an apostle. I'm not lying, as some have said about me.

⁸ Therefore, in every assembly of believers, when you meet together I want you to pray. When the men lift their hands in prayer, I want them all to be doing so as people who are fully dedicated to God—who are free from anger and not involved in quarrels or disputes. ❖ *Paul's "wants" in this context carry the weight of apostolic commands.* ➤ ⁹ Women should be modestly and decently dressed—not in such a way as to offend, distract, or sexually tempt others. They should also not wear elaborate hairstyles, expensive clothes, or expensive jewelry like those who are immoral do. ❖ *This command needs to be understood in the context. Women who did these things were outwardly behaving like prostitutes and it was not considered modest or acceptable. Yet there are other reasons behind the command too, and today, many American women believers should reexamine themselves in light of these apostolic instructions. The principle of not being offensive and not imitating the appearance of those who are worldly or immoral is applicable to any believer—with regard to any aspect of one's outward appearance.* ➤ ¹⁰ Instead, they should spend their time and money helping others—which is what God wants women to do who claim to submit to him in worship.

¹¹ When a man is formally teaching the Scriptures to other men, women should also be allowed to learn in peace along with the men—as long as they are submissive and respectful. ❖ *This was actually a radical permission in that culture, where women generally were not allowed to study the Scriptures.* ➤ ¹² But I do not allow a woman ❖ *Or: wife* ➤ to mentor a man ❖ *Or: husband* ➤ in spiritual instruction, or to exercise spiritual authority over him. Instead, she must have a quiet and submissive demeanor. ❖ *An alternate interpretation of this verse would be: "But I do not allow women to mentor men in spiritual instruction, or to exercise spiritual authority over them. In public meetings, they are to remain quiet during the teaching." The literal text has "woman" and "man" in the singular. These words in Greek are* γυνή *(gunē)—which means either "woman" or "wife" depending on context, and* ἀνήρ *(anēr)—which means either "man" or "husband" depending on context. The traditional interpretation is that Paul was prohibiting women from teaching and having authority over men—which by implication bars women from holding the office of a pastor. An alternate possible interpretation is that while Paul was giving women (literally: a woman) permission to receive instruction, he did not allow a wife to then presume to instruct her husband. If you want to follow the broader traditional interpretation, it should be understood in the context of other commands and examples in Scripture. In a private meeting,*

Priscilla—along with her husband Aquila—taught Apollos. [Acts 18:26] Paul allowed women to prophesy or pray in public meetings. [1 Corinthians 11:5] Believers—whether men or women, both in assembly meetings and outside such meetings—are to encourage each other. [1 Corinthians 14:26-39; Colossians 3:16; Hebrews 3:13; 10:24; 1 Peter 3:15] Some commentators point out that this may have been a command specific to the Ephesian situation where there were false teachers and women were not generally well trained in the Scriptures. [e.g. 2 Timothy 3:6] Also, Romans 16:1-4 and Philippians 4:2-3 suggest that in other situations—where the women were well instructed—he may have allowed them greater freedom to minister. On the other hand, it's possible that their ministry was restricted to teaching other women. There are many woman preachers of the Word today who appear to be bearing good fruit for the Kingdom. A criterion for judging what is of God and what is not was given by Jesus. We can know by the results of their ministry. [Matthew 7:15-20; 12:33; Luke 6:43-45] When discussing this issue, let's keep in mind the commands to not criticize or condemn the Lord's workers. [Matthew 7:1-5; Luke 6:37; Romans 2:1; 14:4-13; 1 Corinthians 4:3-5] ➤ 13 My basis for this is that God created Adam first and then Eve. ❖ Birth order (or in this case—creation order) implied relative status in the biblical cultures. Adam and Eve are also considered "types" of all men and women. Paul assumes that some characteristics of Adam are true of all men and some characteristics of Eve are true of all women. By his reasoning, since Adam had preeminence in the order of creation, all men should have preeminence over women. In addition, Eve was created out of Adam in order to be a helper to him. Hence men are considered the source of woman and the role of women is to help men. These ideas go against modern American cultural values to the point of being offensive to many. But consider that every culture has blind spots and wrong values. If we are humble, we will have to admit that our cultural values are not perfect nor in perfect alignment with what the Scriptures teach is God's will in many areas. Humility will lead us to submit to God's wisdom and will—even though it seems to go against what we would consider common sense or our idea of fairness and justice. Also consider that pretty much every human culture throughout history has assumed this biblical value of women being subordinate to men—except for the past few decades in North American and European cultures. Our cultural values in this area are clearly a historical aberration. So for most cultures throughout history, for women to be allowed to have authority over men would violate cultural norms and be a poor witness. But consider this restriction in the light of biblical examples of exceptions and also the idea that if men voluntarily allow women certain roles, then by filling those roles they are not violating the idea of being submissive to men. There is no argument that woman leadership and teachers are generally acceptable to our culture. The difficult question is if God himself still desires women to be prohibited from these roles today in a culture that would welcome them. Many believers take both sides of this issue. Whichever view we take, we must follow what we believe is God's will according to the Scriptures, and we must not judge and condemn those who take the opposite view—even if we think they are wrong. For these are also principles clearly taught in the Scriptures. God is the one who will judge his people. We are not allowed to do so. ➤ 14 Furthermore, it was the woman Eve who was deceived by Satan and first disobeyed God's command. Adam was not the one deceived. ❖ Since Paul makes this statement, we have to accept it as true. Adam was not deceived—at least not directly by Satan—but he was led astray by his wife, probably with full knowledge of what he was doing. Thus Paul is implying that women are more easily deceived by false teaching, and men are more easily led astray by women. Therefore, women should not have positions of spiritual authority over men. ➤ 15 But even though Eve—the representative woman—was the first human to sin, women will still be saved while they fulfill the roles that women commonly fulfill—such as childbearing, etc.—if they continue to have faith in the Messiah, which will lead them to live lives characterized by love and dedication to God—with decency and moderation. ❖ Note this is exactly the same way that men will be saved while they fulfill the roles men commonly fulfill, if they continue to have faith in the Messiah—which will lead them to live lives characterized by love and dedication to God, with decency and moderation. This is a difficult verse that has been interpreted several ways. The first choice is whether or not Paul is talking about physical preservation through the process of childbearing so they won't die, or about spiritual salvation. This choice is not easy to make. The choice of physical salvation is attractive because it doesn't pose any theological or cultural difficulties. It does pose a practical one, though, that many believing women of apparently strong faith—who have been loving and lived holy lives—have suffered severely in childbirth and also died. If you take the spiritual salvation interpretation, then you have to choose between saying it refers to salvation because of the birth of the Messiah (knowing there is nowhere else in the Scriptures where "salvation through his birth" is referred to), or that it refers to childbearing in general. There are still other interpretations offered. The one given above assumes that "childbirth" is a figure of speech called "metonymy"—where "childbirth" is a specific example *that represents all the roles women typically fill in life. The example given of childbirth does not imply that women without children will not be saved. If this interpretation is correct, Paul was saying that women should be content to fill the common roles allotted to them in this life and not try to assume roles assigned to men. Remember that Paul was writing to a first-century culture—not our own. It is possible that he viewed some roles as culturally defined, and in our culture where roles assigned to women are much broader, perhaps he would have thought that acceptable—even the role of pastor. But despite our uncertainty about Paul's intended meaning, no commentators believe he was saying that women had to bear children in order to be saved.* ➤

3

Qualifications
for Assembly Leaders and Deacons

1 Believers commonly say that if a man wants to become an assembly leader, A he desires a worthwhile role—and this is certainly true. *[Titus 1:5-9]* 2 But an assembly leader needs to live in such a way that no one can truthfully criticize him for doing wrong. He must be totally faithful to his one wife. ❖ *Other interpretations: 1) he may only have one wife at a time (This interpretation is unlikely, as polygamy was uncommon.), 2) he may have only one wife his entire life, i.e., he may not remarry if she dies or divorces him, 3) he must be married. (This view is held by the Eastern Orthodox church.) The Roman Catholic church requires him to be unmarried.* ➤ He must be in full control of himself, not a slave to his feelings, be sensible and moderate in his behavior, respected by others, hospitable and generous, able to teach God's word accurately, 3 not someone who gets drunk, gentle with people, not violent or argumentative, and not someone who is greedy or loves money. 4 He must lead his own family and household well—such that all its members, especially his children, respect, love, and obey him

without coercion, and behave in a way that others respect. 5 For if a man does not know how to properly lead his own family and household so that they love, respect, and willingly obey him, why would you expect him to be the kind of leader that others in the assembly would love, respect, and willingly follow? 6 He must also not be a recent convert to the faith—before he has a chance to mature in his understanding and ways; otherwise he might become proud and conceited and come under God's judgment for pride—just as Satan did. *[James 4:6; 1 Peter 5:5]* 7 He must also have a good reputation among unbelievers in the community so they won't start slandering him. For if that happens, he will be totally ineffective as a witness among them.

8 Those who would be deacons should have similar qualifications. ❖ *A deacon was someone responsible for the physical needs of the members of the assembly. The first deacons—in Acts 6:1-6—had the responsibility of taking care of the financial aspects of the assembly's ministry. They were responsible and trusted leaders who exhibited spiritual maturity, but were not responsible for the spiritual lives of assembly members as the assembly leaders were. Beyond this, we don't know what variety of duties they may have had.* ➤ They must be men of good character and spiritual maturity who are well respected. They must be honest and mean what they say, not people who get drunk, not greedy, and unwilling to seek money by dishonest or disreputable means. 9 They must firmly believe and obey the teachings of our faith—without doubts. 10 Don't appoint deacons quickly. Test them first by giving them responsibilities and observe how they perform them for a time. Only if their character, conduct, and the way they fulfill their responsibilities are beyond reproach, should they be appointed to the position of deacon. 11 Women who are to be

---

A 3:1 ἐπισκοπή (episkopē) means "overseer." This refers to an office that originated in Greek culture and was used to refer to city officials and others in supervisory roles. It is sometimes translated "bishop," but this is misleading because the administrative role of a bishop as we know it today did not exist until the second century AD. During the period when Paul was writing, there were assembly leaders and apostles and nothing in between—unless you count Timothy and Titus and others like them as apostolic

representatives, rather than apostles. (There was also the office of deacon.) Another word used for this same office is πρεσβύτερος (presbuteros)—which means "elder." This refers to an office that originated in Jewish culture and was used for the leaders of synagogues. That these two terms mean the exact same thing in the context of assemblies of believers is seen in Titus 1:5 and 7. In verse 5, Paul calls them "elders," but in verse 7 he refers to them as "overseers."

deacons ❖ *or: the wives of deacons* ➤ must also have good character, be spiritually mature, and well respected. ❖ *Literally: γυνή (gunē)— means either "woman" or "wife" depending on context. It isn't clear if Paul meant the wives of deacons or if he meant women who are deacons. Jewish culture would not allow women to hold such a position, but Romans 16:1 apparently refers to a Gentile woman who did. It's not clear if she would have been equal to a male deacon or only had responsibilities to minister to other women. Another possibility is that this was a position of a female assistant to deacons. Even if it means "wives," it is likely that such wives would also have had some ministry role with their husbands. The arguments on both sides are strong. E.g., there are no requirements given for the wife of an assembly leader, so why would he give requirements for the wife of a deacon? This would imply that he was talking about women holding the position or office of a deacon. By the early second century (AD 112), it's clear that there was a recognized position of "deaconess" among assemblies of believers. This position may not have been common during this period (the AD 60s), but became more common in the following decades.* ➤ They must not gossip or speak maliciously about others. They must be self-controlled, sensible, and moderate in their behavior, and honest and trustworthy in all things. 12 A deacon must be totally faithful to his one wife and clearly lead his children, family, and household well so that everyone is a good example. 13 Those who serve well as deacons will gain recognition and a good reputation. ❖ *Literally: gain "a step," which could mean 1) a good standing in the community, 2) a good standing before God, or 3) promotion to a higher position, possibly to an assembly leader.* ➤ As a result they will be able to speak about their faith in Messiah Jesus with great confidence. ❖ *It might be implied that people will also be more open to listening to them, so they can be more effective for the kingdom.* ➤

Preserve the Core Truths of Our Faith Against False Teaching

14 Even though I hope to return to Ephesus soon, I'm writing these instructions 15 just in case I'm delayed. That way, you will know what to teach about how God wants his people to behave toward each other—since they are his family and part of the larger assembly of all believers who belong to the Living God. ❖ *The expression "living God" sometimes contrasts him with lifeless idols*

and also emphasizes that he is active among his people and the world. ➤ The community of believers vitally support the witness of the truth of God's message by their behavior. If their lives conform to the message they proclaim, it is credible and will accomplish its purpose. If their lives do not conform to the message, it will not be believed. Also, it is the responsibility of all God's people to guarantee that the message proclaimed in the assemblies and by their recognized teachers and leaders, does not contain false claims or teachings. For if we allow the message to be corrupted, it will not accomplish God's purposes. 16 The core of truth in the message that God has revealed to us about the Messiah—which causes us to revere him and which we must preserve uncorrupted—is what we all acknowledge as being true when we sing this hymn: ❖ *or say this creed* ➤

1. He was initially revealed to us as a human being.

2. The Holy Spirit proved he was God's Son—as he said he was—by raising him from death. *[Romans 1:3-4]*

3. He was seen by the angels after his resurrection. *[Matthew 20:2-7, Luke 24:22-23; John 20:11-13; Acts 1:10-11]* ❖ *ὁράω (horaō) – usually translated as "was seen," has many meanings and has to be defined by context, such as to "see, visit, pay attention to, understand, experience, learn about, recognize, take care, cause to happen," etc. Other interpretations of this line are: 1) He was served and cared for by angels while on earth. 2) Angels understood more about him as they watched his life and ministry. The interpretation rendered was chosen because in three other places a similar sequence is expressed, [Philippians 2:9-11; Colossians 2:15; Hebrews 1:6] and it corresponds to these better, as well as retaining a temporal sequence with adjacent lines.* ➤

4. He was taken up to Heaven and restored to his full eternal glory *[John 17:5]* ❖ *This is really line six and has been reordered to this position to put it in chronological order. Commentators offer reasons why it was ordered differently that are too long to explain here.* ➤

5. The message about him was proclaimed to all the peoples of the world.

6. And everywhere he has been proclaimed, people have believed in him.

4

1 We are to guard the truth because the Holy Spirit is frequently telling us through his prophets that during these last days—between Jesus' ascension and his return—some who have previously professed to be believers will be deceived and embrace false teachings that are inspired by demons, abandoning any belief they had in the truth. **2** They teach one thing for their own purposes, but don't believe it themselves. Their consciences are totally numb—so they are not bothered in the slightest by the lies they tell. In fact, there are false teachers like this already teaching their lies.

3 They forbid the people who listen to them to marry, or to have sexual relations, or to eat certain kinds of food—saying that these things defile them in God's sight. But God created ❖ *marriage, sex and* ➤ these foods so that all those who know and believe his message would thank him for them and enjoy them. **4** Everything God created is good, and we shouldn't reject something if we receive it as a gift from him and sincerely thank him for it. **5** For things such as marriage and food are declared good in the Scriptures—and they are set apart for his purposes when we thank him for them and ask him to bless them.

Instructions for Spiritual Leaders

6 Teach all these things to the believers there as a faithful servant of Messiah Jesus. As you teach others and you yourself obey the truths of the faith, you will be spiritually nourished by them. **7** But don't waste your time listening to or refuting false teachings that are myths, fables, and superstitious stories having nothing to do with knowing God. Focus on disciplining yourself to live the way God wants you to live. **8** You know the saying: "Training your body is helpful, but training yourself to do what God wants is better because it benefits you much more—both in this life and the next." **9** Well, that saying is a truth everyone should believe and live by. **10** We work hard, striving **A** to live according to that saying and teaching others to do so too. For we have placed our trust and hope in the Living God who has provided a means of salvation for all humanity—which actually saves only those who trust and submit to the Messiah. **11** So teach all these things to your people and tell them that the Lord expects them to obey them. **12** I will not be pleased if anyone looks down on you or ignores you just because you haven't yet reached 40! ❖ *He was probably in his 30s. That culture expected spiritual leaders to be older than Timothy was.* ➤ But you need to make an effort to set an example and standard in what you say and don't say by always doing what is right, by demonstrating love for others, **B** by always trusting God and never despairing, and by avoiding all sin and impurity. **13** Until I come and take over, I want you to spend most of your time reading the ❖ *Hebrew* ➤ Scriptures in assembly meetings—teaching them what they mean and how God wants them to respond, and exhorting them to obey him. **14** Be sure to actively use the spiritual gift that was imparted to you ❖ *at your ordination* ➤ when the group of assembly leaders laid their hands on you and prophesied how God was intending for you to minister with that gift. **15** Devote all your energy to doing these things so everyone who knows you will observe your progress as you mature spiritually, and then they will be more open to learning from you. **16** Continue to carefully evaluate how your behavior and teaching conform to God's word so you won't go astray. Continue to persevere in obedience and in teaching only the truth—despite persecution or hardships—because you know that God will save you and those who—as a result of listening to you—persevere in obedience. ❖ *Paul is not implying that persevering in obedience earns salvation, or that Timothy is not already saved. When he talks about a future salvation with*

A 4:10 A few manuscripts have "suffer reproach" instead of "strive." These words are very close in spelling and pronunciation in Greek, but the overwhelming textual evidence is that the original was "strive."

B 4:12 Some manuscripts add "in spirit" here, but the oldest and best ones lack this phrase.

regard to people who are already believers, he is referring to the completion of their salvation when they receive the fullness of their eternal inheritance in Heaven. We are saved because God chooses to favor us with salvation for trusting in Jesus as our Savior. But a result of that trust—if it is genuine—is obedience and perseverance in faith to the end of our lives. If we don't persevere, our faith was either not genuine (the Calvinist view) or we have abandoned our faith (the Arminian view) and we will not be saved. Persevering in obedience does not mean we obey perfectly, but that we want to obey and strive to obey—by depending on his enabling power and not our own ability—and repent when we fail. ➤

5

1 When you have to correct people, show them love and respect. Don't act toward an older man like you are his superior, but appeal to him as you would to your own father—and exhort younger men as if they were your brothers. 2 Act toward older women as if they were your mother, and toward the younger women as if they were your sisters—keeping your thoughts about them pure.

Instructions About Widows

3 Show proper respect to widows in the assembly—who have no relative to take care of them—by providing for their needs. 4 But if a widow has children, or grandchildren, or another close relative, those relatives need to put their faith into practice by taking care of their own family—including widows—as a way of repaying those who took care of them when they were small. For this is what God expects of his people and it pleases him. 5 The widows that the assembly as a whole should be taking care of are those who have no relatives and no means of supporting themselves, who are trusting God to take care of them through his people, and who frequently pray for his help—both day and night. 6 But if a widow only does what she wants without regard to God's will, she is spiritually dead and the assembly bears no responsibility to take care of her.

7 Pass on these instructions to the believers so no one will be able to criticize them for neglecting their duty toward widows who are their relatives. 8 Anyone who does

not provide for the needs of his relatives—and especially for close family like a widowed mother or grandmother—is demonstrating that his faith is not genuine. Even unbelievers take care of their relatives, so such a person is worse than an unbeliever. ❖ *They will be judged more harshly because they claim to be believers and have been taught God's will, yet behave worse than those who are ignorant of God's will.* ➤ 9 Only include a widow on the list of those that the assembly cares for if she is at least 60 years old and was faithful to her husband while he lived. ❖ *Younger women had a chance of remarrying and also would be expected to work to earn their living—assuming they were healthy. The following qualifications make it clear that the assembly should not feel obligated to take care of someone who had not clearly demonstrated that she was a true believer who had earned the respect of the assembly. These instructions would also motivate other women to live God-pleasing lives so they would not end up destitute. While in other places the Scriptures urge us to love all people, taking on the complete support of a person takes up a lot of resources. It would be impractical to expect an assembly to take care of anyone who claimed to be a believer—just so she could live off of other people's labor. Most of these believers were poor people or slaves who could barely earn enough to provide for their own families' needs. The principle is that supporting widows is the duty of family. For those widows who have no family and have proven they are committed believers, then the assembly is their family.* ➤ 10 She should have a reputation for doing good deeds like raising her children well, showing hospitality to traveling ministers, and humbly serving the needs of other believers—such as washing their feet, helping people in distress, always helping out and showing kindness wherever she could.

11 But don't put widows under 60 on that list, for those who are put on the list must take a pledge to never remarry and to serve the Messiah full time. But younger widows often will have a desire to marry again and are tempted to forget their commitment to the Messiah. 12 God would then have to discipline them for breaking their promise. 13 Another problem with younger widows who are supported by the assembly is that they are tempted to be lazy. Instead of working, they go from house to house visiting other women, gossiping, sticking their noses in other people's business, and saying things

better left unsaid. 14 That's why I counsel widows under 60 to remarry, to have children if they can, to take care of their husband and family, and so deprive Satan of obvious targets that he can prompt his people to slander. 15 I've learned this through experience—for some such young widows who have been supported have turned away from obeying the Lord and now do the things Satan likes his people to do. 16 This principle applies not only to men with widows as relatives, but to women who are believers that have one or more relatives who are widows. Such women are responsible to take care of their needs so the whole assembly is not burdened with the task. The assembly as a whole should only be responsible for those who have no living relative—male or female—who can take care of them.

Matters Concerning Assembly Leaders

17 Give proper recognition and honor to assembly leaders who do their job well—especially those who preach and teach God's word. You should do this by showing them respect and by helping them with their material needs. ❖ *If they spend a lot of time in these activities, they don't have time to earn their living by other means. The literal text says that we should give them double honor. Most commentators believe this means, 1) respect and 2) financial support. This is deduced from the context of the following verse. Some think it means double the financial support given to others.* ➤ 18 The Scriptures tell us, **"Don't prevent even an ox from benefiting from his work,"** *[Deuteronomy 25:4; 1 Corinthians 9:3-11]* and **"The one who works should be paid."** *[Leviticus 19:13; Deuteronomy 24:15; Matthew 10:10; Luke 10:7]*

19 It's very easy to make false accusations and ruin a reputation—and Satan loves to ruin people's effectiveness for the Lord. So don't believe anyone who accuses an assembly leader of doing wrong unless that accusation can be substantiated by two or three witnesses. ❖ *Anyone who makes such an accusation without the support of witnesses is guilty of slander and should be disciplined.* ➤ 20 If there are witnesses that a leader is guilty of sin, and if you have followed the proper procedure to confront him *[Matthew 18:15-17]* and he has not repented, then rebuke him publicly in an assembly meeting—urging him to repent so that others will see the consequences of sinning. 21 If a leader is guilty of sin and is unrepentant, you are to carry out this procedure with fairness—showing no partiality or favoritism, no matter who it is. I command you to do this and remind you that God and Messiah Jesus and the angels are all watching and will judge if you have done things properly.

22 When you are choosing someone to be an assembly leader, be sure he is a mature believer and proven leader before you lay hands on him to ordain him. For if he turns out to be a poor leader, he will have your endorsement and you will be partly responsible for the sins he does because you approved of him and put him in that position. Also be sure to keep yourself from sinning because you are an example to those under you. 23 But you don't have to be so strict that you don't drink wine. Since you have frequent stomach problems, it's best not to drink only water, but to drink some wine for medicinal purposes. ❖ *In that culture, people usually drank wine (diluted with four or more parts water to one-part wine) when they ate meat. Since assembly leaders were never to get drunk, Timothy may have set a high standard to avoid drunkenness—or even the temptation to drink too much—by totally abstaining. But wine was also considered to have helpful medicinal qualities, so Paul was exhorting him to not be so strict about drinking wine that he didn't take care of himself by drinking a little wine when it would help him. The prohibition in Scripture is always against drunkenness—never that drinking alcohol is forbidden—except for the vow of a Nazirite, which was usually taken for a specific period of time, [Numbers 6:1-4] and for priests while they served in the Tabernacle or Temple. [Leviticus 10:9] Drinking wine and other fermented drink—without getting drunk—was expressly allowed (distilled liquors had not yet been invented in biblical times). [Deuteronomy 14:26]* ➤ 24 The reason you should be careful about choosing leaders is that some people sin openly, and everyone, including you, will know about them before you examine them for their suitability to be leaders. But others sin secretly and their weaknesses are not seen right away. 25 On the other side of the coin, some good deeds people do are quite obvious, but some that people do are not—and may not be known right away—yet eventually they

will come to light. ❖ *There are some who might be qualified to lead, but their good deeds are not obvious—so if you don't observe them over time, you might miss out on some very good humble people.* ➤

6

Instructions for Slaves and Employees

1 All believers who are slaves must have the attitude—reflected in their thoughts, speech, and work—that their masters are worthy of their full respect—regardless of how they treat them. This is because the masters know their slaves are believers who have listened to our teaching, and the slaves' attitude toward their earthly master will affect how he regards our message and our God. Slaves must not be the cause of masters slandering the one true God or what we teach that people should believe and do. 2 If their master is a believer, they should respect and serve him all the more—not less—because he is a brother in the Lord whom they are commanded to love. ❖ *See the notes on slavery in Ephesians 6:18 and 1 Peter 2:18.* ➤

Timothy, teach all the believers to follow these principles. ❖ *From verse 5:3 to 6:2* ➤

Desiring Wealth Leads to Ruin

3 There are those who are teaching things about God and our Lord Jesus the Messiah that contradict or are incompatible with the truths that we apostles have been teaching. Their teachings don't help God's people live the way he wants them to live. 4 Such people are conceited, self-important, and think they know everything, but really have no understanding of spiritual truths. They have a twisted delight in controversies and debates over unimportant nuances of words in the Scriptures. The only fruit they produce among themselves and those who listen to them is jealousy and bitter rivalry with people who take different views—so they speak insults, make insinuations, and even openly slander others. 5 Their arguing is never ending and they have lost all ability to discern between right and wrong or even between truth and lies. They only see teaching about their "ways to please God" as a means to have

people look up to them and pay them for an easy living.

6 They mistakenly think that financial wealth produces happiness. But when we are content to obey God and submit to his will, we gain a great deal such as peace, joy, well-being, and wisdom, as well as the spiritual blessings and eternal rewards stored for us in Heaven. 7 The reason we should be content with what God gives us in this life is that we brought nothing into this world when we were born, and when we die we can't take anything with us into the next life. So why waste time and effort accumulating temporary material wealth that doesn't make us happy in this life, or help us in the next when, instead, we can be accumulating eternal spiritual wealth that we will receive when we go to Heaven? 8 If we have enough food and drink to keep us alive and healthy, and adequate clothing to keep us decently covered and warm, and shelter to protect us from the weather, we should be satisfied that we have all our material needs met in this life. 9 But those who desire riches more than they desire to obey God give in to temptation and get caught in the trap of always wanting more than they have—so they can't be content. They have foolish desires for things that are unwise, wrong, and sinful—and their pursuit of these desires lead them to moral, emotional, social, and spiritual ruin. They will end up in Hell. ❖ *The reader should understand that in the eyes of the people Paul was writing to, even a lower-middle-class American lifestyle would have been viewed as exceedingly wealthy. Examine yourself to see if you have fallen into the trap of not being content with the material wealth you already have—let alone the mere necessities mentioned in verse 8.* ➤ 10 A craving for money produces all kinds of evil effects in a person's life. Some believers have allowed such desires to lead them away from faith in God—resulting in lives filled with emotional pain and misery.

Final Instructions to Timothy

11 But you, Timothy, belong to God—so have a healthy fear of such desires for material wealth and do all you can to avoid falling into that deadly trap. Instead, expend

all your energies wanting what God wants you to want, doing what he wants you to do, trusting him, loving others, always being patient, kind, and gentle with them—and all the while enduring any persecution or difficulty that comes as a result of your obedience, without giving up. 12 Continue to struggle in the spiritual battle to trust God, obey his will, proclaim his message, and oppose false teaching—no matter how difficult it becomes or what the personal cost. For God called you to live in intimate relationship with him forever and ❖ or: when ➤ you accepted his invitation before many witnesses—promising that you would trust and obey him. So diligently seek to experience the reality of that relationship and develop it through prayer, meditating on his Word, allowing him to live his life through you, [Galatians 2:20] and following the leading of the Holy Spirit [Romans 8:1-17; Galatians 5:16, 25]—which will cause him to produce his character [2 Corinthians 3:17-18] and fruit in your life. [Galatians 5:22-23]

13 Now, I have an important command to give you, and I'm calling on God—the source of all life—and on Messiah Jesus— who told Pilate the truth about who he was even though it meant he had to suffer and die—to witness my command to you and to hold you accountable for obeying it. 14 Until our Lord Jesus the Messiah returns, you must obey the commands A of the message of the Good News such that no one can find fault with your faithfulness. ❖ Another interpretation: You must do all you can to guard and preserve the purity of the message of the Good News without corruption. ➤ 15 The Messiah's return will be at a time of God's own choosing. For God— who is worthy of all praise—is the only true self-existing ruler, the highest of all kings, and the most powerful of all lords. [Revelation 17:14; 19:16] 16 He alone has the power in himself to live forever. He is so pure, holy, and good that no sinner can approach him—and no sinner has ever seen him. [Exodus 33:20; John 6:46] May all created beings honor him— acknowledging and submitting to his rule forever! Yes, may it be so!

17 Command believers who are wealthy not to be proud or arrogant because of their wealth and power, and warn them not to trust in their material resources to provide them with security, safety, health, comfort, joy, or for any other purpose. Wealth and it's illusion of power can vanish overnight. They need to trust God to take care of them and help them in all things. He is the true source of all the good things that we have—and he generously provides them for us to enjoy. 18 Tell them that God wants them to use their wealth to do good. Let their good deeds be as plentiful as their money. God expects them to be willing to share generously with those in need. 19 By doing so, they are transforming their temporary earthly wealth into eternal treasures that they will receive in Heaven, and at the same time, they will start to experience the reality and present blessings of the eternal life they already have. ❖ Those who look to material wealth to bless and comfort them will fail to experience many of the spiritual blessings that God wants to give them in this life. ➤

20 Timothy, fulfill the responsibility that God has given you to teach his message— and keep it pure. Don't listen to people who talk about foolish things which don't honor God and contradict the truth. Don't argue or debate with them about their so-called "special knowledge"—for it will only serve to sidetrack you from the things God wants you to do, and it will be a temptation. 21 Some former believers embraced such false teachings and so-called "knowledge"— and in doing so they no longer believe or follow the message of the Good News.

I pray that God will favor all of you far more than you can possibly deserve.

A 6:14 The text literally says "keep the command," and there are many hypotheses about what Paul meant. The interpretation given is just one of many—yet in a general way it covers many of the more specific hypotheses postulated.

Paul's Second Letter to Timothy

See the introduction to Paul's first letter to Timothy for background. Paul wrote this second letter sometime in the period AD 65–67—during his second imprisonment in Rome while he was awaiting execution. All of his companions except Luke had left him.

Timothy was still working in Ephesus, and in this letter Paul urges him to continue serving the Lord—standing firm in his faith no matter what happens. He also requests that Timothy come to see him before he dies.

1

Opening Greetings

¹ I, Paul, was chosen by God to be an apostle of Messiah Jesus for the purpose of proclaiming God's promise of eternal life in union with Jesus for those who believe.

² I'm writing to Timothy—whom I love like a son. I pray that God the Father and Messiah Jesus our Lord will show you great favor and mercy far beyond anything you can deserve—and bless you with peace and well-being.

An Exhortation
to Be Faithful and Willing to Suffer

³ God—whom I learned to faithfully serve **A** in submissive worship with a clear conscience from the examples of my ancestors—hears my prayers for you every day and night as I thank him for you and for what he has done in your life. ⁴ I remember your tears for me when we last parted, and I long very much to see you again so I can be filled with joy.

⁵ I also remember your genuine faith in Jesus—which you learned from your grandmother Lois and your mother Eunice—and I'm sure that you still have that faith. ⁶ Because I'm4 sure of this, I exhort you to remember the spiritual gift that God gave you when I laid hands on you at your ordination—and to stir it to life again by exercising it. ❖ *Some commentators think the word ἀναζωπυρέω (anazōpureō)—"fan into flame"—doesn't imply that he has neglected the use of his gift, but that Paul was only encouraging him to keep using it with the same zeal he had been. The spiritual gift was given to help him in his appointed ministry, but what the precise nature of that gift was, we don't know.* ➤ ⁷ For God gave his people a Spirit of supernatural power, love for others, and self-discipline—not one of timidity and fear. ❖ *This verse and the next may imply that Timothy lacked boldness in his ministry.* ➤ ⁸ So don't be embarrassed to tell others about our Lord Jesus, and don't be embarrassed by your association with me since the reason I'm in prison is for serving him. Instead, depend on God's power to enable you to suffer for the sake of proclaiming the Good News—just as I have.

⁹ For he has saved us from eternal death and called us to **B** a high and holy calling—namely, to be his special people who live holy lives completely dedicated to serve him. He didn't do this for us because of anything we did to merit it, but because it was his eternal plan to favor us in this way through our union with Messiah Jesus. ¹⁰ Now he has revealed this plan to us through the incarnation, death, and

---

A 1:3 λατρεύω (latreuō) can mean either "serve" or "worship." Both were put in since both were true. People today tend to think "worship" is what is done during "worship" services—mainly singing songs or hymns of praise and adoration. These can be means of worship, but they are not the essence of worship—which Paul defines in Romans 12:1. True worship is the offering of our lives in submissive obedience to God's will, direction, and service. So it is possible to worship God through praise—since he has commanded us to do this. But it is also possible to praise him verbally, and adore him in song, and not be submitted to his will—and therefore not be truly worshipping him. So the two possible translations of this Greek word are much closer than the meanings of "serve" and "worship" as they are commonly understood in modern American English. True biblical worship is submissive service or the genuine offering of submissive service. The two concepts are not distinct when properly understood.

B 1:9 κλήσει ἁγία (klēsei hagia) can mean either "with a holy calling" or "to a holy calling."

resurrection of our Savior—Messiah Jesus—who has undone death, forever destroying its power. And through the message of the Good News, he reveals how people can live forever with him.

11 It was this message that God appointed me to proclaim and teach about as his representative. 12 In fact, the reason I've been persecuted and am in prison is because I've been obedient to his commission. I'm not embarrassed or ashamed of being a prisoner because I intimately know the person I've been proclaiming—and I consider it a privilege to suffer for following him. I am fully confident he is able to guarantee that the message of the Good News which he entrusted me to proclaim will continue to be proclaimed until Judgment Day—despite my being in prison.
❖ *The text literally says, "I am convinced he is able to guard my deposit until that day." The two interpretations of "my deposit," are 1) something God has entrusted to Paul, and 2) something Paul has entrusted to God. The word "deposit" also appears in 2 Timothy 1:14 and 1 Timothy 6:20 where it clearly refers to something God has entrusted to Paul, hence the first interpretation was chosen. If interpretation 2) is correct, Paul probably meant something like, "For I am fully confident he is able to guard my life of service that I've entrusted to him, until the day he chooses for me to die and go to be with him."* ➤ 13 So Timothy—exercising faith and love derived from your union with Messiah Jesus—preserve the integrity of the correct teachings which you've heard from me regarding the message of the Good News. 14 Depend on the Holy Spirit who lives in us to help you guard this message that God has entrusted to you to proclaim.

15 You are probably aware that most of my coworkers from Asia Province who I've been depending on have left me since I've been imprisoned—including Phygelus and Hermogenes, whom you know.

16-17 But I pray that the Lord will show special mercy and favor to Onesiphorus and his household because he was not ashamed of my being in prison. Instead, when he came to Rome, he searched until he found me—and since then has often visited and ministered to my needs. 18 I pray that the Lord Jesus will grant him great mercy on Judgment Day. You know the way he is and how he helped me in Ephesus.

2

1 But as for you, my dear Timothy, always depend on the enabling power that is available through your union with Messiah Jesus to keep you spiritually strong and faithful. 2 It's your job to take all the things that you and many others have heard me teach and pass them on to reliable men of faith—who will be competent to pass them on to others and train them to do the same. 3 Be willing to suffer as a spiritual warrior who is under the command of Messiah Jesus—just as many others do. 4 In following him, be like a good soldier who doesn't get involved in business affairs that would distract him from his duties—because he wants to please his commander who enlisted him. 5 In running the race of life, be like an athlete—knowing you will not win the prize unless you compete according to the rules. 6 Be willing to work hard, like a farmer who knows he will be the first one to benefit from the crop he has planted and that his share will be proportionate to his efforts. 7 Think carefully about these three illustrations and the Lord will help you understand how they apply to your life and ministry.

8 As you suffer, think about Jesus and his suffering and death and the fact that God raised him from death—for he is the Messiah, descended from King David as the prophecies foretold. This is the core of the Good News message that I proclaim 9 and for which I am willing to suffer even the indignity, shame, and pain of being shackled in prison as a criminal. But nothing can shackle God's message. It continues to spread and change lives. 10 Since this is true, I am willing to endure any suffering in order to help those whom God has chosen to be his own people—so they can receive salvation and eternal glory by being spiritually united with Messiah Jesus. ❖ *Glory can mean several different things. One aspect of glory which is not often considered is that it refers to God's character. In Exodus 33:19*

and 22, God refers to his "glory" as his "goodness"—referring to his character. In Exodus 34:6, he describes his character as "compassionate and gracious, slow to anger, abounding in gracious love and truth." (The Hebrew word translated "truth" can also mean "faithfulness.") ➤ 11 Another reason I endure suffering is given in the well-known saying which is entirely true: ❖ Many commentators think verses 11-13 may have been a hymn. ➤ Since we have died with the Messiah, we will also live with him forever. [Romans 6:3-5, 8; Galatians 2:20; Colossians 2:20; 3:1-4]

12 If we endure suffering for his sake, we will also reign with him in heavenly glory. [Matthew 19:28; Luke 22:28-30; Romans 8:17-18; Ephesians 2:6; Colossians 3:1-3; Hebrews 10:36; James 1:12; Revelation 2:26; 3:21; 20:4-6]

If we are afraid to suffer for the sake of being identified with him—and therefore deny that we are his followers—he will disown us. [Matthew 10:33; Mark 8:38; Luke 9:26; 12:9] There are other ways of denying him too. [Matthew 7:21-23; Titus 1:16; 1 Timothy 5:8; 1 John 2:22-23. Revelation 2:13]

13 If our faith is weak and we are not entirely faithful to him, he will still always remain faithful to fulfill his promises to us, for he cannot be untrue to his nature— which never changes ❖ Commentators are not agreed on what "if we are unfaithful" (in the literal text) means. Some take it to mean "if we deny the faith," since the verb often means "unbelief." If that is the sense here, many of these commentators think "he remains faithful" means he is faithful to his nature and will punish such people. But that would make this verse entirely parallel with the second half of verse 12— adding little or no new information. ➤

Godly Leaders and False Teachers

14 Continually remind the believers there of all these things I've been reminding you about. And by the Lord's A authority, warn them to stop disputing about words. ❖ Commentators are not agreed on what Paul means by "disputing about words." It might refer to the kinds of things he mentioned in his first letter. [1 Timothy 1:4; 4:7; 6:4] Some think it refers to nuances that don't really affect the overall meaning of a doctrine or teaching. Others think it would be about the real meaning and significance of words—which if interpreted differently would change doctrines and could lead people away from proper faith and understanding. Others think that the disputes are about abstract issues having no

bearing on proper faith and obedience. If they were disputing about words that Paul had taught or written, he always tried to speak and write in a clear easy-to-understand way, so that proper understanding was not based on subtle nuances. [2 Corinthians 1:13; 4:2-3] Certainly Timothy and the Ephesian believers knew what Paul was referring to. ➤ Such disputing doesn't help anyone ❖ and usually doesn't convince anyone ➤ and spiritually harms those who listen and get caught up in it. ❖ Harm comes from: 1) division which destroys unity and love, 2) intellectual confusion, 3) emotional upset resulting in depression, 4) wrong focus, which weakens faith and obedience. ➤ 15 Do your best to teach God's message correctly such that you are confident God will approve of your teaching—and you won't be ashamed when he examines it. 16 But completely avoid participating in or listening to discussions that don't honor God. Because such activity will lead those people further away from him and his truth. ❖ Examples of such discussions could be those where the assumption is that God doesn't exist or is irrelevant, or where a basic assumption in the discussion contradicts truth revealed in the Scriptures or advocates a position contrary to Scriptural teaching. Paul is focusing on such things in the context of warning against false teachers. But it's not totally irrelevant to ask: How many discussions do we participate in, about sports, material possessions, and many other topics—that we totally divorce from how our faith and obedience to God pertain to them, so they would come under the heading of "godless," "worldly," or "empty" chatter? ➤ 17 This kind of false teaching and deadly corruption of the truth will spread among the assembly like gangrene. Two men who have done this are Hymenaeus [1 Timothy 1:20] and Philetus. 18 They have deviated from the truth—saying that the resurrection has already happened—and in doing so have destroyed some people's trust in the truth. ❖ Most commentators think they were teaching that the resurrection happened to the soul at the time of conversion and that there would be no bodily resurrection after death. [1 Corinthians chapter 15] ➤ 19 But in spite of such people, the foundation of God's holy Temple and the Temple itself are in no danger of weakening. ❖ The Temple is the assembly of all God's people—and its foundation is the Messiah and his message as taught by the apostles and the prophets. [Ephesians 2:19-21] ➤ The

---

A 2:14 Many manuscripts have "God" instead of "Lord."

seal of ownership on that foundation has these words engraved on it, **"Yahweh knows who belongs to him,"** *[Numbers 16:5 in the Septuagint, John 10:14]* and also, **"Everyone who claims they believe in Yahweh must turn away from all sin."** ❖ *This is a combination of Joel 2:32 and a reference to verses like Psalm 34:12-14 and Proverbs 3:7. The original Hebrew has "Yahweh," and the Septuagint that Paul quotes has "Lord." Yahweh is the name of the Triune God (Father, Son, and Holy Spirit).* ➤

20 Switching to another figure, in a wealthy person's house, not all the containers ❖ *such as cooking pots, bowls, cups, buckets, garbage containers, chamber pots, etc.* ➤ are of equal value. Some are made of gold or silver and are used for honorable purposes. Others are made of wood or clay and are used for vulgar purposes. ❖ *In the assembly, the different containers reflect two basic kinds of people. There are those who are ready to do noble things for God and those who are not. Those used for vulgar purposes—like garbage containers or chamber pots—particularly represent the false teachers in the context of this letter, though in other contexts, they could be other sorts of ungodly people who claim to be believers. Some containers are kept. Others are disposed of after serving their purpose.* ➤ 21 Therefore, if those used for vulgar purposes spiritually cleanse themselves by repenting and turning from sin, they will become containers that are usable for honorable purposes. Their master will make them holy and ready to do good works so they are useful to him. 22 So, Timothy, whenever you feel a sinful desire that is characteristic of younger people, ❖ *Timothy was probably in his 30s.* ➤ have a healthy fear and immediately turn away from it and turn toward doing what you know God wants you to do. ❖ *Such "youthful" desires include improper sexual desires, selfish ambition, impatience, acting hastily without thinking, being argumentative, selfish indulgence, and everything inconsistent with faith, self-sacrificial love, and peace.* ➤ With the help of others who desire to have a relationship with the Lord Jesus and who want to please him, always do your best to seek his will, be faithful to obey him, and love and live in harmony with others. ❖ *Many commentators think Paul meant: Always do your best to seek his will, be faithful to obey him, love others, and live in harmony with those who desire to have a relationship with the Lord Jesus and who want to please him.* ➤ 23 But completely avoid participating in foolish controversies that are based on ignorance of the truth—because they just produce quarrels and divisions. 24 You know that the leaders of God's people and teachers of his word must not quarrel. Instead, they must be kind and courteous to everyone, competent to teach God's truth and to refute wrong teaching, and not become resentful or bitter toward people who oppose them or who do wrong to them. 25 They must gently correct and instruct those who oppose the truth—hoping and praying that God will enable them to recognize the truth and repent—26 so they can return to clear thinking and escape from Satan's deception which has tricked them into doing what he wants. ❖ *Most commentators say that repentance leads to a recognition of the truth. This is often the case, but in this context of instructing in the truth, repentance is likely to follow—or be simultaneous with—the recognition.* ➤

3

1 But even though we hope for some to return to the truth, be aware that in these last days before the Lord Jesus returns there will be difficult times. ❖ *Some commentators believe the "last days" refers to the entire time since Jesus returned to Heaven until he returns again, and others that it refers to a much-shorter time, just before he returns. But Paul believed that he was living in the "last days" and was making the point that Timothy should not be surprised to see these things happening around him. The difficulties are clarified in the following verses.* ➤ 2 Even people who profess to be followers of Jesus will become selfish—thinking only of themselves, focused on obtaining money and the things it can buy. They will be greedy, proud, boastful, arrogant, overbearing, disrespectful, rude, quick to insult, verbally abusive to others, disrespectful of their parents and disobedient to them, having no sense of gratitude or appreciation. They will be irreverent, profane, holding nothing sacred, 3 heartless and unkind, without love, affection, or tolerance—even for their families. They will be unforgiving gossipers and slanderers who have no self-control or desire to refrain from evil. They will be savage and cruel, hating what God says is good,

4 treacherous betrayers, rash, reckless, conceited, self-important, and they will love pleasure more than they love God. 5 They will make an outward show of being religious and wanting to please God, but there will be no substance or reality to it. For they refuse to acknowledge the miraculous power that God displays and don't allow his power to rid them of their sinful ways. So have absolutely nothing to do with such people! ❖ *This doesn't imply that any one person will exhibit all or most of these characteristics—even though many of them do tend to go together—but that people with major problems in these areas will become more common and increasingly cause problems in the assembly.* ➤

6-7 Some of these people are the kind that prey on others. They visit houses under false pretexts and gain unhealthy influence over women who feel guilty about their sins and are searching for some new teaching to help them. These women always latch onto each new false teaching—hoping they will find something that will give them peace. Yet they will never be able to recognize the truth for they are unwilling to say "no" to their sinful impulses and submit to God's will. They want an easier solution. 8 They are just like Jannes and Jambres who opposed Moses' efforts to represent the truth that Yahweh's power was great and that Pharaoh should fear him—because these false teachers oppose our efforts to represent God's truth to people by teaching false doctrines. Their minds are corrupted with the enemy's lies, and that is why God has rejected their so-called faith as being counterfeit. ❖ *Jannes and his brother Jambres are not mentioned by name in the Hebrew Scriptures, but according to Jewish tradition, they were two of the magicians who performed counterfeit miracles for Pharaoh in Exodus 7:11-22 and 8:7-19.* ➤ 9 But people like that won't be able to deceive others for very long, since their foolishness and falseness will eventually become obvious to all—just as Jannes' and Jambres' claim to have power equal to Yahweh was discredited long ago.

Paul Last Instructions
Concerning Timothy's Ministry

10 But you have carefully observed everything I've taught, the way I've lived, the purposes and intentions behind my words and actions, my trust in God, my patience with the shortcomings of others, my love for others, my persevering in faith and obedience despite persecution and difficulties, 11 and the persecutions and sufferings that I've been willing to bear for the Lord—like those that happened to me in Pisidian Antioch, *[Acts 13:50]* Iconium, *[Acts 14:4-6]* and Lystra. *[Acts 14:19-20]* Such persecutions I endured **A**—yet the Lord brought me through all of them alive! 12 The truth is, *all* who are joined to Messiah Jesus and want to live their lives in such a way as to please him, *will* be persecuted. *[Mark 10:30; John 15:18-20; 16:33; Acts 14:22; 1 Thessalonians 3:3-4; 1 Peter 2:20-21]* 13 But those who live evil lives, and those among them who pretend to be something they are not, will become more and more corrupt in their teaching and depraved in their lives. They themselves have been misled and deceived—and they go on to mislead and deceive others.

14 But as for you, Timothy, continue to believe and trust the things you have been taught and have become convinced are true—for these reasons: 1) you know and trust those who taught you, ❖ *These were his mother Lois, his grandmother Eunice, Paul, and others.* ➤ 15 2) you have known the teachings in the ❖ *Hebrew* ➤ Scriptures since you were a child, 3) and you know from experience that these same Scriptures give you the wisdom to recognize you can only be saved by trusting in Messiah Jesus. 16 God caused everything people wrote in the Scriptures to say what he wanted it to say, and every passage is useful for teaching truth, rebuking those who do wrong, correcting errors, and training people to live in a way that please him. *[Romans 15:4]* ❖ *God doesn't change. [Malachi 3:6] Therefore, if he desired his people to know his truths when these Scriptures were first written, he would still want his*

A **3:11** Since there is no punctuation in the original Greek manuscripts, commentators are not agreed on the

function of the phrase, "what persecutions I endured." Some see it as a restatement of the *[Continued next page]*

*people to know the same truths today—and so would preserve them from significant change or corruption over the centuries. Some people say that we shouldn't derive doctrine from certain books or passages (e.g., the book of Acts). Yet this verse says that **all** Scripture is useful for that purpose.* ➤ 17 For in knowing and rightly understanding the Scriptures, those who serve God will be completely prepared to do every good thing he wants them to do—and will also be proficient in doing them.

4

1-2 Timothy, I'm telling you that your God-appointed ministry is to be prepared and faithful to preach God's message of the Good News—whether you feel like doing so or not, and whether people seem open to hear it or not. Gently correct those whose understanding or actions are wrong; rebuke those who resist correction and persist in sinning; exhort people to believe and obey and encourage them to persist in their faithfulness to the Lord despite difficulties. While you do all these things, be patient with their shortcomings and clearly teach them why they should do as you say. Let me remind you that God is watching you, as well as Messiah Jesus—who will return to judge both those alive when he appears and those who have died, and then he will reign as King over all. The Father and the Son will be the ones who judge if you have adequately fulfilled your ministry or not.

3 For the time will come when people who claim to be followers of Jesus will not tolerate God's truth about what is right and wrong, but will only want to follow their own desires. They will seek out teachers who tell them the kinds of things they want to hear—instead of teachers who confront them for their sins. 4 They will stop listening to the truth in God's word and will pay attention to speculations and myths. 5 But you, Timothy, must think clearly and be self-controlled in every situation. Be willing to endure suffering and hardship as you continue to proclaim

the message of the Good News to those who are not saved, and as you perform all the other duties of your ministry.

6 I'm giving you these instructions and counting on you to continue the work because I will soon be executed. My life has been like a sacrifice offered to please God, and now my life will be poured out like the drink offering that is poured out as the final part of the sacrifice. *[Exodus 29:38-41]* 7 Ever since I first believed, I've contended in the struggle to remain faithful, be obedient, and to further the Kingdom. *[1 Timothy 1:18-19; 6:12]* I've endured in this to the end of my life *[1 Corinthians 9:24; Galatians 5:7; Hebrews 3:14; 12:1]*— and I've not been disqualified from eternal life, but remained loyal and true to my faith. *[1 Corinthians 9:27; Colossians 2:18]* ❖ *Since the first two phrases in the literal text are sports metaphors and in the next verse "crown" (i.e., victory-wreath crown) is also a sports metaphor, it's likely that the third phrase in this verse is too, referring to not being disqualified.* ➤

8 From now on, the victory-wreath prize for having lived a life pleasing to God is waiting for me in Heaven. ❖ *The word* στέφανος *(stephanos) refers to a particular kind of crown made of woven branches used as a victory crown for the winner of an athletic contest. It does not refer to the kind of a crown worn by kings as a symbol of their authority—which is a different word in Greek (i.e. diadem).* ➤ Therefore, I know that on Judgment Day, the Lord Jesus—who always judges fairly—will give me that prize. But I won't be the only one to receive such—for all his people who have longed for his coming and have therefore lived lives that please him will also receive prizes. ❖ *Some commentators believe the "crown of righteousness" is the prize of being made righteous in Heaven. But that prize has already been awarded to us. We have already been justified, sanctified, and glorified. [Romans 5:1, 9; 8:30; 10:10; 1 Corinthians 1:2; 6:11]* ➤

Personal Business

9 Timothy, please do your best to come to me here in Rome as soon as you can. 10 I need you here because Demas has left me to return to Thessalonica (he loves this present life more than he looks forward to

---

first sentence in this verse. Others think it is an exclamation. And others think it should be joined with the following phrase.

the next), Crescens has gone to Galatia Province, and Titus has gone to Dalmatia Province. ❖ *Both Crescens and Titus probably went to minister—since Paul gives no hint that there was anything wrong with their going. Dalmatia Province is the area that is the modern-day country of Albania—northwest of Greece and east of Italy.* ➤ 11 Only Luke is here to help me. Go to Mark and bring him with you since he has been very helpful in my ministry. 12 I'm sending Tychicus to Ephesus to replace you there. ❖ *Tychicus carried Paul's letters to the believers in Ephesus, [Ephesians 6:21] and in Colosse. [Colossians 4:7] Commentators believe it very likely that Paul was sending Tychicus to Ephesus with this letter to replace Timothy. Paul had no one else with him to send the letter, and Tychicus was going to the proper place. He was also one of the people Paul may have sent to replace Titus. [Titus 3:12]* ➤ 13 When you come, please bring my cloak which I left with Carpus in Troas, and also bring my scrolls, especially the ones made of parchment. ❖ *Scrolls were usually made of papyrus, a thick paper-like material made from the papyrus reed. Parchment scrolls—made of animal skins—were more expensive and less commonly available. These scrolls probably contained Scripture. Blank scrolls for writing letters he could have purchased locally.* ➤

14-15 Watch out for Alexander the metal-worker! A ❖ *It's possible this is the same Alexander mentioned in 1 Timothy 1:20.* ➤ He vehemently opposed our message and did me great harm. The Lord will punish him for the evil he has done.

16 In my first court appearance here in Rome—when I was supposed to defend myself against the charges made against me—not a single believer came to witness on my behalf. Everyone who might have helped me has abandoned me from fear. ❖ *The official climate was quite hostile to followers of Jesus at this time.* ➤ I pray that God will forgive them! ❖ *Luke was still with him and others are mentioned in verse 21. He probably meant credible witnesses who could have given testimony that would have helped prove his innocence of the charges had left him.* ➤ 17 But the Lord was with me—strengthening me and making me bold so I could fully proclaim his message

before all those Gentiles present in court when asked about why I was accused. I was rescued from the lion's mouth. ❖ *Commentators are not agreed on the interpretation of this verse. "All Gentiles" (in the literal text) is probably hyperbole (exaggeration). He may have meant all the Gentiles present in the court from many parts of the empire. It may have been a hearing before the emperor himself—with Paul meaning this was the pinnacle of his career to witness before the ruler of the entire empire and the many high officials present. The meaning of "lion's mouth" is also not clear. Some think it refers to being saved from a death by lions in the arena. Others say that as a Roman citizen, he was exempt from this indignity—although not from other forms of execution. It could be a general reference to immediate execution, or a figurative reference to Satan. [1 Peter 5:8] It could mean he was rescued from Satan's temptation to be afraid and not proclaim his message. Given what he says in the next verse and the fact that he expected to be executed "soon," but not immediately, and perhaps not before Timothy could arrive which would take a few months—this last interpretation (i.e., "Lion's mouth" means "Satan's temptation to be afraid and not proclaim his message) fits on the spiritual level and deliverance from immediate execution fits on the physical level.* ➤ 18 And I know that the Lord will continue to rescue me from every evil attack and will ultimately rescue me by taking me to his Kingdom in Heaven. May all people praise and honor our God forever! Yes, may it be so!

Closing Greetings

19 Convey my warm greetings to Priscilla and her husband Aquila for me, and also to all those in Onesiphorus' household. 20 You might want to know that Erastus stayed behind in Corinth, and I left Trophimus in Miletus because he was too sick to travel. 21 Do what you can to get here before winter sets in. Eubulus sends his warm greetings, as do Pudens, Linus, Claudia, and all the other believers here.

22 Timothy, I pray the Lord will always be present to help you in your spirit. And I pray that he will look upon all of you believers in Ephesus with great favor—far beyond anything you can deserve.

A 4:14 Literally, "coppersmith," such craftsmen also worked with other metals.

Paul's Letter to Titus

This letter was written by the Apostle Paul to Titus—who was Paul's representative on Crete Island in the Mediterranean Sea. Titus is mentioned in 2 Corinthians 2:13; 7:6-7, 13-15; 8:6, 16-19, 23; 12:18; Galatians 2:1-3; and 2 Timothy 4:10. Some commentators think he was Luke's brother. Paul wrote this letter while he was in Corinth—sometime in the period AD 63–65—after he wrote his first letter to Timothy.

Paul had preached on Crete after his release from his first time in prison in Rome, and he left Titus there to straighten out the situation among the believers—since there were liars, gluttons, sloths, and immoral people among them.

Outline:

Opening Greetings. [1:1-4]
Qualifications for assembly leaders. [1:5-9]
Paul tells Titus to rebuke false teachers. [1:10-16]
The way to teach and train believers. [2:1—3:11]
Closing Instructions. [3:12-15]

1

Opening Greetings

1 I, Paul, am God's voluntary slave A and an apostle of Jesus the Messiah. I was appointed to this task so I might lead those God has chosen to be his people to know his true teachings—which tell them how to live in a way that pleases him. 2 As a result of knowing these things and responding to them in faith, they will be sure of living forever. Because God—who never lies—promised this to his people based on the plan he determined to accomplish even before he made the world. 3 At the time he chose, he made his plan known to his people through those who proclaimed his message. I am one of those whom God—our Savior—commanded to proclaim it. He has trusted me to do this important work.

4 I'm writing this to Titus—who is like my true son because we both have the same faith. I pray that God the Father and Messiah Jesus our Savior will look upon you with great favor far beyond anything you can deserve—and bless you with peace and well-being.

Qualifications for Assembly Leaders

5 When I left Crete, I asked you to stay because I wanted you to continue to straighten out the problems in the assemblies there. The first thing to do is to appoint assembly leaders in every town. As I instructed you before I left, 6 any assembly leader must be a man who has led such a good life that no one would accuse him of having done anything wrong. He must be faithful to his wife ❖ *or: He must only have one wife.* ➤—whose children and even adult children are all believers, are well behaved and not self-indulgent, immoral, or insubordinate to their parents. ❖ *Paul assumed that a leader would be married since almost all men married. (Marriages were generally arranged and not based on ideas of romance.) But this does not rule out single men (Paul was single), as long as they are celibate and meet his other conditions. Similar instructions on the qualifications of assembly leaders are found in 1 Timothy 3:1-7. 1 Timothy 3:5 gives the reason an assembly leader's children need to be well behaved. If a man cannot raise his children so they are well behaved, then he is not fit to lead other believers. This implies that a father bears a great deal of responsibility for how his children turn out. But very few assemblies today—at least in North America—enforce this apostolic instruction.* ➤ 7 For a person who is given responsibility to carry

---

A 1:1 See the note at Romans 1:1 about his being a voluntary slave.

out God's work in an assembly must have a good reputation. ❖ *Even though Paul uses a different term in the literal text for this office in this verse, he is still talking about assembly leaders. Different translations translate this position as: overseer, church leader, elder, bishop, presbyter, and pastor. But at this early date, there was no administrative hierarchy. Bishops, as they are known today, didn't appear until much later. One difference between this office and the typical pastor today is that there were often more than one assembly leader per assembly—even if the assembly was relatively small by modern standards.* ➤ He must not tend to domineer and always want to have his own way; he must not easily lose his temper, or get drunk, be rough with people, or frequently gets into quarrels and fights. And he must not be greedy for wealth. ❖ *Or: He must not be someone who is willing to do wrong in order to make money.* ➤ 8 He must love to offer hospitality in his own home to traveling believers, and love to do what is right. He must be composed and know what to do in every situation, and be fair and honest in all his dealings. He must be pure and be in full control of his desires and actions. 9 He must firmly believe the message of the Good News that we taught—and know that he can depend on it so he can correctly teach it to others and convince those who have a wrong understanding that they are wrong.

Instructions About False Teachers

10 For there are many who profess to be believers but who rebel against proper authority—especially so-called Jewish converts who insist that all followers of the Messiah be circumcised. They teach nonsense, but they are good at deceiving people and leading them astray. 11 Don't allow them to teach in your meetings because they are destroying the faith of whole households—just in order to get money from them. 12 Long ago, a man from Crete who they call a prophet said, "People of Crete always lie. They are also evil, cruel, lazy, and gluttons." 13 Unfortunately, his statement is still characteristically true of many. Therefore, you will need to firmly rebuke those who are following false teachings so they might return to following the truth 14 and stop paying attention to Jewish myths or to the rules taught by those who have rejected the truth.

15 These false teachers emphasize ritual purity as taught in the Torah. But to those who have been made spiritually pure in heart, all things are ritually pure. But those corrupted unbelievers—who have rejected the truth of the Good News—think nothing is pure, and in fact, their every thought and opinion is corrupted along with their consciences. 16 They claim to know God, but what they do disproves their claims. They don't obey his will and are disgusting in what they do. They are entirely incapable of doing anything good.

2

How Titus Should Teach and Train His People

1 But you, Titus, must only teach those things that are consistent with the true teachings of the Messiah. 2 Teach the older men ❖ *probably those over 50* ➤ to be self-controlled and to live in such a way that others will respect them. They must have a firm faith in God, have a proper understanding of correct teaching, sincerely love others, and continue to be faithful to Jesus in spite of any difficult circumstances that might arise. 3 In the same way, teach the older women to live in such a way that everything they do honors the Lord. They must not gossip, or slander, or say things that are hurtful of others, and must not be controlled by alcohol. ❖ *literally: wine* ➤ But teach them to train children and other women to do what is good. ❖ *Ancient cultures respected older people because of their age and experience. The older women made good teachers because they would be respected. They probably also had more time—as they likely were too weak to do as much physical labor as the younger women.* ➤ 4 They should be good role models and train the younger women ❖ *probably the pre-40 age group* ➤ how to love their husbands and children, 5 how to exercise self-control and use good judgment, to be faithful to their husbands and remain morally pure, to work hard to fulfill their household responsibilities, to be kind, and to willingly submit to their husband's authority. ❖ *The instruction to submit to their husband's*

authority would not surprise or irritate them as it would most 21st-century women from a western culture. Even though there were undoubtedly some women who chafed against this, it was the universally expected norm in the vast majority of the world's cultures at that time (even well into the 20th century) for all wives—and if not yet married, to their fathers. ➤ They must live in this way because their lives are witnesses to the truth of the Good News. It would not be good if their manner of living caused unbelievers to speak evil about God's message—which these women claim to believe.

⁶ Similarly, exhort the young men to be self-controlled and to live in a sensible manner in everything they do. ❖ *Commentators are divided as to whether the final "in everything" is speaking about the young men in this verse, or goes with the instructions for Titus in the next verse.* ➤ ⁷ You yourself should always be a good example for your people in everything you do and say. Be exemplary in doing good deeds. When you teach them, be honest, have unselfish motives, and behave in a way that will cause them to respect you. ⁸ Everything you say must be true, accurate, and such that no one can find a basis for criticizing either you or what you say. This is so those who want to oppose you will not be able to find anything bad to say about us—and so will be frustrated and defeated from the start.

⁹ Teach the slaves who are believers to properly submit to their masters and to try to please them in everything they do. They should not show disrespect by talking back or arguing. ¹⁰ They should never steal, but instead demonstrate that they are honest and can always be trusted—so in everything they do their good behavior will cause people to respect what we teach about God our Savior, and attract them to the faith.

¹¹ Teach the believers to live like this, for God has revealed his undeserved favor by providing a way for all people to be saved and freed from the power of sin—if they will accept it. ¹² Another reason he grants us favor and enabling power is that it teaches us to stop behaving in ways that displease him—and to refuse to follow the strong desires we have for sinful pleasures in this world. This also teaches us to be self-controlled and to live in a way that pleases him as long as we live. ¹³ We are to do this while we wait with expectation for that wonderful day when Jesus—the Messiah who is our great God and Savior—will return in glory and bring us into the fullness of our promised inheritance. ¹⁴ For he allowed himself to die in order to: 1) set us free from the power of sin—so we can refrain from doing evil and 2) to make us entirely pure—so we can belong to him as his own special people who are eager to do what is good in his sight.

¹⁵ These are the things you should be teaching them. Exhort them to live this way—and when they don't listen, rebuke them. As the Messiah's apostle, I have given you the spiritual authority to do this—so don't let anyone get away with ignoring you.

3

¹ Keep reminding your people to respect and submit to secular authorities at all levels and their laws. They should also be ready and willing to do whatever is helpful and good for others. ² They should never slander or criticize anyone, and should strive to live harmoniously with all without arguing, to always be kind and considerate of others—demonstrating genuine humility, courtesy, and gentleness toward everyone.

³ Remind them to live like this toward unbelievers in the hope that they will be saved—for there was a time when we too were ignorant and morally foolish, rebellious against God and disobedient, easily deceived and misguided, controlled by our many passions and desires for all kinds of pleasure. We were mean, cruel, evil, always envious and jealous of others. We freely showed our hatred and disgust of others—so they did the same to us in return. ⁴ But even though we were like that, our Savior God came to us as a human being and demonstrated that he loves all of humanity and is willing to be very generous and kind to us. ⁵ He saved us from the eternal punishment that we deserved—not because of anything good we had done—but simply because of his merciful and compassionate nature and his desire to do so. He did this

through a cleansing of our spiritual nature from all sin by causing our human spirits to be reborn with a new life—his life. ❖ *Literally: "through the washing of regeneration." Some understand this to refer to baptism as a sacrament of regeneration (i.e., rebirth and salvation). [Romans 6:3-4; 1 Corinthians 12:13; Galatians 3:27]* ➤ This was effected in us by the Holy Spirit—6 whom God generously gave to live in us—through our spiritual union with our Savior, Messiah Jesus. ❖ *The text literally talks about the Holy Spirit being "poured out." Water is a common figure representing the Holy Spirit. He is the "river of life," [Revelation 22:1] the "living water," [John 4:10; 7:38-39; Revelation 7:17] who is "poured out" in various measures, [Acts 2:33; 10:45; Romans 5:5] and can "fill us." [Acts 2:4; 4:8, 31; 9:17; 13:9, 52; Ephesians 5:18] Even though he is a person, we can always have "more" of him and his power. [Luke 11:13; John 3:34; Acts 1:8; Ephesians 3:16]* ➤ 7 By means of his great undeserved favor, he declared us righteous in his sight so we would become his children and heirs and live with him forever. 8 You can be sure these things ❖ *in verses 4-7* ➤ are true. I want you to continually emphasize these things when you teach—so those who have trusted God to save them will respond out of love and gratitude for his great mercy by continually focusing on doing only those things which are good in his sight. These teachings are good and helpful for everyone who pays attention to them.

9 But don't allow yourself to get involved in pointless and divisive controversies about genealogies, or other arguments or disputes about the Torah's teachings—because such genealogies and disputes have no spiritual value. They won't help the assembly grow in faith or unity and, at best, are a big waste of time. ❖ *Commentators don't know what the controversies would have been about over genealogies. Some speculate about religious myths. But another possibility—which is common in some societies even today—is the relationship between genealogies and disputes over land ownership and inheritance.* ➤ 10 Give a stern warning to those who cause divisions and dissension in the assembly. Even warn them a second time, but if they persist after that, have the assembly reject them and shun them unless they repent. 11 Such people's thoughts and actions are twisted. They are deliberately sinning—and thus proving to everyone that they are in the wrong.

Closing Instructions and Greetings

12 I'm going to send either Artemas or Tychicus to relieve you there. ❖ *This is the only place Artemas is ever mentioned in the New Testament. Tychicus is probably the same man mentioned in Acts 20:4; Colossians 4:7; Ephesians 6:21; and 2 Timothy 4:12.* ➤ When he arrives, do what you can to meet me in Nicopolis ❖ *on the Greek coast, about 200 miles northwest of Athens* ➤ before winter sets in. ❖ *Ships didn't sail the Mediterranean Sea during winter.* ➤ For that is where I plan to spend it. 13 Do your best to provide the money, clothing, provisions, and anything else that Zenas the lawyer and Apollos will need for their trip onward from there. ❖ *We don't know who Zenas is, or if he was a Roman or Jewish lawyer. It's likely that these men carried this letter to Titus, or else he would have written them greetings too.* ➤ 14 In addition, teach our people there to help out in such things. They must learn to devote themselves to doing good—such as meeting urgent needs people have for food, clothing, etc. If they live this way, their lives will be productive for God's purposes.

15 All the believers here with me send you their warm greetings. Likewise, greet other brothers and sisters in the faith there whom we know and love. I pray that God will look upon you all with great favor far beyond anything you can deserve—and greatly bless you.

Paul's Letter to Philemon

This letter was written by the Apostle Paul, probably during his first imprisonment in Rome [Acts 28:30-31]—sometime in the period AD 60–62. It, along with his letters to the believers in Ephesus, Philippi, and Colosse, are called his "prison letters."

He writes to Philemon in the city of Colosse—who hosted meetings for believers in his home. Philemon had a run-away slave named Onesimus—who somehow met Paul while he was under house arrest in Rome and became a believer under Paul's teaching. Run-away slaves were often killed if caught. Paul asks Philemon to accept Onesimus back as a brother in the Lord and to forgive him any debt or wrong—because Philemon was brought to the Lord by Paul and so was spiritually indebted to him. Paul also offered to pay Onesimus' debt if necessary. It's likely that Philemon did as Paul asked, or the letter would not have been preserved.

This real-life situation illustrates our salvation. Paul acts the role of the Messiah, asking Philemon (a figure for God the Father) to forgive the repentant sinner Onesimus—for Paul's sake. He will pay the debt owed. The law said that Onesimus should die, but he was saved and restored by undeserved favor.

Opening Greetings

1-2 I, Paul, am a prisoner because of my work for Messiah Jesus, and I am writing this letter to Philemon—my dear friend and colleague in the Lord's work—and to our sister **A** in the Lord, Apphia, and to Archippus—our fellow spiritual warrior in the faith ❖ *This implies that Archippus had some association with Paul in his work.* ➤ —and also to all the believers who meet together in your home. ❖ *Many commentators believe that Apphia was likely Philemon's wife, and Archippus may have been his son or a household member.* ➤ Timothy—our brother in the Lord who is here with me—also sends his warm greetings. ❖ *Most commentators believe that Paul was only conveying greetings from Timothy—and not saying that he was involved in writing the letter in any way.* ➤ **3** I pray that God our Father and our Lord Jesus the Messiah will look upon you with great favor far beyond anything you can deserve—and bless you with peace and well-being.

Paul Expresses His Appreciation of Philemon

4 Whenever I mention you in my prayers, Philemon, I always thank God for your life and witness **5** because I keep hearing about your love and loyalty to the Lord Jesus and also to all of his people.

6 I pray that the fellowship **B** you have with other believers ❖ *Paul is thinking of Philemon's future fellowship with Onesimus.* ➤ will deepen your understanding of all the good things that God has given us in our spiritual union with the Messiah. ❖ *This verse has many potential interpretations depending on how you interpret "koinonia" (which can mean "fellowship" or "sharing") and the various other parts of the verse. This results in the many different renderings in the various English translations. A literal translation from the Greek reads: "that the koinonia of your faith may become effective in the knowledge of every good thing in us in the Messiah." The final "in the Messiah" could relate either to "become effective"—in which case it could mean: may this happen to bring honor to the Messiah, or: may this happen to bring us into a closer relationship with the Messiah. Or it could relate to "every good thing" as in the interpretation given above. There are also textual problems with this verse. Some manuscripts have "in us" and some have "in you." And some manuscripts have "Jesus" after "Messiah." The interpretation given above was selected with the purpose of the letter in mind—that Paul was preparing Philemon for what he was going to ask him to do later in the letter.* ➤ **7** My brother, you have refreshed and encouraged God's people with your generosity—and your loving them this way has also greatly encouraged me and causes me to rejoice.

A 1-2 The Byzantine text reads "beloved" rather than "sister."
B 6 Literally, in Greek: κοινωνία (koinōnia)—which means fellowship, sharing, partnership, a close mutual relationship, participation.

Paul Asks Philemon to
Forgive Onesimus and Welcome Him Back

8-9 Philemon, I have a request to make of you. Even though I'm an apostle of the Messiah and am confident that you would obey me if I ordered you to do this, but because I know of your loving and generous ways, I'm only going to ask you to do what is right for a believer in your situation to do. I appeal to you—based on your love for me and all believers. I, Paul, ask that you comfort me—an old man who is a prisoner as a result of serving Messiah Jesus—by 10 forgiving and welcoming back my son in the faith, Onesimus—who became a believer while I've been a prisoner. ❖ *The word πρεσβύτης (presbutēs)— translated "old man"—could instead mean "ambassador." Paul was probably in his 60s. If this is Paul's first imprisonment in Rome, he may have merely been under house arrest and not chained up in a cell. [Acts 28:30-31] If so, he would have been free to meet with people who came to visit him.* ➤ 11 When he was with you before, he didn't live up to his name—but now he really is useful to both me and you. ❖ *Onesimus means "useful, profitable, helpful, beneficial."* ➤

12 I'm sending him back to you—even though I love him like a son and it's like giving up part of myself to let him go. 13 I wish he could stay here so he could help me while I'm held prisoner for preaching the Good News. Since he belongs to you, it would be like you were helping me by assigning him to serve me. 14 But it wouldn't be proper for me to do that without your permission. I want you to be able to offer such help of your own free will and not feel like I've left you no choice.

15 I think that God may have allowed him to run away from you for a while so you could later have him back forever—16 not only as a slave, but as a dear brother in the Lord. He is that to me, but will be even more so to you—both in his relationship to you as a servant and as a fellow believer. 17 So since you regard me as your partner in God's work, welcome him back just like you would welcome me. ❖ *Some commentators believe Paul was strongly hinting that Philemon consider legally setting Onesimus free. If Philemon were to welcome Onesimus the same way as he would Paul, could he continue to treat him as a slave? If he is to treat him as a brother in the Lord, could he allow him to remain a slave? By our cultural standards— no. But it might be the case that such a relationship was possible in that culture.* ➤

18 If—when he ran away—he wronged you in any way or owes you anything, please consider it my debt to you. 19 Having taken the pen from my scribe, I, Paul, am now writing this with my own hand to make me legally responsible. I promise to pay his debt. (Though I will mention that you are more indebted to me than he is to you, because I helped you gain eternal life). 20 So, my brother, I want you to be "useful" to me because of our relationship in the Lord. Encourage and refresh me by doing what I ask—just as you've done for so many other believers with your love and generosity. ❖ *The verb "be useful," is the one from which Onesimus' name is derived and is only used here in the entire New Testament—so it was a deliberate pun, or hint. The benefit, of course, would be for him to send Onesimus back to serve Paul.* ➤

21 As I'm writing this letter, I have every confidence that you will do what I ask—and knowing you, I expect you will do even more than I've asked. 22 I will also ask one more thing at this time—please prepare a place for me to stay with you, for I'm hoping that God will answer your prayers and soon allow me to be released and come to you.

Closing Greetings

23 Epaphras—who is also a prisoner here with me for serving Messiah Jesus—sends you his warm greetings—24 and so do my colleagues Mark, Aristarchus, Demas, and Luke.

25 I pray that our Lord Jesus the Messiah will look upon you with great favor far beyond anything you can deserve—and bless each of you in your spirit.

The Letter to Jesus' Jewish Followers

Also Called "The Letter to the Hebrew

No one knows for sure who authored this letter. The most commonly proposed authors are Paul, Barnabas, and Apollos. It is commonly dated shortly before the destruction of the Temple in Jerusalem in AD 70—since this event is not mentioned in the letter as it most certainly would have been had it already happened. So a likely date is sometime in the decade of the AD 60s.

It was clearly written by a Jewish author to an audience of Jews who believed in Jesus as God's long-promised Messiah. So the author expected the recipients to be thoroughly familiar with the Jewish sacrificial system, the commands in the Torah, and the rest of the Hebrew Scriptures. As a consequence, he makes many brief references to such things without any accompanying explanation. Therefore, background information has been included in places to help the modern reader understand some of what the original readers did when they read the brief references to things they knew well.

The original audience was most likely the Jewish believers of the local assembly in Rome. The purpose of the letter is clear from its contents. Evidently, many Jews who believed that Jesus was the promised Messiah didn't feel comfortable giving up the sacrificial practices taught in the Torah—or they were being pressured to follow these commands by Jewish leaders who did not believe in Jesus, and they feared persecution if they didn't do so. For that reason, the writer goes to great lengths to explain that a New Covenant has superseded the Old Mosaic Covenant—and that God had always intended it to do so when the Messiah came. He also explains that what Jesus accomplished through his death and resurrection replaces the Old Covenant animal sacrifices for sin. In fact, the Tabernacle—and later the Temple—and all the requirements for animal sacrifices were prefiguring "types" of a real Temple in Heaven and the real sacrifice for sin that Jesus made. He demonstrates from the Scriptures that the New Covenant, Jesus' sacrifice, and Jesus' priesthood are all superior to the Old Covenant, the Levitical priesthood, and the animal sacrifices for sin made following the Teachings of Moses. The author warns his readers about the severe consequences of having believed in Jesus as the Messiah and then turning back to the old sacrificial system—because this is a rejection of God and his Messiah which will result in condemnation. So he urges them to remain faithful to the truths they have been taught about Jesus—and not allow pressure from other Jews to weaken their resolve. They need to follow the new revelation of truth brought to them by the Messiah—who is in fact God's Son.

For the modern follower of Jesus, this letter helps clarify the purpose of the sacrificial system in the Torah. In God's overall plan, it was to prepare his people to understand what the Messiah would accomplish when he came. It gives us insight into how the Hebrew Scriptures are to be viewed and interpreted in the light of what we know from the New Testament—and how knowledge of the Hebrew Scriptures can help us understand more deeply and fully some of the things taught in the New Testament. The prefiguring "types" of the Hebrew Scriptures have much to teach us. The writer of this letter talks about such things as the "solid food" that we should be getting out of the Scriptures—and he refers to the basic teachings of the faith as "milk" for spiritual infants. This letter is an introduction into a deeper understanding of God's ways and the teachings of the Scriptures. But it assumes that the reader already knows—through daily practice and experience—the basic principles of the faith and is ready to move on to these deeper truths.

The writer quotes Scriptures from the Septuagint (also known as the LXX), which is the Greek translation of the Hebrew Scriptures that was in common use among Jews and followers of Jesus during the first century—since most of them understood Greek, but little or no Hebrew. There are some variations in wording between the Septuagint and the Hebrew text that we have today. Most of the oldest existing manuscripts of the Hebrew Scriptures existing today—called the "Masoretic" text—only date back about 1,000 years. The oldest existing Hebrew manuscripts—before the discovery of the Dead Sea Scrolls in 1948—were copies of copies of copies, etc., for over 1,000 years. The Dead Sea scrolls proved that very few errors of any kind had crept into the text during all those years. Yet the Septuagint was translated from even earlier manuscripts which may have been different in places, and the Septuagint translators were much closer to the people in the Hebrew Scriptures in time and culture than we are—and they may have made a more accurate translation, in places, than we can get from the Hebrew manuscripts we have today, considering our more limited knowledge of ancient Hebrew compared to theirs. There are also examples of variations among some early Hebrew manuscripts found among the Dead Sea Scrolls—with some small differences between them and the later Masoretic text. Yet English translations of the Hebrew Scriptures are mostly based on the Masoretic Hebrew text—with only occasional use of the Septuagint where the meaning of the Hebrew is not clear. So if you compare the Septuagint Scripture quotations made by the writer of this letter—as well as by Jesus in the gospels and by other New Testament writers—to those verses in your Old Testament which are based on the Masoretic text, you will find some differences in wording. So don't assume that the New Testament writers quoted wrongly.

Furthermore, it was common among Jewish teachers—and New Testament writers—to quote a Scripture text quite loosely compared to modern standards. They did not have the intention of twisting it or deceiving their audience, but they only intended to bring the rest of the passage with its context to the reader's mind. They knew their audience was entirely familiar with the text—much more so than modern believers. So their attitudes toward how to quote Scripture might seem more "loose" than modern attitudes about quotations. The author of this letter quotes Scripture in this looser way following the manner of quotation and argumentation of his time and culture. It was common Jewish practice to build arguments from verses strung together based on words in those verses that were the same. They used means of argumentation that are not commonly accepted as "logically valid" today—and so may seem a bit strange to us. One common assumption was that if God was silent on an issue—particularly concerning something someone did as recorded in the Scripture—then it could be concluded that God did not disapprove. Jesus used this manner of argumentation himself in the gospels. See Matthew 12:3-4; Mark 2:25-27; and Luke 6:3-4 where Jesus argued that since God did not condemn David for disobeying one of the Torah's commands in order to feed his men, he approved of what he did—or at least allowed it. This is an "argument from silence." Yet Jesus expected the Pharisees to have come to the same conclusion on their own. Even though such an "argument from silence" is considered "logically invalid" by western reasoning, it was not used indiscriminately by Jewish teachers. We can therefore assume that where it has been used in the Scriptures, it is inspired by the Holy Spirit.

It is important to realize that the Hebrew Scriptures were written by Hebrews (i.e., Jews and their ancestors) for Hebrews, and that they mainly taught lessons using stories—whereas we mainly teach using logical propositions. That's why so much of the Bible is narrative (i.e., stories) rather than exposition like the New Testament letters are. They weren't meant to be mere stories or just history in the modern sense, but were also meant to be used to teach lessons about God and his expectations of his people. It would be incorrect to assume that the way Jews reasoned and argued from Scripture was in error—since God inspired the Hebrew Scriptures to be written within the context of their culture and he knew their manner of interpretation. If you criticize this kind of reasoning you end up criticizing Jesus and the apostles Peter, John, and Paul in their New Testament writings—for they were all Jews and they all reasoned in this way too. It is, in fact, the modern reader of Scripture who needs to learn to assume—as much as possible— a Hebrew mindset toward the Scriptures to get the fullest possible meaning from them.

In his interpretation of prophecy, the writer of this letter may seem to take verses out of context that clearly related to historical events long before Jesus was born. But the truth is that a prophetic passage may sound like it's speaking about only one event in one time—when it may in fact be speaking about multiple events in widely differing times. One purpose of prophecy is to give a hint beforehand and to verify afterward that God's hand was at work in events. Prophecies concerning the Messiah are like that. They often pertained both to the Messiah who would come hundreds of years after the prophecy was initially given, and to his yet-to-happen second coming thousands of years later, as well as to some event near in time to when the prophecy was originally given. So don't let the apparent looseness of the author's arguments in places put you off. Jesus himself fully explained to his apostles how many seemingly vague prophecies in the Hebrew Scriptures were in fact talking about him. [Luke 24:27; 45-48] So the basis of the author's quoting *them as pertaining to the Messiah comes from the teaching of God's Son himself. While you or I would hesitate to make a strong case from verses that sometimes seem to be ripped from their context, we can trust that God's Son knew what he was talking about when he taught these things to his apostles, and that the Holy Spirit—who inspired the writer of this letter—preserved God's truth in the quotations and the interpretations he assigns them and in the way he uses them in his arguments.*

The majority of the exegetical insights and viewpoints expressed in the interpretation of this letter and its accompanying commentary are based on the analysis in "The Epistle to the Hebrews – An Analytical and Exegetical Handbook" by Neva F. Miller. In giving her the credit she deserves, I only hope any errors of my own will not reflect negatively on her work.

1

The Messiah Is Superior to the Torah and the Prophets Because He Is God's Son

1 Throughout history, God spoke to our Jewish ancestors many times through his prophets, via visions, dreams, audible words, angels, and in other ways too. **A** Through them, he has told us much about himself, his ways, his plans, and his requirements for those who desire a relationship with him. 2 But now, in this period of history before the final judgment, he has spoken to us even more fully and clearly through his eternal Son who became a human being as Messiah Jesus. Through him, God has revealed that his Son was the agent through whom he created the universe—and that it's his plan for all of creation to be brought into submission under his Son's rule. 3 In his human character, Jesus perfectly represented what God is like so we could get to know him. In his deity, the Son is the exact likeness of his Father in every way. He not only spoke the universe into existence, but continues to sustain its existence by the power of his word. *[John 1:3; Acts 17:28; Romans 11:36; 1 Corinthians 8:6; Colossians 1:16-17; 2 Peter 3:7]* He

came into this world to provide a means whereby human sin could be forgiven and permanently eliminated. And when he had accomplished this task, he returned to Heaven—resuming his position of highest rank, enthroned as ruler of all creation at the right hand of his Father, the King of Heaven.

The Messiah Is Superior to Angels

4 Thus it's clear that Jesus is far superior to angels—since his name and rank as God's eternal Son is superior to theirs. ❖ *Jews of the first century considered angels to be very-highly ranked in creation—far above humanity. And there were some Jewish believers who taught that Messiah Jesus was a man who had been elevated to the rank of angels—but was still inferior to God. The writer of this letter sets out to prove from Scripture that this conception is incorrect. To the Hebrew mind, a person's name was not just a convenient label. It reflected the totality of his being and character. Thus the "name" of God's Son—because of who he is—is inherently superior to the "name" of any created creature—no matter how he is addressed.* ➤ 5 This is clear because God spoke about the Messiah in this way, "I am your Father. Today I am publicly revealing that you are my begotten Son." **B** *[Psalm 2:7]* There is nothing in the Scriptures about God saying anything like that to an angel. ❖ *Note that this is an argument from silence—yet it's quite valid. In some*

A 1:1 Also via the Urim and Thumin, [Exodus 28:29–30; Numbers 27:21; Deuteronomy 33:8; 1 Samuel 28:6; Ezra 2:63; Nehemiah 7:65] the casting of lots, [Leviticus 16:8; Joshua 18:6-10; 1 Chronicles 24:31; 25:8; 26:13-16; Nehemiah 10:34; 11:1; Jonah 1:7; Acts 1:26] once through the voice of a donkey, [Numbers 22:28-30] miraculous signs (just a few examples: Exodus 4:1-9; Numbers 17:1-11; Judges 6:36-40; 1 Kings 18:20-40; 2 Kings 20:8-11) and theophanies—i.e., when God appeared in person as a human being. (Some examples: Genesis 18:1-33; 32:22-31; Joshua 5:13–6:5)

B 1:5 The verse in Psalm 2:7 literally says: "You are my son, today I have begotten you." If you think about it, it cannot mean what it literally says, since his Son, the Creator of the universe who became a man, existed before anything was created, thousands of years before he made the prophecy. Nobody takes it literally. There are many Scriptures that don't "mean" exactly what is literally "said." They are figures of speech that need to be understood in the wider context of Scriptural revelation. Translating literally between languages as different as Hebrew and English, or Hebrew and Greek, can often lead to statements that are less clear in translation than they were in the original language and culture.

places in the Hebrew Scriptures, angels are called "sons of God." But the writer is saying that Messiah Jesus is God's Son in a very different sense. He is "begotten" and "like begets like"—i.e., deity begets deity. All of Psalm 2 is prophecy about the Messiah. In the quote above, the word "today" means that at a particular time—clearly at the time of his resurrection and by means of it—God declared that Jesus was no ordinary man but in fact his eternally existing Son. During his ministry on earth, Jesus claimed to be God's Son and essentially equal to him—and God the Father supported that claim by raising him back to life. It would have been clear to any Jew who believed the resurrection actually happened that God would not have done this if Jesus' claims were in any way false. Because such a claim—if not true—would have been blasphemous and offensive to God. ➤ And in another place God said, "I will be his Father and he will be my Son." *[2 Samuel 7:14]* ❖ God said this to King David about his not-yet-conceived son, Solomon—who would become king after him. But this was also a prophecy about another descendant of David—the Messiah who would be born 1,000 years later and who would be God's Son in a more literal sense. In the previous verse, [2 Samuel 7:13] God said he would establish the throne—meaning kingship— of this descendant forever. This was understood at the time as meaning that descendants of Solomon would always be kings over Israel. But it's fuller meaning referred to the Messiah—who will personally reign as king forever. Such is the nature of many prophecies that they have multiple levels of meaning. ➤ 6 And when God brings his firstborn Son into the world again at his second coming, he says about him, "Let all God's angels submit to him in worship."

❖ In the Scriptures, God commands that only he, Yahweh, is to be worshipped—which means to offer yourself in complete submission to him—so this statement clearly implies the deity of his Son and his unity with God the Father. The words in this quote may be from either Psalm 97:7 or from Deuteronomy 32:43, but neither of these verses are quoted exactly. The Septuagint translation of Deuteronomy 32:43 and also the Hebrew Deuteronomy texts found in the Dead Sea scrolls have these words, but the later Masoretic Hebrew text does not. In referring to his "firstborn" Son, Jesus is elsewhere called the firstborn of many sons. But all other sons and daughters are "adopted." God has only one "begotten" Son. ➤ 7 In contrast, when speaking about angels in the Scriptures, God said, "God makes his angels like the wind. They are his servants and like flames of fire." *[Psalm 104:4]* ❖ It isn't particularly clear what this description of angels means—except the point that they are his servants. His Son created everything and is to be submitted to in worship. Angels are servants. There's a clear and vast distinction. ➤ 8 But with regard to his Son, God said, "Your reign as King, O God, will be forever. You will be known for your justice—9 for you love what is right and hate evil. Therefore God—who is your God—has chosen you above all others and has anointed you with the oil of joy." *[Psalm 45:6-7]* ❖ Oil is a symbol of the Holy Spirit, and anointing a person with oil by pouring it over his head was a sign of God's choosing him to be a prophet, priest, or a king—and a sign of receiving the Holy Spirit. God calls his Son, "God." Realize that God very clearly taught and emphasized throughout the Hebrew Scriptures that there is only ONE God. Therefore, it is necessary to conclude that God and his Son—who is also God—are together only one God—not two. From other passages, the same can be said about the Holy Spirit—who is also God. From passages like these, the doctrine (teaching) of the Trinity was formulated—one God existing as three distinct, yet inseparable, persons. ➤ 10 God also said about his Son, "It was you, Lord, who laid the foundations of the earth at the very beginning of time. And with your own hands you made the heavens. *[Psalm 102:25]* ❖ Again, a reference to the Son as the Creator. ¶ First-century Jews had various conceptions of different levels or numbers of heavens, so the plural is intentional. One concept was that the visible night sky was the first heaven, the second Heaven was the invisible spiritual realm where angels live, and the third—or highest—Heaven is where God himself lives. ➤ 11 Their existence is finite in time, but you exist eternally. They will wear out like clothing. 12 You will roll them up, throw them away, and replace them as one would an old coat. But you will remain eternally the same. Your life will never end." *[Psalm 102:25-27]* 13 But God never said to any angel—as he did to his Son, "Sit enthroned at my right hand until I make all of your enemies submit to you." *[Psalm 110:1]* ❖ Again, an argument from silence. ➤ 14 This is because angels are only God's servants. They are spirits that he sends to serve those of us who will be saved.

2

A Warning About Drifting Away from the Faith

1 Since God has spoken to us so clearly through his Son, he will hold us even more responsible for accepting his message about

the way of salvation than he held people previously. So we need to faithfully follow his message—embodied in the Good News—lest we drift away from it and come under condemnation. 2 Consider God's former message as embodied in his Torah which was delivered to Moses by angels for all his people to follow. Whenever our ancestors abandoned his commands, they were justly and severely punished. ❖ *This refers particularly to the Old Covenant as detailed in the Teachings of Moses, and also to all of God's words given to his people in the rest of the Hebrew Scriptures. The authors of the New Testament apparently accepted the Jewish tradition that Moses received the Torah on Mount Sinai from angels representing God, [Acts 7:53; Galatians 3:19] even though the account in Exodus chapters 19—34 says that Yahweh himself spoke to Moses and gave him the Torah. This seems to be emphasized by their interaction in Exodus 33:18-23. ¶ The punishments spoken of in verse 2 were not issued for minor or individual infractions against the Torah's teachings, but rather, when his people as a whole turned away from keeping the conditions of the Covenant. These punishments are detailed in Deuteronomy chapter 28. God's punishment usually took the form of oppression from and being conquered by other kingdoms. Many of the Hebrew Scriptures are about such times—recorded as a warning to us about the seriousness of God's people breaking Covenant with him.* ➤ 3 So if God punished our ancestors so severely for breaking the Old Covenant—instituted through mere angels—what do you expect will happen to us if we break faith with the fantastic message of salvation under the New Covenant, instituted through his own Son? This message was first revealed by the Lord Jesus himself and then passed on to us by those who heard it straight from him. ❖ *This last sentence implies that the writer of this letter did not himself receive the gospel directly from Jesus, which is why many people doubt Paul wrote this letter. See Paul's claim to direct revelation from Jesus in Galatians 1:11-12.* ➤ 4 God affirmed the message spoken by his Son—and later by the apostles—with miraculous signs and supernatural acts showing that God affirmed what they taught. He also affirms the message to us through the supernatural gifts of the Holy Spirit—who distributes them among us as he sees fit.

In the New World Order After Jesus' Return, Humans Will Reign with him

5 The new world that will be established when the Messiah returns will not be ruled by angels. ❖ *First-century Jews commonly believed that angels were the spiritual power behind earthly rulers and were, in effect, the true rulers of nations. There are hints of this in Daniel 10:10-21 concerning the demonic princes of Persia and Greece, and Michael—the prince of Israel.* ➤ 6 Somewhere in the Scriptures David said to God, **"How is it that you are so solicitous of mere human beings or are concerned about us at all? 7 You created human kind a little lower than angels, and now you have exalted us to reign with glory and honor 8 over all you have made."** *[Psalm 8:4-6]* ❖ *The Septuagint says we were created a little lower than "angels." The word in Hebrew is "elohim"—which can refer to any authority, heavenly or earthly, but usually refers to God himself. Since we were made in the very image of God and it was always God's intention to exalt humanity to reign at his side as the bride of his Son, many scholars believe that the Psalm says we were created just a little lower than "God." But since humanity's fall into sinful rebellion against God, we have had a lower position than angels. And Jesus, in his incarnation, was also made like us—lower than the angels in glory and ability before his glory was restored at his resurrection. So both translations of the word are true.* ➤ When the psalm says that God "exalted us to reign over all you made," this clearly includes everything. We haven't seen this happen yet. 9 But we've seen it happen with one man who is our forerunner and who has prepared the way for us. Jesus was made "a little lower than angels" for a time so that he could suffer and die, and now God has exalted him with glory and honor—both as a human being and as his eternal Son—precisely because he suffered and died for all humanity. He did this so God's undeserved favor could be offered to all of humanity. ❖ *Since the incarnation when God's Son became human, humanity has been joined to the Godhead in the person of the Son of God. When God raised Jesus from death and exalted him at his right hand, a human—the God-Man Jesus—was exalted to that position. The Son of God is no longer exclusively deity; he is also fully human. When we are spiritually joined to Jesus in our spiritual rebirth at the time of our salvation, we too are spiritually exalted to where Jesus is in Heaven. [Ephesians 2:6] When we die, we will experience more of this state of glory*

and exaltation in Heaven. And when Jesus returns and we gain our resurrection bodies, we will experience fully what this means. ➤

Jesus the Messiah Is Our Example

10 God made all things for himself and for his own purposes. So it's appropriate that he didn't allow mankind's fall into sin to ruin his original plans to conform many people to his glorious character and make them a bride for his Son. That's why he sent his Son into the world to redeem them. It's also fitting that Jesus had to suffer to bring about our salvation. This was unexpected, but people who are being saved must suffer in this life in order to follow Jesus. And Jesus—in the course of suffering in order to obey his Father's will—became the perfect example for us to follow. ❖ *Since we know that Jesus experienced every suffering and trial we go through (and more), we can have confidence that he sympathizes with us and is willing to help us. He was our trail blazer and is our leader and example in this life. The writer felt a need to explain to his Jewish readers why the Messiah had to suffer—since such an idea was repugnant to them and went against their expectations. The expanded interpretation of this verse (above) brings out the logic implied by the author. There was also the necessity of the Messiah's sacrificial death—which was the largest part of his suffering—and the importance of that is brought out later in the letter. Some of the suffering that all believers must go through is the struggle to reject our sinful desires in order to live in obedience to God's will. Secondly, believers also suffer when we are ridiculed, rejected, persecuted, and sometimes even killed because of our faith.* ➤ 11 He is proud to call his followers his "brothers and sisters" because those that he is in the process of making holy now have the same Father he does. ❖ *When we were spiritually reborn, we became true spiritual children of God the Father. We may not consciously experience the fullness of this reality yet, but in God's eyes we are his true children. He implants his character and nature into our human spirits, and joins our spirits to his Holy Spirit who lives in us—and this spiritually joins us to Jesus and God the Father, since they are all a spiritual unity. The imperfections remaining in us he will eventually eradicate so we will fully reflect his loving character and holiness.* ➤ 12 In fact, in the Scriptures the Messiah said to God, "I will proclaim the greatness of your character to my brothers and sisters. I will sing praise to you among the congregation of your people." *[Psalm 22:22]*
❖ *The writer's point is that the Messiah readily identifies with his followers as his brothers and sisters (literally, "brethren," but it means all his people) and sees himself as a member of the congregation of God's people. He uses the quoted verse to back up his assertion in verse 11 above.* ➤
13 The Messiah also trusts in God, just like we do. He said about God in the Scriptures, "I will trust in him." *[Isaiah 8:17]* He also said, "Here I am, together with God's other children whom he has entrusted to me." *[Isaiah 8:18]* ❖ *Jesus, God's Son, is himself God. Even though we are spiritually joined to him and are adopted as God's children—we are not deity. But Jesus still considers us his brothers and sisters since he is also human and we are spiritual children of his Father. And his role in the Godhead is to fulfill the desires of his Father so he is voluntarily submitted to him. These verses further show that the Messiah identifies himself with his brothers and sisters as being under the Father's authority.* ➤ 14 Since the people that God desired to redeem and make his children had physical human bodies, his Son became a fully physical human too. He did this so that by his death, he could destroy the power Satan had over all humanity—who were otherwise condemned to death. 15 Thus he provided a way that humanity could be set free from its slavery to sin and to the fear of death—which is everyone's master until they are joined to Jesus. ❖ *According to God's holy nature and justice, the penalty for sin was eternal death—i.e., eternal separation from God, the source of all life. Since the guilty people he wanted to redeem were human, a human had to suffer the penalty. That's why his Son had to be fully human. When Adam and Eve sinned, their spirits "died" and they became enslaved to Satan. When God's Son became a human, he resisted Satan's temptations and never succumbed to his power—meaning he was sinless. And when Jesus—as the perfect sinless sacrifice—suffered the penalty of our sin for us by dying and then was raised back to life, he defeated Satan and the power of death. So now, when we believe that he has done this for us and accept him as our Lord and Savior, he creates within us new human spirits that are holy and acceptable to God. Then he spiritually joins us to himself so God considers that we have already been punished for our sins—because we are united with Jesus who was punished for our sins. In that union, we are also joined to his power that is available to enable us to defeat Satan and the power of sin in our lives.* ➤

Jesus the Messiah Is Our High Priest and Is Superior to Moses

16 It's clear that Jesus didn't come to help angels, but to help to those who—because of their faith—are spiritual descendants of Abraham. ❖ *It isn't clear how this verse adds to the writer's argument. One possibility is that his audience considered angels to be more important in God's plan than people. Also, some of them considered the Messiah on equal status to angels and might have thought that he (a man) had actually become an angel for some purpose.* ➤ 17 Therefore, it was necessary for him to become like his people in every way so he could serve us as our High Priest—representing us to God— yet as one who understands our temptation and can show us mercy. He is always faithful to present us to his Father as people whose sins he has paid for and whom he has purified from all sin. A ❖ *This purification from sin is technically called "justification." It means that we have been legally forgiven and declared holy as a result of our union with Jesus—who is holy and who paid the penalty for our sins so we could be forgiven. We are also being "sanctified." This means that the tendency to sin—which we have as long as we remain in these mortal bodies—is gradually being removed. We are becoming holy in experience and character—as well as in legal standing.* ➤ 18 He is able to help us when we are tempted to sin because he also suffered temptation, but without sinning— and he fully understands what our lives in this world are like.

3

1 My brothers and sisters, God called you to be his children and declared you holy in his sight. So carefully consider this man Jesus—who we proclaim is God's special messenger to mankind and our High Priest who represents us to God. 2 He was faithful to complete the work of being our Savior to which God appointed him—just as Moses was faithful in all his appointed work as prophet and Torah giver in the household of God's people. 3 But Jesus deserves far greater honor and praise than Moses—since the one who established God's household deserves greater honor than those who serve in it. 4 For there are many who serve in God's household to build it up, but it was God who established it. 5 It's true that Moses was a faithful servant in God's household, but he was only a servant. ❖ *The Jews revered Moses.* ➤ His life and work were shadows of the things that God would later reveal to his people about Jesus the Messiah. 6 But in contrast, the Messiah was faithful as a Son who is master over all of God's household. And we are members of his household if—in our faith and confident expectation in his promises—we continue to endure until the very end of our lives.

A Warning Against Unbelief

7 Therefore, since the Messiah is superior to Moses and the Messiah taught what God is saying to us today, we had better pay close attention to him. Or else we may end up rebelling against God like our ancestors did. Just as the Holy Spirit says in the Scriptures, **"You must listen to what God is saying today. 8-9 'Don't be obstinate like those who rebelled against me and tried my patience in the Sinai wilderness. Your Israelite ancestors—whom Moses led out of slavery in Egypt—saw me work mighty miracles for forty years and yet they still didn't learn to trust me. 10 That's why I was angry with them and said, "They are always complaining and disloyal to me. They have refused to live according to my commands." 11 So in my anger, I vowed, "These people will never enter my rest." ' "** *[Psalm 95:7-11]* ❖ *God said he would lead the Israelites to the land he had promised to give their ancestor Abraham. It was a fertile land, but was occupied by powerful ethnic groups who were so evil that God had decided he would have the Israelites completely destroy them. This may seem harsh to some people today, but take care that you don't judge God. As an example of their evil, they commonly sacrificed their own children to idols and worshipped their gods with sexual immorality. However, the Israelites had been slaves and were inexperienced in battle. They were afraid and refused to trust God to help them conquer the land—where they would have lived as free people and enjoyed its prosperity after having been slaves for*

A 2:17 The literal text says that he "...made propitiation for the sins of the people." See the footnote at Romans 3:25 about the word "propitiation."

hundreds of years in Egypt. It was a land of "rest." (This is the first meaning of God's "rest." It has a couple of more meanings.) But due to their rebellion against God's commands, he decided they were unworthy of entering that land of rest and enjoying it. So he made them wander in the Sinai wilderness for 40 years—until all the rebellious adults had died and a new generation who would obey him was ready to conquer the land. [Numbers chapters 13—14] The Israelites entering the promised land is also a picture of God's people entering Heaven. (This is the second meaning of God's "rest.") Some commentators think the Israelites who rebelled also didn't enter into God's "rest" in Heaven when they died. But God said in Numbers 14:20 that he pardoned them, so they may have been saved. (There is also a third meaning of "rest" which will be explained later.) ➤ 12 Therefore, my brothers and sisters, take care! It would be tragic if any of you turned away from following the Living God—who keeps his promises and follows through on his threats. 13 To avoid this pitfall, encourage and exhort each other every day as long as you have the opportunity so that none of you will be deceived by sinful lies, become hardened against God's word, and rebel. 14 Do this because we only remain joined to the Messiah and receive all the blessings he has promised if we remain firm in our trusting him just like we did at the beginning—and if we continue until the very end of our lives. 15 Never forget the urgent warning in the Scriptures. It says, **"You must listen to what God is saying today. Don't be obstinate like those who rebelled."** *[Psalm 95:7-8]* 16 Who were the people who heard God speak to them and still rebelled against him? It was almost all of the adult Israelites whom Moses had led out of Egypt and who had seen all the miracles that God had done for them. ❖ *The account of the Israelites leaving Egypt and the miracles God did is found in the book of Exodus. The account continues in the books of Leviticus, Numbers, and Deuteronomy.* ➤ 17 And who made God angry for 40 years? It was the very people he had chosen to be his own special people, but who rebelled and so were sentenced to die in the wilderness. 18 And who was God speaking about when he vowed that they would never enter his "rest?" It was those who rebelled against him. 19 So it's clear that because of their unbelief, God didn't allow them to enter his "rest." They didn't fully trust him.

4

Entering God's "Rest" Means Enjoying the Salvation He Has Already Accomplished for Us

1 God has promised that we can enter into his "rest." But we must take care! It would be tragic if some of us never enter because we fall short of God's requirements. 2 We too have had the Good News of God's promises preached to us, just as our ancestors did. But the promise didn't benefit them because they didn't accept it or trust in the one who made the promise. ❖ *The Israelites had the promise of forgiveness of sin through following the requirements of the Teachings of Moses, and the promise of a fertile land to have as their own. God has promised us that we may enter into the "rest" of knowing that our sins are forgiven and having eternal life in Heaven—through faith in Jesus.* ➤ 3 We, who are true believers, have already entered the "rest" that he referred to when he said, **"So in my anger I vowed, 'These people will never enter my rest.'"** *[Psalm 95:11]* It was possible for them to enter his "rest" because he had finished his work of providing for that "rest" when he created the world. And he has always made it possible for people to enter it. ❖ *God's "rest" refers to his resting after his six days of work creating the world and providing for our salvation. He rested on the seventh day to enjoy what he had accomplished. All his work of creation and also his provision for the salvation of human kind—whom he knew would sin—was finished. Revelation 13:8 indicates that the Messiah was sacrificed for our sins, by plan, even before the world was made. When we enter God's "rest," we join him in his resting and enjoy the salvation that he has already accomplished for us. This doesn't mean that we no longer work. But as we go through life, we are enjoying what God has accomplished and provided for us—especially our salvation—and also enjoying intimate fellowship with him. So once we enter his "rest," we no longer toil in our own strength to please him—but live by allowing his power to do its work in and through us. We are "resting" in the sense that we don't have to strive to accomplish what God has already done for us. We can lean on his strength and power—resting in his arms as we go through life. Ultimately, of course, we will enter into the fullness of his "rest" in Heaven.* ➤ 4 Somewhere in the Scriptures God said this about the seventh day, **"On the seventh day, God rested from all his work."** *[Genesis 2:2]* ❖ *This*

doesn't mean that he rested from all work forever. It means he rested from his work of creation. Jesus said in John 5:17 that his Father is still working—even on the Sabbath. ➤ 5 Again, as quoted above he said, **"These people will never enter my rest."** [Psalm 95:11] ❖ *This "rest" is the same "rest" he made to be available to his people when he first made the world.* ➤ 6 Even so, there are some that he does allow to enter his "rest"—in spite of those in the past who heard good news from God, but didn't enter because they didn't obey him. 7 Many years after those Israelites failed to enter God's "rest," he caused David to write the verse already mentioned that says, **"You must listen to what God is saying today. Don't be obstinate like those who rebelled."** [Psalm 95:7-8] So it's clear that God chose a certain day when people can enter his "rest"—and that day is "today." ❖ *By "today," the writer means every day in the present until a person dies or until Jesus returns. But now is always the best time since no one knows if he will be alive tomorrow, or if Jesus will return tomorrow. Today may be a person's last chance to believe, so it's foolish to wait until later.* ➤ 8 When Joshua later led the Israelites into the promised land, this was part of the "rest" that God had promised them—but not the greatest part. ❖ *See the book of Joshua.* ➤ For if entering the promised land was entering the most important part of God's "rest," then he wouldn't have later talked about another day when his people could enter it. 9 Therefore, there still exists a "rest" for God's people to enter which is like God's Sabbath (seventh-day) "rest" after creating the world. 10 Those who have entered God's "rest" have also ceased working to make themselves acceptable to God, but rather "rest" while enjoying the perfection that God has accomplished in them— just as God rested from his work on the seventh day and enjoyed the perfect world he had made. 11 Therefore, to enter that "rest" we must press in through true faith which results in obedience, lest some of us fail to enter because of unbelief resulting in disobedience. 12 And we must make our decision to enter his "rest" now. Since the Holy Spirit is working through God's word, he causes it to impact us like it's alive and active—helping us recognize his truth. In the same way that a sharp sword can slice us

wide open—exposing the inner recesses of our bodies—God's word can also touch the very center of our hearts and thoughts. When we hear it, it reveals our hidden thoughts and desires to us; and like a judge, it tells us if they are good or evil. So we need to choose to agree with God's word and repent—or else we will end up rejecting it and not enter his "rest." It's impossible to ignore his word. It will either save us or destroy us—depending on how we respond to it. 13 There is nothing we can hide from God. He knows everything we think and do. And at the final judgment, we will all have to answer to him for everything we've done in this life.

Jesus Is Our Great High Priest

14 But don't despair! Instead, cling to what we say we believe, for we have Jesus— God's own Son—as our High Priest. He has entered into the very presence of God in Heaven and represents us favorably to him. 15 He's a High Priest who is able to sympathize with our weaknesses because he was tempted in all the ways we are tempted— yet he didn't sin. 16 So let's boldly come close to our God in prayer and submissive worship, confident that he will warmly welcome us and will grant us his mercy and undeserved favor when we need it. ❖ *God is merciful to his true children, not giving us what we deserve (i.e., punishment) and granting us favor—which means that he treats us with overwhelming kindness and gives us all the help we need, even though we don't deserve it.* ➤

5

1 In the past, every High Priest in Israel was an ordinary man that God appointed to be the only mediator between his people and himself. The High Priest presented the people's gifts and sacrifices for sins to God on their behalf. ❖ *The purpose of this was to instruct people that their sins made them unworthy to be in God's presence. The High Priest had to go through elaborate rituals to make himself ritually acceptable to approach God. These rituals did not, in themselves, remove his sin, but again emphasized the difficulty for sinful man to approach a holy God. Yet it also taught them that God did desire a relationship with people since he provided a way for them to receive*

forgiveness and to approach him—even though it had to be *indirectly.* ➤ 2 The High Priest could be gentle with God's people—even though they were ignorant of God's ways and were constantly led astray into sin—because he had the same inherent sinful weaknesses they had. ❖ *The people—who are here talked about as being "ignorant of God's ways"—understood clearly the way God wanted them to live. Many people today mistakenly think that if they know about God's truth, they have knowledge. But in the biblical sense, they are ignorant unless that intellectual knowledge is manifested in habitual outward—and inward—obedience. True knowledge of God and his ways means that a person intimately knows him because he or she has learned to live humbly in obedience to him. God reveals himself to such people in ways he never does with those who are content with mere intellectual "knowledge."* ➤ 3 That's why the High Priest had to offer sacrifices for his own sins, as well as for the sins of the people he was representing.

4 No one can choose to honor himself by appointing himself as God's High Priest. Only God can call him to this office and give him that honor—just like he called Aaron to be the first High Priest. 5 In the same way, the Messiah didn't decide to grant himself the honor of becoming God's High Priest. It was God the Father who chose him and said, "I am your Father. Today I'm publicly revealing that you are my begotten Son." *[Psalm 2:7]* He never honored any other High Priest in this way. ❖ *To publicly reveal that the man, Jesus, was God's only begotten Son, conferred great honor on him in the sight of people who previously had not known that fact. This probably refers to the public revelation that he was not an ordinary man when he was resurrected from death.* ➤ 6 In another place, God says of the Messiah, "You are a priest forever in the priestly order of Melchizedek." *[Psalm 110:4]* 7 While Jesus lived in this world, he prayed and cried—pleading with God the Father who was able to save him from the death he knew was coming. God answered his prayer because he was completely submitted to the Father. ❖ *This probably refers to Jesus' prayer in Gethsemane. He prayed that God's will would be done, not his own—even though he dreaded the suffering he was facing. The Father answered him by giving him the strength to enable him to do his will.* ➤ 8 Even though Jesus was his Son, it was God's will that he learn to obey even when his obedience caused him to

suffer. ❖ *As long as there is sin in this world, God's people will have to suffer in their efforts to obey him. It was God's will that Jesus learn to obey—even when it caused him to suffer—so that he could fully sympathize with us, be our example, and help us obey when we face suffering as a consequence of obeying.* ➤ 9 Through his obedience, he became qualified to be the perfect High Priest for us—and also the source of eternal salvation for all who are faithful to obey him to the end of their lives. 10 So God appointed him to be our High Priest in the priestly order of Melchizedek.

An Exhortation
for Us to Grow in Our Spiritual Lives

11 There's much more that I would like to say about these things, but it's hard to explain it to you since you have regressed in your faith and have become slow to understand spiritual truth. 12 You've been believers a long time now and should be capable of teaching others about God's truth, but you are not. Instead, you need someone to teach you the basic lessons in God's word all over again. You are like nursing infants who can't yet eat solid food because you can only understand the simplest spiritual truths and are not ready for the deeper ones. 13 Such people are "baby believers." They lack true understanding of the Scriptural teachings about what pleases God, and can only live on "milk" teachings. 14 Solid spiritual food is for those who are more mature in their faith. By that, I mean those who easily discern what is good and evil in God's sight because they've had much experience actually living the way God wants them to live. ❖ *The point being—you can't become mature and really know about God and his ways without daily living in obedience to his word.* ➤

6

1 Therefore, we must go beyond the basic lessons about the Messiah and become mature in our understanding and way of living. We shouldn't have to continually focus exclusively on the basic foundational teachings—such as repenting from evil deeds that lead to eternal death, and trusting in God, ❖ *Another interpretation: repenting from trying to*

depend on your own works for salvation and, instead, trusting in what God has done to save you. ➤ 2 and teachings about different kinds of baptisms (John's baptism of repentance, water baptism for believers, baptism in the Holy Spirit), and the purposes of laying on hands, ❖ *Laying hands on a person (or raising hands over a group of people) is a biblical pattern for conferring a blessing, [Genesis 48:14-15; Leviticus 9:22; Matthew 19:13; Mark 10:16; Luke 24:50] or ordaining someone for service, [Numbers 8:10; 27:18, 23; 1 Timothy 5:22] or healing, [2 Kings 4:34; Mark 5:23; 8:23-25; 16:18; Luke 4:40; Acts 9:12, 17] or for blessing with the gift of the Holy Spirit, [Acts 8:17-19] or conferring a spiritual gift, [1 Timothy 4:14; 2 Timothy 1:6] or transferring sin to a sacrifice. [Leviticus 4:15; 16:21; 24:14; Numbers 8:12]* ➤ about the future resurrection of all who have died, and about God's judging all people on the Last Day and determining their eternal fates. We must go beyond these basic lessons. 3 And we will do this if God allows us—except for those who have gone so far as to reject the Messiah. 4 For people who have truly believed in the Messiah and then later have completely rejected him cannot repent again. *[1 Timothy 1:19; Hebrews 10:26-31]* I'm talking about people who have understood the truth about the Messiah, who have experienced having their sins forgiven, who have experienced the Holy Spirit living in them, 5 who know from experience that God keeps his promises in the Scriptures, and who have seen a little bit of his miraculous power which will be common in the new age after Jesus returns. ❖ *Some commentators believe this refers to the miraculous gifts of the Holy Spirit, but it probably also includes any work of God that they've seen—including answers to prayer.* ➤ 6 People who have experienced all these things and then completely reject the Messiah cannot repent and come back to God again. Because they are nailing God's son to the cross again and exposing him to public humiliation. ❖ *The humiliation may be that of a former follower who has experienced the best God has to offer in this life and then publicly rejects it as not being good enough. Another view, offered by commentator David Stern—a Messianic Jewish believer—is that some former Jewish believers in Jesus were reverting back to animal sacrifices to take away their sins. As long as they were doing this, they were, in effect, declaring that Jesus' sacrifice on the cross was powerless to take away their sins—thus*

implying that they agreed with those Jews who had rejected Jesus and said that his death was merely the shameful death of a common criminal.* ➤ It would be tragic if any of you became like this. 7 Here is an illustration of how God responds to people. They are like land that is cultivated by a farmer and receives frequent rain. ❖ *The farmer represents God, and the rain represents his blessings, teaching, and the Holy Spirit.* ➤ If their lives are like land that produces good produce, then they receive God's blessing. 8 But land that produces thorns and thistles—in spite of the farmer's labor and plentiful rain—is worthless and in danger of being cursed. The farmer will burn it. ❖ *It's true that we are saved because he grants us undeserved favor through our response of faith in his promises—and not by what we do. However, genuine saving faith will inevitably produce a life of obedience and good works—not to earn salvation—but as a result of being forgiven and being filled with the Holy Spirit. Anyone who does not live this kind of life—assuming they have had sufficient time to grow—is not saved and does not have the Holy Spirit living in them—no matter what they profess to believe. Such people are worthless for God's purposes and they will end up in Hell.* ➤ 9 My dear friends, even though I'm giving you these dire warnings, I am convinced that you will not turn out to be among this kind of people who will be condemned. I'm confident that you are producing the good fruit that's the evidence of those who are saved—and that even better things will be forth coming. 10 Because God is entirely fair. He won't forget the work you did for him or the love you showed him in helping his people—just as you continue to do. He will reward you for these things. 11 But I want all of you to continue to be diligent to do the Lord's work out of love for him to the very end of your lives—so that you will receive the Heavenly reward you are expecting. ❖ *If you don't faithfully persevere to the end, there is danger that you will not receive the reward you are expecting. A clear condition in Scripture regarding God's promise of salvation is that we must persevere to the end of our lives in true faith. And true faith always results in obedience to his word.* ➤ 12 So don't become lazy, but try to imitate the lives of those who have already died and gone on to Heaven to receive their promised inheritance from God. I'm talking about those who endured in faith and patience to the very end of their lives.

God Always Fulfills His Promises

❖ *But be aware that many promises are conditional and based on our response to his commands.* ➤

13 For an example of persevering in faith, consider Abraham. When God made his famous promise to Abraham, he swore an oath based on his own integrity—since there was no one greater than himself to swear by. 14 He said, **"I will certainly bless you and cause you to have countless descendants."** [Genesis 22:16-17] ❖ *This is a very partial quote of Genesis 22:17, but the writer knew his readers were intimately familiar with the full quote and context. The oath that God swore is found in Genesis 22:16—which the author didn't quote.* ➤ 15 After waiting patiently a very long time, Abraham finally received what God promised. ❖ *Abraham waited 25 years after this promise was made before Isaac—the son God promised him—was born. And never in his lifetime did he see the complete fulfillment of God's promise that he would have many descendants and inherit the promised land. He only saw the beginning of the promise come true, but he never doubted that God would do what he said.* ➤ 16 When people make an oath, they call on someone greater than themselves to guarantee that they will do what they say—or to punish them if they don't. So the person receiving the promise believes them and, therefore, no further discussion is needed. ❖ *Even in our culture not very long ago, a person's "word," or promise, or a vow before God, was enough to satisfy those who heard it.* ➤ 17 Similarly, God wanted to assure those who will receive what he has promised that his promise is irrevocable and that his plan will never change. That's why he added an oath to his promise. ❖ *God's promises and intentions never change, but we need to understand exactly what those are. It is his intentions that he promises to keep— not whatever free interpretations or misunderstanding of those promises we might have.* ➤ 18 He did this so that we—who have accepted Jesus as our Savior—could be encouraged to know that we really will receive eternal life in Heaven if we continue in true faith and obedience. We know that God cannot lie, so we have two unchangeable things to encourage us to persevere—his promise and his oath. 19 Our looking forward to receiving what he promised us in Heaven is like an anchor in our lives. This keeps us securely tied to Jesus— who is in Heaven where we can't now see him. 20 Jesus has gone ahead of us—on our behalf—into the very presence of God the Father. He is our forerunner, and later we will join him. There, in God the Father's presence, he is our eternal High Priest in the priestly order of Melchizedek—representing us to his Father as those whom he has saved and made holy.

7

Melchizedek's Priesthood Is Greater Than Abraham and the Levitical Priesthood

1 Melchizedek was King of Salem and also a priest of the Most High God. **A** When Abraham was returning home after defeating the armies of four kings in battle, Melchizedek met him and blessed him. ❖ *See the story about Abraham fighting the kings in Genesis chapter 14, and about Melchizedek in Genesis*

A 7:1 Even though the Israelites later came to know that there is only one God, in Abraham's day (approximately 2000 BC), it was commonly thought that there were many gods. So to distinguish the God of Noah, Shem, and later Abraham and his descendants from other so-called gods, he was often referred to as the "most High God"— superior to all others. (His name—"Yahweh"—was only revealed to Moses several hundred years after Abraham's time.) Other gods were usually just man-made idols, although there may have been demonic spirits at work behind many of them. It shouldn't be too surprising that there were still believers in the one true God, since according to biblical chronology the time of this story about Melchizedek is less than 400 years after the flood. Because of the long life spans of Noah and the next few generations, Noah and Abraham overlapped in their life spans by about 50 years—and Abraham overlapped life spans with several other of his long-lived ancestors who were descended from Noah and his son Shem. Shem, who experienced the flood at age 100, died 34 years after Abraham died. So it's very likely that many of Shem's descendants were around who knew about the God of Noah and Shem. Thus the fact that Abraham should meet a priest of the Most High God is not at all surprising. While God chose Abraham and his descendants for a special role in bringing the rest of the world knowledge about him- self—and through which to bring the Messiah into the world—there were likely still other groups of people who knew as much about the Most High God as Noah did and who also still worshipped him.

14:18-20. The name of the city of Salem was later changed to Jerusalem. ➤ ² And Abraham gave Melchizedek one tenth of the spoils he had taken from his defeated enemies. Melchizedek's name means "King of Righteousness." He was the King of the Salem—which means he was "King of Peace." ❖ *Salem means "peace." Note the obvious parallels to the Messiah—who is also both a priest and a king and who bears the title "Prince of Peace" [Isaiah 9:6] and is described as a "king who rules righteously." [Isaiah 32:1; Jeremiah 23:5-6; Revelation 15:3]* ➤

³ There is no record of Melchizedek's father, mother, or genealogy. ❖ *Such records were important and significant for important people in the biblical cultures.* ➤ Nor is there any record of his birth or death. In this, he is like God's Son because he continues to be a priest forever. ❖ *Note the writer's argument from silence. Since there is no record of his dying in the Scriptures (or elsewhere), the writer assumes that he still lives (some 1500 years later) and continues as a priest—thus comparing him in this respect to God's Son. Some people believe that Melchizedek actually was God's Son appearing in the form of a man prior to his incarnation in order to bless Abraham. Such an event is called a "theophany." One Jewish tradition says Melchizedek was a son or descendant of Shem. We don't know if either of these views are correct. But events such as this one with Melchizedek didn't happen by accident, nor was the account included in the Scriptures by accident. Many Hebrew Scripture accounts—even very brief ones like Melchizedek's—are prefiguring "types" that outline spiritual truths. They were placed in the Scriptures by the Holy Spirit for us to learn from, [2 Timothy 3:16] and are best understood in light of the truths recorded in the New Testament.* ➤ ⁴ Now consider the greatness of Melchizedek. Abraham—who is the great patriarch of Israel and also of all who believe in God's promises—gave him the choicest tenth ᴬ of all the spoils he won in battle. ❖ *Abraham is the archetypal example of a man of faith—the revered father of all Israel. Yet the writer is driving home the point that there was someone whom Abraham considered greater than himself.* ➤ ⁵ According to the Teachings of Moses, all the people of Israel must give a tenth of all their income and material increase to those of the tribe of Levi who become priests. The priests collect it from their own people, since they are all descended from Abraham. ❖ *See Numbers 18:25-32 about giving a tenth of all income and material increase to God.* ➤ ⁶ But Melchizedek was not a Levitical priest. Indeed, he was not descended from Abraham because Abraham had not yet had any children. Yet Melchizedek received a tenth of Abraham's spoils and blessed him—the man whom God had honored by giving him great promises of many descendants and a great inheritance. ⁷ Now it's clear to everyone that a person who has the power to bless is greater than the person who receives the blessing. So this proves that Melchizedek was greater than Abraham. ⁸ In the case of the priests of Israel, people pay the tenth part of their income to men who later die. But Melchizedek is greater than they are because he was a priest long before there were Levitical priests—and the Holy Scriptures say that he continues to live. ❖ *The writer of this letter says Melchizedek continues to live because the Scriptures say in Psalm 110:4, "You are a priest forever in the priestly order of Melchizedek." The assumption is that the priestly order of Melchizedek is an order of priests who live and function as priests forever. Since the Holy Spirit inspired the writer of this letter, it is safest to assume this is true.* ➤ ⁹⁻¹⁰ It is possible to think about it like this: Abraham's descendants, the Levitical priests, were genetically still in his body when he paid a tenth to Melchizedek. So in a way, the Levitical priests—who collect the tenth part of the income and material gains of Abraham's descendants—also paid a tenth to Melchizedek. Therefore, Melchizedek's priesthood is greater than the Levitical priesthood. ❖ *It's a common assumption in biblical cultures that an ancestor is greater than his descendants and deserving of greater honor. And a tithe is also paid from one who is lesser to one who is greater.* ➤

ᴬ **7:4** The practice of paying a tenth (also known as a "tithe") to God is an important biblical teaching which was commanded in the Teachings of Moses and is seen here practiced by Abraham hundreds of years before the Torah was given. Many Bible teachers believe that tithing is a principle that God still means for his people to practice today. A proper discussion of this principle is too long to include here. But if you don't know about it, you should study the biblical teachings on tithing. There are also books available on the topic to help you find out why it is important.

God Has Amended the Teachings in His Torah About Who Can Be a Priest

11 The Levitical priesthood was established according to commands that God gave to Moses. But the work these priests did couldn't completely take away people's sins. ❖ *Their work made provision for forgiveness of sins, but not for sanctification—i.e., changing people to rid them of the desire and inclination to sin—making them truly holy.* ➤ They were, in fact, a shadow of a different kind of priest who came later—that is, the Messiah. It's apparent that God didn't consider the Levitical priesthood sufficient for all time because he later spoke about a kind of priest who is like Melchizedek, and who—unlike the Levitical priests—is not descended from Aaron. ❖ *Do not make the mistake of thinking that the Teachings in the Torah and the Levitical priesthood were God's "Plan A" that failed. They served their proper purpose until the time was right for the Messiah to come. The Messiah was in God's plan from the very beginning, but certain things could not be instituted before his death and resurrection. Many things that God told the Israelites to do in the Torah were prefiguring "types" which God would clarify to his people later—through the work of the Messiah. If we properly understand the requirements that God made of his people in the Torah, we can better understand some truths about God, the Messiah, and his work.* ➤

12 And it's clear that God has amended his teachings in the Torah—because now he has made a change in who our High Priest is. ❖ *The implication of this argument is that since the Messiah has come and been appointed as High Priest, God has fulfilled his teachings in the Torah and eliminated the need for the Levitical priesthood. This is not because they failed in any way, but because they have been superseded by a superior priesthood—making theirs no longer necessary. Note that this argument doesn't say that God's teachings in the Torah have been abolished—as some say. But the Torah's regulations* regarding priests and sacrifices have been fulfilled by the Messiah. Whenever God clearly decrees something in Scripture that differs from the Teachings he gave Moses, then it follows that his Torah (teaching) has changed concerning that specific requirement. Therefore, the teachings of the New Testament—and also the rest of the Hebrew Scriptures—are now an integral part of God's amended Torah—with the later revelation clarifying or, in some places, superseding the original revelation in the Torah. ➤ **A** 13 Our Lord Jesus—who is this new High Priest—isn't from the tribe of Levi but from another tribe whose descendants have never served as priests at God's altar. 14 Everyone knows that he is descended from Judah in the line of Israel's kings. And the Teachings of Moses say nothing about priests coming from that tribe. 15 Thus it's clear that God has modified his teachings in the Torah since he has sent us a different kind of priest who is like Melchizedek. 16 The Messiah didn't become a priest based on the usual requirement of physical descent from Aaron. Instead, he became a priest because he has the power of a life that cannot be destroyed. 17 This is clear from the Scripture that says, **"You are a priest forever in the priestly order of Melchizedek."** *[Psalm 110:4]* 18 God has set aside the former commands concerning priests and sacrifices because they were weak in their inability to change people and make them holy. And now that the Messiah has come, there is no longer any need for them. ❖ *But they did accomplish God's purpose for them until the Messiah came.* ➤ 19 For the commands in the Torah that God gave through Moses couldn't make anyone perfect. From the beginning, God only intended them to be over us until the Messiah came *[Galatians 3:19]* to help us to understand about the Messiah's work. But now he has given us a better way

---

A **7:12** With the institution of the New Covenant, God included a relaxation of the Torah's requirement of separation from Gentiles. God doesn't have to issue another formal Torah—as he did with Moses—to alter his commands. All he has to do is do command his people to do something different. That should be all the clue we need to realize that God has made a change. Jesus' commands are all to be included in changes he has made to his Torah. In some areas, he has made his commands stricter. e.g. Now, not only are our actions judged, but also our thoughts. See Matthew 5:27-28 for an example. God himself has not changed in any way, nor have his standards. But because of the different relationship believers have with God through their spiritual union with the Messiah—compared to the relationship with him that believers had before the Messiah came—the outworking of his standards in our lives requires some changes in his Torah. There were also many aspects of the original Torah's requirements that were fulfilled by the Messiah and therefore are no longer needed to serve their purpose—such as the sacrificial system and the Levitical priesthood.

to become acceptable to God so we can live in his presence. That better way is through faith in the Messiah—our new High Priest. 20-21 God used an oath to clarify this modification of the Torah's teachings in making the Messiah High Priest. He never did this for any of the Levitical priests. Only to the Messiah did God say, **"I, Yahweh, have sworn an oath and will not change my mind, 'You are a priest forever.' "** [Psalm 110:4] 22 Because of this oath, we are assured that Jesus oversees a New Covenant that's better than the old one because it and his priesthood will last forever. 23 This reveals another difference between the Levitical priests and Jesus. There were many Levitical priests because they could only serve until they died. 24 But Jesus will live and serve as our priest forever—eliminating the need for any other priests. 25 That's why those who come to God through being joined to him are saved forever. **A** And because he lives and serves forever, he will also forever be interceding for us with God—presenting us to him as those for whom he died to save. 26 He is, in fact, the kind of High Priest we need—one who is holy, innocent of all sin, pure, immune to any evil influence of sinners, and who has been exalted by God to the highest position in Heaven. 27 Unlike previous High Priests, he has no need to offer sacrifices every day—first for his own sins and then for the sins of the people. This is because he is sinless and he has already offered the one sacrifice that is sufficient to pay for the sins of all people forever. That sacrifice was his own life—which he offered on the cross. 28 Those who were previously appointed High Priest under the Teachings of Moses were weak because of their sin. But God—who gave the Torah to Moses—later made an oath which supersedes those Teachings and appointed his Son as High Priest forever. In his wisdom, God made him to become the perfect High Priest for his people. ❖ *He was "made" the perfect priest for us by virtue of his becoming human, enduring temptation, learning*

obedience through suffering, doing it all without sinning, and being able to offer himself as the perfect sacrifice for sins. Thus he is able to fully identify with us and sympathize with our weaknesses—yet he also has the power to help us overcome them. And he can help us change so that we are holy and pure—just as he is—as a result of having perfectly satisfied all of the requirements of God's justice—which says that human sin must be punished by a human death. ➤

8

The Messiah Is Superior to Other High Priests

1 The main point I want to make is this: We have this kind of High Priest who has the place of highest honor and authority at the right hand of God in Heaven. 2 He serves there in the Holy of Holies, that is, in the very presence of God the Father in the true Tabernacle in Heaven—made by God himself. ❖ *The earthly Tabernacle was a portable Temple that God commanded Moses to have made. Later, King Solomon built a permanent Temple modeled on the Tabernacle. But the Tabernacle that God told Moses to build was modeled on the real Tabernacle in Heaven.* ➤ 3 Every High Priest is appointed to offer gifts and sacrifices to God. Therefore, it's necessary that the Messiah— our High Priest in Heaven—also have something to offer. 4 Now if the Messiah were on earth, he wouldn't be allowed to be a priest at all since the Levitical priesthood follows the regulations in the Teachings of Moses. 5 But the Levitical priests serve in a Temple that's only a copy and shadow of the one in Heaven. When God told Moses to make the Tabernacle, he warned him, **"Make sure you make everything according to the pattern that I showed you on the mountain—which follows the pattern of the reality in Heaven."** [Exodus 25:40] ❖ *Many details of the Tabernacle and the requirements in the Teachings of Moses have heavenly or spiritual counterparts. If we fully understand their earthly function and meaning, then we are ready to more fully understand the realities of which they are patterns and "types."* ➤ 6 Now, Jesus—our High Priest—has a ministry in Heaven far superior to the ministry of the Levitical priests. He is also the mediator between God

---

A 7:25 The Greek phrase "to the complete"—here translated "forever"—can also mean "completely." Commentators are divided on which meaning applies here, but the context indicates that we are saved "forever" because Jesus will be our priest "forever."

and his people under a New Covenant—which is superior to the Old Covenant because it's based on better promises. ❖ *This doesn't imply that God's promises under the Old Covenant were not good ones, only that the promises under the New Covenant are even better.* ➤

The New Covenant Is Superior to the Mosaic Covenant

7-8 If the Old Covenant had been fully sufficient for God's ultimate purposes, there would have been no reason for him to make a new one. ❖ *The Old Covenant had no power to help people keep their side of the Covenant. But under the New Covenant, that power is provided through our spiritual union with Jesus and by the Holy Spirit living in us. The writer is addressing Jewish believers who knew beyond a shadow of a doubt that the Old Covenant was good and holy—so they would not mistake his rhetoric in referring to the Old Covenant as literally having "fault." The fault was on the side of people who—because of their sinful natures—could not keep their end of the agreement. The Apostle Paul addresses some of the purposes of the Torah's teachings (i.e., the Old Covenant) in Galatians 3:19-25 and Romans 3:20.* ➤ But because God's people weren't able to keep their side of the agreement, God told the prophet Jeremiah to write, "Yahweh declares, 'The time will come when I will make a New Covenant with the people of Israel in Judah. ❖ *Jeremiah's prophecy in verses 7-8 literally refers to them as "the house of Israel and the house of Judah," sounding to us as if they were two separate groups of people. After King Solomon died, the Israelites split into two nations—one called Israel and one called Judah. About a hundred years before Jeremiah wrote this prophesy, Israel was destroyed by the Assyrian empire and only Judah remained. But they were still known as the people descended from the man Israel (a.k.a. Jacob).* ➤ **A** 9 It will be different from the covenant I made with their ancestors when I took them by the hand and miraculously brought them out of slavery in Egypt. They didn't follow the commands in that Covenant, so I withdrew my protection and blessing from them. ❖ *The punishment mentioned in verse 9 was one of the terms of the Old Covenant.*

[Deuteronomy 28:15-68] ➤ 10 But the New Covenant I will later make with the people of Israel will be like this: I will put my commands in their minds so they will understand them, and I will put my commands in their hearts so they will want to obey them. I will be their God who blesses and takes care of them, and they will be my willingly obedient people who love me. 11 They will not need to exhort their neighbors or relatives to know Yahweh because everyone will already know me—from the lowliest to the most important of them. ❖ *This part of the New Covenant—in which everyone knows Yahweh—has not yet been fully realized. Just as our full experience of our redemption will not come until Jesus returns, this aspect of the New Covenant also will not happen until he returns.* ➤ 12 I will forgive their sins and completely forget **B** they ever did them.' " *[Jeremiah 31:31-34]* 13 When God said he would make a New Covenant, that meant the old one would become obsolete. Anything obsolete is out of date and will soon disappear forever. ❖ *This letter to the Hebrews was probably written only a few years before the Temple in Jerusalem was destroyed by the Roman legions in AD 70. When it was destroyed, the Jews could no longer offer sacrifices for sin according to the teachings of Moses in the Torah—because it didn't allow them to do this anywhere else. Therefore, it's possible that this verse not only talked about the replacement of the Old Covenant with the New—which happened when Jesus was crucified—but was also a prophecy that the practice of animal sacrifices for sin would soon cease.* ➤

9

The Messiah Offers a Superior Sacrifice

1 Now, under the Old Covenant, there were commands regulating worship and there was a holy place here on earth where that worship took place. 2 This was a special tent called the "Tabernacle," constructed according to detailed plans given by God. There were two rooms in the Tabernacle, the

---

A 8:7-8 Another possible interpretation is that the "house of Israel"—which had intermarried with their Gentile conquerors and effectively ceased to exist as a nation—represents the Gentiles who would also be welcomed to enter into this New Covenant.

B 8:12 When God says he will "completely forget" our sins, it means he chooses not to bring them to mind and will treat us as if we had never done those sins. It does not mean that he is incapable of remembering them.

outer one was called the "Holy Place." In this room was a special seven-branched lampstand called a "menorah" and a table with sacred loaves of bread on it. ❖ *Only priests could enter the Holy Place. To learn about the lampstand and the table, read Exodus 25:23-40. To learn about the Tabernacle, see Exodus chapters 25—27.* ➤ 3 Inside the Holy Place was another room, separated from the Holy Place by a thick curtain. This second room was called the "Holy of Holies." 4 Just outside the Holy of Holies, but belonging to it, there was a gold altar for burning incense. And inside the Holy of Holies was the Ark of the Covenant—which was a wooden box covered both inside and out with a layer of hammered gold. ❖ *The Ark was the symbol of Yahweh's presence among the Israelites. Sometimes a bright light—called the "shekinah* **A** *glory"—appeared in the Tabernacle, and later in the Temple, to visibly indicate his presence. [Exodus 40:34-35; 1 Kings 8:10-11; 2 Chronicles 5:13-14; 7:1-3] For the story about the making of the Ark, see Exodus 25:10-22.* ➤ Inside the ark was a jar made of gold with manna in it, ❖ *Manna was the miraculous food which God had provided for his people during their 40 years of wandering in the wilderness. For the story about manna, see Exodus chapter 16. See verses 32-34 about the jar.* ➤ and Aaron's walking stick that

had sprouted leaves, ❖ *For the story about Aaron's stick, see Numbers chapter 17.* ➤ and also two stone tablets with the commands of the Torah carved on them. ❖ *Under the New Covenant, God lives among his people in their hearts. So now the "Holy of Holies"—where God lives in this world—is the hearts of his people.* ➤ **B** 5 On top of the cover of the ark were two statues of a high order of angel called "cherubim"—which symbolized God's glorious presence. Their wings were stretched out over the cover of the ark— which was called the "mercy seat." ❖ *See the footnote at Romans 3:25 about the mercy seat.* ➤ This was the place where blood was sprinkled by the High Priest so that the sins of the people of Israel could be forgiven. But I can't explain the meanings of all of these things at this time. **C**

6 But that is how the two rooms of the Tabernacle were arranged. ❖ *The same arrangement was later made in the Temple in Jerusalem; and at the time of this letter:* ➤ The priests daily enter the first room of the Tabernacle to do their ministry for the people. 7 But only the High Priest is allowed to enter the second room. And he can only do so one day a year—on the Day of Atonement **D**—when he is required to take the blood from an

---

A 9:4a Shekinah is pronounced [shĕh-kē-NAH] in Hebrew, though most English speakers say [shŭh-KĪ-nŭh]. This word does not actually appear in the Hebrew Scriptures, but is used in Jewish writings to talk about the visible cloud of light that represented Yahweh's presence in the Tabernacle and later in the Temple in Jerusalem.

B 9:4b When the Scriptures talk about the "heart," they are rarely referring to the physical organ, nor are they talking about the center of a person's emotions. It is a figure of speech referring to the center of a person's thoughts and being. In Hebrew culture, the center of emotion was the bowels. From a few references in the Scriptures, some people believe that human beings are composed of three parts—spirit, soul, and body (e.g. See 1 Thessalonians 5:23 and Hebrews 4:12 in a literal translation). The body is mortal, but the spirit and soul are immortal. The spirit of an unsaved person is "dead" in relation to God until he or she is spiritually "reborn." The spirit of a believer then becomes "alive" to God, and the Holy Spirit dwells there. It is the "Holy of Holies"—the dwelling place of God in us. Sometimes references in Scripture to the human "heart" are really talking metaphorically about the human "spirit." Because God now dwells in his people, the Scriptures say we are "living Temples"—and corporately, all

believers together form one "living Temple." [Ephesians 2:19-22; 1 Peter 2:5; Revelation 3:12]

C 9:5 The writer wrote about the ark in the past tense because it disappeared hundreds of years earlier during the time of the prophet Jeremiah. It was either hidden just before Jerusalem was conquered by the Babylonians, or it was taken by the Babylonians when they looted the Temple. In any case, after the destruction of Jerusalem by the Babylonians, it is never again mentioned in the Hebrew Scriptures and its whereabouts or existence is unknown.

D 9:7 The Day of Atonement—known in Hebrew as "Yom Kippur"—is on the 10th day of Tishri—the 7th month of the Jewish calendar—which occurs in September and October. The date varies with respect to our calendar because the Jewish calendar is based on the phases of the moon. In modern Jewish observance, Yom Kippur is the last of the "10 Days of Penitence (or Awe)" which begin with Rosh HaShanah—the Jewish New Year's Day. The seeming contradiction in saying that Yom Kippur is the tenth day after the Jewish New Year starts and also in the 7th month of the Jewish calendar, is because the Jews had two calendars—one a civil calendar and one a religious calendar—which were out of phase by half a year.

animal sacrifice with him. He offers this blood to God to take away his own sins and also the sins of God's people that they've done during the previous year without realizing it. ❖ *Other sacrifices were offered at other times for sins that people knew they had done. The commands about these things are in Leviticus chapter 16.* ➤ 8 When the Holy Spirit told them to make the Tabernacle in this way and to follow these commands, he was making clear that due to their sins, people were not permitted to enter God's presence in the Holy of Holies. This continued to be true as long as these commands about the first room and way of worship were still in effect under the Old Covenant.

11 But now, since Jesus has come and returned to Heaven, this new way has been established. And as our Messiah, he is now a High Priest who ministers and officiates over all the good things that God has promised his people under the New Covenant. He has entered into God's presence through the perfect and original Holy of Holies in Heaven—not merely one made by people in this world. 12 And when he entered, he didn't bring the blood of mere goats and calves to God as a sin offering. Instead, he brought his own blood—representing the sacrifice of his own sinless life. He entered into the Holy of Holies in Heaven only one time, and offered the blood of his sacrifice to take away the sins of all people forever. He doesn't need to ever do it again because his one sacrifice is sufficient for all people forever. And now he forever remains in the presence of God the Father to intercede for us. ❖ *God told the Israelites (the ancestors of the Jews) to make the Tabernacle and to follow his commands under the Old Covenant so that they and we could understand exactly what the Messiah did for us in Heaven with his shed blood.* ➤

13 Under the teachings of the Torah that God gave Moses, the blood of goats and bulls and the ashes of a young cow were sprinkled on sinful people in order to make them ritually clean and outwardly acceptable to God. Then they could participate in submissively worshipping him and receive his blessings. ❖ *The ritual cleansing was symbolic only. It pointed to the real cleansing that the Messiah would later accomplish. But when God's people obeyed him in faith by following his commands in the Torah, God forgave them for the sake of Jesus' sacrifice which was yet to come.* ➤

14 But under the New Covenant, the blood **A** of the Messiah does much more than ritual cleansing. He was sinless and was led by the Holy Spirit to offer himself as a sacrifice to God the Father. The offering of his blood actually takes away all our sins and makes our hearts clean and holy so we don't want to do the evil things that previously appealed to us—and which led to eternal death. Instead, we now want to serve God who gives us eternal life.

15 That's why the Messiah is the intermediary of a New Covenant between God and his people. His death paid the price to take away the sins people had done while under the Old Covenant. **B** He did this so that those who God called to be his people can receive

---

A 9:14 God's justice requires that sin be punished by death. The life of a person or animal is in its blood. [Leviticus 17:11] When the blood of a sacrifice is poured out until death, that blood symbolizes the death of the sacrifice. When that blood was sprinkled on people, it was a symbol which meant that the death of the sacrificial animal had been applied to them. The sacrificial animal took their place as a substitute for their own deserved death. So when the Scriptures talk about the Messiah's "blood," they are speaking about his sacrificial death as a substitute for us. His death is applied to us—not by actually being sprinkled with his physical blood (although that picture is used in Hebrews 10:22)—but by our believing that he died for us and by trusting that his death is accepted by God as completely sufficient for forgiving all our sins. When we believe this,

God spiritually joins us to Jesus. He gives us a new living human spirit and his Holy Spirit comes to live in our spirit. The Holy Spirit living in us is a sign that we are truly his people. Then the Holy Spirit helps us and guides us and starts the process of ridding our lives of both sin and the tendency to sin. Those sins are already forgiven, but he is now changing us to become holy and pure—like Jesus himself.

B 9:15 The animal sacrifices under the Old Covenant didn't really take away people's sins. [Romans 3:25-26] Those sacrifices were symbolic of what the Messiah's sacrifice would actually do later. But God accepted their faith and obedience in following his commands to make these sacrifices, and therefore temporarily covered, or ignored, their sins. When The Messiah died, *[Continued next page]*

what he promised them and live with him in Heaven forever.

16 As an example, think about a will. The things promised in a will don't happen until it's clear that the man who made it has died. 17 The stipulations of a will can only be carried out when the man is dead—never while he is still alive. ❖ *The writer is saying that this aspect of a will is like the covenant agreements that God made with his people. The promises that God gave his people in the New Covenant—to forgive their sins and save them—couldn't be fulfilled until the Messiah died. The blood of his death established the New Covenant—just like all ancient covenants were established with blood. And by the establishment of the New Covenant—the Old Covenant was abolished.* ➤ 18 In the same way, the promises that God made in the Old Covenant were also not established until something died. ❖ *That's why animals were sacrificed and their blood—which was used in the Tabernacle to temporarily cover sin—was a sign of the death of the animal. Their sacrifice activated the terms of the Covenant agreement that God would forgive their sins. The sacrificial substitute should have been a man, but God allowed people to kill animals as substitutes until the Messiah came— when he would die as a man for all mankind.* ➤

19 When Moses had told the Israelites all of God's commands under the Old Covenant, he took some blood from sacrificed goats and calves and mixed it with water. He took a branch with red wool wrapped around it and dipped it into the blood. Then he sprinkled the blood on the book of the Torah and on all the people. ❖ *The water kept the blood from coagulating and allowed a relatively small amount of blood to be applied to many people. It may have been symbolic of the Holy Spirit—who is often symbolically represented by water— enabling the "blood" of Jesus in his death to be applied to all who trust in him. Study has revealed no symbolism attached to the hyssop branch used, or to the fact that the wool was red. It's red color may have only been a result of dipping it in the blood water mixture.* ➤ 20 While he did this, he said to them, **"This blood establishes the Covenant God made with you. Now you must follow its requirements."** [Exodus 24:8] ❖ *All ancient covenants between people were established*

by blood—usually the blood of a sacrificed animal. Under the Old Covenant, the blood was from animals—but it was always intended as a symbol of the blood and death of the Messiah who would die about 1500 years after the Old Covenant was first established. The difference between animal sacrifices done by pagans and those done by God's people under the Old Covenant is that those done under the Old Covenant were connected to the Messiah's sacrifice and God's promises and commands. Pagan sacrifices are not based on God's command or the Messiah's sacrifice, and so are worthless in God's eyes. ➤ 21 And in the same way, Moses sprinkled blood on the Tabernacle and on everything inside it to purify them and set them apart for God's use under the terms of the Covenant. 22 Following the Torah's teachings under the Old Covenant, blood was sprinkled to ritually cleanse almost everything, because without a death—represented by the blood—God will not forgive any sins. [Leviticus 17:11] 23 That's why the Tabernacle and all the things in it—which were mere copies of things in Heaven—had to be made ritually clean with blood. The real things in Heaven were also made clean, but with a sacrifice that is superior to the blood of animals.

24 When the Messiah entered the Holy of Holies, it was the real one in Heaven, not the copy made by people in this world. There, he entered into the very presence of God the Father in order to serve as our High Priest— presenting us to God as people he has made holy. 25 The Jewish High Priest enters the Holy of Holies in the Temple once every year with the blood from an animal sacrifice. But the Messiah doesn't repeatedly enter the Holy of Holies in Heaven to offer himself as a sacrifice over and over again. 26 If he entered many times, then he would have had to die many times—ever since God made the world. But that isn't the way it is. Instead, he entered only once. This was the climax of God's plan—accomplished at the end of the ages that existed before the establishment of his New Covenant. He entered

---

all these sins that God had covered were finally punished, taken away, and forgiven. ¶ "Paid the price" means he suffered the necessary punishment for sin which "cost" him great suffering, physical death, and separation from God the Father—in some manner we

can't fathom. Saying that he "redeemed" us or "paid the price" or "bought us" are figures of speech in the Scriptures indicating the "cost" to himself. God did not "pay" Satan to save us—as these terms are sometimes misunderstood.

there to take away all sin, forever, with the blood of his own sacrificial death.

27 Everyone must die once—and then they come before God to be judged. This is the way God has ordered things. ❖ *This verse clearly teaches there is no such thing as reincarnation.* ➤ 28 In the same way, the Messiah also died only once as a sacrifice to take away all the sins of all people. He will come a second time, but not to die to take away sins—since he has already accomplished that. Instead, he will come to his people who are waiting for him to return in order to fulfill all the promises that God has made to those who are saved. ❖ *The writer emphasizes that the Messiah's death takes away the sins of many people. This can be interpreted two ways. Calvinists (i.e., followers of the "Reformed" theology taught by French theologian John Calvin in the first half of the 1500s) say this means his death only paid for the sins of those who will be redeemed. They call this the doctrine of "limited atonement." Non-Calvinists (sometimes called Arminians because of the teachings of Dutch Reformed theologian Jacobus Arminius in the later 1500s—though many non-Calvinists are not really followers of Arminius* **A** *) say his death was sufficient to pay for all of humanity's sins [1 Timothy 4:10]—but is only applied to those who believe. Universalists who believe everyone will be saved (though they have to ignore many clear Scriptures to hold this belief, which indicates their low regard for the authority of Scripture)—might try to read more into this interpretation than the Scriptures mean. There are many clear Scriptures which teach that only a relatively few among all humankind will be saved because most people reject Jesus as their Lord and Savior.* ➤

10

The Messiah's One Sacrifice
Is Sufficient for All People Forever

1 The Teachings of Moses under the Old Covenant are—and were always intended to be—only shadows of the good things that would come under the New Covenant. A shadow resembles the reality, but isn't the reality itself. Therefore, the sacrifices offered year after year under the requirements of the Torah can never make the people who offer them perfect. ❖ *God commanded that these "shadow" sacrifices be made to teach his people about the reality of their sins and their need for a substitute to die for them, and to enable them to recognize the real sacrifice when the Messiah came and established the New Covenant.* ➤ 2 If those sacrifices were able to make God's people perfect and removed their inclination to sin, then they would have accomplished that and the sacrifices would have ceased long ago. For perfect people no longer sin and would, therefore, no longer need to make sacrifices for sin. And if God's people no longer sinned, then they would never feel guilty. But they did sin and they did feel guilty. So instead of removing their inclination to sin, 3 those sacrifices continually reminded them every year that they were still sinners—in need of a sacrificial substitute and forgiveness. 4 That's because it's impossible for the sacrificial death of bulls and goats to really take away human sin. 5-6 Therefore, when the Messiah came into this world, he said to God—as recorded in the prophetic writing of King David, "It was never animal sacrifices and burnt offerings that you required to satisfy your justice regarding human sin. None of these are sufficient. But for that purpose you gave me a human body so I could offer it as an acceptable sacrifice. 7 Then I said, 'Here I am. I have come to do your will by offering my life as a sacrifice for all humanity—just as it's written in the prophecies of the Scriptures that I would.' " [Psalm 40:6-8] 8 In this passage, the Messiah says, "It was never animal sacrifices and burnt offerings that you required to satisfy your justice regarding human sin. None of these are sufficient." He said this even though the Torah's teachings—under the Old Covenant—required people to offer them. 9 But then he added, "Here I am. I have come to do your will by offering my life as a sacrifice for all humanity." In saying this, the Messiah was setting aside the sacrifices for sin required under the Old Covenant in

---

A 9:28 Major denominations that tend to be Calvinistic are Reformed churches, Presbyterians, United Church of Christ, and some Baptist denominations (Primitive Baptist, Reformed Baptist). Major denominations that tend to be non-Calvinistic are Eastern Orthodox, Roman Catholic, Anglican, Episcopal, Lutheran, Methodist, Free-Will Baptist, American Baptist, Pentecostal, Nazarene, and Seventh-Day Adventist.

order to establish the New Covenant—under which it would be his sacrifice that takes away sin. 10 So God's will is that we be made holy through the self-offering of Jesus the Messiah—whose body was sacrificed only once in a sacrifice sufficient to take away all of humanity's sin forever.

11 Under the Old Covenant, priests offered the same kind of sacrifices every day, but these sacrifices could never take away sins. 12 In contrast, the Messiah—who is our High Priest under the New Covenant—offered only one eternally effective sacrifice to remove our sins. Then having completed that work, he sat down **at the right hand of God the Father**—signifying that under his Father, he has the highest rank, honor, and authority in Heaven. 13 He is waiting there **until all of his enemies are conquered, humbled, and brought under his power by God the Father.** [Psalm 110:1] 14 He is resting in that position of authority because by that one offering of his own body, he fully accomplished the work of making his people perfect and holy forever. **A** 15 Now the Holy Spirit also tells us about these things in the Scriptures. First he says, 16 **"Yahweh declares, 'The New Covenant I will make with the people of Israel will be like this: I will put my commands in their minds so they will understand them, and I will put my commands in their hearts so they will want to obey them.' "** ❖ An abridged quote of Jeremiah 31:31-33. ➤ 17 Then he adds, **"I will forgive their sins and completely forget they ever did them."** [Jeremiah 31:34b] 18 Thus it's clear that once sins have already been forgiven and forgotten, there is no longer any need to make further sacrifices to take away sin.

Persevere
in Trusting the Messiah's Finished Work

19 My dear brothers and sisters who have been made one in and with Jesus, we can boldly enter—through prayer and submissive worship—into the very presence of God in the Holy of Holies in Heaven. We can do this without fear of any kind of punishment because of Jesus' sacrificial death offered up on our behalf. 20 For he has opened up the way for us to go through the barrier curtain of sin—which separated us from God—into God's presence. He did this by means of offering his own body as a sacrifice to remove our sin. ❖ Furthermore, since we are also spiritually united with Jesus, we live in God's presence because Jesus lives in his presence. [Ephesians 2:6] ➤ 21-22 And since we have such a superior High Priest who rules over the people of God's household and presents us as his holy and redeemed people, we should, therefore, approach God without fear. We should not be wondering if we need to continue offering animal sacrifices, but instead, be fully trusting in Jesus' sacrifice to make us acceptable. We have been "sprinkled with Jesus' blood" ❖ a picture of his sacrificial death applied to us ➤ so our hearts and consciences have been completely cleansed from guilt and sin. And in the pure water of baptism, we were spiritually joined to Jesus in his death [Romans 6:3-4] and our sins were washed away. ❖ This last sentence is literally, "our bodies were washed with pure water." The washing is clearly a figure, washing indicating a cleansing from sin, and water being symbolic of the Holy Spirit. The interpretational problem is in relating this to a washing of our bodies, or if not our literal bodies, in deciding what our bodies are figurative of. Most translations just render the sentence literally, and most study Bibles don't try to explain

---

A 10:14 Literally, "He has perfected for all time those who are being sanctified." Scholars debate the meaning of the passive present participle of the verb "being sanctified." Some think that the verb is timeless since there is no time reference. Some think that it means a progressive sanctification, as the literal rendering into English would imply. Some think that it is iterative (i.e., that his act of providing perfection in righteousness for all of humanity is complete, but the process of sanctifying people happens each time someone is saved and that perfection is applied to them.) One reason

scholars don't immediately conclude that the participle means "are being sanctified" in the progressive sense that it does in English is because in verse 10 the writer has literally said that we "have been sanctified." There is both a completed aspect to our sanctification and an ongoing aspect. The writer's use of the participle in this verse after using the perfect form of the verb "he has perfected" may suggest that both senses of "have been sanctified" (objectively true from God's perspective) and "are being sanctified" (subjectively true from our perspective) are true at the same time.

what it means. My interpretation is that "our bodies were washed with pure water" is the "washing of regeneration" referred to in Titus 3:5—which some commentators tie to baptism. This tie is also found in Romans 6:3-4 and 1 Peter 3:21. But many believers consider baptism to be merely a symbolic rite of public proclamation of their identification with the Messiah in his death and resurrection—so they don't associate this washing away of sin with it. ➤

23 So let us continue to firmly trust in these things that we've been taught and which we've said we believe—putting aside all doubts—because God is entirely trustworthy and will fulfill his promises to us. 24 Continue to encourage and urge each other to demonstrate love to others and do what's good. 25 Don't fail to gather together with other believers on a regular basis—as some are in the habit of doing. Instead, make it a point to meet together regularly in order to encourage each other. This is more and more important as the Last Day approaches because times will then be difficult for true believers. ❖ *It is Jesus' intention that his followers depend on each other for encouragement and support—and not try to endure the difficulties of this life alone.* ➤

A Warning
for Believers Who Might Reject the Messiah

26 But take care! If a person has understood the truth about how to be saved by trusting in the Messiah and has really believed it, but then continues to choose to live in flagrant sin without repenting—that person is rejecting the Messiah and his sacrifice. There is no longer any sacrifice that is effective for taking away that person's sin—neither Jesus' nor any other sacrifice. *[1 Timothy 1:19; Hebrews 6:4-8]* ❖ *In the context of this letter, the writer was warning Jewish followers of Jesus that they dare not reject the Messiah and go back to their old ways of making animal sacrifices for sin after having chosen to follow him.* ➤ 27 The only thing such a person can expect from God is condemnation, wrath, and punishment in Hell—where all God's enemies will experience eternal ruin. *[Isaiah 26:11]* ❖ *See 2 Thessalonians 1:9 and the note there about what it means to experience eternal ruin in Hell.* ➤ 28 Even under the Old Covenant, when two or three people testified that someone refused to follow God's teachings in the Torah given through Moses, that

person was shown no mercy and was executed. 29 Consider how much more severe the punishment will be for those who despise God's Son and turn away from him. Such people are rejecting the Messiah's blood which was sacrificed on their behalf—by which he established the New Covenant and made them holy. They treat it as if it were worthless! Plus, they are insulting the Holy Spirit who graciously enabled them to know and accept the truth. 30 Certainly we've come to know God and what he is like. He has said, **"Only I have the right to take revenge on those who do wrong—and I will pay them back as they deserve."** *[Deuteronomy 32:35]* He also said, **"Yahweh will judge his people."** *[Deuteronomy 32:36; Psalm 135:14]* 31 It would be a terrifying thing to fall into the hands of the Living God and receive his punishment. So never doubt that he will carry out his threats—just as surely as he fulfills his promises.

Don't Throw Away All You Have Gained,
but Persevere to the End

32 Think back to the days when you first learned about the Messiah. And remember the way that you continued to trust him—even though it resulted in suffering for his sake. 33 Sometimes you were publicly ridiculed and beaten. Other times you helped and encouraged others who experienced these persecutions—thereby sharing their sufferings. 34 You sympathized with people who were put in prison for the sake of the Good News message and helped and supported them. And when all your possessions were stolen, you accepted this with joy instead of bitterness and despair—because you knew that you have better and more permanent possessions waiting for you in Heaven. 35 So don't throw it all away now! Continue to trust in what the Messiah has accomplished for you—for God will greatly reward you if you continue faithfully until the end. 36 You must learn to patiently wait and persevere in doing God's will in order to receive what he has promised. 37 Because the Scripture says, **"In just a little while, he who is coming** ❖ *i.e., the Messiah* ➤ **will come for the final judgment. He will not delay**

much longer. 38 Those who are righteous in God's sight because of their faith in his promises ❖ *particularly the promise of salvation in Jesus* ➤ will continue to live by faith. But if they shrink back from believing and from continued faithfulness, I ❖ *God* ➤ will not be pleased with them." *[Habakkuk 2:3-4]* ❖ *The last sentence of this quote from Habakkuk 2:4 is quoted from the Septuagint and is different from the Hebrew text—which is translated in your English translation of the Hebrew Scriptures.* ➤ 39 But let us not be among those who turn away from Jesus and are destroyed. We must be among those who will persevere in faith to the end and ultimately be saved.

11

God's People Are Examples
of How to Persevere in Trusting God

1 To have faith in God and his promises means that we are entirely confident he will fulfill everything he has promised us in the Scriptures. So we look forward with expectation to receiving them based on our conviction that all his words are true—even though we don't yet see all the things happening that he has promised. It also means that we believe him about unseen and unperceived things which he says are true—even if they contradict our senses and experience. 2 It was precisely by having this kind of unwavering faith in God's words and promises that many of our Jewish ancestors gained God's approval. 3 By faith in what is revealed in the Scriptures, we understand that God spoke this world into existence— and that everything we can see was made from things we can't see. ❖ *Kenneth Taylor— translator of The Living Bible—made an interesting speculation that this might refer to atoms and other physical matter that's too small to be seen. But traditionally it's thought that*

God created matter too—out of nothing. Relativity theory equates matter and energy—meaning that energy can be converted into matter and vice versa. But it is also traditionally thought that all energy as we know it is part of the physical creation that God made from "nothing." ➤

4 By faith in what was revealed about the kind of sacrifice that was acceptable to God, Abel offered a better sacrifice than his brother Cain who ignored God's sacrificial requirements. **A** *[Genesis 4:1-15]* Because of his faith, God accepted his sacrifice—indicating that Abel was accepted as righteous in his sight. Through this act of faith recorded in the Scriptures, Abel's example still teaches us today—even though he died long ago.

5 Enoch's faith enabled him to walk so closely with God in trust and obedience that he was taken up to Heaven without dying. The Scripture says, "No one could find him because God had taken him up" *[Genesis 5:21-24]*—and that before he was taken, he had pleased God. ❖ *The Septuagint says, "he pleased God," and the Hebrew text says, "he walked with God." They both mean essentially the same thing.* ➤

6 If people don't trust God and what he has said in the Scriptures, then God will never be pleased with them. People who want to have a good relationship with him must believe he really exists and that he will reward those who diligently seek to have a personal relationship with him. ❖ *We do this through: 1) studying the Scriptures to know about his character, his ways, and his will, 2) praise and submissive worship, 3) prayer, 4) listening to his Spirit, 5) service in obedience to his word and personal guidance, 6) fellowshipping with other believers and being accountable to them for how we live.* ➤

7 Noah believed God's warning about the flood—even though such a thing had never happened before. So he obeyed God and built the ark ❖ *a large ship* ➤ to save his family. Because he believed God, he

---

A **11:4** Even though it isn't explicitly recorded in the Genesis account, many Bible scholars believe that when God provided Adam and Eve with animal skins to cover the shame of their nakedness as a result of their sin, he also taught them the necessity of a death to pay the penalty for their sins. This would fit in with the understanding that God's people had throughout the Scriptural account—long before the Torah was given to Moses— that animal sacrifices were required for sins to be forgiven. Cain offered farm produce which was the result of his own labor. But God has revealed that there's nothing we can offer him from what we have done that is sufficient to forgive our sins. Only a death will satisfy God's justice. Presumably, both Cain and Abel knew this truth from their parents, but Cain ignored it. Later in Scripture, it became clear that animal sacrifices were signs pointing to the one perfect sacrifice of God's Son—Jesus the Messiah who would remove sin and permanently enable God to justly forgive his people. [1 John 1:9]

was considered righteous in God's sight and was saved not only from the flood, but also eternally. However, all the other people in the world who didn't believe God's warning were condemned to death through the flood—and also eternally in Hell. *[Genesis 6:1—9:17]*

8 God called Abraham to leave his land and go to a faraway country—which he promised to give to him and to his descendants as an inheritance. *[Genesis 12:1-2]* ❖ *Abraham was originally named Abram, meaning "exalted father," and God later changed his name to Abraham, meaning "father of many." [Genesis 17:3-8]* ➤ He believed God and went—even though he didn't know where he was going. 9 Abraham trusted in God's promise and he lived in the country where God told him to go. He was a foreigner there and lived in tents like a temporary visitor—as did his son Isaac and also Isaac's son Jacob. They also believed God's promise that he would give that country to them and their descendants. And they continued to believe in God's promise even though it didn't happen during their lifetimes. 10 Abraham continually trusted in God's promise about the land he would give him—and waited expectantly for it to happen. But he was also looking forward to living in the city in Heaven that God designed and built and which will last forever. He believed in this city because he confidently believed everything God told him. 11 Abraham also fully believed God's promise that he would have a son. So God enabled it to happen—even though it didn't happen until Abraham was 100 years old and his wife, Sarah, was about 90, and she had been barren all her life. **A** 12 His body was so old that it was almost dead as far as

his ability to father a child was concerned. Yet he fathered a son, Isaac, and eventually his descendants became as many as the stars in the sky that are visible to the naked eye, and as uncountable as the grains of sand on a beach—just as God promised. *[Genesis 22:17]* ❖ *The story of Abraham's life is in Genesis chapters 12—25.* ➤

13 Abraham and many of his descendants died while still fully trusting God to give them the land which he had promised to give to them and their descendants. They didn't receive it during their lifetimes—yet they saw that these things would happen in the distant future and they rejoiced. They acknowledged that they were living like foreigners and strangers in this world— with no place here that really belonged to them. 14 It's clear that people who think that way are looking forward to a better place to be their home—namely a place in Heaven. 15 They didn't pine for the country that Abraham originally left behind. If that had been the case, they could have returned there. 16 Instead, they desired a better place in Heaven. Therefore, God is proud to be known as their God and he has prepared a city for them in Heaven to be their true home.

17 Even though Isaac was Abraham's long-promised son, when God tested Abraham's faith, he was willing to offer Isaac as a sacrifice in obedience to God's command. *[Genesis 22:1-18]* 18 He was willing to do this even though Isaac was his only heir and the many descendants that God had promised him were to come through Isaac. **B** *[Genesis 22:12]* 19 So it's clear that Abraham believed God was able to bring Isaac back from death—if necessary—to fulfill his

---

A 11:11 Before the flood, people lived very long lives. But by Abraham's time, 100 years was very old—just like it is today.

B 11:18 Abraham did have an older son, Ishmael, by his wife's servant, Hagar, in an attempt to bring about by his own efforts the son that God promised him—since his wife, Sarah, was barren. But Ishmael was not the son that God had promised to give him by his wife Sarah. So God had him send Ishmael and his mother, Hagar, away—because they were not meant to receive any of Abraham's inheritance. This might seem severe, but God blessed and also provided for Ishmael and his

mother. So at the time, Isaac was Abraham's only heir. Yet when God tested his faith by asking him to offer him up as a sacrifice, Abraham was willing to do so. Abraham's willingness to sacrifice his only son to God demonstrated his complete trust in God's faithfulness in the face of seeming impossibility. Thus Abraham became the archetypal example of a man of faith for all who trust in God. This story is also a foreshadow, or "type," of God's plan to offer up his only Son as a sacrifice to save humanity.

promise. And because God stopped him from killing Isaac at the very last second, in a way, he received his son back from the death that he had planned. **A**

20 Isaac also trusted in God's promises handed down from his father—and so he blessed his sons Jacob and Esau with the inheritance of those promises, trusting that God would honor the blessing and eventually fulfill his promises to them and to their descendants. ❖ *Because he was blind, Isaac blessed Jacob while thinking he was Esau. The blessing he gave is found in Genesis 27:28-29. The story about Jacob and Esau is in Genesis 25:19—36:43.* ➤

21 Jacob, in his old age, leaned on his staff and submitted himself in worship to God whom he trusted and whose promises he trusted. Then, when he was dying, he blessed his grandsons—his son Joseph's two boys—and passed on God's promises to them. ❖ *This story is in Genesis 47:31—49:21. God changed Jacob's name—which literally means "to grasp the heal" and figuratively means "he deceives"—to "Israel," which means "he struggles with God," and his descendants became known as the Israelites. [Genesis 32:28]* ➤

22 Joseph also trusted in God's promises. When he was dying, he talked with certainty about the time when God would lead his people—the Israelites—from out of Egypt to the country he promised to give them long ago. And he made the Israelites promise to take his bones with them when they went. *[Genesis 50:22-26]*

23 Generations later, Moses' parents ❖ *descendants of Israel in the tribe of Levi* ➤ trusted in God to protect them—so they weren't afraid to disobey Pharaoh's command that all Hebrew baby boys be killed. They hid their infant son Moses for three months because they saw that he was a special child. *[Exodus 2:1-10]*

24 When Moses grew up, he trusted in God and refused to be called the son of Pharaoh's daughter (who had adopted him) because he knew that he was really an Israelite and an heir of God's promises. ❖ *Moses grew up in Pharaoh's household and could have*

become an Egyptian prince—but to do this he would have had to worship the Egyptians gods. ➤ 25 Instead, he chose to suffer with God's people rather than enjoy the temporary pleasures of sin living in Pharaoh's household—which would lead to Hell. 26 He considered it better to be oppressed with God's people than to have all the riches of Egypt—because he trusted in God's promise to send the Messiah and was looking forward to the reward that God would give him in Heaven. 27 He trusted in God to protect him—and so was not afraid of Pharaoh's anger when he left Egypt. He endured difficult times, trusting in God even though he could not see him. ❖ *Commentator's disagree about whether this refers to Moses' fleeing Egypt after killing the Egyptian, or if it refers to the time when he led the Israelites out of Egypt. Since everything else is this narrative is told chronologically, the former would seem to be indicated. [Exodus 2:11-15; 12:51]* ➤ 28 On the night of the first Passover, Moses trusted God's promise to protect the Israelites from the angel of death. So he followed God's instructions and told the Israelites how to prepare the Passover meal and to sprinkle blood on the door posts of their houses. As a result of his faith, the firstborn sons of the Israelites were saved from death. *[Exodus 11:1—12:30]*

29 The Israelites trusted God, so they walked on dry land across the middle of the Red Sea—trusting that the water being held back on both sides would not come crashing down and drown them. But when the Egyptian army tried to go across too, they had no faith in the God of Israel and were all drowned. *[Exodus 13:17—14:31]*

30 The Israelites trusted that God would help them defeat their enemies. So in obedience to his instructions, they marched around the city of Jericho for seven days, and the walls of the city miraculously fell. *[Joshua 5:13—6:21]*

31 Rahab of Jericho, the prostitute, trusted in the power and mercy of the God of Israel. So she helped the Israelite spies who were learning about the city's weaknesses, and so didn't die along with all the

---

A 11:19 This part of the story is a foreshadow, or "type," of the Messiah being raised from death. The story is in Genesis chapter 22. Consider that Abraham's faith in God's ability to restore his son was not blind faith. He had already seen God's miraculous power when he enabled Sarah to have Isaac in the first place.

other people of Jericho who refused to follow the one true God. *[Joshua 2:1-24; 6:22-23]*

32 There are many more examples in the Hebrew Scriptures that I could tell you about, but it would take too long to tell you about the stories of Gideon, *[Judges chapters 6—8]* Barak, *[Judges chapter 4]* Sampson, *[Judges chapters 13—16]* Jephthah, *[Judges chapters 11—12]* King David, *[1 Samuel chapters 16—30; all of 2 Samuel, 1 Kings chapters 1—2]* Samuel, and the prophets. You already know all these stories anyway. 33 All these people trusted in God—and as a result: they conquered other countries, they did things that God approved of, they received things that God promised to give them, they were made safe from lions, *[Daniel chapter 6]* 34 fire couldn't harm them even though they stood in the middle of it, *[Daniel chapter 3]* they escaped from being killed by the sword, they were weak but God made them strong, they became powerful in battle and defeated foreign armies, 35 some women received their loved ones raised from death *[1 Kings 17:8-24; 2 Kings 4:8-37]*—all because they trusted in God. Yet others were tortured, but preferred to die and go to be with God rather than turn from him and be set free. 36 Some who trusted in God were despised and whipped, and some were put in prison in chains. 37 Some who trusted in God were stoned to death or sawn in two ❖ *Jewish tradition says the Prophet Isaiah was sawn in two.* ➤ or were tempted to sin or killed with a sword. Many were very poor, starving, persecuted and only had animal skins to wear.

38 Most of the people in this world were not worthy of living in the same world with these special people who trusted in God—even though they were poor and often wandered around in deserts and mountains and lived in caves and holes in the ground. 39 All of these people were righteous in God's sight simply because they trusted in him. Yet none of them received in this life all the things that God promised to give them—40 because he planned to give them something much

better than they expected. But in the wisdom of his plan, they couldn't receive the promise of eternal life in Heaven with him until we too could receive it under the New Covenant and be made perfect by our being spiritually joined to the Messiah.

12

Faithfully Endure in Following the Messiah Despite Persecutions and Difficulties

1 There are so many examples of people who trusted in God's promises. They are like a huge cloud of people everywhere we look in the Hebrew Scriptures. In Heaven, they are looking down on us—watching and cheering us on as we run the race of "living by trusting in and acting upon God's word" in the stadium of this world. Therefore, we should be encouraged to get rid of and avoid everything that tempts us to sin—because those things hinder and distract us from running the race. They can trip us up and even stop us from finishing. In order to finish, we must be determined to persevere in faith and obedience until the very end of our lives. **A** 2 We must keep our attention focused on Jesus, who enabled us to believe and obey in the beginning, and who will continue to help and perfect us if we don't give up and turn away from him. As an example for us, he persevered in trusting and obeying his Father despite the suffering and humiliation of death on the cross that obedience required. He was able to do this because he looked forward to the great joy that awaited him afterward. And now, having completed his race, he is seated in the place of highest honor and authority to the right of the throne of God his Father—King of Heaven. 3 So think about Jesus who patiently persevered in doing God's will—even though many sinners hated and opposed him. Be inspired by his example and ultimate victory. And don't allow yourselves to become discouraged and quit before the

---

A 12:1 We could never "earn" the prize of eternal life. Jesus' death bought it for us. But one condition placed on obtaining it is that we must persevere in trusting and obeying him until the end of our lives. To finish the race is to win the prize that Jesus bought for us; and in this race, all who finish are winners. But if we stop running before we reach the finish line at the end of our lives, we won't receive the prize of eternal life. See also Philippians 3:10-14.

end—no matter how difficult it seems. 4 You have suffered persecution and struggled against the temptation to sin. But despite your difficulties, your struggle to obey God and resist sinning has not yet led to death like Jesus' did. So don't think that God is requiring too much from you. 5 I think you have forgotten the words of encouragement for his children in the Scriptures, "My child, pay attention when Yahweh disciplines you for doing wrong. Don't be discouraged or give up trying to obey him when this happens. 6 Because Yahweh corrects and disciplines everyone he loves. And in love, he administers corrective punishment to everyone he accepts as his child in order to mold their character." [Proverbs 3:11-12] 7 So endure and persevere through difficult times as if they are your Heavenly Father's means of disciplining you. Remember that this shows he considers you his child and heir—because every caring father disciplines his child when needed. 8 If God doesn't discipline you when you've done wrong—as he does all his true children—this means you aren't really his child at all. 9 Most of us had fathers who disciplined us when we needed it so we would grow up to have good character and prosper in this life—and we respected them for it. Therefore, we should be even more willing to submit to our spiritual Father so we can live forever! 10 Our fathers disciplined us for only a few years while we were young—doing the best that they knew how. But God's discipline is always perfectly suited to us and is intended for our own good—to help us become holy like him. 11 No one enjoys being disciplined. But if we allow God's discipline to train us to live holy lives, then later, we will enjoy the results of easily being able to live in perfect obedience to God's will and being at peace with him. 12 Therefore, while running in this race of trusting in God's promises and obeying his commands, strengthen

your tired hands and weak knees by strengthening your determination to persevere to the end. Do this by focusing on Jesus and seeking his help. 13 Keep along straight smooth paths ❖ i.e., live a holy life ➤ so if you are a leader, and the legs ❖ the ability to believe and obey ➤ of those who follow you have been injured by discouragement through stumbling in sin, they will not become worse, ❖ more discouraged or tempted by your stumbling in sin ➤ but instead, can heal and become stronger.

Don't Reject God's Undeserved Favor Offered in the New Covenant

14 Try hard to live in peace with all people—especially with fellow believers. And make it your goal to live a holy life, fully dedicated to God in every way. Because only those who are fully dedicated to submit to God will be saved and live forever in Heaven where they can see the Lord Jesus. 15 Go out of your way to help and encourage each other so that no one turns away from God's freely offered favor and blessing. Take care that no bitterness, resentment, or unbelief is allowed to take root among you—because it will grow, spreading and poisoning attitudes, and cause many problems among you. 16 Make sure there are no sexually immoral or unbelieving people among you—like Esau was. He didn't really believe in God's promised eternal inheritance to Abraham and his descendants which had been taught to him. So as a result of the sin of unbelief, he foolishly sold the right to his inheritance ❖ which was his as the firstborn ➤ to his younger brother Jacob—for the price of a single meal. [Genesis 25:27-34] 17 Later, when he wanted to receive his father's blessing, he was rejected. Even though he begged and cried for the blessing, and wanted to repent over selling his inheritance—it was too late. A [Genesis 27:32-40]

A 12:17 The writer of this letter knew his readers were intimately acquainted with this story so he glossed over some details and compressed the story to make his point. Esau sold his birthright—i.e., inheritance—to Jacob for a bowl of lentil stew when he was very hungry.

[Genesis 25:27-34] He disdained the value of his inheritance because of unbelief, and foolishly focused only on the immediate gratification of his body's desires—which is the root cause of sexual immorality alluded to in verse 16. (Jewish tradition regarded Esau

❖ *The writer's point is: Don't exchange your rightful inheritance of eternal life in Heaven—offered to you by God's undeserved favor—for the fleeting pleasures of sin in this life, and then expect God's blessing. Also realize that there's a point at which regret can come too late to do you any good.* ➤

Differences Between the Two Covenants

18 Your situation now—under the New Covenant—is not the same as it was for the Israelites in the time of Moses when God gave them the First ❖ *i.e., Old* ➤ Covenant. They came to a physical Mount Sinai that could actually be touched. It was blazing with fire and surrounding it were darkness, gloom, and a whirlwind. 19 Then, there was a loud trumpet blast and God's terrifying voice. When your ancestors heard that voice, they begged Moses to ask God not to speak directly to them anymore *[Exodus 20:18-19]*—20 because they were terrified of his voice and of the command he gave that, "Nobody, not even an animal, is allowed to touch the mountain. If they do, then they must be stoned to death." *[Exodus 19:12-13]* 21 To experience those events was terrifying. Even Moses later said, "I'm trembling with fear." *[Deuteronomy 9:19]* ❖ *Meeting God under the Old Covenant was always a frightening experience.* ➤ 22 But you, on the other hand, meet God under the New Covenant which was established on Mount Zion where the Messiah died. You come to meet the Living God in his holy city—the New Jerusalem in Heaven where many thousands of angels celebrate. 23 You've come to join in the joyful gathering of God's people because you are his children whose names are written in the book of life in Heaven. And you ❖ *regardless of your gender* ➤ have all the special privileges that a firstborn son traditionally has in a family—because you are joined to the Messiah who is God's firstborn. You've come to meet God

himself—who will judge all people—yet for you there is nothing to fear. You've come to join with the spirits of those righteous people in Heaven whom God has made perfect and to whom he has given eternal life. 24 And you have come to meet Jesus who is the intermediary between God and his people under the New Covenant—to be sprinkled with his blood which cries to God for your forgiveness, instead of crying out for vengeance like Abel's blood did. *[Genesis 4:10]*

Another Warning

25 Be careful that you don't refuse to listen and obey God who is speaking to you about this New Covenant. Your ancestors didn't escape the punishment of physical and eternal death when they refused to listen to God's warning given through his earthly messenger—Moses. So it's even more certain that we won't escape the punishment of eternal death if we turn away from God's warning given through his heavenly messenger—the Messiah. 26 When God spoke to your ancestors from Mount Sinai, his voice shook the earth. But he also promised, "I will once more shake not only the earth, but also the heavens." *[Haggai 2:6]* 27 The words "once more" mean that God intended to shake and remove those temporary things under the Old Covenant—such as the Levitical priesthood—which could be shaken and destroyed, so that only those things which are eternal and thus "unshakable" under the New Covenant—such as the priesthood of Jesus—would remain. 28 Under the New Covenant, we receive life and blessings as members of God's Kingdom that are eternal and cannot be shaken. Therefore, we ought to show our gratitude by serving God with reverence and awe—doing what pleases him. 29 For our God is like a consuming fire—who will ultimately

---

as a sexually immoral person. And even though this aspect of his life is not detailed in Scripture, the Jewish recipients of this letter would accept the reference.) Later, Jacob stole Esau's blessing as firstborn—which was distinct from his inheritance—by tricking his blind father (Isaac) into thinking he was Esau.

[Genesis 27:32-40] Esau cried over this theft but couldn't receive the blessing because it was already given to another. In this later scene, it's apparent that Esau also regrets selling his birthright, but that too was not recoverable.

destroy everything that doesn't please him. *[Deuteronomy 4:24]*

13

Ways to Please God

[1] So continue to demonstrate unselfish love to other believers. [2] Always be willing to offer hospitality in your homes to strangers—and especially to believers. In doing this, some people have hosted angels who seemed to be ordinary people. **A** [3] Remember to help and pray for those in prison—especially other believers who are there as a result of their obedience to Jesus. Contemplate what it would be like if you were in their situation and respond accordingly. Also remember to help those who are actively persecuted because of their faith and obedience. Identify with their suffering and reach out to help them—since you may be in a similar situation someday. [4] Everyone among you must deeply honor and respect the vows of marriage—both your own and those of others—so that no one breaks the promise to be faithful to their partner. Such must never happen among you because God will judge and eternally condemn those who are guilty of sexual relations outside of marriage—and especially those who break marriage vows in adultery—unless they truly repent and change their ways. ❖ *Note that God's attitude about these sins is much more severe than our culture's attitude—and even the attitude of many believers. Only fools regard lightly what God takes so seriously.* ➤ [5] Don't allow yourselves to fall into the sinful trap of loving money and the things it can buy. Learn to be satisfied with what you have because God has promised, **"I will never leave you and I will never fail to help you."** *[Deuteronomy 31:6, 8]* ❖ *He will provide you with everything you really need and that he wants you to have.* ➤ [6] Therefore, we can confidently say, **"With Yahweh helping me, I'm not afraid of anything people can do to me!"** *[Psalm 118:6 in the Septuagint]* [7] Remember your mentors who first taught you God's word. Think about the good fruit resulting from their lives and imitate their faith and obedience to the Lord's will. [8] Jesus the Messiah is the same yesterday, today, and forever. His holy loving character never changes. [9] So don't allow all kinds of strange teachings to mislead you. A person's strength for faith and obedience comes from accepting God's undeserved enabling favor—not from following regulations about food. Experience should have shown you that following such regulations doesn't really help you to be more faithful or close to God. **B** [10] Those of us who believe in Jesus as the Messiah have benefits under the New Covenant that he procured for us at the altar in the Holy of Holies in Heaven—by means of his sacrifice. But those who continue to offer animal sacrifices for sin under the Old Covenant on an Earthly altar will not receive the benefits he paid for.

[11] Under the Old Covenant, the bodies of sacrificed animals were burned outside the camp—and the High Priest brought their blood into the earthly Holy of Holies as an offering for the people's sins on the Day of Atonement. [12] Therefore, in fulfillment of this Old Covenant "type," Jesus also suffered and died outside the gates of Jerusalem—and in the heavenly Holy of Holies he offered the blood of his own death as the perfect offering, which not only pays the penalty for all sins committed, but also sanctifies—making people completely holy and removing the source of sin in them. [13] If we want to be identified with him in his death and thus receive all the benefits of his sacrifice, we too must share the same shame and rejection that he experienced outside the gates of the city on the cross when those

---

A 13:2 Angels sometimes take on human form to do God's work. The implication of this exhortation is that hosting angels in this way—thinking they are ordinary people—will bring us additional blessings beyond the rewards God promises to give his people in Heaven for the good things we do for people in this life. It's an additional incentive to be hospitable.

B 13:9 The Jewish believers to whom this letter was written were being tempted by others to believe it was essential to continue following all the regulations in the Teachings of Moses regarding animal sacrifices and prohibited foods. They were afraid that if they didn't follow those regulations—as they had before they believed Jesus was the Messiah—God would reject them.

of the Jewish community rejected him—wanting to remain under the Old Covenant. So let's go out to him—outside the camp of Judaism—and endure the same kinds of insults and rejection that he did. **A** For we can't identify with the Messiah and also continue to identify with those who offer sacrifices for sin under the Old Covenant. 14 That's because we, with Jesus, are rejected in this world. We have no city or place in this world that really belongs to us. Instead, we are looking forward to living in the New Jerusalem which will one day come from Heaven.

15 So in our union with Jesus, let us continually offer a sacrifice of praise to God—thanking him and declaring to others that he is our Lord. 16 And do not neglect doing good for others or sharing with those in need—because these are the kinds of sacrifices that please God. 17 Obey your leaders in your local assembly and submit to their spiritual authority—because God has given them the responsibility of helping you to grow strong in your faith. He will hold them accountable for the way they lead you. Therefore, willingly follow their lead so that their responsibility may give them joy and not be a burden. You need to realize that rebellion will not benefit you, but will bring God's discipline. 18 Keep on praying for us. ❖ *The original recipients of this letter knew who the writer was and who else he was talking about. We don't.* ➤ We are sure that we have been following God's will because we've always only wanted to do what he wants of us. Pray that we will continue to do this. 19 And I urge you to pray earnestly that I can come back to you sooner than if you didn't pray. ❖ *Some commentators think the writer may have been writing from prison.* ➤

A Closing Prayer of Blessing

20-21 Now I ask God—who enables us to be at peace with himself and who raised our Great Shepherd, the Lord Jesus, from death—to provide you with every good thing you need to enable you to do his will. And I ask him—who joined us to Messiah Jesus by means of the New Covenant established forever through his blood—to change us into people who always please him. I also ask that he would gain great glory and praise forever because of our union with Jesus. Yes, may it be so!

Final Words

22 My brothers and sisters in Jesus, I urge you to patiently endure my words of exhortation and encouragement in this letter—since I've only written relatively little about these things and much more could be said. 23 I want you to know that Timothy has been released from prison, and if he comes to me soon, both of us will be coming to visit you. 24 Greet all of your leaders and all of God's people there for me. The believers with me here who are from Italy also send you their greetings. 25 I pray that God will grant you all you need of his undeserved enabling favor!

A **13:13** People who blasphemed God and broke the commands regarding the Sabbath day were killed outside of the city. Jesus was wrongly accused of both of these sins. Thus his death was considered shameful—and the priests of the Old Covenant and their followers rejected him completely.

James' Letter

The writer of this letter was the brother of Jesus [Matthew 13:55; Mark 6:3; Galatians 1:19] who became a believer after the resurrection. [1 Corinthians 15:7] James and his brothers waited for the Holy Spirit on Pentecost in Jerusalem with the other believers, [Acts 1:14] and he soon became one of the main leaders of the assembly of believers in Jerusalem. [Acts 12:17; 15:13-21; 21:18; Galatians 2:9, 12] He didn't call himself an apostle, but the early believers considered him and his brother Jude on a level comparable with the apostles. He was later called "James the Just" and was martyred in either AD 62 or 66.

This letter was written to Jewish followers of Jesus who lived outside of Israel sometime in the period AD 46–49, and was probably written before any other book in the New Testament.

James talks about the characteristics of true saving faith. He says "faith without obedience is dead." True faith causes us to submit to God, obey his commands, and control what we say. It helps us resist temptation, to wait patiently without complaining for Jesus to return, and to rejoice even during difficult circumstances.

Key thematic verses in this letter are 1:19-22 and 2:14-17

1

¹ I am James, a voluntary slave to God and also to our Lord Jesus the Messiah. I'm writing to you Jewish believers who are scattered among many countries outside of Judea. Rejoice! ❖ *"Rejoice," was a common greeting in Greek, and as a word play it ties his greeting to the topic of his next sentence.* ➤

Enduring Difficult Circumstances, Persecution, Temptation, and Testing

² My dear brothers and sisters in the Lord, when you find yourself in difficult circumstances or experiencing temptation, you should turn to God and rejoice. ³ You should recognize that such difficulties and temptations are meant to test and prove your faith—to see if you can trust God to take care of you during such times. If your trust doesn't waiver, the result will be an increased ability to persevere in trusting him in even more difficult circumstances. *[Romans 5:3-5; 2 Peter 1:5-8]* ⁴ You need to endure in trusting him until the time of testing is finished. Then you will attain maturity in your spiritual life and in every aspect of your character. Having gotten rid of weaknesses, you will be ready to face any situation.

⁵ But if you aren't sure what God wants you to do in a particular situation, you must ask him for his direction and enabling power. He is always generous and gracious in giving his direction and help to those who ask. He won't begrudge your asking because he wants you to do so. ⁶ But when you do, you must be willing to submit yourself to obey what he tells you to do. To ask when you are not be willing to obey is insincere. ❖ *The figure in the literal text about being driven and tossed by the wind was a common figure of speech among both Jews and Greeks for insincerity—not doubt, as American culture would tend to interpret it.* ➤ ⁷ If you are insincere and unwilling to obey anything at all that he might tell you to do, don't expect to receive any help from him. ⁸ People like that are always wavering and can never make up their mind to do anything. They never stick to any decision. God only promises to help those who fully submit themselves to obey him.

⁹ Believers who are poor or unimportant in the eyes of society should rejoice in the fact that they have high status with God. ¹⁰ And believers who are rich should be glad that God has humbled them—making them believers who now identify with their poor brothers and sisters. They should not put any confidence in their wealth to help them—since it's as temporary as wildflowers. ❖ *Another interpretation is that the rich people are unbelievers and James is speaking against them with irony—because in God's eyes there isn't anything for them to really be glad about. They will die and their wealth will not help them then. This would be understood to encourage the believers who were almost all poor and of no importance. In*

either case, the saying tells people that wealth is meaningless in the face of death. ➤ 11 Just as the sun rises and its heat dries up the grass, causing the wildflowers to wilt and drop off—their beauty gone—in the same way, rich people and their wealth are temporary, disappearing just as quickly from this world even as they go about their business.

12 God will bless those who trust him to take care of them while enduring difficult circumstances and persecutions without complaining. When the duration of the testing of their faith in this life is finished, he will give them eternal life in Heaven. He will also give them a valuable eternal reward for their faithfulness—which he has promised to those who prove their love for him. 13 If you are tempted to sin during difficult circumstances, never think that it is God who is tempting you! For God is incapable of desiring evil and never tempts anyone else to desire it either. 14 Realize that it's your own evil desires that tempt you. They are what draw you to evil and will trap you if give in to them. 15 When you give in to evil desires, you act upon them—committing sin. And if you continue to indulge in sin, it will dominate your life and lead you to eternal death in Hell. 16 So, my dear brothers and sisters in the Lord, don't be deceived by Satan's lies about the source of your temptations, thinking they come from God. 17 What comes from God is: everything that's good. You need not fear—as the heathen do—that the stars rule your fate. For God created every light in the sky and is in control. The stars change position in the sky and astrologers make their fearful predictions, but your Heavenly Father never changes in any way. There isn't even the slightest hint of change or evil in him. 18 He was the one who decided to give us eternal life in union with himself—and he brought it about through the declaration of his Good News message. His purpose was that all who believed his message would become those who—from among all of creation—specially belong to him. ❖ *The first fruits, in the literal text, is a figure of that part of a crop which belongs to God and is dedicated to him. So redeemed humanity belongs uniquely to God.* ➤

The Ways of God's True Children

[Romans 12:1—15:7; 1 Corinthians 13:1-7; Galatians 5:16—6:10; Ephesians 4:1—6:9; Colossians 3:12—4:6; 1 Thessalonians 4:1-12; 5:6-22; James 3:13—4:17; 1 Peter 4:1-11]

19 My dear brothers and sisters in the Lord, remember these truths: Always consider it more important to listen to others than to say what you think. Also, don't allow yourselves to become angry too easily or quickly—20 because anger that comes from your own feelings will not result in words or actions that are in line with God's will. 21 So get rid of everything in your manner of living that defiles you—and all the anger and hatred that leads you to do evil. ❖ *James was writing to people who were tempted to revolt and use violent means to right wrongs.* ➤ Humble yourselves and embrace God's Word that he has placed in your hearts and minds—which is able to save and then transform you. 22 Demonstrate that you are the kind of people who do what God says to do—and not those who merely listen to it and deceive themselves into thinking that they are saved. 23 Those who hear God's message but don't respond with obedience are like people who look in the mirror and see something in their appearance that isn't suitable—yet do nothing. 24 Then they walk away and immediately forget what they've seen. The mirror didn't benefit them at all—just as God's Word does nothing for those who neglect to obey it. 25 But God will think highly of those who continually reflect on his perfect teachings in the Scriptures and diligently remember to follow them. For those teachings will free such people from the power of sin.

26 If you think God is pleased with you, but you don't stop yourself from speaking gossip, criticism, and slander, then you are self-deceived because God is not pleased with you regardless of what other good things you do. You are of no use to him for his purposes. 27 If you really want to please God our Father, you will not defile yourself with such evil talk or any other sinful indulgence, but will demonstrate your love for him by taking care of the helpless—such as widows and orphans. ❖ *Also those*

who are sick, hospitalized, unemployed, poor, desperate, neglected, weary, etc. ➤

2

Don't Favor the Rich and Influential Above Others

1 My brothers and sisters in the Lord, you can't truly believe in our Lord Jesus the Messiah—who has God's glorious character—and at the same time treat some people as more important than others. For he himself lives in all believers—so all people are equally important to him. 2 For example, suppose two strangers come to your worship meeting and you can tell from their clothing that one is rich and the other is poor. 3 If you show more respect to the rich person and offer him the best seat and treat the poor person with less respect—telling her to stand off to the side or sit on the floor—then you have sinned. 4 You have made distinctions among yourselves that some are more important than others—using wrong standards that originate in wrong motives, i.e., desiring the favor of those with money and influence. You are judging wrongly based on outward appearance. 5 My dear brothers and sisters in the Lord, carefully consider this: Isn't it obvious that God mainly chose those who are poor in this world to be the ones whose trust in him is strong and complete, who recognize the Messiah as their King, and who will receive all the blessings he has promised to those who love him? 6 But when you make superficial distinctions like that, you insult the poor whom God has chosen to bless. Isn't it mainly rich people who oppress you and sue you in court? 7 Isn't it usually the wealthy who speak evil about Jesus—to whom you belong? 8 If you are following the "Command of the Kingdom" found in the Scriptures which says, **"You must love and treat others the same way you love and treat yourself,"** then you are doing what is right. *[Leviticus 19:18; Matthew 19:19; 22:39; Mark 12:31;*

Luke 10:27; Romans 13:9; Galatians 5:14] 9 But if you discriminate based on status and wealth, you are sinning and disobeying God's command. 10 Even though you strive to keep almost every-thing the Torah demands, but reject it's authority in only one small part of it, that still means you are as guilty in God's sight as if you had rejected all of his teachings in the Torah. 11 It was the same God who said, **"Don't break the marriage promise,"** and **"Don't murder."** *[Exodus 20:13-14; Deuteronomy 5:17-18]* So even if you strive to always keep your marriage promise, but continue to murder people, you are guilty of rejecting his Torah. **A** 12 So always be aware that God will judge everything you say and do by whether or not it follows his "new" command to love others. He put this command in our minds and hearts and enables us to obey his will. *[Jeremiah 31:33]* 13 He will not show mercy to those who have withheld mercy from others. But those who habitually show mercy to others have nothing to fear when they stand before God as judge.

Faith Without Obedience Is Not True Faith

14 My brothers and sisters in the Lord, if you say that you trust in God's promises but don't obey him—your so-called faith will not save you. 15 If you know about fellow believers who lack adequate food or clothing 16 and you are able to help them—but don't—and instead say, "I will pray that God will give you what you need," your words are meaningless both to the person you spoke to and to God. 17 In the same way, trusting God to save you is useless if you aren't also willing to obey him and do what is right. ❖ *This is not because obedience merits salvation, but because genuine faith necessarily produces repentance from sin—which means that a person turns away from sin and turns toward obeying God. Without repentance and obedience, a person's so-called "faith" is a sham. [Matthew 7:21]* ➤ 18 Someone might ask me, "Do you really believe in Jesus?" And I will respond, "My obedience to him shows that

---

A 2:11 There are various understandings of verses 10-11. I've presented one minority view offered by David Stern in his Jewish New Testament Commentary because I think it deserves consideration and it may not obviously suggest itself from looking at a literal translation.

I believe in him. Can you show me that you believe in him without obeying him? I can only show you I believe by what I do." 19 You claim to believe that there is only one God. That is good, but even the demons know this is true—yet, they are afraid because they also know he will punish them in Hell for their disobedience. So it should be clear that intellectual belief by itself is not enough to save you. 20 Those who only have this kind of faith are foolish. I will show you that trusting God without obeying him is futile. 21 Didn't God say that our ancestor Abraham was considered righteous in his sight because he was willing to offer his son Isaac as a sacrifice in obedience to God's command? *[Genesis chapter 22; especially verse 12]* 22 So it's clear that his faith and his obedience went together. His trust in God was completed by his obedience. ❖ *It was Abraham's trust that God valued, but clearly—if he had not obeyed God it would have indicated that he didn't trust him. Obedience comes from trusting. True faith will always result in obedience. They cannot be separated. There is no conflict between James' teaching here and Paul's teaching in Romans. Paul stresses faith—but also makes it clear that faith implies obedience.* ➤ 23 This is what the Scripture means where it says, **"Abraham believed God's promise—therefore, God considered him righteous in his sight."** *[Genesis 15:6]* Thus he was called "God's friend." 24 So it's clear that people are considered righteous in God's sight because of what they do in obedience as a result of their trusting him—and not by "trusting" him in a way that never produces obedience. 25 It was the same with Rahab the prostitute who offered hospitality to the Israelite spies and sent them safely back by another way so they could escape their pursuers. God considered her righteous because of what she did. *[Joshua 2:4, 6, 15]* 26 Just as a body that doesn't breathe is dead—faith without obedience is dead and worthless.

3

Words Have Power

1 My brothers and sisters in the Lord, it's not appropriate that many of you become leaders who teach God's word. Realize that God will use stricter standards to judge those who teach his people. Their rewards in Heaven will be diminished if their teaching is wrong—or if their lives do not follow their own teaching. 2 We all sin in many ways, but we should always try to speak only what is good and true—because those who never sin in their speaking have attained spiritual maturity and are able to control themselves in every other way as well. 3 Controlling what you say is key. A large horse is entirely directed by means of a small bit in its mouth. 4 Huge ships blown by strong winds are controlled by small rudders, making them go wherever the pilot desires. 5 In the same way, our ability to speak is a small part of us, but can cause big things to happen. Just think how much damage a few words can do—like a small spark can start a forest fire. 6 Our words can be like fire. Evil things we say can destroy entire lives. What we say determines the course of our lives. And if we allow our words to be influenced by Satan, they can destroy like a fire raging out of control. 7 Humans have been able to tame or control all kinds of animals, birds, reptiles, and sea creatures. 8 But without God's help, no one can control the evil words that come out of their mouths. Our mouths are full of deadly poison that can corrupt and destroy the thoughts and lives of others. Evil words slip out—it seems—unrestrained by reason. 9 We praise our Lord and Heavenly Father—and then we turn around and curse people who were made in his image. 10 So we use our words to both bless and curse. My brothers and sisters, this is not appropriate! *[Matthew 12:36-37]* 11 Does a good spring produce both fresh and salt water? 12 Can a fig tree produce olives, or a grapevine produce figs? No—things produce according to their nature. Salt water will never produce fresh water. So when you produce both good and evil words, it means your heart and thoughts are not entirely pure. Repent—and ask God to purify your heart, thoughts, and your words.

God's Wisdom

13 Who among you think they clearly understand—as teachers should—the way

God wants his people to live? Then let your way of life demonstrate it to others through good deeds done in humble obedience to God's command. 14 But if you have any of these things in your hearts and minds: bitterness, envy, jealousy, or selfish ambition, then don't boast and lie about being wise. 15 These things are not produced from having God's wisdom. They are from this sinful world, are not in line with the Spirit, and are characteristic of demons. 16 For wherever there is jealousy and the selfish desire to make yourself greater than others, there will be quarreling and every kind of evil being done. 17 But the wisdom God gives causes us first of all to purify our lives, then it causes us to cooperate harmoniously with others and be considerate of them, to be deferential and compassionate, to produce many good deeds, to love each other impartially, and in all things to be genuine—without hypocrisy. 18 Those who are genuine peacemakers will plant seeds of peace wherever they can—and they will generate a harvest of people living together in peace who follow God's will.

4

Avoid Selfishness

1 What do you think causes the quarrels and fighting among you? Don't you realize that they come from your selfishness—which struggles against the desires of others and against what you know is God's will? 2 You want what you don't have, so you are willing to murder to get it. You covet things that others have and can't get them, so you quarrel and fight to get them. But the reason you don't have what you want is because you don't ask God for them. 3 And if you do ask God for them, but don't get them, it's because you have asked from selfish motives. You just want things for your own pleasure—not because you want to help others as you ought. 4 You aren't following God at all! Don't you realize that if you love the evil ways of this world it's the same as hating God? Therefore, those who choose to partner with people who reject God and with those who indulge in evil—are his

enemies. 5 The Scriptures give warning for a reason when they say that God is jealous of any desires in us that compete with the Holy Spirit he sent to live in us. ❖ *James seems to be quoting in the original text, but there is no Scripture that closely matches what he says. He might be quoting an unknown source or might be referring in general to teaching scattered throughout the Scriptures. [e.g. concerning God's jealous nature: Exodus 20:5; 34:14; Deuteronomy 4:24; 5:9; 6:15; Joshua 24:19; 1 Kings 14:22; Ezekiel 16:38; 23:25; Nahum 1:2] Some commentators understand this verse to mean that God yearns for our human spirits which he created—which is similar to the interpretation given above. Others interpret it to mean that the human spirit God made to live in us has strong envious desires. This last interpretation implies things that can't be reconciled with other Scripture. Unless he is speaking of the unregenerate spirit, it would be hard to find any kind of Scriptural support for the idea. Since James is speaking to believers—and the new human spirit that God has put within us is holy—this last interpretation doesn't make sense.* ➤

God Helps Those Who Are Humble

6 But God gives us all the favor and enabling power we need to overcome these evil desires—if we ask for his help and depend on it. ❖ *See the note after 1 Peter 2:11.* ➤ The Scriptures say, **"God actively opposes those who are proud, but shows his undeserved enabling favor to those who are humble."** *[Proverbs 3:34; 1 Peter 5:5]* 7 Therefore, humble yourselves by admitting you need help—and determine to submit to God's will. Then verbally rebuke and oppose Satan—who amplifies your evil desires—and he will run away from you. ❖ *Jesus showed us how to do this in the accounts of his temptation in the wilderness—where he quoted Scripture to counter Satan's lies, temptations, and twisting of Scripture. [Matthew 4:1-11; Luke 4:1-13.]* ➤ 8 You are sinners and double-minded, trying to follow both your own desires and God's. Instead, try to become intimate with God—and he will make your relationship with him close. You do this by repenting of the evil you've done and starting to obey him. Make it your heart's desire to only follow him. 9 Mourn and cry over your sins. *[Matthew 5:4; Luke 6:21]* Change your laughter and enjoyment of evil into deep grief and tears because of your rebellion. 10 Humble yourselves before the Lord and offer yourselves to him

in submissive worship. As a result, he will spiritually reward you.

Don't Condemn Others

❖ *Another exhortation on how not to speak.* ➤

11 My brothers and sisters in the Lord, take care not to criticize or slander each other. Those who do are—in effect—saying that they are above God's command to love each other. By refusing to obey this command, you are—in effect—saying that you have the right and power to decide for yourself what is good and evil—and that some of God's commands are not fit to be followed. 12 But God is the one who gave his commands and he has reserved the right to judge people for himself alone. Only he has the ability to save people or sentence them to eternal ruin in Hell. ❖ *See 2 Thessalonians 1:9 and the following note about what it means to experience eternal ruin in Hell.* ➤ So who do you think you are that you have the right to criticize, slander, or condemn other people?

Don't Boast About Your Plans

❖ *Another exhortation on how not to speak.* ➤

13 Now pay attention to this: You boast about going to certain places at certain times and what you will do and how you will prosper. 14 But in reality, you know nothing about what will happen tomorrow! Your lives are actually as insubstantial—and potentially as short-lived—as a mist that appears for a while and then disappears. 15 Your attitude and manner of speaking should be, "If the Lord allows it to happen, we will live and do this, or carry out that plan." 16 You have been arrogant and make vain boasts, but all such boasting is evil. 17 Therefore, anyone who knows what God wants—as I've outlined above— and is capable of doing the right thing and doesn't do it—sins.

5

A Warning for the Rich
Who Don't Use Their Power & Wealth for Good

1 You who are rich and are not submitted to God, listen to this: You should be crying and moaning about the punishment that awaits you on Judgment Day! *[Luke 6:24]* 2 Your fine clothing will become moth-eaten and your riches will disappear. 3 Your wealth is corrupt because of the way you got it—and also the way you've spent it. God is aware of that corruption and will punish you for using your wealth wrongly—you will burn in Hell. You have foolishly stored up wealth as if this world will continue forever, but these are the last days and the Messiah will soon return to judge you. 4 You didn't pay the people who worked in your fields. Listen! Do you hear their complaints against you? Almighty God has heard them! 5 You have lived in luxury—spending your wealth only on yourselves to satisfy every desire you've ever had. You've been foolishly indulging your selfish desires—making yourselves fat—all the while unaware that God is ready to start judging you for what you have done. You are like unsuspecting pigs that are about to be slaughtered. 6 You have condemned and executed innocent people and they didn't resist you. ❖ *The interpretation of last phrase is debated. Some think it means they were unable to resist. Others think it was intended as a rhetorical question, meaning—yes, they did resist you and cried out to God for justice.* ➤

Wait Patiently Until the Messiah Returns

7 My brothers and sisters in the Lord, wait patiently without complaining for the Lord Jesus to return. Don't lose hope. Consider farmers as examples of those who wait for their valuable crops to grow. They wait patiently for the rain that comes in the early part of the year, and also for the rain that comes in the later part of the year. ❖ *In Israel, there are two periods of the year when rain is important for a good harvest. They were called the "early rain" and the "later rain." [Deuteronomy 11:14; Joel 2:23] The early rain is in October (the Jewish year begins in September) and the later rain is in April and May. If the later rains don't come, the harvest is small.* ➤ 8 You too must wait patiently without losing hope—for the Lord Jesus will return soon. 9 My brothers and sisters, don't complain about each other. If you do, God will judge that you have sinned. Realize that the Judge is almost ready to start. He is standing in the doorway. 10 Instead of complaining, follow the

example of the prophets who long ago spoke God's words. They suffered for doing good and didn't complain, but waited patiently for God to judge those who persecuted them. [11] We all believe that God approves of those who patiently endured suffering for him. You have heard Job's story and know the way he waited for his suffering to end and continued to trust God. You know that Yahweh finally ended his suffering because he is always compassionate and merciful.

Don't Swear Oaths

❖ *Another exhortation on how not to speak.* ➤

[12] But most importantly, brothers and sisters, never swear an oath by Heaven or Earth—or by anything else in order to affirm your truthfulness. Mean "yes" when you say it, and mean "no" when you say it—so God will not judge that you've lied. *[Matthew 5:33-37]* ❖ *Most commentators do not believe James (or Jesus) was prohibiting official oaths, as in court, but was saying that they were totally inappropriate for affirming every-day truthfulness—since you should always speak truthfully.* ➤

Prayer and Healing

[13] If any among you are suffering, they should pray—asking God to help them. If any among you are happy, they should sing him songs of praise. [14] If there are any among you who are sick, you should call your spiritual leaders to come and anoint you with oil in the name of the Lord Jesus and pray for you to be healed. ❖ *Oil is symbolic of the Holy Spirit. The anointing is a sacramental action—in expectation that the Spirit will come on the sick person with power to heal.* ➤ [15] And their prayer—offered to God in faith that he will heal you—will cause you to recover. ❖ *This doesn't say or imply instantly.* ➤ The Lord will heal you, and if you have committed any sins that caused the sickness, he will forgive them. ❖ *This is a blanket promise of universal healing for those believers who trust God to heal them. It is a teaching sorely neglected among many groups of believers today. But the healing can be inhibited by unbelief [Matthew 13:58; Mark 6:5-6]—and probably by other factors as well.* ➤ [16] So confess your sins to each other and pray for each other so you can all be healed. The prayers of people who are righteous in God's sight—through their spiritual union with Jesus—have power to accomplish much. [17] The prophet Elijah was an ordinary man just like us. He prayed earnestly that it wouldn't rain because of the sins of the Israelites—and it didn't rain for three and a half years. ❖ *Note the "earnestly." Much is implied in this verse, but many people don't receive the answers to their prayers because they pray one quick prayer and don't persevere until the answer is granted. One implication is that who you are doesn't make any difference as to the effectiveness of your prayers.* ➤ [18] Then he prayed again asking for rain—and God sent it. So the ground once again produced crops. *[1 Kings 18:1; 41-45]*

Help Those Who Have Strayed to Return to God

[19] My brothers and sisters in the Lord, if any among you strays from the way God wants us to live, someone should reach out and try to bring him back. [20] Realize that someone who helps such a person turn away from evil will cause many sins to be forgiven—and will save him from eternal death.

Peter's First Letter

Conservative scholars accept that this letter was written by the Apostle Peter near the end of his life while in Rome, probably in the period AD 62–64. Nero was emperor, and some persecution of believers was going on—although the major persecution didn't start until after the fire in Rome in AD 64, which Nero blamed on followers of Jesus. Peter was martyred about AD 67.

He writes to both Gentile and Jewish followers of Jesus scattered around the Roman provinces in the western part of what is today Turkey, but the larger number of believers there were probably Gentiles. It's likely there was persecution going on in Rome—and Peter knew there was also unofficial persecution going on in the provinces, or soon would be. The followers of Jesus lived in the midst of generally hostile unbelievers. Peter writes to encourage them to remain faithful to their Lord—even while enduring persecution and suffering—and teaches them why these things are happening.

For modern-American believers—who have experienced little active persecution and who often hear teaching that prosperity and victory should be the norm—this letter provides a strong counter balance. Believers in many parts of the world face persecution every day. Peter teaches that if we are faithful to God's will, then we will experience persecution. The themes of this letter are 'submitting to authority' and 'suffering for our faith.'

1

Opening Greetings

1 I, Peter, an apostle of Messiah Jesus, am writing to God's people—chosen by him to live as spiritual sojourners who don't belong to this world because their true home is in Heaven—who are scattered throughout the Roman provinces of Pontus, Galatia, Cappadocia, Asia, and Bithynia. ❖ *in western Asia Minor—i.e., present-day western Turkey* ➤ 2 In eternity past, God the Father knew about ❖ *or: predestined* ➤ you and chose you by means of the Holy Spirit's work to set you apart ❖ *or: chose you for the purpose of being set apart by the Holy Spirit, or: chose you and set you apart by the Holy Spirit* ➤ in order to make you pure and acceptable to him. He did this by the application of Jesus' sacrificial death as a substitute for you—bringing you into covenant relationship with himself. His ultimate purpose is to bring you into willing obedience to Messiah Jesus. I pray that he will look upon you with great favor far beyond anything you can deserve—so you will experience complete peace and well-being. ❖ *This verse is theologically packed, but it seems the precise interpretation will inevitably depend on one's theological presuppositions—since the precise logical interrelationships of the phrases are not clearly indicated. Either Calvinistic or Arminian views can be read into it. Some commentators see a reference to baptism because of the word "sprinkling" (in the literal text)—even though it refers explicitly to blood. Note the Trinitarian language—with each person of the Trinity contributing to the process of salvation.* ➤

Our Expectation and Joy
in the Midst of Challenges to Our Faith

3 Let's thank and praise the God and Father of our Lord Jesus the Messiah! ❖ *As a man, Jesus related to God the Father as both his God and his Father. The title "Lord," implies Peter's recognition of Jesus' deity.* ➤ Out of his great compassion for us—and by means of Jesus the Messiah's dying and rising from death—he has enabled us to be spiritually reborn into a new relationship with himself. This relationship causes us to live with increasing expectation 4 of receiving the fullness of the eternal salvation he has promised us as his "legally adopted heirs"—which awaits us in Heaven. That future "inheritance" will never diminish in any way—no matter how long we wait before obtaining it. ❖ *The terminology of "inheritance" does not imply that God has to die before we get it. It is better thought of as a "trust" that one inherits upon attaining a certain age or qualification—in this case, when we enter Heaven.* ➤ 5 As long as you continue to actively trust him and his promises, God's power will protect your relationship with him and your ability to continue to trust him. This protection is effective even

through persecution—and lasts until you enter the fullness of your salvation in Heaven at the time he has appointed.

6 Thus you can inwardly rejoice in anticipation of these things, even if right now you are required to endure the stress and suffering of difficult circumstances—which for a while will test your faith. 7 God's purpose in allowing these challenges to your faith is to both prove its genuineness and to make it stronger and purer. Just as gold's purity is both tested and increased by subjecting it to high temperatures, ❖ *which cause any impurities to be revealed because they float to the surface of the molten gold—causing the gold to become more pure as the impurities are burned or skimmed off* ➤ your faith is tested and purified by the "fire" of challenges put to it. And your faith is far more valuable to him than gold—which is temporary no matter how pure it is. On the Last Day when Messiah Jesus is openly revealed to the entire world, your faith will result in praise, glory, and honor. ❖ *Commentators are divided on which way the praise, glory, and honor are directed. More tend to think they are directed from God to the believer, but it is likely that all three will be directed in both directions.* ➤ 8 Even though you never saw **A** him while he was in this world, you continue to love him. And even though he hasn't yet returned so you still can't see him, you continue to trust him and are filled with a joy beyond your ability to express—which is characteristic of Heaven itself. 9 The end result of your continued trust in him is your experiencing the ongoing process of salvation in your lives. ❖ *The present experience of salvation refers to sanctification. Our salvation is not complete until we receive everything that God has promised us in Heaven. For those who accept the tripartite model of humanity, our human spirits have already been saved (renewed, born again, and sanctified), our bodies will be saved (glorified) at the resurrection, and our souls (mind, will, and emotions) are saved and also are in the process of being saved (being conformed to the character of the Messiah).* ➤

10 The prophets—who prophesied in the Hebrew Scriptures about the results of God's undeserved favor that has come to you through the Messiah—had many unanswered questions about this promised salvation. They sought answers to these question from both God and the Scriptures.

11 When the Messiah's Holy Spirit in them predicted the Messiah's sufferings and the wonderful things that would happen afterward, they wanted to know what period of time **B** these prophesies were about—and what kinds of circumstances would be present in the world when these events would happen. Thus they searched the Scriptures and their own prophecies and the events of their own times to see if their prophecies were to be fulfilled within their lifetimes. 12 God enabled them to realize that their prophecies were not to help them in their time, but to help you who would live after the events mentioned in their prophecies had happened. And now the Holy Spirit—whom the Messiah sent from Heaven—has announced to you that these prophesied events have finally been accomplished. He did this through those who preached the Good News to you. These are things that even the angels have wanted to understand for a long time.

Our Proper Response to God's Favor Is to Dedicate Our Lives to Him

13 Since God has done all this for you, always be prepared to follow the Holy Spirit's leading. To do this, you must be sober and in full control of yourselves. As motivation, keep yourselves focused on obtaining the blessings that Jesus the Messiah has promised to give you when he returns. 14 Since you are now God's children and desire to obey him, don't allow yourselves to follow the evil desires that you had when you didn't yet understand his truth. 15 Instead, you must set yourselves apart as dedicated to live entirely for God. Everything you do should reflect this holy dedication because God—who called you into relationship with himself—is himself uniquely holy and wants your character to

---

A 1:8 A few manuscripts say "knew" him.
B 1:11 The Greek τίς (tis) is ambiguous and could mean "who," (i.e., who these were about), or "which," (i.e., in which time these would happen.) A majority of commentators choose the latter interpretation.

reflect his own. 16 He commands in the Scriptures, **"You must be holy and separate from evil—because I am holy."** *[Leviticus 11:44-45; 19:2; 20:7]*

17 Realize that God—the Heavenly Father to whom you pray for help—judges all people by the same high standards—showing no partiality. He will reward or punish you as you deserve for everything you do in this life. Therefore, during your lives as spiritual sojourners who don't belong to this world, live in awe and fear of his judgment—always considering how he will judge you for what you are doing. 18 Remember that it cost God a lot to set you free from the fate you deserved because you worshiped false gods—as your ancestors taught you to do. ❖ *God did not pay a ransom to Satan or any other being, as some have interpreted the word "redeem" (in the literal text). The cost was the pain to himself.* ➤ The cost was not mere temporary things like gold or silver, 19 but the death of the Messiah ❖ *which the Scriptures often refer to by talking about his "blood"* ➤—who is very precious to God. He was our sacrificial sin offering, our substitute, without flaw or sin, the true sacrifice that the unblemished and spotless Passover lamb pointed to. 20 As part of his original plan, God chose and appointed him to be our sacrificial substitute even before he created this world—because he knew it would be necessary. *[Revelation 13:8]* And in this final period of history, this preordained plan has become manifest—accomplished in time for your eternal benefit. 21 Now—because of what the Messiah has done and through your being joined to him—you have entrusted yourselves to God the Father who raised him back to life and exalted him to be King of Heaven. As a result, your trust and expectations are focused on God and his promises. 22 When you believed the truth of the Good News, you were made clean from every sin that could hinder a genuine affectionate love for each other as brothers and sisters. So make every effort to demonstrate heart-felt Messiah-like love for each other.

23 For you have been given spiritual rebirth into a new life—which is an eternal love relationship with the God of love. This life cannot die, since its source ❖ *literally, "seed"* ➤ is the life essence of the eternal living Word ❖ λόγος *(logos)* ➤ of God himself—the Messiah, the source of all life. ❖ *All commentators that I found believe this verse refers to the written or spoken Word of God because of the connection to the following two verses. But the source of the written and spoken Word of God is the second person of the Trinity—whom John calls the "Word" of God. So the ultimate source of eternal life is the one who is also the Messiah—the Word Incarnate. There is no real dichotomy since the written Word is eternal and effective only because the Living Word—who caused the written Word to be written—continues to cause it to be effective. It is also true that the Holy Spirit was the agent inspiring the writers and is the agent who causes the message of the Word to be effective. But he is the agent of the Living Word.* ➤ 24 For the Scriptures say about the Word of God, **"All human flesh is as temporary as grass, and its splendor is as temporary as that of wildflowers. Grass dries up and flowers drop from their stems.** 25 **But unlike created things, the Word** ❖ ῥῆμα *(rhēma)* = spoken word ➤ **of the Lord is eternal."** *[Isaiah 40:6-8; Septuagint]* ❖ *The quote from Isaiah says "Word of God." So Peter—by saying "Word of the Lord"—is shifting the emphasis to Jesus as Lord.* ➤ It was about this Word of God that you were taught.

2

Crave the Lord Himself

1 Since you have been spiritually reborn, don't allow yourselves to A indulge in—or even contemplate—any kind of evil intent, or any kind of deception, or pretense of holiness, or envy of others, or any kind of insulting or slanderous comments—for these are incompatible with Messiah-like love. 2 Continually crave the spiritual life-giving nourishment of the Messiah himself ❖ *many think this nourishment is delivered through God's written Word* ➤—just as a newborn hungers for his mother's milk. For he ❖ *or it* ➤ will cause you to mature in your experience of what it

---

A **2:1** It is not certain whether the Greek aorist participle ἀποθέμενοι (apothemenoi) "having put away" is a command or an indicative statement of what has been completed. i.e., "you no longer allow yourselves to..."

means to be saved. **A** ❖ *Some commentators believe "growing in salvation" does not refer to growth in maturity, but to our ultimate salvation when we enter Heaven.* ➤ **3 For you have already experienced that the Lord is good, kind, and gracious!** ❖ *This is a modified quote of Psalm 34:8, "Taste and see that Yahweh is good!"* ➤

God's People Are His Temple, His Priests, and a New Chosen Nation

4-5 As you continually become B intimate with the Messiah, he is forming you all together into God's place of residence—his Temple. *[2 Corinthians 6:16]* **You are like living stones that make up that Temple—joined to the Messiah who is the Chief Foundation Stone—rejected by people but precious to God.** *[Daniel 2:34-35; 44-45; Matthew 21:42; Mark 12:10; Luke 20:17; Acts 4:11; Ephesians 2:20-22]* **Not only are you part of his dwelling place, but you also serve him as priests** *[Isaiah 61:6]* **consecrated solely to his service—who offer sacrifices of praise, thanksgiving, worship, and obedience,** *[Romans 12:1; Philippians 4:18; Hebrews 13:15-16]* **and who have been made acceptable to him because of your union with Jesus the Messiah. 6 For the Scriptures say, "I am laying my chosen and precious Chief Foundation Stone in Zion—and those who trust in him will never be disappointed."** *[Isaiah 28:16]* ❖ *The prophecy to place the Stone in Zion hints that it would replace the Temple.* ➤ **7 You believers have this honor. But to unbelievers, the Scriptures say, "The very Stone that the builders rejected** ❖ *"builders" refers to the leaders of Israel who rejected the Messiah [Isaiah 28:14]* ➤ **has become the Chief Foundation Stone in God's plan."** *[Psalm 118:22]* **8 The Scriptures also say that the Messiah is, "a Stone that causes people to stumble, and a Rock that offends them."** *[Isaiah 8:14; Romans 9:33]* **They are presently "stumbling" in unbelief and rejecting the Messiah because they are living in rebellion against God's Word. This current state was predestined by God in eternity past.** ❖ *This verse—along with Jude 4—may speak of the predestination of at least some of those who will perish in Hell. It could*

alternatively be interpreted to mean that the current state of those who were rejecting the Messiah at the time of Peter's writing—and he is probably thinking of fellow Jews—was predestined for God's purposes of opening the message of the Good News to Gentiles—and yet allowed for them to repent later in their lives. ➤ **9 But God chose you to be part of the new race of redeemed humanity, to be priests in the service of Jesus our King, C to be the new spiritual nation of Israel—wholly dedicated to serving God.** *[Exodus 19:6]* **You are to be a people he has created to specially belong to himself—so you can proclaim his excellent character and deeds through your praises. He has called you out of the darkness of existing in sin, unbelief, and spiritual death into the wonderful light of fellowship with himself.** *[Exodus 19:5-6; Isaiah 43:21; Jeremiah 13:11; Malachi 3:17]* **10 Previously, you Gentiles were "not a people," but now you have the highest privilege of being "God's people."** *[Hosea 1:10; 2:23b]* **Previously, you had "not received mercy," but now you have "received his mercy."** *[Hosea 2:23a]* ❖ *All believers are now part of the new redeemed Israel—whether they are Jews or Gentiles. [Isaiah 19:24-25; 56:3-8] Note that the quotations in verses 4-10 come from contexts where God warns that he will reject his people if they persist in rebellion—and he will reject those who reject the "stone" (i.e., Messiah) he has put in Zion.* ➤

How Believers Are to Live in This Unbelieving World

11 My dear brothers and sisters whom I love in the Lord, you are living among unbelievers as spiritual sojourners who don't belong to this world. So I strongly exhort you to continue to actively reject the sinful desires that come from your remaining ingrained sin habits and physical urges which wage all-out war against your true self—which is your perfect human spirit and redeemed mind and will that desire to obey God. *[Romans 7:21-25; Galatians 5:13; 19-21]* ❖ *These things will help you reject sinful desires: 1) Recognize they are not part of your "true self" because: (a) our "old self" was crucified with the Messiah [Romans 6:6], and (b) you are a "new creation" [2 Corinthians 5:17] and are already "sanctified"*

A 2:2 The words "into salvation" (in the literal text) are not in some Greek manuscripts.

B 2:4-5 The present participle προσερχόμενοι

(proserchomenoi) "coming" in Greek, could be interpreted as a command.

C 2:9 or: a Kingdom of priests, or: kings and priests

[1 Corinthians 1:2] and are seated with the Messiah in Heaven. [Ephesians 2:6] 2) When sinful desires come: (a) immediately reject them—rejecting them verbally can help, (b) ask the Lord Jesus to live his life through you, (c) trust that he is doing so, (d) then act in obedience. [Galatians 2:20] 3) Set your mind on pure and good things. [Philippians 4:8] It is important that you not dwell on the temptation. 4) Recognize that temptation is a spiritual attack against you and that "offense is the best defense"—even against Satan. Have on hand a list of people to pray for and their needs, and when you are tempted, start interceding on behalf of those people for salvation, healing, restored relationships, provision, etc. Wage spiritual warfare against the enemy on behalf of your family, friends, colleagues, and acquaintances. Do this out loud if possible. This will distract you from the temptation and will have you actively focusing on God's word, standing on his promises, exercising your faith, strengthening your resolve to oppose the enemy, his temptations, and ways—while actively depending on God's power to overcome on behalf of those for whom you are praying. You will be resisting and opposing Satan—and as a result, he will cease attacking you with temptation, flee, [James 4:7] and leave you alone, at least for a while. [Luke 4:13] 5) If you have established habits of sin over many years, expect that it might take a few years of persistence to fully establish new thought and behavior habits—such as automatically doing steps 1 through 4. ➤

12 As you live among your unbelieving neighbors, your behavior should be so exemplary and praiseworthy that as they observe your good deeds and benevolence over time—even those who have falsely slandered you as undesirables and evil will eventually recognize that the good in your lives comes from your belief in the one true God. ❖ *Pagans often slandered Jews and followers of Jesus living among them because they were different. They tended to keep to themselves to avoid the sexual sins and temptations of their neighbors—so they were seen as anti-social. They were considered to be godless atheists because they refused to worship all the known gods and instead, worshipped one strange God they had never heard about. Believers were also accused of cannibalism because rumors were spread about them eating a body and drinking blood at their meetings (i.e., regarding celebrating the Lord's Supper). In America today, believers are often similarly misunderstood and branded as irrational fundamentalist extremists and hateful, intolerant, narrow-minded bigots—who want to impose their views on everyone else and whose unreasonably oppressive standards are responsible for many of the evils in society. So Peter's advice is still timely.* ➤ Then they will praise him on the day of visitation.

[Matthew 5:16] ❖ *This may refer to the day some of them are converted, or it may refer to Judgment Day.* ➤

Honor the Lord
by Submitting to All Legitimate Authority

13 In order to honor your Lord and obey him, obediently submit yourselves to every legitimate human institution, ❖ *i.e., governmental, social, work, ecclesiastical, family, etc.* ➤ from the Roman Emperor who is the supreme human authority, 14 down to the lower officials who represent him—whose responsibilities are to punish lawbreakers and give public recognition to those who do right. *[Romans 13:3-4]* ❖ *The Scriptures also teach that God does not expect his people to obey commands—from legitimate authorities—to do what God has forbidden. See Exodus 1:17; Daniel 3:13-18; 6:10-23; Acts 4:18-19; 5:27-29; and Hebrews 11:23. But when obedience does not require us to sin, submission is expected—regardless if the authority is pagan, or unjust to the person submitting, or if we disagree with the policy. There may be exceptions where the believer has the option of legitimately removing himself from under certain authorities—such as quitting a job, or moving to a different locality under a different government. But rebellion against authority is never sanctioned by God—except when necessary to submit to a higher authority, especially God himself. At such times, it is usually proper to make clear why you cannot obey, and you should be willing to suffer the consequences—trusting God to take care of you. But Exodus 1:17 is an example of an exception to this—i.e., hen such a declaration would endanger the lives of others.* ➤ 15 For it is God's will that those foolish people—who slander you out of prejudicial ignorance—will eventually notice your proper submission to authority and cease their accusations. 16 Does all this submission sound like bondage? You've been set free from all bondage in your spiritual union with the Messiah. No law can condemn you. But as people who freely offer their lives in service to God—choose to freely submit and obey. And don't think that your freedom from condemnation justifies doing wrong—because it doesn't. 17 Show appropriate honor and respect to everyone. In addition, demonstrate love to your fellow believers, recognize that only God is to be feared and offered complete submission in worship with awe and reverence—and honor the emperor.

Instructions to Slaves
About Submitting to Authority

18 You who are household slaves should submit to your owners and show them every respect—without regard to whether they are kind and considerate of you, or harsh and unreasonable. **A** 19 For if you patiently endure mental anguish for unjust treatment because you know it's God's will for you to submit to authority—you will have his approval. 20 Of course, there is nothing particularly praiseworthy about patiently enduring punishment that you deserve for doing wrong. But if you patiently endure punishment, without protest, which is unjust or a result of your obeying God's will to do right—rather than obeying the authority over you to do wrong—then you have God's favor.

21 The Messiah himself suffered unjustly on your behalf—in submissive patience and silence for the sake of obeying God—and so is an example for us to emulate. In fact, God has called you to be his own for the very purpose of following in the Messiah's footsteps—learning to obey God even when it causes us to suffer. *[Mark 10:30; John 15:18-20; 16:33; Acts 14:22; 1 Thessalonians 3:3-4; 2 Timothy 3:12]* 22 As the Scriptures prophesied about him, **"He had committed no sin and had never uttered a lie."** *[Isaiah 53:9]* ❖ *Some commentators believe verses 22-25 were a hymn because they are composed in sophisticated rhythmic Greek.* ➤ 23 When he was being insulted and verbally abused, he continually refrained from responding in kind. When he was physically suffering, he continually refrained from threatening in return. Instead, he continued to put his trust in God—who always judges fairly—that he was in charge of the situation and would take care of things according to his will. *[Isaiah 53:7]* 24 He suffered the punishment for

our sins when he hung on the cross, so that being spiritually united in his death, we would also die and be set free from the power of sin—and thus could live out his life and be acceptable to God. For by his being physically wounded, your physical healing was provided for. *[Isaiah 53:4-6; Matthew 8:17]* 25 For you were spiritually lost—like sheep having strayed from their shepherd. But now you have turned to God—who takes care of you and protects you like a shepherd does his sheep. *[Isaiah 53:6]*

3

Instructions to Wives
About Submitting to Authority

1 In a way similar to believing slaves submitting to their owners—motivated by obedience to the Lord—wives are to willingly submit to the authority of their husbands. Your manner of submission and service should be so loving that husbands who reject God's word might be converted to the faith without your having to say anything to persuade them. ❖ *In that culture, silence in a woman was considered a virtue. Submission does not imply inferiority in any way—as can be seen in the fact that God the Son willingly submits to the will of God the Father. [Matthew 26:39, 42; Mark 14:36; Luke 22:42; John 8:28-29; 10:37; 12:49-50; 14:31] It's a matter of God-ordained roles and respect for authority.* ➤ 2 They will be attracted to the faith when they observe your pure and reverent behavior toward both them and God. 3 Don't try to attract them to the faith by making yourselves outwardly beautiful. True beauty that attracts the heart is not enhanced by stylish hair, expensive jewelry, or attractive clothing. 4 Instead, let the inner beauty of the Messiah living in you shine through. Character that expresses humility, undemanding gentleness, and calmness is a kind

---

A 2:18 Slaves at this time were often well treated and were often managers, supervisors, doctors, teachers, musicians, skilled artisans, as well as unskilled laborers. There were extensive laws regulating how they were treated and they were generally paid. Many household slaves would be able to save enough to buy their freedom. This is not an attempt to justify their slavery. There were abusive owners and slaves were social inferiors. But knowing their situation helps to understand that it wasn't necessarily a harsh degrading life—and many of them were content with their positions. This was by far the most common form of "employment" at that time. See the footnote at Ephesians 6:9 to understand why leaders among believers did not advocate the abolition of slavery at that time. Also note that slave traders are explicitly condemned in 1 Timothy 1:10.

of beauty that doesn't fade with age—and the kind that God values. 5 That's the way those renowned women of the past made themselves beautiful. They were dedicated to God, trusted in him, and humbly submitted to their husbands' authority. 6 Sarah was always obedient to her husband Abraham and addressed him with utmost respect. ❖ *The Greek word κύριος (kurios), usually translated "lord" (in the literal text) is used with a wide range of meanings. Sarah, who spoke Hebrew, not Greek, used some term of respect whose exact equivalent doesn't exist in English, but perhaps "sir" comes close. Yet this does not at all suggest that a remote or cool formality existed between them. Nor does this mean that a wife today should address her husband as "sir." It does mean that however you interact with your husband, the result should be that he perceives you as respecting him and his authority. [Ephesians 5:33]* ➤ If you do what you know is right and are not afraid to submit to your husbands, you will be like her in having God's favor.

Instructions to Husbands
About Not Abusing Authority

7 In the same way that wives should respect their husbands, you husbands should be considerate of your wives— remembering they are weaker than men— and show them appropriate honor and respect for their equally privileged status and importance as believers—who have received the same undeserved gift of eternal life that you have. This is the way you must treat them if you want God to answer your prayers. ❖ *What did Peter mean by women being weaker than men? He doesn't specify, but no matter which ways they might actually be weaker, or that the culture might consider them weaker, (e.g. physically, in authority, social position, in being more sensitive, or other ways), he implies that husbands should not take advantage of them in those areas. Being considerate of them implies taking care of and protecting them, considering and providing for their needs (physical and emotional), and not placing unreasonable expectations or demands on them. Honoring them includes public and private recognition of their worth, dignity and efforts, showing them respect—and also some level of deference to their desires. There is no hint here or in any other Scripture that having authority over them implies being a domineering master over them. To be the greatest in the God's view or a leader among God's people, a man is instructed to serve others as though they were more important than himself.*

[Matthew 20:26-27; Matthew 23:11; Mark 9:35; Luke 22:25-26] This would certainly also apply to the marriage relationship—for both husbands and wives. ➤

Instructions to All Believers
on Responding to Slander from Unbelievers

8 Finally, all of you should get along well with each other, be sympathetic toward each other, *[Romans 12:15-16]* love each other as brothers and sisters, be humble, and show compassion. ❖ *Note that instructions about how all believers are to treat each other also apply to the marriage relationship.* ➤ 9 Don't retaliate with evil actions or words when people do these things to you. Instead, bless them by interceding for them in prayer because God called you to be his own so you would be a blessing to others— and this is his requirement if you desire to receive blessings from him. *[Luke 6:27-36; Romans 12:14]* 10 The Scriptures say,

"Those who desire true life, who desire to experience love and good times, must keep themselves from speaking evil of others and from telling lies. 11 They must refrain from doing evil—and devote themselves to doing good. They must also make every effort to live in peace with others. 12 For the Lord takes care of those who do what is right and grants their requests. But he actively opposes those who do what he defines as evil."
[Psalm 34:12-16]

13 If you are always eager to do good things for others, no one is likely to want to persecute you. 14 But even if it does happen and you suffer because you have done what is right, God will bless you. *[Matthew 5:10; Luke 6:22]* So as the Scriptures say, "**Don't be afraid of them or their threats—and don't worry about what will happen.**" *[Isaiah 8:12-13]* 15 Instead, revere the Messiah in your hearts—honoring him as your Lord and trusting that he is in complete control. And always be ready to give a clear explanation— to anyone who asks—why your expectation of future reward makes you so different. But be prepared to do so in humility—showing respect and consideration for the person who asks. ❖ *or: showing reverence to God* ➤

16 Live in such a way that your conscience is always clear before God. Then if people slander you for your good behavior and for following the Messiah, God will later cause them to be ashamed. ❖ *either through conviction or on Judgment Day* ➤ 17 For if it's God's will that you suffer for doing what is right, this is much more praiseworthy than suffering for having done wrong. 18 Remember that the Messiah also suffered when he died **A** to pay the penalty of our sins (just the once—which was sufficient for all time) as one who had always done what is right—dying for those who do wrong. ❖ *Therefore you should also be willing to suffer for his sake.* ➤ He did this so he could make us acceptable to bring to God—through his self-sacrificial death ❖ *with us spiritually united with him* ➤ in the physical realm and then being made alive ❖ *through the resurrection* ➤ in the spiritual realm—by the Holy Spirit. ❖ *What Peter intended in the last part of this verse is not clear, making interpretation difficult. This is just one possibility.* ➤ 19 In the Spirit, the Messiah also went and preached through Noah to those whose spirits who are now bound in prison. 20 The Messiah did this when they disobeyed God long ago in Noah's day. He patiently waited for them to repent while Noah built the ark. ❖ *Therefore, you should be willing to witness to the pagans around you like Noah did. Like you, he and his family were only a few against many hostile neighbors. But God will save you—even though you are few in number—just like he did Noah.* ➤ **B** Only eight people were saved in that ark as they went through the flood waters. ❖ *Literally: "they were saved through water." One normal meaning of the preposition διά (dia) (when followed by a genitive noun), here translated "through," is "by means of," and some commentators understand it this way. The difficulty is then to understand how it makes sense that water "saved them." One commentator says the water saved them from the influence of human evil around them. Others interpret the "through" as "locational," as it has been rendered here.* ➤ 21 Their salvation "through water" is a prefiguring "type" that points to baptism, which now saves you. ❖ *Some interpret "baptism now saves you" as a figure of speech called "synecdoche," where a part (i.e., baptism) represents the whole (in this case, the entire process by which people believe the Good News, repent, are spiritually reborn, baptized, sanctified, etc.). This is certainly*

A 3:18 Some texts say "suffered" and others say "died."

B 3:20 There are many speculations about what verses 19-20a mean. Some prominent views: 1) Many Reformers said it meant that the Messiah—via the Holy Spirit—preached through Noah while he was building the ark [2 Peter 2:5] to people who are now imprisoned in Hell. 2) Many "church fathers" (i.e., 2nd-century church leaders) said that after his death and before his resurrection, Jesus preached to those people who had died and whose spirits were in Hades—the realm of the dead. This view comes from tying these verses to 4:6. Two sub-views are: 2a) he offered them a second chance to be saved, or 2b) he proclaimed his triumph and that their condemnation was final. 3) Many commentators today believe that before or after his resurrection, Jesus announced his victory over sin, death, and all of Satan's work to rebellious angels that are bound in Hell. [2 Peter 2:4; Jude 6] The first part of verse 20 is the immediate context of verse 19 (read these in a literal translation), so interpretation 2 is unlikely, in so far as having him preach to everyone in Hell, and if not to everyone, why these in particular? It was a common understanding among some first-century Jews that Genesis 6:1-4 referred to angels who fell into sin during the time of Noah and were imprisoned. See the commentary on Jude 6. But we have no idea if these common (but far-from-uniform) beliefs, derived from non-Scriptural sources such as 1 Enoch, have any basis in reality. And would Gentiles living in Asia Minor (to whom this letter was written) be familiar with these non-Scriptural Jewish books? 4) A Roman Catholic view is that after he died, he went to people from Noah's time who were imprisoned in Purgatory and proclaimed release to those who had repented just before they died in the flood, leading them out of their imprisonment into Heaven. 5) There are also variations on all these views. In any case, while an interesting problem, verses 19-20a don't seem to have any vital implications for our faith or walk, or at least none that we can be dogmatic about. ¶ I highly recommend reading Wayne Grudem's extensive arguments for view 1) in the appendix to his commentary (listed in the bibliography). Interpretation 1) doesn't depend on questionable non-Scriptural sources, it makes more sense as an illustration in the context of Peter's train of thought than the others do, and it doesn't raise theological questions not answered elsewhere in the Scriptures. Grudem believes Peter included this brief passage as an illustration to: a) encourage believers to boldly witness in the midst of hostile unbelievers, giving Noah as an example of someone else who did so, b) reassure them that God will save them—even though they are few in number against such odds—as he did with Noah's family, c) remind them that the coming final judgment is certain—as it was for those who died in the flood—and that the Messiah will ultimately triumph over all who oppose them.

possible, for synecdoche is frequently used in the Scriptures in places where everyone agrees it is synecdoche. Others interpret it literally, meaning that baptism is, in itself, an instrumental means of saving people. ¶ How is this story a "type" pointing to baptism? Peter was most likely thinking of baptism by immersion, in which going under the water was a picture of burying the "old man" that died with the Messiah on the cross, [Romans 6:3-7] and coming out of the water was a picture of rising with the Messiah with a new life, i.e., him living in you. In the process, you leave behind the old life that was enslaved to sin. Noah and his family went "through" the water and came out of it into a new life, having left behind the evil lives of those enslaved to sin, who died in the flood. The flood was a water of judgment upon the sinfulness of humanity. The water of baptism also portrays God's judgment on sin, indicating that the required punishment is death (the going down into the water). While our culture doesn't usually look for figurative types in past events that depict spiritual truths or principles, this was common among ancient peoples. Because we lack practice, it doesn't come easily. We prefer to have our lessons presented in explicit propositional detail. Yet it's apparent that part of what God intends us to learn from the Scriptures depends upon this kind of searching. ➤ Baptism is not a mere external cleansing of the body, but by being baptized you are making an appeal to God for ❖ *or: a promise to God from* ➤ a clear conscience, effected through the resurrection of Jesus the Messiah. ²² Having entered Heaven, *[Hebrews 4:14]* he is now ❖ *with us spiritually united with him* ➤ in the position of highest honor, power, and authority at the right hand of God the Father—with every angel and spiritual authority and power subjected to him.

4

Be Ready to Suffer in Order to Obey

¹ Arm yourselves for spiritual battle by having the same mindset that the Messiah did. He was prepared to suffer physically in order to obey his Father—therefore, you must also be prepared to suffer in order to obey God's will. Those who have succeeding in enduring suffering in order to avoid sinning have succeeded in overcoming the temptation to sin. ² The result of this is that you will no longer be a slave to strong sinful desires, but will spend the rest of your lives following God's will. *[2 Peter 1:6]* ❖ *This does not mean you will never sin, but that you have passed a major*

milestone in your life as a believer so succumbing to sin will be far less frequent—because you are willing to suffer in order to obey and have proved it in experience. ➤ ³ You have already wasted enough of your lives before you believed—doing the things unbelievers do. You routinely practiced extreme immorality, choosing to follow every sinful urge you felt, habitual intoxication, participating in wild immoral parties and drinking parties, and disgusting immoral acts of idol worship that are outlawed even by unbelievers. ⁴ Now your former friends are surprised that you no longer join them in the same sinful excesses, so they have turned against you with insults and slander. ⁵ But on Judgment Day, they will stand before the Messiah who will judge everyone—those who are still alive and those who have already died. They will have to answer to him for everything they did. ⁶ The coming Judgment Day is the reason the Good News was preached to God's people. It was even preached to those believers who have since died. They had to go through the judgment of physical death—just like all people do—but because they first believed the Good News, they are still living in the spiritual realm as God does. ❖ *Their unbelieving neighbors were probably saying that their faith had no value since even those who believe in Jesus die—and some of them violently from persecution. Peter addresses the concerns of those worrying about believing friends and family who have died. They still believed that the Messiah would return during their lifetimes and they hadn't adequately absorbed the message about the state of those who die before he returns.* ➤

How to Live in These Last Days

[Romans 12:1—15:7; 1 Corinthians 13:1-7; Galatians 5:16—6:10; Ephesians 4:1—6:9; Colossians 3:12—4:6; 1 Thessalonians 4:1-12; 5:6-22; James 1:19—2:12; 3:13—4:17]

⁷ The end of this world is near. But don't allow this prospect to pull you away from your daily responsibilities. Therefore, be sober, clear headed, and self-controlled so you can pray effectively. ❖ *to resist temptation, and for guidance* ➤ ⁸ But most important is that you continue to demonstrate your love for each other—because if you really love each other, you are willing to forgive, overlook, and smooth over many sins. *[Proverbs 10:12]*

9 Be willing to generously share your home and food with those who need them—without feeling put out or complaining. ❖ *This command was probably mainly intended for putting up traveling teachers of the Scriptures and other people involved in ministry who were passing through. Today, this would parallel supporting missionaries through sacrificial giving.* ➤ 10 God has given a spiritual gift to every believer. Whatever yours are, you should all be using them to serve each other because God has made you each responsible to administer his favor through those various gifts to those in need of them. 11 Do all things while allowing God in you to do it with his strength and ability. *[Galatians 2:20]* Those who speak, are to speak with careful deliberation as though it is God speaking through them—taking care that they don't say anything contrary to God's Word. ❖ *This does not mean that the speaker is speaking authoritatively as God's mouthpiece—like a prophet in the Hebrew Scriptures or an Apostle did.* ➤ Those who serve others should allow God's strength and ability to do so through them. Live this way so that everything you do will cause people to honor and praise Jesus the Messiah living in you—which also brings honor to God. For all praise, honor, dominion, and power are his forever. Yes, it is so!

Be Encouraged If You Suffer as a Result of Following the Messiah

12 My dear friends, you shouldn't be surprised that this difficult ordeal is happening to you. You should expect such things because God allows them to test and purify your faith. This is nothing unusual in the lives of believers. ❖ *Our "victory" as believers is victory over temptation, and successfully remaining faithful during difficult times. It does not usually enable us to avoid them. Jesus, Paul, and Peter promised that we would suffer difficulties and persecution. [Mark 10:30; John 15:18-20; 16:33; Acts 14:22; 1 Thessalonians 3:3-4; 2 Timothy 3:12; 1 Peter 2:20-21]* ➤ 13 But in so far as your sufferings are because you follow the Messiah—and not for doing evil—you should be rejoicing because these are really his sufferings and you have the privilege of sharing in them. In reality, it's a great honor and proves that you belong to him. Your sharing in his sufferings guarantees that you will also share in his glory when he returns—which will be cause for great rejoicing indeed. *[Matthew 5:10-12; Luke 6:22-23; 21:12-19; 22:28-30; John 15:20; Acts 5:41; Romans 5:3-5; 12:17-18; 2 Corinthians 1:5; 12:9-10; Philippians 1:29; 3:10-11; Colossians 1:24; 1 Thessalonians 3:2-4; 2 Thessalonians 1:4-5; 2 Timothy 1:8; Hebrews 10:32-39; 13:12-13; James 1:2-4; 5:10-11]* 14 If you continue to suffer insults, ridicule, or slander because you follow the Messiah, you are indeed in God's good favor because this is a clear sign that his glorious Holy Spirit rests on you—as he did on Jesus. *[Matthew 3:16; Mark 1:10; Luke 3:22; John 1:32]* ❖ *God's glory is his character. In Scripture, this is often represented by brilliant light—which signifies his purity, holiness, and goodness. [Exodus 33:19, 22] The emphasis on the "Spirit of Glory" in the literal text of this verse means that the Holy Spirit is working to transform your character to be just like God's glorious character.* ➤ 15 But make sure that none of you are suffering as a consequence of committing murder, or for being a thief, or criminal, or even for interfering in matters that aren't your own business. There is no blessing associated with suffering as a result of such things. 16 But if your troubles are because you follow the Messiah, then there is nothing to be ashamed of! Instead, you should praise God that you have the privilege of being identified with him! 17 God has started judging the people of this world and he is starting with his Temple. ❖ *i.e., his people. [Ezekiel 9:6; Amos 3:2] The word "judging" in this verse—κρίμα (krima)—means an evaluation that can result in approval, discipline, or condemnation.* ➤ These troubles that you are experiencing, are a judgment of discipline that acts to purify you. But as it continues from you on toward those not a part of his Temple, ❖ *i.e., unbelievers* ➤ his judgment condemns. If the troubles you are experiencing are his judgment of discipline for the purpose of refining, imagine how much worse his judgment of condemnation will be for those who reject God's message of salvation. 18 As the Scriptures say, "If God makes the road to final salvation in Heaven so difficult—with purifying suffering for those he approves—he will certainly cause those sinners who reject his ways to suffer much more!" *[Proverbs 11:31]* 19 So if you know that your suffering is clearly God's will, entrust yourselves

completely to your trustworthy Creator *[Psalm 31:5]*—and demonstrate this trust by continuing to do those things you know are good and right, even while you suffer.

5

Instructions to Leaders of God's People

1 I have something to say to those who are leaders of God's people. I say this as a fellow leader and as an eyewitness to the Messiah's sufferings and death who testifies about them everywhere—and as one who will also share in his glory and honor when he returns. I urge you to 2 take care of the people God has entrusted to you like a shepherd does his sheep. Exercise your loving leadership voluntarily without begrudging the work—always following God's will—because he has called you to this responsibility. Do it because you want to serve them and not for prestige or from greedy motives. 3 Don't be domineering, manipulative, or demanding with those over whom God has given you responsibility. You are to guide them gently by being a good example for them to follow. *[Matthew 20:25-27; Mark 10:42-44; Luke 22:25-26; Matthew 23:8-12; Mark 9:35]* 4 If you are this kind of leader, then when the Messiah who is leader over us returns, you will receive from him an eternal prize—sharing in his glory and honor.

Instructions for Believers

5 The rest of you who are not leaders should humbly submit to the authority of those God has placed over you. And all of you should always be humble toward each other. For the Scriptures say, **"God actively opposes those who are proud, but shows his undeserved favor to those who are humble."** *[Proverbs 3:34; James 4:6]*

6 Therefore, the wise thing to do is to make yourself submit humbly to God's discipline and to his timing for your deliverance. Then at the time of his choosing, he will honor you. *[Matthew 23:12; Luke 14:11;*

18:14] 7 Take all your worries to God and leave them with him to deal with—because he cares about you and will do what is needed.

8 It's important that you be alert and self-controlled because your enemy—Satan—prowls around looking for those vulnerable to attack so he can try to destroy their faith. He is like a roaring lion who will frighten you if he takes you by surprise. *[Psalm 22:13]* ❖ *Lions were used as figures for enemies of God's people.* ➤ 9 But stand firm in your faith when he roars or attacks. Resist the temptation to be afraid—for he is powerless to ultimately harm you. *[Luke 10:17-19; Ephesians 6:10-18; James 4:7; 1 John 5:18]* He is on a short leash. Remember that you aren't the only ones going through these persecutions and sufferings. Your fellow believers all around the world are going through the same kinds of experiences because they follow the Messiah.

10 Your suffering shouldn't last long because God—who called you to be his own and to share his eternal glory in union with the Messiah—is the source of all mercy and kindness. *[Exodus 3:7; Judges 2:18b, 10:16b]* It won't be long before he will mend and renew you, reestablish you in any position you've lost, strengthen you in any way you need it, and establish you immovably on a firm foundation of trusting him. ❖ *What God means by "a little while" and "soon" is usually significantly longer than what modern Americans normally mean by those terms. Peter might be thinking in terms of months or years, but it does mean it will at some point come to an end.* ➤ 11 For all dominion and power **A** are his forever. Yes, it is so!

Final Words

12 I've dictated this brief letter to Silas **B**—who I highly regard and commend to you as a faithful brother in the Lord. ❖ *The commendation implies that Peter probably also sent Silas to hand-carry this letter to the intended recipients.* ➤ I've tried to encourage you and exhort you to follow all these instructions and to trust that you are in God's will—and

---

A 5:11 Some manuscripts also have "and glory," as in 4:11.
B 5:12 Silas is the Hebrew form of his name, and Silvanus is the Latin form. Luke used "Silas" when he wrote Acts and this is more familiar to many people, hence it is used here—even though literally the Greek text says "Silvanus."

to trust that his favor is with you no matter what happens to you. Hold on strongly to that belief!

13 You have a sister assembly of believers here in Rome **A** who—just like you— were chosen to go through these things. They send you warm greetings and encouragement—as does Mark, my son in the faith. 14 Greet each other warmly as loving family members. I pray that all of you who are in union with the Messiah will experience his peace and well-being.

A 5:13 Literally: "Babylon." Believers called Rome "Babylon" because it was the center of worldly power and opposition to God's message—just as Babylon was in the Hebrew Scriptures. Even though Peter's readers were experiencing opposition and persecution by the unbelieving neighbors, Peter may have been saying that he and their sister assembly were in the central headquarters of such things and so he understood what they were going through. Rome is referred to as Babylon in Revelation 16:19; 17:5; and 18:2;—and 17:9 confirms this identification because Rome is famous for having been built on seven hills.

Peter's Second Letter

This letter was the most disputed of those that were eventually included in the New Testament. The witness of the early believers as to it's being an authentic letter of Peter is weak, (i.e. references to it in the existing writings of leaders in the second to fourth centuries are few), yet much stronger than for any letters that were not accepted. Some scholars believe the Apostle Peter was not the author, but there is no conclusive evidence that he was not. Many conservative scholars accept that Peter wrote it. Even though the style of the Greek is significantly different than that used in 1 Peter, he could have used two different scribes and allowed one or both of them freedom in how they expressed his thoughts.

Assuming the Apostle Peter is the author, it was likely written not long before his death, around AD 61–67 and probably written from Rome. He didn't specify who he was writing to, but recipients in Asia Minor or Egypt are possible, as the letter was known in these areas. We do know that he believed his readers were well-grounded in the faith and had received at least one letter from the Apostle Paul. They were also familiar with the teachings of the prophets in the Hebrew Scriptures and the teachings of the apostles. He mentions that this is his second letter to them, but there is no solid reason to believe that the first letter to these readers was 1 Peter, even though that could be true.

There are obvious similarities between 2 Peter and Jude, and scholars debate if one was based on the other, or if both were based on another source. All of these scholarly debates, as to source, author, date, audience, etc. are mostly irrelevant to the faith of believers today. Believers in the first few centuries after the Messiah returned to Heaven accepted that the evidence for the genuineness of this letter and its inspiration were adequate to include it with the other New Testament books. There is sufficient evidence for accepting it was written by Peter in the AD 60s. What is more important is its message, which is still timely and pertinent to believers today.

This letter has a sense of urgency. Peter knew he would soon die and was concerned to warn his readers about false teachers who would try to make them doubt the things they had been taught and firmly believed. He encourages them to live godly lives, assures them that the things they were taught about Jesus are true and not myths, tells how his readers can identify false teachers, and reminds them of God's punishment that will come upon such people. He then exhorts them to be ready for the Lord's return and to not worry that it hasn't happened yet.

1

Opening Greetings

¹ I, Simon Peter, am a voluntary slave and an apostle of Messiah Jesus. I'm writing to all of you who have the same quality of faith that we apostles have, given to you by Messiah Jesus—who is our God and Savior—because he is fair, showing no partiality. ² I pray that he will look upon you with great favor far beyond anything you can deserve, so you will experience complete peace and well-being as you come to intimately know {God and} **A** Jesus, who is our Lord.

God's Power and Promises Enable Us to Be Like the Messiah

³ He has already given us eternal life and everything we need to live in a way that pleases him. *[Ephesians 1:3]* He called and attracted us to be his people by means of his excellent character—and the almighty power he has as God is available to us as we get to intimately know him and his will. *[Ephesians 1:19]* ⁴ By means of his power—and because of his excellent character—he has

---

A 1:2 Many manuscripts have only "in the knowledge of Jesus our Lord," instead of "in the knowledge of God and Jesus our Lord," which is found in most translations. This fits better with the singular pronoun in verse three and probably reflects the original, as it is more likely that someone expanded the phrase than shortened it. Elsewhere in the letter, only knowledge of Jesus is mentioned, i.e., in 1:8 and 3:18.

made fantastically valuable promises to us that are recorded in the Scriptures. By trusting in them—and because of your union with him—your character will be transformed to be like his own. In this way, you will escape from the moral corruption of your character caused by sinful desires—which is characteristic of unbelievers in this world. 5 Since he has done so much for you, make every effort to trust in his promises and benefit from them. If you do this, excellence will be evident in all areas of your life—which leads to knowing him and his will better. ❖ *Commentators are divided as to whether or not these virtues are simply added to one's life in no particular order, or if it's implied that one leads to the other. I chose to express the latter possibility because it seems to me they are somewhat dependent.* ➤ 6 Knowing him better will make you desire to exercise self-control over all your sinful desires. And success in self-control leads to the ability to persevere in faith and obedience in the face of difficulties—since both require the determination to endure discomfort and suffering in order to obey. *[1 Peter 4:1-2]* Once you are accomplished in enduring discomfort or suffering for the sake of obedience, you will then be able to live in a way that always follows God's will and pleases him. 7 As you live in accordance with his will, you will love all believers as you would your own brothers and sisters—and then you will learn to extend this same self-sacrificial love to all people. ❖ *Despite the chaining effect, in which the perfection of one virtue may depend on previous ones, it is expected that believers strive to exercise all these virtues from the beginning.* ➤ 8 Your union with and intimate knowledge of our Lord Jesus the Messiah will not be wasted or in vain if these virtues are evident in your lives and are continually increasing. *[Romans 5:3-5; James 1:2-3]* 9 Those who don't have these virtues in their lives have shut their eyes to the light of God's truth—so they are spiritually blind. They have deliberately put out of mind the fact that they were saved from their old way of living and made pure from all sin in God's sight. ❖ *In other words, they claim to believe, but they don't obey. They may not be true believers at all—or they may be on the path to denying the faith. Verses 8-9 are reminiscent of the parable of the soils where some professing believers*

allow weeds to choke them so they bear no fruit. *[Matthew 13:22; Mark 4:18-19; Luke 8:14]* ➤

10 Therefore, my brothers and sisters in the Lord, since some people do fall into such blindness, you should do your best to see that these virtues are present in your lives—so the proof of God's calling and choosing you to be one of his own is clear to others and to yourself. If you are diligent to do this, you will never fall away from your relationship to the Messiah. ❖ *Or: fall into serious sin. How can we reconcile the command to "do our best" to exhibit these virtues with Paul's statement in Galatians 2:20? By doing our best to remember to choose to allow the Messiah to live his life through us. We cannot live this way in our own power.* ➤ 11 Another result is that when you enter the eternal Heavenly Kingdom of our Lord and Savior Jesus the Messiah, you will not just merely be allowed to enter, but will be richly welcomed. ❖ *Entrance to Heaven is not earned, it is God's free gift to those who believe in Jesus as their Savior. But the Scriptures also clearly teach that God will reward us for our obedience and good works in this life. Those whose lives are more Messiah-like will be more richly welcomed and rewarded in Heaven than those whose lives did not exhibit his character.* ➤ 12 So even though you already know all these things and firmly believe in the truths of the Good News that were taught to you, I intend to continue to remind you about them because the consequences are so important. 13 For I consider it my duty *[Luke 22:32]*—as long as this temporary body of mine lives—to remind you to focus on them 14 because our Lord Jesus the Messiah has clearly told me I will soon die. 15 So I will also make every effort to ensure that you are able to remember these things after I die. ❖ *Some commentators believe he intended to produce a permanent written reminder of his teachings and that the Gospel of Mark was the result—since tradition says that Peter was Mark's source of information.* ➤

Peter Defends the Authenticity of His Message

16 For when we apostles told you about the power that our Lord Jesus the Messiah exhibited in his ministry and how he will return again in power, we were not simply repeating cleverly crafted fiction—as some have accused us of doing. James, John, and I actually saw him with the visible glory of his divine majesty which he will have when

he returns. *[Matthew 17:2; Mark 9:2-3; Luke 9:29]* ❖ *The synoptic gospels—Matthew, Mark, and Luke—all see the event of the transfiguration as pointing to the Messiah's glory at his second coming. [Matthew 16:28; Mark 9:1; Luke 9:27]* ➤ **17** His body shone as bright as the sun—indicating the glory and honor he received from God the Father. Then the Father in his majestic glory said, "This is my Son whom I love dearly. He pleases me greatly." ❖ *It was the view of both Jews and Gentiles of that time that the Son of God (or son of a god) would also be deity. So this statement by God the Father that Jesus was his Son is an explicit declaration that Jesus was deity. Since Yahweh had clearly taught his people that there is only ONE God, the logical conclusion is that the Father and the Son are together one God—yet in some manner distinct. It is such passages that led to the doctrine of the Trinity. Jesus claimed that he is one (i.e., a unity) with his Father—having the same honor and glory as his Father—and yet is voluntarily subordinate to him in role. [John 5:17-23; 10:30]* ➤ **18** Three of us heard God say this from Heaven with our own ears when we were with Jesus on that holy mountain. ❖ *The phrase "holy mountain" would make his readers think of Mt. Zion (even though the transfiguration took place on a different mountain). Some commentators see the significance of the transfiguration explained in the light of the prophecy in Psalm 2, where Mt. Zion is referred to as "my holy hill." [Psalm 2:6]* ➤ **19** We also have the witness of the prophecies about the Messiah in the Hebrew ❖ *i.e., Old Testament* ➤ Scriptures concerning these matters—which we all know are reliable and true. The things we apostles have told you that we saw in the life of the Messiah can also be discerned to be true because they confirm and fulfill those prophecies. You would be wise to meditate on those prophecies and allow them to illuminate your understanding of what is true—like a light shining in a dark place reveals what is really there. Continue to do this until the day dawns when the Messiah returns and the full light of his truth is revealed to you. ❖ *The phrase "and the morning star rises in your hearts"—in the literal text—has several possible interpretations. ¶ See the partial list of 82 messianic prophecies after the end of 2 Peter in this book.* ➤ **20** It is of utmost importance that you understand this: No prophecy about the Messiah recorded in the Hebrew Scriptures is merely the prophet's own interpretation concerning what God said to him.

❖ *While Peter's focus in this verse was on messianic prophecies in the Hebrew Scriptures, his statement is true about the source of all Scripture. Some commentators interpret this verse differently and say it teaches that individuals cannot properly interpret prophecy without the help of the Holy Spirit. They think Peter said this to oppose false teachers who twisted the Scriptures and came up with their own interpretations.* ➤ **21** For no such prophecy ever originated in the thoughts of a human being. It was the Holy Spirit that caused ❖ *literally: carried along* ➤ the prophets to speak what God wanted them to say. ❖ *Peter was defending both the testimony of the apostles and the Scriptural prophecies about the Messiah because false teachers were saying that the stories the apostles told about the Messiah were fiction. When confronted with the witness of the prophecies in Scripture, they said they were inventions of the prophets. ¶ The Greek word meaning "carried along" was used of the wind driving a ship along in such a way that those on the ship were not in control.* ➤

2

Peter Warns Believers About False Teachers

1 But there were also false prophets among the Israelites in the past—just as there will also always be false teachers among you. These people—who might appear to be true believers—cleverly mix false and destructive elements in their teaching which will lead many people to deny the true faith. They will even renounce the teachings of our Master Jesus—who owns us by right of his purchasing our lives on the cross. ❖ *Some commentators think this means, "they will even teach that the Master did not die to save them." It's unlikely that their denial would be a blatant renouncing of Jesus as Savior since few believers would continue to follow such people. Their denial will usually be more subtle by renouncing key teachings—which is, in effect, the same as renouncing Jesus himself because they are his requirements. Yet many people will be deceived and—not realizing this—will follow a false belief that is totally incompatible with following Jesus—but they will do so thinking they are following him. The Scriptures teach that sincerity of faith is not the same as true faith. We are to be sure that what we believe is what God has really said is true. [e.g. Luke 11:34-36] The Pharisees were very sincere in following what they believed was God's will. Yet Jesus rejected many of them. God's truth is not relative or subject to individual interpretation.* ➤ But in doing so, they will provoke God to suddenly destroy them. ²Many believers will follow their lead in claiming that some of what the Scriptures calls immorality is, in fact, not sin at all and is acceptable to God. Unbelievers will see them living this way and will conclude that this is what our Lord taught—and so the reputation of the truth of the Good News will be ruined. ❖ *This works two ways. Some unbelievers with higher standards will reject Jesus and his followers. Others will choose to follow this false way—thinking they are following Jesus. Their ability to discern what Jesus really taught will have been ruined. Both situations work against God's desire for people to follow his truth.* ➤ ³These false teachers will often be ruled by greed and will attempt to exploit you with their cleverly invented arguments. ❖ *So beware of people who give non-Scriptural reasons for you to give them money. And even when people ask for money for legitimate sounding reasons, check to see if they are telling the truth and how they spend the money that people give them before deciding to support them.* ➤ God decided to condemn and destroy such people long ago. Just because it hasn't happened yet, doesn't mean he's sleeping or unaware of what they're doing. He will certainly destroy them. ⁴We know this is true from the following examples. God did not spare even his own angels from punishment when they rebelled in sin. Instead, he banished them to Hell where they are bound in darkness and waiting for Judgment Day. ❖ *A common understanding is that some of the worst and most powerful angels that rebelled are bound in Hell, while others are allowed some limited measure of freedom (as demons) until Jesus returns. But their ultimate fate will be the same.* ➤ ⁵He also didn't restrain his condemnation and destruction on the people who lived in rebellion of his ways during Noah's time. [Genesis chapters 6—7] Instead, he only preserved Noah—who urged others to follow God's ways and warned of his coming judgment—and seven others in his family. [1 Peter 3:19-20] All others God destroyed in the flood. ⁶He also condemned the people who lived in and around the cities of Sodom and Gomorrah. He destroyed them with fire and reduced them to ashes. [Genesis 18:20-21; 19:1-29] His intention was to make an example of them, to show others in later times what he will do to those who live in rebellion against his commands. ⁷But he made a special effort to

rescue Lot because he followed God's ways and was distressed by the sexually immoral and evil ways of those who lived around him. ⁸Lot is an example for us believers. He was a good man living among evil people. Every day, his sense of what was right was violated by the evil things he heard and saw other people doing. It made him feel distressed. ⁹His story shows that our Lord will rescue his faithful people from their difficult circumstances—just as he also causes those who rebel to experience punishment in this life while they await their final ruin on Judgment Day. ❖ *See 2 Thessalonians 1:9 and the following note about what it means to experience eternal ruin in Hell.* ➤ ¹⁰He will be especially harsh with those who indulge the corrupt passions of their bodies and with those who despise and reject God's authority over them as taught in the Scriptures. These false teachers are reckless and arrogant. They despise and insult glorious ones. ❖ *No one knows for sure what Peter meant by "glorious ones." Some commentators think it may refer to leaders among believers to whom the false teachers refused to submit. Many other hypotheses have been offered, but these words were usually used of angels. It's possible they insulted angels directly. [Jude 8] Another speculation is that they were using a common myth about angels who mated with women (a debated interpretation of Genesis 6:1-4) to justify their own immorality, which, if the myth were not true, would be insulting to angels.* ➤ ¹¹Even angels—who are much greater in strength and power than these false teachers—don't dare to accuse and insult them in the Lord's presence. ❖ *Since commentators are not sure who the glorious ones are in verse 10, they are also not sure who the angels are greater than. Some say the glorious ones are not angels, and the angels are greater than the glorious ones. Others say they are greater than the false teachers, which is a safe and certain fact. Then the question is, who does "them" refer to at the end of verse 11? If the angels are indeed being compared to the false teachers, "them" may refer to the false teachers. Others—who think the glorious ones are not angels—think "them" is the glorious ones. Several permutations are possible, but the two mentioned here are the favored choices. Despite the uncertainties of reference, the point is clear enough. No one should be so arrogant as to insult others in the Lord's presence—and we are always in his presence—even if they are clearly guilty, for even the mighty angels don't dare do this. So these false teachers who do so—and might even be identified as false teachers by their doing so—are showing their true nature. I've heard preachers in the pulpit make fun of the writers of Scripture, saying they didn't know what they were talking about. This principle reveals where they are coming from.* ➤ 12 These false teachers—like animals which are incapable of reason—act by instinct and assault what they don't understand. Just as such animals are born to a fate of being caught and killed, these people—by acting this way—are determining that their own fate will also be destruction. 13 Their eternal destruction will be the just consequence for the harm they have done to the faith of others. Being self-deceived, they shamelessly enjoy indulging every evil desire they have—even publicly in broad daylight. They even shamelessly do these things while feasting with you and so tarnish your good reputation—disgracing you even among unbelievers. 14 They are always on the lookout for illicit sex and are never satiated. They seduce those who aren't well-grounded in the faith and have trained themselves to desire what God has forbidden. They are under his curse. *[Deuteronomy 28:15-68]* 15 They have deliberately rejected God's ways as commanded in the Scriptures and are eternally lost. They have followed in Balaam's footsteps. Balaam, son of Beor, loved what he could obtain through doing evil. ❖ *He led the Israelites into immorality. [Numbers 25:1-3; 16-18; 31:16]* ➤ 16 But God rebuked him for his sin. He caused a donkey to speak with a man's voice to restrain this prophet's insane intention. *[Numbers 22:21-34]* ❖ *The point may be that a dumb animal like a donkey was more adept at discerning God's judgment (the angel in the way) than the prophet who was set on opposing God's will. When a person gives himself over to unrestrained sin, he is blinded to truth and reality.* ➤

17 These false teachers are as useless as springs without water or rain clouds blown away by the wind without delivering water to parched fields. They claim to offer much, but deliver nothing of value. God has prepared them a place in Hell devoid of light for their punishment. ❖ *Where do people get the idea that God or Jesus would never punish anyone in Hell? Not from the Scriptures! Such a God and such a Jesus are not found within the pages of the Bible no matter how hard you look. It's one of the false teachings put forth by these false*

teachers that people latch onto because they don't want to believe the truth. God takes this as a personal rejection. ➤ 18 They speak bold and arrogant words—which when examined closely are pure nonsense. Yet they manage to win people over to their view by appealing to their sinful desires—especially desires for illicit pleasures. ❖ *e.g., drugs and forbidden sexual relationships* ➤ Those who have recently just become believers and have escaped such lifestyles are particularly susceptible to their lies. 19 They promise people "freedom" to do whatever they want—but are themselves bound as slaves to their corrupt desires which will lead them to destruction. *[John 8:34]* For people are slaves to anything that controls them.

20 These false teachers were once unbelievers. Then they believed and knew our Lord and Savior Jesus the Messiah and thus escaped the corrupting ways of unbelievers. But afterward, they then allowed themselves to become entangled in those ways and became enslaved to them again—so they are now worse off than before they believed. *[Hebrews 3:12-18; 6:4-6; 10:26-31; 38-39; Jude 4-5]* 21 Their punishment in Hell would have been less severe if they had never personally known about God's way to be accepted as righteous in his sight—which they received from the apostles. But they accepted it, experienced it, and then turned away from it. 22 The popular proverbs seem to have been written for the foolishness of these false teachers. **"A dog, after having rid himself of his corruption, can't resist returning to his vomit to eat it again,"** *[Proverbs 26:11]* and "A sow that's been washed returns to wallowing in filth."

3

Be Ready for the Lord's Return

1 My dear friends, this is my second letter to you in which I'm reminding you of spiritual truths that you already know—so they will stimulate you to clear uncorrupted thinking about them. 2 I want you to think about the words spoken long ago by the holy prophets and recorded in the Scriptures and also the commands spoken

by the apostles of our Lord and Savior who he put in authority over you. ❖ *Peter is speaking about the apostles' command to live holy lives, and the prophetic warnings about what will happen to those who rebel against God's ways.* ➤

3 It's important to understand that during this period of history since the Messiah ascended to Heaven until he returns again—called the "last days"—some will ridicule both the idea that the Messiah will return and also those who believe that it's true. Having no fear of judgment, they will be controlled by every evil desire that comes to their mind. 4 They will say things like, "He hasn't kept his promise to return yet, has he? In fact, everything keeps going on the same as it always has since the world began. The great 'fathers' of the faith have already died waiting for him to return—and what good did it do them?" 5 But they are ignoring the power of God's words and promises. It was God's word that long ago created this world and the sun and all we see in the night sky— when he made the earth separate from the seas which he caused to surround it. 6 And in Noah's time, he also caused the surface of the Earth to be flooded and destroyed. 7 With this same word of power, he causes everything to continue to exist *[John 1:3; Acts 17:28; Romans 11:36; 1 Corinthians 8:6; Colossians 1:16-17; Hebrews 1:3]* and also declares that on Judgment Day, he will cause fire to destroy all those who have rejected his ways—and also to destroy the heavens and Earth. ❖ *Some commentators speculate that the destruction will be confined to the surface of the Earth and the present atmosphere which will then later be made "new" in the new heavens and New Earth. [2 Peter 3:13; Revelation 21:1]* ➤

8 So don't forget the power of God's word and promises—and also the fact that from the Lord's perspective in Heaven, there is no difference between one day and 1,000 years. *[Psalm 90:4]* ❖ *All time is the same to him. Therefore, one cannot conclude that any length of time having passed means he will not fulfill his promise. Many promises that he made in the Hebrew Scriptures waited thousands of years before they were fulfilled.* ➤ **A** 9 The Lord Jesus is not slow about fulfilling his promise to return—in the way some people think. He is purposely delaying and being patient so more people have the opportunity to be saved. He doesn't desire that anyone be condemned to Hell, but would prefer that everyone would repent and be saved. ❖ *Many say that everyone will be saved—and that all roads lead to Heaven. The Scriptures clearly deny this, and this verse does not mean that the Lord's desire (that all would be saved) will come to pass. It is merely stating his preference. But he himself said that few people find the way to Heaven and that most people choose to follow the many paths to Hell. [Matthew 7:13-14] Notice that repentance goes with salvation. There is no salvation without repentance.* ➤

10 The Day of the Lord—when he returns—will come as unexpectedly as a thief. *[Matthew 24:43; Luke 12:39; 1 Thessalonians 5:2; Revelation 3:3; 16:15]* He will cause the heavens to disappear with a loud roar. It and everything on Earth will be destroyed by fire. **B** ❖ *The reference in the literal text to the elements being destroyed likely means "earth, air, and water"—which according to Greek thought in that day were the basic elemental substances—fire being the fourth element. (Elements defined as different types of atoms have only been known for a few hundred years.) Fire is often seen as a purifying agent in the Scriptures. If a surface "destruction" is what is meant, the fire may be seen as purifying the world so it can start over in a new and pure state.* ➤

11-12 Since the world and those who reject God's ways will be destroyed like this, what kind of people do you think it would be wise to be? While you look forward to the coming

---

A 3:8 Some people believe the saying in this verse means that every 1000 years is like a day to God. He created the world and rested on the seventh day, so they think he may plan to have the world continue for six 1000-year days after creation and then have a 1000-year day of rest, which would be the millennium, (the 1000 years when the Messiah will reign on earth). [Revelation chapter 20] According to Biblical chronology, the world was created approximately 6000 years ago. Exact dating is not possible and by some reckonings, the 6000 years is already past. But if the "last days" mean the last two 1000-year days

which began at Pentecost, [Acts 2:16-17] (in approximately AD 30 plus or minus a year or two), then the end of these last two 1000-year days would be around the year 2030. Since the Lord will return after all the world has heard the Good News, [Matthew 24:14] and when there are believers from every people group, [Revelation 5:9; 7:9] it is possible this could be accomplished in that time frame.

B 3:10 Some Greek manuscripts say εὑρεθήσεται (heurethēsetai) "will be found," which is often translated, "will be laid bare." Some Greek manuscripts say κατακαησεται (katakaēsetai) "will be burned up."

of God's Day, your way of life should be holy and obedient to his will—for this will speed his return. ❖ *The more faithful people are to do his will, the quicker they will accomplish the task of evangelizing the world and the sooner he will return.* ➤ On that day, the sky will burn and the elements will melt in the intense heat. 13 But that won't matter to us because we are looking forward to God's promise that he will make a new Earth and new heavens *[Isaiah 65:17; 66:22]*—where everything and everyone living in it will voluntarily obey God's will.

14 Therefore, my dear friends, since you are looking forward to all these things happening, make every effort to live in a way that pleases him so you will be pure and without fault in his sight. 15 Keep in mind that the Lord's delay in returning is an opportunity for more people to be saved. You know that our dear brother in the Lord—the Apostle Paul—out of the wisdom God has given him has written the exact same thing to you. 16 He talks about these things in all his letters. Now, I know there are some things in his letters that are not easy to understand in places, ❖ *especially when taken out of context* ➤ and some who are ignorant of God's truth and not firmly grounded in the true faith twist what he says—just like they do the other Scriptures. But God will sentence them to eternal ruin in Hell for doing so. ❖ *This verse is the clearest testimony in the New Testament that Paul's writings were considered on par with the Hebrew Scriptures.* ¶ *See 2 Thessalonians 1:9 and the following note about what it means to experience eternal ruin in Hell.* ➤

17 My dear friends, you already know these things, so please take care that you aren't deceived and led astray by the false teachings of those who don't follow God's way. It would not be good if you become uncertain about things that you now firmly believe are true. 18 To prevent this from happening, make every effort to continue to know our Lord and Savior Jesus the Messiah more intimately. And learn to increasingly depend on the power of the undeserved favor he offers—which enables you to obey and please him. May all people praise and honor him in this day—as well as for all eternity! Yes, may it be so! ❖ *Literally: Amen. Some commentators say it's doubtful that the final "Amen" was part of the original manuscript.* ➤

Messianic Prophecies Fulfilled by Jesus

Here is a far-from-exhaustive list of 82 messianic prophecies that were fulfilled in connection with Jesus' first coming (referred to in 2 Peter 1:19). Many others exist, but would require discussion to point out how the Scriptures were fulfilled. There are also many "types" in the Torah pointing to what the Messiah would accomplish and represent, that Jesus fulfilled. (Most of those listed below were taken from the book "The New Evidence that Demands a Verdict" by Josh McDowell, where he also gives further information on many of them.)

Prophecy	Fulfillment
He will crush Satan's head - Gen 3:15	Rom 16:20
He is a descendant of Isaac - Gen 17:19, 21:12	Lk 3:23-34
He is a descendant of Abraham - Gen 22:18	Mt 1:1, Gal 3:16
He is in the line of Judah - Gen 49:10	Lk 3:23-33, Heb 7:14
He is a descendant of Jacob - Num 24:17	Lk 3:23-34
He will be a prophet - Deut 18:18	Mt 21:11, Lk 7:16, Jn 4:19, 6:14, 7:40
He will be a king - Ps 2:6, Jer 23,5, Zech 9:9	Mt 21:5, 27:37, Jn 18,33-38
He is God's Son - Ps 2:7, 1 Chron 17:11-14, 2 Sam 7:12-16	Mt 3:17, 16:16, Mk 9:7, Lk 9:35, 22:70, Jn 1:34,49, Ac 13:30-33
He will be praised by children - Ps 8:2	Mt 21:15-16
He will not rot in the grave - Ps 16:10, 49:15	Mt 28:6, Mk 16:6, Lk 24:46, Ac 2:31, 13:33
God will forsake him - Ps 22:1	Mt 27:46
He will be mocked - Ps 22:2-8	Mt 27:29, 41-43
His heart will be broken - Ps 22:14	Jn 19:34
His hands and feet will be pierced - Ps 22:16, Zech 12:10	Mt 27:35, Lk 23:33, Jn 20:25
They will stare at him - Ps 22:17	Mt 27:36, Lk 23:35
They will divide his garments and cast lots for them - Ps 22:18	Jn 19:23-24
He will commit his spirit - Ps 31:5	Lk 23:46
His bones will not be broken - Ps 34:20, Ex 12:46	Jn 19:33, 36
He will be accused by false witnesses - Ps 35:11	Mt 26:59-60
He will be hated without cause - Ps 35:19, 69:4, Is 49:7	Jn 15:25
His friends will stand far off - Ps 38:11	Mt 27:55-56, Mk 15:40, Lk 23:49
He will be betrayed by a friend - Ps 41:9, 55:12-14	Mt 10:4, 26:49-50, Mk 14:10, Jn 13:21
He will ascend on high - Ps 68:18	Ac 1:9
He will have zeal for God's house - Ps 69:9	Jn 2:15-16
He will be insulted - Ps 69:9	Rom 15:3
He will be shamed and dishonored - Ps 69:19	Mt 27:28
He will suffer thirst - Ps 69:21, 22:15	Jn 19:28
They will offer him gall and vinegar to drink - Ps 69:21	Mt 27:34, Jn 19:28-29
People will offer him gifts - Ps 72:10, Is 60:6	Mt 2:1, 11
He will teach in parables - Ps 78:2, Is 6:9-10	Mt 13:13-15, 34
He will pray for his enemies - Ps 109:4	Lk 23:34
His betrayer will be replaced - Ps 109:8	Acts 1:20
People will shake their heads at him - Ps 109:25, also 22:7	Mt 27:39
He will be called Lord - Ps 110:1	Mt 22:43-45, Lk 2:11
He will sit at the right hand of God - Ps 110:1	Heb 1:3
He will be a priest - Ps 110:4	Heb 3:1, 5:5-6
He will come in the name of the Lord - Ps 118:6	Mt 21:9
He will be rejected - Ps 118:22, Is 8:14, 28:1	Mt 21:42, Rom 9:32-33, 1 Pet 2:7
His people will be blinded to the truth - Is 6:10, 53:1	Jn 12:37-41
He will be born of a virgin - Is 7:14	Mt 1:18, 24-25, Lk 1:26-35
He will be called Immanuel - Is 7:14	Mt 1:23, Lk 7:16
His ministry will begin in Galilee - Is 9:1	Mt 4:12-13, 17
He is heir to the throne of David - Is 9:7	Lk 1:32-33

Prophecy

He is in the line of Jesse - Is 11:1
He will be anointed with the Holy Spirit - Is 11:2, Ps 45:7, 61:1-2

He will be a judge - Is 33:22
He will do miracles - Is 35:5-6a, also 32:3-4

He will be preceded by a messenger - Is 40:3, Mal 3:1
His manner of ministry was predicted - Is 42:1-4
He will be beaten and spit upon - Is 50:6, Micah 5:1
He will be exalted - Is 52:13
He will be disfigured by suffering - Is 52:14, 53:2
He will be hated and rejected by his own people - Is 53:1, 3
He will not be believed - Is 53:1
He will bear people's sicknesses - Is 53:4
He will make blood atonement - Is 53:5
He will be wounded and bruised - Is 53:5, Zech 13:6
He will be our substitute - Is 53:6, 8
He will be brought as a lamb to the slaughter - Is 53:7
He will not respond to his accusers - Is 53:7
He will be buried in a rich man's tomb - Is 53:9
He will save those who believe in him - Is 53:10-11
He will intercede for his persecutors - Is 53:12
He will be numbered with transgressors - Is 53:12
He will be a light to the Gentiles - Is 60:3, also 49:6
He will heal the brokenhearted - Is 61:1-2
He is in the line of David - Jer 23:5

The killing of the children - Jer 31:15
He will come out of Egypt - Hosea 11:1
Darkness will cover the land - Amos 8:9
He will be hit with a rod - Micah 5:1
He existed before creation - Micah 5:2

He will be born in Bethlehem - Micah 5:2
He will enter Jerusalem on a donkey - Zech 9:9
He will be sold for 30 pieces of silver - Zech 11:12
The money would be thrown in God's house - Zech 11:13
The money paid for a potter's field - Zech 11:13
His side will be pierced - Zech 12:10
He will be deserted by his disciples - Zech 13:7
He will be preceded by a messenger - Mal 3:1
He will enter the temple - Mal 3:1
He will be preceded by Elijah - Mal 4:5-6

Fulfillment

Lk 3:23-32
Mt 3:16-17, 12:17-21, Mk 1:10-11, Lk 4:15-21, 43, Jn 1:32
Jn 5:30, 2 Tim 4:1
Mt 9:32-35, 11:4-6, Mk 7:33-35, Jn 5:5-9, 9:6-11, 11:43-47
Mt 3:1-3, 11:10, Lk 1:17, Jn 1:23
Mt 12:14-21
Mt 26:67, 27:26, 30, Lk 22:63
Phil 2:9-10
Mk 15:15-19, Jn 19:5, 14
Mt 21:42-43, Jn 1:11, 7:5, 48, 12:37-38
Jn 12:37
Mt 8:17
1 Pet 1:2
Mt 27:26
Rom 5:6, 8, 2 Cor 5:21
Jn 1:29
Mt 27:12-19
Mt 27:57-60
Jn 3:16, Acts 16:31
Lk 23:33
Mt 27:38, Mk 15:27-28
Ac 13:47-48
Lk 4:18-19
Mt 1:1, 9:27, 15:22, 20:30-31, 21:9,15, 22:41-46, Mk 9:10,10:47-48, Lk 3:23-31, 10:30-35, Ac 13:22-23, Rev 22:16

Mt 2:16
Mt 2:15
Mt 27:45
Mt 27:30
Jn 1:1-3, 17:5, 25, Col. 1:17, Rev. 1:1-2, 1:17, 2:8, 8:58, 22:13
Mt 2:1, 4, Lk 2:4-7, Jn 7:42
Mt 21:6-11, Lk 19:35-37
Mt 26:15, 27:3
Mt 27:5
Mt 27:7
Jn 19:34
Mt 26:31, Mk 14:27, 50
Lk 7:24, 27
Mt 21:12, Jn 1:14, 2:19-21
Mt 11:13-14

John's First Letter

The author of this letter was the Apostle John (Yochanan in Hebrew), the brother of James, the son of Zebedee, [Matthew 4:21] a fisherman, one of Jesus' inner circle, "the disciple whom Jesus loved," [John 13:23] Jesus' best friend and probably his cousin. John's mother Salome was probably Jesus' mother's sister. After Jesus' ascension, he was one of the main leaders of the believers in Jerusalem [Galatians 2:9]—along with Peter and James (the brother of Jesus). He took care of Jesus' mother, Miriam, after Jesus' death. [John 19:25-27] Tradition says that before the destruction of Jerusalem in AD 70, he moved to Ephesus—probably in AD 67. Later, he was exiled by the Romans for a time on the island of Patmos [Revelation 1:9] and died in AD 100. He is also the author of the Gospel of John, Revelation, and John's Second and Third Letters. John probably wrote this letter from Ephesus after writing his Gospel. The exact date is not known, but was probably between AD 85–95 as there is no persecution mentioned in his letter and one started in AD 95 or 96. He wrote this letter to the local assemblies of believers under his care and authority in the Roman Province of Asia (present day Turkey). His purpose was mainly to teach against Gnosticism—which was a theology that taught matter is inherently evil and therefore, God did not become a human being. Gnostics claimed that Jesus was merely a man and that the Messiah—a spirit—came to indwell him at his baptism and left him before he died on the cross. Gnostics believed they had "hidden knowledge" that others lacked—making them a kind of spiritual elite who were above restrictions concerning what was right and wrong. This belief led them into immoral behavior. While the Gnostic heresy is no longer common, the issues John brings up in his letter clarify the eternal divine nature of Jesus and the relationship between salvation and obedience. The content of his letter is very applicable today when many professing followers of Jesus teach universal salvation and the lack of eternal consequences for behavior that the Scriptures condemn. An outline of the topics covered in this letter can be seen in the section headings.

1

Introduction: John's Reason for Writing

1 I'm writing to you about the Messiah— who is God's Message to humanity and who is called the "Word of God." He is the Source of all life—both temporary and eternal—and existed even before the universe or anything in it was created. Yet we apostles have seen him with our own eyes, listened to him with our own ears, extensively observed him—and even touched and embraced him. 2 For the invisible "Life Giver" became a man. A And since we were privileged to be eyewitnesses of his life and ministry, we are compelled to testify about what we've seen. We want to proclaim the truth about this person who in his very essence is "Life Eternal," who has always coexisted with God the Father throughout eternity, and who has clearly revealed himself in human form so that all might come to know him and receive eternal life. 3 Thus, I'm sharing these things that we've seen and heard with you so that you too can join us in the joyful intimate relationship we have with God our Father—and with his son Jesus the Messiah. 4 I hope that as a result of this letter you will share in our joy, making it even greater.

The Theme of John's Letter

God Is Light and Cannot Coexist with Darkness

5 Now this is the message that Jesus told us to proclaim: God is illuminating and self-revealing light—holy and pure with no hint of evil, sin, or darkness existing in him. Nor can evil exist in his presence. 6 So if we claim to have a real relationship with him, but at the same

---

A 1:2 The event of the Word of God becoming a man is commonly referred to as the "Incarnation."

time are living in the spiritual darkness of deliberate rebellion against his commands, or in denial of our sin, then we are liars or are deceived—and have rejected the truth that he has revealed to us. [7] But if we're living in the light of God's truth, submitting ourselves to the sin-exposing light of his Word, shunning sin and seeking to be holy and pure—just as he is—then we will experience joyful fellowship with him and with other believers; and the blood of his son Jesus makes us completely pure from all sin in God's sight. ❖ *"Blood" is a common biblical figure of speech meaning, "the life blood of a being poured out in death as a sacrifice in substitute for another."* ➤ [8] Now, if we claim that we don't sin, we are deceiving ourselves and refusing to accept the truth of God's message. ❖ *This message was given by the Word—Jesus himself—and is written in his Word, the Bible.* ➤ Also, the Truth doesn't live in us. ❖ *This has a double meaning. If we are this kind of person, then we lack all knowledge of God's message which tells us the truth about our sinful state. Jesus also called himself "the Truth," so John is also saying that Jesus does not live in this kind of person.* ➤ [9] But if we confess our sins to God and repent by striving to not repeat them, you can be certain that he keeps his promise to completely forgive us—while remaining entirely just and fully consistent with his holy nature in doing so. Not only will he forgive us, but as we continue to confess and turn away from former sins, he will gradually transform the outward expression of our new nature to make it as holy and pure as he is. [10] So be warned! If we claim we are basically good and not sinners, we are actually calling God a liar and have rejected his Word. (For both his written and living Word say that everyone is a sinner.) And his Word is not in us. ❖ *Again the double meaning: Knowledge of God's word or message, and Jesus who is the living "Word of God."* ➤

2

Even Though We Still Stumble in Sin, We Can Enjoy the Father's Full Favor

[1] My dear friends, I feel as a father toward you so I'm writing these things as a strong exhortation to avoid deliberately sinning at all cost. But if a believer does stumble in sin, Jesus—who is God's Messiah—intercedes for us with his Father. He asks his Father to forgive us and to continue to favor and bless us as his children. And Jesus—who is without any sin—has his Father's full approval. In interceding for us he is actually carrying out his Father's will, for the Father and his Son are always of one mind and purpose. His intercession on our behalf is totally effective because [2] he himself satisfied God's just requirement that human sin be punished by a human death. ❖ *He did this by taking our sin upon himself and dying in our place. If we accept this gift from him by faith—i.e., by trusting that this is true—he spiritually unites us with himself. So when the Father looks at us, he sees us as spiritually one with his Son, and he sees that in our union with him our sins have already been punished. Thus the Father declares us righteous and acceptable in his sight.* ➤ Jesus accomplished this not only for us believers who have joyfully believed and received it, but also for all humanity. His forgiveness is, therefore, freely available to any who would believe and take advantage of the opportunity by faith.

Who Is God's Child? The Test of Obedience

[3] As we examine ourselves, this is the way we can be sure that we know God and have become one of his people. We can be sure it's true if we are joyfully striving to live the way we know he wants us to live. [4] People who say they have a personal saving relationship with God but aren't living the way he has clearly told his people they must live—are liars and are deceived. Jesus the Messiah—who is God's Truth—doesn't dwell in their hearts. [5] But the ultimate effect of God's redemptive love is clearly seen in the person who is living a life of obedience to God's Word that naturally flows out of love for him. If this describes us, then we can be sure that we've been united with him in Jesus—and are saved. [6] So all who claim to have a personal relationship with Jesus and that he is living in their hearts should be living the same kind of holy life that he did.

Who Is God's Child? The Test of Love

The Essence of True Light Is Love
Which Cannot Coexist with Hatred

7 My beloved friends, I'm not writing about something you have never heard before. It's not a new teaching—as some have claimed—that's different from what God commanded in the past. You've all known about it since you first came to the faith. 8 I'm talking about Jesus' command to love one another in the same unconditional self-sacrificial way that he loved us. But our comprehension of the depth and richness of this truth *is* constantly new and fresh. As we experience his never-ending love showered upon us, it is transforming us into his image. Thus the darkness in our own lives—and that in the world—is already being dispelled by the true Light whose love is shining out from us. It's the dawn of the new age to come.

9 So anyone who claims to be living in the light of Jesus' life-transforming love, but hates someone—especially a believer—is obviously still lost in the dark. The Light hasn't penetrated that person's heart. 10 In contrast, those who love fellow believers—merely because they are also one with Jesus—clearly have the Living Light abiding within them. And their love for people keeps them from sinning against them because that inner Light shows them the way to live. 11 But those who hate others—especially if they hate God's people—are clearly still in the dark and don't have a clue. Their hatred distorts how they see other people. They don't realize that it's leading them straight to Hell because their inner darkness has blinded them to the truth.

John Reassures His Friends of His Confidence in Their Faith

12 I'm writing to those of you who are relatively young in the faith—who know that your sins have been forgiven because of Jesus' sacrifice on your behalf. 13 I'm also writing to those who've grown strong in the faith—who've experienced victory over the temptations of the Evil One in your lives.

And I'm also writing to those who've attained true maturity in the faith—who've come to intimately know the Messiah who has always existed.

Yes, the reason I'm writing these things to you new believers is because I recognize that you *have* come to know God as your Father, 14 and to the strong in faith because I recognize that the Word of God *is* vitally alive in you and you *have* defeated the Evil One, and to the mature because I recognize that you *do* have an intimate relationship with the Eternal One.

A Warning Against Loving the Temptations of This Corrupt World

15 Beware of focusing your desires and affections on mere things or on the attractive opportunities available to gain wealth, fame, or power in this life. If any such things are what you seek after most, then it's clear that you don't really love God the Father.
❖ *Because what you seek after most is what you really love. The greatest commandment is: We are to love God with all our heart, mind, soul, and strength!* ➤ 16 For the whole system of this fallen world tries to entice us to be self-oriented, to indulge our sinful desires, to be discontent with what we have, always wanting more things, more power, more recognition, and to see ourselves as superior to others. None of these things come from the Father. He would have us flee from all of them. No, they come from a world system thoroughly corrupted and ruled by Satan. 17 And we know that this corrupt world system with all its temptations and all those who don't separate themselves from it are destined for eternal ruin when Jesus returns. ❖ *See 2 Thessalonians 1:9 and the following note about what it means to experience eternal ruin in Hell.* ➤ But the person whose main desire is to live in obedience to the will of the Father—as revealed in his Word—will live forever.

Who Is God's Child? The Test of Doctrine

A Warning About False Teachers Called Anti-Messiahs

18 Dear friends, the time allotted for this fallen world to exist is nearly over. You've heard that before the end, the "Anti-

messiah" will come, proclaim himself to be the Messiah, and lead people away from the truth. Already, many lesser "anti-messiahs" have brought public attention to themselves who are opposing the truth about the Messiah in their teachings. This is a sign that the time remaining before Jesus returns is short. 19 These lesser anti-messiahs were at one time professing believers in the deity of Jesus, but they were never true believers. If they had been, they would still be with us. Their breaking fellowship with us makes it clear that they were faking it all along. 20 But you are not like them, for God has anointed all of you with the Holy Spirit who now lives in you and gives you spiritual knowledge and insight to discern truth from error. ❖ Anointing with the Holy Spirit under the Old Covenant was reserved for prophets, priests, and kings. It conveyed power, authority, and the ability to hear from God. Under the New Covenant, all of God's people have the Holy Spirit living in them. ➤ 21 So I'm not implying that you don't know the truth or lack discernment. But I want to warn you to be on the alert to discern every error and lie of the enemy. 22 And this one should be obvious—the biggest lie is that Jesus isn't the Messiah, the eternal Son of God who became a man. Anyone who claims this is an anti-messiah and a false teacher. In denying this truth, it's clear that such a person doesn't believe in God the Father or his Son. 23 For anyone who proclaims that Jesus is not the Messiah— God's eternal Son become man—is also rejecting God the Father. The Father clearly testified and affirmed through audible words, through the miracles he enabled Jesus to do via the Holy Spirit, and in raising him from the dead that Jesus is indeed the Messiah and his Son—and that everything Jesus said was true. It is only through the Son that the Father is revealed to us and we are reconciled with the Father. So only those who publicly acknowledge Jesus as the Messiah—God's Son—have a relationship with the Father who sent him. ❖ In Luke 10:16, Jesus said to his followers, "... anyone who rejects me is rejecting God who sent me." ➤ 24 So remain faithful to believe, meditate upon, and obey the message of the Good News preached by Jesus' apostles—which you were taught when you first became a believer. If you do this, you will remain in union and intimate fellowship with both the Son and the Father. You will also not be deceived by false teachings. 25 It's by remaining in this union and fellowship that we obtain and experience the eternal life that Jesus promised us.

26 I wanted to warn you about these anti-messiahs who will try to deceive you. 27 But I am comforted by knowing that the Anointing ❖ i.e., the Holy Spirit ➤ lives in you— so you really don't need anyone else to teach you truth from error. For the Anointing will teach you everything you need to know. You can trust his ability to clearly reveal God's Truth to you and to keep you from all error. So continue to be faithful to what he has revealed to you about living in union with Jesus.

The Standard of Righteousness

28 Now my friends, do all that's necessary to remain in intimate fellowship with Jesus, so when he returns in his glory, we will be able to stand confidently before him—knowing that we are righteous in his sight and not be ashamed to face him because of flagrant sin in our lives. 29 It's correct to expect that children reflect the character of their father. Therefore, if you know that God is righteous in all his ways, you can be sure that only those who consistently live according to his will have been spiritually reborn as his children.

3

1 The immensity of the Father's love toward us is unfathomable! Consider the inconceivable privilege that he has granted us. Not only have we been redeemed from the fate of Hell, not only will we live forever in Heaven, but in addition to this he has made us become his children! This isn't just a figure of speech, but a spiritual reality. ❖ We've been spiritually reborn by his Spirit, so we derive our new spiritual nature from him—even as children derive their physical characteristics from their parents. Note that we are human children that are reborn spiritually. Even though we are now his children and our human spirits are joined to Jesus and the Father and thus joined to deity—we are not ourselves

deity. We were created and remain finite. But the eternal Son of God who became the man Jesus was never created. He was always deity—and this is an important distinction that was clearly understood by the believers to whom John was writing. ➤ But those who do not believe—who love the things of this world rather than God—can't recognize our spiritual family resemblance to the Father because they are incapable of really knowing Him. ❖ *Spiritual truth is only discerned spiritually, so the spiritually dead cannot see, know, or understand him.* ➤ ²My dear friends, try to grasp the reality that we are—right now—God's spiritual children. He hasn't revealed to us exactly what we will ultimately become, but it's clear that this is only the beginning. When Jesus returns in his glory, we will clearly and fully perceive him. And as we behold him in his glory, we will be transformed to have his very character—from glory to glory. ³That is something to look forward to! Everyone who really has this expectation will do their utmost to keep themselves from sin—constantly striving after Jesus' purity and holiness. ❖ *This is, of course, only obtainable by relying on his power. But it's not overly difficult because he lives in us, urges us in this direction, and provides his enabling help to obey.* ➤

⁴Everyone who sins is guilty of rebellion against God's commands and purposes. That's the definition of sin—disobedience to God's commands. ❖ *This means the commands clearly spelled out in his written Word. So every sin is an affront to God himself—even if it might seem that it doesn't involve him at all.* ➤ ⁵And you certainly know that Jesus—who is by nature sinless—came into this world for the express purpose of getting rid of sin altogether. ⁶So all who have the Messiah living in them do not—by habit—consciously choose to sin. Rather, their desires are to obey him and they struggle against sin. But those who habitually and deliberately choose to do things that God has forbidden—with no sense of regret—have never known him at all, despite any claims to the contrary. ❖ *They've never recognized who Jesus really is, or understood the severity of God's*

attitude toward sin. ➤ ⁷Dear friends. Beware of the enemy's deception! Don't follow human reason that leads you away from the clear truth of God's Word! The facts are simple. You can't be righteous without doing what is right. ❖ *This does not mean the converse is true, that doing what is right makes us righteous in God's sight. Righteousness only comes as a free gift from God to those who believe in his promises. But those who have been declared righteous by God—because they've been spiritually joined with his Son Jesus through faith—will do what is right, at least most of the time. True faith results in right living or it is not genuine.* ➤ Those who habitually live in accordance with God's clearly revealed will—because this is the desire of their hearts—are righteous in God's sight just as Jesus is. ⁸But those who habitually live in willful rebellion against God's commands belong to Satan. For he is the originator of sin and is the master of all who live in it. The reason God's Son became a man was to destroy Satan's mastery and undo all that he has done in our lives. ❖ *He broke Satan's power on the cross—and we appropriate that victory in our lives by faith and walking in obedience. So to embrace sin is to be an enemy of Jesus and his work.* ➤ ⁹Those who've become God's children don't live in rebellion against God's will. For he has put his very life and nature in them such that their desire is to obey him and to struggle against temptation to sin. Because God really is their Father, they are incapable of wanting to live in rebellion against him. ¹⁰This is how we can know for sure who are children of God and who belong to Satan: Those who live in willful rebellion against God's commands—or don't love his children—don't belong to him, but to Satan.

More About Love

¹¹The command that we must love one another is an essential part of the Good News message taught by the Messiah's apostles—which you heard from the very start. ❖ *The kind of love John is talking about here is the unconditional self-giving self-sacrificial agape love* **A** *that*

A 3:11 "Agape" [pronounced ah-GAH-pay] is one of three Greek words translated into English as "love." Another is "Eros"—which means "erotic" or "romantic" love and is rarely used in the Bible, although it was the most frequently used term for love in classical Greek. "Phileos" is the third word and means "brotherly Love and affection" or "close friendship." It is used as a verb only 25 times in the New Testament of parental love, of the

Jesus demonstrated to us by dying in our place. ➤ 12 We are to have no part in Cain-like behavior—who belonged to the Evil One and murdered his brother Abel. Why do you think he did this? What was his motive? It was simply because he realized that his own way of life was not pleasing to God and his brother's was. ❖ *It came from jealousy, pride, and self-righteous justification. Everyone who lives in rebellion against God's will hates those who live in obedience. For another person's obedience highlights their own sin and it feels like an accusation against them. They can't stand it. The result is anger and hatred of all that's the opposite of their own behavior. See Genesis 4:1-16 for the story of Cain and Abel. According to non-biblical Jewish traditions, Cain was evil in many ways and was often used as an example of the worst kind of immoral person.* ➤ 13 So, my dear friends, don't be at all surprised that unbelievers hate you when you live godly lives. It's almost inevitable.

Agape Love Is a Sign of Spiritual Life

14 We can know for sure that we've changed from the state of being spiritually dead to God—to being spiritually alive to him and possessing eternal life—when we exhibit agape love toward fellow believers. Anyone who doesn't exhibit this kind of love in their life is still spiritually dead. 15 Those who have hatred in their hearts toward others are murderers, as far as God is concerned. You know that such people do not have eternal life and never will—unless they truly repent and change. 16 We know the true nature of agape love from Jesus' example in his willingness to suffer and die that we might gain eternal life. ❖ *He was willing to do this knowing that most would reject it and that none of us were worthy of it.* ➤ Since we are commanded to love other believers as Jesus loves us, we too must be willing to make selfless sacrifices for unworthy and

ungrateful people—even to the point of being willing to suffer hardship, deprivation, physical suffering, and dying to help them. This is the true nature of Messiah-like agape love. 17 So examine yourselves. If you see someone in genuine need—especially another believer—and you have the means to help them in some way whether through your time, effort, prayer, possessions, or money and do nothing at all, then how can you claim that you have God's love in your heart? You are deceived. If your heart were joined to God's you would feel compelled to help. 18 My dear friends, true love is not merely a matter of talk or sentiment—it's something that always demonstrates its reality through loving deeds.

Knowing That We Demonstrate Agape Love Assures Us of God's Love for Us, Even When We Feel Guilty

19 When we live out our love in this way, we can know for sure that we are being true to the way and nature of God who lives in our hearts ❖ *i.e., in our human spirits* ➤ and we can be confident in his presence. 20 Realize that God knows us better than we do ourselves. ❖ *He is aware of sin in us that never reaches our consciousness—yet he still loves us and accepts us for the sake of Jesus' self-sacrificial death. He has determined that his love for us will eventually overcome all remaining sin in our lives.* ➤ So even when our consciences do bother us, we can be sure that the Father still loves us as his dear children. ❖ *It may be the Accuser bothering us about something we've already confessed and repented of—in which case we can rebuke him. Or it may be the Holy Spirit who is lovingly showing us where we've gone wrong so we can repent and grow.* ➤ Our knowledge that we are God's children and that he loves us can overcome any feelings of guilt, doubt, or fear arising because

---

disciples' love for Jesus, of God's love for his Son and for his people, and once for the disciple whom Jesus loved. [John 20:2] But it's never used of human love for God. "Agape" was chosen by the translators of the Hebrew Scriptures into Greek (the Septuagint) and the writers of the New Testament to represent God's kind of love. In classical Greek it was seldom used. But the writers of the New Testament gave the word a new and richer meaning. In the Bible, agape means love that's freely given, self-sacrificial, and unconditional. It's a desire and

determination to attain what's best for the person being loved, regardless of their response. This doesn't mean that it's independent of emotion. The purest love that a parent has for a child is the closest human equivalent. A good definition is found in 1 Corinthians chapter 13. Agape is a useful word since our culture uses the word "love" to mean many different things—not all of them good. Whenever you see a verse about God loving people, or God commanding his people to love others, it's almost always this kind of agape love that is meant.

of our conscience. So we should never be afraid or too ashamed to come to him in prayer. 21 And when our consciences are clear, we can be even more confident that we are pleasing him and so come boldly into his presence with our requests—knowing that he gladly welcomes us.

Love for God Implies Obedience

22 When we make our requests, we receive whatever we ask from him based on our spiritual union with Jesus. ❖ *i.e., We are asking "in his name" based on our being spiritually one with him.* ➤ He gives us what we ask because he knows we are seeking to do his will and to live in obedience to his commands. ❖ *e.g., Always forgiving others, having faith in him and his faithfulness, not being selfish, and other conditions set upon our prayers in Scripture.* ➤ Since we're trying to please him in everything we do, this promise assumes that our requests are also in line with his will—so he will certainly grant them. ❖ *He answers our prayers as if Jesus himself were asking—just as Jesus promised in John 16:23-24.* ➤ 23 But God's main command and requirement is that we believe Jesus is the Messiah—his eternal Son. ❖ *Out of this faith will flow a trust in his finished work on the cross to save us, and a belief upon which we consequently act in obedience that everything he told us came straight from the Father himself.* ➤ And Jesus' main command was that we continue to live by demonstrating love toward each other in the same way he loved us. 24 The result of all this is that those who strive to obey his commands—because they love God—remain in an intimate relationship with him. He lives in them in their innermost being, and their spirits are joined to his Spirit, and their identities are bound in unity in him. We know that we are among those who are joined to him in this relationship because he gave us the Holy Spirit to be our constant companion. ❖ *We experience the reality of his presence every day as he enables us to have faith, hope, love, and to obey. He prompts and guides us, illuminates the Scriptures, enables discernment of truth and error, convicts of sin, empowers us for service with his spiritual gifts, produces his spiritual fruit in our transformed characters, and comforts and assures us in all situations. If you are a true believer but don't consciously experience the reality of the Holy Spirit living in you, then you are missing out on something*

God intends for you to recognize and experience. [Romans 8:23; 2 Corinthians 1:22; 5:5; Ephesians 1:13-14] ➤

4

Test the Origin of a Person's Teaching by Their Confession of Who Jesus Is

1 Dear friends, be cautious about those you listen to and whose teaching you accept and to whom you submit yourselves. There are many who claim to be teachers, preachers, or prophets of God, but not all of them are true believers. ❖ *Even if they exhibit miraculous signs, this isn't proof that God empowers them or endorses their message. If they don't have the Spirit of God in them, then what they say doesn't come from God. No matter how good it sounds, if it doesn't come from the Spirit of God, then ultimately it comes from Satan and will contain errors that lead people astray.* ➤ You need to use discernment and carefully test them and what they say to be sure that the Spirit of God really lives in them before accepting them. 2 This is one way you can test them. If a person openly teaches that Jesus is the Messiah—the eternal Son of God who became a human being—then that person has the Spirit of God living within. ❖ *Such a person will also claim to trust in Jesus' finished work on the cross alone for their salvation—because this is a necessary corollary implied by this test.* ➤ 3 Any person who will not openly teach this about Jesus or who denies that Jesus is God—is not from God. That person is an "anti-messiah"—a false teacher or prophet and an enemy of the Messiah. You've heard that the Anti-messiah is coming—and already there are many people under the influence of this spirit who oppose the truth. 4 But you, my dear friends, are God's children and have already won the struggle to discern the truth about Jesus for yourselves. You were able to do this because the Holy Spirit—who lives within you—is infinitely more powerful and his wisdom infinitely greater than any demonic spirit that would try to deceive you. 5 These false teachers and prophets are under the influence of demonic spirits that are allies of Satan—the temporary ruler of this world. What they teach appeals to many people because they too are under the influence of the same spirits. 6 But we, who are Jesus'

apostles, have been sent by God. And all who are God's children listen to us and recognize and accept the truth of the apostolic teaching and message proclaimed from the beginning. ❖ *The apostolic teaching is contained in the books of the New Testament.* ➤ Those who are not God's children don't accept our teaching. This is another way you can recognize who has the Spirit of God and who has the spirit of deception.

The Source of Our Love Is God Himself

7 My dear friends, let's continue to demonstrate agape love to each other. Since God is the only source of this kind of love, it's clear that everyone who has agape love flowing out of their lives has been born as a child of God and has an intimate relationship with him. 8 But anyone who doesn't exhibit this kind of love in their life can't possibly have a relationship with him—because agape love is God's essential nature and he imparts it to all his children. ❖ *Nobody can be close to him and remain untransformed by his love.* ➤ 9 The nature and proof of God's love was brought into clear focus when he sent his only eternal divine Son into this sinful world as a man so that we could understand who God is and what he is like, and so we might gain eternal life through believing in him. 10 We understand what agape love *is* by what God *did*. This love caused him to sacrificially send his Son to suffer the necessary punishment that his holy justice demands as a penalty for sinning—which is death. ❖ *The very Source of all Life voluntarily died. He did this for people who hated him so there would be a way that he could—by his own standards—justly forgive us and bring us into an intimate and holy relationship with himself. If we try to conceive of what true love is by looking at the kind of feelings and obedience we're able to produce on our own toward God, then our understanding will fall far short of the real thing. To comprehend true love, we have to realize the immensity of what he did for us and try to understand the high cost to himself. e.g., Think about the sinless one becoming sin, the Father turning his back on his beloved Son, the creator suffering humiliation from his creation. Think about allowing your own child to suffer and die to help people who hate you.* ➤ 11 Dear friends, since God considers each of us so valuable that he lavished his love on us in this way,

how can we dare to not show this same love to each other? ❖ *To withhold love from someone that God loves so much implies that his evaluation of the worth of that person is wrong—and we are in fact judging God's values, not only that person.* ➤

12 No mortal has ever seen the infinite God in all the glorious splendor and majesty of his love and holiness. But if we continue to love each other as he commanded, we remain spiritually united with him and he causes his love to grow in us and to flow out from us—until he has perfectly reproduced his own loving nature in us. 13 As I said before, the fact that he has given us his Holy Spirit to live in us is the proof that God has joined us to himself—and himself to us—in an intimate spiritual relationship. ❖ *It's clear that John assumes people who have the Holy Spirit living in them can recognize this fact. His presence is an experiential reality. [Ephesians 1:14] See the comment in verse 3:24 about how we can recognize his presence in us.* ➤ 14 We apostles are eyewitnesses to the fact that God the Father sent his only Son into this world as a man—to be the means by which anyone can be saved from the power of Satan and from the fate of eternal punishment for their sins. And we continue to openly proclaim this message. 15 All who believe that Jesus is God's Son—and are willing to publicly acknowledge this fact and their faith in him—are only able to do so because God lives in them and has joined them to himself. 16 We've experienced God's love for us and have come to believe it's real and reliable. So we've embraced it and trust it. We've come to comprehend the truth that God's essential nature is unconditional self-giving love. ❖ *Note, though, that God's love is not like human love. His love desires only the very best—by his standards—for those whom he loves. And the very best means that there is no permanent place for sin in the beloved. Ultimately, sin—as he defines it—must be eliminated in those he loves. But God also wants his relationship with his people to be voluntary, and he will not force his holy nature on people who are unwilling to accept it. So his love for such people will not allow him to violate their will—and the necessary consequence is that ultimately, such people cannot remain in his presence. To be banished from God's presence is where Hell is. Also, since God cannot tolerate sin, his justice demands that sin be punished. We would not consider our earthly father loving or just if he failed to punish those who*

harmed us. So God's holy justice is part of his love nature and requires him to punish sin—whereas a popular misconception about love is that it should tolerate and overlook anything and everything. Of course, nobody believes in or practices this kind of love when others do them wrong, but they inconsistently and irrationally expect that a loving God would do this. In summary, the fact that God is love does not mean that he will not punish sin and banish people to Hell. One would be foolish to read one's own definition of love into the statement that God is love. Instead, it is wise to understand what God teaches about himself and his love nature by looking at all he has revealed about himself and his ways in the Scriptures. ➤ Whoever lives out this kind love has to be joined to its source—for we are incapable of this kind of love without God living in us and in spiritual unity with us.

17 As we continue to live in unity with Him, his love in us—which is expressed through us toward others and also back toward himself—becomes more mature and perfect. That's his goal. So we can look forward with confidence and joy to the day when Jesus will return to judge humanity—because we know that the life we've lived in this world was actually his life lived in and through us. **18** In the lives of those who are filled with God's love and have had their own love matured and perfected, there's no fear of punishment from him. ❖ *There is, indeed, no fear of any kind for we know that his love for us and our love for him will overcome, comfort, and sustain us in joy through anything that we might experience.* ➤ Those who are still afraid of God haven't yet adequately experienced his love for them and had his love mature in them. ❖ *If this is true of you, then go back to the basics. Repent, live in obedience to his word, and allow his love to flow through you to others. You will then start to experience his great love for you—and your fear will disappear.* ➤ **19** You must realize that we are only able to have this kind of love at all because God first showered it upon us, and transformed us by it, and filled us with himself. It all comes from him. **20** So if anyone says, "I love God," yet hates one of God's children—that person is a liar. If you can't love one of God's children whom you can see, then it's certainly impossible for you to love a God you can't see. ❖ *As John has said repeatedly, if God lives in us, then we will love as he loves—and he loves all his people. Any lack of love—and especially hatred—is a clear sign that person is not*

living in union with God. And if we're not joined to the source of love, we can't love God or anyone else. Remember that all this discussion is about agape love. Human love could never be focused on an invisible God. Only God's agape love that he put within us can evoke a love response from us toward God himself. ➤ **21** And besides that, Jesus taught us plainly that love for God by definition includes love for his people. That's one of the essential basics of our faith. ❖ *Jesus said in John 14:15, "If you love me, you will obey my commands." And one of his very clear commands in John 15:12 is, "Love each other in the same way I have loved you." See also Matthew 22:37-40; Mark 12:29-31; Luke 10:27-28 and John 13:34 for other commands about loving God and his people. Since Jesus and God are one, what he said about our loving him also applies to our loving God. No other single verse in Scripture explicitly says what John says in this verse, but it is a clear conclusion from Jesus' teachings.* ➤

5

Obedience, Love, and Proper Belief
All Come from God Living in Us

1 All who believe that Jesus is the Messiah—meaning that he is the eternal Son of God—and trust him as their only means of salvation, do so because they are children of God whose spirits have been reborn and are indwelt by the Holy Spirit. And all who've been spiritually reborn as children of God naturally love their Father and all of his other true children. **2** The way we can really know we love God's children is if we love God and obey his commands. ❖ *Since true love comes from God, if we don't love him, his love doesn't live in us—and any so-called love we have toward others is not agape love at all. It's motivated by things such as a need for approval and selfishness. If we obey God's commands—especially regarding other people—then we will be loving them the way God wants us to. If we don't obey his commands, then we clearly aren't loving others because most of his commands teach us the proper way love would have us act toward each other.* ➤ **3** By God's own definition, loving him includes obeying his commands. ❖ *If we hate what he commands, how could we possible love him? This truth is self-evident when we apply it to others in authority over us.* ➤ And God's commands are neither impossible to obey nor overly difficult for his true children. ❖ *This is because he lives in his children to fill them with his love—so they naturally love him in return and want to please him. He also gives them enabling power* through his Holy Spirit to overcome sinful desires so they can obey. ➤ 4 All true children of God overcome the temptations to sin that press in on us in this corrupt world—so that we can obey God and love as he loves. This is accomplished through our faith in Jesus. ❖ *By faith, we trust that he will give us discernment and warning against hidden snares of the enemy. By faith, we draw on his power to obey— trusting that he is living in us and making his power available for that very purpose when we are pulled by temptation. If we rely on his power and ability, we will always find a way to escape the lure of sinful temptations. (See the promise in 1 Corinthians 10:13.) And by faith, we know that he picks us up when we fall, forgives us, cleans us up, and gives us chance after chance to perfect our ability to "walk" by his power to overcome sin in our lives. It's by trusting in his many promises and acting upon them—even when we feel or perceive nothing—that we appropriate his favor and enabling power. Faith is the currency of the Kingdom and the conduit of his power in our lives. Without it, we are bankrupt and power- less. And this faith is generated by the Holy Spirit who lives within us. It's God's gift to his children. Yet we retain the freedom and ability to choose whether or not to use it.* ➤ 5 The only people who can live this kind of life of love and overcome sin and temptation and all the power of the enemy are those whose faith is firmly grounded in the person of Jesus—and in the fact that he is the one and only eternal Son of God. ❖ *This is the most central pillar upon which faith in the Messiah is based. Without it, the rest of the teachings of our faith cannot stand.* ➤

You Can Become God's Child by Accepting His Testimony About Jesus.

6 God proclaimed that Jesus is his only Son when he spoke audibly at Jesus' baptism. *[Matthew 3:16-17; Mark 1:9-11]* "Water" is the first sign—which refers to Jesus' baptism and the Father's audible testimony at that time. God also declared that Jesus is his Son—and not an ordinary man—when he raised him back to life after he died. "Blood" is the second sign—which refers to Jesus' death on the cross and his resurrection. (Without the resurrection, his death wouldn't have been a sign. So the

"blood" refers to both his death and his resurrection.) So God's revelation that Jesus is his Son came by the two signs of water and blood. And the Holy Spirit—who is the Truth—also tells us in our hearts and minds that these things really happened and that Jesus is God's true Son. ❖ *Jesus called himself the Truth in John 14:6 and he calls the Holy Spirit the Spirit of Truth in John 14:17 and 16:13. He also said in John 15:26 that the Spirit of Truth—who comes from the Father—would testify about him. So this third testimony through the Holy Spirit is also from the Father.* ➤ 7 So we have three separate testimonies that Jesus is God's Son **A**—8 the Holy Spirit within us, the sign of water referring to the Father's testimony at his baptism, and the sign of his blood referring both to Jesus' death and the Father's testimony by raising him back to life. These three testimonies all clearly declare the same thing—Jesus is God's eternal Son. 9 We normally accept human testimony about things that have happened and what's true—so we ought to be even more willing to accept the supernatural testimony that God has given. He has clearly testified that Jesus is his Son. 10 All who believe in God's Son have God's testimony about him confirmed in their hearts and minds. All who don't believe God's testi- mony about his Son are, in effect, calling him a liar. ❖ *There is no middle ground, and those who refuse to believe will not be able to deny it when they stand before him at the judgment. They will stand condemned by their own rejection of God's testimony. Nobody will be able to say to his face that his testimony wasn't sufficient—as many try to do now. For he knows the true thoughts and motives of their hearts. They have rejected his testimony because they don't want to believe it. If they believed it, they would have to change their way of living.* ➤ 11 And this is what God has said in his testimony—He offers us the gift of eternal life with him, and this life is only available through faith in his Son. 12 All who have the Son living in them— because they've believed what God has said—have the Source of All Life living within them—and so will live forever. All

---

A 5:7-8 The King James Version has the following for verses 7-8: 7 "For there are three that bear record in heaven, the Father, the Word and the Holy Ghost: and these three are one. 8 And there are three that bear witness in earth, the Spirit and the water and the blood: and these three agree in one." But there are no Greek manuscripts dating before the 16th century that have these words.

who reject God's Son have rejected Life. [13] I've written all these things to you who have accepted God's testimony and have believed in his Son so that you can be completely assured that you really will live forever with him. Eternal life is something you possess right now.

Concluding Assurances and Final Warning

[14-15] Since we are assured of our intimate relationship with God, we can be bold and confident in coming to him with our requests. We know that if we ask for anything that he wants to happen, he gladly hears us and grants our requests. ❖ *So don't be discouraged if the manifestation of his grant is not immediate. Jesus told us to keep on asking until we receive. And if we are asking for something that we know is his will, we can be sure we will eventually receive it. We can even have confidence in interceding for the lives of other believers.* ➤ [16] So if you happen to see a brother or sister in the Messiah stumbling in sin, you should pray for them and God will grant his favor and enabling power to lead them to repentance and renewed life. You should be aware, though, that some sins lead to spiritual death—and we are not to expect that God will answer any requests about such sins. ❖ *Jesus said that blasphemy against the Holy Spirit—i.e., reviling or rejecting him—would never be forgiven. [Mark 3:29; Luke 12:10] This is the unforgivable sin. Yet here John seems to be referring to the major sins he is writing about in this letter—of people who were once believers, or at least professing believers, and who later completely rejected Jesus, denying his deity, and who have rejected their former brothers and sisters in the Messiah and now hate them. This is the sin of apostasy—which is talked about in Hebrews 6:4-6 and 10:26-31. If such people have not rejected the Holy Spirit, it may be possible for them to repent and ask for forgiveness and be restored. But evidently, such sins are so serious that our prayers on their behalf will not—in themselves—be sufficient for God to grant his favor and forgiveness. John implies it may useless for us to pray for such people—or at least he means that we have no promise from God that such a request will be granted. See Jeremiah 7:9-29 (especially verse 16), and 14:10-12 for examples of where God reveals that some of his people have gone too far in rejecting him—such that he will not listen to prayers on their behalf.* ➤ [17] All disobedience to God's commands is sin—and we shouldn't minimize the seriousness of any sin. But while*

many sins can be repented of and therefore, forgiven, there are some that lead far down the road to eternal damnation which are difficult or impossible to repent of. ❖ *If you are in despair over your sin and wish you could change, that is a clear sign that the Holy Spirit has not given up on you. Turn to him in prayer, acknowledge your sin, ask for forgiveness and his help to change your way of life so you won't sin again. Trying to turn away from sin and turn toward obeying God is what repentance is. God will help you—even when you repeatedly fall into the same sin. As long as you have the desire to change, you can repent and he will welcome you. Those who are well on the road to damnation will have no desire at all to acknowledge their sin or change their ways. So if you want to change, but despair of your own ability to change, ask God to help you—and he will. He will not give up on you unless you totally reject him and have no desire at all to seek him. It is not a matter of being worthy. No human is worthy of his attention or help or salvation—as far as God is concerned. It is a matter of whether or not you want God to help you change. There is no one who is too great a sinner for God to love and help—if they are willing to accept his help. To believe that God could not love you and could not forgive you is a lie that demons are putting into your mind. To believe this is to believe that God is a liar—because he says that he does love you, even if he hates what you have done. And he has promised to forgive you and help you if you turn to him and ask for his help. He does not expect you to clean up your act first in your own power. No one can get their act together sufficiently to make themselves worthy of God's love and attention. Only he can change you and transform you. He doesn't love you for the rebellious selfish sinner that you have been (that we all have been). He loves you because he sees the beautiful person he can transform you into—if you will allow him to do so and will cooperate with him. He will give you the desire to do what pleases him. You don't have to work it up in yourself—you can't. He wants you to give up trying to be good in your own power, admit to him that you can't change yourself, and offer him your life so he can change it for you—while you cooperate by repenting and obeying.* ➤ [18] In brief summary, we understand the following things to be true. We know that no one who is spiritually born as a child of God lives in rebellion against his will. ❖ *Even though we all stumble in sin, it's the desire of all true believers to obey God's will. And when we do sin, we are usually fairly quick to repent. The kind of rebellion John is talking about is found in those who habitually and willfully sin without any desire to repent. Such people often won't even admit that what they are doing is wrong.* ➤ God's Son protects them so that Satan cannot harm their faith. *[2 Thessalonians 3:3]* ❖ *Some people interpret this verse to mean that Satan cannot harm believers at all. But the protection that John is talking about applies mainly to our spiritual lives and our faith. There are Scriptural counterexamples to the interpretation that believers are automatically protected from Satan's attacks. 1 Peter 5:8 warns us "Be self-controlled and alert. Your enemy the devil prowls around like a roaring lion looking for someone to devour." Why would Peter give this warning if we are automatically protected in every way? And Paul says in 2 Corinthians 12:7, "To keep me from becoming conceited because of these surpassingly great revelations, there was given me a thorn in my flesh, a messenger of Satan, to torment me."* ➤

19 We are assured that we are God's children, and we understand that everyone who isn't one of his children is under the power and influence of Satan. 20 We also know that God's Son came to give us revelation and understanding about the one true God so we might be united with him and come to know him intimately. So we know that we are living in union with the one true God through our union with his Son—Jesus the Messiah. And this Jesus is himself truly God and Life Eternal.

21 My dear friends, as a final warning, be on your guard against everyone and everything that claims to come from the Truth, but isn't genuine. And take care lest anything takes God's place in your hearts as your first love. ❖ *John's literal exhortation is to guard ourselves from idols. To his original audience, this may have been a reference to worshipping the image of the Roman emperor as a sign of loyalty, or to the influence of pagan gods. But it clearly tells us to guard against worshipping (i.e., submitting ourselves to) anything or anyone that's not the one true God himself. Today, this is much more likely to be wealth, fame, status, power, material possessions, ourselves, our own independence, or other people. Anything that's more important to us than God himself is an idol.* ➤

John's Second Letter

This letter was written by the Apostle John, probably about the year AD 90. See the introduction to John's first letter for more details about him.

John writes figuratively in this letter about a "chosen lady and her children" which represents a local assembly of believers, and "her sister" meaning a sister assembly over which he was also elder. During the first 200 years after Jesus returned to Heaven, many teachers and evangelists traveled from place to place as missionaries and stayed in the homes of believers who would also give them food for their journey to their next destination. False teachers did the same thing. In this letter, John was cautioning the people under his spiritual care to only help true teachers and not help others spread false doctrines. John wrote some of the same things in his first letter—telling his people to remain faithful to the true teachings of the Good News, to love one another, and to not allow false teachers to come and teach in their assembly.

Opening Greetings

1 I am John, the one you call "the elder," and I'm writing to the assembly of those chosen by God to be his own. I love you all because of our common belief in the truth contained in the Good News—and the resulting spiritual unity we share in Jesus. It isn't just I who loves you, but all who believe in the same truth do too. **2** For Jesus—who is the Truth *[John 14:6]*—lives in all of us and will be with us all forever. **3** I pray that God the Father and his son Jesus the Messiah will look upon you with great favor and compassion far beyond anything you can deserve, and enable you to live with each other and with him in peace—experiencing health and well-being in every way because you believe in his truth and because he loves you. ❖ *There are various interpretations of the final phrase "in truth and love" in the literal text, here rendered "because you believe in his truth and because he loves you." Some say: "by believing the truth and by loving others."* ➤

Live in Obedience to the Truth and Live in Love

4 I rejoiced when I heard news about ❖ *or: when I met* ➤ some of your people because it was clear that they were living in obedience to the truth revealed in the Good News—just as the Father commanded us to live. **5** Now, my dear brothers and sisters in the Lord, I exhort you all to also love one another. This is not a new command, but the same one we learned when we first believed. *[Leviticus 19:18; John 13:34-35; 1 John 2:7-8]* **6** And this is what I mean by "love"—We love each other by doing all the things that God commanded us to do in relation to other believers. This is the command that you are to obey—and we all learned it when we first believed. ❖ *The IVP commentary says that in this context, the command to love one another means to stay within the community of believers—since some were dividing and leaving.* ➤

Beware of False Teachers

7 At the same time, watch out for people who are not willing to acknowledge that Jesus the Messiah is the eternally existing Word of God—God's Son who came from Heaven and became fully human. There are many such people about in the world— some of whom come from assemblies of believers *[1 John 2:19]*—who try to deceive true believers with false teachings. They are anti-messiahs and lead people away from him. *[2 Thessalonians 2:3-4; 1 John 2:18, 22; 4:3; Revelation 13]* **8** Take care that those people don't deceive you so that you lose the eternal blessings that we apostles worked to see you gain. We want you to receive your full reward in Heaven. **A** **9** Those who teach

---

A 8 Some manuscripts have: μὴ ἀπολέσητε (mē apolesēte) "you may not lose" and ἀπολάβητε (apolabēte) "you may receive," some manuscripts have μὴ ἀπολέσωμεν (mē apolesōmen) "we may not lose" and ἀπολάβωμεν (apolabōmen) "we may receive." Some manuscripts read εἰργασάμεθα (eirgasametha) "we worked for," some manuscripts have εἰργάσασθε (eirgasathe) "you (plural) worked for." Most

things beyond what the Messiah himself taught, or what we apostles passed on to you, or that contradict those teachings, are not in union with God at all. Such people are not saved. But those who continue to follow the Messiah's teaching are in spiritual union with both the Father and his Son—the Messiah. 10 So if anyone comes to you and teaches something other than the true teachings that have already been passed on to you by the apostles, don't offer them hospitality in your homes and do not allow them to teach in your assembly—as you would those who teach the truth. Don't even greet them as fellow believers or support them in any way. ❖ *Of course, believers would minister to genuine desperate needs to preserve lives—as they would for any unbeliever—although not in such a way as to help them spread their false teaching. But because they pretend to be believers and could confuse true believers, they are much less welcome than unbelievers.* ➤

11 For those who welcome and endorse or support such people become partners with them in the evil they do. ❖ *i.e., false teaching and evil conduct* ➤

Closing Words

12 Even though there are many things I want to tell you, I prefer not to do it in a letter. Instead, I hope to come and see you in person so our **A** mutual joy will be maximized. 13 Those also called by God in your sister assembly here send you their warm greetings!

---

commentators and translations follow the rendering given in the text above. The "we" could include both the apostles and the people he is writing to.

A 12 Many manuscripts have "your joy."

John's Third Letter

This letter was written by the Apostle John, probably around AD 90. See the introduction to John's first letter for more information about the author.

In the first century, believers met in houses, and leaders developed for each house assembly. There were many traveling (i.e., missionary) teachers and evangelists who went from one house assembly to another, and they carried letters of recommendation from recognized leaders to ensure that they would be welcomed and taken care of. There were also false teachers who traveled around in the same way. This is a letter of recommendation for a traveling preacher named Demetrius—probably hand carried by himself— to Gaius. Gaius was either a house assembly leader and Diotrephes was another house assembly leader in the same area, or they were both part of the same assembly. This isn't clear. But Diotrephes had been asserting his own authority and independence and had rejected missionary teachers that the Apostle John had approved. John encourages Gaius to welcome Demetrius. (This Gaius is probably different from others of the same name mentioned elsewhere in the New Testament.)

Opening Greetings

¹ I am John, the one you call "the elder," and I'm writing to Gaius—whom many believers know and love. I love you because of our common belief in the truth contained in the Good News—and the resulting spiritual unity we share in Jesus. ² Dear friend, I pray that God will bless you with material prosperity and good health—just as he has clearly blessed your spiritual life. ³ I greatly rejoiced to hear a report from some brothers in the Lord who told me about your faithfulness in obeying God's truth—just as I know from personal experience that *you* do— unlike some others I could mention. ❖ *In the Greek text, "you" in the last phrase is prominent or emphasized, which some commentators take to mean he is comparing Gaius with someone else, perhaps Diotrephes.* ➤ ⁴ There's nothing that gives me more joy **A** than to hear that believers under my spiritual care are continuing to live in obedience to God's will.

John Praises Gaias' Support of Missionaries

⁵ My dear friend, when you offer hospitality to our missionary brothers who proclaim God's message—and especially when they are strangers to you—you are truly following the way God would have you live. ⁶ These men have told the assemblies about the practical love you have shown them. I hope you will continue to please God by supplying them with food and money and other needs they have as you help them to continue on to their next destination to do his work. ⁷ For these men have gone out so others can learn about the way of salvation through Jesus the Messiah, but they will accept no support from non-believers. ❖ *Since God's favor is always free, they didn't charge to preach the Good News. They also didn't want to be identified with pagan priests who taught for money.* ➤ ⁸ Therefore, we believers should support such men so we can be partners with them in bringing people to know God's truth. ❖ *This is an explicit exhortation to support missionaries—which implies that God will consider you partners with them in their work. This also implies that you will share in the reward they will receive for doing his work. [Matthew 10:41-42]* ➤

Don't Follow Diotrephes' Example

⁹ I wrote a short letter about this to the assembly, but Diotrephes rejects my instructions and authority—as well as the people I send—because he wants independent authority over the entire assembly. ¹⁰ So when I come, I will bring this matter before the assembly about the slanderous charges he makes against me that have no basis in fact. But worse than that, he consistently refuses to offer hospitality to the missionary teachers I've sent—and he forbids others in

---

A 4 Some manuscripts have "grace" instead of "joy."

the assembly from taking them in too. And those who go ahead and offer them hospitality anyway, he expels from the assembly! 11 My dear friend, don't imitate evil practices. Imitate good ones. Recognize that those who do what is good belong to God. But as for those who do evil, do not have fellowship with them—no matter what they may claim.

John's Endorsement of Demetrius

12 Demetrius, who bears this letter, is spoken of highly by all who know him—and his obedience to the truth of the Good News is clearly evident in his life. I too add my endorsement of his ministry—and you know you can rely on what I say.

Closing

13 There are many things I want to tell you, but I prefer not to do it in a letter. 14 I hope to visit you very soon and then we can converse. 15 May God grant you peace and well-being! Your friends here send their warm greetings. Convey my warm greetings to each of our mutual friends there individually. **A**

A 15 Some commentaries and translations include what is in verse 15 inside verse 14 and then have no verse 15.

Jude's Letter

There is some variation among traditions about who wrote this letter, but it's clear that the author assumes he is well-known to his readers and the only prominent Jude with a prominent brother named James was the brother of Jesus. Thus many Bible scholars conclude he was most likely a younger brother of Jesus who didn't become a believer until after the resurrection. [John 7:5; Acts 1:14] Roman Catholics believe that Miriam (Mary) remained a virgin and had no other children—so they believe that Jude was an older brother that Yosef had in a previous marriage. "Jude" is a form of the Hebrew name "Yudah" which in Greek is "Yudas" and in the Gospel accounts of most English translations it's rendered "Judas." [Matthew 13:55; Mark 6:3] His older brother, James, was the leader of the believers in Jerusalem, [Acts 15:13; Galatians 1:18-19] and is not the Apostle James—the brother of the Apostle John and the son of Zebedee—who was the first apostle to be martyred. [Acts 12:1-2] 1 Corinthians 9:5 implies that the Lord's brothers were well-known—along with the apostles—and did missionary work like Paul. James and Jude were not called apostles and did not refer to themselves as such, but believers considered them to be on equal status with the apostles because they were Jesus' brothers and had become major leaders among God's people. The writer of this letter doesn't refer to himself as an apostle— and in verse 17 refers to the apostles as if he were not part of their group. These facts fit well with the view that Jude was Jesus' brother, as opposed to the apostle Judas—son of James—as some have thought.

The situation that Jude addresses in his letter is clearly stated in verses 3 and 4. False teachers had infiltrated some assembly or assemblies and were twisting the Good News message—about salvation by God's freely given favor through faith in Jesus—into permission to indulge in sexual immorality. This kind of false teaching was widespread even in the first century, and today we have no way of knowing to what general geographic location this letter was addressed. In his letter, Jude quotes from and alludes to a story from the book of First Enoch—which was not part of the Hebrew canon (meaning it wasn't considered by Jews to be divinely inspired Scripture). First Enoch claims to have been written by Enoch before the flood, [Genesis 5:19-23] but this is unlikely to be true since it first appeared in the first century BC. Despite this fact, it was a well-respected book that first-century Jews and Jewish followers of Jesus were familiar with. The false teachers claimed divine authority for their teachings based on visions they had. It has been speculated that they may have also claimed support from the book of First Enoch—and that may be one reason why Jude refers to it in order to oppose their teaching.

The situation Jude wrote about is similar to what many assemblies of believers face today. There are professing believers who deny that a loving God would send anybody to Hell—and who teach that sexual lifestyles condemned by the Scriptures as immoral and perverted are to be accepted as normal and acceptable. The false teachers that Jude warns about rejected the authority of the Torah in the Hebrew Scriptures—and modern-day heretics ridicule the reliability and authority of the Old and New Testament Scriptures that condemn their behavior. The situations are entirely parallel, so this letter remains timely.

This letter was clearly intended to be read as a sermon. Some of the content is similar to part of 2 Peter—hence scholars debate whether one letter was based on the other or not and which way. Depending on which view is taken, estimated dates for its composition vary from AD 65–80.

Opening Greetings

¹ Greetings from Jude, a voluntary slave of Messiah Jesus, and a brother of James who leads God's people in Jerusalem. I'm writing to all those who God called to believe the Good News message and have responded with true faith. God the Father enfolds you in his love and protects your faith until Messiah Jesus returns to take you home with him. ² I pray that he will continue to demonstrate his mercy and love to you more and more—so you will remain in perfect peace and unity with him.

A Warning About False Teachers

³ My dear brothers and sisters in Jesus, I very much wanted to write to you about the new life that God has given us through our union with Messiah Jesus. But now I find that because of news I've heard about

certain people, I must instead write an urgent appeal to you to go on the offensive against certain false teachings. These are threatening to undermine the integrity of the Good News message that Jesus and his apostles entrusted to us to preserve and pass on without corruption to others. 4 Certain evil and influential people have infiltrated your assembly, but you have failed to recognize that they are, in reality, refusing to submit to our only true master and Lord—Jesus the Messiah. This can be seen in their teaching and manner of living. They are corrupting God's message of salvation when they teach that it's acceptable for followers of Jesus to live in sexual immorality—and that God will continue to forgive them since he always offers us his favor, even though we don't deserve it. The fate of such people was determined long ago—and the prophets have clearly written in the Scriptures that God will punish such people in Hell because they are unrepentant. ❖ *Jesus gives his undeserved favor and enabling help so that we can have power to overcome sin—not so we can continue to indulge in it. [Romans 6:15-23] We all stumble in sin in this life, but God's true children are always repentant and want to live a life that is holy and pleasing to him—because the Holy Spirit lives in us and prompts us in this direction. But some twist God's Word to say that we can live in immorality without repentance—and God will still always forgive us because of his freely offered undeserved favor. Such people claim there are no eternal consequences for sin, no punishment, and no Hell. These claims are merely wishful thinking and bear no resemblance to the truth that God has revealed about himself and his ways in the Scriptures. God always requires repentance—which includes a turning away from sin. Without repentance, there is no forgiveness—and thus the certainty of eternal punishment in a very real Hell. See Jesus' own words on this subject in Matthew 7:21-23.* ➤

The Scriptures Clearly Teach That God Will Punish Those Who Chose To Live in Sin

5 You already know everything that I want to tell you about how God punished those who sinned long ago, but I'm going to remind you anyway. Remember that even though God saved his chosen people—the Israelites—from being slaves in Egypt, he later destroyed every one of those among them who didn't believe him and obey his commands. ❖ *This refers to Numbers chapter 14, where most of the Israelites didn't believe that God would help them conquer the inhabitants of Canaan—the land he had promised to give them—so they weren't allowed to enter it. Instead, God caused them to wander in the wilderness for 40 years until the entire unbelieving generation died off. Jude's point is that even though people have been saved by God or are apparently saved—as the Israelites had been saved from Egypt—if they later turn away from obeying him, he will punish and reject them. The land of Canaan was—in addition to being a real land—a figurative "type" of Heaven. Not entering the promised land of Canaan was also symbolic of the fact that they didn't enter Heaven when they died.* ➤ 6 Also remember the angels who were created holy but refused to remain submitted to God's authority and abandoned their proper place in Heaven. [Genesis 6:1-4] ❖ *In Jude's time, the Jews and followers of Jesus understood this passage in Genesis to mean that some angels came down from Heaven and made some women pregnant. This was a perversion—violating God's order in creation. The details of this story come from "First Enoch." Rebellious angels came to be called "evil spirits" or "unclean—i.e., defiling—spirits" or "demons." Some have already been confined (as stated below) as these were and possibly also some of the most powerful and evil ones. Others, including Satan—their prince—remain relatively free to roam the earth to tempt and afflict people.* ➤ Therefore, God has already confined some of them in eternal chains in prisons of darkness where they wait for Judgment Day—when they will be cast into the lake of fire in Hell along with all the other angels that rebelled but are still relatively free. 7 Also remember the people of Sodom and Gomorrah and other cities near them. Just like those rebellious angels indulged in perverted sexual relations with human women who were not of their kind, these people indulged in serious immorality and desired perverted sexual relations with the angels that came to Lot. **A** Therefore, God destroyed them and their cities with

---

A 7 Though modern readers of the Bible mainly associate homosexual activity with Sodom and Gomorrah, even conservative evangelical commentators say that particular sin was not the focus of Jude's argument in this verse. I am not deliberately trying to avoid referring to it because of recent cultural [Continued next page]

burning sulfur falling from the sky. ❖ *The burning sulfur was possibly from a volcanic eruption or the blast of an exploding meteorite.* ➤ This story is recorded in the Scriptures as an example and warning of the eternal fire in Hell that will be the punishment of all who are evil. [Genesis 19:1-29]

God Will Punish Those Who Mislead His People

8 These false teachers who have infiltrated your congregation are defiling themselves. They claim they have seen visions from God that justify their immoral practices. But the truth is, they are defiling themselves with immorality and refusing to submit to God's clear commands in Scripture. They show their contempt for God's Torah by insulting angelic authorities. ❖ *When God gave his Torah to Moses on Mount Sinai, he spoke through angels as intermediaries. [Acts 7:38, 53; Hebrews 2:2] Jewish teachers commonly taught that angels were administrators of the Torah and that nations were under angelic authority. (See Daniel 10:13, 20-21, which clearly imply that the princes were angels assigned to some position of authority over the nations mentioned.) But the false teachers thought they were superior to angels and no longer under the requirements of the Torah because of the visions they were having. They also taught that angels maliciously gave the Torah teachings to Moses without God's orders. So when accused of violating the Torah, they would reply that the accusation was only from malicious angels—and that they were superior to angels and thus superior to the Torah too. To demonstrate their contempt for the Torah and angelic authority, they insulted angels.* ➤ 9 This is a serious sin because they think they have the authority to judge God's teachings in the Torah. But even the archangel Michael didn't presume he had this kind of authority when he disputed with Satan over who had the right to take Moses' corpse. Satan correctly accused Moses of murder. [Exodus 2:11-12] But Michael knew he didn't have authority to judge that the Torah's teachings did not apply to this situation—so he did not presume to rebuke Satan. Instead, he said, "I will ask the Lord to rebuke you."

❖ *Jude is talking about a story from a non-Scriptural book called "The Assumption of Moses" in which Satan—a fallen angel who hated Moses—said it was wrong for Michael to bury him because Moses was a murderer. Satan's accusation was true according to God's Torah. But even though Michael knew God had forgiven Moses, he didn't have the authority to judge that the Torah's teachings didn't apply and answer Satan's accusation by saying Moses was exempt from the Torah's penalty. So he asked the Lord to make the judgment and answer Satan's accusation with a rebuke. Jude's point is that if the archangel Michael didn't have the authority to judge the Torah and Satan's accusation—even if he knew that Satan hated Moses—then no human has the authority to judge the Torah when it accuses us of sin, or to say the Torah is wrong. When the false teachers insulted angels, they were judging the Torah. But only God has authority to judge—and the Torah came from him. When they judged the Torah, they were really showing that they had no respect for God.* ➤

10 These people insult anything that they don't understand about the spiritual world. They claim to have true knowledge from their visions, but they behave like unreasoning animals. The only things they really know are their bodies' urges—and these they follow with no self-control. Thus they are earning God's wrath and punishment. 11 And their punishment will, indeed, be harsh! For they are going down the same path as Cain. [Genesis chapter 4] ❖ *In Jewish tradition, Cain was not merely a murderer. From other non-Scriptural stories about him, they believed he was evil in many ways. One tradition says that Cain was a false teacher who led others into immorality and worshipping false gods. It's probably these sins that Jude had in mind, since the false teachers he was writing about weren't murderers.* ➤ They also give themselves over in wanton abandon to Balaam's sin of leading people into immorality for personal gain. [Numbers chapters 22–25; Deuteronomy 23:4-5; Nehemiah 13:2; and especially Numbers 31:16 and Revelation 2:14] ❖ *Jewish tradition said that Balaam deceived Israel into worshipping false gods and practicing immorality because King Balak bribed him to do it. [Numbers 25:1-3]* ➤ And they rebel against proper authority—so God will

---

trends. Homosexual activity is clearly condemned in other Scriptures. [Leviticus 18:22; 20:13; Matthew 5:17-20 (See these verses and the accompanying note to understand Jesus' attitude about the validity of every part of the Mosaic Law, which includes these verses from Leviticus); Romans 1:18-32; 1 Corinthians 6:9-11; 1 Timothy 1:10]

destroy them as surely as he did Korah.
[Numbers chapter 16]

12 These people disrupt your love feasts—when you celebrate the Lord's Supper together—by shamelessly and irreverently partying with each other, thinking only of themselves. ❖ *Early celebrations of the Lord's Supper were full meals.* ➤ You should avoid them like ships avoid treacherous reefs. Their teachings are useless in helping others grow closer to God. Thus they are like clouds without rain *[Proverbs 25:14]*—floating over parched land, promising much but delivering nothing. Like fruit trees that never produce—and so in a sense are dead—they will be uprooted and be doubly dead. ❖ *They are spiritually dead now and will suffer the second death in Hell. [Matthew 7:16-19; Revelation 21:8]* ➤ 13 Like wild waves in a storm that repeatedly splash their foam full of debris and mud on the beach, *[Isaiah 57:20]* others are splattered with their shameful sins and are polluted with their teachings. They are like wandering stars in the sky. ❖ *This might refer to the planets, or the hypothetical situation where stars would not remain in fixed positions relative to other stars.* ➤ Anyone trying to navigate by them will be led astray. They claim to be spiritual guiding lights, but God has reserved them an eternal prison in utter darkness.

14 Enoch—who lived in the seventh generation starting from Adam *[Genesis 5:4-18; 1 Chronicles 1:1-3]*—prophesied about these people. He said, "The Lord is surely coming with many thousands of his angels 15 to judge all of humanity and to punish the wicked for every evil deed and for every evil word they spoke against him." *[Genesis 5:21-24]* ❖ *This prophecy is from "First Enoch." Just because Jude quoted it doesn't mean he regarded "First Enoch" as inspired. He knew the content of the quote was accurate from other prophecies. See Matthew 12:36-37; 16:27; 25:31-32, 41, and 46 for similar prophecies from Scripture. Jude used the word "ungodly" four times in the literal text of verse 15 to make his statement with great emphasis.* ➤

16 These people are continually grumbling about the way God allows things to happen to them—and they are never satisfied. They are always following after their own evil passions—and they speak arrogantly against God's Torah. They don't teach God's truth, but instead, say what they think people want to hear in order to gain their favor. ❖ *See Exodus 16:1-12; 17:1-7; Numbers 11:1; 14:26-29; 16:41—17:10; and 1 Corinthians 10:10 to understand God's attitude toward grumbling against him and his leaders.* ➤

Jude's Main Exhortation

17 But you, my dear brothers and sisters in Jesus, should recall that the apostles of our Lord the Messiah warned you in advance that such evil people would come—and now they are among you. 18 They said that in the end times—before Jesus returns—there will be those who indulge their own evil passions and ridicule people who follow God's ways. 19 And now these are the very kind of people who are causing divisions among you. They are enslaved by their sinful desires—and the Holy Spirit clearly doesn't live in them. ❖ *Romans 8:9 says that anyone without the Holy Spirit doesn't belong to the Messiah.* ➤

20 But you, my dear brothers and sisters, I exhort you to help each other to remember and submit to the teachings of the apostles, and to grow strong in your relationship with Jesus. Allow the Holy Spirit to direct and empower your prayers. ❖ *This includes, but is not limited to, praying in tongues. [1 Corinthians 12:10; 14:1; 14-17; Ephesians 6:18]* ➤ 21 And through submissive obedience, keep close to God—always aware of his love enveloping you as you wait for the day when our Lord Jesus the Messiah will mercifully usher you into eternal life with him in Heaven. 22 Show mercy to those whose faith is weak—not condemning them but helping them to believe. 23 Help to save those assembly members who are listening to false teaching and flirting with sin—and so are in danger of becoming eternally lost—by snatching them away from the brink of the fire of Hell. ❖ *Ways to do this are found in: Matthew 18:15-17; Luke 17:3; Galatians 6:1-2; 2 Thessalonians 3:14-15; 1 Timothy 5:20; Titus 3:10; James 5:19-20; and 1 John 5:16.* ➤ To others who refuse to repent, you must still show mercy and kindness without condescension or condemnation. But at the same time, you must hate their

sinful ways and avoid too close an association with them—lest you too become influenced by their corruption and come under God's condemnation. ❖ *The illustration that Jude used in the literal text implies that we can be corrupted by associating too closely with unrepentant people—in the same way we can have filth rub off on us if we touch a garment covered with filth. We are to avoid associating closely with such people, but at the same time, we are to pray for them and show mercy and kindness. Any time they are willing to listen, we should also share the truth from the Scriptures with them. On the other hand, showing mercy and kindness does not mean that we allow them to remain in the assembly. See Paul's instructions in 1 Corinthians chapter 5.* ➤

Jude's Prayer of Praise

24 Let's praise God—who is able to keep you safe from stumbling in sin leading to unbelief. He will surely enable you to become holy and perfect in every way—and will bring you to stand in his presence in Heaven where you will rejoice exuberantly. 25 Give praise to Yahweh—the one true God who has saved us! By the power of Jesus the Messiah who lives in us, we praise him and declare that he rules in glorious majesty with all power, dominion, and authority! This was true before he created time, is true now, and will be true forever! Yes, He reigns! Hallelujah!

Jesus' Revelation to John About Events to Come

This book was most likely written by the Apostle John. Commentators argue over a date, some saying it was written before AD 70, but most think it was probably written in AD 95–96, during the reign of Domitian Caesar (who reigned from AD 81–96). A thorough understanding the book of Revelation can most easily be obtained by reading several commentaries from different perspectives. The main viewpoints on a Scripture passage can usually be presented concisely for most of the books of the New Testament, but the same cannot be said for Revelation. Since it takes large commentaries to present each viewpoint, this " interpretation" barely scratches the surface in presenting even the major categories of interpretations.

The first difficulty with interpreting this book is that it's a record of a series of visions—which usually convey truth in symbolic form. Not everything in a vision is necessarily symbolic, but much can be. The book itself explains some of the symbolism. Some of the symbols are used and understood in other parts of the Scriptures. Some symbols are understood from knowledge of the culture and period in which it was written. Some symbols remain a mystery and we don't know for sure if John himself understood them or not. This interpretation attempts to explain those symbols on which commentators mostly agree.

Another difficulty is that commentators disagree on the organization of the book. Some believe it's organized in chronological order of when the prophecies will be fulfilled. Others believe it's ordered logically, but that the order in which events are presented does not necessarily correspond with chronological sequence. Some believe there are several visions that describe the same period, either the 3½ years of the tribulation, or over the entire period of history from the time of the Messiah's ascension until his return.

The most common categories of interpretation for Revelation are:

1) The Preterist view—which says that the prophecies were all fulfilled during the time of the Roman Empire. In favor of this view is the fact that the original readers would have interpreted the prophecies in their immediate historical context—and it's likely that Jesus meant for them to do so, at least to some extent. Therefore, it can be helpful to understand how the original readers understood some of the symbolism of the book. Against this view is the fact that much of Revelation speaks of Jesus' second coming—which has not yet happened.

2) The Historical view—which says that the prophecies are about specific historical events that have happened during the past 2000 years, but do not directly pertain to Jesus' second coming. But why would the original readers be interested in such things—and how could they possibly understand them? There is also little or no agreement among those who try to interpret the book this way.

3) The Idealist view—which says that the prophecies are symbolic of the struggle between good and evil that has continued throughout history—and are not meant to represent specific historical events at any time. Against this view is the fact that Revelation depicts an ultimate victory and the return of Jesus. If that isn't about a future historical event, then what does it mean?

4) The Futurist view—which says that the prophecies in this book—starting in chapter 4—are all things that will happen in the future in the few years immediately before the Messiah returns. The weakness of this view is that if it's true, there is little in the book that was immediately relevant to the first readers.

It is helpful to understand that some prophecies in the Scriptures have multiple fulfillments. A simple example is the prophecy of 2 Samuel 7:12-14 which says, "When you (i.e., King David) die, I (God) will cause one of your offspring to be king over your kingdom. He will be the one I've chosen to build a Temple for me, and I will cause the throne of his kingdom to last forever. I will be his Father and he will be my son."

In this prophecy, God spoke to King David about his "son." In Hebrew—depending on context—this can mean a literal son or a descendant. At the time the prophecy was given, he was talking about David's not-yet-conceived son Solomon who would become king after him. God said that he would establish the throne (i.e., kingship) of this son forever. (A Preterist view.) This was understood later as meaning that descendants of Solomon would always be kings over Israel. (An Idealist view.) But this was also a prophecy about a specific descendant of David—the Messiah—who would be born 1,000 years later and who would be God's Son in the full literal sense. His reign as eternal king over Israel started—in a real sense—at his ascension. And the assembly of believers is the spiritual Temple that he is building. (Both a Historical and Idealist view.) At his second coming, there will be the complete establishment of his universally recognized reign over Israel. (A Futurist view.)

Revelation is a prophetic book that also has multiple fulfillments. To fully comprehend the meaning of the prophecy, it must be viewed from multiple views and times. The Lord intended this book to be meaningful and a comfort to John's first-century readers—hence there was a valid Preterist interpretation of parts of it. But since explaining that view takes a lot of space and usually isn't directly pertinent to people today, you won't read much in the way of the Preterist view in this interpretation.

I do not find the Historical view defensible—so you will not find it represented in this interpretation.

The Idealist view—largely held by Amillenarians (who do not believe in a literal 1000-year reign of the Messiah on Earth after his second coming)—does have some very valid points to make, and parts of the prophecies in Revelation can be validly interpreted as truths that pertain throughout the period between Jesus' first and second coming. But saying that this was the primary intended view of the prophecy and that the Futurist view is to be totally discounted leads to almost everything being interpreted symbolically—and leads to a few absurd conclusions in places. An example is the resurrection of the two witnesses in 11:11. The Idealists say that these are not real individuals. They are symbolic of the resumed witness of believers in the world after the total silencing or killing off of all Jesus' followers who had been actively proclaiming the Good News. This leads to the absurd conclusion that an entire hardened world—which has just eliminated most or all of Jesus' followers—would be "terrified" by the reemergence or revival of a few or even many new followers. But since the Idealist view does have valid points to make, their view is sometimes mentioned in this interpretation.

This commentator believes that the Futurist view is probably the primary view intended by the Lord, (along with a divinely intended Preterist interpretation of some prophecies for the first-century readers, and some divinely intended Idealist interpretations too). I also think the Futurist view is the view most pertinent to people living today—even though it is not without its difficulties. As with all the other views, within the Futurist view there are many variations of interpretation given by Futurist commentators. Perhaps surprisingly, I don't mention the Futurist view frequently in the commentary because this view assumes the text is to be taken at face value—once the figures are properly understood (which isn't always easy or possible). The interpretation of the timing and sequence of the events is difficult and has several variations—and I think some of the Idealist views on the ordering of events and the possible simultaneity of some visions should be looked at more carefully by Futurists.

Another difficulty is that there are three main interpretations of the Millennium. [Revelation chapter 20]

Premillennialists mainly take the Futurist view and believe that the Messiah will return and set up a literal Kingdom on Earth that will last 1,000 years before "eternity" begins.

Postmillennialists generally take either the Preterist or the Historical view and believe that the Assembly of Believers in this world will gain in influence until an age of peace, harmony, and knowledge of God will prevail on Earth. This is their symbolic understanding of the 1,000 years. After this age of indeterminate length, the Messiah will return and "eternity" will begin. There are relatively few people who are Postmillennialists these days, and I don't see much in Scripture to support this interpretation of the Millennium. [Luke 18:8; 1 Timothy 4:1; 2 Timothy 3:1-5]

Amillennialists generally take either the Historical or Idealist view and believe that the 1,000 years is symbolic of the period between the Messiah's ascension and his return. When he returns, "eternity" will begin. This is the view of most major denominations and commentators today.

Even though it's possible that there are multiple fulfillments and valid interpretations of many parts of Revelation, these three main interpretations of the Millennium are mutually exclusive. This interpreter thinks the Premillennialists are more consistent in their use of exegetical principles as applied to prophecy and therefore, are generally more correct in their conclusions than Amillennialists. I hope there is a literal Millennium. But even if it happens that there is not, I will be joyfully content with whatever the Lord has *decided to do. I hope my Amillennialists brethren can say the same in the other direction. Because dogmatic attitudes which cause God's people to refuse to fellowship with one another—merely because they disagree about the interpretation of this book or other prophesy—stem from spiritual pride and do not honor the Lord or his command to love one another. [John 13:33-34]*

Even with the explanations I've tried to incorporate—and even if you agree with my interpretation—reading this will bring you to about a number-2 level of knowledge (on a scale from 1 to 10) about the Book of Revelation. That may be all you need as far as understanding the main messages of 1) hope and eventual victory for God's people, and 2) the need to persevere in faith despite persecution and threat of death. But be aware that there is much more to learn about the book of Revelation. The notes on the various views may be confusing the first few times through—since there are so many different views and it may be difficult to keep them sorted in your mind. I highly recommend that you read a commentary (or two or three) from a viewpoint you want to understand to see a more complete and consistent presentation of it. Another reason to read various commentaries is that they propose plausible explanations for difficult verses that this interpretation doesn't include—simply because the explanations are too long or too difficult to condense into a few sentences.

The other major thing that will help you more deeply understand this book is to be thoroughly familiar with the content of the rest of the Bible. There is no substitute for having that background as a basis for understanding this book, its symbolism and its themes.

Outline

A. *A Vision of the Messiah Standing in the Midst of the Assemblies. [chapter 1]*
B. *Messages for the Seven Assemblies. [chapters 2—3]*
C. *A Vision of God on His Throne. [chapters 4—5]*
D. *The Seven Seals. [6:1—8:1]*
E. *The Seven Trumpets. [8:2—11:19]*
F. *The Dragon, the False Messiah, and the False Prophet. [chapters 12—13]*
G. *The Redeemed in Heaven. [14:1-5]*
H. *The Last Proclamation of the Good News and the Harvest of Believers. [14:6-20]*
I. *The Seven Bowls of God's Righteous Wrath. [chapters 15—16]*
J. *Babylon and Her Destruction. [17:1—19:10]*
K. *The Messiah's Second Coming. [19:11-21]*
L. *The Millennium and the Final Judgment. [chapter 20]*
M. *New Jerusalem. [21:1—22:5]*
N. *Final Warnings. [22:6-21]*

1

Preface

1 This book is a revelation that God gave to Messiah Jesus to reveal to his people about things that God has determined must soon happen. Jesus sent an angel to me—his ❖ *prophetic* ➤ servant John—to communicate these matters through symbolic visions. ❖ *Depending on how "he" is interpreted in the original text, it's possible that Jesus himself is the "angel" that communicated the visions to John—since the word ἄγγελος (angelos) can mean either "angel" or "messenger." Thus an alternate* *interpretation would be: He (God) sent a messenger (Jesus) to me—his servant John... However, at least later in the book, the angels who show him visions are clearly not Jesus. [19:9-10; 22:8-9]* ➤ 2 In this book, I've produced a written record of the things I saw and heard in those visions—which contain God's message and instructions for his people and truths about Messiah Jesus. ❖ *Alternatively, the phrase "testimony of Messiah Jesus" (in the literal text) could mean "testimony given by Messiah Jesus" which affirms God's message, or "the witness of God's people concerning Messiah Jesus and the Good News about God's way of saving people."* ➤ 3 Those who publicly **A** read God's words **B** in this book that pertain to

---

A 1:3a Few people in that time could read, so John assumes this book will be read at public meetings.

B 1:3b Literally, "words of prophecy."

both present and future events—and those who listen and obediently submit to them—are in his good favor [Luke 11:28] because his appointed time for these things to happen is near. ❖ *This is the first of seven "beatitudes" in the book. The others are in 14:13; 16:15; 19:9; 20:6; 22:7 and 14.* ➤

A. A VISION OF THE MESSIAH STANDING IN THE MIDST OF THE ASSEMBLIES

❖ *These were seven real assemblies in John's time at the end of the first century AD—and the issues addressed in the letters were real for them at that time. So the seven letters had direct relevance to the specific assemblies addressed. This is the Preterist view and is certainly true. Yet in the Scriptures, the number seven is symbolic of completeness and these seven assemblies are representative of all the assemblies that existed at that time and all the assemblies that have ever existed from the time of these letters until Jesus returns again. The Historical view says that these seven assemblies represent seven periods of history during the past 2000 years—with each of the seven assemblies typical of the assemblies in a particular historical period. There may be some truth to this perspective and there are commentaries that present this idea in detail. The Idealist view says that these seven assemblies were types that are reflected among all assemblies today—as they also were at all times in the past. If that perspective is correct, then we are to consider which of these seven types our own assembly most closely resembles and particularly take to heart our Lord's exhortations to that type. Therefore, these first three chapters had an immediate relevance to the assemblies at the end of the first century, and they have also had relevance to every assembly since then until Jesus returns. Thus Preterist, Historical, and Idealist views can all be seen to shed light on these seven messages.* ➤

Opening Greetings

4-5 I'm writing to the seven assemblies in Asia Province. ❖ *This is the Roman province named "Asia" which was part of present-day Turkey. It's clear in the letters to each assembly that the message is what the Holy Spirit is saying to all the assemblies. [2:7, 11, 17, 29; 3:6, 13, 22]* ➤ May God the Father—who truly exists, has always existed, and will always continue to exist—and the seven Spirits of God who are before his throne, [Isaiah 11:2 in the Septuagint, Revelation 4:5; and maybe 8:2] and Jesus the Messiah continue to look upon you with great favor far beyond anything you can deserve—and grant you peace and well-being. ❖ *The main interpretations of the "seven Spirits" are: 1) The Holy Spirit. 1a) (this is the most popular interpretation) a seven-fold expression of the Holy Spirit, as in Isaiah 11:2 in the Septuagint. The Hebrew text of Isaiah 11:2 lists six aspects of the Spirit; the Septuagint (the Greek translation of the Hebrew Scriptures used by Jews and believers in the first century) adds "godliness" as a seventh aspect. 1b) Others deny that the association of this verse with Isaiah 11:2 as valid, yet still hold that the "seven Spirits" represent the Holy Spirit in the completeness of his ministry with the Messiah. Elsewhere in the Scriptures, "grace and peace" only come from God. This is an argument for concluding that the "seven Spirits" are symbolic of the Holy Spirit. 2) The seven archangels of Jewish tradition listed in the apocryphal book of 1 Enoch. 3) Looking at the references to these Spirits in Revelation 3:1; 4:5; 5:6; (and 8:2) and also Zechariah 4:1-10 (the seven eyes of Yahweh), they might be a group of spirit beings or angels that have a special ministry in connection with the Messiah. Yet aside from these possible references, the word "spirits" in Revelation never refers to good angels, e.g., 16:14. ¶ Concerning the Zechariah 4:1-10 passage, some commentators see the seven-branched lampstand (i.e. menorah) with its seven lamps—which was also in the Tabernacle [Exodus 25:31-40]—as symbolic of the Holy Spirit—as in Zechariah 4:6.* ➤

Jesus the Messiah is the reliable trustworthy revealer **A** [Proverbs 14:5, 25; Jeremiah 42:5] ❖ *He reveals to humanity—through his sacrificial death—the truth about God's love for people and his holy hatred of sin. He gives this revelation throughout the New Testament Scriptures, but John is particularly talking about the revelations made in this book. [John 3:11; 32-33; 8:14; 14:6; 18:37; Revelation 3:14; 22:16]* ➤ and the first human to be permanently raised from death to eternal life—as a pattern for all others who will also be raised. [Romans 8:29; 1 Corinthians 15:20-22; Colossians 1:18; Hebrews 12:23] He is also the sovereign ruler over all kings and authorities in this world. [Psalm 89:27; Philippians 2:9-11; Revelation 17:14; 19:16] His love for us is eternal, and through his self-sacrificial death, he has freed **B** us from the penalty and power of our sins 6 and made us—his people—to be the

---

A 1:4-5a The word μάρτυς (martus) means "witness" and "martyr." In Revelation, it means someone who has been a faithful witness even to the point of suffering a martyr's death. [Revelation 2:13; 11:3, 7; 17:6]

B 1:4-5b Some manuscripts have "washed" instead of "freed," but the weight of textual evidence is for "freed" being the original.

Kingdom over which he reigns. In this Kingdom, we are all priests *[Exodus 19:6; Isaiah 61:6; 1 Peter 2:5, 9]* and kings *[Revelation 2:26; 3:21; 5:10; 20:6]* who serve God—his Father. *[Romans 12:1; Hebrews 13:15]* Therefore, may all people praise and honor him—acknowledging his absolute power and submitting to his rule forever! Yes, may it be so! ❖ *By saying these things about Jesus, John desired to remind his fellow believers—who were suffering severe persecution for their faith—that the Messiah has procured ultimate victory for them through his suffering and death.* ➤ **7** And note this, his return is imminent and will be in this manner: Everyone will see him coming in the sky—surrounded by shining clouds that display his glory and majesty. *[Daniel 7:13; Matthew 24:30; 1 Thessalonians 4:17]* Even those who caused his death will be resurrected and see him, *[Zechariah 12:10-11; John 19:37]* and all who have rejected him—from every people group in this world—will wail in terror at his coming. This is the way it will be. Yes, may it indeed be so! **8** ❖ *In affirmation of what John has just written,* ➤ Yahweh **A** says, "It is I who cause all things to begin and all things to end and have sovereign control over all that happens in between, I, who have always existed just as I exist now and will exist forever—the Omnipotent **B** God." *[Isaiah 44:6; 48:12; Revelation 1:17; 2:8; 21:6]* ❖ *Alpha and Omega, in the literal text, are the first and last letters of the Greek alphabet.* ➤

John's Vision of the Glorified Messiah

9 I, John—your fellow believer in the Messiah—am in union with Jesus, the same as you are, and share the same sufferings in this life for the sake of following him that you do. Together with you, I belong to his Kingdom and wait patiently for his return. In fact, it was because I have faithfully proclaimed God's message about Jesus that I was exiled to Patmos Island where I experienced this vision. ❖ *Tradition says it was the Emperor Domitian that exiled him there.* ➤ **10** It was on a Sunday—the Lord's day—as I was communing with the Lord in my spirit **C** that I heard someone behind me speaking in a voice that projected like the blast of a trumpet. **11** He told me, "Make a written record of the vision you are about to see—and send it to the assemblies in the seven cities of Ephesus, Smyrna, Pergamum, Thyatira, Sardis, Philadelphia, and Laodicea." ❖ *The cities are listed in the order someone would travel to each of them in a roughly circular route.* ➤ **12-13** As I turned around to see who was speaking to me, I saw a being that looked human—but who was obviously more than human *[Daniel 7:13]*—standing in the midst of seven gold stands, each of which supported a burning-wick lamp. *[Zechariah 4:2-6]* He wore a long ❖ *white* ➤ robe that hung to his feet, with a gold band **D** wrapped around his chest. *[Daniel 10:5]* ❖ *The long robe and the band or sash worn high on the chest signified high rank—and may have been symbolic of his being a high priest.* ➤ **14** His hair was white as wool or snow—and his penetrating all-seeing eyes blazed brightly like fire. **E** ❖ *This description in Daniel 7:9 is of Yahweh, "the Ancient of Days." White is also symbolic of purity and holiness.* ➤ **15** His bare feet shined like highly refined bronze that has been polished to a high sheen **F** *[Ezekiel 1:7; Daniel 10:6]* and his voice was as loud as the thundering of a great torrent of rushing water. *[Ezekiel 1:24; 43:2]* ❖ *Commentators variously say that the shining bronze feet symbolize: strength to stamp out all who oppose him, absolute justice, integrity, and splendor. The loud voice indicates awe-inspiring power. John is using a combination of images from the Hebrew Scriptures to describe the overwhelming impression of power, greatness, and awe that this person evoked from him. Fire and a furnace are symbolic of purity attained through undergoing difficulty.* ➤ **16** In the sovereign power of his right hand, he held seven stars; ❖ *Verse 20 says these represent the*

A 1:8a Literally, "lord God," some commentators believe this is referring specifically to the Messiah. "Yahweh" is the Triune God: Father, Son, and Holy Spirit.

B 1:8b "Omnipotent" means "all powerful."

C 1:10 Most commentators believe this word refers to the Holy Spirit rather than to John's human spirit, but they disagree about what John meant by the phrase "in the Spirit."

D 1:12-13 The word ζώνη (zōnē) can also mean "belt" or "sash."

E 1:14 The ancients believed that eyes radiated light to enable them to see, hence the bright blazing eyes symbolize a supernatural ability to see.

F 1:15 Or: like polished bronze that's been heated and made to glow in a furnace. The reference to "made to glow in a furnace" can be taken at face value or could refer to having been refined.

"angels" who look after the assemblies. Their being in his hand indicates that he exercises sovereign control over them—and may also refer to John 10:28. ➤ and coming straight out of his mouth was a double-edged sword blade, representing God's words of judgment. *[Isaiah 11:4; 49:2; Ephesians 6:17; Hebrews 4:12]* ❖ The double edge means his words cut two ways—producing salvation or condemnation—depending on how they are received. ➤ His face **A** was gloriously shining as bright as the noon-day sun. *[Isaiah 60:1; Daniel 10:6; Malachi 4:2; Matthew 13:43; 17:2]* ❖ This light—which is real—symbolizes God's righteousness and his holy glorious character. ➤ 17 The instant I saw him, I was paralyzed with fear, awe, and dread—and collapsed at his feet as if I were dead. *[Exodus 33:20; Isaiah 6:5; Ezekiel 1:28,. 3:23; 43:3; 44:4; Daniel 10:7-9; Acts 9:3-4]* Then I felt him lay his right hand of blessing and power on me—restoring me *[Daniel 8:18; 10:10; Matthew 17:7]*—and heard him say, "There's nothing to be afraid of! *[Genesis 26:24; Matthew 14:27]* I am the first cause and have the last word in all things. I am the eternally existing omnipotent and sovereign God who is in full control over everything. *[Isaiah 44:6; 48:12; Revelation 1:8; 2:8; 21:6; 22:13]* 18 I am the One who has self-existing life and am the source of all that lives. *[Matthew 16:16; John 1:1-3; 6:57; 14:6; Hebrews 3:12; 9:14; 10:31; 12:22]* Even though I once died, I am now alive and can never die again. I have power and authority over death itself and over all who have died. *[Hebrews 2:14]* I can control when people die and I can make the dead alive again—so there is nothing that you need fear. 19 Make a written record of all the visions you have seen and are about to see—which are about the events that are happening now among the assemblies and things that will happen later. 20 The hidden truth of the seven stars you saw in my right hand is that they represent my leaders who watch over the seven assemblies like angels, and the seven lampstands represent the seven assemblies who shine the light of God's truth in the world. *[Matthew 5:14-16]* ❖ The word ἄγγελοι (angeloi), can mean "angels" or "messengers." While it usually means the former, it is unlikely that Jesus would have dictated letters to seven angels. Commentators

have interpreted these messengers to be human leaders in the assemblies who hear from the Lord and pass on his messages of instruction to his people, or perhaps the public reader who would read his message to the people, or the messengers who would carry the letters to the assemblies, or that they represent the "prevailing spirit" or character of the assemblies. The fact that Jesus was standing among the seven lampstands in verse 13 is a comforting message to the assemblies that he is among them and in union with them during the trials they face. ➤

B. MESSAGES FOR THE SEVEN ASSEMBLIES

2

1. Ephesus

1 "Write this to the leader of the assembly in Ephesus to read to his people: I, Jesus, sovereignly control what happens to you leaders over my assemblies and I am spiritually present in the midst of the assemblies. I have this to say to you: 2 I am fully aware of every aspect of your way of life. I know that you work hard in proclaiming the Good News about me, the Messiah, and while doing that you patiently persevere in obeying me and in identifying yourself with me—despite opposition and persecution. I'm aware that you don't allow people whose ways are evil to be part of your assembly, that you examine the teachings and lifestyles of those who claim to authoritatively teach about me, and have determined that many of them are clearly not what they claim to be. 3 I know that you have endured many hardships for remaining loyal to me and that you haven't become discouraged by it all or wanted to renounce me because of it. You continue to trust me. For all this I commend you. 4 But there is one very important area where you have not been faithful. The zealous joyful self-sacrificial love you had for me and for your fellow believers when you first became believers—has died. *[Matthew 24:12]* ❖ Commentators do not agree on

---

A 1:16 The word ὄψις (opsis) can also mean "outward appearance."

whether Jesus was talking about their love for him or for their fellow believers or for both. But genuine love for Jesus is necessarily manifested in love for fellow believers, [John 13:35] so he is talking about both. It's a common situation that believers who are zealous for doctrinal purity and the expelling of heretics from their assembly often lose their proper focus and motive of love for Jesus and his people. ➤ 5 Keep on thinking back to what your love was like in the beginning and realize how far you have fallen from that exalted state of favor and devotion. The solution is to repent and start loving me and each other with the same concern and loving deeds you were doing at that time. If you fail to repent, I will punish you by removing your lampstand from its proper place. ❖ *Commentators do not agree about what this means. Some say it would be a punishment in this world— meaning their assembly would cease to be a light to their pagan neighbors or that it would be disbanded. Others think he meant they would no longer be his people and would be so judged unless they repent. 1 Corinthians 13:2 says that even if believers are excellent in all other areas but are lacking in love, they are useless for God's purposes. They cannot be spiritual lights to this world. And if they have no love for Jesus that is demonstrated to other believers, [John 13:34-35; 14:15, 23] then they are like the Pharisees whose hearts were far from God despite their knowledge and outward zeal. Love for God and his people is an essential part of our faith.* ➤ 6 But you do have this in your favor—that you hate the idolatry and immoral ways of those who follow the teaching of Nicolaus, just as I do. ❖ *It seems that the Nicolaitan sect was short-lived and our only certain knowledge of it comes from this book. Commentators believe this sect taught that it was acceptable for believers to engage in idolatry—such as the formal acknowledging of the emperor as divine in order to avoid persecution. They also taught that the body wasn't important—so sexual immorality was not something that defiled you in God's sight.* ➤ 7 If your hearts are attuned to God, heed what the Holy Spirit is saying to the assemblies in these messages! Those who remain faithful and obedient to me to the very end of their lives—despite difficulties and persecution—will obtain from me the right to eat from the tree of life and live forever in perfect fellowship with my Father and me in Heaven." *[Genesis 2:9; Revelation 22:2]* ❖ *Tradition says that the assembly in Ephesus did heed this warning and repent.* ➤

2. Smyrna

8 "Write this to the leader of the assembly in Smyrna to read to his people: I, who am the first cause and have the last word in all things, *[Isaiah 44:6; 48:12; Revelation 1:8, 17; 21:6]* who once died but am now alive and can never die again, have this to say to you: 9 I am fully aware of your suffering under persecution and your resultant physical poverty—though spiritually you are rich. I am also aware of those who slander and denounce you to the authorities—who think they are true Jews and thus God's people but are not—for they are a synagogue that unknowingly serves Satan. *[John 8:44-47; Romans 2:28-29; Philippians 3:3]* ❖ *Σατανᾶς (Satanas) "Satan" means "adversary." Satan is also frequently called the Devil, which means "slanderer" or "false accuser"—which is what some Jews were doing to the believers in Smyrna. When Jews denounced the followers of Jesus—who were originally considered to be a Jewish sect—to the Roman authorities as not being true Jews, they no longer had the legal exemption that Jews had to not worship the Emperor. Without that protection, the believers were persecuted as atheistic traitors.* ➤ 10 I want you to trust me and not fear the suffering that you are about to go through in the near future. I will allow Satan to have some of you put into prison—awaiting execution—to test if your faith in me will endure, and you will suffer this persecution for a short period. But continue to trust and obey me—even if they execute you—and I will give you eternal life as a prize. ❖ *Commentators do not agree about the meaning of "ten days" in the literal text. Some think it means "a short limited period of time." Some think it's an allusion to the "short test" in Daniel 1:12— which was followed by more major trials later. Others think that it means a severe persecution since for some it ended in death. But if it ended in death, the period of suffering was short. Imprisonment was usually only for the purpose of awaiting trial or execution—and not seen as a punishment in itself. They would most likely be tried for not worshipping the emperor as a god. If they submitted to doing this, they could be freed. The test was to see if they would remain totally loyal to Jesus and refuse to worship a false god—even if it meant a painful death. Many such executions took place in Smyrna— the most famous one being Bishop Polycarp's, some decades later. Tradition says that Polycarp was a disciple of the Apostle John.* ➤ 11 If your hearts are attuned to God, heed what the Holy Spirit is saying to the

assemblies in these messages! Those who remain faithful and obedient to me to the very end of their lives—despite difficulties and persecution—will in no way experience the 'second death' in Hell, eternally separated from 'true life.' *[Revelation 20:14; 21:8]*

3. Pergamum

12 "Write this to the leader of the assembly in Pergamum to read to his people: I—who speak God's words of judgment—have this to say to you: 13 I'm aware that you live in the center of Emperor worship in Asia Province—where Satan's influence dominates everything. ❖ *Commentators suggest that the reference to "Satan's throne," in the literal text, was the temple dedicated to the worship of the Roman Emperor. Pergamum was also known for its worship of the serpent god Asclepius (a god of healing) and for a giant altar overlooking the city dedicated to Zeus, the chief of the Roman gods. Other explanations have also been offered. Some believe that the higher-ranking "princes" among demons rule over certain geographic areas. Satan, the chief of these princes, is a finite being who can only be in one place at a time. He might have chosen to locate his center of influence at that time in Pergamum.* ➤ I know that you refused to renounce your sole allegiance to me, even when your lives were at stake and they martyred Antipas who—through his words and deeds—faithfully witnessed to the reality of my being Lord in his life. ❖ *Nothing is known about this Antipas, but a legend about him from centuries later says that he was slowly roasted to death in a bronze bowl because he refused to worship the emperor. Jesus referred to him in the literal text as his "faithful witness"—which is Jesus' own title—indicating that Antipas was in some way very much like himself. [Revelation 1:5]* ➤ And you remain faithful to me—even in that city where Satan himself dominates many of the inhabitants and makes your lives difficult. 14 But there are some important areas where you have not been faithful. You have allowed people to remain in your assembly who follow the ways of the prophet Balaam—as in the days of Moses. He showed Balak, King of Moab, how to entice the Israelites to sin by participating in feasts with pagans to honor and worship of their false gods, and by indulging in sexual immorality. *[Numbers 22:5, 7; 25:1-3; 31:16; Deuteronomy 23:4]* ❖ *See the notes at 2 Peter 2:15 and Jude 11*

about Balaam. Commentators believe there were false teachers among them who were saying that believers could compromise and get along with their pagan neighbors who worshipped the emperor—and still be faithful to Jesus.* ➤ 15 You've also been tolerating some in your assembly who follow the teachings of Nicolaus. ❖ *See the note at Revelation 2:6. Those who followed the teachings of the Nicolaitans and those who followed the ways of Balaam were very similar in promoting compromise by offering worship to the emperor and engaging in sexual immorality.* ➤ 16 So you had better repent and rid your assembly of these people, *[1 Corinthians 5:12-13]* or I will come soon to fight against them with pronouncements of God's judgment. ❖ *Jesus' words have power to create or curse. See Deuteronomy chapter 28 for the kinds of punishments he might have inflicted on them. It seems to be implied that those in the assembly who have not been active followers of Nicolaus or participators in idolatry or immorality—but have tolerated them—will in some way also be punished, though the brunt of the punishment would be against those who taught and did evil.* ➤ 17 If your hearts are attuned to God, heed what the Holy Spirit is saying to the assemblies in these messages! To those who remain faithful and obedient to me to the very end of their lives—despite difficulties and persecution—I will give some of the unseen manna. *[John 6:30-51]* ❖ *Jesus himself is the unseen manna—the Bread from Heaven which imparts eternal life. To have the hidden manna is to have a vital relationship with him—being spiritually joined to him and to his eternal divine life.* ➤ I will also give them each a white stone with a new unique name for the person who receives it—and only that person and I will know what that new name is. ❖ *Commentators variously say a white stone is symbolic of: 1) a verdict of innocence, 2) divine favor, 3) victory, and 4) admission into his banquet in Heaven. The new unique name is indicative of the believer's uniqueness and probably means that they will each receive a special promise or blessing—as happened to people in the Scriptures whose names God changed (i.e. Jacob, Abram, Sarai, and Simon). [Genesis 17:5-8; 15-16; 32:28-29; Isaiah 62:2; Mark 3:16; Luke 6:15; John 1:42]* ➤

4. Thyatira

18 "Write this to the leader of the assembly in Thyatira to read to his people: I, God's Son—who sees everything and stamps out all who oppose me—have this to say to you: 19 I'm aware that your ways are good, that

out of love for me and your fellow believers you continue to be loyal to me and lovingly meet the needs of others—despite persecution—and I know that you are excelling in these things even more than you did when you first became my followers. For these things I commend you. 20 But there is one important area where you have not been faithful. You tolerate that influential woman in your assembly with her false prophecies. Like evil Queen Jezebel of old, she seduces my people to participate in idolatrous pagan feasts and sexual immorality. *[1 Kings 16:31; 21:25-26; 2 Kings 9:22, 30]* 21 She has refused to repent of her immoral ways—even though I've given her ample time. 22 So observe her punishment as I make her bedridden with serious illness so she can't continue to deceive my people. And unless they repent, I will also afflict great suffering upon all who have committed adultery with her. ❖ *"Committed adultery with her" could possibly refer to unfaithfulness to Jesus, as well as sexual sin related to idol worship.* ➤ 23 I will, in fact, kill off all who have followed her so all the assemblies will realize that I closely examine the hidden thoughts and desires A of my people to see if they are faithful to me or reject my commands—and I reward or punish them accordingly. *[Job 34:33; Psalm 7:9-10; 62:12; Proverbs 24:12; Isaiah 40:10; 59:18; 62:11; Jeremiah 17:10; Matthew 16:27; 25:31-46; Romans 2:6; 2 Corinthians 5:10; Galatians 6:7-8; 2 Timothy 4:14; Revelation 2:23; 20:13]* 24-25 But to my people in Thyatira who have rejected her evil teachings and ways and have not delved into the so-called 'deep and secret things' that are really Satan's teachings, I commend you and have no further requirement to place on you—except to continue faithfully as you have been doing until I return. ❖ *It's possible that the "deep things of Satan" (in the literal text) is what they actually called them, and that this false prophet was saying a believer's spiritual life is not affected by what they do with their bodies—so they should experience the deepest evils taught by Satan to demonstrate that they are unable to affect their trust in God's undeserved favor. This was the teaching of Gnostic heretics in the second century. Another view is that she called her teachings the "deep things of God," and Jesus*

was saying they were really of Satan. ➤ 26-27 Those who remain faithful and obedient to me to the very end of their lives—despite difficulties and persecution—will share with me the authority my Father has given me over all the peoples of this world. **They will have absolute power to shatter all opposition to God's will—like an iron rod smashes a clay pot.** ❖ *This is a loose quote of Psalm 2:8-9. The expression to "rule with an iron rod" (in the literal text) means to "destroy"—not to "rule with absolute power" as most English speakers would guess. [Isaiah 30:14; Jeremiah 19:11; Revelation 12:5; 19:15]* ➤ 28 They will also receive the Morning Star. ❖ *The Morning Star is the planet Venus—which is often seen just before dawn as the beautiful herald of the end of darkness and the beginning of a new day. This is figurative of the end of the reign of sin and the start of the new age when the Messiah rules and all is in conformity to his will. [Luke 1:78; 2 Peter 1:19; 1 John 3:2] Some think this is a symbol of victory and domination. But Jesus declares himself to be the Morning Star. [Revelation 22:16] And this promise probably means that those who receive the Morning Star will experience an intimate relationship with him. There is no greater gift anyone could receive, for in him is everything. All the promises in all of these letters apply to all believers who make it to Heaven.* ➤ 29 If your hearts are attuned to God, heed what the Holy Spirit is saying to the assemblies in these messages

3

5. Sardis

1 "Write this to the leader of the assembly in Sardis to read to his people: I who have the fullness of God's Holy Spirit *[Revelation 1:4-5]* and sovereignly control what happens to my assemblies *[Revelation 1:16]*—have this to say to you: I'm fully aware of your ways. You have a good reputation among the pagans in your community, but the way you live proves to me that you are all near spiritual death.

2 "You are supposed to be vigilantly alert for Satan's schemes to deceive you, but you are guilty of sleeping on duty. So wake up and revive what little faith you have left—for you are on the verge of becoming totally useless to me. None of your ways are

---

A 2:23 The Greek idiom—which originally comes from Hebrew, e.g., Psalm 7:9—is literally, "search kidneys and hearts." It means to closely examine a person's inner thoughts and desires.

completely faithful to God's will—for you have compromised with the enemy by trying to fit in with the pagan community around you. 3 Review the teachings that you heard and gladly received when you first believed in me, then repent of your ways and obey all those things you were taught. [Acts 20:20-21; 2 Timothy 1:13-14; Titus 1:9] If you fail to respond to this warning, I will come to you suddenly—catching you off guard as a thief would—and punish you for your rebellion. [Matthew 24:42-44; Mark 13:33-37; Luke 12:39-40; 1 Thessalonians 5:2-4; 2 Peter 3:10; Revelation 16:15] 4 There are a few individuals in my assembly in Sardis who have not defiled themselves with sinful compromise and rebellion against my will. They remain pure and worthy of my favor because of their continued union with me. They will continue to have intimate fellowship with me as they faithfully minister in moral purity and triumph over temptation. 5 Those who remain faithful and obedient to me to the very end of their lives—despite difficulties and persecution—will become like those few among you who have remained faithful. They too will be pure and have my favor because of their union with me—and I will not delete their names from the official list of those who will live forever in Heaven. A [Exodus 32:32-33; Psalm 69:28; Revelation 20:12] And on Judgment Day, I will acknowledge to my Father and his angels that they truly belong to me. [Matthew 10:32; Luke 12:8] 6 If your hearts are attuned to God, heed what the Holy Spirit is saying to the assemblies in these messages!"

6. Philadelphia

7 "Write this to the leader of the assembly in Philadelphia to read to his people: I—who am the Holy One [Mark 1:24; John 6:69] ❖ This was a title for God in the Hebrew Scriptures. [Isaiah 40:25; Habakkuk 3:3] ➤ and the Genuine Messiah B—am faithful to my promises and have total control over the royal household in Heaven. I am the only one who determines who will enter and who will not. [Job 12:14; Isaiah 22:22] I have this to say to you: ❖ The Jewish community in Philadelphia had expelled believers in Jesus from their synagogue, thus depriving them of the legal protection that Jews had to not worship the emperor and to practice their faith unmolested. Jesus was reassuring them that it was he—not the local Jewish community—who determined who was and was not part of God's people. ➤ 8 I'm fully aware of your ways. I want you to know that I have opened the door to Heaven so you can enter—and no one can keep you out. ❖ Another interpretation is that the open door is an opportunity for ministry in their city. ➤ I know you are few and so have little influence in your city, but you have remained obedient to my will and have never hesitated to proclaim that you belong to me. 9 Watch, for I will cause those Jews who falsely claim to be my people—but who actually serve Satan by persecuting you—to humble themselves before you and acknowledge that you are my beloved people. [Isaiah 45:14; 60:14] ❖ This is interpreted two ways. 1) On Judgment Day, God will force them to do this. Or 2) God will cause them to become believers and they will join those whom they had previously persecuted. ➤ 10 Since you have remained faithful and obedient while patiently enduring persecution—just as I commanded you to do [Matthew 10:22; 24:13; Mark 13:13; Romans 2:7; 1 Timothy 4:16; 2 Timothy 2:10-12; Hebrews 10:36; James 1:12]—I will protect your faith from Satan's attacks [John 17:15; 2 Thessalonians 3:3; 1 Peter 1:5; 1 John 5:18] during the period of suffering and testing that is about to happen to all in the world. ❖ There are two main interpretations of this—which are not necessarily mutually exclusive: 1) There would shortly be a time of persecution that they and all believers in the world would experience in their lifetime. 2) This refers to the Great Tribulation that will happen just before Jesus returns. There are also two interpretations pertaining to the Great Tribulation that he would 2a) protect them "during" that time (i.e., they would live through it), or 2b) protect them "from" that time (i.e., by removing them from this world via the "rapture"). See the footnote at 1 Thessalonians 4:17. ➤ 11 I will return soon. [Revelation 22:7] ❖ What does Jesus mean by "soon"? Clearly, first-century believers believed that he would return during their

---

A 3:5 This seems to say that from Jesus' point of view, it is possible for someone who is already saved—with their name already written in the Book of Life—to lose their salvation.

B 3:7 "Holy and true" (in the literal text) are also ascribed to God the Father in Revelation 6:10.

lifetimes—and nearly every generation of believers since has thought the same. Perhaps this is what he intended his people to think so we would always live prepared for his immediate return. [Matthew 24:42; 44; Mark 13:35; Luke 12:40; 1 Thessalonians 5:2; 2 Peter 3:10] The meaning of the word "soon" in God's thinking—to whom 1,000 years is like a day [Psalm 90:4; 2 Peter 3:8]—does not have to match our normally much-shorter interpretation of the word. ➤ Keep clinging to your correct understanding, faith, obedience, and confident expectation—as you have been doing—so no one can lure you away from them and thus cause you to be disqualified for obtaining the prize of eternal life. 12 Those who remain faithful and obedient to me to the very end of their lives—despite difficulties and persecution—I will establish as important permanent parts of God's living Temple which is composed of his people. They will always enjoy being in his presence and never leave it. I will make it clear to all that they belong to my God and are citizens of New Jerusalem—which will come down from Heaven to the New Earth [Isaiah 62:2; Revelation 21:2]—and that they have a special relationship with me and fully share every aspect of my holy character which will be revealed when I return. 13 If your hearts are attuned to God, heed what the Holy Spirit is saying to the assemblies in these messages!"

7. Laodicea

14 "Write this to the leader of the assembly in Laodicea to read to his people: I, who am the 'Amen,' ❖ This could refer to Isaiah 65:16 where God calls himself "elohim amen" which means "the God whose name is 'Amen'" (as in the New English Bible and the Revised English Bible), but is usually translated "God of truth" or "the faithful God." Or, it could mean that Jesus is the one who affirms the truth about God. ➤ the reliable trustworthy revealer, ❖ See the last note in Revelation 1:5 and the first footnote in Revelation 1:5. ➤ the first cause and supreme ruler of God's entire creation, [Colossians 1:15-18; Revelation 1:17-18] have this to say to you: 15 I am fully aware of your ways. Like the tepid lukewarm water that flows into your city—which you always complain about—you are neither cold enough to spiritually refresh my people nor hot enough to spiritually heal the sick, like

hot medicinal springs heal the body. Your deeds are useless for my purposes. I sincerely wish you were more refreshing or healing in your so-called 'ministry.' ❖ The other interpretation is that "cold" and "hot" refer to their spiritual state of being hostile or zealous. The difficulty is to know why he might prefer them "cold" or hostile. Perhaps because such people are often easier to bring into the Kingdom than those who are merely indifferent. ➤ 16 But because you are neither hot nor cold—but are disgustingly useless and 'lukewarm'—you are about to make me vomit, and that will be the end of our relationship. 17 You claim to have attained both material and spiritual wealth by your own efforts—and think that you lack nothing. But your true spiritual condition is that you are pathetically impoverished in faith and proper understanding, you are blind to the truth, and are also embarrassingly naked with respect to righteousness. 18 My advice is that you should come to me to obtain spiritual riches—such as faith that has passed through the fire of persecution and has thus been purified so it's more precious than gold. [1 Peter 1:7] And also obtain the pure white garment of my righteousness—which is the only thing that can cover your sinful shame and humiliation. And come for my healing salve to restore your spiritual insight and understanding—so you can perceive the truth. [Psalm 119:18] These are obtainable without cost by those who recognize their need and entrust themselves to me to provide them. [Isaiah 55:1] 19 My reprimand and disciplining punishment are actually a sign of my genuine love for you. [Job 5:17; Psalm 94:12; Proverbs 3:11-12; 1 Corinthians 11:32; Hebrews 12:5-6, 10] My love for all my people causes me to do this—so they may become pure and have intimate fellowship with me. So repent and become zealous to obey me. It's not too late. ❖ God's love is not a blind sentimental love that moves him to be tolerant of sin—which is rebellion against his will. His love means that he intends the best eternal outcome for those he loves—and that best means that they must be transformed into people he can have an eternal intimate relationship with. This love moved him to send Jesus to suffer the eternal consequences of sin in our place. But people who refuse to accept the opportunity he offers to be changed into people that he can accept for eternity are, in effect, rejecting *his loving outreach and saying that they either believe Jesus' death was not needed or is not wanted—which is a rejection of all that God is. And God will honor this rejection by sending them to the only place in the universe where he will tolerate such people existing for eternity—which is a place totally separated from his presence in Hell.* ➤ 20 I'm waiting for you to fully open your hearts to me. If you are able to hear my request and respond by asking me to come in and be the center of your life, I will enter and we will experience joyful intimate fellowship together. 21 Those who remain faithful and obedient to me to the very end of their lives despite difficulties and persecution—just as I overcame temptation and the power of sin and death—will share my authority to rule, just as I share my Father's authority to rule. 22 If your hearts are attuned to God, heed what the Holy Spirit is saying to the assemblies in these messages!"

C. A VISION OF GOD ON HIS THRONE

❖ *This section relates a vision of God sitting on his throne, and the seven seals that only the Lamb (Jesus) is worthy to open. From an Idealist viewpoint, this section appears to span the entire age from the time of the vision [4:1] until the Judgment Day [6:16-17] when the saints will be in glory in Heaven after the Great Tribulation. [7:13-17] They see the opening of the six seals in chapter 6—and also the trumpets in chapters 8 and 9—to be descriptive of judgments spanning the entire period between Jesus' first and second coming. But Futurists see the judgments of the seals as sequentially preceding the judgments of the trumpets in chapter 8, and as happening shortly before Jesus returns to judge the world.* ➤

4

The Throne Room in Heaven

1 After he finished saying these things, I looked up and saw an open doorway into Heaven. Then I heard the same person with the trumpet-like voice speak to me again. He said, "Come up here. A I want to show you some things that will happen later on." 2 Instantly, I was in total communion with the Lord in my spirit and had a vivid vision. I saw a glorious throne in Heaven with an even more glorious Divine Being sitting on it. *[Ezekiel 1:26-28; 10:1]* 3 The Divine Being shone in brilliant multicolored light like precious jewels, and a rainbow as brilliant as an emerald encircled B the throne.

❖ *Some commentators say the "rainbow" was a single color, emerald green, which symbolizes hope and God's undeserved favor. Ladd speculates that it alludes to the rainbow in Genesis 9:12-17—which was a sign of God's covenant to never again destroy the world with water. As such, it could be a sign of God's mercy and patience in judgment until the Last Day.* ➤ 4 Also surrounding the throne were 24 subordinate thrones, each with an elder sitting in them. ❖ *These may represent the twelve tribes of Israel and the twelve apostles, symbolic of the leaders of God's people—who themselves represent all of his redeemed people. The IVP commentary says they are the heavenly counterparts of the 24 orders of priests that served in the earthly Temple. [1 Chronicles chapters 24—25] Other commentators think they are angelic beings and not redeemed humanity. Many other possibilities are also offered by commentators.* ➤ They were dressed in pure white robes ❖ *representing the Messiah's righteousness that covered their sins (if they are human, otherwise they just represent purity and holiness)* ➤ and each also wore a gold victory-wreath crown. ❖ *The crowns and thrones may be symbolic of redeemed humanity's sharing of Jesus the Messiah's rule, or just symbols of heavenly rulers. Since they wore victory-wreath crowns (symbols of victory) rather than diadems (crowns symbolizing the authority to rule), this interpreter leans toward the view that these elders were among the redeemed. This same kind of victory-wreath crown is mentioned in 1 Corinthians 9:25; Philippians 4:1; 2 Timothy 4:8; James 1:12; 1 Peter 5:4; and Revelation 2:10; and it usually—though not always—symbolizes victory or a prize, as opposed to authority to rule.* ➤ 5 Frightening bolts of lightning and peals C of thunder emanated from the throne. *[Exodus 19:16; Revelation 11:19; 16:18]* ❖ *These symbolize the awesome unapproachable majesty and power of God.* ➤ Directly in front of the throne were seven burning torches which are the seven spirits of God.

❖ *See the note in Revelation 1:4 about the seven spirits.* ➤ 6 Surrounding the throne was

---

A 4:1 Some dispensationalists take this command to refer to the rapture, but many do not.

B 4:3 Or possibly arched over the throne.

C 4:5 The word φωναί (phōnai) can also be translated "voices" or "sounds."

spread a completely transparent shiny surface like an immense sea, bright as crystal. **A** *[Ezekiel 1:22]* ❖ *There are many interpretations of this sea. e.g., Caird interprets it as a barrier that those who are saved must pass through to enter Heaven. Osborne says this sea "alludes to the waters in Genesis 1:7 and the bronze 'sea' (pool) in Solomon's Temple, [1 Kings 7:23-26] and also the 'expanse, sparkling like ice and awesome,' above the living creatures in Ezekiel 1:22. It is a major metaphor for the majesty of God." So some see it as a symbol of God's majesty and transcendence, others that it shows the separation between his holiness and sinful humanity. These interpretations are not necessarily mutually exclusive.* ➤ Arrayed closely **B** on four sides of the throne were four unique beings covered all over with eyes. *[Isaiah 6:2-3; Ezekiel 1:4-21; 10:1-17]* ❖ *There are many posited interpretations of these four beings, but they may be a high order of angels who attend the throne. They may be the cherubim, although the description John gives differs at points with the description of the cherubim in Ezekiel. The vision may be symbolic and the differences may not be important.* ➤ **7** The first unique being was like a lion, the second like a young bull, the third had a face like a man, and the fourth was an eagle that was flying. ❖ *Some commentators think these descriptions were characteristic of their entire bodies while others think they only describe their heads. Hughes thinks they represent all living created beings, symbolized by the "king" of their kind (i.e. wild beasts, domesticated beasts, human beings, and birds) and their eyes indicate God's all-seeing interest in and awareness of everything all creatures do. However, this leaves out sea creatures. Mounce says they represent strength, ability to serve, intelligence, and swiftness to serve. [Psalm 103:20] Other commentators have other explanations. In short, no one knows for sure what they may represent.* ➤ **8** These beings each had six wings with eyes all over their bodies, even under their wings. ❖ *They also resemble the seraphim described in Isaiah 6:2-3 and the cherubim in Ezekiel 10:12. Their eyes are probably symbolic of an all-seeing ability.* ➤ They repeatedly proclaim, day and night, "Holy, holy, holy is Yahweh, the Omnipotent God, who has always existed just as he is now—and will continue to exist forever!" *[Isaiah 6:3; Revelation 1:8]* **9** And every time these unique beings honor the eternally living God in this way— proclaiming their praise and thanks to him as he sits on his throne—**10** the 24 elders prostrate themselves and lay **C** down their victory-wreath crowns before his throne as they worship him and acknowledge that their authority comes only from him. They say, **11** "Only you, our Lord and God, are worthy to be praised and honored and to have every living being willingly acknowledge and submit to your omnipotent power. For you are the creator of everything that exists—and everything continues to exist only because you so will it." ❖ *Those who worshipped the Roman emperor Domitian used the words "you are worthy," and called him "our lord and god." This vision was telling the believers in John's time that these words were only to be used of the one true God.* ➤

5

Worshipping God and the Lamb in Heaven

1 Then I saw that God, sitting on his throne, was holding out a scroll in his right hand. The scroll had writing on both sides of the material, filled with his decrees about what must happen, but was tightly rolled and held closed with seven seals so no one could read it. ❖ *Commentators say the seven seals indicate it was sealed by God and that his decrees in it are complete and unchangeable. They do not agree about what the scroll represents—though many think it contains God's plans for judgment and the events that usher in the new age—or whether all seven seals had to be broken before the contents of the scroll could be read or not. But seals on a scroll would normally be along the exposed straight edge of the scroll—meaning that all seven would need to be broken before the scroll could be opened. [Ezekiel 2:9-10; Isaiah 29:11]* ➤ **2** An angel of great power announced with a voice that reached the limits of creation, "Is there anyone morally worthy and qualified to break the seals and open the scroll that proclaim God's decrees for mankind?" **3** But there was no created being in Heaven, on Earth, among the dead, or anywhere in creation who was worthy to

---

A **4:6a** The word κρύσταλλος (krustallos) can also be translated "ice."

B **4:6b** One commentator thinks these beings may be an integral part of the throne itself.

C **4:10** The word βάλλω (ballō) has a wide range of meaning, including: "throw," "put," "give," "offer," etc.

open the scroll or read it. ❖ *Angels have no right to be involved in the judgment of humanity; and because of sin, no human is worthy.* ➤ 4 Then I was overcome with grief and began to cry since no one was found worthy to open the scroll or read it. ❖ *Mounce suggests that John wept because this meant God's plan for creation would be frustrated. Hughes thinks he grieved over humanity's unworthiness.* ➤ 5 But one of the 24 elders told me, "There's no need to cry. The one called the 'Lion of Judah' [Genesis 49:9] and the 'Root ❖ i.e., descendant ➤ of David' [Isaiah 11:1, 10] ❖ These are both Messianic titles.* ➤ has defeated the power of sin and death—and so is worthy to break the seven seals and open the scroll." [John 5:22] 6 Then I saw a Lamb [Isaiah 53:7; John 1:29, 36; 1 Corinthians 5:7; 1 Peter 1:19] ❖ who is the Messiah, God's sacrificial sin offering for humanity ➤ standing in the midst of the throne—inside the circle of the four unique beings and the outer circle of the 24 elders. ❖ The throne is evidently more than an ornate chair. God the Father is still seated in it, yet the Lamb is clearly right next to him in the center of the throne area which is bounded by the four unique beings. ➤ This Lamb was clearly alive, but looked as though he had been killed as a sacrifice. He had seven horns [Daniel chapter 8] ❖ which symbolize his omnipotent power A [Matthew 28:18] ➤ and seven eyes which are the seven spirits of God [Revelation 1:4] that he sends out to every part of the Earth. [Zechariah 3:9; 4:10] ❖ That the Holy Spirit is the Spirit of the Messiah himself—not just of God the Father—is seen in Acts 16:7; Romans 8:9; and Galatians 4:6. The sending of the seven spirits throughout the Earth speaks of his omniscience B and also of the outpouring of the Spirit to the ends of the Earth. [Acts 1:8] ➤ 7 He approached and took the scroll from God the Father's right hand. ❖ God's hand represents his power [Psalm 17:14; 21:8; 44:2; 74:11] and his right hand represents the righteous use of his omnipotent C power. [Psalm 48:10; Isaiah 41:10] The transfer of the scroll indicates the Lamb's right to judge and rule over all of creation. [Matthew 28:18; John 17:1-2] ➤ 8 Then the

four unique beings and the 24 elders all prostrated themselves before the Lamb in submissive worship—each of them holding a lyre ❖ which was used for singing praises and thanksgiving and prophesying [1 Samuel 10:5; 1 Chronicles 25:1, 3, 6; 2 Chronicles 5:12; 29:25; Nehemiah 12:27; Psalm 33:2; 43:4; 150:3] ➤ and a gold bowl filled with burning incense which symbolizes the prayers of God's people. [Psalm 141:2; Revelation 8:3] ❖ The prayers of God's people—in addition to being efficacious for accomplishing God's work—are like sweet-smelling incense that is pleasing to him. Burning incense was a prescribed part of Jewish worship. [Exodus 30:1-8; 34-38; Deuteronomy 33:10; Luke 1:10] Though symbolism can be abused, Jewish worship abounded with it. Why do many assemblies today shy away from the use of symbolism, incense, or other pleasing fragrances and even musical instruments to enhance the beauty and richness in worship? All these things were commanded by God for his people to use in worship in the Hebrew Scriptures. ➤ 9 They spontaneously sang this new song: [Psalm 33:3; 40:3; 96:1; 98:1; 144:9; 149:1; Isaiah 42:10] ❖ Note that it was a new song, probably inspired at that moment by the Holy Spirit with whom they were in perfect union and unhindered communication. ➤ "You alone are worthy to take the scroll and break the seals because at great personal cost, you saved people from every tribe, language, ethnic group, and culture D from the fate of eternal death by your own self-sacrificial death. E [1 Corinthians 6:20; 1 Peter 1:18-19] 10 You have transformed them [2 Corinthians 5:17; Revelation 21:5] to be holy citizens of God's Kingdom who serve him as priests [Exodus 19:6; 1 Peter 2:9; Revelation 1:6; 20:6] and who will rule with you on Earth forever." [Genesis 1:26-28; 2 Timothy 2:12; Revelation 20:6]

11 Then I noticed uncountable millions F of angels surrounding the circle of elders and the unique beings and the throne. [Daniel 7:10] 12 In roaring response, they proclaimed, "The Lamb who was killed in sacrifice is worthy to be praised, honored, and exalted

---

A 5:6a Passages where horns depict power are: Deuteronomy 33:17; 1 Kings 22:11; Psalm 18:2.

B 5:6b Omniscience means that he knows everything.

C 5:7 Omnipotent means that he is infinitely powerful.

D 5:9a The word ἔθνος (ethnos)—usually translated "nation"—does not have the meaning usually assigned to that word today. It means unique people group, whether defined by language, ethnicity, or culture.

E 5:9b The literal phrase "by your blood" means "by your substitutional sacrificial death." [Leviticus 17:11] See the note about this phrase at Ephesians 2:13.

F 5:11 The largest single number in Greek is 10,000. The text literally says, "10,000 of (i.e., times) 10,000 and thousands of thousands." This is not meant to be calculated out, but merely indicates a huge uncountable number.

for his power, wealth, wisdom, strength, and glorious character!" *[1 Chronicles 29:10-13]* ❖ *Creatures can praise, honor, and exalt him, but he already possesses all power, wealth, wisdom, strength and glory. [Matthew 28:18; John 1:14; 17:5; 1 Corinthians 1:24; 2 Corinthians 8:9; Ephesians 3:8]* ➤ 13 Then every created being in Heaven, on Earth, under the Earth, **A** on the sea, and under water also responded, "May it be forever true that all of creation will praise and honor God and the Lamb—and will recognize their glory and joyfully submit to their dominion!" ❖ *The timing of this acclamation is uncertain. When every created being on Earth will do this is in the next age after the judgment—when all evil has been removed from creation. Yet the seven seals are not yet broken—which is before the judgment and next age. The timing of prophecy often spans different times. It's possible the first part of this vision depicts a scene in Heaven before the seals are broken and the later part—starting at verse 11—could depict a time in the next age. The phrases "and I looked," "then I looked," "and I saw," and "then I saw" (in the literal text) often mark transitions between visions in this book. Ladd considers this verse to be merely poetic language expressing the universality of Jesus' rule.* ➤ 14 The four unique beings kept affirming each assertion with, "Yes, may it be so!" And the elders again prostrated themselves in submissive worship before God and the Lamb.

D. THE SEVEN SEALS

6

Seal 1: The White Horse of War and Conquest

1 Then the Lamb broke the one of the seven seals on the scroll and one of the four unique beings thunderously commanded, "Come forth!" **B** ❖ *The scroll itself could not be unrolled and read until all seven seals were broken. So the events associated with the breaking of the seals precede the reading and execution of the divine decrees written on it.* ➤

2 Suddenly, a white horse appeared with a rider who held a bow. He received a victory-wreath crown and went to Earth to fight and conquer. ❖ *Commentators are divided on what this horse and rider represent. Some have thought it was the Messiah because of the similarities to Revelation 19:11. Hendriksen also sees the Messiah here because of the bow and the images in Psalm 45:3-5; Habakkuk 3:8-9; and Isaiah 41:2. Lenski and others think it represents the message of the Good News, with the bow and crown representing victory. But the Word of God is usually symbolized by a sword—i.e., the sword of the Spirit. Ladd says the symbolism of the four horses is based on Zechariah 6:1-8, (see also Zechariah 1:7-11) and arguing from the symbolism of the color white throughout the Scriptures representing good, also concludes that the white horseman represents the message of the Good News being spread throughout the world and it's eventual conquest. Some interpret the white horseman as the anti-messiah. Others say all four horsemen are human enemies of God to whom he gives permission to wreak death and destruction on Earth as part of his punishment for sinful humanity's rebellion. (Some draw a parallel with Luke 21:9-11 where Jesus predicts wars, revolutions, plagues, and famines. See also Jeremiah 15:2 and Ezekiel 5:12.) With this latter interpretation, the bow is a weapon of violence, the crown is permission to rule—however corruptly—and the white horse symbolizes victorious conquest. Roman readers of John's time would have identified the rider on the white horse as a Parthian archer—Rome's most-dreaded enemy—and clearly a symbol of war and conquest.* ➤

Seal 2: The Red Horse of Civil War and Bloodshed

3 Then the Lamb broke the second seal on the scroll and the second unique being commanded, "Come forth!" 4 A bright red horse appeared whose rider received a large sword and the power to cause civil wars in which people slaughter each other on a large scale. ❖ *Hendriksen—an Idealist—says this represents religious persecution and that the sword could be a sacrificial knife. Others say the red horse represents international war or bloodshed.* ➤

A 5:13 Since this is a future where everyone on Earth will praise God and the Lamb, it's not clear what "under the Earth" means unless it means animals that live underground. In other contexts, it means the "world of the dead," but that doesn't fit the context here. Will living animal also have the intelligence to praise God? Perhaps, or maybe this is just a figurative way of expressing the universal response of all creatures

capable of it. Some think that "under the Earth" refers to Satan and his demons and those in Hell.

B 6:1 Some commentators believe that the shout, "Come!" (in the literal text) is a plea to the Messiah to come—and not a command to the horsemen. Some believe the command was to John to "come and see," but John was already observing and the words "and see" are only in a few manuscripts.

Seal 3: The Black Horse of Famine and Death

5 When the Lamb broke the third seal on the scroll, the third unique being commanded, "Come forth!" And a black horse appeared whose rider held a balancing scale used for weighing food. 6 I heard a voice coming somewhere from among the four unique beings announcing, "A quart of wheat flour or three quarts of barley flour will cost a full-day's pay. ❖ *These were high prices such that a common laborer could barely feed himself and a small family if they ate all he earned. But most families were not small—so many would starve. This was between 8-16 times the normal cost for these staples (commentators give various figures).* ➤ But you are not allowed to harm the olive trees and grape vines that produce oil and wine." ❖ *Lenski argues that there was plenty of food available to the rich, but it was not affordable to the common man. So this horse represents the unequal distribution of wealth and food in the world. The rich would be comfortable while many of the poor starve because of famine. Oil and wine were also staples—not luxuries—but the poor could no longer afford them. Hendriksen agrees and sees the poor as mainly representing believers.* ➤

Seal 4: The Pale Greenish-Gray Horse of Death

7 When the Lamb broke the fourth seal on the scroll, the fourth unique being commanded, "Come forth!" 8 And a pale greenish-gray horse appeared ❖ *the color of a Caucasian corpse* ➤ whose rider was Death itself—with Hell **A** following close behind. They received permission to kill a quarter of the Earth's population through fighting, starvation, epidemic disease, and wild animals. *[Leviticus 26:25-26; Deuteronomy 32:24-25; Jeremiah 14:12; 21:6; 24:10; 27:8; Ezekiel 5:17; 6:11-12; 7:15; 12:16; 14:12-13, 21; 33:27]* ❖ *Even though permission is given to these horsemen so that punishment for evil and rebellion against God may be executed, certain limits are set in the hope that those who survive will take these events as warnings to repent.* ➤

Seal 5: Martyrs for the Faith

9 When the Lamb broke the fifth seal on the scroll, I saw in a vision all the people who had been killed because of their faithful obedience to God's word and their witness and loyalty to Jesus the Messiah. God considered their deaths to be pleasing self-sacrifices offered up to him. *[Romans 12:1; 2 Timothy 4:6]* ❖ *For many, their loyalty took the form of refusing to acknowledge the Roman emperor as a god and refusing to offer even perfunctory worship to him just to save their own lives. The meaning of being "under the altar"—in the literal text—is that their deaths were considered holy sacrifices.* ➤ 10 They all called out to God, "Lord of the universe, you are sovereign over all things, you are holy and always keep your promises! How much longer will it be before you execute your end-time judgment against those of Earth whose citizenship will never be in Heaven? When will our faith in you be vindicated for all to see?" *[Genesis 4:10]* ❖ *They are not seeking personal vengeance, but vindication. Any revenge will be the Lord's for offenses to him. [Romans 12:19] The martyrs themselves are in a place of safety, glory, and delight—and it was their joy to die for their Lord. [Revelation 14:13] Some commentators say it is a cry for vengeance, but believers in Heaven will desire only what God wants—and personal vengeance is not within his will.* ➤ 11 Each of them received a white robe symbolizing the purity and righteousness of the Messiah and their eternal victory over death. ❖ *While they will also be vindicated before their murderers at the final judgment, their robes of righteousness are themselves the clearest sign of the vindication of their faith. Some commentators believe the robes symbolize glorified bodies that are awarded earlier to the martyrs than other believers. This may be contradicted by Revelation 7:9, but these visions are not necessarily in chronological order. Many commentators believe these "souls" have no bodies in Heaven—and won't until the resurrection. Yet "soul" is often used in the Scriptures to refer to the whole person. The vision could be entirely symbolic—including the apparent bodies the people have that John sees—or they may have temporary glorified bodies different from the ones we will all receive at the resurrection. All pictures of Heaven in John's visions and in Jesus' stories seem to depict people with bodies, but how else could they be depicted?* ➤ Then they were told that they should enjoy their Heavenly rest awhile longer because the final judgment would not happen until the complete number of their fellow believers joined them—who would be martyred for their faith as they had been.

A 6:8 Literally, "Hades"—the place of the dead. Since believers go to Heaven when they die, Hades is the place unbelievers go—which is commonly referred to as Hell.

❖ *Some commentators believe God has predetermined that there will be a certain number of martyrs in Heaven.* ➤

Seal 6: Terror in the Last Days

12 I saw the Lamb break the sixth seal on the scroll—and the Earth and the entire universe were shaken. The sun became black and the moon dimmed to a dark blood red. *[2 Samuel 22:8; Isaiah 13:10; 24:23; Jeremiah 4:23-24; Ezekiel 32:7-8; Joel 2:10; 30-31; 3:15; Amos 5:18; 8:9; Haggai 2:6; Matthew 24:29-30; Mark 13:24-26; Luke 21:25-27; Acts 2:19-20; Hebrews 12:26; Revelation 11:13; 16:18]* ❖ *Whether or not these things will literally happen or not, the way the people of John's time would have interpreted them was that these events mean the very end of the world was at hand—and also the imminent return of the Messiah in glory. Some commentators interpret these events symbolically such as the failure of major economic systems, but such interpretations would hardly account for the terror described in verse 16 below.* ➤ 13 The universal shaking was such that the very stars fell from the sky, like a strong wind causes unripe figs to fall from a tree. *[Isaiah 34:4]* ❖ *This could be an incredible meteor shower, but again, whether or not it literally happens, this phenomena is symbolic of the universal extent of God's imminent judgment. Symbolically, significant changes in the stars always portended major events in the world—and often disasters.* ➤ 14 The visible sky was rolled back like a stage backdrop, revealing a hidden reality behind it. Everything that people had assumed was permanent and unchangeable—such as mountains and islands—were shaken, changed, and moved, some of them disappearing. *[Isaiah 34:4; Nahum 1:5; Revelation 16:20]* 15 Then every unbeliever, whether ordinary people, or the rich and powerful, or military personnel, or government authorities and rulers, from the least to the greatest—all were terrified and tried to hide themselves in caves and under rock overhangs in the mountains. *[Isaiah 2:10; 19-21; 13:6-9]* 16 Their only thoughts and desires were that the shaking would cause rocks to fall and cover the mouths of the caves and their hiding places—to hide them from the terrifying sight of God on his throne and from the wrathful retribution of the Lamb. *[Hosea 10:8; Luke 23:30]* ❖ *Some commentators believe they were desiring death as a means of escape—rather than mere hiding—and considered death preferable to facing God and*

his righteous anger. ➤ 17 For they recognized that the Judgment Day—which they had scorned and refused to believe would happen—had finally arrived, and none of them would escape God's righteous anger and punishment for their rejection of his Messiah. *[Job 41:10; Psalm 1:5; 76:7; 130:3; Joel 2:11; Nahum 1:5-6; Zephaniah 1:14-18; Malachi 3:2]*

7

The Marking of 144,000 as God's People

1 Then in another vision I saw four angels at the four corners of the Earth. They were preventing the four compass-point winds from blowing so they couldn't cause destruction on land or sea or affect any tree. ❖ *Some commentators say they only prevented destructive winds (from verses 7:2-3). Others say they caused a complete ceasing of all wind. [Jeremiah 49:36; Daniel 7:2] Some commentators see 7:1-8 as a flashback prior to the release of God's judgments on unredeemed humanity.* ➤ 2 And a fifth angel rose from the east, holding God's royal seal. He called to the four who had power to release the winds—causing destruction on land and sea—3 "Don't release them until we've marked God's people on their foreheads with his seal of ownership and protection from his judgments." ❖ *The protection is from God's judgments, but not from martyrdom. [Ezekiel 9:2-4; 2 Corinthians 1:22; Ephesians 1:13-14; 4:30] The angels and the four winds are not mentioned again. Some commentators believe these four winds correspond to the four horsemen of the first four seals. This sealing of God's people might take place before the sixth seal on the scroll is broken, and possibly before the first. Others say the seals correspond to the judgments released with the seven trumpets in the next chapter.* ➤ 4 Then I heard how many they sealed, 144,000 Israelites of every tribe, 5-8 12,000 from each of the twelve tribes: Judah, Reuben, Gad, Asher, Naphtali, Manasseh, Simeon, Levi, Issachar, Zebulun, Joseph, and Benjamin. ❖ *The order of the list is arbitrary, and the order of these tribes listed in the Hebrew Scriptures varies considerably. We don't know why Dan is left out and Joseph is listed. Usually Joseph is listed as the two half tribes of Manasseh and Ephraim (his two sons) and Levi is not listed because they didn't own land. Some commentators speculate that Dan was omitted here because of that tribe's association in extra-biblical literature with idolatry. ¶ Most commentators*

agree that the number 144,000 is symbolic of completeness. They differ as to whether it refers to all believers, or all Jews who become believers in the last days (the view of many Messianic Jews today), or all the martyrs that come out of the tribulation. Many commentators say that all believers are now part of the New Israel (as is indicated in Romans 11:16-24), but Dispensationalists believe Israel remains distinct from the assembly of believers that began at Pentecost. [Revelation 14:1-5] ➤

The Uncountable Throng in White Before God's Throne

⁹ After seeing these things, I saw an immense uncountable throng of people from every ethnic group, culture, tribe, and language. ❖ *Some commentators see 7:9-17 as a flash forward to a time after the great tribulation when all of those who died during the tribulation are in Heaven. Some also see this uncountable throng as representing the same group as the 144,000.* ➤ They were all clothed in white robes—representing victory and the Messiah's righteousness—waving palm branches in joyous celebration, and were arrayed before God's throne and the Lamb. ¹⁰ As with a single thundering voice, they proclaimed, "Our salvation and victory comes entirely from our sovereign God and the Lamb!" ¹¹ Then all the angels that were standing around the throne and the 24 elders and the four unique beings prostrated themselves in submissive worship toward God on his throne ¹² and proclaimed, "Yes, it is true! All praise, thanks, honor, glory, wisdom, power, and capability belong to our God forever! Yes, it is true!" ¹³ Then one of the elders asked me, "Do you know who these people in white are and where they've come from?" ¹⁴ I replied, "No, sir, **A** will you tell me?" He said, "These are the people who came to Heaven through the Great Tribulation. They have received the Lamb's righteousness because they trusted in his death on the cross to save them. *[Daniel 12:1; Matthew 24:21; Mark 13:9]* ❖ *Futurists say the "great tribulation" is the period just before Jesus returns; Idealists say it represents the tribulations that all believers throughout*

history have endured since the time of Jesus. ➤ ¹⁵ Since they are now righteous, they never cease to serve God. They are continually in his presence and he protects them from all harm. ¹⁶ Never again will they experience unfulfilled hunger, thirst, discomfort, or unfulfilled desire of any kind. *[Psalm 121:5-7; Isaiah 49:10]* ¹⁷ For the Lamb in the center of the throne ❖ *i.e., in total harmony with God the Father who sits on the throne* ➤ will take care of them like a loving shepherd takes care of his sheep. He will lead them to the source of eternal-life-giving water—which is God himself—who will fill them with joy and remove all the hurt from anything they have ever suffered." *[Psalm 23:1-2; 36:8-9; Ezekiel 34:23; Isaiah 25:8; 40:11]*

8

Seal 7: The Scroll Can Now be Opened

¹ When the Lamb broke the last seal on the scroll so it could be opened and read, for about half an hour there was an ominous silence in Heaven—anticipating the dreadful judgments about to be released. ❖ *Though there is no explicit further mention of the scroll, the purpose of breaking the seals is so it could be opened and read. The implication is that all the judgments that follow, beginning with the seven trumpets and following with the bowls, were written in the scroll. The actions described in verses 2-6 may have been going on during the silence.* ➤

² Then I saw seven angels standing in God's presence, ready to serve him. They were each given a trumpet to herald the coming cataclysmic events. ❖ *First century Jews believed there were seven archangels who are named in the apocryphal book of 1 Enoch. (Their names are Uriel, Raphael, Raguel, Michael, [Daniel 12:1; Jude 9] Saraqâêl, Gabriel, [Luke 1:19, 26] and Remiel.) They stand in the presence of God. [Luke 1:19; 1 Thessalonians 4:16] In the canonical Scriptures, only Michael is explicitly called an archangel. These seven angels may be the same ones mentioned in Revelation 15:1, 6-8; 16:1; 17:1; and 21:9.* ➤ ³ Another angel came forward and stood at the gold incense

---

A 7:14 Literally "sir" is "my lord," although some manuscripts lack "my." Some commentators see this as a confirmation of their view that the 24 elders are angels, rather than representing saved humanity or elders among saved humanity. But the Greek word translated "lord" was also commonly used as a respectful form of address among people.

altar in front of the throne. He held a gold censer ❖ *an instrument which holds burning coals and in which incense is burned* ➤ and was given a large quantity of incense to offer up to God—which was the prayers of God's people. ❖ *Many interpret the verse as meaning that the incense was mixed with the prayers of God's people, but elsewhere they are identified as being one and the same. [Psalm 141:2; Revelation 5:8] Hendriksen sees this as a mixing of Jesus' intercessions with the prayers of his people.* ➤ 4 The pleasant-smelling smoke from the burning incense ascended from the censer in the angel's hand up to God on his throne—symbolizing his acceptance and approval of the sacrificial prayers of his people. 5 Then the angel filled the censer with burning coals from the altar and threw the fiery coals of God's righteous wrath down from Heaven to Earth in response to the prayers of his people for vindication. Along with the fire went flashes of lightning and rumblings of thunder—and the Earth shook. *[Ezekiel 10:1-2; Revelation 11:19; 16:18]* 6 The seven angels—each holding a trumpet—readied themselves to herald the coming of God's warning judgments to the inhabitants of Earth.

E. THE SEVEN TRUMPETS

❖ *Idealists see the seven trumpets as being simultaneous with the breaking of the seals, and that both sets of seven cover the whole span of time from Jesus' ascension until his second coming. In this view, the different calamities described are not events that happen in sequence, but are judgments that happen throughout this age at any time and place. The horror of the descriptions of the judgments heralded by the seven trumpets must be greatly diminished, though, to interpret these judgments as having taken place throughout the past 2000 years. Ladd sees the seven trumpets as the content of the seventh seal, and that the first six seals span the 2000 years of this age and that the trumpets are the start of the end of this age. This is a mixture of Idealist and Futurist views, placing the trumpets in the future. Futurists interpret these trumpets as specific horrifying events to happen shortly before the Messiah returns again. Unless the seven trumpets and seven bowl judgments follow sequentially after some clear revelation like the sixth seal, how would people on Earth—unbelievers and those who follow other religions—have a clue that the catastrophes are in fact judgments from the God of the Bible? And if these judgments are just like catastrophic events that have*

happened over the last 2000 years—and not greatly worse like they are literally depicted in this book, but are greatly diminished as described by Idealists in their commentaries—how could anyone know they were in fact judgments from God and not just natural occurrences? Natural occurring disasters do not convince atheists and Muslims and Hindus and followers of other religions that the God of the Bible is real and that they need to turn to Jesus to save them. Only a very clear revelation like the sixth seal could give them the proper context to view subsequent calamities as punishments from the one true God. ➤

Trumpet 1: A Third of the Land Is Burned

7 The first trumpet was blown and a blood-red storm of hail and fire rained over the land on Earth—burning up about a third of the vegetation and trees everywhere, and all the green grass. *[Exodus 9:23-25; Ezekiel 38:22]* ❖ *The judgments associated with the trumpets are partial and preliminary, with the intent of warning those who survive that they need to repent before the final judgment. Some Futurists take the descriptions of these first four trumpets very literally. Others try to think how these descriptions could be connected with natural type events. For example, Osborne says the blood in the literal text is thought by some to be a red-colored rain caused by red dust particles in the atmosphere. This does occasionally happen in the Mediterranean area. Volcanic eruptions have also turned the sky red. They, of course, see these natural explanations as still being caused by God.* ➤

Trumpet 2: A Third of All Sea Life Is Destroyed

8 The second trumpet was blown and a fiery mountain-sized asteroid plunged into the sea—turning a third of the sea blood red. ❖ *We don't know for sure what this refers to. This is simply a possible interpretation.* ➤ 9 All the ships and sea life in that area were destroyed.

Trumpet 3: A Third of All Rivers and Springs Are Poisoned

10 The third trumpet was blown and a great flaming shooting star plummeted from the night sky—fragmenting into many smaller pieces and poisoning the sources of a third of the rivers and natural springs. ❖ *Many rivers and springs have their source in the mountains. Another possibility is that this is a description of a comet which can look like a flaming torch in the sky (see the literal text).* ➤ 11 This falling star was called Wormwood—which means bitterness—

because it made a third of the freshwater sources bitter and poisonous—like Wormwood does—causing many people who drank from them to die. *[Jeremiah 9:15; 23:15]*

Trumpet 4: The Sun, Moon, and Stars Are Struck

12 The fourth trumpet was blown and the sun, moon, and stars were struck, such that for a third of the day there was no light from the sun and a third of the night had no light from the moon or stars. *[Isaiah 13:10; Ezekiel 32:7; Joel 2:10, 31; 3:15] ❖ This resembles the plague of darkness in Exodus 10:22-23. Some commentators interpret it as a reduction of intensity of these lights— which is much easier to imagine. If it occurs as literally described, this will clearly not be due to any known natural phenomenon. ➤* 13 Then I saw an eagle A flying and loudly proclaiming, "It will be terrible indeed for those still living on Earth when the last three trumpets are blown!"

9

Trumpet 5: The Plague of Locusts from Hell

1 Then the fifth trumpet was blown and I saw that a fallen angel was given the key to the bottomless pit of Hell with divine permission to open it. *❖ Most commentators agree that the "star" in this verse is a spiritual being, but what kind is debated. Some say it's Satan, [Isaiah 14:12] some that it's the same angel mentioned in Revelation 20:1, and others as is rendered above. ➤* 2 When he opened it, smoke shot up out of it as from an enormous furnace, such that the atmosphere was darkened—dimming the sun's light. *[Genesis 19:28]* 3 Then demonic locusts swarmed out of the smoke and they were given power and permission to sting people like scorpions. 4 But they were forbidden from harming vegetation or trees or people who bore God's seal of ownership on their foreheads. *[Revelation 7:3]* 5 They were also forbidden to kill anyone, but were allowed to torment people with intense agony from their scorpion-like stings for five months. 6 During that period, people who are suffering from the stings will long to die to escape their agony. They will

even try to kill themselves, but will discover they can neither die nor escape their punishment. *[Job 3:21]* 7 The demonic locusts looked like war horses with intelligent human-like faces and something like gold wreath-crowns on their heads. 8 They had long savage-like unkempt hair and fierce lion-like fangs. *[Joel 1:6; 2:4-5]* 9 Their chests were as impregnable as iron breastplates, and the din of their wings was like the roar of many horses and chariots charging into battle. 10 They had tails with scorpion-like stings whose venom could cause people agony for five months. *❖ Whether agony from one sting would last for five months or they would live to repeatedly sting people for five months, we don't know. There are natural creatures, e.g., centipedes and sea urchins, whose sting causes such great agony for days that people sometimes wish for death. ➤* 11 The king of these demonic locusts is a fallen angel who lived in the bottomless pit of Hell. His name in Hebrew is *"Abaddon"* and in Greek it's *"Apollyon"*— both meaning "Destroyer." *❖ Some commentators think this is Satan, others think he is not. The Roman Emperor when John wrote this book was Domitian—who considered himself the Greek god Apollos in human form. One of Apollos' symbols was the locust. Apollyon was not a real name in use at that time and some commentators believe it was a hint that Domitian was in league with a demon from Hell. ➤* 12 The vision of the first calamity afflicting God's enemies associated with the fifth trumpet is finished, but there are two more calamities to follow. *❖ Some commentators think this is a highly symbolic description of a severe and terrifying demonic attack and that the physical description of these demonic locusts is not to be taken literally. ➤*

Trumpet 6: Plague of the Demonic Army

13 Then the sixth trumpet was blown, and I heard a voice coming from the horns on the four corners of the gold incense altar that stands in front of God's throne. *[Exodus 30:1-3] ❖ Commentators think the voice from the altar is symbolic of God's response to the prayers of his people—indicating that much of what he does in this world is done in response to prayer. ➤* 14 It commanded the angel who had just blown the sixth trumpet, "Release the four fallen angels *❖ i.e., demons ➤* of

---

A **8:13** The word ἀετός (aetos) could alternately be translated "vulture."

destruction who have been held bound at the great Euphrates River." 15 So those four fallen angels—who had been kept bound for release at this exact moment—were loosed for their intended purpose—which was to kill a third of all the people remaining on the face of the Earth. 16 The demonic cavalry which they commanded numbered twice 10,000 times 10,000. I heard the sound of this immense number of horses. ❖ *Literally, this would calculate out to 200 million. But see the footnote at Revelation 5:11 about uncountable millions.* ➤ 17 In this vision of the army of demonic horses and their riders, the riders wore breastplates that were fiery red, deep blue, and sulfurous yellow. The horses' heads resembled lions—and fire, blue smoke, and burning sulfur streamed out of their mouths. ❖ *Burning sulfur is often called brimstone, and in the Scriptures it is often a symbol of divine punishment. [Genesis 19:24; Psalm 11:6; Isaiah 30:33; 34:9; Ezekiel 38:22]* ➤ 18 The fire, smoke, and burning sulfur coming from the horses' mouths were three afflictions A that kill a third of the people remaining on Earth. 19 The ability of these horses to kill was not only in their mouths but also their tails, which were like biting poisonous snakes. 20 Despite these clear judgments from God, those unbelievers who are not killed by these afflictions will refuse to repent of the evil things they do or to submit to the Living God. They continue to worship demons, lifeless man-made idols, and false gods. *[Psalm 115:4-7; 135:15-17; Daniel 5:23; 1 Corinthians 10:19-20]* 21 They continue to murder, practice occult arts, indulge in sexual immorality, and steal. ❖ *Hendriksen, an Idealist, interprets this plague as simply symbolic of war, i.e., all wars. Wilcock sees it symbolic of any kind of disastrous death or destruction, not limited to wars.* ➤

10

The Angel with the Small Scroll

1 Then I saw another angel B of great power and size descend from Heaven to Earth. It was like his body was clothed in a cloud, and he wore a rainbow on his head. His face shone brilliantly like the sun and his legs looked like pillars of fire. ❖ *The cloud and the pillars of fire were symbols of God's presence and glory in Exodus 13:21-22, and the rainbow was a symbol of God's promise and mercy. [Genesis 9:12-17] The bright light from his face shining through water particles in the cloud would produce the rainbow (this is the way rainbows are produced by refracting light in nature). ¶ For the sake of a young generation unfamiliar with history, let me add that the current meaning of a rainbow representing the LGBT movement only started in 1978. There is no connection between that meaning and its meaning in Scripture.* ➤ 2 He descended until his right foot stood on the sea and his left foot stood on land and he held a small unrolled scroll in one hand. ❖ *The positioning of his feet symbolizes that his authority and message was for the entire planet. Osborne, along with other commentators, thinks this scroll is the same one that had been sealed with the seven seals, even though they are referred to by totally different words in the Greek. Its small size could merely be relative to the size of the angel.* ➤ 3 This being made a deafening shout like the roar of a lion, which was answered by the replies of the seven thunders. ❖ *We don't know what the seven thunders are, but thunder in other places in this book always precedes the execution of God's punishment. [Revelation 8:5; 11:19; 16:18]* ➤ 4 I was about to record what the seven thunders said when I heard a voice from Heaven command me, "Don't record what they said, for you may not report it to others." *[2 Corinthians 12:2-4]* 5 Then this angel of great power—who was standing with one foot on the sea and one on land—raised his right C hand toward Heaven *[Deuteronomy 32:40; Daniel 12:7]* 6 and swore an oath in the name of the eternal God—creator of Heaven, Earth, and sea D and everything in them *[Exodus 20:11; Psalm 146:6]*—that this message from God was true, "There will be no more delays. E 7 In the period of time that will commence with the blowing of the seventh trumpet, all of God's purposes for his restored creation that were hidden until the Messiah first came

---

A **9:18** The word πληγῶν (plēgōn) can also mean "plagues" or "wounds."

B **10:1** Because of the description of this angel, many commentators think it may be the Messiah himself.

C **10:5** Some manuscripts lack the word "right."

D **10:6a** Some manuscripts lack the phrase "the sea and everything in it."

E **10:6b** The word χρόνος (chronos) can mean "delay" or "time," and some manuscripts take it in the latter sense.

will be fulfilled—just as he had announced as Good News to his prophets and through their writings in the Scriptures." [Amos 3:7] **8** Then I again heard the voice from Heaven command me, "Go and take the scroll from the hand of the angel who stands with one foot on the sea and one on land." **9** So I went and asked the angel for the small scroll and he told me, "Take it and eat it. You will find that it tastes as sweet as honey, [Psalm 19:10; 119:103; Jeremiah 15:16; Ezekiel 2:8—3:3] but it will upset your stomach." ❖ *God's words are sweet for his servants to receive, especially that there would be no more delay and that God's people would ultimately be victorious. But digesting the message and proclaiming it can sometimes be unpleasant. Commentators think that the unpleasantness is either the message of judgment for unbelievers in the rest of this book, or the message for the assemblies that they must yet face a difficult time before they experience their complete victory— i.e., the message in Revelation 11:1-13.* ➤ **10** I took the small scroll from the angel and ate it. Indeed, it did taste sweet as honey, but after I had eaten it my stomach became upset. **11** Then I was instructed, "You must once again prophesy what God has shown you about **A** many kings, ethnic groups, and language groups." ❖ *Commentators think this refers to the rest of the content of this book.* ➤

11

God's Witnesses will Prophecy for 1260 Days

1 Then I was handed a long stiff reed of a determined length to use as a measuring stick and was commanded, "Go measure God's Temple and the altar, and count how many are worshipping in it. [Ezekiel 40:3-5; Zechariah 2:1-2] ❖ *Some commentators say that measuring was done in preparation for repairing, restoration, or preservation of a building. So the measuring is symbolic of preserving God's Temple—which is symbolic of God's people who are his living Temple. [1 Corinthians 3:16; 6:19; 2 Corinthians 6:16; Ephesians 2:19-22] The preservation does not mean physical protection from persecution, but spiritual protection of their faith. The only altar so far mentioned is the incense altar which is associated with the prayers of God's people. Measuring it may mean protecting their access to him in prayer. The*

IVP commentary says measuring it is a way of pointing out its greatness, which brings God praise. This would seem to apply more to the measuring in Revelation 21:15-17 than in this context. Lenski interprets the measuring as determining who is saved and who is not. Ladd and some other commentators interpret this chapter as prophesying about God's preserving of his people—the physical descendants of Israel—and their salvation. ➤ **2** But don't measure the outer court of the Gentiles, for it has been turned over to unbelievers. They will persecute my holy city ❖ *another symbol for God's people (though some commentators take it to specifically mean Jerusalem, and hence Israel)* ➤ for 42 months. [Luke 21:24] ❖ *3½ years = 42 months = 1260 days (assuming 30-day months). These numbers all refer to the same period. The measuring is similar to the sealing of Revelation 7:3-4. Not measuring the outer court may correspond to excluding all who profess to be believers but who in reality are not, or it may refer to all unbelievers in general. According to Futurists, the 3½ years are part of the tribulation period. According to Idealists, it corresponds to the entire period between the Messiah's first and second comings.* ➤ **3** I will send my two witnesses dressed in sackcloth, ❖ *a symbol of mourning and repentance, and often the apparel of prophets [2 Kings 1:8; Isaiah 20:2; Zechariah 13:4]* ➤ and for 1260 days they will prophesy my warnings to repent." ❖ *No one knows who these two witnesses are, but there have been many guesses. A popular one is that they are Moses and Elijah. Idealist commentators don't believe they are real men, but think that they symbolize God's witness that exists in this world until Jesus returns—through his people and the message of the Good News. According to the Torah, two witnesses in agreement were always required to establish the truth of what was said.* ➤ **4** These two witnesses are the two lampstands and the two olive trees that stand in the presence of the Lord of all the Earth. ❖ *Read Zechariah 4:1-14 for the context of this reference. Oil from the two olive trees kept the lamps burning. These lamps (i.e., the witnesses) are fueled by the oil of the Holy Spirit and provide spiritual light to the world.* ➤ **5** Anyone who tries to harm these witnesses are destroyed by fire that comes out of their mouths. ❖ *Futurists take this verse and most others fairly literally, so I need not always point out that fact. Idealists say the fire is symbolic of God's words of judgment and refers to the same figure as in Jeremiah 5:11, 14. God's people are not immune to physical harm, but as to their faith and eternal life, nothing can harm them. It's possible*

A 10:11 The word ἐπί (epi) has many possible meanings. Most commentators interpret it to mean "about" in this context, but some say it means "against."

that there has been a figurative fulfillment of these witnesses since Pentecost and that there will also be a literal fulfillment in the last-days tribulation. ➤ 6 During the period when these witnesses prophesy, they are able to punish unbelievers by preventing any rain from falling—causing famine—they can turn water to blood, and can cause any plague or affliction to come upon the world. They can do these things as often as they believe the Lord wants them to do so. *[1 Kings 17:1; Exodus 7:14-21; 1 Samuel 4:8; Luke 4:25; James 5:17]* ❖ *These are abilities that were given to Moses and Elijah. Idealists say this means God's people have the same resources that Moses and Elijah did. But these resources are further symbolized to say that they represent the believer's ability to pronounce God's judgments on those who reject the Messiah. This seems to stretch things. Most believers certainly have never had these powers literally, and the Scriptures forbid us from pronouncing judgment or punishment on anyone. At most, we can proclaim what the Scriptures say about the coming judgment for those who don't repent.* ➤ 7 When God's appointed time for their witnessing is over, the False Messiah **A** from the bottomless pit of Hell will attack, overcome, and kill them. *[Daniel 7:7, 21; Revelation 13:5-7; 17:8]* ❖ *Now Idealists shift their interpretation of the witnesses from representing all of God's people since Pentecost to a specific group—i.e., all the remaining believers that are killed in the last days. Otherwise, how could Satan overcome God's people? Jesus promised it would never happen. [Matthew 16:18] Those who hold to this symbolic interpretation of the two witnesses believe there will be a time when all witness on the Earth to God's truth ceases—if only for a short time.* ➤ 8 Their corpses will be left to rot in disgrace in the street of the great city where their Lord was crucified. This city is figuratively referred to as Sodom for its great immorality, and as Egypt for the stubbornness, oppression, and idolatry of Pharaoh during the time of the Exodus. *[Isaiah 1:9-10]* ❖ *Commentators disagree over what is meant by "the great city." Some say it's Jerusalem, where the Messiah was crucified. Others say "the great city" clearly refers to Rome seven other places in this book. [16:19; 17:18; 18:10, 16, 18-19, 21] Rome was the "system" that crucified Jesus. Some say it is a figure representing no specific location, but the entire pagan world that opposes God and his people.* ➤ 9 Then for three and a half days, people from every tribe, language, ethnic group, and culture

will be able to see and despise those corpses. For the authorities will show their scorn by not allowing them to be buried. ❖ *In the past, Futurist commentators said that representatives of all these people groups would be present in that city and would see these bodies. Now, the technology exists for literally the entire world to see them.* ➤ 10 There will be rejoicing and celebrating all over the world—even going so far as sending gifts to each other to celebrate the death of the two prophets who had made life miserable for them for three and a half years. ❖ *Idealists interpret these as responses toward the believers in the world who had preached the message of repentance, but were now exterminated—or at least if there are remaining believers, their witness is silenced from fear.* ➤ 11 But at the end of three and a half days, these bodies suddenly stood up, for God had restored the two prophets to life. All who saw them alive again were terrified. *[Ezekiel 37:10]* ❖ *Idealists variously interpret this as a restoration of remaining believers to boldness for witnessing again—though that would hardly terrify the world—or they say it refers to the resurrection and rapture of believers—which would terrorize, if witnessed by the unbelieving world. ¶ Note that the narrative changes to past tense in this verse. Typically in prophecy, the past tense indicates certainty that the events stated will happen—and does not mean that they have already happened. Also, a change in tense here might be a device to indicate the climax of the story being told.* ➤ 12 Then the two prophets heard a loud command from Heaven, "Come up!" And they ascended into Heaven in a cloud as their enemies watched. 13 Within the same hour that they ascended, there was a strong earthquake that destroyed a tenth of the city's buildings and killed 7000 people. The rest of the people in that city were terrified and offered praise to God who reigns from Heaven. ❖ *Some Idealists interpret the earthquake figuratively—as a shaking of the structures of society—and see the tenth and 7000 as referring to a partial judgment. (It's odd and inconsistent that they don't say the 7000 is symbolic of completeness.) Some believe it might refer to a literal earthquake. Some believe the praise offered was a panic reaction and not a true change of heart. Others think it indicates true conversion, but then they can't be the same people who interpret the city as a figure for the entire world. Many interpretations are not consistent. If 7,000 people corresponds to a tenth of the great city's population, it would*

A 11:7 The False Messiah is introduced in chapter 13.

more likely to be Jerusalem than Rome in the first century. Rome had nearly a million inhabitants. ➤ **14** The vision of the second calamity afflicting God's enemies that is associated with the sixth trumpet is finished, but there will soon be a third calamity to follow.

Trumpet 7: The Proclamation of God's Reign over the Earth

❖ *Some commentators think that the seventh trumpet is the "last trumpet," heralding the return of the Messiah. [Matthew 24:31; 1 Corinthians 15:52; 1 Thessalonians 4:16-17] Others think it introduces the final period of time which includes the period of the seven bowl judgments and is the beginning of the end, but not yet the visible return of the Messiah. Ladd sees the seventh trumpet as introducing the third calamity, which he believes is the seven bowl judgments that start in chapter 16.* ➤

15 Then the seventh trumpet was blown and I heard many voices in Heaven loudly proclaim, "The rebellious kingdom **A** of Earth—ruled by Satan—has been completely subjugated and placed under the irresistible rule of our Lord God and his Messiah. His sovereign reign over all things will never end." *[Exodus 15:18; Isaiah 9:7; Daniel 2:44; 7:14, 27]* ❖ *This is an angelic proclamation ("his Messiah," not "our Messiah") stating what has been declared in Heaven and is about to be manifest on Earth. As in many other places, something declared in Heaven means it will certainly happen, but it doesn't mean that it is necessarily instantaneously manifest in this world. However some commentators do take it to mean that the proclamation is being sung while the events of Revelation 19:11-12 are happening.* ➤ **16** Then once again, the 24 elders—who were sitting on their thrones before the throne of God—prostrated themselves before him in submissive worship **17** and proclaimed, "Thank you, our omnipotent sovereign Lord and God. You have always been the sovereign Lord of the universe—as you are now. But we thank you because you are now demonstrating your omnipotent power and exercising your sovereign rule over those who have rebelled against you. ❖ *Again, some commentators interpret the 24 elders literally, others as representing all of redeemed humanity, and others as representing an angelic order.* ➤ **18** Unbelievers

have always been defiantly furious at you, but the appointed time has finally arrived when you demonstrated your wrath over their sin and rebellion. Judgment Day has arrived when you will judge all who have died. You will reward all who have served you—your prophets and holy people who have honored and obeyed you—from the least important ones to the great ones. You will also destroy those who have been destroyers on Earth." *[Psalm 2:1-12; 46:6]* ❖ *There is no leeway here for the idea of universal salvation.* ➤ **19** Then I saw the sanctuary of God's Temple in Heaven opened and the Ark of his holy Covenant revealed. Then great flashes of lightning appeared—along with roaring thunder, an earthquake, and a devastating hailstorm. *[Revelation 8:5; 16:18, 21]* ❖ *The Ark of the Covenant was symbolic of God's throne and was associated with his Torah. The Torah declared many curses for those who failed to keep the commands in God's Torah. The Ark also would remind his people that he keeps his covenant promises, both to judge (the ark contained a copy of the Torah) and to save (the mercy seat). [Exodus 25:17-22; 30:6; Leviticus 16:2-16] Its being revealed is symbolic of the intimate relationship that God now has with his people. [Exodus 25:22] The lightning, thunder, earthquake, and hail appear several times in Revelation—always preceding an expression of God's wrath and judgment against those who rebel against him. They also represent his awesome power and majesty.* ➤

F. THE DRAGON, THE FALSE MESSIAH, AND THE FALSE PROPHET

The Sign of the Woman, the Child, and the Dragon

❖ *Symbols in the Scriptures are often fluid and change their meaning in different contexts. Here, the woman symbolizes the true Israel (God's chosen people in the Hebrew Scriptures). The child is the Messiah and the Dragon is Satan. While John probably saw these visions in the order he writes them, the contents of some of them may not all be in chronological order. This vision and the next are like flashbacks, painting a backdrop for the future events he also records. This vision depicts the spiritual background and battle behind the persecution of believers in this world throughout history.* ➤

A 11:15 Some manuscripts have the plural "kingdoms."

12

¹ Then I saw a vision of an important sign appearing in Heaven. I saw a woman who looked like she was clothed with the sun, had the moon under her feet, and was wearing a wreath crown of twelve stars. ² She cried out in pain as she was about to give birth. ³ Then I saw another sign appear in Heaven, an immense fiery-red Dragon with seven heads and ten horns, with a crown on each head. *[Daniel 7:7]* ❖ *The Dragon represents Satan. The horns symbolize power, and the seven heads represent the completeness of his rule over those in rebellion against God.* ➤ ⁴ The Dragon's tail had long ago swept a third of the stars out of the sky and knocked them down to Earth. *[Isaiah 14:12-15; Ezekiel 28:11-17; Daniel 8:10]* ❖ *Many commentators think this refers to Satan's initial rebellion against God before humanity sinned—when he led a third of the angels in rebellion against God and they were expelled from Heaven and confined to Earth. Stars were often thought of as angels. This sentence was a further flashback, and the next returns to the time of the Messiah's birth.* ➤ Now it stood in front of the woman so it could consume the child immediately after its birth. ❖ *This is commonly understood to refer to Herod's attempt to kill the Messiah by ordering all the infants in the vicinity of Bethlehem to be killed. [Matthew 2:16] But it also refers to Satan's attempts to destroy the Messiah during his ministry—especially at the crucifixion.* ➤ ⁵ The woman gave birth to a son who was destined to destroy all the peoples of the world who are his enemies. *[Revelation 2:27; 19:15] To "rule with an iron rod" (in the literal text) is an idiom meaning "to destroy," not "to rule with absolute power"—as it would seem to modern English speakers. [Psalm 2:9]* ➤ Before the Dragon could harm the child, he was safely whisked away and taken to God on his throne. ❖ *Some commentators see this "birth" and whisking away as representing not only his birth, but also his life on Earth, death, resurrection, and ascension.* ➤ ⁶ Then the woman ❖ *who now symbolizes the assembly of all believers still in the world* ➤ ran away into the wilderness, where God prepared a safe place for her to stay so she would be nourished and sustained during the 1260 days. ❖ *Idealists*

note parallels between Israel's 40 years in the Sinai wilderness with the experiences of believers in this world between the Messiah's first and second comings. Futurists interpret this as protection for people who are on Earth as believers during the 3½ years of tribulation. ➤

⁷ Then there was a battle in Heaven **A** where the archangel Michael—chief angelic protector of Israel—attacked the Dragon and his minions. Though the Dragon and his angels fought back, ⁸ they were defeated and permanently cast out of Heaven. ❖ *Some commentators see this as a further flashback to the time of verse 12:4a, but many commentators today interpret this battle as occurring after the exaltation of the Messiah to the right hand of the Father.* ➤ ⁹ It was in this way that the great Dragon, who was the serpent in the Garden of Eden, *[Genesis 3:1-5]* who is called the Devil (meaning slanderer) and Satan (meaning accuser), and who deceived all of humanity, was cast down to Earth along with his demons. ❖ *There are hints that prior to this—though in some sense previously cast out, (assuming this casting out happened at the exaltation of the Messiah in Heaven)—Satan still had some kind access to Heaven as in Job 1:6-11; Zechariah 3:1; and as referred to in the next verse.* ➤ ¹⁰ Then I heard proclaimed in Heaven, "At last, God has brought about salvation for his people, the public demonstration of his power, the establishment of his rule on Earth, and acknowledgement of his Messiah's authority. For the one who used to continually accuse our fellow believers of their sins before our God, has been cast down.

¹¹ "His people have also overcome the power and accusations of Satan by trusting in the sacrificial death of the Lamb—and by proclaiming what the Lamb has done to save them. They loved him more than their own lives and so were willing to be faithful and loyal to him—even if it meant they had to die. ¹² So everyone who lives in God's presence in Heaven has great reason to rejoice! But it will be terrible for those living on the Earth and sea, because Satan has been cast down to their habitat. Knowing that his time before the final judgment is short, he intends to unleash his fury against them."

A 12:7 The word οὐρανός (ouranos) can mean either "Heaven" or "sky."

13 When the Dragon realized that he was confined to the Earth, he persecuted the woman from whom the Messiah had come. ❖ *The woman represents the true Israel, which now includes all of God's redeemed people—whether Jews or Gentiles.* ➤ 14 But she was given two wings like those of an eagle so she could fly back to safety in the wilderness [Exodus 19:4; Deuteronomy 32:11; Isaiah 40:31] where she was nourished, provided for, and protected from the Dragon for three and a half years. [Daniel 7:25; 12:7] ❖ *Idealists interpret this period as between the Messiah's first and second comings. The wilderness is our sojourn in this life. Our protection relates to our faith, not to our physical life. Futurists interpret it as a literal 3½ years during the Great Tribulation.* ➤ 15 The Dragon caused a flood of persecution to flow from his mouth in an attempt to drown the woman. 16 But God caused the Earth to help her by opening up and absorbing the flood before it reached her. ❖ *Floods are symbolic of persecution and evil in the Hebrew Scriptures. [Psalm 18:4; 32:6; 69:15; 124:2-5; Isaiah 43:1-2]* ➤ 17 The Dragon was furious over his failure to destroy the woman, and went off to try to destroy her children who obey God and proclaim the Good News about Jesus. ❖ *Some commentators say the woman here represents the early first-century assembly of believers in and near Jerusalem—who were almost entirely Jews. The flood was his early attempts at eradicating the believers, e.g. through Saul of Tarsus. The woman's children would be the Gentiles who became believers as the message of the Good News spread outside of Palestine. Others see this event as something that happens during the Great Tribulation, which makes sense in that it is recorded in the context of verse 14 as happening during the three and a half years.* ➤

13

The First Monster, Which is the Anti-Messiah

1 Then I saw the Dragon standing on the seashore. A He summoned a monster out of the sea who had seven heads and ten horns—just like the Dragon. [Revelation 12:3] Unlike the Dragon, the ten horns each had a crown on them (instead of the heads). On each head was written a name that blasphemed God. [Daniel 7:3-25; 11:6; Revelation 17:3; 7-12] ❖ *This monster (traditionally called the "beast" in most translations) is the Anti-messiah, the personal agent of Satan himself—though some Idealists interpret him as not an individual but as a "spirit" of antagonism against believers and the message of the Good News that has been at work in the world since Jesus' ascension to Heaven. In John's first letter, he does speak about many anti-messiahs. [1 John 2:18, 22; 4:3; 1 John 1:7] But Paul writes in a clearly non-figurative manner about the "man of lawlessness" in 2 Thessalonians 2:1-10—which many commentators identify with the same Anti-messiah talked about here—who I refer to as "the monster" in this interpretation. Given Paul's description, it's likely that this monster represents a real human being, more in line with the descriptions given by Futurists. Horns represent power, and crowns represent the right to rule.* ➤ 2 The monster's body resembled a leopard's, but his paws were like a bear's and his mouth like a lion's. The Dragon gave it his authority to rule over the world, [Luke 4:6; John 12:31; 16:11; Ephesians 2:2] and his own power to use. ❖ *This monster is a combination of the four beasts described by Daniel in his vision recorded in Daniel 7:3-7. The beasts in Daniel represented four empires in history that persecuted God's people. Thus this seven-headed monster is being portrayed as the ultimate evil person who blasphemes God and tries to destroy his people. Though this Anti-messiah will come in the final years before Jesus returns, the believers in John's time would probably have identified him with the Roman empire. The seven heads have been historically interpreted as seven emperors over Rome—the city of seven hills. As John says in his first letter, there are many anti-messiahs and have been throughout history. That truth does not negate the fact that this ultimate Anti-messiah will also appear at the end of history. The fact that the Anti-messiah is referred to as a monster is a comment on his spiritual nature—which is a gross perversion of good. But it is likely that the actual person will be an attractive person with a charismatic personality.* ➤ 3 One of the monster's heads looked as if it had suffered a fatal wound and then was healed. All the unbelievers in the world were amazed by the monster's coming back to life—and therefore became the devoted followers of this False Messiah. ❖ *Futurists interpret this as meaning the Anti-messiah will become prominent, then apparently be killed and come back to life again—which will*

A 13:1 Many translations put this first sentence as 12:18, rather than as part of 13:1.

convince those who reject the true Messiah that this man is a god, worthy of their submissive worship. So he is henceforth referred to in this interpretation as the False Messiah. ➤ 4 They worshipped the Dragon because he was the source of the False Messiah's authority, and they also worshipped the False Messiah himself, exclaiming, "There is no one as great as he is. He is so powerful that no one could possibly hope to defeat him." 5 God allowed the False Messiah to make arrogant claims and blaspheme Jesus. God also allowed him to exercise his Satanic authority over the world for 42 months. 6 He said terrible things about our God—blaspheming him and his character and those he indwelled who died while remaining loyal to him and who now live in Heaven. ❖ *The believers in Heaven (and on Earth) are God's Temple, his dwelling place. [1 Corinthians 3:16; 6:19; 2 Corinthians 6:16; Ephesians 2:19-22]* ➤ 7 God allowed him to gain authority over every tribe, language, ethnic group, culture, and country in the world—and also allowed him to officially persecute and kill believers every-where. 8 The Lamb—whose sacrificial death was fore-ordained from before the world was created **A**—has a book in Heaven called the Book of Life. Everyone in Heaven and on Earth who belongs to him has their name written in it. They are the only people on Earth who do not worship the False Messiah. 9 If your hearts are attuned to God, listen carefully and clearly understand the following: 10 Those of God's people who are predestined to be arrested, will be arrested. Those of God's people who are predestined to die, will die. **B** If you belong to God, you must patiently endure this persecution and be faithful to him to the very end of your life. *[Jeremiah 15:1-4; 43:11]*

The Second Monster,
Which Is the False Prophet

11 Then I had a vision of another monster, but this one came up out of the Earth. He had two small horns like a lamb does, **C** but spoke the Dragon's words. ❖ *Some commentators note an unholy anti-trinity with the Dragon (i.e., Satan—the antithesis of the Father), who gives his authority to the False Messiah (the antithesis of the Son—the True Messiah), and the False Prophet (the antithesis of the Holy Spirit)—who urges people to worship the False Messiah.* ➤ 12 He exercised all the authority of the False Messiah as an agent on his behalf. His goal was to make everyone in the world worship the False Messiah who had died and come to life again. 13 He was able to perform spectacular miraculous signs, and people even witnessed him causing fire to come out of the sky upon his command. *[Mark 13:22; 2 Thessalonians 2:9-10]* ❖ *Some Idealists interpret this figure as false prophets who work from within the assemblies of believers.* ➤ 14 With the power given to him by the False Messiah to perform these miraculous signs, he is able to deceive everyone in the world who does not belong to Jesus. He had an image of the False Messiah made which showed the fatal wound he had received and from which he had recovered. 15 Then the False Messiah gave the False Prophet the power to make the image appear to live and breathe and speak. The image also had the ability to kill anyone who refused to submissively worship both it and the False Messiah. 16 The False Prophet also forced everyone in the world—regardless of social or financial status—to accept a permanent mark on their right hand **D** or on **E** their forehead. 17 The mark is the numerical equivalent of the name of the False Messiah, and signifies a person's allegiance to him.

A 13:8 The phrase in Greek "from the foundation of the world" can be interpreted as applying either to the Lamb's death or to the names of the saved written in the book of life. In Greek, the phrase follows "the Lamb who was slain" and ends the verse. Even though I've attached it to "the Lamb who was slain" in this verse, the same phrase is clearly attached to "names written in the book of life" in Revelation 17:8.

B 13:10 Some manuscripts indicate an alternate interpretation— that this verse is a warning to unbelievers that all who persecute

believers in this way will suffer the same fate themselves. A third interpretation is that the first statement means believers must accept their God-ordained fate, and the second statement means "those believers who fight back will be killed"—so is a warning against believers using violence to defend themselves.

C 13:11 Many species of sheep do have horns, including those in Palestine.

D 13:16a The Greek word translated "hand" can also include the wrist and forearm. This is true in many languages.

E 13:16b The preposition ἐπί (epi) *[Continued next page]*

Those without the mark will not be able to purchase or sell anything. 18 One needs God's wisdom to understand this. Such a person may calculate the number of the False Messiah, for that number is the number of a particular man. **A** His number is six hundred sixty-six. ❖ *In Greek and Hebrew, letters also represent numbers, and the values of letters in a name were often added up to give a number. Many guesses have been made as to what name is meant, but if the False Messiah is a particular person who has not yet become prominent in the world, then we would not yet know his name to be able confirm his number. We also don't know if the sum should be done with his name in Greek or Hebrew. Others think the number is symbolic of the imperfection of humanity (6 being one short of 7 which represents perfection) and not the value of anyone's name. What most modern commentators forget is that in John's day, numbers were indicated by the sums of values of letters, or by words, or by Roman Numerals (DCLXVI = 666). Commentators and teachers often talk about 6 6 6—as if three distinct number sixes is what is talked about in this verse. But 666 is an Arabic representation of the number that didn't come into common use until centuries later (the numbers we use today are called Arabic numerals). The number is not "six, six, six," as people often say today. It is a sum that has a value of six hundred sixty-six—and representing this value in the form of three sixes was not even conceived of in John's day. So beware of interpretations that depend on it being depicted as three separate sixes. That concept never occurred to John. ¶ If this prophecy about the "mark" and buying and selling is to have a literal fulfillment, the technology exists today to implement it. Miniature electronic chips implanted beneath the skin—that can be scanned so information on the chip about the person can be read—are in actual use today. Some think something along this line could very well be the "mark of the beast (monster)" and eventually be required for all financial transactions. ¶ Hendriksen, an Idealist, interprets the False Messiah as the power of Satan working through governments and nations to persecute believers, and the False Prophet as representing false religions and philosophies. He interprets the mark of the monster as being figurative of the spirit of those who oppose God and the true Messiah in thought (forehead) or deed (hand). ¶ It seems that Idealist explanations of the prophecy about the inability to purchase and sell anything without the mark of the monster are weak. Hendriksen says it simply means that unbelieving merchants and rulers will make it*

difficult for believers in their business pursuits. This is a much weaker statement than what the prophecy actually says. Idealist interpretations of the False Messiah and False Prophet reflect obvious truths, known from the first decades after Jesus ascended—i.e. that believers will be persecuted. Jesus promised this and it is mentioned explicitly in Jesus' letters to the assemblies. This is so obvious that it hardly needs restating, and thus is highly unlikely to be the main intended meaning of this chapter of prophecy. ➤

G. The Redeemed in Heaven

14

1 Then I saw the Lamb in a vision, standing on Mount Zion with the 144,000 who had his name and his Father's name on their foreheads—signifying their allegiance to them. ❖ *Commentator's disagree on whether this is Mount Zion is in Heaven or on Earth, but the location before the throne in verse 3 below seems to indicate they were in Heaven, or at least in the Heavenly Zion (New Jerusalem) that has descended to New Earth after the judgment. [Psalm 2:6; Isaiah 59:20; Joel 2:32; Micah 4:7] The 144,000 again are understood by most commentators to figuratively represent the total number of humanity that have been redeemed—the uncountable throng of Revelation 7:9. But see the note at the end of Revelation 7:8. [Ezekiel 9:4; Revelation 7:3-4]* ➤ 2 I heard voices from Heaven singing as loud as a roaring waterfall or like rolling thunder. They also sounded as beautiful and majestic as the lyres played in God's Temple as part of the worship there. [1 Samuel 10:5; 2 Samuel 6:5; 1 Chronicles 13:8; 15:16, 28; 16:4-5; 25:1, 6; 2 Chronicles 5:11-12; 20:28; 29:25-26; Nehemiah 12:27; Psalm 33:2; 43:4; 71:22; 81:2; 92:3; 98:5; 147:7; 149:3; 150:3-5; Revelation 5:8; 15:2] 3 They were singing a new song in the presence of God on his throne and before the four unique creatures and the 24 elders. No creature could sing this song except the 144,000 who had experienced redemption, for it sprang forth from their experience and gratitude. 4 These are the ones among humanity who have remained spiritual virgins **B** [2 Kings 19:21; Jeremiah 18:13; Lamentations

---

translated "on (before "hand" and before "forehead"), could just as validly be translated "in."

A 13:18 The Greek text can also be read to mean "for that

number is the number of man."

B 14:4 Or: spiritually chaste (the spiritual adjective is implied). There are commentators who believe that this

1:15; Amos 5:2; 2 Corinthians 11:2; Ephesians 5:25-27; Revelation 21:9]—for they have kept themselves pure from worshipping false gods. Wherever the Lamb leads, they follow [John 10:4; 1 Peter 2:21] and so are always in his presence. They were redeemed from fallen humanity and have been offered to God and the Lamb as their own special possession. [Jeremiah 2:3; Ephesians 1:11, 18; James 1:18] ❖ The sense of "first fruits" in the literal text in this context, is not that they are the first of more to follow, but that they are the portion of humanity that has been dedicated to God as his special possession, the rest not having been saved. ➤ 5 In their union with the Lamb and his righteousness, no one can say they are guilty of lying or of any sin. [Zephaniah 3:13] ❖ This is in contrast with those who are not saved, as in Revelation 21:27 and 22:15. ➤

H. THE LAST PROCLAMATION OF THE GOOD NEWS, AND THE HARVEST OF BELIEVERS

❖ This previous vision is probably after the judgment, since all 144,000 believers, i.e., all redeemed believers, are portrayed as being with God. If this interpretation is correct, the next vision is clearly out of temporal sequence, flashing back to a time before the judgment. Even Idealists like Hendriksen see this next vision as pertaining to the time immediately before the second coming of the Messiah. ➤

6 Then I saw another angel flying everywhere, proclaiming the eternal message of the Good News to every tribe, language, ethnic group, and culture in the world. [Matthew 24:14] ❖ Some commentators think this is a gospel (which means "Good News") of judgment and not an offer of salvation. But how can it be the eternal message of Good News unless salvation is offered? [1 Timothy 2:3-4] ➤ 7 He proclaimed in a loud voice that everyone could understand, "This is your last chance to repent and voluntarily submit to the one true God and honor and praise him, because Judgment Day is about to begin! Worship the Creator of Heaven and Earth and sea and fresh water!" [Acts 14:15] 8 This angel was followed by a second who proclaimed, "The Great Babylon—who has seduced all peoples into reveling in immorality and idolatry—

has fallen in defeat!" [Isaiah 21:9; Jeremiah 51:8; Revelation 18:2] ❖ Lenski summarizes that Preterists interpret Babylon as the Roman empire and its pagan worship, Idealists interpret it as all the systems that have opposed believers and their assemblies since the Messiah ascended to Heaven, and Futurists interpret it as the False Messiah's capital (probably Rome) and his government. ➤ 9 Then a third angel followed the second, loudly proclaiming, "Those who worship the False Messiah or his image and willingly receive his mark on forehead or hand as a sign of their allegiance to him 10 will experience God's full unrestrained righteous wrath and fury! They will suffer shame and agony in the fire of burning sulfur in the presence of the Lamb and his holy angels! [Matthew 5:22; 8:12; 10:28; 13:42, 50; 18:9; 22:13; 24:51; 25:30; Mark 9:47-48; Luke 13:28; 16:24; Jude 7; Revelation 19:20; 20:10; 21:8] 11 They will experience agonizing punishment in Hell fire, night and day, without relief, forever! [Isaiah 34:10; 2 Thessalonians 1:9] 12 Therefore, those who belong to God—who obey his commands and trust in Jesus—must patiently endure every persecution and remain faithfully loyal and obedient to him even if it means their death—lest they join the fate of those who reject him!" [Revelation 13:10] 13 Then a voice from Heaven commanded me, "Record this: 'Contrary to what it seems during their suffering, the Lord will greatly bless those—who die from persecution during this particularly difficult time and afterward—for their loyalty to him.'" ❖ This does not imply that those who were martyred previous to this would be in any way less blessed. ➤ The Holy Spirit responded to this statement, "This is certainly true! In Heaven, they will enjoy eternal rest from their laborious toil and troubles—and eternal rewards for their good deeds on Earth." [Psalm 62:12; Proverbs 24:12; Matthew 6:1-6; 16-18; 12:35-37; 16:27; John 4:36; Acts 17:31; Romans 2:6; Ephesians 6:8; 2 Corinthians 5:10; Revelation 22:12]

The Judgment Harvest

14 Then I saw the Messiah in a vision— the "Son of Man" [Daniel 7:13-14] sitting on a

---

refers to physical virgins, but then their interpretation of the 144,000 is different, and this would be a highly select subgroup among all those who are redeemed. The interpretation of "virgins" as referring to physical virgins is unlikely because there is no special virtue attached to sexual abstinence in the Scriptures. [Matthew 19:10-12]

white cloud. He wore a gold wreath-crown and held a sharp sickle. ❖ *The sickle is symbolic of harvesting. In Jesus' parables, the harvest was the time of judgment when the saved are separated from the unsaved and taken to Heaven—while the unsaved are burned. [Matthew 3:12; 13:30; 37-42; Luke 3:17] Some commentators interpret "one who was like a son of man" to mean a being that looked human, but was not the Messiah himself, because in the next verse he seems to take an order from an angel. That could be correct, but the angel coming from the Temple is probably carrying a command from God the Father.* ➤

15 Another angel came out of God's presence in the Heavenly Temple and in a loud voice called out to the One on the cloud, "The harvest of saved souls on Earth is finally ready. The time has come to gather in the harvest." *[Joel 3:13]* 16 Then the One on the cloud swung his sickle over the Earth and the harvest of his righteous people was taken up into Heaven. ❖ *Commentators disagree on whether this was the harvest of the righteous or the wicked. (Some see both harvests mentioned in this section as pertaining only to the harvest of the wicked.) In Matthew 13:30, the weeds are harvested first. But both the parable and this vision are symbolic and do not necessarily restrict the reality to being in the exact order of either account. This "harvest" could be the "rapture." [1 Thessalonians 4:17] Some Futurists believe the rapture occurs before the tribulation, some believe it happens in the middle of it, and some believe it happens at the end.* ➤

17 Another angel came out of the Heavenly Temple and he too had a sharp sickle. 18 Yet another angel—the one who has authority over the altar fire ❖ *perhaps the same angel as in Revelation 8:5* ➤—came from the altar and in a loud voice called out to the angel with the sickle, "Harvest the unrighteous grapes that are ripe for God's righteous punishment." ❖ *Fire is associated with judgment, and the altar is associated with the prayers of God's people.* ➤ 19 The angel swung his sickle over the Earth and gathered the clusters of unrighteous grapes and threw them into the winepress of God's holy fury against sin. *[Joel 3:13]* ❖ *Crushed grapes resemble and represent human blood.* ➤ 20 The grapes are smashed in the winepress of God's fury—which is his holy war against them outside the Holy City of Jerusalem. Blood flowed from that massacre in a chest-high flood for

a distance of 1600 A stadia. ❖ *Commentators variously calculate this length as corresponding to 165-200 miles, but it is most likely symbolic of a worldwide judgment. It also corresponded to an ancient estimate of the length of Palestine (from Syria to Egypt). The horse's-bridle height—for which I've substituted "chest height" as more easily grasped by modern urban dwellers—is also symbolic of a huge quantity, rather than to be taken literally. [Isaiah 63:3; Lamentations 1:15; Revelation 19:15]* ➤

I. THE SEVEN BOWLS OF GOD'S RIGHTEOUS WRATH

❖ *The vision of the seven bowls of God's righteous wrath—introduced in Revelation 15:1—follows the preceding visions, but may not be sequential in time. (This can be said of several of the visions.) Some commentators think that together, the seven bowls are the third calamity [Revelation 11:14] associated with the seventh trumpet, and that they are still warnings of the eternal punishment in Hell to come—implying that there might still be an opportunity for some to repent, though some commentators believe that the opportunity to repent is gone since they are poured out on those with the mark of the False Messiah. Yet in Revelation 16:11, the text says "but they refused to repent"—as if prompting repentance was the purpose behind the judgments. In Revelation 14:8, the second angel proclaimed that Babylon had fallen, and in 14:14 the "harvest begins." It's possible that the bowls of wrath are poured out before the angel in 14:6-7 gave his "last chance" message, or before the second angel proclaimed the defeat of Babylon. Or it could happen between the harvest of believers and the harvest of the unrighteous "grapes"—which might be suggested by 15:2 where the all the righteous are already in Heaven. Or the seven bowls could be a clarifying expansion of what is involved in the figure of the winepress in 14:20. Hendriksen (an Idealist) believes these seven bowl judgments are also poured out throughout this age. He sees the trumpet judgments as warnings to unbelievers and the bowl judgments as punishments for those who do not repent—though in his examples of how this happens, he has to significantly weaken the descriptions of the judgments in order to make his point.* ➤

15

1 Then I saw a vision of another important and wondrous sign in Heaven. There were seven angels carrying seven

---

A **14:20** There are some manuscripts that say 1606, which is probably due to an error in copying, and some that say 1200. But the manuscript evidence points toward 1600 as being the original number.

last afflicting judgments in bowls. These are the final warnings in this age of God's righteous wrath that awaits people in Hell if they refuse to repent. ❖ *It's unlikely that this verse literally means that with these seven afflictions God's wrath is completed (in the literal text), unless it only means as it will be expressed on Earth before the final judgment—since his wrath against rebellious sinners will be eternal in Hell itself.* ➤

The Song of Moses and the Lamb

2 I also saw something like a sea of transparent fiery crystal. *[Revelation 4:6]* All those who had victoriously resisted worshipping the False Messiah or his image and had refused to receive the mark with the number representing his name were standing by **A** this crystal-like sea—holding lyres that God had given them. *[Revelation 5:8; 14:2]* ❖ *Some commentators associate the fire mixed in the transparent crystal-like sea as pertaining to the fire of persecution that these believers have successfully come through, or the fire of God's judgments that are taking place in the world below, or the lake of fire. [Revelation 9:20] Hendriksen sees verse 2-4 as a vision in Heaven after the judgment—in a situation similar to the victory celebration of the Israelites on the far side of the Red Sea after the defeat of the Egyptians. He interprets the fire mixed with the transparent sea as representing God's judgments that demonstrate his righteous wrath upon those who reject him.* ➤ 3 They were singing a song of victory and deliverance modeled after the song of Moses *[Exodus 15:1-18]* ❖ *Jews sang this song in their synagogues on Sabbath evenings, so it was very familiar to Jewish believers.* ➤ who was God's servant, in honor of the victory and redemption that the Lamb had obtained for them. They sang, "Omnipotent Lord and God, *[Amos 4:13]* everything you do is grand and wonderful! *[Psalm 92:5; 111:3; 139:14]* King over all that happens throughout the ages, **B** your ways are righteous and just! *[Deuteronomy 32:4]* 4 There is no one who will not fear, honor, and praise you, Lord! *[Jeremiah 10:7]* For you are uniquely holy and set apart—no one else is even remotely like you! *[Exodus 15:11]* All redeemed peoples will come and worship you because they have seen your righteous redemptive deeds!" *[Psalm 86:9-10]*

The Seven Bowls

5 After this, I saw in a vision the Holy of Holies in the Heavenly Temple *[Hebrews 8:1-5; 9:11-12]*—which is the Heavenly Tabernacle of the Testimony—and it was opened, allowing me to see in. *[Exodus 38:21; 40:20-21; Numbers 17:7; 18:2]* ❖ *The Testimony refers to the tablets of the Torah that God gave to Moses which were kept in the Ark of the Covenant. [Exodus 32:15-16; Deuteronomy 10:5]* ➤ 6 Seven angels came out of the Temple with God's commission to deliver the seven last afflicting judgments to the Earth. They were dressed in pure-white shining linen and wore a gold band around their chests. *[Revelation 1:12-13]* ❖ *The linen [Exodus 28:4-8] and the gold band (or sash or belt) may be symbolic of a priestly function. [Revelation 1:13]* ➤ 7 Then one of the four unique beings gave each of the seven angels a gold bowl full of the everliving God's righteous wrath. ❖ *24 gold bowls in Revelation 5:8 were associated with the prayers of God's people. Some commentators see a tie here.* ➤ 8 The Heavenly Temple was filled with clouds of dense smoke of the intense presence of God's power and glory *[Exodus 19:18; 40:34; 1 Kings 8:10-11; 2 Chronicles 5:13-14; Isaiah 6:4]* such that no one was able to enter it until the seven angels were finished delivering their seven afflicting judgments.

16

1 Then I heard God's voice thunder from the Temple, telling the seven angels, "Now is the time to pour out the seven bowls containing my righteous wrath upon the people of Earth." ❖ *Note the similarities between these afflicting judgments and the plagues that Moses delivered in Egypt.* ➤

Bowl 1: Boils and Ulcerous Sores

2 The first bowl was poured out upon Earth—and those who had the mark of the False Messiah and submissively worshipped his image broke out in foul painful boils and open ulcerous sores. *[Exodus 9:8-10]*

A 15:2 The preposition ἐπί (epi) translated "by" is ambiguous and could just as validly be translated "on" or "in," as far as we know.

B 15:3 Many manuscripts say "King of the nations" rather than "King of the eons."

Bowl 2: The Seas Turn into Blood

3 The second bowl was poured out into the salt-water oceans and seas—and they all turned into blood that coagulated and stank like a dead body. Every living organism in them died. [Exodus 7:19-24; Revelation 8:8-9]

Bowl 3: All Freshwater Sources Turn into Blood

4 Then the third bowl was poured out into all the rivers, springs, and sources of fresh water in the world—and they too turned into blood. [Psalm 78:44] 5 I heard the angel who had authority over the Earth's water respond, "O Holy God, you are now—as you always have been—righteous and just in sending this afflicting judgment on those who hate you. 6 They have shed the blood of your people and prophets—so it's appropriate and fair that you give them blood to drink." 7 Then I heard the voices of the martyrs A from the altar say, "Yes, our omnipotent Lord and God. We acknowledge that your judgments and punishments are righteous and fair." [Revelation 6:9-10]

Bowl 4: The Sun Gets Hotter

8 Then the fourth bowl was poured out on the sun—causing it to flare up and severely burn people. 9 Everyone on Earth was painfully scorched by the intense heat, but instead of repenting and praising Him, they cursed and blasphemed God who they knew was sending these afflictions.

Bowl 5: Total Darkness

10 Then the fifth bowl was poured out on the False Messiah's center of power—and his kingdom was plunged into total darkness. [Exodus 10:21-23] People bit their tongues in the agony 11 from their sores, but they refused to repent of their evil ways and continued to curse and blaspheme God in Heaven for afflicting them.

Bowl 6: The Euphrates River Dries Up

12 Then the sixth bowl was poured out on the mighty Euphrates river—and its water completely dried up. This provided an easy invasion route for the pagan rulers in the east B to send their troops. [Isaiah 11:15-16] ❖ Note the parallel with the sixth trumpet. [Revelation 9:13-15] ➤ 13 The vision also showed me three demonic spirits that looked like frogs, one each coming out of the mouths of the Dragon, False Messiah, and the False Prophet. ❖ According to Leviticus 11:10-12, frogs are ritually unclean, repulsive, and detestable—so their appearance may emphasize that aspect of these demons. They may also allude to the plague of frogs in Exodus 8:1-6. ➤ 14 These demons had the power to perform miraculous signs [Mark 13:22; 2 Thessalonians 2:9-10; 1 Timothy 4:1] which they used to engage the support of every king and ruler in the world—convincing them to gather their armed forces in preparation for the battle that was about to begin on Almighty God's Great Day. ❖ On that day, God will come in the person of Jesus the Messiah to subdue all opposition to his rule and to judge everyone who has ever lived. This battle is the same one described in Revelation 19:11-21 and—according to Amillennialists—also the one in Revelation 20:7-10. ➤

15 Jesus said, "Take care, for my return will be unannounced and will be as unexpected as a thief. I will bless those who are alert for my return and keep themselves spiritually pure so they will not be exposed to public shame at the judgment." [Matthew 24:43-44; Luke 12:39-40; 1 Thessalonians 5:2-10; Revelation 3:3] 16 Then the demons had the world rulers deploy all their forces in the valley of Megiddo (pronounced "Har Magiddon" in Hebrew, meaning "Magiddo Mountain"). [Zechariah 12:11; Revelation 19:19] ❖ The exact meaning of the reference to Harmageddon (or Armageddon) and its location is debated. There was a city named Megiddo on a hill overlooking a plain in the Jezreel Valley—which is the site many commentators think this refers to. Hendriksen sees the story in Judges chapters 4 and 5 as the place to find the proper interpretation of this battle. Some commentators think the reference to a mountain is rooted in Ezekiel 38:8, 21; 39:2, 4, 17. This final battle is predicted in Ezekiel chapters 38—39; Joel 2:11; 3:2; Zechariah chapters 12—14; and 2 Thessalonians 2:8 ➤

Bowl 7: The Final Destruction of Babylon

17 Then the seventh bowl was poured out on the air—and God's voice thundered

---

A 16:7 This is one guess. Other commentators say it is the voice of the angel who serves at the altar.

B 16:12 In the first century, this might have meant the Parthians, some of Rome's most-feared enemies.

from his throne in the Heavenly Temple, "It is accomplished!" *[John 19:30]* **18** Then there were tremendous flashes of lightning, roaring thunder, and the most severe earthquake that has ever occurred during Earth's existence. *[Hebrews 12:26-27; Revelation 8:5; 11:13, 19]* ❖ *It's the end of the world as we have known it.* ➤ **19** The great city of Rome **A** was split into three parts, and it—along with every other city on Earth—was completely destroyed by the quake. God had not forgotten the great sins of the people loyal to Babylon. Just as she had made the world drink from her cup of immorality and idolatry, God made her drink of the cup of his righteous wrath. *[Isaiah 51:17]* ❖ *Drinking from a cup is a figure of speech meaning to participate in and experience the contents of whatever is mentioned in the cup. See a literal translation of Revelation 14:8 to understand the reference. Babylon is a figurative reference to both the city of Rome—the center of the False Messiah's power base—and the worldwide system of false religion and the people that worshipped him.* ➤ **20** Every island sank and every mountain was leveled by the quake. *[Revelation 6:14]* **21** Tremendous hailstones weighing up to a hundred pounds fell from the sky, killing and destroying. *[Exodus 9:23-25]* ❖ *Hail was a common figure in the Hebrew Scriptures for God's punishment—as well as a real means to deliver that punishment. [Joshua 10:11; Job 38:22-23; Isaiah 28:2, 17; Ezekiel 13:11-13; 38:22-23]* ➤ But the people who remained on Earth cursed and blasphemed God, instead of acknowledging their sin and the righteousness of his judgment.

J. BABYLON AND HER DESTRUCTION

A Flashback about Babylon, the Great Spiritual Prostitute

❖ *The things that John reports from a vision in chapters 17 and 18 are clearly not sequential in time with the events of chapter 16. It's purpose is to give more background and details about this Babylon [Revelation 16:19] which John*

has just seen destroyed. The title of "prostitute" or "harlot" in the Hebrew Scriptures usually refers to Israel being unfaithful to Yahweh by worshipping false gods. But there are also references to the pagan cities of Nineveh [Nahum 3:4] and Tyre [Isaiah 23:15-18] where they are referred to as prostitutes because they lure people and nations into desiring luxury, pleasure, and power at the expense of all that is moral and right—a charge that might be leveled against much of US and Western culture today. Hendriksen gives the following references that should be studied as a foundation for understanding the symbolism of Babylon as the great spiritual prostitute: Genesis 10:10; 11:1-9; Isaiah chapters 13—14; 21; 46—48; Jeremiah chapters 25; 50—51; Daniel chapter 2; 4:30; and chapter 7, Habakkuk chapter 3; and Ezekiel chapter 27 about the fall of the city of Tyre. Wilcock—in his book (see the bibliography)—has a very insightful discussion on "the identifying of symbols" on pages 151-157 that is worth studying. ➤

17

1 Then one of the angels—whom I had seen pour out one of the seven bowls of God's righteous wrath—came to me and said, "Come with me and I will show you more about that great spiritual prostitute **B** who sits on many waters *[Jeremiah 51:12-14]* and the punishment that awaits her. **2** Earth's rulers had immoral spiritual relationships with her, and Earth's people got drunk on the intoxicating effects of indulging in her sins." *[Jeremiah 51:7]* **3** The angel transported me in spirit to an uninhabited area. There I saw a woman sitting on a terrifying scarlet-colored monster whose hide was covered with names that were blasphemous of God. This monster had seven heads and ten horns. *[Revelation 13:1]* **4** The woman was dressed in luxuriously expensive purple and scarlet cloth **C** and was extravagantly adorned with gold, gemstones, and pearl jewelry. She held a beautiful gold cup full of enticing intoxicating drink—which represented the vile, disgusting, shameful,

---

A 16:19 Rome is thought to be the place where the False Messiah will center his base of power. But if he centers his government in some other city, then that is the city which would be meant. The literal text says, "the great city," which most commentators take to mean, "Babylon," but they also interpret this name as symbolic of a world center of evil.

B 17:1 The word here translated "prostitute" and in other translations as "harlot" is πόρνη (pornē) from which we get the English word "porn." It is also the root of the Greek word for "fornication."

C 17:4 Osborne notes that purple was the color of royalty and scarlet was the color of wealth.

and obscene immoralities, corruptions, and blasphemies she lured her lovers to participate in. ❖ *The literal text says her cup is full of abominations, which Ladd points out is associated with idolatry (the worship of false gods) in the Hebrew Scriptures.* ➤ 5 A name with symbolic meaning **A** was visible on her forehead,

"THE GREAT BABYLON,
THE MOTHER AND SOURCE OF ALL PROSTITUTES AND LOATHSOME PRACTICES ON EARTH."

6 She drunkenly reveled in the killing of God's people **B**—and especially of those who died because they boldly proclaimed their loyalty to Jesus. I was amazed, appalled, dumbfounded, and mystified at the sight of her.

An Angel Interprets Some of the Symbolism

7 The angel asked me, "Why are you so amazed? I will explain the symbolism of the woman and the monster she rides with the seven heads and ten horns. 8 The monster once lived, is no longer alive, but will once again emerge alive from the bottomless pit of Hell—and eventually be destroyed. ❖ *This is the monster of chapter 13—the False Messiah—described before the bowls of God's righteous wrath have been poured out.* ➤ Those on Earth whose names have not been written in the Book of Life in Heaven since the creation of all things, will be amazed when they see this False Messiah—because he lived, died, and will come back to life again. 9 One needs God's wisdom to understand this. The seven heads of the monster are the seven hills that the woman sits on. ❖ *Rome was originally built on seven hills.* ➤ 10 They also represent seven kings, five of which have fallen, one which currently exists, and one that has not yet come. But when he does come, he must endure for a short while. ❖ *Preterists assign these kings to seven particular Roman emperors of the first century. Traditionally, Futurists have understood these kings as referring to the empires of Egypt, Assyria,*

Babylon, Persia, and Greece—which had opposed God's people and had ceased to exist with any power at the time of this vision—Rome, which was still in existence, and the one to come as the worldwide empire of the Anti-messiah—the monster which is the False Messiah. Some commentators have noted that other empires have come and gone since Rome—such as Nazi Germany and the Soviet Union—which aspired to world domination and persecuted God's people, both Jews and Gentile believers. Idealists interpret the seven kings symbolically—which might be more believable if there was less description in this verse and if their symbolic interpretations were more vague. ➤ 11 The False Messiah who lived, but is now not alive, will himself be an eighth king—and is also one **C** of the seven. He will be destroyed. 12 The ten horns on the monster are ten future kings who will have their authority to rule for the same brief time that the False Messiah rules. *[Daniel 7:24]* ❖ *Idealists take the number 10 to be symbolic of completeness. But according to them, so are the numbers 4, 7, 12, 12,000, 144,000, etc. That doesn't mean there's no validity to this symbolism, but they don't seem to take any number literally—and they all mean the same thing!* ➤ 13 These ten kings all rule with the same purpose, to support the False Messiah with their power and authority. 14 They will marshal their armed forces to wage war against the Lamb *[Revelation 16:14; 19:11-21]* and his glorified resurrected people— whom he called and chose and who remained his faithful followers to the end. But the Lamb will effortlessly defeat them because he is— in name, authority, and power—Lord over all lords and King over all kings." *[Deuteronomy 10:17; Psalm 136:3; Daniel 2:47; 1 Timothy 6:15; Revelation 19:16]* 15 The angel also told me, "The waters on which the prostitute sits *[17:1]* represent the large numbers of people from every language and people group who support Babylon—the spiritual prostitute. ❖ *Ladd explains that the prostitute sitting on the waters represents her relationship with what the waters represents, (i.e., she is supported by the many peoples) and her sitting on the monster represents her relationship with what the monster represents (i.e., she is supported by Satan). Osborne says that "waters" is a metaphor in the Hebrew*

A 17:5 The meaning is that she represents the capital city of the False Messiah, as well as the worldwide system of government, religion, and economics that supports the False Messiah.

B 17:6 Ladd says that the literal text, "drunk with blood," was a common ancient idiom where a sword that has

killed is said to be "drunk with blood." [Isaiah 34:5-7; 49:26; Jeremiah 46:10; Ezekiel 39:18-19]

C 17:11 Some translators would eliminate the word "one," and say, "is also of the seven," understanding the "of" in a difference sense. Their explanations of that sense are vague.

Scriptures for inhabitants, and gives the following references: *[Isaiah 8:7; 17:12-13; Jeremiah 46:7-8; 47:2]* ➤ 16 But the ten horns and the seven-headed monster will hate the prostitute—and ultimately they will turn on her, strip her of all her glory, eat her flesh, and consume her with fire. ❖ *This may happen when they see that they are going to lose the war against the Lamb, but the timing is not clear. Osborne sees this as civil war within the False Messiah's empire, and says that such an end-time civil war is predicted in Ezekiel 38:21 with details that match this verse in Ezekiel 23:25-29. (In the Ezekiel 23 passage, it is Jerusalem which is being destroyed by the Babylonian empire.)* ➤ 17 For in reality, God is in full control and accomplishes his purposes through them—first in having them give their support to the False Messiah until his prophecies are accomplished, and then in putting it in their minds to turn on the prostitute. 18 And the woman you saw—the spiritual prostitute Babylon—is that great city of Rome that dominates the Earth's rulers."

18

Babylon's Destruction

1 Then I saw another angel of very high rank A descend from Heaven—and the brilliant light of his glory illuminated the entire world. 2 He proclaimed in a voice that was clearly heard by everyone on Earth, "It is decreed in Heaven that the Great Babylon will fall in defeat! *[Isaiah 21:9; Jeremiah 51:8; Daniel 5:26; Revelation 14:8]* It will become so desolate and uninhabitable that only demons and carrion birds will be found there. ❖ *The pronouncement in the original text is in the past tense—which is typical of prophecies whose future fulfillment is certain. The rest of the chapter is mostly in the future tense, mixed with some past tense. This interpretation tries to make it conform to consistent English style as a future description that is certain to happen.* ➤ 3 All the peoples of Earth have enthusiastically participated in her immoralities and idolatry. The world's rulers have supported and duplicated her evil deeds. The world's businessmen have profited and become wealthy by participating in her immoral exploitations."

4 Then I heard another voice from Heaven speaking for God, "My people,

separate yourselves from all association with Babylon and all her immoral ways. If you participate in her sins, then you will also share in her punishment! *[Isaiah 48:20; Jeremiah 51:6, 45; 2 Corinthians 6:14-17]* 5 Her vile sins have become so many that it's impossible for me to further delay the accumulated punishment she deserves. She will soon see that I have neither forgotten nor failed to notice her crimes against me. *[Genesis 18:20; Jeremiah 51:9; Romans 2:5-6; Revelation 16:19]* 6 I will treat her in the same way she has abused my people—and I will double the punishment each of her evil deeds deserves. I will, in effect, force her to drink a double portion of punishment consisting of the same kinds of sufferings she has caused others to experience—which she has enjoyed drinking so much from her own cup. *[Psalm 137:8; Jeremiah 50:29]* ❖ *Hendriksen and some other commentators interpret "double" to mean the matching of punishment to the crime—not that the punishment itself will be double that which would normally be deserved. Other commentators also say that the phrase about repaying double for deeds is an idiom in the Hebrew Scriptures—which means punishment in full measure, not twice the punishment. [Jeremiah 16:18; 17:18] In reality, their punishment is eternal suffering in Hell, so the idea of doubling the punishment in terms of quantity is meaningless—unless it refers only to the amount or intensity of suffering they will experience in this life before their deaths or the final judgment. Even if this is sometimes an idiom—though this is debated—the Scriptures do sometimes mean a literal double retribution, or more. [Exodus 22:4, 7, 9; Psalm 79:12]* ➤ 7 I will give her as much pain, anguish, and grief as she enjoyed luxury and riches and proudly ascribed praise and glory to herself. She self-deceptively thinks, 'As Queen, I'm the supreme ruler. I'm safe from the afflictions that can affect widows—and I will never have to mourn over the death of my children. Nothing can touch me!' *[Psalm 10:4, 11, 13; Isaiah 47:5-9; Obadiah 3-4; Zephaniah 2:15]* 8 Because of her arrogant pride, I will destroy her in a single day with death, anguish, and famine. Fire will consume her and all that she boasts about, for Yahweh—who judges her—is all powerful.

9 "The world's rulers who depended on her for their luxury and wealth and who participated in her immorality and idolatry,

---

A **18:1** Or of great authority or power.

will mourn in anguish for their own loss when they see her destruction. 10 Terrified by the prospect of sharing in her fate, they will distance themselves from her as much as they can and exclaim, 'How utterly dreadful is Babylon's destruction! She was so powerful and majestic, but in such a short time God's judgment has made her desolate!' [Ezekiel 26:16-17]

11 "The world's businessmen will also lament her destruction—since the economy and their livelihood will have been destroyed along with her. [Ezekiel 27:12-36] 12 Her empire is the main market for the luxuries of gold, silver, gemstones, pearls, fine fabrics, exotic wood, and all kinds of expensive quality artifacts made of ivory, rare woods, marble, bronze, and iron, 13 and exotic spices, perfumes and incense, wine, olive oil, flour, wheat, livestock, weapons, slaves, and even people condemned to be killed as entertainment for the masses. 14 All the exotic luxuries she longed for will no longer be available. All her wealth and glory will have evaporated—never to be restored.

15 "Those who became rich by supplying her with these things will distance themselves from her and disavow any connection—out of fear that they too will suffer her fate. But they will mourn what they've lost as a result of her downfall. 16 They will lament, 'What a wretched shame that this terrible fate should come upon such a grand city, adorned with gorgeous expensive fabrics and gold, gemstones, and pearls. 17 In such a short time, all that wealth was demolished!'

"Every merchant-ship's captain and sailors and all who profited from transporting those rich cargos will distance themselves from their association with her 18 when they see her smoldering ruins. They will exclaim, 'There was never a more glorious city than she was!' 19 They will display their mourning for all to see and lament, 'What a terrible thing to happen to such a magnificent city which made us all rich. In such a short time she's been utterly devastated!'

20 "But you who live in Heaven—my holy people and apostles and prophets—will rejoice because her destruction will have vindicated your faith and God's holiness! I will have paid her back for what she did to you." [Deuteronomy 32:43; Jeremiah 51:48-64; Romans 12:19]

21 Then an angel of great might picked up a boulder as large as a big millstone and hurled it into the sea. He proclaimed, "In the same way that boulder disappeared beneath the sea, the great city Babylon will be violently hurled down and never seen again. 22 Where there was music and celebration, there will be utter silence. There will be no industry or workers to make the slightest sound—and no food. 23 There will be utter darkness without even a single glimmer of light. Never again will there be a marriage there, nor love or joy. This is the fate of her businessmen—the richest and most powerful in the world. They—along with all the world's peoples—were deceived by her demonic miracles into thinking she was invincible. [Isaiah 24:8; Jeremiah 7:34; 25:10] 24 For she and all associated with her are held responsible for the deaths of all God's prophets and the rest of his holy people and also everyone else killed on Earth—because she was its ruler."

19

Heaven Rejoices over
the Destruction of Babylon,
and the Coming Wedding of the Lamb

1 Then I heard what sounded like an immense assembly of the redeemed A in Heaven—loudly proclaiming in unison, "Praise Yahweh! He is our God who saves and redeems, whose power and glory and majesty are unequaled! 2 His judgments and punishments are righteous and fair! He has righteously condemned the great spiritual prostitute who corrupted Earth's peoples with her immorality and idolatry! He has avenged her killing of his people!" [Deuteronomy 32:35, 43; 2 Kings 9:7; Psalm 19:9; Romans 12:19; Hebrews 10:30-31] 3 Then a second time I heard them proclaim,

---

A 19:1 Some commentators believe this is an assembly of angels, not the redeemed. But see Revelation 7:9.

"Praise Yahweh! For her destruction is final and eternal!" *[Isaiah 34:10]* 4 And the 24 elders and four unique beings around the throne prostrated themselves in worship before God and responded, "Yes, it is so! Praise Yahweh!" *[Psalm 106:48]* ❖ *If the reader accepts the interpretation that the immense assembly in verse 1 is all those who have been redeemed, then the interpretation that the 24 elders are symbolic of all of redeemed humanity is unlikely. See the note at Revelation 4:4.* ➤

5 Then an angel's voice came from the throne, exhorting, "Let us praise our God, everyone of every rank who serves, honors, and fears him!" 6 In response, I heard the united voice of an immense assembly which was as loud as the roar of a great waterfall or a deafening clap of thunder. It proclaimed, "Praise Yahweh! For our omnipotent Lord and God has begun to visibly and openly reign over all creation! *[Psalm 93:1; 97:1; 99:1]* 7 Let us exult and celebrate and mightily praise him! For the time is finally at hand when the Lamb will marry his bride—which is the Assembly of all those who have made themselves ready for him. *[Ephesians 5:25-32; 2 Corinthians 11:2]* 8 By his enabling power and the righteousness he has bestowed on her in his spiritual union with her, his bride **A** has dressed herself in fine white linen." ❖ *which represents the good deeds that his holy people have done in obedience to his will.* ➤ 9 Then the angel instructed me, "Record this: Those who are invited to the Lamb's wedding banquet in Heaven are truly blessed. These very words come from God himself." ❖ *The marriage of the Messiah and his "bride"—which is the Assembly of All Believers—is symbolic of the start of a new intimate relationship between them. This relationship starts when we are saved, but the consummation of that relationship in Heaven will be so much more than we have in this life that it will seem quite new and wonderful. Some commentators see a difference between those believers who compose the "bride" and those who are the wedding guests. Most commentators see the two as referring to the same group of people—with the symbolism being fluid.* ➤

10 I was so overwhelmed with awe that I prostrated myself in worship before the angel, but he immediately admonished, "Don't worship me! I'm only a fellow servant—along with you and your fellow believers who remain faithful to Jesus. God is the only one you should worship, for it's the Spirit-inspired prophetic ministry of all God's servants to testify about what Jesus has done—not to glorify themselves or other servants."

K. THE SECOND COMING

The Messiah's Return and His Enemies' Destruction

11 Then I saw in a vision a perspective from Earth where I could see Heaven openly visible in the sky. A rider on a white horse came out of Heaven whose titles are "Faithful," "Dependable," and "True to his Word." He came to make war against the False Messiah and his followers—and his decision to do so is righteous, just, and holy. *[Psalm 96:13; Isaiah 11:4; 2 Thessalonians 1:7-10]* 12 His penetrating all-seeing eyes blazed brightly like fire *[Daniel 10:6; Revelation 1:14]* and he wore many crowns **B**—indicating his supreme sovereignty over all rulers. On his forehead is a name unknown by anyone except himself. *[Revelation 2:17]* ❖ *A person's name is his unique identity and character. No finite being can fully know or comprehend the identity and character of the Son of God.* ➤ 13 His garment is dipped in blood ❖ *Commentators don't agree whether the blood is symbolic of his own death or the blood of those he is fighting—as in [Isaiah 63:1-6].* ➤ and he is the Living Expression of God to his creation. 14 Following behind him—also on white horses—are his Heavenly warriors, dressed in pure white linen. ❖ *Commentators don't agree whether his army is composed of angelic warriors, the redeemed, the martyrs, or all of the above.* ➤ 15 The words he speaks have all the power necessary to defeat his enemies. *[Isaiah 11:4; 2 Thessalonians 2:8; Revelation 1:16; 19:21]* With his absolute power, he will completely destroy them *[Psalm 2:9]* ❖ *To "rule with an iron scepter," in the literal text, does not mean to rule*

A 19:8 The word here is "wife," not "bride," but a woman who was betrothed was often called a "wife," even if the actual wedding had not yet taken place.

B 19:12 The word here is διαδήματα (diadēmata) which means "diadems" or "crowns," not the victory-wreath type of crown.

strictly from power, but to destroy. *[Revelation 2:27; 12:5]* ➤—and motivated by the fierce wrath of Almighty God against sin, he will crush them like grapes in a winepress. *[Isaiah 63:3; Joel 3:13; Revelation 14:19]* 16 He has this title boldly written on his robe at thigh level:

"LORD OVER ALL LORDS,
AND KING OVER ALL KINGS."

*[Deuteronomy 10:17; Psalm 136:3; Daniel 2:47;
1 Timothy 6:15; Revelation 17:14]*

17 Then I saw an angel standing in front of the sun, commanding all birds capable of flight, "Come and gorge yourselves on the slaughter provided for you by God. *[Ezekiel 39:17-20]* 18 Eat the dead flesh of all God's enemies who have been destroyed—from kings and generals on down to ordinary people and slaves."

19 Then I saw more details in a vision. I saw the False Messiah and all of Earth's rulers who were his allies and their armed forces—deployed to engage in war against the One on the white horse and his army. *[Revelation 16:16]* 20 I saw the False Messiah and his False Prophet—who had performed miraculous signs for him that had deceived all those who had accepted the False Messiah's mark of loyalty and had worshipped his image. *[Revelation 13:1-8]* They were both helplessly seized by the Lord's forces and thrown alive and conscious into the stinking lake of burning sulfur in Hell. *[Revelation 20:10; 14-15; 21:8]* 21 The Rider on the white horse killed the rest of God's enemies simply by speaking *[Isaiah 11:4; 2 Thessalonians 2:8; Revelation 1:16; 19:15]*—and the birds gorged themselves on their dead bodies.

L. THE MILLENNIUM AND THE FINAL JUDGMENT

20

The Millennium when Satan is Bound

1 Then I saw an angel in a vision, descending from Heaven to Earth, holding the key that locks the entrance to the bottomless pit of Hell, and holding a massive chain. ❖ *This is the start of a new vision and it's time frame is unknown relative to the previous vision. Idealist interpreters say this took place after Jesus' ascension, and Futurist interpreters say it will happen after Jesus' second coming—in sequence with the previous vision.* ➤ 2 This angel seized the dragon who is Satan—the serpent in the Garden of Eden *[Genesis 3:1]* also known as the Devil. Then he bound Satan with the massive chain. This binding was to last for 1,000 years. 3 Then Satan was cast into the bottomless pit of Hell and the entrance was closed and securely locked—so he would be unable to deceive people on Earth during the 1,000 years of his imprisonment. After the 1,000 years is up, he must be freed again, but only for a short period of time. ❖ *The Amillennialist Idealist interpretation is that Satan has been bound since his defeat at the cross—and that the 1,000-year period is symbolic of the period between Jesus' earthly ministry and his second coming. The difficulty with this view are verses like the following: [Acts 5:3; Romans 16:20; 1 Corinthians 5:5; 7:5; 2 Corinthians 2:11; 4:3-4; 12:7; Ephesians 4:27; 6:11; 1 Thessalonians 2:18; 1 Timothy 1:20; 3:7; 5:15; 2 Timothy 2:26; James 4:7; 1 Peter 5:8; Revelation 2:10, 13] All of these verses—written by Luke, Paul, James, Peter, and John—talk about the Devil as if he is an active agent in this age. All five of those authors would have to have been speaking figuratively of the Devil's demons in those verses—and not about Satan himself—if the Amillennialist view is correct. But if these authors are speaking figuratively of all demons by referring to the Devil or Satan in all those verses, then why would it be any different in this verse? It would seem to be consistent that this verse too would refer not only to Satan, but to all his demons as being bound—since they too deceive. But it's clear that demonic activity and deception are still prevalent in this age. Amillennialists also say that Satan is restricted in his being bound, but is still active to a degree in this world. In particular, his being bound means he cannot prevent the spreading of the message of the Good News in this age. But his being cast into the Abyss (bottomless pit) of Hell and locked in there is an odd way of indicating a partial restriction of his activities instead of a complete restriction of them. The verse also says he is "unable to deceive" during this period. Deception is Satan's main means of working—and is clearly rampant in this age. Amillennialists do have counter arguments to all this, but space prohibits detailing them here. The interested reader should have no problem finding a commentary with this view since they are in the majority. But if the past 2,000 years is the glorious millennial age when Satan is bound—it's certainly not something to be excited about! What were the believers in John's*

time to be looking forward to? Is deception, temptation, and sin really significantly restrained now compared to what it was like before Jesus came? I don't think so. ¶ The Premillennialist Futurist interpretation is that this is a 1,000-year period (a few would interpret the 1,000 years as figurative, but most take it literally) that will start after Jesus returns. Osborne says a possible purpose of the millennium is to demonstrate the necessity of eternal punishment for Satan—who will never change his ways—and for those who reject the salvation the Messiah offers. This will be seen when the unsaved peoples that live during the millennium still choose to follow Satan and to rebel against the Messiah—after having experienced 1,000 years of his benevolent rule. ➤

4 Then I saw thrones in a vision—and those sitting on them have been given authority to judge. ❖ *Commentators disagree as to who these judges are. Are they all believers, the apostles, the 24 elders, the martyrs from the tribulation, all martyrs, all of the redeemed? The text doesn't tell us.* ➤ I also saw those who had been executed for their faith—for proclaiming the Good News about Jesus and the truth of God's Word. They had refused to worship the False Messiah or his image and had refused to receive his mark on their foreheads or hands. Jesus had raised them back to life, and they shared his rule for 1,000 years. *[Daniel 7:22; 1 Corinthians 6:2-3]* ❖ *Amillennialists say this is a spiritual resurrection—not a physical one—and that they rule now in Heaven. Premillennialists say this is a physical resurrection and that they will rule on Earth over a remnant of unbelievers that are not destroyed in the Great Tribulation. There is some disagreement among Premillennialists as to who is included in this first resurrection that rule during the 1,000 years on Earth. Some say just the martyrs from the Tribulation, others that it includes all who have been saved.* ➤ 5 This is the first resurrection. (The rest of the dead do not come back to life until the 1,000 years have passed.) ❖ *Many Premillennialists say that the "rest of the dead" refers to the unsaved, and that all who are saved participate in the first resurrection.* ➤ 6 Those who participate in the first resurrection are indeed specially set apart and blessed. None of them will experience the "second death"—which is eternal damnation in Hell. Instead, they will be priests who serve God and the Messiah and will share in his rule for 1,000 years.

Satan's Last Stand and Defeat

7 But when the 1,000 years have passed, Satan will be set free from his prison. 8 He will be allowed to roam everywhere on Earth and once again deceive many peoples for the purpose of assembling them together to once again fight God and his people. Those he deceives are called Gog and Magog—and their number is immense, like the grains of sand on a beach. *[Ezekiel 7:2; 38:2; 8-9; 14-16]* 9 This mighty army will spread out on a wide plain surrounding Jerusalem—the city God loves and where his people live. But God will send down fire from Heaven on them and completely consume them. *[Ezekiel 38:22; 39:6]* 10 Then Satan—who deceived those peoples—will be permanently confined to the stinking lake of burning sulfur in Hell where the False Messiah and False Prophet also exist. *[Revelation 19:20]* There, they will suffer agonizing punishment, night and day, without relief, forever.

The Great White Throne Judgment

❖ *Amillennialists interpret this as the only physical resurrection and the only judgment. Premillennialists interpret this as a second resurrection and judgment—involving only those who have not been saved—which takes place after the rule of the Messiah on Earth for 1,000 years.* ➤

11 Then in a vision I saw a huge white throne and One who sat on it. *[Daniel 7:9-10]* ❖ *This is the throne of both God the Father and Jesus the Lamb. [Revelation 22:1, 3] We know that the Father has given all authority to judge humanity to his Son. [John 5:22; 26-27] We also know that the Son does not judge on his own, but listens to his Father. [John 5:30; 8:16, 28]* ➤ Earth and sky **A** will disappear, for there will no longer be a place for them. ❖ *The meaning of this last sentence is obscure. Some think the present Earth and sky—and possibly Heaven too—will evaporate, to be replaced by a new Heaven and a new Earth. Others think Earth and its sky will be purified by fire that completely destroys the surface and atmosphere, but the planet will remain and be renewed as New Earth. The new "heaven" could simply be a new atmosphere, or a new Heaven, or a renewed Heaven. The details are simply ambiguous—and it really won't matter to us which version is accurate. Some commentators think this*

A 20:11 The word οὐρανός (ouranos) can mean either "Heaven" or "sky."

could be what is described in more detail in Revelation 6:12-14 at the breaking of the sixth seal. ➤ **12** I saw every human who had ever died—from the most exalted to the least important—standing before the throne awaiting judgment. And the books with the records of their lives, words, and deeds were opened for examination and judgment. There was another book also open—the Book of Life—in which are written the names of all who are saved. *[Daniel 12:1-2; Luke 10:20; Philippians 4:3; Revelation 3:5; 13:8; 21:27]* **13** This crowd of resurrected humanity included all those who had died—regardless if their bodies had been buried or lost at sea, or buried in the earth, or destroyed by fire or other means—and included those who had been sent to Hades (the place of those who die and do not go to Heaven). Everyone will be judged and given punishments or rewards based on what they did during their lives on Earth. *[Psalm 28:4; 62:12; Proverbs 24:12; Isaiah 40:10; 59:18; 62:11; Jeremiah 17:10; Matthew 16:27; 25:31-46; Romans 2:6; 14:12; 1 Corinthians 3:12-15; 2 Corinthians 5:10; Galatians 6:7-8; 2 Timothy 4:14; 1 Peter 1:17; Revelation 2:23; 20:13]* **14** Then Hades and Death itself were permanently cast into the lake of fire in Hell. This lake of fire is the second and eternal death. *[Daniel 7:9-11; Isaiah 66:24; Matthew 3:12; 24:51; Mark 9:43-48]* ❖ *Hades, the place of the unsaved dead, has no further purpose. It is united with Hell. Death is destroyed in Hell, so Death will no longer exist outside of Hell. [Isaiah 25:8; Hosea 13:14; 1 Corinthians 15:26]* ➤ **15** All those whose names were not written in the Book of Life were also permanently cast into the lake of fire in Hell.

M. NEW JERUSALEM

21

All Things are Made New

1 Then I saw New Heaven and New Earth in a vision, for the first ones had ceased to exist. *[Psalm 102:25-26; Isaiah 34:4; 65:17; 66:22; Matthew 24:35; 2 Peter 3:7; 10-13]* ❖ *Other Scriptures hint that it will be a renewed creation, rather than an entirely new one from scratch. [Romans 8:19-22;*

2 Corinthians 5:17 (by analogy)] ➤ And New Earth has no sea. ❖ *Some commentators say that the sea in Revelation is symbolic of evil, so the absence of a sea in New Earth symbolically represents the idea that evil is absent.* ➤ **2** I saw New Jerusalem—a truly holy city— descending from New Heaven to New Earth. *[Isaiah 2:1-5; 18:7]* This city was magnificently adorned as a bride ready to be wed. *[Isaiah 52:1; 61:10; 65:18; Galatians 4:26; Hebrews 11:10; 12:22; 13:14; Revelation 3:12]* ❖ *"Jerusalem" can refer to the city itself, i.e., the structures, or to its inhabitants, or to both. The inhabitants of New Jerusalem are corporately the "bride" of the Messiah. They are also the "Temple of the Holy Spirit" which is God's dwelling place. So Jerusalem is also God's dwelling place, and his people are his Temple in one sense, and are the bride of God's Son. Some commentators believe the description is of a literal city, others that it is a symbolic description of the bride, God's people.* ➤ **3** I heard a voice from God's throne proclaim, "The glorious presence of God will now permanently be among redeemed humanity— where he will live in **A** them. They will be his special people, and he will be their God who lives in, with, and among them. *[Exodus 29:45; Leviticus 26:11-12; Jeremiah 31:33; Ezekiel 37:27; 43:7-9; Zechariah 2:11; 8:8]* **4** He will completely heal all past grief and hurts. Death will no longer exist—and pain, grief, and crying will no longer occur. The corruption of humanity and creation's fallen state have ceased to exist." *[Isaiah 25:8; 35:10; 51:11; 65:16-19; Revelation 7:16-17]* **5** Then God said from his throne, "Observe, I am now restoring and making everything renewed and perfect." *[Romans 8:21; 2 Corinthians 5:17]* Then he commanded me, "Record the words I have just spoken—for they can be trusted and will really happen." **6** Then he told me, "From my eternal perspective, these things have already been accomplished. I am the first cause that starts all things, I am in sovereign control at all times, and I have the last word in the final fate of all things. *[Isaiah 44:6; 48:12; Revelation 1:8, 17; 2:8; 22:13]* Those who seek to satisfy their spiritual thirst—who long to have a relationship with me—I will allow to freely drink from the Heavenly Source—whose water gives eternal life. *[Psalm 23:2; 36:8-9; 42:1-2; 46:4;*

A 21:3 The preposition μετά (meta) can mean either "with," "in," or "among."

63:1; Isaiah 12:3; 41:17; 44:3; 49:10; 55:1; Jeremiah 2:13; 17:13; Matthew 5:6; John 4:14; 7:37-39] ❖ *Water is a symbol of life, of eternal life, and of the Holy Spirit who imparts eternal life. God himself is the source of all these.* ➤ 7 Those who remain faithful and obedient to me to the very end of their lives—despite difficulties and persecution—will be my children who inherit all that I have [Acts 20:32; Romans 8:17; Galatians 3:29; 4:7; Ephesians 1:14; 3:6; Titus 3:7; 1 Peter 1:4]—and I will be their God who loves and takes care of them. [Genesis 17:7; 2 Samuel 7:14; Revelation 2:7, 11, 17, 26; 3:5, 12, 21] 8 But as for those who are too afraid to remain faithful to me in the face of persecution, those who reject my Messiah, those who participate in things I've forbidden as abominations, those who commit murder, those who give themselves over to sexual immorality, those involved in the occult or sorcery, those who worship false gods, and all habitual liars—unless they turn to me and repent, changing their ways—their fate will be the burning lake of sulfur in Hell which is the second and eternal death." [Romans 6:16; 1 Corinthians 6:9-10; Galatians 5:19-21; 6:7; Ephesians 5:5-6]

New Jerusalem Described

9 Then an angel who had poured out one of the seven bowls of God's righteous wrath came for me and said, "Come with me. I will show you the pure and holy bride of the Messiah—the woman who has an intimate relationship with the Lamb as his wife." ❖ *This vision seems to be a description of the bride after her marriage with the Lamb. A newly married woman may still be called a bride.* ➤ 10 He transported me in spirit to the top of a high mountain from where he enabled me to see the holy city—New Jerusalem—as God sent it down from Heaven to New Earth. [Ezekiel 40:2; Revelation 21:2] 11 It was shining with the brilliant light of God's glory—like a bright sparkling priceless gemstone. 12 It was surrounded by an unbreachable high wall with twelve gates, each with an angel stationed by it. Each gate is named after one of the twelve tribes of Israel. 13 Each of the four sides of the city wall had three gates, with the four walls

facing the four cardinal compass directions. [Ezekiel 48:30-34] 14 Its wall was built on twelve foundation stones, each of which had a name of one of the Lamb's twelve apostles. [Ephesians 2:20] 15 The angel who showed me the city had a gold measuring rod which he used to measure the city, its walls, and gates. ❖ *The purpose behind measuring the city is to point out its magnificence, beauty, symmetry, and perfection.* ➤ 16 The city is in the form of a perfect cube ❖ *like the Holy of Holies in the earthly Temple* ➤ with the length of each side 12,000 stadia, as measured by the angel. ❖ *The figure is given in stadia since many commentators assume the number and description are purely symbolic. 12,000 stadia is roughly equivalent to 1400-1500 miles, according to different sources. Some commentators have noted that a pyramid could also fit the literal description.* ➤ 17 According to his measurements, the wall is 144 cubits. ❖ *This number may also be symbolic but translates to 216 feet or 72 yards. Whether it indicates the wall's thickness or height, we don't know, but the former is more likely given the dimensions of the city.* ➤ 18 The wall is made of precious stone, and the city inside is made of pure gold, like pure glass. [Isaiah 54:11-12] ❖ *Commentators don't know if this means transparent like glass, or as perfectly reflective as a mirror. The main purpose of the description is to depict great beauty, grandeur, and perfection—reflecting the glory of God himself.* ➤ 19 The foundations of the wall are adorned with many kinds of gemstones, each **A** a different kind. Jasper, sapphire, chalcedony, emerald, 20 sardonyx, carnelian, chrysolite, beryl, topaz, chrysoprase, jacinth, and amethyst. ❖ *It's not clear if the foundation stones themselves are each a huge precious stone, or if they are merely inlaid with these different stones. The names of these precious and semiprecious stones don't necessarily agree with their modern equivalents in every case, and their exact color and appearance is purely secondary in importance to the fact that they were precious, rare, and beautiful.* ➤ 21 Each of the twelve gates was carved out of a single huge pearl and the city streets are made of pure gold that's as transparent as glass. 22 There is no Temple, as such, in the city where God is specially present—for Almighty Yahweh and the Lamb are its Temple and are everywhere in the city, in and among its people. 23 There's no need for light from the sun and

---

A 21:19 "Each" or "each adorned with."

moon to illuminate the city, for the light of the glory of God and the Lamb provides all the light it needs. *[Isaiah 60:3, 11; 19-20]* ❖ *This doesn't necessarily mean the sun and moon no longer exist, merely that their light is not needed to see by, and may be eclipsed by the light of God's glory.* ➤ 24 All the redeemed peoples of the world that live in this city will live in harmony with the light of God's glorious character. Those of high rank in the Kingdom, similar to what kings were on Old Earth, will also live there, and their glorious rewards from God will add to the splendor of the eternal city. ❖ *The meaning of this verse and verse 26 is debated. Some see the "nations" and "kings" referring to earthly inhabitants that are not part of the redeemed—among several other explanations. The interpretation given above is certainly true, but whether or not it expresses the intended meaning of this verse is not known.* ➤ 25 There will be no night in that city, so its gates will never be closed. 26 And all the redeemed peoples who live there will bring the city honor and glory. 27 Things that are impure and people who tell lies or do shameful things will never enter it, only those who belong to the Lamb—whose names are recorded in his Book of Life. *[Isaiah 52:1; Ezekiel 44:9]*

22

1 Then the angel showed me the River of Life whose water gives eternal life. *[Psalm 36:9; 46:4; Isaiah 12:3; 44:3; 55:1; Jeremiah 2:13; Joel 3:18; John 4:14; 7:37-39; Revelation 7:17; 21:6]* It's source is the throne from which God and the Lamb reign. The river is sparkling-crystal clear and flows 2 down the middle of the city's main street. *[Ezekiel 47:1; Zechariah 14:8]* All along the river on both sides, grow the Tree of Life. *[Genesis 2:9; 3:22; Ezekiel 47:12]* ❖ *Some commentators interpret the verse as saying there's only one Tree of Life, rather than many, all of the same variety. Another interpretation is that there is a wide boulevard with the street on one side and the river on the other, with the tree (or line of trees) between them. The River of Life is figurative of the Holy Spirit, and its originating at the throne means that God the Father and the Son are the source of the Holy Spirit.* A *That doesn't exclude*

the likelihood that the River of Life is also literally real. ➤ This tree bears twelve kinds of fruit every month of the year. ❖ *Some commentators take this to mean it bears a different kind of fruit each of the twelve months.* ➤ It's fruit sustains eternal life and its leaves heal and restore all the redeemed peoples living in the city. *[Ezekiel 47:12]* ❖ *Perhaps the leaves refer to their shade, though most take it to mean a medicinal use of the leaves. But in either case, it's not clear what the significance is in pointing this out about the leaves—in this city where there is no sickness, pain, weakness, or dysfunction, either physical, emotional, or spiritual—unless it's symbolic of the fact that none of these exists there.* ➤ 3 The curse that God placed upon all of creation and humanity when Adam sinned will no longer be in effect. *[Genesis 3:16-19; Zechariah 14:11; Romans 8:19-22]* God the Father and the Lamb will live in that city and rule from it, and his redeemed people will joyfully and freely serve and worship him. 4 His people will live in his presence and enjoy his attention and favor, *[Exodus 33:20; Matthew 5:8; 1 Timothy 6:16; 1 John 3:2]* ❖ *The expression "see his face," in the literal text, is an idiom meaning "having his favor." It will, of course, also be literally true in that city.* ➤ and his name will be on their foreheads. ❖ *God's "name" is his character. It will be clear to all living beings that each and every citizen of this city has a special intimate relationship with him and shares his holy loving perfect character. [2 Corinthians 3:18; Revelation 3:12]* ➤ 5 Never again will there be any night, nor will they have a need for any artificial light or the sun because Yahweh will be their light. *[Isaiah 60:19; 2 Corinthians 4:6]* ❖ *This is not only speaking of physical light, but also the light of true knowledge of God and of how to live according to his will and ways.* ➤ And they will share in his sovereign rule over the universe for the rest of eternity. *[Daniel 7:18; Luke 22:28-30; Romans 5:17; 8:17; Ephesians 2:6; 2 Timothy 2:12; Revelation 2:26; 5:10]*

N. FINAL WARNINGS ABOUT THE PROPHECIES IN THIS BOOK

6 Then the angel told me, "The words and message that you have seen, heard, and recorded can be trusted and will really

---

A 22:2 Thus the figure in verse 1 supports the theology that the Holy Spirit proceeds from both the Father and the Son—as expressed in the Nicene Creed. John 15:26 explicitly only says that the Spirit proceeds from the Father. This issue, among others, divided the eastern and western church in AD 1054.

happen. *[Revelation 21:5]* Yahweh—who is the God that inspires all true prophets *[2 Timothy 3:16; 2 Peter 1:21]*—sent his angel to you, who are his voluntary slave, to show you these important events that will soon happen."

❖ *The Heavenly perspective concerning what is "soon" is often very different from our human view in this age. [Psalm 90:4; 2 Peter 3:8-9]* ➤

7 I heard Jesus say, "Be alert, for I am returning soon! *[Matthew 24:42; 25:13; Romans 13:11-12; Hebrews 10:37; Revelation 1:1; 22:20]* Those who pay attention to the prophetic message in this book and remain obedient and faithful to me will be truly blessed and have no regrets." *[Revelation 1:3]*

8 I, John—who have written this book—am the person who actually saw and heard all the things recorded in it. ❖ *i.e., This book is not a secondhand account.* ➤ When I saw and heard these things, I was so overwhelmed with awe that I prostrated myself in an attitude of worship in front of the angel who had showed me these visions. *[Revelation 19:10]* 9 But he immediately admonished, "Don't worship me! I'm only a fellow servant—along with you and others who are God's prophets and your fellow believers who pay attention to the message in this book and remain obedient and faithful to Jesus. God is the only being you should submit to in worship!"

10 Then he commanded me, "Don't keep the prophetic message of this book hidden from your fellow believers, for the time when all this will happen is near. ❖ *From the Preterist viewpoint, there was a near-term historical fulfillment of many of the prophecies within years or decades of when John wrote this book. That should never be discounted. From the Idealist viewpoint, the symbolic message of many of the prophecies is true for every generation and should also not be discounted. From the Futurist viewpoint, many today believe that the ultimate fulfillment of all these prophecies really is near, in the next few years or decades. There are many signs that indicate this for those who are familiar with the Scriptures and have discernment.* ➤ 11 Those who do wrong and indulge in moral filth may continue to do so—unless they want to avoid the consequences of God's righteous wrath. ❖ *Until Jesus returns or a person dies—or until they receive the mark of the False Messiah—there is always opportunity to repent and be saved.* ➤ But those who have been united with Jesus' righteousness

should continue to submit to him and do what they know is right until the very end of their lives—if they want to live with him forever in New Earth." *[Daniel 12:10]*

12 Jesus says, "Be alert, for I am returning soon! When I do, I will reward or punish every person based on what they have done during their lives on Earth. *[Psalm 28:4; 62:12; Proverbs 24:12; Isaiah 40:10; 59:18; 62:11; Jeremiah 17:10; Matthew 16:27; 25:31-46; Romans 2:6; 2 Corinthians 5:10; Galatians 6:7-8; 2 Timothy 4:14; Revelation 2:23; 20:13]* ❖ *Many understand this as meaning we will be judged based on what we allow Jesus to do through us by his power, [Galatians 2:20] not merely on what we do in our own strength according to what we think his will is.* ➤ 13 It is I who cause all things to begin and all things to end. I am the first cause and have the last word in all things. From the beginning of time, until the end of eternity, I am in sovereign control over everything that happens. *[Isaiah 44:6; 48:12; Revelation 1:8, 17; 2:8; 21:6]* 14 Those who have received my righteousness because they trusted in my death on the cross to save them, *[Revelation 7:14]* and who remain faithful to me their entire lives despite persecution so they can enter and live in New Jerusalem and eat from the Tree of Life and live forever—they are truly in God's good favor. *[Matthew 10:22; 24:13; Mark 13:13; Romans 2:6-7; 1 Timothy 4:16; 2 Timothy 2:11-12; Hebrews 10:36; James 1:12; Revelation 14:13; 16:15; 22:7]* 15 But those who are spiritually corrupt, *[Deuteronomy 23:17-18; Matthew 7:6; Philippians 3:2]* ❖ *In the biblical cultures, dogs (referred to in the literal text) were considered vicious detestable animals, and figuratively sometimes referred to heathen Gentiles, God's enemies, and prostitutes.* ➤ or indulge in sexual immorality, or the occult, or sorcery, or murder, or the worship of false gods, or love to lie and deceive—they will be outcasts who are never allowed in the holy city. *[Revelation 21:8]*

16 "I, Jesus, have sent my messenger angel to all of you—so that this prophetic message can be proclaimed to all the assemblies of my people. I am the Messiah, the One prophesied to come from the line of King David, *[Isaiah 11:1-10; 53:2; Romans 1:3]* ❖ *The prophecy speaks of the root of "Jesse"—who was David's father.* ➤ the bright Morning Star that signals the imminent start of a new day. *[Numbers 24:17; Luke 1:78-79; John 1:4-5, 9; 2 Peter 1:19; Revelation*

2:28; 22:16] ❖ *The morning star is Venus—which often appears just before dawn. This term is symbolic of the descendant of David who would be the Messiah. In this context, the star heralds not merely a new day, but the coming of a new eternal age—where spiritual darkness and all the evil attached to it cease to exist and everything exists in the unhidden brilliant light of God's glory. Jesus was this Morning Star at his first coming, for the star is not the dawn itself, but a sign of the dawn shortly to follow.* ➤

17 "The Prophetic Holy Spirit and those who are already part of my Bride urge you to, 'Come to Jesus and obtain eternal life!' And those who respond to this invitation must also urge others who have not yet responded, 'Come to Jesus and obtain eternal life!' *[Isaiah 55:1; Romans 10:12-13; 2 Corinthians 5:20]* ❖ *Some take the literal "come" to be an urging to Jesus that he quickly return and fulfill his plan and promises—as in verse 20 below.* ➤ Those who have a spiritual thirst that needs satisfying may come to me and receive the satisfying and refreshing water of eternal life—without earning or deserving it. *[Revelation 21:6]* ❖ *Eternal life is offered as a free gift. There is no cost—in the sense that there is nothing you must do or can do to earn it. Yet there is a cost, because it is only obtainable by coming to Jesus and having a proper relationship with him. This means trusting him to save you, trusting everything he has said in the Scriptures, turning away from all sin, living in submission to him, and not being ashamed to be identified with him no matter what sort of persecution that brings, and remain faithful to him until*

you die. Yet the price you pay in doing this is nothing compared to what you receive in return—and in no sense earns what you receive. ➤

18 "I, Jesus, warn everyone who reads or hears the prophetic message in this book: If anyone dares to distort the purity and accuracy of the message it proclaims by adding their own prophecies or false teaching to it, God will punish such a false prophet with the afflictions recorded in this book. 19 And if anyone dares to distort the purity and completeness of the message it proclaims by subtracting any part that they find inconvenient or distasteful, God will punish such a false teacher by taking away his or her right to enter the holy city and eat of the Tree of Life. *[Deuteronomy 4:2; 12:32]*

20 "I, Jesus—who have revealed these things to you—tell you that yes, it is true that I will return soon."

We—his people—pray in response to this promise, "Yes, may it be so! Lord Jesus, come quickly!" ❖ *This was a common prayer of the early believers—in Aramaic, "Marana tha" meaning "Our Lord, come." [1 Corinthians 16:22] Addressing him as "Lord" is an acknowledgment of his deity.* ➤ 21 I, John, pray that the Lord Jesus will look upon all of you with great favor far beyond anything you can deserve—and always be with you to help you. Yes, may it be so! **A**

A 22:21 The final "amen" (translated "Yes, may it be so!") is probably a later addition to the text, as it is not found in some early manuscripts.

Bibliography
of Exegetical Resources Consulted

General Works on the New Testament

Analytical Greek New Testament Plus – with Tyndale Interlinear Translation and links to lexicons. Greek New Testament text (Fourth Revised Edition), Deutsche Bibelgesellschaft, 1998. / Friberg, Barbara and Timothy Friberg, Eds. AGNT grammatical tags and lemmas from the Analytical Greek New Testament, Second Edition pre-publication version, 2001. / Douglas, J.D. Ed. Tyndale Interlinear Translation from The New Greek-English Interlinear New Testament. Tyndale House, 1990. / Lexical information and contextual links to lexicons. Dallas, TX: SIL International, 2002.

Barnwell, Katharine, Paul Dancy, and Anthony Pope. Key Biblical Terms in the New Testament – An aid for Bible translators. Dallas, TX: SIL International, 1995.

Deibler, Ellis. An Index of Implicit Information in the New Testament.

Keener, Craig S. The IVP Bible Background Commentary. InterVarsity Press, 1993.

Louw, Johannes P., and Eugene A. Nida, Eds. Greek-English Lexicon of the New Testament based on Semantic Domains. New York: United Bible Societies, 1988.

Newman, Barclay M. Jr. A Concise Greek-English Dictionary of the New Testament. New York: United Bible Societies, 1971.

Stern, David H. Jewish New Testament Commentary. Clarksville, MD: Jewish New Testament Publications, Inc., 1996.

Matthew

Allen, Jerry. Translator's Notes on Matthew 1-14. International Translation Department, Dallas, TX: Summer Institute of Linguistics, 2002.

Exegetical Helps on the Gospel of Matthew – SIL in-house publication, 1976. Compiled by Matthew Ulrich, David Mason, Leo Skinner. Edited by John Beekman.

Morris, Leon. The Gospel according to Matthew. (Pillar New Testament Commentary Series). Grand Rapids, Michigan: Wm. B. Eerdmans Publishing Co., 1992.

Newman, Barclay M. and Philip C. Stine. A Translator's Handbook on the Gospel of Mathew. New York: United Bible Societies, 1988.

Tasker, R.V.G. The Gospel According to St. Matthew. (Tyndale New Testament Commentaries). Leicester, England: InterVarsity Press, Grand Rapids, Michigan: William B. Eerdmans Publishing Company, 1961.

The Translator's Reference Translation of Matthew. Dallas, TX: SIL International 2002.

Mark

Bratcher, Robert G. and Eugene A Nida. A Translator's Handbook on the Gospel of Mark. New York: United Bible Societies, 1961.

Cole, R. Alan. The Gospel According to St. Mark. (Tyndale New Testament Commentaries). Leicester, England: InterVarsity Press, Grand Rapids, Michigan: William B. Eerdmans Publishing Company, 1961.

Exegetical Helps on the Gospel of Mark – SIL in-house publication, 1981. Compiled by Richard C. Blight. Edited by Robert E. Smith.

Lane, William L. The Gospel of Mark. (The New International Commentary on the New Testament). Grand Rapids, Michigan: William B. Eerdmans Publishing Company, 1974

Gundry, Robert H. Mark – A Commentary on His Apology for the Cross. Grand Rapids, Michigan: Wm. B. Eerdmans Publishing Co., 1993.

The Translator's Reference Translation of Mark. Dallas, TX: SIL International 2001.

Luke

Allen, Jerry. Translator's Notes on Luke. International Translation Department, Dallas, TX: SIL International, 2000.

Bailey, Kenneth E. Finding the Lost – Cultural Keys to Luke 15. St. Louis, MO: Concordia Publishing House, 1992.

Bailey, Kenneth E. Jacob & the Prodigal. Downers Grove, IL: InterVarsity Press, 2003.

Bailey, Kenneth E. Poet & Peasant and Through Peasant Eyes (combined edition) – A Literary-Cultural Approach to the Parables in Luke. Grand Rapids, Michigan: Wm. B. Eerdmans Publishing Co., 1983.

Exegetical Helps on the Gospel of Luke – SIL in-house publication, 1985. Compiled by Richard C. Blight. Edited by Robert E. Smith.

Marshall, I. Howard. The Book of Luke – A Commentary on the Greek Text. (The New International Greek Testament Commentary on the New Testament). Wm. B. Eerdmans Publishing Co., 1978.

John

Carson, D.A. The Gospel According to John. (Pillar New Testament Commentary Series). Grand Rapids, Michigan: Wm. B. Eerdmans Publishing Co., 1991.

Morris, Leon. The Gospel According to John. (The New International Commentary on the New Testament). Grand Rapids, Michigan: William B. Eerdmans Publishing Company, 1971.

Newman, Barclay M. and Eugene A. Nida. A Translator's Handbook on the Gospel of John. New York: United Bible Societies, 1980.

Tasker, R.V.G. John. (Tyndale New Testament Commentaries). Leicester, England: InterVarsity Press, Grand Rapids, Michigan: William B. Eerdmans Publishing Company, 1960.

The Translator's Reference Translation of John. Dallas, TX: SIL International, 2003.

Acts

Blood, David. Translator's Notes on Acts 1-14. International Translation Department, Dallas, TX: Summer Institute of Linguistics, 2000.

Bruce, F. F. The Book of the Acts. (The New International Commentary on the New Testament). Grand Rapids, Michigan: William B. Eerdmans Publishing Company, 1988.

Marshall, I. Howard. The Acts of the Apostles. (Tyndale New Testament Commentaries). Leicester, England: InterVarsity Press, Grand Rapids, Michigan: William B. Eerdmans Publishing Company, 1980.

Newman, Barclay M. and Eugene A. Nida. A Translator's Handbook on the Acts of the Apostles. New York: United Bible Societies, 1972.

The Translator's Reference Translation of Acts. Dallas, TX: SIL International, 2002.

Wagner, C. Peter. Lighting the Word. Acts 9-15 (The Acts of the Holy Spirit Series). Ventura, CA: Regal Books, 1995.

Romans

Deibler, Ellis W. Jr. A Semantic and Structural Analysis of Romans. Dallas, TX: Summer Institute of Linguistics, 1998.

Exegetical Helps on Romans – SIL in-house publication, 1973. Compiled by Richard C. Blight. Edited by John Beekman.

Morris, Leon. The Epistle to the Romans. (Pillar New Testament Commentary Series). Grand Rapids, Michigan: Wm. B. Eerdmans Publishing Co., 1987.

Murray, John. The Epistle to the Romans. (The New International Commentary on the New Testament). Grand Rapids, MI: Wm. B. Eerdmans Publishing Co., 1968.

Newman, Barclay M. and Eugene A. Nida. A Translator's Handbook on the Paul's Letter to the Romans. New York: United Bible Societies, 1973.

1 Corinthians

Arichea, Daniel C. Jr. The Silence Of Women In The Church: Theology And Translation In 1 Corinthians 14.33b-36. The Bible Translator, Vol. 46 No. 1 (January, 1995): 101-112.

Barrett, C.K. The First Epistle to the Corinthians. (Black's New Testament Commentary). Peabody, MA: Hendrickson Publishers, 1968.

Ellingworth, Paul, and Howard A. Hatton. A Translator's Handbook on Paul's First Letter to the Corinthians. New York: United Bible Societies, 1993.

Fee, Gordon D. The First Epistle to the Corinthians. (The New International Commentary on the New Testament). Grand Rapids, Michigan: William B. Eerdmans Publishing Company, 1987.

Grosheide, F.W. The First Epistle to the Corinthians. (The New International Commentary on the New Testament). Grand Rapids, Michigan: William B. Eerdmans Publishing Company, 1953.

Lenski, R.D.H. The Interpretation of St. Paul's First and Second Epistles to the Corinthians. Minneapolis, Minnesota: Augsburg Publishing House, 1937 and 1963.

Miller, Neva F. and Michael Martens. Translator's Notes on 1 Corinthians Chapters 1 through 7 (Preliminary Version). International Translation Department, Dallas, TX: Summer Institute of Linguistics, 1998.

Morris, Leon. The First Epistle of Paul to the Corinthians – An Introduction and Commentary. (Tyndale New Testament Commentaries). Leicester, England: InterVarsity Press, Grand Rapids, Michigan: Wm. B. Eerdmans Publishing Co., 1958.

Trail, Ronald. An Exegetical Summary of 1 Corinthians 1-9. Dallas, TX: Summer Institute of Linguistics, 1995.

2 Corinthians

Abernathy, David. An Exegetical Summary of 2 Corinthians. Dallas TX: Summer Institute of Linguistics, 2001.

Exegetical Helps on Second Corinthians – SIL in-house publication, 1975. Compiled by E. Clay Johnston (chapters 1—5) and Steward Hussey (chapters 6—13). Edited by Richard C. Blight.

Furnish, Victor Paul. II Corinthians. (The Anchor Bible). New York: Doubleday, 1984.

Hughes, Philip E. Paul's Second Epistle to the Corinthians. (The New International Commentary on the New Testament). Grand Rapids, MI: Wm. B. Eerdmans Publishing Co., 1962.

Lenski, R.D.H. The Interpretation of St. Paul's First and Second Epistles to the Corinthians. Minneapolis, Minnesota: Augsburg Publishing House, 1937 and 1963.

Omanson, Roger L. and John Ellington. A Translator's Handbook On Paul's Second Letter To The Corinthians. New York: United Bible Societies, 1993.

Tasker, R.V.G. The Second Epistle of Paul to the Corinthians. (Tyndale New Testament Commentaries). Leicester, England: Inter-Varsity Press, Grand Rapids, MI: Wm. B. Eerdmans Publishing Company, 1963.

Galatians

Arichea, Daniel C. and Eugene A. Nida. A Translator's Handbook on Paul's Letter to the Galatians. New York: United Bible Societies, 1976.

Bruce, F.F. The Epistle to the Galatians. (New International Greek Testament Commentary). Grand Rapids, Michigan: Wm. B. Eerdmans Publishing Co., 1982.

Larsen, Iver. Translator's Notes On Galatians. (Preliminary Version) International Translation Department, Dallas, TX: SIL International, 1999.

Longenecker, Richard N. Galatians. (Word Biblical Commentary). Dallas, TX: Word Books, 1990.

Ephesians

Bratcher, Robert G. and Eugene A. Nida. A Translator's Handbook on Paul's Letter to the Ephesians. New York: United Bible Societies, 1982.

Bruce, F.F. The Epistles to the Colossians, to Philemon and to the Ephesians. (The New International Commentary on the New Testament) Grand Rapids, Michigan: Wm. B. Eerdmans Publishing Co., 1988.

Exegetical Helps on Ephesians – SIL in-house publication, 1974. Compiled by Edna Jane Travis. Edited by John Beekman.

Graham, Glenn H. An Exegetical Summary of Ephesians. Dallas, TX: Summer Institute of Linguistics, 1997.

Thomas, Elaine. Translator's Notes On Ephesians. International Translation Department, Dallas, TX: SIL International, 1998.

Philippians

Allen, Jerry. Translator's Notes On Philippians. International Translation Department, Dallas, TX: SIL International, 2002.

Banker, John. A Semantic and Structural Analysis of Philippians. (Preliminary Edition). Dallas, TX: Summer Institute of Linguistics, 1996.

Fee, Gordon D. Paul's Letter to the Philippians. (The New International Commentary on the New Testament) Grand Rapids, Michigan: Wm. B. Eerdmans Publishing Co., 1995.

Greenlee, Harold J. An Exegetical Summary of Philippians. Dallas, TX: Summer Institute of Linguistics, 1992.

Loh, I-Jin. and Eugene A. Nida. A Translator's Handbook on Paul's Letter to the Philippians. New York: United Bible Societies, 1977.

O' Brian, Peter T. The Epistle to the Philippians. (New International Greek Testament Commentary). Grand Rapids, Michigan: Wm. B. Eerdmans Publishing Co., 1991.

Colossians

Bratcher, Robert G. and Eugene A. Nida. A Translator's Handbook on Paul's Letter to the Colossians. New York: United Bible Societies, 1977.

Bruce, F.F. The Epistles to the Colossians, to Philemon and to the Ephesians. (The New International Commentary on the New Testament) Grand Rapids, Michigan: Wm. B. Eerdmans Publishing Co., 1988.

Callow, John. A Semantic and Structural Analysis of Colossians. (Preliminary Edition). Dallas, TX: Summer Institute of Linguistics, 2002.

Gray, Sharon. Translator's Notes On Colossians. International Translation Department, Dallas, TX: SIL International, 2001.

King, Martha. An Exegetical Summary of Colossians. Dallas, TX: Summer Institute of Linguistics, 1998.

Wright, N.T. Selections from Colossians and Philemon. (Tyndale New Testament Commentaries). Leicester, England: Inter-Varsity Press, Grand Rapids, MI: Wm. B. Eerdmans Publishing Company, 1986.

1 Thessalonians

Blight, Richard. An Exegetical Summary of 1 & 2 Thessalonians. Dallas, TX: Summer Institute of Linguistics, 1989.

Ellingworth, Paul. and Eugene A. Nida. A Translator's Handbook on Paul's Letters to the Thessalonians. New York: United Bible Societies, 1976.

Gray, Sharon. Translator's Notes On 1 Thessalonians. International Translation Department, Dallas, TX: SIL International, 2002.

Morris, Leon. The First and Second Epistles to the Thessalonians. (The New International Commentary on the New Testament) Grand Rapids, Michigan: Wm. B. Eerdmans Publishing Co., 1991.

Sterner, Robert H. A Semantic and Structural Analysis of 1 Thessalonians. (Preliminary Edition). Dallas, TX: Summer Institute of Linguistics, 1998.

2 Thessalonians

Blight, Richard C. An Exegetical Summary of 1 & 2 Thessalonians. Dallas, TX: Summer Institute of Linguistics, 1989.

Callow, John. A Semantic and Structural Analysis of 2 Thessalonians. Dallas, TX: Summer Institute of Linguistics, 2000.

Ellingworth, Paul. and Eugene A. Nida. A Translator's Handbook on Paul's Letters to the Thessalonians. New York: United Bible Societies, 1976.

Gray, Sharon. Translator's Notes On 2 Thessalonians. International Translation Department, Dallas, TX: SIL International, 2002.

Morris, Leon. The First and Second Epistles to the Thessalonians. (The New International Commentary on the New Testament) Grand Rapids, Michigan: Wm. B. Eerdmans Publishing Co., 1991.

1 Timothy

Arichea, Daniel C. and Eugene A. Nida. A Handbook on Paul's Letters to Timothy and to Titus. New York: United Bible Societies, 1995.

Bean, Mark Ellis. Translator's Notes On 1 Timothy. (Preliminary Version). International Translation Department, Dallas, TX: SIL International, 2001.

Knight, George W. III. The Pastoral Epistles. (New International Greek Testament Commentary). Grand Rapids, Michigan: Wm. B. Eerdmans Publishing Co., 1992.

2 Timothy

Andrews, Henrietta. Translator's Notes On 2 Timothy. International Translation Department, Dallas, TX: SIL International, 2002.

Arichea, Daniel C. and Eugene A. Nida. A Handbook on Paul's Letters to Timothy and to Titus. New York: United Bible Societies, 1995.

Knight, George W. III. The Pastoral Epistles. (New International Greek Testament Commentary). Grand Rapids, Michigan: Wm. B. Eerdmans Publishing Co., 1992.

Titus

Arichea, Daniel C. and Eugene A. Nida. A Handbook on Paul's Letters to Timothy and to Titus. New York: United Bible Societies, 1995.

Banker, John. A Semantic and Structural Analysis of Titus. Dallas, TX: Summer Institute of Linguistics, 1994.

Boswell, Freddy. Translator's Notes On Titus. International Translation Department, Dallas, TX: SIL International, 2000.

Greenlee, Harold J. An Exegetical Summary of Titus and Philemon. Dallas, TX: Summer Institute of Linguistics, 1989.

Knight, George W. III. The Pastoral Epistles. (New International Greek Testament Commentary). Grand Rapids, Michigan: Wm. B. Eerdmans Publishing Co., 1992.

Philemon

Allen, Jerry. Translator's Notes On Philemon. International Translation Department, Dallas, TX: SIL International, 2000.

Banker, John. A Semantic and Structural Analysis of Philemon. Dallas, TX: Summer Institute of Linguistics, 1999.

Bratcher, Robert G. and Eugene A. Nida. A Translator's Handbook on Paul's Letter to Philemon. New York: United Bible Societies, 1997.

Bruce, F.F. The Epistles to the Colossians, to Philemon and to the Ephesians. (The New International Commentary on the New Testament) Grand Rapids, Michigan: Wm. B. Eerdmans Publishing Co., 1988.

Greenlee, Harold J. An Exegetical Summary of Titus and Philemon. Dallas, TX: Summer Institute of Linguistics, 1989.

Wright, N.T. Selections from Colossians and Philemon. (Tyndale New Testament Commentaries). Leicester, England: Inter-Varsity Press, Grand Rapids, MI: Wm. B. Eerdmans Publishing Company, 1986.

Hebrews

Bruce, F.F. The Epistle to the Hebrews. (New International Commentary on the New Testament). Grand Rapids, Michigan: Wm. B. Eerdmans Publishing Co., 1990.

Ellingworth, Paul. The Epistle to the Hebrews, A Commentary on the Greek Text. (The New International Greek Testament Commentary). Grand Rapids, Michigan: Wm. B. Eerdmans Publishing Co., 1993.

Ellingworth, Paul and Eugene A. Nida. A Translator's Handbook on the Letter to the Hebrews. New York: United Bible Societies, 1983.

Exegetical Helps on Hebrews – SIL in-house publication, 1975. Compiled by Brian and Helen Geytenbeek, Larry Clark and Ronald Olson. Edited by Richard Blight. General Editor: John Beekman.

Greenlee, J. Harold. An Exegetical Summary of Hebrews. Dallas, TX: Summer Institute of Linguistics, 1998.

Lane, William L. Hebrews. (Word Biblical Commentary). Dallas, TX: Word Books, 1991.

Miller, Neva F. The Epistle to the Hebrews – An Analytical and Exegetical Handbook, Dallas, TX: Summer Institute of Linguistics, 1988.

James

Adamson, James. The Epistle of James. (The New International Commentary on the New Testament). Grand Rapids, Michigan: Wm. B. Eerdmans Publishing Co., 1976.

Davids, Peter H. The Epistle of James. (The New International Greek Testament Commentary on the New Testament). Wm. B. Eerdmans Publishing Co., 1982.

Exegetical Helps on James – SIL in-house publication, 1968. Compiled by James Rupp. Edited by John Beekman.

Hart, George and Helen. A Semantic and Structural Analysis of James. Dallas, TX: Summer Institute of Linguistics, 2001.

Greenlee, Harold J. An Exegetical Summary of James. Dallas, TX: Summer Institute of Linguistics, 1993.

Loh, I-Jin and Howard A. Hatton. A Translator's Handbook on the Letter from James. New York: United Bible Societies, 1997.

Moo, Douglas J. The Letter of James. (Tyndale New Testament Commentaries). Leicester, England: InterVarsity Press, Grand Rapids, Michigan: Wm. B. Eerdmans Publishing Co., 1985.

Pope, Anthony G. Translator's Notes On James. (Preliminary Version). International Translation Department, Dallas, TX: SIL International, 1998.

1 Peter

Abernathy, C. David. An Exegetical Summary of 1 Peter. Dallas, TX: Summer Institute of Linguistics, 1998.

Arichea, Daniel C. and Eugene A. Nida. A Translator's Handbook on the First Letter From Peter. New York: United Bible Societies, 1980.

Bigg, Rev. Charles. A Critical and Exegetical Commentary on the Epistles of St. Peter and St. Jude. (The International Critical Commentary). Edinburgh: T & T Clark, 1902.

Exegetical Helps on the First Letter From Peter – SIL in-house publication, 1971. Compiled by Robert E. Meader. Edited by Richard C. Blight. General Editor: John Beekman.

Goppelt, Leonhard. A Commentary on I Peter. Translated and augmented by John E. Alsup. Göttingen, Germany: Vandenhoeck & Ruprecht, 1978, Grand Rapids, Michigan: William B. Eerdmans Publishing Company, 1993.

Grudem, Wayne A. The First Epistle of Peter, An Introduction and Commentary. (Tyndale New Testament Commentaries). Leicester, England: InterVarsity Press, Grand Rapids, Michigan: Wm. B. Eerdmans Publishing Co., 1988.

Kelley, J.N.D. The Epistles of Peter and of Jude. (Black's New Testament Commentary). Peabody, MA: Hendrickson Publishers, 1969.

Michaels, J. Ramsey. 1 Peter. (Word Biblical Commentary). Waco, TX: Word Books, Publisher, 1988.

Stibbs, A.M. and A.F. Walls. The First Epistle General of Peter. (Tyndale New Testament Commentaries). Leicester, England· InterVarsity Press, Grand Rapids, Michigan: Wm. B. Eerdmans Publishing Co., 1959.

2 Peter

Arichea, Daniel C. and Howard A. Hatton. A Translator's Handbook on the Second Letter From Peter. New York: United Bible Societies, 1993.

Bauckham, Richard J. Jude, 2 Peter. (Word Biblical Commentary). Waco, TX: Word Books, 1983.

Bigg, Rev. Charles. A Critical and Exegetical Commentary on the Epistles of St. Peter and St. Jude. (The International Critical Commentary). Edinburgh: T & T Clark, 1902.

Exegetical Helps on Second Peter – SIL in-house publication, 1981. Compiled by Edna Jane Travis. Edited by John Beekman.

Green, Michael. The Second Epistle General of Peter and the General Epistle of Jude. (Tyndale New Testament Commentaries). Leicester, England: InterVarsity Press, Grand Rapids, Michigan: Wm. B. Eerdmans Publishing Co., 1987.

Johnson, Edna. A Semantic and Structural Analysis of 2 Peter. Dallas, TX: Summer Institute of Linguistics, 1988.

Kelley, J.N.D. The Epistles of Peter and of Jude. (Black's New Testament Commentary). Peabody, MA: Hendrickson Publishers, 1969.

Thomas, Elaine. Translator's Notes on 2 Peter. International Translation Department, Dallas, TX: SIL International, 1999.

1, 2, 3 John

Anderson, John L. An Exegetical Summary of 1, 2, and 3 John. Dallas, TX: Summer Institute of Linguistics, 1992.

De Jonge, C. Hass M. and J. L. Swellengrebel. A Translators' Handbook on the Letters of John. New York: United Bible Societies, 1972.

Marshall, I. Howard. The Epistles of John. (The New International Commentary on the New Testament). Grand Rapids, Michigan: Wm. B. Eerdmans Publishing Co., 1978.

Persson, Andrew. Translator's Notes On 1, 2, and 3 John. International Translation Department, Dallas, Texas: SIL International, 2000.

Sherman, Grace E. and John C. Tuggy. A Semantic and Structural Analysis of the Johannine Epistles. Dallas, Texas: Summer Institute of Linguistics, 1994.

Smalley, Stephen S. 1, 2, 3 John. (Word Biblical Commentary). Waco, Texas: Word Books, 1984.

Stott, John R. The Epistles of John – An Introduction and Commentary. (Tyndale New Testament Commentaries). Leicester, England: InterVarsity Press, Grand Rapids, Michigan: Wm. B. Eerdmans Publishing Co., 1960.

Jude

Arichea, Daniel C. and Howard A. Hatton. A Translator's Handbook on the Letter from Jude. New York: United Bible Societies, 1993.

Bauckham, Richard J. Jude, 2 Peter. (Word Biblical Commentary). Waco, Texas: Word Books, 1983.

Bigg, Rev. Charles. A Critical and Exegetical Commentary on the Epistles of St. Peter and St. Jude. (The International Critical Commentary). Edinburgh: T & T Clark, 1902.

Exegetical Helps on the Letter from Jude – SIL in-house publication, 1972. Compiled by Ian Gardner and Richard C. Blight. Edited by John Beekman.

Green, Michael. The Second Epistle General of Peter and the General Epistle of Jude. (Tyndale New Testament Commentaries). Grand Rapids, Michigan: Wm. B. Eerdmans Publishing Co., 1987.

Greenlee, J. Harold. An Exegetical Summary of Jude. Dallas, TX: SIL International, 1999.

Kelley, J.N.D. The Epistles of Peter and of Jude. (Black's New Testament Commentary). Peabody, MA: Hendrickson Publishers, 1969.

Revelation

Bratcher, Robert G. and Howard A. Hatton. A Translator's Handbook on the Revelation to John. New York: United Bible Societies, 1993.

Caird, G.B. A Commentary on the Revelation of St. John the Divine. (Black's New Testament Commentaries). London: Adam & Charles Black Ltd., 1966.

Green, Oliver B. The Revelation – Verse by Verse Study. Greenville, South Carolina: The Gospel Hour Inc., 1963.

Hendriksen, William. More than Conquerors, Grand Rapids, Michigan: Baker Book House, 1940, 1967.

Hughes, Philip Edgcumbe. The Book of the Revelation – A Commentary. (Pillar New Testament Commentary Series). Grand Rapids, Michigan: Wm. B. Eerdmans Publishing Co., 1990.

Ladd, George Eldon. A Commentary on the Revelation of John. Grand Rapids, Michigan: Wm. B. Eerdmans Publishing Co., 1972.

Lenski, R.C.H. The Interpretation of St. John's Revelation. Minneapolis, Minnesota: Augsburg Publishing House, 1943 and 1963.

Morris, Leon. The Book of Revelation. (Tyndale New Testament Commentaries). Leicester, England: InterVarsity Press, Grand Rapids, Michigan: Wm. B. Eerdmans Publishing Co., 1987.

Mounce, Robert H. The Book of Revelation. (The New International Commentary on the New Testament). Grand Rapids, Michigan: Wm. B. Eerdmans Publishing Co., 1997.

Osborne, Grant R. Revelation. (Baker Exegetical Commentary on the New Testament). Grand Rapids, Michigan: Baker Academic, 2002.

Swete, Henry Barclay. Commentary on Revelation. Grand Rapids, Michigan: Kregel Publications, 1977.

Trail, Ronald L. An Exegetical Summary of Revelation 1-11. Dallas, TX: SIL International, 2003.

Wilcock, Michael. I Saw Heaven Opened – The Message of Revelation. Downers Grove, Illinois, 1975.

Glossary

Here are a few definitions of words and phrases used in the Bible, whose meanings are different in the Bible from how they are commonly used in everyday speech.

Body – The body refers to everyone who truly believes that Jesus is the Messiah—God's eternally begotten Son—and has the Holy Spirit living within them. The body is one picture of the relationship believers have with Jesus. Just as a body is united to and follows the commands of the head, so the body of Jesus is spiritually joined to him and follows his directions.

Church – In common use, this word refers to a building, a particular assembly, parish, denomination, or organization. But in the New Testament, it literally means " assembly" or "gathering" and refers to all true believers. The assembly of all believers is also the "bride of Jesus." This means that believers have an intimate (but non-sexual) relationship with Jesus, as a bride does with her husband.

Epistle – This is a Greek word meaning "letter." Epistles usually followed a fixed formal format with an opening—where the writer identifies himself and those he is writing to—a body and a closing. The New Testament letters are traditionally referred to as "epistles" in church contexts.

Glory and *glorify* – have different meanings in different contexts. "Glory" can refer to God's magnificent beauty, or to the brilliant light that signifies his presence. It can also refer to his good, holy, loving, righteous, and just character—which is pictured and implied when referring to his light and beauty. Or it can mean to bring praise by revealing the beauty of his character to others (e.g. I will bring God glory). As a verb, "glory" means to "rapturously enjoy" (e.g. I glory in the Lord.) or "to praise his character" (e.g. I will glorify God). As an adjective (e.g. glorious prize) it means something that reflects God's character or reveals it such that people will praise him.

Holy – means "set apart and dedicated for God's use." It sometimes has the connotation of being pure and without sin, but this isn't its primary meaning.

Hope – has two meanings, one the common meaning of "aspiration, desire, or wish," but in the New Testament it is used with an older meaning not commonly used today of "confident expectation," as in 2 Corinthians 1:10.

Perfect – To be perfect does not mean to be without sin—which none of us can achieve in this life. It can mean to "have undivided devotion," as in Matthew 5:48. Or it can mean "maturity" as in James 1:4.

Pure in heart – A pure heart is not one that is without sin—as many tend to think—but is a heart and mind that has a single, undivided, dedication and commitment toward obeying God, with no desires that detract from that commitment. See 1 Timothy 1:5. If you are pure in heart, everything you do is an act of submissive worship.

Righteous – This has several different senses. To be "righteous in God's sight" means he considers you acceptable to him. Your sins are forgiven and you have entered into a close relationship with him. When referring to God or Jesus, it means "sinless perfection" and their fair and just judgment. "Righteous living" means living in conformity with God's will.

Saint – means "a person who is a true believer and follower of Jesus." It never means a person who is more dedicated, sinless, or close to God than most believers—as it does in common usage. Literally, it means "holy one"—a person who has been set apart and dedicated to serve God. This is true of all believers. So, "assembly" (i.e., church), "the body," (i.e., of Jesus) and "the saints" are all basically synonymous terms that focus on different aspects our relationship with God and each other.

Seek or See God's face – This is a figure of speech that many readers mistakenly take literally. To seek or see God's face—as in 2 Chronicles 7:14, Hosea 5:15, and Revelation 22:4—means to seek or have God's favor. For if you can "see his face," this means he is looking at you with favorable attention.

Worship – Today, most people use this word to mean "to praise, honor, and adore God," usually with music and singing or clapping or raising one's hands. And certainly any of these can be valid means of expressing worship, but none of them are the core of worship. In fact, all these things can be done while not truly worshipping at all. Biblical worship is the genuine intentional offering of your life and resources in submissive obedience and service to God. See Romans 12:1. God encourages us to honor and praise people who deserve such, (see Romans 12:10 and 13:7)—but true worship is reserved for God alone (see Deuteronomy 6:13 and Luke 4:8). Many people participate in "worship services," but remain unrepentantly rebellious against one or more of God's commands in their daily life (e.g., they may habitually lie, cheat, criticize, gossip, slander, hate, be selfish or unkind, participate in sexual relationships forbidden by God, view pornography, refuse to forgive someone who has wronged them, or some other sin)—so are not truly submitted to him. And their so-called worship is counted as worthless by God (see Isaiah 29:13-14 and Matthew 15:7-9). In the Bible, submissive worship is most frequently symbolized by physically bowing or prostrating oneself before someone. Fake worship is hypocrisy and is also idolatry—i.e., submission to something as more important than God. This can be anything at all, including money, fame, power, a person, a feeling, or one's own desires. God views idolatry and fake worship as a personal rejection of himself. The more you know about God, the more serious the consequences become for rejecting him and not submitting to him in true worship.

Appendix – About Salvation

1. God's Original Plan and Ultimate Purpose

When God decided to create the physical universe and humanity, he created people to be like himself in many ways. He made them capable of love and other emotions, reasoning, creativity, appreciation of beauty, enjoyment of God and his creation, and capable of interacting with him. His intention was to create human sons and daughters who, though finite, would be like himself. He wanted to multiply the love and joy that existed within the Godhead between the Father, Son, and Holy Spirit. He also intended people to be eternal companions for his Son. Since we are finite, we can only interact on a deep level with a few people at a time. But the infinite God can easily interact intimately with billions of people simultaneously—without stretching his infinite capabilities. While humans need one mate to be a companion and complete them, an infinite God desires at least hundreds of millions—if not billions—of finite humans who perfectly share his holy loving character to adequately complement his Son.

2. The Fall of Humanity, and Original Sin

God is holy, pure, loving, selfless, and just. All that is in any way good or excellent in this physical universe is a dim reflection of some aspect of the creator—who is perfectly and entirely good. All good things come from him—however indirectly. All good things that people are capable of come from the capability that he created in human beings. God's being and character define what is good. Anything in conflict with his character is defined as sin—which he hates. He will not have a close relationship with beings that imperfectly reflect his character, and he will not tolerate beings who are not in perfect agreement with him—and in perfect submission to him—to live with him forever in Heaven. God created all angels and humanity without any inclination at all to rebel against him. They were perfect, sinless, and holy. But he did give them the ability to choose for themselves because they couldn't have a genuine love relationship with him unless they had the freedom to reject him. This ability to choose is commonly called "free will."

Lucifer, the highest angel, became proud and chose to love himself rather than God. He convinced about a third of the angels in Heaven to join him in rebellion against their creator. Their knowledge of God must have been far from complete. Even we know from the Scriptures that God is all powerful—so no finite created being could be any match for the Creator. Even Lucifer's greater power—which is very great by human standards—is nothing at all to God. Yet Lucifer thought that he was as great or than God and could take his place. When he was cast out of Heaven along with the other angels who followed him, he decided to attempt to thwart God's plans for humanity. Some people speculate that Lucifer—who we now call Satan (which means "Adversary")—was jealous of humanity because of God's plan to bring humanity into a closer relationship with himself than the angels have, and he also planned to give us a higher rank than angels. So Satan tempted the first humans, Adam and Eve—even before they started procreating—and lured them into choosing to distrust and disobey God. This is commonly called "the Fall" of humanity into sin and rebellion.

We don't know exactly what would have happened had Adam and Eve resisted that temptation. But the Scriptures teach that God knew ahead of time that they would choose to sin. Some theologians speculate that God exists outside of time—and that time itself is part of the physical universe that he created. Thus from his perspective outside of time, all of time is visible simultaneously before him—like we could see a long scroll spread out before us and look at any part of it. He sees the start of time at creation, just as he sees the end of this age and the final judgment. He sees all years in between as present. Yet he is able to enter time and interact with people within time. Angels are finite beings who also exist in time.

There are two major theological schools of thought about the way God saves people. They both agree that Satan's rebellion and Adam and Eve's sin did not take God by surprise. They also agree that he had a plan to redeem a portion of humanity who would fulfill his original purpose for them in relationship to himself and his Son. He had this plan in mind even before he created humanity because he knows all things. When he created time, he saw it all from beginning to end. His intelligence is at such a high level that all possibilities of cause and effect are transparent and comprehensible to him, no matter how complex.

John Calvin and many who hold to his understanding (called Calvinists) say that God foreordained some people to be saved. He chose who he was going to save, even before he created the universe. It was all his decision. Humanity freely decided to sin and reject God, and God sovereignly decided to save some of them and make them love him. He decided not to save all of humanity. He has his reasons. Those he chose to be saved, will be saved, and nothing can stop them from being saved. These lucky people are called his "elect," and they were predestined to be saved. There are a number of passages in the Scriptures that seem to support this understanding.

The other theological school of thought is called Arminian. They say that God not only originally gave humanity free will, but continues to fully respect our free will. After Adam and Eve sinned, they and their descendants could not of their own ability freely choose to love and obey God, for they were enslaved to the power of sin. But God sends his Holy Spirit to work in the hearts and minds of all people to woo them to himself, and enables them to freely choose to submit themselves to God. If they so choose after his enabling, then God creates a new perfect spirit within them that loves God, and he sends the Holy Spirit to live in them to continue to help them (but not force them) to continually choose to love and serve God who has saved them. But they always have freedom of choice and they may choose to disobey God and turn away from him, and eventually reject him, thus rejecting the salvation that was granted them. This is called apostasy. Arminians say that God "calls" all people and desires that all people will be saved, but "chooses" only those who—once given the ability—freely choose him. Those who remain faithful to the end of their lives are his "elect" who will live with him in Heaven forever. Since God lives outside of time, he knew even before he created humanity who would choose to love him and who would remain faithful to him to the very end of their lives. This is his foreknowledge. There are also passages in the Scriptures that seem to support this understanding.

Since this author is Arminian in outlook, I admit that I might not be able to represent the Calvinist viewpoint 100% accurately. There are also some variations on details among both Calvinists and Arminians in their theologies of salvation. If you happen to go to an assembly of believers that teaches the Calvinist viewpoint, your pastor will be able to instruct you more completely and accurately regarding this viewpoint.

But both schools of thought say that when Adam and Eve sinned, they became estranged from God. They died spiritually. They could no longer have an intimate relationship with God. Those who hold to the tripartite nature of human beings—i.e., that we are composed of spirit, soul, and body—say that our human spirits died, and that our souls and bodies were corrupted with sin. This condition was passed on to all of Adam and Eve's offspring and descendants because spiritually dead and corrupt humans cannot procreate spiritually alive and perfect offspring. Even before children are capable of understanding and reason, they are self-oriented—not God oriented. They are incapable—in their own power—of choosing to properly submit to God and love him in the way that he intended humanity to be able to do. They are spoiled and unacceptable to him. Theologians call this condition "original sin."

All people are born in a state of sinfulness that is unacceptable to God and therefore, must eventually be completely removed from his presence for all eternity—unless they are changed and transformed into the perfection that he originally planned for them. To be completely removed from the presence of the infinite omnipresent God and all his goodness and blessings is what is commonly called "Hell." It is a place God originally created for Satan and the angels that rebelled with him. But once humanity sinned, they were destined to the same fate. Only those who choose to allow God to transform them (or whom God sovereignly chose to transform)—so they can be made to perfectly reflect his glorious character—can be saved from damnation in Hell. God will not tolerate sinful humans for eternity, but he will tolerate them for a time to give many an opportunity to be saved. Many believers think that God has a set time frame when he will end this age and rid his universe of sin and those people who reject him. Some think he may have a certain number of people he wants to be saved before he ends this age. We do know that he intends to wait until some people from every people group in the world have been saved—whether those groups are defined by language, ethnicity, culture, or other factors.

Every human is in this state of "original sin" from the time of conception. Calvinists have a doctrine called "total depravity." This means that because of original sin, no human can in any way contribute to saving themselves. Only by God's initiation and work can a person be saved. As an Arminian, I agree with this doctrine—at least as I have described it here. This "total depravity" does not mean that from a human point of view, people are incapable of any good. We were created in God's image and if properly taught, we are all capable of much love, kindness, goodness, and greatness—at least by human standards. But we are also all tainted with sin, are self-oriented, and are capable of much selfishness, hatred, and evil. In our natural state, even our love and good deeds are tainted with sin—and are as acceptable to God as if someone tried to impress us with a gift that was covered in excrement. We can't see our sins the way God sees them. We have never known sinless perfection, and before we are saved, we have never known perfect love and submission to God. In our natural state, we are incapable of helping ourselves to be saved. God has to be the one to reach out to us, and draw us to himself, and save us.

For most practical purposes, the differences between Calvinists and Arminians are minor in what they say our human response to God is supposed to be. They don't teach different ways of being saved—as far as what we are to believe and do in order to have a proper relationship with God. It's more that they disagree about the way God acts on his part in calling those who become saved. We will all find out about that for sure once we reach Heaven.

3. God's Plan of Salvation

Even though—according to God's standards—we all are worthy of eternal damnation, God's plans and purposes cannot be thwarted. He may not tolerate sinful humanity for eternity, but God is patient—and will suffer sinful humanity's existence for a few thousand years until he has saved enough people for his purpose. Evidently it is not his plan or purpose to save everyone. He says it is his desire to see all people choose to repent and turn to him so he can save them, [1 Timothy 2:3-4] but he will not violate their free will by forcing them to do so. I cannot present the Calvinist view on this issue as I don't understand it. But this non-Calvinist believes that God's purpose is to save at least a certain number of people who freely choose to have an eternal love relationship with him. I believe he has predestined that a certain minimum number will be eventually saved for his purpose, but I don't believe he has predetermined who each individual is, like the Calvinists do. When the Israelites rejected God, he told Moses that he was willing to reject them, and start all over again with Moses' descendants. He wants everyone to repent, but he will go with whoever does repent—and allow the others their freedom to reject him. I believe he has known from the beginning of time—and possibly even before that— who will be saved; but I don't believe he sovereignly chose to save certain people and not save others—without giving them each an opportunity and the ability to choose. I admit that Calvinists are correct when they say that God would be entirely just to do so. All people deserve eternity in Hell, so if he doesn't save some, he is still being just. And he is being gracious to those he would decide to save—even if he only offered salvation to a few. But my reading of the Scriptures leads me to believe that God is also fair and impartial—not arbitrary—and gives everyone the ability and opportunity to freely choose to respond to him properly so they will be saved. I think Calvinists will agree that from our human perspective, it appears to us that this is the case, and that we can't know ahead of time who will be saved and who will not. But the sad fact is that the majority of human beings reject him—even when given a clear opportunity.

A. Grace

All conservative believers—those who believe the Scriptures are the reliable message from God to all people, and that no errors have crept in that change the teachings he wants all his people to know and believe—say that if a person is saved, it is purely by God's grace. Grace, in the Scriptures, means God's unmeritable favor and enabling power. He saves people because he wants to do so—not because of anything people can do to earn his favor. Even from the Arminian view that some of us freely choose to submit to him, that is only because he first sent his Holy Spirit to 1) enable us to choose, and 2) to woo us so that we would want to choose to submit to him. After we are saved, we look back and say it was all his doing. There was nothing inherent in us that was worthy of his attention or salvation. It was his enabling us to freely choose—because in our fallen state we are not capable of that choice on our own—and it was his wooing or drawing us to himself that made us want to choose to be saved. And then when he does save us, he is the one who puts a new living spirit in us which is holy and perfect and loves him and desires to obey him. He also gives us his Holy Spirit to live in our human spirit—who guides us, and continues to woo us, and enables us to obey him. We merit nothing by choosing.

It's a common mockery by nonbelievers to say that religion is a crutch. Actually, our salvation is more like being fully dependent upon a respirator that enables us to breathe because we are incapable of doing so on our own. We who have been saved are as dependent on God's grace and help through the Holy Spirit as someone fully dependent on a respirator to breathe. We are incapable of properly responding to God on our own power. We are, moment by moment, dependent on the power of his enabling favor—which is commonly referred to as his "grace"—for our continued relationship with him.

Because of his great grace toward us, once we are saved, he chooses to see us not only as we are in our current thoughts and actions, but as we will be when our transformation is complete into people who are exactly like his Son in having his holy, loving, selfless character. This will happen when we die and go to Heaven.

We are saved by his grace, and we continue to have a relationship with him by depending on his grace. He gets all the credit and praise—and we merit nothing. But his grace goes even beyond this. During this life while we struggle to choose to submit to his will and do what he wants us to do—which for most of us is not always easy, even though we do want to obey him—he promises us eternal rewards for our obedience to him in this life. It would be ridiculous to think that we merit those rewards. They are pure grace, pure unmerited favor. But he offers them as additional incentives for us to strive toward his goals for us and for others. Some people teach that we should obey purely because it is the right thing to do—not to gain rewards. And they are correct. But Jesus himself urges us to work for eternal rewards, so having that as a motivation is not wrong. Most of us need that additional incentive.

God has requirements for his people to be saved and to gain rewards. But our fulfilling those requirements does not in any sense merit anything and is only possible because he enables us to do so. He enables us to choose to obey his requirements—and he woos us to make the right choice. When we do, he rewards us. But we

certainly have not earned that reward—let alone our salvation.

For an analogy to God rewarding his children for obedience, consider a rich father who promises his son that he can accompany him on a month-long all-expenses-paid trip to Europe—if he will just fill out his passport application in time and be ready to accompany him at the proper time. In order to travel overseas, having a valid passport is a requirement, and being ready to board the plane when the plane is ready to depart is a requirement. Fulfilling these requirements can in no way be seen as meriting the all-expenses-paid month-long trip to Europe. Meeting requirements is not the same as meriting a reward. In the same way, meeting God's requirements to obey him in certain ways in no way merits the eternal rewards he gives us for meeting those requirements. The rewards are pure grace and are unmerited. But they are not given unless requirements are met.

B. How to be Saved

From a human viewpoint—being unaware of what exactly God is doing behind the scenes in calling us—requirements for salvation include:

1) A recognition that you have sinned against a holy God, and that you deserve to be punished in Hell. Those who are ready to be saved already recognize this fact about themselves.

2) An admission—usually called a "confession"—to God that you are a sinner, that you can't save yourself because you are not already perfect and sinless, and therefore you need his help to be saved.

3) An acknowledgment that Jesus the Messiah (a.k.a. Jesus Christ) is God's Son, and that he suffered the punishment for your sins—which you deserve—when he died on the cross. You must also believe that God raised him physically back to life after he died as proof that he is God's Son, and as proof that everything he said while he was on this planet in human form—and recorded in the Bible

about him—`is true. This is your profession of "faith."

4) Your willingness and determination to do your best—while depending on God's help—to stop living in ways that God disapproves of, and to start living in ways he does approve of. This is called "repentance."

5) Your asking Jesus to save you and come into your life as your Lord and Master.

6) Your trusting that he has heard your prayer and has saved you—because he has promised in the Bible to do this for **anyone** who fulfills these requirements. This trusting him to do what he has said he would do is called "living by faith"—i.e., in what he has promised.

You must believe and accept that you are not too evil to be saved. If you at all desire to be saved, it is because the Holy Spirit is working in you to give you that desire—and therefore he is willing to save you no matter what you have done in the past. You can never get your act together sufficiently to deserve being saved. No one can. We all deserve eternal punishment in Hell. Salvation is not about what you deserve, it's about what God is offering you that no human—no matter how good—could ever deserve. Don't dwell on how bad and undeserving a sinner you are. Dwell on how great God is, who is willing and able to transform the worst sinners into people he can be proud of. But he starts doing this after you are saved—not before.

There are many implications of the above requirements—especially of your repentance. Repentance is turning away from sin and turning toward God in obedience. One of the first things he requires of you is to be baptized. *[Acts 2:37-38]* You can go to your local assembly of believers (church) to be instructed about this requirement. You can't baptize yourself. You have to allow someone else to do it for you. Get used to the idea of needing help from other believers. God does not intend for you to live your new life on your own—without emotional support and counseling support and prayer support of other believers. Loners will never thrive spiritually.

If you really want to obey Jesus—and any truly-saved person does—then you will want to know what he wants you to do and what he wants you to stop doing. To discover what these things are, you need to carefully read and study the Bible—especially the New Testament—but don't neglect the Hebrew Scriptures (Old Testament) either. You will discover that one of the most important things he wants you to do is to gain a thorough knowledge of his message in the entire Bible. This will take time and effort. If you aren't familiar with the Bible, I recommend that you read through the introduction to this book and the Harmony of the Gospels. That will give you a good basic (but very minimal) introduction. Even after you have gained a good knowledge of the teachings in the Bible, it's good to memorize Scripture and think about it deeply every day—contemplating what it means and how it applies to your life. This is one way to help you maintain a vital relationship with your new Lord and Savior. There will always be distractions, business, and temptations that will lure you away from thinking about God's teaching, so you have to constantly work to refresh his teachings in your mind. This is one way that he transforms your character—for what you constantly think about will affect the way you live.

You can fulfill the above requirements at any time. Just talk to God like you would to another person. The exact words don't matter. What matters is that you are completely honest in what you say. God knows all your thoughts and if you are holding back or not. If you want help, go to a church or to someone you know is a believer and ask for help. If the first person you ask isn't absolutely thrilled to help you, then find someone else.

C. How to Allow Jesus to Live through You

The goal of your salvation is to have a new intimate relationship with God that starts immediately—and will continue on forever once your earthly body dies. Assuming you are a believer and have fulfilled the requirements in the previous section, you have eternal life right now—and a new desire to please God. This desire to please him is the surest sign that he has saved you. He has given you a new spiritual life source—his very own eternal life essence in your new human spirit that has been spiritually "reborn" (born again). It doesn't matter if you didn't "feel" anything. One of the main things you have to learn is that as wonderful as feelings can be, they are not to be depended on. We are to live and make decisions based on what we "know" from the Scriptures—not on what we "feel" or see or even think we know of the natural world.

Trust that he has given you the Holy Spirit to live in your spirit. Again, if you now want to obey God and to get to know him, this is the surest sign that you are saved— since these desires come from the Holy Spirit. Before you were saved, you did not have these desires. The Holy Spirit will help you to understand his message in the Bible, and will urge you to obey, and will enable you to obey when you find it difficult—if you ask for and consciously depend on his help. He has redeemed your will, so you are now capable of freely choosing to obey him—as well as capable of freely choosing to disobey him. He is starting to transform your mind. This will continue the rest of your life and is aided by your studying and thinking about his message in the Bible, and by choosing to believe everything he says is true—despite some things that seem to make it hard to believe. For example, he promises that he is always with you, will always help you, always loves you, and is in full control of your life. But if something bad happens to you, you will be tempted to disbelieve that he is in control of the situation or that he has allowed it to happen to you. Or you will be tempted to believe he doesn't love you. You need to learn to base your beliefs on what he says in the Bible as being more reliable than what circumstances and your emotions are telling you. He is also starting to heal your emotional

responses and past emotional hurts in your life. This healing will usually take time, and until you get to Heaven, you will always have to struggle with emotions that don't always act the way you want them to act. So your transformation in your mind and emotions is gradual in this life. While it can progress rapidly with your cooperation and obedience, the transformation will never be complete in this life. Your body's redemption has been paid for, but you will not be free of this weak body until you die. Eventually, you will gain a new glorified body that will not tempt you as your current body always will in this life. Your experiencing the redemption of your body waits until you die.

So how do you live your new life? Many believers struggle most or all of their lives and never learn the key—mainly because they have never been taught it or have been taught wrongly. Jesus lives in you now through his Holy Spirit. It is his spiritual life force that is now empowering your life. Your old "dead" spirit was done away with. He wants you to allow him to live his life through you. He doesn't want you to try to live this new life by your own efforts. You won't succeed by your own power. You may succeed just a little, but you will continually fail and become discouraged if you try to do it yourself. Only he can live the kind of life that pleases God. You cannot, even with your new spirit and redeemed will. You will be tempted by bodily desires and by external sources—including lies from demons cleverly placed in your mind to make you think that the thoughts originated with you. You cannot withstand these temptations much at all on your own. God doesn't intend for you to do so. So how do you allow Jesus to live his life through you?

1) You need to know what he wants you to do. That is why it's important to know what his general will is for all people as revealed in the Scriptures. We will cover how to know what he wants you to do in circumstances not explicitly covered by teaching in the Scriptures in the next section.

2) Once you know what he wants you to do:

   a) Trust that he is always living in you, that you are spiritually joined to Jesus, that you are therefore already accepted as perfect and righteous in God's sight—because you are spiritually joined to Jesus who is perfect and righteous—and that all his infinite resources are waiting to help you do his will.

b) Act in obedience to what you know he wants you to do, all the while trusting that he is empowering you to do it. You can't be passive. You have to step out and act, but you also have to be consciously depending on him in you to do it through you. Ask for him to live his life through you by his power. Do this moment by moment—and especially when you feel tempted to disobey.

c) Trust that he is doing it through you, and trust that the results that happen are what he intends for you to experience. Assuming you were obedient and were trusting him to help you, even if it appears you were a failure— e.g., you did poorly on a test or in some project you attempted—trust that he was doing it through you and that he wanted you to experience that apparent failure. He wants you to learn to depend on him and believe that he is present and helping you—regardless of what results. Some of the apparent failures will be just to test you and train you to trust him. Some of the apparent failures may in fact be what he wanted to happen for reasons you cannot imagine at that time. I have seen what I considered to be major failures in my life to in fact lead to God's major success later on. I later realized that had I succeeded when I wanted to, it would have resulted in greater overall failure later on. Trust that his willingness to help you is not dependent on your previous obedience—nor is it hampered by your past disobedience. He is always willing to help you obey him—even if you just deliberately sinned. Of course he wants you to repent of your sin too, but he will not for any reason withhold his help to obey if you desire it. He wants to live his life through you. He wants you to practice and cultivate a moment by moment awareness of his presence within you and your need to depend on him. For many, cultivating this habit and remembering to depend on him is the hardest part.

d) Thank him for the results. They are his results—if you were trusting him to do it through you and you were obedient. Don't judge based on outward appearances. If you were trying to obey his will and were trusting him to help you, believe that is what was happening and that the results are his doing for his purpose. So relax and thank him that he is in control. For many, this is a difficult attitude to adopt, but you may as well give in and do it because he will eventually get you there one way or another. In general, the more quickly you learn to thank him in all circumstances, the more rapid progress you will make in becoming spiritually mature.

3) If you have trouble remembering to depend on him, then as often as you do remember, ask him to help you remember and cultivate that awareness and dependence. It will take a while to change your habits and become fully dependent most of the time. For most people, it will probably take several years to establish a more or less automatic habit—so don't give up after only a few weeks or months. Dig in and prepare for the long haul. The more you do it, the easier it becomes.

4) As you develop the habit to constantly, moment by moment, turn to Jesus to depend on him to live through you, you will find yourself talking to him, and seeking his advice and wisdom all through the day. You can do this either aloud, or just by thinking. He knows your thoughts. This is a very important kind of prayer. This is the relationship he wants with you. The more you do this, the easier it will become to know what he wants. He will become your constant companion and intimate friend. That's your goal in

this life, to become intimate with him on a moment by moment basis as much of the time as you are able to do so. This will lead to great peace, contentment, and joy.

5) When you do stumble in sin, ask for forgiveness immediately—and trust that he has forgiven you as he has promised. *[1 John 1:9]* Don't go by your feelings of failure and lack of worthiness. Satan will try to keep you from turning to God and asking Jesus to live through you. He will try to strengthen those bad feelings. Decide to ignore them! Then get on with allowing Jesus to live through you. Act as if that stumble in sin was just like a baby trying to learn how to walk. Get right up and forget about the failure that just happened and try again. He wants you to turn to him after sinning. He does not want you sulking and avoiding him from shame. That doesn't help your relationship at all. He has already forgiven you, and his love and acceptance is not based on your obedience, but on your spiritual union with Jesus.

6) Cultivate the habit and attitude to be thankful in all circumstances. *[1 Thessalonians 5:16-18]* Focus on the joy of being saved and knowing that you will spend eternity in Heaven. Don't allow circumstances to control your attitudes. Always thank God that he is in control of all the circumstances he has allowed you to experience—and that he is using those circumstances to transform you into the character of his Son. The sooner you learn to humbly accept that and rejoice in all circumstances, the quicker you will get through with that difficult lesson and learn to enjoy life—though there will always be some occasional difficulties to be faced.

7) It is also very important to understand that God does not expect you to live this way on your own. He commands his people to get together and help each other. At a bare minimum, every week you should meet together with other believers for worship, prayer, and study of the Scriptures. Get to know a few believers well, so they will know when

you are struggling and will pray with you, and for you, and encourage you. You are to help them in the same way. Believers are to love each other and help each other just like brothers and sisters—both in their faith and in all aspects of their lives. God never intended any believer to be a "Lone Ranger" who tries to live as he wants us to live—all on our own. We need the help and accountability that close relationships with other believers can offer us. Watching Bible teachers on TV just won't hack it. Don't be put off by believers who are less than perfect. That describes all of us—and you too. Remember that Jesus will never let you down, even though his people will. You, too, will sometimes let other people down—so don't let the imperfections of God's people keep you from the joy of fellowship and strength of unity that you can have with them.

Choose the assembly of believers to which you will commit yourself with care. Make sure that they believe the same things that you see the Bible teaches. There are, unfortunately, many assemblies that don't believe much that is in the Bible. If they believe there is no Hell and that God saves everyone, run! If this were true, there would be no need for the Bible or for the existence of assemblies of believers. If they believe that all ways lead to God, run! All beliefs do not lead to God any more than all roads lead to New York City. Anyone who believes that has turned off their brain. They believe such things because they want to do whatever they want and not be responsible to a very real God for their behavior. If they believe that Jesus is not God (as the Jehovah's Witnesses do not), or that someone is more important that Jesus (like Joseph Smith—this is what Mormons believe), run! Find some other group to associate with. You are seeking people who believe what the Bible teaches, for the Bible contains the truth about God. He caused people to write what is in it and he has preserved that message for us today. If someone thinks he didn't write it or preserve it, then the Bible must be worthless to them. Why bother reading it at all? Only if it is entirely true and trustworthy is it worth reading. If it isn't all true, then we can't know what is true and what is not true in it—and the book is worthless. But there is a lot of evidence that the Bible is true and that God preserved it so we would know his truth. So find others who believe the same. It's not that hard to do.

Also understand that most of what the Bible teaches is easy to understand and straightforward. It was written so simple uneducated people can understand it. So if someone tells you that a passage in the Bible doesn't mean what it seems to plainly mean, then be careful. Not all passages are easy to understand, but the bulk of the book is easy enough. The reason some parts are difficult for us to understand today is because we live in a different culture, time, and place than the first readers. It was much easier for them to understand certain expressions than us because it was their everyday way of talking at that time. But overall, the main message is still usually clear and straightforward.

D. How to Learn What He Wants You to Do

As I said before, a thorough knowledge of his general will for all people as revealed in the Scriptures is essential. He will never lead you in a way that will contradict what he has taught in the Bible. But there are many everyday things not explicitly covered by the instructions in the Bible. For example, who to marry, what job to accept, what house to buy, how to prioritize your time, how to spend your money, how to encourage a particular person, etc.

First, you should always follow the clear commands and general principles that are revealed in the Bible. Here are a few Scripture passages that list some of the important teachings about the way God wants his people to live. *[1 Corinthians 13:1-7; Galatians 5:16—6:10; Ephesians 4:1—6:9; Colossians 3:12—4:6; 1 Thessalonians 4:1-12; 5:6-22; James 1:19—2:12; 3:13—4:17; 1 Peter 4:1-11]*

1) Fulfill your responsibilities and promises. Therefore, you get up and take care of your family duties, and get to work or school on time, and fulfill your assigned duties, and obey the law. Don't bother asking the Lord if it's OK to drive five miles over the speed limit like everyone else around you. He has already said in the Scriptures to submit to all governing authorities. You know what is right to do. Don't make it a habit to justify what you want to do by other people's behavior. You will never learn to please God doing that. As long as no one is demanding that you do something the Scriptures prohibit, if they are in authority over you, then it is God's will for you to obey that authority over you—even if it is unjust toward you. Practice consciously depending on Jesus' living through you in every mundane daily thing you do and say. If you make little exceptions—even when they have no consequences (like driving five miles per hour over the speed limit)—you will eventually make big exceptions and develop the very bad habit of rationalizing anything you want to do. That is not the way to please your Lord and grow in maturity and intimacy with him.

2) Everything you do and say reflects on the reputation of your Lord. So do and say everything in a loving and humble manner to the best of your ability—while relying on him to do it through you. Apologize and ask for forgiveness when you mess up. And you will mess up. We all do. If you don't choose to be humble and admit that you messed up, realize that God opposes those who are proud. You don't want him to make you humble. It will not be a pleasant lesson. So just admit you are not perfect and you make mistakes and genuinely apologize for messing up. It's so much easier that way.

3) Ignore feelings that you recognize are pulling you in a direction that is not God's will. Depend on his help to ignore those demanding feelings and desires that you know are contrary to his will. It's not a sin to feel any particular way. Sin is choosing to do or say or think what you know is wrong. It is not a sin to feel tempted. It is a sin to contemplate that temptation and not immediately reject it. It is NOT hypocritical to do what you know is

right—like showing your Lord's love to someone—even though you don't at all feel like it. It is allowing Jesus to live his life through you in spite of inappropriate feelings over which you have little or no control. If you are humble, you won't be a hypocrite in God's eyes. It is a common lie from Satan that it is hypocritical to do something that you don't feel like doing, such as, "It would be hypocritical to be nice to that person because I don't like them." God commands you to be nice, regardless of your feelings. It is never hypocritical to obey God. It is hypocritical to pretend you are better than you are. If you are humble, you will never be a hypocrite.

4) If you are not sure what you are supposed to do in a situation, ask God to give you wisdom. He has promised that he will give you wisdom if you ask for it. *[James 1:5-8]* If you do this, you have to be willing to obey whatever he shows you, or else he will not give it to you. Assume he is giving you wisdom. If an idea comes to mind after you ask—and it is not in conflict with his general will or principles as revealed in the Scriptures—then assume it is from him and act on it. You may make mistakes, but if you really want to obey him, he will really want to reveal his will to you—and he will teach you to recognize your mistakes. Don't do anything you don't feel right about. If no new or clear idea comes to mind, do what seems best to you according to your understanding. Trust that he is working through your ordinary intelligence and understanding. If it is a very important matter and you feel that you need God's clear guidance before making a decision, he is rarely in a hurry. So you may ponder the matter, and pray, and take as much time as you need to be confident you have his leading before acting. Again, God is never in a hurry. If someone is pressing you for a decision quickly and you aren't sure the Lord is saying go ahead, then default with a NO. If it's something important and it is his will, God will give you the time you need to seek his will. He will also confirm his leading through other believers. Ask for their advice.

5) For important decisions where you feel you need clear guidance, spend time in quiet and prayer. Calm your emotions and be open to doing something that you don't feel like doing—if he seems to lead in that direction. Strong emotions make it difficult to discern God's quiet prompting. Fasting and prayer may be necessary. If you would spend several hours seeking human advice over a matter, consider it worth spending at least as much time in prayer and waiting on the Lord for his leading. When you think you have discerned his will, you will feel a peace. Your decision must, of course, not violate his general will as revealed in the Scriptures. Reading and thinking about the Scriptures can help clear your mind while you wait on him—and he may bring the answer to your mind while you are doing this. You can also spend time in praise and worship and thanksgiving to help you focus on him, and to strengthen your desire to obey him no matter what he reveals to you.

6) For important decisions where human wisdom and knowledge might be helpful, seek counsel from people who are close to the Lord, and spiritually mature, and who know you.

7) Don't assume that God will want you to do something that you simply can't contemplate doing—like becoming a missionary. If he wants you to do such difficult things, he will give you a desire to do it. Psalm 37:4 says that if we delight in God, i.e., if we love him, and are happy to do what he wants of us, then he gives us the desires of our hearts. He puts his desires in us, and then grants them. He doesn't want us to be miserable and he won't call us to a career or major commitment that will make us miserable.

8) If you really want to do something or make a decision in a certain direction, examine that desire. Is it a desire that you would have had before you believed? If not, then there's a strong possibility that desire comes from God—as long as it is

not in conflict with his revealed will in the Scriptures.

9) If you have strong feelings about something—and those feelings could be motivated by pride or selfishness—be extra cautious. Strong emotions—unless they are clearly selfless—can easily mislead us. If at all possible, wait until those emotions are not so strong and ask God to take them away—if they are not of him—so you can more easily discern his will.

10) Don't just allow circumstances to always lead you—though they may be a factor. Sometimes God wants us to persevere and overcome difficult circumstances. Sometimes he wants us to ignore an easy "open door."

11) You may ask for some kind of sign. Some people teach you should not do this, and it shouldn't be your main everyday means of discerning the Lord's will. But there is biblical precedent, and it is sometimes warranted.

12) Some people believe that God will only speak to you through the Scriptures. Therefore, memorizing Scripture is very helpful—as it makes it easier for God to bring a specific one to mind. Others believe that he will "speak" directly to you through your spirit—to your mind. This is not an audible voice but is often a thought or impression, or the leading of your conscience. He will also never lead you in a direction that violates his will as revealed in the Scriptures. If you want to learn to "hear" God's leading in this way, there are many books available on the subject. It is best to also seek help from someone who easily hears from God in this way.

E. More about Living as One Who is Saved

Now that you are truly saved, you will want to do what God wants you to do. If this isn't true of someone, then they haven't really been saved. But living this new life isn't always easy because unbelievers will make fun of you, discriminate against you, make life more difficult for you, and even persecute or kill you. Believers are not openly persecuted yet in the US, but they are in many countries of this world, and some are killed for their faith. Jesus requires that we not be ashamed of belonging to him. If we deny that he is our Savior and master— even if it's just to avoid ridicule, persecution, or death—then he will deny that we belong to him and we won't get to Heaven. So believers have to be prepared and willing to suffer in order to follow Jesus. We have to suffer in minor ways—like giving up things our bodies enjoy doing that we know are sinful and forbidden to us. And we may have to suffer external persecution or even death for his sake. Start cultivating the mindset that you are willing to suffer for Jesus any way that is necessary. He has promised that you will gain eternal rewards in Heaven for enduring suffering because you belong to him, and for refusing to disown him or be ashamed of him. The eternal rewards you will gain far outweigh the temporary sufferings in this life that you experience.

Believers are to do their best to study the Scriptures, and learn to live the way he wants us to live, and to live that way every day. This is commonly called being a disciple—or student-follower—of Jesus. We also have the privilege and responsibility to tell others about Jesus and the way of salvation. We are to share with others the ways he has helped us and answered our prayers—as evidence that he is real. We are to help bring others to salvation through our prayers, words, deeds, and lifestyle of honesty, integrity, purity, and love. Jesus commands this of every believer. If you help bring someone to saving faith, you might also have the responsibility to teach them what they need to know and help them to become mature in their faith. So you have to become prepared to be able to do this.

Jesus has set us free from the power of sin. Sinful desires can no longer force us to sin—but they can tempt us. Experiencing temptation is not sinning. But entertaining sinful thoughts and desires without rejecting them is sin. Believers have the ability to reject sinful thoughts and desires—and God wants you to make it a habit of doing this—so that actual sinning in your life becomes more and more rare.

These Things Can Help You Reject Sinful Desires

1) Recognize they are not part of your "true self" because our "old sinful self" was crucified with Jesus, *[Romans 6:6]* you are a "new person," *[2 Corinthians 5:17]* you are already "holy" *[1 Corinthians 1:2]* and are spiritually united with the Messiah in Heaven. *[Ephesians 2:6]*

2) When sinful desires come, immediately reject them—aloud if necessary—immediately ask Jesus to help you, trust that he is doing so, then do what you know is right. *[Galatians 2:20]*

3) Focus your thoughts on things that are good and holy. *[Philippians 4:8]* Take your mind off of the temptation by focusing on Jesus though songs of praise and adoration.

4) Recognize that temptation is a spiritual attack against you, and that "offense is the best defense"—even against Satan. Have on hand a list of people to pray for and their needs; and when you are tempted, start interceding on behalf of those people for salvation, healing, restored relationships, provision, etc. Wage spiritual warfare against the enemy on behalf of your family, friends, colleagues, and acquaintances. Do this aloud if possible. This will distract you from the temptation and will have you actively focusing on God's word, standing on his promises, exercising your faith, strengthening your resolve to oppose the enemy, his temptations, and ways—while actively depending on God's power to overcome on behalf of those for whom you are praying. You will be resisting and opposing Satan, and as a result—he will cease attacking you with temptation, flee, *[James 4:7]* and leave you alone, at least for a while. *[Luke 4:13]*

True believers who will end up in Heaven must persevere in their faith and obedience until the end of their lives—or until Jesus returns. Those who turn away from him and start living in unrepented sin again—will not enter Heaven. Therefore,

you need to work at your relationship with Jesus and keep it strong at all times. Also meet with other believers who will help you, pray for you, keep you accountable, and encourage you.

One important principle in the life of a believer is called the principle of "sowing and reaping." This simply means that what you do in your life is like planting seeds. Later, those seeds will sprout and produce what you planted. If you sow love, generosity, integrity, and purity in your life, then God will cause these good things to come back to you and benefit you. But if you sow sins like dishonesty, impurity, hypocrisy, selfishness, or other evils in your life, then God will cause you to suffer the consequences of those sins. You will not get away without his discipline because he desires to see you become exactly like Jesus in his holy character. When you give generously to those in need, God will give back to you and will reward you. If you are merciful to others, God will be merciful to you. If you are stingy with others, God will be stingy in blessing you. If you are impatient and criticize others, God will judge you strictly and not be lenient with you. *[2 Samuel 22:21; Psalm 18:20; Proverbs 13:21; 22:4; Jeremiah 31:16; Hosea 10:12; Matthew 7:2; 10:40-42; 16:27; Mark 4:24; 9:41; Luke 6:37-38; Romans 2:5-10, 16; 1 Corinthians 3:8-15; 2 Corinthians 5:10; 9:6-8; Galatians 6:7-8; Ephesians 6:8; Colossians 3:23-25; Hebrews 4:12; 11:6; Revelation 2:23; 20:12; 22:12]* These things may not affect your salvation, but they will affect the rewards you will receive in Heaven. There will be rank and riches in Heaven—and your status there is determined by how you live in this life.

F. Forgiving Other People

One extremely important requirement that God places upon you is that you have to freely forgive others who have done wrong against you—in the same way that God has freely forgiven you. You did not earn God's forgiveness, so you are not allowed to require others to earn your forgiveness either. This is difficult for people who have been seriously abused, or who have had a major wrong done to them, who feel betrayed or violated, or taken advantage of, or who are proud (this is a sin, by the way). But this is a major requirement for all believers. And you cannot grow in your faith or in your relationship with God if you are unwilling to forgive someone else. If you refuse to forgive someone, God will not forgive you. It is a condition of his continued forgiveness. And if God does not forgive you, that means you will go to Hell. Is your holding onto anger and hurt worth going to Hell for?

We are commanded to forgive, even if the person who sinned against us is not sorry or repentant—even if we know they will do it again. There are many sins that you are unaware of and have never repented of—yet God forgives you anyway. So you are required to forgive others, even if they are unaware of their sin against you, or even if they are aware and are not sorry.

Many people feel that they can't forgive someone because it is too hard for them to overcome their feelings. But it often helps to understand what forgiveness is, and what it is not.

Forgiveness **Does Not Mean** that

1) what the person did was OK or is of no consequence to you.
2) there will be no consequences for them.
3) you were not harmed by it.
4) you no longer feel taken advantage of, hurt, abused, betrayed, or violated.
5) you have neutral or positive feelings toward them
6) you have forgotten about it.
7) you will accept them back into your life and not avoid them.
8) the previous relationship is restored.
9) you now trust that person.

Forgiveness **Does Mean** that you will

1) not try to seek revenge or punish them in any way—such as speaking evil to them or about them to others, or doing wrong to them to "teach them a lesson."
2) not bring the matter up with them—unless they do. Bringing the matter up again is a form of punishment—which you give up the right to do when you forgive.
3) give the matter and the offender into God's hand for him to deal with in his own way and in his own time—trusting that he will punish them appropriately if they are unrepentant. It is his job—not yours—to punish. God's real punishment will not come until that person dies, because in this life he will try to bring that person to repentance. But his punishment in Hell will be much greater than anything you could impose in this life as payback or revenge. And God may cause the person to experience consequences for his sin in this life to teach him, and to show him his need to repent—just as he does to us.
4) try to let go of the anger, and remind yourself that you have decided not to punish that offender. You will not continually remind yourself of what they did wrong.

We are commanded to pray for our enemies and bless them—and we are forbidden to curse them. If you have anger towards someone, they are your enemy. And it can help you get rid of your anger—over time—if you pray for them and ask God to bless them—every time you feel that anger. You can ask God to bring them to repentance and salvation, and help them to recognize that what they did is wrong, and to change them so they won't do it again to you or to anyone else. This is a way of blessing them.

Forgiveness is a decision to not punish the person yourself, and to let God take care of the situation. It is not a decision that you will be able change your feelings toward that person right away. You may need to make the decision to forgive that person over and over and over again until the anger doesn't keep coming back to you. It may take a long time for the feelings to fade, but that should not affect your decision to forgive—which is to give up the right to punish.

Forgiveness means that you will be willing to give the person another chance if they do repent and admit they were wrong and ask for your forgiveness. To not be willing to give a person another chance if they do repent is to punish them—and in forgiving them you decided to give up that right.

Trust and close relationships are earned. If someone who sinned against you repents and desires a relationship with you and desires your trust, they will have to earn it. It is not automatically granted. But you have to be willing to give them that chance. Trust that God will restore what was taken from you, and that he will heal all your hurts—physically, emotionally, and mentally. That is his job—not the person's who harmed you. God's complete righting of the wrong done to you may or may not happen until you go to heaven, but he will do it.

Forgiveness is letting go of the right to revenge, but if the offender is not repentant, you are not required to be around them and be a friend or a target of further abuse. If they are unrepentant and likely to sin against you again, you would be wise to set up barriers and avoid them so you don't give them opportunities to harm you again. But if they do repent, you have to be willing to show God's love to them—as you would to any stranger, or even to an enemy—and give them another chance to have a relationship with you. It doesn't mean you have to feel love, or kindness, or any positive feeling toward them right away, only that you will demonstrate God's love for them by doing what is good for them, and will refuse to nurture and reinforce any negative feelings and thoughts that you have toward them.

Forgiveness doesn't mean that you will not report a crime to the proper authorities or refuse to testify against them. If you are in authority over that person—such as an employee, or someone you supervise, or a child—forgiving them does not mean that you withhold proper consequences that would be appropriate for any authority to enforce in such a situation. But you do need to take care that any penalties you impose are not motivated by anger or revenge, but are just and fair. For God will later judge your behavior towards those under you. It would be wise to seek counsel in some situations so you don't end up sinning against the person you are over.

It also helps to realize that many people we are angry at and who we find it difficult to forgive are oblivious to our feelings or to the fact that they hurt us. And some of them don't care. But by holding on to your anger and resentment, you are not really punishing them, you are not making the situation better, you are not helping yourself—you are just making yourself miserable. Unforgiveness can become bitterness—which is like a cancer in your mind, emotions, and personality. Bitterness will destroy your ability to enjoy anything in life, it will destroy your character, and can even make you physically ill. Some think it can even cause real cancer—though clearly not all cancer is due to bitterness. Someone said that refusing to forgive is like drinking poison and hoping it will harm the one who hurt you. Your anger and unforgiveness mainly hurts yourself—and often does not bother the other person at all. By forgiving someone and letting go of your anger, and allowing God to handle the other person, you are only helping yourself and cutting the emotional tie that has you and your thoughts in bondage to the person who hurt you. As long as you refuse to forgive and you hold on to anger, that person—or what they did—has you in an emotional prison that will make your life miserable—and that misery will ultimately destroy you. By forgiving the offender you are not letting them off the hook, you are putting them on God's hook and letting yourself off of their hook.

Because of strong emotions, it can still be difficult for people to forgive in some situations. Read Luke 17:3-6 in this book with the accompanying notes. Those verses deal with repeat offenders who are repentant, but the principle is the same with those who are not repentant. If you have even a small amount of faith, God will give you all the power you need to help you make the decision forgive—if only you will trust him and obey him by trying to do so. But you have to be willing to try.

4. The Great Exchange

The work Jesus did in saving us is sometimes called the "Great Exchange."
He came to earth so we could go to
  Heaven. [John 6:38-39, 51]
He gave up all he had in Heaven so we
  could gain everything he has. [Philippians
  2:6-7, John 14:12-14, Romans 8:17]

He became human so we could become
God's children. *[1 John 3:1-2]*

He made himself humble so we could share
God's greatness. *[Philippians 2:8, Romans 8:17]*

He became physically weak so we could
become spiritually strong. *[1 Corinthians 1:25,
16:13; 2 Corinthians 12:9; 13:4; Hebrews 11:33]*

He became poor so that we could become
rich in Heaven. *[2 Corinthians 8:9; Galatians 3:13-14]*

He became like us physically so we could
become like him in character. *[Colossians 2:9;
John 13:34; 1 Corinthians 1:2; Ephesians 1:4; 1 Peter 1:15-16]*

He became hated by men so we could
be loved by God. *[Isaiah 53:3; Romans 1:7;
Acts 15:8; Romans 15:7]*

He was rejected by God so we could be
accepted by God. *[Matthew 27:46;
Mark 15:34; Ephesians 3:1-6]*

He was punished so we could be
forgiven. *[1 John 1:9; 1 Peter 3:18]*

He took our sins upon him so we could
receive his righteousness. *[Isaiah 53:5]*

He was beaten so we could be physically
healed. *[Isaiah 53:4-5]*

He experienced sadness and grief so we
could experience eternal joy.
[Isaiah 61:3; John 15:11]

He was cursed so we could receive
God's blessings. *[Galatians 3:13-14]*

He died so we could live forever. *[Romans 6:23]*

5. The Upside-Down Life

If you want to gain eternal life, you have
to give up all claim to running your
own life in this world. *[Matthew 16:24-25]*

If you want God's power to be manifested
in and through you, you must fully
surrender your will to him. *[John 14:31]*

If you want to be victorious over sin in
your life, you have to be willing to
suffer. *[1 Peter 4:1]*

If you want to be rich in Heaven, you have
to give away your earthly riches to
those in need—and not spend them on
yourself. *[Matthew 19:21]*

If you want to become great in God's Kingdom, you have to become a humble
servant of others. *[Matthew 20:25-27]*

If you want to be first in God's estimation,
you have to consider yourself the least
important of all people. *[Mark 10:42-44]*

6. Common Errors About Salvation

A. Universalism

Many people today believe that a loving
God will not send anyone to Hell. They
believe all people will live in Heaven, and so
they reject the idea of a God who hates sin
and will punish many people in Hell forever.
This idea comes from a desire to make up a
God according to their own design. They feel
more comfortable with a much-less-
demanding God than the one described in
the Bible—because it allows them more freedom to do what they want in this life. They
latch on to the Biblical teaching that God is
love—and conveniently ignore all the other
teachings about God's character in the Bible.
They think a God who is love could never
punish anyone forever.

However logical this sounds to some
people, it doesn't match up with what the
Bible teaches. God's love is a holy righteous
love, not a sappy-tolerate-anything kind of
love. He desires the best for people—and is
not content to allow people to do what they
want when it violates his holy character. He
is more loving than any human being. But
he is also much more holy than any human,
and he hates sin because of the evil and
suffering it inevitably produces. He cannot
tolerate sin in his presence. He is merciful
and patient, and gives everyone adequate
opportunity and help to be changed into
someone he can accept. But he cannot
violate his own character by allowing sinful
people to live with him in Heaven. He also
will not violate a person's free will by
forcing them to submit to his will when they
don't want to do so. He will save anyone
who wants to be saved and is willing to meet
his conditions. Those who end up in Hell are
those who of their own free will reject him
and his Son Jesus and his conditions. Jesus
said that relatively few people will reach
Heaven. *[Matthew 7:13-14]*

It's impossible to read the New
Testament, believe it's true, and come to the
conclusion that Hell doesn't exist and that
God doesn't send people to Hell. Those who
come to this conclusion have to ignore most

of what the New Testament teaches. Jesus himself talked about Hell more than anyone else. The idea that all people will be saved is totally foreign to the Bible, and is simply wishful thinking. *[Matthew 3:9-12; 5:22; 29-30; 7:13-14, 19, 21; 8:12; 10:28; 11:23; 13:41-42, 50; 18:8-9; 23:15, 33; 25:41; Mark 9:43-48; 16:16; Luke 3:8-9, 17; 12:5; 16:23-24; John 3:16, 36; 17:12; Acts 8:20; 18:6; Romans 1:32; 8:13; 1 Corinthians 11:32; 15:17; 2 Corinthians 2:15; Galatians 1:8-9; 2 Thessalonians 2:10-12; 2 Peter 2:4-12; Revelation 20:11-15]*

The Scriptures talk over and over about being saved, and urgently urges people to repent, to turn away from sin, and trust Jesus to save them. This makes no sense unless people are saved from something—namely Hell. If there is no Hell, there is nothing to save people from. If God intends to bring all people to Heaven automatically—no matter what they do or believe—then all churches should disband since they serve no real function. The Bible serves no function. There's nothing for anyone to worry about. Forget about God and do what you want—because he will take care of everything for you.

But we all instinctively know there is right and wrong, and have an innate sense of justice that says wrong should be punished. To say that God should never punish people in Hell makes as much sense as saying we should stop punishing criminals and release everyone from prison. Heaven wouldn't be Heaven if it were full of evil people like this world is.

B. All Religions Lead to God

Many people today—including some professing believers in Jesus—say that all religions lead to God. They say it doesn't matter if you are Christian, Jewish, Buddhist, Muslim, or follow any other religion. All roads lead to Heaven. This clearly doesn't make sense in this physical world. All roads don't lead to the same place. So the only thing that would make someone think this is true of going to Heaven is wishful thinking. Certainly nothing in anyone's experience in this world would support that conclusion. And certainly the Bible doesn't teach it.

Except for the Baha'i faith, all religions make exclusive claims. Christians, religious Jews, and Muslims who believe what their historical faiths and holy books teach, believe that their way is the only way to Heaven, if they believe in a Heaven. Jesus said he was the only way to the Father in Heaven. *[John 14:6]* Either the Bible is completely wrong, or the people who say all religions lead to God and Heaven are wrong. Every religion can't be right because they all teach incompatible things as being true. There is nothing in this life that could lead people to believe that multiple contradictory facts are all equally true. It certainly doesn't work with math, science, or other non-religious matters. The teaching that contradictory religious beliefs are all equally valid, good, and true is pure nonsense. It was invented by people who have no true religious beliefs, and was intended to avoid conflict. But it doesn't ever work to avoid conflict because not everyone is stupid enough to buy into this lie. This belief is again merely wishful thinking and a variation on the wrong belief that all people will end up in Heaven. There is simply no evidence in the Bible that this is the case.

Those who hold to the belief that all will get to Heaven are in a dangerous position. If they are right, we all win and we don't need to worry about following their politically-correct belief because it won't make any difference if we do or don't. But if they are wrong—and all common sense in this world says their belief is nonsense—then they will have missed their chance. Logically, the odds are heavily against them, and they would be wiser to hedge their bets. But such people aren't really interested in knowing truth. They only want to think thoughts that make them happy right now, and want to ignore what the future might hold. The Bible calls this "foolishness." They are like doped-up drug addicts, lost in their own temporary world, blissfully unaware of the real world around them, and uncaring about the unpleasant consequences and reality that they will have to face when they become sober again. Foolish people who ignore God and his Word are unaware of the harsh reality they will face when they stand before an all-knowing, holy and righteous God to be judged for every thought, word, and deed they have ever done in this life.

C. Works Righteousness

Every person in this world who believes in God has the idea that if they are good enough, God will be pleased with them. If they are good enough, then they can gain eternal life in Heaven. If their good works outweigh their bad works, then they will get to Heaven. If they are better than others, then God must be pleased with them. Most religions teach this in some form. But the Bible teaches that all people are tainted with sin. Therefore, no one is worthy of going to Heaven. From a human point of view, certainly some people are much better than others. Unfortunately, the Bible says God's standards are perfection. Just one sin and you are not fit to spend eternity with God. He won't tolerate any sin or impurity in his presence. So there's nothing you can do to earn Heaven. No one is good enough. There's not even anything we can do to gain his favor, for sinners can't please him. All our good deeds are tainted. Our good works are like doing our best to prepare a fantastic banquet feast to serve God, but sprinkled throughout the good food in minute bits are pieces of dung. Those little bits spoil the whole feast. None of it is edible, and none of our good deeds are pure enough to be acceptable to him.

That's why God sent his Son to become the man Jesus. He lived a perfect sinless life and is acceptable to God. If we trust in his death to pay the penalty for our sins, then God spiritually joins us to Jesus, and we gain his holy perfection. No, we don't see that perfection in this life. But it is there on a spiritual level—which in reality is the most important and permanent level—and God gradually transforms us in this life to make it more manifest in our character and actions. When we die, he completes the transformation—eliminating all traces of sin in us as we enter Heaven. In this life, he is favorably disposed toward us, not because of anything good we do, but only because we are spiritually joined to Jesus—and thereby share his holiness and righteousness. Our sins are forgiven. When we sin, that doesn't lessen God's favor toward us—since his favor is not based on what we do. It is based on who we are in our spiritual union with his Son.

So don't think that God will be more favorable toward answering your prayers because you've been good this week—or less favorable toward you because you've been bad. His favor toward you—if you are a believer—is unwavering because it's based on your union with Jesus—not on what you've done. If you've been bad this week, don't be too ashamed to approach God in prayer or worship. Of course he wants you to acknowledge your sin and repent. But he then immediately welcomes you in full acceptance because of your union with Jesus. So never let your sins keep you from God—and don't proudly think that your good works give you an "in" with him either. The Bible says God will actively oppose you if you are proud and self-righteous; but if you are humble and acknowledge your sin and dependence on Jesus' righteousness, he will greatly favor you. *[James 4:6]*

D. Abuse of Grace

It is unfortunately a common and serious error that some people think God is always willing to forgive, therefore it doesn't matter if they willingly sin. Jesus saved us from the dominion of sin so that we could choose to live holy lives. God still hates sin. He is willing to forgive if we have an attitude of repentance. Repentance means we are sorry we have sinned and are striving to depend on his power to live a holy life and not sin. If a person deliberately and continually chooses to sin and has no desire to repent, then such a person is not saved. If they were saved at one time, then they are hardening their hearts against God and eventually the Holy Spirit will give up on them—and they will be apostate and lost forever.

The Scriptures clearly warn against this kind of attitude and this false teaching—that it's OK to live a sinful lifestyle condemned by the Scriptures. The Scriptures warn that such people will not be saved. It is one thing to repeatedly fall into sin yet be truly repentant and wanting to please God by changing your ways and trying not to repeat that sin. God knows your heart. If you desire to change and be made pure, he will forgive you and help you—no matter how many times you fail. But if you willingly embrace what you know the Bible condemns as sin, and have no desire to change—thinking God won't mind, or at least he will always forgive you—you are wrong. *[Hebrews 10:26-31]* You will go to Hell. *[Jude 4-16]*

7. Two Difficult Questions about Salvation

A. Salvation of
Young Children and the Mentally Challenged

If people must believe in Jesus and repent, how can infants and retarded people be saved? First, we must trust God's Word where he says that he loves children and infants—which most people would agree includes the mentally immature, like retarded people—and that he is fair. He will do the right thing. King David believed that he would eventually be reunited with his infant that died. Many people think this shows that infants of believers will go to Heaven. The apostle Paul said that the children of a believer are holy. Many believe this means all infants and young children of believers are saved. Some people believe that all infants and young children are saved.

Jews circumcise baby boys, and this is a sign that they are under God's covenant and will receive all the blessings of that covenant. Baptism has replaced circumcision as the main rite of initiation into the Assembly of all Believers and into spiritual union with Jesus, so some denominations teach that baptism saves infants. Christian denominations and Messianic Jewish congregations who don't baptize infants usually dedicate them to God and teach that God will save them if they die before they are old enough to understand and believe. The Scriptures don't explicitly say anything about retarded people, but God

loves them too. Most believers think that if they are the children of believers, they will be saved. Most retarded people can consciously believe and trust in Jesus. There are only a very few who cannot. But the Scriptures say that the ability to believe is a gift from God; it is not something we can do in our own power. So God can give saving faith even to retarded people and infants.

B. Those Who have Never Heard the Good News

The Scriptures do not explicitly tell us what God will do to those people who have never heard the Good News. But it does say some things. Ezekiel 3:16-19 says: **16 After the seven days had passed, Yahweh spoke to me. 17 He said, "Mortal man, I am making you a watchman for the nation of Israel. You will pass on to them the warnings I give you. 18 If I tell you that someone evil is going to die as punishment for his sins, but you don't warn him to change his ways so that he can be saved, he will die with his sin unforgiven, but I will hold you responsible for his death. 19 If you do warn such a person and he doesn't change his ways, he will die—still condemned—but you will not be held responsible."**

This Scripture shows God's attitude. Every person is responsible for their own sin, and God will punish them for that sin—no matter if they are warned or not. But we —who know the message of the Good News— have the responsibility to tell it to people. If we have the chance to do so and do not do it, then God will hold us responsible for those people not hearing it.

Romans 1:18-23 says God has made it clear to every person that he exists. If they do not turn to him and try to know him, then they will be punished for their rejecting him.

All people are born condemned to Hell. So if God saves anyone, he is being kind and merciful. He is not being unfair to punish those who are punished in Hell.

But God is merciful and fair to all people. *[Deuteronomy 32:4; Psalm 9:4; 19:9; 119:137-138]* He gives everyone a chance to turn to him. Romans 2:12-16 says that God will not punish people for things they do wrong that they did not know were wrong. He will punish them for violating their own understanding of what is right and wrong. Jesus said in Luke 12:47-48 that the punishment God gives is worse for people who know what is right and wrong, and less for those who didn't know they did wrong. Therefore, all punishment in Hell is not equal.

I believe God is fair and gives everyone a chance to be saved—even if they have never heard the Good News. There are true stories about people who lived in a country where there were no believers in Jesus, and a person recognized there is a God who created the world and the stars—so he prayed to God. God told the person he would send someone to tell him about the one true God. Then he sent a missionary to that person to tell him about the Good News.

So we—who know the Good News message—have the responsibility to tell it to people who don't know it—whenever we have the chance. God calls some to go to places where people don't know him. If he calls you, you must be willing to go. But we must trust that God is fair and loves those people who have never heard the Good News. We must trust that he will do what is just. 1 Timothy 2:4 says: It is his desire that everyone would come to know and believe his message of truth and be saved. He has already revealed his existence to everyone through his creation—and no one has a valid excuse not to recognize this and seek him. If he sends someone to tell them the message of the Good News about his freely offered salvation through faith in Jesus, that is a bonus outreach on his part. We have to trust that he is more loving and fairer than we are, and therefore he gives everyone an adequate chance to repent and believe. But if we are saved and now have his desires concerning unsaved people, we will strongly want to give them that added advantage of hearing the Good News message.

The question of what God does with those who have never heard the salvation message is usually brought up by unbelievers—mainly as an attempt to side-track any discussion of their own response to God. If you are such a person, realize that you have heard his message—so God will hold you accountable for accepting or rejecting it. Your rejecting it won't help anyone else who hasn't heard the message. If your question and concern for such people is genuine, then become one of those who works to make sure everyone possible does hear. God is not accountable to explain to you what he will do with such people. He has made his plan of salvation known to you, and the issue right now is, how will you respond? God's answer to you about those who have not yet heard can wait until you have responded in submission to him. Then he will show you what he wants you to do.

What Is God's Name
in the Hebrew Scriptures?

Disclaimer

This is *not* an issue touching on salvation or any other major doctrine. There is *no reason* for any division among believers to arise from it. In fact, if any division does arise from people holding strong views about it, they are sinning against His Name. This is an issue of tertiary importance only. However, it is an issue of truth versus a false tradition of men. It is also an issue of love.

My Question

I write this assuming that you either do not know the facts I will present, or that you have not been challenged to seriously consider the facts. Is your love for God big enough that you would be willing to turn aside from a long-standing church tradition if you were shown it is in error?

The Facts

In the original Scriptures of the Old Testament, the proper name of the one true God is rendered in Hebrew by four consonants, which are often transliterated into the following four Roman letters: YHWH or JHWH. This is referred to as the "Tetragrammaton." You should be aware that in Hebrew, the meaning of a word is defined by the consonants, and the vowels in between the consonants often change depending on grammatical context. (This is a characteristic of Semitic languages.) So the fact that the name of God was written without vowels does not mean it wasn't pronounceable, it just means that they weren't written, as is true of **all** words in Hebrew. Several centuries after Jesus, some Hebrew scholars added some marks—called "vowel points"—to the Hebrew text of the Old Testament, which were meant to indicate which vowels were to be pronounced in the word. This was needed because Hebrew was essentially a dead language—only used in Jewish worship and used by biblical scholars, much

like Latin is today. But since Hebrew wasn't written with vowels, it was difficult for people to remember how to pronounce the Hebrew words, and so the vowel points were added. (They are called "vowel points" because many of them are literally dots, as well as other marks, which are written below and above the consonants and not in line with them—as normal vowel letters are written in English and other languages using a Roman alphabet.)

At some point in the history of the Jews—and certainly by the time of Jesus—the Jews had developed a tradition to never say the name of God aloud. This was intended to show great respect. And since the language of the Jews became other than Hebrew (by Jesus' day most of them spoke Aramaic—a language related to Hebrew) eventually the exact pronunciation became unknown to many. However, there were early translations of the Old Testament into other languages in that part of the world that used vowels in their alphabets, and from studying how the name of God was transliterated into those languages—plus knowledge of how the sounds of languages work and change when words and names are borrowed or transliterated from other languages—scholars have a very high degree of confidence that the name of God was pronounced "Yahweh." But this was not known to the western church until the 20th century.

Going back to the story of the Hebrew scholars who added the vowel points to the Hebrew Old Testament text, when they added vowel points to the name of God, they did not use the vowel points for "Yahweh." Since they were Jews, they still believed that readers should not say the name of God aloud. Their custom was to substitute the Hebrew equivalent of the English word "lord"—which in Hebrew is "Adonai"—when reading the Scriptures aloud. So they added the vowel points for the word "Adonai" under the consonants of the name of God to remind the reader to say

"Adonai" and not pronounce the actual name of God when reading the text. At some point in history, Christian scholars who were ignorant of this custom read the name of God with the vowel points of "Adonai" and came up with the pronunciation "Yehovah." At that time in history, the letter of the Latin alphabet used to represent the sound made by the consonant "y" (the consonant sound in yoyo) was "j." So they spelled the name of God as "Jehovah," but remember that the "j" was pronounced like "y" and pronounced "Yehovah." Over the years in English, the letter "j" came to have a different sound. But instead of changing the spelling of Bible names that begin with the letter "j" to "y," the spelling was kept the same and the pronunciation was changed. All names that begin with the letter "j" in the Old Testament are really pronounced with a "y" sound in Hebrew, their language of origin.

So up until the 20th century, Christian scholars thought that the name of God was "Jehovah." But Jewish scholars insist that there never was such a name. It is a mistake made long ago by someone who didn't know about the Jewish custom of using the vowel points for "Adonai" with the consonants of the name of God. We now know better. It is well attested that the pronunciation of the name of God around the time of Jesus was something very close to "Yahweh." Yet many Christians persist in using "Jehovah," which was a mistake and is an alteration of God's name. (Jehovah came into popular use among Christians because the American Standard Version translation of the Bible in 1901 used Jehovah for the name of God—the first major English translation to restore the name of God to the Old Testament Scriptures.). The excuse people give for still using Jehovah is that we have a number of hymns and songs we enjoy singing that use "Jehovah" and we don't want to give them up. This is a clear indication that some people love their comfortable tradition of calling God by this false name above their love and respect for his true name. Our God is gracious, and because most people use this false name in ignorance, he is not offended. There are many languages in the world that

cannot say his name as it was said in Hebrew because they have a different set of consonants and vowels in their languages, and I'm sure God doesn't mind. Nobody's salvation is in jeopardy because of using the false name Jehovah. Yet for English speakers who have no difficulty saying "Yahweh," and who know the truth about his name, there is no valid excuse for preferring the mistaken tradition over the truth. *It is a sign of lack of respect for anyone to know the proper way to pronounce a person's name, and to insist on mutilating it to the point where it hardly resembles the original.* Yet many people assume God doesn't mind, even when they know what his real name is.

It is true that when the Scriptures speak about the "name" of God, they are speaking of more than the sounds of the spoken name. They are speaking of his character and being and authority. Yet common sense tells us that the pronunciation of a name is still an important part of any name. The Scriptures teach that God is jealous of his name (See Ezekiel 39:25. But some modern translations—e.g. the TEV and NIV—translate the word 'jealous' differently). Again, that may primarily refer to the broader sense of his character. But can we assume that it has nothing at all to do with his literal name as well? We will certainly not earn any favor with God by using the correct name—for no sinner can "earn" his favor. But to know the truth and to love a false tradition above the truth is certainly not helpful. How can we say we love someone and not care if we pronounce their name correctly? Jehovah is so far from Yahweh, that it isn't even a mispronunciation. It is a different name. Would you call your spouse or child by an improper name? The name Jehovah has been taken by a non-Christian religion—the Jehovah's Witnesses. If that name were correct, this would not stop me from using it. But since Jehovah is not God's name, and since Jehovah's Witnesses have taken it as their identity, why do we want anything to do with it?

Since the name Jehovah is not in widespread use among Christians today—except in a few songs—it wouldn't even take much effort to make the change, i.e., to never use Jehovah and instead use Yahweh. Why don't we? For those who love God, why doesn't it matter that people call him by a false name?

The name of God is not extremely familiar to most English-speaking Christians because of another long-standing human tradition. The translators of the English Bible decided to follow the Jewish custom of not saying the name of God in order to show respect. Instead, they substituted the word "LORD" for God's name thousands of times in the Old Testament. Many English translations use small capital letters for the "ORD" when LORD stands for the name of God, and use lower case letters "ord" when lord is translating the Hebrew word "Adonai." Many modern translations continued this tradition, citing as a reason that English-speaking people felt no devotional or emotional value attached to the name Yahweh, as they did to the word "Lord." This is not surprising since most of them have never seen that name in the Bible. Yet these modern translators—unlike the KJV translators—knew the truth about the name of God and decided to hold this tradition of men above the truth and hide the truth from common Christians. In reality, they were probably more concerned about how well their translation would sell if it deviated from the tradition of the KJV than they were about anything else. Putting Yahweh in their translation—especially when most Christians still used the KJV—would have likely meant rejection of their translation by many people.

The irony of this tradition is that it does not at all follow the tradition of the Jews. Orthodox Jews have such a high respect for the Word of God that they would never dream of removing God's holy name from their written scrolls. They may not pronounce his name aloud, but their eyes behold it in print every time they read. Many conservative Christians often strongly criticize even the smallest changes in wordings in new translations, yet they don't seem to care that the name of God has been removed from over 6000 places in the Bible they use. The original inspired writings contained his name, but almost every English translation follows a tradition that has removed God's name from the Bible entirely—such that present-day Christians are mostly unaware of it.

Try reading the Old Testament in an English translation that keeps Yahweh in the Old Testament—such as the Jerusalem Bible. You will be surprised at how much you were missing by his name being removed.

People often complain that God is robbed of many things like tithes, respect, etc., but almost never do they complain that he has been robbed of his name in the Bible and among his people.

What can you do about this? Buy and use a translation that retains the name Yahweh in it. Write to the publishers of your favorite translations and tell them you want to see them put God's name back in them in a future edition or you will not buy it. That is the only thing that will change existing translations—the threat of losing market share. Write to your favorite Christian singers or their recording companies and ask them to use Yahweh instead of Jehovah in their lyrics. Bring up the issue—in a non-divisive manner—with your pastor and elders. Point out in a non-threatening manner the wrongness of using Jehovah and of removing the name of God from Scripture. They may have never thought about it seriously before. Ask them to educate your church about Hebrew names and particularly God's name. Use the name of Yahweh in your family devotions and correct the translation you use by reinserting "Yahweh" for "the Lord" when reading aloud in the Old Testament. But above all, honor His Name by not creating divisions in the church about this issue, and beware of spiritual pride. It is not a sin to use "Lord." Yet honor him by using Yahweh when you can and personally decide to never use the name Jehovah again. Learn to pronounce "Jehovah Jirah" and other commonly used names for God correctly as they are pronounced in Hebrew (i.e., Yahweh Yireh[year-eh]) or at least as close as you are able to do it. And share this knowledge with others.

A Scriptural Study of God's Statements and Commands Regarding His Name

YHWH

I quote quite a few Scriptures below because repetition in Scripture is understood by Bible scholars to be an indication of God's emphasis on a subject. The sheer quantity of pertinent Scriptures should also make an impression upon the reader.

The issue of this appendix concerns God's most-frequently-used name in the Hebrew Scriptures, represented by the Tetragrammaton **YHWH**—which has been deleted from almost every English translation over 6000 times. I believe the Scriptures quoted below clearly indicate that God intends and even commands his people to know his name, to use it, and to make it known.

All Scriptures quoted below are from the New American Standard Bible (because it is a very literal translation and widely accepted as accurate by conservative believers), except for the re-insertion of the Tetragrammaton, i.e., **YHWH**—the name of God—for "The LORD" where it appears in the original Hebrew text. The issue of an appropriate pronunciation of the name **YHWH** is discussed later in this appendix.

The Scripture quotations below are listed in the order they occur in the Bible rather than being organized by topic.

Exodus 3:13-15 Then Moses said to God, "Behold, I am going to the sons of Israel, and I will say to them, 'The God of your fathers has sent me to you.' Now they may say to me, 'What is His name?' What shall I say to them?" **14** God said to Moses, " I AM WHO I AM"; and He said, "Thus you shall say to the sons of Israel, 'I AM has sent me to you.' " **15** God, furthermore, said to Moses, "Thus you shall say to the sons of Israel, 'YHWH, the God of your fathers, the God of Abraham, the God of Isaac, and the God of Jacob, has sent me to you.' This is My name forever, and this is My memorial-name to all generations. ❖ *"all generations" includes this generation.*

Exodus 6:2-3 God spoke further to Moses and said to him, "I am **YHWH**; **3** and I appeared to Abraham, Isaac, and Jacob, as God Almighty, but by My name, **YHWH**, I did not make Myself known to them.

Exodus 9:16 But, indeed, for this reason I have allowed you to remain, in order to show you My power and in order to proclaim My name through all the earth. ❖ *God wants his name known by everyone on earth.*

Exodus 15:3 YHWH is a warrior; **YHWH** is His name. ❖ *His name is NOT "Adonai" (used by Jews) because "Adonai" is a title—not a name. It is translated into English as the title "LORD."*

Exodus 20:24 You shall make an altar of earth for Me, and you shall sacrifice on it your burnt offerings and your peace offerings, your sheep and your oxen; in every place where I cause My name to be remembered, I will come to you and bless you. ❖ *God wants his name to be remembered—not forgotten.*

Exodus 33:19 And He said, "I Myself will make all My goodness pass before you, and will proclaim the name of **YHWH** before you;

Exodus 34:5 YHWH descended in the cloud and stood there with him as he called upon the name of **YHWH**. ❖ *He did not call upon "Adonai" or "the Lord." He called upon "YHWH."*

Numbers 6:23-27 "Speak to Aaron and to his sons, saying, 'Thus you shall bless the sons of Israel. You shall say to them: **24 YHWH** bless you, and keep you;

25 YHWH make His face shine on you, And be gracious to you; **26 YHWH** lift up His countenance on you, And give you peace.' **27** So they shall invoke My name on the sons of Israel, and I then will bless them." ❖ *This is a clear direct command. "Thus you shall bless" means "you will bless using these exact words." To substitute "Adonai" or "the Lord" for the name YHWH violates the command. In the KJV it says, "On this wise ye shall bless..." which in modern English means, "In this way, you will bless..."*

Deuteronomy 6:13 You shall fear only **YHWH** your God; and you shall worship Him and swear by His name. ❖ *To swear by his name means you have to say it. You cannot swear by his name without saying it, or by substituting "Adonai" or "the Lord."*

Deuteronomy 10:8 At that time **YHWH** set apart the tribe of Levi to carry the ark of the covenant of **YHWH**, to stand before **YHWH** to serve Him and to bless in His name until this day.

Deuteronomy 21:5 Then the priests, the sons of Levi, shall come near, for **YHWH** your God has chosen them to serve Him and to bless in the name of **YHWH**; ❖ *To bless in his name means you have to say it, as in Numbers 6:23 above.*

Deuteronomy 28:9 YHWH will establish you as a holy people to Himself, as He swore to you, if you keep the commandments of **YHWH** your God and walk in His ways. **10** So all the peoples of the earth will see that you are called by the name of **YHWH**, and they will be afraid of you. ❖ *For people to see that you are called by the name of YHWH, you can't always substitute "Adonai" or "the Lord" for the Name. The Name itself has to be used and known.*

Deuteronomy 28:58-61 "If you are not careful to observe all the words of this law which are written in this book, to fear this honored and awesome name, **YHWH** your God, **59** then **YHWH** will bring extraordinary plagues on you and your descendants, even severe and lasting plagues, and miserable and chronic sicknesses. **60** He will bring back on you all the diseases of Egypt of which you were afraid, and they will cling to you. **61** Also every sickness and every plague which,

not written in the book of this law, **YHWH** will bring on you until you are destroyed. ❖ *One of his commands is that the name YHWH be used and made known.*

Deuteronomy 32:3 For I proclaim the name of **YHWH**; Ascribe greatness to our God!

2 Samuel 6:2 And David arose and went with all the people who were with him to Baale-judah, to bring up from there the ark of God which is called by the Name, the very name of **YHWH** of hosts who is enthroned above the cherubim.

2 Samuel 6:18 When David had finished offering the burnt offering and the peace offering, he blessed the people in the name of **YHWH** of hosts.

2 Samuel 7:25-26 Now therefore, O **YHWH** God, the word that You have spoken concerning Your servant and his house, confirm it forever, and do as You have spoken, 26 that Your name may be magnified forever, by saying, '**YHWH** of hosts is God over Israel'; and may the house of Your servant David be established before You. ❖ *Note the "forever" and the "by saying."*

2 Samuel 22:50 Therefore I will give thanks to You, O **YHWH**, among the nations, And I will sing praises to Your name. ❖ *One cannot sing praises to his name without saying the Name.*

1 Kings 8:41-43 "Also concerning the foreigner who is not of Your people Israel, when he comes from a far country for Your name's sake **42** (for they will hear of Your great name and Your mighty hand, and of Your outstretched arm); when he comes and prays toward this house, **43** hear in heaven Your dwelling place, and do according to all for which the foreigner calls to You, in order that all the peoples of the earth may know Your name, to fear You, as do Your people Israel, and that they may know that this house which I have built is called by Your name. ❖ *God's purpose—that all peoples of the earth might know his Name—has been thwarted by Jewish and Christian custom, which violates his command. Yes, his Name includes his reputation and character, but those are* *to be associated with his Name, not with some generic title like "Adonai" or "the Lord."*

2 Kings 21:7 Then he set the carved image of Asherah that he had made, in the house of which **YHWH** said to David and to his son Solomon, "In this house and in Jerusalem, which I have chosen from all the tribes of Israel, I will put My name forever. ❖ *If he put his name in Jerusalem forever, it cannot have been lost (as some claim) and he intends it to be known.*

1 Chronicles 16:2 When David had finished offering the burnt offering and the peace offerings, he blessed the people in the name of **YHWH**. ❖ *David used the name YHWH. The Jewish Encyclopedia of 1901, Vol. 1, pg 201-202 says that even as late as the early period of the Second Temple [i.e. after the Babylonian captivity around 500 BC] the name YHWH was still in common use by Jews. Since God's people commonly used the name YHWH for nearly 1000 years in obedience to God's clear commands, it cannot be wrong to use it today. The later Jewish and Christian traditions violate God's Law and command. Therefore it is wrong to NOT use his name.*

1 Chronicles 16.8 Oh give thanks to **YHWH**, call upon His name; Make known His deeds among the peoples.

1 Chronicles 17:24 Let Your name be established and magnified forever, saying, '**YHWH** of hosts is the God of Israel, even a God to Israel; and the house of David Your servant is established before You.'

1 Chronicles 23:13 The sons of Amram were Aaron and Moses. And Aaron was set apart to sanctify him as most holy, he and his sons forever, to burn incense before **YHWH**, to minister to Him and to bless in His name forever.

Nehemiah 9:5 Then the Levites, Jeshua, Kadmiel, Bani, Hashabneiah, Sherebiah, Hodiah, Shebaniah and Pethahiah, said, "Arise, bless **YHWH** your God forever and ever! O may Your glorious name be blessed And exalted above all blessing and praise!

Psalm 7:17 I will give thanks to **YHWH** according to His righteousness And will sing praise to the name of **YHWH** Most High.

Psalm 8:1, 9 O **YHWH**, our Lord, How majestic is Your name in all the earth, ❖ *His name should be known in all the earth, but it is not because of Jewish tradition, and because the tradition of translation in English Bibles has followed this tradition.*

Psalm 9:10 And those who know Your name will put their trust in You, For You, O **YHWH**, have not forsaken those who seek You.

Psalm 22:22 I will tell of Your name to my brethren; In the midst of the assembly I will praise You.

Psalm 34:3 O magnify **YHWH** with me, And let us exalt His name together. ❖ *"Together" means the use of his name is to be done corporately and in public—not exclusively in private.*

Psalm 68:4 Sing to God, sing praises to His name; Lift up a song for Him who rides through the deserts, Whose name is **YHWH**, and exult before Him.

Psalm 74:18 Remember this, O **YHWH**, that the enemy has reviled, And a foolish people has spurned Your name. ❖ *This originally refers people who rejected YHWH, the God of Israel, but it also speaks a truth about those who have spurned YHWH's name.*

Psalm 83:18 That they may know that You alone, whose name is **YHWH**, Are the Most High over all the earth.

Psalm 99:6 Moses and Aaron were among His priests, And Samuel was among those who called on His name; They called upon **YHWH** and He answered them. ❖ *They did not call on "Adonai" or "the Lord", they called on "YHWH". Who will dispute this fact?*

Psalm 102:12 But You, O **YHWH**, abide forever, And Your name to all generations. ❖ *His name is supposed to be known by all generations—including this one.*

Psalm 102:21 That men may tell of the name of **YHWH** in Zion And His praise in Jerusalem, ❖ *The Name YHWH is NOT told in Jerusalem, at least not by Jews or Jewish believers, nor even by Christians, because of tradition.*

Psalms 105:1-3 Oh give thanks to **YHWH**, call upon His name; Make known His deeds among the peoples. **2** Sing to Him, sing praises to Him; Speak of all His wonders. **3** Glory in His holy name; ❖ *This is a Scriptural command that is not being obeyed by most* *believers, because of a tradition perpetuated in English translations.*

Psalm 113:3 From the rising of the sun to its setting The name of **YHWH** is to be praised. ❖ *All day long the Name YHWH is to be praised. Evidently the Psalmist did not consider the frequent use of the name to diminish it in any way. This answers the objection that frequent use of his name diminishes it and makes it common and less meaningful.*

Psalm 119:5 O **YHWH**, I remember Your name in the night, And keep Your law.

Psalm 124:8 Our help is in the name of **YHWH**, Who made heaven and earth.

Psalm 129:8 Nor do those who pass by say, "The blessing of **YHWH** be upon you; We bless you in the name of **YHWH**."

Psalm 135:3 Praise **YHWH**, for **YHWH** is good; Sing praises to His name, for it is lovely. ❖ *This is clearly talking about the Name itself, not God as a person, for God is not "it." This answers the objection that references to "the Name" refer mainly to God's character and reputation, and not to the actual name itself.*

Psalm 135:13 Your name, O **YHWH**, is everlasting, Your remembrance, O **YHWH**, throughout all generations.

Psalm 145:21 My mouth will speak the praise of **YHWH**, And all flesh will bless His holy name forever and ever.

Psalm 148:13 Let them praise the name of **YHWH**, For His name alone is exalted;

Isaiah 12:4 And in that day you will say, "Give thanks to **YHWH**, call on His name. Make known His deeds among the peoples; Make them remember that His name is exalted." ❖ *This is a command.*

Isaiah 42:8 I am **YHWH**, that is My name; ❖ *Because the Name YHWH has been removed from English Bibles, most believers think God's name is "the Lord." "Lord" is not a name. It is a title also given to men. This diminishes God's name, not by assigning him the title "Lord" itself (as the Scripture does in many places), but by assigning him this human title in total exclusion of his Name YHWH—which he commanded be known—such that almost no one now knows it. Diminishing God in any way is called—in Scripture—"blasphemy."*

Isaiah 48:2 For they call themselves after the holy city And lean on the God of Israel; **YHWH** of hosts is His name.

Isaiah 50:10 Who is among you that fears **YHWH**, That obeys the voice of His servant, That walks in darkness and has no light? Let him trust in the name of **YHWH** and rely on his God.

Isaiah 51:15 For I am **YHWH** your God, who stirs up the sea and its waves roar (**YHWH** of hosts is His name). ❖ *This is repeated so often in Scripture because God didn't want his people to forget it. Repetition in Hebrew culture and in the Scripture was a form of emphasis, and a measure of importance.*

Isaiah 52:6 Therefore My people shall know My name; therefore in that day I am the one who is speaking, 'Here I am.' "

Isaiah 54:5 For your husband is your Maker, Whose name is **YHWH** of hosts; ❖ *Israel was YHWH's spiritual wife. It is not presumptuous for a wife to call her husband by his name, especially when he repeatedly commands her to do so. This answers the objection that it is inappropriate for us to call our heavenly Father by his name in the same way it is inappropriate to call our earthly father by his name.*

Isaiah 56:6 "Also the foreigners who join themselves to **YHWH**, To minister to Him, and to love the name of **YHWH**, ❖ *We are to love his name, not be reluctant to speak it.*

Isaiah 59:19 So they will fear the name of **YHWH** from the west And His glory from the rising of the sun,

Jeremiah 3:17 At that time they will call Jerusalem 'The Throne of **YHWH**,' and all the nations will be gathered to it, to Jerusalem, for the name of **YHWH**; nor will they walk anymore after the stubbornness of their evil heart.

Jeremiah 10:16 The portion of Jacob is not like these; For the Maker of all is He, And Israel is the tribe of His inheritance; **YHWH** of hosts is His name.

Jeremiah 12:16 Then if they will really learn the ways of My people, to swear by My name, 'As **YHWH** lives,' even as they taught My people to swear by Baal, they will be built up in the midst of My people. 17 But if they will not listen, then I will uproot that nation, uproot and destroy it," declares **YHWH**.

Jeremiah 16:21 "Therefore behold, I am going to make them know—This time I will make them know My power and

My might; And they shall know that My name is **YHWH**."

Jeremiah 23:6 In His days Judah will be saved, And Israel will dwell securely; And this is His name by which He will be called, '**YHWH** our righteousness.'

Jeremiah 31:35 Thus says **YHWH**, Who gives the sun for light by day And the fixed order of the moon and the stars for light by night, Who stirs up the sea so that its waves roar; **YHWH** of hosts is His name:

Jeremiah 32:18 who shows lovingkindness to thousands, but repays the iniquity of fathers into the bosom of their children after them, O great and mighty God. **YHWH** of hosts is His name;

Jeremiah 33:2 "Thus says **YHWH** who made the earth, **YHWH** who formed it to establish it, **YHWH** is His name,

Jeremiah 33:16 In those days Judah will be saved and Jerusalem will dwell in safety; and this is the name by which she will be called: **YHWH** is our righteousness.'

Jeremiah 46:18 As I live," declares the King Whose name is **YHWH** of hosts,

Jeremiah 48:15 Moab has been destroyed and men have gone up to his cities; His choicest young men have also gone down to the slaughter," Declares the King, whose name is **YHWH** of hosts.

Jeremiah 50:34 Their Redeemer is strong, **YHWH** of hosts is His name;

Jeremiah 51:19 The portion of Jacob is not like these; For the Maker of all is He, And of the tribe of His inheritance; **YHWH** of hosts is His name.

Jeremiah 51:57 "I will make her princes and her wise men drunk, Her governors, her prefects and her mighty men, That they may sleep a perpetual sleep and not wake up," Declares the King, whose name is **YHWH** of hosts.

Ezekiel 39:7 "My holy name I will make known in the midst of My people Israel; and I will not let My holy name be profaned anymore. And the nations will know that I am **YHWH**, the Holy One in Israel.

Ezekiel 39:25 Therefore thus says the Lord GOD, "Now I will restore the fortunes of Jacob and have mercy on the whole house of Israel; and I will be jealous for My holy name.

Hosea 12:5 Even **YHWH**, the God of hosts, **YHWH** is His name.

Joel 2:32 And it will come about that whoever calls on the name of **YHWH** will be delivered;

Amos 4:13 For behold, He who forms mountains and creates the wind And declares to man what are His thoughts, He who makes dawn into darkness And treads on the high places of the earth, **YHWH** God of hosts is His name.

Amos 5:8 He who made the Pleiades and Orion And changes deep darkness into morning, Who also darkens day into night, Who calls for the waters of the sea And pours them out on the surface of the earth, **YHWH** is His name.

Amos 9:6 The One who builds His upper chambers in the heavens And has founded His vaulted dome over the earth, He who calls for the waters of the sea And pours them out on the face of the earth, **YHWH** is His name. ❖ *I hope the repetition is not too boring, but rather that it demonstrates God's desire for his people to know this name. YHWH is his name. Not "the LORD," not "God," not "Adonai." These three words are titles, not names. "The LORD" is NOT his name! "Adonai" is NOT his name. It is a gross misrepresentation of God's Word and a lie to say that "The LORD" or "Adonai" is his name. Yet this lie is frequently proclaimed because of tradition—at least among English speakers. I know the tradition is not intended to be a lie, but because of the universal substitution of "the Lord" or "Adonai" for the Name, it really is a lie that a majority of believers, both Jewish and Gentile, believe.*

Zephaniah 3:9 For then I will give to the peoples purified lips, That all of them may call on the name of **YHWH**,

Zephaniah 3:12 But I will leave among you A humble and lowly people, And they will take refuge in the name of **YHWH**.

Zechariah 13:9 And I will bring the third part through the fire, Refine them as silver is refined, And test them as gold is tested. They will call on My name, And I will answer them; I will say, 'They are My people,' And they will say, '**YHWH** is my God.' "

Malachi 2:1-2 "And now this commandment is for you, O priests. **2** If you do not listen, and if you do not take it to heart to give honor to My name," says **YHWH** of hosts, "then I will send the curse upon you and I will curse your blessings; and indeed, I have cursed them already, because you are not taking it to heart. ❖ *I would be afraid to be among those who do not give honor to the Name YHWH in the way he has commanded. Jewish tradition supposedly honors his Name by not uttering it. But despite this declared motivation, it violates God's clear command concerning his name, thus from God's viewpoint, it is actually dishonoring it.*

Malachi 3:16 Then those who feared **YHWH** spoke to one another, and **YHWH** gave attention and heard it, and a book of remembrance was written before Him for those who fear **YHWH** and who esteem His name. ❖ *His name cannot be esteemed if it is unknown and never uttered, for these acts violate his revealed will in the Torah and in the rest of the Hebrew Scriptures.*

If the Jewish tradition to not speak God's name did not exist, there is no way anyone would be able to conclude from the above passages—or any other Scripture passages—that God intended the title "Adonai" (or in English, "the Lord") to be substituted for his name **YHWH,** and for his name to never be pronounced. It is only coming from indoctrination in the Jewish tradition that the plain intent of these Scriptures could be obscured. Unfortunately, the tradition to substitute "The LORD" in almost every English translation (which originally came directly from a Christian translator following the Jewish tradition) helps obscure the clear intent of these and other verses. Unless one thinks about it, it never occurs to people that "The Lord" has been substituted for an actual name, which is a serious violation of the text. Or else they think that "The Lord" is a name itself—which it is not. If you don't think "The Lord" violates the text, then it would also not be a violation of the New Testament text to everywhere remove the name of Jesus and substitute something else that is not a name, such as "the Master."

Jeremiah 23:26-27 How long? Is there anything in the hearts of the prophets who prophesy falsehood, even these prophets of the deception of their own heart, **27** who intend to make My people forget My name by their dreams which they relate to one another, just as their fathers forgot My name because of Baal?

Isaiah 29:10-13 For **YHWH** has poured over you a spirit of deep sleep, He has shut your eyes, the prophets; And He has covered your heads, the seers. **11** The entire vision will be to you like the words of a sealed book, which when they give it to the one who is literate, saying, "Please read this," he will say, "I cannot, for it is sealed." **12** Then the book will be given to the one who is illiterate, saying, "Please read this." And he will say, "I cannot read." **13** Then the Lord said, "Because this people draw near with their words And honor Me with their lip service, But they remove their hearts far from Me, And their reverence for Me consists of tradition learned by rote... ❖ *The Jewish tradition to not say God's name is not one that he commanded. It is a tradition of men—and however noble the motivation sounds, it violates God's command to make his name known and to use it.*

Mark 7:9, 13 He *(Jesus)* was also saying to them, "You are experts at setting aside the commandment of God in order to keep your tradition..... **13** thus invalidating the word of God by your tradition which you have handed down; and you do many things such as that." ❖ *Jesus condemned this kind of pharisaic (and later rabbinic) tradition of building a fence around the Law and setting aside God's clear command in favor of man-made tradition.*

In Deuteronomy 31:11-13, it is clear God commanded that his people hear his Torah read to them and to observe **all the words of his Torah,** which includes his Name. (See also Joshua 8:34-35, 2 Kings 23:2, 2 Chronicles 34:30, and Jeremiah 36:4-6.) There was no instruction to not say his Name while reading it to them. Therefore, he intended for his Name to be read as it is written. (And it most certainly was read aloud until the current Jewish tradition came into being after the Babylonian captivity.) To substitute 'Adonai' for his Name while doing so would be to CHANGE the words of the Torah, thus

CHANGING God's Word, and disobeying his direct command.

The commandment to not take (use) God's name in vain (Exodus 20:7 *"You shall not take the name of YHWH your God in vain, for YHWH will not leave him unpunished who takes His name in vain.")*—which, by the way, refers to the name YHWH, NOT to the word "God"—ASSUMES that people will know and speak his Name. Otherwise the commandment would have explicitly forbidden people to speak his Name at all. But it does not say this. Clearly he intended that his people know, speak, and use his Name in a reverent manner, and that all the nations would know his Name and character.

Have you read every Scripture above?

Can you conclude that when reading the Scriptures in public, God does not want people to:

> know that his name is **YHWH**?
> use his name **YHWH** for blessing?
> swear by his name **YHWH**?
> sing to his name **YHWH**?
> call on his name **YHWH**?
> speak his name **YHWH** ?

God has clearly revealed his will, but both Jewish and Christian custom has essentially caused his name to be forgotten—as God condemned in Jeremiah 23:27. To the uninitiated in Messianic congregations it would seem God's name is actually "Adonai," for this title is used exactly as a name is used. In effect, Jews and Messianic Jews have changed God's name to "Adonai," as far as actual use is concerned. YHWH is generally not known, either among Jews or among most Christians. And because of the tradition of English translations, most believers don't even know that his name YHWH occurs in the Hebrew manuscripts over 6800 times. The actual title "Lord" or "Adonai" occurs only a few hundred times in the Hebrew Scriptures. God's Word has been VIOLATED by removing it. This is as serious as if a translation were to remove the name Jesus from the New Testament and substitute "Lord" or "Master" or something else that is not his Name. No one would question that doing so would be a violation of the Scriptures. Yet it is considered

acceptable in the Hebrew Scriptures because it is a long-standing tradition.

Pronunciation of God's Name

If we were to restore the use of the Name, how should we pronounce **YHWH**?

Does it really matter? Yes and no. Languages change over time. **YHWH's** name was in use for over 1000 years before the Jewish tradition came into being that essentially wiped out the common knowledge and use of his Name. Over that period of time, the pronunciation of **YHWH** undoubtedly changed. **ALL** words in ALL living languages change over time—**even highly revered names**. The English name "Jesus" was originally "Yesus" (Yay-soos) from the Greek translation of his name. Over hundreds of years, the pronunciation changed in English, as it also has changed in other languages (e.g. Jesus in Spanish is pronounced Hay-soos). His name was really *"Yeshua"* in Aramaic, but God allowed it to be translated into Greek as "Yesus" (Yay-soos). Therefore, the exact pronunciation of Yeshua's name was not important to God. Even though I prefer to say "Yeshua" (the name that his parents and disciples called him) over "Jesus," I know that the name "Jesus" is acceptable to God, as is every other version of his name used in the world, because demons fear it and people are healed and saved by this name. **Therefore, the exact pronunciation is not important to God.**

Some Jewish rabbis claim that the correct pronunciation was lost. Actually, several early Christian writers who wrote in Greek said that the name was pronounced 'Yahweh' (ιαουε) [yah-owe-way]. Though there are also some other minor variations in evidence, 'Yahweh' is the top choice of scholars as the most likely form of the name (at least at the end of the 1000-year period when it was commonly used). **Even Jewish scholars** write that they are SURE the pronunciation was either 'Yahweh' or something very close to it. This is stated in the Jewish Encyclopedia of 1901, Vol. 12, pg. 119; also in the

Modern Judaica Encyclopedia, Vol. 7, pg. 69; also in the 20th Century Schaff-Herzog Encyclopedia, pg. 1194-1195; and in The Encyclopedia Judaica, 1972, Keter Publishing House, Jerusalem, Vol. 7, pg 680.

However, while the exact pronunciation is not important (Yahweh, Yahuweh, Yahveh), the name "Jehovah" is KNOWN to be totally inaccurate. It is not even close. In my opinion, it should NOT be used (though it is not a sin to use it) because it isn't his name. Do you think it would OK to substitute any old name for "Jesus" that isn't even remotely similar? (Would you think that calling him "George" might be disrespectful?) Scholars and Greek manuscripts with "Yahweh" written in them transliterated into Greek spelling have given us a reasonably close approximation with "Yahweh." Why would we consider anything else?

What about the fact that there is no "W" in Hebrew? Sounds of letters change over time. In current Hebrew pronunciation, there is no "W" sound. But it is clear that the sounds of at least some of the consonants in Hebrew have changed over time. Otherwise there would not be sets of two consonants that are pronounced exactly the same (i.e. Chet and Kaf, Kaf and Kof, Tet and Tav, Samech and Sin, Aleph and Ayin—not to mention the different vowel points that are no longer pronounced differently). Linguist scholars know how they were pronounced separately in the past. This is not a mystery. Jewish Hebrew scholars know about the history of the Hebrew language, and THEY say the original pronunciation of **YHWH** was most likely "Yahweh" (with a "W", not a "V") or "Yahuweh." Those are their top two choices. Even if it was "Yahveh," it should be clear from the way God allowed Yeshua's name to be written as "Yesus" in Greek that **the exact pronunciation is not important to him.** God inspired the writing of the New Testament in Greek. There is no basis to say that he inspired any translation, such as

the Septuagint, which started the violation of God's Word by substituting the Greek word "kurios" (lord) for YHWH in that translation.

Some people think that **YHWH** is God the Father's name—and that it is too holy to use. This idea clearly contradicts the teaching of the Scriptures quoted above. These people say they would never call their own father by name. This is a valid point with regard to human fathers. But Scriptural command with regard to God is different than human tradition. And is it really true that **YHWH** is only the name of God the Father?

Actually, **YHWH** is the name of the Triune God. This is easily proven from Scripture.

Joel 2:32 says, "And it will come about that whoever calls on the name of **YHWH** will be delivered (i.e. saved)." But Acts 4:12 says, *"And there is salvation in no one else; for there is no other name under heaven that has been given among men by which we must be saved."* This clearly refers to Jesus. Therefore Jesus must be **YHWH.**

Exodus 3:13-15 quoted earlier in this appendix says that **YHWH's** name is I AM. Jesus claimed to be "I AM" in John 8:58. Therefore he was claiming to be **YHWH.**

John the Baptist—in speaking about the coming of Jesus the Messiah—said, [John 1:23] *"I am A VOICE OF ONE CRYING IN THE WILDERNESS, 'MAKE STRAIGHT THE WAY OF THE LORD,' as Isaiah the prophet said."* This "Lord" he was referring to was clearly Jesus. In Isaiah's prophecy which John was quoting, [Isaiah 40:3] in Hebrew the prophecy speaks of the coming of **YHWH.** Hence Jesus is **YHWH.**

Amos 4:13 and 5:8 say the creator's name is **YHWH.** We know from John 1:1-3, that the Word of God—who became Jesus the Messiah—is the creator of all things. Therefore Jesus is **YHWH.**

When the apostles and Paul said "Jesus is Lord," [Romans 10:9, 1 Corinthians 12:3] as Jews—who called **YHWH** "Lord," (or "Adonai")—they were actually making the claim that Jesus is **YHWH.**

On the other hand, in the following Scripture it is clear that **YHWH** refers to God the Father:

Psalm 110:1-4 YHWH says to my Lord *(the Messiah)*: "Sit at My right hand Until I make Your enemies a footstool for Your feet." **2 YHWH** will stretch forth Your strong scepter from Zion, saying, "Rule in the midst of Your enemies." **3** Your people will volunteer freely in the day of Your power; In holy array, from the womb of the dawn, Your youth are to You as the dew. **4 YHWH** has sworn and will not change His mind, "You are a priest forever according to the order of Melchizedek."

The Shema in Deuteronomy 6:4 declares that our God **YHWH** is One (i.e., a unity). The Father is God—therefore, he is **YHWH**. The Son is God—therefore, he is **YHWH**. The Holy Spirit is God—therefore, he is **YHWH**.

Jesus said in John 5:22-23, "For not even the Father judges anyone, but He has given all judgment to the Son, **23** so that all will honor the Son even as they honor the Father. He who does not honor the Son does not honor the Father who sent Him."

Therefore, it is appropriate for us to honor God the Father the exact same way we honor God the Son, i.e. Jesus. It goes in both directions. Some say it diminishes Gods name to speak it familiarly. It does not diminish Jesus' name to use it familiarly and frequently, and Jesus is God, one with the Father. We magnify and exalt Jesus' name as we loudly proclaim it and use it frequently in praise and worship. It does not diminish his name in our eyes or the eyes of others. The opposite is true. It aids our worship and makes us feel closer to him. The same is true among Christians who use the name "Yahweh" in praise and worship. We want Jesus' name to be publicly proclaimed. If **YHWH** is the Father's name (and it is, but not his exclusively) then we should be able to honor him using that name in the same way we honor his Son's name. Using **YHWH** in worship enhances worship. It does not show disrespect or over-familiarity. God intended—according to many of the above

Scriptures—for people to verbally bless his name, and to bless in his name, to sing to his name, to use it in public, and to let everyone know that we are associated with this name. To forbid or discourage people from doing so is a violation of God's commands in Scripture. It is following a TRADITION OF MEN and establishing that tradition as being MORE IMPORTANT than God's Word—thus enabling us to ignore God's command. If this tradition is correct, then according to John 5:23—which says that the Father wants us to honor the Son in the same way we honor the Father—we must also refrain from using Jesus' name. This is clearly wrong.

What do you value most? A tradition of men or God's will as revealed in his Word? It really comes down to that.

A counter argument given to me: The name of Yahweh was not used by the apostles or Jesus.

Jesus condemned "many" traditions of the Pharisees that trumped their obeying God's Word. He did not bring this one up specifically—probably because he knew that the Jewish leadership and the common Jew of his time would have wrongly considered this an issue of blasphemy for those who spoke the name. To have made an issue of this point would have immediately closed the mind of almost every Jew of his day. His desire was to reach them—not turn them off.

The apostles were steeped in this tradition, and since Jesus didn't bring the issue up, they were unlikely to be aware of it—unless the Holy Spirit clearly prompted them on it. But there was another reason. They didn't call their savior "Jesus." They called him "Yeshua"—which in Hebrew and Aramaic clearly means "Yahweh saves." The short form of Yahweh—"Yah"—was still commonly used in Hebrew names and in "hallelujah"—which means, "Praise Yah(weh)." They recorded that Jesus claimed to be "I am" and they identified his name, Jesus/Yeshua, as the name above all names, the name to call upon to be saved—which in the Old Testament is clearly Yahweh himself. Since

"Yahweh saves" was the name of their Lord and Savior, when his name was being used, they were exalting the name of Yahweh as the Old Testament Scriptures command, and they did so in a way that did not offend the Jews of their day.

What has changed is that English speakers use "Jesus", not "Yahweh saves" as the name of their Lord and Savior. The knowledge of the name has been lost. Jews had the name before their eyes in the Hebrew scrolls. The name is no longer seen by English speakers who do not read Hebrew because it has been omitted from almost every English translation (except the Jerusalem Bible). God's commands concerning his name are now violated, except with regard to the name of Jesus/Yeshua.

Evidently, it is not a major issue with God, or Jesus would have confronted it. But it is still an issue of obedience and truth. While we merit nothing by being obedient, we should desire to be obedient to clear commands of Scripture, and not allow human tradition to deter us. Those who are obedient to the command to use and proclaim the name "Yahweh" are blessed. Those who don't, miss out on this aspect of blessing that he desires to give his people. This is true of many blessings in many areas. By missing out on them, we don't lose our salvation, and we don't cancel the blessings we do have. But we are missing out on something that God has clearly commanded us to do. Why try to avoid it?

The Name Is "Yeshua"

What is the Name above every name, the only Name given under heaven by which people may be saved? I know that many will reprove me for bringing this up, but that Name is "Yeshua."

Now before you refuse to read further, let me reassure you that I know people who call upon the name of "Jesus" will be saved. I will make several disclaimers so you will know that I am not attacking common Evangelical Christian theology. I don't really want to raise controversy, dissension, or cause division. I know the Scriptures forbid it and Jesus (Yeshua) will not be pleased with me if I do. So let me make my disclaimers first, and then let me make my point which I do not intend to be divisive, but a matter of love.

First, my disclaimers. I believe that when the writers of Scripture refer to the name of Jesus, they are not referring only or even primarily to the literal name that we say. In the Hebrew mind, the name of God, or Jesus, refers to his character and being and authority. It is not just a verbal label. I accept that. When people pray to Jesus and call on his name, the person to whom they are referring hears and understands and responds. The English name of Jesus is efficacious. Demons yield to its authority. And there is the clear evidence that the Holy Spirit did not think it was important for people to read and pronounce the name of our Savior exactly as he was known among his Jewish contemporaries, since he moved the writers of the New Testament to write in Greek and render his name as "Yesus" (yay-soos), which is not particularly close to his name in Hebrew, "Yeshua" (yeh-SHOO-ah). So I am not saying that the "correct" pronunciation of his name is very important to our Lord. It evidently is not. And I believe Jesus would not want any of us to quarrel over it. So I won't. I'll just make my point and let you think about it. And I'll accept you and love you even if you still persist in calling Yeshua by the name "Jesus."

Just so some readers won't misunderstand, all the Old Testament Bible names that start with the letter "j" are correctly pronounced in Hebrew with a "y" sound. The Roman letter "j" originally was pronounced like "y" is in the word "yes." When Bible names were first transliterated into Roman letters into Latin from Hebrew, "j" was used for the sound "y." Later the pronunciation of "j" changed to what it is today, but the spellings of the names were not revised. The pronunciation of the vowels in English also changed in what is called "the great English vowel shift" and that is why English vowels are pronounced differently than in most European languages—which did not go through that shift (e.g., Spanish). The changes in pronunciation of "j" and also the vowels in English results in the fact that the way most Old Testament names are pronounced in English is significantly different from the way they were originally pronounced in Hebrew.

It is common for names that originate in one language to change pronunciation somewhat as they are borrowed into another language. This is because every language does not have the same inventory of sounds and it is not always possible for a speaker of one language to say a word or a name exactly as it is said in another language. For example, in some languages in the Pacific, there is no "j" sound in the language, and all syllables have to end with a vowel. There are no words in these languages that end in a consonant, so it is difficult for the people to say such a word. They automatically add a vowel at the end. So in one of these languages, the English name "Jesus" became "Tisasi" (TEE sah see) which is as close as they can get with the inventory of sounds their language has and the way it works. Is that OK with you, or does it leave you uncomfortable? I'm sure the Lord doesn't mind. After all, he created their language and knows its limitations. Many languages don't have the sound made by "sh" in English and "s" is as close as they come. That is why Yeshua (Yeh SHOO ah) comes out in Greek as "yay-soos" (Yesus). (Don't ask me why the final sound is "s" rather than "ah" in Greek, I don't know, nor is it important.)

So it is apparent that the Lord isn't particularly concerned about the pronunciation of his name, since the Holy Spirit didn't go to any lengths to have it preserved better in Greek. Who am I to argue with the Holy Spirit? Not I. You go ahead and pronounce Jesus' name any way you like. So what is my point?

I heard years ago in Sunday school that Jesus' name and Joshua's name were actually the same in Hebrew. Yehoshua (Yeh HOE shoo ah) is a close approximation of this Hebrew name in English, and it is often shortened to Yeshua. (It is also sometimes transliterated "Yahvashua" or "Yahshua.") In Hebrew it literally means "Yah(weh) saves." That was interesting, but didn't make any impact on my thinking. In later years I heard that many or most Jews who have come to accept "Jesus" as their Messiah call him by the name "Yeshua." This was also interesting, but again didn't make any significant impact on my thinking. I was quite comfortable with the name Jesus, and it would be terribly difficult to change years of habit—and for what reason? It was unlikely that anyone else would change just because I did, and who wants to be an oddball or stir up controversy?

So what has brought about a change in my thinking? Why do I now value the name "Yeshua"—although I don't in the least despise the name "Jesus"—and why should you care? Several things wove together in my life. I'm not sure they will mean anything to you, but they might.

First, was my observation that many people are bound by tradition to the detriment of their knowing truth. Not that I'm against tradition. Many traditions are good and necessary. But some are neither, and they actually hold people back from something much better. It was easy to fall into the trap of thinking myself superior, but then the Lord brought to mind ways that I too was bound by unnecessary traditions. Some of these traditions made it hard for me to draw close to the Lord and have the intimacy of relationship I desired. Whether it was from the Lord or not, one of the things that became clear to me was that I knew his name was not really Jesus, yet I was reluctant to change to using Yeshua.

Secondly, some years ago I heard teachings and exhortations on having an intimate and passionate relationship with Jesus. These teachings struck a strong chord of yearning in me. I knew I wanted much more in my relationship with him, which was rather matter of fact and dry at the time. As I desired to know him more, it also became clear that as someone I loved dearly I wanted to know his name and use it rightly. I have from time to time been mildly annoyed when people mispronounce my own name, when they are well able to pronounce it correctly—especially when they don't seem to care how I pronounce it. It is just a label to them. But to me it is more than a label. It is a part of me, and it feels like a lack of respect when people don't care how or if they garble it. While our Lord is much more gracious and forgiving than I, as I sought to know him more, I began to be more cognizant of the fact that he had been a real physical person, whose parents, relatives, friends, disciples and enemies called him by one particular name. And that name wasn't Jesus. It was Yeshua, or something fairly close to that. He is still human, as well as divine. I know it will earn me no merit to use his proper name, but it might please him that I went to the trouble, as it would please me. I would never dream of distorting a friend's or loved one's name, except for giving an affectionate nickname. So why am I content to use a severely distorted name for my Lord, when I have been privileged to learn his true one and am able to pronounce it fairly closely—at least much more closely than "Jesus" is to his real name. Not that Jesus is a bad name. To me it is now like a name that an infant first learning to talk uses when he can't quite pronounce a family member's real name. It is quite acceptable, and even endearing. And sometimes those infant names become family nicknames that stick. But the infant grows and also learns to say the family member's name properly, and knows that at times a nickname is not appropriate. I grew up using the name Jesus and will probably never totally rid myself of using it in this life. Yet as I grow closer to my Savior, his real name, the same one Mary and Joseph (uh—Miriam and Yosef) called him, the same one the twelve apostles called him in their own language, that is the name that I want to call him as well. I don't know what we will all call him in heaven. Will we all continue to use our own languages, or will we have one in common? I know it is speculation at best. But somehow, I tend to think that his birth name will be learned and used by all of us. I'm starting now.

Thirdly, a trip to Israel—and also reading some books written by Jewish Christians—brought home forcefully to me the fact that Jesus was a Jew. Now we all know that as an intellectual fact, but I think we tend to think that the Jews gave up their right to him and he is "Christian" now. But I believe Jesus' Jewishness was a very integral part of his identity and still is. The Jews are God's chosen people. Jesus himself said that salvation comes from the Jews. This is more than just mere happenstance. It was part of God's purpose and plan. Christians through the centuries have tended to despise Jews and their traditions—to the detriment of our insight concerning some of the finer points in the Bible. Not that Christians have missed any major doctrinal truths, but they do miss out on some significant knowledge. These days, as many Christians are looking forward to Jesus' second coming and events that may unfold in Israel, and since many Jews are becoming "Messianic Jews" or "believers in Yeshua," it is becoming more acceptable to study and learn from the Jewish traditions of our new Jewish brothers and sisters in Christ. This is all to say that the reality of Jesus' Jewishness has been heightened for me, and my use of his Jewish name is an aid to me in keeping this aspect of his identity in mind.

So again, why am I sharing this with you? What is my point? Well, even though he is your Lord and Savior, he is also mine. I won't be argumentative and insist that you call him by his rightful birth name, but I want to be sure that you are aware of what his true name is. Just like I would inform someone who said my spouse's name incorrectly, I'm telling you his real name is "Yeshua." That's my point. You don't have to use it. Yeshua doesn't want me to make a big issue of it and cause problems. That is not his way. But I just wanted to make it clear to you that the name "Jesus" is a distortion that comes down to us through history due to changes in languages, and is maintained by tradition despite the fact that many people know better. I may be wrong, but I think Yeshua wanted me to point that out to you, just so you could think about it.

CPSIA information can be obtained
at www.ICGtesting.com
Printed in the USA
LVHW050529030822
725075LV00004B/118

9 781948 048255